Assessing Adolescent and Adult Intelligence

Second Edition

Alan S. Kaufman
Yale University

Elizabeth O. Lichtenberger
The Salk Institute

Allyn and Bacon
Boston   London   Toronto   Sydney   Tokyo   Singapore

Executive editor: Rebecca Pascal
Manufacturing buyer: JoAnne Sweeney
Cover designer: Suzanne Harbison
Production coordinator: Pat Torelli Publishing Services
Editorial-production service: Chestnut Hill Enterprises, Inc.
Electronic composition: Omegatype Typography, Inc.

Library of Congress Cataloging-in-Publication Data
Kaufman, Alan S.
     Assessing adolescent and adult intelligence / Alan S. Kaufman, Elizabeth O.
Lichtenberger. — 2nd ed.
        p.   cm.
     Includes bibliographical references and indexes.
     ISBN 0-205-30527-X
       1. Wechsler Adult Intelligence Scale.   2. Intelligence tests.   3. Teenagers—Intelligence testing.   I. Lichtenberger, Elizabeth O.   II. Title.

BF432.5. W4 K38 2001
153.9'3—dc21

                                                                                2001046379

Printed in the United States of America
10   9   8   7   6   5   4   3   2   1   05   04   03   02   01

MIMI:

Sono andati? Fingevo di dormire
perchè volli con te sola restare.
Ho tante cose che ti voglio dire,
o una sola,
ma grande come il mare,
come il mare profonda ed infinita.
Sei il mio amor e tutta la mia vita.

Have they left us? I was pretending to sleep
to be alone with you.
So many things to tell you,
but really just one,
that is as huge as the ocean,
and as deep and infinite.
You are my love and my whole life.

RODOLFO:

O mia bella Mimi!

My beautiful Mimi!

MIMI:

Son bella ancora?

Am I still beautiful?

RODOLFO:

Bella come un'aurora.

Beautiful as the dawn in Springtime.

A. S. K.

For everyone on this earth,
there will always be
one special someone to love.
For me,
there will always be
You.

E. O. L.

CONTENTS

v

PART II
Individual Differences on Age, Socioeconomic Status, and Other Key Variables

PART V
Additional Measures of Adolescent and Adult IQ

CHAPTER 13 Kaufman Adolescent and Adult Intelligence Test (KAIT)   522

The second edition of *Assessing Adolescent and Adult Intelligence* covers the same general scope of material and is intended for the same group of readers as the first edition. The first edition presented comprehensive coverage of clinical and neuropsychological assessment of intelligence, particularly as measured by the Wechsler Adult Intelligence Scale—Revised (WAIS-R), and the second edition provides similar comprehensive coverage, but this time focuses on the third edition of the Wechsler Adult Intelligence Scale (WAIS-III). However, since publication of the first edition of this book, the number of comprehensive and brief tests of intelligence and related abilities available for assessing adolescents and adults has greatly increased, and the second edition reflects these exciting advancements in the field. In addition to our coverage throughout the book of the highly popular WAIS-III, we integrate research and clinical use of additional instruments, most notably the Kaufman Adolescent and Adult Intelligence Scale (KAIT), Woodcock-Johnson—Third Edition (WJ III), and brief tests such as the Wechsler Abbreviated Scale of Intelligence (WASI) and Kaufman Brief Intelligence Test (K-BIT).

Similar to the first edition of this book, our approach to assessment in this edition represents a dynamic integration of (a) thousands of research investigations on the WAIS-III, its prede-cessors, and other pertinent tests of intelligence; (b) an empirical approach to WAIS-III IQ, Index, and subtest profile interpretation that can be applied at a sophisticated level by the psychometrically orientated professional, or via simple rules of thumb by the mathematically insecure; (c) a clinical, neuropsychological, and psychoeducational approach to the WAIS-III and other intelligence tests that facilitates interpretation of significant profile fluctuations; (d) the application of theories of intelligence whenever the theories are clinically or neuropsychologically relevant; and (e) adherence to the intelligent testing philosophy, which elevates clinicians above the test they use and places less emphasis on the IQs than on the peaks and valleys in the total test profile.

Because of the increased number of intelligence tests for adolescents and adults now available to clinicians and researchers, we have sharpened the focus of the second edition to some extent. We now attend almost exclusively to individually administered, clinical measures of intelligence. Separate chapters and sections from the first edition on comprehensive neuropsychological batteries, adaptive behavior inventories, and individual achievement tests have been eliminated. Research findings based primarily on group-administered tests (such as the Scholastic Aptitude Test) have usually been eliminated, although we made an exception with some crucial aging studies such as Schaie's cross-sequential investigations with the Primary Mental Abilities Test.

This abridgment in the type of specific instruments covered in depth allowed us to attend more closely to the WAIS-III and its new four-scale structure, to the array of new brief and comprehensive tests, and to the burgeoning literature on adolescent and adult IQ that has increased exponentially during the past decade. However, the elimination of specific instruments did not alter the major focuses of the book. For example, we eliminated the chapter on two comprehensive neuropsychological test batteries (Halstead-Reitan and Luria-Nebraska) but retained the crucial emphasis on the neuropsychological interpretation of IQ tests, especially the WAIS-III.

There are several new topics and topics covered with new breadth in this addition. Some of those include the heritability of IQ and attacks on the IQ construct, including the learning disabilities challenge; IQ differences across the lifespan; ethnic differences (white-African American and white-Hispanic) and the WAIS-III and Kaufman tests; factor analysis of the four factor WAIS-III; new theories such as those of Cattell-Horn-Carroll and Baltes; new tests such as the KAIT, WJ III, WASI, and K-BIT; and arguments against using short forms of Wechsler's tests and in favor of using well-normed brief tests of intelligence.

ACKNOWLEDGMENTS

Numerous individuals made valuable contributions to the second edition of *Assessing Adolescent and Adult Intelligence*. We are extremely grateful to Drs. Kevin McGrew, Laurie Ford, and Richard Woodcock for their excellent chapter on the Woodcock-Johnson—Third Edition, which helped enhance our text by offering in-depth coverage of this recently revised and restandardized instrument; Drs. McGrew and Woodcock are two of the WJ III authors, making this chapter an authoritative approach for the interpretation of the WJ III for adolescents and adults. We would also like to thank Dr. Debra Broadbooks for her contribution to the chapter on the Kaufman Adolescent and Adult Intelligence Test (KAIT), which facilitated our comprehensive discussion of another recent test of adult intelligence. We are indebted to Dr. Aurelio Prifitera of The Psychological Corporation, and to the publisher itself: (a) for generously sharing WAIS-III data with Alan, permitting him to conduct the key studies on aging across the lifespan that were previously published and are featured in Chapter 5; (b) for arranging to have Dr. Robert Heaton and his colleagues share with us the results of their excellent analyses of WAIS-III and Wechsler Memory Scale—Third Edition (WMS-III) demographic data for inclusion in our book, greatly enhancing several key topics in Chapter 4; and (c) for sending each of us complimentary copies of several tests such as the WASI. Indeed, we are most grateful to Dr. Heaton and his collaborators—Drs. Jennifer Manly, Michael Taylor, and David Tulsky—for conducting an ingenious set of analyses on age, gender, and ethnic differences on the WAIS-III and WMS-III; for sharing the results of their analyses in preliminary drafts of manuscripts, and for being so responsive to our follow-up questions (e.g., sample sizes of each separate educational group).

Dr. James McLean provided invaluable assistance in analyzing WAIS-III data for our discussion of factor analysis and Dr. Joseph Glutting kindly sent each of us complimentary copies of the WRIT. We are also grateful to several graduate students from the California School of Professional Psychology—San Diego from Liz's Intelligence Testing courses who sent copies of their case reports on adolescents and adults for us to use; we are especially grateful to Douglas Johnson and Megan Lucas, whose reports were selected for inclusion in this book. One student, Susan Stumph, who served as Dr. Lichtenberger's research assistant, was vital in locating and copying numerous research articles and completed many other tasks that allowed us to finish this text on time.

We owe our respective spouses and families a great deal of appreciation for all of their support and encouragement. Alan is especially grateful to Drs. Nadeen and James Kaufman, and Dr. Jennie Kaufman Singer, for their helpful insights on many of the topics that are included in this book. James merits an extra special thank you for providing invaluable research assistance, especially with conducting numerous literature searches and for his tireless efforts in locating hard-to-find references. Liz would like to thank Mike for his assistance with quick data entry and number checking, as well as his understanding about many late nights and providing extra help with little Hannah whenever necessary; and Liz's little Hannah for reminding her of what is most important.

Alan S. Kaufman

Elizabeth O. Lichtenberger

CHAPTER 1

IQ Tests: Their History, Use, Validity, and Intelligent Interpretation

The field of intelligence, particularly of adolescent and adult mental development, has dominated the psychological literature for decades, and now encompasses a diversity of domains within cognitive psychology, clinical psychology, psychobiology, behavioral genetics, education, school psychology, sociology, neuropsychology, and everyday life. Excellent handbooks are available with chapters written by experts in many aspects of intellectual theory, measurement, and development (e.g., Flanagan, Genshaft, & Harrison, 1997; Groth-Marnat, 2000), and even these texts cover only a portion of the territory and quickly become outdated. Consequently, in writing this text on the assessment of adolescent and adult intelligence, we have had to make several decisions about which areas to include and how thoroughly to cover each topic.

First, this book focuses on the clinical assessment of intelligence, and every topic must bear, either directly or indirectly, on the clinical aspect of mental measurement. Because clinical assessment within the fields of neuropsychology, special education, and clinical, school, and counseling psychology involves individual evaluations, research on group-administered tests is subordinated to the more pertinent research on individual intelligence tests. The 1990 version of this text covered group-administered intelligence tests to some extent. However, the adolescent and adult assessment scene has changed during this past decade, with clinicians having options beyond Wechsler's tests. Whereas the Wechsler Adult Intelligence Scale—Third Edition (WAIS-III; Psychological Corporation, 1997; Wechsler, 1997) is still the most used test, and is clearly the featured instrument in this revised text, the availability of a variety of new in-depth and brief intelligence tests, and a proliferation of research on these instruments, has impelled us to focus on individually administered intelligence tests.

For example, the monumental efforts of Schaie (1958, 1983b, 1994) and his colleagues (Hertzog & Schaie, 1988; Schaie & Labouvie-Vief, 1974; Schaie & Strother, 1968; Schaie & Willis, 1993) to understand the development of adult intelligence have been based on the group-administered Primary Mental Abilities Test. The key findings from these innovative cross-sequential studies are of interest to psychology in general, but have limited applicability to the work of clinical and neuropsychological practitioners. Consequently, investigations by Schaie will only be discussed in the context of aging studies on clinical instruments (e.g., Kaufman, 2000b, 2001; Kaufman & Horn, 1996), especially the WAIS-III, WAIS-R (Wechsler, 1981) and Kaufman Adolescent and Adult Intelligence Test (KAIT; Kaufman & Kaufman, 1993).

Consistent with the focus on clinical tests of intelligence, we have also eliminated sections and chapters from the first edition on clinical tools that are only tangentially related to IQ assessment, most notably neuropsychological instruments, adaptive behavior surveys, and individual achievement tests.

OUTLINE OF THE BOOK

Assessing Adolescent and Adult Intelligence (2nd ed.) has five parts:

I. Introduction to the Assessment of Adolescent and Adult Intelligence (Chapters 1–3)

II. Individual Differences on Age, Socioeconomic Status, and Other Key Variables (Chapters 4–5)

III. Integration and Application of WAIS-III Research (Chapters 6–9)

IV. Interpretation of the WAIS-III Profile: IQs, Factor Indexes, and Subtest Scaled Scores (Chapters 10–12)

V. Additional Measures of Adolescent and Adult IQ (Chapters 13–15)

Part I includes: Chapter 1, which discusses pertinent historical information, issues regarding validation of the IQ construct, and our philosophy of intelligent testing; Chapter 2, which discusses pressing issues and challenges to the IQ concept (e.g., heritability and malleability of the

IQ); and Chapter 3, which provides the rationale for the WAIS-III subtests for adolescents and adults and traces the empirical and logical continuity from the Wechsler-Bellevue to the WAIS to the WAIS-R and to the WAIS-III.

Part II presents research on individual differences in intelligence associated with pertinent background variables on the WAIS-III and other instruments, notably gender, ethnicity, socioeconomic status, and urban–rural residence (all treated in Chapter 4), and aging across the adult lifespan (Chapter 5).

Parts III and IV are devoted to the WAIS-III and, occasionally, its predecessors (e.g., WAIS-R) or "alternate-form" at age 16 (WISC-III). In Part III, the focus is on research, delving into topics such as administration and scoring (Chapter 6), factor analysis (Chapter 7), and Verbal Performance (V-P) IQ differences, especially as they pertain to lateralized brain lesions (Chapter 8) and other clinical disorders (Chapter 9). The three chapters of Part IV (Chapters 10, 11, and 12) are all devoted to an empirical and clinical approach to interpretation of the WAIS-III multiscore profile.

Part V is composed of three chapters; each focuses exclusively on additional (non-Wechsler) measures for adolescent and adult assessment and integrates them with the WAIS-III: the KAIT (Chapter 13), the Woodcock-Johnson—Third Edition or WJ III (Chapter 14, authored by McGrew, Woodcock, and Ford), and a variety of brief tests of intelligence (Chapter 15). The tests discussed in the latter chapter, for example, the Peabody Picture Vocabulary Test—Third Edition (PPVT-III), the Kaufman Brief Intelligence Test (K-BIT), and the Wechsler Abbreviated Scale of Intelligence (WASI), may be used as supplements to the WAIS-III, KAIT, or WJ III, or may be used instead of comprehensive intelligence tests in certain circumstances (e.g., screening or research purposes).

The discussion of non-Wechsler tests in Part IV is essential to round out the cognitive assessment scene, but the WAIS-III, like the WAIS-R, WAIS, and Wechsler-Bellevue before it, remains the key tool for clinical and neuropsychological evaluation of adolescents and adults and, hence, the focus of all sections of the book. The chapters on clinical applications of intelligence tests, along with the previous parts of the book, place the focus of this text squarely on the WAIS-III.

Wechsler's Scales

Even a casual observer of the clinical or neuropsychological assessment scene is aware that Wechsler's scales are uncontested as the primary cognitive measures of adolescent and adult intelligence. Individuals in their teens and adults of all ages are invariably administered the Wechsler Intelligence Scale for Children—Third Edition (WISC-III; Wechsler, 1991) or the WAIS-III when they are referred to a competent professional for a thorough assessment of their intellectual abilities, usually as part of a clinical, vocational, neuropsychological, or psychoeducational evaluation. The WISC-III is used for adolescents as old as 16 years, while the WAIS-III is used for individuals aged 16 to 89. Therefore, they overlap at age 16, giving clinicians a choice of Wechsler test for that age group.

Using the WISC-III as a clinical and psychometric tool has been discussed elsewhere in a comprehensive text (Kaufman, 1994a). For practical purposes, then, this book is primarily devoted to the WAIS-III, child of the WAIS-R (Wechsler, 1981), grandchild of the WAIS (Wechsler, 1955), and great-grandchild of the Wechsler-Bellevue Form I (Wechsler, 1939).

Clinical Relevance of Theory

To be included in this book in any depth, a topic needs to contribute to a psychologist's understanding of intelligence in the clinical arena, not in the laboratory. For example, the Cattell-Horn-Carroll (CHC; McGrew & Flanagan, 1998) theory—an amalgam of Horn's (1989) expansion of Horn-Cattell Gf-Gc theory and Carroll's (1993, 1997) model of intelligence—is treated throughout the book because it is instrumental in explaining changes in verbal and nonverbal abilities with advancing age, and it (or Horn-Cattell theory) underlies three tests of adolescent and adult intelligence: the Woodcock Johnson Psycho-Educational Battery—Third Edition (WJ III; Woodcock, McGrew, & Mather, 2000), the Stanford-Binet Intelligence Scale, Form IV (Thorndike, Hagen, & Sattler, 1986a), and the KAIT (Kaufman & Kaufman, 1993). In contrast, Sternberg's (1985) three-pronged triarchic theory of intelligence, though popular and widely discussed, is not emphasized because of its limited application to clinical assessment and the interpretation of the WAIS-III and other individual intelligence tests. Currently the Sternberg Triarchic Abilities Test (Sternberg, 1993), a group-administered measure, is available as an unpublished research instrument available from its author. However, if it is ever adapted as an individually administered, commercially published, standardized measure that translates laboratory principles to the domain of the clinical psychologist, neuroclinician, and psychoeducational diagnostician, the theory may become even more popular.

In addition, other theories of intelligence such as Gardner's (1993a, 1993b) theory of multiple intelligences—which defines intelligence as the ability to solve problems, or to create products, that are valued within one or more cultural settings—is also not emphasized in this book. The theory of multiple intelligences calls for measuring intelligences by asking individuals to solve problems in the contexts in which they naturally occur. Although the multiple intelligences theory has attracted much attention in the fields of cognition and education (Kornhaber & Krechevsky, 1995), thus far its practical application to clinical assessment and the interpretation of the WAIS-III and other major standardized individual intelligence tests is limited.

A Short History of IQ Tests

The history of intellectual assessment is largely a history of the measurement of the intelligence of children or retarded adults. Sir Francis Galton (1869, 1883) studied adults and was interested in giftedness when he developed what is often considered the first comprehensive individual test of intelligence (Kaufman, 2000a). But despite Galton's role as the father of the testing movement (Shouksmith, 1970), he did not succeed in constructing a true intelligence test. His measures of simple reaction time, strength of squeeze, or keenness of sight proved to assess sensory and motor abilities, skills that relate poorly to mental ability, and that are far removed from the type of tasks that constitute contemporary intelligence tests.

The Binet-Simon Scales

Alfred Binet and his colleagues (Binet & Henri, 1895; Binet & Simon, 1905, 1908) developed the tasks that survive to the present day in most tests of intelligence for children and adults. Binet (1890a, 1890b) mainly studied children; beginning with systematic developmental observations of his two young daughters, Madeleine and Alice, he concluded that simple tasks like those used by Galton did not discriminate between children and adults. In 1904, the Minister of Public Instruction in Paris appointed Binet to a committee to find a way to distinguish normal from retarded children. But 15 years of qualitative and quantitative investigation of individual differences in children—along with considerable theorizing about mental organization and the development of a specific set of complex, high-level tests to investigate these differences—preceded the "sudden" emergence of the landmark 1905 Binet-Simon intelligence scale (Murphy, 1968).

The 1908 scale was the first to include age levels, spanning the range from III to XIII. This important modification stemmed from Binet and Simon's unexpected discovery that their 1905 scale was useful for much more than classifying a child at one of the three levels of retardation: moron, imbecile, idiot (Matarazzo, 1972). Assessment of older adolescents and adults, however, was not built into the Binet-Simon system until the 1911 revision. That scale was extended to age level XV and included five ungraded adult

tests (Kite, 1916). This extension was not conducted with the rigor that characterized the construction of tests for children, and the primary applications of the scale were for use with school-age children (Binet, 1911).

Measuring the intelligence of adults, except those known to be mentally retarded, was almost an afterthought. But the increased applicability of the Binet-Simon tests for various child-assessment purposes dawned on Binet just prior to his untimely death in 1911: "By 1911 Binet began to foresee numerous uses for his method in child development, in education, in medicine, and in longitudinal studies predicting different occupational histories for children of different intellectual potential" (Matarazzo, 1972, p. 42).

Terman's Stanford-Binet

Lewis Terman was one of several people in the United States who translated and adapted the Binet-Simon scale for use in the United States, publishing a "tentative" revision (Terman & Childs, 1912) 4 years before releasing his painstakingly developed and carefully standardized Stanford Revision and Extension of the Binet-Simon Intelligence Scale (Terman, 1916). This landmark test, soon known simply as the Stanford-Binet, squashed competing tests developed earlier by Goddard, Kuhlmann, Wallin, and Yerkes. Terman's success was undoubtedly due in part to heeding the advice of practitioners whose demand "for more and more accurate diagnoses …raised the whole question of the accurate placing of tests in the scale and the accurate evaluation of the responses made by the child" (Pintner & Patterson, 1925, p. 11).

But, like Binet, Terman (1916) saw intelligence tests useful primarily for the detection of mental deficiency or superiority in children and for the identification of "feeblemindedness" in adults. He cited numerous studies of delinquent adolescents and adult criminals, all of which pointed to the high percentage of mentally deficient juvenile delinquents, prisoners, or prostitutes, and concluded that "there is no investigator who denies the fearful role played by mental deficiency in the production of vice, crime, and delinquency" (p. 9). Terman also saw the potential for using intelligence tests with adults for determining "vocational fitness," but, again, he emphasized employing "a psychologist…to weed out the unfit" or to "determine the minimum 'intelligence quotient' necessary for success in each leading occupation" (p. 17).

Perhaps because of this emphasis on the assessment of children or concern with the lower end of the intelligence distribution, Terman (1916) did not use a rigorous methodology for constructing his adult-level tasks. Tests below the 14-year level were administered to a fairly representative sample of about 1,000 children and early adolescents. To extend the scale above that level, data were obtained from 30 businessmen, 50 high school students, 150 adolescent delinquents, and 150 migrating unemployed men. Based on a frequency distribution of the mental ages of a mere 62 adults (the 30 businessmen and 32 of the high school students above age 16), Terman partitioned the graph into the following MA categories: 13–15 (inferior adults), 15–17 (average adults), and above 17 (superior adults).

The World War I Tests

The infant field of adult assessment grew rapidly with the onset of World War I, particularly after U.S. entry into the war in 1917 (Anastasi & Urbina, 1997; Vane & Motta, 1984). Psychologists saw with increasing clarity the applications of intelligence tests for selecting officers and placing enlisted men in different types of service, apart from their generation-old use for identifying the mentally unfit. Under the leadership of Robert Yerkes and the American Psychological Association, the most innovative psychologists of the day helped translate Binet's tests to a group format. Arthur Otis, Terman's student, was instrumental in leading the creative team that developed the Army Alpha, essentially a group-administered Stanford-Binet, and the Army Beta, a novel group test composed of nonverbal tasks.

Yerkes (1917) opposed Binet's age-scale approach and favored a point-scale methodology, one that advocates selection of tests of specified, important functions rather than a set of tasks that fluctuates greatly with age level and developmental stage. The Army group tests reflect a blend of Yerkes's point-scale approach and Binet's notions of the kind of skills that should be measured when assessing mental ability. The Army Alpha included the Binet-like tests of Directions or Commands, Practical Judgment, Arithmetical Problems, Synonym-Antonym, Dissarranged Sentences, Analogies, and Information. Even the Army Beta had subtests resembling Stanford-Binet tasks: Maze, Cube Analysis, Pictorial Completion, and Geometrical Construction. The Beta also included novel measures like Digit Symbol, Number Checking, and X-O Series (Yoakum & Yerkes, 1920).

Never before or since have tests been normed and validated on samples so large; 1,726,966 men were tested (Vane & Motta, 1984)! Point-scores on the Army Alpha or Army Beta were converted to letter grades ranging from A to D- (the Beta was given only to illiterate and non-English-speaking candidates). Validity was demonstrated by examining the percent of A's obtained by a variety of Army ranks, for example, recruits (7.4%), corporals (16.1%), sergeants (24.0%), and majors (64.4%). In perhaps the first empirical demonstration of the Peter Principle in action, second lieutenants (59.4% A's) outperformed their direct superiors—first lieutenants (51.7%) and captains (53.4%)—while those with ranks above major performed slightly worse than majors (Yoakum & Yerkes, 1920, Table 1). Can there be any more compelling affirmation of the validity of the Army intelligence tests? Another intelligence scale was developed during the war, one that became an alternative for those who could not be tested validly by either the Alpha or Beta. This was the Army Performance Scale Examination, composed of tasks that would become the tools-of-trade for clinical psychologists, school psychologists, and neuropsychologists into the twenty-first century: Picture Completion, Picture Arrangement, Digit Symbol, and Manikin and Feature Profile (Object Assembly). Except for Block Design (developed by Kohs in 1923), Wechsler's influential Performance Scale was added to the Army battery, "[t]o prove conclusively that a man was weakminded and not merely indifferent or malingering" (Yoakum & Yerkes, 1920, p. 10).

Wechsler's Creativity

David Wechsler assembled a test battery in the mid-1930s that comprised subtests developed primarily by Binet and World War I psychologists. His Verbal Scale was essentially a Yerkes point-scale adaptation of Stanford-Binet tasks; his Performance Scale, like other similar nonverbal batteries of the 1920s and 1930s (Cornell & Coxe, 1934; Pintner & Patterson, 1925), was a near replica of the tasks and items making up the individually administered Army Performance Scale Examination.

In essence, Wechsler took advantage of tasks developed by others for nonclinical purposes to develop a clinical test battery. He paired verbal tests that were fine-tuned to discriminate among children of different ages with nonverbal tests that were created for adult males who had flunked both the Alpha and Beta exams—nonverbal tests that were intended to distinguish between the nonmotivated and the hopelessly deficient. Like Terman, Wechsler had the same access to the available tests as did other psychologists; like Terman and Binet before him, Wechsler succeeded because he was a visionary, a man able to anticipate the needs of practitioners in the field.

While others hoped intelligence tests would be psychometric tools to subdivide retarded individuals into whatever number of categories was currently in vogue, Wechsler saw the tests as dynamic clinical instruments. While others looked concretely at intelligence tests as predictors of school success or guides to occupational choice, Wechsler looked abstractly at the tests as a mirror to the hidden personality. With the Great War over, many psychologists returned to a focus on IQ testing as a means of childhood assessment; Wechsler (1939), however, developed the first form of the Wechsler-Bellevue exclusively for adolescents and adults.

Most psychologists saw little need for nonverbal tests when assessing English-speaking individuals other than illiterates. How could it be worth 2 or 3 minutes to administer a single puzzle or block-design item when 10 or 15 verbal items can be given in the same time? Some test developers (e.g., Cornell & Coxe, 1934) felt that Performance scales might be useful for normal, English-speaking people to provide "more varied situations than are provided by verbal tests" (p. 9), and to "test the hypothesis that there is a group factor underlying general concrete ability, which is of importance in the concept of general intelligence" (p. 10).

Wechsler was less inclined to wait a generation for data to accumulate. He followed his clinical instincts and not only advocated the administration of a standard battery of nonverbal tests to everyone but placed the Performance Scale on an equal footing with the more respected Verbal Scale. Both scales would constitute a complete Wechsler-Bellevue battery, and each would contribute equally to the overall intelligence score.

Wechsler also had the courage to challenge the Stanford-Binet monopoly, a boldness not unlike Binet's when the French scientist created his own forum (the journal *L'Année Psychologique*) to challenge the preferred but simplistic Galton sensorimotor approach to intelligence (Kaufman, 2000a). Wechsler met the same type of resistance as Binet, who had had to wait until the French Ministry of Public Instruction "published" his Binet-Simon Scale. When Wechsler's initial efforts to find a publisher for his two-pronged intelligence test met failure, he had no cabinet minister to turn to, so he took matters into his own hands. With a small team of colleagues, he standardized Form I of the Wechsler-Bellevue by himself. Realizing that stratification on socioeconomic background was more crucial than obtaining regional representation, he managed to secure a well-stratified sample from Brooklyn, New York.

The Psychological Corporation agreed to publish Wechsler's battery once it had been standardized, and the rest is history. Although an alternative form of the Wechsler-Bellevue (Wechsler, 1946) was no more successful than Terman and Merrill's (1937) ill-fated Form M, a subsequent downward extension of Form II of the Wechsler-Bellevue (to cover the age range 5 to 15 instead of 10 to 59) produced the wildly successful WISC (Wechsler, 1949). Although the Wechsler scales did not initially surpass the Stanford-Binet in popularity, serving an apprenticeship to the master in the 1940s and 1950s, the WISC and the subsequent revision of the Wechsler-Bellevue, Form I (WAIS; Wechsler, 1955) triumphed in the 1960s. "With the increasing stress on the psychoeducational assessment of learning disabilities in the 1960s, and on neuropsychological evaluation in the 1970s, the Verbal-Performance (V-P) IQ discrepancies and subtest profiles yielded by Wechsler's scales were waiting and ready to overtake the one-score Binet" (Kaufman, 1983b, p. 107).

Irony runs throughout the history of testing. Galton developed statistics to study relationships between variables—statistics that proved to be forerunners of the coefficient of correlation, later perfected by his friend Karl Pearson (DuBois, 1970). The ultimate downfall of Galton's system of testing can be traced directly to coefficients of correlation, which were too low in some crucial (but, ironically, poorly designed) studies of the relationships among intellectual variables (Sharp, 1898–99; Wissler, 1901). Similarly, Terman succeeded with the Stanford-Binet while the Goddard-Binet (Goddard, 1911), the Herring-Binet (Herring, 1922), and other Binet-Simon adaptations failed because he was sensitive to practitioners' needs. He patiently withheld a final version of his Stanford revision until he was certain that each task was appropriately placed at an age level consistent with the typical functioning of representative samples of U.S. children.

Terman continued his careful test development and standardization techniques with the first revised version of the Stanford-Binet (Terman & Merrill, 1937). But 4 years after his death in 1956, his legacy was devalued when the next revision of the Stanford-Binet comprised a merger of Forms L and M, *without a standardization* of the newly formed battery (Terman & Merrill, 1960). The following version saw a restandardization of the instrument, but without a revision of the placement of tasks at each age level (Terman & Merrill, 1973). Unfortunately for the Binet, the abilities of children and adolescents had changed fairly dramatically in the course of a generation, so the 5-year level of tasks (for example) was now passed by the average 4½-year-old!

Terman's methods had been ignored by his successors. The ironic outcome was that Wechsler's approach to assessment triumphed, at least in part because the editions of the Stanford-Binet in the 1960s and 1970s were beset by the same type of flaws as Terman's competitors in the 1910s. The newest Stanford-Binet (Thorndike, Hagen, & Sattler, 1986a, 1986b) attempted to correct these problems and even adopted Wechsler's multisubtest, multiscale format. However, these changes in the Fourth Edition of the Binet were too little and too late to be much threat to the popularity of the Wechsler scales, to offer much contribution to the field of intelligence testing, or to merit the linkage with the Binet tradition.

SURVEYS OF TEST USAGE FOR ADULTS

Surveys of test use in the United States have appeared increasingly in the literature in the past decade. These surveys are usually based on data from clinical agencies and hospitals (Lubin, Larsen, & Matarazzo, 1984; Petrowski & Keller, 1989), school systems (Goh, Teslow, & Fuller,

1981; Hutton, Dubes, & Muir, 1992; Wilson & Reschly, 1996), industry (Swenson & Lindgren, 1952), military settings (Lubin, Larsen, Matarazzo, & Seever, 1986), forensic settings (Lees-Hayley, Smith, Williams, & Dunn, 1996), or private practitioners (Archer, Maruish, Imhof, & Piotrowski, 1991; Camara, Nathan, & Puente, 2000; Harrison et al., 1988; Lubin et al., 1986; Watkins, Campbell, Nieberding, & Hallmark, 1995). Data from such studies of test use are becoming increasingly important in light of the role that managed-care companies play in reimbursement for assessment services. Data from surveys that help determine which are the typical instruments used for various types of assessment and the amount of time practitioners usually spend on an assessment may serve a function in setting standard approved rates for practitioner compensation by managed-care companies. Thus, we reviewed the recent literature to attempt to discover which instruments are most commonly used by practitioners with a variety of backgrounds and find out how much time is typically spent on assessments.

Has Test Use Changed over the Years?

Overall, little substantive change has occurred in the most popular instruments used in the last several decades (Camara et al., 2000). Test usage was first documented by Louttit and Brown (1947), with data collected spanning the mid-1930s to the mid-1940s. Since that early survey, subsequent surveys have shown that the most commonly used tests have not changed much over the years. The Wechsler family of tests has remained on the top of the assessment list for most psychologists, across a variety of settings (Ball, Archer, & Imhof, 1994; Brown & McGuire; 1976; Camara et al., 2000; Harrison et al., 1988; Lubin et al., 1971). The WAIS and WAIS-R have consistently been mentioned in surveys as the most often used adult intelligence tests by clinical psychologists, school psychologists, neu-

ropsychologists, and forensic psychologists, and the WAIS-III will surely follow suit in future surveys.

Many studies of test usage lump together tests from all areas of assessment, including intellectual assessment, personality assessment, adaptive functioning assessment, achievement assessment, and neuropsychological assessment. Nonetheless, even when considering all these different types of assessment, the Wechsler tests remain ranked in the top 10.

Because the WAIS-III is fairly new, we were unable to find any published surveys that reported on the latest adult Wechsler test. The most recent survey at the time that this book went to press had a 2000 publication date, but the authors collected their data in late 1994, before the WAIS-R was revised (Camara et al., 2000). However, it is safe to assume that the WAIS-III will maintain the high ranking enjoyed by the WAIS-R.

Test Usage of 1,500 Psychologists and Neuropsychologists

Camara et al.'s (2000) collected survey data on test usage and assessment from 933 clinical psychologists and 567 neuropsychologists who were randomly selected from the American Psychological Association (APA) and the National Association of Neuropsychology (NAN). The authors were interested in data from practitioners who conducted assessments on a regular basis, so they ultimately conducted their analyses on data from respondents who engaged in 5 or more hours per week of assessment-related services. Thus, the final sample used for ranking test usage comprised 179 clinical psychologists (19% of the clinical psychologist respondents) and 447 neuropsychologists (79% of the neuropsychologist respondents). Table 1.1 displays the hours spent administering, scoring, and interpreting psychological tests during a typical week, for the total number of respondents to the survey ($N = 1,500$).

TABLE 1.1 Hours spent administering, scoring, and interpreting psychological tests during a typical week

	Clinical Psychologists		Neuropsychologists	
Hours	**n (%)**	**Cumulative %**	**n (%)**	**Cumulative %**
0–4	755 (80.9)	100.0	116 (20.5)	100.0
5–9	62 (6.6)	18.7	62 (10.9)	78.8
10–14	39 (4.2)	12.1	92 (16.2)	67.9
15–20	36 (3.9)	7.9	105 (18.5)	51.7
More than 20	37 (4.0)	4.0	188 (33.2)	33.2
No response	4 (<1)	<1	4 (<1)	<1
Total	**933 (100.0)**		**567 (100.0)**	

NOTE: Data are from "Psychological Test Usage in Professional Psychology," by W. J. Camara, J. S. Nathan, & A. E. Puente, 2000, *Professional Psychology: Research and Practice, 31,* 141–154. Copyright © by the American Psychological Association. Reprinted with permission.

Interestingly, the sample of neuropsychologists spent many more hours per week doing assessments than did the sample of clinical psychologists. Among neuropsychologists, almost 80% spent at least 5 assessment hours per week and about half spent at least 15 hours a week conducting assessments. For clinical psychologists, the corresponding values were about 20% and 8%.

According to Camara et al. (2000), of the clinical psychologists who performed assessments 5 or more hours per week, the majority of their assessment time was spent conducting intellectual or achievement testing (34%) and personality testing (32%). For neuropsychologists, their assessment time was fairly equally divided between neuropsychological assessment (26%), intellectual or achievement assessment (20%), and personality assessment (20%). Watkins et al. (1995) reported that 8% of a clinical psychologist's total time practicing was spent on intellectual assessment, and 12% of the total time was spent on personality assessment ($N = 412$). In a study examining assessment practices of school psychologists ($N = 389$), respondents reported that they spent about one half of their time in assessment-related activities (*Mdn* = 50%) (Hutton et al., 1992).

How Frequently Are Tests Used?

As mentioned, the Wechsler tests have held on strongly to their place at the top of the heap of tests administered by practitioners over the years. In Camara et al.'s (2000) study, clinical psychologists ranked the WAIS-R the number one test administered and neuropsychologists ranked it number two. Other Wechsler tests were also at the top of the list: clinical psychologists rated the WISC-III number 3 and neuropsychologists rated the Wechsler Memory Scale—Revised number 3. Camara et al. (2000) did not separate children's tests from adults' tests, or measures of intelligence from other measures, such as personality functioning. Clinical psychologists ranked the Minnesota Multiphasic Personality Inventory—Second Edition (MMPI-II) as the number 1 most frequently used test and neuropsychologists ranked it as number 2. Other studies report similar findings: in a survey tapping tests administered by psychologists to adolescent clients, the Wechsler scales were the number one most frequently used tests (Archer, Maruish, Imhof, & Piotrowski, 1991); in a survey of tests administered by forensic neuropsychologists, the WAIS-R, MMPI-II, and WMS-R were ranked numbers 1, 2, and 3, respectively (Lees-Hayley et al., 1996); and school psychologists also reported the Wechsler scales as the most frequently used assessment tools (Hutton et al., 1992; Wilson & Reschly, 1996).

Administration Time and Implications for Reimbursement

Camara et al. (2000) also examined the mean time to administer, score, and interpret a battery of tests. The median number of minutes reportedly spent by clinical psychologists on the WAIS-R was administration (75), scoring (20), and interpretation (30), for a total time of a little over 2 hours; similar values were reported by neuropsychologists. Considering that the WAIS-R (or WAIS-III now) is only one component of a full battery, the total time to administer, score, and interpret an entire battery is significantly greater. Clearly, the time varies depending on the type of testing necessary to answer the referral questions. That being said, Camara and colleagues found that, on average, psychologists spent about 3.5 to 4.25 hours on administering, scoring, and interpreting an assessment battery. However, the authors concede that some areas of assessment take substantially longer than these average times, especially intellectual and neuropsychological assessment.

The results from Camara et al.'s (2000) study have implications for the reimbursement of assessments by third parties, especially managed-care companies. The authors note that assessment services are often limited to 2 hours of reimbursable time, the approximate time the psychologists in Camara et al.'s (2000) study spent administering, scoring, and interpreting the WAIS-R. However, because the Camara data demonstrated that trained practitioners require at least 4 hours to complete a comprehensive assessment, it is clear that clinicians are limited in what types of assessments they can provide, if they want to be reimbursed for their time. The consequences of limited reimbursement for assessment may be that the number of psychologists conducting assessments will diminish. Already, Camara and colleagues note that almost 90% of clinical psychologists spend less than 10 hours a week on assessments (see Table 1.1).

For What Purposes Are Adults Given Intelligence Tests?

It is clear that the WAIS-R and WAIS-III are widely used in the field of assessment today, but why are these and other intelligence tests typically administered to adults? Harrison et al. (1988) asked that question specifically of a group of 277 clinical psychologists. In a survey, respondents were asked to rank seven purposes for which they would administer an intelligence test. The number 1 purpose was to measure the potential or cognitive capacity of a person. Table 1.2 lists the seven purposes and how important respondents felt each was. Although nearly 40–50% of psychologists ranked educational and vocational placement or interventions as a purpose for assessing adults, very few felt these are the main reasons for conducting an assessment (6–17%). Clearly, the data show that clinicians think that the most important reasons for assessing adults are to measure cognitive potential, obtain clinically relevant information, and assess functional integrity of the brain.

Conclusions

The Camara et al. (2000) survey results indicate that the WAIS-R, and, intuitively, the WAIS-III, is supreme among assessment tools used to assess adolescent and adult functioning by clinical psychologists and neuropsychologists. These results, in combination with results of other studies, show that the Wechsler tests are equally

TABLE 1.2   Purposes for using intelligence tests when assessing adults

Purpose	% of Psychologists Who Assess Adults for This Purpose	% of Psychologists Who Rank This Purpose as Very Important
Measure potential of capacity	85.2	58.5
Obtain clinically relevant information	85.2	53.1
Assess functional integrity of brain	77.6	43.3
Determine educational placement	48.4	17.0
Determine vocational placement	45.5	12.3
Develop educational interventions	44.0	10.8
Develop vocational interventions	39.4	5.8

NOTE: Data are from Harrison et al. (1988), based on 277 respondents asked to list all the purposes for which "you generally use a standardized intelligence test in your assessment battery" and "then rank the ones you checked in order of their importance with a 1 as the most important." The "*% of psychologists who rank this purpose as very important*" equals the percentage of the total group of 2,787 who assigned each purpose a ranking of 1 or 2.

popular in other domains such as forensic psychology, school psychology, hospital settings, and outpatient clinics. The percentage of clinical time spent conducting assessments varies across specialties within psychology (e.g., clinical, school, neuropsychology). However, the typical amount of time necessary to conduct an assessment is similar across domains, although it fluctuates depending on the type of assessment necessary. The inconsistency between the amount of time typically allowed to be reimbursed for assessment services and the actual amount of time spent in assessment-related services was pointed out by Camara et al. (2000). Such inconsistency may affect the types and numbers of assessments performed by clinicians. Notwithstanding the fees and reimbursement issues, the popularity of the Wechsler scales and the primary reasons for assessing adults remain unchanged. There appears to be a strong need for tools to assess cognitive capabilities and obtain related clinical information in adults, and the WAIS-III is there to meet those needs for those who choose to conduct assessments. However, clinicians would be wise to consider theory-based alternatives to

Wechsler's scales, such as the KAIT and WJ III Tests of Cognitive Ability for adolescents and adults, and the Cognitive Assessment System (CAS; Naglieri & Das, 1997a, 1997b) for adolescents. Also, in view of time constraints imposed by managed-care criteria, reliable and valid brief intelligence tests may need to be weighed as possible assessment options (see Chapter 15).

VALIDITY OF THE IQ CONSTRUCT FOR ADOLESCENTS AND ADULTS

Matarazzo (1972, Chapters 6, 7, and 12) devoted most of three chapters to support the validity of the IQ construct, Jensen (1980) addressed the issue from both theoretical and empirical perspectives (his Chapters 6 and 8, respectively), and Brody (1985) published a thought-provoking chapter on "The Validity of Tests of Intelligence." These three esteemed psychologists concluded, in essence, that the IQ construct, as measured by contemporary intelligence tests, is valid when defined within the societal context and when the IQ's limitations are kept fully in mind. In a survey of psychologists and educational specialists with expertise in areas related to intelligence testing, Snyderman and Rothman (1987) found that, overall, experts hold positive attitudes about the validity and usefulness of intelligence and aptitude tests. Although the validity of the IQ construct and the tests purported to assess it are important to this text, we treat it cursorily here because it has been thoroughly discussed elsewhere. Our focus is on the following aspects of IQ's validity: prediction of academic achievement, relationship to educational attainment, relationship to occupational membership, and prediction of job performance.

Prediction of Academic Achievement

The age-old IQ criterion of prediction of school achievement has been explored in thousands of studies across the age range, and Matarazzo (1972) concluded a generation ago that a correlation of about .50 exists between IQ and school performance. Coefficients are typically a bit higher in elementary school and lower in college (Brody, 1985). The overall value of .50 is high enough to support the validity of the IQ for the purpose that Binet originally intended it, but low enough to indicate that about 75% of the variance in school achievement is accounted for by factors other than IQ. Some more recent studies with newer, theory-based intelligence tests have reported higher coefficients in the .60–.70 range for the Horn-based WJ-R (McGrew, Werder, & Woodcock, 1991) and for the Luria-based K-ABC and CAS (Naglieri, 1999, Table 5.5) between intelligence and achievement. In fact, these coefficients for the theory-based tests are similar in magnitude to the values obtained with the Third Editions of the WISC and WAIS, using WIAT scores as the criteria (Psychological Corporation,

1992, Table D.6). Hence, more recent studies with new and revised instruments suggest that IQ may explain as much as 50% of school achievement; however, even that substantially higher value still leaves 50% for other variables.

For adults, the IQ-achievement correlations are illustrated by correlations between the WAIS-III and the Wechsler Individual Achievement Test (WIAT; Psychological Corporation, 1992). Overall the correlations between the WAIS-III IQs and the WIAT Composites (Reading, Math, and Language) range between .53 and .81, with most correlations in the .60s and .70s, and a median value of .70 (Psychological Corporation, 1997). The correlations between the WAIS-III Indexes and the WIAT Composites were slightly lower than those with the IQs, with rs ranging from .42 to .77 with a median value of .61.

Wechsler's Verbal IQ consistently correlates more strongly with achievement than does the Performance IQ. Correlations between the WAIS-III and WIAT exemplify that fact: V-IQ correlations range from .70 to .81 with the WIAT Composites, whereas P-IQ correlations range from .53 to .69 with the WIAT. Data from the WAIS-III indexes also mirror the IQ data. In WAIS-R studies (e.g., Ryan & Rosenberg, 1983; Spruill & Beck, 1986), mean correlation coefficients were .65 for Verbal and .54 for Performance. In five WAIS studies cited by Matarazzo (1972, p. 284), V-IQ correlated higher than P-IQ with high school rank (.63 versus .43) and college grade-point average (GPA) (.47 versus .24). Numerous WISC-III investigations summarized by Gridley and Roid (1998) have also shown stronger correlations between achievement ability and Verbal IQ than between Performance IQ and achievement.

In general, the use of the WAIS-III for predicting college achievement is likely to produce coefficients lower than the values in the .60s observed when standardized achievement tests are the criteria. Matarazzo (1972, p. 284), for example, cited a coefficient of .44 between WAIS FS-IQ and GPA for 335 college students with a mean IQ of 115, and Jensen (1980, p. 330) reported a median correlation of .40 between the General Intelligence test of the General Aptitude Test Battery (GATB) and college grades in 48 different samples (comprising 5,561 students).

Even if correlation coefficients involving the WAIS-R or WAIS-III account for only 15% to 20% of the variability in college students' grades (compared to 25–50% for elementary and high school), such values nonetheless strongly support the Wechsler scales' validity for educational purposes. Correlations for college students are attenuated substantially, having nothing to do with the quality of the instrument because of (1) the restricted range of IQs found in highly selected samples, (2) the questionable reliability and validity of the GPA criterion (it, too, is usually restricted to a 5-point scale from A to F, and college grading systems fluctuate notoriously from instructor to instructor), and (3) the increasing role played by nonintellective factors such as motivation and study habits.

Relationship of IQ to Education

For children's intelligence tests, correlations between IQ and school achievement are among the best evidences of validity, but those coefficients are less valuable for adult tests. The best arguments for the validity of an adult test are the relationships between IQ and formal education and between IQ and occupational level (a variable that correlates substantially with years of schooling; Kaufman, 1990). Success in school is a key task of children and adolescents; life accomplishments are the goals of an adult.

Logically, people who score higher on a so-called intelligence test should advance higher within the formal education hierarchy and should assume positions within the more prestigious occupations. Which is cause and which is effect is not relevant to this point. Perhaps individuals score higher on IQ tests because of what they learn in school; perhaps they proceed to higher levels of education because they are smart to begin with; or perhaps these two variables combine in some way. In any case, a strong relationship between education and IQ supports the construct that underlies tests that purport to measure intelligence.

This relationship is explored in depth for the WAIS-III in Chapter 4, and again in Chapter 8 regarding V-P differences and brain damage. The present discussion gives only an overview of the relationship between years of schooling and WAIS-III scores in order to illustrate the overwhelming validity support for the WAIS-III when educational attainment is the criterion.

Educational data that are available for the WAIS-III Full Scale IQ are age-corrected z scores, predicted by education; these data were kindly provided by Heaton, Manly, Taylor, and Tulsky (personal communication, September, 2000), with the permission of The Psychological Corporation, and are discussed more fully in Chapter 4. Briefly, mean Full Scale IQs for 16- to 89-year-olds with different formal education levels ranged from 80.5 for individuals with 0–7 years of schooling to 116.8 for those with 17 or more years.

The two extreme educational groups differ by about 36 points, more than two standard deviations! These differences tend to be larger for Verbal than Performance subtests, but they are nonetheless substantial even for tasks like Block Design or Digit Symbol-Coding that are not specifically taught in the classroom. The mean scaled-score differences for those with 17 or more years of schooling versus those with 7 or less years of schooling (for ages 20 to 89) on two selected WAIS-III subtests, one closely related to the specific content taught in school (Vocabulary) and one unrelated to curriculum (Block Design), are 6.60 and 4.47. Specifically, on Vocabulary the mean scaled score for those with 17+ years of schooling was 13.33, whereas it was only 6.83 for those with seven or fewer years of schooling. In contrast, on Block Design mean scaled score for those with 17+ years of schooling was 11.92, yet it was only 7.45 for those with seven or fewer years of schooling. Thus, the very highly educated adults scored 2.2 *SD* higher than relatively uneducated adults on Vocabulary and 1.5 *SD* higher on Block Design.

These data show that relatively uneducated people perform poorly on both school-related and school-unrelated tasks, and that both types of tests are substantially related to formal education. As indicated, however, highly educated adults have a greater advantage on crystallized than on fluid tasks (i.e., on Information or Vocabulary than on Block Design). Data from the Fels Longitudinal Study (McCall, 1977) reveal that childhood IQs correlate about .50 (±.10) with both adult educational and occupational attainment, stabilizing at that relatively high level at ages 7 to 8 for males and females.

The strong relationship between IQ and formal education should not obscure the considerable *variability* of IQs earned by individuals with the same educational attainment. Fluctuations in WAIS-R IQ by education level were shown by Reynolds et al. (1987), and are presented in Table 4.5. These results indicate that each level of educational attainment is accompanied by a wide range of Full Scale IQs. For example, individuals with some college education have a higher mean IQ by about 11 points than those with some high school, but their IQ ranges are fairly similar: 76–139 for those with 13–15 years of schooling compared to 59–146 for those with 9–11 years of schooling.

IQ and Occupation

For ages 20 to 54, WAIS-R data provide additional validation evidence for Wechsler's IQs by examining mean scores earned by adults actively engaged in different levels of occupation (Reynolds et al., 1987). Adolescents have been eliminated from consideration because occupational data are based on their parents' occupation, and the 55–74-year-olds have been eliminated because two thirds are categorized as "Not in Labor Force."

Occupational data are treated in depth in Chapter 4, and are summarized here to illustrate

the validity of the IQ construct. Mean Full Scale IQs are shown in Table 1.3 for five categories of occupation, listed in order of the average educational level (from high to low) that typifies each category. These values range from about 87 for unskilled workers to 112 for professionals and technical workers.

The 25-point difference between professionals and unskilled workers, combined with the educational data, gives strong support to the construct underlying Wechsler's Full Scale IQs for adult samples; occupational and educational data presented in Chapter 4 give substantial validity support for the separate Verbal and Performance IQs as well.

In general, the relationship between occupation, education, and WAIS-R IQs for persons 75 years and older was similar to that found by Reynolds et al. (1987) for persons 16 to 74 (Ryan, Paolo, & Dunn, 1995). When past occupation was measured in an elderly sample (ages 75+), individuals who were retired professionals or managers earned WAIS-R Full Scale IQs that were 15.78 points higher than those who were retired

TABLE 1.3   Mean WAIS-R Full Scale IQs for 20- to 54-year-olds employed in different levels of occupation

Occupational Group	Mean WAIS-R Full Scale IQ
1. Professional and technical	112.4
2. Managers and administrators, clerical workers, and sales workers	103.6
3. Skilled workers (craftsmen and foremen)	100.7
4. Semiskilled workers (operatives, service workers—including private household—farmers, and farm managers)	92.3
5. Unskilled workers (laborers, farm laborers, farm foremen)	87.1

NOTE: Data are from Reynolds et al. (1987).

laborers or operatives. Education was also an important variable in this elderly sample, as it accounted for 30% to 43% of the variance in the WAIS-R IQs. Similar to results with younger adults, there were substantial differences (17.05 points) between those with the most education (12 or more years) and those with less formal schooling (0 to 11 years). As the relationship between education and occupation is known to be quite strong, Ryan et al. (1995) performed analyses to determine whether preretirement occupation would explain an additional amount of variance in IQ over and above age and education. Occupation did, in fact, contribute significantly to all WAIS-R IQs, explaining an additional 3% to 6% of the variance in the Verbal, Performance, and Full Scale IQs, beyond that of age and education.

When IQs are provided for specific jobs instead of general categories, even wider discrepancies emerge between diverse occupations. For example, Matarazzo (1972, pp. 178–180) cites numerous studies and his own considerable clinical experience to show that physicians, medical students, dentists, university professors, psychiatrists, executives in industry, scientists, and attorneys have consistently averaged IQs of 125 on the Wechsler-Bellevue and WAIS. In a study of 35 medical students, Mitchell, Grandy, and Lupo (1986) reported mean Full Scale IQs in the same range on both the WAIS (124.5) and WAIS-R (120.8).

The wide range of mean scores by people in different occupations is further illustrated by a comprehensive (N = 39,600) 1970 U.S. Department of Labor study cited by Jensen (1980, pp. 341–342). Mean IQs on the GATB General Intelligence scale were provided for 444 specific occupations, and ranged from 55 for Tomato Peeler to 143 for Mathematician. Although the GATB General Intelligence score correlated .89 with the WAIS (Jensen, 1980), the two scales have different standard deviations. When the GATB scores for Tomato Peelers and Mathematicians are converted to the Wechsler metric, the means become 66 and 132, respectively. This discrepancy is not as impressive as the 88-point

difference on the GATB scale (mean of 100, SD of 20), but it nonetheless provides additional evidence of the IQ construct's validity.

Figure 1.1, adapted from Matarazzo (1972, p. 178) and Jensen (1980, p. 113) and modified based on WAIS-R data reported by Reynolds et al. (1987), presents graphically the educational or occupational referents of different IQ levels. However, these values are just the averages for different jobs or educational accomplishments. As Matarazzo (1972) and Jensen (1980) stress, adults in each occupation or educational category vary considerably in IQ range. Table 4.5 presents pertinent data that reveal the fairly wide range of IQs for individuals from the same occupational category (as mentioned previously, this same table shows the wide IQ ranges for people with different levels of education). For occupational groups, the range is relatively small for people employed in routine, menial jobs usually reserved for the mentally retarded, but substantial IQ ranges characterize members in jobs as diverse as physicians or policemen or even unskilled construction workers.

The strong relationship depicted here between IQ and occupation may be an artifact of the even stronger relationship described previously between IQ and educational attainment. Occupation and education correlate substantially, particularly because advanced formal education is frequently a prerequisite for many high-prestige occupations. Gottfredson and Brown (1981) observed an interesting age-related finding in the occupation–education relationship in their large-scale longitudinal study. Occupational status correlated a modest .17–.20 with years of schooling at ages 18–20 years, but increased at age 22 (.45) and age 24 (.60) before plateauing in the mid-.60s for 26- and 28-year-olds. Gottfredson and Brown interpreted these age-related findings as a function of the facts that (1) the later entrants into the work force are brighter and better educated, and (2) among those already employed, the smarter and more educated adults advance from low-level to high-level positions.

Crawford and Allan (1997), studying a group of 200 adults ages 16 to 83 (M = 44.3 years) from

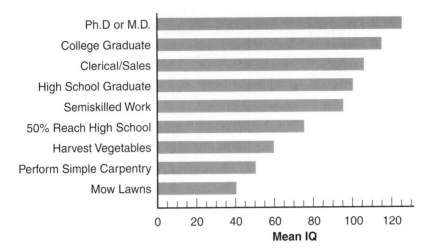

FIGURE 1.1

Mean Wechsler adult IQs that correspond to different educational and occupational accomplishments (based on data on Table 7–3 of Matarazzo, 1972, p. 178; data in Table 4.5 in Jensen, 1980, p. 113; WAIS-R standardization data reported by Reynolds et al., 1987).

the United Kingdom, found that occupation was a slightly stronger predictor of WAIS-R IQ than was education. The correlations for this sample between occupation and FS-IQ (.65), education and FS-IQ (.58), and education and occupation (.65) are within the ranges of what has been previously reported. However, Crawford and Allan found that occupation was the single best predictor of IQ for all three scales in a stepwise regression. Occupational classification accounted for 42%, 43%, and 25% of the variance in FS-IQ, V-IQ, and P-IQ, respectively. Education and age significantly increased the variance predicted, with final models predicting 32% to 53% of the variance in the IQs. Thus, it appears that occupation in and of itself is an important demographic variable contributing to IQ.

Regardless, years of schooling "is the single most important determinant of occupational status in United States society" (Brody, 1985, p. 361). Brody states further that the results of path analysis in several studies indicate that IQ has "a large influence on educational attainment and *relatively little indirect influence on occupational status*" (pp. 361–362, italics ours)—that is, separate from the IQ–education relationship.

Prediction of Job Performance

Average correlations between general intelligence and job proficiency are traditionally in the .20s (Ghiselli, 1966, 1973). However, because the predictors and criteria are typically restricted in variability due to selection factors and other practical limitations of test validation in industrial settings, some have argued that such coefficients require statistical correction to reflect more accurately the "true" relationship between IQ and job success (Hunter & Hunter, 1984). For the purpose here (i.e., to determine the validity of the *theoretical* construct underlying intelligence tests), the corrected values seem more appropriate.

In an ambitious meta-analysis of hundreds of studies relating intelligence to job performance, Hunter (1986) concluded that "general cognitive ability has high validity predicting performance ratings and training success in all jobs" (p. 359). He organized data from three major sources, correcting coefficients for restriction of range in all cases, and for attenuation (imperfect test reliability) in the first two sets of studies: (1) Ghiselli's lifework, involving several summaries of a quarter-century's worth of validity studies in industry on the prediction of job proficiency and success in training programs; (2) 515 validation studies conducted by the U.S. Employment Service with the GATB, 425 on job proficiency ($N = 32,124$) and 90 on training success ($N = 6,496$); and (3) U.S. military studies of training success in mechanical, clerical, electronic, and general technical fields (828 studies totalling 472,539 subjects).

Coefficients of correlation between intelligence and job proficiency (performance ratings) were consistently higher for complex jobs than for those demanding less complexity. The Ghiselli studies produced substantial corrected correlations for the complex jobs of manager (.53), clerk (.54), and salesperson (.61). Coefficients in the mid-.40s were obtained for jobs of medium complexity (e.g., crafts and trades), while values in the high .20s and .30s were typical of low complexity jobs like vehicle operator. Similar averages emerged when Hunter (1986) grouped the U.S. Employment Service studies by complexity: high complexity (r = .58), medium (.51), and low (.40). Gottfredson (1997) suggested that general intelligence (g) has pervasive utility in work settings because it is related to one's ability to deal with cognitive complexity. She noted that the more complex a work task, the greater the advantages that higher g confers in performing it well.

Intelligence correlated even more impressively with success in training than it did with job performance. Further, the coefficients obtained for various training programs were about equally good, regardless of job complexity. The average corrected coefficient for the 828 studies of training success conducted by the U.S. military was .62, with values hovering around that overall value for each of the four job families (i.e., me-

chanical, clerical, electronic, and general technical). Coefficients from the Ghiselli summaries ranged from .37 (vehicle operator) to .87 (protective professions) with a median correlation of .65 across seven categories of jobs. The 90 training studies carried out by the U.S. Employment Service yielded average values of .50 to .65 (median = .56) for jobs grouped into four categories.

Hunter showed further that validity coefficients are even higher when objective work samples of job performance are used instead of subjective supervisor ratings. Based on a handful of particularly well-designed investigations that used objective criteria to evaluate job proficiency, corrected correlations were .75 in civilian data and .53 in military data.

In a more recent synthesis of the vocational data, Schmidt and Hunter (1998) reviewed 85 years of research in personnel selection, focusing on the results of the best meta-analyses, including much of the data reviewed in the preceding paragraphs. They concluded once again that IQ (referred to as general mental ability or GMA) had strong validity, and that the validity could be increased substantially when other predictors are considered as well: .63 (GMA + work sample or GMA + structured interview) or .65 (GMA + integrity test). Based on their review, Schmidt and Hunter concluded: (1) "of all procedures that can be used for all jobs, whether entry level or advanced, [GMA] has the highest validity and lowest application cost" (p. 264); (2) "the research evidence for the validity of GMA measures for predicting job performance is stronger than that for any other measure" (p. 264); and (3) "GMA has been shown to be the best available predictor of job-related learning" (p. 264).

Jensen's (1980) analysis of some of the same data summarized by Hunter (1986) presents a more sobering view of the ability of intelligence tests to predict job performance and training success. Coefficients reported by Hunter were corrected for restriction of range and, usually, for attenuation as well; these corrections inflate the correlations by estimating their magnitude in "what-if" situations. The correction for attenuation (test unreliability) is particularly questionable, however, because, by definition, tests are not perfectly reliable. Jensen (1980, pp. 347–350) notes that Ghiselli's actual coefficients were in the .20 to .25 range, on the average, and that the median coefficient for the GATB General Intelligence score for 537 U.S. Employment Service studies was .27.

Similarly, Jensen demonstrates that correlations are greater for more complexions but that the values for jobs with high complexity are in the .35 to .47 range. Jensen also notes that the average correlation between IQ and success in training programs is close to .50, not the values of about .60 reported by Hunter. These criticisms apply as well to the more recent review by Schmidt and Hunter (1998).

Data from both Hunter (1986) and Jensen (1980) support the IQ construct as reasonably valid in its role as predictor of job success, although the claims made by Hunter may be exaggerated by his incautious and, perhaps, overzealous correction of obtained coefficients. From a theoretical perspective, the data set evaluated by Hunter and Schmidt and Hunter (1998) give excellent support of the construct validity of IQ in vocational settings. In a practical sense, however, the obtained correlations are often the most pertinent. In all instances, readers are wise to heed the cautions of two expert statisticians and psychometricians, Lloyd Humphreys and Robert Linn, regarding Hunter's correction procedures. Humphreys (1986), in his commentary on Hunter's article (and other papers as well) in a special issue of the *Journal of Vocational Behavior*, wrote, "Given the heterogeneity among the many studies to be aggregated, corrections for measurement error and restriction of range of talent are rough estimates at best" (p. 427). In a similar commentary, Linn (1986) asserted that "adjustments for range restriction and attenuation are nontrivial[;]... correlations that are changed dramatically by adjustments should always be viewed with caution" (pp. 440–441).

Although IQ seems to be a valid predictor of job performance, the general findings from this line of research indicate that a relatively small amount of the variance in job performance is ac-

counted for by IQ. At worst, the average validity coefficient between measures of cognitive ability and measures of cognitive ability is .20 (Ghiselli, 1966; Wigdor & Garner, 1982), accounting for only 4% of the variance, and, at best, the average validity coefficient is about .5 (Hunter & Hunter, 1984; Schmidt & Hunter, 1998), accounting for 25% of the variance in job performance. As Sternberg, Wagner, Williams, and Horvath (1995) point out, these values leave at least three-quarters of the variance unexplained. Sternberg et al. suggest that practical intelligence (common sense) is a variable that may contribute to the prediction of job performance, above and beyond what traditional IQ contributes. Practical intelligence, or "tacit knowledge," has only a small relationship to general intelligence (Sternberg et al., 1995). When tasks of tacit knowledge are used to predict managerial performance, tacit knowledge accounts for substantial and significant increases in variance above and beyond IQ (Wagner & Sternberg, 1990). Using measures of traditional intelligence in conjunction with measures of tacit knowledge may more effectively predict job performance than reliance on one of these measures alone (Sternberg et al., 1995), although reliable and construct-valid measures of tacit knowledge are not yet available.

THE INTELLIGENT TESTING PHILOSOPHY

One's philosophy regarding the interpretation of individually administered clinical tests should be an intelligent one. The approach we will be describing has been spelled out in detail for various Wechsler tests (Kaufman, 1979a, 1994a; Kaufman & Lichtenberger, 1999, 2000), applied to the K-ABC (Kamphaus & Reynolds, 1987), and applied to a variety of other clinical and neuropsychological instruments (Reynolds & Fletcher-Janzen, 1989). Consequently, our goal here is only to summarize the assumptions underlying the approach and the basic methodology that characterizes it. The essential method is the same, whether applied to tests for children, adolescents, or adults. Intelligent testing rests on five assumptions, discussed in the sections below:

1. IQ tasks measure what the individual has learned.
2. IQ tasks are samples of behavior and are not exhaustive.
3. IQ tests like the WAIS-III, KAIT, and WJ III assess mental functioning under fixed experimental conditions.
4. IQ tests are optimally useful when they are interpreted from an information-processing model.
5. Hypotheses generated from IQ test profiles should be supported with data from multiple sources.

IQ Tasks Measure What the Individual Has Learned

This concept comes directly from Wesman's (1968) introduction of the intelligent testing approach. The content of all tasks, whether verbal or nonverbal, is learned within a culture. The learning may take place formally in the school, casually in the home, or incidentally through everyday life. As a measure of past learning, the IQ test is best thought of as a kind of achievement test, not as a simple measure of aptitude. Like the SAT, IQ tests assess "*developed abilities*, broadly applicable intellectual skills and knowledge that develop slowly over time through the individual's experiences both in and out of school…[that are] not tied to the content of any specific course or field of study" (Anastasi, 1988, p. 330).

The interaction between learning potential and availability of learning experiences is too complex to ponder for any given person, making the whole genetics–environment issue of theoretical value, but impractical and irrelevant for the interpretation of that person's test profile. Even the sophisticated scientific challenges to the IQ construct issued by Lezak (1988a) and Siegel (1999) or the emotional, less informed indictments of IQ tests handed out by members of the public, become almost a side issue when the tests are viewed and interpreted simply as measures of accomplishment. The term *achievement* implies a societal responsibility to upgrade the level of those who have not attained it; the term *aptitude* implies something inborn and personal and can justify a withdrawal of educational resources (Flaugher, 1978).

Issues of heredity versus environment and the validity of the IQ construct are meaningful for understanding the multifaceted intelligence construct; the accumulating research helps test developers, practitioners, and theoreticians appreciate the foundation of the tests used to measure intelligence; and the IQ tests, as vehicles for the research, are essential sources of group data for use in scientific study of these topics. But all of the controversy loses meaning for each specific person referred for evaluation when the clinician administers an IQ test to study and interpret just what the person has or has not learned and to help answer the practical referral questions.

IQ Tasks Are Samples of Behavior and Are Not Exhaustive

The individual Wechsler subtests, or the subtests that compose the KAIT or WJ III, do not reflect the essential ingredients of intelligence whose mastery implies some type of ultimate life achievement. They, like tasks developed by Binet and other test constructors, are more or less arbitrary samples of behavior. Teaching people how to solve similarities, assemble blocks to match abstract designs, or repeat digits backward will not make them smarter in any broad or generalizable way. What we are able to infer from the person's success on the tasks and style of responding to them is important; the specific, unique aspect of intellect that each subtest measures is of minimal consequence.

Limitations in the selection of tasks necessarily mean that one should be cautious in generalizing the results to circumstances that are removed from the one-on-one assessment of a finite number of skills and processing strategies. Intelligence tests should, therefore, be routinely supplemented by other formal and informal measures of cognitive, clinical, and neuropsychological functioning to facilitate the assessment of mental functioning as part of psychodiagnosis. The global IQ on any test, no matter how comprehensive, does not equal a person's total capacity for intellectual accomplishment.

IQ Tests Like the WAIS-III, KAIT, and WJ III Assess Mental Functioning under Fixed Experimental Conditions

Standardized administration and scoring means conducting an experiment with $N = 1$ every time an examiner tests someone on an intelligence test. For the results of this experiment to be meaningful, the experimenter–examiner must adhere precisely to the wording in the manual, give appropriate probes as defined in the instructions, time each relevant response diligently, and score each item exactly the way comparable responses were scored during the normative procedure. Following these rules prevents examiners from applying a flexible clinical investigatory procedure during the administration (like Piaget's semistructured *méthode clinique*), from teaching the task or giving feedback to a person who urgently desires this intervention, or from cleverly dislodging from the crevices of a person's brain his or her maximum response to each test item.

It is necessary to be an exceptional clinician to establish and maintain rapport and to weave the standardized administration into a natural, pleasant interchange between examiner and subject. Clinical skills are also essential when observing and interpreting a person's myriad behaviors during the examination and during interpretation of all available information and data when interpreting the profile of test scores. But it is vital for an examiner to follow the standardized procedures to the letter while administering the test; otherwise, the standard scores yielded for the person will be invalid and meaningless. To violate the rules is to negate the value of the meticulous set of norms obtained under experimental conditions by most major test-publishing companies for their tests.

The testing situation has a certain built-in artificiality by virtue of the stopwatch, the precise words to be spoken, and the recording of almost everything spoken by the examinee. A person with excellent visual–spatial and manipulative skills might perform slowly and ineffectively on Object Assembly because of anxiety caused by the time pressure; or a person with an impressive store of general knowledge and a good common-sense understanding of social situations may fail several Information and Comprehension items because of failure to understand some of the questions. It is tempting to give credit to a puzzle solved "just 2 or 3 seconds overtime" or to simplify the wording of a question that the person "certainly knows the answer to." But the good examiner will resist these temptations, knowing that the people in the reference group did not receive such help. Testing the limits on a subtest can often give valuable insight into the reasons for failure or confusion, so long as this flexible, supplemental testing occurs *after* the score has been recorded under appropriate conditions.

In an experiment, the empirical results are of limited value until they are interpreted and discussed in the context of pertinent research and theory by a knowledgeable researcher. By the same token, the empirical outcomes of an IQ test are often meaningless until put into context by the examiner. That is the time for a clinician's acumen and flexibility to be displayed.

IQ Tests Are Optimally Useful When They Are Interpreted from an Information-Processing Model

One of the examiner's jobs in an assessment is to identify specific areas of dysfunction. One model that has been particularly useful to clinicians in delineating areas of dysfunction is the information-processing model (Silver, 1993). The information-processing model is applicable to the learning process in general and any given cognitive task. The four components of the model are shown in Figure 1.2.

The information-processing model can be used as a conceptual framework for interpreting IQs, Factor Indexes, and scaled scores that extends beyond the specific areas obtained (Kaufman, 1994a). With the help of this model, scores can be reorganized and translated into fundamental areas of strength and weakness within the cognitive profile.

Generally, the input of WAIS-III Verbal subtests tends to be auditory, while that of the Performance subtests is visual. Although it is perhaps simplistic to reduce the input of WAIS-III subtests into a verbal–visual dichotomy, in a rudimentary way, all subtests can be categorized as having one or the other types of input. For the KAIT and WJ III, there is no simple relationship between scales and modalities. For example, the KAIT Logical Steps subtest is on the Fluid Scale (akin to Performance Scale), but it requires good verbal comprehension for success.

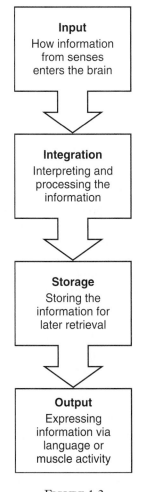

FIGURE 1.2

Information-Processing Model

Hypotheses Generated from IQ Test Profiles Should Be Supported with Data from Multiple Sources

Test score profiles are optimally meaningful when interpreted in the context of known background information, observed behaviors, and approach to each problem-solving task. Virtually any examiner can deduce that WAIS-III Verbal IQ, KAIT Crystallized IQ, or WJ III Comprehension-Knowledge standard score is not a very good measure of the crystallized intelligence of a person raised in a foreign culture, a person who understands Spanish or Vietnamese far better than English, or a person with a hearing impairment, and that Wechsler's Performance IQ or KAIT Memory for Block Designs does not measure nonverbal intelligence very well for a person with crippling arthritis or a visual handicap. The goal of the intelligent tester is to deduce when one or more subtests may be an invalid measure of a person's intellectual functioning for more subtle reasons: distractibility, poor arithmetic achievement in school, subcultural differences in language or custom, emotional content of the items, suspected or known lesions in specific regions of the brain, fatigue, boredom, extreme shyness, bizarre thought processes, inconsistent effort, and the like.

Being a great detective, able to follow up leads and hunches about peaks and valleys in a profile, is the hallmark of an intelligent tester. Such a tester will integrate IQ test profiles with background information, clinical observations of behaviors, and other tests administered in order to more fully understand the examinee's profile.

Tying Together the Tenets of Intelligent Testing

The principles discussed in the preceding sections direct our attention to one important point: the focus of any assessment is the person being assessed, not the test. Many psychological reports stress what the scales or subtests measure instead of what aspects of the person are particularly well developed or in need of improvement; many reports are so number-oriented that the reader loses sight of the person's uniqueness. Current IQ tests for adolescents and adults enable psychologists to better understand a person's cognitive functioning, but other facets of an individual are also revealed during an assessment and should be fully integrated to represent that person as a whole. Although the section of an assessment report that systematically reports and interprets the IQs, cluster scores, and subtest scores is valuable, the behavioral observations section of a case report is often more revealing, and ultimately of more value, if it helps to explain how or why examinees arrived at the scores that they did. The content of the responses and the person's style of responding to various types of tasks can be more important as a determiner of developmental level and intellectual maturity than the scores assigned to the items or tasks.

When several tests are administered to a person (intelligence, language, achievement, personality, visual–motor), the results must be integrated from one test battery to the other. Intelligent testing does not apply only to the interpretation of intelligence tests. The examiner's main role is to generate hypotheses that pertain mostly to assets and deficits within the informa-

tion-processing model, and then confirm or deny these hypotheses by exploring multiple sources of evidence. This integrative, flexible, clinical–empirical methodology and philosophy, as outlined in the preceding tenets, represents the approach taken in this book for the interpretation of the WAIS-III, KAIT, WJ III, and other tests for adolescents and adults. The guidelines for interpreting IQ test profiles and the illustrative case reports throughout this book rest solidly on the intelligent testing framework.

SUMMARY

This chapter first delineates the goal of this book to serve as a text on individual, clinical assessment of intelligence and then outlines the five sections that make up the book: (1) introduction to the assessment of adolescent and adult intelligence; (2) individual differences on age, socioeconomic status, and other key variables; (3) integration and application of WAIS-III research; (4) interpretation of the WAIS-III profile; and (5) additional measures of adolescent and adult IQ. The remainder of the chapter sketches a brief history of the IQ, gives survey data of test usage, presents evidence for the validity of the IQ construct, and introduces the intelligent testing philosophy.

Alfred Binet was truly the pioneer of IQ testing. His concepts and approach dominated the field for years, and Terman's adaptation, the Stanford-Binet, became the criterion of intelligence in the United States. The nonverbal Performance tests developed during World War I to assess non-English-speaking recruits, low-functioning individuals, and suspected malingerers joined with the verbal-oriented Binet tradition to pave the way for David Wechsler's creative contribution of a dual Verbal and Performance approach to intellectual assessment. Wechsler went on to become a proponent of clinical, not just psychometric, assessment. The need for multiscore measurement that accompanied the learning disabilities movement in the 1960s catapulted the Wechsler series of scales ahead of the Binet as the most popular intelligence test.

The results of recent surveys on test usage show that the Wechsler tests still are strongly popular in clinical psychology, neuropsychology, forensic psychology, school psychology, hospital settings, and outpatient clinics. The percentage of clinical time spent conducting assessments varies across specialties within psychology (e.g., clinical, school, neuropsychology), with fluctuations depending on the type of assessment necessary. The inconsistency between the amount of time typically allowed to be reimbursed for assessment services and the actual amount of time spent in assessment-related services may affect the types and numbers of assessments performed by clinicians. Notwithstanding the fees and reimbursement issues, the popularity of the Wechsler scales and the primary reasons for assessing adults remain unchanged. A strong need for tools to assess cognitive capabilities and obtain related clinical information in adults will undoubtedly keep the WAIS-III in its place at the top of the heap of assessment measures.

The validity of the IQ construct was explored for adolescents and adults. Empirical evidence supports the IQ as a good predictor of academic achievement for college students and clinical referrals, and as a strong correlate of educational attainment; IQ also relates substantially to the status of an occupation and correlates significantly with job performance, especially with success in training programs. In general, validity evidence is provided for both verbal and nonverbal measures of intelligence.

The intelligent testing philosophy, which considers the clinician's expertise and training to be more important an aspect of the assessment process than the specific instruments administered or the scores obtained, embodies the following principles: (1) IQ tasks measure what the individual has learned; (2) IQ tasks are samples of behavior and are not exhaustive; (3) IQ tests like the WAIS-III, KAIT, and WJ III assess mental functioning under fixed experimental conditions; (4) IQ tests are optimally useful when they are interpreted from an information-processing model; and (5) hypotheses generated from IQ test profiles should be supported with data from multiple sources.

CHAPTER 2

Heritability and Malleability of IQ and Attacks on the IQ Construct

Chapter 1 presented evidence for the validity of the IQ construct, particularly for adolescents and adults. This chapter treats topics that are generally controversial and that relate either directly or indirectly to the utility and validity of the IQ construct. The topics of heredity, environment, and IQ malleability are discussed, exploring questions such as "How important are genetics and environment in determining a person's IQ?" Next, Flynn's (1984, 1987, 1998a, 1998b, 1998c) analysis of cross-cultural investigations of the intelligence of people from numerous nations leads to an interesting question that is addressed: "Do nations differ in their IQ gains from generation to generation?" Finally, two key challenges to the value of IQ tests are presented, accompanied by our rebuttals to these challenges: Lezak's (1988a) dismissal of the IQ construct, as articulated in the eulogy for the IQ that she delivered to the International Neuropsychological Society; and the gathering momentum from some leaders in the field of specific learning disabilities (SLD) who

are demanding the elimination of IQ tests from the SLD assessment process (e.g., Siegel, 1999; Stanovich, 1999; Vellutino, Scanlon, & Lyon, 2000).

THE HERITABILITY AND MALLEABILITY OF IQ

Heritability

Although laypeople and professionals alike have long argued whether IQ is determined almost exclusively by genetics or by environment, and whether IQ tests are fair or hopelessly biased, the scientific issues involved are complex and the answers are not simple. Excellent technical, empirical, logical, and objective treatments of the genetic question are available (e.g., Bouchard, 1998; Grigorenko, 2000; McArdle & Prescott, 1997; McGue, Bouchard, Iacano, & Lykken, 1993;

Neisser et al., 1996; Sternberg & Grigorenko, 1997) and should be consulted for in-depth treatment of the topic. In this section, the concept of heritability is discussed within the context of accumulated research findings by behavior geneticists, and the point is stressed that the key question to consider is *not* genetics versus environment but genetics versus *malleability* of the IQ (Angoff, 1988).

Evidence for the Roles of Both Genes and the Environment

Different types of evidence bear on the association between genetics and IQ, such as the characteristic intellectual profiles displayed by individuals with single-gene abnormalities (e.g., PKU, Tay Sachs disease) or an abnormal number of either nonsex chromosomes (Down's syndrome) or sex chromosomes (Klinefelter's or Turner's syndrome) (Vandenberg & Vogler, 1985). In addition, McKusick (1986) reports the identification of more than 100 rare single-gene mutations involving intellectual retardation. In fact, the recessive gene that causes the chromosomal condition of fragile X syndrome (Madison, George, & Moeschler, 1986) appears, according to Plomin (1989), "to be a major reason for the excess of mild mental retardation in males" (p. 106). The one-gene, one-disorder hypothesis (referred to as "OGOD" by Plomin, 1997) applies to adult dementia as well as to childhood disorders such as PKU and fragile X syndrome. A rare type of Alzheimer's disease (AD) known as FAD, which appears in middle adulthood, displays a dominant single-gene pattern of inheritance; most FAD cases have been found to be linked to a gene on chromosome 14, although a few cases of FAD are associated with a mutated protein gene on chromosome 21 (Plomin, 1997). Although this line of research is provocative, this section focuses on the accumulated evidence obtained from studies of normal individuals, specifically the correlations between the IQs earned by people who differ in their degree of genetic similarity. Identical twins have the same genetic makeup, whereas fraternal twins are no more similar genetically than any two siblings born at different times.

Correlational Studies

Table 2.1 summarizes pertinent coefficients from a plethora of studies conducted for about three-quarters of a century by investigators throughout the world. As indicated, the average correlation for identical twins reared together is .86, not very different from the test-retest reliability coefficient of about .95 for Wechsler's most recent tests for children and adults (.94 for the WISC-III and .96 for the WAIS-III for the same person tested twice over about a 1-month interval). Because many of the IQ tests used in these diverse studies do not match the stability coefficients of the third editions of Wechsler's batteries, the correlation for identical twins probably closely approximates the coefficient that would have been obtained if either twin had been tested twice. In contrast, the coefficient for fraternal twins reared together—though a substantial .55—is not nearly as high as the value of .86, nor does it compare to the correlation obtained for identical twins reared *apart* (.76). Further, the high coefficient for identical twins raised together has been resistant to change over time.

The coefficient in the .70s for identical twins reared apart is quite an impressive testimony to the importance of genetics in having an influence on children's and adults' IQs. However, this unusually high relationship between the IQs of individuals raised in different environments has been the subject of some controversy. Initially, data were derived from three studies conducted between 1937 and 1980 based on a total of 65 pairs of identical twins reared apart; in the original Table 2.1 in the first edition of this book (Kaufman, 1990), the correlation for those 65 pairs of twins was .72. That substantial degree of correlation was criticized as bogus by Kamin (1974) and others because of reasons such as contact between the twins and placement of the twins in similar types of homes. However, two

TABLE 2.1   Average correlations, from numerous studies, between the IQs of people differing in their degree of genetic relationship

Relation	Number of Pairs	Correlation
Same Person (Tested Twice)[a]	747	.95
Identical Twins—Reared Together[b]	4,672	.86
Identical Twins—Reared Apart[c]	158	.76
Fraternal Twins—Reared Together[c]	8,600	.55
Fraternal Twins—Reared Apart[c]	112	.35
Virtual Twins—Reared Together (unrelated siblings, same age, reared together from early infancy)[d]	90	.26
Siblings—Reared Together[b]	26,473	.47
Siblings—Reared Apart[b]	203	.24
Unrelated Siblings—Reared Together–CHILDREN (adopted/natural or adopted/adopted)[e]	689	.28
Unrelated Siblings—Reared Together–ADULTS (adopted/natural or adopted/adopted)[e]	398	.04
Half-siblings[b]	200	.31
Cousins[b]	1,176	.15
Parent/child—Living Together[b]	8,433	.42
Parent/child—Living Apart[b]	814	.22
Adoptive Parent/child—Living Together[b]	1,397	.19
Mid-Parent/child—Living Together[b]	992	.50
Mid-Adoptive Parent/child—Living Together[b]	758	.24
Unrelated Persons—Reared Apart[b]	15,086	−.01

[a]Data from Wechsler (1991, pp. 170–172) for the WISC-III ($N = 353$; mean $r = .94$) and The Psychological Corporation (1997, pp. 58–61) for the WAIS-III ($N = 394$; mean $r = .96$).

[b]Data from Vandenberg and Vogler (1985, Figure 7), based on data originally summarized by T. J. Bouchard and M. McGue in 1981.

[c]Data from Scarr (1997, p. 28).

[d]Data from Segal (2000).

[e]Data from Bouchard (1998, p. 265).

more recent studies conducted in the 1990s, based on a total of 93 twin pairs reared apart, yielded virtually identical IQ correlations in the .70s (Bouchard, 1996, Table 1), and, importantly, addressed the criticisms of the previous investigations. Neither the criticism regarding the degree of contact (which was measured) nor the criticism that the similarity in the home placements inflated the correlations, was borne out; the substantial coefficients could not be explained by these alleged confounding variables. The precise overall correlation of the IQs of identical twins reared apart, based on the five separate studies that were conducted, differs based on which behavioral genetic expert is reporting the data; the value is .76 according to Scarr (1997), .75 according to Bouchard (1996), and .72 according to Plomin and Petrill (1997). These small differences are due to different statistical procedures for combining data across IQ measures (as many as three in one of the studies) and across studies. But the big picture that emerges is that genetics plays an important role in how individuals perform on conventional IQ tests, and this role does not seem to be diminished by the role of possible confounds.

There are other intriguing aspects of Table 2.1 that attest both to the importance of genetics and to the key role played by environmental circumstances. The IQ correlation for fraternal twins reared together (.55) is substantially higher than their "reared-apart" value (.35), suggesting that the role of environment is quite considerable. Very similar results for "reared-together" versus "reared-apart" coefficients likewise support the vital impact played by environment in contributing to one's IQ: Siblings (.47 together versus .24 apart) and Parent–Child (.42 versus .22). Also, the coefficient for fraternal twins, who share a more similar environment than siblings of different ages, is notably higher than the correlation for natural siblings in general. In addition, the .28 correlation for unrelated siblings reared together, when the siblings are tested during childhood, demonstrates the importance of a shared family environment on children's IQs.

However, the importance of genetics is revealed by some interesting research conducted by Segal (1997, 2000) with what she has termed "virtual twins," i.e., unrelated siblings of the same age who are reared together from early infancy. She has studied 90 of these unique sibling pairs, which mimic "twinness" but without genetic relatedness (65 pairs included two adoptees, 25 were composed of one adoptee and one biological child; mean age = 8 years, SD = 8.5

years). Though she found a significant correlation of .26 (p < .01) between the IQs of the virtual twins, supporting the environmental contribution, this value is not nearly as high as the coefficients obtained for identical twins (.86), fraternal twins (.55), or even siblings of different ages (.47) (see Table 2.1). Segal (2000) concluded that her results with virtual twins "support explanatory models of intelligence that include genetic factors, demonstrating that shared environments have modest effects on intellectual development" (p. 442). In addition, the higher correlations of the IQs of birth parents than adoptive parents with the adopted children's IQs reinforces the importance of genetics; this topic is addressed more fully in the next section on adoption studies, which also offer additional findings that stress the value of environment. For an insightful and thorough treatment of twin studies and their implications, see the recent book by Segal (1999).

The correlations shown in Table 2.1 should not be interpreted as fixed and unchangeable. Plomin and DeFries (1980) have shown convincingly that coefficients for various degrees of genetic relationship have changed substantially when comparing data obtained prior to 1963 to data obtained in the late 1970s. For example, the IQs of a parent and child living together correlated .50 (pre-1963) versus .35 (late 1970s). Coefficients for fraternal twins changed in the opposite direction, though, interestingly, coefficients were exactly the same whether the fraternal twins were the same gender or different genders, regardless of when the data were obtained (Plomin & DeFries, 1980).

Adoption Studies

Adoption studies have contributed much to our understanding of the relative roles of genetics and environment (Scarr & Carter-Saltzman, 1982). Interestingly, one adoption study conducted by Scarr and Weinberg (1976) has been widely interpreted as supporting the importance of environment on IQ, whereas a second adoption study by the same investigators (Scarr & Weinberg, 1978) supports the role of heredity.

In the 1976 investigation, African American and interracial children (N = 130) adopted at an average age of 18 months by socially advantaged Caucasian families in Minnesota earned an average global IQ of 106.3 on the 1949 WISC, 1972 Stanford-Binet, or WAIS, about 20 points higher than the typical mean IQ earned by African Americans, and about 1 *SD* above the mean earned by African American children from the North Central region of the United States (Scarr & Weinberg, 1976). These exciting findings are tempered to some extent by the finding that the natural children of the adoptive parents earned a weighted mean IQ of 116.6, about 10 points higher than the adopted African American children. Caucasian adopted children in Scarr and Weinberg's (1976) study had an average IQ of 111.5, and African American children with one Caucasian parent outscored African American children with two African American parents 109.0 to 96.8. Importantly, however, Scarr and Weinberg (1976) showed that the 12-point discrepancy in favor of African American adoptees with one Caucasian parent can largely be accounted for by differences between the two subsamples in their placement histories and in the natural mother's education. The main point here is that the issues involved are complex and multifaceted, and cannot be resolved by a single study or set of studies. Extremists of either the environmental position or the genetic approach can find data to support their position.

Scarr and Weinberg's (1978) second adoption study examined the role of environmental variables in predicting adolescents' IQs in 120 biological and 104 adoptive families (average age at adoption was 2.6 months). Parents and children were given a four-subtest short form of the WAIS. Variables like parental education and income produced a much higher multiple correlation for biological families (.33) than adoptive families (.14). The IQ of the mother rearing the adolescent increased the correlation substantially only for the biological families. In fact, the

one variable that raised the multiple correlation most for the adoptive families was the *natural* mother's educational attainment. Again, however, the complexity of the issues precludes simple answers.

The Texas Adoption Study (Horn, Loehlin, & Willerman, 1979; Loehlin, Horn, & Willerman, 1994, 1997) is a particularly well-designed investigation that sheds further light on the heredity–environment controversy. The project began with 300 Texas families who adopted children, mostly in the 1960s, through a church-related home for unwed mothers. Both birth and adoptive families were largely Caucasian and middle class. Birth mothers were typically tested on the Revised Beta (a nonverbal paper-and-pencil IQ test), but occasionally on a Wechsler scale. Adoptive parents were administered both the Revised Beta and the WAIS; preschool children were tested on the old Stanford-Binet, those ages 5 and above were given the WISC (mean age at original testing was about 8 years with a range of 3–14). About 10 years later, the children from 181 families were retested, this time on the WISC-R or WAIS-R (some families had more than one adopted child, so more than 240 adoptees were tested during the follow-up).

Table 2.2 summarizes correlational data from the Texas Adoption Study, providing relationships between the IQs of the adopted children and the IQs of their (1) birth mothers, (2) adoptive mothers, and (3) adoptive fathers. The results are both provocative and interesting. The correlations with the birth mother are substantially higher than the correlations with the adoptive parents, suggesting the greater contribution of genetics than environment to the children's IQs; this finding is especially noteworthy because, "These birth mothers had no contact with their children after the first few days of life; in fact, many of the infants went directly from the hospital to their adoptive families" (Loehlin et al., 1997, p. 113). Second, the differential between the correlations for the birth mother versus adoptive parents was substantially greater when the children were older than when they were younger, a topic treated later in this

TABLE 2.2   The Texas Adoption Study: Average correlations, across IQ tests, between adopted children and both their birth mother and their adopted parents, at two points in time

Adoptive Father with Adoptive Child	Adoptive Mother with Adoptive Child	Birth Mother with Adoptive Child
Parent and Child—Original Testing		
.14	.12	.32
(range: .08 to .19)	(range: .10 to .13)	(range: .23 to .36)
Parent (Original Testing) with Child (about 10 Years Later)		
.10	.02	.48
(range: .07 to .15)	(range: −.02 to .07)	(range: .26 to .78)

NOTE: Based on coefficients of correlation presented by Loehlin et al. (1997, Table 4.2). Data are averaged for two combinations of tests at original testing (Wechsler/Wechsler and Beta/Wechsler for parent/child) and four combinations of tests at the 10-year follow-up. All means were computed using Fisher's logarithmic *z* transformation.

chapter in "Heritability and Age." Overall, Loehlin et al. (1997) concluded that their findings were consistent with the results of other behavior–genetic methodologies, such as the identical versus fraternal twin studies or the studies of twins reared apart.

Broad Heritability of IQ

The broad heritability of a trait such as intelligence corresponds to "the proportion of the total variance that is due to heredity" (Vandenberg & Vogler, 1985, p. 14). Falconer's (1960) formula for estimating broad heritability is fairly simple (the difference between intraclass correlations for identical versus fraternal twins, times 2), and is widely used (Vandenberg & Vogler, 1985), but more sophisticated formulas and approaches are used as well. Regardless of the statistical technique applied, heritability "is a descriptive statistic like a mean or variance that refers to a particular population at a particular time" (Plomin & Petrill, 1997, p. 57); "estimates of heritability" differ from population to population as

genetic and environmental variances change as proportions of the total variance" (Scarr & Carter-Saltzman, 1982, p. 820).

Probably the best overall estimate of the heritability of IQ is 50%, a value proposed as the most sensible summary of the results from the diversity of behavioral genetic research (Plomin & Petrill, 1997). The value of 50% derives from, "Model-fitting analyses that simultaneously analyze all of the family, adoption, and twin data…, suggesting that about half of the variance of IQ scores in these populations can be attributed to genetic differences among individuals" (Plomin & Petrill, 1997, p. 59). The value of 50% is similar to the heritability for weight, but not nearly as high as the value for height. Weight demonstrated a broad heritability estimate of 48%, versus 80% for height, in one investigation that explored those two noncognitive variables (Garfinkle, 1982).

As noted, the heritability estimate of 50% for IQ represents an overview of values derived from different types of studies and for different kinds of populations. These estimates are a function of numerous variables, several of which are summarized briefly in the following sections.

Heritability and Type of Cognitive Ability

Different cognitive abilities have different heritabilities. For example, in a study of 8-year-olds on the 1949 WISC, the heritability was higher for Verbal IQ (76%) versus Performance IQ (52%) (Scarr & Carter-Saltzman, 1982, Table 13.5). Higher Verbal than Performance heritabilities have also been reported on Wechsler's scales in other studies with various age groups. For example, the Minnesota twin study obtained WISC-R short-form data on identical and fraternal twins ages 11–12 years and WAIS-R data, minus Similarities, for adult identical and fraternal twins ages 17–18, 30–59, and 60–88 years. Heritabilities for Verbal abilities were much higher than heritabilities for Performance abilities at ages 11–12 (mid-.50s vs. mid-.20s) and ages 60–88 (mid-.80s vs. mid-.60s); data for the two middle-age groups were based on insufficient sample sizes to produce reliable data (McGue et al., 1993). In an analysis of specific cognitive abilities, Bouchard (1998, Table 2) compiled data from the Swedish Adoption/Twin Study of Aging, and reported heritabilities for this adult sample of .58 for verbal ability and perceptual speed, .46 for spatial ability, and .38 for memory. In a summary of data compiled from other sources, Bouchard (Table 4) reported values ranging from .48 for verbal ability and memory to the low .60s for spatial ability and perceptual speed. In a review of a diversity of studies, Kaufman (1990, Table 2.2) noted heritabilities in the .40s for social studies achievement, language achievement, and WISC Verbal-Performance discrepancy; values in the mid- to high-.30s for number ability, crystallized intelligence tasks, fluid intelligence tasks, and receptive vocabulary (PPVT); values in the low .30s for memory, verbal fluency, and natural science achievement; and values in the low .20s for Raven's Progressive Matrices and tests of creativity. At least two important conclusions stem from

the Bouchard (1998) and Kaufman (1990) data summaries: (1) different cognitive abilities tend to have decidedly different heritabilities; and (2) diverse measures of Gf and Gc seem to have approximately equivalent heritabilities (a finding noted, as well, by Horn, 1985), arguing against the common misperception that Gf is primarily genetic and Gc is mainly environmental.

Heritability and Social Class

Fischbein (1980), in a study of twins, divided his samples into three groups categorized by social class. He found that heritability estimates increased with increasing social class. The estimate of broad heritability from the intraclass correlations for identical and fraternal twins was .78 for the highest social class, but only .30 for the lowest. Extremely similar results were obtained from a large-scale study of 1909 non-Hispanic Caucasians and African American sibling pairs (identical twins, fraternal twins, full and half siblings, cousins in the same household, and biologically unrelated siblings) from the National Longitudinal Study of Adolescent Health who were tested on Wechsler's Vocabulary subtest (Rowe, Jacobson, & Van den Oord, 1999). When categorized by parental education, the heritability for the most highly educated families averaged .74 versus a value of .26 for the less well-educated families (Rowe et al.). In a twin study conducted in Russia, Grigorenko and Carter (1996) evaluated the parenting styles of the mothers of identical and fraternal twins, and analyzed these relationships as a function of the family's social class. They found parenting styles to differ for the two types of twins (e.g., mothers of identical twins employed more infantilization, invalidation, and authoritarianism than mothers of fraternal twins), and for different social classes. Regarding the latter point, Grigorenko and Carter found that Russian mothers with less education and lower occupational status were more likely than their more educated, higher status counterparts to use authoritarian approaches, to view their children's behavior less positively, and to invalidate and infantilize their twins' behavior. The latter two styles were also associated with lower children's IQs.

Heritability and Ethnicity

Scarr and Carter-Saltzman (1982, Figure 13.12) demonstrate substantial differences among three ethnic groups in the relationships between the cognitive scores obtained by children and their parents. Regressions of mid-child on mid-parent for verbal, spatial, perceptual speed, and visual memory factors averaged about .70 for Koreans, .50 for Americans of European ancestry living in Hawaii, and .35 for Americans of Japanese ancestry living in Hawaii.

Heritability and Age

Despite occasional statistical arguments to the contrary (e.g., Devlin, Daniels, & Roeder, 1997), it has become widely accepted among behavior geneticists that heritabilities are substantially larger in adulthood than childhood (Bouchard, 1996, 1998; McGue et al., 1993; Neisser et al., 1996; Plomin & Petrill, 1997). Based on data from the Colorado Adoption Study, Plomin, Fulker, Corley, and DeFries (1997) concluded that "genetic influence increases monotonically from infancy to childhood to adolescence" (p. 446). The substantially greater role of genetics in adulthood than in childhood is evident in Table 2.1 from a comparison of the correlations between unrelated siblings reared together when they are tested as children (.28) as opposed to when they were tested as adults (.04). The same age-related inference can be drawn from Table 2.2, regarding the results of the Texas Adoption Study: The differential between the correlations for the birth mother versus adoptive parents was substantially greater when the children were older than when they were younger (a difference in coefficients of about .40 at the 10-year follow-up compared to a difference of about .20 at the original assessments). Furthermore, high heritabilities for Wechsler's Full Scale—in the low- to mid-.80s, well above the average of about .50 for

studies of children—have been obtained for adult samples, such as the ones tested in twin studies conducted in Norway (Tambs, Sundet, & Magnus, 1984), Sweden (Pederson, Plomin, Nesselroade, & McClearn, 1992), and Minnesota (McGue et al., 1993). All of these findings suggest that the role of genetics increases as children become adolescents and then adults, at the same time that the modest effect of family environmental factors may be decreasing.

The increase in heritability with age has been demonstrated as well in studies that cover a relatively small age span. In a study of Dutch twins tested at age 5 ($N = 209$ pairs) and again at age 7 ($N = 192$), the heritability increased dramatically from .27 at age 5 to .62 at age 7 (Boomsma & van Baal, 1998). Remarkably, the influence of heredity on infant "intelligence" increased steadily from age 14 months to 36 months in a longitudinal study of identical and fraternal twins selected for high cognitive ability on the Bayley Scales of Infant Development (Bayley, 1969) at ages 14, 20, and 24 months, and on the original Stanford-Binet (Terman & Merrill, 1973) at age 36 months (Petrill et al., 1998). Heritabilities in the Petrill et al. study increased in value from .00 to .28 to .40 to .64 as age increased from 14 to 36 months for these high-scoring infants. At the same time, the role of group common environment (i.e., shared family environment, usually abbreviated c2) decreased from an average of .39 at 14–24 months to .07 at 36 months.

McGue et al. (1993, Figure 2) graphed the heritabilities derived from "reared-together" twin studies, along with the values of c2 (shared home environment) as well as environmental influences other than those derived from growing up in the same family (nonshared environment). Heritabilities rise from the low .40s at ages 4–6 years to the mid-.50s at ages 6–20 to the mid-.80s for adults aged 21 and older. Corresponding to this increase in heritabilities is a decrease in c2 for the same three age groups, from the mid-.30s to about .30 to near-zero. In contrast to these substantial age changes, the proportions for nonshared environment across this broad age range remained nearly a constant of about .15–.20. These striking findings (especially the near-zero variance for family environment on adult IQ) are mitigated by three factors: (1) the two extreme age groups—the ones showing the substantial deviations in heritability and c2—comprised *small* samples of twin pairs (124 identical and 213 fraternal for ages 4–6; 190 identical and 178 fraternal for ages 21+), compared to sample sizes that averaged more than 2,000 identical twin pairs and more than 2,200 fraternal twin pairs for each of ages 6–12, 12–16, and 16–20; (2) the values of heritability and c2 virtually plateaued between ages 6–12 and 16–20, not at all reflecting the monotonic increase in heritability from infancy to childhood to adolescence observed by Plomin et al. (1997); and (3) the data are derived only from twins reared together, using the relatively crude Falconer formula, excluding the variety of other behavior genetic data and not relying on the more sophisticated model-fitting analyses.

The potentially small role of the shared home environment on older children's and adults' IQs, a notion that has had empirical support for three-quarters of a century (Burks, 1928), is a shocking, counterintuitive result. As Neisser et al. (1996) observed in their thorough review article, "These findings suggest that differences in the lifestyles of families—whatever their importance may be for many aspects of children's lives—make little long-term differences for the skills measured by intelligence tests" (p. 88). However, the conclusions reached about heritability and aging by McGue et al. (1993) based on twin studies, and by others (e.g., Loehlin et al., 1997) based on adoption studies, need to be considered tentative and not conclusive for the reasons mentioned in the preceding paragraph about adult studies, and because of an important caveat stressed by Neisser et al. for childhood and adolescent studies:

We should note, however, that low-income and non-White families are poorly represented in existing adoption studies as well as in most twin samples. Thus it is not clear whether these surprisingly small values of (adoles-

cent) c2 apply to the population as a whole. It remains possible that, across the full range of income and ethnicity, between-family differences have more lasting consequences for psychometric intelligence. (p. 88)

The Rowe et al. (1999) study mentioned previously, which included substantial numbers of African American twin pairs and a variety of income levels, is relevant to this general point, even though it has nothing to do with the "age" issue. In this study, the value of c2 was .00 for highly educated families, but it was a substantial .23 for less well-educated families, nearly identical to the heritability value of .26 for the latter families (Rowe et al., 1999). In addition, before reaching firm conclusions about the role of family environment on IQ across the lifespan, it is important for researchers to emulate the methodology of Grigorenko and Carter (1996), described previously, who specifically measured parenting styles and examined how these styles interacted with type of twin (identical vs. fraternal) and social class.

There is some evidence that the so-called increase in heritability of IQ with age applies to adults up to age 70, but that the heritability then drops for elderly adults (Bouchard, 1996). In a study that combined data from Sweden and Minnesota (Finkel, Pederson, McGue, & McClearn, 1995), the heritability was .81 and c2 was virtually zero for ages 27–50 and 50–65 years. For the Swedish sample, the heritability dropped to .54 for adults ages 65–85 years (Finkel et al.), and, more recently, it was .62 for same-gender twins ages 80 years and older with no major cognitive or related impairments (McClearn et al., 1997). However, similar drops in heritability were not observed for the Minnesota sample of elderly adults (Bouchard, 1998). Results from a 21-year longitudinal investigation of aging in twins aged 60 and above (Jarvik & Bank, 1983) are consistent with the notion that heritabilities drop in the elderly. Based on data from several Wechsler-Bellevue subtests and the Binet Vocabulary task, Jarvik and Bank observed that the intelligence scores of fraternal twins were no more disparate than the scores of identical twins, as "the genetically identical MZ [monozygotic] twins tended to show increasing dissimilarities over the years." (p. 46).

Maternal Environment

Two interesting lines of research involve what has been termed the "maternal environment," which refers specifically to the environment in the womb during pregnancy: (1) Devlin, Daniels, and Roeder (1997) model-fitting approach, which gives great credence to the importance of maternal environment for siblings, and, especially, for twins; and (2) the interesting findings from genetic research that has distinguished whether identical twins shared a placenta or had separate placentas (e.g., Rose, Uchida, & Christian, 1981).

Maternal Effects and Statistical Models

Devlin et al. (1997) takes issue with the common assumption by genetic researchers that maternal environment effects are trivial. They argue that the mother's womb provides an important early environment, one that witnesses substantial *in utero* brain growth, and that a huge number of perinatal factors, such as the mother's ingestion of alcohol, drugs, or lead, may lower the child's IQ, whereas other factors (e.g., dietary supplements) can raise a child's IQ. Therefore, maternal environmental effects on twins' IQs are likely to be rather large for twins and notable for siblings (because the mothers' physiological status and personal habits during pregnancy are likely to be similar, but not identical, from one pregnancy to another). Devlin et al. tried to fit four competing models to a large database composed of correlations between pairs of relationships that differed in genetic overlap (e.g., identical twins, fraternal twins, parent–child, siblings, adopting parent–child). The data set derived from a meta-analysis of 212 studies (204 correlations based on more than 50,000 distinct pairings). The researchers posited four models, two of which assigned a value of zero to maternal effects. The model that fit the data best (i.e., was the best at accurately predicting the array of weighted mean correla-

tions from the 212 studies) attributed a large maternal environment effect for twins (20%) and a substantial effect for siblings (5%).

The important implication of Devlin et al.'s (1997) conclusions is that variance formerly attributed to genetics may actually be attributable to environment (namely, maternal environment). The unusually high correlations obtained between identical twins reared apart (averaging .76; see Table 2.1) translate to a heritability of 76% for these twins who have 100% genetic overlap and allegedly a 0% environmental overlap. However, according to Devlin et al., they do have a substantial environmental overlap, namely, about 20% by virtue of sharing the same womb. When that 20% is subtracted from the 76%, the heritability falls into line with the typical estimates of 50%. Bouchard (1998) disagrees with Devlin et al.'s conclusions about maternal effects, and also with their conclusions that heritability does not increase with age. Bouchard argued that Devlin et al. were incorrect to discount the relationship of heritability of IQ to age, and stated that the higher heritability values for identical twins reared apart were not due to maternal effects, but were a direct function of the higher heritabilities for adults than children (because identical twins reared apart were typically tested as adults). Bouchard (1998) argued his point cogently, also emphasizing that research is more supportive of the notion that far from being overestimated, genetic effects are usually underestimated. Nonetheless, Bouchard (1998) conceded that: "None of the research cited by Devlin et al. (1997) regarding possible in utero effects on IQ is unimportant; it simply does not support their narrow argument that maternal effects create excessive similarity in twins" (p. 270). However, their "narrow" argument has at least some support from the results of the placentation research discussed in the next section.

Maternal Effects and Placentation Research

Identical twins either share one placenta (when the zygote divides 4 to 7 days after fertilization) or they have separate placentas (when division occurs within 72 hours); about two thirds of identical twins share one placenta (Rose et al., 1981). This placentation (also known as "chorion") effect relates significantly to identical twins' birth weight, cord blood cholesterol level, adult personality, and cognition, and it impacts as well on correlations among abilities (Rose et al.). The dramatic chorion differences in the correlations for identical twins are shown in Table 2.3 for Canadian adults (ranging in age from about 20–44) on the WAIS (Rose et al.) and for French 8- to 12-year-old children on the WISC-R (Spitz et al., 1996). Adult identical twins, regardless of chorion status, correlated .95 in their scores on WAIS Vocabulary. In great contrast, however, are their correlations on Block Design: a value of .92 was obtained for identical twins who shared one placenta (and, hence, had essentially identical maternal environments), but a coefficient of only .48 was obtained for identical twins who had separate placentas. When Falconer's (1960) popular heritability formula is applied, the values of heritability are markedly different for monochorionic identical twins (.96) and dichorionic identical twins (.08). The trivial heritability for twins with separate placentas reflects the fact that the correlation for those particular identical twins was nearly the same as the value of .44 for fraternal twins.

These findings were cross-validated by Spitz et al. (1996) for children on the French WISC-R. Whereas the correlations for monochorionic and dichorionic twins on Vocabulary (.78 and .89) did not differ significantly, the values for these two types of identical twins did differ significantly on Block Design (.84 vs. .61, $p < .01$). When the Falconer formula is used to compute heritabilities for the French children's sample, the value for identical twins who shared a placenta is .66, quite a bit higher than the value of .20 for identical twins with separate placentas. Though the results in the Spitz study are not as dramatic as the Rose findings, they are consistent with the initial results, providing solid cross-validation of the specific maternal environmental effects on Block Design performance. Whereas U.S. hospitals typically do not systematically record chorion differences for identical twins, the fact that other countries sometimes note this information meticulously allowed this fascinating research to be conducted.

When the chorion research is interpreted alongside the Devlin et al. (1997) model-building research, the Devlin hypothesis about the importance of maternal effects takes on added validity. Indeed, Devlin et al. did not even consider there to be different maternal environments for *fraternal* twins, much less identical twins with different numbers of placentas. The chorion re-

TABLE 2.3   Identical twins and placentation: Correlations on IQ tests

	Toronto, Canada: WAIS			Paris, France: WAIS		
	Number of Pairs	*Vocabulary*	*Block Design*	*Number of Pairs*	*Vocabulary*	*Block Design*
Identical Twins						
One Placenta	17	.95	.92	20	.78	.84
Identical Twins						
Two Placentas	15	.95	.48	24	.89	.61
Fraternal Twins	28	.55	.44	24	.62	.51

NOTE: Data for adults tested on WAIS Vocabulary and Block Design are from Rose, Uchida, and Christian (1981). Data for children tested on WISC-R Vocabulary and Block Design are from Spitz et al. (1996).

search suggests that the maternal environment may be more potent and more subtle than Devlin even conceived. If Devlin, Rose, and their colleagues are correct, then it is possible that a substantial portion of variance that has routinely been assigned to genetics may actually be due to environmental differences that occur before children are born.

Nonetheless, there are caveats to the research on maternal effects. Bouchard's (1998) intelligent critique of Devlin's methodology provides an alternate explanation to the influence of maternal environment. Also, the sample sizes of both chorion studies are small, and the results seem fairly specific to Wechsler's Block Design (Spitz et al., 1996, did not obtain the same results with K-ABC subtests, even though a few of them seem to measure the same visual–spatial abilities as Block Design). As Kaufman (1999) states about the two chorion studies:

> *Ironically, the greatest effect seems to be on a nonverbal measure of an ability believed to be closely aligned with neurological development, rather than with the verbal, education-dependent Gc subtest. The results require additional replication and generalization to be accepted as scientific findings; furthermore, some significant findings in the chorion studies indicate greater similarities among dichorionic than monochorionic MZ twins. The findings are, however, sufficiently provocative to challenge all known heritability estimates pertaining to intelligence and personality because pertinent studies failed to control for the chorion effect. (pp. 627–628, emphasis ours)*

Overview

The bulk of behavior genetic research from a diversity of methodologies converges on the fact that genetics are an important determinant of IQ, and its role conceivably becomes greater as people age, except, perhaps, among the very elderly. This finding, even in light of the possibility that maternal effects account for a considerable portion of the variance that has previously been attributed to genetics, should not be minimized or underplayed. Plomin and Petrill (1997) state:

"Regardless of the precise estimate of heritability, the point is that genetic influence on IQ test scores is not only statistically significant, it is also substantial. It is rare in the behavioral sciences to explain 5% of the variance. For example, despite the interest in birth order, it accounts for less than 1% of the IQ variance. Finding that heredity accounts for 50% of the variance is a major discovery about intelligence" (p. 59).

Indeed, specific environmental variables rarely account for very much variance by themselves. Bouchard and Segal (1985) concluded, based on an exhaustive review of a plethora of environmental variables (anoxia, malnutrition, family income, family configuration, and many more): "The principal finding in this review of environmental effects on IQ is that no single environmental factor appears to have a large influence on IQ. Variables widely believed to be important are usually weak" (p. 452). The environmental influence update by Neisser et al. (1996) basically concurs with that conclusion. Although environmental variables such as amount of formal schooling and occupational status relate substantially to IQ, genetics and environment interact dynamically with such global indexes, and separating their respective influences is often futile. Nonetheless, some findings regarding the influence of school attendance are compelling: For example, when children of about the same age go to school a year apart because of admission criteria involving birth dates, children with the extra year of school score higher on IQ tests; and when one Virginia county closed its schools in the 1960s, preventing most African American children from obtaining formal education, a controlled study indicated that each lost year of school was worth 6 IQ points (Neisser et al.).

Environmental contributions are complex, varying from culture to culture and within heterogeneous cultures as well. Despite disappointing results in their evaluation of the impact of environmental variables on IQ when taken one at a time, Bouchard and Segal (1985) were not discouraged by the findings, recognizing "that environmental effects are multifactorial and largely unrelated to each other" (p. 452). When the impact of aggregated (but unspecified) cultural or environmental influences on IQ are evaluated (Vandenberg & Vogler, 1985, Table 6), the estimates vary more than do heritability estimates, but they "are usually of similar magnitude" (p. 34). Further, it is conceivable (Bouchard & Segal, 1985)—perhaps even likely (Scarr & Grajek, 1982)—that the correlation between genotype and environment is considerably larger than usually believed. For example, siblings may be treated significantly differently by their parents, as was suggested in Grigorenko and Carter's (1996) study of parent–child variables in samples of Russian identical and fraternal twins; in fact, the maternal effects research suggests that this "different treatment" may be biochemical, affecting children's future intelligence before they are even born. In addition, the cross-cultural research on IQ changes from generation to generation conducted by Flynn (1987), discussed later in this chapter, attests to the vital impact of environmental factors on IQ. Flynn points out that "the fact that the factors are unknown does not mean that when identified, they will prove exotic or unfamiliar" (p. 189).

And the general finding of a 50% heritability for IQ is not nearly as high as estimates from the past; furthermore, it also means that up to 50% of the IQ variance is due to known and unknown environmental factors, quite a respectable percentage, and sufficiently high to challenge the controversial conclusions about race differences and social policy reached by the authors of *The Bell Curve* (Herrnstein & Murray, 1994). As Neisser et al. (1996) appropriately conclude regarding the difference of approximately one standard deviation in the mean IQs earned by Caucasians and African Americans (see Chapter 4), based on an extensive review of pertinent research: "Several culturally based explanations of the Black/White IQ differential have been proposed; some are plausible, but so far none has been conclusively supported. *There is even less empirical support for a genetic interpretation.* In short, no adequate explanation of the differential be-

tween the IQ means of Blacks and Whites is presently available" (p. 97, emphasis ours). Weinberg (1989) adds that one needs to accept the role of genes in helping to shape IQ, along with a multitude of environmental and "organic" factors (such as a mother's taking drugs or exposure to excessive radiation during pregnancy), such that acceptance of our "genetic heritage…need not be pessimistic nor bode evil for social and educational policy" (p. 102). More than a decade ago, Plomin (1989) wisely cautioned: "As the pendulum swings from environmentalism, it is important that the pendulum be caught midswing before its momentum carries it to biological determinism" (p. 110). More recently, Plomin and Petrill (1997) continued this metaphor: "The reason for hoping that the pendulum is coming to rest at a point between nature and nurture is not merely that we want everyone to be happy. It is what genetic research on intelligence tells us" (p. 55).

MALLEABILITY

Angoff (1988) has argued that the wrong question has continually been asked by those trying to determine the relative influences of heredity and environment on IQ variability. Researchers have insisted that "genetic does not mean immutable" (Plomin, 1983, p. 253), and have deplored the fact that "[t]he myth of heritability limiting malleability seems to die hard" (Scarr, 1981, p. 53). Yet Angoff argues that intelligence is "thought by many to be largely innate…and to a considerable extent inherited, and therefore unchangeable both within a given lifetime and across generations" (p. 713). Certainly that generalization seems to summarize the viewpoint expressed implicitly by Herrnstein and Murray (1994).

To Angoff, *"The real issue is whether intelligence can be changed, an issue that does not at all go hand in hand with the issue of heritability"* (p. 713, emphasis in original). "Whatever the 'true' heritability coefficient for intelligence is…, whether it is high or low..., the essential point is that in the context of group differences and what these differences connote, its numerical value is irrelevant. What is relevant is whether these group differences can be changed, with what means, and with what effect" (p. 716).

Angoff (1988) uses a simple but powerful illustration to show that a variable with unusually high heritability, such as height, can and does change markedly from generation to generation. Adolescents in the United States and Great Britain gained about 6 inches in average height in the course of a century (Tanner, 1962). Within Japan, Angoff notes, the average height of young adult males increased by 3 to 4 inches from the mid-1940s to the early 1980s, a change that is "not inconsiderable by anyone's standards" (p. 714). As further evidence of the powerful role played by environment in modifying a trait with very high heritability, Angoff cites a 1957 study by Greulich showing that U.S.-born Japanese children were taller, heavier, and more advanced in skeletal development than their contemporaries in Japan.

In fact, Angoff did not have to go so far afield to bring his point home. The malleability of intelligence has been demonstrated dramatically by two very different research approaches: Flynn's (1984, 1987, 1998a, 1998b, 1998c) investigations of generational gains in IQs, as well as the results of various intervention studies. The first section summarizes research on the so-called Flynn effect. The second section discusses the results of early intervention studies, featuring the highly successful Abecedarian Project (Campbell, Pungello, Miller-Johnson, Burchinal, & Ramey, in press; Campbell & Ramey, 1986, 1994, 1995).

The Flynn Effect

In an ambitious undertaking to study IQ gains by different countries over time, Flynn (1987) contacted 165 scholars in 35 countries who were known to be interested in IQ trends. To assess changes in IQ within each country from one generation to the next, he set up unusually strin-

gent standards, applying four criteria (derived from Jensen's suggestions) to each data set he received:

- Were the samples comprehensive (e.g., composed of draft registrants), to eliminate sampling bias?
- Were the tests unaltered from one generation to the next, and was it possible to estimate trends based on raw score differences?
- Were at least some of the available data based on culturally reduced tests like Raven's Matrices, which provide more valuable information than tests of acquired knowledge composed of items that might be specifically learned?
- Are the data at least partially based on mature subjects, those who have reached their "peak" raw score performance?

Flynn used the first two criteria (the quality of the samples and the continuity of the tests) to categorize each data set into four statuses:

Status 1 = verified evidence of IQ gains

Status 2 = probable evidence

Status 3 = tentative evidence

Status 4 = speculative evidence

He used the last two criteria in his discussions of the implications of the results he obtained. These criteria are rigorous, as supported by the statuses he assigned to data that he previously reported from 73 studies (sample size of nearly 7,500) in the United States (Flynn, 1984) and by the statuses that he assigned to Lynn and Hampson's (1986a) impressive data sets in Japan and Great Britain. Flynn (1987) assigned status 2 to his U.S. data for subjects aged 2–18 and status 3 to a set of U.S. data for adolescents and adults; he assigned status 3 to the British data and status ¾ to the Japanese data.

Flynn applied sophisticated logical and empirical treatment of the data to determine the number of IQ points that each country has gained per year, focusing on the generation from about 1950 to 1980. His results are presented in the following sections, along with updated findings from studies conducted after his 1987 paper (Flynn, 1998a, 1998b, 1998c).

Gains in IQ from One Generation to the Next

Figure 2.1 summarizes data that are included in Flynn's (1987) Table 15. He presented the amount of gain per year and per generation (30 years), but we have converted his results to IQ gain per decade. He also presented his results

grouped by type of test (nonverbal, verbal, or both), and he kept samples separate if they differed in age range or geographic location within the country. We took averages across samples to provide data for each country as a whole. When data sets for a given country differed in status, we used only the data with the highest status; for example, we preferred not to risk contaminating the verified (status 1) data for Canada from Edmonton with the probable/tentative (status ⅔) data from Saskatchewan.

Figure 2.1 indicates that each of the 14 nations showed gains in IQ from the previous to

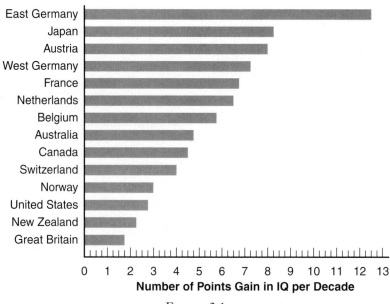

FIGURE 2.1

Gains in IQ per decade by 14 nations (Flynn, 1987, Table 15). Flynn categorized data from each country by its status: 1 = verified, 2 = probable, 3 = tentative, 4 = speculative. For each country, the status of the data is given below in parentheses, along with the measures used. When data were available from more than one type of test (verbal, nonverbal, mixed), the different rates of IQ gain were averaged. If data differing in status were available for the same nation, only the highest status data were included in the figure. Whenever possible, verbal and nonverbal measures were weighed equally. The tests used, and status of the data, are as follows: East Germany (Raven, status ½), Japan (Wechsler, status ¾), Austria (Wechsler, status 4), West Germany (Wechsler, status ¾), France (Raven + Verbal–math, status 3), Netherlands (Raven, status 1), Belgium (Raven, shapes and Verbal–math, status 1), Australia (Jenkins Nonverbal, status 3), Canada (Raven + CTMM, status 1), Switzerland (Wechsler, status 4), Norway (Matrices + Verbal–math, status 1), United States (Weschler-Binet, status 2), New Zealand (Otis, status 1), and Great Britain (Raven, status 3).

the present generation, and in some countries these gains have been quite large. Japan joins six Western European countries (East Germany, Austria, West Germany, France, Netherlands, Belgium) in gaining more than 5 points per decade (more than a standard deviation per generation!). Of the 14 nations listed in the figure, only data from the following countries are status 1, or verified evidence of generational IQ gains: Netherlands (6.7 points), Belgium (5.8), Canada (4.6), Norway (3.2), and New Zealand (2.4). Consequently, all evidence of extreme gains in Figure 2.1 (half a standard deviation or more) is either tentative or speculative.

As impressive as the three-point gain per decade for people in the United States has seemed to readers of Flynn's (1984) article, the United States has outgained only two of the nations studied by Flynn (1987)—New Zealand and Great Britain—and the latter country showed gains of 5.4 points per decade in a subsequent study of adults from 1942 to 1992 (Raven, Raven, & Court, 1993) that used the same test (Raven's Matrices) that was administered in Flynn's (1987) study. In addition, the United States has been outgained by four nations with verified data—the Netherlands, Belgium, Norway (barely), and neighboring Canada. And, to add insult to injury, the U.S. gain of three points seems to have dwindled to 2.5 points in Flynn's (1998c) recent study of WISC-III and WAIS-III data from 1972 to 1995. Nonetheless, all comparisons among nations must remain highly speculative because the data presented in the figure are not directly comparable. They have different statuses as scientific evidence, different tests were generally used in different countries, the samples were not comparable in age or background from one country to the next, and so forth.

Gains on Verbal versus Nonverbal Tests

As Flynn (1987) points out, gains on tests of fluid intelligence like Raven's Progressive Matrices have more theoretical meaning than gains on crystallized tests like Wechsler's Information subtest. Gains on the former imply true improvement in abstract problem-solving ability; gains on the latter may merely reflect greater mastery of the specific content of the items (i.e., improved achievement, not cognitive ability). As Flynn reminds us, "[t]he average person today would outscore Aristotle or Archimedes on general information, but this hardly shows greater intelligence" (p. 184).

In fact, Flynn (1987) showed fairly consistently that gains were greater on fluid tests than on crystallized tests, indicating a true increase in problem-solving ability. For all nations studied by Flynn (1987), the median gain on the Raven and related tests was 5.9 points per decade, compared to 3.7 points per decade on verbal tests (either the Otis, tests of verbal and math ability, or a Binet-like test), as shown in Table 2.4. A value about midway between these extremes (5.2) was obtained by taking the median of the gains on tests with both verbal and nonverbal content

TABLE 2.4   Separate nonverbal and verbal gains for countries in Figure 2.1

| Nation | Gain in IQ points per decade | | |
	Nonverbal	Verbal	Overall
France (status 3)	10.0	3.7	6.9
Belgium (status 1)	7.6	4.1	5.8
Norway (status 1)	4.2	2.2	3.2
Mean	7.3	3.3	5.3

(invariably a Wechsler scale), using data from Flynn's (1987) Table 15, which included nine samples representing seven nations. Separate gains are shown in Table 2.4 for the countries in Figure 2.1 whose gains were averaged from fluid and crystallized tests. Of the countries using the Wechsler scales for which separate data were available for the Verbal and Performance Scales, a similar pattern emerged for the post-1950 generation (table adapted from Flynn, 1987, Table 17), shown in Table 2.5. Table 2.6 supplements Figure 2.1 by showing the gains in IQ per decade by various nations on tests of nonverbal, usually fluid, ability, and also on verbal tests. This table includes data from Flynn's (1987) initial comparative study plus additional data from his more recent summary (Flynn, 1998a). The median gain on nonverbal tests was 6.4, compared to a median of 4.1 on tests of verbal and mathematical ability. The following nations scored at or above the median gain on both verbal and nonverbal measures: Japan, Austria, Belgium. The United States earned gains well below the median on both types of tests. France showed a striking difference in gains on the nonverbal Raven test (10.0) and on the verbal–math test (3.7). An extremely similar finding was also reported for

France from the "speculative" Wechsler data cited previously, offering good cross-validation of the results for that country.

Persistence of Gains through Adulthood

The IQ gains across generations, to be truly meaningful, must persist into adulthood until adults reach their full mental maturity. If these gains are temporary and short-lived, they would only show that citizens of a particular nation reached peak ability at an earlier age but did not raise their ultimate level of performance.

For this analysis, Flynn (1987) focused on tests of fluid intelligence, a vulnerable ability that peaks in late adolescence and declines during most of the adult life span (see Chapter 5) whose "growth and decline closely parallels measures of physical strength, air capacity of the lungs…, and brain weight" (Jensen, 1980, p. 235). Crystallized intelligence, by contrast, does not peak until the 50s or 60s, preventing Flynn (1987) from applying his extensive data sets to the important theoretical question that he raised.

Flynn's data suggest that IQ gains are not temporary, but instead persist to maturity. His

TABLE 2.5 Separate performance and verbal gains on the Wechsler scales for countries after 1950

Nation	Gain in IQ points per decade		
	Performance	Verbal	Full Scale
Japan (status ¾)	7.3	6.7	8.4
Austria (status 4)	9.3	6.7	8.2
West Germany (status ¾)	9.3	4.0	7.4
France (status 4)[a]	6.3	1.0	3.7
United States (status 2)[b]	3.3	2.7	3.0
Mean	7.1	4.2	6.1

[a]Data for France do not match the data in Figure 2.1; these Wechsler data are status 4 data that were excluded from that figure.
[b]Data for the U.S. are just WISC vs. WISC-R in order to hold generation (post-1950) constant.

TABLE 2.6   Gains in IQ per decade for numerous nations, based either on verbal or nonverbal tests

Nation	Gain on Nonverbal Tests	Nation	Gain on Verbal Tests
East Germany (Leipzig)	12.5	Japan	6.7
France	10.0	Austria (Vienna)	6.7
Austria (Vienna)	9.3	Canada (Saskatchewan)	4.9
West Germany	9.3	Scotland	4.3
Belgium	7.6	Belgium	4.1
Japan	7.3	West Germany	4.0
Netherlands	6.7	France	3.7
Israel	6.0	New Zealand	2.4
Australia	4.9	Norway	2.2
China	4.4		
Norway	4.2		
Canada (Edmonton)	4.0		
Great Britain	3.6		
United States	3.3		
Median Nonverbal Gain	**6.4**	**Median Verbal Gain**	**4.1**

NOTE: All data are from Flynn (1987, Tables 15 & 17), except for recent data summarized by Flynn (1998a, Figure 3, p. 43 & p. 49) for China (Raven's Matrices), Israel (Raven's Matrices), Scotland (Binet-type test), and Great Britain (Raven's Matrices). The value presented for Great Britain is the mean of the values reported by Flynn (1987) and Flynn (1998a). Nonverbal tests from Flynn's initial study (1987) are the Raven for East Germany, France, the Netherlands, Canada (Edmonton), and Great Britain; the Raven and a Shapes test for Belgium; an adapted Raven for Norway; matrices and other "fluid" tests for Australia; and Wechsler's P-IQ for Japan, Austria, West Germany, and the U.S. Data for Canada (Saskatchewan) are status ⅔ that were excluded from Figure 2.1 in favor of the status 1 data from Edmonton. Status 4 Wechsler data are excluded from this table.

status 1, or verified data, on tests of fluid intelligence for Belgium, Netherlands, and Norway reveal unequivocally that the IQ gains persist to full mental maturity. In the United States, the adult data were based on different instruments (WAIS and WAIS-R), and, hence, classified by Flynn (1987) as status 3, or tentative, data. Focusing on Wechsler Full Scale IQ analyses (it is unclear why Flynn did not use P-IQ, which more closely resembles fluid ability), Flynn showed that gains per decade in the United States were 1.85 points for adults below age 35, and 3.4 points for adults ages 35–75. When contrasted to the rate of 3 points per decade for school chil-

dren, Flynn (1987) concluded from these results that "American gains on Wechsler tests appear to persist into late adulthood" (p. 186). Additional support for his tentative conclusion comes from research findings that show that the peak raw-score performance of people in the United States on Wechsler's subtests has risen from age 22 in the mid- to late-1930s to age 30 in the late 1970s to nearly 40 in 1995. And about a decade after his tentative conclusions, Flynn (1998a) synthesized the results of an array of studies on the "Flynn effect" to state more definitively: "More often than not, gains are similar at all IQ levels. Gains may be age-specific, but this has not yet been established *and they certainly persist into adulthood*" (p. 61, emphasis ours).

Implications of the Flynn Effect for the Malleability of Intelligence

Flynn (1998b) concluded: "Data from twenty nations show not a single exception to massive IQ gains over time. The escalation of whatever skills are involved probably began no later than the onset of the industrial revolution" (p. 106). Likely explanations for the increases in U.S. IQs from the 1930s and 1940s to the late 1970s and to the mid-1990s are the advent of television, the increasing reach of the mass media in general, changing attitudes toward parenting (including better understanding of stimulation in infancy), improved perinatal care, nutrition, and so forth. *The Rising Curve*, edited by Neisser (1998), offers a multifaceted look at possible explanations and analyses of generational gains in IQ and related measures such as academic achievement. Regardless of the precise reasons "why," the changes are clearly related to cultural factors, not to modifications in specific test items or subtests or administration procedures. For example, the large differences in IQs yielded by a test and its successor occurred even when the test had *not* been revised, such as the 1972 Binet (Thorndike, 1975) and most of the studies from other countries (Flynn, 1987), and when analyses of the WISC and WISC-R IQ differences were based only on the core of items that was common to both batteries (Doppelt & Kaufman, 1977; Kaufman, 1979a).

These IQ gains are certainly due to environment, not heredity, and reflect the malleability of intelligence. Flynn (1987) states: "Massive IQ gains cannot be due to genetic factors. Reproductive differentials between social classes would have to be impossibly large to raise the mean IQ even 1 point in a single generation (Flynn, 1986; Vining, 1986)" (p. 188). When evaluating the 20-point Dutch gain in a generation (about 7 points per decade), Flynn (1987) was able to conduct further analyses of this exceptional data set to apportion the 20 points into specific environmental components. He was able to attribute 1 point of the increase to formal education, 3 points to socioeconomic status (estimated by father's occupation), and 2 points to test sophistication. Overall, he estimated that 5 of the 20-point Dutch IQ gain from the 1950s to the 1980s was accounted for by the three variables indicated previously (he did not simply add the 1+3+2 points per variable because of confounding), leaving 75% of the difference due to unknown environmental variables. The potency of environmental variables, despite the difficulty in identifying the contributions of each one separately, echoes the problem of the relationship of environment to IQ.

The average intelligence of the Japanese people has increased at the impressive rate of 8 IQ points per decade since World War II (Flynn, 1987; Lynn & Hampson, 1986a; see Figure 2.1), based on large samples of data from numerous sources. Flynn interprets the results of the studies from Japan more cautiously than do Lynn and Hampson, but both sets of investigators agree that the rise of IQ in postwar Japan has been substantial. Within Japan, the rapid industrialization of "a relatively undeveloped country in the 1930s…[one that] suffered considerable disruption and deprivation in and immediately after World War II" (Lynn & Hampson, 1986a, p. 31) should logically lead to great improvement in the people's intelligence. As might be predicted, the gains in Japan were more rapid just after the war (10–11 points per decade) and decelerated to about 5 points per decade since 1960.

Overall, Lynn and Hampson's (1986) and Flynn's (1984, 1987, 1998a, 1998b, 1998c) data support the concept of the malleability of intelligence for whole cultures and confirm the fact that the level of intelligence seems to be in continual flux. This line of research joins with intervention studies, discussed in the next section, to provide broad-based support for intelligence's considerable malleability.

The Abecedarian Project

The malleability of IQ based on direct interventions has traditionally produced conflicting results. Positive findings emerged in several studies from the 1940s (e.g., Honzik, Macfarlane, & Allen, 1948; Tuddenham, 1948) that Angoff (1988) cited regarding the issue of the IQ's changeability. But studies attempting specific interventions, usually in the early years of life and sometimes with the treatments spanning several years, have sometimes been unsuccessful. Reviews from a generation ago (Jensen, 1969), and even more recently (Brody, 1985), were quite pessimistic. For example: Studies to raise the IQs of retarded children (Spitz, 1986) generate "the dismal conclusion that they have been uniformly failures" (Angoff, 1988, p. 718). Or: "there is little evidence that short-term interventions will lead to enduring changes in intelligence" (Brody, 1985, p. 371). Furthermore, like Sir Cyril Burt's questionable or fraudulent heritability data, which cast doubt on the validity of other researchers' genetic studies as well, a scandal involving Heber and Garber's (1970) Milwaukee Project (Reynolds, 1987b; Sommer & Sommer, 1983) cast doubt not only on that study's dramatic positive findings, but also on gains shown in other studies.

However, the doom-and-gloom conclusions reached by some reviewers of intervention studies, and the cynicism that accompanied reports of possibly fraudulent data in Milwaukee, which tended to characterize opinions expressed in the 1980s, is not congruent with more recent reviews. Barnett (1995) concluded from a review of 15 well-designed early childhood intervention studies that most could boast positive gains years after the treatment ended. Academic gains frequently occurred initially (e.g., Bryant & Maxwell, 1997), and sometimes lasted into middle childhood (Jester & Guinagh, 1983; Johnson & Walker, 1991; Lally, Mangione, & Honig, 1988) or mid-adolescence (Berrueta-Clement, Schweinhart, Barnett, Epstein, & Weikart, 1984). Long-lasting *behavioral* gains have also been observed in the school setting (Lally et al., 1988; Seitz, Rosenbaum, & Apfel, 1985). Perhaps no data can better illustrate the malleability of children's intelligence than the strongly positive gains, through age 21 years, from arguably the best intervention study ever conducted—the

Abecedarian Project (Burchinal, Campbell, Bryant, Wasik, & Ramey, 1997; Campbell, Pungello, Miller-Johnson, Burchinal, & Ramey, in press; Campbell & Ramey, 1986, 1994, 1995; Ramey & Campbell, 1984; Ramey, Campbell, & Ramey, 1999).

Description of the Project

The Abecedarian Project was a true experimental study as 57 infants were randomly assigned to the treatment group and 54 were randomly assigned to the control group. The full scope of the early childhood program appears in Ramey and Campbell (1984) and is summarized briefly here. Infants (98% African American, all from low-income families) averaged 4.4 months of age when attendance began at the child care center. The treatment program—designed to promote cognitive, language, perceptual-motor, and social development—was developed especially for the Abecedarian Project (Sparling & Lewis, 1979); the child care center was open 8 hours per day, 5 days per week, 50 weeks per year, and the treatment was maintained for five years. The teacher–child ratios were low (ranging from 1:3 for infants to 1:6 for children age 5). For preschool children, the focus of the curriculum switched to language development and preliteracy skills (Ramey, McGinesss, Cross, Collier, & Barrie-Blackley, 1982; Sparling & Lewis, 1984).

The infants who were randomly assigned to the control group received enhanced nutrition to ensure that any gains observed for the treatment group were not a function of their better nutrition (iron-fortified formula for the first 15 months), and social work services were made available to families in both the treatment and control groups, as needed. Additionally, many control children did attend other child care centers, some starting in infancy and others in the preschool years.

Because infants in the treated group received much of their nutrition at the center, infants in the control group received iron-fortified formula for the first 15 months. This was done in an effort to reduce the likelihood that cognitive differences between the groups were due to better early nutrition in treated children. In addition, families of control children received disposable diapers until the child was toilet trained as an incentive for participation. Social work services were made available to both groups as needed. Many children in the control group attended child care centers, some beginning in infancy and others beginning in the preschool years (Campbell et al., in press).

The 57 experimental and 54 control infants, all healthy and believed to be free of any biological conditions potentially associated with retardation, were included in one of four cohorts between 1972 and 1977. All 111 infants were identified as "high risk" based on factors such as maternal education (which averaged grade 10) and family income; mothers were 20 years old, on average, and 53% of the infants were female.

IQ was assessed with different instruments at different points in time: Stanford Binet (Terman & Merrill, 1973) at ages 3–4; WPPSI at age 5; WISC-R at ages 6.5, 8, 12, and 15 years; and WAIS-R at age 21. Reading and math were measured with the Woodcock-Johnson Psychoeducational Battery—Achievement at ages 8, 12, and 15 years (WJ; Woodcock & Johnson, 1977) and at age 21 years (Woodcock & Johnson, 1989). The sample varied at each age due to attrition (and occasionally to children who returned to the area); at age 15, and again at age 21, the sample was a respectable 104 (53 treatment and 51 control).

IQ and Achievement Gains through Age 21

Campbell et al. (in press) report IQ gains from age 3 to 21 years, and achievement gains from age 8 to 21 years, for the treatment sample relative to the control group (data for ages 3 to 15 were also reported in numerous previous publications). The results are phenomenal. The authors utilized a sophisticated analytic procedure (Hierarchical Linear Models) with both the IQ and achievement data to describe the patterns of change over time and to identify the variables associated with the change. However, the effectiveness of their well-designed and well-controlled longitudinal study is evident by just examining the mean IQ and achievement scores for the treatment and control groups at different points in time (Campbell et al., in press, Table 1). During the preschool years, the treatment group outscored the controls by about 16.5 points (age 3), 12.5 points (age 4) and 7.5 points (age 5). Gains for the treatment group relative to the control sample on the WISC-R were about 4 to 6 points (4 points at age 8, and 6 points at ages 6.5, 12, and 15). At age 21 on the WAIS-R, the gain was still a significant 4.42 points (about .30 SD), with the treatment group earning an average Full Scale IQ of 89.66 versus a value of 85.24 for the controls.

Gains on the achievement tests at ages 8 to 21 years for the treatment sample relative to the controls exceeded the IQ gains for those ages. At age 8, the gain was almost 9 points, and it leveled off to about a constant 6 points (.40 SD) for ages 12, 15, and 21. For math, the gains were about 5 points at ages 8, 12, and 21, and nearly 7 points at age 15.

According to Cohen (1977), effect sizes of at least .25 have practical, educational significance. All of the effect sizes at ages 3–21 for IQ and ages 8–21 for achievement exceeded .25, as did the effect sizes computed by Campbell et al. (in press) for other comparisons between treatment and control subjects based on a diversity of sophisticated analyses. The very large gains in IQ at ages 3 and 4 may have been spuriously high because of the use of the highly verbal Stanford-Binet with children whose treatment stressed language development. However, the gains of about 4 to 6 IQ points on the WISC-R and WAIS-R, and about 5 to 7 standard-score points on Woodcock-Johnson reading and math, which maintained throughout childhood, adolescence, and young adulthood, are a testimony to the intellectual and academic gains that resulted from an intensive and carefully conceived early childhood intervention program. And, more importantly, they illustrate the malleability of cognitive ability. For a more detailed study of the IQ and achievement gains, as well as the factors that mediate these gains and the growth curves that define the gains over time, consult Campbell et al.

The amazing endurance of the treatment effects of the Abecedarian Project into early adulthood was not matched by either the Early Training Project (Gray, Ramsey, & Klaus, 1982) or the High/Scope Perry Preschool Project (Berrueta-Clement et al., 1984; Schweinhart, Barnes, & Weikart, 1993), both of which reported post-high school results. According to Campbell et al. (in press), the success of the Abecedarian Project relative to these other excellent programs may be due to reasons such as: (1) beginning treatment in early infancy in contrast to ages 3 or 4 years, which characterized the other two programs as well as numerous others; (2) providing five years of treatment instead of the 1 to 2 years provided by the other two programs; and (3) offering an intensive year-round 8-hour-a-day program instead of half-day programs that were in operation for part of a year. It may be that many of the programs that did not show long-term gains failed to do so because they provided too little too late, and not because of a lack of malleability in intellectual development.

Overview of Malleability of IQ

To Brody (1985), the relative constancy of the IQ from early childhood through adulthood (Conley, 1984; Pinneau, 1961) and the failure of most intervention studies to demonstrate a malleable IQ "suggest that intelligence tests are valid measures of the construct intelligence" and are "congruent with our ordinary intuitions about the meaning of the construct" (p. 371). He is probably right in that sense. The stability data do support the validity of the IQ construct. For example, IQs at age 5 have been shown to correlate .50–.60 with IQ at age 40, and IQs at age 9 to correlate about .70 (McCall, 1977); the average of children's IQs at ages 10 through 12 have been shown to predict average IQ at ages 17 and 18 to the tune of .96 (Pinneau, 1961); and 101 retarded children tested four times on Form L-M of the Binet, with 1-year intervals between as-

sessments, obtained rather constant IQs, producing a median correlation of .85 (Silverstein, 1982b).

But these are group data, which obscure individual differences, and which do not take into account the malleability of the IQ for individuals who are given early intensive intervention to "kill" the prediction of low IQs for low-income infants (e.g., Abecedarian Project). As Anastasi and Urbina (1997) point out, "Studies of individuals…may reveal large upward or downward shifts in test scores" (p. 326). They also cite research suggesting that one can improve prediction of a person's future intellectual status by combining current IQ with "measures of the individual's emotional and motivational characteristics and of her or his environment" (p. 327). Additionally, the group data presented by researchers studying intelligence across generations (Flynn, 1984, 1987, 1998a, 1998b, 1998c; Lynn & Hampson, 1986a) demonstrate that IQ is indeed malleable based on environmental changes, despite the stability of the rank ordering of people over time or the substantial heritability coefficient for the trait of intelligence.

Research conducted systematically on different cultures over time (or retrospectively) may help isolate specific sets of environmental variables that are most associated with the largest gains in intelligence. Because the average intelligence of people in the United States (and, especially, Europeans and Asians) seems to be increasing at a steady, measurable, and rather substantial rate, researchers can investigate possible answers to these pressing questions, answers that might be a precursor for developing successful interventions to reduce group differences among ethnic groups and across social classes (see Neisser, 1998, and, especially, the overview by Flynn, 1998a, for an in-depth, diverse look at the issues associated with the Flynn effect). Similar intervention strategies may be developed based on research on motivation and emotional stability, as well as environmental variables "that can effectively alter the course of intellectual development in the desired directions" (Anastasi & Urbina, 1997, p. 327).

Angoff (1988) has argued that researchers and other professionals should focus more on the IQ's changeability than on dividing its variance into genetic and environmental components. As he pointed out, the prevalent focus has led to controversy, unscientific arguments and assertions about a scientific issue, name-calling, and claims that intelligence tests are invalid or useless. A shift in focus is a step toward reducing the difference in the IQs of groups of Caucasians and African Americans. To close the IQ gap, "such an effort will have to be buttressed by a broad program of educational, psychological, cultural, and economic types of interventions targeted not only at the child but also at the child's parents, his or her extended family, and indeed, the entire community" (Angoff, 1988, p. 719). The persistent findings of the Flynn effect over time and across nations, as well as the success of many early intervention programs such as the Abecedarian Project, both speak to the need for innovative research and for an optimistic outlook regarding the potential applications of such studies.

ATTACKS ON THE IQ CONSTRUCT

The IQ construct has been in the line of fire for controversy from the moment of its inception. Two of these controversies are presented in the sections that follow: (1) the clinically based challenge issued by Lezak (1988a) as a result of her practical experience as a neuropsychologist, and (2) the research-based and decision-making-based challenge issued by leaders in the field of learning disabilities assessment (e.g., Siegel, 1999). Both of these anti-IQ approaches are described and rebutted in the sections that follow.

Lezak's Eulogy

Muriel Lezak announced to the professional world that the IQ concept was dead in an address

to the International Neuropsychological Society in January 1988, which she subsequently published as "IQ: R.I.P." in the *Journal of Clinical and Experimental Neuropsychology* (Lezak, 1988a). However, she delivered a funeral oration for a corpse that has been dead for at least 10 to 15 years (Kaufman, 1988; Reynolds, 1988), thus demonstrating that some leaders in the field of neuropsychology may be oblivious to the research and philosophy that characterize the related fields of clinical and school psychology together with special education.

Because of Lezak's (1995) deserved influence on the clinical assessment scene, the provocativeness of the comments in her eulogy, the relevance of the topic for any text on intellectual assessment, and the fact that her criticisms echo those of many other neuropsychologists, we have treated the issues in some depth. First, we summarize the key points of her funeral oration; after each point, we respond from the vantage point of the intelligent testing philosophy (described in Chapter 1) and research base that have typified our approach, and that of others in the field, to the interpretation of diverse instruments. The rebuttal arguments include many of the points raised by Dean (1988), Hynd (1988), Reynolds (1988), and Kaufman (1988) in the invited responses to Lezak's paper that appeared in a special section of the *NASP Communique* organized by Telzrow (1988).

Lezak (1988a) eulogized "a concept that, when young, served psychology well by giving it a metric basis that made it less of a speculative philosophy and more like a science…. [But the] IQ—as concept and as score—has long ceased to be a useful scientific construct for organizing and describing our increasingly complex and sensitive behavioral observations…. [T]he IQ became senescent soon after its brilliant adolescence, and should have been put to rest by now" (pp. 351–352). Basically, Lezak's specific criticisms can be grouped into two general categories: the meaninglessness and impurity of global IQs, and the misuse and abuse that commonly accompany psychologists' interpretation of IQs.

The Global IQs Are Impure and Meaningless

CRITIQUE

Lezak (1988a): "When the many and various neuropsychological observations elicited by so-called 'intelligence' tests are lumped and leveled into a single IQ-score—or even three— the product of this unholy conversion is a number that, in referring to everything, represents nothing" (p. 352).

REBUTTAL

Worship or overinterpretation of global IQs has not existed among the mainstream of clinical and school psychologists for at least two decades, probably longer. For clinical purposes, IQs exist as midpoints of the person's overall performance, providing reference points for ipsative profile interpretation. Practitioners have become accustomed to following the interpretive strategy that psychologists and trainers have urged for about a quarter of a century (e.g., Kaufman, 1979a): "[T]he Full Scale IQ serves as a target at which the examiner will take careful aim.... Large V-P differences, numerous fluctuations in the scaled-score profile, or inferred relationships between test scores and extraneous variables (e.g., fatigue, anxiety, subcultural background) greatly diminish the importance of the Full Scale IQ as an index of the [person's] level of intelligence" (p. 21).

Global IQs are useful summaries and provide a concrete starting point for profile interpretation. When the search for strengths and weaknesses proves fruitless, as it sometimes does, then the V-P IQ discrepancy or even the "unholy conversion" into the FS-IQ becomes quite meaningful. In those instances, the empirical validation of the IQ construct based on data obtained for groups comes into play, enabling the clinician to interpret the scores with meaning. Even multiscore professionals like us can appreciate the extensive empirical sup-

port for the g construct (e.g., Jensen, 1987, 1998), which justifies the combination of diverse mental abilities into one, two, or three global ability scales.

Indeed, the V and P IQs provide an exceptional summary of abilities for many individuals, and the difference between them may have important diagnostic or remedial implications. Lezak (1988a) seemed to acknowledge this benefit herself when she noted that "as we all know, persons with left hemisphere damage tend to have relatively lowered scores on the more verbally demanding subtests compared to their better scores on several of the less verbally dependent subtests" (p. 358). (Ironically, this generalization does not hold up very well; see the discussion in Chapter 8.)

For individuals, global IQs are frequently nothing more than overviews of a person's total ability spectrum that mask substantial variability among the subtest scores; but for groups, the summative scores have abundant meaning. How can one summarily dismiss a construct that produces discrepancies of 36 IQ points between adults with at least 17 years of schooling and individuals who failed to graduate from elementary school (see Table 4.10)? Yet, nowhere in her funeral oration does Lezak make the important distinction between the IQ construct for individuals and for groups.

Lezak (1988a) also seems to believe that wide profile fluctuations reside within the domain of neuropsychology, "where most examinations are conducted on persons whose mental functioning is only partially impaired" (p. 352). Much research shows emphatically that the Wechsler profiles of normal, intact individuals are characterized by a striking amount of inter- and intra-scale variability (Kaufman, 1976a, 1976b, 1990; Psychological Corporation, 1997, Appendix D; Wechsler, 1991, Appendix B; 1997, Appendix B). Competent clinical and school psychologists are aware of this normal scatter; as Reynolds (1988) notes, "Lezak has set up the IQ in an archaic, once used manner that has been antithetical to good practice for at least a decade" (p. 6).

CRITIQUE

Lezak (1988a): "Perhaps Wechsler's VIQ and PIQ concepts would have had a greater chance for independent survival if they had been not only theoretically attractive but psychologically sound. However, hundreds of factor analytic studies…have repeatedly and consistently demonstrated that not all Verbal Scale subtests measure verbal functions, that one Performance Scale subtest has a considerable Verbal loading, and that other important aspects of cognitive behavior—particularly attention and concentration, mental tracking, and response speed—contribute variously to both Wechsler's VIQ and PIQ scores without being recognized or measured in their own right" (p. 355).

REBUTTAL

Lezak is correct that the Wechsler subtests do not always behave in a predictable manner, but she is off the mark in labeling the Verbal and Performance Scales as psychometrically unsound. Probably nowhere in the psychometric literature has there been more support than for the constructs underlying Wechsler's V and P IQs. Although Wechsler developed the scales from an armchair, the empirical validity of the Verbal Comprehension and Perceptual Organization dimensions has been affirmed by factor analysis for a multitude of samples, between the ages of 3 and 89 years, differing in gender, ethnic group, and presence and type of exceptionality.

When two factors are rotated for the WISC-R and WAIS-R, the tests in use when Lezak eulogized the IQ, the match of the rotated factors to Wechsler's V and P scales borders on the astonishing for normal and clinical samples (Kaufman, 1990, Tables 8.1 and 8.2; Kaufman, Harrison, & Ittenbach,

1990, Tables 2 and 3); the support is just as strong for Wechsler's preschool scale and for predecessors of the WISC-R and WAIS-R (Silverstein, 1969; Wechsler, 1989, Tables 17 and 18). Even with the addition of subtests to the WISC-III and WAIS-III, and the organization of the scales into four factors, the two-factor rotated solutions of Wechsler's Third Editions match the V-P split fairly closely. For the WISC-III, two-factor solutions produce clear-cut Verbal and Performance factors, with each of the six Verbal and seven Performance subtests loading higher, usually much higher, on its designated factor (Wechsler, 1991, Table 6.2). For the WAIS-III, the split is not as decisive, but it is nonetheless compelling: All seven Performance tests loaded higher on the Performance factor and five of the seven Verbal subtests—all but Letter–Number Sequencing and Digit Span—loaded higher on the Verbal factor (Kaufman, Lichtenberger, & McLean, in press; also see Chapter 7). Even when three or four factors are rotated for the legion of Wechsler tests, past and present, the support for the construct validity of Wechsler's V and P IQs is still overwhelming.

Lezak's criticism that noncognitive variables affect test scores represents a strength of the tests, not a weakness. Wechsler did not consciously develop a neuropsychological test or even a psychometric test; he constructed a clinical test intended to measure an aspect of the total personality structure. The assessment of what Wechsler (1950) terms "conative" or nonintellective factors, "necessary ingredients of intelligent behavior" (Wechsler, 1974, p. 6), is essential because general intelligence is simply a multifaceted construct. Wechsler (1974) states that "such traits as persistence, zest, impulse control, and goal awareness[,]…[l]ike enzymes,…serve to direct and to enhance (sometimes also to demean) the utilization of other capacities" (p. 6). To criticize the role of personality traits on mental measurement is, in effect, to blame Binet for having the vision to go beyond Galton's psychophysical tests of intelligence.

When Lezak states that these nonintellective factors are neither "recognized nor measured in their own right," she is only partly correct. They certainly are recognized by any clinical or school psychologist who has completed even a halfway decent training program, and are incorporated completely into the interpretation of the person's profile. They are not specifically measured because there are no empirical criteria for determining which subtest scores are depressed due to anxiety or inattention. Even if identifiable, will those particular subtests be subject to the influences of distractibility (or impulsivity, or anxiety, or shyness, and so forth) for each person tested? Some people interpret the third Wechsler factor (WMI on the WAIS-III) as a behavioral dimension (Freedom from Distractibility, Freedom from Disruptive Anxiety), but how reasonable is it to believe that distractible or anxious people will perform poorly on Arithmetic, Digit Span, Letter–Number Sequencing, or even Coding/Digit Symbol primarily or exclusively because of these behavioral variables? In sum, Lezak's criticisms of the failure of IQ tests to specifically measure behavioral traits is both impractical and antithetical to the clinical interpretation of test profiles.

CRITIQUE

Lezak (1988a): "Not surprisingly, IQ scores do not do a very good job at predicting success in real life" (p. 356).

REBUTTAL

What does?

CRITIQUE

Lezak (1988a): "One major problem that from its inception has dogged the IQ, whether score or concept, is its questionable conceptual basis" (p. 356).

REBUTTAL

This is a valid criticism, one that has impelled Kaufman and Kaufman (1983a, 1993) to develop the K-ABC from a sequential versus simultaneous processing model and to base the KAIT on the Cattell-Horn distinction between broad fluid and broad crystallized intelligence. It also led Thorndike et al. (1986a) to apply a modified Cattell-Horn crystallized versus fluid intelligence model to the Stanford-Binet Form IV and was the impetus for Woodcock (1990) to apply Horn's (1985) expansion and refinement of the Gf-Gc theory to the revised Woodcock-Johnson Psycho-Educational Battery and its successor, the Woodcock-Johnson III (see Chapter 14). But the criticism does not mitigate the value of Wechsler's scales for clinical, neuropsychological, or educational assessment, nor does it diminish the value or meaning of the global IQs yielded by his scales.

Despite a list of definitions for intelligence that exceeded 90 in the early 1960s (Lezak, 1988a) and that has, perhaps, "doubled in the last quarter century" (p. 357), the Wechsler system is not threatened by an unclear theoretical model underlying Wechsler's batteries, by an inadequate conceptual framework for the construct of intelligence, or by a lack of unanimity in its definition. The validity evidence from thousands of research investigations indicates the practical and clinical utility of the tests and the scores they yield.

CRITIQUE

Lezak (1988a): "[N]europsychological studies have repeatedly failed to identify neuroanatomic or neurophysiologic correlates of IQ" (p. 357).

REBUTTAL

The call for a search for neuroanatomic correlates for a construct so deliberately multifaceted and complex as a global IQ scale seems naive coming from an expert in the specificity of neuropsychological function. In any case, we do not see the necessity for an intelligence test to have a clear-cut neurophysiological correlate.

CRITIQUE

Lezak (1988a): "IQ scores and all their conceptual trappings have been built on the unstable sands of arbitrary and shifting item selection" (p. 357).

REBUTTAL

Lezak bases this statement on research (including a study she conducted) showing that the WAIS-R yields lower scores than the WAIS by about a half a standard deviation. She attributes the lower IQs to the "effects of relatively small changes in the tests" (p. 357). But here she is simply wrong. As discussed previously in this chapter, Flynn's (1984, 1987, 1998a, 1998b, 1998c) research has shown real changes in the abilities of children and adults from generation to generation at the quantifiable rate of 3 points per decade within the United States. These shifts in the norms occur even when no items are modified (as in 1972, when the 1960 Binet was restandardized but not revised) and have nothing to do either with the specific items that are included or excluded, or with the arbitrary choice of "tasks chosen or devised by test makers according to their notions of what is intelligent behavior" (Lezak, 1988a, p. 357).

Misinterpretation of What IQ Measures

CRITIQUE

Lezak (1988a): "[P]sychometricians have dug their own grave by misusing mental ability tests and thereby limiting children's opportunities for objective evaluation of their ability potential" (p. 358).

REBUTTAL

In reaching this conclusion, Lezak (1988a) referred specifically to the Larry P. case and to the increase in the plaintiff's IQ by 38 points when retested by an African American examiner. She is evidently unaware of decisions in similar cases or of the absurdity of taking the 38-point gain at face value. As Reynolds (1988) states: "The Larry P. decision is a judicial anomaly. Related cases have been decided in just the opposite direction, the most prominent, and more recent, at the Federal level being PASE v. Hannon and Marshall v. Georgia" (p. 6). He continues: "The 'black examiner' example of 38-point IQ gains is simply ludicrous. Examination of the Larry P. transcript indicates that wholly inappropriate answers were given credit in an attempt to increase the IQ of the so-called Larry P. Furthermore, the extant research literature demonstrates that white examiners do not impede the performance of black children (e.g., Sattler & Gwynne, 1982)" (p. 6).

Elliott (1987), in a thorough and insightful treatment of IQ tests in the courtroom, showed how West, the examiner of Darryl L. ("Larry P."), violated standard testing procedures: "He accepted 'acting bad' as the definition of 'nonsense'.... When West asked Darryl why criminals should be locked up, Darryl seemed not to understand the question, so he rephrased it, identifying criminals as people who sometimes break the law" (p. 33). Elliott further described how Judge Peckham of the Larry P. case differed from Judge Grady of Chicago's PASE decision regarding the alleged bias of test items, even though the "tests and testimony were much the same" (p. 148):

One very significant difference in these two trials was in the willingness of the judges to accept a broad range of social science data. Judge Peckham... adopted the strategy of other government agencies ...confronting test differences that threaten opportu-

nities for minorities: He particularized the validation requirements so much…that the large quantity of data available generally on the prediction of black school achievement became almost irrelevant…. Judge Grady, on the other hand, pleaded with both sides to give him any and everything they had on race differences in item passing rates. (p. 187)

In his summation, Elliott indicated that the impetus for his book "was the outcome in Larry P., which violated the scientific consensus, and the contrary outcome in PASE, which added inconsistency to perversity in the adjudication of a scientific issue in psychology" (p. 194).

CRITIQUE

Lezak (1988a): "[T]oday, most psychologists, psychiatrists, educators, judges, the United States Social Security Administration, among others, think, write, talk, and make decisions as if an IQ score represented something real and essentially immutable with a locus somewhere in the cranium" (p. 356).

REBUTTAL

Not since 1961, when J. McV. Hunt published his landmark book *Intelligence and Experience*, has any self-respecting psychologist regarded the IQ as fixed, immutable, or imprinted indelibly somewhere beneath the dura mater in the cerebral cortex. Lezak can legitimately criticize judges or federal agencies or members of the Mensa Society or state departments of education or medically trained professionals. She would also be justified in criticizing those neuropsychologists who still administer the obsolete Wechsler-Bellevue or WAIS, who ignore the available base-rate data on the magnitude of V-P IQ discrepancies, or who conduct study after study on patients with lateralized brain damage without reporting their subtest scores. Perhaps, as Hynd (1988) states, "clinical-

psychometric-legal issues that have so impacted on school psychologists are just now beginning to impact on the perspectives employed in clinical neuropsychology" (p. 4). But Lezak is wrong to criticize the clinical and school psychologists who administer and interpret the tests, or the educators who apply the test results in a practical setting, for reasons that Dean (1988), Hynd (1988), Reynolds (1988), and Kaufman (1988) have all echoed in our rebuttals to Lezak.

For example, Kaufman (1988) stated:

Rigidly interpreted IQs for individuals referred for assessment have been embalmed for nearly a generation by psychologists and educators who realized in the early 1960s that one, two, or three summative scores are far less useful for psychodiagnosis than a profile of abilities…. Is Dr. Lezak aware of the strong focus on intraindividual differences that accompanied the rise of the learning disabilities movement in the 1960s (Bannatyne, 1971)? Or of the legal responsibilities of psychologists, educators, and other multi-disciplinary team members who endeavor to meet the stipulations of PL 94-142, which prohibits overemphasis on global IQs?… Does Lezak understand the "intelligent testing" approach that many clinical psychologists, school psychologists, and special educators apply in their psychological or psycho-educational evaluations and teach to their students in graduate programs? (p. 5)

To her credit, Lezak (1988b) candidly admitted that "I have little acquaintance with the literature and current teaching in school psychology and special education" (p. 6).

CRITIQUE

Lezak (1988a): "Psychologists who take IQ scores at face value without taking account of the patient's status or subtest variations, tend to interpret an IQ score that has been lowered by virtue of some specific neurologic deficit to be an indicator of the patient's overall ability level" (p. 358).

REBUTTAL

The intelligent testing approach is specifically designed to put the global scores aside if neurological, behavioral, or other factors suggest that one or more subtests do not validly assess a person's intelligence. This technique has been available to clinicians for 20 to 30 years (Kaufman, 1979a; Sattler, 1974) and has been studied and applied by numerous clinicians around the world (Kaufman & Kaufman, 2001b).

Some of the basic tenets of the intelligent testing approach (Kaufman, 1979a, 1994a; Kaufman & Lichtenberger, 1999, 2000), summarized in Chapter 1, are repeated here to emphasize that this philosophy is not new:

> Global scores are deemphasized, flexibility and insight on the part of the examiner are demanded, and the test is perceived as a dynamic helping agent rather than as an instrument for placement, labeling, or other types of academic oppression (p. 1).... The burden is on test users to be "better" than the tests they use (p. 11).... The value of the scores increases when the examiner functions as a true experimenter and tries to determine why the [person] earned the particular profile revealed on the record form; the IQs become harmful when they are unquestioningly interpreted as valid indicators of intellectual functioning and are misconstrued as evidence of the [person's] maximum or even typical performance. (p. 13)

In addition: "It is during the process of clinical interpretation of the test profile of any given individual referred for evaluation—someone who may have depressed scores on one or more subtests due to sensory, motor, emotional, attentional, neurological, motivational, or cultural factors—that the global IQs have, for many years, resided in a coffin six feet below the foundations of schools and clinics throughout the country" (Kaufman, 1988, p. 5).

Lezak's Proposed Alternative to the IQ

Lezak (1988a): "Rather than equating mental abilities with intelligence and thinking of them as aspects of a unitary phenomenon that can be summed up in an IQ score, we need to conceptualize them in all their multivariate complexity and report our examination findings in a profile of test scores" (p. 359).

Lezak wants examiners to treat the results of an intelligence test as a multiplicity of scores representing an enchanting array of disparate abilities. Eliminate "IQ" from one's vocabulary, and study the peaks and valleys in the scaled score profile. The good part of her suggestion is that she is able to damn the IQ concept without cavalierly discarding the instruments altogether. The bad part is that her suggestion, if followed assiduously, represents a return to a clinical interpretation approach that was once popular but is now out of favor. That approach treated each subtest as a discrete entity, with each task a measure of a long string of traits and abilities. Books typifying that approach often devoted a separate chapter to each of Wechsler's subtests, with few chapters devoted to their integration (e.g., Glasser & Zimmerman, 1967).

Such books were quite informative, but they often encouraged young professionals to interpret the Wechsler scales one subtest at a time, thus losing the global perspective. For example, a person scoring low in Picture Completion was typically reported to be deficient in visual alertness and in distinguishing essential from nonessential details. That same person may well have earned a high score in Picture Arrangement (which also requires close attention to visual detail), but the examiner is not likely to have integrated the data across subtests. Why? Because too much focus on the uniqueness of each subtest in a profile (including its unique neurological correlates) can work against a more integrated treatment of the total picture. And, despite Lezak's arguments to the contrary, the global IQs, as well as the results of factor analysis, are just as much a part of the totality of test interpretation as the profile of 10 or 11 or 12 Wechsler subtests. As Dean (1988) notes, "the aggregate IQ offers the psychologist a stable baseline from which to consider profile points" (p. 4).

We agree with Lezak's focus on the subtest profile and on the potential neuropsychological (not to mention clinical, subcultural, educational, behavioral) impact on selected subtests for a given individual, whether that person has an intact brain or not; we have spent most of our professional life arguing for that type of flexibility in test interpretation. We have, at the same time, opposed methods of interpretation that fragment intelligence tests into their component parts, ignoring the empirical or rational foundations that the test authors used, either implicitly or explicitly, when they developed their tests. Such approaches lead to interpretation of findings in isolation; they lead to the use of pairwise comparisons (do Object Assembly and Similarities differ significantly from each other?) instead of a systematic, empirically defensible method of determining strengths and weaknesses; and they often lead examiners to ignore statistical significance to focus on what seem like high or low scores in the profile. ("Her 13 on Block Design is her best performance, indicating well developed spatial visualization and visual–constructive ability. In contrast, her lowest score, a 9 on Information, indicates a relatively poor range of general knowledge.")

We prefer to take into account profile fluctuations—but in sequence, going from the most global (i.e., most reliable) scores to the most specific (generally, the least reliable) scores, as we have detailed in Chapters 11 and 12 and elsewhere (Kaufman & Lichtenberger, 1999, 2000).

Ultimately, we agree with Lezak's eulogy of the IQ concept, except that she missed the funeral, which was held more than 20 years ago by clinical and school psychologists. We disagree with her dismissal of IQs altogether, and her failure to distinguish between their different types of value for group versus individual interpretation. We disagree with many of her arguments regarding intelligence tests and their use/abuse by the professionals who are trained to administer them. And we see her proposal to return to the multi-subtest profile in place of the IQs as a regressive suggestion, one that will be no more helpful for neuropsychology than for clinical, school, or educational psychology, or for special education.

The Learning Disabilities Challenge

A different challenge to the IQ construct has come full force from experts in the field of learning disabilities, who propose, either explicitly or implicitly, to eliminate IQ from the learning disabilities (LD) or specific learning disabilities (SLD) assessment process because it is nothing more than a vestige, an unwanted relic from the past. Though these arguments have filled recent pages of the *Journal of Learning Disabilities* (Siegel, 1999; Stanovich, 1999; Vellutino, Scanlon, & Lyon, 2000), neither the anti-IQ special educators, nor their seek-and-destroy mission, has changed much from a decade earlier (Siegel, 1989; Stanovich, 1989), when the same LD journal published a special issue devoted to the IQ controversy.

In this section, we present the anti-IQ arguments of a few of the leading spokespersons in the field of LD or SLD assessment, notably Siegel (1999), Stanovich (1999), and Vellutino et al. (2000). All of these critics propose the elimination of the IQ-achievement discrepancy from the SLD definition and two (Siegel, Stanovich) propose not using IQ tests at all for SLD assessment. We briefly present rebuttals to their arguments, highlighting and synthesizing points made by Kaufman and Kaufman (2001a; 2001b), Nicholson (1996), Kavale and Forness (2000), Flanagan, McGrew, and Ortiz (2000, Appendix H), and Flanagan, Ortiz, Alfonso, and Mascolo (in press). For a richer, more complete discussion of the issues surrounding this complex controversy, consult the aforementioned sources. For a thorough, thoughtful delineation of the opposing perspective, consult Stanovich's (2000) excellent book on reading.

The Anti-IQ Sentiments

Stanovich (1999) wants to eliminate the aptitude–achievement discrepancy from the LD definition and, in the process, to sack the IQ test altogether: "LD advocacy will always be open to charges of 'queue jumping' as long as the field refuses to rid itself of its IQ fetishism, refuses to jettison aptitude achievement discrepancy, and fails to free clinical practice from the pseudoscientific neurology that plagued the field in the 1970s" (p. 359). Siegel (1999), in agreement with Stanovich's goals, unequivocally states: "Scores on IQ tests are irrelevant and not useful and may even be discriminatory" (p. 304).

Vellutino et al. (2000) concede that, "there may be something important about a child's IQ, particularly with respect to how it interacts with that child's emotional and behavioral response to failure" (p. 236). They state further that, "because of the widespread belief that IQ and reading ability are related, it might well be the case that more resources would be brought to bear to support the reading development of a child who scored high on an intelligence test as compared with a child who scored in the average or low average range on the test" (p. 236). In other words, they don't think too much of IQ tests, but they may have indirect value either clinically or because of people's misperceptions about its importance.

The reasons for eliminating IQ tests and simultaneously eliminating the IQ-achievement discrepancy from the LD definition stem primarily from the results of research studies that show that IQ is unrelated to reading ability or remedial progress, from arguments that the aptitude–achievement discrepancy is unnecessary for diagnosing LD, from insistence that there are no conceptual or practical differences among poor readers with high versus low IQs, and from a deep-seated belief that IQ tests are hopelessly flawed. These and related arguments in support of all of these points are expanded on by Siegel (1999), Stanovich (1999), and Vellutino et al. (2000), and, especially, in the recent book by Stanovich (2000).

Stanovich's (1986) Matthew Effects, or "reciprocal causation effects involving reading and other cognitive skills" (Stanovich, 2000, p. 356), are seen by Siegel as dooming the value of IQ tests and of the aptitude–achievement discrepancy: "[T]he validity of using a discrepancy-based criterion [is undermined] because children

who read more gain the cognitive skills and information relevant to the IQ test and consequently attain higher IQ scores. Children with reading problems read less and, therefore, fail to gain the skills and information necessary for higher scores on IQ tests" (Siegel, 1999, p. 312).

Siegel (1999) also finds many other flaws with IQ tests, for example: (1) "A person with a slow, deliberate style would not achieve as high a score as an individual who responded more quickly" (p. 311); and (2) "IQ tests consist of measures of factual knowledge, definitions of words, memory, fine motor coordination, and fluency of expressive language; they do not measure reasoning or problem-solving skills" (p. 311). Similarly, she makes claims about IQ tests that defy both logic and the results of a plethora of research studies: "One assumption behind the use of IQ tests is that the scores predict and set limits on academic performance, so that if a person has a low IQ score, we should not expect much from him or her in the way of academic skills" (Siegel, 1999, p. 311).

Siegel (1999) cites many references to document that "there are no differences between individuals with dyslexia and poor readers on measures of the processes most directly related to reading" (p. 312). Vellutino et al. (2000) add: "In independent studies…, it was found that poor readers who manifested no significant IQ-achievement discrepancy performed no differently on independent measures of reading achievement than poor readers who did manifest such discrepancies. More important is the finding in both studies that these two groups also performed no differently on tests of the cognitive abilities believed to underlie one's ability to learn to read" (p. 225). And the results of Vellutino et al.'s (2000) remediation study indicated that "the IQ-achievement discrepancy does not reliably distinguish between disabled and nondisabled readers…. Neither does it distinguish between children who were found to be difficult to remediate and those who were readily remediated, prior to initiation of remediation, and it does not predict response to remediation" (p. 235).

The conclusion apparently reached by the opponents of IQ and the aptitude–achievement discrepancy for LD assessment is to advocate a diagnostic approach that does not attempt to distinguish between LD and low achievement, but instead lumps all low-achieving students into a single package, without concern for the presence of neuropsychological intactness in unaffected domains. For example, Siegel (1999) discusses identification of specific learning disabilities in terms of what specific cutoff to use on *achievement* tests, with no need at all to weigh the individual's cognitive profile. Kaufman and Kaufman (2001b) note about Siegel:

> *She discusses the merits of identifying as SLD all students who score below the 25th percentile, but notes that the 20th or 15th percentiles might also be acceptable cut-off criteria. She acknowledges that there are some exclusionary criteria, namely "ruling out" inadequate education, sensory deficits, serious neurological disorders, and social/emotional difficulties as causes of low academic achievement. Yet, though she perceives these exclusionary criteria as "reasonable"…, she is not convinced that they are necessary. She endorses a deficit model that has no room for systematic evaluation of exclusionary criteria or for the need to demonstrate the student's neuropsychological, cognitive, or academic intactness. (p. 436)*

Stanovich (1999) likewise would use achievement tests to diagnose reading disability, most notably measures of word attack (pseudo-word reading) and word recognition. He states: "Intelligence would play no part in the diagnosis…. [T]he 25th-percentile criterion discussed in Siegel's commentary…would likely be too liberal. I would probably opt for a more stringent criterion such as the 15th percentile, or even the 10th, on at least one of the tests" (p. 351).

Nicholson (1996) summarizes Stanovich's key role in seeking to destroy the concept of dyslexia: "Stanovich reasons that that poor phonological skills result in poor reading regardless of IQ, and therefore IQ is irrelevant to the definition of reading disability (Stanovich, 1991), and then fi-

nally that dyslexia may not exist as a separate syndrome (Stanovich, 1994)" (p. 195).

A Response to the Critics

The critics are experts in the field of LD, especially reading, but they do not demonstrate expertise in the area of intellectual assessment and they are not current in their knowledge of contemporary instruments. They cite research to buttress their points, especially that IQ is unrelated to reading ability and to successful remediation, but they ignore other pertinent research that supports differences between individuals with LD versus low achievement (LA). These and related points are addressed here in summary fashion.

SELECTIVE EXAMINATION OF PERTINENT RESEARCH. The critics do present an impressive compilation of research to support their claims that IQ does not discriminate between individuals with LD and LA in reading. However, they ignore other lines of research that support the opposite position. Kavale and Forness (2000), for example, cite several studies that show "that students with LD and LA could be reliably distinguished with the population with LD being the lowest of the low on the achievement distribution but equivalent to the LA population on the ability (i.e., IQ) distribution" (p. 248). Nicholson takes Stanovich and other antidiscrepancy theorists to task for (1) switching the focus from research on the causes of dyslexia to research on the causes of poor reading; and (2) treating the much acclaimed notion of phonological deficit as the cause, rather than as a symptom, of dyslexia. Nicholson (1996) provides a well-reasoned logical attack on Stanovich's line of thinking, strongly disputing his conclusions about the irrelevance of IQ for diagnosing reading disability as well as his dismissal of the term *dyslexia*. Furthermore, genetic research conducted with identical and same-gender fraternal twins, when at least one member of each pair was diagnosed with a reading disability (RD), found different heritabilities for individuals based on their WISC-R or WAIS-R Full Scale IQs (Wadsworth, Olson, Pennington, & DeFries, 2000). The heritability was .43 for those with IQs below 100 and .72 for those with IQs 100 and greater, a significant difference. Wadsworth et al. concluded: "The results of the current study support the hypothesis of a differential genetic etiology of RD as a function of IQ, suggesting that genetic influences may be more important as a cause of RD among children with higher IQ scores.... [They] suggest that knowing a child's IQ may tell us something about the causes of the reading deficit, which could possibly help focus intervention and remediation efforts" (p. 198).

A more complete picture of relevant research, one that extends beyond the litany of studies cited by Siegel, Stanovich, and others, provides a more balanced view of the issues and does not quickly condemn the IQ to irrelevance in the LD or RD assessment process. For example, in a recent neuropsychological investigation, poor readers did, indeed, differ from those with dyslexia (i.e., those with an IQ-achievement discrepancy) on phonological and related tasks—as Stanovich, Vellutino, and Siegel have claimed—but the dyslexics and poor readers differed significantly and notably on tests of static cerebellar function (Fawcett, Nicolson, & Maclagan, 2001). These investigators concluded from their findings, "that there are indeed theoretically valid reasons for distinguishing between poor readers with IQ discrepancy and those without" (p. 132).

IQ IS NOT A SYNONYM FOR WECHSLER. The critics unabashedly equate "IQ test" with "Wechsler test." Siegel's (1999) criticisms about bonus points penalizing individuals with slow, deliberate styles, and about the failure of IQ tests to measure problem-solving ability are all targeted at Wechsler's tests. Stanovich (1999) dismisses as unimportant the professional disagreements concerning whether verbal or nonverbal scales provide the best IQ criterion for a child assessed for possible LD as if Wechsler's nontheoretical dichotomy is the only available subdivision of intel-

ligence. These LD experts show no awareness of the many theoretically derived intelligence tests that offer more meaningful divisions of global IQ than Wechsler's armchair dichotomy, created more than 60 years ago.

Yes, Wechsler's tests are the most commonly used instruments for LD assessment in the United States, but that is not an acceptable reason for these LD professionals to fail to consider well-validated options in the face of their uncompromising dismissal of the IQ construct—broadly defined—from LD assessment. These leading spokespersons should consult the cross-battery approach for supplementing Wechsler's scales with tests that measure abilities not covered by the WISC-III or WAIS-III (Flanagan et al., 2000) or for focusing on a variety of alternatives to Wechsler's tests for learning disabilities assessment (Flanagan et al., in press). They should familiarize themselves with the growing number of alternative instruments, such as the CHC-based Woodcock-Johnson III Tests of Cognitive Ability (Woodcock, McGrew, & Mather, 2000), the Horn-Cattell-based KAIT (Kaufman & Kaufman, 1993), the Luria-inspired Cognitive Ability Scales (CAS; Naglieri & Das, 1997), the Differential Ability Scales (DAS; Elliott, 1990), to name a few of the more recent Wechsler alternatives.

Kaufman and Kaufman (2001a), citing the fluid and planning abilities measured by the aforementioned tests, as well as by neuropsychological tests, state: "Consider Siegel's (1999) criticism that IQ tests fail to measure reasoning or problem-solving skills. If one departs from the Wechsler system and examines the available well-constructed, well-designed, theory-driven test batteries (both cognitive and neuropsychological), one finds an abundance of scales or subtests that measure the kinds of abilities that Horn would classify as fluid and Piagetians would consider dependent on formal operational thought" (p. 442). They add, on a related topic:

In addition to the Wechsler tests' shortage of high-level reasoning tasks, the channels of communication mea-

sured by the various Wechsler subtests fall into one of only two categories: auditory–vocal (Verbal subtests) and visual–motor (Performance subtests). These are important channels, but clinicians who evaluate individuals suspected of SLD will often benefit by assessing other channels of communication. For example, the K-ABC includes subtests for school-age children within the auditory–motor channel (Word Order) and the visual-vocal channel (Gestalt Closure, Faces & Places) as well as the two channels measured by Wechsler's scales.... Similarly, the WJ-R... includes two visual–vocal subtests (Picture Vocabulary, Visual Closure) and the CAS...includes an auditory–motor subtest, Verbal-Spatial Relations. (Kaufman & Kaufman, 2001a, pp. 442–443)

For an in-depth treatment of these and other alternative instruments for use in SLD assessment, with most chapters written directly by each test's authors, consult Kaufman and Kaufman (2001b). For a thorough discussion of the application of the cross-battery approach to enhance greatly the IQ's validity for predicting achievement and for its utility for issues concerning LD assessment in general, consult Flanagan's texts (Flanagan, McGrew, & Ortiz, 2000; Flanagan & Ortiz, 2001; Flanagan et al., in press).

IQ AS A MEASURE OF *g*.   The array of studies used to criticize the IQ construct for LD assessment treats IQ as if it is Spearman's (1904) century-old "*g*" factor, supported by some researchers in the present (most notably, Jensen, 1998), but contrary to most modern theories of intelligence such as Horn's (1989) expansion and elaboration of the Horn-Cattell Gf-Gc theory, or the Luria-based PASS model that Naglieri and Das (1997) used as the foundation of the CAS (Naglieri, 1999). The LD experts show no awareness that the Full Scale IQ is the least interesting and least valuable score yielded by IQ tests. Horn's expanded theory, as well as its integration with Carroll's (1993, 1997) theory to form Cattell-Horn-Carroll or CHC theory (Chapter 14), has been quite influential for the development of new and revised intelligence tests (Kaufman & Kaufman, 1993; Woodcock & Mather, 1989; Woodcock, McGrew, & Mather, 2000) and has

greatly impacted interpretation of Wechsler's scales (Flanagan et al., 2000; Kaufman, 1994a; Kaufman & Lichtenberger, 1999, 2000).

Consider the various studies cited by Siegel (1999), Stanovich (2000), and Vellutino et al. (2000) that feature Full Scale IQ's dismal failure at discriminating among reading groups or remediation groups. Might these groups have differed on other IQ-related scales, such as the Attention or Planning Scales on the CAS, the K-ABC Sequential or Simultaneous Processing Scales, the KAIT Fluid Scale, the DAS Nonverbal Reasoning Ability Scale, or any of the seven Horn-based clusters that comprise the WJ III Tests of Cognitive Ability? Might they have differed on "new and forthcoming neuropsychologically-based instruments that are designed to go beyond conventional profiles of scores on IQ tests, such as the WISC-III as a Process Instrument (WISC-III—PI) or the Delis-Kaplan Test of Executive Functions"? (Kaufman & Kaufman, 2001a, pp. 445–446).

Stanovich (1999) states that, "Intelligence has played a major role in the conceptual muddle surrounding the notion of reading failure. The confusion arises because it makes no sense to say that low intelligence…*causes* reading difficulties, given what is currently known about reading disabilities" (p. 352).

ELIMINATING THE IQ-ACHIEVEMENT DISCREPANCY DOES NOT MEAN THROWING OUT IQ TESTS.   The IQ critics join two issues at the hip when they are quite separate: eliminating the IQ-achievement discrepancy from the LD definition and jettisoning IQ tests from the entire LD assessment process. These topics are not cause–effect, even if the critics act as if deleting the discrepancy criterion from the definition leads directly to getting rid of the IQ test from the assessment process.

It is easy to see why the anti-IQ LD experts have no need for the IQ. Apart from their equation of IQ test with Wechsler test, and their failure to appreciate the last two decades' growth, both in the publication of new and revised IQ alternatives and in theory-based approaches to clinical interpretation and test selection, they no longer view LD as anything but an achievement deficit.

In fact, there are some excellent reasons to eliminate the discrepancy criterion from the LD definition. For example, as Shepherd (2001) indicates from her own clinical experience and that of her colleagues, data are frequently ignored when diagnostic decisions are made, replaced by practical variables such as available resources and the needs of the parents and teachers. MacMillan and Speece (1999), in a review of three studies conducted after PL 94-142 was enacted, discovered that more than 50% of the students in each study identified with SLD failed to meet relevant diagnostic criteria; they concluded that tests were given mostly to conform to legal requirements, but data from the tests were often ignored. Similarly, Kavale and Forness (2000) reviewed several other pertinent studies that found that "large-scale investigations of LD populations show that only about 50% of students actually classified as LD demonstrate a significant aptitude-achievement discrepancy" (p. 249). Kaufman and Kaufman's (2001a) response to the real-life practices:

> *What a waste! Why bother having trained psychologists administer 90-minute IQ tests and have other professionals administer time-consuming achievement, adaptive behavior, or processing tests, if these measures are just given so the professionals can cover their own backs? One does not need to weigh the carefully-reasoned (though occasionally flawed) arguments of Siegel (1999), Stanovich (1999), or Vellutino et al. (2000) against the use of the IQ-achievement discrepancy for SLD diagnosis. Their attacks on IQ tests, however motivated, are far less impressive evidence for abandoning the IQ-achievement discrepancy than are the apparent everyday realities of differential diagnosis: The discrepancy is often not used when diagnosing SLD, even though the pertinent test data are invariably obtained. Given the realities of clinical practice, at least in schools, why not delete the IQ-achievement discrepancy from the definition of SLD? (p. 437)*

But giving up the discrepancy criterion does not mean abandoning IQ tests from the LD diagnostic process. Nor does it mean giving up the *concept* of discrepancy, a notion that is intricately woven into the LD fabric at many levels of the definition (Kavale & Forness, 2000; Mather & Woodcock, 2001; Nicholson, 1996), even if it means giving up a formulaic, rigid approach to discrepancies. Kaufman and Kaufman (2001a) state:

> *The acceptance of error as a necessary prerequisite for measuring IQ, embraced by David Wechsler,...has persisted from one century to the next and continues into the new millennium. Error is a fact of assessment life, a fundamental tenet of a psychologist's clinical training, and antagonistic to the use of any discrepancy formulas or cut-off points.... One does not have to be a special educator or learning disabilities specialist to criticize the psychologist's tools. We have historical reasons to acknowledge—even embrace—their limitations. One does not need to read Siegel's (1999) or Stanovich's (1999) criticisms of IQ tests to discover that these measures are imperfect.... Verbal tasks overlap with the content of achievement tests; process deficits are just as likely to impair performance on IQ tests as on tests of academic skills; neither verbal nor nonverbal measures of IQ are necessarily better or more valid (or valid at all) of the intelligence of an individual with SLD; IQ does not effectively provide a measure of a person's potential; and so forth.... The real problem resides in the federal and state guidelines that mandate the use of these formulas (even if their use is illusory in many real-life situations). (p. 439)*

One needs to be creative, and function as a blend of a psychometrician and clinician, to identify appropriate discrepancies between ability and achievement, discrepancies that highlight cognitive strengths as well as deficient basic cognitive processes that contribute to academic failure. Consult the innovative and clever approaches to computing ability–achievement discrepancies described by Mather and Woodcock (2001), as well as the in-depth treatment of the topic by Flanagan and her colleagues (Flanagan et al., 2000, Appendix H; Flanagan et al., in press).

Perhaps the best conceptual argument for keeping the notion of discrepancy in the definition of LD and SLD comes from M. J. Shepherd (personal communication, October 14, 1999), who was Nadeen Kaufman's mentor in the Learning Disabilities program at Teachers College, Columbia University, and who was directly responsible for the intra-individual approach to Wechsler interpretation that Alan Kaufman adopted for his intelligent testing approach:

> *Siegel and Stanovich's claim that phonological reading disability occurs at all IQ levels is "déjà vu all over again"—Cruikshank, Kephart et al. claimed that specific learning disability (meaning visual–perceptual deficit) occurred at all IQ levels.... If we accept the hypothesis that mental activity is specific (unique) to the task being performed, it makes sense that all children having difficulty with a particular task (word recognition and spelling) will have similar cognitive deficits. This means (to me) that we will not achieve a full understanding of specific learning disabilities by looking at deficits alone. In neuropsychological terms we have to document the cognitive traits that have been "spared." This is the point that Stanovich and Siegel aren't making because (a) they insist on working with a limited conception of reading (word recognition) and/or (b) they have a political agenda—protect the poor against the rich.*

The task for professionals involved with the assessment of LD or SLD, whether they are in psychology or special education, is to embrace new research programs (see, for example, Nicholson, 1996) and to make use of novel and better approaches to assessment as part of the diagnostic process. The definition and diagnosis of LD, SLD, dyslexia, and so forth, are complex; the disorders are real, and qualitatively—not quantitatively—different from low achievement; the answers to the pressing practical and theoretical issues facing the field require careful study, not simple, knee-jerk solutions.

SUMMARY

This chapter discusses the heredity, environment, and malleability of the IQ, and attacks on the IQ construct by Lezak and experts in the field of learning disabilities. A variety of investigations, especially studies of twins and adoption, indicate that the role of genes in determining intelligence is considerable, probably about 50%, and that the role of genetics may increase as people age. However, even a heritability percentage as high as 50 leaves about half of the variance for environmental factors. Furthermore, the findings from interesting studies that pertain to "maternal effects" (womb environment) suggest that dramatic environmental effects (prenatally) may have been mistakenly attributed to genetics in previous studies.

Angoff has argued that the malleability of the IQ is more important than the issue of heredity versus environment. There have been important studies demonstrating just how malleable the IQ seems to be. Flynn's analysis of the intelligence of many developed nations has shown substantial generational gains in the intelligence of people in the United States (about 3 points per decade), and even greater gains by individuals in many other countries (e.g., 6–7 points in Belgium and the Netherlands). Evidence indicates that gains are greater on fluid than crystallized tests, and that these gains persist into adulthood. In addition, the dramatic results of the Abecedarian program, an intensive early intervention program from infancy to age 5 that has produced substantial, enduring cognitive and academic gains through age 21, speak to the impressive malleability of human intelligence.

Lezak eulogized the IQ construct, arguing that it has outlived its usefulness and should be buried. Her main criticisms concern the meaninglessness and impurity of global IQs and the misuse and abuse that have accompanied psychologists' interpretation of them. Major arguments against Lezak's position include: (1) the fact that worship of the global IQ gave way to an intelligent testing model of profile interpretation many years ago within the fields of clinical and school psychology; (2) IQs for groups have considerable validation; (3) the impact of nonintellectual factors on obtained IQs is a strength, not a weakness, of intelligence tests; (4) her citation of the Larry P. case ignores other, contradictory evidence as well as testing errors made by "Larry P.'s" examiner; (5) the learning disabilities movement begun in the 1960s, and pertinent legislation since that time, have elevated the interpretation of profiles above the rigid treatment of precise IQ scores; and (6) Lezak's proposals to focus exclusively on the separate subtests represent a return to an older, less sensible, approach to Wechsler interpretation.

Experts in the field of learning disabilities (LD), notably Siegel, Stanovich, and Vellutino, have argued for the elimination of IQ from the LD assessment process. They cite research on reading and remediation, and point out flaws in IQ tests, that they interpret as evidence both for eliminating the aptitude–achievement discrepancy from the LD definition and for dropping IQ tests from the whole LD assessment process. Arguments against these LD experts focus on the following points: (1) the experts have examined the pertinent research in a selective manner; (2) IQ tests are not synonymous with Wechsler tests; (3) IQ needs to be interpreted from the vantage point of multiple theories, not exclusively as a measure of "*g*"; and (4) eliminating the IQ-achievement discrepancy does not mean throwing out IQ tests.

CHAPTER 3

From the Wechsler-Bellevue I to the WAIS-III

The WAIS-III is the most popular test for assessing adult intelligence (Camara, Nathan, & Puente, 2000) and, as discussed in Chapter 1, it is used in most clinical, educational, and vocational evaluations of individuals aged 16 through old age. The WAIS-III contains substantial revision from the WAIS-R, including the updating of norms, extension of the age range to 89 years, addition of three new subtests, decreased reliance on timed performance, and the addition of factor indexes. The WAIS-R was basically a slight modification of the 1955 WAIS (Kaufman, 1985a), a cleaner WAIS with a new standardization sample. The WAIS was, in turn, a modified and restandardized version of the 1939 Wechsler-Bellevue, Form I (W-B I), so the evolution of the WAIS-III from the W-B I through the WAIS and WAIS-R is direct and of importance to present-day clinicians. This importance is not merely historical, although the history of intellectual assessment, and of David Wechsler's role in it, is both fascinating and illuminating. Rather,

the value of studying the W-B I, WAIS, and WAIS-R, even though the former two are virtually historical relics, concerns interpretation of the WAIS-III.

Thousands of research investigations have been conducted during the past half century on the WAIS-III's predecessors. These studies have ranged from the banal and repetitive to the ingenious and vital; the better endeavors have revealed much about intellectual development, mental functioning, and neuropsychological processing of different types of information. But how many of these insights are test-specific, valid for the W-B I, WAIS, or WAIS-R, but not necessarily for the WAIS-III? The answer lies in the continuity of measurement from one test battery to another. The degree of change in test content, in reliability coefficients, in standardization samples, and in underlying constructs all bears on the question of continuity. Major changes from one revision to another, especially in the construct validity of the respective batteries, would greatly limit generalization of research findings from the W-B I, WAIS, or WAIS-R to the present-day adult battery; empirical evidence of similarity, however, would argue for the direct application of many previous research findings to the WAIS-III. However, we want to make clear when the WAIS-R research may have questionable application to the WAIS-III because of the considerable structural changes that accompanied the latest version of the Wechsler's adult tests.

This chapter compares the W-B I, WAIS, WAIS-R, and WAIS-III and attempts to answer the theoretical question of continuity of measurement and the practical question of generalizability of W-B I, WAIS, and/or WAIS-R findings to the WAIS-III.

SELECTION OF THE SUBTESTS

Wechsler selected tasks for the Wechsler-Bellevue from among the numerous tests available in the 1930s, many of which were developed to meet the assessment needs of World War I. Although Wechsler chose not to develop new subtests for his intelligence battery, his selection process incorporated a blend of clinical, practical, and empirical factors. His rationale for each of the well-known subtests is discussed in the sections that follow. The WAIS-III also contains three new subtests that were not part of the earlier Wechsler batteries: Letter-Number Sequencing, Symbol Search, and Matrix Reasoning. These subtests are discussed in separate sections.

Verbal Scale

Information

Wechsler (1958) included a subtest designed to tap a subject's range of general information, despite "the obvious objection that the amount of knowledge which a person possesses depends in no small degree upon his [or her] education and cultural opportunities" (p. 65). Wechsler had noted the surprising finding that the fact-oriented information test in the Army Alpha group examination had among the highest correlations with various estimates of intelligence: "It correlated… much better with the total score than did the Arithmetical Reasoning, the test of Disarranged Sentences, and even the Analogies Test, all of which had generally been considered much better tests of intelligence.… The fact is, all objections considered, the range of a [person's] knowledge is generally a very good indication of his [or her] intellectual capacity" (p. 65). Wechsler was also struck by a variety of psychometric properties of the Army Alpha Information Test compared to other tasks (excellent distribution curve, small percentage of zero scores, lack of pile-up of maximum scores), and the long history of similar factual information tests being "the stock in trade of mental examinations, and…widely used by psychiatrists in estimating the intellectual level of patients" (p. 65).

Always the astute clinician, Wechsler was aware that the choice of items determined the value of the information subtest as an effective measure of intelligence. Items must not be chosen whimsically or arbitrarily, but must be developed with several important principles in mind, the most essential being that, generally, "the items should call for the sort of knowledge that an average individual with average opportunity may be able to acquire for himself" (p. 65). He usually tried to avoid specialized and academic knowledge, historical dates, and names of famous individuals, "[b]ut there are many exceptions to the rule, and in the long run each item must be tried out separately" (p. 66). Thus, he preferred an item like "What is the height of the average American woman?" to ones like "What is iambic tetrameter?" or "In what year was George Washington born?" but occasionally items of the latter type appeared in his information subtest. Wechsler was especially impressed with the exceptional psychometric properties of the Army Alpha Information Test "in view of the fact that the individual items on [it] left much to be desired" (p. 65).

Although Wechsler (1958) agreed with the criticism that factual information tests depended heavily on educational and cultural opportunities, he felt that the problem "need not necessarily be a fatal or even a serious one" (p. 65). Similarly, he recognized that certain items would vary in difficulty in different locales or when administered to people of different nationalities: "Thus, 'What is the capital of Italy?' is passed almost universally by persons of Italian origin irrespective of their intellectual ability" (p. 66). Yet, he was extremely fond of information, considering it "one of the most satisfactory in the battery" (p. 67).

Digit Span

Memory Span for Digits (renamed Digit Span) combines in a single subtest two skills that subsequent research has shown to be distinct in many ways (Costa, 1975; Jensen & Figueroa, 1975): repetition of digits in the same order as they are spoken by the examiner, and repetition of digits in the reverse order. Wechsler (1958) combined these two tasks for pragmatic reasons, however, not theoretical ones: Each task alone had too limited a range of possible raw scores, and treating each set of items as a separate subtest would have given short-term memory too much weight in determining a person's IQ, ⅙ instead of ⅟₁₁.

Wechsler was especially concerned about overweighing memory because Digit Span proved to be a relatively weak measure of general intelligence (*g*). He gave serious consideration to dropping the task altogether, but decided to retain it for two reasons. First, Digit Span is particularly useful at the lower ranges of intelligence; adults who cannot recall 5 digits forward and 3 backward are mentally retarded or emotionally disturbed "in 9 cases out of 10" (p. 71), except in cases of neurological impairment (Wechsler, 1958). Second, poor performance on Digit Span is of unusual diagnostic significance, according to Wechsler, particularly for suspected brain dysfunction or concern about mental deterioration across the life span.

Digit Span also has several other advantages that may account for Wechsler's (1958) assertion that "[p]erhaps no test has been so widely used in scales of intelligence as that of Memory Span for Digits" (p. 70): It is simple to administer and score, measures a rather specific ability, and is clinically valuable because of its unusual susceptibility to anxiety, inattention, distractibility, and lack of concentration. Wechsler noted that repetition of digits backward is especially impaired in individuals who have difficulty sustaining concentrated effort during problem solving. The test has been popularly "used for a long time by psychiatrists as a test of retentiveness and by psychologists in all sorts of psychological studies" (p. 70); because Wechsler retained Digit Span as a regularly administered subtest on the WAIS-R but treated it as supplementary on the WISC-R, it is evident that he saw its measurement as a more vital aspect of adult than of child assessment.

Vocabulary

"Contrary to lay opinion, the size of a [p]erson's vocabulary is not only an index of his schooling, but also an excellent measure of his general intelligence. Its excellence as a test of intelligence may stem from the fact that the number of words a [person] knows is at once a measure of his learning ability, his fund of verbal information and of the general range of his ideas" (Wechsler, 1958, p. 84). The Vocabulary subtest formed an essential component of Binet's scales and the WAIS but, surprisingly, this task, which has become prototypical of Wechsler's definition of verbal intelligence, was not a regular W-B I subtest. In deference to the objection that word knowledge "is necessarily influenced by...educational and cultural opportunities" (p. 84), Wechsler included Vocabulary only as an alternative test during the early stages of W-B I standardization. Consequently, the W-B I was at first a 10-subtest battery and Vocabulary was excluded from analyses of W-B I standardization data such as factor analyses and correlations between subtest score and total score. Based on Wechsler's (1944) reconsideration of the value of

Vocabulary and concomitant urging of examiners to administer it routinely, Vocabulary soon became a regular W-B I component. When the W-B II was developed, 33 of the 42 W-B I words were included in that battery's Vocabulary subtest. Because many W-B I words were, therefore, included in the WISC when the W-B II was revised and restandardized to become the Wechsler children's scale in 1949, Wechsler (1955) decided to include an all-new Vocabulary subtest when the W-B I was converted to the WAIS.

This lack of overlap between the W-B I Vocabulary subtest and the task of the same name on the WAIS, WAIS-R, and WAIS-III is of some concern regarding the continuity of measurement from the W-B I to its successors. Wechsler himself (1958) noted: "The WAIS list contains a larger percentage of action words (verbs). The only thing that can be said so far about this difference is that while responses given to verbs are easier to score, those elicited by substantives are frequently more significant diagnostically" (pp. 84–85). This difference in diagnostic significance is potentially important because Wechsler (1958) found Vocabulary so valuable, in part because of its qualitative aspects: "The type of word on which a subject passes or fails is always of some significance" (p. 85), yielding information about reasoning ability, degree of abstraction, cultural milieu, educational background, coherence of thought processes, and the like.

Nonetheless, Wechsler was careful to ensure that the various qualitative aspects of Vocabulary performance had a minimal impact on quantitative score. "What counts is the number of words that he knows. Any recognized meaning is acceptable, and there is no penalty for inelegance of language. So long as the subject shows that he knows what a word means, he is credited with a passing score" (1958, p. 85).

Arithmetic

Wechsler (1958) included a test of arithmetical reasoning in an adult intelligence battery because such tests correlate highly with general intelligence; are easily created and standardized; are

deemed by most adults as "worthy of a grownup" (p. 69); have been "used as a rough and ready measure of intelligence" (p. 69) prior to the advent of psychometrics; and have "long been recognized as a sign of mental alertness" (p. 69). Such tests are flawed by the impact on test scores of attention span, temporary emotional reactions, and of educational and occupational attainment. As Wechsler notes: "Clerks, engineers and businessmen usually do well on arithmetic tests, while housewives, day laborers, and illiterates are often penalized by them" (p. 69). However, he believed that the advantages of an arithmetical reasoning test far outweighed the negative aspects. He pointed out that adults "may be embarrassed by their inability to do certain problems, but they almost never look upon the questions as unfair or inconsequential" (p. 69). He took much care in developing the specific set of items for the W-B I and the WAIS and believed that his particular approach to constructing the Arithmetic subtest was instrumental in the task's appeal to adults. Wechsler constructed items dealing with everyday, practical situations such that the solutions generally require computational skills taught in grade school or acquired "in the course of day-to-day transactions" (p. 70), and the responses avoid "verbalization or reading difficulties" (p. 69). Whereas the WISC-R and W-B I involve the reading of a few problems by the subject, all items on the WAIS, WAIS-R, and WAIS-III are read aloud by the examiner. Bonus points for quick, perfect performance are not given to children on the WISC-R, but Wechsler considered the ability to respond rapidly to relatively difficult arithmetic problems to be a pertinent aspect of adult intelligence; bonus points are given to two items on the W-B I Arithmetic subtest, to four items on the WAIS task, to five items on WAIS-R Arithmetic, and to two items on WAIS-III Arithmetic.

Comprehension

Measures of general comprehension were plentiful in tests prior to the W-B I, appearing in the original Binet scale and its revisions, and in group examinations like the Army Alpha and the

National Intelligence Test. However, the test in multiple-choice format, though still valuable, does not approach the contribution of the task when subjects have to compose their own responses. "Indeed, one of the most gratifying things about the general comprehension test, when given orally, is the rich clinical data which it furnishes about the subject. It is frequently of value in diagnosing psychopathic personalities, sometimes suggests the presence of schizophrenic trends (as revealed by perverse and bizarre responses), and almost always tells us something about the subject's social and cultural background" (Wechsler, 1958, p. 67).

In selecting questions for the W-B I Comprehension subtest, Wechsler (1958) borrowed some material from the Army Alpha and the Army Memoirs and included a few questions that were also on the old Stanford-Binet, "probably because they were borrowed from the same source" (p. 68). He was not bothered by overlap because of what he perceived to be a very small practice effect for Comprehension: "It is curious how frequently subjects persist in their original responses, even after other replies are suggested to them" (p. 68).

The WAIS Comprehension subtest was modified from its predecessor by adding two very easy items to prevent a pile-up of zero-scores and by adding three proverb items "because of their reported effectiveness in eliciting paralogical and concretistic thinking" (p. 68). Wechsler found that the proverbs did not contribute to the subtest exactly what he had hoped; they were useful for mentally disturbed individuals, "but 'poor' answers were also common in normal subjects…[and] even superior subjects found the proverbs difficult. A possible reason for this is that proverbs generally express ideas so concisely that any attempt to explain them further is more likely to subtract than add to their clarity" (1958, p. 68). Despite the shortcomings of proverb items, particularly the fact that they seem to measure skills that differ from prototypical general comprehension items (Kaufman, 1985a), Wechsler (1981) retained the three proverb items in the WAIS-R Comprehension subtest.

Because these three items are relatively difficult (they are among the last five in the sequence), they are instrumental in distinguishing among the most superior adults regarding the abilities measured by WAIS-R Comprehension. Only two of the proverb items were retained on the WAIS-III (again the last items of the subtest).

According to Wechsler (1958), Comprehension was termed a test of common sense on the Army Alpha, and successful performance "seemingly depends on the possession of a certain amount of practical information and a general ability to evaluate past experience. The questions included are of a sort that the average adult may have had occasion to answer for himself at some time, or heard discussed in one form or another. They are for the most part stereotypes with a broad common base" (pp. 68–69). Wechsler was also careful to include no questions with unusual words "so that individuals of even limited education generally have little difficulty in understanding their content" (p. 69). Comprehension scores are, however, dependent on the ability to express one's thoughts verbally.

Similarities

Unlike the other subtests in Wechsler's Verbal Scale, "similarities questions have been used very sparingly in the construction of previous scales …[despite being] one of the most reliable measures of intellectual ability" (1958, p. 72). Wechsler felt that this omission was probably due to the belief that language and vocabulary were necessarily too crucial in determining successful performance. However, "while a certain degree of verbal comprehension is necessary for even minimal performance, sheer word knowledge need only be a minor factor. More important is the individual's ability to perceive the common elements of the terms he is asked to compare and, at higher levels, his ability to bring them under a single concept" (p. 73). A glance at the most difficult items on the W-B I, WAIS, WAIS-R, and WAIS-III Similarities subtests (fly–tree, praise–punishment) makes it evident that Wechsler was successful in his goal of increasing "the difficulty of test items without resorting to esoteric or unfamiliar words" (p. 73).

Wechsler (1958) saw several merits in the Similarities subtest: it is easy to administer, has an interest appeal for adults, has a high *g* loading, sheds light on the logical nature of the person's thinking processes, and provides other qualitative information as well. Regarding the latter point, he stressed the "obvious difference both as to maturity and as to level of thinking between the individual who says that a banana and an orange are alike because they both have a skin, and the individual who says that they are both fruit.... But it is remarkable how large a percentage of adults never get beyond the superficial type of response" (p. 73). Consequently, Wechsler (1958) considered his 0-1-2 scoring system to be an important innovation to allow simple discrimination between high-level and low-level responses to the same item. He also found his multipoint system helpful in providing insight into the evenness of a person's intellectual development. Whereas some individuals earn almost all 1's, others earn a mixture of 0, 1, and 2 scores. "The former are likely to bespeak individuals of consistent ability, but of a type from which no high grade of intellectual work may be expected; the latter, while erratic, have many more possibilities" (p. 74).

Performance Scale

Picture Completion

This subtest was commonly included in group-administered tests such as the Army Beta. A variant of this task, known as Healy Picture Completion II, which involves placing a missing piece into an uncompleted picture, was given individually in various performance scales, including the Army Performance Scale Examination; however, individual administration of Picture Completion, though conducted with the Binet scale for an identical task named Mutilated Pictures, was less common. Wechsler (1958) was unimpressed with the group-administered versions of Picture Completion because the subject

had to draw in (instead of name or point to) the missing part, too few items were used, unsatisfactory items were included, and items were chosen haphazardly (such that a typical set of items incorporated many that were much too easy and others that were unusually difficult).

Wechsler nonetheless believed that the test's "popularity is fully deserved" (1958, p. 77); he tried to select an appropriate set of items while recognizing the difficulty of that task. "If one chooses familiar subjects, the test becomes much too easy; if one turns to unfamiliar ones, the test ceases to be a good measure of intelligence because one unavoidably calls upon specialized knowledge" (p. 77). He thought that the W-B I set of items was generally successful, although he had to increase the subtest length by 40% when developing WAIS Picture Completion to avoid a fairly restricted range of obtained scores. Although Wechsler was critical of the group-administered Picture Completion tasks, it is still noteworthy that four of the W-B I and WAIS items were taken directly from the Army Beta test, and an additional four items were clear adaptations of Beta items (using the same pictures, with a different part missing, or the same concept).

The subtest has several psychometric assets, according to Wechsler (1958), including brief administration time, minimal practice effect even after short intervals, and good ability to assess intelligence for low-functioning individuals. Two of these claims are true, but the inconsequential practice effect is refuted by data in the WAIS-III Manual (Psychological Corporation, 1997), which shows test-retest gains for WAIS-III Picture Completion over a 2- to 12-week interval to be about 2 scaled-score points for 16- to 29-year-olds and 30- to 54-year-olds and 1 to 1.5 points for those ages 55–74 and 75–89; this gain led to an average practice effect of about 6.5 points for P-IQ (compared to only 2.4 points for V-IQ). Limitations of the task are that subjects must be familiar with the object in order to have a fair opportunity to detect what is missing, and the susceptibility of specific items to sex differences. Wechsler (1958) notes that women did better in finding the missing eyebrow in the girl's profile and that men did better in detecting the missing thread on the electric light bulb. Similarly, on the WISC-R, about two thirds of the boys but only about one third of the girls across the entire 6–16 age range were able to find the missing "slit" in the screw; in contrast, many more girls than boys detected the sock missing from the girl who is running.

Because a person must first have the basic perceptual and conceptual abilities to recognize and be familiar with the object pictured in each item, Wechsler (1958) saw Picture Completion as measuring "the ability of the individual to differentiate essential from non-essential details," and "to appreciate that the missing part is in some way essential either to the form or to the function of the object or picture." But because of the total dependence of the assessment of this skill on the person's easy familiarity with the content of the item, "[u]nfamiliar, specialized and esoteric subject matter must therefore be sedulously avoided when pictures are chosen for this test" (p. 78).

Picture Arrangement

Tests requiring the examinee to arrange a set of pictures presented in mixed-up order so that they tell a sensible story were first used in France by DeCroly (1914). Similar items were developed for the Army Beta group examination but were found inadequate before a different set of items emerged as a component of the individually administered Army Performance Scale Examination (Wechsler, 1958). Yet this task was not used much by the Army and was not popular in the United States except for its inclusion on the Cornell-Coxe Performance Ability Scale (Cornell & Coxe, 1934). Wechsler believed that its relative unpopularity was due to difficulty in scoring the items (because of numerous alternative solutions that are conceivably worthy of full or part credit) and in finding good sequences. However, "[c]artoons appear to have an international language of their own" (p. 75), and the task has some positive features: "[I]t effectively measures a subject's ability to comprehend and size up a total situation…[and]…the subject

matter of the test nearly always involves some human or practical situation" (p. 75).

Consequently, Wechsler considered it worthwhile to develop a Picture Arrangement subtest for the W-B I despite unavoidable limitations inherent in the test itself. He borrowed three items from the ill-fated Army group-administered version of the task and added four new items taken from Soglow's "Little King" series of cartoons (Wechsler, 1958). For the WAIS, he dropped one W-B I item and added two by new cartoonists. He selected items based on "interest of content, probable appeal to subjects, ease of scoring, and discriminating value." Yet Wechsler was never satisfied with the result, noting that "the final selection leaves much to be desired" (p. 75). He spent much time and statistical analysis trying to discern which alternative responses deserved credit and even called in a team of four judges; yet, the final system for assigning credit for alternative arrangements "turned out to be more or less arbitrary" (p. 76).

The problems with Picture Arrangement concern the important role that content must play for each item, which introduces variables regarding cultural background, urban versus rural upbringing, sex differences, interests, and so forth. Yet this limitation is also the subtest's greatest asset, because it is the unique content of each item that gives the task its clinical power. Although Wechsler (1958) did not believe in social intelligence (considering it merely the application of general intelligence to social situations), he conceded that comprehension of the Picture Arrangement items "more nearly corresponds to what other writers have referred to as 'social intelligence'" (p. 75). When individuals perform well on Picture Arrangement, despite poor performance on other tasks, they "seldom turn out to be mental defectives" (p. 76). Furthermore, Wechsler stressed the clinical information obtainable from listening to the subject explain the story behind his or her arrangement, whether the sequence is correct, arguably correct, or plain wrong. "Consistently bizarre explanations are suggestive of some peculiar mental orientation or even psychotic trend." Wechsler considered the explanations given to various arrangements to be "[m]ore interesting than the question of credits allowed" (p. 76), and recommended that examiners routinely ask for verbal explanations of their arrangements when time permits. To avoid violating the norms, these explanations should not be elicited until the entire subtest is completed; then the items of interest can be placed in front of the subject in the order that he or she gave.

The emphasis on speed changed from the W-B I to the WAIS to the WAIS-R to the WAIS-III. Bonus points for quick, perfect performance were allotted for more items on the WAIS than the W-B I, increasing the range of possible subtest scores and enhancing the role played by speed of performance on the obtained score. However, Wechsler (1981) reversed this trend for the WAIS-R and deemphasized speed greatly by not allowing bonus points for any of the Picture Arrangement items. Test publishers (Psychological Corporation, 1997) honored Wechsler's wishes by continuing to avoid bonus points on WAIS-III Picture Arrangement.

Block Design

Kohs (1923) developed the Block Design test, which used blocks and designs that were red, white, blue, and yellow. His test was included in numerous other tests of intelligence and neuropsychological functioning before Wechsler adapted it for the W-B I. Wechsler (1958) shortened the test substantially, used designs having only two colors (although the W-B I blocks included all four colors, unlike the red and white WAIS and WAIS-III blocks), and altered the patterns that the examinee had to copy. Block Design has been shown to correlate well with various criterion measures, to be a good measure of g, and to be quite amenable to qualitative analysis (Wechsler, 1958). It intrigued Wechsler that those who do very well on this subtest are not necessarily the ones who treat the pattern as a gestalt, but are more often the individuals who are able to break up the pattern into its component parts.

Wechsler (1958) believed that observation of individuals while they solve the problems, such as their following the entire pattern versus breaking it into small parts, provided qualitative, clinical information about the subject's problem-solving approach, attitude, and emotional reaction that is potentially more valuable than the obtained scores. "One can often distinguish the hasty and impulsive individual from the deliberate and careful type, a subject who gives up easily or becomes disgusted, from the one who persists and keeps on working even after his time is up" (p. 80). He also felt that the Block Design subtest is most important diagnostically, particularly for persons with dementia or other types of neurological impairment. From Goldstein's (1948) perspective, those with brain damage perform poorly on Block Design because of loss of the "abstract approach," although Wechsler preferred to think that most "low scores on Block Design are due to difficulty in visual-motor organization" (1958, p. 80).

Object Assembly

Two of the three W-B I Object Assembly puzzles (Manikin and Feature Profile) are slight adaptations of items developed by Pintner and first used in the Army Performance Scale Examination before appearing in performance tests devised by Pintner and Patterson (1925) and by Cornell and Coxe (1934); Wechsler developed the third W-B I item (Hand) and the new item added to the WAIS (Elephant). Wechsler (1958) was dissatisfied with the popular formboard tests, especially for assessing adults, but he "wanted at least one test which required putting things together into a familiar configuration" (pp. 82–83). He included Object Assembly, but only "after much hesitation" (p. 82) because of its known liabilities: (1) relatively low reliability and predictive value, (2) large practice effects, and (3) low correlations with other subtests.

The assets of Object Assembly that impelled Wechsler (1958) to include it in the battery despite its considerable shortcomings were partly psychometric (it contributed something unique to the total score), but mostly clinical and qualitative. Observing individuals solve the puzzles offers great insight into their thinking and work habits and allows the examiner to view several different approaches to the task: "an immediate perception of the whole, accompanied by a critical understanding of the relation of the individual parts[;] ...rapid recognition of the whole but with imperfect understanding of the relations between the parts [;...or a response] which may begin with complete failure to take in the total situation, but which after a certain amount of trial and error manifestation leads to a sudden though often belated appreciation of the figure" (p. 83).

The special clinical value of Object Assembly, according to Wechsler, therefore derives from the examiner's opportunity to observe firsthand "the subject's mode of perception, the degree to which he relies on trial and error methods, and his manner of reaction to mistakes" (1958, p. 84).

Digit Symbol-Coding

"The Digit Symbol or Substitution Test is one of the oldest and best established of all psychological tests. It is to be found in a large variety of intelligence scales, and its wide popularity is fully merited" (Wechsler, 1958, p. 81). The W-B I Digit Symbol subtest was taken from the Army Beta, the only change being the reduction in response time from 2 minutes to 1½ minutes to avoid a pileup of perfect scores. For the WAIS, the number of symbols to be copied was increased by about one third, although the response time remained unchanged.

Wechsler's (1958) main concern regarding the use of Digit Symbol for assessing adult intelligence involved its potential dependency on visual acuity, motor coordination, and speed. He discounted the first two variables, except for people with specific visual or motor disabilities, but gave much consideration to the impact of speed on test performance. He was well aware that Digit Symbol performance drops dramatically with increasing age and is especially deficient for older individuals, who "do not write or handle objects as fast as younger persons, and what is perhaps equally important, they are not as easily motivated to do so. The problem, how-

ever, from the point of view of global functioning, is not merely whether the older persons are slower, but whether or not they are also 'slowed up'" (p. 81). Because correlations between Digit Symbol performance and total score remain high (or at least consistent) from age 16 through old age, Wechsler concluded that older people deserve the penalty for speed, "since resulting reduction in test performance is on the whole proportional to the subject's over-all capacity at the time he is tested" (p. 81). Although neurotic individuals also have been shown to perform relatively poorly on Digit Symbol, Wechsler attributed that decrement to difficulty in concentrating and applying persistent effort, i.e., "a lessened mental efficiency rather than an impairment of intellectual ability" (p. 82).

Compared to earlier Digit Symbol or Substitution tests, Wechsler saw particular advantages to the task he borrowed from the Army Beta and included on his scales: It includes sample items to ensure that examinees understand the task, and it requires copying the unfamiliar symbols, not the numbers, lessening "the advantage which individuals having facility with numbers would otherwise have" (1958, p. 82).

Optional procedures have been added to the WAIS-III Digit Symbol-Coding subtest (previously named Digit Symbol), which were developed to help examiners assess what skills (or lack thereof) may be impacting examinees' performance on the subtest. These optional procedures involve recalling shapes from memory (Pairing and Free Recall) and perceptual and graphomotor speed (Digit-Symbol Copy).

ITEM CONTENT CHANGES FROM THE W-B I TO THE WAIS TO THE WAIS-R AND TO THE WAIS-III

Table 3.1 presents a summary of changes in the item content of the 11 subtests when the W-B I was first revised to produce the WAIS, the WAIS was revised a generation later to become the WAIS-R, and finally the WAIS-R was revised to produce the WAIS-III in 1997, fully 16 years after Wechsler's death. Although now in its final form, the WAIS-III has 14 rather than 11 subtests, Table 3.1 discusses the subtests that are common among all versions of the WAIS. This table was constructed from helpful tables in the WAIS, WAIS-R, and WAIS-III manuals (Wechsler, 1955, 1981, 1997). A glance at the first three columns shows that the number of items was increased for 9 of the 11 subtests when the W-B I was revised; however, when the WAIS was revised the overall number of items remained about constant, as increases in four subtests were offset by reductions in the length of three subtests. In its final form now, the WAIS-III has increased the subtest length in 9 of the 11 subtests that are the same across the versions. Overall, Vocabulary has become progressively shorter, whereas Comprehension, Similarities, Picture Arrangement, Block Design, and Digit Symbol have increased in length. In addition to the lengthening of these subtests, there are also now three additional subtests in the WAIS-III, plus supplemental procedures. Therefore, the length of the test itself has been increased by the new Letter-Number Sequencing, Symbol Search, and Matrix Reasoning subtests, as well as the supplementary procedures that were added to Digit Symbol-Coding to enhance its neuropsychological value.

The development of three entirely new subtests for the WAIS-III was the largest change in the test since its inception. This change allowed the development of four factor indexes, and also led to a change in the composition of subtests that comprise the IQs. The WAIS-III's four indexes include: Verbal Comprehension (Vocabulary, Similarities, Information), Perceptual Organization (Picture Completion, Block Design, and Matrix Reasoning), Working Memory (Digit Span, Arithmetic, and Letter-Number Sequencing), and Processing Speed (Digit Symbol-Coding and Symbol Search). The Verbal IQ is comprised of the following subtests: Vocabulary,

Similarities, Arithmetic, Digit Span, Information, and Comprehension. The Performance IQ is comprised of Picture Completion, Digit Symbol-Coding, Block Design, Matrix Reasoning, and Picture Arrangement. Letter-Number Sequencing is not included in the Verbal IQ unless clinicians choose to substitute its score for Digit Span. Symbol Search is not included in the Performance IQ unless clinicians choose to substitute it for Digit Symbol-Coding. Object Assembly is not included in the Performance IQ unless clinicians choose to substitute it for a spoiled Performance subtest for individuals ages 16–74.

One of the largest changes in the content of original Wechsler subtests was in the development of an entirely new set of Vocabulary items in the development of the WAIS. In general, however, there has been a rather substantial turnover in the Verbal items from the W-B I to its successors as only 46.5% of the W-B I Verbal items were retained in the WAIS and only 36.2% were still in the WAIS-R. Excluding Vocabulary and Digit Span (which have not changed at all), the remaining four WAIS Verbal subtests include an average of about two thirds of the W-B I items, and the four WAIS-R tasks include an average of about one half of the W-B I items. For the Performance Scale, the changes have been more modest, as 93.1% of W-B I items are on the WAIS, and 85.1% are on the WAIS-R. However, those percentages are inflated by Digit Symbol; content changes for Picture Completion, Picture Arrangement, and Block Design resemble closely the changes characterizing the Verbal subtests.

Across all subtests, about two thirds of 217 W-B I items were on the WAIS, and nearly three fifths remained on the WAIS-R. In contrast, item changes from the WAIS to the WAIS-R were generally minor; 81.4% of the WAIS Verbal items and 92.5% of the WAIS Performance items (87.2% overall) appeared on the WAIS-R. Beyond the addition of new subtests, other changes from the WAIS-R to the WAIS-III were also notable; 81.8% of the WAIS-R Verbal Items and 72% of the Performance items remained on

TABLE 3.1 Changes in the item content from the Wechsler-Bellevue I to the WAIS to the WAIS-R to the WAIS-III

Subtest	Number of Items on				Percent of W-B I Items Retained on WAIS	Percent of WAIS Items Retained on WAIS-R	Percent of WAIS-R Items Retained on WAIS-III	Percent of New Items Written for		
	W-B I	WAIS	WAIS-R	WAIS-III				WAIS	WAIS-R	WAIS-III
Verbal										
I	26	29	29	28	61.5	69.0	65.5	44.8	31.0	32.0
DSp	14	14	14	15	100.0	100.0	100.0	0.0	0.0	7.1
V	42	40	35	33	0.0	82.5	71.4	100.0	5.7	24.2
A	10	14	14	20	50.0	85.7	100.0	64.3	14.3	30.0
C	12	14	16	18	66.7	85.7	75.0	42.9	25.0	33.3
S	12	13	14	19	83.3	76.9	78.6	23.0	28.6	42.1
Performance										
PC	15	21	20	25	73.3	66.7	50.0	47.6	30.0	60.0
PA	7	8	10	11	85.7	75.0	50.0	25.0	40.0	54.5
BD	9	10	9	14	77.7	90.0	100.0	30.0	0.0	35.7
OA	3	4	4	5	100.0	100.0	60.0	25.0	0.0	40.0
DSy	67	90	93	133	100.0	100.0	100.0	25.6	3.2	0.0[a]
Total										
Verbal	116	124	122	133[b]	46.5	81.4	81.8	57.3	17.2	28.1
Performance	101	133	136	188[b]	93.1	92.5	72.0	29.3	9.6	47.6
Full Scale	217	257	258	321[b]	67.7	87.2	77.3	42.8	13.2	35.9

[a]Three supplementary procedures were added to WAIS-III Digit Symbol: Pairing, Free Recall, and Digit Symbol-Copy.
[b]These totals do not include the new subtests on the WAIS-III: Letter-Number Sequencing, Symbol Search, and Matrix Reasoning
The percent of items retained from the Wechsler-Bellevue I or WAIS includes items that were modified slightly by rewording, redrawing, or reduction in size.

In addition, the blocks used for Block Design were red, white, blue, and yellow for the W-B I, but were just red and white for the WAIS and WAIS-R. The new items written for the WAIS are expressed as a percentage of the number of items on the WAIS, the new items written for the WAIS-R are expressed as a percentage of the number of items on the WAIS-R, and the new items written for the WAIS-III are expressed as a percentage of the number of items on the WAIS-III.

the WAIS-III. Four of the WAIS-III subtests retained all items from the WAIS-R: Digit Span, Arithmetic, Block Design, and Digit Symbol-Coding. The remaining seven subtests include less than 80% of the WAIS-R items: Information, Vocabulary, Similarities, Comprehension, Picture Completion, Picture Arrangement, and Object Assembly. The changes in content between the WAIS-R and its successor is also evident from the percentage of WAIS-III items that are totally new—35.9%—a far cry from the 13.2% of the WAIS-R items that were newly written. The majority of the new WAIS-III items were from the Performance scale, with 47.6% of the items being written expressly for that scale.

Thus, relatively major content changes occurred when the W-B I was revised to become the WAIS, and fairly minor content changes accompanied the metamorphosis of the WAIS into the WAIS-R. Now with the WAIS-III, we again see some major changes in the battery. Modifications in the W-B I were made by Wechsler (1955) primarily because "[r]estriction of range of item difficulty was the principal inadequacy… [leading to] less than the desired reliability for some of the single tests" (p. 1), and because some items were ambiguous. Content changes were made from the WAIS to the WAIS-R (Wechsler, 1981) primarily to remove or modify dated or ambiguous items, to include more Verbal and Performance items relevant to women and minority group members, and to eliminate very easy items. In addition, administration and scoring changes were made to conform more closely to WISC-R procedures.

The WAIS-III manual (Wechsler, 1997) outlines several issues that were considered in the revision of the WAIS-R: updating the norms, extending the age range because individuals are living longer, removing outdated and biased items, modernizing and enlarging artwork, extending the floor of the test to more adequately discriminate among examinees with mental retardation, decreasing reliance on timed performance, organizing the test into four factors, and linking

other measures statistically to the test. However, despite these changes, the continuity of the W-B I through its most recently revised and restandardized edition, the WAIS-III, is demonstrated by the fact that more than half of the W-B I items are still administered to adults evaluated in the last decade of the twentieth century, despite sweeping cultural and technological changes.

RELIABILITY COMPARISONS OF THE W-B I, WAIS, WAIS-R, AND WAIS-III

Reliability of a scale is directly related to the number of items in that scale (holding other variables constant), such that longer versions of tests tend to be more reliable than shorter versions of those same tests. Based on the increased test length of most W-B I subtests when the WAIS was constructed, one would logically assume that the reliability of the WAIS would outstrip that of its predecessor.

Table 3.2 presents the best reliability estimates available for the W-B I, WAIS, WAIS-R, and WAIS-III. Although the same psychometric procedures were not applied uniformly to the four batteries, preventing simple or direct comparisons from test to test, the table reveals that the WAIS is indeed more reliable than the W-B I. As Wechsler had intended when he lengthened the W-B I, the reliabilities of V-IQ and P-IQ rose from the mid-80s on the W-B I to the mid-90s on the WAIS; the coefficient for Full Scale likewise jumped from 90 to 97. Two of the three subtests that were most lengthened when the WAIS was developed (Arithmetic, Digit Symbol) showed the biggest jumps in reliability. Surprisingly, Picture Completion evidenced the same coefficient on the\W-B I and WAIS, even though it was increased from 15 to 21 items; nonetheless, the increase served the useful function of raising the maximum scaled score obtainable on Picture Completion from 15 on the W-B I to 18 on the WAIS.

TABLE 3.2   Reliability and stability coefficients for the Wechsler-Bellevue I, WAIS, WAIS-R, and WAIS-III

Subtest/IQ/Index	W-B I (Test-Retest)	WAIS (Split-Half)	WAIS-R (Split-Half)	WAIS-R (Test-Retest)	WAIS-III (Split-Half)	WAIS-III (Test-Retest)
Verbal Subtests						
Information	.86	.91	.89	.91	.91	.94
Digit Span	.67	.68	.83	.86	.90	.83
Vocabulary	.88	.95	.96	.92	.93	.91
Arithmetic	.62	.82	.84	.85	.88	.86
Comprehension	.74	.78	.84	.81	.84	.81
Similarities	.71	.86	.84	.84	.86	.83
Letter-Number Sequencing	—	—	—	—	.82	.75
Performance Subtests						
Picture Completion	.83	.83	.81	.88	.83	.79
Picture Arrangement	.64	.67	.74	.73	.74	.69
Block Design	.84	.84	.87	.86	.86	.82
Object Assembly	.69	.68	.68	.70	.70	.76
Digit Symbol	.80	.92	.82	.84	.84	.86
Matrix Reasoning	—	—	—	—	.90	.77
Symbol Search	—	—	—	—	.77	.79
Factor Index						
Verbal Comprehension	—	—	—	—	.96	.95
Perceptual Organization	—	—	—	—	.93	.88
Working Memory	—	—	—	—	.94	.89
Processing Speed	—	—	—	—	.88	.89
IQs						
Verbal	.84	.96	.97	.96	.97	.96
Performance	.86	.93	.93	.90	.94	.91
Full Scale	.90	.97	.97	.96	.98	.96

NOTE: Data for the Wechsler-Bellevue I are from a test-retest study conducted by Derner, Aborn, and Cantor (1950) with 158 normal individuals. Wechsler (1958, p. 102) and Matarazzo (1972, p. 239) feature these data, apparently considering them as the best estimates of W-B I reliability. Data for the WAIS are the means of the values provided in the WAIS Manual (Wechsler, 1955, Table 6) for ages 18–19 ($N = 200$), 25–34 ($N = 300$), and 45–54 ($N = 300$). The value for WAIS Digit Symbol was based on a test-retest study of 59 female nursing applicants aged 18–19, who were tested on the WAIS and W-B I Digit Symbol subtests. Split-half data for the WAIS-R are the means provided in the WAIS-R Manual (Wechsler, 1981, Table 10) for the nine age groups between ages 16 and 74. The values for the WAIS-R Digit Symbol and Digit Span are test-retest coefficients based on four age groups (Ns of 48–80). Test-retest data for the WAIS-R are the means of the values for the two groups presented in the WAIS-R Manual (Wechsler, 1981, Table 11) at ages 25–34 ($N = 71$) and 45–54 ($N = 48$). When the mean split-half values for the WAIS-R are based only on ages 18–19, 25–34, and 45–54 to make them directly comparable to the mean split-half values for the WAIS, the results are highly similar to the WAIS-R split-half means based on all nine age groups; values for the three IQs are identical and values for the subtest are within .03 of each other. Data for the WAIS-III are from the WAIS-III/WMS-III Technical Manual (Psychological Corporation, 1997, Tables 3.1 and 3.11).

Reliability coefficients for the WAIS-R and WAIS-III are similar, especially for the IQs. For most of the subtests on the WAIS-R and the WAIS-III, the reliability coefficients differ only by .01–.02. The largest increase in subtest reliability (.07) between these two versions of the test was for Digit Span. Historically, Digit Span's reliability increased the most between the WAIS and WAIS-R, probably because of the administrative change requiring examiners to give both trials to all individuals, even if they pass the first trial. This difference from WAIS and W-B I procedures, which required second trials only for those who failed the first time, effectively increased the number of items in the WAIS-R subtest, even though technically each battery contains the same 14 items.

Overall, the reliability coefficients for the three batteries generally show improvement with each revision and restandardization, although the relative lack of gain from the WAIS-R to the WAIS-III is quite surprising in view of The Psychological Corporation's (1997) extensive efforts to extend the floors of several subtests, modernize and enhance the art, remove biased items, and so forth. Despite notable increases in the reliability coefficients from the W-B I through the WAIS-R, the values are sufficiently similar for the three batteries on both the global scales and separate subtests to support the continuity of consistent measurement from the W-B I to the WAIS to the WAIS-R to the WAIS-III.

STANDARDIZATION OF THE W-B I, WAIS, WAIS-R, AND WAIS-III

The standardization samples of the Wechsler adult batteries have improved significantly with each successive norming program. The initial standardization of the W-B I was conducted by Wechsler and his colleagues before he received financial backing from a test publisher, so a nationwide norming was not feasible; consequently the W-B I was standardized on a population that was "mostly urban from the City and State of New York" (Wechsler, 1958, p. 92). The W-B I normative sample was also all Caucasian, excluding African Americans and other non-Caucasian groups "because it was felt at the time that norms derived from a mixed population could not be interpreted without special provisions and reservations… [which] appears now to have been an unnecessary concern" (Wechsler, 1958, p. 90).

Although the W-B I sample (which ranged from ages 7 to 70) included males and females, it was not systematically stratified by gender. The W-B I adult normative population was roughly stratified by education level, but not occupational group. Hence, the W-B I was stratified by age and education, but not on variables that today are considered essential for an intelligence test: gender, race, geographic region, occupation, and urban versus rural residence. Yet, the stratification on age was an important contribution to psychometrics, because "the practice for a long time was to treat all individuals over 16 years as constituting a single age group" (Wechsler, 1958, p. 86). In addition, the choice of education as a rough stratification variable was a good one because of its correlations in the .50s to low .70s with IQ (Matarazzo, 1972; Reynolds et al., 1987).

The WAIS was normed on a nationwide sample of African Americans and Caucasians and was systematically stratified for ages 16 to 64 on the variables of age, gender, race, geographic region, urban versus rural residence, educational attainment, and occupational group. This sample was far superior to the W-B I sample, but it did not include a stratified sample of older individuals. Norms for ages 65–69, 70–74, and 75 and over were derived from 359 individuals included in a sample of 475 elderly Kansas City residents. Although this elderly sample was carefully selected using probability sampling techniques, it was not stratified on the major variables used to stratify the WAIS for all other age groups and is, therefore, not ideal. In contrast, the WAIS-R was stratified on all of the same key variables as the

WAIS through age 74. Like the WAIS-R, the WAIS-III was stratified on age, gender, ethnicity, education level, and geographic region. An additional 200 African American and Hispanic individuals were administered the WAIS-III without discontinue rules for item-bias analyses. Further oversampling was completed so that at least 30 participants would be included in each educational level within each age group for research on the relationship between cognitive abilities and education level. The WAIS-III represents the ultimate in adult norming of a Wechsler battery.

The W-B I sample included 50 to 70 children at each year of age between 7 and 14, and 100 children at age 15. Sample sizes for the age groups between 16 and 39 ranged from 100 to 135 (Wechsler, 1958). After age 39, the size of each of the age groups decreased and was inconsistent, ranging from $N = 50$ at ages 55–59 to $N = 91$ at ages 40–44. Clearly, the younger half of the age range (16–39, $N = 830$) was far better represented than the older half (40–70, $N = 351$). In the WAIS, WAIS-R, and WAIS-III these unusual disproportions were eliminated. The WAIS included 200 individuals aged 16–17, 18–19, 20–24, and 55–64, and 300 subjects aged 25–34, 35–44, and 45–54; the sample of 1,700 included exactly equal numbers of males and females at each of the seven age groups. The WAIS-R sample included 1,880 individuals spread across nine age levels between 16 and 74. The WAIS-III standardization sample consisted of 2,450 individuals, ages 16–89 years, divided into 13 age bands (each group included 200 subjects, except for the 80–84 and 85–89 age groups, which contained 150 and 100 participants, respectively).

Wechsler (1955, 1981) did not provide a rationale for having larger samples at the younger ages or for having narrower age bands at the extremes of the age range (16–24 and 65–74 years). Presumably, the age bands are narrower for the younger and older ages because of the more rapid intellectual change (whether increasing or declining) associated with adolescence and old age. The larger samples of younger than older subjects probably reflects the relative ease or difficulty of obtaining volunteers for testing from the different age groups.

One interesting difference between the WAIS and WAIS-R samples is the inclusion of one male and one female institutionalized mentally retarded individual at each of the seven WAIS age groups (Wechsler, 1955), although the sample did not include any other "known hospital or mentally disturbed subjects" (Wechsler, 1958, p. 92); for the WAIS-R, the normative sample excluded "institutionalized mental defectives, individuals with known brain damage or severe behavioral or emotional problems, or individuals with physical defects which would restrict their ability to respond to test items" (Wechsler, 1981, p. 18). However, this difference in the two samples involves too few individuals to be of much practical consequence. For the WAIS-III, a separate sample of 108 individuals with mental retardation was collected to assess the clinical sensitivity of the test.

Because the W-B I, WAIS, WAIS-R, and WAIS-III standardization samples were each stratified on education level, this variable is a good way of comparing the three samples. Table 3.3 presents the proportion of the subjects in each sample attaining different levels of education. The total sample for the W-B I matched the best available Census data for the 1930s reasonably well, and the total samples for the WAIS, WAIS-R, and WAIS-III matched best estimates of Census data for the 1950s, 1970s, and 1990s, respectively. Hence, differences in proportions of the samples for each educational level reflect real differences in the population as a whole at the time of each standardization.

Overall, the data in Table 3.3 reveal that each level of educational attainment was appropriately represented in all four standardization samples. In view of the importance of this variable in terms of its impact on IQ compared to most other variables (Reynolds et al., 1987), the state of the art regarding the psychometrics underlying test standardization in the 1930s versus the 1950s, 1970s, and 1990s, and the cultural influences of

TABLE 3.3   Comparison of education levels characterizing the total standardization samples of the W-B I, WAIS, WAIS-R, and WAIS-III

Education level (Years of School Completed)	Percent in W-B I Sample	Percent in WAIS Sample	Percent in WAIS-R Sample	Percent in WAIS-III Sample
16 or more (college graduate)	5.1	4.9	11.4	17.8
13–15 (some college)	3.8	8.6	13.4	22.9
12 years (high school graduate)	10.8	23.3	34.7	34.4
9–11 years (some high school)	18.8	27.8	25.1	12.1
8 or less	61.6	35.5	15.5	12.8

NOTE: Data for the W-B I and WAIS are from Wechsler (1958, Tables 9 and 10). Data for the WAIS-R are based on sample sizes for the total standardization group provided in Table 1 by Reynolds et al. (1987). Data for the WAIS-III are from the WAIS-III/WMS-III Technical Manual (Psychologi-cal Corporation, 1997, Table 2.6). The group listed as "8 or less" for the W-B I is actually a combination of percentages provided for elementary school graduates, those with some elementary school, and illiterates.

the time (which would have made it understandable to omit non-Caucasians from the W-B I sample), it is reasonable to conclude that the standardization samples of the four adult Wechsler batteries are appropriately comparable.

COMPARISON OF THE CONSTRUCT VALIDITY OF THE W-B I, WAIS, WAIS-R, AND WAIS-III

Construct validity, which determines the degree to which a test measures the traits or constructs it was developed to measure, is considered by Messick (1980) to be the only real type of validity. More than a comparison of reliability coefficients, content changes, or standardization samples, a comparison of the constructs underlying the three adult Wechsler test batteries is instrumental in deciding whether the bulk of research obtained on the W-B I, WAIS, and WAIS-R is legitimately generalizable to the WAIS-III. Three of the types of acceptable evidence in support of a test's construct validity (Anastasi & Ur-

bina, 1997) will be examined for the W-B I, WAIS, WAIS-R, and WAIS-III: internal consistency (correlations between each subtest and total score on the battery), factor analysis, and developmental changes (progression of mean Verbal, Performance, and Full Scale scores across the age range).

Internal Consistency

Table 3.4 presents correlations between subtest scores and total scores on each of the three test batteries based on age groups that are roughly comparable, after correction for contamination due to the subtest's overlap with total score. The column of WAIS-III coefficients also includes those for the three new subtests: Letter-Number Sequencing, Matrix Reasoning, and Symbol Search. These coefficients are good estimates of the internal consistency of each battery. (The value for W-B I Vocabulary had to be estimated by Wechsler, 1958, from research conducted after standardization because Vocabulary was merely an alternative test during the early standardization testing.) Overall, the coefficients for the 11 W-B I subtests ranged from .48 to .75, slightly lower than the ranges of .56 to .84 for the

TABLE 3.4   Coefficients of correlation between the subtests and Full Scale Score on the W-B I, WAIS, WAIS-R, and WAIS-III

Subtests	W-B I (Ages 20–34)	WAIS (Ages 25–34)	WAIS-R (Ages 25–34)	WAIS-III (Ages 25–34)
Verbal				
Information	.67	.84	.79	.77
Digit Span	.51	.56	.57	.57
Vocabulary	(.75)	.84	.82	.81
Arithmetic	.63	.66	.72	.77
Comprehension	.66	.71	.74	.77
Similarities	.73	.74	.72	.75
Letter-Number Sequencing	—	—	—	.70
Performance				
Picture Completion	.61	.72	.72	.57
Picture Arrangement	.57	.69	.65	.68
Block Design	.71	.79	.74	.67
Object Assembly	.48	.58	.59	.61
Digit Symbol	.67	.63	.52	.45
Matrix Reasoning	—	—	—	.69
Symbol Search	—	—	—	.63
Mean Verbal	.66	.72	.73	.74[a]
Mean Performance	.61	.68	.64	.59[a]
Mean Full Scale	.64	.70	.69	.67[a]

[a]Mean WAIS-III correlations are based on the 11 subtests that are common to the previous versions of the WAIS. With all 14 WAIS-III subtests, the mean correlations for the scales were .71 for Verbal, .62 for Performance, and .66 for Full Scale. The coefficients for the Wechsler-Bellevue I are between each subtest's total score minus the particular subtest, based on $N = 355$. The value for Vocabulary was estimated by Wechsler (1958, pp. 84–85) from studies conducted subsequent to the W-B I standardization, because correlations with Full Scale were not computed for Vocabulary, an alternative test in the early stages of the W-B I standardization. The coefficients for the WAIS ($N = 300$), WAIS-R ($N = 300$), and WAIS-III ($N = 400$) between each subtest and total score were corrected for contamination due to overlap. Data for the W-B I and WAIS are from Wechsler (1955, Table 17), data for the WAIS-R are from Wechsler (1981, Table 15), and data for the WAIS-III are from The Psychological Corporation (1997, Tables A.4 and A.5).

WAIS and .52 to .82 for the WAIS-R. The coefficients for the 11 WAIS-III subtests common to the earlier versions of the test ranged from .45 to .81. The mean coefficient for all W-B I subtests was .64, compared to a mean of about .70 for the WAIS and WAIS-R. The mean coefficient for the WAIS-III was slightly lower at .67. Because all validity coefficients are a function of reliability, it is likely that the slightly attenuated W-B I values are merely a reflection of the lower reliability of most subtests and all IQ scales of that battery.

For the W-B I through WAIS-R, Vocabulary, Information, and Block Design were among the highest correlates of Full Scale. With the WAIS-III, however, the highest correlates of Full Scale are Vocabulary, Information, and Similarities. For all four batteries, Object Assembly and Digit Span were among the lowest correlates. When the task-total correlations are rank-ordered from high to low for each of the three batteries, the following rank-order correlations (rho) are obtained: W-B I with WAIS (.78, $p < .02$), with WAIS-R (.63, $p < .05$), and with WAIS-III (.73, $p < .02$); WAIS with WAIS-R (.90, $p < .01$) and with WAIS-III (.83, $p < .01$); and WAIS-R with WAIS-III (.88, $p < .01$). These results attest to the similar construct validity of the W-B I, WAIS, WAIS-R, and WAIS-III—especially the last three—when applying the internal consistency criterion.

Factor Analysis

Historically, factor-analytic investigators of Wechsler's adult scales have not agreed on the number of meaningful factors or constructs underlying the batteries. Silverstein (1982a) frequently argued for two, corresponding fairly closely to the intended constructs of verbal and nonverbal intelligence, while others opted for factor solutions that interpret three or more meaningful dimensions (Berger, Bernstein, Klein, Cohen, & Lucas, 1964; Matarazzo, 1972; Wechsler, 1958). With development of the WAIS-III, some differences in the factor structure were expected, as one of the goals for this version of the test was to strengthen the theoretical basis by creating hypothesized third and fourth factors. Letter-Number Sequencing and Symbol Search were added to the WAIS-III with hopes of producing a Working Memory and a Processing Speed factor to supplement the familiar, robust verbal comprehension and perceptual organization dimensions. The issue of the number of meaningful WAIS-III factors and possible theoretical interpretations is treated at length in Chapter 7. Whereas the factor analyses of the WAIS-III showed that there are four dimensions comprising the test, three dimensions have emerged

fairly consistently for the W-B I, WAIS, and WAIS-R. On these older versions of the test, for a wide variety of normal and special samples using an even greater variety of psychometric techniques, the two main, omnipresent factors were Verbal Comprehension and Perceptual Organization, and the third, smaller dimension was assigned labels like Freedom from Distractibility, Memory, Sequential Ability, and Number Ability. The four dimensions of the WAIS-III (Verbal Comprehension, Perceptual Organization, Working Memory, Processing Speed) are similar to those found on the earlier versions of the test, and contain slightly different subtests, as shown in Table 3.5.

Exploratory and confirmatory factor analyses were performed on the WAIS-III standardization data. The results of these analyses, which included all subtests but Object Assembly (now an optional subtest), clearly supported a four-factor solution. The Verbal Comprehension factor had its highest loadings by Vocabulary, Information, Similarities, and Comprehension; Perceptual Organization had its highest loadings by Block Design, Matrix Reasoning, Picture Completion, and Picture Arrangement. The third factor, Working Memory, had its highest loadings by Digit Span, Letter-Number Sequencing, and Arithmetic, and the final factor, Processing Speed, was made up of Digit Symbol-Coding and Symbol Search.

Confirmatory analyses were performed on the WAIS-III standardization sample to determine how well the four-factor model would fare in comparison to one-factor, two-factor, three-factor, and five-factor models (Psychological Corporation, 1997). All of these factor models were evaluated according to a variety of goodness-of-fit indexes. The results showed that the four-factor model, indeed, provided the best fit for the data for the WAIS-III sample, although the results for ages 75–89 did not conform to the neat four factors for ages 16–74 (see discussion in Chapter 7).

On the Wechsler-Bellevue, the WAIS, and the WAIS-R, when two factors were rotated, the six Verbal subtests tended to load highly on the

TABLE 3.5 Comparison of the Verbal Comprehension (VC) and Perceptual Organization (PO) factors of the W-B I, WAIS, WAIS-R, and WAIS-III

| | Rotated Factor Loadings | | | | | | | | Rank Order of Factor Loadings | | | | | | | |
| | WB-I | | WAIS | | WAIS-R | | WAIS-III | | Verbal Comprehension | | | | Perceptual Organization | | | |
Subtest	VC	PO	VC	PO	VC	PO	VC	PO	W-B I	WAIS	WAIS-R	WAIS-III	W-B I	WAIS	WAIS-R	WAIS-III
Verbal																
I	**63**	-02	**79**	**42**	**79**	31	**80**	31	1	2	2	2	9	6	11	10
DSp	02	-03	**52**	34	**47**	37	**44**	29	10	7	6	6.5	10	11	8	11
V	**61**	-08	**83**	35	**84**	32	**84**	32	2	1	1	1	11	9.5	10	9
A	27	04	**61**	**40**	**58**	**47**	**61**	**40**	6	5	5	5	6.5	7	4	5.5
C	**55**	00	**70**	35	**73**	34	**74**	35	3	4	3	3	8	9.5	9	8
S	**54**	04	**71**	38	**69**	39	**73**	39	4	3	4	4	6.5	8	7	7
Performance																
PC	34	**43**	**48**	**63**	**44**	**55**	33	**61**	5	8.5	8	9.5	3	3	3	3
PA	18	**42**	**48**	**57**	**45**	**45**	**44**	**50**	7	8.5	7	6.5	4	4	6	4
BD	02	**59**	35	**72**	33	**72**	33	**72**	8	10	10	9.5	2	1	1	1
OA	-08	**73**	28	**70**	22	**69**	24	**71**	11	11	11	11	1	2	2	2
Dsy	01	23	**54**	**44**	39	**46**	36	**40**	9	6	9	8	5	5	5	5.5

NOTE: Decimal points are omitted. Loading of .40 and above are in bold print. Data for the Wechsler-Bellevue I are the means of the oblique-rotated loadings from three-factor solutions reported by Cohen (1952a) for three neuropsychiatric groups, each composed of 100 hospitalized male veterans between the ages of 20 and 40: psychoneurotic, schizophrenic, brain-damaged. The data for the WAIS and WAIS-R are the means of the varimax-rotated loadings from two-factor solutions reported by Silverstein (1982a) for the standardization samples of each instrument. For the WAIS, means are based on three age groups (18–19, 25–34, and 45–54) comprising a total of 800 subjects; for the WAIS-R, means are based on all nine age groups between 16 and 74, comprising 1880 subjects. The data for the WAIS-III are from a two-factor varimax-rotated principal factor solution for the WAIS-III (ages 16–89) based on the 11 subtests included in both the WAIS-R and WAIS-III as reported by Kaufman, Lichtenberger, and McLean (2001). Rank-order correlations of subtest ranks between pairs of Verbal Comprehension (VC) factors are as follows: W-B I and WAIS, rho = .81; W-B I and WAIS-R, rho = .85; WAIS and WAIS-R, rho = .93; W-B I and WAIS-III, rho = .85; WAIS and WAIS-III, rho = .95; WAIS-R and WAIS-III, rho = .98. Rank-order correlations of subtest ranks between pairs of Perceptual Organization (PO) factors are as follows: W-B I and WAIS, rho = .91; W-B I and WAIS-R, rho = .91; WAIS and WAIS-R, rho = .78; W-B I and WAIS-III, rho = .96; WAIS and WAIS-III, rho = .90; WAIS-R and WAIS-III, rho = .92.

first or Verbal Comprehension factor, and the five Performance subtests primarily defined the Perceptual Organization dimension (a factor more accurately described as Visual Organization) (Kaufman, 1990). The two-factor structure for the WAIS-III also reflects a nearly flawless split of the six verbal subtests and five Performance subtests when only the 11 subtests shared with the WAIS and WAIS-R were analyzed (Kaufman, Lichtenberger, & McLean, 2001). In fact, the coefficients of congruence between the WAIS-R and WAIS-III two-factor solutions were .998 for Verbal Comprehension and .996 for Perceptual Organization (Kaufman et al., 2001). Table 3.5 presents the Verbal Comprehension and Perceptual Organization factors for the W-B I, WAIS, WAIS-R, and WAIS-III. These results are taken from two-factor solutions for the latter three test batteries, based on the entire standardization samples; for the W-B I, the best available data were the first two factors from three-factor solutions of abnormal populations.

Despite these differences in samples and procedures (including the fact that correlated factors were obtained for the W-B I, whereas independent factors were extracted for the WAIS, WAIS-R, and WAIS-III), the three Verbal factors are quite similar to each other, as are the three Performance dimensions. Table 3.5 shows factor loadings as well as the rankings of each subtest on each factor (where 1 denotes the highest loading and 11 signifies the lowest).

For each adult Wechsler battery, the best measures of Verbal Comprehension are Vocabulary, Information, Comprehension, and Similarities, and the best measures of Perceptual Organization are Block Design, Object Assembly, and Picture Completion. The note to Table 3.5 gives the rank-order correlations between pairs of factors assigned the same name on the three test batteries. These values, averaging .86 for the Verbal factors and .87 for the Performance factors, are all statistically significant ($p < .05$).

Also of interest is a comparison of the nature of the relationships between the Verbal and Performance IQs on the W-B I, WAIS, WAIS-R, and WAIS-III. The following V-P IQ correlations from available standardization data are observed: W-B I ($r = .71$ for ages 20–25); WAIS ($r = .78$, mean of ages 18–19, 25–34, and 45–54); WAIS-R ($r = .74$ for the total sample ages 16–74); and WAIS-III ($r = .75$ for the total sample ages 16–89). These values are similar to each other, again affirming the comparability of the two major constructs underlying the four adult Wechsler batteries. "These correlations are fairly high but not sufficiently high that substantial differences in the separate IQ's obtained by any individual may not occur" (Wechsler, 1958, p. 102).

Table 3.6 presents data on the third factor extracted from three-factor solutions of the W-B I, WAIS, WAIS-R, and WAIS-III (Kaufman, 1990; Kaufman et al., 2001) and again the similarity from battery to battery is remarkable. For the earlier three versions of the test, the prototypical triad of distractibility subtests (Digit Span, Arithmetic, Digit Symbol) had the highest loadings on each of the dimensions. However, on the WAIS-III, the three-factor solution had loadings from the traditional three "distractibility" tasks plus strong loadings from the new tasks on the Working Memory Index (Letter-Number Sequencing) and the Processing Speed Index (Symbol Search). The third factor on the WAIS-III, being a combination of Working Memory and Processing Speed tasks, seems to stress working memory in both the visual and verbal modalities (Kaufman et al., 2001). The three-factor solutions in the WAIS-R and the WAIS-III are quite reasonably congruent (.984) when comparing the third WAIS-R dimension with the third WAIS-III factor obtained from an analysis of only the 11 subtests shared with the WAIS-R (Kaufman et al., 2001).

Developmental Trends

With the publication of the WAIS-III, which raised the upper age range of the test to 89, came interesting questions about cognitive abilities across the age range. Prior to the development of

TABLE 3.6   Comparison of the Working Memory/Freedom from Distractibility factors of the W-B I, WAIS, WAIS-R, and WAIS-III

	Rotated Factor Loadings			
Subtests	W-B I	WAIS	WAIS-R	WAIS-III
Verbal				
Information	.03	.07	**.30**	**.34**
Digit Span	**.55**	**.71**	**.64**	**.58**
Vocabulary	.01	.12	**.34**	**.34**
Arithmetic	**.30**	**.32**	**.55**	**.64**
Comprehension	.00	−.06	.27	.27
Similarities	.06	.10	.27	.28
Performance				
Picture Completion	−.09	−.07	.17	.21
Picture Arrangement	.02	.08	.23	.25
Block Design	.18	.04	**.30**	**.35**
Object Assembly	.00	.03	.17	.14
Digit Symbol	**.37**	.24	**.36**	**.36**

NOTE: Loadings of .30 and above are in bold print. Data for Wechsler-Bellevue I are the means of the oblique-rotated loadings from three-factor solutions reported by Cohen (1952a) for the three groups described in the note to Table 3.5. Data for the WAIS are oblique-rotated loadings from three-factor solutions reported by Fowler, Richards, and Boll (1980) based on the mean intercorrelation matrix for the three standardization age groups in the WAIS Manual (ages 18–19, 25–34, 45–54). Data for the WAIS-R are the means of the varimax-rotated loadings reported by Parker (1983) for the nine standardization groups, ages 16–74; three-factor solutions were used for seven age groups, but four-factor solutions had to be used to obtain the desired three factors for ages 18–19 and 45–54. Data for the WAIS-III are from the three-factor varimax-rotated principal-factor solutions (ages 16 to 89) based on the 11 subtests included in both the WAIS-R and WAIS-III reported by Kaufman, Lichtenberger, and McLean (2001).

Rank-order correlations of subtest ranks between pairs of Freedom from Distractibility/Working Memory factors are as follows: W-B I and WAIS, rho = .83; W-B I and WAIS-R, rho = .84; W-B I and WAIS-III, rho = .88; WAIS and WAIS-R, rho = .85; WAIS and WAIS-III, rho = .80; WAIS-R and WAIS-III, rho = .97.

the third edition of the WAIS, scaled scores for each of the three earlier versions of the battery were based on a reference group of individuals aged 20–34. Although the WAIS-III's method of deriving scaled scores separately by age groups has clinical superiority, the old method of using the 20- to 34-year-old reference group allowed comparisons of the relative ability level of separate age groups via an examination of sums of scaled scores (not IQs, which are adjusted for age). Thus, in order to complete analyses of age-

related trends on the WAIS-III, scaled scores derived from the reference group were needed for each subtest at each age, and educational attainment was controlled. For the W-B I, data are incomplete, as mean scores are only available through age 59 for the Verbal and Full Scales, and through age 49 for the Performance Scale (Wechsler, 1958, Table 13). In view of the small sample sizes for the older half of the W-B I sample, one cannot have too much confidence in the generalizability of the developmental trends across the entire age range. Nevertheless, mean scaled scores were computed for W-B I age groups having 150 or more cases to permit some comparisons to the WAIS, WAIS-R, and WAIS-III. (Mean scaled scores allow direct comparison because the W-B I sums of scaled scores are based on only 10 subtests, not 11, and because the Verbal and Performance scales have different numbers of subtests on the WAIS, WAIS-R, and WAIS-III. Note that even though the WAIS-III sum of scaled scores contains 11 subtests, like the WAIS and WAIS-R, it includes Matrix Reasoning rather than Object Assembly.) The W-B I mean scaled scores are shown in Table 3.7, and the WAIS, WAIS-R and WAIS-III mean scaled scores are shown in Table 3.8. As is evident in these data, on the W-B I individuals aged 16–19 performed not quite as well as those aged 20–24; verbal scores began to decline after age 29, and nonverbal scores began to descend after age 24. Table 3.8 presents similar data for the WAIS and WAIS-R for seven age groups within the 16- to 64-year age range, and the data for the WAIS-III extend the age range to age 89 with 5 additional age groups.

The data in Table 3.8 are quite revealing. On the WAIS and WAIS-R, Verbal scores increased gradually from ages 16 through 34 and did not really begin to decline until after age 44. However, on the WAIS-III, the Verbal scores did not begin to decline until the mid-50s, and the decline was gradual until after the 70s. For the WAIS, WAIS-R, and WAIS-III, Performance scores likewise increase gradually, but only

through age 24 before plunging after age 34. Verbal scores begin to decline slightly during the 30s and more rapidly in the 40s, and Performance scores begin an early decline on both the W-B I and the WAIS during the mid-20s.

Note that the changes in mean scores with age cannot be interpreted as meaningful developmental fluctuations because the various cross-sectional age groups differed on other key variables such as educational attainment. This topic is addressed in detail in Chapter 5.

Problems with Adolescent Data

The data for the WAIS-R are in accord with the W-B I, WAIS, and WAIS-III data for adults ages 20 and above, but not for adolescents. Indeed, the mean scaled scores for the WAIS, WAIS-R, and WAIS-III Full Scales are virtually identical for the age groups between 20–24 and 25–34. The WAIS-R data for ages 16–19, however, do not correspond well to those of the WAIS or the WAIS-III, a point raised previously concerning the WAIS (Kaufman, 1985a, 1990; Gregory, 1987).

The older adolescents in the WAIS-R sample performed very poorly compared to their age-mates in previous standardization samples, scoring strikingly lower on the Verbal and Full Scales and substantially lower on the Performance Scale. Even more inexplicable is the failure of 18- and 19-year-olds to outperform the 16- and 17-year-olds on the WAIS-R, even though they have more education. The WAIS-R shows mean scaled scores for the 11 subtests of 8.9, 9.0, and 10.0 for the three youngest age groups in the standardization sample. The net result for the WAIS-R was to produce a set of "soft" norms that spuriously inflated their IQs.

Unlike the WAIS-R, the 16- to 17-year-olds performed as one would expect in comparison to the 18- to 19-year-olds on the WAIS-III; the older, more educated group performed better. However, on the WAIS-III, the 18- to 19-year-olds performed at a level identical to 20- to 24-year-olds. This finding is surprising given the

TABLE 3.7 Mean scaled scores computed for W-B I age groups having 150 or more cases

Age Group	Verbal	Performance	Full Scale
16–19	9.3	10.2	9.7
20–24	9.4	10.2	9.8
25–29	9.4	9.7	9.5
30–39	9.2	8.8	9.0
40–49	8.8	7.7	8.3

TABLE 3.8 Mean scaled scores on the Verbal, Performance, and Full Scales of the WAIS, WAIS-R, and WAIS-III earned by different age groups across the 16–89 year range

Age Group	Verbal			Performance			Full Scale		
	WAIS	**WAIS-R**	**WAIS-III**	**WAIS**	**WAIS-R**	**WAIS-III**	**WAIS**	**WAIS-R**	**WAIS-III**
16–17	9.1	8.5	9.5	9.8	9.5	10.0	9.4	8.9	9.7
18–19	9.6	8.6	9.7	9.9	9.4	10.2	9.7	9.0	10.0
20–24	9.9	9.8	9.9	10.1	10.2	10.1	10.0	10.0	10.0
25–34	10.1	10.2	10.2	9.9	10.0	10.0	10.0	10.1	10.1
35–44	10.0	9.6	10.3	9.2	9.1	9.5	9.4	9.3	9.9
45–54	9.7	9.7	10.8	8.2	8.4	8.9	9.0	9.1	9.9
55–64	9.3	9.3	10.4	7.4	7.6	8.4	8.4	8.5	9.4
65–69			10.6			7.7			9.1
70–74			10.2			7.2			8.7
75–79			10.0			6.6			8.3
80–84			9.5			6.2			7.9
85–89			9.2			5.9			7.5

NOTE: Data for the WAIS and WAIS-R were computed from data provided in the test manuals by Wechsler (1955, Table 19; 1981, Table 7). Data for the WAIS-III are from Kaufman (2000a). WAIS-III data are based on the reference group, ages 20–34 years, and values for ages 20–89 years are adjusted for the educational attainment of age groups 25–29 and 30–34.

fact that more than 50% of the 20- to 24-year-olds have attended at least one year of college (Kaufman, 2000a). The result of this similarity across subjects in the 18- to 24-year-old range is that the same level of performance on the WAIS-III at ages 18 or 19 versus 20 through 24 will produce virtually identical IQs.

Possible Explanations of Questionable WAIS-R Adolescent Norms

Why do the WAIS-R 16- to 19-year-old norms look so different from WAIS and WAIS-III adolescent norms? As discussed in the previous edition of this book (Kaufman, 1990), the only sensible conclusion is that the WAIS-R norms for ages 16–19 included some type of unknown, systematic bias that limited their value. Different procedures were used to select 16- to 19-year-olds and 20- to 74-year-olds for the WAIS-R standardization sample. For the older adoles-

cents, occupation of the subject's head of household was used to stratify the sample; for the adults, their own occupation was used. Additionally, all age groups matched Census proportions on years of school completed, based on divisions into the following educational categories: 8 years or less, 9–11 years, 12 years, 13–15 years, and 16 or more years.

The categories of 9–11 years of education and high school graduate (12 years) are quite different for adolescents and adults. For adults, those categories usually reflect a person's ultimate educational attainment, whereas for 16- to 19-year-olds they may just be intermediate points in their education. Paradoxically, the stratification difference resulting from the variable of education should have produced a bias that was opposite to the one that apparently occurred; that is, individuals with 9 to 11 years of education who are destined to go on to college should perform better than those who will never graduate from high school.

Thus, the explanation of the problem is not simple or obvious. Yet, there certainly seems to be some connection to the occupational and educational variables, as evidenced by the relationships of IQ to these socioeconomic variables at ages 16–19 (see Chapter 4 for further discussion). For example, educational attainment correlated only .19 with WAIS-R Full Scale IQ at ages 16–17, compared with coefficients of .50–.67 for other age groups, suggesting a problem with the sampling at ages 16–17.

However, the fact that the stratification variables of occupational group and educational attainment operated differently for 16- to 19-versus 20- to 74-year-olds may well be related to the seemingly wrong norms for the youngest two age groups in the WAIS-R sample. Further, the lack of a clear-cut explanation did not vitiate the severity of the problem when the WAIS-R was the test of choice from the early 1980s to late 1990s.

In contrast to the WAIS-R 16- to 19-year-old norms that appear too soft, are the WAIS-III norms, which yield spuriously low IQs for those in their late teens. The explanation for the steep norms for ages 18–19 on the WAIS-III may be related to how The Psychological Corporation gathered the data (Kaufman, 2000a). For ages 16–19, the parents' education was used, but for individuals aged 20 or above, a person's own educational attainment was used. Whereas the parents of older adolescents included nearly 20% college graduates, the 20- to 24-year-olds only included 11% college graduates. The relatively high level of educational attainment of the 16–19 year olds' parents may have given them an unfair advantage relative to the 20- to 24-year-olds who are still in the process of obtaining their higher education.

Clinical Implications of the WAIS-III Norms at Ages 16–19

The lack of gain from ages 18–19 to 20–24 on the WAIS-III should be internalized by clinicians. The norms for individuals ages 16–19 are likely to be slightly inflated relative to young adults. How-

ever, these norms do increase from ages 16–17 to 18–19, as would be expected. Although these findings suggest that the WAIS-III norms for older adolescents should be considered valid, examiners should keep in mind that norms for the older version of the test, the WAIS-R, are suspect. Even though the WAIS-R is an outdated test, examiners need to understand the peculiarities of the 16- to 19-year-old norms (1) when interpreting a client's WAIS-R IQs obtained at ages 16–19 with his or her WAIS-III IQs obtained during adulthood, and (2) when interpreting research studies that compare the WAIS-R and WAIS-III based on samples that include a substantial proportion of adolescents.

Overview of Developmental Trends

The present discussion supports the construct validity of the W-B I and WAIS inasmuch as the developmental trends observed for these instruments conform to what research has shown to characterize adolescent and adult intellectual development when no effort is made to control for cohort differences (see Chapter 5). The construct validity of the WAIS-R and WAIS-III is supported for the adult age range. Consequently, the W-B I, WAIS, WAIS-R, and WAIS-III are sufficiently comparable in the constructs they measure across the adult age ranges, when developmental changes are used as the criterion, but the data for ages 16–19 are not very similar across the four instruments.

CORRELATIONS BETWEEN THE W-B I AND WAIS, WAIS AND WAIS-R, AND THE WAIS-R AND WAIS-III

The various construct validation approaches described previously are instrumental in determining whether research findings on the W-B I, WAIS, and WAIS-R can be applied to the WAIS-III. Just as valuable as these theoretically based approaches is a simple, pragmatic procedure: correlations between the scores yielded by one test battery and the test battery that was developed to replace it.

Relationship of the W-B I and WAIS

Zimmerman and Woo-Sam (1973, Table 2.1) and Matarazzo (1972, Table 10.21) present data summarizing the relationships between W-B I and WAIS IQs found in diverse studies published from 1956 to 1964. In five of these studies, both instruments were administered to groups ranging in size from 28 college students (Duncan & Barrett, 1961) to 179 brain-damaged patients (Fitzhugh & Fitzhugh, 1964a); the total number of subjects in the five studies was 356.

Correlations between the W-B I and WAIS Verbal IQs ranged from .72 to .95 with a mean value of .83. Performance IQ correlations ranged from .25 to .84 with a mean of .48, and Full Scale coefficients ranged from .46 to .87 with a mean of .72. These values, however, are attenuated greatly by an unusual degree of range restriction in the obtained IQs of three of the four groups; standard deviations in the 8 to 12 range were found for the IQs of the two samples of college students, and standard deviations of 6 to 9 points were obtained for a group of Air Force psychiatric patients. When variability of the IQs is far less than the designated standard deviation of 15, lower correlations are the predictable result. Hence, the observed correlations, particularly for the Verbal and the Full Scale IQs, are large enough to support the continuity of measurement from the W-B I to its successor.

Fitzhugh and Fitzhugh (1964a) assessed the one group that had normal-sized standard deviations and that also produced the highest correlations between the W-B I and WAIS IQs (.84 to .95). Yet, they were skeptical about the compara-

bility of the two instruments because their group of 179 brain-damaged patients displayed different V-P IQ discrepancies on the W-B I and WAIS. Their caution is sensible, but because about 2 years had elapsed between the administrations of the W-B I and the WAIS, it is possible that changes occurred in the verbal and nonverbal abilities of those patients.

In reviewing a number of different types of studies pertaining to this issue, Matarazzo concluded "that in a very general and gross sense, the Verbal versus Performance differential on the WAIS has as much potential to differentiate left- from right-hemisphere lesions as does such a differential on the W-B I.... Nevertheless,...[the] Verbal versus Performance differences which the practitioner obtains with an individual patient might be a function of the Wechsler Scale employed, rather than reflecting an underlying brain dysfunction in such a patient" (1972, p. 398).

Matarazzo, therefore, agreed that W-B I research is generalizable to the WAIS, but he cautioned that, for any given client or case, the clinician must be alert to the influences of precisely which battery was administered. This issue becomes particularly important when comparing the results of Wechsler-Bellevue studies of brain-damaged individuals with similar studies that used the WAIS or WAIS-R (see Chapter 8).

Relationship of the WAIS to WAIS-R

In the WAIS-R Manual, Wechsler (1981, Table 17) provided correlations between the WAIS and WAIS-R for 72 adults aged 35–44, tested on both instruments in a counterbalanced order with an interval of 3 to 6 weeks between administrations. He reported WAIS versus WAIS-R coefficients of .91 for the Verbal Scale, .79 for the Performance Scale, and .88 for the Full Scale.

Ryan, Nowak, and Geisser (1987, Table 2) summarized the results of eight groups, including the one cited by Wechsler (1981), that were tested on both the WAIS and WAIS-R. These samples ranged in size from 29 mildly and moderately retarded adults (Simon & Clopton, 1984) and 29 medical and psychiatric patients (Warner, 1983) to 88 college students (Mishra & Brown, 1983). Table 3.9 summarizes the correlations between IQ scales and subtests of the same name on the WAIS and WAIS-R based on the results of these eight samples, which totaled 420 individuals. Median coefficients are reported, rather than means, because of several uncharacteristically low values reported by R. S. Smith (1983) for 70 college students. Mean test-retest reliability coefficients for the WAIS-R, obtained from data on two samples provided by Wechsler (1981, Table 11), are also shown in Table 3.9 to

serve as a reference point for evaluating the WAIS/WAIS-R coefficients.

Overall, the corresponding WAIS and WAIS-R IQs correlated quite substantially (.84 to .92) and not much lower than the respective WAIS-R IQs correlated with each other in a test-retest situation (.90 to .96). The correlation of .87 between V-IQ on the W-B I and WAIS-R, reported by Stewart (1981) for 44 normal Caucasian, middle-class adults (median age = 31.5), is wholly consistent with the coefficients observed for the W-B I and WAIS and for the WAIS and WAIS-R.

Five of the 11 subtests on the WAIS and WAIS-R correlated about as high with each other as one could reasonably expect in view of WAIS-R

TABLE 3.9 Summary of correlations between WAIS and WAIS-R IQs and scaled scores for eight samples tested on both instruments

Subtest or Scale	Range of Correlations	Median Correlation	Mean WAIS-R Stability Coefficient
Verbal			
Information	.47 to .94	.88	.91
Digit Span	.66 to .86	.76	.86
Vocabulary	.26 to .95	.92	.92
Arithmetic	.27 to .88	.80	.85
Comprehension	.51 to .85	.72	.80
Similarities	.33 to .90	.82	.84
Performance			
Picture Completion	.30 to .83	.68	.88
Picture Arrangement	.15 to .80	.58	.72
Block Design	.74 to .89	.82	.86
Object Assembly	.14 to .80	.60	.70
Digit Symbol	.29 to .94	.78	.84
IQ Scales			
Verbal	.73 to .96	.92	.96
Performance	.76 to .89	.84	.90
Full Scale	.85 to .94	.92	.96

NOTE: Data for the WAIS/WAIS-R comparisons are based on Table 2 in a summary article by Ryan et al. (1987). Mean WAIS-R stability coefficients, provided for comparison purposes, are computed from data provided by Wechsler (1981, Table 11) for 71 people aged 25–34 and 48 individuals aged 45–54.

stability coefficients: Information, Vocabulary, Arithmetic, Similarities, and Block Design each correlated within .05 of the test-retest coefficient. If .10 is selected as an arbitrary "allowable" discrepancy between WAIS/WAIS-R correlation and WAIS-R stability coefficient, then only two subtests, Picture Completion and Picture Arrangement, show an inadequate relationship. The WAIS and WAIS-R Picture Completion subtests correlated .68, well below its WAIS-R stability coefficient. The two Picture Arrangement tasks correlated a moderate .58, not nearly as high as its test-retest coefficient of .72 on the WAIS-R.

The three IQs yielded by the WAIS and WAIS-R correlated so well that their comparability is axiomatic. Nine of the 11 subtests also correlated sufficiently well to support their comparability on the WAIS and WAIS-R. However, the two Picture Completion and the two Picture Arrangement subtests do not relate well enough to support their continuity of measurement from the WAIS to the WAIS-R. Not coincidentally, these two subtests were modified substantially when the WAIS was revised (Wechsler, 1981). They retained only 60% to 70% of the WAIS items; among other subtests, only Information rivaled that percentage (see Table 3.1).

Relationship of the WAIS-R to WAIS-III

The *WAIS-III/WMS-III Technical Manual* (Psychological Corporation, 1997) provided data on a sample of 192 adults who were administered both the WAIS-R and WAIS-III. The sample was administered the two tests in counterbalanced order with a 2- to 12-week interval between the tests (median = 4.7 weeks). The correlation coefficients were calculated in a two-step process to account for differential practice effects; the results of the analysis are presented in Table 3.10. As shown in the table, which also includes WAIS-III stability coefficients for comparison purposes, the correlation between tests was .94 for Verbal IQ, .86 for Performance IQ, and .93 for Full Scale IQ.

Overall, the corresponding WAIS-R and WAIS-III Verbal subtests correlated better than the Performance subtests of the two versions of the test. However, this finding is to be expected, given that the test-retest coefficients for the WAIS-III are generally more stable for the Verbal subtests (range =.75-.94; median = .83) than the Performance subtests (range = .69-.86; median = .78). Six of the 11 WAIS-III subtests that are the same for the two versions of the test correlated strongly with one another (given what one could reasonably expect based on their WAIS-III stability coefficients). Digit Span, Vocabulary, Comprehension, Similarities, Picture Completion, and Block Design each correlated within .05 of the test-retest coefficient. Only one subtest, Information, had a discrepancy between the correlation and stability coefficient that was larger than 0.10 (correlation = .83, stability coefficient = .94). Of the Verbal subtests, Information retained the lowest amount of items from its previous version (65.5%). However, given the very high stability coefficient, the .83 correlation between the two Information subtests is still relatively strong. The two subtests that had the lowest correlations between the WAIS-R and WAIS-III were Picture Completion (.50) and Picture Arrangement (.63). However, this lack of continuity is not surprising given that only 50% of the items from the WAIS-R were retained on the WAIS-III for each of these two subtests (see Table 3.1). Like the relationships between subtests on the WAIS and WAIS-R, most coefficients obtained for the WAIS-R and WAIS-III were impressive.

COMPARISON OF SYSTEMS FOR CLASSIFYING INTELLIGENCE ON THE W-B I, WAIS, AND WAIS-III

Although the classification systems used to describe IQs do not relate to the comparability of the instruments, it is still worthwhile to examine

TABLE 3.10   Summary of correlations between WAIS-R and WAIS-III scaled scores, indexes, and IQs along with stability coefficients

	WAIS-R & WAIS-III correlation	Mean WAIS-III stability coefficient
Verbal Subtests		
Information	.83	.94
Digit Span	.82	.83
Vocabulary	.90	.91
Arithmetic	.80	.86
Comprehension	.76	.81
Similarities	.79	.83
Letter-Number Sequencing	—	.75
Performance Subtests		
Picture Completion	.50	.79
Picture Arrangement	.63	.69
Block Design	.77	.82
Object Assembly	.69	.76
Digit Symbol-Coding	.77	.86
Matrix Reasoning	—	.77
Symbol Search	—	.79
Index		
Verbal Comprehension	—	.95
Perceptual Organization	—	.88
Working Memory	—	.89
Processing Speed	—	.89
IQs		
Verbal	.94	.96
Performance	.86	.91
Full Scale	.93	.96

NOTE: Correlational data are based on Table 4.1 of the *WAIS-III/WMS-III Technical Manual* (Psychological Corporation, 1997). Stability data are from Table 3.9 of the *WAIS-III/WMS-III Technical Manual* (Psychological Corporation, 1997).

the changes in the system espoused by Wechsler for his adult intelligence tests. These systems and their modifications are indicated in Table 3.11.

Note that the IQ ranges for the W-B I differ a bit from the more familiar ranges used for the WAIS, WAIS-R, and WAIS-III; the differences are relatively sizable for the Mentally Retarded and Borderline categories, as a cutoff for retardation of 65 (rather than the more typical 69) was used for the W-B I. Examination of Table 3.11 reveals that the IQ ranges were modified when the W-B I was revised, and the labels applied to some IQ ranges were altered when the WAIS was revised. The only label that changed when the WAIS-R was revised was for the lowest category, which changed from Mentally Retarded to Extremely Low.

The lesson here is that classification systems are necessarily arbitrary and can change at the whim of test authors, government bodies, or professional organizations. They are statistical concepts and do not correspond in any real sense to the specific capabilities of any particular person with a given IQ. The classification systems provide descriptive labels that may be useful for communication purposes in a case report or conference, and nothing more.

COMPARISON OF IQS YIELDED BY THE WAIS-R AND WAIS-III

The number of studies employing both the WAIS-R and WAIS-III is smaller than the numerous studies available for comparing earlier versions of the test. The *WAIS-III/WMS-III Technical Manual* (Psychological Corporation, 1997) provided data on a large sample ($N = 192$) that was administered both tests in counterbalanced order (interval = 2–12 weeks). The mean IQs differed very slightly, with the WAIS-III Full Scale IQ being 2.9 points less than the WAIS-R Full Scale IQ. The Verbal and Performance IQs were

TABLE 3.11   Classification systems used for W-B I, WAIS, WAIS-R, and WAIS-III IQs

| WAIS-III Classification | Corresponding IQ Range | | | | Theoretical % |
	W-B I	WAIS	WAIS-R	WAIS-III	
Very Superior	128+	130+	130+	130+	2.2
Superior	120–127	120–129	120–129	120–129	6.7
High Average (Bright-normal on W-B I & WAIS)	111–119	110–119	110–119	110–119	16.1
Average	91–110	90–119	90–119	90–119	50
Low Average (Dull-normal on W-B I & WAIS)	80–90	80–89	80–89	80–89	16.1
Borderline	66–79	70–79	70–79	70–79	6.7
Extremely Low (Defective on W-B I & WAIS; Mentally Retarded on WAIS-R)	65 & below	69 & below	69 & below	69 & below	2.2

NOTE: The classification systems for the W-B I and WAIS are from Wechsler (1958, Tables 2 and 3); the system for the WAIS-R is from Wechsler (1981); and the system for the WAIS-III and the theoretical percentages are from The Psychological Corporation (1997). The theoretical percentages correspond to the IQ ranges for the WAIS, WAIS-R, and WAIS-III, but not the W-B I ranges.

only 1.2 and 4.8 points less, respectively, on the WAIS-III in comparison to the WAIS-R. According to Flynn (1984, 1987), U.S. norms become outdated at the rate of about 3 points per decade, although the current rate may be closer to 2½ points (Flynn, 1998a, 1998c). Thus, these differences are what one would expect (Flynn, 1984, 1987, 1998a, 1998c), given the lower scores that occur when an individual's performance is referenced to outdated norms.

Practical Implications of WAIS-R/WAIS-III IQ Differences

There are several practical implications of the differences in the mean IQs yielded by the WAIS-R and WAIS-III. Many of these implications affect when or whether clinicians switch from using the older version of the test to the WAIS-III. Tulsky and Ledbetter (2000) outlined some of the factors that clinicians and researchers may consider when deciding whether to use a new version of the test: The WAIS-R has a large body of accumulated research behind it which may or may not be generalizable to the WAIS-III; interpreting score discrepancies between the two versions of the test is difficult in a clinical situation; and, in research, switching midstream to the new version of the test may cause a threat to the internal validity of the study.

The most pressing reason to utilize the newest version of the WAIS is to have an updated normative group to which you can compare your clients' scores. Examiners can make inaccurate conclusions about an individual's functioning if no adjustments are made once a test's norms become outdated (Tulsky & Ledbetter, 2000). Clearly this is an ethical as well as clinical issue for psychologists (see the AERA, APA, and NCME *Standards for Educational and Psychological Testing*, 1999). The IQ differences between the WAIS-R and the WAIS-III provide information on just how "outdated" the WAIS-R norms had become. The overall differences of about 1.2 to 4.8 points between the WAIS-R and WAIS-III

IQs are roughly consistent with Flynn's (1984, 1987) expected discrepancies between tests normed about 16 years apart. The WAIS-R was standardized between 1976 and 1980 and the WAIS-III in 1995 and 1996, so one would predict that the WAIS-III would yield IQs that are about 4.5 points lower than the WAIS-R IQs. The WAIS-R/WAIS-III discrepancies for the three IQs, especially the value of 2.9 points for Full Scale IQ, impelled Flynn (1998) to speculate that the rate of change in the United States may have dropped from 3 points to 2½ points.

The IQ discrepancy findings provide good and bad news for WAIS-R/WAIS-III users, as they affirm the similarity between the WAIS-R and WAIS-III standardization samples as well as elucidate some of the changes in the samples. It appears that the only differences between them are the predictable, "real" differences in intellectual performance that characterize successive generations in the United States. It does not appear that they are due to changes in the items from the WAIS-R to the WAIS-III in view of the significantly high correlations between the tests. These lawful findings reinforce the continuity from the WAIS-R to the revised test that replaced it.

Nonetheless, the differences in the IQs yielded by the two test batteries have practical consequences for examiners. Those who still cling to the WAIS-R for some or all of their evaluations should recognize that the WAIS-R IQs are very out-of-date and, therefore, incorrect. Matarazzo delineates some of the issues at hand: "[I]t is imperative that such (age) norms be periodically updated lest they be less than fully efficient for the re-examination of individuals living in a social-cultural-educational milieu potentially very different from the one which influenced the individuals constituting the norms for that same age group in an earlier era" (1972, p. 11). As Gregory (1987) has stressed: "[T]he failure to use the modern test and norms can throw the IQ score off by as much as 8 points. In selected cases, 8 points could make the difference between recommending a college instead of a technical school or placing an individual in a group home instead of in an institution" (p. 140).

Clinicians who give the WAIS-III to adults who have previously been tested on the WAIS-R should anticipate lower WAIS-III scores (except, perhaps, for retarded or gifted individuals). Even discrepancies of about ½ standard deviation between them (i.e., about twice the expected difference between WAIS-R and WAIS-III IQs) may not indicate loss of intellectual function. Such determinations are especially crucial in instances of brain damage or dementia; examiners should guard against making inferences about deterioration when the decrease in IQ accompanies a switch from the WAIS-R to the WAIS-III. Supplementary support for a loss of function is necessary in such circumstances.

GENERALIZATION FROM THE W-B I, WAIS, AND WAIS-R TO THE WAIS-III

The preceding sections have typically supported the continuity of measurement from the W-B I to the WAIS to the WAIS-R to the WAIS-III. In general, research findings on the older Wechsler adult batteries may be considered fairly applicable to the current instrument. There are, however, some qualifications and these are discussed in the following sections.

Studies at Ages 16–19 Years

The lack of construct validity for the WAIS-R's 16- to 19-year-olds based on the developmental change criterion is the finding of greatest concern, along with the unusual pattern observed on the WAIS-III (equal performance by ages 18–19 and 20–24). These problems with the WAIS-R norms at ages 16–19, and concern about the WAIS-III norms for older adolescents, call into question attempts to generalize any research findings from the W-B I or WAIS to the WAIS-R

and the WAIS-R to the WAIS-III when the samples are composed exclusively or primarily of older adolescents.

Studies Focusing on Picture Completion, Picture Arrangement, or Object Assembly

The item content changes from the WAIS-R to the WAIS-III may have affected the continuity of the Picture Completion, Picture Arrangement, and Object Assembly subtests. Only 50% of the content of Picture Completion and Picture Arrangement was retained from the WAIS-R, and only 60% of the Object Assembly items were retained. In addition, the correlations between the WAIS-R and WAIS-III versions of these subtests are relatively low (r's of .59–.63). Although the effects of these differences in subtests between versions of the test are not fully known, we must be cautious in assuming that studies that focus on these particular subtests are generalizable.

We also know that significant changes occurred in Picture Arrangement and Picture Completion when the WAIS was revised to become the WAIS-R, thereby making research investigations on the W-B I or WAIS that were devoted to one or both of these subtests of questionable generalizability to the WAIS-R as well as the WAIS-III. For example, Fogel (1965) found WAIS Picture Arrangement to be a better discriminator of "organics" than five other WAIS subtests, including Block Design; introverts scored significantly lower on Picture Arrangement than did extroverts, as selected by the MMPI Social Isolation scale (Schill, 1966); and Blatt and his colleagues concluded that WAIS Picture Arrangement was a measure of anticipation and planning by relating subtest performance to criteria like punctuality versus procrastination or subscores on the Thematic Apperception Test (Blatt & Quinlan, 1967; Dickstein & Blatt, 1967). Because of the content changes in Picture Arrangement, it is dubious whether findings such as these with WAIS Picture Arrangement are generalizable to the WAIS-R or the WAIS-III.

Factor Analysis Studies

Although there are similarities in the factor structures for the four adult Wechsler batteries, there are some differences in the WAIS-III that one should consider before generalizing from W-B I, WAIS, or WAIS-R investigations of the two or three constructs that underlie the test batteries. The Verbal and Performance IQs continue to denote the two major factors, but, with the WAIS-III, the Object Assembly subtest is no longer a part of the Performance IQ and the new Matrix Reasoning subtest stands in its place. Although the mean scores on these two subtests have been shown to be almost identical across most age groups (Kaufman, 2000a; Kaufman & Lichtenberger, 1999), these two subtests are likely measuring quite different abilities, and may impact the meaning of the Performance IQ. Whereas Matrix Reasoning is a prototypical measure of Horn's fluid ability (Gf), Object Assembly requires speed and visual–motor problem solving in addition to Gf. Therefore, any studies that explored V-P IQ differences on the W-B I, WAIS, or WAIS-R for diverse samples, such as those with known brain damage (Matarazzo & Herman, 1985; see Chapters 8 and 9), should be examined with careful consideration before deciding whether they are generalizable to the WAIS-III. Similarly, studies using the WAIS and WAIS-R Freedom from Distractibility factor may be generalizable to the WAIS-III's Working Memory factor; however, the WAIS-III's addition of Letter-Number Sequencing to the traditional Digit Span-Arithmetic dyad adds much uncertainty to the meaningfulness of earlier versions of this factor to the current one. Research is needed simply to answer the question of whether the WAIS or WAIS-R results are applicable to the WAIS-III, especially because the neurological "seat" of Matrix Reasoning (Horn,

1989) may be quite different from the right-hemisphere damage that has long been associated with loss of functioning on Wechsler's traditional Performance subtests (see Chapter 8).

Because the WAIS-III commonly produces a four-factor, rather than three-factor result, the typical factor-analytic findings for the W-B I, WAIS, and WAIS-R on diverse clinical and normal samples are not always going to be directly applicable to the WAIS-III. In particular, the specific nuances of the loadings of particular subtests will likely appear quite different, and the previous versions simply had no analogs for Letter-Number Sequencing, Symbol Search, and Matrix Reasoning.

The specific loadings of any given subtest are subject to the influences of variables such as sample size, geographic location of the subject pool, and simple chance error, as well as variables having to do with modifications in the test battery itself. Hence, when generalizing research findings from the W-B I, WAIS, or WAIS-R to the WAIS-III, it is better to focus on key results dealing with the two or three global constructs or with the general factor underlying overall performance (e.g., Full Scale IQ) than to dwell on subsidiary results or relatively minor details.

Short Form Studies

Short form studies on the W-B I, WAIS, or WAIS-R should *not* be generalized to the WAIS-III. These studies usually capitalize on chance relationships between pairs of subtests and total score in selecting the best dyads (or triads, or tetrads, etc.). The best Verbal dyad on the WAIS-R may be the tenth best WAIS-III dyad owing to myriad factors related to sample selection, content changes in the subtests, differences in reliability coefficients, differences in the correlation matrixes, and chance error. As we discuss in Chapter 15, we do not advocate use of short forms with the WAIS-III because there are so many other brief tests available for measuring intellectual ability, for example, the Wechsler Abbreviated Scale of Intelligence (WASI; Psychological Corporation, 1999), and the Kaufman Brief Intelligence Test (K-BIT; Kaufman and Kaufman, 1990).

Correlational Studies

The numerous correlational studies involving the WAIS-R and other instruments are generally applicable to the WAIS-III, but only if the correlations involving the IQs are examined and if the other instrument has not also been revised. However, correlations involving the W-B I and WAIS are invariably with older tests, and therefore of little current relevance. Even with the correlational studies, however, some caution is advised when interpreting values for the P-IQ and FS-IQ because of the unknown effects of replacing Object Assembly with Matrix Reasoning.

In no instance should mean differences between WAIS-R IQs and the overall scores on the "other" test be generalized to the WAIS-III. The differences in the IQs yielded by the WAIS-R and WAIS-III are, on average, one-fifth of a standard deviation and the WAIS-R standard deviations for sums of scaled scores differ significantly from each other (Lindemann & Matarazzo, 1984). Obviously, the difference in the IQs produced by the WAIS-R and any other instrument will not characterize the differences between the WAIS-III and that test. Hence, the correlations between the WAIS-R and another measure are likely to generalize to the WAIS-III reasonably well, but not the differences in the global scores they yield.

Group versus Individual Interpretation

The studies and variables discussed in this chapter address the issue of comparability to discern whether the body of research accumulated on the W-B I, WAIS, and WAIS-R is applicable to the most recent version, the WAIS-III. As indicated, the answer to this question is generally yes, with some areas of caution. However, this continuity concerns the generalizability of group data obtained on one instrument to group data on another instrument.

In the case of specific individuals, one would not immediately assume, for example, that a person with a significant V-P IQ difference on the WAIS-R when evaluated 5 or 10 years ago will necessarily have that same significant difference when tested again on the WAIS-III. Test scores for an individual are too variable and are much less stable than group data. Any given person's ability spectrum may have changed over time, or chance factors may have been operating; he or she may not have displayed a significant V-P difference if retested 6 months later on the same instrument (the WAIS-R).

Thus, one cannot make predictions about a specific person's obtained scores on any of the adult Wechsler scales. But one can be reasonably assured, based on the literature review analyzed in this chapter, that, apart from the exceptions noted, a clinician who gives the WAIS-III to anyone will be measuring the same constructs that Wechsler intended to measure when he first developed the W-B I, and that he continued to measure with the WAIS and WAIS-R.

Conclusions

Most comparisons and analyses discussed in this chapter support the comparability and continuity of the W-B I, WAIS, WAIS-R, and WAIS-III. Comparisons of item content revealed that a core of items from the W-B I was retained in the WAIS, a majority of WAIS items were retained on the WAIS-R, and a solid core of WAIS-R items can be found on the present-day WAIS-III. Although there is a core of items that journeyed from one version of the test to the next, modification in content during the WAIS, WAIS-R, and WAIS-III revisions was the rule rather than the exception. These content changes, however, did not usually affect the constructs underlying the test batteries, the exceptions being that the WAIS-III now provides a clear measure of processing speed in its new indexes and the Perceptual Organization factor now provides a stronger measure of fluid reasoning with the addition of Matrix Reasoning. Reliability, construct validity, and correlational analyses generally revealed similarities in the values observed for the four adult Wechsler scales; any changes typically reflected refinement and improvement in the revision and restandardization process. The two global constructs forming the foundation of the four test batteries seem particularly robust to the changes in item content.

SUMMARY

The goal of this chapter was to relate the WAIS-III to its predecessors, the WAIS-R, WAIS, and Wechsler-Bellevue I, primarily to determine the degree to which W-B I, WAIS, and WAIS-R research results are generalizable to the current battery. First, Wechsler's rationale was explored for selecting each of the 11 subtests for the original W-B I; the four Wechsler adult scales were then compared on their test content, reliability coefficients, standardization samples, and construct validity.

Wechsler selected his tasks from other available tests of the day, especially the series of instruments developed by the U.S. Army during World War I. He chose Information despite its obvious relationship to education, because similar tasks displayed excellent psychometric properties and correlated exceptionally well with various measures of intelligence. Digit Span, despite being a weak measure of *g*, was included because of its value with low-functioning individuals and its diagnostic significance. Vocabulary was originally a W-B I alternate (Wechsler's concession to its educational and cultural dependency); however, its great clinical value and excellence as a measure of

g led to its ultimate inclusion on the regular W-B I and core membership on subsequent Wechsler batteries. Arithmetic shares many of the pros and cons of Information and Vocabulary, but is subject to the influences of attention span and temporary emotional states; nonetheless, such tasks are easily created and are perceived as face valid by adults. Comprehension, though heavily dependent on verbal expression, invariably contributes rich clinical information (especially concerning the diagnosis of psychopathology). Similarities is the only verbal subtest to have appeared sparingly in previous tests; Wechsler selected it primarily for its ease of administration and interest to adults, and for providing insight into a person's logical thinking process.

Wechsler selected Picture Completion for the Performance Scale, despite the difficulty in constructing hard items that are not too specialized, because it is both short and easy to administer and is effective for measuring the intelligence of low-functioning individuals. He included Picture Arrangement because of its interpersonal content and enormous clinical value despite nearly insurmountable obstacles in developing unambiguous items. Block Design affords examiners direct observation of a person's problem-solving strategy and has important neurological implications; Wechsler found little to criticize with this task, unlike the other subtests. In contrast, Object Assembly was included in spite of difficulties regarding reliability and low correlations with other measures because of its clinical value and its use of familiar stimuli. Digit Symbol, though perhaps too reliant on motor coordination and speed, was one of Wechsler's favorites as a good, quick measure of nonverbal intelligence.

Major item content changes occurred when the W-B I was revised to become the WAIS, including the lengthening of numerous subtests and the development of a new set of Vocabulary words. Changes from the WAIS to the WAIS-R, by contrast, were relatively minor as 87% of the WAIS items were retained. For the WAIS-III, 36% of the items were newly written, in addition to adding three brand-new subtests. In the earlier revisions of Wechsler's adult test, more item changes characterized the Verbal than Performance subtests. However, with the WAIS-III more changes were made to the Performance subtests than the Verbal. Nonetheless, continuity of content is supported from the old W-B I to the present-day WAIS-III by virtue of the inclusion, in the current battery, of a substantial amount of the original W-B I items.

One of Wechsler's key goals in revising the W-B I was to obtain better score distributions and greater reliability for most subtests, and the substantial increase in reliability from the W-B I to the WAIS demonstrates his success. In general, reliability has improved with each revision (though only slightly from WAIS-R to WAIS-III), although the magnitudes of the coefficients for the four batteries are similar enough to support the continuity of consistent measurement from one scale to the other.

Like the reliability coefficients, Wechsler aimed to improve the quality of the standardization samples with each successive revision. The W-B I sample (ages 7–70 years) was composed mostly of Caucasian, urban New Yorkers; it was roughly stratified on education, but not on gender, race, or occupational level. In contrast, the WAIS (ages 16–64 years) and WAIS-R (ages 16–74 years) were carefully stratified on many important variables. Old-age norms for the WAIS were developed from a nonrepresentative sample; the key improvement in the WAIS-R norms was the inclusion of a stratified elderly population. The WAIS-III expanded the age range of its standardization sample from 16 to 89 and even included oversampling of some groups for additional study. Each of the standardization samples matched Census proportions on the crucial variable of educational attainment; in addition, each sample represented the state of the art for its era. Consequently, the samples are reasonably comparable.

The continuity of the constructs measured by the W-B I, WAIS, WAIS-R, and WAIS-III has been documented amply by the techniques of internal consistency, factor analysis, and correlational analysis. The method of inferring construct validity from developmental changes in mean scores, however, suggested the continuity of constructs for adults aged 20 and above, but not for 16- to 19-year-olds.

WAIS-R and WAIS-III IQs correlate extremely highly with each other, indicating excellent continuity of measurement of Wechsler's major constructs; further, WAIS-R/WAIS-III correlations are adequate for 9 of the 11 overlapping subtests, all but Picture Completion and Picture Arrangement. Wechsler modified his system for classifying IQs on the W-B I, WAIS, WAIS-R, and WAIS-III although such changes do not affect the continuity of measurement from one battery to another.

The IQs yielded by the WAIS-III are 1.2 to 4.8 points lower than the corresponding values on the WAIS-R. This finding seems to reflect real changes in the ability levels of the generations, with present-day individuals scoring better than adults in the past (hence, producing "steep" WAIS-III norms). These IQ changes indicate the need to restandardize tests fairly frequently, but they do not imply a lack of consistency in the constructs measured by the WAIS-R and WAIS-III.

Overall, these comparisons support the continuity of measurement from the W-B I to the WAIS to the WAIS-R to the WAIS-III. In general, one may legitimately generalize research results from the older scales to the WAIS-III. There are important exceptions, however (e.g., factor analysis, in view of the four-factor structure for the 14-subtest WAIS-III), and clinicians need to understand the distinction between generalizations made for groups versus those made for individuals.

CHAPTER 4

Individual Differences
for Adolescents and Adults
on Gender, Ethnicity,
Urban–Rural Residence,
and Socioeconomic Status

Large, nationwide, carefully stratified standardization samples almost always represent the best samples of normal individuals obtained at one point in time on that test. Such samples serve the vital function of providing a representative normative group for determining an individual's accurate profile of IQs and scaled scores, but they can also serve the equally important function of understanding individual differences on key background variables like occupational group, urban versus rural residence, and race. Subsequent studies with new samples can also address these issues (and occasionally do), but such investigations are usually conducted with nonrandom samples of individuals who are referred for intellectual assessment for diverse reasons, or with essentially random samples of normal subjects who are typically small in number and who reside in the same geographic region.

The sections that follow explore IQ, standard-score, and scaled-score differences for people who differ on the kinds of crucial background variables that serve to stratify the samples of intelligence tests. We explore the relationships of IQs and other scores to the variables of gender, race, urban versus rural residence, occupational group, and education level, focusing on data obtained on individually administered clinical tests of intelligence for adolescents and adults, most notably the WAIS-III, WAIS-R, Stanford-Binet IV, and Kaufman tests (e.g., Kaufman Adolescent and Adult Intelligence Test or KAIT).

GENDER DIFFERENCES

Global Scales

Gender differences on the WAIS-III at ages 20–89 years were examined by Heaton, Manly, Taylor, and Tulsky (2001) by computing age-corrected and education-corrected z scores on each WAIS-III IQ, index, and scaled score in a sample of 2,250 individuals collected during WAIS-III standard-ization (2,028 standardization cases plus 222 cases from an "education oversampling"). Males scored higher by about 5 points on V-IQ, ½ point on P-IQ, and 3 points on FS-IQ. On the indexes, men outscored the women by about 3½ points on both the VCI and WMI and about 2½ points on the POI; in contrast, women surpassed men by about 5½ points on the PSI. All of these differences correspond to relatively small effect sizes, all below 0.4 *SD;* the largest difference observed was the female superiority of 0.37 *SD* on PSI, which is a direct function of their better performance on both PSI subtests, as discussed in the next section.

The small differences in favor of males on the WAIS-III IQs resemble WAIS-R data obtained for the total standardization sample of 1,880 adults, ages 16–74 years (Reynolds et al., 1987), and for a sample of 230 above-average, middle- to upper-middle class adults ages 16–71 (mean age = 35 years; mean FS-IQ = 110) tested by Arcenaux, Cheramie, and Smith (1996). Within the standardization sample, males scored higher than females by 2.2 points on V-IQ and FS-IQ and 1.4 points on P-IQ (Reynolds et al., 1987). For the above-average adult sample, males again out-

scored females by a few points, namely 3 to 3½ points on the three IQ scales (Arcenaux et al., 1996). The small gender differences also characterized the 1955 WAIS standardization sample, with males scoring higher by about 1 IQ point on the Verbal and Full Scales, with no IQ difference evident on the Performance Scale (Kaufman, 1990; Matarazzo, 1972). Another WAIS study of normal adults (264 male and 257 female adoptive parents, mean age = 39 years, mean FS-IQ = 113.5) produced similar results: Males earned a higher FS-IQ by 2.6 points (Turner & Willerman, 1977).

Non-Wechsler tests have likewise yielded very small gender differences on their global scales for adult samples. At ages 17–94 years on the KAIT (Kaufman & Kaufman, 1993), less than 1 IQ point separated the education-adjusted IQs earned by 716 men and 784 women on the Fluid and Crystallized Scales (Kaufman & Horn, 1996), as shown in Table 4.1. Also, at ages 12–23 on the Stanford-Binet IV (Thorndike et al., 1986b, Table 4.5), the standard-score differences between 800 males and 926 females was 1 point or less for the Composite and for three of the four area scores (females scored 2.2 points higher on Short-term Memory).

TABLE 4.1 Mean differences between males and females on the KAIT Fluid IQ, Crystallized IQ, and selected subtests at ages 17 to 94 years, adjusted for educational attainment ($N = 1,500$)

KAIT IQ or Subtest	Males N = 716	Females N = 784	Mean Difference	Difference in *SD* units
Fluid IQ	100.4	99.6	+0.8	+0.05
Crystallized IQ	99.8	100.1	−0.3	−0.02
Memory for Block Designs (Fluid subtest)	10.5	9.3	+1.2	+0.40
Famous Faces (Crystallized subtest)	10.6	9.9	+0.7	+0.23
Logical Steps (Fluid subtest)	10.1	9.5	+0.6	+0.20
Mystery Codes (Fluid subtest)	10.2	9.8	+0.4	+0.13
Auditory Comprehension (Crystallized subtest)	10.5	10.1	+0.4	+0.13

NOTE: Mean difference = mean for males minus mean for females. These data are from Kaufman and Horn (1996), who computed means and *SD*s based on a special set of "all-adult" norms for ages 17–94 years, and adjusted these means for edu-cational attainment in analyses of covariance. Data for Famous Faces and Auditory Comprehension are based on 767 women and 705 men.

The similarity in the results of gender-difference studies for adults from instrument to instrument extends to studies of gender differences for children. For example, on Wechsler's children's scales, boys outscored girls with slightly higher IQs on the WISC (Seashore, Wesman, & Doppelt, 1950), WISC-R (Kaufman & Doppelt, 1976), and WISC-III (Slate & Fawcett, 1996); on the Stanford-Binet IV (Thorndike et al., 1986, Table 4.5) and Kaufman Assessment Battery for Children (K-ABC; Kaufman & Kaufman, 1983b, Table 4.33), girls scored a bit higher at the preschool ages, but boys and girls performed equally at the school-age level.

The overall trend on the WAIS-III and other tests is for males to score slightly higher than females on global IQ scales, though there are notable exceptions (e.g., processing speed), but these gender differences are of no practical consequence. With large sample sizes, like those found in the standardization samples, even differences of 2 points are likely to be statistically significant when each variable is treated separately. However, such small differences are not of practical significance. Furthermore, the results of gender differences on major intelligence tests are of limited generalizability regarding a theoretical understanding of male versus female intellectual functions. The results are contaminated because test developers have consistently tried to avoid gender bias during the test development phase, both in the selection of subtests for the batteries and in the choice of items for each subtest. Matarazzo (1972) pointed out: "From the very beginning developers of the best known individual intelligence scales (Binet, Terman, and Wechsler) took great care to *counterbalance* or *eliminate* from their final scale any items or subtests which *empirically* were found to result in a higher score for one sex over the other" (p. 352; Matarazzo's italics). According to Wechsler (1958): "The principal reason for adopting such a procedure is that it avoids the necessity of separate norms for men and women" (p. 144).

Gender Differences on Separate Subtests

Gender differences on the separate WAIS-III subtests (Heaton et al., 2001) were notable (about 0.5 SD) on three subtests: Males outscored females on Information and Arithmetic and females scored higher on Digit Symbol. Smaller effect sizes of about 0.2–0.3 were observed on Comprehension, Block Design, and Picture Arrangement, with males scoring higher in each case. Females scored higher on Symbol Search (0.15 SD), but the remaining seven subtests produced trivial effect sizes (less than 0.1 SD).

KAIT subtests (Kaufman & Horn, 1996) that showed more than trivial differences are presented in Table 4.1. Males scored higher by .13–.40 SD on five of the eight KAIT subtests, with the largest differences observed on Memory for Block Designs, Famous Faces, and Logical Steps. Overall, the strongest gender differences favored males on WAIS-III Information (0.51 SD), WAIS-III Arithmetic (0.47 SD), and KAIT Memory for Block Designs (0.40 SD), and favored females on WAIS-III Digit Symbol Coding (0.50 SD).

Kaufman, Chen, and Kaufman (1995) examined gender differences on six Horn abilities for 587 males and 559 females ages 15–93, based on categorizations of subtests from three tests developed by Kaufman and Kaufman (1993, 1994a, 1994b). Two Horn abilities produced standard-score differences that exceeded 1 point, with males scoring higher in both instances: Gv or Broad Visualization (0.45 SD), measured by Gestalt Closure from the Kaufman Short Neuropsychological Procedure (K-SNAP), and Gq or Quantitative Thinking (0.24 SD), measured by Arithmetic from the Kaufman Functional Academic Skills Test (K-FAST).

Mathematics Ability

Regarding the higher WAIS-III Arithmetic and K-FAST Arithmetic scores, males have consistently outperformed females in quantitative ability (Halpern, 2000), although the advantage does not emerge until early adolescence, about age 12 or 13 (Hyde, 1981; Maccoby & Jacklin, 1974). That research finding may account for the notable gender difference on WAIS-III Arithmetic, and also on WAIS-R Arithmetic (0.32 *SD*, based on data presented by Kaufman et al., 1988), but not on Wechsler's children's scales (e. g., Jensen & Reynolds, 1983). Interestingly, the math superiority for males is evident on standardized tests, but not in classroom grades; research on math performance in school has generally reported no differences, or differences favoring females, even in high-level mathematics courses (Bridgeman & Wendler, 1991; Kessel & Linn, 1996). The reasons for the gender differences observed in math are subtle and sometimes controversial (Gallagher & DeLisi, 1994; Gallagher et al., 2000; Kessel & Linn, 1996). Whereas some investigators (Benbow & Stanley, 1980, 1982, 1983) have implicated biological factors as causing the gender differences in mathematics, Jacklin (1989) cites the lack of evidence for biological causation; she focuses instead on a series of investigations indicating "that math anxiety, gender-stereotyped beliefs of parents, and the perceived value of math to the student account for the major portion of sex differences in mathematical achievement" (p. 127). More recent models take less extreme positions about causality, recognizing that societal and biological factors interact systematically to create gender differences in cognitive abilities such as mathematics (Halpern, 2000).

Clerical Speed

The substantially better score by females on Digit Symbol-Coding, and the mildly higher score on Symbol Search (which places less demand on fine-motor coordination than does Digit Symbol-Coding), combined to produce the much higher PSI for females mentioned previously. Female superiority on Digit Symbol Coding and symbol-digit substitution tasks (rapidly

copying the digit rather than the symbol) is well documented in the literature, although the reason for this female advantage is less apparent; numerous experimental psychologists have systematically explored explanations for this persistent gender difference. Estes (1974) hypothesized that females outperform males on these psychomotor tasks because of a greater ability to verbally encode the abstract symbols. This hypothesis has received support from Royer (1978), who devised three forms of the symbol-digit substitution task. One form used the easily encoded WAIS symbols, while the others used symbols of greater spatial and orientational complexity (ones not readily encoded verbally). Females outperformed males significantly on the WAIS symbols, as expected, but males significantly outscored females on the most complex symbol set. Additional support for the Estes verbal encoding hypothesis comes from Majeres's (1983) experiment indicating female superiority on matching and symbol-digit tasks that utilize verbal material, contrasted with male superiority on symbol-digit substitution tasks employing spatial stimuli.

However, arguments against the Estes hypothesis persist. Delaney, Norman, and Miller (1981) also used symbol sets that varied in their degree of verbal encodability and concluded that the female advantage seems due to a perceptual speed superiority rather than a verbal encoding strength. Laux and Lynn (1985) also challenged the encoding hypothesis, but, unlike the previous investigations, Laux and Lynn's correlational and componential analyses and experimental design did not provide a direct test of the pertinent question.

Although the female advantage in Digit Symbol and other tests of clerical speed has emerged in numerous investigations, including cross-culturally, Feingold (1988) noted that the size of the discrepancy had fallen substantially from the mid-1940s to mid-1980s. Contrary to Feingold's (1988) observations, the WAIS-III versus WAIS-R data do *not* support a decrease in the female superiority in clerical speed through the mid-1990s, when the WAIS-III was normed. If anything, the discrepancy increased during the almost two decades that separated the standardizations. On the WAIS-R, females earned scaled scores that averaged 0.92 points higher than males, across four age groups between 16–19 and 55–74 years (Kaufman, McLean, & Reynolds, 1988), a discrepancy of 0.31 *SD*, not nearly as large as the discrepancy of 0.50 *SD* observed on WAIS-III Digit Symbol-Coding (0.50 *SD*).

Spatial Visualization

The higher scores by males than females on WAIS-III Block Design, KAIT Memory for Block Designs, KAIT Logical Steps, and K-SNAP Gestalt Closure undoubtedly reflects the well-documented male advantage in visual–spatial ability, or *Gv* from Horn's (1989) theory, a skill that is measured by all of these subtests. Jensen (1980) states: "The largest and most consistently found sex difference is spatial visualization ability, especially on spatial tests that require analysis, that is mentally breaking up a gestalt into smaller units in ways that facilitate spatial problem solving (e.g., the Block Designs test)…[;] the sex difference in spatial ability is not established consistently until puberty, and it persists thereafter. Generally, in studies of adolescents and adults, only about one-fourth of the females exceed the male median on various tests of spatial visualization" (p. 626).

Related to this topic, Chastain and Joe (1987) performed a canonical correlation analysis using data from the entire WAIS-R standardization sample. They entered the 11 subtests and a variety of background variables into the analysis, interpreting as meaningful three canonical factors, one of which, labeled Manual Dexterity, included a .72 loading by Gender (males were coded as 1, females as zero). Block Design (.49) and being in a skilled occupation like carpentry (.38) also related substantially to this dimension; other tasks with moderate loadings were Picture Completion, Object Assembly, Picture Arrangement, and Arithmetic. This canonical factor, de-fined primarily by "maleness," reiterates other findings of men generally outperforming women on visual–spatial tasks.

Hyde (1981) calculated that about 4% of the variation in visual–spatial abilities is attributed to gender differences, versus only about 1% each for verbal ability and quantitative ability. According to Deaux (1984), similar small effect sizes for the variable of gender have been identified for noncognitive factors as well, such as aggression and social influence. She states that, "although additional evidence remains to be gathered, 5% may approximate the upper boundary for the explanatory power of subject-sex main effects in specific social and cognitive behaviors" (p. 108).

Clinical Implications of Gender Differences on Mental Tasks

The results of gender differences on major intelligence tests are of limited generalizability regarding a theoretical understanding of male versus female intellectual functions. The results are contaminated because, as noted, test developers have avoided gender bias whenever possible when selecting tasks and items.

Thus, the mean gender differences in global IQs are undoubtedly an artifact of the specific subtests included in the WAIS-III, KAIT, and other tests; to some extent, differences in subtest scores (such as WAIS-III Information or KAIT Famous Faces) may be an artifact of the specific items chosen for each subtest. However, it is possible to reach some hypotheses about "true" male–female differences on some of the subtests (Kaufman et al., 1988). It is hard to imagine how any Block Design or Digit Symbol items could have been eliminated due to gender bias (or any other kind of bias) because of the abstract, non-meaningful nature of the stimuli; similarly, Arithmetic items are far more dependent on the computational process than on the verbal content, and therefore are not reasonably subject to the potential impact of bias. Consequently, it seems reasonable to conclude that adult males are superior to adult females in the skills assessed by WAIS-III Block Design and Arithmetic and KAIT Memory for Block Designs, and that adult females clearly outstrip adult males in the ability measured by Digit Symbol. All of these conclusions are quite consistent with the bodies of research discussed in the previous sections. However, even the WAIS-III and KAIT subtests that yielded the largest gender differences produced differences of about 0.40 to 0.50 *SD*, which reflect small (or, at best, moderate) effect sizes (McLean, 1995). Consequently, even the tried-and-true gender differences produce discrepancies on adult intelligence tests that are too small to be of very much clinical value.

ETHNIC DIFFERENCES IN IQ

This section reports data on ethnic differences, focusing on the groups for which there are ample data based on research with the WAIS-III and other individually administered intelligence tests for adolescents and adults: Caucasians, African Americans, and Hispanics.

Differences between Caucasians and African Americans

The difference of about 1 standard deviation in the IQs earned by Caucasians and African Americans, identified for numerous samples with a wide variety of tests (Hauser, 1998; Lichtenberger, Broadbooks, & Kaufman, 2000; Puente & Salazar, 1998) and seemingly impervious to time, also is similar to the trends seen on the WAIS-III.

WAIS-III IQs and Factor Indexes

With a statistical adjustment for age, but not for educational attainment, Caucasians outscored African Americans on the four WAIS-III indexes at ages 20–89 years by about .80 *SD* to nearly 1.0 *SD* (Manly, Heaton, Taylor, 2000), differences of about 12 to 15 standard-score points. When cor-

rected for age, gender, and education in a subsample of the standardization sample, ages 20 to 89 years, based on data for 1,734 whites and 282 African Americans (Heaton, et al., 2001), the following differences were observed: Caucasians outscored African Americans by 0.73 of a standard deviation on V-IQ, .83 of a standard deviation on P-IQ, and .86 of a standard deviation on FS-IQ, discrepancies of about 11 to 13 IQ points. When corrected for age, gender, and education, Caucasian–African American differences on the factor indexes ranged from .66 *SD* on WMI to .84 *SD* on POI, differences corresponding to 10 to 12½ standard-score points.

The age-, gender-, and education-adjusted mean IQs and Indexes for African Americans spanned the narrow range of about 89 to 92, when the *z* scores presented by Heaton et al. (2001) are converted to standard scores with mean = 100 and *SD* = 15. In contrast, WISC-III means at ages 6–16 years for a sample of African Americans matched to a sample of Caucasian on age, gender, parental education, and other variables spanned the much wider range of 88.8 on POI to 96.9 on PSI and 97.0 on FDI (Prifitera, Weiss, & Saklofske, 1998, Table 1.2). The effect sizes for Caucasian-African American differences on the WISC-III for the P-IQ, FS-IQ, and POI are similar to the values reported for the WAIS-III, ranging from 0.73 to 0.85, but the WISC-III effect sizes are smaller for V-IQ and VCI (0.59), and much smaller for FDI (WMI) and PSI (0.27–0.37) (Prifitera et al., 1998).

In general, then, discrepancies between Caucasians and African Americans on the Wechsler IQs and indexes are larger for adults than for children and adolescents. Prifitera et al. (1998, Table 1.4) divided their matched samples into two broad age groups (6–11 years, *N* = 143 African Americans; 12–16, *N* = 109), and presented IQ and index differences between Caucasians and African Americans for these two broad groups. Their results, when juxtaposed with Heaton et al.'s (2001) findings, reveal changes in effect sizes from childhood to adolescence to adulthood. The effect sizes for all three IQs and for VCI and POI are much higher at ages 12–16 than at ages 6–11, and the adolescent values are even higher than the adult values. For FDI (WMI) and PSI, the effect sizes increased with increasing age.

WAIS-R IQs

WAIS-R IQ differences for Caucasians and African Americans, uncorrected for education, were quite similar to uncorrected WAIS-III index differences reported by Manly et al. (2000), as Cau-

casians scored higher on WAIS-R IQs by about 1½ points on V-IQ, 14 points on P-IQ, and 14½ points on FS-IQ. Table 4.2 presents interesting data for WAIS-R IQs—Caucasian–African American IQ differences for groups differing in age, gender, education, and occupation—provided by Reynolds et al. (1987) and presented here because comparable data are not available for the WAIS-III.

The Caucasian-African American differences on the WAIS-R are a virtual constant across age

TABLE 4.2 Differences in the mean WAIS-R IQs earned by Caucasians and African Americans, by age, gender, education, and occupation

Variable	Verbal IQ			Performance IQ			Full Scale IQ		
	Caucasians	African Americans	Diff.	Caucasians	African Americans	Diff.	Caucasians	African Americans	Diff.
Age									
16–19	100.7	88.0	+12.7	100.7	87.2	+13.5	100.8	86.9	+13.9
20–34	101.5	88.4	+13.1	101.9	87.5	+14.4	101.8	87.0	+14.8
35–54	101.3	87.2	+14.4	101.4	87.2	+14.2	101.4	86.6	+14.8
55–74	101.3	87.8	+13.5	101.0	87.3	+13.7	101.4	87.0	+14.4
Gender									
Male	102.3	88.2	+14.1	101.9	87.9	+14.0	102.4	87.3	+15.1
Female	100.2	87.6	+12.6	100.6	86.8	+13.8	100.3	86.4	+13.9
Education									
0–8 Years	87.9	80.9	+7.0	91.0	81.0	+10.0	88.6	80.2	+8.4
9–11 Years	97.4	87.8	+9.6	99.5	86.4	+13.1	98.0	86.3	+11.7
12 Years	101.1	91.9	+9.2	101.2	90.9	+10.3	101.1	90.7	+10.4
13+ Years	112.1	95.8	+16.3	108.4	97.5	+10.9	111.6	95.8	+15.8
Occupation									
Prof./Tech./Mgr./Cler./Sales/Skilled	105.2	94.9	+10.3	104.7	93.1	+11.6	105.4	93.5	+11.9
Semiskilled and Unskilled	93.9	84.8	+9.1	96.0	85.3	+10.7	94.4	84.2	+10.2
Not in Labor Force	100.8	86.5	+14.3	100.0	85.6	+14.4	100.5	85.3	+15.2

NOTE: Diff. = Difference. Difference scores equal the mean earned by Caucasians minus the mean earned by African Americans. Data are from "Demographic characteristics and IQ among adults: Analysis of the WAIS-R standardization sample as a function of the stratification variables," by C. R. Reynolds, R.L. Chastain, A. S. Kaufman, & J. E. McLean, 1987, *Journal of School Psychology, 25,* 323–342. Copyright 1987 by Elsevier Science. Reprinted with permission.

groups and for males and females, as African Americans consistently earned mean V-, P-, and FS-IQs between 86½ and 88½. For education level, unlike for the variables of age and gender, the WAIS-R IQs of African Americans varied by about 1 standard deviation, ranging from a low of 80–81 for those with less than 9 years of education to 96–97 for those with at least some college experience. Caucasian–African American differences were smallest for individuals with 0–8 years of schooling (7 to 10 points), and only reached the traditional 1 standard deviation discrepancy for the most educated group. However, the data for individuals with 13 or more years of education are tentative at best because the entire sample of African Americans totaled only 20. (No other cell in Table 4.2 is based on a sample size of less than 41.)

The results of ethnic difference analyses in Table 4.2 indicate that, within middle-class occupations, Caucasians outscored African Americans by about 10 to 12 IQ points on the WAIS-R, and they outscored African Americans by about 9 to 11 points within working-class occupations. It is only for the group of adults not in the labor force that the familiar 15-point difference emerged. When one looks at occupational group WAIS-R IQ differences within each ethnic group, the middle-class workers outscored the working-class subjects by about 9 to 11 points for Caucasians, and by about 8 to 10 points for African American adolescents and adults. Thus, the impact of occupational group on IQ is comparable for both ethnic groups. However, as Reynolds et al. (1987) have pointed out, the mean WAIS-R IQs for African American middle-class individuals are of the same order of magnitude as the mean IQs of Caucasian working-class people. Data are not presented in Table 4.2 for ethnic differences by urban versus rural residence because of small sample sizes for rural African Americans (N = 25). Reynolds et al. (1987) have reported, however, that the mean IQs for the small sample of rural African Americans were trivially lower than the means for urban African Americans (1 point on the Full Scale).

Stanford-Binet IV and the Kaufman Tests

Thorndike, Hagen, and Sattler (1986b) reported data for African Americans and Caucasians in the Binet-4's standardization sample, and observed ethnic differences for their adolescent and adult sample (ages 12–23) that are similar to the ones found for the WAIS-III and WAIS-R. Caucasians (N = 1,303) outscored African Americans (N = 210) by 17.4 points (1.16 SD) on the Composite (means of 103.5 and 86.1 based on standard scores having a mean of 100 and SD of 16), and demonstrated a comparable discrepancy on the Verbal Reasoning, Abstract/Visual Reasoning, and Quantitative Reasoning Area scores; African Americans earned mean standard scores of 85.4 to 87.7 on these three area scores. In Short-Term Memory, Caucasians scored about 11 points (0.73 SD) higher, 102.1 versus 91.2.

Results on two tests developed by the Kaufmans have shown similar patterns in Caucasian–African American group differences. On the Kaufman Adolescent and Adult Intelligence Test (KAIT; Kaufman & Kaufman, 1993)—without an education adjustment—differences between Caucasians (N = 1,547) and African Americans (N = 241) were 11–12 IQ points at ages 11–25 years, and 13–14 IQ points at ages 25–94 years, on the Crystallized, Fluid, and Composite Scales (effect sizes ranging from .73–.93 SD) (Kaufman, McLean, & Kaufman, 1995). After covarying for educational attainment, the differences reduced to 8–9 points for the Crystallized and Fluid IQs at ages 11–24 and to 10 points for ages 25–94, corresponding to effect sizes of 0.58 SD and 0.68 SD, respectively (A. Kaufman, McLean, et al., 1995). Differences were similar on both the Crystallized and Fluid Scales for both age groups, both with and without an educational adjustment; A. Kaufman, McLean, et al. (1995) did not report an education-adjusted KAIT Composite IQ.

On the Kaufman Brief Intelligence Test (K-BIT; Kaufman & Kaufman, 1990), at the ages of 20–90 years with standard scores adjusted for educational attainment, Caucasians (N = 391) performed better than African Americans (N = 52) by 14.6 points on the K-BIT Composite, an effect size of 0.97 SD.

Wechsler and Kaufman Subtest Profiles

When ethnic differences are examined on global scales, specific differences in the subtest profile tend to be masked. In this section, Caucasian–African American differences are examined on the separate subtests of the WAIS-III, WAIS-R, and several Kaufman tests.

On the WAIS-III, Heaton et al. (2001) found that, when they corrected for age, gender, and education, the largest differences between African Americans and Caucasians were on Block Design, Object Assembly, Symbol Search, and Vocabulary (effect sizes of 0.7–0.8 SD), and the smallest differences were on Digit Span, Picture Arrangement, Information, and Letter-Number Sequencing (effect sizes of 0.3–0.6 SD).

Kaufman et al. (1988) conducted MANOVAs and follow-up univariate ANOVAs on the 11 WAIS-R subtests for each of four age groups and found that Caucasians significantly outscored African Americans on each of the 11 subtests for all age groups. WAIS-R Block Design and Vocabulary produced the most substantial differences, with effect sizes of about 1.0 SD; smallest effect sizes, of about 0.50 SD, were yielded for Digit Span and Picture Arrangement. The results were similar for each age group between ages 16–19 and 55–74 years. These WAIS-R results are remarkably similar to Heaton et al.'s (2001) WAIS-III findings. For both the WAIS-III and WAIS-R, the categories of subtests producing the largest and the smallest Caucasian–African American difference are each composed of *both* Verbal and Performance subtests. The subtests that produced the smallest differences are interesting in the wide array of abilities they cover. On both the WAIS-III and WAIS-R, relatively small differences are produced by tests that measure short-term memory (Digit Span) and reasoning (Picture Arrangement), at opposite ends of Jensen's (1980) Level I

and Level II ability continuum. On the WAIS-III, the four smallest differences occurred for one subtest associated with each of the four factor indexes: VCI (Information), POI (Picture Arrangement), WMI (Letter-Number Sequencing), and PSI (Symbol Search). Although Picture Arrangement is not technically on the POI, it has traditionally loaded on PO factors, including the WAIS-III PO factor (see Chapter 7). Information, often considered the most culture-loaded Wechsler subtest, is unexpectedly among the WAIS-III group with relatively small effect sizes; its effect size of 0.51 SD is notably lower than its mean effect size (0.78 SD) in the WAIS-R analyses (Kaufman et al., 1988), perhaps because of the extensive use of bias panels and bias analyses by The Psychological Corporation (1997) during the item development and item selection phase of constructing the WAIS-III.

A. Kaufman, McLean, et al. (1995) analyzed subtest profiles as well as KAIT IQs in their education-controlled investigation of ethnic differences. The following KAIT subtests produced the *smallest* differences between Caucasians and African Americans (age group and effect sizes are in parentheses):

- Famous Faces (11–24, 0.15 SD, not significant at $p < .05$);
- Rebus Learning (11–24, 0.33 SD and 25–94, 0.38 SD);
- Definitions (11–24, 0.43 SD);
- Auditory Comprehension (11–24, 0.48 SD and 25–94, 0.55 SD); and
- Logical Steps (11–24, 0.50 SD) (A. Kaufman, McLean, et al., 1995).

Largest Caucasian–African American differences were on:

- Mystery Codes (11–24, 0.74 SD);
- Logical Steps (25–94, 0.70 SD);
- Memory for Block Designs (11–24, 0.66 SD and 25–94, 0.69 SD);
- Definitions (25–94, 0.69 SD); and

- Famous Faces (25–94, 0.65 *SD*) (A. Kaufman, McLean, et al., 1995).

As with the Wechsler results, the array of subtests in the "large difference" and "small difference" categories is wide, with both the Fluid and Crystallized Scales represented in each category for both age groups.

In addition, two subtests that produced among the smallest differences at ages 11–24 (Famous Faces, Logical Steps) yielded among the largest differences at ages 25–94. For both age groups, Rebus Learning (a Fluid test of learning ability) and Auditory Comprehension (a Crystallized test) produced relatively small differences. Also, for both age groups, a Fluid subtest yielded the largest Caucasian–African American discrepancy, Mystery Codes at ages 11–24 and Logical Steps at ages 25–94. The nonsignificant difference at ages 11–24 on Famous Faces, a measure of general factual knowledge, is consistent with the WAIS-III findings for Information, although Famous Faces did produce substantial differences for the older sample. Also, the relatively large differences on KAIT Memory for Block Designs coincides with substantial differences on WAIS-III and WAIS-R Block Design.

At ages 20–90 years on the Kaufman Brief Intelligence Test (K-BIT; Kaufman & Kaufman, 1990), with standard scores adjusted for educational attainment, Caucasians (*N* = 391) performed better than African Americans (*N* = 52) on both a crystallized task (Vocabulary) and a fluid task (Matrices) by 0.87 *SD* and 0.91 *SD*, respectively (Kaufman & Wang, 1992), differences that are inexplicably larger than those observed for the KAIT subtests.

As mentioned in the discussion of gender differences on specific subtests, J. Kaufman et al. (1995) investigated individual differences at ages 15–93 years on six Horn abilities, as measured by subtests included on three Kaufman tests. After adjustment for educational attainment, Caucasians (*N* = 956) scored significantly higher than African Americans (*N* = 128) on all six Horn abilities. *Largest* differences were on the measure of

Gq (Quantitative Thinking, assessed by K-FAST Arithmetic, effect size = 0.79) and on one of the two measures of *Glr* (Long-term Retrieval, assessed by KAIT Auditory Delayed Recall, effect size = 0.64). Considerably *smaller* differences were found for the other Horn abilities:

- *Gf* (Fluid Reasoning, assessed by K-SNAP 4-Letter Words, effect size = 0.31),
- *Gsm* (Short-term Memory, assessed by K-SNAP Number Recall, effect size = 0.36),
- The second measure of *Glr* (assessed by KAIT Rebus Delayed Recall, effect size = 0.45),
- *Gv* (Broad Visualization, assessed by K-SNAP Gestalt Closure, effect size = 0.46), and
- *Gc* (Crystallized Knowledge, assessed by K-FAST Reading, effect size = 0.50).

The most interesting finding reported by J. Kaufman et al. (1995) on the six Horn abilities is the relatively small effect size of .31 (less than 5 standard-score points when education is covaried, and less than 6 points without a covariate) for the measure of *Gf*, a novel test of fluid reasoning that emphasizes problem solving in a different way from Wechsler's POI subtests. The K-SNAP 4-Letter Words subtests does measure speed of problem solving, but using linguistic stimuli and emphasizing mental, not visual-motor, processing speed. In contrast, all Wechsler nonverbal subtests use pictures or designs, most measure *Gv* as well as *Gf*, and most rely on visual–motor speed for success. Chen, Kaufman, and Kaufman (1994) posit that the uniqueness and novelty of the K-SNAP's fluid task (4-Letter Words) may have influenced the results, thereby producing findings different from previous research, including research on the apparently similar KAIT measures of *Gf* and *Gc* (A. Kaufman, McLean, et al., 1995). The greatly reduced Caucasian–African American differences on this novel test of abstract, fluid reasoning should encourage test developers to pursue a variety of other new tasks in the effort to construct tests that are fairer to diverse ethnic groups.

Differences between Caucasians and Hispanics

Each of the studies cited in the previous sections, except for Reynolds et al.'s (1987) and Kaufman et al.'s (1988) WAIS-R investigations, reported data for samples of Hispanics in addition to samples of Caucasians and African Americans. In this section, we summarize discrepancies observed between Caucasians and Hispanics and also between African Americans and Hispanics.

WAIS-III IQs and Factor Indexes

In addition to providing comparisons of WAIS-III scores for Caucasians and African Americans, Heaton et al. (2001) also presented comparisons for Caucasians versus Hispanics. They corrected for age, gender, and education in a subsample of the standardization sample, ages 20 to 89 years, based on data for 1,734 Caucasian and 163 Hispanics. We converted the z scores provided by Heaton et al. (2001) to standard scores with mean = 100 and SD = 15. When adjusted for background variables, Hispanic adults earned mean IQs of about 96–99, with V-IQ higher than P-IQ by 3.3 points. The profile of indexes reveals a wider range, from a low of about 94 on WMI to a high of about 100 on PSI. Interestingly, the VCI-POI discrepancy is a trivial 1.2 points, even smaller than the P > V difference. When the Caucasian–Hispanic comparisons were only corrected for age (not education and gender), the ethnic differences were larger: Caucasians scored about 6–7 points higher on POI and PSI (0.4 to 0.5 SD) and about 11–12 points higher on VCI and WMI (0.7 to 0.8 SD) (Manly et al., 2000), indicating a POI > VCI profile of about 5 points (no data for IQs were presented).

P > V profiles for Hispanic individuals reflect the language demands and cultural content of the Verbal scale on the Wechsler tests, which may unduly depress scores for those whose first or second language is Spanish and whose cultural and subcultural influences are from the nondominant culture. The small P > V and POI > VCI WAIS-III profiles, especially with education and gender controlled, are contrary to the bulk of literature in this area (e.g., Valencia & Suzuki, 2001), although much of the previous research has been with children. A comparison of WISC-III and WAIS-III data likewise shows a more pronounced P > V profile for children and adolescents than for adults. On the WISC-III, the P > V difference within the standardization sample averaged 5.6 IQ points, with differences larger for children from lower socioeconomic backgrounds (8.6 points for children whose parents had 0–8 years of schooling versus 1.9 points for 13+ years of schooling) (Prifitera et al., 1998, Table 1.8). POI > VCI profiles were similar in magnitude, averaging 5.2 points for the total sample; 8.7 points for parental education < 9 years; and 1.1 points for 13+ years.

The largest effect size, by far, when comparing Caucasian and Hispanic adults on the WAIS-III IQs and indexes is the value of 0.58 SD for WMI. Small effect sizes of 0.29–0.39 SD were obtained for the verbal scores (V-IQ and VCI) and trivial effect sizes of 0.12–0.22 SD were obtained for the nonverbal scores (P-IQ, POI, and PSI). By way of contrast, effect sizes for matched Caucasian and Hispanic samples on the WISC-III for ages 6–16 years (Prifitera et al., 1998, Table 1.3) are as follows: FDI, akin to WMI (0.29 SD); V-IQ and VCI (0.20–0.24 SD); and P-IQ, POI, and PSI (–0.0–0.15 SD). Though the pattern of effect sizes is the same for children and adults, the magnitude of the effects is consistently lower for the 6–16 year range, as summarized by the values for FS-IQ (0.19 SD for WISC-III vs. 0.32 SD for WAIS-III).

Stanford-Binet IV and the Kaufman Tests

The Binet-4 *Technical Manual* (Thorndike et al., 1986b, Table 4.5) presented mean standard scores, uncorrected for education, for 1,303 Caucasian and 111 Hispanic 12–23-year-olds. The Hispanic individuals earned a mean of 99.0 on the Abstract/Visual Reasoning scale (nonverbal) and a mean of 93.1 on Verbal Reasoning, a discrepancy of 5.9 points. Effect sizes for Caucasian–Hispanic differences were 0.22 *SD* for the nonverbal scale and 0.69 *SD* for the verbal scale. The Short-term Memory scale, akin to FDI and WMI, produced an effect size of 0.44 *SD*.

On the KAIT (Kaufman & Kaufman, 1993), Hispanics scored 3.9 points higher on Fluid IQ than Crystallized IQ at ages 11–24 (*N* = 76 Hispanics) and 5.7 points higher at ages 25–94 (*N* = 64 Hispanics), without an adjustment for education (A. Kaufman, McLean, et al., 1995). These differences resemble the magnitude of P > V differences on the WISC-III and WAIS-III, although Fluid IQ is not the same as P-IQ; they load on separate factors (Kaufman, Ishikuma, & Kaufman, 1994), and the Fluid subtests require verbal ability for success, including verbal responding for Rebus Learning and verbal comprehension for Logical Steps. With educational attainment covaried, Caucasians outscored Hispanics on the Crystallized Scale by about 6 points at ages 11–24 and 9 points at ages 25–94 (A. Kaufman, McLean, et al., 1995). In contrast, differences for both groups on the Fluid Scale were only about 3–4 IQ points. Across ages, effect sizes were about 0.50 *SD* for Crystallized IQ versus .25 *SD* for Fluid IQ with education controlled (A. Kaufman, McLean, et al., 1995).

Findings on the K-BIT (Kaufman & Kaufman, 1990) supported the KAIT results for the fluid–crystallized distinction. At ages of 20–90 years, with standard scores adjusted for educational attainment, Caucasians (*N* = 391) performed better than Hispanics (*N* = 37) by 15.3 standard-score points on Vocabulary (a measure of *Gc*), versus 6.6 points on Matrices (a measure of *Gf*), corresponding to effect sizes of 1.02 *SD* and 0.44 *SD*, respectively (Kaufman & Wang, 1992). Hispanics earned education-adjusted mean Matrices standard scores that were 7.8 points higher than their Vocabulary scores. Interestingly, the Matrices–Vocabulary K-BIT discrepancy was smaller for children at ages 4–7 (5.4 points), 8–12 (2.3 points), and 13–19 (1.4 points) (Kaufman & Wang, 1992). The Kaufman Assess-

ment Battery for Children (K-ABC; Kaufman & Kaufman, 1983), which was specifically designed to minimize the impact of language and culture on its IQ scale (the Mental Processing Composite), yields virtually no differences in intellectual performance for Caucasian versus Hispanic children ages 2½ to 12½ years (Lichtenberger, Broadbooks, & Kaufman, 2000).

Wechsler and Kaufman Subtest Profiles

Based on Heaton et al.'s (2001) age-, gender-, and education-adjusted analyses, the largest differences between Caucasians and Hispanics were on the three WMI subtests and Similarities (effect sizes of 0.38–0.48 *SD*) and the smallest differences were mostly on Performance subtests (Digit Symbol, Picture Arrangement, Block Design, Object Assembly) plus the Information subtest (effect sizes of 0.02–0.15 *SD*). Although the three WMI subtests all involve verbal comprehension and oral responding, it is nonetheless surprising that the WMI subtests produced larger discrepancies between Caucasian and Hispanic adults than any of the VCI subtests. Two other notable findings when comparing Caucasian–African American differences to Caucasian–Hispanic discrepancies: (1) the culturally loaded Verbal subtest, Information, produced among the smallest differences for *both* Hispanics and African Americans; and (2) the subtest profiles for Hispanics and African Americans were dramatically different. Regarding the latter point, two subtests that produced among the smallest Caucasian–African American differences (Digit Span and Letter-Number Sequencing) yielded relatively large differences between Caucasians and Hispanics, whereas two subtests that yielded relatively large Caucasian–African American discrepancies (Object Assembly and Block Design) were among the group of subtests that produced very small Caucasian–Hispanic differences.

The education-controlled study of ethnic differences on KAIT scales and subtests (A. Kaufman, McLean, et al., 1995) yielded small effect sizes for Caucasian–Hispanic comparisons on all

KAIT subtests at ages 11–24, and all but two at ages 25–94. Differences on the four Fluid subtests were uniformly small for both age groups, ranging from 0.08–0.30 *SD* for the younger sample and from 0.15–0.36 *SD* for the older sample. For both groups, the lowest effect size was for Rebus Learning—which also produced quite small effect sizes for Caucasians versus African Americans—and the highest was for Memory for Block Designs (which, oddly, is the only KAIT Fluid subtest that does *not* depend on verbal ability for success). Among the four Crystallized subtests, the culturally loaded, factual-knowledge Famous Faces task produced the lowest effect size for both age groups (a nonsignificant 0.02 *SD* for ages 11–24 and 0.27 *SD* for ages 25–94). The only two subtests with moderate effect sizes (> .50) were Double Meanings (0.72 *SD*) and Auditory Comprehension (0.59 *SD*), both for the older group, with Double Meanings also yielding the highest effect size (0.49 *SD*) for the younger sample. Double Meanings requires verbal reasoning, flexibility, and knowledge of the subtleties of language concepts, and Auditory Comprehension measures verbal comprehension and verbal memory for meaningful information told as part of a mock news broadcast. Both of these subtests probably produced the largest effect sizes among KAIT subtests because of their heavy linguistic and cultural demands. Though Definitions, a Crystallized subtest, and Logical Steps, a Fluid measure, also require excellent linguistic skills for success, both of these tasks produced relatively small Caucasian–Hispanic discrepancies for both age groups (effect sizes in the 0.20–0.35 range).

The very small Caucasian–Hispanic differences on Famous Faces accords well with similar findings in the comparison of Caucasians to African Americans and these results are also congruent with the finding that WAIS-III Information produced among the smallest ethnic differences for both African Americans and Hispanics. Bias reviewers and bias analyses were conducted during the development of the KAIT, just as such procedures were followed for the WAIS-III,

which may pertain to the relatively small differences that were observed on such culturally loaded subtests, but these results are, nonetheless, unexpected. Interestingly, K-ABC Faces & Places, a children's analog to Famous Faces, yielded fairly small differences between Caucasians and both Hispanics and African Americans (Kaufman & Kaufman, 1983b, Table 4.35).

The previously mentioned investigation of differences on six Horn abilities (J. Kaufman et al., 1995) also investigated Caucasian–Hispanic differences (*N* = 62 Hispanics). All effect sizes were moderate (0.04–0.40 *SD*), and only two reached statistical significance: *Gq* (K-FAST Arithmetic) and *Gsm* (K-SNAP Number Recall). The Arithmetic subtest requires verbal comprehension and, because the test measures functional math, the items were placed with a U.S. cultural context. Number Recall—like the WAIS-III WMI and its separate subtests, Binet-4 Short-term Memory, and KAIT Memory for Block Designs—yielded relatively large effect sizes suggesting that Caucasians may perform better than Hispanics on some tests of immediate memory. In contrast, Caucasian–Hispanic differences were small on both measures of long-term retrieval (KAIT Delayed Recall subtests) in the J. Kaufman et al. (1995) investigation.

The pattern of performance across the Wechsler and Kaufman tests, plus the Binet-4, indicates that Hispanic adolescents and adults perform better, in general, on fluid than crystallized tasks, and they perform better on nonverbal visual–spatial and highly speeded tasks than they do on measures of short-term and working memory, especially those with a verbal component. Clearly, if an adolescent or adult of Hispanic descent is raised as bilingual or is less acculturated into U.S. society, then tests that tap verbal skill or knowledge of the dominant culture do not provide unbiased estimates of their capabilities. When testing individuals from a nondominant culture, clinicians must use caution in interpreting performance on tests that are school-related or require acculturation (Lichtenberger, Broadbooks, & Kaufman, 2000).

URBAN–RURAL
RESIDENCE DIFFERENCES

WAIS-III and KAIT data on the relationship of IQ to urban versus rural residence have not been reported, so this discussion is limited to analyses of the WAIS-R (Reynolds et al., 1987) and other older tests. WAIS-R IQs for the total WAIS-R standardization sample revealed that urban–rural differences were small and nonsignificant: Urban residents outscored their rural counterparts by a trivial 2½ points on V-IQ, less than 1 point on P-IQ, and 2 points on FS-IQ. For males, urban–rural IQ differences on the Verbal, Performance, and Full Scales were 2, 0, and 1½ points, respectively; for females, urban residents scored higher by 3 points, 2 points, and 2½ points. Residence differences were nonsignificant for males and females, and the interaction between gender and residence was nonsignificant as well, as were the interactions between residence and all other stratification variables examined by Reynolds et al. (1987). Consequently, no further urban–rural IQ data are presented here.

Further, urban versus rural residence had loadings of approximately zero on all three canonical factors rotated by Chastain and Joe (1987), derived from an analysis of the WAIS-R subtests and pertinent background variables. Therefore, coming from an urban or rural background was independent of a person's general intelligence, nonverbal ability, and manual dexterity.

Generational Changes
in Urban–Rural Differences

Urban versus rural residence IQ discrepancies gradually declined from the 1930s to late 1970s; the urban superiority on the old Stanford-Binet at ages 2–18 years ranged from 6 to 12 points for different age groups tested in the 1930s (McNemar, 1942). For children aged 5 to 15 tested on the WISC in the late 1940s, the urban advantage was

4 to 6 IQ points (Seashore et al., 1950), and for preschool and primary grade children tested on the WPPSI in the mid-1960s the difference was only 3½ points.

Urban children, adolescents, and adults still retained a slight advantage over rural individuals into the 1970s, scoring 1½ to 2 points higher on the WISC-R (Kaufman & Doppelt, 1976), normed in the early 1970s, and on the WAIS-R, normed in the mid- to late-1970s. However, as noted, the WAIS-R difference did not reach statistical significance, and it is conceivable that even the 2-point urban advantage on the WISC-R and WAIS-R would disappear if other variables were controlled. The reduction to zero of the urban–rural difference on WPPSI is precisely what occurred when urban and rural children were matched carefully on age, gender, race, region, and father's occupation (Kaufman, 1973).

Data for the Binet-4 (Thorndike, Hagen, & Sattler, 1986a, 1986b) are consistent with the trend of reduced urban superiority. Thorndike et al. (1986b) presented data for rural individuals and for people from cities of various sizes. At ages 2 to 6 years, urban children (those living in cities with populations of 2,500+) outscored rural youngsters by 2.6 points; at ages 7 to 11 and 12 to 23, however, rural individuals earned higher mean Composite scores on the Binet-4 by 1.1 and 3.2 points, respectively. The elimination of the urban superiority from earlier years is obvious, but the Binet urban–rural data are undoubtedly contaminated by the socioeconomic variable, which was poorly stratified in the Binet-4 norming program.

The best explanation of the steady reduction, and perhaps elimination, of residence differences over the past 50 years is the impact of mass media on people living anywhere in the United States. Television and other means of communication, along with improved educational facilities and opportunities and the advent of the Internet, have ended the relative isolation of people living in rural areas, making the kinds of facts and problems assessed by intelligence tests readily accessible to almost everyone.

Residence Differences on the WAIS-R Subtests

Urban–rural residence differences on the 11 separate WAIS-R subtests were nonsignificant at ages 16–19, 20–34, and 35–54 in the MANOVAs conducted by Kaufman et al. (1988), but reached significance at the .01 level for the 55- to 74-year-olds. Table 4.3 shows the mean scaled scores on the 11 WAIS-R subtests earned by urban and rural adults aged 55–74 and indicates the four tasks that reached statistical significance, all favoring urban elderly adults: Information, Digit Span, Vocabulary, and Arithmetic.

As Kaufman et al. (1988) point out, three of these subtests (not Digit Span) measure what Bannatyne (1968) has termed Acquired Knowledge—school-related, crystallized abilities. The impli-

cation is that those individuals who were born from the early 1900s to the mid-1920s (and were therefore 55 to 74 years old when the WAIS-R was normed), and who were raised in rural areas, did not have the opportunity to benefit from improved education and more accessible mass media; hence, they did not perform as well on school-related tasks as did their urban contemporaries.

One would anticipate that growing up in a rural environment in the first quarter of the twentieth century would not adversely affect success on nonverbal subtests, and that is precisely what is revealed in Table 4.3. Urban–rural residence is probably not a meaningful variable for elderly people per se, but just for those individuals who grew up before World War II. If this interpretation of the interaction between age group and residence found in the WAIS-R subtest data is

TABLE 4.3 Mean scaled scores on the WAIS-R subtests earned by urban and rural adults ages 55–74

Subtest	Urban Mean	Rural Mean	Difference
Verbal			
Information	9.5	8.7	+0.8*
Digit Span	9.0	8.0	+1.0*
Vocabulary	9.6	8.4	+1.2**
Arithmetic	9.2	8.3	+0.9*
Comprehension	9.3	9.1	+0.2
Similarities	8.1	7.5	+0.6
Performance			
Picture Completion	7.4	7.0	+0.4
Picture Arrangement	6.9	6.7	+0.2
Block Design	7.0	7.1	−0.1
Object Assembly	7.1	7.4	−0.3
Digit Symbol	5.9	5.8	+0.1

**$p < .01$; *$p < .05$

NOTE: Difference equals urban mean minus rural mean. Data are only presented for adults aged 55–74 because this is the only age group for which a significant main effect for residence was obtained in the MANOVAs investigating urban–rural differences on the 11 subtests (Kaufman et al., 1988). Data are from *Journal of School Psychology, 25*, Reynolds et al., "Demographic characteristics and IQ among adults," pp. 323–342, 1987, with permission from Elsevier Science.

correct, then only the very oldest WAIS-III or KAIT age groups (75 and above) would be predicted to show significant urban–rural differences on the more crystallized subtests. Unfortunately, those data are not available because neither test used urban–rural residence as a stratification variable.

OCCUPATIONAL DIFFERENCES

Like residence, occupational group was not used as a stratification variable for either the WAIS-III or KAIT, so data relating IQ to occupation are based on WAIS-R analyses (Reynolds et al., 1987). Occupational category is an important variable to understand because, like educational attainment, it is often used as an index of socioeconomic status. In Table 4.4, occupation differences are provided for the total WAIS-R sample, revealing a steady decline in mean IQs from professional and technical workers through unskilled laborers. The IQ ranges for these extreme occu-

pational groups are from 17½ to 22½ points, with the Verbal Scale producing the largest discrepancies. Examination of occupation differences for different age groups within the WAIS-R age range is essential because of the changing nature of this background variable: For ages 16–19, occupational group corresponds to the adolescent's head of household, but for ages 20 and above it relates to the person's own job. The group labeled "not in labor force" becomes quite substantial (67% of the sample) for ages 55–74. To conduct an occupational group by age analysis, the four broad age groups had to be reduced to three (by merging ages 20–34 with ages 35–54) so that no mean IQs would be based on a sample size smaller than 20 (Reynolds et al., 1987). The results of this analysis appear in Table 4.4.

Best Estimate of IQ Differences for Adults in Different Occupations

Because the 16- to 19-year-old group included occupations of the head of household, and the

TABLE 4.4 Mean WAIS-R IQs earned by different occupational groups for three broad age groups

Occupational Group	Ages 16–19			Ages 20–54			Ages 55–74		
	V	P	FS	V	P	FS	V	P	FS
Professional and Technical	108	105	107	113	110	112	115	109	114
Managers, Clerical, Sales	103	103	103	104	103	104	110	106	109
Skilled Workers	97	99	98	99	103	101	99	102	100
Semiskilled Workers	93	95	93	92	94	92	94	96	95
Unskilled Workers	93	92	92	87	90	87	—	—	—
Not in Labor Force	—	—	—	99	98	99	99	99	99

NOTE: V = Verbal, P = Performance, FS = Full Scale. Means are provided for samples with fewer than 20 subjects ($N = 0$ for 16- to 19-year-olds whose head of household is Not in Labor Force; $N = 9$ for Unskilled Workers aged 55–74). For ages 16–19, sample sizes ranged from 24 (Unskilled Workers) to 120 (Semiskilled Workers); for ages 20–54, sample sizes for the five occupational groups ranged from 35 (Unskilled Workers) to 248 (Managers, Clerical, Sales), and for ages 55–74 sample sizes ranged from 20 (Professional and Technical) to 59 (Semiskilled). At ages 20–54, the Not in Labor Force category comprised 265 people; for ages 55–74 this group was composed of 315 subjects. Data are from *Journal of School Psychology, 25*, Reynolds et al., "Demographic characteristics and IQ among adults," pp. 323–342, 1987, with permission from Elsevier Science.

55- to 74-year-olds included less than 60 adults per occupational group (except for the huge unemployed or retired sample), the data for ages 20–54 are the most representative and typical for generalizing about IQ differences by occupational category. The following mean WAIS-R IQ range seems to best exemplify workers in the five different occupational categories used by Wechsler (1981) to stratify the WAIS-R standardization sample.

Occupational Category	IQ Level
Professional and Technical	110–112
Managers, Clerical, Sales	103–104
Skilled Workers	100–102
Semiskilled Workers	92–94
Unskilled Workers	87–89

The difference in the mean WAIS-R IQs for the two extreme occupational groups at ages 20–54 equals 26 points for Verbal IQ, 20 points for Performance IQ, and 25 points for Full Scale IQ. This discrepancy is huge, approaching 2 standard deviations for the Verbal and Full Scales, and is far greater than the IQ discrepancy in favor of Caucasians over African Americans discussed previously. As noted in the discussion of Table 4.2, the mean difference in WAIS-R IQs between those in middle-class occupations and those in working-class occupations is comparable in magnitude for Caucasians and African Americans. The impact of a person's occupational group on intelligence test scores is a consideration that clinicians need to keep in mind during the interpretive process, regardless of which IQ test is administered.

The IQ ranges of 20 to 26 points between professionals and unskilled workers found for 20- to 54-year-olds actively engaged in occupations are considerably larger than the ranges of 13–15 IQ points for the 16- to 19-year-olds whose father or mother was employed. Comparable analyses with the 6- to 16-year-old WISC-R sample (Kaufman & Doppelt, 1976) produced ranges across the oc-

cupational groups of 21 points on the Verbal Scale, 17 points on the Performance Scale, and 21 points on the Full Scale. These values for the WISC-R are substantially higher than the ranges of only 13 to 15 points found for the 16- to 19-year-olds. Indeed, the values of slightly less than 1 standard deviation are a bit small when compared with similar data from numerous other investigations (Anastasi & Urbina, 1997), and with data obtained on the parents of preschool children: IQ ranges between extreme occupational groups equaled 15 to 18 points for the WPPSI (Kaufman, 1973), and the McCarthy General Cognitive Index range equaled 16½ points (Kaufman & Kaufman, 1975).

Because of an insufficient sample size of elderly unskilled workers, an IQ range could not be computed for the 55- to 74-year-olds. However, the range in mean Full Scale IQ between professionals and semiskilled workers equaled 19 points for ages 55–74. Reynolds et al. (1987) point out the importance of the finding that the group of individuals not in the labor force earned mean IQs of about 100 for ages 20–54 (means of 98–99 with SDs of 16) and ages 55–74 (means of 99 with SDs of 15); they also earned normative values of 100 and 15 when data were analyzed separately for males and females, and Caucasians and African Americans not in the labor force earned means and SDs close in magnitude to the values obtained for each total ethnic group (Reynolds et al., 1987). The unemployed or retired members of the WAIS-R standardization sample were thus incredibly representative of adults in general.

Had the group not in the labor force been obtained unsystematically or without extreme care (e.g., by testing an overabundance of former professionals, a group that is often easier to get to volunteer for standardization testing), the mean IQs of that group would have been skewed and a biased set of norms, especially for elderly people, would have resulted. However, the obtained data suggest that the group labeled "Not in Labor Force" was probably employed previously in occupational groups in proportions closely similar to U.S. Census proportions (Reynolds et al., 1987).

IQ Variability within Occupational Groups

The sizable differences in mean WAIS-R IQs corresponding to different occupational levels should not be used to mask the considerable range of IQs earned by individuals within the same occupational category. Fluctuations in IQ by occupational category (and also by education level) are shown in Table 4.5, and also in Figure 4.1, based on data compiled (but not published) by Reynolds et al. (1987).

Table 4.5 shows the range of Full Scale IQs for adults (ages 20–74) in the WAIS-R standardization sample from each of six occupational groupings. Also presented are the FS-IQs corresponding to the bottom 5% and top 5% for

each category. Figure 4.1 presents a bar graph depicting the IQ range of the middle 50% (semi-interquartile range) of adults in different occupational groups.

Despite the substantial differences in mean WAIS-R IQs already noted for the occupational categories, the wide variability within each level is quite evident in both the table and the figure. In Table 4.5, the ranges (both the lowest and the highest scores) tend to increase steadily with occupational status, although the overlap in IQ distributions is still enormous. Some professionals score in the low 80s; some white-collar workers (managers, clerks, salespersons) score in the low 70s; and a number of semiskilled workers (e.g., factory workers, truck drivers, domestics) earn IQs in the superior and gifted ranges. Figure 4.1

TABLE 4.5 Range of intelligence (WAIS-R Full Scale IQs) corresponding to different levels of educational attainment and occupational category

	Sample Size	WAIS-R Full Scale IQs		
		Range	5th %ile	95th %ile
Education (Years of Schooling)				
16+ (college graduate)	214	87–148	96	136
13–15 (some college)	227	76–139	89	124
12 (high school graduate)	549	63–141	81	121
9–11 (some high school)	224	59–146	72	117
8 (elem. school graduate)	140	65–125	76	111
0–7 (some elem. school)	126	53–139	59	106
Occupational Group				
Professional and Technical	144	81–148	92	136
Managers, Clerical, and Sales	301	73–137	86	125
Skilled Workers	127	72–131	81	119
Semiskilled Workers	284	56–135	70	117
Unskilled Workers	44	53–126	65	115
Not in labor force	580	55–146	75	124

NOTE: These data are based on adults (ages 20–74) in the WAIS-R standardization sample from data compiled, but not published, by Reynolds et al. (1987). Adolescents (ages 16–19) were eliminated because (1) data were only available for their parents' occupations, and (2) many had not yet completed their formal educations.

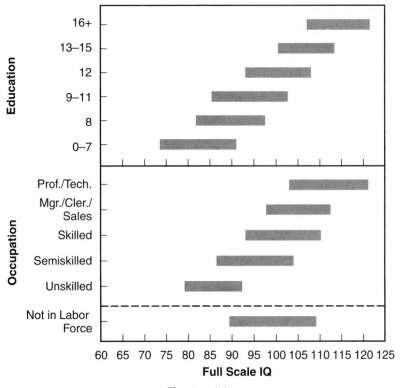

FIGURE 4.1

WAIS-R Full Scale IQs earned by the middle 50% of adults (aged 20–74) in the WAIS-R standardization sample, categorized by educational attainment and occupational category.

shows differences as well as similarities in the distributions of the "middle 50%." The average unskilled worker, for example, falls within a "middle 50%" IQ range that is completely below the range for white-collar workers and professionals.

Additionally, Matarazzo (1972, pp. 175–181) presents distributions of scores earned by several diverse groups who demonstrated the following range of Full Scale IQs on the WAIS: (1) 243 police and firemen applicants (86 to 130, median = 113); (2) 80 medical students at the University of Oregon (111 to 149, median = 125.5); and (3) 148 faculty members at the University of Cambridge (110 to 141, mean 126.5).

As Table 4.5, Figure 4.1, and Matarazzo's (1972) distributions show, however, even the lowest scoring individuals in professions requiring much advanced education are still well above the average of adults in general. The lowest scores among professors (110) and medical students (111) correspond to percentile ranks of 75 and 77, respectively. More generally, people are found at all levels of the IQ distribution in low-level occupations, but the reverse does not hold; low IQ individuals are rarely members of high-status occupations (Gottfredson, 1984), a generalization supported from the WAIS-R standardization data summarized in Table 4.5 and Figure 4.1.

Brody (1985) concluded from this relationship that "intelligence test score acts as a threshold variable for occupational success. Individuals with low scores have a low probability of being found in prestige occupations" (p. 362).

Occupational Status and Canonical Factors

No data have been published to examine mean scaled-score differences on the 11 separate WAIS-R subtests for individuals in different occupational groups. However, Chastain and Joe (1987) included membership in each of the five occupational categories as variables, along with the 11 subtests and a variety of other background factors, in their canonical correlation analysis of the WAIS-R standardization sample. Being in a professional occupation such as engineering was associated with the General Intelligence canonical factor (.37 loading); so was *not* being in a semi-skilled job like driving a taxi cab or bus (–.33 loading). However, neither of these occupational variables was nearly as related to the general factor as years of education or success on the Vocabulary or Information subtests (loadings of .80+).

Holding a job as an electrician or being in other skilled occupations was meaningfully related to the Manual Dexterity dimension; the "skilled worker" variable helped define this canonical factor, as did two other variables with high loadings: being a male and performing well on Block Design.

EDUCATIONAL ATTAINMENT

Recent data (late 1980s to mid-1990s) on the WAIS-III, KAIT, and K-BIT that relate educational attainment to intelligence are featured in this section. As mentioned previously, educational data are quite important for examiners to internalize because, like data on occupational groups,

these data are closely associated with socioeconomic status and are often used to estimate SES.

WAIS-III Mean Scores Earned by Adults Differing in Educational Attainment

The data featured in this section are based on WAIS-III analyses conducted by Heaton et al. (2001), although, whenever possible, WAIS-III data are compared to pertinent data for the WAIS-R and WAIS. In some cases, data from earlier Wechsler adult scales are emphasized because comparable WAIS-III data are unavailable.

WAIS-III IQs

Huge IQ differences are evident for the total WAIS-III standardization sample when individuals are grouped by education level, defined as years of school completed. We converted the z scores to standard scores with mean = 100 and SD = 15. Across the broad 20- to 89-year range, notable jumps in IQ points are evident with nearly every additional year of education. The age-corrected educational data we report here are from Heaton et al. (2001). These data are probably the best ever presented for educational attainment because of the quality of the WAIS-III sample (N = 2,312) and the relatively large sub-samples (ranging from 68 to 736) for very homogeneous educational groups: 11 groups ranging from ≤ 7 to ≥ 17 years of schooling.

The data reveal substantial differences in IQs for those who have graduated college versus those who have only minimal education (less than 8th grade). We converted the age-corrected z scores provided by Heaton et al. (2001) to standard scores with mean = 100 and SD = 15. The 36.3-point difference in Full Scale IQ for those who graduated college (mean FS-IQ = 116.8) versus those with minimal formal education (mean = 80.5) corresponds to a huge effect size of 2.42 standard deviations, and is a larger range, by far, than was found for any other stratification variable. The corresponding ranges for Verbal IQ and Performance IQ are 35.7 points (2.38 *SD*) and 30.5 points (2.03 *SD*), respectively. Not surprisingly, in terms of the item content and language skills assessed, the Verbal IQ is more associated with educational attainment than is Performance IQ. The same finding was obtained for the WAIS-R, which produced a 33-point IQ range (2.20 *SD*) for Full Scale IQ, as college graduates (16+ years of schooling) averaged 115 while those with minimal formal education (0–7 years of schooling) averaged 82 (Reynolds et al., 1987). For V-IQ and P-IQ, corresponding ranges were 34 points (2.27 *SD*) and 27 points (1.80 *SD*), respectively.

Consequently, the relationship between education and IQ is monstrous in magnitude. Although the relationship is stronger for verbal than nonverbal intelligence, the steady, huge drop in Performance IQ with decreasing educational attainment makes it clear that the strong education–IQ correlation is not merely a direct function of being formally taught specific facts and school-related skills (see Chapter 1 for a comparison of Information and Block Design).

Examining the IQ shifts between each year of education, the biggest jumps of 6–7 IQ points occurred for the transitions from 0–7 to 8 years of education (means of about 80–82 for elementary school dropouts versus means of about 88–90 for elementary school graduates), and from 11 to 12 years of education (91–93 for high school dropouts versus 98–100 for high school graduates). The next biggest jump of 5–7 IQ points occurred between 16 and 17+ years of education (108–111 for college graduates versus 113–117 for those with some graduate school). Interestingly, however, those who completed elementary school but dropped out of high school (those with 9, 10, or 11 years of education) did not differ in their IQs. In other words, if you had "some high school," but did not graduate, IQ was not related to when you dropped out. In contrast, the exact number of years spent in college does appear to affect IQ. Each year of college was as-

sociated with about 3 points of Verbal IQ, 2 points of Performance IQ, and 2.5 points of Full Scale IQ.

Regardless of the strong relationship between years of formal schooling and IQ, especially Verbal IQ, it is important to remember that one cannot attribute causality to these relationships. Although increased education may increase IQ, especially Verbal IQ, it is also feasible that smarter people continue to attend school longer than those who are not as smart.

WAIS-III Indexes

Heaton et al. (2001) also presented age-corrected educational data for the WAIS-III indexes (effect sizes in *SD* units, based on a comparison of the means for ≥ 17 years and ≤ 7 years, are in parentheses): VCI (2.37), POI (1.89), WMI (1.71), PSI (1.54). Once again, the largest differences in indexes occurred for the VCI when comparing adults with at least one year of graduate school with those who did not complete elementary school. The effect size of almost 2.4 *SD* for the VCI was virtually identical to the value for V-IQ. Substantially smaller differences were found on the other three indexes, most notably the PSI, but even differences of 1½ to 1¾ *SD*s are considerable.

WAIS-III Subtests

Data on the WAIS-III subtests, adjusted for age by Heaton et al. (2001), were based on a slightly smaller sample than the sample used for the IQs and indexes (2,250 instead of 2,312). When comparing the mean scaled scores for the most and least educated on each subtest, the three VCI subtests plus Comprehension yielded the only effect sizes greater than 2 *SD* (2.06–2.20 *SD*), with Vocabulary ranking number 1 with a value of 2.20 *SD*, and Arithmetic ranking just behind the VC quartet. The POI subtests plus Picture Arrangement were in the middle of the pack with effect sizes of about 1.5 *SD*, while the supplementary Object Assembly subtest was at the bottom of the pile with an effect size of 1.0 *SD.* Near the bottom were two new subtests (Letter-Number Sequencing, Symbol Search) and Digit Span with values of about 1.25 *SD.* To illustrate the meaning of these effect sizes, adults with ≥ 17 years of schooling earned an average scaled score of 13.3 on Vocabulary compared to a mean of 6.7 for those with ≤ 7 years of schooling. In contrast, the corresponding values for Digit Span are 11.6 and 7.9, respectively. Subtest data are entirely consistent with the data for the IQs and indexes.

WAIS-R IQ Variability within Educational Groups

IQ and education are closely related, but there is still considerable variability in the IQs earned by individuals with the same educational attainment. Fluctuations in WAIS-R IQ by education level are shown in Table 4.5, and also in Figure 4.1, based on data compiled (but not published) by Reynolds et al. (1987). This table and figure have already been discussed regarding the variability of WAIS-R IQs within occupational categories.

Table 4.5 presents the range of Full Scale IQs for adults (ages 20–74) in the WAIS-R standardization sample, categorized by educational attainment; also shown are IQs corresponding to the bottom 5% and top 5% for each level. Figure 4.1 depicts the IQ range of the middle 50% of adults completing varying numbers of years of education.

Despite the substantial differences in mean IQs already noted for education levels, there is nonetheless wide variability within each level. College graduates, for example, ranged in WAIS-R FS-IQ from 87 to 148, while high school graduates ranged from 63 to 141. The ranges for the four lowest educational levels do not differ very much from each other; the ranges for the highest levels differ only at the low end, as no college graduate scored more than 1 standard error of measurement below the Average category, and no one with some college scored below 75.

If the values of WAIS-R FS-IQ corresponding to the 5th and 95th percentiles are thought of as a range, they cut off the middle 90% of adults achieving each education level. All of these ranges overlap substantially. The top 5% of people with seven years of education or less outscore considerably the bottom 5% of college graduates. Figure 4.1 depicts the IQ ranges for each educational group corresponding to the middle 50% (the semi-interquartile range). Again, the substantial degree of overlap from level to level is evident. However, Figure 4.1 also reveals, for example, that the WAIS-R IQs of the middle 50% of adults who failed to graduate from elementary school do not overlap at all with the IQs earned by the middle group of adults with at least a high school education.

WAIS-III Correlations with Educational Attainment

Table 4.6 provides a different kind of quantification of the relationship between intelligence and education, presenting coefficients of correlation between educational attainment and WAIS-III IQs, indexes, and scaled scores. These data are taken from Heaton et al. (2001), who conducted multiple regression analysis to predict educational attainment from age-corrected z scores on each WAIS-III IQ, Index, and scaled score for individuals ages 20–89. Correlations for the WAIS-R IQs and subtests (Kaufman et al., 1988; Reynolds et al., 1987) appear in parentheses after the pertinent WAIS-III coefficients.

As shown, the correlations are moderate in magnitude for all WAIS-III IQs and Indexes, ranging from 0.40 for PSI to .58 for V-IQ and VCI. In terms of the amount of overlapping variance between educational attainment and global WAIS-III scores, the range is from 16% to 34%, with verbal scores overlapping with education more so than the nonverbal P-IQ and POI; based on coefficients in the .40s with education, the nonverbal scores shared about 20% variance with years of schooling. As mentioned previously, no causality can be inferred from any of these relationships.

TABLE 4.6 Correlation coefficients of WAIS-III IQs, indexes, and subtest scaled scores with years of education (N = 2,250)

IQ	r	Index	r
Verbal	.58 (.60)	VCI	.58
Performance	.47 (.44)	POI	.42
Full Scale	.57 (.57)	WMI	.43
		PSI	.40

Verbal Subtests		Performance Subtests	
Vocabulary	.55 (.60)	Matrix Reasoning	.41
Information	.53 (.58)	Digit Symbol	.37 (.44)
Similarities	.51 (.52)	Symbol Search	.36
Comprehension	.49 (.54)	Picture Arrangement	.34 (.38)
Arithmetic	.44 (.50)	Block Design	.33 (.40)
Letter-Number Sequencing	.34	Picture Completion	.30 (.38)
Digit Span	.32 (.42)	Object Assembly	.25 (.28)

NOTE: These WAIS-III coefficients are from Heaton, Manly, Taylor, and Tulsky (2001), who conducted multiple regression analysis to predict educational attainment from age-corrected z scores on each WAIS-III IQ scale, Index, and scaled score. The sample of 2,250 includes 2,028 standardization cases plus 222 cases from an "education oversampling." Values in parentheses are for the WAIS-R. Coefficients for the WAIS-R IQs (Reynolds et al., 1987) are for the adults in the standardization sample, ages 18–74 (N = 1,680); coefficients for the subtests (Kaufman et al., 1988) are median values for four age groups between 16–19 and 55–74.

Comparison of IQ Correlations for WAIS-III, WAIS-R, and WAIS

A comparison of the coefficients for the WAIS-III and WAIS-R IQs, shown in Table 4.6, reveals extreme similarity; both FS-IQs correlated .57 with education, the V-IQs correlated close to .60, and the P-IQs correlated in the mid-.40s. In contrast, correlations between education and IQ were higher for the WAIS than the WAIS-R or WAIS-III. Wechsler (1958, p. 251) reported coefficients between years of schooling and WAIS sums of scaled scores for ages 18–19, 25–34, and 45–54; he found correlations of .66–.73 for the Verbal Scale, .57–.61 for the Performance Scale, and .66–.72 for the Full Scale. Matarazzo's (1972) statement that a correlation of .70 best summarizes the relationship between IQ and education, though applicable to the WAIS, is much

too high for the WAIS-R or WAIS-III. Thus, education accounts for about one third of the variance in WAIS-R and WAIS-III Full Scale IQ, substantially less than the 49% value for WAIS Full Scale IQ. We have no explanations for the change, although, in view of the great similarity in the constructs measured by the WAIS, WAIS-R, and WAIS-III (see Chapter 3), we feel confident that the change is related to generational differences rather than modifications in the test batteries.

Interestingly, the correlation of .57 between education and both WAIS-R and WAIS-III FS-IQ is about the same as the correlation of .58 between IQ at age 12 and subsequent educational attainment obtained by Bajema (1968) from retrospective interviews of 437 adults who were 45 years old. In addition, correlations between educational attainment and IQ were similar in magnitude for 157 workers from Mexico City who were referred for psychological or psychiatric evaluation and administered the Spanish WAIS, or Escuela de Inteligencia para Adultos (Kunce & Schmidt de Vales, 1986). For this clinical sample of men and women, which had a mean age of 38.5, a mean educational level of 10.0, and mean IQs of 93–94, years of schooling correlated .66 with V-IQ, .51 with P-IQ, and .61 with FS-IQ. Also, WAIS-R Full Scale IQ correlated .52 with highest grade completed for a U.S. clinical sample of 45 male and 45 female psychiatric inpatients (mean age = 29.2, mean educational attainment = 9.7, mean FS-IQ = 86.5) (Thompson, Howard, & Anderson, 1986).

Comparison of Subtest Scaled-Score Correlations for WAIS-III, WAIS-R, and WAIS

Relationships between education and WAIS-III subtest scaled scores were generally highest for the Verbal subtests, especially the four measures of Verbal Comprehension, and lowest for auditory memory and Perceptual Organization subtests. Coefficients ranged from .25 for Object Assembly (6% overlap with education) to .55 for Vocabulary (30% overlap). Again, coefficients for WAIS-R subtests are similar to the corresponding WAIS-III values, ranging from .28 for Object Assembly to .60 for Vocabulary.

Birren and Morrison (1961) presented correlations between educational attainment and WAIS subtest scores for a sample of 933 native-born Caucasian males and females spanning the 25- to 64-year age range. They obtained coefficients that are quite consistent with the values shown in Table 4.6 for the WAIS-III and WAIS-R: correlations in the .60s for Information and Vocabulary, and in the .50s for Digit Symbol, Similarities, and Comprehension; the lowest value reported by Birren and Morrison was .40 for Object Assembly. As was true for the IQs, these WAIS coefficients are higher than the values obtained subsequently for the WAIS-R and WAIS-III.

Kunce and Schmidt de Vales (1986), in their study of 157 clinical referrals tested on the Spanish WAIS in Mexico City, found that educational attainment correlated highest with Information (.60) and lowest with Object Assembly (.29). In addition, Bornstein (1983a) reported essentially the same findings for 55 elderly patients with carotid artery disease: WAIS Information correlated highest (.56) with years of formal education, while Object Assembly correlated lowest (.05). Hence, the *pattern* of the relationships of subtest performance to years of education (not the *magnitude* of the coefficients) is rather comparable for the WAIS, WAIS-R, and WAIS-III, and even generalizes to medical patients in the United States and to psychological and psychiatric referrals in Mexico.

WAIS-R IQ Correlations by Age, Gender, and Ethnicity

Reynolds et al. (1987) reported an interesting breakdown of coefficients with education, examining the values separately by age, gender, and ethnicity. Table 4.7 summarizes their results, though we have used three broad age groups rather than the homogeneous age groups (e.g., 18–19, 70–74) that they reported.

Correlations for Verbal IQ and education are substantially higher for ages 25–54 and 55–74 (rs of .67–.68) than for the young adults, ages 18–24 (r = .54); the latter group includes a number of individuals still completing their education, which may account for the lower relationship. However, the lower correlation for Performance IQ for the young adults (r = .42 versus values of .48–.50) is less easy to explain. Relationships between education and IQ are stronger for Caucasians than African Americans on the Verbal and Full Scales, but not on the Performance Scale; correlations were about .05 higher for males than females on each IQ scale. Higher correlations with education for males than females were also reported for the six Horn abilities (represented by subtests included in three Kaufman tests) studied by J. Kaufman et al. (1995) for 587

TABLE 4.7 Coefficients of correlation between educational level and WAIS-R IQ at ages 18–74 years, by age, ethnicity, and gender (N = 1,680)

Group	N	Verbal IQ	Performance IQ	Full Scale IQ
Age				
18–24	400	.54	.42	.53
25–54	800	.67	.50	.64
55–74	480	.68	.48	.63
Ethnic Group				
African American	166	.44	.43	.45
Caucasian	1,492	.60	.42	.56
Gender				
Female	840	.57	.42	.54
Male	840	.63	.47	.59

NOTE: Data are from Reynolds et al. (1987), with permission from Elsevier Science.

males and 559 females aged 15 to 93 years. Coefficients averaged .42 for males and .33 for females with a higher correlation for males emerging for each separate Horn ability by .07–.13. Highest coefficients were obtained for both males and females on measures of crystallized knowledge and quantitative thinking (.55 for males vs. .44–.47 for females) with lower values obtained for the two main Horn abilities that are believed to be measured by Wechsler's Performance Scale: Fluid Reasoning (.39 vs. .32) and Broad Visualization (.30 vs. .17). These correlations are not directly comparable to the Wechsler coefficients because J. Kaufman et al. (1995) merged data for parental education (ages 15–24) with self-education (ages 25–93), but the pattern of higher values for males than females supports the gender difference found for the WAIS-R.

Interestingly, the correlations of V-IQ and P-IQ with education were about equal for African Americans, in contrast to the notably higher coefficients with V than P IQ (by .12 to .18) for all other samples shown in Table 4.7. Nonetheless, the data in the table support the strong relationship between obtained WAIS-R IQs and educational attainment, regardless of age, gender, or ethnicity.

Relationship of Intelligence to Education on the Kaufman Tests

Tables 4.8 and 4.9 present unpublished KAIT data on educational attainment provided by Kaufman and Kaufman (2000) for the IQ scales and subtest scaled scores, respectively. Tables 4.10 and 4.11 summarize K-BIT educational data (Kaufman & Wang, 1992).

KAIT IQs and Subtests

Mean KAIT IQs are shown in Table 4.8 for ages 25–94 years for five educational categories ranging from ≤ 8 years of schooling to ≥ 16 years. The ranges are a bit larger for Crystallized IQ than Fluid IQ (1.81 vs. 1.44 SD), with the differ-

TABLE 4.8   Mean KAIT Crystallized, Fluid, and Composite IQs for normal adults by years of education for adults ages 25 to 94 years ($N = 1,200$)

Years of Education	N	Crystallized IQ	Fluid IQ	Composite IQ
≤ 8	175	83.9	88.6	85.7
9–11	148	93.4	95.8	93.8
12	454	99.6	99.1	99.5
13–15	194	104.8	102.8	104.2
≥ 16	229	111.0	110.2	112.1
Range (Mean for ≥ 16 minus Mean for ≤ 8)		1.81 *SD*	1.44 *SD*	1.76 *SD*

NOTE: Data are for the KAIT standardization sample, ages 25 to 94 years (Kaufman & Kaufman, 2000, unpublished data). Ages 11–24 years are excluded from the analysis because they were stratified by *parental* education.

ence between the correlations for the two KAIT IQs (0.37 *SD*) resembling closely the difference in the coefficients for WAIS-III Verbal and Performance IQs (0.37 *SD*). The magnitude of the effect sizes is substantially smaller for the KAIT IQs than for the WAIS-III IQs (e.g., values for global IQ are 1.76 for KAIT and 2.42 for WAIS-III), but this discrepancy is due to the more homogeneous educational categories used by Heaton et al. (2001) for the WAIS-III (e.g., ≥ 17 years) than the ones used for the KAIT. When the WAIS-III *SD* ranges reported by Heaton et al. (2001) are recomputed for the same educational categories used for the KAIT, the following ranges emerge for each WAIS-III IQ (V-IQ = 1.74 *SD*, P-IQ = 1.43 *SD*, FS-IQ = 1.75 *SD*). These recomputed values are uncannily close to their respective KAIT values, cross-validating the long history of Wechsler data with data from an entirely different comprehensive measure of adult intelligence.

Table 4.9 presents educational data for KAIT subtests, and these results also conform closely to the WAIS-III data. Effect sizes are uniformly higher for Crystallized than Fluid subtests with the highest values of about 2 *SD* obtained for

Definitions and Famous Faces, analogs to Wechsler's Vocabulary and Information, respectively.

K-BIT

Mean K-BIT standard scores earned by adults, ages 20–90 years, categorized by education (Kaufman & Wang, 1992) are shown in Table 4.10. The pattern of a stronger relationship with the verbal–crystallized measure (Vocabulary) than with the nonverbal–fluid measure (Matrices) conforms to the patterns found for the KAIT and the various Wechsler adult scales. The magnitude of the effect sizes for the three K-BIT scores (2.06 to 2.45 *SD*), however, is substantially higher than the magnitude for the more comprehensive IQ tests. Perusal of Table 4.10 indicates that the principal difference is the very low mean standard scores (mid- to high-70s) earned by the group with the lowest education level. Because this subsample was small ($N = 49$), that value may be an atypically low estimate for the population.

Table 4.11 presents correlations between K-BIT standard scores and educational achievement for the total sample, ages 20–90 years, and separately by age and ethnicity. The overall coefficient

TABLE 4.9   Mean KAIT subtest scaled scores, by education, for adults ages 25 to 94 years

Subtest	Mean 16+ Years	Mean 0–8 Years	Difference in *SD* Units
Crystallized			
Definitions	12.9	6.8	2.03
Auditory Comprehension	12.4	7.1	1.77
Double Meanings	12.2	7.0	1.73
Famous Faces	12.6	6.7	1.97
Fluid			
Rebus Learning	12.0	8.0	1.33
Logical Steps	12.0	7.9	1.37
Mystery Codes	11.6	7.9	1.23
Memory for Block Designs	11.1	8.7	0.80
Delayed Recall			
Rebus Delayed Recall	11.9	8.0	1.30
Auditory Delayed Recall	12.3	7.7	1.53

NOTE: Data are for the KAIT standardization sample, ages 25 to 94 years (Kaufman & Kaufman, 2000, unpublished data). Ages 11–24 years are excluded from the analysis because they were stratified by parental education. Sample sizes are: 16+ years, $N = 229$; 0–8 years, $N = 175$.

TABLE 4.10   Mean K-BIT standard scores, by education, for adults ages 20 to 90 years ($N = 500$)

Years of Education	N	Vocabulary	Matrices	IQ Composite
≤ 8	49	74.7	79.9	75.1
9–11	46	92.8	88.6	89.6
12	177	98.9	96.6	97.4
13–15	114	103.7	103.4	103.9
≥ 16	114	110.3	110.8	111.8
Range (Mean for ≥ 16 minus Mean for ≤ 8)		2.37 *SD*	2.06 *SD*	2.45 *SD*

NOTE: Data are for the adult portion of the K-BIT standardization sample, ages 20 to 90 years (Kaufman & Wang, 1992).

TABLE 4.11 Coefficients of correlation between K-BIT standard scores and educational attainment, by age and ethnicity, for adults ages 20 to 90 years ($N = 500$)

Group	N	Vocabulary	Matrices	IQ Composite
Age				
20–29	146	.61	.57	.65
30–49	205	.72	.63	.72
50–90	149	.65	.62	.69
Ethnicity				
White	391	.56	.58	.63
African American	52	.77	.61	.74
Hispanic	37	.67	.33	.61
Total	500	.64	.59	.67

NOTE: Data are for the adult portion of the K-BIT standardization sample, ages 20 to 90 years (Kaufman & Wang, 1992, Table 6).

of .67 for K-BIT Composite for the total adult sample is higher than the values of .57 for the WAIS-III and WAIS-R FS-IQs, perhaps, in part, because of the unusually low scores earned by the least-educated group. The difference in the coefficients for Vocabulary (.64) and Matrices (.59) is in the predicted direction, but the difference between these values is smaller than typically found in studies of Wechsler's adult tests. Interestingly, the coefficient for Matrices (.58) was about equal to the coefficient for Vocabulary (.56) for the Caucasians in the sample, whereas Vocabulary correlated much higher with education than did Matrices for the African Americans (.77 vs. .61). In contrast, for the WAIS-R (Table 4.7), it was the sample of African Americans that failed to display the characteristically higher coefficient for V-IQ than P-IQ. Also, the coefficient of .33 with Matrices for Hispanics is surprisingly low, just as the difference in coefficients in favor of Vocabulary (.67) for Hispanics is notably high. The latter finding has potentially important practical implications, but first it must be cross-validated

with a much larger sample of Hispanic adults and with more comprehensive measures of Gf and Gc.

Clinical Implications of Educational Data

The strong impact of education on intelligence test performance must be kept in mind when interpreting IQ test profiles. For example, a Full Scale or Composite IQ of 110 has quite a different meaning for individuals from varying educational backgrounds. Quite obviously, given the data presented throughout this section on educational attainment, an IQ of 110 will correspond to a much higher percentile rank for someone with 0–7 years of education than someone who is a college graduate!

The relationship of socioeconomic status, as measured by occupational group or educational attainment, is profound. However, as noted, the substantial correlations between WAIS-III, WAIS-R,

KAIT, and K-BIT scores and education should not be used to infer causality. Clearly, a decisive relationship exists between the two variables, but the reason underlying the relationship is unclear. Do people score higher on intelligence tests because of their long years of education? Or do people stay in school longer because they are smarter to begin with? Unquestionably, the answer to both questions is "yes," but the relative variance attributed to each aspect of the education–IQ entanglement is unknown, and "surprisingly few studies have attempted to distinguish between these two possibilities" (Bouchard & Segal, 1985, p. 448). Of the investigations that have attempted to answer the questions posed here, one found that additional education did not enhance IQ (Bradway, Thompson, & Cravens, 1958), but four other investigations reached opposite conclusions (Harnqvist, 1968; Husen, 1951; Lorge, 1945; Newman, Freeman, & Holzinger, 1937).

Certainly, formal education should logically facilitate performance on crystallized tasks such as WAIS-III or WAIS-R Information/Vocabulary and KAIT Definitions/Famous Faces, and scaled scores on those tasks consistently displayed the strongest relationships with an adult's educational attainment. Yet the highly significant relationships between education and nonacademic tasks like WAIS-III Digit Symbol and Block Design, KAIT Logical Steps, and K-BIT Matrices argue that it is not just educational experience per se that leads to high IQs. In addition to the studies cited previously suggesting that additional years of education enhance IQ is an often-cited study by Dillon (1949) that is consistent with the reciprocal notion that intelligence level limits educational attainment.

Dillon investigated 2,600 seventh-grade students and found seventh-grade IQ to be an excellent predictor of when students dropped out of school. For example, only 16.5% of the 400 students with IQs below 85 entered grade 11 and only 3.5% graduated from high school. The corresponding percentages for IQs of about 100 are 75.8% and 63.4%; 92.2% of those with IQs of 115 and above entered eleventh grade and 86.0% graduated from high school.

Naturally, even Dillon's study does not prove causality because education prior to seventh grade may have had a vital impact on the children's IQs. Further, that study involved IQs obtained during childhood on group-administered tests; the results may not be generalizable to individually administered tests or to IQs measured during adulthood. But Dillon's results do reinforce current data and findings from numerous other studies suggesting a powerful relationship between educational attainment and intelligence.

For clinical purposes and for neuropsychological assessment (e.g., estimating premorbid IQ), it is essential for examiners to internalize the strikingly different IQs earned by adults based on their educational background and, further, to internalize the different relationships to education displayed by a diversity of measures of crystallized knowledge, fluid and nonverbal reasoning, short-term and working memory, and processing speed. Heaton et al. (2001) provide numerous important tables and valuable guidelines for directly applying the relationships between educational attainment and WAIS-III IQs, indexes, and scaled scores to neuropsychological decision making and test interpretation.

SUMMARY

This chapter examines individual differences in intelligence on the important background variables of gender, ethnicity, urban–rural residence, occupational category, and educational attainment; it then relates these differences to comparable findings in the literature. Recent data on the WAIS-III are featured, along with recent data obtained on the KAIT and other Kaufman tests, and the current data are integrated with data obtained in earlier generations on the WAIS-R and WAIS, and, when pertinent, with Stanford-Binet IV data for adolescents and adults. Males scored slightly higher than females on the three WAIS-III IQs, a finding consistent with the results of previous Wechsler studies but of no practical consequence. Across the age range, and based on variables from Wechsler's adult scales and several Kaufman tests, males consistently outperformed females on measures of arithmetic and spatial visualization; on the WAIS-III and other Wechsler scales, females have consistently outscored males on measures of clerical and processing speed, such as Digit Symbol Coding and the PSI. The mathematical and visual–spatial advantage of males, and the psychomotor speed advantage of females, conform to a wide array of prior investigations; however, researchers disagree on the explanations of these gender differences.

Across the various Wechsler and Kaufman tests, and on the Binet-4, Caucasians scored substantially higher than African Americans, even when corrections are applied for background variables such as educational attainment. However, some tests have yielded quite small differences in the scores earned by Caucasians and African Americans, including tests that are extremely culture-loaded, such as WAIS-III Information and KAIT Famous Faces, as well as a new measure of fluid reasoning on the K-SNAP. Caucasians outscored Hispanics by a smaller margin than was found in the Caucasian–African American studies, with the largest differences usually observed on verbal, crystallized, and memory tests rather than on nonverbal, fluid, and highly speeded tests. However, the traditional P > V profile for Hispanics was not found on the WAIS-III. With education controlled, the P > V IQ difference was only about 3 points, and the POI > VCI difference was only 1 point.

Data from the WAIS-R indicated that urban individuals outscored those living in rural areas by about 2 points, a small difference that reflects a trend toward less urban–rural difference over the years. The urban advantage was substantial in the 1930s, but has virtually disappeared since then. Subtest differences were significant only

for the oldest sample (ages 55–74) and primarily on tasks of school-related learning; this finding is related to generational change because elderly rural individuals were born in the first quarter of the twentieth century.

The relationship of socioeconomic status to adult intelligence was explored by examining data based on occupational group and educational attainment, although only the latter set of data are available for recent tests like the WAIS-III and KAIT. Therefore, the occupational group analysis was limited to data from the WAIS-R. Mean WAIS-R IQs earned by members of different occupational categories differ strikingly, ranging from about 87–89 for unskilled workers to 110–112 for professional and technical workers; however, there is considerable variability within each of the five categories studied, and much overlap in the distributions.

On the WAIS-III, even larger IQ differences were observed for educational category (a mean of about 117 for individuals with more than a 4-year college degree versus 81 for elementary school dropouts). Overall, educational attainment correlated .58 with V-IQ, .57 with FS-IQ, and .47 with P-IQ. Correlations for the indexes were generally lower (.40 to .43), with the exception of VCI, which correlated .58 with education. These overall results were quite consistent with the relationships observed between WAIS-R IQ and education, although both the WAIS-III and WAIS-R did not relate as strongly to educational attainment as did their predecessor, the WAIS. Consistent with much previous research on the WAIS and WAIS-R, however, is the finding that the best correlates of educational attainment were WAIS-III Vocabulary and Information, while the worst was Object Assembly. Analyses of the relationships between educational attainment and the KAIT Fluid and Crystallized scales and subtests provide strong cross-validation of the Wechsler findings, including the consistent result that correlations with education tend to be higher for verbal, crystallized measures than for nonverbal, fluid tests. Data with the K-BIT, composed of one crystallized and one fluid subtest, likewise conform to the findings with the more comprehensive IQ tests. Data obtained on the WAIS-R and K-BIT support the relationship between intelligence and education for different ages, genders, and ethnic backgrounds, although there is some evidence that the association is stronger for males than females.

The substantial relationships between intelligence and the background variables of ethnicity and socioeconomic status (i.e., occupational group and educational attainment)—as well as the small but consistent findings for gender and the lack of difference for urban–rural residence—are important, and must be fully taken into account by clinicians when they interpret IQ and subtest profiles on any test they administer.

CHAPTER 5

Age and Intelligence across the Adult Life Span

Research on the relationships between aging and intelligence had its inception nearly 100 years ago in comparisons between adults and children (Kirkpatrick, 1903). The topic has captivated researchers in theoretical and clinical disciplines for over half a century (Jones & Conrad, 1933; Lorge, 1936; Miles & Miles, 1932; Willoughby, 1927). Whether intelligence declines with increasing age has long been the subject of research and debate by experts in the field (Baltes & Schaie, 1976; Botwinick, 1977; Horn & Donaldson, 1976), with both the research investigations and the controversies continuing to the present (Bengtson & Schaie, 1999; Birren, Schaie, Abeles, Gatz, & Salthouse, 1996; Craik & Salthouse, 2000; Kaufman, 2000a, 2001; Lawton & Salthouse, 1998; Lindenberger & Baltes, 1997; McArdle, Prescott, Hamagami, & Horn, 1998; Park & Schwarz, 2000). The nature of the complex relationship between aging and changes in intellectual functioning is of prime concern to clinicians who test clients across a wide age span,

inasmuch as proper WAIS-III, KAIT, and WJ III interpretation demands understanding of normal, or expected, differential fluctuations in a person's ability spectrum from late adolescence and young adulthood to old age. Distinguishing between normal and pathological development is often the essence of competent diagnosis in clinical and neuropsychological assessment.

Probably the most comprehensive and cleverly conceived set of studies has been the life's work of K. Warner Schaie (e.g., 1958, 1983b, 1994) in collaboration with numerous colleagues (e.g., Hertzog & Schaie, 1988; Schaie & Labouvie-Vief, 1974; Schaie & Strother, 1968; Schaie & Willis, 1993). His results have transformed the preconceptions of professionals throughout the world regarding the inevitability of declines in mental functioning along the path to old age. Although some of Schaie's findings are controversial, it is incontestable that his clever sequential combination of cross-sectional and longitudinal research designs has shown the importance of considering cohort (generational) effects when conducting research on aging. Further, Schaie's research program suggests that, when declines in intelligence do occur with age, they do so at far later ages than was formerly believed.

But Schaie consistently used the group-administered, speeded Primary Ability Tests (PMA; Thurstone & Thurstone, 1949), based on Thurstone's theory of intelligence and normed only through age 18 years. As valuable as his findings are, they cannot replace research results based directly on the WAIS-III, its predecessors (Wechsler, 1939, 1955, 1981), and other intelligence tests for adults in helping clinicians understand the kinds of changes to anticipate during clinical, neuropsychological, or psychoeducational assessment. Evaluation of adolescents and adults depends on the WAIS-III or other individually administered clinical instruments as its primary or exclusive measure of intellectual functioning. Age changes on the PMA, Army Alpha (Yoakum & Yerkes, 1920), or other group instruments do not necessarily generalize to the profile changes to anticipate when testing the same person several times during his or her lifetime, or when comparing the subtest profiles of individuals or groups who differ in chronological age.

For these reasons, the studies conducted on the WAIS-III (Heaton, Manly, Taylor, & Tulsky, 2001; Kaufman, 2000a, 2001; Kaufman & Lichtenberger, 1999, pp. 187–200; Manly, Heaton, & Taylor, 2000), WAIS-R (Kaufman, 1990, pp. 212–222; Kaufman, Reynolds, & McLean, 1989), WAIS (Birren & Morrison, 1961; Botwinick, 1967, 1977), and Kaufman tests (Kaufman & Horn, 1996; Kaufman, Kaufman, Chen, & Kaufman, 1996; Wang & Kaufman, 1993) provide the most valuable research findings for the clinical interpretation of aging and intelligence. Especially valuable are data for the WAIS-III, based on both cross-sectional comparisons of education-adjusted IQs and longitudinal analyses of independent samples (Kaufman, 2001). Taken together, these recent analyses offer insight into aging and IQ for a contemporary sample that spans the broad 16–89-year age range. These WAIS-III analyses are discussed later in this chapter, and are integrated with the results of similar analyses conducted on the WAIS-R (Kaufman, 1990, pp. 212–222; Kaufman et al., 1989) and Kaufman tests (Kaufman & Horn, 1996; Kaufman et al., 1996; Wang & Kaufman, 1993), to gain insight into generational differences in the relationship of IQ to the aging process and into theoretical perspectives on these changes. The findings from Schaie's (1983b) landmark 21-year cohort-sequential Seattle longitudinal study, though based on the nonclinical PMA test, are also integrated into this discussion. However, to be consistent with the focus of this text, this chapter consistently emphasizes aging data obtained from studies of Wechsler's and Kaufman and Kaufman's individually administered intelligence tests for adults. In contrast to these tests, group-administered instruments like the PMA are subject to individual differences in test-taking behaviors, such as motivation level, attention span, and so forth; these variables are often important in testing elderly individuals. All data on tests like the WAIS-III and KAIT were obtained by well-trained psychologists who ensured the maintenance of rapport and motivation level throughout the testing session.

DOES IQ DECLINE WITH ADVANCING AGE? A CROSS-SECTIONAL APPROACH

To answer the crucial questions that pertain to the relationship between adults' IQs and the aging process, we have integrated the results of both cross-sectional and longitudinal investigations of this relationship. These different types of studies are treated in the sections that follow, with emphases on the pros and cons of each style and on an integration of the findings from both kinds of empirical investigation.

Cross-Sectional Investigations of Wechsler's Adult Scales

The existence of large-scale standardization data on Wechsler's scales has provided clinicians and researchers with an impressive body of Census-representative data on the intelligence of adult samples at a wide cross-section of chronological ages. However, inferring developmental changes from cross-sectional data is a risky business. Groups that differ in chronological age necessarily differ on other variables that may confound apparent age-related differences. A child growing up in the 1940s had different educational and cultural opportunities from one growing up in the 1970s. When tested in the mid-1990s as part of the WAIS-III standardization sample, the former child was in the 45- to 54-year-old category, while the latter individual was a member of the 25- to 34-year-old group. Differences in their test performance may be partially a function of their chronological ages during the 1990s, and partially a function of the generational or cohort differences that characterized their respective periods of growth from childhood to adulthood.

Cohort differences, even seemingly obvious ones like the greater number of years of education enjoyed by adults born in more recent years, were mostly ignored by clinicians and researchers through the 1950s and even the 1960s. Wechsler (1958) himself inferred an early and rapid decline in intelligence by uncritically accepting changing mean scores across the adult age range as evidence of a developmental trend: "What is definitely established is...that the abilities by which intelligence is measured do in fact decline with age; and...that this decline is systematic and after age 30 more or less linear" (p. 142). Although such interpretations were prevalent 40 to 50 years ago, researchers on aging are now thoroughly familiar with the impact of cultural change and cohort differences, including educational attainment, on apparent declines in intelligence with age, and have greatly

revised the pessimism of Wechsler's conclusions. Indeed, when examining mean IQ test performance for different age groups across the adult life span, the results can be sobering.

Table 5.1 presents mean IQs for various adult age groups on the W-B I, WAIS, WAIS-R, and WAIS-III. Whereas mean IQs on Wechsler's scales are necessarily set at 100 for each age group, the data in Table 5.1 base the mean IQs on common yardsticks (see note to Table 5.1) to permit age-by-age comparisons. Overall, the striking apparent age-related changes in intelligence from the 20s through old age, especially in P-IQ, are so overwhelming (and depressing, if taken at face value) that it is easy to understand why Wechsler and others concluded that the path to old age is paved by a steady, unrelenting loss of intellectual function. Also intriguing in Table 5.1 is the incredible similarity in the cross-sectional data for the four adult Wechsler batteries that were normed in 1937, 1953, 1978, and 1995. In particular, the mean P-IQs (relative to a common yardstick) for the WAIS, WAIS-R, and WAIS-III are uncannily similar for each age group between 20–24 and 65–69, never differing by more than three IQ points. Considering that each corresponding age group in the WAIS, WAIS-R, and WAIS-III samples was subject to huge generation or cohort effects, the similarities in the cross-sectional data seem quite remarkable. (Forty-year-olds in the WAIS sample, for example, were born just before World War I, while their age contemporaries in the WAIS-R sample were born just prior to World War II, and those in the WAIS-III sample were born just after the Korean War). Though the mean scores for adults over age 70 in the three standardization samples differ more substantially than the means for ages 20–69, the accumulated data over a 40-year span (1955 to 1995) indicate that adults who are in their 70s also earn mean Performance IQs in the 70s.

However, the data for separate age groups cannot be interpreted in isolation. Table 5.2 presents data for the WAIS, WAIS-R, and WAIS-III

TABLE 5.1   Mean IQs across the adult lifespan on the W-B I, WAIS, WAIS-R, and WAIS-III for designated cross-sectional age groups

Age Group	*Verbal IQ*				*Performance IQ*				*Full Scale IQ*			
	W-BI	WAIS	WAIS-R	WAIS-III	W-BI	WAIS	WAIS-R	WAIS-III	W-B I	WAIS	WAIS-R	WAIS-III
20–24	100	98	96	97	105	102	101	99	103	100	97	98
25–34	100	100	98	100	100	100	99	99	103	100	97	100
35–44	98	99	94	102	93	95	93	97	95	98	94	100
45–54	95	97	95	104	86	89	89	92	91	93	92	99
55–64	93	95	93	99	83	84	84	86	88	90	88	94
65–69	—	91	91	98	—	80	79	81	—	86	84	90
70–74	—	85	90	97	—	72	76	79	—	78	82	89
75+	—	80	87	93	—	66	72	74	—	73	78	83

NOTE: W-B I data for ages 55–64 are based only on adults ages 55–59. All sums of scaled scores for all scales are based on scaled-score norms for ages 20–34. Mean IQs for the WB-I, WAIS, and WAIS-R are based on the IQ conversion table for ages 25–34; mean IQs for the WAIS-III are based on the IQ conversion table for all ages. WAIS data for ages 65–69 through 75+ are for the stratified elderly sample tested by Doppelt and Wallace (1955). WAIS-R data for ages 20–74 are from Kaufman, Reynolds, and McLean (1989). WAIS-R data for ages 75+ are for the stratified elderly sample tested by Ryan, Paolo, and Brungardt (1990), and were kindly provided by Ryan (personal communication, March, 1998) for 115 individuals ages 75–89. WAIS-III data for all ages are from Kaufman (2001). Standardization data of the Wechsler Adult Intelligence Scale: Third Edition. Copyright © 1997 by The Psychological Corporation. Used by permission. All rights reserved.

TABLE 5.2   Percents of the standardization samples of the WAIS, WAIS-R, and WAIS-III with 0–8 and 13+ years of schooling, by age group

Age Group	*0–8 Years of Schooling*			*13+ Years of Schooling*		
	WAIS (1953)	WAIS-R (1978)	WAIS-III (1995)	WAIS (1953)	WAIS-R (1978)	WAIS-III (1995)
20–24	22	4	4	20	40	51
25–34	25	5	4	20	44	51
35–44	40	10	4	18	32	56
45–54	54	16	8	14	26	49
55–64	66	28	14	11	19	36
65–69	—	38	18	—	19	30
70–74	—	45	16	—	16	29
75–79	—	—	19	—	—	29
80–89	—	—	32	—	—	22

NOTE: Data are from the manuals for the WAIS (Wechsler, 1955), WAIS-R (Wechsler, 1981), and WAIS-III (Psychological Corporation, 1997).

standardization samples, showing the percent in each sample with 0–8 years of schooling and the percent with 13 or more years of schooling (at least one year of college). This table reveals the folly of interpreting changes in mean scores from age to age as evidence of developmental change. Good standardization samples match the U.S. Census proportions on key background variables, and some variables, like educational attainment, differ widely from age group to age group. With each passing decade, an increasing proportion of adults stay longer in elementary and high school, and more and more people attend college. Consequently, the younger adult age groups will tend to be relatively more educated than the older adult age groups. Similarly, any age group tested in the early 1950s on the WAIS will be considerably less educated than that same age group tested in the late 1970s on the WAIS-R, which, in turn, will be less educated than its age-mates in the mid-1990s WAIS-III sample. These facts are quite evident in Table 5.2; comparable data for the Wechsler-Bellevue I (Wechsler, 1939) were not available, although the lower level of education for the total adolescent and adult W-B I sample (Matarazzo, 1972, Table 9.3) was evident from the low percentage of high school graduates (10.8).

When Tables 5.1 and 5.2 are viewed together, it is evident that the lower IQs earned by older adults, relative to younger adults, mirror the older adults' lower level of education. For example, for the WAIS-R sample, 45% of adults ages 70–74 had less than 9 years of schooling, compared to only 5% of those ages 25–34; for the WAIS-III sample, the corresponding percentages were 16 and 4 (see Table 5.2). In 1995, virtually all age groups had more formal education than comparable age groups in 1978, yet the fewer years of education for older than younger samples remains a fact of life at any point in time.

Maybe the entire "decline" in mean IQs across the adult lifespan is illusory, reflecting nothing more than the higher level of educational attainment for the younger age groups relative to the older ones. That possibility was

explored with WAIS standardization data about 40 years ago in the United States (Birren & Morrison, 1961) and about 30 years ago in Puerto Rico (Green, 1969). Interestingly, these two cross-sectional studies gave different answers to the question. However, subsequent studies with the WAIS-R (Kaufman et al., 1989), WAIS-III (Kaufman, 2000a, 2001), and Kaufman tests (e.g., Kaufman & Horn, 1996) have provided more definitive data for answering the aging-IQ questions via cross-sectional methodology.

Birren and Morrison's (1961) Study of Caucasian Adults on the WAIS

Birren and Morrison (1961) controlled education level statistically by parceling out years of education from the correlation of each WAIS subtest with chronological age, using standardization data for 933 Caucasian males and females aged 25–64.

KEY FINDINGS.   Scores on each of the 11 subtests initially correlated negatively with age, with all Performance subtests correlating more negatively (–.28 to –.46) than did the Verbal tasks (–.02 to –.19). After statistically removing the influence of educational attainment from the correlations, four of the six Verbal subtests produced *positive* correlations, with the highest coefficients obtained for Vocabulary (.22) and Information (.17). The two Verbal subtests that remained negative (Similarities, –.04, and Digit Span, –.08) are not very dependent on formal schooling, in stark contrast to the two Verbal subtests with the highest positive coefficients. On the Performance Scale, the removal of education level did not erase the negative correlations between IQ and age; partial correlations were only slightly lower (about .10) than the original coefficients, and they remained statistically significant. Some of the partial correlations were strongly negative, even after the statistical removal of education, notably Digit Symbol (–.38) and Picture Arrangement (–.27).

Although Birren and Morrison (1961) did not conduct these analyses with the three IQ scales, their study did show the decrease in mean V-IQ with age—but not the decrement in P-IQ—to be an artifact of education level. In fact, the positive correlations with some Verbal subtests suggest an *increase* in test scores with increasing age.

Green's (1969) Spanish WAIS Study for Education-Balanced Groups

Green approached the problem differently in his analysis of the Puerto Rican standardization data for the Spanish WAIS. He added and subtracted subjects from each of four age groups (25–29, 35–39, 45–49, and 55–64) until they were balanced on educational attainment. Each of the education-balanced samples comprised about 135 adults (total sample = 539), with mean years of education ranging from 7.6 to 7.8.

KEY FINDINGS. Before balancing for education, Verbal scores increased through the early 40s and then began a slight decline; Performance scores started to decrease in the 20s, with a more dramatic decline beginning during the 40s. The unbalanced samples differed widely in education level, but even the youngest sample averaged only about 8 years of education (the oldest averaged a third-grade education). Green's equated samples demonstrated an increase in Verbal sums of scaled scores and only a slight decrement in Performance scores, as shown in Table 5.3. (The mean values have been adjusted for education level and urban–rural residence, and are from Green's Table 4.) Green concluded from his analyses that "Intelligence as measured by the WAIS does not decline in the Puerto Rican population before about age 65.... [T]he same con-

clusion is almost certainly true for the United States" (p. 626).

Despite Birren and Morrison's (1961) contradictory finding with the WAIS Performance Scale, for years Green's assertions have been tacitly accepted by writers such as Labouvie-Vief (1985), who praised his work as the "most careful study thus far of education-related effects on patterns of intellectual aging" (p. 515), but failed to point out the limited generalizability of his results. Whether the increment in V-IQ with age, coupled with the apparent lack of a sizable decrement in P-IQ, generalizes to samples that are higher in education is surely not intuitive; Green's (1969, Tables 1 and 2) groups averaged less than 8 years of education, with 43% having between 0 and 5 years of formal education.

Kausler (1982) correctly stated that Green's study has high internal validity, but low external validity. Hence, one can generalize the causative role played by education to other samples, but "the age differences found for his balanced groups no longer estimate accurately the age differences extant for the entire population of adults living in Puerto Rico" (p. 73). Kausler might have added that one ought to be cautious in generalizing Green's results to more educated samples.

Kaufman, Reynolds, and McLean's (1989) Study of the WAIS-R

Kaufman et al. analyzed the WAIS-R standardization data for ages 20 to 74 years ($N = 1,480$), a sample that was carefully stratified on gender, race (Caucasian–non-Caucasian), geographic region, educational attainment, and occupation. In

TABLE 5.3 Mean Verbal and Performance scores earned by Green's education-balanced samples on the Spanish WAIS

	Ages 25–29	Ages 35–39	Ages 45–49	Ages 55–64
Verbal Sum	56.0	61.9	64.7	65.7
Performance Sum	45.9	47.1	44.7	43.4

one analysis, using ANOVA methodology, they equated for education by a weighting technique that matched each group's educational attainment to a "target" age; ages 25–34, the age group with the highest level of education, served as the target. On the WAIS-R (as on the WAIS and W-B I), scaled scores for all adults are based on a reference group of 20- to 34-year-olds. To compare one age group to another, all sums of scaled scores were first weighted to control for education and then entered into the IQ table for ages 25–34 (thereby providing a common yardstick). In a second analysis, multiple regression methodology was applied to study the relative contributions of age and education to IQ, especially to determine whether age added significantly and substantially to the prediction of IQ obtainable from education alone (Kaufman et al., 1989; McLean, Kaufman, & Reynolds, 1988).

KEY FINDINGS OF EQUATING STUDY.   Table 5.4 shows the mean sums of scaled scores (based on the norms for ages 25–34, the reference group) for each separate educational category, by age. Regardless of chronological age (and, hence, when people were educated), adults with the same amount of formal education earned about the same mean sum of scaled scores on the Verbal Scale. Adults with 0–8 years of education earned Verbal sums of about 40; those with 9–11 years scored about 50; high school graduates scored 55–60; adults with some college earned means of approximately 65; and college graduates scored in the 70–75 range. This relationship maintained whether the adult was 25, 50, or 65, and whether he or she was educated in the 1910s, 1930s, or 1950s. Unlike Verbal sums, Performance sums decreased steadily within each educational category, although the decrements were relatively small for the least educated samples.

The overall results of this WAIS-R study are depicted in Figures 5.1 and 5.2, which show the mean V-IQs and P-IQs, respectively, for seven adult age groups, both with and without a control for education. After controlling for education, the decline in Verbal IQ disappeared, but the decline in P-IQ remained substantial. On the Verbal Scale, the peak IQ (99.8) occurred for ages 55–64 after equating for education level; even at ages 70–74, the weighted mean V-IQ was nearly 98. In contrast, education-controlled means in P-IQ dipped below 90 at ages 55–64, and below 80 for 70- to 74-year-olds. The weighted Verbal means did not differ significantly from each other, based on ANOVA results, but the weighted Performance means differed at the .001 level.

These results are entirely consistent with Birren and Morrison's (1961) WAIS data, but not with Green's (1969) results. Green observed increments in Verbal scores and only trivial decrements in Performance scores for his education-balanced age groups in Puerto Rico. The key to the discrepancy may reside in the low education level of the Puerto Rican education-balanced samples. Consider Table 5.4. For adults with 0–8 years of education, the category closest to Green's sample, WAIS-R Verbal sums of scaled scores rose steadily and substantially between ages 25–34 and 55–64 (the ages most resembling Green's youngest and oldest samples); WAIS-R Performance scores dropped only trivially between these ages for the least educated group. These results parallel Green's findings almost identically. However, these relationships do not maintain on the WAIS-R for more educated samples: Within each age category between 9–11 and 16+ years of education, Verbal sums of scaled scores are approximately equal regardless of age, and Performance sums decrease substantially between ages 25–34 and 55–64. As Kaufman et al. (1989) point out, differences between the results of the two studies may also be a function of cohort differences (1960s versus 1970s), instrument differences (WAIS versus WAIS-R), language differences (Spanish versus English), and cultural differences (Puerto Rico versus the United States). Yet, the education hypothesis remains a viable and strong explanation (or partial explanation) for the discrepancies observed.

Matarazzo (1972) was cautious in interpreting Green's findings, primarily because he wondered

TABLE 5.4   Mean WAIS-R Verbal, Performance, and Full Scale sums of scaled scores for adults completing different numbers of years of education, by age

Years of Education	Age group						
	20–24	25–34	35–44	45–54	55–64	65–69	70–74
Verbal Scale							
0–8	41.6	31.9	37.3	41.8	42.3	42.4	43.0
9–11	51.1	50.8	45.8	51.4	52.7	52.2	51.1
12	55.5	57.6	58.2	60.0	59.9	59.4	55.6
13–15	65.0	67.7	63.6	65.4	65.0	62.2	66.0
16+	69.5	74.3	72.8	74.2	75.3	73.8	72.9
Weighted mean	59.5	61.4	60.2	62.4	62.8	61.6	60.6
Performance Scale							
0–8	37.0	33.1	31.9	31.0	28.9	28.3	27.7
9–11	47.7	44.0	38.0	40.2	37.6	35.8	30.8
12	49.5	47.6	46.1	43.8	42.1	36.0	31.7
13–15	54.3	53.6	50.0	44.4	42.6	37.4	35.9
16+	58.7	57.2	53.7	50.2	47.9	41.8	38.0
Weighted mean	51.8	49.9	47.0	44.4	42.4	37.2	33.7
Full Scale							
0–8	78.6	65.0	69.2	72.8	71.2	70.7	70.7
9–11	98.8	94.8	83.7	91.6	90.3	88.0	81.8
12	105.0	105.3	104.4	103.8	101.9	95.5	87.3
13–15	119.2	121.2	113.5	109.8	107.7	99.6	101.9
16+	128.2	131.5	126.5	124.4	123.2	115.6	110.9
Weighted Mean	112.2	111.3	107.2	106.8	105.1	98.9	94.3

NOTE: Weighted means were obtained by using as weights the proportions of adults in each educational category at ages 25–34 years. Data are from Kaufman et al. (1989).

whether years of formal education is "a variable with identical meaning across generations" (p. 115). Matarazzo's question obviously has no definitive answer, although his criticism is refuted to some extent by the provocative data in Table 5.4, which show that, regardless of age, and with only mild aberrations, individuals with a comparable amount of education earned simi-

lar scores on the WAIS-R Verbal Scale. Quite clearly, the Verbal Scale measures skills (e.g., general information, word meaning, and arithmetic ability) that bear a logical relationship to one's formal education.

Similar analyses were conducted for the 11 separate WAIS-R subtests (McLean et al., 1988). After equating for education, the declines in Verbal

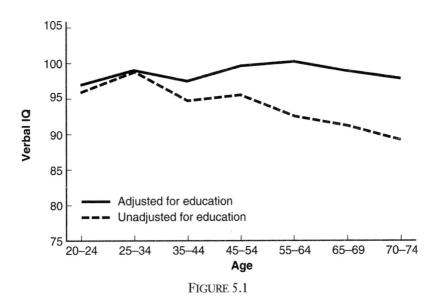

FIGURE 5.1

Change in WAIS-R Verbal IQ across the 20- to 74-year age range, both with and without a control for education; IQs were based on norms for ages 25–34 (data from Kaufman, Reynolds, & McLean, 1989).

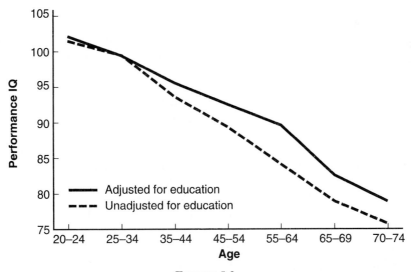

FIGURE 5.2

Change in WAIS-R Performance IQ across the 20- to 74-year age range, both with and without a control for education; IQs were based on norms for ages 25–34 (data from Kaufman, Reynolds, & McLean, 1989).

means disappeared and were replaced by gradual increments into the mid- to late 60s for Information, Vocabulary, and Comprehension. Arithmetic produced nearly equal weighted means (9.9–10.4) for each of the seven age groups. Only Digit Span and Similarities showed a declining trend (in the mid-50s), but it was small in magnitude. In contrast, each Performance subtest (like the total Performance Scale), continued to reveal striking decrements in mean scaled scores, even after balancing the groups on education. Mean education-adjusted scaled scores for ages 70–74 were about 7 for all subtests except Digit Symbol, which dipped to 5.5. These WAIS-R subtest findings are remarkably similar to Birren and Morrison's (1961) correlational results with the WAIS subtests, on both the Verbal and Performance scales.

All of the WAIS-R findings give clear-cut support to Botwinick's (1977) classic intellectual aging pattern, which posits maintenance of performance on nontimed tasks versus decline on timed tasks. The results also support Horn (1985, 1989) and his colleagues' (Horn & Hofer, 1992; Horn & Noll, 1997) interpretation of the classic pattern from the fluid/crystallized theory of intelligence: Crystallized abilities remain stable through old age ("maintained" abilities), while fluid abilities (and other abilities such as visualization and speed) decline steadily and rapidly, starting in young adulthood ("vulnerable" abilities). The distinction in the adult development literature of fluid versus crystallized abilities was first made by Horn and Cattell (1966, 1967) in the 1960s and remains one viable theoretical model for understanding the aging process (Berg, 2000). Fluid intelligence (Gf), manifested by the ability to solve novel problems, is presumed to increase with neurological maturation during childhood and adolescence and to decline throughout adulthood concomitantly with neurological degeneration. In contrast, crystallized intelligence (Gc), knowledge and skills dependent on education and experience) is expected to continue to increase during one's life, reflecting cultural assimilation.

Finally, the results of these cross-sectional analyses accord well with Baltes's (1997) two-component (mechanics–pragmatics) lifespan the-ory of intellectual development. The pragmatics component resembles crystallized ability and is believed by Baltes to be maintained across the adult lifespan. P-IQ does not correspond to a unitary ability in Horn's modern Gf–Gc theory, but is a blend of tasks that require Gf, processing speed (Gs), and visual processing (Gv). This array of abilities corresponds closely to the broad "mechanics" component of cognition in Baltes's theory. In contrast to the pragmatics component, the mechanics component is vulnerable to the effects of normal aging and subsumes reasoning, spatial orientation, memory, and perceptual speed (Baltes, 1997; Baltes, Staudinger, & Lindenberger, 1999; Lindenberger & Baltes, 1997). This computer analogy refers to the mind's hardware (mechanics) and software (cognitive pragmatics).

KEY FINDINGS OF MULTIPLE REGRESSION ANALYSIS. When entered first in the multiple regression analysis, education accounted for nearly half the variability in WAIS-R V-IQ and FS-IQ, and about one third of the variance in P-IQ. Table 5.5 summarizes the results of the regression analysis for IQs and scaled scores. The strong relationships of education to IQ shown in Table 5.5 were never at issue; instead, the key was whether chronological age would add substantially to the prediction of intelligence when entered as the second predictor in the regression equations. ("Substantial" was defined as meeting two requirements: statistical significance at the .01 level, and accounting for an additional 2% or more of the total variance. Significance was not enough, because a sample size of nearly 1,500 yields significance with very small increments; the increment had to be of practical, not just statistical, significance.)

Adding age as a predictor led to a striking increment of nearly 13% for P-IQ but only a trivial increase of 0.3% for V-IQ (see Table 5.5). None of the increments for the Verbal subtests reached the 2% criterion, whereas each of the Performance subtests easily met the requirement. Age improved the prediction of scaled score by at least 5% for every Performance task, ranging from 5.6% for Picture Completion to 14.4% for Digit Symbol.

TABLE 5.5   Multiple regression analysis, using education and age as predictors of WAIS-R scores: the amount of variance accounted for by age over and above the contribution of education

	Percentage of variance accounted for by		
WAIS-R Criterion	**Education Alone**	**Education and Age Combined**	**Increment Due to Age**
Sum of Scaled Scores			
Verbal	45.1	45.4	0.3%*
Performance	32.9	45.6	12.7%**
Full Scale	45.5	47.5	2.0%**
Verbal Scaled Score			
Information	34.7	35.8	1.1%**
Digit Span	21.4	21.5	0.1%
Vocabulary	37.0	38.6	1.6%**
Arithmetic	27.9	28.2	0.3%
Comprehension	31.0	31.8	0.8%**
Similarities	33.0	33.6	0.6%**
Performance Scaled Score			
Picture Completion	21.2	26.8	5.6%**
Picture Arrangement	20.7	28.6	7.9%**
Block Design	24.3	31.2	6.9%**
Object Assembly	15.2	23.8	8.6%**
Digit Symbol	28.9	43.3	14.4%**

*$p < .01$; **$p < .001$
NOTE: Table is adapted from Kaufman et al. (1989, Table 2).

These results support Botwinick's (1977) classical aging pattern: Age was shown to be a substantial correlate of intelligence, over and above the contribution of educational attainment, for the timed Performance subtests and for P-IQ, but not for the nontimed components (Arithmetic is an exception) of the Verbal Scale. The results also support Horn's (1989) distinction between maintained and vulnerable abilities and Baltes's (1997) mechanics–pragmatics dichotomy.

Table 5.5 reveals the interesting finding that the combination of education and age accounts for almost the precise amount of variance in V-IQ (45.4%) as in P-IQ (45.6%). However, the relative contributions of each variable are quite different when age and education are treated separately, as shown in Table 5.6.

Heaton's Age–Education Gradients for the WAIS, WAIS-R, and WAIS-III

Heaton, Grant, and Matthews (1986) considered the impact of both age and education on test scores in their WAIS investigation of 553 adults (64% male), ages 15–81 years (mean = 39.3), who were tested as normal controls at several neuropsychological laboratories. The groups were divided by age (<40, 40–59, 60+) and education

TABLE 5.6   Relative contributions of age and education to WAIS-R IQs

Criterion	Amount of Variance Accounted for by	
	Age Alone	Education Alone
Verbal IQ	3.1%	45.1%
Performance IQ	28.2%	32.9%
Full Scale IQ	13.4%	45.5%

NOTE: Data are from Kaufman et al. (1989).

(<12, 12–15, 16+), although as a group they were a highly educated sample (mean years of education = 13.3). Heaton et al. computed an age–education gradient for each WAIS subtest by subtracting the amount of variance accounted for by education from the amount accounted for by age; positive values denote the more age-related subtests, while negative values indicate the tasks more heavily dependent on education.

Kaufman (1990) computed this gradient for WAIS-R subtests, using data yielded by Kaufman et al.'s (1989, Table 2) multiple regression analysis. And Heaton et al. (2001) conducted a series of interesting analyses with the WAIS-III at ages 20–89 years, using data from both the standardization sample (n = 2,028 of the 2,050 cases at ages 20–89) and an "education oversample" (n = 222) for a total N = of 2,250, which permitted the computation of age–education gradients. Heaton et al. (2001, Tables 3 & 4) correlated education to age-corrected WAIS-III z scores and also correlated chronological age to education-corrected WAIS-III z scores, thereby providing the pertinent percentages of variance needed to compute age–education gradients.

KEY FINDINGS.   Heaton et al.'s initial study of age–education gradients for WAIS subtests showed Picture Arrangement, followed closely by Digit Symbol and Object Assembly (each with values in the +5 to +10 range), as the most age-related WAIS tasks; in contrast, Vocabulary and

then Information (with values close to –40) were the most education-related. Table 5.7 presents the age–education gradients for WAIS, WAIS-R, and WAIS-III subtests; the 11 subtests that are included in all three Wechsler adult scales have ranks in parentheses next to their gradients where one equals the most age-dependent subtest and 11 equals the most education-dependent. Kendall's W (coefficient of concordance) was computed to determine the consistency in the ranks from one adult scale to another. A near-perfect W = .976 was obtained, with an average pairwise rank-order correlation = .964 ($p < .01$). These coefficients denote striking consistency in the subtests' age–education gradients over time and despite substantial item revisions from scale to scale.

Of the three new WAIS-III subtests, Symbol Search is virtually tied with Digit Symbol as the most age-dependent task in the battery. Letter-Number Sequencing and Matrix Reasoning are exactly in the middle of the pack, with each having nearly equal percentages of variance due to age versus education. Perusal of Table 5.7, which is ordered by the WAIS-III age–education gradients, reveals that the first seven subtests listed (the most age dependent) are on the Performance Scale, followed by the seven Verbal subtests. Indeed, the subtests also align by Index. The two PS subtests are at the top of the list, followed by the five subtests that are either included on the PO or have been shown by factor analysis to load on PO factors. Next are the three WM subtests followed by the four subtests that have consistently loaded on VC factors.

Based on Heaton et al.'s (2001, Tables 3 and 4) data, the following age–education gradients emerge for the Indexes, again with the most age-dependent listed first: PSI (+22), POI (+7), WMI (–10), VCI (–34). For the IQs, the order is: P-IQ (+13), FS-IQ (–21), V-IQ (–34).

Kaufman's (2000a, 2001) Equating Studies of the WAIS-III

Kaufman analyzed data from the WAIS-III standardization sample of 2,450 individuals at ages 16 to 89 years, focusing on the four Indexes and

TABLE 5.7   Age–education gradients on WAIS-R subtests

Wechsler Subtest	WAIS-III % Variance: Age	WAIS-III % Variance: Educ.	WAIS-III Age–Educ. Gradient	WAIS-R Age–Educ. Gradient	WAIS Age–Educ. Gradient
Digit Symbol	35	14	+21 (1)	+0.3 (2)	+7 (2)
Symbol Search	33	13	+20	—	—
Object Assembly	20	06	+14 (2)	+1.5 (1)	+5 (3)
Picture Arrangement	25	12	+13 (3)	–3.2 (3)	+8 (1)
Block Design	18	11	+07 (4)	–7.1 (5)	–5 (4)
Picture Completion	14	09	+05 (5)	-6.8 (4)	–6 (5)
Matrix Reasoning	21	17	+04	—	—
L-N Sequencing	15	12	+03	—	—
Digit Span	04	10	–06 (6)	–18.2 (6)	–11 (6)
Arithmetic	01	19	–18 (7)	–26.2 (8)	–24 (7)
Similarities	03	26	–23 (8)	–25.8 (7)	–28 (8)
Comprehension	<01	24	–24 (9)	–29.9 (9)	–29 (9)
Information	02	28	–26 (10)	–33.7 (10)	–39 (10)
Vocabulary	01	31	–30 (11)	–36.2 (11)	–40 (11)

NOTE: Educ. = Education; L-N = Letter-Number; age–education gradient equals age variance minus education variance. Positive values denote the more age-related subtests, while negative values indicate the tasks more heavily dependent on education. Subtests are listed in order of gradients for the 14 WAIS-III subtests. Numbers in parentheses denote the rank order of the age–education gradients for the 11 subtests common to the three Wechsler adult scales. WAIS-III data are from Heaton et al. (in preparation). WAIS-R data are from Kaufman et al. (1989) and Kaufman (1990). WAIS data are from Heaton et al. (1986); values are estimated from Heaton et al.'s (1986) Figure 3.

14 scaled scores in one study (Kaufman, 2000a) and on the three IQs in a second study (Kaufman, 2001). The WAIS-III sample was subdivided into 13 separate subsamples between ages 16–17 and 85–89. Each of the 11 subsamples from 16–17 through 75–79 was composed of 200 individuals; ages 80–84 had $N = 150$ and ages 85–89 had $N = 100$. The number of males and females was equal through age group 55–64, but matched Census proportions at ages 65+, when females are more numerous. The sample was also stratified on the variables of race/ethnicity, geographic region, and educational attainment (Psychological Corporation, 1997, pp. 19–39).

For the WAIS and WAIS-R, scaled scores for all adults were based on a reference group of adults ages 20 to 34 years. Though that method left much to be desired for clinical purposes (e.g., the means and *SD*s for subtests varied from age to age and from subtest to subtest within each age group), the use of a reference group facilitated aging research by providing a yardstick for age-to-age comparisons. The WAIS-III manuals (Psychological Corporation, 1997; Wechsler, 1997) do not directly provide data for comparing age groups; however, The Psychological Corporation generously provided mean scaled scores, for each age, on the 14 WAIS-III subtests, based on the reference group of 400 adults ages 20 to 34 years. These data permitted direct comparisons across the 16- to 89-year age range on all subtests, Factor Indexes, and IQs.

However, comparisons of mean scores by age, even on the common metric of reference-group scaled scores, is confounded by cohort effects. The one cohort effect that is large and pervasive is educational attainment, as discussed previously and illustrated in Tables 5.1 and 5.2. Fortunately, this cohort variable is capable of being controlled because the WAIS-III (like the WAIS-R) was stratified by education and each person's years of formal schooling were obtained as part of the standardization process. In order to equate the age groups on education, as was done by Kaufman et al. (1989) for the WAIS-R, it was necessary to know the mean test scores earned by adults in each of the five educational categories (i.e., 0–8, 9–11, 12, 13–15, and 16+ years of schooling) for every WAIS-III age group. Again, these age X education data were kindly provided by The Psychological Corporation. For the WAIS-R, ages 25–34 was selected as the target age group because that group was the most educated. From Table 5.2, it is evident that the most educated WAIS-III group is ages 35–44, with 56% having at least one year of college and 4% with less than 9 years of schooling. Nonetheless, to be comparable to the procedure used in the WAIS-R study, Kaufman (2000, 2001) equated educational attainment to the education level of ages 25–34 (the midpoints of the educational attainment percents for ages 25–29 and 30–34; Psychological Corporation, 1997, Table 2.6). This equating procedure was used for IQs, Indexes, and scaled scores for each age group between 20–24 and 85–89 years. Scores for ages 16–19 years were not equated for educational attainment because only parents' education was provided and many of these older adolescents had not yet completed their formal education; nonetheless, mean WAIS-III scores for ages 16–19 years were obtained based on the reference group to permit a rough comparison to adults ages 20 to 89.

Though the WAIS-III standardization sample represents a "normal" sample, this sample is, nonetheless, unusual because of the many exclusionary criteria that were applied. When selecting the sample for testing, The Psychological Corporation (1997, Table 2.1) excluded three categories of adults: (1) individuals with sensory or motor deficits that might compromise the validity of the obtained test scores (e.g., color-blindness, uncorrected hearing loss); (2) individuals undergoing current treatment for alcohol or drug dependency, those who consumed more than three alcoholic beverages more than two nights per week, and those currently taking certain medications (e.g., anti-depressants); and (3) adults with a known or possible neuropsychological disorder, those who see a doctor or other professional for memory problems or problems with thinking, and those with related problems (e.g., suffering a head injury that required hospitalization for more than 24 hours, or having a medical or psychiatric condition that could affect cognitive functioning, such as epilepsy or Alzheimer's dementia).

The standardization sample, therefore, may be *normal*, but it is not *typical*. The third exclusionary category, in particular, is age-related; both the number and severity of cognitive/neurological pathologies accelerate in old age (Rabbitt, Bent, & McInnes, 1997). More older than younger individuals, therefore, will have been excluded from the WAIS-III standardization sample, an important fact to consider when interpreting the aging-IQ data. The sample of adults ages 80–84, for example, is undoubtedly higher functioning than a random sample of 80- to 84-year-olds in the population. Any cognitive deficits with increasing age are probably "lower-bound" estimates of the actual deficits within the population. Yet, the liberal exclusion of adults with suspected or known thinking impairments has an upside for aging research: Any observed declines in cognitive function are likely to be "real" declines, not artifacts of the inclusion of increasing numbers of cognitively impaired adults with increasing age.

KEY FINDINGS. Horn's (1989) and Baltes's (1997) notions of maintained and vulnerable abilities during the adult aging process are supported by the results of both the cross-sectional and longitudinal analysis of WAIS-III data, much more so than Schaie's (1984) belief in the maintenance of various intellectual abilities. V-IQ was maintained and P-IQ was vulnerable, consistent with previous research involving the WAIS-R, WAIS, and other measures. Table 5.8 shows education differences from age to age, as well as both the unadjusted and education-adjusted mean V-IQs, P-IQs, and FS-IQs for each age group between 20–24 and 85–89 years. Figure 5.3 presents the strikingly different age-related patterns for V-IQ versus P-IQ from ages 16–17 through 85–89 years (unadjusted means for ages 16–19, education-adjusted means for ages 20–89). V-IQ was basically maintained throughout the life span, declining only during the 80s and dipping as low as 96 only at ages 85–89. In contrast, P-IQ peaked in young adulthood, then declined steadily and dramatically across the age range (especially at ages 45 and above); education-adjusted mean P-IQs

were below 80 for adults in their 80s. On the Verbal Scale, education-adjusted mean V-IQs were lowest at ages 85–89, but note in Table 5.8 that the values for adults in their 80s were closely similar to the values for young adults ages 20–24. From Figure 5.3, it is evident that the adjusted means for 85- to 89-year-olds were comparable in magnitude to the unadjusted mean for ages 18–19 and substantially higher than the mean for ages 16–17.

The familiar P-IQ decline is especially noteworthy in view of the exclusion from the standardization sample of many low-functioning adults, that is, those with known or suspected memory/cognitive disorders. The decline in mean P-IQ is evidently "real" and not an artifact of having increasing numbers of patients in older age groups. However the observed declines are probably lower-bound estimates of the "true" declines that exist within the adult population.

TABLE 5.8   Education level and mean WAIS-III IQs of each standardization age group (mean IQs adjusted for educational attainment are in parentheses)

Age Group	Percent High School Dropout	Percent College Graduate	Mean WAIS-III IQs		
			Verbal	Performance	Full Scale
20–24	15.0	11.0	97.1 (98.1)	99.4 (100.0)	98.5 (99.4)
25–29	14.0	23.5	99.4 (99.5)	99.9 (99.9)	99.9 (100.0)
30–34	14.0	23.0	101.0 (100.9)	98.4 (98.4)	99.9 (99.9)
35–44	9.5	29.0	102.4 (101.2)	97.3 (96.3)	100.1 (98.9)
45–54	17.5	25.0	103.8 (104.4)	91.8 (92.4)	99.0 (99.7)
55–64	26.5	18.0	98.9 (102.1)	86.3 (89.0)	93.8 (97.0)
65–69	32.0	14.0	98.2 (102.9)	80.9 (84.8)	90.2 (94.9)
70–74	31.5	14.0	97.1 (101.1)	78.8 (82.3)	88.7 (92.8)
75–79	34.0	13.5	96.0 (100.3)	76.2 (79.7)	86.8 (91.1)
80–84	49.3	11.3	91.4 (97.8)	72.9 (78.2)	81.0 (87.4)
85–89	50.0	12.0	89.8 (96.3)	69.9 (75.9)	78.6 (85.3)

NOTE: Percentages of high school dropouts and college graduates for the WAIS-III standardization sample are from The Psychological Corporation (1997, Table 2.6). Mean WAIS-III IQs for all ages are based on sums of scaled scores for ages 20–34. Education-adjusted IQs (values in parentheses) are adjusted to match the educational attainment of adults ages 25–34. Mean IQs and adjusted IQs are from Kaufman (2001). Standardization data of the Wechsler Adult Intelligence Scale: Third Edition. Copyright © 1997 by The Psychological Corporation. Used by permission. All rights reserved.

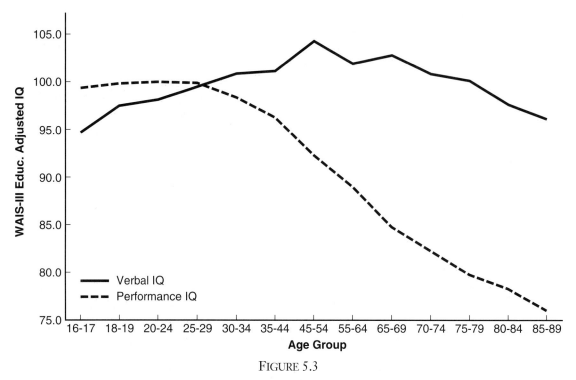

FIGURE 5.3

Mean "reference group" (ages 20–34) WAIS-III Verbal and Performance IQs, by age, for adults ages 16–17 to 85–89 years, adjusted for educational attainment (values for ages 16–19 are unadjusted).

SOURCE: Standardization data of the Wechsler Adult Intelligence Scale: Third Edition. Copyright © 1997 by The Psychological Corporation. Used by permission. All rights reserved. Reprinted from Kaufman (2001) with permission.

Figure 5.4 (Verbal IQ) and Figure 5.5 (Performance IQ) compare the results of cross-sectional analyses of the WAIS-III with the WAIS-R (Kaufman et al., 1989), including Ryan and Paolo's extension of WAIS-R data to elderly samples ages 75 and older (Paolo & Ryan, 1995; Ryan, personal communication, March, 1998; Ryan, Paolo, & Brungardt, 1990; Ryan, Paolo, & Dunn, 1995). The WAIS-III and WAIS-R education-adjusted results are congruent for P-IQ across the 20- to 89-year range but not for V-IQ. The P-IQ results suggest a generation-to-generation continuity in the observed decline in nonverbal intelligence with increasing age.

The most important difference in the education-adjusted V-IQ graphs for WAIS-R versus WAIS-III concerns their different shapes, denoting different ages of peak performance. Peak performance was at about age 60 (ages 55–64) on the WAIS-R and peaks in the 60s have been reported by Horn (1989) and colleagues (Horn, Donaldson, & Engstrom, 1981; Horn & Hofer, 1992; Horn & Noll, 1997). However, an earlier peak emerged for the WAIS-III, a decisive elevation at ages 45–54. Heaton and colleagues' WAIS-III analyses for five-year age intervals (Heaton et al., 2001; Manly et al., 2000) make it clear that the elevation is for ages 45–49, *not* 50–54 years.

The WAIS-III results for V-IQ probably reflect a real generational change. Horn's conclusions are based on WAIS and WAIS-R Verbal IQ

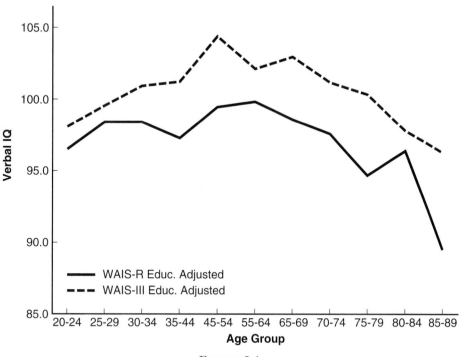

FIGURE 5.4

Comparison of mean "reference group" (ages 20–34) Verbal IQs, by age, on the WAIS-R versus WAIS-III for adults ages 20–24 to 85–89 years, adjusted for educational attainment.

SOURCE: WAIS-R IQs for ages 20–74 are from Kaufman et al. (1989). WAIS-R IQs for ages 75–89 for the stratified elderly sample tested by Ryan, Paolo, and Brungardt (1990), and were kindly provided by Ryan (personal communication, March, 1998) for the age groups shown. Standardization data of the Wechsler Adult Intelligence Scale: Third Edition. Copyright © 1997 by The Psychological Corporation. Used by permission. All rights reserved. Reprinted from Kaufman (2001) with permission.

and on studies of other measures of crystallized intelligence, with all data collected prior to 1980. In addition to WAIS-III results, other recent data suggest peak performance well before age 60; indeed, measures of *Gc* ability on several Kaufman tests (discussed later in this chapter) all peaked in the early- to mid-40s (Kaufman & Horn, 1996; Kaufman, Kaufman, Chen et al., 1996; Wang & Kaufman, 1993), and the recently normed WJ III *Gc* scale peaked at about age 45 (although those data were not adjusted for education; see Chapter 14). There is an apparent generational shift toward an earlier peak in *Gc* ability, although explanations for this shift are not obvious.

The four WAIS-III Indexes display patterns of age-by-age means that are decidedly different from each other (see Figure 5.6), with each one corresponding to different Horn abilities: VCI = *Gc*, POI = *Gf/Gv*, WMI = short-term memory (*Gsm*), PSI = *Gs*. In contrast, none of the WAIS-III IQs correspond to Horn's theoretical constructs. FS-IQ is an atheoretical amalgam from the vantage point of Horn's modern *Gf–Gc* theory. V-IQ and P-IQ correspond to broad *Gc* and broad *Gf*, respectively, consistent with the original Horn-Cattell conception of these global abilities (Cattell, 1963; Horn & Cattell, 1966, 1967) and with Baltes's (1997) two-component mechanics–pragmatics life span theory of intellectual devel-

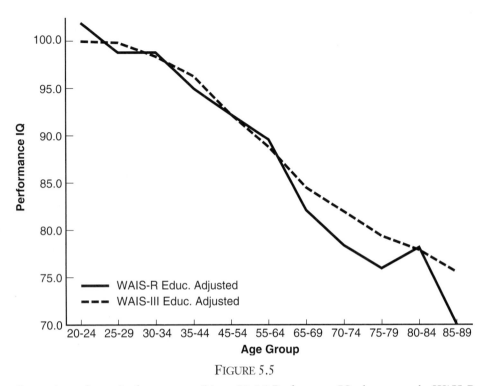

FIGURE 5.5

Comparison of mean "reference group" (ages 20–34) Performance IQs, by age, on the WAIS-R versus WAIS-III for adults ages 20–24 to 85–89 years, adjusted for educational attainment.

SOURCE: WAIS-R IQs for ages 20–74 are from Kaufman et al. (1989). WAIS-R IQs for ages 75–89 for the stratified elderly sample tested by Ryan, Paolo, and Brungardt (1990), and were kindly provided by Ryan (personal communication, March, 1998) for the age groups shown. Standardization data of the Wechsler Adult Intelligence Scale: Third Edition. Copyright © 1997 by The Psychological Corporation. Used by permission. All rights reserved. Reprinted from Kaufman (2001) with permission.

opment. But the separate IQs are too impure to denote pure abilities in Horn's (1989) expanded and refined *Gf–Gc* theory. Note in Figure 5.6 that the peak age is at ages 45–54 for *both* Indexes composed of Verbal subtests (VCI and WMI), consistent with the peak age observed for the entire V-IQ. In the analyses by Heaton and colleagues (Heaton et al., 2001; Manly et al., 2000) for five-year age groups, it is once again evident that the peak occurs at ages 45–49, not 50–54 years. However, for VCI, Heaton et al. (2001) observed dual peaks at 25–29 and 45–49 years. The somewhat different results reported by Kaufman (2000a, 2001) and Heaton and colleagues are probably due to the slightly different

samples used by the investigators and the different techniques used to adjust for education.

P-IQ is basically composed of two major components, nonverbal and spatial problem solving (fluid intelligence and visual processing, Horn's *Gf* and *Gv*) and speed of problem solving (Horn's processing speed or *Gs*). Each of these components is represented by a Factor Index, POI and PSI, respectively. Therefore, examination of the age-by-age changes on the POI and PSI, in conjunction with age patterns on P-IQ, might offer insight into the nature of the well-known dramatic decline on P-IQ during adulthood with increasing age. Figure 5.7 juxtaposes these three aging patterns. Interestingly, the age-

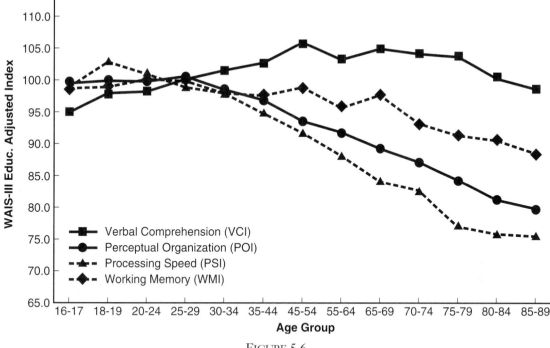

FIGURE 5.6

Mean "reference group" indexes on the four WAIS-III factors for adults ages 16–17 to 85–89 years, adjusted for educational attainment (values for ages 16–19 are unadjusted).

by-age pattern of education-adjusted mean IQs on the WAIS-III P-IQ is closely similar to the pattern of Indexes on the POI during its period of early stability (ages 16–44), but they overlap with the pattern for PSI during the period of rapid decline with increasing age (especially ages 55–74). The rapid decline of P-IQ with increasing age, therefore, may be more a function of the highly speeded nature of some of its subtests than of their *Gf* or *Gv* component. (In this chapter, we are using *Gf–Gc* terminology and abbreviations that are consistent with the more recent amalgamation of the Horn, Horn-Cattell, and Carroll, 1993, theories known as Cattell-Horn-Carroll or CHC theory; see Flanagan, McGrew, & Ortiz, 2000, and Chapter 14. The actual stud-

ies that are summarized and integrated in this chapter, however, usually used the original Horn, 1989, terminology and abbreviations.)

Aging patterns for the 14 WAIS-III subtests are grouped into four sets of graphs: Figure 5.8 (VCI plus Comprehension), Figure 5.9 (WMI), Figure 5.10 (POI plus Object Assembly), and Figure 5.11 (PSI plus Picture Arrangement). Three of the four subtests that measure verbal comprehension and expression (Figure 5.8) demonstrate a maintained-ability profile, but the age changes for Similarities denote a blend of maintained and vulnerable abilities, in keeping with its presumed blend of *Gc* and *Gf* components. From Figure 5.9, it is striking that each component WMI subtest has its own character-

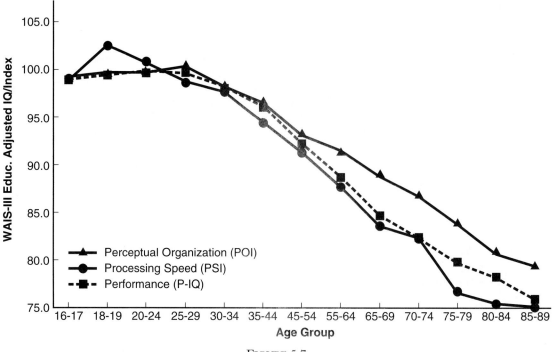

FIGURE 5.7

Mean "reference group" (ages 20–34) WAIS-III Indexes/IQs for scales composed of Performance subtests (Performance IQ, POI, PSI), by age, for adults ages 16–17 to 85–89 years, adjusted for educational attainment (values for ages 16–19 are unadjusted).

SOURCE: Standardization data of the Wechsler Adult Intelligence Scale: Third Edition. Copyright © 1997 by The Psychological Corporation. Used by permission. All rights reserved. Reprinted from Kaufman (2001) with permission.

istic age-by-age pattern of means. Digit Span, a prototypical measure of Horn's *Gsm* (also referred to as SAR), evidences the moderate degree of vulnerability associated with short-term memory ability (Horn & Hofer, 1992). Arithmetic, though considered to measure *Gsm* by Horn (1985, 1989), also measures school achievement and displays a maintained ability (*Gc*). Letter-Number Sequencing, in stark contrast to the other WMI tasks, displays a vulnerability that resembles closely the aging patterns for the Performance subtests. In contrast to the "within-Index" variability that characterizes the age-by-age graphs of the VCI and WMI subtests, the graphs for the four subtests that assess nonverbal reasoning and visual–motor coordination (in-

cluding the three that make up the POI) are nearly identical (Figure 5.10), as are the graphs for the two PSI subtests (Figure 5.11).

Table 5.9 on page 151 presents, for each of the 14 WAIS-III subtests, the ages at which education-adjusted scaled scores were highest ("peak" ages) and lowest ("weak" ages), and also shows the difference (in *SD* units) between the extreme values. Peak ages for the separate Verbal subtests tended to mirror V-IQ and VCI (about age 50), although the aberrant, vulnerable subtests of Digit Span and Letter-Number Sequencing peaked at age 22, and the education-oriented Information subtest did not reach its peak until age 67. Weak ages for Verbal subtests were age 87 except for the two subtests with the most ex-

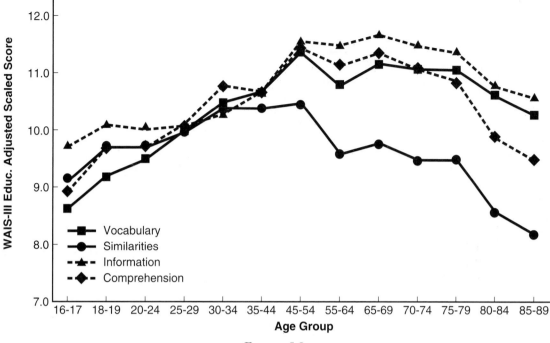

FIGURE 5.8

Mean "reference group" scaled scores on the Verbal Comprehension subtests, plus Comprehension, for adults ages 16–17 to 85–89 years, adjusted for education (values for ages 16–19 are unadjusted).

SOURCE: Standardization data of the Wechsler Adult Intelligence Scale: Third Edition. Copyright © 1997 by The Psychological Corporation. Used by permission. All rights reserved. Reprinted from Kaufman (2000, Figure 4) with permission.

tremely negative age–education gradients (Vocabulary and Information; see Table 5.7) that produced their lowest scaled scores at age 22. The most vulnerable subtests—all seven Performance subtests plus Letter-Number Sequencing—tended to peak early (age 22 or 27) and produce their lowest scores at age 87. These eight very vulnerable subtests also produced huge differences between peak and weak ages (about 1.5 *SD*) compared to moderate differences for the remaining six Verbal subtests (about 0.67 *SD*). Peak ages for the WJ III scales are generally consistent with the WAIS-III data (see Chapter 14, especially Figures 14.1–14.3), although the WJ III data were not adjusted for education.

The results depicted in Figures 5.10 and 5.11 and in Table 5.9 are also important for theoretical and clinical reasons. From Horn's theory, the POI is composed of subtests that are primarily measures of *Gv* (Picture Completion), *Gf* (Matrix Reasoning), or both *Gv* and *Gf* (Block Design). Nonetheless, all three subtests have aging patterns that are virtually identical. Additionally, Matrix Reasoning and the subtest it replaced on the regular Performance Scale and on the POI—Object Assembly—have nearly identical aging patterns. At least from the perspective of age-to-age changes in ability across the life span, the substitution of Matrix Reasoning for Object Assembly in the WAIS-III is given empirical justification.

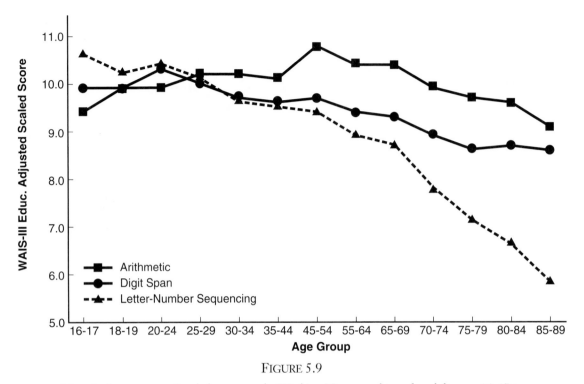

FIGURE 5.9

Mean "reference group" scaled scores on the Working Memory subtests for adults ages 16–17 to 85–89 years, adjusted for education (values for ages 16–19 are unadjusted).

SOURCE: Standardization data of the Wechsler Adult Intelligence Scale: Third Edition. Copyright © 1997 by The Psychological Corporation. Used by permission. All rights reserved. Reprinted from Kaufman (2000, Figure 5) with permission.

Even more important is the fact that, unlike all other Wechsler Performance subtests, ever since their inception in 1939, Matrix Reasoning is untimed—no bonus points, no time limits, no stopwatch needed. Yet, its aging pattern is virtually the same as the highly speeded Block Design and Object Assembly subtests. That finding argues against Botwinick's (1977) speeded–nonspeeded hypothesis and in favor of Horn's vulnerable–maintained hypothesis.

Parker's (1986) Studies of Global IQ Peak Performance on Wechsler's Scales

Peak performance with education controlled on V-IQ and P-IQ and their respective subtests has

been discussed previously. Also of interest is peak performance on Wechsler's FS-IQ without a control for education to address the issue of which age group scores highest on an IQ test, ignoring cohort differences and focusing on peak global IQ performance across generations. Parker studied this "peak" phenomenon for global intelligence using as his data sources the three Wechsler standardizations (W-B I, WAIS, WAIS-R) plus three additional fairly representative samples tested between 1916 and 1931: Terman (1916), Jones and Conrad (1933), and Miles and Miles (1932).

KEY FINDINGS. Parker observed the following ages of peak global performance on IQ tests (we

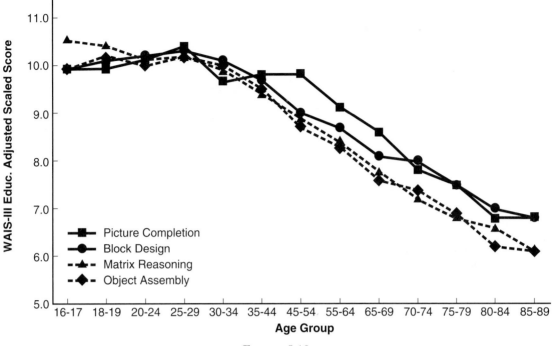

FIGURE 5.10

Mean "reference group" scaled scores on Perceptual Organization subtests, plus Object Assembly, for adults ages 16–17 to 85–89 years, adjusted for education (values for ages 16–19 are unadjusted).

SOURCE: Standardization data of the Wechsler Adult Intelligence Scale: Third Edition. Copyright © 1997 by The Psychological Corporation. Used by permission. All rights reserved. Reprinted from Kaufman (2000, Figure 2) with permission.

added 1995 data for the WAIS-III based on the uncorrected values of WAIS-III FS-IQ reported by Kaufman, 2001, and shown in Table 5.8):

Year Tested	Peak Age
1916	16
1926	20
1931	18.5
1937	22
1953	27
1978	30
1995	39.5

These results show that global intelligence, uncorrected for cohort variables such as educa-

tional attainment, tends to reach a peak later in life with each succeeding generation. WAIS-III data—added to Parker's data on the WAIS-R, WAIS, W-B I, early editions of the Stanford-Binet, and related IQ tests from the early part of the twentieth century—suggest a steady increase in the peak performance of adolescents and adults between 1916 and 1995. This generational pattern reinforces findings by Flynn (1984, 1987) that scores on intelligence tests are increasing in the United States at the rate of 3 points per decade (see Chapter 2). However, the continuing generational trend is not conclusive for two reasons. First, from Table 5.8, it is evident from the column of unadjusted FS-IQs that the means are trivially larger for ages 35–44 than for ages 25–29 and 30–34 (101.1 vs. 99.9). In addition,

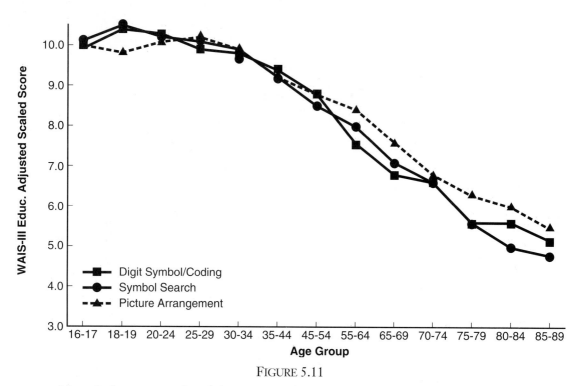

FIGURE 5.11

Mean "reference group" scaled scores on the Processing Speed subtests, plus Picture Arrangement, for adults ages 16–17 to 85–89 years, adjusted for education (values for ages 16–19 are unadjusted).

SOURCE: Standardization data of the Wechsler Adult Intelligence Scale: Third Edition. Copyright © 1997 by The Psychological Corporation. Used by permission. All rights reserved. Reprinted from Kaufman (2000, Figure 3) with permission.

the observed pattern may not generalize to intelligence tests that are theory-based or otherwise do not conform to the Binet-Wechsler model of IQ tests. On the KAIT, for example, whose standardization data were obtained about 1990, Composite IQ peaked at age 22 (Kaufman & Kaufman, 1993, Table 8.6). KAIT Composite IQ is a blend of Fluid IQ and Crystallized IQ.

Cross-Sectional Investigations of Kaufman and Kaufman's Adult Tests

Kaufman and his colleagues conducted a series of studies to examine the patterns of education-corrected mean scores across the adult life span on

the Kaufman Adolescent and Adult Intelligence Test (KAIT; Kaufman & Kaufman, 1993), Kaufman Brief Intelligence Test (K-BIT; Kaufman & Kaufman, 1990), Kaufman Functional Academic Skills Test (K-FAST; Kaufman & Kaufman, 1994a), and Kaufman Short Neuropsychological Assessment Procedure (K-SNAP; Kaufman & Kaufman, 1994b). Consult Chapter 13 for a thorough treatment of the KAIT and Chapter 15 for discussions of the K-BIT, K-FAST, and K-SNAP.

Kaufman and Horn's (1996) KAIT Investigation at Ages 17 to 94 Years

The KAIT standardization sample at ages 17–19 through to 75–94 years (N = 1,500) served as the data source for Kaufman and Horn's (1996) study

TABLE 5.9 "Peak" and "Weak" ages of performance on the 14 WAIS-III subtests, based on scaled scores adjusted for educational attainment

Subtest	Peak Age	Weak Age	Peak Age Group	Weak Age Group	Scaled-Score Range (*SD* units)
			Mean Education-Adjusted Scaled Score		
Verbal					
Vocabulary	49.5	22	11.4	9.5	1.9 (0.63 *SD*)
Similarities	49.5	87	10.5	8.2	2.3 (0.77 *SD*)
Arithmetic	49.5	87	10.8	9.1	1.7 (0.57 *SD*)
Digit Span	22	77 & 87	10.3	8.6	1.7 (0.57 *SD*)
Information	67	22	11.7	10.0	1.7 (0.57 *SD*)
Comprehension	49.5	87	11.5	9.5	2.0 (0.67 *SD*)
Letter-Number Sequencing	22	87	10.4	5.8	4.6 (1.53 *SD*)
Performance					
Picture Completion	27	84.5	10.4	6.8	3.6 (1.20 *SD*)
Digit Symbol—Coding	22	87	10.3	5.2	5.1 (1.70 *SD*)
Block Design	27	87	10.3	6.8	3.5 (1.17 *SD*)
Matrix Reasoning	27	87	10.2	6.1	4.1 (1.37 *SD*)
Picture Arrangement	27	87	10.2	5.5	4.7 (1.57 *SD*)
Symbol Search	22	87	10.2	4.8	5.4 (1.80 *SD*)
Object Assembly	27	87	10.2	6.1	4.1 (1.37 *SD*)

NOTE: Peak Age and Weak Age equal the *midpoint* of the age group (or adjacent age groups) having the highest (or lowest) mean scaled scores (adjusted for educational attainment) earned by the 11 separate age groups between 20–24 and 85–89 years. Scaled scores are based on the reference group ages 20–34 years. Values for ages 20 to 89 years are adjusted for the educational attainment of age groups 25–29 and 30–34 years.

Data are from Kaufman (2000a). Standardization data of the Wechsler Adult Intelligence Scale: Third Edition. Copyright © 1997 by The Psychological Corporation. Used by permission. All rights reserved.

of age changes in women and men on the KAIT IQ scales and subtest scores. The sample was subdivided into 13 age groups with sample sizes ranging from 86–150. Of particular interest are the results for Fluid IQ and Crystallized IQ, which served as dependent variables in a MANCOVA in which Age and Gender were independent variables and Educational Attainment was the covariate. To permit comparisons across age groups, a special "All-Adult" norms table was developed for all adults between ages 17 and 94 years.

KEY FINDINGS. A significant *F* value was obtained for Age, but not for Gender or for the Age × Gender interaction in the MANCOVA. In follow-up univariate ANCOVAs, the *F* values for Age were significant for both Fluid IQ and Crystallized IQ. The education-adjusted and gender-adjusted mean Fluid and Crystallized IQs from ages 17–19 to 75–94 years are shown in Figure 5.12. As for Wechsler's adult scales, the *Gc*-IQ is a maintained ability and *Gf*-IQ is vulnerable to the effects of age. Similar to the data for the WAIS-III, KAIT

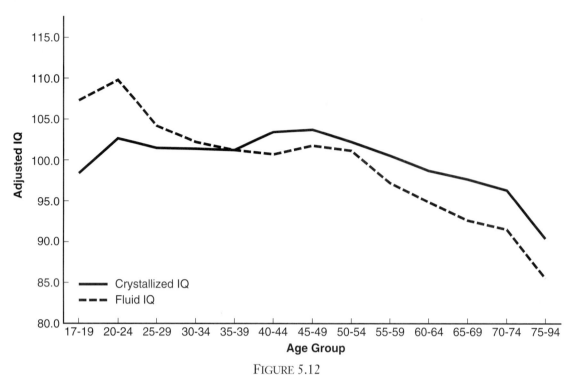

FIGURE 5.12

Mean KAIT Crystallized and Fluid IQs (based on norms for ages 17–94 and adjusted for gender and education) for adults aged 17–94 years.

SOURCE: Reprinted from Kaufman and Horn (1996, Figure 1) with permission.

Gc-IQ peaked at ages 45–49 and *Gf*-IQ peaked at ages 20–24.

Based on Tukey's Honestly Significant Differences (HSD) test, mean KAIT *Gc*-IQ increased significantly from ages 17–19 to 20–24, but the means did not differ significantly between ages 20–24 and 55–59. The most noteworthy drop in mean scores occurred in the mid-70s. On the KAIT *Gf*-IQ, means dropped significantly in the mid-20s, but then reached a plateau between ages 25–29 and 50–54. As of ages 55–59, decreases in mean scores with increasing age were steady, reaching a low point of 85.4 for the oldest sample (ages 75–94). The plateau from ages 25 to 54 on KAIT *Gf*-IQ did not occur for WAIS-R or WAIS-III P-IQ or for WAIS-III POI and PSI. This difference in the results for KAIT versus

Wechsler adult scales may be related to the fact that speed of visual–motor performance is highly rewarded on the Wechsler scales but not on the KAIT Fluid subtests. However, the fact that the aging profile for the untimed WAIS-III Matrix Reasoning subtest did *not* display a plateau between the mid-20s and mid-50s weakens that hypothesis. Furthermore, the similarities in the vulnerable profiles for the Wechsler and Kaufman adult *Gf* scales are far more compelling than any differences in the shapes of the graphs. Results from *Gf* and *Gc* scales on both comprehensive IQ tests, KAIT and WAIS-III, are strongly supportive of Horn's theory.

The three regularly administered KAIT *Gc* subtests and the alternate *Gc* subtest (Famous Faces) displayed extremely similar maintained aging patterns, as did all four KAIT *Gf* subtests, including the alternate (Memory for Block Designs), and displayed extremely similar vulnerable aging patterns (Kaufman & Kaufman, 1993, Tables 8.1 and 8.2). However, the ANCOVA for two of the *Gc* subtests (Definitions and Auditory Comprehension and Definitions) produced significant Age X Gender interactions; aging patterns for the *Gc* subtests differed to some extent—especially below age 30—for separate groups of women and men (Kaufman & Horn, 1996, Figures 2 and 3).

Wang and Kaufman's (1993) K-BIT Investigation at Ages 20 to 90 Years

The adult portion of the two-subtest K-BIT standardization sample (N = 500) was divided into eight age groups between 20–24 and 70–90 years for Wang and Kaufman's aging study. Sample sizes ranged from 43 to 79. The Vocabulary subtest was the measure of *Gc* and the Matrices subtest assessed *Gf*. Two two-way ANCOVAs (one for each subtest) were conducted with Age and Gender serving as independent variables and educational attainment as the covariate. To achieve a common adult norm, standard scores for all individuals were based on the norms for ages 25–34 years.

KEY FINDINGS. A significant F value was obtained for Age, but not for Gender or for the Age X Gender interaction in each ANCOVA. In follow-up univariate ANCOVAs, the F values for Age were significant for both Fluid IQ and Crystallized IQ. Figure 5.13 shows the age-by-age patterns for both the *Gc* and *Gf* subtests. Once again, *Gc* displays a maintained ability pattern, peaking at ages 40–49 years, and *Gf* reveals a vulnerable pattern with peak performance at age 25–29 years.

Tukey's HSD analysis showed that none of the mean *Gc* scores for ages 20–24 through 60–69 differed significantly from each other; only the oldest group—ages 70 to 90 years—"tailed off." In contrast, Tukey's HSD analysis produced nu-

merous significant discrepancies between pairs of mean scores. The six age groups between 20–24 and 50–59 did not differ significantly from each other, but these groups, in almost every instance, outscored adults ages 60–69 and 70–90. Like the KAIT *Gf*-IQ (but unlike Wechsler's P-IQ), the K-BIT measure of *Gf* demonstrated a decided plateau during the middle of the life span.

Kaufman, Kaufman, Chen, and Kaufman's (1996) Investigation of Six Horn Abilities at Ages 15 to 94 Years

To investigate age-by-age patterns of mean education-corrected standard scores on a broad array of abilities from Horn's (1989; Horn & Noll, 1997) expanded and refined *Gf–Gc* theory, Kaufman, Kaufman, Chen et al. (1996) used the standardization data from 1,193 adolescents and adults (ages 15–94 years) who were administered the K-FAST, K-SNAP, and two of the supplementary subtests from the KAIT Expanded Battery. They investigated seven subtests from these tests to measure six Horn abilities: *Gc* (K-FAST Reading), *Gf* (K-SNAP Four-Letter Words), *Gq* or quantitative knowledge (K-FAST Arithmetic), *Gv* or visual processing (K-SNAP Gestalt Closure), *Gsm* or short-term acquisition and retrieval (K-SNAP Number Recall), and *Glr* or long-term storage and retrieval (KAIT Rebus Delayed Recall and Auditory Delayed Recall). The sample was subdivided into 14 age groups from 15–16 to 75–94 years; sample sizes ranged from 60 to 124. Data from the entire sample of 15- to 94-year-olds were pooled to provide norms for all individuals. A two-way MANCOVA was conducted with Age and Gender as independent variables, the seven subtests as dependent variables, and educational attainment (mid-parent's education for 15–24, self-education for 25–94) as the covariate. Age and Gender were significant main effects but the interaction was not (gender differences are interpreted in Chapter 4). F values for all seven subtests were statistically significant in the follow-up univariate ANCOVAs. In addition, multiple regression analysis was conducted

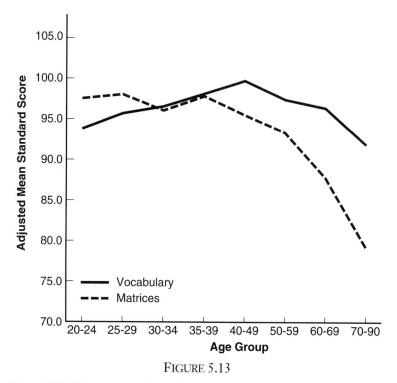

FIGURE 5.13

Mean K-BIT Vocabulary (*Gc*) and Matrices (*Gf*) standard scores (based on norms for ages 25–34), adjusted for education, for eight groups of adults between the ages of 20 and 90 years.

SOURCE: Reprinted from Wang and Kaufman (1993, Figure 1) with permission.

with educational attainment (self-education) and age as predictors of each of the seven subtests. The results of these regression analyses (based on *N* = 860 adults ages 25–94) permitted computation of age–education gradients, similar to the gradients reported by Heaton et al. (1986), shown in Table 5.7 for Wechsler's adult scales.

KEY FINDINGS. The measures of *Gc* and *Gq* displayed maintained age-by-age patterns (see Figure 5.14), consistent with Horn's (1989; Horn & Hofer, 1992) predictions and with results on Wechsler's V-IQ, VCI, and Arithmetic subtest. In contrast, but in keeping with Horn's predictions, the tests that measure *Gf* and *Gv* demonstrated quite vulnerable aging patterns. Though the *Gv* subtest (K-SNAP Gestalt Closure) is a Wechsler-

like measure of Perceptual Organization, most resembling Picture Completion, the *Gf* subtest (K-SNAP Four-Letter Words) is totally different from Wechsler's Performance subtests. This novel task requires no visual–spatial ability, but, instead, measures fluid reasoning ability with semantic stimuli. Note in Figure 5.14 that the graph for the *Gf* subtest has a plateau during the middle of the adult life span, similar to KAIT Fluid IQ and K-BIT Matrices, but different from the steady decline (after age 34) of the Kaufman measure of *Gv* and the steady decline of Wechsler's Performance subtests.

On the maintained abilities, *Gc* and *Gq*, Tukey's HSD test revealed that mean scores increased significantly from the adolescent years (ages 15–19) to the young adult groups. Then,

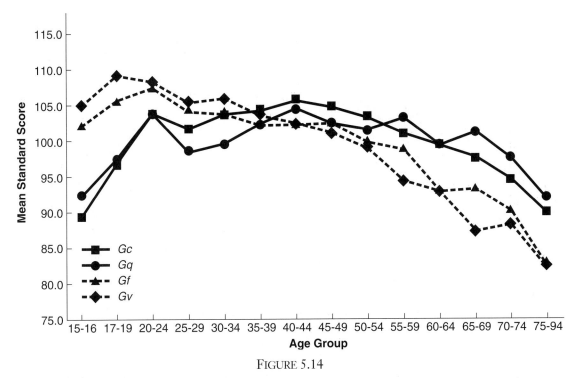

FIGURE 5.14

Mean *Gc* (K-FAST Reading), *Gf* (K-SNAP Four-Letter Words), *Gq* (K-FAST Arithmetic), and *Gv* (K-SNAP Gestalt Closure) standard scores (based on norms for ages 15–94 years), adjusted for education, for 14 groups of adults between the ages of 15 and 94 years.

NOTE: *Gc* = (K-FAST Reading); *Gq* = (K-FAST Arithmetic); *Gf* = (K-SNAP Four-Letter Words); *Gv* = (K-SNAP Gestalt Closure).

SOURCE: Graphs developed from data presented by Kaufman et al. (1996, Tables 4, 5, and 7) with permission.

abilities were maintained through the late 60s before scores declined in the 70s, notably at age 75 and older. Peak performance was at ages 40–44 on both *Gc* and *Gq*. On the vulnerable abilities of *Gf* and *Gv*, adults ages 50–54 scored nearly 0.5 *SD* (6–7 IQ points) higher than adults ages 60–64 and about 1.0 *SD* (14–17 IQ points) higher than the oldest sample (ages 75–94). Peak performance was at ages 20–24 on *Gf* and at ages 17–19 on *Gq*.

Horn and Hofer (1992) classified *Glr* (also called TSR, long-term storage and retrieval) as a maintained ability, as opposed to short-term memory, which they consider vulnerable: "several studies showing that in the same samples in which *Gsm* declines with age in adulthood, *Glr* does not decline and, in some samples, increases"

(p. 69). However, Horn and his colleagues have typically studied *Glr* with tasks that involve words and verbal learning. The KAIT measures of *Glr* include one task (Auditory Delayed Recall) that resembles Horn's tasks and one that does not (Rebus Delayed Recall). Figure 5.15 displays age-by-age education-adjusted means for these two measures of long-term retrieval and the graphs are quite different from each other. The Auditory task displayed a maintained pattern across the life span, but the Rebus task revealed a vulnerable pattern. Both tasks measure recall of information learned about 30–45 minutes earlier in the KAIT administration. The Delayed Auditory subtest measures retention of information presented as part of a mock news

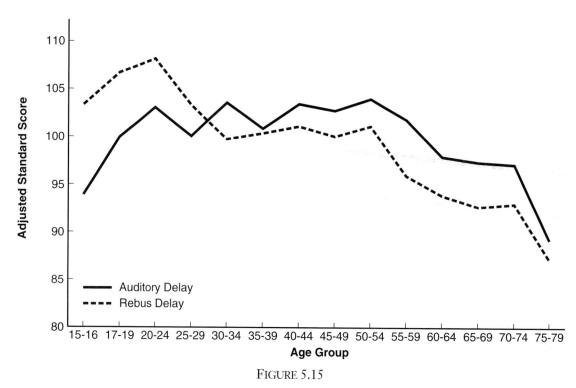

FIGURE 5.15

Mean standard scores on two measures of *Glr* (KAIT Rebus Delayed Recall and KAIT Auditory Delayed Recall), based on norms for ages 15–94 and adjusted for education, for 14 groups of adults between the ages of 15 and 94 years.

SOURCE: Reprinted from Kaufman et al. (1996, Figure 1) with permission.

broadcast in the Crystallized Auditory Comprehension subtest; the Delayed Rebus task assesses how well individuals remember the words that are paired with unfamiliar symbols (rebuses) in the Fluid learning task known as Rebus Learning. Even though the initial subtests are administered a few minutes apart, as are the two delayed-recall tasks, how much a person remembers from each initial subtest is quite dependent on his or her age.

As Figure 5.15 indicates, adolescents ages 15–16 earned mean scores that were about 9 points *higher* on Rebus Delayed Recall than on Auditory Delayed Recall; in contrast, elderly adults (ages 65 and above) scored about 3 points *lower* on the Rebus subtest than on the Auditory subtest. Horn (personal communication, September 1994) con-

sidered the different patterns for the two *Glr* tasks suggestive of "intriguing hypotheses" about the storage, consolidation, and retrieval of information. In the Kaufman, Kaufman, Chen et al. (1996) study, the aging pattern for long-term retrieval tasks depended on the material to be recalled: When the stimuli were learned during a *Gc* task, the amount of retention displayed a *Gc*-like maintained pattern; when the stimuli were learned during a *Gf* task, the pattern of retention was vulnerable to the effects of aging. Data for the WJ III *Glr* scale, which measures long-term retrieval with tasks that resemble KAIT's Fluid subtest (Rebus Learning), are consistent with Kaufman et al.'s finding: This WJ III scale demonstrates a vulnerable pattern (see Chapter 14), although the data are tentative because education was not controlled. The results with the KAIT and WJ III require cross-validation, especially with longer delays between initial learning and later recall. Though the KAIT interval of 30 to 45 minutes clearly qualifies as measuring *Glr* and not *Gsm* from a Horn standpoint, it is nonetheless true that Horn and colleagues (e.g., Horn & Hofer, 1992; Horn & Risberg, 1989) have been primarily interested in storage for hours, weeks, or years when investigating and theorizing about *Glr*. Furthermore, the use of Horn's terminology to define memory tasks is one of many theoretical approaches that can be taken. For example, in the next section, the aging patterns observed for WMS-III scales are interpreted within an episodic versus semantic memory context (Tulving, 1983), and there are numerous other ways of categorizing distinctions among memory tasks, and of interpreting changes due to aging from cognitive and neuropsychological perspectives (Craik & Salthouse, 2000).

Age–education gradients were computed for each of the seven subtests investigated by Kaufman, Kaufman, Chen et al. (1996) based on a multiple regression analysis conducted for ages 25–94 years. Table 5.10 presents these gradients, listed from the most age-related to the most education-related subtest. The measure of *Gv* was easily the most related to age, followed by the measure of *Gf*, whereas *Gq* and *Gc* were most related to education. These results are quite similar to the findings for the WAIS, WAIS-R, and WAIS-III subtests (see Table 5.7). The age–education gradients show again how different the two *Glr* tasks were, with the gradient for the Rebus task fairly similar to the gradient for the *Gf* measure and the gradient for the Auditory task close to the value for the *Gc* test.

TABLE 5.10   Age–education gradients on Kaufman and Kaufman subtests that measure different Horn abilities

Horn Ability (Kaufman Subtest)	% Age Variance	% Education Variance	Age–Education Gradient
Gv—Broad visualization (K-SNAP Gestalt Closure)	32.0	15.5	+16.5
Gf—Fluid reasoning (K-SNAP Four-Letter Words)	26.4	21.9	+4.5
Glr—Long-term storage & retrieval (KAIT Rebus Delayed Recall)	18.0	22.2	−4.2
Gsm—Short-term acquisition & retrieval (K-SNAP Number Recall)	13.0	20.0	−7.0
Glr—Long-term storage & retrieval (KAIT Auditory Delayed Recall)	13.0	31.8	−18.8
Gc—Crystallized knowledge (K-FAST Reading)	17.5	40.9	−23.4
Gq—Quantitative thinking (K-FAST Arithmetic)	8.7	38.1	−29.4

NOTE: Age–education gradient equals age variance minus education variance. Positive values denote the more age-related subtests, while negative values indicate the tasks more heavily dependent on education. Subtests are listed in order of gradients for the seven Kaufman and Kaufman subtests.

Heaton and Colleagues' Cross-Sectional Investigation of Wechsler Memory Scale—III

In addition to analyzing education-controlled aging data for the WAIS-III, Heaton and colleagues (Heaton et al., 2001; Manly et al., 2000) conducted similar analyses for the major memory indexes yielded by the WMS-III. In each WMS-III study, data were analyzed for ages 20 to 89 years, although sample sizes, composed of standardization cases and additional "education oversampling" cases differed in the two reports: $N = 885$ for Heaton et al. (2001) and $N = 1,089$ for Manly et al. (2000). To permit age-by-age comparisons, all standard scores were based on norms for ages 20–34 years and statistically corrected for education.

KEY FINDINGS.   Heaton et al. (2001) compared z scores for the age group earning the lowest education-corrected mean index (ages 85–89 in each case) and the highest mean index (usually ages 20–24), as well as the difference between these indexes in SD units. The fact that the peak age is 20–24 years for six of the indexes (Auditory Delayed Recognition and Working Memory were exceptions) indicates the vulnerability of these abilities to the normal aging process. The differences between high and low means in SD units, which exceeded 1.5 SD for five indexes and ranged from 1.20 to 1.76 SD, further illustrates the vulnerability of both the immediate and delayed recall scales on the WMS-III, although the three measures of delayed recall were clearly the most vulnerable: The largest effect sizes (about 1.6–1.7 SD) were obtained for General Memory, Auditory Delayed, and Visual Delayed. Compare the WMS-III effect sizes with the values of the WAIS-III indexes, also reported by Heaton et al. (2001) using analogous techniques: PSI (1.9), POI (1.5), WMI (1.1), and VCI (0.6). The values for most WMS-III indexes are commensurate with the value for POI.

The delayed recall indexes, both auditory and visual, are both quite vulnerable to the effects of age. In contrast, the auditory delayed recognition index is a more maintained ability, as depicted in graphs presented by Manly et al. (2000). The auditory delayed recall and delayed recognition tasks are a combination of performance on delayed memory of a story (which has a Gc component) and delayed recall of paired associates (which is a learning task with a Gf component). The visual delayed recall test is a combination of memory of faces and memory of family pictures, both with a substantial Gv component, resembling Gv subtests on the Woodcock-Johnson Tests of Cognitive Ability, both the WJ-R and WJ III (see Chapter 14). The immediate and delayed conditions are separated by about 25 to 35 minutes, similar to the interval for the KAIT Delayed Recall subtests.

The findings for the WMS-III reinforce the findings for the KAIT delayed memory subtests and the WJ III Glr scale (see Chapter 14). Contrary to Horn's prediction that long-term retrieval is unilaterally a maintained ability, the nature of the material to be recalled is instrumental in determining the shape of the aging curve. When the initial learning involves a vulnerable ability like Gf or Gv, then the long-term retrieval likewise displays a vulnerable pattern.

A comparison of the aging patterns for the highly vulnerable auditory delayed recall index versus the moderately maintained auditory delayed recognition index also suggests an additional amendment to Horn's predictions: Even when the content of the tasks is held constant, different aging patterns may emerge whether adults are asked to recall the material or recognize it.

Finally, Heaton et al. (2001) data indicate that the WMS-III immediate memory indexes generally have substantially larger high–low differences in SD units (1.3–1.5) than the WAIS-III WMI (1.1). The mildly vulnerable pattern found for the WAIS-III WMI, akin to Horn's Gsm, is a blend of three distinctly different patterns for each of the three component subtests (as mentioned earlier and depicted in Figure 5.9). The subtest that most captures the essence of Horn's Gsm is WAIS-III Digit Span. None of the WMS-III subtests is very similar to the basically simple Digit Span. The auditory paired associates task, for example, requires learning ability and Gf, and is not really an immediate recall task in the true sense of the term. Other WMS-III subtests, as indicated, have components of Gc and Gv and are far more complex than Digit Span. Interestingly, both the WAIS-III and WMS-III yield Working Memory Indexes, yet they are quite different from each other even though *both* include Letter-Number Sequencing. On the WAIS-III, the WMI reflects a blend of skills, whereas the two-subtest Index of the same name on the WMS-III includes Spatial Span—which, like Letter-Number Sequencing, measures Gv as well as Gsm—leading to the extreme vulnerability of the WMS-III Working Memory Index.

The WMS-III results are consistent with the literature on memory and aging, which is often interpreted within the context of Tulving's (1983) distinction between episodic and semantic memory. *Episodic memory* refers to personally experienced events or episodes and is assessed experimentally with immediate or delayed recall of word lists, geometric designs, text, faces, and so forth (as well as with more personally oriented tasks requiring individuals to recall things that occurred to them at a particular time or within a specific context). In contrast, *semantic memory* reflects general world knowledge and is often assessed with tests of information, naming ability, or vocabulary. All of the WMS-III tasks and scales fit into the category of episodic memory. The vulnerability of the WMS-III scales is consistent with the burgeoning literature on age changes in episodic memory that usually reports notable declines with aging on immediate recall, delayed recall, and delayed recognition of a variety of verbal and nonverbal stimuli (e.g., Korten et al., 1997; Souchay, Isingrini, & Espagnet, 2000). Even an elite sample of elderly professors at Berkeley (ages 60–71) performed much more poorly than middle-aged professors (ages 45–59) and young professors (ages 30–44) on a verbal paired-associate learning task (Shimamura, Berry, Mangels, Rusting, & Jurica, 1995). In contrast, semantic memory displays a maintained pattern with little variability across most of the adult life span before declining systematically and gradually in very old age (Backman, Small, Wahlin, & Larsson, 2000).

In general, the experimental psychology literature on memory and aging mimics the findings of the studies of the Wechsler and Kaufman tests: Episodic memory—like fluid intelligence, processing speed, visualization, and the memory abilities assessed by the WMS-III and KAIT—is quite vulnerable to the effects of aging, in contrast to semantic memory and the related construct of crystallized intelligence, both of which are maintained abilities that do not decline appreciably until old age. There also seems to be a maintained aging pattern for tasks that might technically fall within the episodic-memory domain, but have a clear-cut Gc component such as recalling the main facts in a mock news broadcast (KAIT Auditory Comprehension and Delayed Auditory Recall) or repeating prose passages that contain factual content. Both of the KAIT memory tasks displayed maintained aging patterns (Kaufman & Horn, 1996; Kaufman et al., 1996). Also, the elderly Berkeley professors who performed so poorly on a paired-associate memory task performed as well as young and middle-aged professors when repeating prose passages about a woman who was robbed (WMS-R Logical Memory), the elements that make up the earth's atmosphere, and the tribal cultures in the Mississippian period (Shimamura et al., 1995).

Overview of Cross-Sectional Investigations

The Wechsler adult scales have been in use for more than 60 years, and data on several versions of these scales have been analyzed cross-sectionally, with controls for cohort differences in education, for several generations. Though occasionally the results of an investigation have led to conclusions that suggested little or no decline in P-IQ with advancing age (e.g., Green's, 1969, study of Puerto Rican adults with very limited formal education), the preponderance of evidence accumulated over time has supported a steady and sometimes dramatic decline in P-IQ as individuals age from adolescence to old age. This decline has been accompanied by maintenance of V-IQ through middle age and occasionally the 60s, before a notable decrease in verbal ability as adults reach their seventh and eighth decades of life.

These aging patterns have been interpreted from a Horn-Cattell (Horn & Cattell, 1966, 1967) standpoint as denoting the vulnerability of fluid intelligence or *Gf* in the face of maintenance of crystallized intelligence or *Gc*. Some researchers, notably Woodcock (1990) and Flanagan and McGrew (1997), insist that Wechsler's P-IQ denotes *only Gv*, with virtually no *Gf* at all, but that position is arguable (Kaufman, 1994a, 2000b). Horn believes that Wechsler's Performance subtests (except for highly speeded tasks like Digit Symbol-Coding) measure a blend of *Gf* and *Gv* (Horn & Hofer, 1992), and that interpretation is consistent both with the accumulated research and with examiners' clinical observations of the clear-cut problem-solving components of tasks like Block Design and Picture Arrangement. Yet, the tasks, including WAIS-III Matrix Reasoning, definitely involve visual–spatial ability also. P-IQ and POI seem to be dependent on both *Gf* and *Gv*, and untangling them seems futile.

Data from the Kaufman and Kaufman tests clarify the issue to some extent. The KAIT includes measures of *Gf*, notably Mystery Codes and Logical Steps, that emphasize reasoning ability without stressing visualization. K-SNAP includes one measure of *Gf* (Four-Letter Words) that has no discernible *Gv* component at all and includes one measure of *Gv* (Gestalt Closure) that apparently requires no *Gf*. All of these Kaufman subtests demonstrated extremely vulnerable patterns for measures that are primarily *Gf* and for measures that are primarily *Gv*; these findings are also reinforced by the growth curves for WJ III cognitive scales, although those curves were not adjusted for educational attainment (see Chapter 14, especially Figures 14.1–14.3). The WMS-III immediate and delayed scales, which include subtests that are dependent on *Gv*,

also evidenced extreme vulnerability to aging. Therefore, the best conclusion is that the aging declines observed for WAIS, WAIS-R, and WAIS-III P-IQ—and for WAIS-III POI—reflect the vulnerability of *both Gf* and *Gv* from Horn's theoretical perspective. Even more dramatically, a decline occurs for *Gs* or broad speediness. From Baltes's theory, the "mechanics" component is vulnerable to the effects of normal aging and subsumes all of these Horn abilities: reasoning, spatial orientation, and perceptual speed (Baltes, 1997; Baltes, Staudinger, & Lindenberger, 1999).

Taken together, the data from the Kaufman tests (KAIT, K-BIT, K-SNAP, K-FAST) and the Wechsler adult scales offer broad-based support for the increase and then maintenance of *Gc* ("pragmatics" to Baltes) across much of the life span before notable declines occur during the 70s and 80s. At the same time, this accumulation of data from the Wechsler and Kaufman tests offers equally pervasive support for the peaking of *Gf* and *Gv* abilities in early adulthood (usually 20–24 years) followed by declines that continue throughout adulthood and old age. The findings of maintained *Gc* abilities and vulnerable *Gf* abilities—including the approximate magnitude of the declines in *Gf* ability with increasing age, and the ultimate decline in *Gc* in very old age—are also consistent with age-related changes in intelligence observed in well-designed, large-scale, cross-sectional studies conducted in Europe (i.e., Rabbitt's, 1993, investigation of more than 6,000 adults ages 50–96 in the United Kingdom, and Baltes & Lindenberger's, 1997, study of 687 adults ages 25–103 in Germany). Data collected prior to 1980 suggest that *Gc*, once adjusted for educational differences among age groups, peaks in the 60s. However, the more recent data integrated in this chapter from the Kaufman tests (late 1980s and early 1990s) and WAIS-III (mid-1990s) indicate an earlier peak in the 40s. Why this generational shift has occurred is not clear.

The overall findings for IQ versus memory variables, regarding patterns of maintenance and vulnerability, can be interpreted jointly. As noted, *Gc* and semantic memory tasks display maintained aging patterns across most of the life span (with both declining in old age), while *Gf*, *Gv*, and episodic memory tasks are extremely vulnerable to the normal aging process. "There are interesting parallels with regard to the cognitive processes involved during task performance, with semantic memory and crystallized intelligence drawing largely on prior knowledge and episodic memory and fluid intelligence requiring new learning and flexible adjustments to new situational demands" (Backman, Small, Wahlin, & Larsson, 2000, p. 503). In addition, tasks akin to episodic memory are included—along with tests of fluid reasoning, processing speed, and visualization—as measures of mechanics from Baltes's pragmatics–mechanics dichotomy (Lindenberger & Baltes, 1997). The evidence is conflicting on whether the parallel declines in old age on *Gf* and episodic memory are due to the same cause or set of causes. There is some evidence from a study by Isingrini and Taconnat (1998) with 318 adults (aged 20–40 and 60–85) that the simultaneous declines on *Gf* and episodic memory tasks are two fairly separate phenomena. In addition, data from a longitudinal study of 387 healthy old people (ages 70–88 years) who were retested four years later revealed differences in prediction from time 1 to time 2 for measures of fluid ability (matrices) versus episodic memory (Wechsler's Logical Memory) (Deary, Starr, & MacLennan, 1998). Demographic variables, blood pressure, and measures of premorbid IQ accounted for nearly 40% of the reliable variance in fluid intelligence compared to 12% of the memory variance; also, blood pressure at the initial testing was related to subsequent fluid ability but not to episodic memory differences (Deary et al., 1998). In contrast to the studies that suggest separate explanations for the vulnerability of *Gf* and episodic memory is a series of studies with adults in their 70s and 80s by Backman, Hill, and their colleagues (e.g., Backman et al., 1998) that report substantial correlations between measures of *Gf* and both verbal and nonverbal episodic recall (though the heavy speed component of the *Gf* tasks in the Backman-Hill studies clouds the nature of the relationship to some extent).

Cautions Associated with Cross-Sectional Investigations

Despite the careful experimental designs of the cross-sectional investigations conducted on Wechsler's and Kaufman's adult scales, this type of study has a few built-in problems that must be considered, namely issues concerned with (1) equating on educational attainment, (2) cohort and time-of-measurement effects, and (3) internal and external validity.

Equating on Educational Attainment

All of the results discussed and integrated in this section are based on the interpretation of cross-sectional data that were matched or otherwise equated on adults' educational attainment. Matarazzo (1972) wondered whether years of formal education is "a variable with identical meaning across generations" (p. 115), and his concern has merit (Kaufman, 2001). Equating groups that differ substantially in age on educational attainment is an inexact science and must be considered as approximate correction for a changing society's inequalities. For example, schooling beyond high school, commonplace now, was enjoyed primarily by the elite in the 1950s. Indeed, about 50% of each age group between 20–24 and 45–54 had at least one year of college (see Table 5.2), making post-high school education "average" for young and middle-age adults in the WAIS-III sample. In contrast, only about 15–20% of adults ages 20–54 in the early 1950s (when the WAIS was standardized) had some college, as shown in Table 5.2. The meaning of "attended college" or "graduated college," therefore, is not a constant across generations; analogously "high school dropout" has a far greater stigma for younger than older adults in the 2000s than a half-century earlier.

"Years of formal schooling" is clearly not a perfect yardstick. Nonetheless, despite logical arguments to the contrary, there is some empirical evidence that this term may have a fairly constant meaning across the adult age range. Consider the provocative data in Table 5.4, which show that, regardless of age, and with only mild aberrations, individuals with a comparable amount of education earned similar scores on the WAIS-R Verbal Scale. Certainly Verbal skills are closely related to formal education; other things being equal, the greater the years of schooling, the greater the success on tests of general information, word meaning, and arithmetic ability. As shown in Table 5.4, mean Verbal sums of scaled scores for those with 0–8 years of schooling averaged about 40 *regardless of age*, and similar consistency across age was obtained for other educational categories as well. Thus, Verbal IQ, long known to be a maintained ability across much of the adult age range (Horn & Noll, 1997), was maintained within each of five different levels of educational attainment. Although this finding does not trivialize the concern of the inequality of the educational attainment yardstick, it does provide some empirical support for statistically controlling for education in the various cross-sectional investigations.

Cohort and
Time-of-Measurement Effects

Regardless of consistencies across studies, instruments, and generations, inferences from cross-sectional studies about developmental (ontogenetic) changes in intelligence are speculative at best. As long as different individuals compose the separate age samples, one can only guess at the nature of the age-related changes in intelligence in the same individuals over time. When education level is controlled, one aspect of cohort differences is eliminated to some extent. However, numerous other nonage and noneducation variables associated with growing up at a given period of time are either unknown, unmeasured, or unquantifiable. Yet such variables as motivation level, historical events, social customs and mores, the availability of television and personal computers, child-rearing techniques,

nutrition, the quality and extent of prenatal care and knowledge, and the impact of mass media will affect apparent age-related changes in scores on mental tests.

In addition, time-of-measurement effects interact with performance on intelligence tests. Real changes either in mental ability or in test-taking ability could affect how every group of adults (regardless of cohort) performs on a given test. These sweeping cultural changes could affect individuals aging from 25 to 35 in much the same way that they affect others who age from 40 to 50 during the same time frame. For example, in the 1920s, tests were uncommon for everyone, and scores would likely be relatively low for a person of 20 or 40 or 60 tested on unfamiliar items like verbal or figure analogies; people of the same ages tested in the 1960s or 1970s would likely score relatively higher on these same tests because such tests had become a familiar part of U.S. culture. This type of control for cultural change was used by Owens (1966) in his landmark longitudinal study (discussed later in this chapter).

Not all cultural changes relate to test-taking ability, however, as Flynn (1984, 1987) has made abundantly clear (see Chapter 2). Indeed, Flynn has probably come as close as anyone to quantifying these cultural or time-of-measurement effects by using cross-sectional data to show systematic IQ gains across generations. That these gains differ dramatically from country to country stresses their cultural–environmental origin. Because differences in IQs earned in different eras by individuals of the same age reflect both time-of-measurement and cohort effects, Kausler (1982, 1991) prefers to use the term *time lag* to denote these changes in intelligence scores.

Internal and External Validity

By controlling for education level in various cross-sectional studies, the investigators have conducted studies high in internal validity, permitting both the identification of causative factors and the generalization of these causative factors to other samples (Kausler, 1982, 1991).

Thus, apparent age-related declines in verbal intelligence may be attributed to educational attainment; declines with age in mean *Gs*, *Gf*, *Gv*, and *Gsm* scores are due partly to education, but mostly to age differences plus an unknown proportion of cohort variation. The downside of the high internal validity of the Wechsler and Kaufman age–education studies is low external validity, meaning poor generalization of the "adjusted" age differences to the population at large; in fact, in the real world, older individuals are less well educated than younger adults. Consequently, the actual, unadjusted values come closer to describing true differences in the mean scores of different age groups. With the WAIS-III, though, even the unadjusted values may not validly describe true differences in the population at large in view of the unusual number of exclusionary criteria applied to the selection of the standardization sample. However, unadjusted values cannot be used to infer causality of the differences, and they have limited value for implying developmental change. But education-balanced groups, according to Kausler (1982), "give a truer picture of ontogenetic change than our previous contrasts between educationally imbalanced age groups that were, nevertheless, representative of their respective populations" (p. 67). Because of the very nature of the limitations of cross-sectional research, it is essential that any conclusions about aging and IQ be buttressed by the results of longitudinal research.

DOES IQ DECLINE WITH ADVANCING AGE? A LONGITUDINAL APPROACH

Inferring developmental trends from cross-sectional data is risky, partly because of cohort effects and partly because of the failure to test the same individuals more than once. Longitudinal investigations of aging and intelligence solve both problems by holding constant cohort vari-

ance (each individual is, in effect, his or her own cohort control), and by observing developmental changes within the same person over time. In fact, longitudinal investigations of the Wechsler-Bellevue (Berkowitz & Green, 1963) and WAIS (Eisdorfer & Wilkie, 1973) have generally shown little age-related decline in ability, far less than has been revealed by cross-sectional analysis, with or without an education control. Unfortunately, longitudinal studies of intelligence and aging are beset by problems different from the disadvantages of cross-sectional studies but nonetheless potentially debilitating.

In the next sections we discuss some of these pitfalls, especially in studies using Wechsler's adult tests. We then treat two of the best designed and most influential longitudinal studies: Owens's (1953, 1966) Army Alpha investigation of adults tested originally in 1919 as Iowa State freshmen; and Schaie's (1983b) 21-year Seattle longitudinal study with the PMA that utilized sophisticated cohort-sequential methodology. We conclude this section with Kaufman's (1990, 2001) longitudinal investigations of Wechsler's scales using independent samples.

Problems in Investigating Aging Longitudinally

Ideally, the alleged early and rapid decline in P-IQ—and other measures of *Gf*, *Gv*, and *Gs*—with increasing age could be verified or disproved by the continual retesting of the same individuals. Some excellent longitudinal investigations using the WAIS, or a portion of it, have been conducted (Schaie, 1983a), but the results have not answered the question. The main difficulty lies less with the research studies than with the WAIS itself.

Practice Effects and Progressive Error on Wechsler's Performance Scale

With all tests, the effects of using the same instrument repeatedly introduce unwanted error into the analysis, a confounding known as *progressive error* (Kausler, 1982, 1991). This type of error is important for any studies involving Wechsler's Performance Scale because of the nature of the items and the enormous practice effect associated with them. Adults who are retested on the WAIS or WAIS-R after about a month will gain only about 2 to 3 points on the Verbal Scale, versus 8 to 9 points on the Performance Scale (Kaufman, 1994b). This profound practice effect on P-IQ extends for at least 4 months (Catron & Thompson, 1979). On the WAIS-III, the P-IQ practice effect seems to be a function of age, with the typical 8-point gain found for ages 16–54 years, but with smaller gains found for ages 55–74 (6 points) and 75–89 (4 points) (Kaufman & Lichtenberger, 1999). Even if the practice effect dissipates after a year or two and is smaller for elderly adults than young and middle-aged adults, this variable still looms large in longitudinal investigations. The practice effect may not impede the results of the first retest in a longitudinal study, but it surely will not disappear by the third, fourth, or fifth retest, and may be quite large even for elderly individuals.

In the first of two Duke longitudinal studies, comprising an initial sample of 267 adult volunteers between the ages of 59 and 94 from North Carolina (who matched the age, sex, race, and socioeconomic characteristics of the community), 42 "survivors" were tested up to 11 times on the WAIS between 1955 and 1976! The second Duke study involved a four-subtest WAIS short form administered to an initial sample of 502 adults, aged 46–70, from the same general area; the 331 survivors were given the short form four times between 1970 and 1976 (Siegler, 1983). The two Duke longitudinal investigations were exceptional studies, uncovering fascinating relationships among the cognitive, memory, personality, sensory, and motor variables administered repeatedly to the subjects. But it is impossible to make inferences about changes in P-IQ over time for samples that are so overexposed to the five Performance subtests. Eisdorfer and Wilkie (1973), for example, found decrements of 3.2

points on the Verbal sums of scaled scores, and a similar 4.4 points on the Performance sum, for 50 of the Duke subjects in the first study who were tested in both the first wave in the late 1950s and the seventh wave in 1972. The Verbal data are reasonably interpretable because of the small practice effect for V-IQ, but the Performance data are meaningless for individuals tested five, or six, or seven times over a 15-year span.

The Performance subtests, even the ones that seem to be more dependent on *Gv* or *Gs* than *Gf*, are novel tasks that assess a person's adaptability and flexibility when faced with new problem-solving situations. These tasks are new the first time they are given, but the novelty wears off quickly. College students tested back-to-back on the WAIS with no time interval at all improved their P-IQ by 14.2 points, versus a 3.1-point gain on V-IQ (Catron, 1978). A different retest sample found little novelty in the Performance tasks after a 4-month interval, showing an 8-point gain (compared to less than a 1-point gain in V-IQ). When people are retested after a few weeks or months, they seem to remember only a few specific nonverbal items; even if they recall many of the puzzles or pictures, no feedback for correctness is given either during or after the test. What people do tend to remember is the type of items they faced and the kinds of strategies and attack modes that seemed successful. When individuals are tested repeatedly on Wechsler's Performance tasks, they no longer measure the kind of intelligence that thrives on novel problem-solving tasks with visual–spatial stimuli, and it becomes questionable whether they measure intelligence as opposed to a combination of mental ability, long-term memory, and the ability to apply learning sets.

The progressive error from the practice effect could have been neutralized to some extent by testing fresh samples during each "wave" of the study (matched on age and other relevant variables to the longitudinal sample at each point in time) to provide "base-line" data. But this type of control was not included in the Duke design. Similarly, the design of the excellent Bonn longitudinal study, utilizing the Hamburg-Wechsler (German WAIS), did not permit identification of the impact of practice on the successive Performance scores of adults tested as many as six times between 1965 and 1980 (Schmitz-Scherzer & Thomae, 1983). The investigators tested two cohorts simultaneously, initially composed of 222 men and women aged 60–65 (1900–1905 cohort) or aged 70–75 (1890–1895 cohort).

Schmitz-Scherzer and Thomae (1983) presented mean Hamburg-Wechsler sums of scaled scores on the Verbal and Performance Scales for each cohort tested in 1965, 1967, 1969, 1972, and 1976–1977. The younger cohort performed fairly constantly on the Verbal Scale over the 12-year period, while the older cohort dropped significantly (almost five weighted score points) as they aged from the 70s to mid-80s. On the Performance Scale, both cohorts either maintained or improved their scores between the 1965 and 1972 testings (four administrations) before showing a sizable drop in 1976–1977. The Verbal changes are consistent with the results of other cross-sectional and longitudinal investigations, including the decrement by the older cohort during their late 70s and early 80s (Botwinick, 1977; Jarvik & Bank, 1983). The Performance changes imply virtually no loss of function for the older cohort between the ages of about 72 to 79, and small gains in Performance scores for the younger cohort between ages 62 and 66. However, such interpretations of Performance abilities are fanciful, based on the considerable practice effect inherent in the separate nonverbal subtests.

Botwinick (1977) showed how failure to consider the differential practice effect can confound studies based on a single retest. He criticized the faulty conclusions reached by Rhudick and Gordon (1973), who retested an initial sample of 58- to 88-year-old men and women using intervals of 1 to 8 years. They concluded that the adults showed improvement in their V, P, and FS scores over 1- to 8-year intervals. Yet when the authors divided their samples by length of interval, "Full and Verbal scale scores were found unchanged, but the Performance scores changed in a way to

emphasize the importance of the length of the test-retest interval. The interval of 2 or less years showed a significant age-increase while the interval of 6–8 years showed a significant age-decrease" (Botwinick, 1977, pp. 595–596). Botwinick explored explanations for this "paradoxical pattern," opposite to the classical aging pattern, but he missed the most obvious (and probable) explanation: the powerful effect of practice on P-IQ.

The practice effect undoubtedly colored the results of a fascinating study of twins, aged 60 and above, over a 20-year span (Feingold, 1950; Jarvik & Bank, 1983). Selected Wechsler-Bellevue subtests were administered along with Binet Vocabulary and a motor test in 1947–1949 to an initial sample of 134 pairs of twins. Consistent with other longitudinal results, Vocabulary and W-B Similarities scores maintained into old age, contrasting with notable declines in Block Design and Digit Symbol. However, even performance on the latter two tasks failed to show a significant decrement when the elderly twins (mean age = 67.5) were retested the first time less than 1 year later at the age of 68.4 (Jarvik, Kallmann, & Falek, 1962). Jarvik and Bank (1983) indicate that "given an elderly non-test-wise group of subjects, one would expect artificially low initial scores and substantial practice effects on subsequent retests" (p. 44). These authors were apparently unaware, however, of the practice differential for verbal versus nonverbal tests.

It should be noted, however, that not everyone interprets practice effects as an artifact. Flynn (1998b), discussing the results of Rabbitt's ongoing longitudinal aging study in Manchester, England, suggested that, "decline after age 50 for fluid intelligence is less than we once believed; the elderly show a surprisingly robust gain from practice effects, which may not boost our estimate of their IQs but does show a lively ability to learn in old age" (p. 106).

Selective Attrition

A second major problem of longitudinal aging research is selective attrition of subjects. When using volunteer subjects, "at all ages in adulthood, those who do not volunteer initially and those who do not show up in retesting tend to be lower scorers on ability tests than those who do cooperate" (Horn & Donaldson, 1976, p. 717). The Duke longitudinal study was especially valuable in generating research to help quantify this effect. Analysis of data from the first 10 years of the first Duke study (Eisdorfer & Wilkie, 1973) revealed "a substantial loss of *S*s, with the lowest IQ group sustaining a loss of 72 percent; the middle IQ group, a loss of 51.4 percent; and the high IQ group, a loss of only 36.8 percent" (p. 28). Even more dramatic evidence of the selective attrition factor came from Siegler and Botwinick's (1979) analysis of data from all 11 "waves" of the first Duke study. Individuals who continue to be retested over time are more intelligent than those who drop out early. Among 60- to 74-year-olds in the Duke study, the relationship is

nearly linear between IQ at the initial assessment and the number of times the person returned to be tested, as depicted in Figure 5.16. Of the 179 individuals tested on the WAIS in the first wave, only 18 returned to be tested at all 10 subsequent assessments. Overall, the 60- to 74-year-olds who came once or twice earned mean sums of scaled scores on the Full Scale of 85 to 90, compared to means of close to 110 for those who came to be tested 10 or all 11 times!

Obviously some of the elderly subjects died or were too ill to be tested, but many simply chose not to be retested for whatever reason; the selective attrition factor occurs as well for younger adults, although the effect seems to increase with age (Horn & Donaldson, 1976). Research has been divided over the level of initial intelligence and the rate of IQ decline over time, with some investigators showing no significant interaction (e.g., Owens, 1959), and others (including Sie-

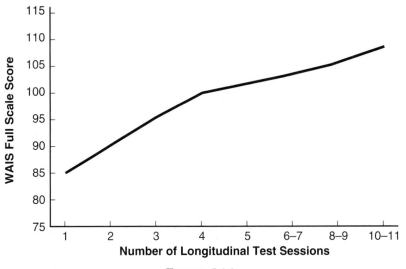

FIGURE 5.16

Mean WAIS Full Scale scores earned by adults (aged 60–74 years) on the initial assessment, shown as a function of the number of longitudinal test sessions in which the subjects participated.

SOURCE: Data points, based on samples ranging in size from 43 to 179, are weighted means for ages 60–64 and 65–75, obtained from Table 1 and Figure 1 in Siegler and Botwinick, 1979.

gler and Botwinick, 1979) finding different patterns of decline for the more and less able subjects. Nonetheless, all such analyses are based on people who return at least once to be tested. Those who drop out very early in a study (and whose IQ changes are never evaluated) may be a breed apart from the low IQ subjects who keep coming back. Hence, generalizations from longitudinal studies must be made quite cautiously because of the considerable selective attrition factor. At the very least, it is essential for researchers to partly compensate for this problem by following Eisdorfer and Wilkie's (1973) advice: "The appropriate analysis of longitudinal data should use data only from the same subjects across time, whether *S*s are lost secondary to death or drop out" (p. 28).

Other potential difficulties with longitudinal research, and with cross-sectional research, have been treated in depth by experts on aging (e.g., Kausler, 1991; Nesselroade & Labouvie, 1985; Salthouse, 2000); the reader is referred to these sources for a more thorough and technical treatment of the topic.

Two Groundbreaking Longitudinal Investigations of IQ and Aging

We now turn to two of the most influential and well-designed investigations of IQ and aging: Owens' Iowa State Army Alpha Study and Schaie's 21-Year Seattle Cohort-Sequential Study.

The Iowa State Army Alpha Study

Owens (1953) administered the Army Alpha test in 1950 to 127 men, age 50, who had previously been among 363 Iowa State University freshmen who had been administered the same test in 1919 at age 19. These initial results "were important in stimulating a critical reexamination of the inevitability of intellectual decline in adulthood" (Schaie, 1983c, pp. 13, 15); the study "ushered in

an era of new ideas in research on adult development and intelligence" (Cunningham & Owens, 1983, p. 20). The study continued in 1961 when 96 of these men were tested once more, at age 61 (Owens, 1966); Owens also tested a random sample of 19-year-old Iowa State freshmen on the Army Alpha in 1961–1962 to permit a time-lag comparison, thereby estimating the impact of cultural change on the obtained test scores. The Army Alpha, one of Wechsler's primary sources for selecting Verbal subtests, comprises eight tasks, including tests of Information, Practical Judgment (Comprehension), Arithmetical Problems, and Synonyms–Antonyms (Vocabulary). For simplicity of interpretation, Owens (1966) focused on age changes in the three factors that Guilford (1954) identified for the Army Alpha: Verbal, Numerical, and Relations (or Reasoning).

KEY FINDINGS.   Results of the Iowa State longitudinal investigation for the 96 men tested three times on the Army Alpha reveal improvement in Verbal and Total scores between ages 19 and 50, followed by a slight decline from age 50 to 61. Reasoning displayed small increments from one testing occasion to the next, while Numerical evidenced the opposite profile. The most noteworthy changes were the improvement in Verbal scores from age 19 to 50 and the sudden decrease in Numerical scores from age 50 to 61.

Owens then corrected the data for cultural change, based on the better performance (especially in Reasoning) by the 19-year-olds tested in the early 1960s compared to the 19-year-olds tested in 1919. Following this time-lag correction, what had appeared to be slight increments in Reasoning were actually steady decrements in performance. Despite the correction for cultural change, Verbal factor scores continued to show gains between ages 19 and 61; numerical scores showed a loss across this same age span, but a smaller loss than was observed for Reasoning.

IMPLICATIONS OF RESULTS.   Botwinick (1977) concluded that the Reasoning "factor score was based more on the speeded test items than the other factor scores: in this way it was more similar to the WAIS Performance subtests than the Verbal" (p. 593). Cunningham and Owens's (1983) overall conclusion from the Iowa State study: "The results suggest peak performance and the beginning of declines of overall intellectual functioning roughly in the decade of the 50s for this elite sample. The losses appear to be small and probably are not of much practical significance until at least age 60" (p. 34).

All eight subtests of the group-administered Army Alpha involve verbal and/or numerical ability. Even the Reasoning factor, although interpreted by Owens (1966) as a measure of fluid ability, is defined by verbal tests like Analogies (e.g., *fear* is to *anticipation* as *regret* is to?). Thus, the findings from Owens's longitudinal investigation and Cunningham and Owens's overall conclusions are quite consistent with the Wechsler and Kaufman cross-sectional studies holding education constant.

Both the Iowa State Longitudinal data and the Wechsler/Kaufman cross-sectional sets of data indicate *Gc* skills that increase slightly with age during adulthood and that are still strong into the 60s.

Schaie's 21-Year Seattle Cohort-Sequential Study

Schaie's (1983b) sophisticated combination of cross-sectional and longitudinal designs was predicated on the contributions of three variables to the scores obtained by adults on intelligence tests: chronological age, cohort (year of birth), and time-of-measurement (the year the tests were administered). He conducted four independent cross-sectional studies with the group-administered Primary Mental Abilities (PMA) test, starting with his 1956 sample of 500 adults. This group was divided into seven ages, with means ranging from 25 to 67 (cohorts 1889–1931); subsequent independent samples were tested in 1963 ($N = 996$, ages 25–74, cohorts 1889–1938), 1970 ($N = 705$, ages 25–81, cohorts 1889–1945),

and 1977 ($N = 609$, ages 25–81, cohorts 1896–1952). All samples comprised approximately equal numbers of men and women, with the groups tending to be relatively well educated for the 1960s and 1970s (about 50% with one or more years of college).

Coinciding with the last three cross-sectional studies were longitudinal investigations ranging from 7 to 21 years. Three 7-year studies included the retesting of as many subjects as possible from the 1956 ($N = 303$), 1963 ($N = 420$), and 1970 ($N = 340$) cross-sectional investigations. In addition, two 14-year studies included 162 adults followed from 1956 to 1970, and 337 individuals tested in 1963 and 1977; finally, one sample of 130 was followed for the 21-year interval between 1956 and 1977. These rigorous cross-sequential, cohort-sequential, and longitudinal designs permitted Schaie and his colleagues to identify cohort and time-of-measurement variation in an attempt to understand "true" intelligence differences due to aging.

KEY FINDINGS. His 1968 investigation (Schaie & Strother, 1968) was widely publicized in popular texts at that time (Cronbach, 1970; Matarazzo, 1972) because it showed dramatic differences in the aging-IQ growth curve from cross-sectional data alone (his 1956 sample of 500) and the curve obtained from his first 7-year longitudinal study (the 303 members of the 1956 sample retested in 1963). The cross-sectional data for ages 20–70 revealed the same type of plunge in abilities with age that characterized the WAIS, WAIS-R, or WAIS-III Full Scale IQ prior to an adjustment for education (see Table 5.1); the mix of cross-sectional and longitudinal data for the smaller sample (a sequential analysis) demonstrated growth curves showing virtually no decline across the age range, not unlike the education-corrected patterns for the various Wechsler and Kaufman measures of *Gc*. These findings applied to the separate components of the PMA, whether measuring verbal ability (Verbal Meaning, a multiple-choice vocabulary test) or skills akin to Wechsler's Performance subtests, especially tasks like Block

Design with a strong *Gv* component (Space, a match-to-sample spatial orientation test).

IMPLICATIONS OF RESULTS.   These data became the subject of controversy, with Horn and Donaldson (1976) and Botwinick (1977), for example, citing variables such as selective attrition to account for the apparent maintenance of both fluid and crystallized abilities through old age. Regardless of the arguments and counterarguments (Baltes & Schaie, 1976; Horn & Donaldson, 1977), the early Schaie data show both consistency and inconsistency with Wechsler and Kaufman cross-sectional results. In Schaie's findings, scores on the nonverbal, *Gf/Gv* tasks (Space, along with a measure of inductive reasoning) clearly began a decline much later in life than was found for Wechsler's Performance subtests. Yet, like the Wechsler findings, scores on Space and Reasoning peaked far earlier than the more crystallized PMA subtests (Verbal Meaning and Number). Interestingly, the later decline for the PMA Space and Reasoning subtests is consistent with the relatively late decline (after age 54) observed for the *Gf* tasks on the Kaufman adult tests (KAIT, K-BIT, and K-SNAP).

Subsequent analyses (e.g., Schaie & Hertzog, 1983) revealed Schaie's responsiveness to the criticisms and the concomitant efforts by his research team to refine their methodologies and analyses. Schaie and Hertzog (1983) admitted that their original cross-sequential design was ill-suited to evaluate age changes; further, the results of the two 14-year longitudinal studies they reported indicated earlier declines in intelligence (i.e., prior to age 60) than were previously observed in Schaie's laboratory. In Schaie and Hertzog's (1983) analysis, however, the pattern of decline for the 14-year longitudinal samples was quite similar for both verbal and nonverbal PMA subtests. Schaie and Labouvie-Vief's (1974) generalization about aging and intelligence, that "most of the adult life span is characterized by an absence of decisive intellectual decrements" (p. 15), summarizes well the overall results of their many PMA studies.

The best integration of the numerous analyses appears in Schaie's (1983b) thorough treatment of the 21-year Seattle project. Among other syntheses of the data, he organized the findings of the three 7-year longitudinal studies into two tables, each comparing the performance of every age group to age 25; the average score was set at 100. The first table showed these comparisons without correction for potentially confounding variables, while the second one corrected all values for time-of-measurement effects, attrition, and cohort differences (Schaie, 1983b, Tables 4.17 and 4.18). Figure 5.17 depicts Schaie's results for Verbal Meaning, Space, and Reasoning, where these values are corrected for the three variables noted previously. For these three tasks, the uncorrected and corrected values were quite similar for each age, usually disagreeing by only 1 to 3 points.

In Figure 5.17, Verbal Meaning increases steadily until age 53, with a notable decline occurring between ages 67 and 74. Space peaks earlier than Verbal Meaning (age 46), but has its first sizable decline between the same 67- to 74-year period. Nonetheless, its decline is more dramatic than that of the vocabulary test. Reasoning declines substantially after age 60, plunging to 73 by age 81.

These results are basically in agreement with the differential results for the measures of maintained abilities (*Gc*, *Gq*) versus vulnerable abilities (*Gf*, *Gv*, *Gs*, *Gsm*) on the various Wechsler and Kaufman scales. Unlike the popular interpretations of the initial findings reported by Schaie and his colleagues, intelligence does, indeed, decline with chronological age, and that decline becomes precipitous; however, the use of longitudinal data juxtaposed with cross-sectional results on the PMA suggest that the decrements may not begin until relatively late in life.

SHOULD CORRECTIONS BE MADE FOR COHORT EFFECTS?   We have excluded Number from Figure 5.17, despite its similarity to Wechsler's Arithmetic subtest, because its corrected and uncorrected values were so disparate. Prior to correction, peak performance on Number was at age

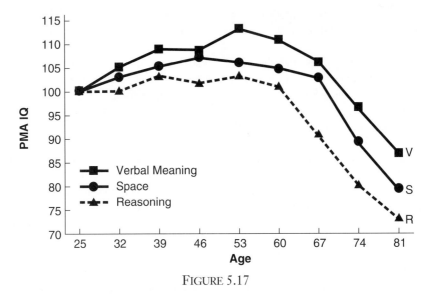

FIGURE 5.17

Performance on three Primary Mental Abilities (PMA) subtests at ages 25–81 as a proportion of age 25 performance (set at 100), corrected for time-of-measurement, attrition, and cohort efforts (from Schaie, 1983b, Table 4.18, based on 7-year longitudinal data).

32 (a score of 111), with scores declining to 91 at age 60 and 55 at age 81. After correction, peak performance on Number was an astonishing 126 at age 60, and 74-year-olds outperformed 32-year-olds. We have difficulty accepting the validity of corrected results when the changes are so dramatic (rather like seeing a correlation of .15 jump to .70 after correcting it for range restriction). In general, we are not totally in agreement with the idea of correcting IQs for cohort differences, which may be the main culprit in the Number data. Selective attrition certainly requires correction to the degree possible, and so do time-lag effects, so long as these effects can be shown to apply to virtually every group of adults living at the time. If an entire group of people responds to cultural changes by performing differently at time 1 and time 2 (perhaps because of some type of generic change in society that affects nearly everyone), then correction makes sense. How can one attribute developmental significance to a change that occurs for everyone within that same time

frame, even if some part of the change is due to cohort effects? If variables like familiarity with standardized tests or the availability of television tend to improve each person's score (on average) between 1940 and 1980, it would be foolish to attribute the gain to "mental growth."

But specific cohort effects are different. These variables are assumed to affect intelligence differently for people born in different years. Adults who were raised in a time of parental enlightenment about infant stimulation or prenatal care are likely to outscore those who were born at other times. Children reared during the Depression or the world wars might not develop their intellect at the same rate as children born during other historical periods. However, we are not sure that it always makes sense to correct IQs for such factors. At what point do chronological age and the time one is reared become separable? We certainly favor controlling for educational attainment when exploring age differences in IQ. Because education is a cohort-related variable, we can see some value in keeping cohort factors out of the developmental picture. But education is separate from most other cohort effects. Its impact on IQs is known, quantifiable, and profound. It is commonly a variable that is considered along with intelligence for vocational selection and placement, and in other real-life situations associated with intellectual assessment. As Reese and Rodeheaver (1985) have noted: "Performance on cognitive tasks is often correlated more highly with education than with age.... The issue of education is critical in assessing adult age differences in problem solving" (p. 479).

The specific attitudes toward child-rearing and the social and historical environment associated with any particular group of years are intrinsically interwoven with the person's chronological age such that separation can become artificial; indeed, "cohort and age are inseparable" (Botwinick, 1977, p. 583). For gerontological research, we grant that the identification and quantification of the impact of cohort effects on intelligence is crucial; one must try to separate ontogenetic factors from cohort variables as causations of age differences in IQ to understand life span development of intelligence. From a practical standpoint, however, most cohort differences closely resemble the kinds of differences that characterize one subculture versus another or one family versus another within a single cohort. Yet, we do not ordinarily adjust a person's IQ because of a disadvantaged home life or other deprivations, or for growing up within the different cultures associated with the United States. As clinicians, such factors enter into test interpretation, but we do not infer that the person should have a few points added to his or her score to be "fair." Nor do intelligence tests provide separate norms for individuals based on ethnic group, social class, region, residence, or income level; supplementary norms are sometimes provided to facilitate clinical or neuropsychological interpretation, but the global intelligence scores are necessarily derived from representative national norms.

In the extreme, the view that cohort differences are of vital concern and must be controlled to truly measure intelligence implies that norms for any intelligence test are not generalizable to other cohorts. WAIS-III norms, for example, obtained in 1995–96, might be viewed as suitable for 60-year-olds born in the 1935–36 (Depression time), but not the early 1940s (war time). Restandardizations would be needed every 5 years or so, a nice ideal but not a very practical one. Schaie and Schaie (1977), using Wechsler's adult tests as examples, have even suggested that "tests which have been constructed for a given cohort...may not be valid for successive cohorts" (p. 695). For the most part, we agree with Botwinick's (1977) view of cohort effects: "In the world outside the laboratory where abstractions differentiating between cohort and age do not exist, age and cohort are one. Age is not synonymous with biology, nor is cohort synonymous with sociocultural influences" (p. 583).

Schaie's research has been quite valuable in helping us understand intelligence and aging and in stimulating research. Surely the simple cross-sectional data do not have important ontogenetic implications, and declining intelligence for a given person undoubtedly occurs far later in the life span than ever conceptualized prior to Schaie's and Owens's series of studies. Yet it is unclear to what degree findings with group tests generalize to the Wechsler scales, and it is at least arguable whether correction for all variance attributable to cohort effects is justifiable, except as a basis for enhancing our theoretical understanding of intellectual development across the life span.

Kaufman's (1990, 2001) Longitudinal Investigations of Wechsler's Adult Scales Using Independent Samples

Schaie's research "substantiated the position that cohort differences exert profound effects in observed patterns of intellectual development in adulthood" (Dixon, Kramer, & Baltes, 1985, p. 318). Perhaps IQs earned by different cohorts should be adjusted for these effects and perhaps not, but the key question that remains unanswered from cross-sectional investigations of Wechsler's series of scales is whether the rapid decline in Wechsler's Performance IQ, even after control for the cohort effects attributable to years of formal education, is an artifact of other unknown cohort variables. Another important question based on the WAIS-III cross-sectional data (Kaufman, 2001) and WAIS-R cross-sectional data for elderly samples ages 75 and older (Ryan, personal communication, March, 1998; Ryan, Paolo, & Brungardt, 1990) is whether the substantial decline in Verbal IQ after age 74 is an artifact of uncontrolled cohort variables. Do the descending mean P-IQs evident in Figure 5.5 apply only to different age groups at a fixed point in time, or do these results have at least some implications for ontogenetic changes? What about the descending mean V-IQs for ages 75 and older in Figure 5.4?

Certainly the evidence necessary to answer these questions was not available in the existing Wechsler literature when the first edition of this book went to press in 1990. Most longitudinal studies of the Wechsler-Bellevue or WAIS focused on older subjects, even at the initial assessment, and none of these studies adequately handled the issue of practice effects or progressive error on the Performance subtests. While writing the aging chapter in the first edition of this book, Kaufman (1990, Chapter 7) was troubled by the lack of an answer to the important question about P-IQ decline and conducted a study that was inspired by the methodologies of Owens (1966), Schaie (1983b), and Parker (1986), and by Kausler's (1982, 1991) detailed discussions of the pros and cons of diverse methodologies.

Parker (1986) had the clever idea of examining the comparative performance of year-of-birth cohorts by equating the standardization samples of the Wechsler-Bellevue I, WAIS, and WAIS-R. However, he focused solely on the Full Scale IQ, when it is the separate V- and P-IQs

that are of the greatest theoretical interest for analyses of aging. But Parker's article made Kaufman (1990) realize the analogy between the WAIS and WAIS-R standardization samples and Schaie's repeated cross-sectional analyses between 1956 and 1977. In fact, the WAIS standardization sample, tested in 1953–1954, and the WAIS-R sample, tested between 1976 and 1980, correspond closely to the dates of Schaie's first and fourth cross-sectional analyses. The two Wechsler standardization samples were quite comparable, allowing longitudinal interpretation of data obtained by independent samples from the same cohort. Schaie (1983b) also conducted several longitudinal analyses based on comparable independent samples, in part to answer criticisms of the selective attrition associated with conventional longitudinal analysis, and concluded that the results were "generally quite comparable" (p. 106).

The use of independent samples or "cohort substitution" (Kausler, 1982), if they are truly comparable and random, makes it "possible to compute age-change estimates that are controlled for the effects of testing and experimental mortality" (Schaie, 1983b, p. 106). Kaufman (1990) used the cohort substitution method with the WAIS and WAIS-R normative samples serving as the data source, primarily to determine whether longitudinal data would replicate the cross-sectional finding of rapidly declining P-IQ across most of the life span. He then used the same method with the WAIS-R and WAIS-III standardization samples (Kaufman, 2001) to cross-validate the WAIS/WAIS-R finding for P-IQ and to determine whether the cross-sectional decline for V-IQ between ages 75 and 89 emerges with longitudinal data.

Kaufman's (1990) Study of WAIS and WAIS-R Samples

The WAIS and WAIS-R standardization samples are quite similar to each other, each matching relevant Census data on numerous key variables. They differ in that the data were collected 25 years apart, in approximately 1953 and

1978. Thus, several cohorts in the WAIS sample are also represented in the WAIS-R sample. For example, adults born in the 1909–1913 cohort were tested at ages 40–44 in 1953 (on the WAIS), and again at ages 65–69 in 1978 (on the WAIS-R). To the degree that the two samples are comparable, a comparison of the test performance of 40- to 44-year-olds on the WAIS with that of the 65- to 69-year-olds 25 years later on the WAIS-R represents a longitudinal comparison of adults from the same cohort.

There are four adult cohorts represented within both the WAIS and WAIS-R standardization samples, as shown in Table 5.11. In essence, Kaufman (1990) followed each of four cohorts longitudinally from 1953 to 1978 to see if individuals born in the same era gained or lost IQ points over the course of a generation. Before making the comparisons, he verified empirically that the independent samples were extremely well matched and comparable within each of the four cohorts on the important variables of gender, race (Caucasian–non-Caucasian), geographic region, and educational attainment. Then, he had to convert sums of scaled scores on the WAIS and WAIS-R to a common yardstick to permit age-by-age comparisons, and chose to use the norms for ages 25–34 for all adults in the study. Next, he had to control for the fact that different tests (WAIS vs. WAIS-R) were administered at the two points in time. Conceptually, these two adult scales are interchangeable (see Chapter 3), but because of the "Flynn effect" the WAIS-R yields lower IQs. Kaufman added 6 to 6½ points to each

WAIS-R IQ (the median IQ differences from 20 studies totaling over 1,300 subjects) (Kaufman, 1990, Table 3.13) to convert these IQs to WAIS IQs. These "corrections" to the WAIS-R IQs helped answer the crucial question, "How many IQ points higher would adults have scored had they been administered the WAIS instead of the WAIS-R in 1978?" Finally, he applied a time-lag correction to control for cultural change during the 25-year span, just as Owens (1966) did in his Iowa State study. Adjustment for cultural change requires a comparison of the IQs earned by each cohort in 1953 with the IQs earned by adults of the *same age* in 1978. The 1909–1913 cohort, for example, was 40 to 44 years old in 1953. This group was compared to adults aged 40–44 in 1978 to determine how cultural changes have affected test scores for this age group. Similar time-lag comparisons were conducted for each of the other three cohorts who, in 1953, were ages 20–29, 30–39, and 45–49. The analyses showed that cultural change affected each of the four cohorts about equally, producing about a 3-point IQ gain on the Verbal and Full Scales and about a 5½-point gain on the Performance Scale, presumably due to some type of culture-related change between 1953 and 1978 that affected all adults who were between the ages of 20 and 49 in 1953. Kaufman (1990) adjusted the estimated WAIS IQs earned by each cohort in 1978 for these time-lag effects to remove the influence of cultural change.

KEY FINDINGS.   The changes in WAIS IQs over a 25-year period from 1953 to 1978 for four

TABLE 5.11   The four adult age cohorts represented in the WAIS and WAIS-R standardization samples

Cohort (Year of Birth)	Age in 1953 (WAIS Standardization)	Age in 1978 (WAIS-R Standardization)
1924–1933	20–29	45–54
1914–1923	30–39	55–64
1909–1913	40–44	65–69
1904–1908	45–49	70–74

cohorts tested twice via the cohort-substitution technique are shown in Table 5.12, along with the effect sizes corresponding to these changes. When corrected for time-lag effects, all cohorts earned lower IQs in 1978 than they did in 1953. The most striking finding in the data is the difference between the Verbal and Performance Scales. Decrements in V-IQ produced small effect sizes for each cohort, (the average decrease was .24 *SD*). In contrast, P-IQ decrements produced moderate effect sizes for each cohort, ranging from 11.6 to 13.5 IQ points (an average decrease of 12.6 points or .84 *SD*). Substantial decreases in P-IQ occurred for each cohort whether they advanced in age from 24.5 to 49.5 (on the average) or from 47 to 72. These results support the findings from the cross-sectional analyses of Wechsler's and Kaufman's scales, with or without a control for education.

IMPLICATIONS OF RESULTS. Technically, it is methodologically incorrect to construct age gradients from a combination of longitudinal and cross-sectional data: "the use of cross-sequential results to evaluate age changes [is] ill considered" (Schaie & Hertzog, 1983, p. 532). Nonetheless, we believe that the best way to show relationships between the WAIS/WAIS-R longitudinal and WAIS-R cross-sectional data is to graph the age gradients from each study simultaneously, which we have done for P-IQ (Figure 5.18). The data graphed for the longitudinal analysis represent two data points for each of the four cohorts; cross-sectional data are the education-adjusted WAIS-R values shown in Figure 5.2.

The P-IQs from each study form nearly identical curves, emphasizing the consistency of the dramatic decrease in mean Performance IQ with increasing age, starting early in adult life. Neither curve can rightfully be considered a growth curve, and ontogenetic changes should either be inferred with caution or not at all. Yet the fact that adults within each of the four cohorts showed sizable decrements across a 25-year period reinforces the notion that adults do decline in nonverbal intelligence with advancing age, and this decline begins far earlier on Wechsler's scales than on the Army Alpha or PMA. The

TABLE 5.12   Effect sizes (in *SD* units) of the mean change in WAIS/WAIS-R IQs for four cohorts over a 25-year span (1953 to 1978), controlling for instrument and time-lag effects

Cohort (Year of Birth)	Verbal IQ		Performance IQ		Full Scale IQ	
	Adj. Change	Effect Size	Adj. Change	Effect Size	Adj. Change	Effect Size
1924–1933 (Age 24.5 to 49.5)	−1.5	.10	−11.6	.77*	−6.2	.41
1914–1923 (Age 34.5 to 59.5)	−3.3	.22	−12.5	.83*	−8.2	.55*
1909–1913 (Age 42 to 67)	−3.9	.26	−12.9	.86*	−8.5	.57*
1904–1908 (Age 47 to 72)	−5.5	.37	−13.5	.90*	−10.1	.67*
Median Effect Size		.24		.84*		.56*
Mean Effect Size		.24		.84*		.55*

*Moderate Effect Size

NOTE: Adj. = Adjusted. Standardization data of the Wechsler Adult Intelligence Scale: Third Edition. Copyright © 1997 by The Psychological Corporation. Used by permission. All rights reserved. Reprinted from Kaufman (2000, Figure 5) with permission.

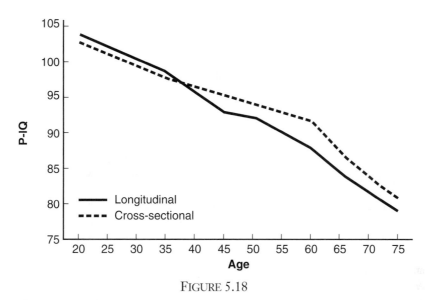

FIGURE 5.18

Changes in Wechsler Performance IQ with chronological age using two different experimental designs: cross-sectional (controlling for education) and longitudinal (controlling for instrument and time-lag effects).

shape of the precise growth curve remains elusive, but longitudinal analysis suggests that the lower P-IQs for successive age groups is not just a cross-sectional phenomenon.

Kaufman's (2001) Study of WAIS-R and WAIS-III Samples

Kaufman (2001) used Parker's (1986) and Kaufman's (1990) methodology to replicate the WAIS/WAIS-R cohort-substitution study with data from the WAIS-R and WAIS-III standardization samples. He examined changes on the three IQs for seven cohorts over the 17-year span from 1978 to 1995. These cohorts, summarized in Table 5.13, range from individuals born between 1954 and 1958 (tested at age 22 and again at 39) to adults born between 1904 and 1908, who were 72 during the WAIS-R standardization and 89 when the WAIS-III was normed. Kaufman (2001) demonstrated that the pairs of independent samples within each of the seven

cohorts matched adequately on the variables of gender, geographic region, educational attainment, and race/ethnicity. The key difference between the instruments, apart from the 17 years between standardizations, is the substitution of Matrix Reasoning for Object Assembly for computing P-IQ and FS-IQ. However, WAIS-R and WAIS-III P-IQs correlated .86 and the FS-IQs correlated .93 in a counterbalanced study of 192 adults, ages 16–74 years, tested twice (Psychological Corporation, 1997, pp. 78–79). These values are comparable to the coefficients of .84 and .92 for the WAIS and WAIS-R Performance and Full Scales, respectively (Ryan, Nowak, & Geisser, 1987), supporting the publisher's claim "that the WAIS-III measures essentially the same constructs as does the WAIS-R" (Psychological Corporation, 1997, p. 78).

To correct for the difference in the IQs yielded by the two instruments, constants of 1.2, 4.8, and 2.9 were added to mean WAIS-III Verbal, Performance, and Full Scale IQs, respectively, to make

TABLE 5.13 The seven adult cohorts represented in the WAIS-R and WAIS-III standardization samples

Cohort (Year of Birth)	Age in 1978 (WAIS-R Standardization)	Age in 1995 (WAIS-III Standardization)
1954–1958	22 (20–24)	39 (37–41)
1944–1953	29.5 (25–34)	46.5 (42–51)
1934–1943	39.5 (35–44)	56.5 (52–61)
1924–1933	49.5 (45–54)	66.5 (62–71)
1914–1923	59.5 (55–64)	76.5 (72–81)
1909–1913	67 (65–69)	84 (82–86)
1904–1908	72 (70–74)	89 (87–91)

NOTE: Standardization data of the Wechsler Adult Intelligence Scale: Third Edition. Copyright © 1997 by The Psychological Corporation. Used by permission. All rights reserved. Reprinted from Kaufman (2001) with permission.

these IQs comparable to WAIS-R IQs; these constants were derived from IQ differences obtained in the WAIS-R/WAIS-III counterbalanced study (Psychological Corporation, 1997, Table 4.1). For both instruments, all IQs were based on reference group norms (ages 20–34 years) to provide a common yardstick for comparisons from age to age. To control for cultural change or "time lag" to ensure that any observable changes over the 17-year interval for each cohort are truly due to development and not to other factors, Kaufman (2001) compared the IQs earned by each cohort in 1978 with the IQs earned by adults the same age in 1995. The time lags were smallest for the two youngest cohorts, averaging about 1 point for Verbal IQ, 4.5 points for Performance IQ, and 2.5 points for Full Scale IQ. For the older five cohorts, time lags averaged about 6 to 9 points for each IQ.

KEY FINDINGS. Table 5.14 shows the IQ changes from 1978 to 1995 for each of the seven cohorts, adjusted for instrument and time lag, along with effect sizes (based on $SD = 15$) for each adjusted change. Except for the two youngest cohorts, each cohort lost IQ points on each scale. Effect sizes are small in magnitude for Verbal IQ except for the two oldest cohorts. By contrast, the effect sizes for Performance IQ are moderate, and similar in value, for the five oldest cohorts. Over the 17-year period, adults born before 1944 lost 10 points (±1) of Performance IQ, or about 2/3 of a SD, whether they were about 60, 70, 80, or 90 years of age in 1995. For the oldest two cohorts, Full Scale IQ losses were larger than either separate loss reflecting the more generalized loss of function in both verbal and nonverbal domains that occurs during the decade of the 80s.

IMPLICATIONS OF RESULTS. Kaufman (2001) presented WAIS-III education-adjusted cross-sectional analyses, discussed previously, alongside these cohort-substitution analyses, and the similarity in results for these two alternate approaches to IQ and aging is remarkable. In both analyses, Verbal IQ emerged as a maintained ability for most of the life span (peaking at ages 45–54), with the only notably lower mean Verbal IQs occurring for adults in their 80s. Performance IQ was a vulnerable ability in both cross-sectional and longitudinal analyses, with peak performance occurring at ages 20–24. Figure 5.19 graphs the decline in P-IQ during the adult life span for mean IQs obtained cross-sectionally and longitudinally. As was true for the cross-sectional and

TABLE 5.14   Effect sizes (in *SD* units) of the mean change in WAIS-R/WAIS-III IQs for seven cohorts over a 17-year span (1978 to 1995), controlling for instrument and time-lag effects

Cohort (Year of Birth)	Verbal IQ		Performance IQ		Full Scale IQ	
	Adj. Change	Effect Size	Adj. Change	Effect Size	Adj. Change	Effect Size
1954–1958 (Age 22 to 39)	+6.3	.42	−2.1	.14	+1.6	.11
1944–1953 (Age 29.5 to 46.5)	+3.2	.21	−5.8	.39	−0.6	.04
1934–1943 (Age 39.5 to 56.5)	−1.0	.07	−9.3	.62*	−4.7	.31
1924–1933 (Age 49.5 to 66.5)	−5.6	.37	−10.9	.73*	−8.8	.59*
1914–1923 (Age 59.5 to 76.5)	−2.9	.19	−10.1	.67*	−7.0	.47
1909–1913 (Age 67 to 84)	-7.4	.49	−9.2	.61*	−10.2	.68*
1904–1908 (Age 72 to 89)	-8.3	.55*	−10.1	.67*	−11.4	.76*
Median Effect Size		.37		.62*		.47
Mean Effect Size		.33		.55*		.42

*Moderate Effect Size

NOTE: Adj. = Adjusted. Standardization data of the Wechsler Adult Intelligence Scale: Third Edition. Copyright © 1997 by The Psychological Corporation. Used by permission. All rights reserved.

longitudinal WAIS-R P-IQ data (Figure 5.18), the graphs for WAIS-III P-IQ overlap remarkably for most ages (age 72 is an exception). Again, Figure 5.19 is only offered for comparison purposes, as it is inappropriate to evaluate age changes with cross-sequential data (Schaie & Hertzog, 1983). The major developmental inferences come from the 17-year cohort comparisons (Table 5.12): The 10-point P-IQ decrements for the five oldest cohorts denote a fairly constant loss of nonverbal intellectual function over a 17-year period for individuals born between 1904 and 1943, and the 7- to 8-point Verbal IQ losses for the two oldest cohorts (those aging from 67 to 84 and from 72 to 89) reflect loss of verbal skills for adults in their 80s.

Combining WAIS-III cross-sectional and longitudinal data suggests a loss of about 0.5 points per year in Performance IQ, or 5 points per decade, which is precisely Horn's (1985; Horn, Donaldson, & Engstrom, 1981) best estimate of the adult decline in fluid intelligence

based on his reviews and results of numerous studies. That degree of loss in P-IQ also mirrors precisely the results of Kaufman's (1990) WAIS/ WAIS-R cohort-substitution study, which found an average decrease over a 25-year period of about 12½ P-IQ points for the four cohorts (see Table 5.12).

The two Wechsler cohort-substitution studies provide results that agree remarkably well with the cross-sectional data provided for Wechsler's adult scales and for the Kaufman and Kaufman tests. Taken together, the two cohort-substitution studies offer broad support to the developmental reality of a loss in nonverbal intellectual function (*Gf, Gv, Gs*) across virtually the entire adult life span as well as a loss in verbal function (primarily *Gc*) during the decade of the 80s. These meaningful declines on the WAIS-III, in particular, are dramatic in view of the systematic exclusion of so many potentially low-functioning adults from the normative sample, for example, adults who merely went to a doctor or other professional for

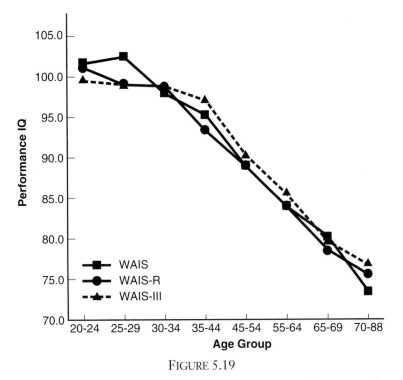

FIGURE 5.19

Mean "reference group" (ages 20–34) Performance IQs, by age, on the WAIS-R or WAIS-III for adults ages 22 to 88 years—comparison of cross-sectional and longitudinal data.

SOURCE: Standardization data of the Wechsler Adult Intelligence Scale: Third Edition. Copyright © 1997 by The Psychological Corporation. Used by permission. All rights reserved. Reprinted from Kaufman (2001) with permission.

memory problems or problems with thinking. The consistency in the P-IQ decrease with increasing age for U.S. men and women born during the first half to three-quarters of the twentieth century—from cross-sectional and longitudinal data on the WAIS, WAIS-R, and WAIS-III—is simply phenomenal.

Comparison of Wechsler and PMA Results

Taken together, the Wechsler cohort-substitution longitudinal studies suggest that declines in P-IQ with age start at about age 50. In the WAIS/WAIS-R study, the change in P-IQ for the youngest cohort in 1953 was a striking 11.6-point drop between ages 24.5 and 49.5 (Table 5.13). In the WAIS-R/WAIS-III study, the cohort that turned 46.5 in 1995 dropped a modest 5.8 points in P-IQ, compared to a more substantial drop of 9.3 points for the cohort that turned 56.5 (Table 5.15). These sizable decrements in P-IQ during the decade of the 50s are not matched by declines in V-IQ, which remained fairly constant over time for the above-mentioned cohorts in both Wechsler longitudinal studies.

To compare these results with Schaie's findings, his most pertinent analyses were sought. Of the various analyses reported by Schaie and his colleagues, the one that most resembles the two Wechsler longitudinal studies is his analysis of data for a 21-year span, based on scores earned by independent samples from the same cohorts (Schaie, 1983b, Table 4.14). This span is exactly midway between the 25-year span for the WAIS/WAIS-R study and the 17-year span for the more recent study. Also, Schaie's initial data point was 1956 and his final data point was 1977, closely resembling the dates for the first Wechsler cohort-substitution study conducted by Kaufman (1990).

We have converted the 21-year changes (reported by Schaie in *T*-score units) to units corresponding to Wechsler's *SD* of 15. We have also averaged data for the PMA Verbal Meaning and Number subtests, offering an analog to Wechsler's V-IQ, and have similarly averaged data for Space and Reasoning, the best P-IQ counterpart. Each of the five cohorts listed showed decrements across the 21-year span on each subtest. (Data for two of Schaie's cohorts were merged—32/53 and 39/60—to enable the PMA cohorts to match the Wechsler cohorts more closely). The pattern of decline for the verbal and nonverbal combinations is shown in Table 5.15.

In general, the PMA trends do not resemble the Wechsler findings. Declines on the PMA verbal and nonverbal tasks are similar to each other: small for the youngest cohort and increasing steadily through the cohort that turned 74 in 1977 (reaching .81 *SD* for verbal and .64 *SD* for nonverbal), before declining in magnitude for the oldest cohort to .71 *SD* for verbal and .47 *SD* for nonverbal. The PMA decline is approximately one half of a standard deviation for the cohort aged 46 years in 1956, and this sizable decrement occurs at that time for both verbal and nonverbal tasks. There is some PMA evidence that the nonverbal decline is larger for the two younger cohorts, but this finding is offset by a reverse trend for the three older cohorts. At its peak (ages 53 to 74), the nonverbal PMA decline of nearly 10 points is commensurate with most of the P-IQ declines observed in both Wechsler cohort-substitution studies for adults turning 50 or older, but even this peak decline in PMA nonverbal ability is notably smaller than the verbal decline of about 12 points for the same cohort. The main similarity in the Wechsler and PMA data concerns the declines in *both* verbal and nonverbal abilities for cohorts turning 80 or above. The two oldest WAIS-R/WAIS-III cohorts that turned 84 years and 89 years, respectively, lost 7 to 10 IQ points on the Verbal and Performance Scales (Table 5.14); the PMA cohort that turned 81 lost a similar 7 to 10 IQ points in both verbal and nonverbal domains (Table 5.15). The main differences between the data sets are that PMA verbal scores decline at *earlier* ages than Wechsler's V-IQ and are larger in magnitude than declines in PMA nonverbal

TABLE 5.15   Decline in PMA verbal and nonverbal scores across a 21-year span for independent samples included in Schaie's Seattle Longitudinal Study

Age in 1956	Age in 1977	Change in PMA Verbal Standard Score (Verbal Meaning, Number)	Change in PMA Nonverbal Standard Score (Space, Reasoning)
25	46	−0.7	−3.1
35.5	56.5	−1.8	−5.7
46	67	−7.9	−7.0
53	74	−12.2	−9.6
60	81	−10.6	−7.1

NOTE: Change equals standard score in 1956 minus standard score in 1977. Standard scores have a standard deviation equal to 15.

scores for the three oldest cohorts. Schaie's data were uncorrected for time-lag and cohort effects, but these adjustments to his data invariably reduce declines, not increase them.

The comparisons between Wechsler and PMA longitudinal data suggest that (1) the same striking differential V-IQ/P-IQ pattern observed on the Wechsler is not observed for the PMA tasks, and an opposite pattern may prevail for the PMA; (2) the large, early decline in P-IQ does not occur for the PMA, although an earlier verbal decline is evidenced; and (3) if Schaie had used a Wechsler adult scale instead of the PMA in his research, it is unlikely, regardless of his adjustments to the data, that P-IQ would have maintained itself into the 50s or 60s before declining substantially.

The reasons for the difference in the relationships of age to P-IQ and the PMA nonverbal tests may relate to the visual–motor components of Wechsler's tasks and the cognitive complexity that defines virtually each Performance subtest. This complexity makes Wechsler's nonverbal subtests very sensitive to brain damage and psychiatric disorders (see Chapters 8 and 9), as well as aging, and adds to the clinical richness of the scales.

INTERPRETATION OF THE AGING PATTERNS FOR V-IQ VERSUS P-IQ: SPEED OR FLUID/ CRYSTALLIZED ABILITY?

The accumulated cross-sectional and longitudinal data obtained on several versions of Wechsler's adult scales, when coupled with data on the Kaufman and Kaufman tests and on other pertinent data such as the comprehensive cross-sectional findings reported in the United Kingdom (Rabbitt, 1993; Rabbitt, Donlan, Watson, McInnes, & Bent, 1995) and Germany (Baltes & Linden-

berger, 1997; Baltes & Mayer, 1999), create a clear picture of aging and cognition. Adults' performance on tests of crystallized ability (Horn) or pragmatics (Baltes) is maintained during much of the life span and does not decline appreciably until the mid-70s or 80s; in contrast, their performance on tests of fluid–visualization–speed abilities (Horn) or mechanics (Baltes) declines early in the life span and continues the steady descent throughout middle and old age. On the WAIS-III, this dichotomy is depicted by the maintenance of V-IQ and VCI and the vulnerability of P-IQ, POI, and PSI.

The Horn and Baltes theoretical explanations of the "classic aging pattern" stand in opposition to Botwinick's (1977) speeded–unspeeded rationale for the tasks that decline with normal aging versus those that are maintained throughout most of the adult life span. In this section we examine the evidence for these competing hypotheses, especially to evaluate whether the age-related decline on Wechsler's P-IQ, KAIT's Fluid IQ, and on other similar tasks is primarily a function of diminished cognitive capacity or of diminished speed. Numerous investigators have interpreted the classical pattern from Botwinick's perspective, for example, Jarvik and Bank (1983) in their longitudinal analysis of aging among elderly twins.

Indeed, the decline in speed with advancing age is a fact. This slowing "is not only an acknowledged laboratory result but also of considerable practical importance.... [A]ge-related slowness is evident in tasks of daily living such as zipping a garment, dialing a telephone, picking up coins, unwrapping a band-aid, cutting with a knife, and even putting on a shirt" (Salthouse, 1985, p. 400). It is also evident from the WAIS-III cross-sectional data that the tests that depend the most on visual–motor speed, the ones that comprise the PSI, show declines with aging that are steeper than the declines for vulnerable subtests that are less speed-dependent (see, for example, Figure 5.6). However, the bulk of evidence supports a decline in ability, not just a more generalized difficulty with timed tasks.

Age-Related Declines on Untimed Tasks such as Matrix Reasoning

As noted previously, the aging pattern for the untimed Matrix Reasoning subtest is virtually identical to highly speeded subtests such as Block Design and Object Assembly (see Figure 5.10). That finding, coupled with the similar finding of a vulnerable pattern for the analogous K-BIT Matrices subtest (Wang & Kaufman, 1993), also untimed, argues strongly against Botwinick's (1977) speeded–unspeeded hypothesis and in favor of Horn's hypothesis that it is the abilities themselves, and not just the speeded nature of tasks, that fosters decline with aging. Also consistent with this view are the substantial declines with increasing age across the adult life span on K-SNAP Gestalt Closure, a reasonably pure measure of *Gv* that is untimed (see Figure 5.14).

Age-Related Changes on Wechsler's Arithmetic, Picture Completion, and Picture Arrangement Subtests

Further fuel for the Horn perspective comes from the extreme vulnerability of Picture Completion (Figure 5.10), the close similarity of the aging pattern for Picture Arrangement to the highly speeded PSI subtests (Figure 5.11), and the maintained pattern for Arithmetic (Figure 5.9). That is to say, Picture Completion and Picture Arrangement are both vulnerable subtests, even though neither WAIS-III subtest utilizes bonus points, and Arithmetic is a maintained subtest even though all items are timed and the more difficult items are scored with bonus points. Whereas Picture Completion and Picture Arrangement items are timed, the time limits for these items, other Performance items (i.e., Block Design and Object Assembly), and Arithmetic items are usually generous enough to permit correct solutions for those adults who are able to solve the problems.

Doppelt and Wallace's (1955) "Old-Age" WAIS Study

Doppelt and Wallace administered WAIS Arithmetic and all Performance subtests to an "old-age" sample aged 60 and above under standard conditions and also under "irregular" conditions, when elderly adults were allowed to solve each item with unlimited time (bonus points were not considered in their analysis). The subjects improved their scores only trivially on all tasks except Block Design. Storandt (1977), in a similar investigation with 40 young and 40 elderly adults matched on verbal ability, supported Doppelt and Wallace's results. The elderly group improved their raw scores significantly on only one of the five WAIS subtests, this time Picture Arrangement, while the younger subjects (ages 20–30) failed to improve their scores significantly on any of the tasks. The 20-second time limit for Picture Completion items was adequate in both studies because none of the groups of subjects improved their Picture Completion raw scores significantly with unlimited time. In fact, trivial gains of less than a half point were observed for all subsamples in the two studies.

Aging Patterns on WAIS-R and WAIS-III Arithmetic Subtest

Visual–motor speed, rather than mental processing speed *per se*, seems to be the most vulnerable to normal aging. In fact, when vocal answers are required rather than motor responses, the relationship between speed and aging no longer holds (Salthouse, 1985). This consistent research finding was supported by the age trends for the WAIS-R Arithmetic subtest in McLean et al.'s (1988) investigation and for WAIS-III Arithmetic in Kaufman's (2000a) study. On the WAIS-R, when education was controlled, each adult age group between 20–24 and 70–74 earned a mean scaled score of about 10 (range of 9.9 to 10.4, with ages 70–74 averaging 10.3; Kaufman, 1990, pp. 398–399). Yet, all WAIS-R Arithmetic items are timed (the first nine items allow only 15–30 seconds apiece) and the last five items award 1 bonus point apiece for quick, perfect performance. On the WAIS-III, mean values ranged from 9.9 to 10.8 at ages 20–24 to 70–74, peaking at ages 45–54; not until ages 85–89 did the education-adjusted mean Arithmetic scaled score dip below 9.6. And processing speed is rewarded even more on the WAIS-III than the WAIS-R Arithmetic subtest, as the final two WAIS-III items award *two* possible bonus points for rapid solutions. Clearly, the speeded component of Arithmetic did not impair the performance of elderly adults on this Wechsler subtest.

Data from the
Bonn Longitudinal Study

Zimprich (1998) used a statistical technique called *latent growth curve methodology* to investigate the contention that the loss of speed during aging leads directly to decrements in fluid ability. Using data from the Bonn Longitudinal Study of aging (N = 127; mean age = 67) at four measurement points, Zimprich analyzed data on two markers of mental speed (WAIS Digit Symbol and a simple psychomotor task) and two measures of *Gf* (WAIS Object Assembly and Block Design, both of which actually measure *Gf* and *Gv*). After analyzing separate and combined Latent Growth Curve Models for speed and *Gf*, Zimprich concluded that the results were not supportive of the speed hypothesis as changes in *Gf* within each individual did not relate to change in mental speed.

Speed versus Cognitive
Ability on Digit Symbol

On Wechsler's adult scales, Digit Symbol/Coding produces the most dramatic age declines (along with the highly speeded Symbol Search subtest; see Figure 5.11), and this task is a strong measure of psychomotor speed. However, cognitive research suggests that poor Digit Symbol performance is not just a function of speed of responding.

Whereas Zimprich (1998) used WAIS Digit Symbol as a marker of mental speed, Storandt (1976) examined the speed and cognitive components of this Performance subtest. First, Storandt tested the pure motor speed of young and elderly adults by simply having them copy symbols as rapidly as possible without the matched pairs. Younger adults far outstripped the elderly in this task. However, when these groups were also given the standard WAIS Digit Symbol subtest, a clear-cut cognitive differential was evident as well; the superior performance by the younger subjects could not be explained by the speed differential alone. In fact, the cognitive and speed components contributed about equally to the differential.

Storandt (1977) studied bonus points as well and discovered that the young earned more bonuses than the elderly on all tasks, with the mean difference relatively small on Arithmetic (1.7 versus 1.2), and striking on Block Design (3.5/0.6) and Object Assembly (7.0/2.2). That analysis might implicate speed as the culprit in the sharp age-related decline in scores, except that "even when this advantage in favor of the young is eliminated, the old still exhibit poorer performance than the young" (Storandt, 1977, p. 177).

Creative Works

Creative contributions of men and women provide indirect support for the early decline in fluid ability. Table 5.16 presents the average ages when people in diverse fields made their greatest innovations (adapted from Matarazzo, 1972, Table 7.4, based on Lehman, 1953, 1954). Virtually all of these creative works, the products primarily of fluid intelligence, were contributed by men and women in their 20s and 30s. The only field in which the most creative works were developed by people in their 40s was literature (when authors wrote their "best" books); this endeavor seems to relate to crystallized intelligence more so than writing poetry, coming up with practical inventions, or making discoveries in science and mathematics.

TABLE 5.16 Average ages of men and women in diverse fields when they contributed their most creative works

Late 20s	Early 30s	Mid 30s	Late 30s	Early 40s
Literature (poetry)	Mathematics	Literature (fiction)	Geology	Literature (best books)
Baseball	Physics	Genetics	Bacteriology	
Boxing	Electronics	Entomology	Astronomy	
Racing	Practical inventions	Psychology	Physiology	
Chemistry	Botany	Surgical techniques	Pathology	
	Classical descriptions of disease		Medical discoveries	
			Philosophy	

NOTE: Adapted from Table 7.4 in Matarazzo (1972, p. 186), based on work by H. C. Lehman (1953, 1954).

Integration of Speed, Fluid Ability, and Other Factors

The preceding sections have argued for the hypothesis of an age-related decline in fluid ability that is not due solely to a decline in speed. Whereas the evidence for that contention is quite strong, it may be more sensible to try to integrate the Botwinick and Horn explanations for the classic aging pattern rather than trying to support one and deny the other. Indeed, the close relationship between perceptual speed and cognitive decline is congruent with the finding that sensorimotor variables are extremely predictive of intellectual functioning in old age (70–103 years) (Lindenberger & Baltes, 1997).

Sensory Acuity

Furthermore, sensory variables (with no motor involvement) may be related to declines on all three Horn factors (*Gf*, *Gv*, and *Gs*) in view of compelling evidence of substantial correlations between measures of sensory processes and measures of intellectual processes (Baltes & Lindenberger, 1997; Lindenberger & Baltes, 1994, 1997). In one large-scale study, both visual and auditory acuity were substantial correlates of IQ in old age (70–103) much more so than during the earlier adult years (25–69), with fluid abilities correlating substantially with sensory functioning in both age groups (Baltes & Lindenberger,

1997). These researchers have found that, within very old samples, more than 90% of the age-related variance in IQ can be accounted for by differences among the elderly individuals in their sensory acuity. Although Baltes and Lindenberger found higher correlations for older than younger adult cohorts, quite substantial correlations between sensory and intellectual variables have been reported for younger adult samples as well by Salthouse and his colleagues (Salthouse, Hambrick, & McGuthrey, 1998; Salthouse, Hancock, Meinz, & Hambrick, 1996).

All Wechsler Performance subtests are heavily dependent on visual acuity for interpreting the pictures and designs, and on auditory acuity for understanding the examiner's instructions. These sensory variables have generally been overlooked when trying to account for declines in Performance IQ across the entire adult life span. It is inconceivable that the dramatic declines on *Gf*, *Gv*, and *Gs* tasks across the life span are actually *caused* by declines in vision and hearing, regardless of how high the correlations are between the two. It is quite possible, however, that there is a common cause for the age-related declines in intellectual and sensory function (Lindenberger & Baltes, 1994; Salthouse et al., 1996), a hypothesis that requires empirical research to "explore what the common factor actually represents" (Backman et al., 2000, p. 505).

Processing Speed

Two other large-scale studies accord well with the interface of speed and cognition regarding cognitive decline with normal aging. Hertzog (1989) controlled for perceptual processing speed (using measures such as rapidly finding As in strings of letters) and found that the age-related variance in performance on other cognitive tasks was reduced by an average of 92%. Salthouse, Kausler, and Saults (1988) evaluated the influence of processing speed (time required to make simple comparisons) on measures believed to assess *Gf*, although by Horn's (1989) expanded *Gf–Gc* theory the measures were either primarily *Gf* (e.g., series completion) or primarily *Gv* (e.g., geometric analogies). For both *Gf* and *Gv* tasks, between 13% and 32% of the age differences in test performances were associated with age differences in processing speed. The best synthesis of the research is probably provided by Salthouse's (1992) review and summarized by Berg (2000): "The results from a large number of studies…now provide moderate support for speed of processing as a resource responsible for some of the age-related differences in cognitive tasks" (p. 126). Deficits in processing speed, therefore, contribute to the vulnerability displayed by measures of *Gv* and *Gf*, but that contribution is best thought of as "moderate." For a thorough treatment of the role of information processing speed as a basic processing component needed for the performance of complex cognitive tasks, consult Salthouse (1996).

Working Memory

Another variable that may contribute mightily to the vulnerability of *Gf* and *Gv* variables on the Wechsler and Kaufman tests is working memory. Though this construct is used to label the WAIS-III WMI, in actuality working memory is crucial for all cognitive tasks. This variable has been assessed with auditory and visual tasks alike, and is best thought of as the "mental scratch pad" that people use to temporarily store information while solving a variety of cognitive problems. One's working memory capacity refers to the amount of information that each person is able to have access to on that scratch pad. Salthouse (1992) used a "computation span" as the measure of working memory for adults ages 18 to 83 years; these adults were also administered measures of *Gf* (e.g., Raven's Matrices) and *Gv* (e.g., paper folding). Salthouse concluded that working memory is associated with about 50% of the age-related variance in the various measures of *Gf* and *Gv*.

However, these findings about speed and working memory need to be interpreted within a broader context, not one that focuses primarily on the decline on fluid or visual–spatial tasks. For example, Arithmetic is dependent on *both* speed and on working memory; indeed the ability to solve oral arithmetic problems quickly and without pencil and paper is a prototypical "mental scratch pad" test of working memory. Therefore, the emphasis on both speed and working memory would lead one to predict that scores on Arithmetic would be extremely vulnerable to age. Yet, that is simply not the case, as discussed previously for both WAIS-R and WAIS-III Arithmetic.

Executive Functions
and Frontal Lobe Functioning

Age-related declines have repeatedly been observed on measures of executive functions, such as the Wisconsin Card Sorting Test (WCST; Heaton, Chelune, Talley, Kay, & Curtis, 1993), which have been shown to depend on the integrity of the prefrontal cortex (e.g., Tien, Schlaepfer, Orr, & Pearlson, 1998). Raz (2000), for example, reported effect sizes as large as 1 *SD* in the relationship of age to perseverative errors on the WCST in three independent samples of healthy adults between the ages of 18 and 81. Similarly, Isingrini and Vazou (1997) assessed 107 adults (ages 25–46 and 70–99) on executive functions ("frontal lobe functioning") with the WCST and two verbal fluency tests, as well as on measures of

Gf (matrices), *Gc* (WAIS Information and Vocabulary), and a mixture of *Gf* and *Gc* (WAIS Similarities). They noted significant age differences in favor of the young adults on both *Gf* tasks (including Similarities) and on all measures of executive functions; within the elderly sample, the measures of frontal lobe functioning correlated significantly only with the *Gf* tasks. Conceivably, it is the decline in executive functions (such as inhibition) that may relate directly to age-related declines on measures of *Gv* and *Gf*, and on tests of working memory and episodic memory. Indeed, the "executive control of cognitive processes is a necessary component of virtually all cognitive activity, and its breakdown may underlie many of the age-related deficits in information processing when modality-specific functions are still intact" (Raz, 2000, p. 63). Parkin and Java (1999) also observed significant deterioration in tests of frontal lobe executive functions for adults ages 65–74 and 75+, relative to a younger adult sample, and analyzed these data alongside measures of *Gf*, *Gc*, and *Gs*. They concluded that much of the age-related variance on the executive function measures may be due to a more general factor defined by both fluid ability and speed.

Physical Health

The negative impact of health problems and medications on cognitive performance has been extensively studied: Circulatory system diseases such as hypertension in adults age 55 and older have been considered to account for much of the variance in age-related cognitive decline (Breteler, Claus, Grobbee, Hofman, 1994); the incidence of diabetes mellitus increases in very old age and the duration of the disease has been associated with cognitive loss at all ages, including among the elderly (Croxon & Jagger, 1995); medications taken more frequently by elderly individuals (e.g., benzodiazepines, anticholinergic medicines) may affect—sometimes dramatically—the cognitive performance by very old persons (Foy et al., 1995; Kurlan & Como, 1988); and so forth for thyroid diseases, vitamin deficiencies, and other illnesses.

Many of the health–cognition studies use memory tasks and diverse measures of information processing and cognitive ability, often with self-reported health status as the independent variable. These studies have reported mixed results regarding the relationship of health to IQ, usually reporting significant relationships (e.g., Hultsch, Hammer, & Small, 1993), but occasionally not (Hultsch, Hertzog, Small, & Dixon, 1999; Salthouse, Kausler, & Saults, 1990). A few researchers have used clinical measures of IQ. For example, Field, Schaie, and Leino (1988) assessed health via self-reports from interviews and related this variable to the WAIS IQs earned at two points in time (mean ages of 69 and 83) by individuals included in the Berkeley Older Generation Study. There was some evidence that health was more related to intellectual functioning for the oldest individuals, and that self-reported health related more strongly to Performance than to Verbal scores. However, most relationships between health status and either present or future intelligence test performance were not significant; Field et al. (1988) concluded that "[s]elf-assessed health was not found to be as strong a correlate of cognitive functioning as was anticipated" (p. 390). In another WAIS study, Perlmutter and Nyquist (1990) used an extensive set of measures of self-reported health with a sample of 127 adults, in age groups of 20s, 40s, 60s, and 80s. They obtained significant relationships between health status and both fluid intelligence and memory span, but *not* crystallized intelligence. Also, health accounted for more variance in older than younger adults, especially on tasks of fluid intelligence. Though Hultsch et al. (1993) did not use Wechsler's scales, their results, based on testing 484 adults ages 55–86, were consistent with the fluid–crystallized distinction found by Perlmutter and Nyquist. They found meaningful health–cognition relationships for basic information processing variables but not for measures of *Gc* such as vocabulary and verbal fluency.

Overall, health problems generally contribute a relatively small amount of variance toward declining intelligence once socioeconomic status, cohort effects, and other pertinent variables are controlled (Willis, 1985), and even this small relationship may be due to other causes such as limited stimulation or activity following disease (Schaie & Willis, 1986). However, research on the relationship between health and IQ has revealed some fascinating findings, including great individual variation in the relationship between physical health and mental test performance. This work supports the view that the "stereotype of inevitable frailty in old age...is yielding in the face of evidence from longitudinal studies" (Field et al., 1988, p. 390).

Although occasional researchers feel confident of a cause–effect relationship between illnesses in old age and cognitive decline, probably the most prudent interpretation of the bulk of research findings in this area is offered by Backman et al. (2000): "Given that health conditions increase in very old age, the failure to assess these conditions will inevitably overestimate the size of normal age-related changes in late-life cognitive performance" (p. 521).

Overview

When integrating the mass of data on aging and various cognitive processes, it is quite difficult to attribute cause and effect and, sometimes, even to understand which is cause and which is effect. Most typically, aging researchers have examined two competing hypotheses to explain age-related declines in Gf: (1) decline in processing speed mediates the decline in Gf, and (2) atrophy in frontal lobe structures with increasing age diminishes executive functions, thereby leading to a decline in Gf. Schretlen et al. (2000) analyzed data for 197 normal adults ages 20–92 and concluded that each theory is partially correct and that they are complementary, not mutually exclusive.

However, even the focus on Gf, speed, frontal lobe functions, sensory acuity, working memory,

and health does not nearly reflect a complete perspective on the diversity of theories and variables that have been studied and proposed as possible causative or mediating factors regarding cognitive and memory loss across the life span, especially during old age. Other variables have also appeared front and center in the aging literature, for example, attention. "Attentional processes are involved in a variety of other cognitive functions;... A number of broad theories of cognitive aging in the information-processing tradition have pointed to attentional deficits as the source of most age-related changes in cognition" (McDowd & Shaw, 2000, p. 254). However, attentional processes are related to the inhibition associated with executive functions as well as to working memory, short-term memory, and behaviors such as distractibility and anxiety. Numerous aspects of attention decrease with increasing age (for a summary of research and theory, consult McDowd & Shaw, 2000), but implicating attention as the primary cause of Gf decline during the life span (e.g., Stankov, 1988) is premature. Untangling attentional processing from a diversity of interrelated variables is simply a difficult task.

The variables to consider and evaluate when studying the cognitive decline that occurs during the normal aging process are multiple, complex, and interactive. Probably the best approach to true understanding will come from studies of the brain. Indeed, research and theory about the aging brain and the relationship of declining abilities to brain deterioration have expanded exponentially within the neuropsychology and neuroimaging literature during the past decade and there is no let-up in sight. The range of the research is vast, spanning the global to the specific. From a global perspective, atrophic changes in whole brain volume across the 16- to 65-year range, determined by magnetic resonance imaging (MRI) techniques, showed rates of decline that were remarkably similar to that of WAIS-R P-IQ (Bigler, Johnson, Jackson, & Blatter, 1995). On the more specific side, Phillips & Della Sala

(1998) reviewed pertinent neuropsychological and neuroimaging findings involving aging, cognition, and the frontal lobes, and concluded that changes in cognition with advancing age are more easily interpreted in terms of functions subsumed by dorsolateral regions of the frontal lobe rather than orbitoventral regions. Even more specific are findings that older adults show reduced activation, relative to younger adults, in the left inferior prefrontal cortex (area 47) and in the anterior cingulate gyrus (Grady et al., 1995). A large body of data from a variety of disciplines and samples and using a diversity of standardized and informal tests supports the notion that certain constructs are fairly resistant to the aging process across most of the adult life span, before declining in very old age (notably measures of *Gc*, *Gq*, and semantic memory), in contrast to other constructs that are extremely vulnerable to normal aging and begin their decline in early adulthood (measures of *Gf*, *Gv*, episodic memory, working memory, sensory acuity, executive functioning, and speed). Though brain–behavior explanations answer some questions about the reasons for the maintenance versus vulnerability of different abilities, the new wave of high-tech studies has also raised many questions that researchers will continue to address during the twenty-first century. For a thorough review and integration of the vast neurological literature on the aging brain and cognition, consult the excellent chapter by Raz (2000).

Can Cognitive Decline Be Slowed Down?

Data from a 5-year longitudinal study that compared the intelligence and memory of 69 eminent academics (aged 70 and older) with 30 elderly blue-collar workers led the researchers to reach two sobering conclusions: (1) slower rates of decline are *not* associated with high ability, and (2) cognitive deterioration on nonverbal IQ tests is *universal* (Christensen, Henderson, Griffiths,

& Levings, 1997). Although the authors of another study of eminent adults, Berkeley professors, included the optimistic phrase "evidence for successful aging" in their title (Shimamura et al., 1995), their results (discussed, in part, on pp. 159) belie their optimism. Their oldest sample of professors, who averaged only 64.7 years of age, performed about equally to middle-aged and young professors in their ability to recall factual passages that were read to them. Tasks such as that those load highly on *Gc* factors (Kaufman & Horn, 1996), and maintenance of ability on crystallized tasks through the decade of the 60s is a well-known finding for adults who are not elite. On all other tasks in the study, however, the elderly professors scored significantly and substantially lower than the other groups of professors. These tasks included a paired-associate task, resembling the KAIT Rebus Learning subtest, which loaded substantially on a *Gf* factor for adults of all ages (Kaufman & Horn, 1996), as well as measures of reaction time and working memory. If elderly professors in these two studies show basically characteristic patterns of age-related decline on measures of *Gf*, speed, and memory, are these losses in cognitive functioning inevitable, or can they be slowed down?

Pertinent Theories

Several theories have been advanced concerning the attenuation of cognitive decline in aging, with two theories receiving perhaps the most attention: Salthouse's (1991) "disuse" theory and Schooler's (1987) environmental complexity hypothesis. The disuse theory posits that the changing activity patterns that accompany the aging process lead to disuse and subsequent atrophy of the skills needed to perform some cognitive activities, for example, information-processing speed (Salthouse, 1996). Support for this theory has come from cognitive training research that has been interpreted as evidence that the decline in *Gf* can be reversed. Elderly people can be trained to improve their fluid and spatial skills, such as the ones measured by the PMA Space and Reasoning subtests (Baltes & Willis, 1982; Schaie, 1996; Schaie & Willis, 1986), and they can be trained to improve their episodic memory (Kliegl, Smith, & Baltes, 1990; Verhaeghen, 1993).

Reviews of the bulk of literature in this area show that even minor interventions can lead to significant performance gains (Labouvie-Vief, 1985). The results are interesting, and do, indeed, suggest the need for an educational psychology of the older adult learner (Willis, 1985). Whether the ability to reverse a decline casts "grave doubts" on the "irreversible decrement models that assume normative patterns of intellectual decline" (Schaie & Willis, 1986, p. 224) is another matter. We don't believe that norms make any such assumption of irreversibility. They describe what is, not what might be under different circumstances. Fluid intelligence implies the ability to solve new problems in adaptive, flexible ways. Once training intervenes, these problems are no longer new. Transfer of training has been supported (Baltes & Willis, 1982), but such studies neither imply a universal gain in fluid intelligence nor do they offer meaningful support to Salthouse's (1991) disuse theory. Further, young adults also show improvement when trained on fluid ability tasks (Denney, 1982), and the results of "studies in which elderly adults have been compared with younger adults [indicate] that there is a *decrease* in plasticity with increasing age" (p. 817, italics ours). The key question is whether individuals who are trained on tasks like the PMA fluid subtests will improve substantially on the WAIS-III P-IQ or POI six months after the training (controlling for a Wechsler practice effect). We doubt it, but that is the type of research result that would make us share the optimism of investigators like Schaie and Willis (1986) regarding the importance of the training studies and make us reconsider the possible validity of Salthouse's disuse theory.

Schooler's (1987) theoretical approach to maintenance of intelligence concerns the complexity of a person's environment. More complex environments comprise diverse stimuli and re-quire complex decisions; complex activities that take place in such environments will enhance and maintain related cognitive skills, in contrast to activities that do not place significant demands on a person's cognitive skills. The theory predicts that elderly adults who participate regularly in demanding activities will maintain their intellect more so than those who do not, perhaps forestalling or attenuating the inevitable decline. This prediction, however, is also consistent with the underlying concepts of Salthouse's disuse theory. The research summarized briefly in the next section addresses the relationship of active engagement in cognitive activities to maintenance of cognitive ability in old age.

Engagement in Cognitive Activities and Maintenance of Intelligence

Evidence does exist that lifestyle is related to decline in intellectual functioning. Much of the research on participation in diverse activities and cognitive performance has been cross-sectional; hence, one cannot attribute causality to these relationships because they tend to be reciprocal. How can one distinguish whether engagement in the activities helped maintain intelligence or whether the more intelligent people sought out the stimulating activities? Nonetheless, in summarizing the findings from many cross-sectional investigations, Hultsch, Hertzog, Small, & Dixon (1999) conclude that, generally, "these studies have reported that greater participation in physical, social, and intellectual activities is associated with higher levels of cognitive performance on a wide range of cognitive tasks" (p. 246). In addition, cross-sectional data from Hultsch, Hammer, and Small (1993) suggest that the relationship between engagement and cognitive performance may become stronger in old age.

Longitudinal data from the Seattle Longitudinal Study (Schaie, 1984, 1996) suggest that people who pursue much environmental stimulation and who continue their formal and informal educations throughout their life spans tend to display strong mental functioning in later years (Gribbin, Schaie, & Parham, 1980). Being involved in a stimulating early work experience has also been associated with IQ maintenance (Willis, 1985), as has coming from high socioeconomic status and remaining fully engaged with their environment (Schaie, 1984). In contrast, the largest declines tend to be shown by older adults (most notably by intelligent females) who have faced family dissolution or personal disengagement (Willis, 1985); widowed women who were never in the workforce and who were disengaged were particularly vulnerable to cognitive decline (Schaie, 1984). Additionally, longitudinal data obtained on World War II veterans tested twice (40-year interval) revealed significant relationships between participation in cognitive activities (and health, and education) and maintenance of intelligence (Arbuckle, Gold, Andres, Schwartzman, & Chaikelson, 1992).

However, as Hultsch et al. (1999) pointed out, both the Schaie and Arbuckle data used lifestyle criteria that are confounded with numerous factors such as socioeconomic status and education, raising the possibility that differences in initial ability level were largely responsible for producing the apparent maintenance of intellectual ability in old age. Consequently, many of the longitudinal findings, like the cross-sectional findings, prevent a clear understanding of cause versus effect. Probably the best data for addressing the causality issue are provided by the Victoria Longitudinal Study of 250 middle-aged and older adults tested three times in six years (the initial sample at time 1 comprised 487 adults ages 55–86) (Hultsch et al., 1999). The investigators administered a battery of tests that measured nine hypothesized latent variables, three of which involved crystallized intelligence (vocabulary, story recall, reading comprehension) with the rest emphasizing memory or processing speed. In a very well-designed and well-controlled study, they assessed activity lifestyle in a variety of areas such as physical fitness, social activities, and novel information processing activities (e.g., playing bridge, learning a language), while also measuring the self-reported health and personality of the sub-

jects. They identified a significant relationship between intellectually related activities (but not social and physical activities) and change in cognitive functioning, but overall their hypotheses involving health, personality, and lifestyle were not supported. Furthermore, the results of Hultsch et al.'s (1999) structural equation modeling were just as supportive of the hypothesis that intelligent people lead intellectually stimulating lives as vice versa. In addition, their failure to include *Gf* tasks in their design prevented a possible understanding of differences in the maintenance of *Gf* versus *Gc*.

Overall, the huge amount of cross-sectional and longitudinal literature that either directly or indirectly pertains to the question of whether cognitive decline can be attenuated or eliminated is inconclusive. Ideally, future studies will use the sophisticated statistical methodology and longitudinal design employed by Hultsch et al. (1999) with clinical instruments, such as the WAIS-III, KAIT, or Woodcock-Johnson Tests of Cognitive Ability III (see Chapter 14), that include construct valid *Gf* and *Gc* scales.

SUMMARY

The relationship between aging and intelligence is reviewed in this chapter, with the key question being the nature of the relationship between measures of crystallized ability (such as V-IQ and VCI) and fluid ability (such as P-IQ and POI) to the normal aging process. Although Schaie and his colleagues have conducted the most exhaustive and excellent investigations of this topic, their general conclusion of small declines occurring relatively late in life were based on the group-administered, highly speeded, and old PMA test. Of more importance for clinicians are the relationships to advancing age of the scores yielded by individually administered tests of intelligence such as the WAIS-III and KAIT (and the WJ III; see the section on "CHC Abilities across the Life Span" in Chapter 14).

Consequently, the degree to which scores on these clinical tests of intelligence change across the life span based on cross-sectional and longitudinal data, as well as possible explanations for these changes, are the focus of this research-based chapter.

When uncontrolled for educational attainment, mean scores on Wechsler's IQ scales, factor indexes, and scaled scores decrease with age in diverse cross-sectional investigations. With education controlled, however, V-IQ, VCI, and most Verbal scaled scores are maintained throughout most of the adult age range before declining substantially in the mid-70s and 80s. In contrast, even with a control for educational attainment, P-IQ, POI, PSI, and all Performance subtests (plus the new Letter-Number Sequencing subtest on the Verbal Scale) are extremely vulnerable to the effects of normal aging. These results are remarkably consistent for the WAIS, WAIS-R, and WAIS-III, and conform to Horn's predictions from his expanded and refined *Gf–Gc* theory. The findings are also supported in cross-sectional analyses of pertinent scales and subtests in tests developed by Kaufman and Kaufman (KAIT, K-BIT, K-SNAP, K-FAST). Taken together, the Wechsler and Kaufman cross-sectional data reveal maintenance for several Horn abilities (*Gc, Gq,* and *Glr* when the stimuli to be recalled are school-related) and extreme vulnerability for other Horn abilities (*Gf, Gv, Gs,* and *Glr* when the stimuli to be recalled are novel). From Baltes's theory, "pragmatic" abilities were maintained and "mechanics" abilities were vulnerable. When controlled for education, vulnerable abilities peak in the early 20s on nearly all measures. The peak for maintained abilities with education controlled has shifted in recent generations. With data gathered before 1980, the peak was in the 60s; more recent data suggest that peak performance is reached in the late 40s to early 50s. WMS-III scales, both immediate and delayed recall, demonstrate extreme vulnerability, consistent with the literature on episodic memory.

Longitudinal investigations of the relationship between aging and IQ were conducted by several researchers using the WAIS, but the findings are difficult to interpret because of the highly selective attrition that accompanies any longitudinal investigation and the practice effect that differentially influences scores on the Verbal and Performance Scales (with gains in P-IQ being far more substantial) when the same individuals are tested over and over again. Owens's longitudinal investigation of the Army Alpha, which resembles Wechsler's Verbal Scale, provided interesting data when he controlled for time lag (cultural change); overall, his findings are in agreement with the results of the Wechsler and Kaufman studies.

The comprehensive series of studies conducted by Schaie and his colleagues both agree and disagree with the Wechsler/Kaufman results. The PMA subtests that are the most "fluid" show earlier declines than the more "crystallized" tasks. However, unlike the Wechsler and Kaufman findings, sizable decrements with age begin relatively late in life (the decade of the 60s). Part of the difference between Schaie's and the Wechsler/Kaufman findings may result from the control for cohort effects that Schaie traditionally applies, a control that is arguable.

To gain more insight into the relationship between aging and IQ on Wechsler's scales, Kaufman conducted two longitudinal studies with independent samples, the first using four cohorts from the WAIS and WAIS-R standardization samples (25-year interval) and the second using seven cohorts from the WAIS-R and WAIS-III normative samples (17-year interval). In each study, the cohorts at time 1 and time 2 were shown to be comparable on meaningful background variables. To compare gains or losses in intelligence, scores were corrected for instrument and time lag (cultural change). Both studies gave results similar to each other and to the bulk of cross-sectional data: maintenance of V-IQ and extreme vulnerability of P-IQ.

The existence of an age-related decline on Wechsler's Performance, but not Verbal, Scale is a well-validated finding that constitutes Botwinick's classic intellectual aging pattern. Botwinick's explanation of the pattern from a speeded–nonspeeded perspective, however, differs from Horn's interpretation of the same pattern from a fluid–crystallized model. Much research was reviewed regarding these competing hypotheses, with the Horn perspective providing a better fit to the data. However, age changes in processing speed are quite important and need to be interpreted in concert with the age-related decline of *Gf* and *Gv* tasks. Also, the interpretation of maintained and vulnerable abilities needs to incorporate research and theory on numerous other factors as well, such as working memory, executive functions, sensory acuity, and physical health; in addition, neuropsychological and neuroimaging findings, often involving the frontal lobe, are crucial for understanding the normal aging process. Although much cross-sectional and longitudinal research has been conducted on attenuating the decline on vulnerable abilities (e.g., by engaging in intellectually stimulating activities), the results of these studies are equivocal.

CHAPTER 6

Research on Administration, Scoring, and Relationships between Wechsler Scales

This chapter discusses studies on the following topics: administration time, scoring errors, and two types of WAIS-III stability—test-retest and a special case of alternate forms reliability (the relationship of the WAIS-III to its cousin, the WISC-III, at age 16). The remaining chapters in this section of the book likewise treat WAIS-III research on important clinical and theoretical topics, each forming part of the foundation of WAIS-III interpretation, the focus of Part IV of this text.

ADMINISTRATION AND SCORING

Prior to the interpretation of any test battery, the intricacies of administration and scoring must be mastered. Without correct techniques for obtaining the data, any interpretation of test pro-

files is meaningless. This section integrates WAIS-R and WAIS-III research with the topics of administration time and scoring errors. Examiners who desire a more clinical discussion of WAIS-III and scoring that focuses on specific guidelines and pitfalls on a subtest-by-subtest basis should consult Kaufman and Lichtenberger (1999, Chapters 2 and 3).

Administration Time

According to the WAIS-III Manual (Wechsler, 1997), the 11 tests of the WAIS-III that are needed to obtain the three IQs typically require from 60 to 90 minutes to administer ($M = 75$ minutes); administration of the 11 subtests to obtain the four Indexes requires approximately 45–75 minutes ($M = 60$ minutes); and administration of the 13 subtests needed to obtain both the IQs and Indexes requires about 80 minutes (ranging from about 65 to 95 minutes). Ryan,

Lopez, and Werth (1998) recorded the administration times for the WAIS-III subtests, IQs, and indexes in a sample of 62 patients at a Veterans Affairs Medical Center who were referred for routine psychological or neuropsychological assessment. The primary diagnosis for this group of patients was substance abuse disorder, followed by a small number of patients with psychiatric disorders, medical illnesses, and neurological conditions. The sample was nearly all male (2 women) and the mean age was 46.87 (*SD* = 11.68). On average, the 11 subtests that yield the three IQs took 91 minutes to administer to this clinical sample, and the 11 subtests that yield the four WAIS-III indexes took 77 minutes to administer; the 13 subtests that permit computation of the IQs *and* indexes averaged 100 minutes of administration time. All of these values are a little higher than the *upper range* of estimates reported in the WAIS-III Manual, and substantially higher than the mean values estimated in the manual.

The subtests that yield the Verbal IQ took 51 minutes to administer, and the Performance subtests took about 11 minutes less. The Verbal Comprehension and Perceptual Organization indexes were nearly identical in their administration times (27 and 26 minutes, respectively), and the Working Memory and Processing Speed Indexes took the least amount of time to administer (16 and 7 minutes, respectively). Table 6.1 lists the administration time of each of the WAIS-III individual subtests. The most lengthy subtests to administer were Vocabulary (*M* = 14 minutes) and Comprehension (*M* = 12½ minutes), followed by Block Design (*M* = 12 minutes) and Picture Arrangement (*M* = 10½ minutes). These four subtests were also the most lengthy to administer on the WAIS-R (Ryan & Rosenberg, 1984a; Ward, Selby, & Clark, 1987).

Thus, in contrasting estimates of WAIS-III administration times from the WAIS-III manual to those of Ryan et al.'s (1998) clinical population, it appears that the times from the standardization sample may not generalize to a clinical population. There are a number of possible explanations for these differences. Although many of the VA patients ultimately had IQs falling in the Average range (*M* Full Scale IQ = 94.31), the 61% of the patients who had Full Scale IQs $\geq$ 90 took approximately 14 minutes longer to complete the three IQs than the patients who had Full Scale IQs $\leq$ 89. In addition to IQ level, patient characteristics such as severity of illness, ability to concentrate, and level of cooperation were also likely some of the variables that affected the differences in administration times between this clinical sample and the standardization sample. Experimenter variables such as level of experience, tendency to query verbal responses, and fluidity with the testing materials may also influence the administration time. Finally, administration times in the WAIS-III manual may be underestimates of the actual administration times. The WAIS-III standardization battery was substantially longer than the final battery. Therefore, the administration time had to be estimated for the standardized sample in light of numerous items that were deleted from the WAIS-III prior to its publication. In contrast, Ryan et al. (1998) reported precise administration times for the final version of the WAIS-III.

Camara, Nathan, and Puente (2000) conducted a survey of psychologists and neuropsychologists and obtained information from them about how long they typically spend on administering, scoring, and interpreting testing data. They reported data from a variety of practice areas including: intellectual-achievement, neuropsychological, adaptive-functional behavior assessment, personality psychopathology, and others. The areas of direct relevance to the topics of this book are intellectual-achievement and neuropsychological. Although the time required to administer, score, and interpret was not gathered according to specific tests, we can infer from Camara et al.'s (2000) other data, which clearly ranked the Wechsler Intelligence Scales at the top of the list of measures administered, that the values they present likely include administration of a

TABLE 6.1   Means, standard deviations, and ranges for administration time of WAIS-III subtests and optional procedures in a VA Sample (*N* = 62)

Variable	*M*	*SD*	Range
Standard Subtests			
Vocabulary	14:09	3:30	5:52–25:04
Similarities	6:59	2:17	3:25–13:31
Arithmetic	7:00	1:58	2:55–11:10
Digit Span	4:20	1:31	1:56–9:20
Information	6:11	2:29	1:48–15:54
Comprehension	12:29	3:10	6:04–23:07
Picture Completion	5:41	1:21	3:34–11:10
Digit Symbol-Coding	3:37	0:48	2:29–6:15
Block Design	12:12	2:42	4:37–17:15
Matrix Reasoning	7:55	4:03	2:15–20:10
Picture Arrangement	10:32	2:58	3:05–17:59
Supplementary Subtests			
Letter-Number Sequencing	4:52	1:55	1:45–14:32
Symbol Search	3:49	0:56	2:08–9:13
Digit Symbol-Optional Procedures			
Incidental Learning[a]	3:18	1:11	1:12–10:52
Copy[b]	2:05	0:27	1:43–4:25

[a]*n* = 58.

[b]*n* = 47.

NOTE: Adapted from "Administration time estimates for WAIS-III subtests, scales, and short forms in a clinical sample," by J. J. Ryan, S. J. Lopez, & T. R. Werth, 1998, *Journal of Psychoeducational Assessment, 16,* pp. 315–323.

Wechsler scale. Clinical psychologists reported spending an average of 115 minutes administering intellectual or achievement tests, 31 minutes scoring them, and 65 minutes interpreting them. Neuropsychologists reported similar values: 122 minutes to administer, 33 minutes to score, and 61 minutes to interpret. The amount of time spent on a neuropsychological battery was substantially more: clinical psychologists spent on average 208 minutes administering, 59 minutes scoring, and 99 minutes interpreting, and neuropsychologists on average spent 304 minutes administering, 79 minutes scoring, and 135 minutes interpreting. The increased amount of time to administer a neuropsychological battery in comparison to a battery of intellectual tests is not surprising as often many more detailed tasks comprise a neuropsychological battery in comparison to a single IQ measure that is often the key instrument in assessing global cognitive functioning.

Ryan and Rosenberg (1984a) obtained systematic data on administration time, subtest by subtest, for a clinical population of 50 male neurological and psychiatric patients at a Veterans Administration Medical Center. This group was composed of 36 Caucasians and 14 African Americans with a variety of diagnoses, averaging 42.5 years of age (*SD* = 11.5), a WAIS-R Full Scale IQ of 90.7 (*SD* = 13.0), and 13.3 years of schooling (*SD* = 1.9). The group's average age was near the middle of the WAIS-R age range, the education level was a bit higher than average, and the IQ was at the low end of average. Hence, the obtained data were probably not too different from data that would be obtained for a group of normal individuals.

The data provided by Ryan and Rosenberg (1984a) should generalize nicely to the typical types of subjects who are referred for evaluation on the WAIS-R. Table 6.2 shows the administration time data for Ryan and Rosenberg's (1984a) sample of clinical patients. Overall testing time averaged about 1½ hours, which is at the upper end of Wechsler's (1981) estimate of 60–90 minutes to administer the WAIS-R. For Ryan and Rosenberg's sample, the Verbal Scale took 7 minutes longer to give than the Performance Scale. Four subtests required an average administration time in excess of 10 minutes: Vocabulary, Comprehension, Picture Arrangement, and Block Design. In contrast, Digit Span, Arithmetic, Similarities, Picture Completion, and Digit Symbol each took less than 6 minutes to administer. The

TABLE 6.2   Average WAIS-R administration time as determined by Ryan and Rosenberg (1984a) for 50 clinical patients, and by Ward et al. (1987) for 60 low-functioning clients

Subtest/Scale	Ryan & Rosenberg (1984a) Time (in min. and sec.)			Ward et al. (1987) Time (in min.)		
	Mean	*SD*	Range	Mean	*SD*	Rank
Vocabulary	13:20	4:21	6:00–26:10	6.65	2.99	5
Block Design	12:42	3:43	6:00–20:00	9.85	2.84	1
Comprehension	12:00	4:22	2:20–23:51	7.18	3.06	4
Picture Arrangement	11:45	3:29	5:38–21:00	9.20	3.42	2
Object Assembly	9:03	2:43	4:02–14:54	9.00	2.71	3
Information	7:51	2:27	2:12–13:05	5.62	2.66	7
Similarities	5:33	1:52	2:00–10:30	4.15	2.03	9
Arithmetic	5:28	1:59	2:00–12:00	4.65	2.19	8
Picture Completion	5:04	1:29	2:00–10:00	5.93	2.52	6
Digit Span	4:59	1:43	2:55–10:00	3:45	1.32	10
Digit Symbol	3:46	2:03	2:00–15:00	3.17	0.96	11
Verbal Scale	49:09	9:45	30:00–79:40	31.70	—	—
Performance Scale	42:15	8:06	26:49–69:00	37.15	—	—
Full Scale	91:24	14:15	61:00–133:00	68.85	—	—

NOTE: Subtests are listed in the order of their mean administration time (longest to shortest) in the Ryan and Rosenberg (1984a) study. The column labeled "rank" in the Ward et al. (1987) study refers to a ranking of administration times in which 1 equals the longest subtest to administer and 11 equals the shortest. Note that Ryan and Rosenberg reported their data in minutes and seconds, whereas Ward et al. reported theirs in minutes. Hence, the value of 9.85 minutes observed by Ward et al. for Block Design corresponds to 9 minutes, 51 seconds.

range of testing time for each subtest and scale was rather large. Using a range of plus or minus 2 *SD*s from the mean administration time, the complete WAIS-R legitimately takes between 1 and 2 hours to give to patients who are of about average intelligence. Note that the average administration time for the WAIS-R in Ryan and Rosenberg's (1984a) study of clinical patients with IQs in the low 90s (on average) is strikingly similar to the mean administration time for the 11 "regular" WAIS-III subtests in Ryan et al.'s (1998) study of a different "low 90s" clinical sample.

A similar administration time study (Ward, Selby, & Clark, 1987) used 30 patients at a Veterans Administration Hospital (70% Caucasian, 97% male) and 30 private practice "Social Security evaluation" clients (37% Caucasian, 50% male). Because these groups were comparable in age (early to mid-40s) and ability level (FS-IQs in the mid to upper 70s), data for both subsamples are combined in Table 6.2 to show the mean administration times for 60 low-functioning individuals whose average ages are almost identical to those of Ryan and Rosenberg's sample of clinical patients.

There are some similarities in the time it takes to administer the WAIS-R subtests to low-functioning and average patients. For both groups, the five longest subtests to give are identical (although they do not appear in the same order), and the two subtests with the shortest administration time are Digit Symbol and Digit Span. However, the WAIS-R is clearly a shorter test to give to low-functioning patients than to those with average intelligence, with the largest discrepancy occurring on the Verbal Scale (see Table 6.2). The three longest subtests to administer to low-functioning patients are all on the Performance Scale (Block Design, Picture Arrangement, Object Assembly, each with an administration time of 9 to 10 minutes); in contrast, Vocabulary and Comprehension are two of the three longest tasks to give to patients of average intelligence.

On the average, the WAIS-R took nearly 70 minutes to administer to Ward et al.'s (1987)

sample of low-functioning private practice clients and hospitalized patients. The mean administration time was 22½ minutes longer for Ryan and Rosenberg's (1984a) group, with most of the difference (17½ minutes) accounted for by the Verbal Scale. Conceivably, the WAIS-R is shorter to give to people with low IQ than those with average IQ. Thompson, Howard, and Anderson (1986) tested 90 psychiatric patients on the WAIS-R whose average Full Scale IQ was 86.5. Not only was this group's Low Average mean IQ in between the average IQs of the samples tested by Ward et al. (1987) and Ryan and Rosenberg (1984a), but so, too, was their average administration time for the complete WAIS-R (76.9 minutes). Thompson et al. did not, unfortunately, report times for the separate subtests or scales.

Despite the evidence, one must be hesitant before concluding that the differences between the administration time data in the three studies are primarily a function of the ability levels of the respective samples. Individual examiners differ substantially in their rates of test administration, the degree of questioning verbal responses, and the like. Possibly the data from the three studies differ, in part, because of examiner variables. This hypothesis has some support if one examines Ward et al.'s (1987) administration time data separately for the examiner who conducted the Social Security evaluations and the examiner who tested the patients at the Veterans Administration Hospital. Total average administration time for the former examiner was 77 minutes (Verbal = 36, Performance = 41), while for the latter examiner it was 61 minutes (Verbal = 28, Performance = 33). Note, however, that even the slower examiner was considerably quicker than the six examiners used by Ryan and Rosenberg (1984a) to test patients with average ability. Also, both of Ward et al.'s (1987) examiners took about 5 minutes longer to give the Performance than the Verbal Scale, whereas the examiners in Ryan and Rosenberg's (1984a) investigation took 7 minutes longer to administer the Verbal Scale.

It is reasonable to generalize the findings from these WAIS-R studies to the WAIS-III, especially to the 11 WAIS-III subtests that are used to compute the IQs. One reason in support of the generalization is the very similar administration time results Ryan and Rosenberg (1984a) and Ryan et al. (1998) obtained for the WAIS-R and WAIS-III, respectively, for fairly comparable clinical samples.

Administration Errors

Research as well as experience in working with graduate students and professionals in psychological assessment clearly reveals the prevalence of administration errors on Wechsler batteries (Kaufman & Lichtenberger, 1999; Moon, Blakey, Gorsuch, & Fantuzzo, 1991; Slate, Jones, & Murray, 1991; Thompson & Hodgins, 1994). Such errors in administration can ultimately impact the final IQ (Slate et al., 1991). Training of psychologists in test administration varies widely, with some programs using a self-instruction approach (Moon et al., 1991) and others emphasizing the importance of numerous practice administrations (Slate et al., 1991). Each type of training has some merit. However, without good supervision, a checking approach, and correction of errors via a structured approach, the number of errors is unlikely to diminish (Thompson & Hodges, 1994).

The Nature and Frequency of Administration Errors

Moon et al. (1991) and Slate et al. (1991) both examined the errors made in the administration of the WAIS-R or WISC-R. The results of both studies generalize to the WAIS-III. A sample of 33 doctoral students in an APA-approved clinical psychology program provided the data for Moon et al.'s study. Thirteen of these students had already completed their formal coursework in psychological testing, and the remaining 20 students were enrolled in a required course on psychol-

ical testing during the study. Using a checklist of 177 items, each assessing a specific WAIS-R administration error, Moon et al. tabulated the error percentages for the subjects in two conditions: (1) after subjects studied the manual on their own, and (2) after subjects completed 8–10 hours of additional structured training. The general types of errors included: timing errors, neglecting to record responses, not repeating specific parts of the directions verbatim, mishandling stimuli objects, and neglecting to query or overprompting. The results showed that there were 20 administration requirements specifically referenced in the manual that were failed by at least 50% of the test administrators after self-instruction. However, even though accuracy improved after additional structured training, the number of administration errors was remarkable: 11 specific administration requirements were failed by at least 24% of the test administrators. Ultimately, even after the structured training, the administration accuracy rate was only 67%, with errors in the standardized procedures being committed by 21% to 97% of the trainees. Although Moon et al.'s sample was relatively small and they looked at only a circumscribed set of administration errors, their results send red flags up about how successful training in test administration is.

Slate et al. examined 150 WAIS-R protocols completed by 20 graduate students to study the effect of practice administrations in teaching the WAIS-R. Their subjects were master's-level students in counselor education in an intelligence testing course. To help determine the effect of practice generalization between the WAIS-R and WISC-R, subjects administered either 5 WISC-R batteries and 10 WAIS-R batteries or 10 WISC-R batteries and 5 WAIS-R batteries. After each administration, they received oral and written feedback on every protocol. Errors in administration (failure to record responses), mechanical errors (misaddition, incorrect transferring of raw scores, incorrect age calculation), and scoring errors were tabulated. Errors were found on all 150 protocols with a decrease in average error rate from 30.4 to 22.3 errors per protocol across ten administrations. The most errors were made on Digit Span, Vocabulary, and Picture Completion. The most frequent error, across the board, was a failure to record the subject's response and the next most frequent error was assigning too many points to an examinee response. In fact, students were nearly five times more likely to give too many points than too few points on Verbal items. The next most common error was failing to question an examinee when the test manual called for a response to be queried. Failure to query occurred three times more often than querying too often. When the effect of the number of practice administrations was examined, Slate et al. found that "practice does not make perfect," as the only significant reduction in errors with practice was a reduction in the failure to record responses. The authors suggested that, rather than becoming proficient in test administration, subjects often practiced errors. In applying their findings to practitioners, they speculated that, over time, in the absence of feedback, the types of errors that are frequent among students will also adversely affect practitioners.

Scoring Errors

A number of studies have demonstrated that experienced and inexperienced examiners alike make clerical and other errors when scoring Wechsler protocols (Sattler, 1988). Investigations of scoring accuracy have been conducted with the WAIS-R. Ryan, Prifitera, and Powers (1983) conducted a prototypical study of the different scores obtained when the same record forms are scored by numerous subjects who vary in their level of experience, and Jaffe (1983) conducted an innovative study that tried to determine the source of scoring errors that appear repeatedly on the three subjectively scored Verbal subtests.

The Nature of Scoring Errors

Ryan et al. (1983) compared the scoring accuracy of 19 Ph.D. psychologists averaging 7.3 years experience with that of 20 psychology graduate students. Each subject was asked to score two actual test protocols, one of a male and one of a female middle-aged vocational counseling client. The record forms were unchanged and, therefore, did not include an unusual number of ambiguous responses. Nonetheless, both groups of subjects made errors in scoring that produced a large degree of variability in the obtained IQs, which are summarized in Table 6.3. Although the mean IQs for each protocol were almost identical to the actual IQs earned by the clients, the ranges of the IQs were huge, reflecting an abominable number of scoring errors. According to Ryan et al., examination of the separately scored protocols "revealed that IQ variability resulted from mechanical errors in scoring, such as incorrectly converting scaled scores to IQs, giving incorrect credit to individual items, and calculation errors in adding raw scores of subtests" (p. 149). Although this result is consistent with previous research (Sattler, 1988), it is nevertheless disheartening that the experienced examiners performed just as miserably in this scoring exercise as did the novices; there were no significant group differences for any IQ or scaled score for either protocol when focusing on mean values. However, mean scores are less important than the variability in the scores in a study like this one, and Ryan et al. reported that the experienced examiners had greater variability than did the novices in the Performance IQs of both protocols; hence, the Ph.D. psychologists were more likely to make errors in computing Performance IQs than were the graduate students. This greater degree of variability is evident in Table 6.3; the experienced examiners ranged from 119 to 129 in their computations of Performance IQ of protocol 1 and from 88 to 105 for protocol 2; this carelessness far exceeded that of the graduate students, who produced corresponding "reasonable" ranges of 122–126 and 98–102, respectively.

Across both protocols, the percentages of perfect agreement with the actual IQs are shown in Table 6.4. When both levels of examiners are combined, the percentages of subjects who com-

TABLE 6.3 The mean and range of the IQs assigned to two actual WAIS-R protocols by experience and inexperienced examiners

Experience Level of Examiners	Verbal IQ		Performance IQ		Full Scale IQ	
	Mean	(Range)	Mean	(Range)	Mean	(Range)
Protocol 1						
Experienced (19 Ph.D.'s)	99.4	(96–105)	122.5	(119–129)	110.1	(107–115)
Inexperienced (20 Students)	99.1	(97–105)	122.2	(122–126)	109.9	(108–117)
Combined (N = 39)	99.2	(96–105)	122.3	(119–129)	110.0	(107–117)
Actual IQs	99		122		110	
Protocol 2						
Experienced (19 Ph.D.'s)	108.5	(104–116)	98.5	(88–105)	103.8	(101–108)
Inexperienced (20 Students)	107.2	(98–116)	99.2	(98–102)	103.2	(98–110)
Combined (N = 39)	107.8	(98–116)	98.8	(88–105)	103.5	(98–110)
Actual IQs	108		99		103	

NOTE: Data are from Ryan et al. (1983).

TABLE 6.4 Percentage of perfect agreement with actual IQs in Ryan et al.'s (1983) investigation of WAIS-R scoring accuracy

	Verbal IQ	Performance IQ	Full Scale IQ
Experienced	40%	69%	32%
Inexperienced	38%	88%	35%

puted IQs within 1 standard error of measurement of the actual IQs were 89% for Verbal IQ, 95% for Performance IQ, and 83% for Full Scale IQ. Yet, how encouraging is it to find out that trained professionals can usually compute a score within 1 *SEm* of the actual score? The standard error of measurement doesn't even include examiner variability as anything more than a minor source of error because, during standardizations, the test protocols are scored and rescored by statistical clerks who check each other's accuracy. In that sense, scoring errors constitute fluctuations in the IQs that are not

fully taken into account by the *SEm*, and, therefore, represent additional errors over and above the known or "built-in" chance errors.

The degree of error found in the Ryan et al. (1983) study of the WAIS-R is of the same order of magnitude as the scoring errors found in previous studies of other Wechsler scales (Sattler, 1988), including the WAIS (Franklin, Stillman, Burpeau, & Sabers, 1982), but that fact provides little comfort. If 39 subjects in a study that is obviously concerned with scoring accuracy (including about half with considerable clinical experience) come up with a Verbal IQ ranging from 98 to 116 for a person having a V-IQ of 108, and with a Performance IQ ranging from 88 to 105 for a person having a P-IQ of 99, what type of accuracy can one expect when the pressure to be careful is not present? Someone may argue that examiners are more careful with their own cases that "count." However, our personal examination of files of "official" cases given by highly trained examiners has revealed many careless (often striking) errors; clerical accuracy does not seem to correlate highly with clinical ability, and errors seem to be an unfortunate, built-in aspect of individual assessment that is often resistant to training or spontaneous improvement.

Professors who teach graduate-level assessment courses should strongly consider adopting a comprehensive and well-thought-out automated package for training clinicians and students to administer and score the WAIS-III (Blakey, Fantuzzo, Gorsuch, & Moon, 1987; Blakey, Fantuzzo, & Moon, 1985; Moon, Fantuzzo, & Gorsuch, 1986). Blakey et al. (1985), for example, showed that 11 hours of systematic training and just two test administrations led to striking improvement in their subjects' WAIS-R administration and scoring accuracy (pretest error rate of 62% versus posttest error rate of 94%).

Slate and Hunnicutt (1988), in an intelligent and persuasive article on the sources of examiner errors, make a strong case for the inadequate training of psychological examiners. Lack of quality graduate-level instruction, a problem that may be more pervasive in clinical psychology than in school psychology training programs (Oakland & Zimmerman, 1986), may produce examiners who lack knowledge of the specifics in the manual, fail to appreciate the need for applying rigorous standardized procedures, and dislike testing—often because they failed to administer enough tests during the training process. Slate and Hunnicutt cite several surveys in the literature that find clinical psychology graduate students and interns to have deficient assessment and diagnostic skills due to a combination of factors: (1) superficial teaching; (2) disparaging, critical, condemning attitude about standardized

testing by clinical faculty; (3) lack of knowledge of psychometric procedures; and (4) poor supervision during internships.

Most of the other sources of examiner error cited by Slate and Hunnicutt (1988)—ambiguity in test manuals, carelessness, examiner–examinee relationships (e.g., "halo" effect, coldness or warmth of examiner), and job concerns (e.g., examiners trying to deal with excessive caseloads)—are probably reducible to the initial inadequacy of the examiners' training in psychodiagnostics.

The Sources of WAIS-R Scoring Errors

Jaffe (1983) explored possible reasons for examiner error when scoring the WAIS-R Similarities, Vocabulary, and Comprehension subtests, free response tasks "which according to Wechsler (1955) demand 'considerable judgment by the examiner,' a caveat reduced to 'some judgment' in the recent [WAIS-R] manual (Wechsler, 1981)" (p. 1). Unlike Ryan et al. (1983), who used actual protocols as stimuli, Jaffe used ambiguous responses to assess scoring errors. Consequently, Jaffe's results are not typical or directly generalizable to everyday clinical occurrences, but they are nonetheless revealing; they also generalize directly to the WAIS-III Similarities, Vocabulary, and Comprehension subtests. He examined four variables that potentially contribute to examiner error: ambiguity of scoring criteria, specific instructions given to the examiner regarding the most efficient way to score the responses, the level of the examiner, and the personality attributes of the examiner. In this regard, Jaffe was investigating systematically several of the inferred sources of error enumerated by Slate and Hunnicutt (1988).

Jaffe's (1983) study included 63 subjects organized into three groups, each with about an equal number of males and females: 20 with "low experience" (graduate students having classroom, but no clinical, experience with the WAIS or WAIS-R), 26 with "medium experience" (graduate students with at least 1 year of clinical experience administering the WAIS or WAIS-R on a regular basis), and 17 with "high experience" (licensed clinical psychologists who regularly administer at least 12 tests per year). Jaffe felt it was important to establish specific criteria for level of experience, because previous studies evaluating this variable have differed markedly in their definitions of *experienced*.

Subjects were asked to score two responses to each of 42 items: all 14 Similarities items, 14 of the 16 Comprehension items (excluding numbers 3 and 4, which require two separate ideas for full credit), and 14 randomly selected Vocabulary items. For each item, one response was verbatim from the scoring system provided by Wechsler (1981), and one was from clinical test results. All responses required judgment to score, based on the opinions of a six-member panel. Wechsler's (1981) specific scoring guidelines for the 42 items were given to each subject, along with the general scoring guidelines for each subtest; the only modification in Wechsler's list of specific illustrative responses was exclusion of one response per item, taken from the sample responses, that the subject was asked to score.

Subjects were randomly assigned to two groups. One experimental group was given a cover sheet explaining precisely what they had to do, i.e., score the two responses to each of 42 items using the general and specific scoring criteria that were provided. The second group was given additional information in the cover sheet advising them of the possible ambiguity of responses and the need for referring to the general rules for each subtest; they were told that the study was concerned with scoring difficulties and they were to minimize guessing. The self-report Eysenck Personality Inventory was administered to all subjects to explore the relationships between scoring errors and two personality dimensions: introversion/extraversion and neuroticism/stability. Jaffe computed two types of error scores, total error and bias error. Total error was simply the sum of all errors, regardless of whether the errors were due to leniency (giving more credit than was legitimately earned) or strictness (assigning a lower score than was deserved); bias error allowed lenient and strict errors to cancel each other out, and equaled the net error rate, the degree to which all errors combined to lower or raise the "person's" total score on the items. The latter error score was included because of research findings (e.g., Sattler & Winger, 1970) showing that examiners' errors tend to reflect a "halo" effect rather than occurring randomly.

Jaffe (1983) obtained the following results:

1. Subjects made numerous errors, both on the manual responses and the clinical responses. Across all subtests and items, subjects made errors on an average of nearly half of the responses.

2. The three subtests were differentially susceptible to scoring errors, with significantly more errors occurring on Vocabulary than on Similarities or Comprehension.

3. Bias errors were in the direction of leniency for all subtests, with Comprehension producing the strongest halo effect.

4. Experimental subjects who were given extra precautions to be aware of ambiguities in the responses, to check the general scoring guidelines, and so forth, generally did not differ significantly in their scoring accuracy from subjects who did not receive a special instructional set. The only significant finding was that subjects given the precautions made fewer bias errors.

5. The subjects' level of experience was unrelated to scoring accuracy. This finding reinforces similar results from other studies (Kasper, Throne, & Schulman, 1968; Slate & Hunnicutt, 1988).

6. Contrary to Jaffe's hypothesis, high neuroticism subjects made more scoring errors than low neuroticism subjects.

7. Males with high extraversion scores made fewer total errors, whereas females with high extraversion scores made more total errors.

Ryan et al.'s and Jaffe's studies of scoring error on the WAIS-R reinforce numerous previous findings with Wechsler's scales, showing that it is very common for examiners to make scoring errors, and that level of experience is unrelated to scoring accuracy. Jaffe has given some evidence that an examiner's personality is related to his or her scoring accuracy, and that it may be quite difficult to teach or urge examiners to be more careful, unless trainers adopt comprehensive, systematic programs for teaching the WAIS-R and similar tests (Blakey et al., 1987; Fantuzzo, Sisemore, & Spradlin, 1983).

Implications for Administering and Scoring the WAIS-III

The research we have cited, as well as our own experience with training graduate students and working with seasoned practitioners, paints a less than desirable picture about the administration and scoring accuracy of newly trained and highly trained test administrators. Although structured training does increase administration and scoring accuracy, there is still room for improvement after training and practice. In addition to training and supervision, employing a structured checking procedure can be effective for further reducing administration and scoring errors (Thompson & Hodgins, 1994). We developed a list of common pitfalls of WAIS-III subtest administration (Kaufman & Lichtenberger, 1999, pp. 54–56), which can be used as a checklist in administration. A list of tips for scoring the WAIS-III is also available in Kaufman and Lichtenberger (1999, pp. 71–75). Sattler and Ryan (1999, pp. 1228–1235) also provide a helpful administrative checklist for the WAIS-III. Using such tools provides additional means for examiners or supervisors to increase the accuracy of WAIS-III administration and scoring.

WAIS-III STABILITY

This section covers two main topics, both of which pertain to the stability of the WAIS-III: (1) WAIS-III test-retest reliability, including an in-depth study of practice effects and a thorough

integration of the pertinent literature on WAIS and WAIS-R; and (2) correlations between the WAIS-III and WISC-III at age 16, the age at which the two tests overlap, which provides a special type of alternate-forms reliability.

WAIS-III Test-Retest Reliability and Practice Effects

Practice effects on Wechsler's scales tend to be profound, particularly on the Performance Scale, although many examiners ignore this fact when interpreting profiles. Matarazzo and his colleagues have studied this variable extensively for the WAIS (Matarazzo, Carmody, & Jacobs, 1980) and the WAIS-R (Matarazzo & Herman, 1984a), stressing the importance of understanding the predictable retest gains in IQs when interpreting clinical data; they have applied the practice effect to research as well, showing how consideration of normal or base rate data on retesting forces re-evaluation of the supposed gains in intelligence that accompany surgical removal of placque from the carotid artery (Matarazzo, Matarazzo, Gallo, & Wiens, 1979).

Stability of the WAIS-III IQs and Indexes

The Psychological Corporation (1997, Tables 3.6, 3.7, 3.8, and 3.9) presented WAIS-III stability data for a total of 394 adults divided into four age groups: 16–29, 30–54, 55–74, and 75–89; all groups of normal individuals (Ns of 88–104) were retested after intervals ranging from 2 to 12 weeks. Test-retest reliability coefficients averaged .96 for Verbal and Full Scale IQs and .91 for Performance IQ. Stability coefficients averaged .95 for the Verbal Comprehension Index and .88–.89 on the other three indexes.

Table 6.5 summarizes the gains from one testing to the next on the IQs and indexes based on data provided by The Psychological Corporation (1997, Tables 3.6, 3.7, 3.8, and 3.9). Average gain scores (practice effects) were 2.4 points on Verbal IQ, 6.5 points on Performance IQ, and 4.5 points on Full Scale IQ. However, these

TABLE 6.5   WAIS-III test-retest reliability for the IQs and indexes, by age

	POINT GAIN FROM FIRST TO SECOND TESTING				
	Age Group				
IQ or Index	16–29	30–54	55–74	75–89	Mean
IQ Scale					
Verbal	+3.2	+2.0	+2.1	+2.4	+2.4
Performance	+8.2	+8.3	+5.7	+3.7	+6.5
Full Scale	+5.7	+5.1	+3.9	+3.2	+4.5
V-P Difference in Gains	**+5.0**	**+6.3**	**+3.6**	**+1.3**	**+4.1**
Factor Index					
Verbal Comprehension	+2.5	+2.1	+1.9	+3.2	+2.4
Perceptual Organization	+7.3	+7.4	+4.0	+2.7	+5.4
Working Memory	+2.9	+3.1	+2.2	+1.3	+2.4
Processing Speed	+6.0	+4.6	+3.8	+1.3	+3.9

NOTE: Data are adapted from Tables 3.6, 3.7, 3.8, and 3.9 of the *WAIS-III and WMS-III Technical Manual* (Psychological Corporation, 1997).

overall values do not tell the whole story because of clear-cut age changes that are evident in the data, with practice effects found to be smaller, in general, for the two older samples. Traditionally, practice effects are much larger on the Performance than Verbal Scale. For the WISC-III (Wechsler, 1991, Tables 5.3, 5.4, and 5.5), the average gain score on V-IQ was 2 to 2½ points versus 12 to 12½ points on P-IQ, a net change of 10 points in a person's V-P IQ discrepancy. On the WAIS-R (Wechsler, 1981, Table 11), for ages 25–34 and 45–54, gains were about 3 points on V-IQ, and about 8½ points on P-IQ, a net change of 5½ points in the V-P IQ discrepancy.

WAIS-III data are quite similar to WAIS-R data for the two youngest ages tested, 16–29 and 30–54, but the P-IQ gain reduces to 5.7 points at ages 55–74 and to only 3.7 points at ages 75–89 (see Table 6.5). These age effects were not observed on the WAIS-R because the oldest sample tested in the retest study was 45–54 years. However, the full picture indicates that the sometimes huge practice effect on Wechsler's Performance

subtests is modest for ages 55 and above, and even resembles the magnitude usually associated with the Verbal Scale for ages 75 and above. The net result is that the V-P IQ difference, on a retest, is an interpretive concern primarily for ages 16–54 years, when an average gain (in favor of P-IQ) due to practice is 5–6 points. However, this net gain is only about 3½ points for ages 55–74, and 1 to 1½ point for ages 75–89 (see Table 6.5). The smaller practice effect on the Performance Scale for the oldest age group is undoubtedly related to the higher stability coefficient for P-IQ at ages 75–89 (.93) relative to ages 16–29 (.88).

The differential between the gains in the Verbal and Performance scales is certainly related to the lower reliability of most Performance than most Verbal subtests and the concomitant lower reliability of the Performance than Verbal IQ; the less stable a score, the greater the changes from test to retest. However, the fact that the changes in Performance IQ from test to retest tend to be gains far more often than losses is undoubtedly due to the relative unfamiliarity of the

Performance items. Verbal tasks tend to be similar to the kinds of problems presented in school or magazines such as *Readers Digest*, and even for adults who are far removed from school such verbal-oriented items will be familiar. In contrast, Performance items are far less related to the real world and everyday situations and require a little getting used to. This orientation to the task and learning what is expected occurs during the first testing session; an additional habituation period is not needed on a retest, allowing examinees to proceed more quickly (always a benefit on the Wechsler Performance Scales) and with more assurance (a benefit on any test). In the case of Object Assembly, improvement may be related as well to recall of specific puzzles.

Stability of the WAIS-III Subtests

Test-retest reliability coefficients, based on the same samples discussed previously for the IQs and indexes (Psychological Corporation, 1997, Tables 3.6–3.9) ranged in their mean values from .69 for Picture Arrangement to .94 for Information. For Verbal subtests, the "mean of the means" was .85, substantially higher than the mean of .78 for Performance subtests. Letter-Number Sequencing (.75), Object Assembly (.76), Matrix Reasoning (.77), Picture Completion (.79), and Symbol Search (.79) all had mean coefficients below .80. In contrast, the following tasks had means of .85 or higher: Vocabulary (.91), Arithmetic (.86), and Digit Symbol-Coding (.86).

Table 6.6 was prepared from the *WAIS-III/WMS-III Technical Manual* to show at a glance which subtests are the most subject to the influence of practice. The three WAIS-III subtests producing the largest gains from test to retest are Picture Completion, Object Assembly, and Picture Arrangement, all of which are on the Performance Scale. However, the subtest data do not conform to a simple V-P split; the task showing the smallest gain is also a Performance subtest (Matrix Reasoning), followed by Vocabulary and Comprehension. There doesn't appear to be a simple explanation for the rank ordering of tests that show the smallest and largest practice

effects. Matrix Reasoning is perhaps the most "pure" measure of fluid reasoning, and reexposure to this novel task does not appear to help subjects. Although Block Design has a fluid component as well, it is also strongly impacted by speed, and on second exposure subjects may be able to respond more quickly, thereby gaining in their score. Many, but not all, of the subtests with the strongest split-half reliabilities are among those with the smallest practice effects (4 out of 5), and 2 of the 3 subtests with the lowest split-half reliabilities are among those with the largest practice effects. However, there isn't a clearly delineated relationship between split-half reliability and practice effects that provides a clear explanation for the pattern of gains on WAIS-III subtests.

Once again, gains on some subtests were a function of age. Among Verbal subtests, only Digit Span showed an age effect; for ages 16–74, the gain was 0.4–0.5 scaled-score points, but for ages 75–89, there was no practice effect at all (–0.1). Most Performance subtests had a larger practice effect for ages 16–54 than for the two older groups (Matrix Reasoning is an exception). Picture Completion, for example, produced a gain of 2.3–2.4 points for ages 16–54, versus values of 1.6 and 0.9 for ages 55–74 and 75–89, respectively. Block Design showed a substantial gain of 0.7–1.0 for the youngest two ages, compared to a negligible gain (0.2–0.3) for the older two samples.

Matarazzo's Research on WAIS and WAIS-R Stability

Matarazzo and his colleagues, as noted previously, conducted investigations on WAIS and WAIS-R stability, and also entered into debates with other researchers regarding the impact of stability data on research findings. Many of these issues generalize to some extent for the WAIS-III, and all pertain to test interpretation.

STABILITY OF THE WAIS.   With the WAIS, Matarazzo et al. (1980) reviewed 11 retest studies with intervals ranging from 1 week to 13 years, sample sizes ranging from 10 to 120, and mean

TABLE 6.6 WAIS-III test-retest reliability for the 14 subtests, by age

Subtest	Mean Difference	Ages 16–29 (N = 100)			Ages 30–54 (N = 102)			Ages 55–74 (N = 104)			Ages 75–89 (N = 88)		
		First Testing	Second Testing	Difference	First Testing	Second Testing	Difference	First Testing	Second Testing	Difference	First Testing	Second Testing	Difference
Vocabulary	(+0.2)	10.6	10.8	0.2	9.9	10.0	0.1	9.8	10.0	0.2	9.8	10.2	0.4
Similarities	(+0.5)	10.3	10.9	0.6	10.1	10.4	0.3	10.1	10.5	0.4	9.6	10.3	0.7
Arithmetic	(+0.4)	10.2	10.8	0.6	10.0	10.3	0.3	9.6	9.9	0.3	10.1	10.6	0.5
Digit Span	(+0.3)	10.2	10.7	0.5	9.6	10.0	0.4	9.7	10.1	0.4	9.7	9.6	-0.1
Information	(+0.6)	10.1	10.7	0.6	10.0	10.6	0.6	10.2	10.7	0.5	10.1	10.7	0.6
Comprehension	(+0.2)	10.5	10.9	0.4	10.1	10.2	0.1	10.1	10.2	0.1	9.9	10.2	0.3
Letter-Number Sequencing	(+0.4)	10.6	10.7	0.1	9.9	10.6	0.7	10.1	10.4	0.3	10.0	10.5	0.5
Picture Completion	(+1.8)	10.6	12.9	2.3	10.3	12.7	2.4	10.0	11.6	1.6	10.1	11.0	0.9
Digit Symbol-Coding	(+0.9)	10.2	11.4	1.2	9.6	10.7	1.1	10.2	11.0	0.8	9.6	10.2	0.6
Block Design	(+0.6)	10.3	11.3	1.0	10.2	10.9	0.7	9.9	10.1	0.2	9.7	10.0	0.3
Matrix Reasoning	(+0.1)	10.2	10.3	0.1	10.1	10.4	0.3	9.5	9.7	0.2	10.2	10.1	-0.1
Picture Arrangement	(+1.1)	10.3	11.5	1.2	10.0	11.2	1.2	10.0	11.2	1.2	10.1	10.8	0.7
Symbol Search	(+0.4)	10.1	11.1	1.0	10.2	10.7	0.5	10.2	10.7	0.5	10.1	9.9	-0.2
Object Assembly	(+1.4)	10.2	12.5	2.3	10.0	11.6	1.6	10.0	11.0	1.0	9.9	10.8	0.9
Average	**(+0.6)**	**10.3**	**11.2**	**0.9**	**10.0**	**10.7**	**0.7**	**10.0**	**10.5**	**0.6**	**9.9**	**10.4**	**0.4**

NOTE: Adapted from The Psychological Corporation (1997).

ages ranging from 19 to 70. Across this heterogeneous group of studies, the authors found Verbal, Performance, and Full Scale IQs to have median stability coefficients of .89, .85, and .90, respectively. Average gains were 2 points for V-IQ, 8 points for P-IQ, and 5 points for FS-IQ. Catron (1978; Catron & Thompson, 1979) explored the relationship of WAIS retest gains to the interval between test administrations for college undergraduates and found a smaller retest effect for Performance and Full Scale IQs as the interval was increased. Gain scores ranged from 1 to 5 points on the Verbal Scale; the practice effect was only 2 points after 1 or 2 months, and less than 1 point after 4 months. On the Performance Scale, however, a gain of about 1 standard deviation was observed when the second testing immediately followed the first administration (no interval), and a difference of about ½ of a standard deviation was still evident after a 4-month interval. For Full Scale IQ, the gain gradually decreased from 8 points with no interval to 4 points for a 4-month interval.

Matarazzo stressed that all these findings are for groups, and are, therefore, important to internalize, but that information of perhaps equal value to clinicians is the distributions of test-retest changes for specific individuals within the various groups. Whereas his detailed analyses of individual and group retest differences for the WAIS (Matarazzo et al., 1979, 1980) and WAIS-R (Matarazzo & Herman, 1984a; Wechsler, 1981) are of interest, these data do not especially generalize to the WAIS-III. However, some of the WAIS-R data may be pertinent, and will be elaborated in the sections that follow.

PRACTICE EFFECTS ON THE WAIS-R. Matarazzo and Herman (1984a) combined the two WAIS-R stability samples (Wechsler, 1981, Table 11) into a single group of 119 normal adults, ages 25–54, to study the distributions of changes in IQ on retesting after an interval of about 1 month. The largest losses for anyone in the sample were 12 points on each IQ scale; largest gains were 15 points in V-IQ, 28 points in P-IQ, and 20 points in

FS-IQ. Their analyses showed that meaningful losses in IQ on retesting were rare, occurring less than 10% of the time for Verbal IQ and less than 5% of the time for Performance and Full Scale IQs. Indeed, the practice effect on WAIS-R IQs was so profound that nearly half the adults tested twice improved notably (i.e., more than the error of measurement) on the Verbal Scale, and almost three-quarters of the sample improved substantially on the Performance and Full Scales. Whereas gains in Verbal IQ tended to be modest, improvement on the Performance Scale was typically large and was sometimes dramatic.

WAIS-R STABILITY FOR CLINICAL PATIENTS. Gains in intelligence that are sometimes attributed to recovery from an illness or operation or to any intervention designed to improve cognitive abilities may be nothing more than a demonstration of the Wechsler practice effect. The most notable instance of such an occurrence concerns patients who had undergone carotid endarterectomy, surgery for the removal of arteriosclerotic deposits that partially block blood flow in the artery leading from the heart to the brain. Several investigators (e.g., Juolasmaa et al., 1981) interpreted pre- to post-surgery gains on the WAIS as clear-cut evidence of cognitive improvement following the surgery. As optimistic as such a finding would be, Matarazzo et al. (1979) argued that the gains demonstrated by the surgical patients on the retest were not appreciably different from the gains shown by nonpatients. Although Shatz (1981) called the conclusion of no discernible intellectual gains following surgery premature because of uncontrolled variables in the available test-retest studies, a subsequent well-controlled investigation by Parker, Granberg, Nichols, Jones, and Hewett (1983) concluded that gains in test scores of surgical patients after a 6-month interval were not significantly greater than gains displayed by the control groups.

WAIS-R stability data for 21 psychiatric and neurological patients (retest intervals ranging from 2 to 144 weeks with a mean of 38 weeks), revealed test-retest coefficients that were substantial in magnitude: .79 for V-IQ, .88 for P-IQ, and .86 for FS-IQ (Ryan, Georgemiller, Geisser, & Randall, 1985). However, these values were lower than the values obtained for the normal samples (Wechsler, 1981): .96 for WAIS-R Verbal and Full Scale IQs and .94 for WAIS-R Performance IQs. The practice effect for Ryan et al.'s sample was 3 points for the Verbal Scale, 4½ points for the Performance Scale, and about 4 points for the Full Scale.

In a more recent sample of 21 psychiatric inpatients (Hawkins & Sayward, 1994), stability data revealed WAIS-R scores that were fairly consistent with the WAIS-R standardization retest sample (Wechsler, 1981). The retest interval was 15 months, on average. Test-retest coefficients for the Verbal, Performance, and Full Scale IQ were .90, .89, and .91, respectively. The average gains were slightly higher Performance IQ (5 points) than for Verbal IQ (3 points).

WAIS-R stability data for 60 head-injured patients (mean test-retest interval of 8.5 months), revealed stability coefficients that were: .91, .84, and .92 for the Verbal, Performance, and Full Scale IQs, respectively (Moore et al., 1990). These values were also fairly consistent with the WAIS-R's normative data, but still were not as strong as in the normal group. On retest, the mean improvement in the head-injured sample was 4, 8, and 6 points for the Verbal, Performance, and Full Scale IQs, respectively.

Overview of Matarazzo's Findings and Generalization to the WAIS-III

The following rules of thumb concerning practice effects on the WAIS-R could be deduced from the important work done by Matarazzo and his associates:

1. Decreases in IQ are very unusual when a person is retested on the WAIS-R. Any decrease in IQs from test to retest is cause for some concern, and a loss of just 5 points is significant. These findings for WAIS-R are reasonable to generalize to the WAIS-III until

similar data for the WAIS-III are made available by the publisher.

2. Substantial increases in WAIS-R IQ from test to retest are common. An increase of at least 1 standard deviation (15 points) in Full Scale IQ is usually necessary to justify inferring a significant improvement in general intelligence. Matarazzo et al. (1980) suggested using this 15-point rule of thumb for each of the three IQs on the WAIS, but the WAIS-R analyses suggested that 15 points is fine for Full Scale IQ and even Verbal IQ, but that a 20- to 25-point gain is needed for Performance IQ. The latter recommendation would seem to apply to the WAIS-III for ages 16–54, based on the extreme similarity of the data for those ages to the WAIS-R data at similar ages. However, for ages 55 and above, a 15-point gain on P-IQ is undoubtedly sufficient.

3. The practice effect is much stronger for the Performance than the Verbal Scale. Increases in Performance IQ will typically be about twice as large as increases in Verbal IQ. Again, this generalization applies to the WAIS-III at ages 16–54, but not 55 and above.

Examiners must be careful not to apply the above rules of thumb to instances when the WAIS-R was administered first, followed by the WAIS-III. The rules hold only when both the test and retest use the WAIS-III. The WAIS-R norms are long out-of-date, and they do not produce IQs that are comparable to WAIS-III IQs (as discussed in Chapter 3). WAIS-III IQs are known to be 1 to 5 points lower than WAIS-R IQs. Consequently, increases due to the practice effect are negated to a large extent by the steeper WAIS-III norms when a person who was tested on the WAIS-R is retested on the WAIS-III.

It is not known precisely how the practice effect relates to intervals of different lengths and to individuals of different ages. The data provided by Matarazzo and Herman (1984a) and summarized here are most generalizable to retest intervals of 1 or 2 months and the ages of 25–54. The WAIS-III data (Psychological Corporation, 1997) are most generalizable to retest intervals of half a month to 3 months and to adults aged 16 to 89. With the WAIS, a substantial practice effect was still in evidence for intervals as long as 4 months (Catron & Thompson, 1979) or longer, and for individuals across virtually the entire WAIS age range (Matarazzo et al., 1980).

But, once the intervals reach 1 year or longer, the practice effect is far less pronounced or even nil, especially with older subjects (Shatz, 1981). As a general rule, retest intervals should not be much longer than 6 months in order to apply the present stability findings. However, we need much additional data on the WAIS-III before we can infer the degree to which the data discussed here are applicable to a broad spectrum of retest intervals, and to better understand the changes in practice effect with increasing age for those ages 55 and above. Other variables may be relevant as well. Ryan et al. (1985) found that WAIS-R IQ gain or loss for their 21 clinical patients was not significantly related to age at initial testing, initial intelligence level, days between tests, or diagnosis (brain damage versus psychiatric disorder); however, these investigators found a significant correlation ($r = .55$) between gain score and years of education.

Generalization of Data from Normal Individuals to Neurological Patients

Seidenberg, O'Leary, Giordani, Berent, and Boll (1981) and Shatz (1981) believe that practice effects based on largely or exclusively normal subjects are not particularly generalizable to neurological patients. But if the WAIS-III norms (which systematically excluded brain-damaged patients, and even individuals who were referred to a physician for forgetting) are considered applicable to neurological patients, "norms" regarding the WAIS-III practice effect must also be applicable. Norms are just that: reference points for comparison to determine whether something abnormal exists.

If neurological patients truly have smaller practice effects than normal, as Shatz (1981) contends, based on a review of pertinent studies, that finding is made possible only by the existence of test-retest norms for a random group of adults. However, the finding that a neurological patient has made significant gains in IQ compared to other patients is not impressive. That patient's IQs were computed from norms derived from normal individuals, not brain-damaged patients; consequently, any significant change in that patient's IQs should be relative to the expected gains made by normal individuals. With the WAIS-III, it is especially important to take the patient's age fully into account when interpreting gains on a retest.

Seidenberg et al. (1981) seem to present especially specious arguments regarding the "significant" gains made by epileptic patients. They divided the WAIS gains made by the patients into three categories: no gain, little gain, and high gain. Those with high gains also made significant gains on the Halstead-Reitan (the other two groups did not), but this may simply indicate that those individuals who are able to benefit from practice can do so on more than one test. The authors emphasize the "significant" finding that the "high gain" group had larger WAIS gains than the typical gain demonstrated by Matarazzo and Herman's (1984a) controls. But the high gain group was identified solely by the magnitude of their WAIS gains. Naturally, that group will have a larger than normal practice effect. So will any group that is retested—normal, epileptic, or otherwise—if they are selected based on the size of their retest gain! Nonetheless, Seidenberg et al. (1981) did have one provocative finding: When they divided their epileptic sample into two subgroups, one that had improved in their seizure activity and one that had not improved, the group that had improved in seizure activity showed significantly larger test-retest gains in Verbal and Full Scale IQ (not Performance IQ) than the group showing no improvement in seizure activity. This result is consistent with Matarazzo's mandate to support substantial IQ gains with external validating evidence before attributing meaningfulness to the apparently large gains. However, the result is also consistent with the finding that substantial gains in Performance IQ are normal and expectable and not necessarily a function of meaningful variables such as improvement in an epileptic's seizure activity.

Clinical and Research Implications of Practice Effects

The impact of retesting on test performance, whether using the WAIS-III, WAIS-R, other Wechsler scales, or similar tests, needs to be internalized by researchers and clinicians alike. Researchers should be aware of the routine and expected gains of about 2½ points in V-IQ for all ages between 16 and 89 years. They also should internalize the relatively large gain on P-IQ for ages 16–54 (about 8 to 8½ points), and the fact that this gain in P-IQ dwindles in size to less than 6 points for ages 55–74 and less than 4 points for ages 75–89. These values should always be used as base-rate or control statistics, whenever a suitable control group is unavailable for comparisons in a study employing a test-retest paradigm.

Clinicians must keep these age-related average gains in mind for assessment purposes because of the frequency with which psychiatric, medical, and neurological patients are retested in the course of treatment. The possible loss of function over time by an Alzheimer's patient, or gain in cognitive function by a recovering stroke patient, has to be inferred to make important medical, legal, educational, or vocational decisions. The age of the patient and the base rates of the WAIS-III practice effect must always be considered when making determinations about a relative change in function.

Research on the WAIS-III and WAIS-R has shown that decreases in IQ are very unusual when a person is retested. Any decrease in IQs from test to retest is cause for some concern, and a loss of just 5 points may be significant. The practice effect is much stronger for the Performance than the Verbal Scale up to age 55. Increases in Performance IQ will typically be about twice as large as increases in Verbal IQ for individuals ages 16 to 54. Changes in IQs by themselves are only of potential clinical importance, even if such changes are unusually large. Matarazzo et al. (1980) warn that, "unless other corollary clinical or behavioral evidence also is available to corroborate that patient's change in WAIS score(s)…, the burden of proof that the change is mirroring a clinically significant effect quite likely has not been met" (p. 103). Matarazzo and Herman (1984a) expand this appropriately conservative position by stressing that, if a large WAIS-R IQ change from test to retest "is a truly meaningful finding, it typically also will be corroborated in one or more of the other neuropsychological tests which were administered to this patient" (p. 359). Both of these quotes regarding the WAIS-III's ancestors suggest crucial clinical cautions that apply to the WAIS-III as well.

Alternate Forms Reliability and Stability: WAIS-III versus WISC-III

Wechsler used three separate test batteries to cover the age span from 3 to 89 years: the WPPSI-R (ages 3 to 7), the WISC-III (ages 6 to 16), and the WAIS-III (ages 16 to 89). At the ages of overlap, the Wechsler Scales are, in effect, alternate forms, and their correlations should be treated as alternate forms reliability coefficients. This section assesses the magnitude of the coefficients between the WISC-III and WAIS-III at age 16 to determine the alternate forms reliability of Wechsler's batteries. In addition, stability of the test scores over time is examined, because, typically, the WAIS-III is given to young adults or older teenagers who previously were tested on the WISC-III as young adolescents, perhaps at age 13 or 14. The stability of the scores, and the difference in the means yielded by the two instruments, are of practical importance; the continuity of measurement is likely to have a vital impact on placement decisions, for example, of retarded adolescents who were identified with the WISC-III and are reevaluated with the WAIS-III.

The major practical issue addressed in this section, however, is whether an examiner would be wiser to select the WAIS-III or WISC-III when testing individuals at the age of overlap: 16 years 0 months through 16 years 11 months.

The extreme similarity in the factor structures of the WAIS-III and WISC-III is discussed in Chapter 7. Indeed, the WAIS-III is a descendant of Form I of the Wechsler-Bellevue, and the WISC-III is the offspring of its alternate form, the Wechsler-Bellevue II. One would, therefore, anticipate comparable underlying structures for the two tests; a simple examination of the items composing each of the subtests that the WAIS-III and WISC-III share (all but Matrix Reasoning, Letter-Number Sequencing, and Mazes) reveals that each set of items comes from essentially a common item pool. The next sections evaluate the statistical comparability of the WAIS-III and WISC-III by studying the relationships between the scores yielded by their respective IQ scales and subtests.

Counterbalanced WAIS-III/WISC-III Study of a Normal Sample

The Psychological Corporation (1997, Table 4.3) presented data from a carefully counterbalanced study of 184 16-year-olds of average intelligence who were administered the WAIS-III and WISC-III with a time interval of 2 to 12 weeks. Correlations between Verbal IQs were .88, Performance IQs .78, and Full Scale IQs .88. Mean Verbal IQs and Performance IQs were virtually identical (0.5 points different), with the WAIS-III producing mean Full Scale IQs that were quite similar to WISC-III IQs (0.7 points different). Because the WAIS-III was standardized about 5 to 6 years later than the WISC-III, one would have predicted lower WAIS-III IQs by about 1½ points, based on Flynn's (1998) analyses of changes in intelligence test performance across generations. However, that prediction was

not borne out with this particular sample, and, as Flynn (1998) points out, "sampling error can easily create a difference between two standardization samples of that magnitude" (p. 1236).

In addition to the IQs, the WAIS-III and WISC-III scaled scores correlate quite substantially in normal samples (Psychological Corporation, 1997). The mean IQs and scaled scores on the two tests are quite similar in magnitude. As shown in Table 6.7, in a sample of 184 16-year-olds who were administered both the WISC-III and WAIS-III within a 2- to 12-week interval, the mean difference between subtest scaled scores was .05 and the median correlation between the subtests was .71. These findings, along with the magnitude of the IQ correlations, indicate that the two instruments are measuring the same, or very similar, constructs.

Counterbalanced Studies of Exceptional Samples

Although no data on both the WISC-III and WAIS-III, other than those reported in the WAIS-III manual, are available, Sandoval, Sassenrath, and Penaloza (1988) conducted an earlier counterbalanced study of the WISC-R and WAIS-R. They used a small sample ($N = 30$; 15 males, 15 females; 18 Caucasian, 12 Hispanics) of learning-disabled 16-year-olds with Full Scale IQs between 87 and 116. WISC-R IQs were higher than WAIS-R IQs by about 1 point on the Full Scale and nearly 3 points on the Performance Scale; WAIS-R V-IQ was about 1 point higher than the corresponding WISC-R IQ. None of these differences reached significance at the .05 level. The Verbal and Full Scale IQs each correlated .96 and the Performance Scale correlated .82, mirroring the pattern of correlations found by Wechsler (1981) for normal adolescents.

As was true for normal individuals, the learning-disabled adolescents tested by Sandoval et al. (1988) manifested high correlations for some subtests (the four Verbal Comprehension subtests on the WAIS-R correlated .82–.93 with their WISC-R counterparts) and abysmally low

TABLE 6.7   Mean Scores, *SD*s, and Correlations between WISC-III and WAIS-III for 16-year-olds

| Subtest | WISC-III | | WAIS-III | | WAIS-III vs. WISC-III | |
	Mean[a]	SD	Mean[a]	SD	Difference	r_{12}[b]
Vocabulary	10.0	2.6	10.3	3.0	0.3	0.83
Similarities	11.1	3.4	10.9	3.3	−0.2	0.68
Arithmetic	10.4	3.3	11.0	3.3	0.6	0.76
Digit Span	10.4	3.4	10.3	2.8	−0.1	0.73
Information	10.3	2.9	10.6	3.2	0.3	0.80
Comprehension	10.5	3.5	10.3	3.0	−0.2	0.60
Picture Completion	11.3	2.9	10.6	3.0	−0.7	0.45
Digit Symbol-Coding	10.9	3.6	10.8	2.9	−0.1	0.77
Block Design	10.4	3.4	11.0	3.1	0.6	0.80
Picture Arrangement	10.2	2.9	10.7	3.0	0.5	0.31
Symbol Search	11.3	3.2	10.6	2.8	−0.7	0.67
Object Assembly	10.4	3.3	10.7	2.7	0.3	0.61
Scale						
V-IQ	103.0	15.2	103.5	15.6	0.5	0.88
P-IQ	104.5	15.1	104.9	14.2	0.4	0.78
FS-IQ	103.9	15.2	104.6	15.1	0.7	0.88
Index						
VCI	103.0	14.8	103.6	16.2	0.6	0.87
POI	104.0	14.7	104.4	14.7	0.4	0.74
WMI[c]	102.8	16.2	101.1	16.2	−1.7	0.80
PSI	106.4	15.4	103.7	14.4	−2.7	0.79

[a]The values in the Mean columns are the average of the means of the two administration orders.
[b]The weighted average was obtained with Fisher's *z* transformation.
[c]For WMI, *N* = 44
NOTE: Adapted from *WAIS-III/WMS-III Technical Manual* by The Psychological Corporation, 1997, Table 4.3, p. 81, San Antonio, TX: Author. *N* = 184. Correlations were computed separately for each order of administration in a counterbalanced design and corrected for the variability of the WAIS-III standardization sample.

coefficients for other subtests (Arithmetic, Picture Completion, Block Design, and Object Assembly produced correlations of only .28–.54). These results may not necessarily generalize to other samples because of a substantial P > V profile of 11 points on the WAIS-R (15 points on the WISC-R). This nonverbal superiority is likely a combination of the nature of the group's exceptionality (learning disabled) and ethnic background (40% were Hispanics).

Other researchers have also conducted carefully counterbalanced WAIS-R/WISC-R investigations of small samples of exceptional 16-year-olds, for example, 37 hearing-impaired residential students (Meacham, 1985), 30 low-functioning males enrolled in special education programs (Sisemore, 1985), and 30 males in gifted programs (Sisemore, 1985). Mean Performance IQs of the hearing-impaired sample did not differ significantly for the two instruments, with the WAIS-R producing a higher value than the WISC-R by 1⅓ point (Meacham, 1985). Similarly, the mean WAIS-R and WISC-R IQs for the special education and gifted students did not differ significantly, except for the 4.4-point advantage in favor of the WAIS-R Verbal IQ for low-functioning 16-year-olds (Sisemore, 1985).

Grace (1986) administered the WAIS-R ($N = 30$) or WISC-R ($N = 25$) randomly to 16-year-old male delinquents. The two groups were well matched on age, race (each group was composed of approximately equal numbers of African Americans and Caucasians), and prior exposure to the tests. Overall, the subjects earned about equal FS-IQs on both tests (WAIS-R mean was ½ point higher). Otherwise, the results of the study were quite unusual and inexplicable: (1) WAIS-R produced a 4-point higher V-IQ but a 5-point lower P-IQ; (2) WAIS-R Full Scale IQ was 9½ points higher for Caucasians, but 5½ points lower for African Americans; and (3) as detailed in Chapter 9 regarding P > V profiles for delinquent populations, a substantial characteristic profile emerged for both African Americans and Caucasians on the WISC-R, but for neither race on the WAIS-R.

Longitudinal Relationship of WISC-R to WAIS-R

Studies conducted with experimental rigor, using normal subjects of average intelligence and diverse exceptional populations, are essential to understand the equivalence (or lack of it) for two instruments that overlap and that are intended to provide continuous measurement across the life span. However, in real life the WISC-III is administered first and the WAIS-III is later given to exceptional populations who must be reevaluated by law, to clinical patients who have outgrown the WISC-III, and so forth. To date, the research available in the literature remains focused on the older versions of these tests: the WISC-R and WAIS-R. Table 6.8 summarizes several studies that examined the longitudinal relationship of the WISC-R and WAIS-R for clinical samples of deaf and low-functioning adolescents.

The intervals between the WISC-R and WAIS-R administrations were 3 to 4 years for all studies listed in Table 6.8, long enough to minimize or negate the impact of any practice effect. Coefficients of correlation between the three WISC-R and WAIS-R IQs were quite substantial, despite the lengthy interval between testings. The median values of .78 for V-IQ, .82 for P-IQ, and .84 for FS-IQ compare favorably to coefficients obtained for children with school learning problems tested twice on the WISC-R with a 3-year interval: correlations of .78–.85 for 367 Caucasian, African American, and Mexican American children (Elliott et al., 1985); and correlations of .70–.74 for 150 students (Oakman & Wilson, 1988). In Elliott et al.'s (1985) study, coefficients were significantly higher for Caucasians (.83–.90) than for either African Americans (.61–.70) or Mexican Americans (.66–.81).

Neither study of exceptional children tested twice on the WISC-R produced meaningful differences in mean IQs. Oakman and Wilson (1988) found a 1½-point gain on the second testing, while Elliott et al. (1985) obtained identical mean WISC-R Full Scale IQs of 77 on each administration; Caucasians, African Americans, and Mexican Americans earned virtually identical IQs on both the test and retest. In marked contrast, each WISC-R/WAIS-R study listed in Table 6.8 produced higher IQs on the WAIS-R, although the differences failed to reach significance in the studies by Sattler, Polifka, Polifka, and Hilsen (1984) and Braden and Paquin (1985).

TABLE 6.8   Longitudinal comparison of WISC-R and WAIS-R IQs for clinical populations

Authors	Nature of Sample	N	Mean Age WISC-R	Mean Age WAIS-R	Mean IQ WISC-R	Mean IQ WAIS-R	Difference	r
Sattler et al. (1984)	In LD or MR Classes	30	13.8	17.5	V 81.0	81.3	+0.3	.76
					P 84.7	86.5	+1.8	.82
					FS 81.1	82.7	+1.6	.86
Zimmerman et al. (1986)	Special Ed. Referrals (white)	50	13.7	17.9	V 75.8	81.2	+5.4	.84
					P 79.7	83.3	+3.6	.85
					FS 75.9	81.2	+5.2	.88
	Special Ed. Referrals (black)	40	13+ (est.)	16.8	V 70.6	75.3	+4.7	.57
					P 72.6	72.3	−0.3	.75
					FS 69.6	73.0	+3.4	.70
Rubin et al. (1985)	TMR & EMR (residential)	41	15.1	18.3	V 58.8	70.0	+11.2	.80
					P 60.7	65.5	+4.8	.82
					FS 55.8	66.9	+11.1	.83
Vance et al. (1987)	Special Ed. Students	28	14.2	17.0	V 72.4	77.9	+5.5	—
					P 77.2	79.5	+2.3	—
					FS 72.4	77.5	+5.1	—
Braden & Paquin (1985)	Deaf (residential)	32	14.7	18.1	P 94.9	97.2	+2.3	.74
Median Values			14.0	17.7	V		+5.4	.78
					P		+2.3	.82
					FS		+5.1	.84

NOTE: Difference equals WAIS-R IQ minus WISC-R IQ.

The WAIS-R produced higher Verbal IQs than the WISC-R by an average of 5.4 points (range of 0.3 to 11.2), higher Performance IQs by an average of 2.3 points (range of –0.3 to 4.8), and higher Full Scale IQs by an average of 5.1 points (range of 1.6 to 11.1).

These discrepancies are opposite in direction to what one would anticipate, inasmuch as tests normed more recently invariably produce lower mean scores than their predecessors (Flynn, 1984). Although regression to the mean will tend to increase IQs for the low IQ adolescents who are retested on the WAIS-R, the differences of 5 to 5½ points for the Verbal and Full Scale IQs are larger than one would expect from a simple re-

gression effect. These findings accord with similar results of nearly a dozen WISC/WAIS or WISC-R/WAIS investigations in the literature (Carvajal, Lane, & Gay, 1984).

The difference in the scores yielded by the WAIS-R and WISC-R may be primarily due to the problems cited previously with the WAIS-R norms at ages 16–19, to the instability of norms for low IQ levels because of the few individuals at those levels who are included in the standardization samples, to the lack of "bottom" for several WAIS-R subtests, to a real gain in intelligence for low-functioning individuals over time, or some other reason. Because the identical results occurred with the 1955 WAIS, the problem is not likely to be the problematical WAIS-R adolescent norms.

The possibility of the gain truly reflecting improved ability was given some support by Carvajal et al.'s (1984) WISC/WAIS study. They analyzed data for 66 retarded individuals tested on the WISC at an average age of 11 years, 9 months and on the WAIS at 17 years, 6 months. The group gained 9½ points in FS-IQ on the retest. But Carvajal et al. were able to retest 21 subjects on the WAIS at a mean age of 28 years, 6 months. This subsample showed a gain in mean IQ from 64 on the WISC at time 1 to 73 on the WAIS at time 2 to 79½ on the WAIS at time 3; the gain from older adolescence to adulthood for this sample of individuals with mental retardation held the instrument constant. However, the sample was small and contained only those willing to be tested; conclusions are tentative and not generalizable. The only conclusion is that the WAIS-R (like the WAIS before it) tends to yield higher IQs than the WISC-R, especially on the Verbal and Full Scales, for low-functioning individuals who are retested on the WAIS-R after several years.

WAIS-R versus WISC-R
for Individuals with Mental Retardation

When Zimmerman, Covin, and Woo-Sam (1986) combined data from their two subsamples of referrals, they found that the discrepancies in favor of WAIS-R were largest for mentally retarded individuals and virtually disappeared for subjects with average or near-average IQs. Based on WISC-R Full Scale IQ, they found the following discrepancies with WAIS-R IQ by IQ level:

IQ Level	N	Mean Difference
40–59	11	+14.4
60–69	23	+5.5
70–79	32	+2.7
80–89	15	+1.1
90 and above	9	+1.3

These results are highly similar to the results reported by Zimmerman et al. for the separate Verbal and Performance Scales.

Rubin, Goldman, and Rosenfeld (1985) divided their institutionalized sample of individuals with mental retardation into subgroups of trainable mentally retarded (N = 21) and educable mentally retarded (N = 20), using a WISC-R Full Scale IQ of 55 as the cutoff. Like Zimmerman et al. (1986), Rubin et al. found the difference in Full Scale IQs for the group with lower IQs to be larger than the WAIS-R/WISC-R discrepancy for the EMRs (14 versus 7 points). Also, Carvajal et al. (1984) found slightly larger gains from WISC to WAIS over a 6-year interval for retarded people with IQs below 70 (10½ points) than for those with IQs of 70 and above (8 points). Again, the direction of the relationship between the size of the IQ discrepancy and level of intelligence is predictable based on the known impact of the phenomenon of regression to the mean; however, the magnitude of the relationship is more than one would anticipate from the statistical artifact.

The consequence of the higher WAIS-R than WISC-R IQs for low-IQ individuals is a different intelligence classification on reevaluation, which occurred frequently in Zimmerman et al.'s (1986) study, and dramatically in the investigation by Rubin et al. (1985). The former group of researchers state: "Such dramatic changes in classification may have ominous repercussions for school personnel" (Zimmerman et al., 1986, p. 150). Rubin et al. (1985) add that the reclassification in their study of nearly all TMRs as EMRs based on the WAIS-R IQs "could shift placement from one type of class or school to another, with a totally different educational plan and available resources, and perhaps also even present a major shift in funding base" (p. 395).

These concerns are legitimate. However, such consequences are primarily a function of rigid federal, state, and local guidelines that emphasize the specific IQs earned by an individual, and that adhere rigidly to specific IQ cutoff points. The differences in the norms of any two instruments at the extremes of the IQ distribution, even two instruments that are intended to be comparable, can be expected in view of the state of the art of test development. The main problem for clinicians is to try to coordinate their sophisticated knowledge of psychometrics and the intelligence construct with rigid, unsophisticated decision-making guidelines.

Interestingly, results for learning-disabled (LD) individuals also suggest potential classification differences on a retest, but these results are opposite to the findings for retarded adolescents and adults. McQuaid and Spreen (1989) followed up a group of learning-disabled individuals over a 15-year period; a sample of 81 was tested on the old WISC at age 10 and on the WAIS-R at age 24. These adults with learning disabilities obtained significantly lower IQs on the WAIS-R than WISC, even after the investigators included a control for the outdated WISC norms. Approximately equal decrements were noted for all three IQs; however, the largest IQ decreases on all scales were found for LD individuals without soft or hard neurological signs when assessed as children. In contrast, the smallest decrements resulted for those who evidenced hard signs in a childhood neurological examination (McQuaid & Spreen, 1989; Spreen, 1987).

The differences in IQs yielded by the two Wechsler instruments at their ages of overlap are provocative and have serious practical implications, especially for individuals whose diagnosis and possible placements depend on their obtained IQs. However, the results of studies on outdated instruments like the WAIS-R and WISC-R *do not generalize to the WAIS-III and WISC-III*. Observed mean differences are always likely to be due to difference in the normative samples for the specific instruments, differences that may be subtle, are likely to be unknown, and will conceivably be observed at the lower and upper tails of the distributions (where sample sizes are relatively small). All conclusions about mean differences on the WAIS-III and WISC-III for clinical populations must be based on future studies that address the question directly.

Selecting the WAIS-III or WISC-III at Age 16

To decide whether the WAIS-III or WISC-III is a better instrument for adolescents ages 16-0 to 16-11, several factors must be considered: the reliability of each subtest, the ceiling of each subtest, and the recency of the tests norms. When each of these factors are considered, we recommend the following:

Estimated ability level of adolescent	Wechsler test to administer
Below Average	WISC-III
Average	WAIS-III
Above Average	WAIS-III

For adolescents with Below Average cognitive ability, the WISC-III will allow them to better demonstrate what they are capable of answering. In contrast, on the WAIS-III there is a risk of a floor effect for individuals who are functioning at a low level. On the opposite end of the spectrum, a 16-year-old with Above Average intelligence may not be able to adequately demonstrate his or her knowledge on the WISC-III because of a ceiling effect. However, there are more difficult items available to a 16-year-old on the WAIS-III, so the ceiling effect can be averted by choosing the WAIS-III over the WISC-III for an adolescent whose cognitive ability is estimated to be Above Average. The data in the WAIS-III and WISC-III manuals give strong support for the WAIS-III having a better ceiling than the WISC-III for 16-year-olds, where "ceiling" is defined as the scaled score that corresponds to a perfect raw score. The ideal ceiling is a scaled score of 19. Of the 12 subtests in common, the WAIS-III has a higher ceiling for 7 subtests (3 Verbal, 4 Performance), a considerable number. The difference is usually 1 scaled-score point (19–18 for 5 subtests, 18–17 for Picture Completion), but was 2 points (19–17) for Information. The data from the manuals give moderate support that the WISC-III has a better floor than the WAIS-III at age 16 years, where "floor" is defined as the scaled score that corresponds to a raw score of 3 or fewer points. The ideal floor is a scaled score of 1. Of the 12 subtests in common, the WISC-III has a lower floor for five subtests. Whereas the scaled score equivalent for WISC-III raw scores of 3 or below was 1 for all subtests, on the WAIS-III, Block Design has a scaled score equivalent of 2 for raw scores of 3; Information, Comprehension, and Object Assembly have scaled score equivalents of 3 for raw scores of 3; and Picture Arrangement has a scaled score equivalent of 4 for raw scores of 3.

For those adolescents who do not fall at either end of the ability spectrum, and are best described as Average in their cognitive abilities, the WAIS-III is preferable because its norms are more recent. Because of the Flynn effect (Flynn, 1987, 1998), which has demonstrated that the norms in the United States become outdated at the rate of 2½ to 3 points per decade, newer norms are generally preferable to older ones (see Chapter 2). However, as previously stated, we make an exception for adolescents with Below Average cognitive ability. A better "floor" is provided on the WISC-III than the WAIS-III, which outweighs the advantage of having more recent norms than the WISC-III.

There are other circumstances in which our WISC-III versus WAIS-III recommendations may not be followed. For instance, if an adolescent who has recently been tested on the WAIS-III needs to be reassessed, then the adolescent may be retested using the WISC-III, as long as he or she has not yet turned 17. Administering an alternate form (i.e., WISC-III rather than WAIS-III) in this instance may minimize any practice effects. Of course, the same benefit of using different Wechsler tests can be obtained when an adolescent has been tested on the WISC-III and needs retesting, which can then be completed with the WAIS-III.

SUMMARY

This chapter reviews research studies pertaining to WAIS-III administration time, scoring errors,

and "alternate forms" reliability of the WAIS-III and WISC-III as well as the WAIS-R with the WISC-R. Studies of administration time for clinical samples suggest that groups of average intelligence require about 90 minutes of testing time, with shorter administration times (about 70–80 minutes) observed for low-functioning samples. Vocabulary is the longest subtest to administer (6 to 25 minutes), while Symbol Search and Digit Symbol-Coding are the shortest (2 to 9 minutes).

Although we have to rely on our clinical experience in teaching graduate students, rather than on empirical data on WAIS-III scoring errors, our impression is that scoring errors due to mechanical mistakes and other types of carelessness are just as common for the WAIS-III as they have been for other Wechsler batteries. On the WAIS-R, huge numbers of errors are made by examiners, regardless of their scoring experience, and inadequate training in individual assessment may be the chief problem. A well-designed study of scoring errors on the three WAIS-R Verbal subtests with subjective scoring systems yielded the following results:

- Subjects made errors on nearly half the ambiguous responses they had to score, whether these responses were taken from the manual or from clinical cases.

- More errors were made on Vocabulary than on Comprehension or Similarities.

- Errors tended to be biased toward leniency for all three tasks.

- Neither specific cautions to be careful nor the experience level of the examiner was related to scoring accuracy.

- An examiner's personality was significantly related to accuracy.

WAIS-III test-retest reliability indicates quite good stability for the IQs and indexes and for most Verbal subtests; stability for the Performance subtests is adequate. Practice effects are larger for Performance IQ than for Verbal IQ at ages 16–54, but the customary strong relationship does not hold for adults above age 54, especially at ages 75–89. WAIS and WAIS-R stability was thoroughly reviewed and investigated by Matarazzo and his colleagues, leading to the following conclusions about practice effects when the two administrations surround an interval of 1 or a few months: P-IQ increases substantially more than V-IQ, decreases in IQ on a retest are quite rare, FS-IQ gains of at least 15 points are necessary to infer a meaningful gain in general intelligence or verbal intelligence, with gains of 20–25 points needed for P-IQ. These findings generally apply to the WAIS-III as well, especially at ages 16–54. For ages 55 and older, gains of 15 or more points probably denote a meaningful gain on all three IQ scales. Any changes in IQ are meaningful only if interpreted in the context of base-rate data concerning the practice effect, along with clinical and behavioral inferences. Some researchers have applied strong cautions regarding generalizations from Matarazzo's work, but his findings seem to have serious implications for the interpretation of both clinical and research data. Among separate WAIS-III subtests, the largest practice effects were observed for Picture Completion, Object Assembly, and Picture Arrangement; the smallest were noted for Matrix Reasoning, Vocabulary, and Comprehension.

WAIS-III and WISC-III IQs correlate substantially for normal and clinical samples, although the corresponding subtests on the two batteries often do not. When 16-year-olds are tested on both tests, mean IQs have been quite similar in magnitude. Longitudinal investigations of the WISC-R and WAIS-R, administered in that order about 3 to 4 years apart, show substantial correlations between the IQs yielded by the two Wechsler batteries. Typically, the WAIS-R IQs earned on the retest have averaged about 5 FS-IQ points higher than the WISC-R IQs for the various samples, most of which were composed of low-functioning subjects. Some evidence suggests a real gain in intelligence over time for retarded individuals, but the results are speculative; other evidence suggests that WAIS-R IQ gains over time are larger the lower the mean IQ of the sample of individuals with mental retardation. These gains, whatever their cause, have important practical implications for clinicians regarding changes in classification from test to retest.

For 16-year-olds, use the WISC-III for individuals functioning in the Below Average Range; the WAIS-III has an insufficient "bottom" for low-functioning 16-year-olds. The WISC-III lacks a sufficient "top" on several tasks and therefore makes the WAIS-III a wiser choice when assessing adolescents who are of Above Average intelligence. For those 16-year-olds of Average intelligence, the WAIS-III is a better choice of instrument because it has newer norms.

CHAPTER 7

Factor Analysis of the WAIS-III

There seems to be nothing more irresistible to a psychometric researcher than factor analysis of a Wechsler battery—except, possibly, developing or validating short forms. The passion for factor analysis reached its height with the WISC-R, WISC-III, and WAIS-R, but the WAIS-III seems to be generating a number of investigations as well (e.g., Caruso & Cliff, 1999; Kaufman, Lichtenberger, & McLean, 2001; Tulsky, Zhu, & Prifitera, in press). This chapter addresses WAIS-III psychometric research related to factor analysis; the concepts of the g factor and subtest specificity, both dependent on factor analysis, are also covered.

Chapter 3 presented the basic three-factor structure of the WAIS-III to show the similarities with the factor structures of its predecessors, the Wechsler-Bellevue I, the WAIS, and the WAIS-R. As noted, the Verbal Comprehension, Perceptual Organization, and so-called Freedom from Distractibility (or Working Memory) factors were highly similar for each adult Wechsler

scale, reinforcing the continuity of the constructs measured by the original adult battery and its three subsequent revisions. In this chapter, the factor structure of the WAIS-III is reexamined to aid interpretation of the test. This discussion is limited to techniques such as principal factor analysis followed by orthogonal or oblique rotations and to confirmatory factor analysis. This chapter concludes with a systematic treatment of the strengths and weaknesses of the instrument, based on the comments of reviewers.

THE WAIS-III AS A ONE-FACTOR TEST

Does just one factor (general intelligence, or g) underlie the WAIS-III? Both The Psychological Corporation (1997) and Ward, Ryan, & Axelrod (2000) attempted to answer that key question with confirmatory factor analysis, a sophisticated empirical approach that pits various possible factor solutions against each other to see which one emerges victorious. The Psychological Corporation considered the five alternative solutions listed in Table 7.1 and Ward et al. considered the six solutions listed in Table 7.2. The two sets of models that were analyzed by The Psychological Corporation and Ward et al. were largely similar, but with some slight variations. The Psychological Corporation's five models ranged from 1-factor to 5-factors and Ward et al.'s models included only 1- to 4-factors with variations in the 2- and 3-factor models. In addition to studying the models underlying the 13 subtests, as The Psychological Corporation did, Ward et al. also investigated corresponding models with the 11 WAIS-III subtests that are used in the IQ calculations.

Both The Psychological Corporation and Ward et al. investigated their competing models

using data from the total standardization sample, ages 16 to 89 years, as well as five age groups (ages 16 to 19, 20–34, 35–64, 65–74, and 75 to 89). Both sets of authors also used several statistics to compare the various models (e.g., chi-square, adjusted goodness-of-fit index, comparative-fit-index). When the multiple-factor models are compared to the one-factor model, the multiple-factor models come out clearly ahead. Significant improvements in fit were found with the two-, three-, and four-factor models over the one-factor model. This finding was supported across the age groups. Based on practical and empirical considerations, neither The Psychological Corporation (1997) nor Ward et al. (2000) consider the WAIS-III to be primarily a one-factor test. The evidence is too compelling in support of multiple factors underlying the WAIS-III.

TABLE 7.1 Organization of 13 WAIS-III subtests in The Psychological Corporation's (1997) confirmatory factor analysis models

Subtest	Model 1 (1 Factor)	Model 2 (2 Factors)	Model 3 (3 Factors)	Model 4 (4 Factors)	Model 5 (5 Factors)
Vocabulary	g	V	VC	VC	VC
Similarities	g	V	VC	VC	VC
Information	g	V	VC	VC	VC
Comprehension	g	V	VC	VC	VC
Picture Completion	g	P	PO	PO	PO
Block Design	g	P	PO	PO	PO
Matrix Reasoning	g	P	PO	PO	PO
Picture Arrangement	g	P	PO	PO	PO
Arithmetic	g	V	VC	WM	Q
Digit Span	g	V	WM	WM	WM
Letter-Number Sequencing	g	V	WM	WM	WM
Digit Symbol-Coding	g	P	WM	PS	PS
Symbol Search	g	P	WM	PS	PS

NOTE: *g* = general factor; P = Performance; V = Verbal; VC = Verbal Comprehension; PO = Perceptual Organization; FD = Freedom from Distractibility; WM = Working Memory; PS = Processing Speed; Q = Quantitative Ability. Based on The Psychological Corporation's analyses of the total standardization sample, ages 16–89 years (N = 2,450), the best solution is Model 4.

TABLE 7.2 Organization of 13 WAIS-III subtests in Ward, Ryan, and Axelrod's (2000) confirmatory factor analysis models

Subtest	Model 1	Model 2A	Model 2B	Model 3A	Model 3B	Model 4
Vocabulary	g	V	VC	VC	VC	VC
Similarities	g	V	VC	VC	VC	VC
Information	g	V	VC	VC	VC	VC
Comprehension	g	V	VC	VC	VC	VC
Picture Completion	g	P	P	PO	PO	PO
Block Design	g	P	P	PO	PO	PO
Matrix Reasoning	g	P	P	PO	PO	PO
Picture Arrangement	g	P	P	PO	PO	PO
Arithmetic	g	V	P	FD	FD	WM
Digit Span	g	V	P	FD	FD	WM
Letter-Number Sequencing	g	V	P	FD	FD	WM
Digit Symbol-Coding	g	P	P	FD	PO	PS
Symbol Search	g	P	P	FD	PO	PS

NOTE: g = general factor; P = Performance; V = Verbal; VC = Verbal Comprehension; PO = Perceptual Organization; FD = Freedom from Distractibility; WM = Working Memory; PS = Processing Speed. Based on Ward et al.'s (2000) analyses of the two-factor solutions, the best solution is Model 2B; based on analysis of the three-factor solutions, Models 3A and 3B were equally viable; and based on comparison of the two-, three-, and four-factor solutions, both the three- and four-factor models were equally viable and provided better fits than the two-factor models.

THE WAIS-R AS A TWO-FACTOR TEST

Kaufman, Lichtenberger, & McLean (2001) examined the two- and three-factor solutions of the WAIS-III. Although The Psychological Corporation (1997) reports the comparisons between various factor solutions, it only presents factor loadings for the four-factor solution. Kaufman et al. used the data from the standardization sample to conduct a principal factor analysis of the 14 WAIS-III subtests and specified two- and three-factor varimax and oblimin solutions in advance. Their findings showed easily identifiable Verbal and Performance factors. Four of the seven Verbal subtests (Vocabulary, Similarities, Information, and Comprehension)

loaded much higher on the Verbal than the Performance factor. However, the three Verbal subtests that define the Working Memory Index loaded either on both factors or more decisively on the Performance Scale. Specifically, Arithmetic loaded about equally on each factor and Digit Span and Letter-Number Sequencing loaded higher on the Performance factor (in the oblimin solution, these two subtests loaded much higher on the Performance factor; see Table 7.5, which presents the two- and three-factor oblimin solutions). In contrast, all seven subtests on the Performance scale loaded higher on the Performance than the Verbal factor. However, Picture Arrangement did have a secondary loading on the Verbal factor (.30). In all, the two-factor solution reported by Kaufman et al. supports the usual division of the subtests into the Verbal and

Performance scales. The visualization (*Gv*) component of Digit-Span and Letter-Number Sequencing may have made their association stronger with Performance subtests, which are typically thought to measure broad visualization and fluid abilities (*Gf*). Kaufman et al. also conducted a factor analysis with just the 11 subtests that comprise the WAIS-R, and found that, when the variables are limited to these subtests, the Verbal–Performance split of the factor loadings is precisely in the predicted direction. Table 7.3 presents Kaufman et al.'s WAIS-III two-factor varimax-rotated solutions using 11 and 14 subtests.

Caruso and Cliff (1999) used a different procedure to analyze the scale placement of the WAIS-III subtests. The method that they used, reliable-component analysis (RCA), emphasizes the extraction of reliable orthogonal components and produces factor solutions that are a bit different from conventional techniques. Their RCA solution (using all subtests but Object Assembly) found that the three Verbal subtests that define the Working Memory Index loaded higher on the Performance factor. In addition, two of the Performance subtests were misplaced, with Picture Arrangement loading more strongly on the Verbal factor and Picture Completion loading about equally on both factors. Thus, Caruso and Cliff's RCA solution did not offer as good support for the WAIS-III's Verbal–Performance

TABLE 7.3   Two-factor varimax-rotated principal factor solution for the 14 WAIS-III subtests and two-factor varimax-rotated principal factor solution for the 11 WAIS-III subtests that are also on the WAIS-R

Subtest	14 Subtests in Solution		11 Subtests in Solution	
	Factor I (POI)	**Factor II (VCI)**	**Factor II (POI)**	**Factor I (VCI)**
Vocabulary	.35	**.82**	.32	**.84**
Similarities	.39	**.74**	.39	**.73**
Arithmetic	**.52**	**.53**	**.40**	**.61**
Digit Span	**.45**	.34	.29	**.44**
Information	.34	**.79**	.31	**.80**
Comprehension	.34	**.76**	.35	**.74**
Letter-Number Sequencing	**.53**	.38	—	—
Picture Completion	**.57**	.34	**.61**	.33
Digit Symbol-Coding	**.61**	.22	**.40**	.36
Block Design	**.66**	.35	**.72**	.33
Matrix Reasoning	**.58**	**.44**	—	—
Picture Arrangement	**.48**	**.45**	**.50**	**.44**
Symbol Search	**.75**	.24	—	—
Object Assembly	**.55**	.31	**.71**	.24

NOTE: Loadings of .40 and above are in bold print. Data are from Kaufman et al. (2001) based on analyses of the total standardization sample, ages 16–89 years (*N* = 2,450).

dichotomy as did the principal factor analyses with varimax and oblimin rotation reported by Kaufman et al. (2001).

THE WAIS-III AS A THREE-FACTOR TEST

Kaufman et al.'s (2001) examination of the three-factor structure revealed interesting differences in results of their analyses of 11 versus 14 subtests, primarily in the structure of the third factor. As shown in Table 7.4, which presents the varimax solutions, the third factor on the WAIS-III when 11 subtests are analyzed is simply an Arithmetic-Digit Span dyad (Digit Symbol-Coding failed to load meaningfully). However, when the 14 subtests are analyzed by either a varimax (Table 7.4)

or oblimin (Table 7.5) rotation, the third factor is characterized by a robust dimension of five subtests: Arithmetic, Digit Span, Letter-Number Sequencing, Symbol Search, and Digit Symbol-Coding. These five subtests are those that comprise the WAIS-III's Working Memory Index and the Processing Speed Index.

When Kaufman et al. coupled the robustness of the third factor with both the orthogonal and oblique rotations with the results of a screen test that suggested no more than three meaningful WAIS-III factors, the authors questioned whether The Psychological Corporation overfactored to produce the WAIS-III's four-factor solution. Similar questions were raised by Sattler (1992) about the WISC-III's fourth factor, the Freedom from Distractibility Index. However, Sattler's analysis did not show a strong third factor; in contrast, the third WAIS-III factor has strong load-

TABLE 7.4   Three-factor varimax-rotated principal factor solution for the 14 WAIS-III subtests and three-factor varimax-rotated principal factor solution for the 11 WAIS-III subtests that are also on the WAIS-R

Subtest	14 Subtests in Solution			11 Subtests in Solution		
	Factor I (POI)	Factor II (VCI)	Factor III (WMI)	Factor II (POI)	Factor I (VCI)	Factor III (WMI)
Vocabulary	.28	**.78**	.33	.29	**.79**	.34
Similarities	.36	**.70**	.27	.37	**.71**	.28
Arithmetic	.29	**.48**	**.54**	.28	**.41**	**.64**
Digit Span	.12	.28	**.61**	.17	.24	**.58**
Information	.27	**.75**	.30	.27	**.74**	.34
Comprehension	.32	**.73**	.25	.33	**.71**	.27
Letter-Number Sequencing	.19	.30	**.67**	—	—	—
Picture Completion	**.57**	.29	.26	**.59**	.30	.21
Digit Symbol-Coding	.37	.16	**.52**	.34	.23	.36
Block Design	**.66**	.29	.31	**.66**	.24	.35
Matrix Reasoning	**.49**	.39	.38	—	—	—
Picture Arrangement	**.47**	**.41**	.25	**.48**	**.40**	.25
Symbol Search	**.51**	.18	**.56**	—	—	—
Object Assembly	**.72**	.25	.11	**.73**	.23	.14

NOTE: Loadings of .40 and above are in bold print. Data are from Kaufman et al. (2001) based on analyses of the total standardization sample, ages 16–89 years ($N = 2,450$).

TABLE 7.5   Two- and three-factor oblimin-rotated principal factor solutions for the 14 WAIS-III subtests at ages 16 to 89 years (*N* = 2,450)

WAIS-III Subtest	Two-Factor Solutions		Three-Factor Solutions		
	I	II	I	II	III
Verbal					
Vocabulary	.01	**.89**	−.02	**.86**	.06
Similarities	.11	**.75**	.13	**.74**	.09
Arithmetic	**.41**	.39	.05	.37	**.45**
Digit Span	**.42**	.18	−.10	.13	**.65**
Information	.00	**.85**	−.01	**.83**	.05
Comprehension	.03	**.81**	.08	**.80**	−.03
Letter-Number Sequencing	**.52**	.17	−.04	.12	**.71**
Performance					
Picture Completion	**.59**	.09	**.53**	.14	.10
Digit Symbol-Coding	**.72**	−.10	.26	−.07	**.53**
Block Design	**.71**	.05	**.62**	.10	.15
Matrix Reasoning	**.55**	.22	.36	.25	.24
Picture Arrangement	**.41**	.30	.37	.33	.07
Symbol Search	**.90**	−.16	**.42**	−.09	**.54**
Object Assembly	**.59**	.06	**.77**	.09	−.10

NOTE: Loadings of .40 and above are in bold print. Data are from Kaufman et al. (2001). Factors I and II in the two-factor solution correlated .75. In the three-factor solution, the following correlations among factors emerged: I X II = .61; I X III = .55; II X III = .64.

ings from the three Working Memory subtests and the two Processing Speed Subtests (ranging from .52 to .67; see Table 7.4), suggesting that it represents a meaningful psychological construct. However, as discussed below, there is strong theoretical support for the four-factor solution.

THE WAIS-III AS A FOUR-FACTOR TEST

The four-factor solution of the WAIS-III has been the most heavily researched of all the factor solutions (Psychological Corporation, 1997; Sattler & Ryan, 1999; Ward et al., 2000). The Psychological Corporation (1997) conducted exploratory and confirmatory factor analyses in developing the four-factor WAIS-III. In exploratory factor analyses they compared the factor solutions for the total standardization sample as well as those for five separate age groups ranging from 16–19 to 75–89 years. Throughout most of the analyses, a four-factor solution was supported. Tables 4.18, 4.19, 4.20, and 4.21 in the *WAIS-III/WMS-III Technical Manual* (Psychological Corporation, 1997) provide the four-factor solutions for the five age groups. Table 7.6 shows the exploratory factor pattern for four-factor obliquely rotated solutions on the total standardization sample. The first factor is Verbal Comprehension, with highest loadings by Vocabulary, Information, Similarities, and Comprehension. The second factor is Perceptual Organization, with the highest loadings by Block

TABLE 7.6   Four-factor solutions with an oblique rotation of the WAIS-III from exploratory analyses of the total standardization sample, ages 16–89 ($N = 2,450$)

Subtest	Verbal Comprehension	Perceptual Organization	Working Memory	Processing Speed
Vocabulary	**.89**	–.10	.05	.06
Similarities	**.76**	.10	–.03	.03
Information	**.81**	.03	.06	–.04
Comprehension	**.80**	.07	.01	–.03
Picture Completion	.10	**.56**	.13	.17
Block Design	–.02	**.71**	.04	.03
Matrix Reasoning	.05	**.61**	.21	–.09
Picture Arrangement	.27	**.47**	–.09	.06
Arithmetic	.22	.15	**.51**	–.04
Digit Span	.00	–.06	**.71**	.03
Letter-Number Sequencing	.01	.02	**.62**	.13
Digit Symbol-Coding	.02	–.03	.08	**.68**
Symbol Search	–.01	.16	.07	**.63**

NOTE: Loadings of .40 and above are in bold print. The inter-factor correlations ranged from .60 to .77, magnitudes indicating that the amount of shared variance between any two factors is equal to or less than 60%. From *WAIS-III WMS-III Technical Manual* (p. 105) by The Psychological Corporation, 1997, San Antonio, TX: Author. Copyright 1997 by The Psychological Corporation. Reproduced with permission.

Design, Matrix Reasoning, Picture Completion, and Picture Arrangement. The third factor, Working Memory, is defined by the highest loadings from Digit Span, Letter-Number Sequencing, and Arithmetic. The fourth factor was defined by Digit Symbol-Coding and Symbol Search, and reflects processing speed. For the four youngest age groups, the overall sample is nearly identical; however, there are some important discrepancies in the structure for the oldest age group, which we discuss in depth in the section of this chapter on age-related findings.

HOW MANY FACTORS UNDERLIE THE WAIS-III?

Researchers and clinicians using the WAIS tended to interpret many factors when trying to explain adult intellectual performance. Cohen typically interpreted as meaningful four or five WAIS factors for various normal and clinical samples (Berger et al., 1964; Cohen, 1957a, 1957b). Wechsler (1958) delighted in finding clinical interpretations of small, exotic factors. For example, he interpreted Cohen's Factor D, defined by Picture Completion and little else, as a dimension of "relevance": "By relevance we mean appropriateness of response. This is perhaps illustrated by instances when appropriateness is lacking. For example, many schizophrenics and other subjects, instead of noting the called for and essential missing part of a picture, respond with an irrelevant detail" (p. 126).

Cohen's statistical sophistication was vitally necessary during the 1950s to impose some psychometric order on the clinical "art" of profile interpretation, and Wechsler's clinical genius is axiomatic. In retrospect, however, Cohen grossly overfactored in most of his landmark factor-analytic studies of Wechsler's scales, and Wechsler attempted to assign clinical meaning to statistical artifacts.

Wechsler was a consummate clinician who developed the Wechsler-Bellevue as a clinical tool to be used for measuring cognition within the broader domain of personality. However, the fact that Cohen overfactored and Wechsler overinterpreted WAIS dimensions should not impel researchers or clinicians to take a position that is diametrically opposite. Yet, that is exactly what some professionals have done in arguing strenuously that Wechsler's scales are nothing but one-factor instruments (e.g., O'Grady, 1983). Reducing the WAIS-III to a one-score instrument and cautioning clinicians to beware of the separate Verbal and Performance IQs because of their statistical overlap, which makes it "not surprising that both researchers...and practitioners...have been unable to employ a Verbal–Performance discrepancy index with any degree of power as a diagnostic tool" (O'Grady, 1983, p. 830), effectively cripples clinical artistry. As Leckliter, Matarazzo, and Silverstein (1986) stress, the main reason for factor-analyzing a Wechsler battery is "to provide the basis for hypothesis testing by the examiner" (p. 341). With that as a rationale, the real issue is whether the WAIS-III is best interpreted as a two-, three-, or a four-factor test battery.

ARE THERE TWO, THREE, OR FOUR WAIS-III FACTORS?

The data we have presented thus far in this chapter have shown that the one-factor model of the WAIS-III is not the best statistical fit. However, the two-, three-, and four-factor models all seem to have some merit. The confirmatory maximum likelihood factor analyses (Psychological Corporation, 1997; Ward et al., 2000) compared and contrasted various multiple-factor models of the WAIS-III to determine which was the most statistically sound and clinically useful (see Tables 7.1 and 7.2). In the total sample, as well as across most of the five age groups studied, The Psychological Corporation (1997) found significant successive improvements in model fit moving from two to three to four factors. The conclusion was that the four-factor model best fits the data for the total sample and most age groups. Ward et al. (2000) found that the three-factor models statistically fit better than the two-factor model; however, the advantage was very minimal. An important observation made by Ward et al. was that their alternative two-factor model, which assigns the three Working Memory subtests to the Performance Scale (see Table 7.2, Model 2B) afforded a better fit in the younger groups than did the traditional dichotomy of Verbal–Performance subtests. In comparing the three- and four-factor models, Ward et al. found that, overall, there were no important differences between the three- and four-factor models. The fit differences were negligible between three- and four-factor models, and the three-factor models were somewhat more parsimonious in a statistical sense. The Ward et al. finding of near-equivalence of three- and four-factor models is interesting in light of the robust and meaningful three-factor solution reported by Kaufman et al. (2001). However, to this point, each of the findings has been presented in statistical isolation, without regard to the psychological meaningfulness or possible theoretical underpinnings of the factor models. To best discern which model has the best fit, we have to start with statistics but move on to integrate how these factors may be interpreted psychologically.

Beginning with the statistics, it seems that the question boils down to whether the three- or four-factor model is the best for the WAIS-III. The two-factor model does fit with the Verbal–Performance dichotomy, but the numbers show that there is an advantage (albeit perhaps small) for interpreting at least three factors (Kaufman et al., 2001; Psychological Corporation, 1997; Ward et al., 2000). The Psychological Corporation ultimately argues for four factors and Kaufman et al.

and Ward et al. provide some evidence for three. Perhaps a look at theoretical explanations will help to resolve the matter. The third factor in the three-factor solution comprises both the Processing Speed subtests and the Working Memory subtests. Kaufman et al. and Ward et al. recognize that all five subtests may be reflecting working memory, executive functioning, or attention. Both Processing Speed subtests and all three Working Memory subtests tax the working memory, as they require the temporary storage of material that is in an active state. Thus, it seems there are valid psychological interpretations of this third five-subtest factor. In addition, the merger of Processing Speed and Working Memory seems to be particularly meaningful for elderly adults, ages 75–89. As stated previously, when four factors are evaluated for this sample, most Performance subtests load highest on the Processing Speed factor instead of the Perceptual Organization factor. Whereas that is the main difference in the factor structure for the 75–89 versus 16–74 age groupings, the Working Memory factor also produces an important difference—namely, the two Processing Speed subtests both have secondary loadings in the high .30s on this factor (see Table 7.9)—creating the psychologically meaningful five-subtest dimension discussed above.

Choosing the WAIS-III three-factor model over the four-factor model implies that the two Processing Speed subtests are best interpreted with the three Working Memory subtests as primarily tapping short-term or working memory, rather than speed, per se. However, choosing the four-factor solution as the most conceptually meaningful opens up the door to considering Digit Symbol-Coding and Symbol Search as uniquely common in their measurement of visual scanning or perceptual processing speed (Ward et al., 2000). Kaufman et al. note that Horn's (1985, 1989, 1991) theoretical model would view the five-subtest third factor as two distinct abilities: short-term memory (SAR) and speed (Gs). Also, from the CHC model (see Chapter 14), the distinct abilities measured would be Short-Term

Memory (Gsm—Digit Span and Letter-Number Sequencing), Quantitative Knowledge (Gq) and Fluid Intelligence (Gf—Arithmetic), and Processing Speed (Gs—Symbol Search and Digit Symbol-Coding). These distinct processing speed and short-term memory (and quantitative and fluid) abilities merit separating the Digit Symbol-Coding and Symbol Search dyad from the triad of Working Memory subtests, thereby offering strong theoretical support for the four-factor model. The Horn abilities, SAR and Gs, have distinctive aging patterns (see Chapter 5): Processing speed is much more vulnerable than short-term memory to the aging process. Ward et al. also recognize that the Processing Speed Index is established empirically as a valuable clinical tool in and of itself because it is sensitive to brain pathology. Thus, as confirmatory factor analyses do provide empirical support for the four-factor solution in the total sample and across separate age groups, and there are viable theoretical explanations for the four-factor solution, the WAIS-III's publishers were on solid ground to interpret four factors.

Notwithstanding the empirical and theoretical support for interpreting four factors, the robustness of the five-subtest third factor in the three-factor model, and its emergence for elderly individuals, ages 75–89, in the four-factor model, also reflects a meaningful construct that might merit interpretation in some cases. When individual clients score consistently high or low on *both* the Processing Speed and Working Memory indexes, interpreting them as a unit may be considered. For example some groups of children with Attention-Deficit Hyperactivity Disorder or learning disabilities have displayed consistently low scores on the WISC-III Freedom from Distractibility Index and Processing Speed Index (Kaufman, 1994a; Kaufman & Lichtenberger, 1999; Schwean & Saklofske, 1998). Preliminary evidence from the WAIS-III also shows that ADHD adolescents have lower mean indexes on both the Working Memory Index and the Processing Speed Index (Psychological Corporation, 1997). In such groups, the hypothesized construct of deficient executive functioning (Barkley, 1997) may be responsible for lower scores on the five-subtest third factor, just as it might merit such an interpretation for any individual above age 75 who scores relatively low on both WMI and PSI.

Differences in WAIS-III Factor Structure Due to Ethnicity

Tulsky, Zhu, and Prifitera (in press) tested the stability of the WAIS-III factor structure on different ethnic groups by conducting exploratory analyses separately for groups of African Americans (*N* = 279), Hipanics (*N* = 181), and Caucasians (*N* = 1925) from the standardization sample. Overall, the results of the solutions with an oblique rotation across the separate ethnic groups were similar to those presented for the total sample (see Table 7.7). The main difference concerned the pattern of loadings for Arithmetic. For the African Americans, Arithmetic's loadings were split between Verbal Comprehension and Working Memory, and, for Hispanics, Arithmetic's loadings were split between Verbal Comprehension and Perceptual Organization. We calculated the coefficients of congruence between the ethnic groups, taken two at a time, and found the factors to be highly congruent (see Table 7.8). Values ranged from .90 to .99 (median .965), with the greatest congruence shown for Verbal Comprehension and Processing Speed. These results offer strong support for the construct validity of the WAIS-III for all three ethnic groups studied by Tulsky et al.

Age Differences in the WAIS-III Factor Structure

Based on separate factor analysis for five age groups, The Psychological Corporation (1997) recognized that the structure was quite similar for each of the four youngest groups: 16–19, 20–34, 35–54, and 55–74 years. However, the overall structure was quite different for the oldest group. Namely, the 75- to 89-year-old sample had different subtests loading on the Processing Speed and Perceptual Organization factors than did all other age groups, and both Processing Speed subtests had secondary loadings (.37–.39) on the Working Memory factor. Regarding the nonverbal factors, many Performance subtests loaded primarily on the Processing Speed factor: Picture Completion, Block Design, Picture Arrangement, Digit Symbol-Coding, and Symbol Search. Only one subtest had a loading above .40 on the Perceptual Organization factor, Matrix Reasoning, which is an untimed test. Block Design had a secondary loading on the Perceptual Organization factor of .39, but loaded higher on Processing Speed (.51). The test publisher hypothesized that the time limits on the Performance subtests led to a heavier weighting on processing speed for the oldest age group. However, that explanation is not consistent with the results of the four-factor solution when Object Assembly is included in the analysis, alongside the 13 other WAIS-III subtests analyzed by the test publisher. Sattler and Ryan (1999, pp. 1216–1217) included Object Assembly in their four-factor solutions for each of the 13 separate standardization age groups and found that this subtest (which is not intended for ages 75–89) loaded substantially (.54–.81) on the Perceptual Organization factor for all age groups, and had only one loading above .14 on the Processing Speed factor (.26 at ages 65–69). Object Assembly places a very heavy emphasis on speed and is included with the PSI subtests in Dean's Visual-Motor Speed category (see Chapter 10), which is contrary to the publisher's contention about the effect of time limits on the elderly sample's success on nonverbal subtests.

Overall, the small Perceptual Organization factor for ages 75–89 probably should not be interpreted. The most sensible conclusion is that only three factors are meaningful for elderly individuals: Verbal Comprehension, Working Memory (the five-subtest version, akin to Barkley's, 1997, executive functioning construct), and

TABLE 7.7 Four-factor solutions with an oblique rotation of the WAIS-III from exploratory analyses with African American, Hispanic, and Caucasian subjects in the standardization sample

Subtest	Verbal Comprehension			Perceptual Organization			Working Memory			Processing Speed		
	A-A	H	W	A-A	H	W	A-A	H	W	A-A	H	C
Vocabulary	**.85**	**.80**	**.92**	-.01	-.15	-.11	.03	.26	.04	.09	.08	.05
Similarities	**.75**	**.73**	**.74**	.05	.04	.09	-.03	-.01	-.01	.11	.07	.03
Information	**.82**	**.76**	**.81**	-.01	.11	.02	.09	-.07	.07	-.07	-.01	-.03
Comprehension	**.77**	**.70**	**.80**	.09	.14	.06	-.06	.02	-.01	-.01	.03	-.02
Picture Completion	.02	.17	.12	**.57**	**.39**	**.49**	-.09	-.01	-.10	.13	.10	.21
Block Design	.05	-.04	-.03	**.52**	**.72**	**.68**	.05	.11	.08	.12	.01	.07
Matrix Reasoning	.02	.14	.07	**.56**	**.54**	**.60**	**.34**	.05	.22	-.03	.14	-.06
Picture Arrangement	.22	**.36**	.27	**.51**	**.37**	**.41**	.00	.00	-.03	-.02	.04	.09
Arithmetic	**.38**	.25	.22	-.02	**.31**	.20	**.51**	**.32**	**.47**	.09	.10	-.01
Digit Span	.05	-.09	.02	.06	.11	.01	**.67**	**.67**	**.66**	.00	.10	.04
Letter-Number Sequencing	-.02	.18	.01	.07	.02	.01	**.68**	**.55**	**.63**	.22	-.04	.10
Digit Symbol-Coding	.05	.01	.04	.01	-.01	-.05	-.01	-.07	.07	**.76**	**.81**	**.70**
Symbol Search	.01	.00	-.02	.12	.03	.15	.13	.14	.06	**.66**	**.73**	**.69**

NOTE: A-A = African American (N = 279); H = Hispanic (N = 181); W = white (N = 1,925); loadings of .30 or above are bolded. From "Assessing adult intelligence with the WAIS-III" by D. S. Tulsky, J. Zhu, and A. Prifitera, in press. In G. Goldstein (Ed.), *The handbook of psychological assessment*, Boston, MA: Allyn & Bacon.

TABLE 7.8 Coefficients of congruence for the WAIS-III factors obtained for three ethnic groups

WAIS-III Index	African Americans and Hispanics	African Americans and Whites	Hispanics and Whites
Verbal Comprehension	.97	.99	.99
Perceptual Organization	.90	.96	.97
Working Memory	.91	.99	.93
Processing Speed	.94	.97	.96

NOTE: These coefficients are based on the oblique-rotated four-factor solution presented by Tulsky et al. (in press). (See Table 7.7.)

Performance (i.e., a blend of Perceptual Organization and Processing Speed).

Another finding for the oldest group is that a five-factor solution had a slightly better fit than a four-factor solution. The five-factor solution was identical to the four-factor solution except for Arithmetic, which was placed on its own factor (labeled Quantitative). The slightly better fit for the five-factor solution was not significantly better than the four-factor solution, and both the four- and five-factor solutions probably reflect overfactoring, at least from a clinical or practical standpoint. Although the publisher's final conclusion from the overall analyses was that the four-factor solution, which best fit the younger age groups, was a valid structure for an older adult population, we believe that three factors represent the best fit for ages 75–89 years.

Sattler and Ryan (1999) conducted a principal axis factor analysis on each of the 13 age groups of the WAIS-III standardization sample. They specified a four-factor solution and used all 14 WAIS-III subtests (unlike The Psychological Corporation, which excluded Object Assembly from their analyses). Though there were some slight variations in the oblimin-rotated factor loadings across the 13 age groups, for the most part Sattler and Ryan thought that the findings were consistent with those reported by The Psy-

chological Corporation (1997). Sattler and Ryan recognized that there are various explanations for the variations in the structure: sampling differences, measurement error, or an unknown factor related to developmental trends. Those explanations notwithstanding, interesting structural differences were apparent throughout the four factors. For example, three Performance subtests (Picture Arrangement, Matrix Reasoning, and Picture Completion) had secondary loadings ($\geq$ .30) on the Verbal Comprehension factor at one or more ages. In particular, Picture Arrangement loaded .30 or above on Verbal Comprehension at nine age groups and Arithmetic loaded $\geq$ .30 at eight age groups.

Letter-Number Sequencing had a rebel loading on the Perceptual Organization factor in the 25- to 29-year-old age group, and the Working Memory factor had loadings of .30 or above by three Performance subtests (Matrix Reasoning, Picture Arrangement, Object Assembly) at one or more age groups. Similarly, the Processing Speed factor had loadings of .30 or above by four subtests (Letter-Number Sequencing, Picture Completion, Digit Span, Block Design) at one or more age groups.

Interestingly, the three age groups that comprise the 75- to 89-year-old age group in The Psychological Corporation's analyses (ages 75–79,

80–84, and 85–89) look different when their data are examined separately than when they are combined as a single "elderly" sample. Table 7.9 provides the average factor loadings for these three groups together and separately. Several of the Perceptual Organization subtests that loaded aberrantly on the Processing Speed factor in The Psychological Corporation's (1997) analysis of the combined 75- to 89-year-old sample did not load on the Processing Speed factor when analyzed as three separate age groups (Sattler & Ryan, 1999). In fact, most of the loadings of the Performance subtests on the Processing Speed factor seemed to be driven by the oldest age group, the 85- to 89-year-olds; the 75- to 79-year-olds had only Digit Symbol-Coding and Symbol Search load on the Processing Speed factor (as was typical for those under age 75), and the 80- to 84-year-olds had only Block Design load above .30 on the Processing Speed factor. There were also a couple of rebel Verbal subtests that loaded on the Processing Speed factor for the 75- to 79-year-old group: Letter-Number Sequencing had a .44 loading and Digit Span had a .37 loading. In addition, as noted previously, the Working Memory factor included secondary loadings by the two Processing Speed subtests for ages 75–89, providing some support for the interpretation of this five-subtest factor in terms of Barkley's (1997) executive functioning construct. However, examination of Table 7.9 indicates that this five-subtest dimension emerged for the total sample of elderly adults, but *not* for any of the three subsamples; the best support for this executive functioning factor was provided for ages 80–84, as four of the five subtests had loadings above .60.

The reasons for the variability in the three oldest age groups are not entirely clear. It seems plausible that the effects of the speeded nature of the Performance subtests do not impact older adults until they reach the age of 85. However, the reason for the lack of strong loadings for Digit Symbol-Coding and Symbol Search on the Processing Speed factor at ages 80–84 is unclear.

In that age group, both of those subtests loaded heavily (above .60) on the Working Memory factor, but in the other two old-age samples the loadings of Digit Symbol-Coding and Symbol Search were solely on the Processing Speed factor.

Table 7.9 does reveal a few interesting developmental trends for the Verbal Comprehension factor that may have theoretical implications: (1) the loadings for Similarities descend with increasing age, from .91 (ages 75–79) to .59 (ages 85–89); (2) Arithmetic loads ≥ .40 at ages 75–79 and 80–84, but loads negligibly at ages 85–89; (3) Picture Arrangement's loadings increase steadily from ages 75–79 (.21) to 85–89 (.44); and (4) Picture Completion loads negligibly at ages 75–79 and 80–84, but loads .45 for the oldest group. These results may all relate to the striking declines of several abilities with age. Similarities and Arithmetic both require considerable *Gf* for success, in addition to *Gc*, unlike the other Verbal subtests. The rapid decline in both *Gf* and *Gc* from 75 to 89 years (see Chapter 5) may alter the strategies that elderly adults use to solve the problems as they age from the mid-70s to late 80s. The increase in the Verbal Comprehension loadings for Picture Completion and Picture Arrangement, especially for the 85- to 89-year-old group, may be partly a function of the very rapid decline of both *Gf* and *Gv* for elderly individuals. Adults in their late 80s may rely on verbal strategies to solve these items because their reasoning and visualization strategies are not at a high enough level to insure success.

These are merely speculations about the reasons for the age-related findings evident in Table 7.9. What is more certain is that the factor structures for the three elderly age groups differ in many ways, undoubtedly because of the rapid development that is occurring from age 75 to 89. The combination of these subsamples into a single age group, therefore, may produce factor-analytic results that represent nothing more than an average of disparate factor loadings, suggesting caution in interpreting the data obtained for the 75- to 89-year-old sample.

TABLE 7.9 Four-factor solutions of the WAIS-III for adults ages 75–79, 80–84, and 85–89, and for the total sample of elderly individuals (ages 75–89)

Subtest	Verbal Comprehension				Perceptual Organization				Working Memory				Processing Speed			
	Ages 75–79	Ages 80–84	Ages 85–89	Total: 75–89	Ages 75–79	Ages 80–84	Ages 85–89	Total: 75–89	Ages 75–79	Ages 80–84	Ages 85–89	Total: 75–89	Ages 75–79	Ages 80–84	Ages 85–89	Total: 75–89
Vocabulary	**90**	**90**	**77**	**86**	–07	–08	07	–06	06	04	13	08	08	08	–06	00
Similarities	**91**	**79**	**59**	**68**	14	–02	24	04	01	08	–01	02	14	10	09	18
Arithmetic	**40**	**58**	13	27	01	–03	25	21	**40**	25	**50**	**44**	11	20	06	–09
Digit Span	29	15	19	16	–04	–15	08	01	–25	**62**	**55**	**58**	37	–11	–08	–09
Information	**85**	**92**	**76**	**83**	02	01	–07	05	–06	–11	10	01	–01	–10	20	07
Comprehension	**82**	**78**	**80**	**77**	14	14	08	07	–01	–04	11	03	–13	–08	–07	–03
Letter-Number Sequencing	19	12	02	06	14	16	–08	–03	–06	**73**	**71**	**62**	**44**	–28	17	11
Picture Completion	12	05	**45**	22	**56**	**73**	04	02	15	25	–11	–12	15	–20	**41**	**62**
Digit Symbol-Coding	04	04	02	–06	–01	08	17	–06	10	**64**	29	39	**80**	25	**57**	**52**
Block Design	–01	22	03	–01	**66**	**42**	**62**	39	–16	11	09	–06	06	38	17	**51**
Matrix Reasoning	06	**41**	–01	06	**42**	29	**62**	**42**	–29	12	14	02	05	18	05	30
Picture Arrangement	21	35	**44**	30	32	29	08	05	–03	18	00	–05	20	04	37	**47**
Symbol Search	–13	–06	00	15	14	21	26	04	–12	**72**	14	37	**76**	19	**63**	**59**
Object Assembly	02	04	25	—	**75**	**65**	**54**	—	08	–08	–31	—	–02	10	–01	—

NOTE: Decimal points are omitted. A principal axis method with an oblique rotation was used in these analyses. Loadings of .40 or above are in bold print. N = 200 for 75–79-year-olds. N = 150 for 80–84-year-olds. N = 100 for 85–89-year-olds. Data for separate ages are from *Assessment of children: Revised and updated third edition: WAIS-III Supplement* (pp. 1216–1217), by J. Sattler & J. J. Ryan, 1999, La Mesa, CA: Jerome M. Sattler. Copyright 1999 by Jerome M. Sattler. Data for the total sample, ages 75–89, are from *WAIS-III WMS-III Technical Manual* (p. 109) by The Psychological Corporation, 1997, San Antonio, TX: Author. Copyright 1997 by The Psychological Corporation. Reproduced with permission.

COMPARISON OF **WAIS-III** AND **WAIS-R** FACTORS

Some researchers argued that the WAIS-R is just a one-factor test, while other investigators, using diverse techniques, insisted on either two or three significant factors (Kaufman, 1990). As noted, a one-factor WAIS-R solution is fairly meaningless for clinical assessment; two- or three-factor solutions are each defensible as the best reduction of WAIS-R data (Lecklitter et al., 1986). Kaufman (1990) concluded that examiners may choose to interpret either two or three WAIS-R factors, depending on the profile obtained by any given individual (i.e., the decision should rest on whether the small third dimension is interpretable for a given person).

In the first edition of this book, Kaufman (1990) reported that two-factor solutions of the WAIS-R offer outstanding support of the construct validity of the WAIS-R for normal and clinical samples, for males and females, for African Americans and Caucasians, and for different age groups spanning adolescence and old age. The WAIS-R's Verbal Comprehension dimension is defined by all six Verbal subtests, although the loadings for Digit Span are not as decisive as the loadings for the other five tasks. Similarly, the WAIS-R's Perceptual Organization is defined by the five Performance subtests. Two Performance subtests (Picture Completion and Picture Arrangement) have substantial loadings on the Verbal factor as well, but this tendency is stronger for the normal standardization sample than for the diverse clinical groups.

A third WAIS-R factor, historically labeled Freedom from Distractibility, but sometimes called Sequential Ability, Short-term Memory, Number Ability, Attention/Concentration, or Working Memory, was identified for various abnormal samples and for normal groups differing in gender, ethnic background (African Americans, Caucasians, Hispanics), and age (Kaufman, 1990). This third factor is composed of two WAIS-R subtests: Digit Span and Arithmetic.

Although Digit Symbol (-Coding) is associated with the third factor for the WISC-R, there is only weak and inconsistent support for its inclusion on the third WAIS-R factor. When three WAIS-R factors are rotated, Verbal Comprehension is defined by four subtests (all but the two "distractibility" tasks), and Perceptual Organization is defined by three: Block Design, Object Assembly, and Picture Completion. Neither Picture Arrangement nor Digit Symbol is consistently associated with any of the three factors, although both evidence interesting age-related trends for males and females (Kaufman, 1990).

Kaufman, Lichtenberger, and McLean (2001) compared the factor structure of the 11 subtests that are on both the WAIS-R and the WAIS-III to examine the continuity between the two versions of the test. As discussed in Chapter 3, the latest two versions of the WAIS are strikingly similar when only the 11 shared subtests are analyzed. Tables 3.5 and 3.6 in this book present the two- and three-factor solutions of both the WAIS-R and WAIS-III. The coefficients of congruence are striking, ranging from .984 to .996 on the three-factor solutions and surpassing .995 when two factors are rotated. With the addition of the new WAIS-III subtests, the four-factor model dominates the latest version of the test; however, like the WAIS-R, there is still strong support for the three-factor model of the WAIS-III (Kaufman et al., in press; Ward et al., 2000).

COMPARISON OF **WAIS-III** AND **WISC-III** FACTORS

Just as it was important to establish the continuity between the WAIS-III constructs and the constructs defining its predecessors—the Wechsler-Bellevue I, WAIS, and WAIS-R—so, too, is it necessary to evaluate the continuity between the WAIS-III factors and the WISC-III factors. Both tests are intended for essentially adjacent age ranges, and are organized into four highly similar factor indexes. Examiners who test children and adolescents within the 6- to 16-year age range on the WISC-III may conceivably assess these same individuals on the WAIS-III when they are too old for the children's battery. Rather than assuming that the two batteries measure identical constructs, which is done implicitly whenever a clinician compares a person's WISC-III scores to his or her subsequent WAIS-III scores to detect either growth or decline, it is essential to demonstrate empirically that the constructs are the same.

Table 7.10 presents factor-analytic data for both the WAIS-III and the WISC-III, showing four-factor solutions with oblique rotations for the total standardization samples of each battery. Although the age-related trends in the WAIS-III factor structure are reasonably pronounced (unlike the WISC-III, which produced quite similar patterns across the 6- to 16-year range), it still seemed most efficient to compare the factor structures obtained for the entire normative groups. Hence, Table 7.10 examines the continuity of WISC-III and WAIS-III constructs in a global fashion.

From Table 7.10, it is easily inferred that the WAIS-III and WISC-III measure highly similar constructs across their respective age ranges.

TABLE 7.10 Four-factor solutions with an oblique rotation of the WAIS-III and WISC-III for each test's entire standardization sample

Subtest	Verbal Comprehension		Perceptual Organization		Working Memory		Processing Speed	
	WAIS-III	WISC-II	WAIS-III	WISC-III	WAIS-III	WISC-III	WAIS-III	WISC-III
Vocabulary	**.89**	**.89**	−.10	−.07	.05	.01	.06	.06
Similarities	**.76**	**.76**	.10	.12	−.03	−.02	.03	.01
Information	**.81**	**.82**	.03	−.03	.06	.09	−.04	−.03
Comprehension	**.80**	**.79**	.07	.09	−.01	.01	−.03	−.06
Picture Completion	.10	.13	**.56**	**.56**	−.13	.11	.17	.13
Block Design	−.02	−.04	**.71**	**.70**	.04	.19	.03	−.03
Matrix Reasoning	.05	—	**.61**	—	.21	—	−.09	—
Picture Arrangement	.27	.32	**.47**	.39	−.09	−.05	.06	.07
Object Assembly	—	−.01	—	**.80**	—	−.04	—	−.05
Arithmetic	.22	.26	.15	.04	**.51**	**.52**	−.04	.04
Digit Span	.00	.11	−.06	−.07	**.71**	**.45**	.03	.15
Letter-Number Sequencing	.01	—	.02	—	**.62**	—	.13	—
Digit Symbol-Coding	.02	.02	−.03	−.05	.08	.02	**.68**	**.73**
Symbol Search	−.01	−.04	.16	.17	.07	.07	**.63**	**.65**
Coefficient of Congruence	.99+		.98		.87		.98	

NOTE: Loadings of .40 and above are in bold print. Total WISC-III standardization sample is ages 6–16 (N = 2,200). Total WAIS-III standardization sample is ages 16–89 (N = 2,450). For the coefficients of congruence computations, loadings for Letter-Number Sequencing were deleted from the analyses because Letter-Number Sequencing appears only in the WAIS-III; in addition, WISC-III Object Assembly and WAIS-III Matrix Reasoning were treated as if they were the same subtest, because Matrix Reasoning replaced Object Assembly as a regular WAIS-III subtest. Data are adapted from *WAIS-III WMS-III Technical Manual* (p. 105) by The Psychological Corporation, 1997, San Antonio, TX: Author. Copyright 1997 by The Psychological Corporation. Reproduced with permission.

The four familiar factorial dimensions are defined by the same set of subtests. We calculated the coefficients of congruence between the factors given the same verbal label and found them to be quite high (.98+) for three factors: Verbal Comprehension, Perceptual Organization, and Processing Speed. The coefficient of .98 for Perceptual Organization is especially impressive in that we treated WAIS-III Matrix Reasoning and WISC-III Object Assembly as if they were the same subtest (because the former subtest replaced the latter as a regular WAIS-III subtest). To compute the coefficients, we excluded Letter-Number Sequencing because this new WAIS-III subtest has no analog on the WISC-III. The WAIS-III Working Memory factor, which includes this subtest, correlated only moderately well (.87) with the similar WISC-III Freedom from Distractibility factor. Despite the similarity in constructs measured by the WAIS-III and WISC-III, the differences in the IQs that the two instruments yield for low-IQ adolescents create interpretive and other practical difficulties for clinicians and educators (see Chapter 4).

Kaufman, Lichtenberger, and McLean (2001) jointly analyzed two-factor and three-factor solutions of the WISC-III and WAIS-III, including only the 12 subtests that they share. Like the four-factor solutions, the two- and three-factor solutions of the two tests were highly similar. The two-factor varimax-rotated solution had coefficients of congruence of .998 and .982 for the Verbal Comprehension and Perceptual Organization factors, respectively. The WISC-III and WAIS-III three-factor varimax-rotated solutions also had a high level of correspondence with coefficients of .994, .980, and .945 for the Verbal Comprehension, Perceptual Organization, and Working Memory/Processing Speed factors, respectively.

THE GENERAL FACTOR (g)

The unrotated first factor of principal factor analysis is commonly used as an estimate of the g factor that presumably underlies cognitive functioning. The loadings of the different subtests on this large, unrotated dimension reveal the degree to which the tasks are related to g. By convention, g loadings of .70 and above denote subtests that are good measures of g; loadings of .51 to .69 characterize fair measures of g; and loadings of .50 and below are typical of poor measures of g (Kaufman, 1975).

Table 7.11 presents g loadings for the WAIS-III and also for the WISC-III to permit comparisons across tests and ages. Overall, the following WAIS-III subtests (listed in order of their g loadings) are good measures of g: Vocabulary, Similarities, Information, Comprehension, Arithmetic, Block Design, Matrix Reasoning, and Symbol Search. The remaining six subtests are all fair measures of g, having mean loadings in the .60s, as no WAIS-III tasks came close to being poor measures of general ability.

On the WISC-III, five subtests are good measures of g (Vocabulary, Information, Similarities, Arithmetic, and Block Design), five subtests are fair measures of g (Comprehension, Object Assembly, Picture Completion, Symbol Search, and Picture Arrangement), and two subtests are poor measures of g: Digit Span and Coding. Differences between the magnitude of the WAIS-III and WISC-III g loadings occurred across the board as all subtests loaded higher on the WAIS-III than WISC-III; the differences were substantial (.15 or more, on the average) for Comprehension, Symbol Search, Picture Arrangement, Digit Span, Arithmetic, and Digit Symbol-Coding. Nonetheless, the general factors for children and adults were quite comparable, as evidenced by a .91 rank-order correlation between the subtest g loadings for the 12 subtests included in both the WISC-III and WAIS-III.

The generally higher g loadings for the WAIS-III than the WISC-III represent an age-related trend wherein the same Wechsler task seems to be more dependent on general intellectual ability for adults than for children and adolescents. This tendency was also noted in the 1977 edition of the Woodcock-Johnson Cognitive Battery (Kaufman & O'Neal, 1988a) and the Stanford-Binet, Fourth

TABLE 7.11   Loadings on the general factor (*g*) for the WAIS-III (ages 16–89) and WISC-III (ages 6–16)

Subtest	WAIS-III *g* loadings	WISC-III *g* loadings
GOOD Measures of *g* on WAIS-III		
Vocabulary	.83	.80
Similarities	.80	.77
Information	.80	.78
Comprehension	.78	.68
Arithmetic	.77	.76
Block Design	.75	.71
Matrix Reasoning	.75	—
Symbol Search	.72	.56
FAIR Measures of *g* on WAIS-III		
Picture Arrangement	.69	.53
Letter-Number Sequencing	.68	—
Picture Completion	.68	.60
Object Assembly	.65	.61
Digit Symbol Coding	.62	.41
Digit Span	.60	.47

NOTE: *g*-loadings are listed from highest to lowest according to WAIS-III *g*-loadings. WAIS-III values are from *Essentials of WAIS-III Assessment* (p. 79), by A. S. Kaufman and E. O. Lichtenberger, 1999, New York: Wiley. Copyright 1999 by Wiley. WISC-III values are from *Essentials of WISC-III and WPPSI-R Assessment* (p. 83), by A. S. Kaufman and E. O. Lichtenberger, 2000, New York: Wiley. Copyright 1999 by Wiley.

Edition (Reynolds, Kamphaus, & Rosenthal, 1988), suggesting that the constructs influencing test performance change systematically during the aging process. The finding was much more pronounced for Processing Speed and Freedom from Distractibility subtests than for Perceptual Organization or Verbal Comprehension tasks on the Wechsler scales.

The high *g* loadings by WAIS-III subtests are a primary reason for the relatively small (in terms of variance accounted for) factors in the WAIS-III factor analyses; the outcome was generally low eigenvalues in the principal components analysis and legitimate debate over whether or not it is feasible to interpret four significant WAIS-III factors. Simply put, when a subtest is heavily dependent on general ability, it will be less dependent on smaller group factors.

For the purpose of WAIS-III interpretation, all subtests are at least fair measures of *g* across the 16–89 age range, and most subtests are good measures of general ability. Table 7.11 groups the WAIS-III subtests into "good" and "fair" measures of *g*.

Subtest Specificity

For half a century clinicians have interpreted the specific abilities or traits believed to be measured by the separate Wechsler subtests. Case reports are typically filled with an individual's strength or weakness in commonsense understanding of social situations or the ability to distinguish essential from nonessential details or psychomotor speed or attention span, based on strong or weak performance on a single subtest. Yet, implicit in the interpretation of a person's score on any particular subtest is the presumption that the task in question has an adequate amount of reliable specific variance, which Cohen (1952b) has termed "subtest specificity."

Definition of Subtest Specificity

Basically, a subtest has three types of variance: common variance, which is the portion that is shared with other subtests in the battery (e.g., each Verbal subtest shares variance with the other Verbal subtests, as evidenced by robust Verbal Comprehension factors); specific variance, which is the portion that is both reliable and unique to that subtest (a subtest's unique contribution to a Wechsler battery); and error variance (which equals 1 minus the reliability coefficient).

In order to legitimately interpret the abilities supposedly measured by any subtest, that task must have a reasonable amount of reliable specific variance (subtest specificity), and the specificity should exceed the subtest's error variance. How large is reasonable? Clearly, the median of 14% that characterized WAIS subtests (Cohen, 1957b) does not qualify. Cohen states: "Thus, on the average, only one-seventh of the subtests' variance is not attributable to common factors and error. Under these circumstances, the attribution of specific measurement functions to the subtests, as has been done by such clinicians as Rapaport (1945) in connection with the Wechsler-Bellevue, is clearly unjustified" (p. 289). However, the results with the WISC were a bit more promising (Cohen, 1959), and Cohen seemed to treat 25% as the amount of specific variance that is large enough (as long as it exceeds error variance) to warrant subtest specific interpretation. The application of Cohen's (1959) informal rules to the

WISC-R showed that subtest-specific interpretation is feasible for nearly every subtest across the age range (Kaufman, 1979b, Table 4.2).

Adequate, as opposed to ample, specificity occurs when a subtest comes close to meeting Cohen's empirical criteria but doesn't quite make it: (1) the specific variance exceeds error variance but is consistently less than 25%; or (2) the specific variance is at least 25% but the error variance tends to be a bit more.

Computation of subtest specificity is easy. The reliability coefficient equals the percentage of reliable variance for a subtest (no, it does not have to be squared, as some psychologists have tried to insist at our workshops). Subtract from the reliability coefficient the best estimate of common or shared variance, and the remainder is the subtest specificity. Cohen (1957b, 1959) used the commonality from factor analysis as the best estimate of common variance, but Silverstein (1977a) has argued in favor of the multiple-squared correlation between a subtest and all remaining subtests. Silverstein's arguments are sensible; he points out that the commonality varies as a function of the number of factors that are extracted, but R^2 is totally determined by the correlation matrix.

Subtest Specificity of WAIS-III Subtests

Table 7.12 presents subtest specificities for the WAIS-III subtests at ages 16 through 89. These values are from Kaufman and Lichtenberger (1999). Table 7.12 also presents the error variance for the subtests; these values were obtained by subtracting the mean reliability coefficient from 1.0. The subtests are grouped into categories based on their specificity and error variance.

These empirical findings justify clinicians in continuing their half-century-old practice of interpreting the specific abilities or traits presumed to be measured by each WAIS-III subtest, with the exception of Symbol Search and Object

TABLE 7.12 WAIS-III subtests categorized by their specificity

	Reliable Unique Variance	Subtest Error Variance
Ample Specificity		
Digit Span	.50	.10
Matrix Reasoning	.39	.10
Digit Symbol-Coding	.38	.16
Picture Completion	.35	.17
Letter-Number Sequencing	.34	.18
Arithmetic	.30	.12
Adequate Specificity		
Picture Arrangement	.31	.26
Block Design	.27	.14
Information	.23	.09
Comprehension	.20	.16
Similarities	.20	.14
Vocabulary	.19	.07
Inadequate Specificity		
Symbol Search	.21	.23
Object Assembly	.24	.30

NOTE: WAIS-III specificity values are for the entire standardization sample ages 16–89 and are from *Essentials of WAIS-III Assessment* (p. 80), by A. S. Kaufman and E. O. Lichtenberger, 1999, New York: Wiley. Copyright 1999 by Wiley.

Assembly. Symbol Search should be treated primarily as a measure of Processing Speed, as it has an insufficient amount of specificity compared to its level of error variance. Similarly, Object Assembly should be treated primarily as a measure of Perceptual Organization; it has an insufficient amount of specificity, compared to its large dose of error variance, to permit interpretation of any presumed unique abilities or traits. To understand the distinction between interpretation of subtests with ample versus adequate specificity,

as well as instances when even Symbol Search's or Object Assembly's unique variance is interpretable, see Chapters 11 and 12.

EVALUATION OF THE WAIS-III

This chapter on factor analysis has produced a variety of interesting findings, both theoretically and clinically. However, the most compelling finding that echoes throughout the analyses is the strong construct validity support provided for the WAIS-III IQs. The strong *g* loadings for the subtest supports the construct validity of the Full Scale IQ. The two-factor solutions support the construct validity of the Verbal IQ–Performance IQ dichotomy, and the four-factor solutions—both exploratory and confirmatory—support the constructs that are believed to underlie the four-factor indexes.

Indeed, the evidence of the WAIS-III's construct validity constitutes perhaps its biggest strength as a psychometric instrument. For that reason, we chose this factor analysis chapter as the most suitable place to discuss the pros and cons of the WAIS-III. We end this chapter with a thorough evaluation of the instrument.

To help evaluate the WAIS-III, Table 7.13 summarizes the advantages and disadvantages of the instrument as extrapolated from three WAIS-III reviews: Kaufman and Lichtenberger (1999), Sattler and Ryan (1999), and Groth-Marnat, Gallagher, Hale, and Kaplan (2000).

Groth-Marnat, Gallagher, Hale, and Kaplan (2000)

The development of indexes for the WAIS-III [and WISC-III] have been a clear strength that allows for more detailed interpretations of particular relevance among the neuropsychological populations.... One of the strongest assets of the Wechsler intelligence scales is the extensive re-

TABLE 7.13   Summary of the advantages and disadvantages of the WAIS-III
(G = Groth-Marnat, Gallagher, Hale, & Kaplan, 2000; K/L = Kaufman & Lichtenberger, 1999;
S/R = Sattler & Ryan, 1999)

Area	Advantage	Disadvantage
Test Development	• The addition of Symbol Search allows a similar four-factor structure for the WISC-III, providing valuable continuity. (G, K/L) • The new Processing Speed index is particularly sensitive to neuropsychological impairment. (G) • The addition of Matrix Reasoning enhances the assessment of fluid reasoning on both the Performance Scale and Perceptual Organization Index. (K/L) • Matrix Reasoning provides opportunity for those examinees who are not inclined to perform well on speeded visual motor tasks to demonstrate their non-verbal abilities on a "power" test. (K/L, S/R) • Artwork, manual with built-in easel, and overall appearance of materials are updated and improved. (K/L) • There is an extension of the age range for which the test was normed from 74 to 89 years. (K/L) • There is a reduced emphasis on bonus points on some subtests, which appears to be an asset in testing elderly examinees. (S/R)	• Some of the artwork on the Picture Completion section is too busy and can be distracting (e.g., Items #5, 11, 24). (K/L) • There is great emphasis on the symmetry of items and trivial detail on Picture Completion, which may be subtly biased against disadvantaged individuals (e.g., Item 16, 17, 21). (K/L) • Matrix Reasoning colors can be distracting, and are potentially unfair to color blind individuals. (K/L) • Theories of intelligence have undergone significant changes, but such changes in the more current views of intelligence have not been reflected in the development of the test. (G)
Administration and Scoring	• Scoring rules and reverse rules are consistently implemented. (K/L) • The procedures that require the examiner to ask for another reason when they give only one reason for Comprehension items ensure that the test does not penalize examinees for failing to understand the demands of the questions. (S/R) • The inclusion of practice items on some subtests is desirable. (S/R) • Beginning the battery with Picture Completion rather than Information is less anxiety producing for many clients. (K/L) • Digit Symbol and other tasks on which the examinee has to use a pencil are all located in one convenient response booklet.	• Some of the Vocabulary, Similarities, and Comprehension items seem to be arbitrarily marked to query (e.g., several 1-point responses on Vocabulary #13 & 17; Similarities #11 & 15; Comprehension #11 & 12). (K/L) • Three verbal tests still require complex judgments to be made in scoring (e.g., Similarities, Vocabulary, Comprehension). (G, K/L) • The Digit Symbol supplementary procedures utilize the word "symbols" whereas the Digit Symbol-Coding directions switch terms and refer mostly to "special marks" or "marks" which can be confusing for low functioning individuals. (K/L)

(Continues)

TABLE 7.13   (Continued)

Area	Advantage	Disadvantage
Administration and Scoring (continued)	• The record form is well designed with ample space to write responses and to note incorrect block design constructions, and the new rebus symbols are easy to follow. (K/L) • The manual is easy to read as the instructions are printed in a different color from that of other text material. (S/R) • The presentation of Vocabulary words a few items at a time is very useful, as it avoids the frustration felt by those with poor vocabularies (who previously had to see the entire list they were going to be administered). (K/L) • The presentation of scoring criteria concurrently with the directions for administration for Similarities, Vocabulary, and Comprehension is convenient. (K/L) • The scoring guidelines for the Vocabulary, Similarities, and Comprehension subtests are supplemented with many typical responses and several examples demonstrate application of the scoring principles. (S/R) • For Picture Completion, the list of queries to prompt the examinee (when they have either named the object pictured, mentioned a part of the picture off of the page, or mentioned an unessential part) has been handily written right on the record form. (K/L)	• In the Digit Symbol-Coding response booklet, it is confusing to differentiate the two rows of Pairing from the blank space on which examinees are to respond for Free Recall. (K/L) • Because of the need to differentiate colors to determine the correct response on some Matrix Reasoning items, adults and adolescents who are color blind may be at a disadvantage on these items. (K/L) • The proverb items on Comprehension measure a different type of reasoning skill (generalization) than the other items but were still retained in this newest version. (K/L) • The artwork in Picture Arrangement contains too many fine details, sometimes obscuring what is important (e.g., DREAM & SHARK items). (K/L) • The templates for scoring the Digit Symbol-Coding and Symbol Search subtests are poorly constructed and may tear and disintegrate quickly. (S/R)
Reliability and Validity	• Split-half reliability coefficients and standard errors of measurement are outstanding for the V-IQ, VCI, and FS-IQ, and are excellent for the P-IQ, POI, and WMI. (G, K/L, S/R) • Overall, split-half reliabilities are excellent for all subtests across the 13 age groups except Object Assembly and Picture Arrangement. Of the spit-half reliability values for the Verbal subtests, 79% were at or above .85. However, for the Performance subtests, excluding OA, only 43% of the reliability values were at or above .85. (K/L)	• Split-half reliability for Object Assembly at ten of the 13 age levels is below .75; the four oldest age groups are below .70. For Picture Arrangement, six groups have split-half reliability below .75, and two of those are below .70. (G, K/L, S/R) • Test-Retest stability is not excellent for Letter-Number Sequencing, Picture Arrangement, or Object Assembly (average stability coefficients were .75, .69, and .76, respectively). (K/L)

(Continues)

TABLE 7.13   (Continued)

Area	Advantage	Disadvantage
Reliability and Validity (continued)	• Statistically linked to the WIAT and the WMS-III, providing more information about the interrelationships among a wider array of cognitive abilities. Co-norming also enables examiners to "predict" an examinee' S/R achievement scores on the basis of his or her IQ. (K/L, S/R) • Strong counterbalanced studies of the WAIS-III with the WAIS-R (*N*= 192) and the WISC-III (*N*=184). (G, K/L) • The amount of data from validity studies in the WAIS-III Manual was greatly improved from what was available in the WAIS-R Manual. Multiple criterion-validity studies are presented (e.g., WAIS-III FS-IQ correlated .64 with Standard Progressive Matrices, .88 Stanford-Binet-IV Composite, and ranged from .53 to .81 with WIAT composites). (G, K/L, S/R) • Construct validity was demonstrated with factor analysis studies. The four-factor structure was supported for all age groups except ages 75–89. In the oldest age group, many PO subtests loaded on the PS factor. (K/L)	• The Perceptual Organization and Processing Speed factors do not emerge as separate constructs for the 75–89 year old age group. (K/L)
Standardization	• The standardization sample was well stratified for many key variables. (G, K/L, S/R) • Oversampling was completed to conduct research on educational level and cognitive abilities. An additional 437 individuals were tested so that at least 30 participants would be included in each educational level within each age group. (K/L) • Oversampling was done for African American and Hispanic individuals to perform item bias analyses. An additional 200 individuals from these two ethnic groups were administered the WAIS-III without discontinue rules. (K/L) • Care was taken to ensure that qualified examiners collected the standardization data; only examiners with extensive testing experience were recruited. (K/L)	• Data on the mean IQ and Indexes for various ethnic groups are not included in the tables. (K/L) • The 18–19 year olds performed very similarly to the 20–24 year olds, which raises questions about the norms for the youngest age groups. (K/L)

(Continues)

TABLE 7.13 (Continued)

Area	Advantage	Disadvantage
Standardization (continued)	• The standardization sample for older individuals contained more women than men, consistent with Census data. (K/L) • Range of FS-IQ was extended to 45–155 from 46–150. (G, K/L)	
Test Interpretation	• The new four factor indexes allow the examiner to more easily interpret cognitive abilities underlying P-IQs and V-IQs. (G, K/L) • The record form contains a new area for calculation of strengths and weaknesses, as well as discrepancy comparisons for the global scales. (G, K/L) • The descriptive categories are conveniently listed right on the record form. (K/L) • The comparison between the backward and forward span on Digit Span is encouraged by the record form. (K/L) • The new supplemental measures for Digit Symbol-Coding allow easier evaluation of errors on Digit Symbol-Coding. Digit-Symbol Pairing and Free Recall allow further examination of visual memory, and Digit-Symbol Copy allows examination of graphomotor speed without the element of matching the symbol to a digit. (K/L) • The removal of the reference group (ages 20–34) to determine everyone's scaled scores eases profile interpretation across the age groups, and also within each individual's profile (because all subtests have a mean = 10 and SD=3 for each separate age group, which was not so on the WAIS-R). (K/L) • The WAIS-III Technical Manual provides some interpretive guidelines for profile interpretation (pp. 181–216). For example, it discusses how to calculate discrepancy scores, how to use the supplementary tables, and how to compare scores on different indexes. (K/L) • The WAIS-III Technical Manual provides guidelines for comparing the WAIS-III and the WMS-III or the WIAT (pp. 211–216). It reviews the simple difference method and the predicted-difference method for comparing ability with memory or achievement. (K/L, S/R)	• The manual provides little research on minority assessment. When interpreting a profile of a minority individual, it is important to know how other members of minority group perform, on average, and that data is not available in the manual. (K/L) • Caution needs to be exercised in interpreting profiles for gifted individuals because the highest possible scaled score is different for various tests at different ages (e.g., for age 20–34, Picture Arrangement is 17 and Block Design is 19). (K/L) • Picture Arrangement may not offer a sufficient floor for low functioning individuals (e.g., raw score of 0 = scaled score of 5 for ages 85–89, a scaled score of 4 for 75–84, and scaled score of 3 for ages 65–74). Some reverse items should have been added. (K/L, S/R) • Because the range of scaled scores is less than 19 on some subtests, there may be minor problems in profile analysis in some age groups at the lower and upper extremes of scores. (S/R) • The four factors do not perfectly match the WISC-III factors, especially the Verbal Comprehension and Perceptual Organization Indexes, which include 3 subtests on the WAIS-III, one less than the corresponding WISC-III factors. (K/L) • Three-subtest VC and PO provides limited measurement of these important constructs; no good rationale was provided for eliminating Comprehension and Picture Arrangement; Object Assembly (for ages 16 to 74) would have provided more continuity with WISC-III. (K/L)

(Continues)

TABLE 7.13   (Continued)

Area	Advantage	Disadvantage
Test Interpretation	• Addition of Letter-Number Sequencing and the Digit Symbol Supplemental procedures provide excellent new neuropsychological data. (K/L) • The addition of extra items to lower the floor of the test is quite helpful in the assessment of lower functioning individuals. (K/L) • Addition of Symbol Search allows measurement of Processing Speed Index. (K/L) • Addition of Letter-Number Sequencing enhances the "Freedom from Distractibility" factor, broadening the construct it measures and justifying its new name of Working Memory. (K/L)	• Replacing Object Assembly with Matrix Reasoning on the Performance Scale alters the meaning of the P-IQ, perhaps jeopardizing the continuity of the P-IQ construct from the Wechsler Bellevue-I to WAIS to WAIS-R to WAIS-III. Hence research on this construct for previous adult Wechsler measures may not generalize to the WAIS-III, especially the important neuropsychological research with unilateral brain damage. (K/L) • With norms for the three IQs based on 11 standard subtests, there is no way of knowing precisely what scores mean when you substitute one of the supplementary subtests (Letter-Number Sequencing and Symbol Search) or the optional subtest (Object Assembly) for a regular subtest. (S/R)

search that has been done with or on them.... This research base allows practitioners to more fully understand the meanings behind the performances of individuals as well as various population groups.... However, theories of intelligence have undergone significant changes (see Harrison, Flanagan, & Genshaft, 1997) and these changes generally have not been reflected in the structure or strategies underlying the Wechsler scales.... The Wechsler scales have not responded to many of the more current views of intelligence. (pp. 141–143)

Kaufman and Lichtenberger (1999)

There are several major strengths that we found on the WAIS-III, but not any weaknesses that we considered major. Significant strengths that we feel are important to highlight include the following: excellent standardization sample, high reliability and stability of the IQs, elimination of the reference group from the scaled score computation, four-factor structure with Working Memory and Processing Speed, addition of Matrix Reasoning and Letter-Number Sequencing to the overall battery,

extending the "bottom" by adding reverse-items, and enhanced neuropsychological interpretations made possible with supplemental data tables for Digit Span and Digit Symbol-Coding.

The changes made in this latest revision of the WAIS have made it a much stronger instrument. There are several abilities, such as fluid reasoning and working memory, that were not possible to measure with confidence in the earlier versions of the WAIS. With all of these strengths highlighted, it is also important to note that the WAIS-III does not measure every possible construct that underlies intelligence. (p. 164)

Sattler and Ryan (1999)

The assets of the WAIS-III include its excellent standardization, excellent reliability, adequate validity, good administrative procedures and excellent test manuals.... The limitations of the WAIS-III include limited range of IQs, low reliability of some subtests, difficulty in interpreting norms when you substitute one or both supplementary subtests for standard subtests, difficulty scoring some subtests, and poor quality of some test materials.

Overall, the WAIS-III represents a major contribution to the field of intelligence testing of adolescents and adults. It serves as an important instrument for this purpose. (p. 1262)

SUMMARY

This chapter reviews factor analysis of the WAIS-III for the normal standardization sample, a variety of clinical populations, for males and females, and for different age and ethnic groups across the 16- to 89-year range. Because the factor analyses reported here strongly support the WAIS-III's construct validity—a very positive feature of the test—we ended the chapter with a summary of the WAIS-III's pros and cons. A table at the end summarizes the advantages and disadvantages of the WAIS-III as delineated in three major reviews of the battery.

Investigators have disagreed on the appropriate number of factors underlying the WAIS-III, and empirical techniques have also yielded different factor solutions depending on the criterion employed. There is consensus that the one-factor solution does not best fit the WAIS-III data. The two-factor solution provides validation for the Verbal–Performance split. The three-factor solution is viewed as a quite viable model, with statistical and theoretical backing for the third factor that is comprised of both Processing Speed and Working Memory subtests. The four-factor solution is deemed the most clinically use-

ful and statistically sound solution, which verifies the publisher's choice of creating a four-index test.

Factor analyses for different ethnic groups and different age groups have shown general consistency with the overall four-factor structure. However, some variations in the structure are apparent. In African American and Hispanic groups the Arithmetic subtest has loadings split on two factors, but the two factors are different for these ethnic groups. In the oldest age group of the WAIS-III standardization sample, many more of the Performance subtests load on the Processing Speed index than the two that typically comprise the Processing Speed index. These variations in the factor structure aside, overall, the four-factor indexes hold up well in factor analysis of different ethnic and age groups.

The factor analyses also provide data pertaining to each subtest's relationship to the g factor and to the degree of subtest specificity (reliable unique variance) that each task possesses. The best measures of g are Vocabulary, Similarities, and Information; lowest g loadings are consistently obtained by Digit Span and Digit Symbol-Coding, but no WAIS-III subtests have poor g loadings. All WAIS-III subtests have adequate or ample specificity, except for Symbol Search and Object Assembly, permitting examiners to make subtest-specific interpretations for nearly all tasks. The subtests that share the least variance with other WAIS-III tasks and that have the highest subtest specificities are Digit Span, Matrix Reasoning, and Digit Symbol-Coding.

Verbal–Performance
IQ Discrepancies:
A Neuropsychological Approach

Wechsler (1939) published the first edition of the Wechsler-Bellevue about a half century ago, and clinical interest in Verbal–Performance IQ (V–P) discrepancies probably surfaced a few minutes after publication. Just as Wechsler researchers enjoy nothing more than factor-analyzing or abbreviating a battery, Wechsler clinicians have a difficult time satisfying their craving for interpreting V–P IQ discrepancies and relating such differences to neurological impairment, psychopathology, and diverse variables encompassing nearly every aspect of human behavior. Because of the extensive literature on group differences in verbal and nonverbal functioning and the clinical value of Wechsler's dichotomy for any particular individual, this book treats the topic of V–P IQ differences in two chapters.

Chapter 8 deals with five major areas, all pertaining to a neuropsychological understanding of V–P IQ discrepancies: (1) an overview of V–P studies of neurological patients having damage confined to the left or right hemisphere; (2) the

nature of brain damage; (3) subtest patterns for left- and right-lesions patients; (4) the interaction of gender and race with V–P discrepancies in brain damage; and (5) the interaction of age and education with V–P discrepancies in brain damage. Chapter 9 focuses on a more clinical understanding of V–P IQ differences. Although the WAIS-III offers an additional way to examine verbal–nonverbal differences, namely the discrepancy between the Verbal Comprehension and Perceptual Organization indexes, Chapters 8 and 9 focus primarily on V-IQ and P-IQ because WAIS-III literature on discrepancies is sparse.

V–P DISCREPANCIES AND BRAIN DAMAGE

Research in neuropsychology has consistently supported the notion that lesions in the left cerebral hemisphere are associated with diminished verbal and language abilities, whereas lesions in the right cerebral hemisphere are accompanied by visual–spatial deficits (Reitan, 1955c). Consequently, a logical hypothesis is that people with left-brain lesions will demonstrate P > V profiles, and those with documented right-brain lesions will show V > P discrepancies. This hypothesis has been tested in dozens of research investigations with the Wechsler-Bellevue, WAIS, and WAIS-R, and the results of these many studies are summarized and integrated in this section. The one WAIS-III study was reported in the WAIS-III technical manual (Psychological Corporation, 1997), but only a partial seven-subtest battery was administered to small samples of adults with temporal lobe epilepsy; these data are integrated with the large body of data on previous Wechsler adult scales. The latter half of this chapter treats numerous issues regarding the literature on brain damage, such as the controversial topic of gender differences in the relationship between localization of lesion and V–P differences.

Right- versus Left-Brain Lesions

The predicted interaction between the nature of a brain-damaged patient's V–P IQ discrepancy and the location of his or her lesion has been investigated with a diversity of samples, for example, those with head injuries (Mattis, Hannay, Plenger, & Pollock, 1994; Uzzell, Zimmerman, Dolinskas, & Obrist, 1979), those wounded by a missile (Black, 1973, 1976), patients with epilepsy undergoing temporal lobectomies (Chelune, Naugle, Luders, Sedlak, & Awad, 1993; Ivnik, Sharbrough, & Laws, 1987; Meier & French, 1966), and patients with strokes or tumors (Haaland & Delaney, 1981; Mattis, Hannay, & Meyers, 1992). Most samples, however, are heterogeneous regarding the cause of the brain damage and are best labeled "mixed" (Matarazzo & Herman, 1985).

Table 8.1 summarizes pertinent studies with the Wechsler-Bellevue, Table 8.2 summarizes the numerous WAIS studies, and Table 8.3 summa-

rizes the WAIS-R studies. Many of the Wechsler-Bellevue and WAIS references were compiled by Matarazzo and Herman (1985, pp. 902–905) and Inglis and Lawson (1982), although we tracked down the original source for every study in both tables. The few studies available on brain injury employing the WAIS-III used subjects with diffuse brain injury (or the authors did not specify the brain region that was affected); thus, we were not able to include data from the WAIS-III on right- and left-hemisphere lesions.

Tables 8.1 and 8.2 also include studies that have previously been excluded from past summaries because the investigators failed to provide Verbal and Performance IQs for the brain-damaged samples. These include studies that provided just the V–P IQ discrepancy, but not the actual V- and P-IQs (Goldstein & Shelly, 1973; Lansdell, 1968; Reitan & Fitzhugh, 1971), as well as investigations that provided just the subtest scaled scores (Reitan, 1955c) or weighted sums of scaled scores (Smith, 1966b, 1966c) for the brain-damaged patients. Because several of these studies have been widely cited in the literature (especially Reitan, 1955c and Smith, 1966b) it seemed important to include their data in the computations to determine the relationship between V–P discrepancies and location of brain lesion.

For Reitan's (1955c) and Smith's (1966b, 1966c) studies, it was necessary to determine the best estimate of the Wechsler-Bellevue IQs for the brain-damaged samples. For his samples, Smith (1966b, 1966c) provided the weighted sums of Verbal scores (excluding Vocabulary) and Performance scores. We entered these sums into the Wechsler-Bellevue IQ conversion table using the mean age of each sample to determine the appropriate column to enter (i.e., the column for ages 45–49 for 46- and 47-year-olds; the midpoint of the columns for ages 40–44 and 45–49 for his 45-year-olds). Reitan (1955c) provided a graph of scaled scores on the separate subtests. To estimate V- and P-IQs, we determined the scaled score on each subtest (excluding Vocabulary) from his graph, computed the weighted Verbal and Performance sums, and entered these

TABLE 8.1 V–P IQ discrepancies on the Wechsler-Bellevue I or II for adult patients with lesions localized in the left or right hemisphere of the brain

Authors	Total N	% Males	Mean Age	Mean Educ.	Mean V-IQ minus mean P-IQ (sample size in parentheses)	
					Left Lesions	*Right Lesions*
Reitan (1955)	31	—	40	11	−7.0 (14)	+6.5 (17)
Meyer & Jones (1957)						
Temporal lobe epileptics (postoper.)						
Males	16	100	30	—	−10.8 (11)	+3.2 (5)
Females	15	0	24	—	−1.9 (9)	+7.0 (6)
Klove (1959)	79	84	36	10	−10.0 (42)	+11.9 (37)
Doehring et al. (1961)	38	—	38	11	−9.0 (19)	+17.0 (19)
Fitzhugh et al. (1962)						
Recent	43	84	38	8	−9.1 (18)	+15.0 (25)
Chronic	45	42	32	5.5	−3.9 (20)	+2.1 (25)
Dennerll (1964)						
Temporal lobe epileptics	60	55	21	8	−10.3 (29)	+12.5 (31)
Meier & French (1966)						
Temporal lobe epileptics (postoper.)						
Sample I	30	60	28	—	−8.7 (14)	+2.7 (16)
Smith (1966b)						
Tumor (Generalized)	99	—	46	10.5	0.0 (48)	+6.8 (51)
Smith (1966c)						
Tumor (Frontal lobe)	41	59	46	10.5	−1.4 (18)	+3.8 (23)
Lansdell (1968)						
Temporal lobe epileptics (postoper.)						
Males	24	100	33	—	−8.8 (11)	+2.2 (13)
Females	28	0	33	—	−4.9 (8)	+3.4 (20)

Reitan & Fitzhugh (1971)					
Stroke	30	100	51	10.5	−19.8 (15)	+10.8 (15)
Leli & Filskov (1981a)	71	—	53	12	−4.4 (38)	+12.1 (33)
Reitan (1985)	56	—	30	11.5	−10.1 (25)	+7.8 (31)
Herring & Reitan (1986)						
Tumor (2/3) & Stroke (1/3)						
Males	48	100	46	11	−8.0 (24)	+8.8 (24)
Females	48	0	46	11	−4.1 (24)	+3.2 (24)
Weighted Mean					**−7.5 (369)**	**+8.1 (392)**

NOTE: mean V–P IQ differences for several samples are estimated from graphs presented in the articles (Doehring et al., 1961; Herring & Reitan, 1986) or from weighted sums of scaled scores (Reitan, 1955c; Smith, 1966b). For Reitan's sample, weighted sums were computed from graphs of scaled scores on each subtest (excluding Vocabulary). Dennerll (1964) used one of four Wechsler scales: Wechsler-Bellevue, Form I or II, WAIS, WISC. Data for Smith's (1966c) sample with frontal lobe tumors are excluded from the computations of mean V–P IQ discrepancies because 31 of the 41 patients were also included in Smith's (1966b) sample of 99 tumor patients.

TABLE 8.2 V–P IQ discrepancies on the WAIS for adult patients with lesions localized in the left or right hemisphere of the brain

Authors	Total N	% Males	Mean Age	Mean Education	Mean V-IQ minus mean P-IQ (sample size in parentheses)	
					Left Lesions	Right Lesions
WAIS Studies						
Fitzhugh & Fitzhugh (1964b)						
Chronic seizure activity	52	48	37	5.5	–4.8 (28)	+4.5 (24)
Meier & French (1966)						
Temporal lobe epileptics (postoper.)						
Sample II	40	55	30	—	–3.7 (15)	+8.4 (25)
Satz (1966)	30	—	43	—	–10.3 (12)	+7.5 (18)
Satz et al. (1967)	47	—	—	—	–12.6 (23)	+10.5 (24)
Warrington & James (1967)	65	58	44	—	–6.0 (29)	+13.0 (36)
Parsons et al. (1969)	49	—	48	9.5	–7.5 (24)	+10.4 (25)
Zimmerman et al. (1970)	54	100	40	—	–1.0 (23)	+5.4 (31)
Simpson & Vega (1971)	44	—	48	10	–3.6 (21)	+12.8 (23)
Black (1973)						
Missile wounds	40	100	21	12	–1.8 (20)	+3.5 (20)
Goldstein & Shelly (1973)	48	—	45	11.5	+5.9 (26)	+7.9 (22)
Black (1974a)						
Missile wounds	60	100	21	12	–6.0 (30)	+7.4 (17)
Black (1974b)						
Missile wounds	86	100	21	12	–3.4 (50)	+4.5 (36)
Buffery (1974)						
Temporal lobe epileptics (postoper.)	30	73	24	—	–4.6 (13)	+7.4 (17)
Landsdell & Smith (1975)						
Mostly missile wounds & closed head injuries	150	100	24	—	+0.3 (76)	+10.9 (74)
Black (1976)						
Missile wounds to frontal lobes	44	100	21	11.5	–3.3 (28)	–1.1 (16)
Munder (1976)						

Blacks	50	100	—	—	+5.7 (25)	+10.4 (25)
Whites	50	100	—	—	−5.2 (25)	+15.1 (25)
Todd et al. (1977)	114	63	38	12	+6.0 (68)	+7.7 (46)
McGlone (1978)						
Stroke (2/3) & tumor (1/3)						
Males	40	100	48	11	−11.2 (23)	+13.5 (17)
Females	37	0	48	11	−0.1 (20)	+4.2 (17)
Uzzell et al. (1979)						
Head injury	21	95	30	11	−8.7 (8)	+17.5 (13)
Haaland & Delaney (1981)						
Tumor	29	—	46	11.5	0.0 (14)	+3.0 (15)
Stroke	43	—	56	12	−7.0 (26)	+12.0 (17)
Inglis et al. (1982)						
Stroke						
Males	40	100	67	10	−15.3 (20)	+19.6 (20)
Females	40	0	71	10	+0.2 (20)	+4.5 (20)
Snow & Sheese (1985)						
Stroke						
Males	28	100	63	11.5	+13.9 (14)	+19.8 (14)
Females	17	0	66	10.5	+8.0 (5)	+22.7 (12)
Ivnik et al. (1987)						
Temporal lobe epileptics (postoper.)	63	54	28	13	−7.6 (28)	+1.9 (35)
Whelan & Walker (1988)						
Tumors (anterior or posterior)						
Males	34	100	47	10.5	+2.7 (13)	+10.5 (21)
Females	30	0	47	11.5	+0.8 (16)	+13.9 (14)
Turkheimer et al. (1993)						
Males	33	100	—	—	−1.3 (16)	+23.9 (17)
Females	31	0	—	—	+6.3 (11)	+10.5 (20)
Weighted Mean of WAIS Studies					**−2.0 (692)**	**+10.1 (703)**

TABLE 8.3 V–P IQ discrepancies on the WAIS-R for adult patients with lesions localized in the left or right hemisphere of the brain

Authors	Total N	% Males	Mean Age	Mean Education	Mean V-IQ minus mean P-IQ (Sample size in parentheses)	
					Left Lesions	Right Lesions
WAIS-R Studies						
Bornstein (1983)	44	—	39	11	-4.9 (20)	+10.7 (24)
Bornstein (1984)						
Males	33	100	37	11.5	-4.9 (17)	+10.6 (16)
Females	30	0	39	11	-5.5 (15)	+11.1 (15)
Massad et al. (1988)	32	62	49	12.2	-0.6 (16)	+13.1 (16)
Bornstein & Share (1990)	79	43	33	11.6	-0.9 (43)	-2.7 (36)
Temporal lobe epileptics						
Mattis et al. (1992)	63	55	41	14.3	+1.0 (34)	+11.1 (29)
Tumors (generalized or posterior)						
Paniak et al. (1992)						
Head injury	20	79	32	11.4	+6.3 (11)	+2.1 (9)
Mattis et al. (1994)						
Head injury	35	73	—	13	-0.3 (20)	+9.8 (15)
Chelune et al. (1993)						
Temporal lobe epileptics (postoper.)	96	63	29	13	-6.6 (47)	-3.6 (49)
Perez et al. (1996)	40	55	61	12.2	-6.8 (20)	+19.0 (20)
Ryan et al. (1996)	67	100	58	11.4	+2.0 (32)	+10.8 (35)
Weighted Mean of WAIS-R Studies					**-2.2 (275)**	**+6.7 (264)**

NOTE: Unless otherwise indicated, the brain-damaged samples are "mixed," composed of a variety of etiologies.

weighted sums into the Wechsler-Bellevue IQ conversion tables, using the midpoint of the values in the columns for ages 35–39 and 40–44 (the average age of subjects in his samples was 40 years).

We did not believe that these estimates introduced any substantial error into the magnitude of the mean V–P IQ discrepancies for Reitan's or Smith's samples. To check out this hunch, we followed the same procedure for data provided by Klove (1959) and Klove and Reitan (1958). Because these investigators gave the mean IQs and the mean weighted sums for their samples, we were able to see how close the estimated V- and P-IQs were (i.e., the values obtained by entering the mean weighted sums into the columns for the average age of each sample) to the actual, reported IQs for the various samples. For Klove and Reitan's (1959) three samples and Klove's (1959) four samples, the estimated Verbal IQs were within 1 point of the actual values for each of the seven groups. Estimated Performance IQs were within 1 point of actual Performance IQs for three samples and were within 3 points for all seven groups of brain-damaged patients. Consequently, we feel confident in our estimates of the V–P IQ differences for Reitan's and Smith's samples summarized in Table 8.1. We would have liked to have followed similar estimation procedures for Andersen's (1951) samples of brain-damaged groups, because Andersen (1950, 1951) was truly the pioneer of the type of Wechsler research presented in Tables 8.1, 8.2, and 8.3. Unfortunately, his findings cannot be included because of the peculiar nature of the subtest scores he used.

Wechsler-Bellevue Studies

The results presented in Table 8.1 for a total of 761 patients (369 with left damage and 392 with right damage) generally conform to the predictions from neuropsychology, in which patients with left-brain lesions had higher mean P- than V-IQs in all but one Wechsler-Bellevue study, and patients with right-hemisphere lesions likewise had mean V > P profiles for 17 of the 18 samples. Overall on the Wechsler-Bellevue, left-brain-damaged adults had an average P > V superiority of 7.5 points, and right-brain-damaged had a mean V > P advantage of 8.1 points. By contrast, patients with diffuse brain damage (spanning both hemispheres) had a mean V–P IQ discrepancy of approximately zero (–0.1 points) with values ranging from –5.2 to +3.5, based on data included in five of the studies cited by Matarazzo and Herman (1985, Table 1), in two of Reitan's studies not included in their table (Reitan, 1985; Reitan & Fitzhugh, 1971), and in studies by Reitan (1955c) and Smith (1966b), which required estimation of V- and P-IQs.

WAIS Studies

The results with the WAIS, shown in Table 8.2 for 1,395 patients (692 with left damage and 703 with right damage), are not as decisive as the Wechsler-Bellevue data. The predicted P > V profile for left lesions was found, but barely (2-point discrepancy), in contrast to the substantial V > P profile of 10.1 points identified for patients with right-hemisphere lesions. Of the 32 WAIS samples summarized in Table 8.2, a total of 19 (or 59%) displayed both the characteristic V > P pattern for right-brain lesions and P > V pattern for left-brain lesions, using a mean V–P IQ discrepancy of ± 1 point or more as necessary for satisfying the criterion. However, if one insists on a 6-point difference between mean V- and P-IQs in the predicted directions, only 9 of the 32 samples (28%) behaved as predicted. For the 18 Wechsler-Bellevue samples summarized in Table 8.1, 16 (89%) showed the predicted V–P patterns using the liberal ± 1 criterion, and 8 samples (44%) displayed the hypothesized pattern applying the more stringent ± 6 criterion. These percentages are clearly higher than the corresponding values for the WAIS.

Overlapping Samples of Patients

Several of the samples summarized in Tables 8.1 and 8.2 are not independent but used some of the same patients in more than one study. About three-fourths of Smith's (1966c) group of patients with frontal lobe lesions were included in his larger group of patients with generalized lesions (see Table 8.1). Overlap also characterized the WAIS research conducted by McGlone (1977, 1978) and Black (1973, 1974a, 1974b, 1976), reported in Table 8.2. Whereas Smith (1966c) noted the overlap with his previous study (Smith, 1966b), Black and McGlone, unfortunately, did not make readers aware of the contamination in their respective samples until they evidently were contacted for clarification by Bornstein and Matarazzo (1982, 1984).

Data from Vega and Parsons (1969) for groups with minimal and maximal sensory–motor deficit have typically been included in summaries of WAIS brain lesion studies (Matarazzo & Herman, 1985). However, Vega and Parsons reported that their total sample was essentially identical to the sample used by Parsons, Vega, and Burn (1969), so only the Parson et al. data are included in the table. Similarly, because McGlone's (1977, 1978) samples were "largely overlapping" (Bornstein & Matarazzo, 1984, p. 707), only data from her 1978 sample are included in Table 8.2. (Bornstein and Matarazzo used only data from McGlone's 1977, larger sample. They were evidently unaware that McGlone provided mean Verbal and Performance IQs for different samples in her 1977 article. Verbal IQs were given just for nonaphasic patients; Performance IQs were presented for all left-lesion and right-lesion patients.)

Data from all of Black's studies are included in Table 8.2, however, because the amount of overlap from sample to sample is unclear. Nonetheless, as indicated in the notes to Table 8.1, the known contamination in the brain-damaged samples listed in each table is accounted for in the procedure used to compute the mean V–P discrepancies. Hence, the overall values shown for the Wechsler-Bellevue and WAIS P > V and V > P discrepancies are presumably corrected for the overlap in samples.

WAIS-R Studies

The results with the WAIS-R for 11 samples (total N = 539, composed of 275 with left lesions and 264 with right lesions), shown in Table 8.3, are similar to WAIS data; patients with left lesions showed a small P > V profile whereas patients with right lesions demonstrated a more noteworthy (though not as extreme) V > P profile. Of the 11 WAIS-R samples, 9 (87%) displayed the characteristic V > P pattern for right-brain lesions, using a mean V–P IQ discrepancy of ± 1 point more as necessary for satisying the criterion. For left-brain lesions, 5 of the 11 WAIS-R samples (45%), displayed the characteristic V > P pattern by ± 1 point. Overall, of the 11 WAIS-R samples, only 2 (18%) displayed *both* the characteristic V > P pattern for right-brain lesions and P > V pattern for left-brain lesions. If one insists on a more rigorous 6-point difference between mean V- and P-IQs in the predicted directions, only 1 of the 11 WAIS-R samples (Perez, Schlottmann, Holloway, & Ozolins, 1996) behaved as predicted for both the right- and left-hemisphere lesion subjects.

Comparison of Results for Wechsler-Bellevue versus WAIS versus WAIS-R

The mean P > V discrepancy for patients with left lesions is only about 2 points on the WAIS and WAIS-R. That value is quite a bit lower than the comparable value of 7.5 found for the Wechsler-Bellevue. However, the mean value of V > P on the WAIS (10 points) for those with right-brain damage is higher than the means of about 7-8 obtained for the Wechsler-Bellevue and WAIS-R.

Hence, the failure of most studies summarized in Tables 8.2 and 8.3 to display characteristic P > V and V > P profiles by 6 or more points is a function of the insensitivity of the WAIS and WAIS-R V–P IQ discrepancy to *left*-hemisphere lesions. Examination of Tables 8.2 and 8.3 reveals that of 32 WAIS samples (some overlapping) in Table 8.2, 23 of the patient samples with right-brain damage had V > P discrepancies of 6 or more points (72%), versus only 10 of the left-brain damage samples having mean P > V discrepancies of 6 or more points (31%). Of 11 WAIS-R samples in Table 8.3, the comparable percents are 73 and 18, respectively. In contrast, for the Wechsler-Bellevue (see Table 8.1), the comparable value is 61% for *both* categories of brain-damaged samples. Hence, the V–P IQ discrepancy is sensitive to lesions of the right hemisphere for all adult Wechsler scales, but only the data for the old Wechsler-Bellevue suggest sensitivity to left-hemisphere lesions.

Todd, Coolidge, and Satz's Large-Scale Study with the WAIS

Most of the groups shown in Tables 8.2 and 8.3 include relatively small numbers of patients with localized brain damage in the left or right hemispheres. Todd, Coolidge, and Satz (1977) published the only study with more than 100 patients having a well-defined lesion in either the left (*N* = 68) or right (*N* = 46) hemisphere. (Lansdell and Smith, 1975, had a larger sample, but included some patients with bilateral lesions.) These researchers found V > P profiles for patients having lesions in either hemisphere, as well as for additional samples of adults having diffuse brain damage localized in both hemispheres (*N* = 69), nonspecific brain damage evidencing no clear-cut localization (*N* = 74), or psychiatric problems with no known brain involvement (*N* = 78). These five groups showed the following mean V–P IQ differences:

Left Damage +6.0

Right Damage +7.7

Diffuse Damage +7.6

Nonspecific Damage +4.6

Psychiatric Controls +4.5

Smith's Large-Scale Investigations Using the Wechsler-Bellevue

Smith (1966a, 1966b) also found results contrary to the predicted patterns. In his large-scale study of 92 left-brain-damaged and 99 right-brain-damaged adults using the Wechsler-Bellevue, Smith (1966a) reported that V > P IQs characterized both groups; only about one third of the left-brain-damaged patients he studied at several medical centers had the predicted P > V profile. Although Smith's (1966a) sample was criticized for varying "dramatically in the type and the duration of their brain damage" (Todd et al., 1977, p. 450), he obtained similar results for a segment of his larger sample, a rather homogeneous group of 99 patients with acute tumors lateralized to the left (*N* = 48) or right (*N* = 51) hemisphere; less than half of the left-hemisphere patients (43.8%) demonstrated the predicted P > V profile (Smith, 1966b). Smith's (1966a, 1966b) results were considered not too generalizable to most types of brain damage (e.g., Reitan & Fitzhugh, 1971), or applicable only to chronic (as opposed to acute) lesions (Russell, 1972).

The controversies surrounding Smith's negative findings, and methodological issues in general, were among the reasons why Todd et al. (1977) conducted their large-scale study. As indicated, Todd and his colleagues duplicated Smith's (1966a, 1966b) results of V > P profiles, but this time with samples that were carefully defined on key variables. Todd et al. not only failed to find a relationship between V–P IQ discrepancy and left–right lateralization of brain lesions, but found no significant relationship between V–P difference and acuteness versus chronicity of the lesions, or even between V–P discrepancy and the presence or absence of brain damage. As is evident from the preceding discussion, Todd et al.'s psychiatric controls and the four brain-damaged groups were not distinguishable on the basis of their V–P profiles.

Smith's (1966a, 1966b) studies included large samples, but his data have been excluded from tables summarizing V–P/localization studies (e.g., Matarazzo, 1972; Matarazzo & Herman, 1985) because he failed to present mean Verbal and Performance IQs for his brain-damaged groups, as discussed previously.

Like Todd et al.'s (1977) findings, and the general results of WAIS and WAIS-R studies summarized in Tables 8.2 and 8.3, Smith's data do support lowered Performance IQ for patients with brain damage to the right hemisphere. Only 18.2% of his heterogeneous sample of right-damaged adults and 23.5% of his homogeneous group of patients with acute brain tumors had P > V IQ. Again, like the bulk of previous research, his results do not reveal a consistent P > V profile for adult patients with damage to the left hemisphere. We have included Smith's (1966b) study in Table 8.1 because we were able to estimate mean V- and P-IQs for that sample. Unfortunately, this procedure could not be followed for his larger, more heterogeneous sample of 191 adults with lateralized lesions (Smith 1966a) because he did not supply the requisite raw data.

Bilateral Brain Damage

As indicated, Todd et al. (1977) identified a V > P profile on the WAIS for patients having lesions in both cerebral hemispheres. Smith (1966a) also found V > P patterns on the Wechsler-Bellevue for 55 patients with bilateral damage; only 27.3% had P > V patterns. In fact, the nine studies cited by Matarazzo and Herman (1985, Table 2) that included patients with diffuse brain damage spanning both cerebral hemispheres produced a WAIS V > P profile by an average of 6.2 points (range = −1.8 to 13.4). Munder (1976) found WAIS V > P profiles of similar magnitude for both of her samples with diffuse brain damage,

25 African American patients (+4.5 points) and 25 Caucasian patients (+6.3).

WAIS-R and WAIS-III V–P IQ Studies

We compiled a set of recent data that included samples of patients with bilateral and diffuse brain damage tested on either the WAIS-R or the WAIS-III (see Table 8.4). Of the 13 WAIS-R and 2 WAIS-III bilateral/diffuse brain damage samples, 11 (73%) displayed V > P patterns (± 1 point), with 5 (33%) showing that pattern with the ±6-point criterion. Of the WAIS-III studies, one displayed the V > P pattern, the other did not. Of the four samples that failed to yield low P-IQ (by at least 1 point), one was an all-female sample and two of the other three included patients with mild to moderate brain injuries. Thus, the majority of WAIS-R and WAIS-III bilateral/diffuse brain damage samples conform to the V > P pattern that was found on the WAIS.

WAIS-III Factor Index Studies

Two WAIS-III V-P IQ studies are reported in Table 8.4, and a third was excluded because the authors (Martin, Donders, & Thompson, 2000) failed to report IQs for their samples. However, all three sets of authors did report a complete factor index profile for their samples, and the results are quite revealing, as shown in Table 8.5.

All four of the small samples tested (*N*s of 22–31) were diagnosed with traumatic brain injury (TBI), three with mild injuries and one with moderate to severe injuries. The sample reported by The Psychological Corporation (1997) in the test manual displayed the so-called characteristic V > P IQ profile (+5.1 points), as indicated in Table 8.4. The index profile, however, provides fascinating information that renders the V > P profile meaningless. This sample of patients with mild TBI earned their *highest* standard score (92.1) on the Perceptual Organization index and their *lowest* (73.4) on the Processing Speed index, thereby revealing no deficit whatever in the ability presumed to be reflected in the Performance

TABLE 8.4 V–P IQ discrepancies for adult patients with bilateral or diffuse brain damage

Author	Year	Test	N	% Males	Mean Age	Mean Education	V-IQ	P-IQ	Mean V-P Discrepancy
Massad et al.	(1988)	WAIS-R	33	62	49	12.2	86	78	+8.5
Paniak et al.	(1992)	WAIS-R	9	79	32	11.4	95	90	+4.4
Mattis et al. (bilateral)	(1994)	WAIS-R	29	73		13	87	79	+8.3
Mattis et al. (diffuse)	(1994)	WAIS-R	15	73		13	90	88	+1.6
Sherman et al. (mild to moderate)	(1995)	WAIS-R	260	70		11.5	94	98	−4.4
Kraiuhin et al. (moderate to severe)	(1996)	WAIS-R	25	72	28	10.5	95	96	−1.3
Little et al.	(1996)	WAIS-R	77	100	33		84	79	+4.6
Perez et al.	(1996)	WAIS-R	20	90	37	11.9	87	82	+5.1
Ryan et al.	(1996)	WAIS-R	28	100	52	11.9	87	81	+6.2
Iverson et al.	(1997)	WAIS-R	138	70	29	12.1	91	89	+2.7
Ryan et al.	(1997)	WAIS-R	152	0	44	12.6	87	87	+0.5
Ingram et al.	(1998)	WAIS-R	61				85	78	+7.0
Leahy & Lam	(1998)	WAIS-R	58	83	33	13	90	83	+6.6
The Psychological Corporation	(1997)	WAIS-III	22	64	27	13.3	90	85	+5.1
Fisher et al. (mild TBI)	(2000)	WAIS-III	23	52	36	12.9	96	100	−3.7
Weighted Mean of WAIS-R Studies			905						**+1.5**
Weighted Mean of WAIS-III Studies			45						**+0.6**
Weighted Mean of WAIS-R and WAIS-III Studies			950						**+1.4**

TABLE 8.5 Mean WAIS-III factor indexes for samples with traumatic brain injury

Study/Severity of Injury	Background Information				Mean Factor Index			
	N	% Males	Mean Age	Mean Education	Verbal Comprehension	Perceptual Organization	Working Memory	Processing Speed
The Psychological Corporation (1997)—Mild	22	64	27	13.3	89.6	92.1	89.8	73.4
Fisher et al. (2000)—Mild	23	52	36	12.9	95.8	104.6	96.1	95.3
Martin et al. (2000)		52	34	12.9				
Mild	29				99.5	100.3	100.3	100.9
Moderate to Severe	31				92.7	98.0	95.4	88.1
Weighted Mean	**105**				**94.6**	**98.8**	**95.7**	**90.1**

IQ. Instead, their marked deficiency was specifically in their ability to process information quickly.

Three of the four samples summarized in Table 8.5 earned their highest standard score on Perceptual Organization and their lowest on Processing Speed. The fourth sample, the group with mild TBI studied by Martin et al. (2000) displayed a totally flat profile, standard scores of 100–101. Because of the small sample sizes in each study, the most meaningful set of mean indexes is the one provided for the total of 105 patients with TBI: POI (99), WMI/VCI (95-96), and PSI (90). This overall index profile suggests intact Perceptual Organization and weak Processing Speed. Indeed, for three of the four samples, the discrepancy between these indexes was at least 9 points.

Hawkins (1998) examined the clinical samples tested during the WAIS-III standardization to determine if there were any indicators of brain dysfunction that could be derived from study of the WAIS-III IQs and indexes; his results also support the sensitivity of the PSI. The clinical groups included: Alzheimer's disease ($N = 35$), Huntington's disease ($N = 15$), Parkinson's disease ($N = 10$), traumatic brain injury (TBI; $N = 22$), chronic alcohol abuse ($N = 28$), Korsakoff's syndrome ($N = 10$), and schizophrenia ($N = 42$), in addition to 25 patients with Multiple Sclerosis. For all seven clinical populations, the PSI was the low point in the WAIS-III profile (on average, nearly one standard deviation below the high point on each profile). Despite the clinical lore regarding the sensitivity to general brain dysfunction of fluid reasoning and visuo-constructional abilities, the POI did not tend to be depressed for this diversity of clinical samples. Hawkins's (1998) data suggest that Verbal Comprehension–Processing Speed comparisons will better facilitate screening of brain injuries than Verbal–Performance IQ comparisons.

The relatively unaffected performance by the subjects with diffuse TBI on the Perceptual Organization index (as well as some of the other clinical samples studied by Hawkins) may be par-

tially explained by the inclusion of the new Matrix Reasoning subtest; in post hoc analyses, Martin et al. (2000) determined that this subtest, in fact, was not affected by increased injury severity. Thus, the overall impact of the inclusion of Matrix Reasoning in the 5-subtest P-IQ, and, especially, in the 3-subtest POI, may be a lessening of sensitivity to diffuse brain injury. Future neuropsychological research is vital, especially for samples with injuries other than TBI, and with injuries lateralized to one hemisphere. The prospect of the index profile rendering the WAIS-III V–P IQ profile obsolete for the clinical analysis and research investigation of brain damage is both exciting and provocative. We urge researchers to report both IQs and factor indexes, however, to permit comparisons between the two approaches, as was done by both The Psychological Corporation (1997) and Fisher, Ledbetter, Cohen, Marmor, & Tulsky (2000), but not Martin et al. (2000).

Overview of Results

The V > P pattern on the WAIS, WAIS-R, and WAIS-III for patients with bilateral damage or diffuse brain injury conforms to Wechsler's (1958) original clinical observation that patients with "organic brain disease" usually display depressed Performance IQs. However, the WAIS-III Processing Speed Index may be even more sensitive than the global measures of V-IQ and P-IQ on the WAIS-III or on any of its predecessors. That possibility is partially due to the addition of Matrix Reasoning to the WAIS-III Performance Scale, and, perhaps equally, to the elimination of the highly-speeded Object Assembly subtest from all global measures of nonverbal ability on the WAIS-III.

General Conclusions regarding Studies of Brain Damage

Three general conclusions seem warranted based on the numerous WAIS and WAIS-R studies of patients having left-, right-, and bilateral hemisphere disease, and the small number of WAIS-III studies on bilateral/diffuse brain damage:

1. Patients with damage to the right hemisphere, whether the damage is unilateral or accompanied by damage to the left hemisphere as well, are very likely to manifest a substantial V > P profile.

2. Patients with unilateral damage to the left hemisphere may show a slight P > V profile, but not of a magnitude that is large enough or displayed consistently enough to be of much diagnostic benefit; indeed, they are almost as likely to show V > P or no V–P discrepancy.

3. Patients with bilateral or diffuse brain injury may show a V > P profile on the W-B, WAIS, and WAIS-R. However, on the WAIS-III such a pattern will likely not be as pronounced, and, instead, the most evident pattern will be in the factor indexes with the Processing Speed index being the most depressed, especially in comparison to the Perceptual Organization index.

For the present, concerning lateralized brain damage, let's ignore the subtleties of the study-to-study differences in the brain-damaged samples, or in the neuropsychological procedure employed, and combine data from all relevant investigations. In the absence of ideal, well-controlled studies using large numbers of patients with unilateral brain damage, a compilation of data from the existing literature with the Wechsler-Bellevue, WAIS, and WAIS-R provides the best guess at the relationship between V–P IQ difference and lateralized brain lesions. This overview of 2,695 adult patients (combining data from Tables 8.1, 8.2, and 8.3) is as follows:

Left Lesion ($N = 1,336$)	Right Lesion ($N = 1,359$)
P > V = 3.6	V > P = 8.9

The interacting effects of other variables on the relationship between V–P IQ discrepancy and location of a brain lesion, for example, of acuteness versus chronicity of lesion, age of onset, gender, race, and the role played by each separate subtest, are discussed later in this chapter.

THE NATURE OF BRAIN DAMAGE

When Smith (1966a, 1966b) reported the first major negative findings regarding left- versus right-brain damage and direction of V–P IQ discrepancy, he also speculated on the intervening variables that may have led to the contradictory findings. He pointed to methodological problems in most studies, including his own, stressing that "lumping together younger and older patients with different types of lesions in various parts of the two hemispheres obscures possible significant differences in effects as a function of the nature, age, extent, dynamics, and specific locus of the lesion within arbitrarily defined cortical and subcortical gross structures" (Smith, 1966a, p. 121).

Bornstein and Matarazzo (1984) also tried to reconcile McGlone's (1977, 1978) negative findings for females with the bulk of positive findings for other patient samples by focusing on the nature of the brain damage in her samples. They note: "[R]eview by us of McGlone's actual data in her published studies reveals that right lesion females did demonstrate the expected pattern of VIQ greater than PIQ; and that, among the left lesion women, patients'…vascular symptoms did demonstrate the expected pattern of VIQ less than PIQ, but women patients with tumor did not" (p. 707).

Bornstein and Matarazzo (1984) went one step further in this "sub-analysis" to emphasize that "[a]mong the left tumor females…, more than 50 per cent had meningiomas…which tend to be slowly progressive [and] may allow the brain to compensate" (pp. 707–708). Herring and Reitan (1986) further noted that the males in

McGlone's (1977) samples of tumor patients had more intrinsic tumors than did the females (who had more extrinsic tumors), at least raising to Herring and Reitan (1986) "the possibility that the men had more malignant, destructive, and extensive lesions" (p. 537).

The issue of whether V–P discrepancies and side of lesion are more or less related for different types of brain lesion is crucial and is commonly discussed; we have not, however, seen a systematic treatment of this topic in the literature. Most investigators have combined a variety of etiologies to form their "left-lesion" and "right-lesion" samples, and even then they usually come up with groups that are small by research standards. It is impractical to expect researchers to identify samples whose lesions are due to tumors or stroke and are restricted to the anterior left or right parietal lobes.

Such control would be useful, because much clinical experience by neuropsychologists like Reitan has led to detailed understanding of brain–behavior relationships. For example, Reitan (1974) states that, "Block Design is especially sensitive to posterior right hemisphere involvement and especially to right parietal and occipital damage whereas Picture Arrangement is more sensitive to anterior right temporal lesions" (p. 45); other researchers have verified these findings (e.g., Long & Brown, 1979). But that degree of control is not feasible in research. Even if it were, other variables would impinge on the interpretation of the findings of a very specific type of brain damage: severity of the lesion, cause of the brain damage, acuteness or chronicity of the lesion, age at onset, education of patient, and so forth.

In the absence of the ideal, we have accumulated findings from the available studies that used reasonably homogeneous samples. Table 8.6 summarizes the results of 27 studies, comprising eight samples of stroke victims, six patient groups with generalized or posterior tumors, twelve samples with temporal lobe epilepsy, three groups with head injuries, one with missile wounds, and three

samples whose injuries were confined to the frontal lobes. The results are interesting.

Lesions Caused by Stroke, Head Injury, and Tumors

Stroke victims show substantial V–P discrepancies. Because the composite samples are relatively large (about 125 with lesions in each hemisphere), we can have confidence in the generalizability of the results: P > V by 6½ points for left-lesion patients, and V > P by 13½ points for patients with right-hemisphere lesions. These hypothesized findings are even more dramatic for male stroke victims—V–P differences of about –10 and +17 points for patients with left and right lesions, respectively. For females, however, only strokes to the right hemisphere produced the predictable V > P pattern (by a substantial 9½ points); for left-lesion female patients who have had strokes, the V–P discrepancy was zero.

The direct impact of stroke on differential V–P performance, more so than other lesions, follows logically from the nature of cerebrovascular accidents: They feature "the disruption of the supply of nutrients—primarily oxygen and glucose—to the brain as a result of disrupted blood flow. The inability of the nervous tissue of the brain to survive more than several minutes of oxygen deprivation accounts for the rapidity with which irreversible brain damage takes place (Lezak, 1995, pp. 194–195). Further, "[s]ince each carotid artery supplies blood to one cerebral hemisphere, lateralized deficits are common among stroke victims" (Brown, Baird, & Shatz, 1986, p. 387).

No other type of lesion, besides stroke, showed such dramatic results. In the first edition of this book, stroke was joined by head injury in producing striking and predictable P > V and V > P findings, but data were based on a single study with small sample sizes (Uzzell et al.'s, 1979, almost all-male sample of patients with hematomas, hemorrhagic contusions, or cerebral swelling). However, additional data on head-injured samples are now available and are included in Table 8.6. As

TABLE 8.6 Mean V–P IQ discrepancies on various Wechsler scales for adults having different types of brain lesions

Type of Lesion/Study	N	Left Lesions			N	Right Lesions		
		Mean V-IQ	Mean P-IQ	V-P Diff.		Mean V-IQ	Mean P-IQ	V-P Diff.
Stroke								
Reitan & Fitzhugh (1971/W-B)								
Male	15	—	—	−19.8	15	—	—	+10.8
McGlone (1978/WAIS)								
Males	15	—	—	−16.0	11	—	—	+16.0
Females	13	—	—	−3.0	11	—	—	+4.0
Haaland & Delaney (1981/WAIS)	26	87	94	−7.0	17	111	99	+12.0
Inglis et al. (1982/WAIS)								
Males	20	84	99	−15.3	20	107	88	+19.6
Females	20	90	90	+0.2	20	101	96	+4.5
Snow & Sheese (1985/WAIS)								
Males	14	104	90	+13.9	14	104	84	+19.8
Females	5	97	89	+8.0	12	102	79	+22.7
Tumors (Generalized or Posterior)								
Smith (1966b/W-B)	48	94	94	0.0	51	98	92	+6.8
McGlone (1978/WAIS)								
Males	8	—	—	−7.5	6	—	—	+14.0
Females	7	—	—	+3.5	6	—	—	+5.0
Haaland & Delaney (1981/WAIS)	14	94	94	0.0	15	100	97	+3.0
Whelan & Walker (1988/WAIS)								
Posterior	21	93	90	+2.4	24	103	88	+14.7
Mattis et al. (1992/WAIS-R)	34	94	93	+1.0	29	96	85	+11.1
Temporal Lobe (Epileptics)								
Meyer & Jones (1957/W-B)								
Males	11	87	98	−10.8	5	97	94	+3.2
Females	9	80	82	−1.9	6	110	103	+7.0

Dennerll (1964/W-B)	29	86	96	−10.3	31	106	94	+12.5
Meier & French (1955/W-B)								
Sample I	14	92	101	−8.7	16	102	99	+2.7
Lansdell (1968/W-B)								
Males	11	—	—	−8.8	13	—	—	+2.2
Females	8	—	—	−4.9	20	—	—	−3.4
Meier & French (1966/WAIS)								
Sample II	15	90	94	−3.7	25	100	91	+8.4
Buffery (1974/WAIS)	13	89	93	−4.6	17	103	95	+7.4
Ivnik et al. (1987/WAIS)	28	94	102	−7.6	35	103	101	+1.9
Fedio & Mirsky (1969/WISC)								
Children (age 10½)	15	96	98	−2.4	15	104	100	+4.0
Bornstein & Share (1990/WAIS-R)	43	82	83	−0.9	36	85	88	−2.7
Chelune et al. (1993/WAIS-R)	47	89	95	−6.6	49	93	97	−3.6
Head Injury								
Uzzell et al. (1979/WAIS)	8	72	81	−8.7	13	96	79	+17.5
Paniak et al. (1992/WAIS-R)	11	85	79	+6.3	9	93	91	+2.1
Mattis et al. (1994/WAIS-R)	20	84	84	−0.2	15	89	79	+9.8
Missile Wounds								
Black (1947b/WAIS)	50	95	98	−3.4	36	98	94	+4.5
Frontal Lobe Lesions								
Smith (1966b/W-B)								
Tumors	18	90	91	−1.4	23	103	99	+3.8
Black (1976/WAIS)								
Missile wounds	28	99	102	−3.3	16	99	100	−1.1
Whelan & Walker (1988/WAIS)								
Tumors	8	90	90	−0.4	11	105	99	+5.6

(Continues)

TABLE 8.6 (Continued)

Type of Lesion/Study	Left Lesions				Right Lesions			
	N	Mean V-IQ	Mean P-IQ	V-P Diff.	N	Mean V-IQ	Mean P-IQ	V-P Diff.
Totals								
Stroke	128			-6.4	120			+13.5
Males	64			-10.1	60			+16.8
Females	38			+0.1	43			+9.5
Tumors (Generalized or Posterior)	132			+0.4	131			+9.0
Temporal Lobe Epilepsy								
Including children	243			-5.8	268			+2.4
Excluding children	228			-6.0	253			+2.3
Head Injury	39			-0.1	37			+10.6
Missile Wounds	50			-3.4	36			+4.5
Frontal Lobe lesions	54			-2.2	50			+2.6

shown in the "totals" portion of Table 8.6, the weighted mean V–P IQ discrepancy for right lesions due to head injuries is much less dramatic (+10.6) than the 17.5-point difference reported by Uzzell et al., and the V–P discrepancy for left lesions is nonexistent (–0.1).

Patients with generalized or posterior tumors do not demonstrate clear-cut laterality findings. As shown in Table 8.6, tumors to the left hemisphere produced no V–P difference for the composite sample of 132 patients; right-brain tumors for about an equal number of patients produced V > P, as predicted, but the mean value of 9 points is substantially less than the sizable discrepancy found for patients who have had strokes.

Temporal Lobe Epilepsy

The most frequent group of homogeneously defined patients with lateralized lesions has been patients with temporal lobe epilepsy. Data are presented for 12 separate samples in Table 8.6, most of whom were tested postoperatively following removal of the afflicted temporal lobe. For some of these samples, data were presented that permitted evaluation of V–P discrepancies both before and after the lobectomy.

Basic Findings for More than 400 Patients with Epilepsy

Patients with temporal lobe epilepsy displayed predictable V–P differences based on the side that the lesion was located. Because one sample comprised only children with epilepsy (Fedio & Mirsky, 1969), aggregated data are presented both with and without this young sample. Regardless of the inclusion of children, patients with left lesions had P > V by about 6 points, and those with right lesions had V > P by about 2½ points. Because these composite values are based on about 500 patients, the results are probably generalizable to other samples of patients with temporal lobe epilepsy.

These studies have the advantage of being confined to a reasonably specific part of each

hemisphere, and most of the samples were tested following the surgical removal of the affected temporal lobe. Consequently, it is sensible to conclude from Table 8.6 that the left temporal lobe has a clear impact on verbal ability, as measured by Wechsler's Verbal Scale, and the right temporal lobe has a small, but decided impact on a person's success on Wechsler's Performance Scale in comparison to the Verbal scale. Data for separate groups of patients with temporal lobe epilepsy suggest that the findings may hold true for males but not females; however, the small samples of men and women prevent anything other than tentative hypotheses.

WAIS-III Data

The Psychological Corporation (1997, Tables 4.40 and 4.42) included postoperative data on 4 Verbal and 3 Performance subtests for 27 patients with temporal lobe epilepsy, 15 who had a left lobectomy (mean age = 32.5; 73.3% female; 93.3% Caucasian; 73.3% with at least some college) and 12 who had a right lobectomy (mean age = 30.5; 50% female; 58.3% Caucasian, 33.3% African American, 8.3% Hispanic; 75% with at least some college). The following WAIS-III subtests were administered to the 27 patients: Verbal (Vocabulary, Similarities, Digit Span, Letter-Number Sequencing) and Performance (Digit Symbol-Coding, Block Design, Matrix Reasoning). The patients with left lesions, who had a left lobectomy, earned a mean Performance scaled score of 10.0 compared to a mean of 8.3 on the Verbal subtests. This substantial difference is in the predicted direction of P > V. The patients with right lesions who had a right lobectomy averaged 9.8 on Verbal subtests and 10.2 on Performance subtests, a slight V > P pattern that is opposite to prediction. The predicted finding for patients with left lobectomy is consistent with previous research, as is the more pronounced result for patients with epilepsy who have left versus right temporal lesions. However, the opposite profile for patients with right lobectomies is not consistent with most previous research, though it does mirror Chelune et al.'s (1993) results.

The Psychological Corporation (1997) administered two subtests from three of the factor indexes plus a single Processing Speed task. Mean scaled scores were computed for each of the three indexes for each patient sample; these means are shown below, with the mean Digit Symbol-Coding scaled score serving as the estimate of PSI.

	VCI	POI	WMI	PSI
Left Lobectomy	7.8	10.3	8.8	9.4
Right Lobectomy	9.6	10.4	10.0	9.8

Note that the patients with right lesions performed better on all four factors. However, the differences were substantial for VCI and WMI (consistent with predictions, because both of these scales are composed of Verbal subtests) and trivial for POI and PSI. The Psychological Corporation (1997) also administered the WMS-III to the patient sample and found predictable patterns for both groups: Patients with left lesions had higher scores on visual than auditory tasks, both immediate and delayed, whereas patients with right lesions performed better on auditory than visual memory tasks.

Preoperative versus Postoperative V–P Discrepancies

Table 8.7 shows the results of three studies of patients with temporal lobe epilepsy that permitted a comparison of preoperative and postoperative scores on the Wechsler Verbal and Performance scales. The samples differed greatly in the mean interval between the temporal lobectomy surgery and the posttest (means of about 1 month, 1 year, and 3 years). Nevertheless, in nearly all samples V–P differences prior to surgery were in the predictable directions based on the side of the lesion, but these discrepancies were small; subsequent to surgery, V–P differences were still mostly in the predicted directions, but the re-

moval of the left or right temporal lobe apparently led to a substantial increase in mean V–P discrepancies.

Across samples, with about 100 subjects in each group (left and right lobectomies), the V–P differences changed from about 2 points before surgery to about 6½ points after surgery for the left-brain patients and changed from less than one point change before surgery to about 1½ points after surgery for the right-brain patients. Following the lobectomies, left-brain patients dropped about 2 points in Verbal IQ and gained 2½ points in Performance IQ, and right-brain patients evidenced virtually no change in their Performance IQs and gained only 1 point in their Verbal IQs.

Meier and French (1966) noted that Picture Arrangement scores were especially depressed due to right temporal lobectomy. Lezak (1995) and Milner (1954) observed the opposite in their clinical observations, namely, that patients with temporal lobe lesions did poorly on Picture Arrangement but that this poor performance was present prior to surgery and did not worsen from the lobectomy.

Lezak (1995) seemed to support Milner's (1954) conclusion that abnormally functioning tissue may lead to greater deterioration of test performance than the absence of the tissue. The data in Table 8.7, however, provide an empirical contradiction to Milner's inference, at least regarding the relationship of V–P discrepancies to the removal of the left or right temporal lobe in patients with epilepsy.

Chelune et al. (1993) had alternative explanations for the modest retest effect that was present in both of their right- and left-lesion samples. They agreed that, on the surface, the findings were generally consistent with what commonly appears to be "improvement" in IQs after surgery. However, Chelune et al. had an additional control group sample of epilepsy patients who had not received surgery that shed new light on the retest effects seen in the IQs. When contrasting the left- and right-brain temporal lobe patients that had surgery to the control group

TABLE 8.7 V–P IQ discrepancies obtained by patients with temporal lobe epilepsy, both before and after temporal lobectomies

Study	Postoperative Interval	Preoperative			Postoperative			Change	
		V-IQ	P-IQ	V–P	V-IQ	P-IQ	V–P	V-IQ	P-IQ
Meyer & Jones (1957; W-B)									
Left Lesion (N = 20)	1 mo.	94	99	–5.1	84	91	–6.8	–9.8	–8.1
Right Lesion (N = 11)	1 mo.	102	100	+2.4	104	99	+5.3	+1.8	–1.2
Meier & French (1966)									
Sample I (W-B, pre and post)									
Left Lesion (N = 14)	10 mo.	94	95	–1.6	92	101	–8.7	–1.5	+5.6
Right Lesion (N = 16)	11 mo.	100	98	+1.8	102	99	+2.7	+2.6	+1.7
Sample II (W-B, pre; WAIS, post)									
Left Lesion (N = 15)	3.2 yr.	91	93	–1.7	90	94	–3.7	–0.9	+1.1
Right Lesion (N = 25)	3.6 yr.	100	97	+2.7	100	91	+8.4	–0.3	–6.0
Chelune et al. (1993)									
Left Lesion (N = 47)	11 mo.	87.8	89.0	–1.2	88.7	95.3	–6.6	+0.9	+6.3
Right Lesion (N = 49)	11 mo.	91.8	94.1	–2.3	93.1	96.7	–3.6	+1.3	+2.6
Weighted means									
Left Lesion (N = 96)				–2.1			–6.5	–1.9	+2.4
Right Lesion (N = 98)				+0.1			+1.3	+1.1	–0.1

NOTE: *V–P* stands for Verbal IQ minus performance IQ. "Change" refers to change in Verbal IQ and Performance IQ preoperatively to postoperatively. It equals postoperative IQ minus preoperative IQ; therefore, negative signs refer to lower postoperative IQs. Mean differences between V- and P-IQs, and between preoperative and postoperative IQs, were computed from mean IQs rounded to the nearest tenth. Buffery's (1974) and Ivnik et al.'s (1987) preoperative and postoperative data for temporal lobe epileptics are excluded from this table because their pre and post samples did not contain the same patients.

265

that had not had surgery, they found that the un-operated sample had similar mean IQ improvements. Because the improvements were similar across groups that had surgery and that did not, the observed improvements are most likely attributable to a positive practice effect. Indeed, the most measurable improvements in Chelune et al.'s samples were in the P-IQ, which typically has more substantial practice effects than the V-IQ (see Chapter 6).

Temporal Lobe versus Parietal Lobe Lesions

Warrington and James (1967) divided their 36 right-lesion and 29 left-lesion patients into the following groups, each composed of 16 or 17 patients: right temporal, right parietal, left temporal, left parietal. The two right-damage groups overlapped by two patients who had damage to both areas, and the two left-damage groups overlapped by three patients; 62% of the patients had tumors.

Warrington and James found no difference between the right temporal and right parietal groups regarding V–P discrepancy, with both showing a substantial 15-point difference favoring Verbal IQ. However, left temporal damage seemed more sensitive than left parietal damage to a verbal deficit; the former group had P > V by 6½ points, compared to P > V of 3 points for the latter sample. The P > V pattern of nearly 7 points for the patients with left temporal damage (composed of 10 with tumors, 3 with strokes, 2 with abscesses, and 1 each with a missile wound and lobectomy) is similar to the P > V discrepancy reported in Table 8.6 for patients with left temporal lobe epilepsy.

Frontal Lobe Lesions

In contrast to the temporal lobe's relationship to the differential cognitive functioning of the two hemispheres, the frontal lobe seems to be external to the cerebral asymmetry. Combining data

from Smith's (1966c) and Whelan and Walker's (1988) studies of tumors confined to the frontal lobes, and Black's (1976) study of missile wounds that were similarly confined, Table 8.6 reveals very slight V–P differences for patients with left- or right-brain lesions. Although the differences are both in the predicted direction, they are too small (2 to 2½ points) to be of consequence.

Frontal versus Posterior Lesions

When WAIS scores of missile wound patients with frontal lesions are compared to the scores of missile wound patients with posterior lesions, the frontal lobe sample earned IQs of about 100, significantly higher than the mean IQs of about 90 earned by patients with posterior lesions (Black, 1976). Also, Lansdell and Smith (1975) found that nonverbal factor scores were significantly related to side of lesion in the predicted direction; however, "Scores for patients with damage limited to the frontal lobes showed small side differences, suggesting that damage other than to the frontal lobe on the right caused the impairment shown by the nonverbal scores" (p. 923).

All of these results are consistent with Teuber's (1964) conclusions from a review of pertinent literature that (1) lesions in the frontal lobes affect cognitive performance less than lesions in other parts of the brain, and (2) there are no apparent differences between the effects of right and left lesions of the frontal lobes on higher intellectual functions. The present results are also consistent with the findings of other investigations of missile wounds to the frontal lobes (Newcombe, 1969; Schiller, 1947) and of frontal lobe tumors (Pollack, 1955).

Although Smith (1966c) did not detect a laterality pattern in the V–P differences of patients with left versus right frontal tumors, he did observe two findings that are at variance with Black's (1976) results with missile wound patients and with Teuber's (1964) conclusions. First, he found that patients with left frontal tumors had lower

Full Scale IQs than those with right frontal tumors (90 versus 101); second, he found that patients with frontal lobe tumors in one of his subsamples (but not in the other) earned similar mean Full Scale IQs to patients with lesions in nonfrontal regions of the brain. Smith (1966c) attributed these aberrant findings to differences in his samples from many previous samples on variables such as age (his group was older than most samples, with a mean age of 46) and the acuteness of the lesions in his samples (they were tested immediately before or just after surgery).

Interestingly, Whelan and Walker (1988) replicated Smith's (1966c) results almost exactly with their male and female tumor patients. Like Smith's group, Whelan and Walker's patients had an average age of 47 and were tested within 1 month of surgery (48 presurgery, 16 postsurgery). In Whelan and Walker's investigation, men and women with right frontal lobe tumors achieved WAIS IQs of about 100, but those with left frontal lobe tumors had depressed Verbal and Performance IQs of 90, paralleling the lowered IQs of patients with left posterior tumors.

Whelan and Walker (1988) further demonstrated that tumors in the right hemisphere are more likely to produce the expected large V > P discrepancy if they are located in the posterior regions of the brain (14.7 points) than in the anterior, frontal regions (5.6 points). This finding held true for separate samples of men and women. Patients with lesions in the left hemisphere, however, failed to produce P > V patterns regardless of the location of the tumors.

Table 8.6 shows that patients with missile wounds in various portions of the brain (Black, 1974b) showed predictable V–P discrepancies depending on which side the wound was on, but that the differences were a rather small 4 points. Black (1974b) noted, however, that most (about 85%) of the patients with missile wounds in his sample had frontal lobe injuries, although the injuries often affected other regions as well. Hence, the V–P discrepancies that he found for missile wound patients were probably attenuated by the preponderance of frontal lobe lesions. By

way of contrast, only about 20% of his right- and left-lesion samples had temporal lobe lesions, about 35% had lesions of the occipital lobe, and about 10% had parietal wounds. (The percentages exceed 100 because many patients had damage to multiple areas.)

ACUTE VERSUS CHRONIC LESIONS

The impact of the recency of the lesion on cognitive impairment has been discussed by early researchers of V–P differences in patients with unilateral lesions as a likely intervening variable in many studies (Fitzhugh, Fitzhugh, & Reitan, 1961; Klove & Fitzhugh, 1962). These investigators felt that failure to control for the acuteness versus the chronicity of the left or right lesions probably accounted for the negative findings in the literature. Specifically, they hypothesized that acute (new) lesions are more likely than chronic (long-standing) lesions to lead to predictable V–P discrepancies for patients with unilateral brain damage. This hypothesis is consistent with a bulk of clinical and research findings (Lezak, 1995) that stress that "the recency of the insult may be the most critical factor determining the patient's psychological status" (p. 282).

Fitzhugh et al.'s Study

Fitzhugh et al. (1962) systematically evaluated the acute–chronic dimension and found significant V–P discrepancies in the predicted direction only for their sample of patients with acute lesions; the differences for the chronic patients, though in the anticipated direction, were just 2 to 4 points.

Although Fitzhugh et al.'s study is often cited as evidence for the impact of the recency of brain damage on Wechsler test patterns, their samples of acute and chronic patients differed on numerous other variables as well: institution (acute patients were at a university medical center, chronic patients at a state hospital); gender (acute patients were predominantly male, chronic patients included a majority of females); nature of brain damage (acute injuries were almost all strokes, tumors, or head injuries, whereas chronic patients had convulsive disorders due to a wide variety of causes); education level (acute patients had an average of 8 years of education; chronic patients had an average of 5½ to 6 years); and IQ level (acute patients had mean FS-IQs of about 85; chronic patients had mean FS-IQs of about 70). Based on the previous discussion of gender differences, that variable alone might have accounted for the different V–P findings for the acute and chronic patients.

Aggregated Data from Several Samples

Table 8.8 was compiled from Fitzhugh et al.'s (1962) investigation and two additional studies (comprising four samples in all) that examined acuteness versus chronicity as an independent variable. The combination of data from these diverse samples should give more insight into the importance of this variable than is provided by Fitzhugh et al.'s unmatched samples. The data

from the two samples of patients who have had strokes investigated by Inglis, Ruckman, Lawson, MacLean, & Monga (1982) are of particular value because the samples of acute and chronic patients were carefully matched on the variables of gender (by treating males and females separately), age, education (exception: chronic males with left lesions were much more educated than acute males with left lesions), familial lefthandedness, and severity of lesion.

Fitzhugh et al. (1962) did not specify how soon after the brain lesion the group with "recently developed symptoms of cerebral dysfunction" (p. 306) were tested, but they noted that the chronic sample was tested about 25 years following the first noted seizure. Todd et al. (1977) used a 1-year cutoff to determine acuteness and chronicity; all patients who were tested on the WAIS within 1 year of brain damage were designated as acute, while those tested 13 or more months following damage were classified as chronic. In Inglis et al.'s (1982) study, the acute samples had suffered a stroke within 6 months of testing (mean = 3 months), and the chronic groups had had a stroke 1–12 years prior to testing (mean = 4 years).

As indicated in Table 8.8 for the composite samples, left-brain-damaged patients with acute lesions and with chronic lesions both had a P > V difference of about 2½ points. Among right-

TABLE 8.8   V–P IQ discrepancies for patients with acute and chronic lesions lateralized to the right or left hemisphere

| | Acute Lesions | | | | Chronic Lesions | | | |
| | Left | | Right | | Left | | Right | |
Study	N	V–P	N	V–P	N	V–P	N	V–P
Fitzhugh et al. (1962)	18	–9.1	25	+15.0	20	–3.9	25	+2.1
Todd et al. (1977)	15	+12.7	11	+10.5	26	+2.2	20	+6.3
Inglis et al. (1982)								
Males	10	–10.2	10	+24.0	10	–20.3	10	+15.2
Females	10	–5.3	10	+6.6	10	+5.8	10	+2.4
Weighted Mean	**53**	**–2.4**	**56**	**+14.2**	**66**	**–2.5**	**65**	**+5.5**

hemisphere patients, however, acute subjects showed a far more substantial V > P discrepancy than chronic patients (14 versus 5½ points). Both right-lesion groups showed the predicted pattern, but only the acute group showed a sizable discrepancy. Thus, the data in Table 8.8 suggest that left-lesion patients do not vary in their V–P differences as a function of the recency of the lesion, but that acuteness–chronicity is a key variable for patients with right-hemisphere damage.

Generally, the most neurobehavioral recovery from traumatic brain injury is made in the first years after the injury. The most rapid recovery typically occurs within the first 3–6 months and then a plateau occurs around 2 years (Jones, 1992). Within these broad parameters, some abilities recover more quickly than others, and improvement from traumatic brain injury is a heterogeneous process.

The relative improvement, over time, in right-brain cognitive functioning by patients with damage to that side of the brain attests to the recuperative powers of brain-injured people. Lezak (1995) states: "Cognitive functions, particularly those involving immediate memory, attention and concentration, and specific disabilities associated with the site of the lesion generally continue to improve markedly during the first six months or year, and improvement at a progressively slower rate may go on for a decade or more following a stroke or other single-event injury to the brain" (p. 283). Nonetheless, it is still consistent with previous research and clinical experience to find a V > P discrepancy of 5½ points in chronic right-lesion patients beause full recovery is rare, even for apparently slight injuries (Brodal, 1973; Schachter & Crovitz, 1977).

Correlational Studies

Snow, Freedman, and Ford (1986) correlated the absolute value of the V–P differences for several samples of left- and right-lesion patients with the number of months following the onset of the damage. They obtained a strong negative relationship (–.83) based on data from Wechsler-Bellevue investigations, showing once again that larger V–P IQ discrepancies are more likely to emerge for patients who recently became brain injured than for those with long-standing injuries. Because Snow et al. (1986) grouped the left-lesion and right-lesion samples together for their correlational analysis, it was possible neither to deny nor confirm the hypothesis proposed here that acuteness versus chronicity is a more important variable for lesions to the right hemisphere. Paniak, Silver, Finlayson, and Tuff (1992) examined the time from injury to WAIS-R testing in a sample of head-injured patients and found that longer time from injury to testing was associated with higher Performance IQ ($r = .29$, $p < .01$). Like Snow et al., Paniak et al. did not provide data on the duration of injury across separate left- and right-hemisphere lesion patients.

SUBTEST PATTERNS FOR LEFT- AND RIGHT-LESION PATIENTS

The diverse studies of brain-damaged patients suggest that the Wechsler V–P discrepancy seems to be a better indicator for those with right lesions than for those with left focal damage. This section examines the separate Wechsler subtests to see if observable patterns are evident that help make sense of the accumulating data on brain damage.

Mean Scaled Scores for Patients with Focal Brain Damage

Table 8.9 presents mean scaled or weighted scores on the 11 Wechsler subtests for all of the unilaterally brain-damaged patient samples that provided these data for all or most subtests. The table includes five samples tested on the Wechsler-Bellevue and eight assessed with the WAIS. Typically, the mean scores for right-lesion samples on the tests of verbal ability were in the average range (9–11); exceptions were for the two tasks that are more associated with the Freedom from Distractibility/Working Memory factor than the Verbal Comprehension factor (Arithmetic, Digit Span) and for the two groups (samples 12 and 13 in Table 8.9) with low overall functioning. Mean scores for right-lesion patients were in the average range for four W-B/WAIS samples (samples 1, 3, 7, 8) on Block Design, and for three W-B/WAIS samples on Object Assembly (samples 1, 3, 7). However, samples 1, 3, and 8 are limited to patients with temporal lobe epilepsy; lesions to the temporal lobe are not associated with poor performance on Block Design and Object Assembly, both of which are sensitive to lesions in the more posterior regions of the right hemisphere (Lezak, 1995; Reitan, 1986).

Left-lesion samples generally scored higher on Performance than Verbal tasks, as many hypothesize. However, they usually scored below the average range on *all* subtests (except for left-lesion samples 3 and 6 in Table 8.9, who scored in the average range on nearly all Performance subtests).

Table 8.10 presents mean age-based scaled scores on the WAIS-R subtests for three unilaterally brain-damaged patient samples that provided these data for all or most subtests. Because sample sizes are small, only the weighted means for 69 patients with left lesions and 61 patients with right lesions will be addressed. Those with left lesions performed comparably (and poorly) on all subtests, with no Verbal–Performance distinction evident. However, the right-lesion samples demonstrated their highest scores on Verbal subtests and their lowest scores on Performance tasks, as predicted, with only Picture completion behaving more like a Verbal than Performance subtest.

Discrimination between Right-Lesion and Left-Lesion Patients

Table 8.11 summarizes the data in Table 8.9 by presenting mean scaled scores for left- and right-lesion patients tested on the Wechsler-Bellevue and the WAIS. These mean values, as well as the mean difference in scaled scores for patients with left versus right lesions, are presented separately for each test as well as together. Table 8.12 then pools the W-B and WAIS data with the WAIS-R subtest data from Table 8.10 to provide a broad overview of the left lesion versus right lesion discrimination ability of each of the 11 subtests common to the three WAIS-III predecessors.

Overall comparison of the subtest performance of left- and right-lesion patients on the Wechsler-Bellevue, WAIS, and WAIS-R indicates the following: Right-lesion patients outscored left-lesion patients by an average of 1 to 2½ points on all Verbal subtests; left-lesion patients outperformed right-lesion patients on all Performance subtests except Digit Symbol by 1 to 1½ points; the patient samples did not differ in their scores on Digit Symbol.

Only three subtests functioned markedly differently on the Wechsler-Bellevue, WAIS, and WAIS-R: Picture Completion, Arithmetic, and Similarities. Whereas Picture Completion discriminated effectively between left- and right-lesion samples on the Wechsler-Bellevue, it did not do so on the WAIS or WAIS-R. Both Arithmetic and Similarities discriminated adequately for both the Wechsler-Bellevue and WAIS, but not for the WAIS-R.

When subtest data were combined for all 16 samples (Table 8.12), Digit Symbol and Picture Completion failed to discriminate effectively between left- and right-lesion patient groups. The three remaining Performance tasks all discriminated in the predicted direction between the two patient samples, and they all discriminated about equally well. The six Verbal subtests discriminated effectively between left- and right-lesion samples in the predicted fashion. Digit Span, Vocabulary, and Comprehension were the best discriminators, followed by Information, Similarities, and Arithmetic, which were about equally good at it.

If the subtest means are examined for only left-lesion patients and only for right-lesion patients to determine which tasks produce the largest differences within each group, the following

TABLE 8.9 Mean scaled or weighted scores on the Wechsler-Bellevue and WAIS subtests by patients with lesions localized in the left or right hemisphere

Subtest	Wechsler-Bellevue study									WAIS study			
	1	2	3	4	5	6	7	8	9	10	11	12	13
Left Lesion													
I	7.0	8.1	8.3	8.0	7.7	8.0	8.2	8.1	—	9.2	9.3	7.8	6.8
C	8.4	8.5	8.6	6.7	7.5	6.8	7.6	8.8	—	8.6	8.2	7.4	6.6
A	7.4	5.8	7.7	5.0	5.0	7.8	8.2	9.1	9.6	8.8	8.7	6.6	6.3
S	6.7	7.8	9.2	5.0	8.1	7.4	9.5	8.8	8.9	6.7	8.9	7.5	4.9
DSp	7.8	5.0	6.4	2.8	5.5	7.2	8.4	8.5	8.1	7.5	7.8	7.1	5.2
V	7.2	7.6	7.0	6.5	8.0	7.5	8.2	7.0	9.1	8.1	8.6	6.8	6.5
DSy	8.5	6.7	8.0	5.8	5.8	—	—	8.1	—	5.5	6.6	4.9	2.5
PC	8.7	8.5	10.4	9.0	8.8	10.8	9.2	10.1	10.6	8.9	10.8	8.4	6.8
BD	9.6	9.0	10.2	8.7	7.6	9.6	7.4	10.3	10.4	8.0	9.8	5.6	5.8
PA	8.9	7.9	9.4	7.3	8.5	10.2	8.7	8.9	8.9	8.0	9.4	6.7	5.9
OA	9.9	9.5	10.6	8.1	8.2	9.0	8.2	8.5	8.6	7.3	9.3	5.7	5.7
Right Lesion													
I	10.6	10.2	9.8	10.3	9.4	11.4	10.3	9.6	—	9.9	10.4	8.0	8.4
C	11.4	10.1	11.8	10.1	10.5	10.8	10.3	10.9	—	11.0	11.4	8.2	9.1
A	10.2	8.3	7.1	7.1	7.8	11.0	9.1	9.9	9.3	9.2	10.2	7.4	7.8
S	10.5	9.5	10.8	8.2	10.5	11.0	9.8	10.6	9.7	8.9	11.3	6.6	7.5
DSp	10.5	7.4	8.5	5.1	7.5	11.4	10.4	9.0	10.9	8.9	9.3	7.7	7.6
V	10.6	9.6	9.1	10.1	10.0	11.8	11.0	9.6	10.4	9.7	11.0	7.4	8.7
DSy	8.2	6.0	9.6	4.8	6.5	—	—	8.2	—	6.6	6.8	4.0	3.8
PC	8.8	8.1	9.8	8.5	6.4	9.8	10.8	9.1	9.2	9.3	8.8	7.0	7.3
BD	9.1	6.2	9.9	5.8	5.8	7.3	9.4	9.8	7.5	8.0	8.4	5.0	5.5
PA	8.9	6.5	7.5	6.0	6.5	8.0	8.6	6.9	6.9	7.6	8.0	5.6	5.7
OA	9.2	7.8	10.2	7.0	6.0	7.0	9.0	7.9	6.3	7.3	7.2	5.2	4.7

NOTE: The numbers in the heading correspond to the following studies: 1. Dennerell (1964); 2. Klove (1959); Meier & French (1966, Sample I); 4. Reitan (1955c); 5. Doehring et al. (1961); 6. Inglis et al. (1982, Males); 7. Inglis et al. (1982, Females); 8. Meier & French (1966, Sample II); 9. Warrington & James (1967); 10. Zimmerman et al. (1970); 11. Munder (1976, Whites); 12. Munder (1976, Blacks); 13. Simpson & Vega (1971). Sample sizes for the patients with left and right lesions are presented in Table 9.6 for studies 1–5, and in Table 9.7 for studies 6–13.

TABLE 8.10 Mean age-based scaled scores on the WAIS-R subtests by patients with lesions localized in the left or right hemisphere

Subtest	Left Lesion			Right Lesion			Weighted Mean		Mean Diff.
	Study 1 (N=16)	Study 2 (N=19)	Study 3 (N=34)	Study 1 (N=16)	Study 2 (N=16)	Study 3 (N=29)	Left Lesion (N=69)	Right Lesion (N=61)	Left–Right
I	6.6	6.9	9.9	9.8	8.7	10.1	8.3	9.6	–1.3
DSp	6.5	—	—	8.6	—	—	6.5	8.6	–2.1
V	6.1	—	—	9.6	—	—	6.1	9.6	–3.5
A	6.8	7.6	8.8	8.3	8.7	8.5	8.0	8.5	–0.5
C	6.7	6.6	8.2	9.3	8.1	9.2	7.4	8.9	–1.5
S	6.6	7.5	9.0	8.0	7.8	9.0	8.0	8.4	–0.4
PC	6.5	8.2	9.9	7.0	7.7	9.0	8.6	8.1	+0.5
PA	6.6	8.4	8.8	5.9	6.5	7.5	8.2	6.8	+1.4
BD	6.6	7.7	9.4	5.7	7.0	7.2	8.3	6.7	+1.6
OA	6.4	7.8	9.2	5.7	6.2	7.2	8.1	6.6	+1.5
Dsy	4.8	—	—	5.8	—	—	4.8	5.8	–1.0

NOTE: The numbers in the heading correspond to the following studies: Study 1 = Massad et al. (1988); Study 2 = Mattis et al. (1994); Study 3 = Mattis et al. (1992). Weighted means equal the Study 1 means for Digit Span, Vocabulary, and Digit Symbol.

TABLE 8.11   Differences between the weighted means earned on the 11 Wechsler-Bellevue and WAIS subtests by patients with left and right lesions

Subtest	Wechsler-Bellevue			WAIS			Total		
	Left Lesion N=118	Right Lesion N=120	Mean Diff.	Left Lesion N=178	Right Lesion N=205	Mean Diff.	Left Lesion N=296	Right Lesion N=325	Mean Diff.
C	8.1	10.7	−2.6	7.7	10.3	−2.6	7.9	10.5	−2.6
V	7.4	9.9	−2.5	7.8	9.9	−2.1	7.6	9.9	−2.3
DSp	5.7	8.0	−2.3	7.5	9.4	−1.9	6.8	8.9	−2.1
I	7.8	10.1	−2.3	8.2	9.7	−1.5	8.0	9.9	−1.9
S	7.4	9.9	−2.5	7.8	9.4	−1.6	7.7	9.6	−1.9
A	6.2	8.4	−2.2	8.2	9.2	−1.0	7.4	8.9	−1.5
DSy	7.0	7.0	0.0	5.4	5.9	−0.5	6.3	6.4	−0.1
PC	8.9	7.3	+1.6	9.3	8.9	+0.4	9.2	8.3	+0.9
BD	9.0	7.3	+1.7	8.4	7.6	+0.8	8.6	7.5	+1.1
OA	9.4	8.1	+1.3	7.8	6.8	+1.0	8.4	7.3	+1.1
PA	8.3	7.2	+1.1	8.3	7.1	+1.2	8.3	7.1	+1.2

NOTE: Mean Diff. = mean for patients with left lesions minus the mean for patients with right lesions. Subtests are listed in the order of their mean differences for the total sample, going from the most negative to the most positive.

These weighted means are based on data presented in Table 8.9 for five Wechsler-Bellevue and eight WAIS studies. Sample sizes shown are for all subtests except Information, Compre- hension, and Digit Symbol, which had missing data for some samples tested on the WAIS. The sample sizes for Information and Comprehension were as follows: WAIS—left lesions = 149, right lesions = 169; Total—left lesions = 267, right lesions = 289. For Digit Symbol, the corresponding WAIS and Total sample sizes were 109, 129, 227, and 249, respectively.

results emerge. On the Wechsler-Bellevue, left-lesion patients did best on Object Assembly and Block Design and worst on Digit Span and Arithmetic; on the WAIS, they did best on Picture Completion and Block Design and worst on Digit Symbol and Digit Span. On the WAIS-R, left-lesion patients did best on Picture Completion and worst on Digit Symbol.

For patients with right-hemisphere lesions, the following dyads are highest and lowest: on the Wechsler-Bellevue, Comprehension/Information versus Digit Symbol/Picture Arrangement; on the WAIS, Comprehension/Vocabulary versus Digit Symbol/Object Assembly; on the WAIS-R, Vocabulary/Information versus Digit Symbol/Object Assembly.

The Psychological Corporation (1997) pre-sented WAIS-III data for 27 patients with tem-poral lobe epilepsy who had undergone either a left or right lobectomy, but they administered only four Verbal and three Performance subtests. The patients with right lesions scored higher on all subtests except Block Design, which pro-duced nearly equal means (10.4, left lesion; 10.2 right lesion). Consistent with expectancies based on location of the lesion, the patients with right lesions (N = 12) scored much higher than pa-tients with left lesions (N = 15) on the four Ver-bal tasks (means of 9.8 and 8.3, respectively), but only slightly higher on Performance subtests (10.2 vs. 10.0). In order of magnitude, the differ-ences in favor of the patients with right lesions

TABLE 8.12   Differences between the weighted means earned on the 11 Wechsler-Bellevue, WAIS, and WAIS-R subtests by patients with right and left lesions

Subtest	Left Lesion Weighted Mean (N = 365)	Right Lesion Weighted Mean (N = 386)	Left–Right Difference
C	7.8	10.2	–2.4
V	7.3	9.7	–2.4
DSp	6.7	8.8	–2.1
I	8.1	9.8	–1.7
S	7.7	9.4	–1.7
A	7.5	8.8	–1.3
DSy	5.8	6.2	–0.4
PC	9.0	8.3	+0.7
BD	8.6	7.4	+1.2
OA	8.4	7.2	+1.2
PA	8.3	7.1	+1.2

NOTE: Left–Right Difference = mean for patients with left lesions minus the mean for patients with right lesions. Subtests are listed in the order of their mean differences for the total sample, going from the most negative to the most positive. Separate total sample sizes for patients with left lesions on W-B, WAIS, and WAIS-R are 118, 178, and 69, respectively, and for patients with right lesions, sample sizes are 120, 205, and 61, respectively. Sample sizes for some subtests, notably Digit Symbol, are a bit smaller.

were as follows: Similarities (+2.2), Digit Span (+2.0), Vocabulary (+1.3), Letter-Number Sequencing (+0.5), Matrix Reasoning (+0.5), Digit Symbol-Coding (+0.4), and Block Design (–0.2).

Hemispheric Functioning: Process versus Content

The results summarized in Tables 8.11 and 8.12 are quite revealing and may relate to the reason why patients with left-hemisphere lesions do not display the predicted P > V profile in most studies. For both the Wechsler-Bellevue and WAIS, the deficiencies shown by left-lesion patients are on the third or distractibility factor, not on the Verbal Comprehension dimension—namely the

triad of Digit Span, Arithmetic, and Digit Symbol. (The results from the WAIS-R are not quite as clear-cut. However, only one of the samples included scores from most of the Freedom from Distractibility factor.) The Freedom from Distractibility factor has been interpreted as sequential or successive processing (Bannatyne, 1971, 1974; Kaufman, 1979b, 1994a; Kaufman & Kaufman, 1983b), the type of mental processing that has been associated with the left hemisphere by cerebral specialization researchers (Levy, 1972; Sperry, 1968). Hence, damage to the left hemisphere may disrupt a person's ability to process sequentially, not necessarily his or her ability to handle verbal content.

Conversely, left-lesion patients generally performed best on the three Wechsler-Bellevue,

WAIS, and WAIS-R subtests that are the best measures of the Perceptual Organization factor: Picture Completion, Object Assembly, Block Design. These are precisely the Wechsler subtests that provide measurement of simultaneous or holistic processing, the problem-solving style associated with the right hemisphere.

Left-lesion patients are able to process relatively well with their right hemispheres, and they score adequately on the Wechsler Performance subtests that are excellent measures of simultaneous processing. However, they have more difficulty with a Performance subtest that has a decided sequential component, namely Digit Symbol. Just as their weakness may be sequential processing, so, too, their strength may be simultaneous processing; this process distinction is different from the content distinction that is examined whenever the Verbal and Performance IQs are compared. WAIS-III studies are needed with patients known to have lateralized lesions to follow up on this process-based hypothesis derived from data on its predecessors. The factor index profile is especially well suited to such an analysis. If the process interpretation is correct, then one would anticipate large discrepancies for patients with left-hemisphere lesions when subtracting the WMI from the POI, larger than the differences obtained when comparing VCI and POI.

Support for a process approach to brain functioning also comes from an investigation of the reading achievement of 86 left-lesion and 76 right-lesion patients averaging 40 years of age and 13 years of education (Heaton, Schmitz, Avitable, & Lehman, 1987). Both groups were deficient, compared to a control group of 100 normal adults, in Reading Recognition and Reading Comprehension on the Peabody Individual Achievement Test (PIAT). However, the left-lesion group performed significantly worse than the right-lesion sample only on the recognition (oral reading) task. Consequently, the two brain-damaged groups did not differ significantly in reading per se but in the subtest requiring sequential, linear analysis of letters and syllables.

Should V–P Discrepancies Be Used for Assessing Brain Damage?

Some neuropsychologists are opposed to the use of the V-IQs and P-IQs because they are too heterogeneous and global. Smith (1966a) felt that "[t]he arbitrary lumping together of all WB verbal subtests into a hypothesized dimension of 'verbal' intelligence, and of all Performance subtests into another hypothesized dimension… confounds efforts to define the specific effects of specific brain lesions" (p. 121). Lezak (1995) echoes these sentiments: "IQ scores…represent so many different kinds of more or less confounded functions as to be conceptually meaningless" (p. 24).

We respect the message conveyed by these clinicians, but feel that it is unwise to take such an extreme stance. Wechsler's combination of tasks into two scales was not "arbitrary," and the results of factor analysis point to the impressive commonalities among Verbal Comprehension subtests and among Perceptual Organization subtests. Table 8.12, summarizing subtest patterns from 16 studies with three different versions of Wechsler's tests for adults, shows that the six Verbal subtests are about equally good at discriminating right-lesion from left-lesion patients, perhaps excepting Arithmetic, and the same can be said for the Performance subtests of Block Design, Object Assembly, and Picture Arrangement.

The use of a regrouping of the 11 subtests into three categories, corresponding to the three factors that dominated the literature prior to the WAIS-III enhanced interpretation, especially concerning a process versus content distinction for patients with left lesions. However, the three factors helped refine the Verbal and Performance Scales, not necessarily invalidate them for clinical interpretation. Similarly, the four indexes reflect a refinement of the global V and P scales, especially because they pair up, such that two are composed only of Verbal subtests and two only of Performance subtests. Quite obviously, WAIS-III studies with patients having lateralized lesions are an essential adjunct to the research literature. But, as stated, the researchers would be wise to report a full set of global scores, IQs alongside indexes, to permit interpretation of the new data alongside the older data obtained on the WB, WAIS, and WAIS-R.

Until factor index profiles are shown to be more valuable than IQ profiles in their relationships to unilateral brain damage—just as preliminary evidence with four TBI samples with nonfocal lesions (Table 8.5), and with several diverse samples such as schizophrenics and Alzheimer's patients (Hawkins, 1998), has demonstrated the primacy of the indexes—the V–P IQ discrepancy cannot be summarily dismissed. The V–P differences remain important because of the bulk of clinical and neuropsychological research that has been conducted with these IQs. However, as stressed throughout this book and elsewhere (Kaufman, 1990, 1994a; Kaufman & Lichtenberger, 1999, 2000), the global IQs are merely the starting point of profile analysis. The next stages involve systematic, empirical evaluation of subtest profiles, a process that should help pinpoint the specific cognitive deficits that accompany specific localized brain lesions to either hemisphere.

The V–P difference has great potential utility for understanding the cognitive assets and deficiencies of adults with unilateral brain damage; the index profile has even greater potential. Examiners who test patients with neuropsychiatric and neurological disorders should almost always go beyond the IQs and incorporate the WAIS-III factor indexes into their interpretation of the client's strengths and weaknesses. But we consider the reliance on global scores, whether IQs or Indexes, a far more sensible procedure than relying on just a few isolated subtests or on a set of "signs" such as Picture Completion > Arithmetic or Information > Object Assembly (Simpson & Vega, 1971) to assess lateralized brain damage.

GENDER OF PATIENTS WITH LATERALIZED LESIONS

Males and females are believed to differ in various aspects of brain functioning (Witelson, 1976), and they have demonstrated differences in cerebral organization in experiments with normal individuals using techniques such as dichotic listening and assessment of the superiority of the left or right visual fields for verbal versus visual–spatial stimuli (Bryden, 1979). Lezak (1995) concludes that "lateral asymmetry is not as pronounced in women as in men" (p. 297). Yet this variable has been ignored by many researchers despite the likelihood, or at least the conceivability, of gender differences in the relationship between the localization of a lesion to the left or right hemisphere and the direction of the V–P discrepancy.

Lansdell's Initial Observations

Over a quarter of a century ago, Lansdell (1962) observed gender differences concerning the impact of temporal lobe neurosurgery on epileptic patients' verbal and nonverbal behavior. Removal of the right temporal lobe affected the visual perception of males, who demonstrated a significant reduction in their artistic aptitude following the surgery; similarly, removal of the left temporal lobe, as predicted by lateralization research on brain function, resulted in men scoring significantly lower on a test of proverbs after surgery than before. In marked contrast, these hypothesized reductions in visual–spatial and verbal performance following right and left temporal lobe surgeries, respectively, failed to occur for women. Lansdell (1968) subsequently obtained similar findings with the Wechsler-Bellevue, concluding that "the results suggest that perceptual abilities are to some extent represented differently in the brains of men and women" (p. 266).

Regardless of Lansdell's (1962, 1968) suggestions of gender differences in cerebral lateralization and the similar sentiments of other neuropsychologists (Buffery & Gray, 1972), the issue of male–female differences in Wechsler studies of patients with unilateral lesions was mostly ignored until McGlone's (1977, 1978) research was published, including a literature review that she claimed supported the existence of these differences (McGlone, 1980).

Dennerll (1964), following Lansdell's (1962) lead, found that he was better able to classify males than females according to location of lesion when using subtest scores as "predictors" in regression analyses. But researchers largely ignored his early cross-validation of Lansdell's preliminary work. Samples of males and females were simply combined in most studies, and it was common for investigators not to bother to even tell the reader how many men and women comprised the left-lesion and right-lesion samples (e.g., Doehring, Reitan, & Klove, 1961; Leli & Filskov, 1981a; Satz, 1966). As recently as 1985, Reitan failed to give the gender breakdown of his 56 patients with left- or right-hemisphere lesions.

McGlone's Research

McGlone's (1977, 1978) clear demonstration of gender differences gave new impetus to this line of investigation. In her first study, males and females with right lesions both showed the expected pattern, but the V > P difference of 15.8 points for males far exceeded the value of 5.1 for females. McGlone (1977) did not provide enough data to compute V–P differences for her left-lesion patients (Verbal IQs were provided only for half of her male sample and three fourths of her female sample—the nonaphasics—but Performance IQs were presented only for the total left-lesion samples); nevertheless, she gave evidence that a low V-IQ characterized the male nonaphasics (mean = 87) but not the female nonaphasics (mean = 99).

McGlone (1978) then reported the following results in her second study: Males with left lesions

had P > V of 11.2 points, and males with right lesions had V > P of 13.5 points; females with left-hemisphere lesions had a V–P IQ discrepancy of approximately zero (–0.1), and females with right-brain lesions had a V–P difference of +4.2. These findings were rather compelling, but they were also misleading because McGlone failed to inform readers that the samples in her two studies were "largely overlapping," a fact that Bornstein & Matarazzo (1984, p. 707) uncovered in a personal communication from McGlone in 1983. Thus, rather than providing an independent cross-validation of her first set of results, McGlone's (1978) follow-up investigation was just a restatement of her initial findings.

However, McGlone's (1980) review helped ignite interest in the gender-difference topic. Her review was handicapped by a relative paucity of pertinent data because "the sex composition of neurological patient samples has traditionally been biased by the inclusion of a greater proportion of males" (p. 216); nonetheless, McGlone helped place the issue of neuropsychologically meaningful gender differences before the professional forum; commentary from 37 of her peers appeared in response to her review in the same 1980 issue of *Behavioral and Brain Sciences*. Many contributors were skeptical of her findings (e.g., Kinsbourne, 1980; Sherman, 1980), but significant research efforts followed.

Basically, McGlone's lead was pursued by researchers who investigated the gender difference issue either by (1) reviewing numerous previous investigations of patients with unilateral brain damage who were tested on the Wechsler scales (Bornstein & Matarazzo, 1982, 1984; Inglis & Lawson, 1982; Lawson & Inglis, 1983), or (2) systematically investigating gender differences with new samples of brain-damaged adults that included groups of men and women matched on key variables like age, education, and severity of lesion (Bornstein, 1984; Herring & Reitan, 1986; Inglis et al., 1982; Snow & Sheese, 1985; Turkheimer, Farace, Yeo, & Bigler, 1993; Whelan & Walker, 1988).

Well-Controlled Investigations

Other well-controlled studies have differed in their findings. Inglis et al. (1982) and Turkheimer et al. (1993) confirmed the dramatic gender differences reported by McGlone (1977, 1978). Other investigations, however, failed to find significant interactions between gender and V–P IQ discrepancy for patients with left lesions and right lesions tested on the Wechsler-Bellevue (Herring & Reitan, 1986), the WAIS (Snow & Sheese, 1985; Whelan & Walker, 1988), and the WAIS-R (Bornstein, 1984).

Bornstein (1984) and Whelan and Walker (1988) truly found identical results for male and female patients, but the results of the other two studies were less decisive. Herring and Reitan (1986) did, indeed, observe the predictable V–P differences for patients of both sexes with lateralized lesions, but they failed to stress that the magnitude of the discrepancies was about twice as large for males than females. Further, Snow and Sheese (1985) found no gender difference of consequence, but they neglected to point out just how atypical their findings were in comparison to previous brain lateralization research: They found V > P for all samples (even left lesion), with the discrepancies equal to about 1 standard deviation or more for three of the groups (males and females with right lesions, and males with left lesions).

Inglis and Lawson's Study of Gender Differences

As noted previously, Inglis et al. (1982) found results that closely paralleled McGlone's (1977, 1978) dramatic gender-related interaction. They controlled for type of brain damage by including in their sample only right-handed, nonaphasic patients who had experienced a single thrombotic cerebrovascular accident (stroke), whose medical condition had stabilized, and who had experienced no other neurological disorder. Each group (i.e., males with right-brain lesions, females with left-brain lesions, etc.) was equally divided among new patients (the stroke occurred within the last 6 months) and old patients (the stroke occurred 1 to 12 years prior to testing). The groups were matched with each other and with a control group of 20 medical patients (10 males and 10 females with no symptoms or signs of neurological disorders) on the variables of age, education, and familial history of left-handedness. Further, the brain-damaged samples were matched almost exactly on an index of severity.

The well-matched groups of stroke victims yielded striking gender differences. For males, V–P discrepancies exceeded 1 standard deviation for the left- and right-damaged samples, in the precise directions predicted by cerebral organization research. Females with left-hemisphere lesions showed no V–P discrepancy, while those with right-hemisphere lesions displayed only a small (4½ point) V > P difference. The interaction involving scale (V vs. P), gender, and side of lesion proved to be highly significant ($p < .0001$). As expected, the control group had V–P discrepancies of approximately zero.

Turkheimer et al.'s Study of Gender Differences

Turkheimer et al. (1993) analyzed WAIS data from 17 males with right-hemisphere lesions and 16 with left-hemisphere lesions, and 20 females with right-hemisphere lesions and 11 with left-hemisphere lesions. The mean age was 55 years, 36% had a college degree or higher, 41% had high school degrees, and the rest had less than a high school degree. The sample was required to have a lesion that was visible on CT scan and that was limited to one hemisphere. The etiologies of the lesions consisted of stroke, tumor, focal trauma, and abscess.

Turkheimer et al.'s sample produced results that were similar to those found by earlier researchers; namely, that males with unilateral brain lesions show greater differences between V-IQ and P-IQ than females. Males with left-hemisphere lesions produced the expected P > V profile, but the magnitude was only 1.3 points; females with left-hemisphere lesions had the opposite profile, V > P of 6.3 points. The right-hemisphere lesions produced an even larger gender difference: Males had a V > P pattern of 23.9 points and for females the value was 10.5 points.

Inglis and Lawson's Meta-Analysis of Gender Difference Studies

In their meta-analysis of gender differences, Inglis and Lawson (1982) identified numerous Wechsler-Bellevue and WAIS studies of patients with unilateral brain damage that reported the proportions of males and females constituting the samples. They identified 15 such publications, including 3 that provided separate data for males and females. The authors then studied the 22 samples reported on in the 15 studies, computing the percentage of males in each group. These percentages ranged from zero for the all-female samples to 100 for the all-male samples and were spread fairly well across the entire range.

Inglis and Lawson (1982) hypothesized that P > V for left-damaged patients would be higher for males than females, and that V > P for right-damaged patients would likewise be higher for males than females. Consequently, they predicted significant positive correlations between the percentage of males in left-lesioned samples and the mean P > V discrepancies for those samples. Analogously, they anticipated significant positive correlation between the percentage of males in right-lesioned samples and the mean V > P discrepancies for those samples. Their reasoning was sensible: If males tend to show the predicted relationship between V–P IQ difference and left-versus right-brain damage, but females do not, the samples with many females should evidence smaller V–P differences in the predicted direction than the samples with few females.

Inglis and Lawson's (1982) meta-analysis supported their hypotheses. For left-brain-damaged adults, mean P > V discrepancies correlated .53

with percentage of males in the samples; for right-brain-damaged patients, mean V > P difference scores correlated .46 with percentage of males. When the patient samples are combined, V–P differences correlated .48 with the percentage of males. All of these correlations are statistically significant. The results indicate that gender of the brain-damaged patients accounts for about 25% of the variance in the V–P IQ discrepancy scores. In view of the impact of other variables on the size of V–P discrepancy for adults with unilateral brain damage (e.g., age, precise location of lesion, cause of damage), the relationships found by Inglis and Lawson for the variable of gender are substantial, noteworthy, and clinically valuable.

Bornstein and Matarazzo's Review of Gender Difference Studies

Bornstein and Matarazzo (1982) reviewed a large number of Wechsler-Bellevue and WAIS studies with patients having unilateral brain damage, paying particular attention to Inglis and Lawson's (1982) conclusions about gender differences, but also addressing other variables like location of the lesion and diagnostic etiology. They concluded that there is support for lowered V-IQ in patients with left damage, and a corresponding lower P-IQ for right-damaged adults. However, they conceded that "these laterality findings will more likely be seen in male patients than in female patients" (p. 329).

Bornstein and Matarazzo (1982) pointed out that two of the major negative studies regarding laterality of brain damage and V–P difference, the large-scale investigations conducted by Smith (1966a, 1966b) and by Todd et al. (1977), had proportions of females that were in the 35–40 age range. They hypothesized that the high percentages of females in these studies may have been partially responsible for the negative findings, although they noted that data provided by Todd et al. (1977) make the "gender" explanation for that study unlikely. Indeed, Todd et al. conducted an analysis of variance using gender as an independent variable and found a nonsignificant interaction between gender and discrepancy score.

Bornstein and Matarazzo's (1984) second review of Wechsler studies of brain-damaged adults replicated Inglis and Lawson's (1982) methodology and computed correlations between the percentage of males and mean V–P IQ discrepancies. They also included additional samples not identified by Inglis and Lawson and made some decisions different from those of Inglis and Lawson regarding the elimination of overlapping data and the exclusion of patients with evidence of bilateral damage.

Overall, Bornstein and Matarazzo computed coefficients based on 28 samples of patients with unilateral brain damage. They obtained significant coefficients, but their values were lower than the correlations of about .50 reported by Inglis and Lawson. They found a coefficient of .42 between the percentage of males and mean P > V for left-damage samples and a correlation of .39 for the right-lesion groups. Bornstein and Matarazzo concluded from their results that only about 15% of the variance in the V–P discrepancies of adults with unilateral brain damage can be attributed to the patient's gender, rather than the estimate of 25% that emerged from Inglis and Lawson's (1982) meta-analysis. Bornstein and Matarazzo stood by their earlier statement that lateralization of brain lesion is more associated with predictable V–P differences in men than women, but they cautioned against overinterpretation of the significant correlations found in the retrospective studies conducted by them and by Inglis and Lawson.

They noted that the percentage of men in each sample is but one of numerous variables on which the samples differ; they also vary on the etiology of the lesions (with most samples composed of heterogeneous groups of patients), acuteness versus chronicity of lesions, inclusion or exclusion of dysphasic patients, and nature of the neurodiagnostic criteria for selecting patients. Regarding the latter point, Bornstein and Matarazzo (1984) stress that the more recent studies have had the benefit of modern technology, such as application of computerized axial tomography (CAT) scans, which has cast some doubt on the accuracy of the classification of patients as "purely" right or left damaged in some of the earlier investigations.

Snow, Freedman, and Ford's Review of Gender Differences

Snow, Freedman, and Ford (1986) entered into the debate over gender differences, concluding that such differences tended to characterize Wechsler-Bellevue but not WAIS studies. They reported a nonsignificant .37 correlation between the percentage of males and the size of V–P IQ discrepancy for 16 samples tested on the WAIS, compared to a significant (.05 level) correlation of .58 for 12 samples tested on the Wechsler-Bellevue. However, their conclusion is unwarranted. Appropriate methodology does not depend on one coefficient falling just short of statistical significance and the other one emerging as significant. The coefficients must be shown to be significantly different from each other to support their conclusion. The values do not differ sufficiently to justify Snow et al.'s interpretation of the data.

Nonetheless, Snow et al. are correct in trying to understand variables that might interact with gender to account for the male–female differences observed in the literature. These authors also showed that the percentage of males correlated about .90 with age, education, and chronicity in Wechsler-Bellevue studies, although these findings were not replicated in the WAIS investigations. The ultimate impact of Snow et al.'s results is to remind researchers and clinicians that the best way to study the relationship of any variable to the impact of unilateral brain damage is to hold as many other variables constant as is reasonably possible, given the practical constraints on neuropsychological research.

Turkheimer and Farace's Meta-Analysis of Gender Difference Studies

Turkheimer and Farace (1992) more recently conducted a meta-analysis of gender-difference studies to follow up on the data presented by Inglis and Lawson (1982), Bornstein and Matarazzo (1982), Snow et al. (1986), and Kaufman (1990). Turkheimer and Farace examined the Verbal and Performance IQs in 12 studies by conducting a repeated-measures analysis of variance with three dichotomous independent variables: gender, hemisphere of lesions, and type of Wechsler scale (Verbal or Performance). They conducted their analyses with both weighted and unweighted means and found the results to be highly similar for both.

The results of their repeated-measures analysis revealed a significant main effect for laterality, with left-hemisphere lesions producing greater deficits (M = 91.9) than right-hemisphere lesions (M = 96.1; p < .008), across gender and Verbal and Performance scales. However, when examining the effects of lesion across genders in the *separate* Verbal and Performance scales, the V-IQ versus P-IQ difference produced by the right lesions was substantially larger than the V–P difference produced by left lesions (1.7 point discrepancy vs. an 11.2 point discrepancy).

The main effect for gender was also significant, as female patients had lower IQs than did males across type of scale and laterality. The final main effect of type of scale (V or P) showed that the mean V-IQ of 96.3 was significantly higher than the mean P-IQ of 91.6. Most important was the significant three-way interaction found between gender, type of scale, and laterality. Male and female patients showed roughly equivalent scores on V-IQ following left hemisphere lesions, but female patients with left-hemisphere lesions had lower P-IQs (note that P-IQ is *not* supposed to be associated with left hemisphere functions). Male and female patients with right hemisphere lesions had roughly equal P-IQs, but female patients had lower V-IQs; again, V-IQ is not ordinarily associated with the right hemisphere.

Turkheimer and Farace conclude that the primary effect appears to be that female patients are more sensitive to lesions in the hemisphere *opposite* to that thought to be "dominant" for a function. The sets of means presented in Table 8.13 reveal that males and females with unilateral lesions did *not* differ in their means on the IQ (either V or P) that is supposed to be associated with a specific hemisphere (shown in bold print),

TABLE 8.13   Results of Turkheimer and Farace's (1992) meta-analysis for male and female subjects with left and right brain lesions

	Left Lesion			Right Lesion		
	V-IQ	*P-IQ*	*V–P Diff.*	*V-IQ*	*P-IQ*	*V–P Diff.*
Males (M)	**91.1**	94.6	−3.5	104.0	**90.3**	+13.7
Females (F)	**91.0**	90.8	+0.2	99.3	**90.7**	+8.6
IQ Difference						
(M minus F)	**+0.1**	+3.8		+4.7	**−0.4**	

NOTE: Diff. = Difference. V–P Difference equals mean Verbal IQ minus mean Performance IQ. The IQ scale (V or P) that is believed to be associated with each type of lesion (left or right) is in bold print, as are the mean IQs earned by males and females on that IQ scale, and the difference between them.

TABLE 8.14 V–P IQ discrepancies for separate groups of males and females displaying lesions localized in the left or right hemispheres

	Females				Males			
	Left Lesions		Right Lesions		Left Lesions		Right Lesions	
Study	N	V–P	N	V–P	N	V–P	N	V–P
Wechsler-Bellevue								
Meyer & Jones (1957)								
Temporal lobe epileptics (postoperative)	9	–2.0	6	+7.0	11	–11.0	5	+3.0
Herring & Reitan (1986)								
Tumor (2/3) and Stroke (1/3)	24	–4.1	24	+3.2	24	–8.0	24	+8.8
Lansdell (1968)								
Temporal lobe epileptics (postoperative)	8	–4.9	20	–3.4	11	–8.8	13	+2.2
WAIS								
McGlone (1978)								
Stroke (2/3) and Tumor (1/3)	20	–0.1	17	+4.2	23	–11.2	17	+13.5
Inglis et al. (1982)								
Stroke	20	0.0	20	+5.0	20	–15.0	20	+19.0
Snow & Sheese (1985)								
Stroke	5	+8.0	12	+22.7	14	+13.9	14	+19.8
Whelan & Walker (1988)								
Tumor	16	+0.8	14	+13.9	13	+2.7	21	+10.5
Turkheimer et al. (1993)	11	+6.3	20	+10.5	16	–1.3	17	+23.9
WAIS-R								
Bornstein (1984)	15	–5.5	15	+11.1	17	–4.9	16	+10.6
Weighted Mean	**128**	**–0.9**	**148**	**+7.2**	**149**	**–5.6**	**147**	**+13.2**

NOTE: V–P equals mean V-IQ minus mean P-IQ.

but they differed in the "opposite" IQ. And, once again, the, "predicted" profiles of P > V for left lesions and V > P for right lesions are stronger for males than females.

Two main hypotheses are given for the gender differences: differences in the degree of hemispheric lateralization (McGlone, 1980) and differences in problem solving (Inglis & Lawson, 1982).

Research Issues in the Investigation of Gender Differences

We concur with Bornstein and Matarazzo's (1984) plea for "a comprehensive prospective study that, at the very least, controls for a number of potentially important lesion-related variables" as a means of delineating the role of gender in V–P discrepancies in patients with unilateral brain damage. However, in the absence of such a landmark study and of "a large-scale retrospective study with enough patients in the sample to permit statistical control of such potentially relevant variables…by involving a number of large medical centers in a single, coordinated effort" (p. 709), we must try to understand the variable of gender as best we can based on the considerable database available. We disagree emphatically with Jacklin's (1989) strong suggestion to stop conducting research on gender-related cognitive differences.

Meta-analysis (Bornstein & Matarazzo, 1984; Inglis & Lawson, 1982; Snow et al., 1986; Turkheimer & Farace, 1992) provides one useful research technique. Another is to compare the V–P differences of males and females only from those reasonably well-controlled investigations that included both sexes in approximately equal numbers. Inglis and Lawson (1982) did compare V–P discrepancies for separate groups of male and female patients, combining data from several studies. However, they failed to match the male and female samples on any pertinent variables. For example, their aggregated sample of male patients included data from studies comprising only males. Consequently, the sample of 170 males included a group like Black's (1974a) 21-year-old veterans with missile wounds; no similar group was included among the 55 female patients. The latter sample was composed only of patients with temporal lobe epilepsy (spanning a wide age range) or elderly stroke victims. Inglis and Lawson's (1982) male–female comparisons were therefore contaminated by nearly all the intervening variables noted by Bornstein and Matarazzo (1984).

Aggregated Data from Gender Difference Studies

Table 8.14 presents data from nine studies that included males and females in approximately equal proportions. Most of these studies were extremely well designed, controlling for differences between the genders on variables like age, education, nature of lesion, and recency of lesion. Despite Snow et al.'s (1986) cautions to the contrary, data were combined across instruments, as the Wechsler-Bellevue, WAIS, and WAIS-R were all used for one or more studies. The instrument given has, nonetheless, been held constant because the same Wechsler test was administered to men and women in each separate study.

To a reasonable degree, the variables of concern to Bornstein and Matarazzo (1984) and Snow et al. (1986) were controlled in the male–female comparisons presented in Table 8.14. The neurodiagnostic criteria that were used in each study, whether primitive or high-tech, were applied equally to males and females. Similarly, variables such as age, education, recency of lesion, and etiology were not appreciably different for the men and women within each separate investigation. Therefore, the data shown in Table 8.14 come as close as is presently feasible to the type of coordinated effort that Bornstein and Matarazzo have urged.

As shown in Table 8.14, each gender is represented by more than 125 patients with left-hemisphere lesions and more than 145 patients with right-hemisphere lesions; data are based on

276 women and 296 men with unilateral brain damage. Taken separately, six of the nine studies showed apparent gender differences in the V–P discrepancies for patients with lesions in each hemisphere; only the investigations by Snow and Sheese (1985), Bornstein (1984), and Whelan and Walker (1988) failed to discern meaningful gender-related findings.

Taken together, P > V was 5.6 points for males with left lesions but only 0.9 points for females with left lesions. Similarly, patients with lesions in the right hemisphere evidenced larger V > P differences if they were male (13.2 points) than if they were female (7.2 points). We believe that the accumulated data in Table 8.14 show strong support for the alleged gender-related interaction between side of lesion and direction of V–P difference. For both genders, damage to the right hemisphere produced more striking V–P discrepancies than damage to the left hemisphere. But for males, the V > P of about 13 points for right-lesioned patients is nearly twice the value of 7 points for females.

The 5½-point P > V difference for left-damaged adult males does not measure up to the opposite discrepancy for right-damaged adult males, but the observed difference still gives good support to the predicted hypothesis of depressed Verbal IQs for patients with lesions in their left hemispheres. For females, however, the P > V discrepancy of less than 1 point for those with left-hemisphere lesions does not support the old hypothesis. In sum, women apparently have a different cerebral organization than men, and may differ in the asymmetry of their brains. However, the reason for the interaction with gender is far less obvious than the fact of it.

Proposed Explanations of the Interaction with Gender

McGlone's Asymmetry Hypothesis

McGlone (1977) found a much greater proportion of aphasics among her male than female patients with left-hemisphere damage (48% versus

13%), a result that characterized both her tumor and strokes patients; she also found greater verbal intelligence deficits and verbal memory loss in her male than female patients following left-brain lesions. Further, McGlone discovered that females with left lesions and females with right lesions performed about equally well on visual–spatial and perceptual tasks usually associated with right-hemisphere function: Block Design, Thurstone's (1938) Spatial Relations test requiring mental rotations, and a test of immediate memory of photographed faces.

In marked contrast, males with right-brain damage were far outstripped on these spatial tasks by nonaphasic males with left-hemisphere lesions. McGlone (1978) concluded: "For the women, cognitive deficits tended to be less severe and less specific compared to men" (p. 126). Her proposed explanations for the gender-related findings in her investigations (McGlone, 1977) are (1) a "greater degree of bilateral speech representation in women" (p. 787) than in men, (2) "sex differences in the underlying neural organization of speech processes within the left hemisphere" (p. 789), and (3) greater control of the right hemisphere in women (compared to men) over certain verbal functions.

McGlone's (1977) conclusion is "that asymmetrical specialization of the two cerebral hemispheres is less characteristic of adult female right-handers than adult male right-handers" (p. 790). She reiterated this conclusion in her review and analysis of pertinent investigations (McGlone, 1980), although a number of her peers disputed predictions that follow logically from her explanation of the gender differences in brain-damaged patients (e.g., Hier & Kaplan, 1980; Kinsbourne, 1980).

Inglis and Lawson's Emphasis on Female Processing of Performance Tasks

Inglis and Lawson (1982) disagree with McGlone's (1977, 1978, 1980) explanations of the gender differences based on the results of empirical analyses that they conducted as part of their meta-analysis of pertinent Wechsler studies. They developed regression equations to predict the V- and P-IQs of male and female adults with left or right lesions, based on the association of the percentage of men in each study to the magnitude of the separate IQs. Table 8.15 presents the results of these analyses.

As shown in Table 8.15, the predicted Verbal IQs of men and women with right-hemisphere damage are about equal, as are the predicted Verbal IQs of men and women with left-hemisphere damage. In striking contrast are the predicted Performance IQs of the neurological patients: Among left-lesion cases, men outscored women by 6 points on the Performance Scale; among right-lesion cases, women outscored men by the same amount.

Inglis and Lawson (1982) then attempted to cross-validate these findings by comparing the V- and P-IQs of all-female samples with unilateral brain damage to the V- and P-IQs of all-male samples with unilateral brain damage; the results of this second type of analysis fully supported the results of the regression analysis. They interpreted their double-barreled findings as contradicting McGlone's assertions, and instead favor a quite different explanation of the gender differences observed in the Wechsler V–P studies of patients with lesions to the left or right hemisphere.

Inglis and Lawson cite the equal Verbal IQs of males and females having the same localization of brain damage (i.e., left or right hemisphere) as providing strong support for the similarity of how the two genders process information when solving Wechsler's Verbal subtests. Males and females differ, according to these researchers, in how they apply strategies to Wechsler's Performance tasks. They believe that their analyses suggest "that the functional organization of the cerebral hemispheres in women may not be more symmetrical than it is in men" (p. 679). Inglis and Lawson offer the following model to explain the gender differences in the Wechsler V–P/lesion studies:

> *The Verbal Scale items are left hemisphere, verbal problems for both men and women. The Performance Scale items, however, tend to be processed as left hemisphere tasks (i.e., more verbally) by women, whereas men use mainly right hemisphere (i.e., more spatial, nonverbal) processing in their solution. Because women may solve the items in the Performance Scale through the use of a more verbal strategy than men, left lesion women show a greater deficit on this scale. As right brain-damaged women also process these items verbally, and because their verbal skills remain relatively intact, they thus show a lesser impairment on the Performance Scale (p. 680).*

Inglis and Lawson (1982) further argued against McGlone's (1977) "less asymmetry for women" hypothesis by refuting her finding of more aphasics among male than female patients with left-brain damage. They cited evidence from Hier and Kaplan (1980), who claim that McGlone's (1977) findings with a small sample are inconsistent with the clinical experience of most neurologists or speech pathologists. Hier and Kaplan also presented data from three large-scale studies (total $N = 767$) that showed male aphasics

TABLE 8.15   Results of Inglis and Lawson's (1982) regression analyses for male and female subjects with left and right brain lesions

	Predicted Verbal IQ		Predicted Performance IQ	
	Left Lesion	*Right Lesion*	*Left Lesion*	*Right Lesion*
Males	84	98	94	87
Females	86	97	88	93
Difference	−2	+1	+6	−6

to outnumber female aphasics only slightly. Inglis and Lawson also believed that McGlone's stress on the gender-related nature of aphasia should lead to clear-cut male–female differences on the Verbal Scale for patients with left-hemisphere lesions. As indicated in the previous summary of Inglis and Lawson's data, this does not seem to be the case.

Inglis and Lawson's Failure to Focus on V–P Discrepancies

Regardless of Inglis and Lawson's (1982) careful, intelligent analyses and the cogent arguments put forth by them and other respected researchers (Bryden, 1979, 1980; Harris, 1980; Sherman, 1978, 1980) in support of the "different strategies" used by men and women, we disagree with their conclusions. First, we do not believe that it is particularly meaningful or appropriate to compare just the Verbal IQs (or Performance IQs) of males and females having brain damage lateralized to one hemisphere. We have no knowledge of premorbid intelligence and, therefore, cannot evaluate how much the Verbal or Performance IQ has fallen as a result of the brain lesion. The males and females with left-hemisphere damage may have equal Verbal IQs, but that tells us little about the specific impact of the neurological impairment on verbal intelligence for men and women.

We believe that it is essential to consider both the Verbal and Performance scales when estimating the deleterious effects of brain lesions on intellectual functioning. The use of both scales provides a built-in control regarding a patient's relative loss of mental function. In effect, the V–P IQ comparison allows each patient to serve as his or her own control. We simply begin with the assumption that the mean premorbid difference between the Verbal and Performance IQs equals zero for any particular patient group. The mean V–P discrepancy for a sample then provides a simple index of loss of function in verbal or nonverbal intelligence, a loss that is presumably due to the brain damage.

This index measures relative loss, because it is possible (indeed likely) that brain damage to either hemisphere will affect intellectual performance, at least to some extent, on both of Wechsler's scales. Yet, in the absence of good estimates of premorbid intelligence, and in view of the great difficulty in applying ideal experimental design to these studies (you can't exactly assign patients to undergo left or right brain lesions, and finding good non-neurological controls is almost impossible), the V–P IQ index of relative loss of function becomes quite valuable.

Looking at Verbal and Performance IQs separately has too many experimental pitfalls to merit much interpretive generalization. Also, Inglis and Lawson (1982) compared the Verbal IQs of males and females with left lesions using two questionable techniques: (1) one set of data used estimates of these IQs, via regression equations, where the predictor (percentage of males) accounted for much less than 50% of the variance in the criterion; and (2) the second set of data compared unequal samples of men and women, samples that differed in key variables besides gender, such as age and type of lesion (see p. 307). Furthermore, Inglis and Lawson's results were *not* cross-validated by the data compiled by Turkheimer and Farace (1992) in their meta-analysis of 12 studies. If the Turkheimer-Farace data (Table 8.13) are reorganized to conform to the Inglis-Lawson data (Table 8.15), then males and females with right lesions did not earn about equal V-IQs, regardless of localization. Rather, among patients with right lesions in the Turkheimer-Farace meta-analysis, males scored almost 5 points *higher* than females on the Verbal scale. Neither was the other Inglis-Lawson prediction borne out by the more recent analysis: Males did not outscore females on P-IQ, regardless of location of the lesion; among patients with right-hemisphere lesions, the two genders earned virtually identical P-IQs.

Premorbid V–P IQ Differences of Brain-Damaged Samples

There is a legitimate question regarding our assertions of the value of comparisons based on the V–P discrepancy: Is it reasonable to assume that the mean premorbid V–P difference of any given sample equals zero? Certainly that assumption would not hold for any particular individual. As discussed at length in Chapter 11 concerning unusual or abnormal discrepancies, it is quite common for normal individuals to have substantial differences in their V- and P-IQs. But it's a different story for groups. The entire WAIS-III normative sample of 2,450 earned a mean Verbal sum of scaled score of 60.2 and a mean Performance sum of 50.1 (Psychological Corporation, 1997, Table 4.12). When entered into the WAIS-III IQ conversion tables, these sums of scaled scores equal a mean V-IQ = 99.2 and a mean P-IQ of 99.1. That equality is predictable because the test was normed to have mean Verbal IQs and mean Performance IQs of approximately 100.

However, the equal V- and P-IQs also hold for separate groups of males and females in the WAIS-III standardization sample that were corrected for age and education (Heaton et al., 2001): males (mean V-IQ = 102.7, mean P-IQ = 100.3, mean V–P discrepancy = +2.4); females (means of 97.8, 99.7, and –1.9, respectively). Data were similar for the WAIS-R standardization sample (Matarazzo, Bornstein, McDermott, & Noonan, 1986): Males had a mean V–P discrepancy of +0.3, and for females the discrepancy was –0.5.

As shown above, the expected WAIS-III V–P IQ difference for such samples is, at most, 2 points in favor of Performance IQ for females and 2½ points in favor of Verbal IQ for males. For the WAIS-R, the expected differences for both genders are between zero and 1 point. Therefore, it is a most logical and empirically defensible assumption to expect brain-damaged samples with a moderate amount of education to have had a mean premorbid V–P IQ discrepancy of about zero; the V–P difference for patients with left or right damage is, thus, a good estimate of a group's relative loss of function following neurological impairment.

The Inglis/Lawson Hypothesis and Subtest Profiles

Even if one grants that the V–P difference, not a simple comparison of one IQ at a time, is the es-

sential unit of study, it is still necessary to refute Inglis and Lawson's contention that the Performance Scale alone accounts for the different V–P findings for men and women with lateralized lesions. Some evidence against their notion comes from subtest data that they presented for male and female stroke victims (Inglis et al., 1982). These data are presented in Table 8.16, which compares the scaled-score profiles of males and females with left lesions, and of males and females with right lesions.

As indicated, men and women with left lesions differed consistently and systematically on Verbal as well as Performance subtests: Women with left-hemisphere damage scored about 1 scaled-score point higher than men with the same type of damage on Verbal tasks, but scored about 1½ points lower than the men on Performance subtests. The identical pattern of identical magnitude—but in reverse—occurred for men and women with right-brain lesions. Thus, men and women differed a bit more on Performance than Verbal subtests, but only slightly more. Table 8.16 clearly shows that subtests on both of Wechsler's scales are instrumental in leading to smaller than predicted P > V IQ discrepancies for females with left lesions, and smaller than predicted V > P differences for females with right lesions.

These findings are more in agreement with McGlone's (1977, 1978, 1980) interpretation that female brains are organized with less cerebral asymmetry than are the brains of males than with Inglis and Lawson's (1982) conclusions that women depend on verbal strategies to solve Performance subtests. Also inconsistent with Inglis and Lawson's reasoning are the results of some analyses conducted with the normal standardization sample.

Evidence from Correlational and Factor Analyses, by Gender

If Inglis and Lawson (1982) are correct in their hypothesis that women and men solve nonverbal problems differently, with women demonstrating "a preference for verbal, left hemisphere approaches to problem solving…, even when these

TABLE 8.16   Mean scaled scores on the WAIS earned by males and females with unilateral brain damage due to stroke

	Left Lesion			Right Lesion		
Subtest	Males (N=20)	Females (N=20)	Mean Diff.	Males (N=20)	Females (N=20)	Mean Diff.
Verbal						
I	8.0	8.2	−0.2	11.4	10.3	+1.1
C	6.8	7.6	−0.8	10.8	10.3	+0.5
A	7.8	8.2	−0.4	11.0	9.1	+1.9
S	7.4	9.5	−2.1	11.0	9.8	+1.2
DSp	7.2	8.4	−1.2	11.4	10.4	+1.0
V	7.5	8.2	−0.7	11.8	11.0	+0.8
Performance						
PC	10.8	9.2	+1.6	9.8	10.8	−1.0
BD	9.6	7.4	+2.2	7.3	9.4	−2.1
PA	10.2	8.7	+1.5	8.0	8.6	−0.6
OA	9.0	8.2	+0.8	7.0	9.0	−2.0
Mean						
Verbal	7.4	8.4	−1.0	11.2	10.2	+1.0
Performance	9.9	8.4	+1.5	8.0	9.4	−1.4

NOTE: Mean Diff. = mean for males minus mean for females. Data are from Inglis et al. (1982). Digit Symbol was not administered to any of the patients.

problems are intended, by the examiner, to be nonverbal, right hemisphere tasks" (p. 681), then other logical hypotheses would follow. First, the Inglis/Lawson hypothesis suggests that Verbal and Performance IQs should be more correlated in women than men, because women presumably apply similar strategies for tasks on both scales. A higher correlation for women would mean that V–P discrepancies should tend to be smaller for women; their base rates of occurrence should be substantially different than for men. Second, it follows from Inglis and Lawson's speculations that the factor structure for males and females should differ markedly. Clear-cut, separate verbal and nonverbal dimensions should emerge for men, but the distinction should be cloudy for

women; in particular, Performance subtests would have far higher loadings on the Verbal Comprehension factor for women than men.

To address the Inglis/Lawson hypothesis by correlational techniques, Kaufman, McLean, and Reynolds (1990) computed coefficients of correlation between V- and P-IQs for separate groups of men and women from the standardization sample. They divided the normative group into four age levels and discovered that V-IQ and P-IQ correlated about equally well for men (average $r = .72$) and women (average $r = .73$). Coefficients ranged from .69 to .77 for males and from .68 to .77 for females; none of the comparisons at the four age groups reached statistical significance. These findings clearly contradicted

Inglis and Lawson's hypothesis that women tend to use verbal processing to solve nonverbal problems.

Table 8.17 summarizes base-rate data for V–P IQ discrepancies separately for men and women, based on comprehensive tables provided by Matarazzo et al. (1986) for the total WAIS-R standardization sample. As indicated, the base rates for males and females are rather similar. For example, about 19% of males and 17% of females have V–P differences (regardless of direction) of 15 points or more; about 3% of each sex have discrepancies of 25 or more points. Although the small differences in percentages for men and women are all in the direction predicted by Inglis and Lawson's (1982) hypothesis, the similarities in the distributions far outweigh the slight differences. The results in Table 8.17 are contrary to Inglis and Lawson's suggestion that women, more so than men, use verbal strategies to solve nonverbal problems.

Separate factor analyses of the WAIS-R for men and women suggested that females (more so than males) do tend to apply verbal strategies to tasks intended by Wechsler to be nonverbal (Kaufman, 1990, Chapter 8). Such a finding would support Inglis and Lawson's claims. But those factor analyses were based on a wide age range (16–74 years), perhaps masking age-related trends in the data.

Table 8.18 shows the results of WAIS-R factor analyses conducted for separate groups of men and women at four age levels: 16–19, 20–34, 35–54, and 55–74 (Kaufman, McLean, & Reynolds, 1990). Overall, the factor structures for men and women across the age range were extremely similar. Coefficients of congruence for males and females across the four age groups ranged from .972 to .995 for the Verbal Comprehension and Perceptual Organization factors (Kaufman et al., 1990), astonishingly high values.

The most pertinent test of the Inglis/Lawson hypothesis concerns the loadings of the WAIS-R Performance subtests on the Verbal Comprehension factors. Their hypothesis predicts that nonverbal tasks should have higher Verbal loadings for females than males, because women purportedly use verbal strategies to solve nonverbal problems. These crucial loadings (shown in boxes in Table 8.18) are, indeed, higher for females at ages 16–19 and 20–34. For women in this age range, WAIS-R Picture Arrangement is decidedly a verbal task, and WAIS-R Picture Completion has a strong verbal component.

However, on the WAIS-R, women at ages 16–34 do not differ from men in the application of verbal strategies during Block Design, Object Assembly, and Digit Symbol. Furthermore, an opposite trend is observed at ages 35–54: Men use verbal strategies far more than women when

TABLE 8.17   Verbal–Performance IQ discrepancies of a given magnitude or greater, for separate groups of males and females

Size of V–P Discrepancy (Regardless of Direction)	**Males (*N*=940)**		**Females (*N*=940)**	
	N	*%*	*N*	*%*
5	631	67.1	615	65.4
10	368	39.1	343	36.5
15	176	18.7	156	16.6
20	89	9.5	82	8.7
25	28	3.0	27	2.9

NOTE: Data are based on tables presented by Matarazzo, Bornstein, McDermott, and Noonan (1986).

TABLE 8.18 Varimax rotated two-factor WAIS-R solutions for males and females at four age groups

	Ages 16–19				Ages 20–34				Ages 35–54				Ages 55–74			
	Males		Females		Males		Females		Males		Females		Males		Females	
Subtest	VC	PO	VC	PO	VC	PO	VC	PO	VC	PO	VC	PO	VC	PO	VC	PO
Verbal																
I	81*	32	84*	20	80*	33	80*	27	74*	36	80*	36	80*	26	78*	38
DSp	35	48*	48*	23	50*	25	51*	34	57*	29	52*	42*	52*	36	41*	50*
V	82*	37	85*	28	85*	30	88*	31	89*	28	87*	31	90*	25	82*	36
A	54*	51*	64*	39	64*	37	59*	46*	59*	43*	54*	57*	61*	37	55*	53*
C	72*	32	71*	36	72*	34	73*	33	70*	26	80*	32	75*	33	78*	36
S	72*	33	76*	30	57*	46*	70*	36	68*	39	76*	35	71*	42*	67*	49*
Performance																
PC	34	47*	43*	44*	34	66*	48*	62*	52*	52*	49*	53*	39	62*	45*	65*
PA	31	37	49*	26	35	55*	61*	34	52*	41*	51*	50*	44*	60*	36	53*
BD	22	76*	28	85*	36	72*	29	80*	42*	73*	30	78*	30	76*	34	79*
OA	23	62*	18	58*	21	69*	25	72*	26	87*	21	67*	17	78*	23	65*
DSy	39	52*	42*	45*	38	37	34	37	56*	38	33	58*	39	63*	40*	52*

NOTE: VC = Verbal Comprehension; PO = Perceptual Organization. Decimal points are omitted. Asterisks mark loadings of .40 and above. Data are from Kaufman et al. (1990a). The loadings shown in boxes indicate the degree to which each performance subtest has a verbal component of males and females across the 16- to 74-year range.

solving nonverbal items. (Three of the five WAIS-R Performance subtests loaded in the .50s on Verbal Comprehension for these middle-aged men.) In addition, at ages 55–74, neither sex applied verbal strategies to WAIS-R Performance tasks to any marked degree.

Thus, an overview of the WAIS-R factor structures for males and females attests to the similarity of these patterns. Where differences occur, they are as likely to disagree as to agree with predictions made on the basis of Inglis and Lawson's (1982) hypothesis. In fact, only one instance gives the Inglis/Lawson hypothesis good support: African American females, compared to African American males, a topic that is treated in the section on race differences in brain-damage studies.

Correlation coefficients between WAIS-III V-IQ and P-IQ, separate by gender, are not available, and neither are separate factor analyses of the WAIS-III. Therefore, the WAIS-R data will have to suffice for the discussion of the Inglis/Lawson interpretation of gender differences among patients with lateralized lesions. However, as indicated previously, the pertinent neuropsychological investigations of unilateral brain damage on Wechsler's Verbal and Performance scales have been conducted with the WAIS-R and its predecessors, not with the WAIS-III.

Turkheimer et al.'s Evaluation of the McGlone Hypothesis versus the Inglis/Lawson Hypothesis

Turkheimer et al. (1993) recognized that the question remains unresolved concerning why gender differences occur in the effects of lateralized lesions. They noted that two of the major explanatory hypotheses are those we discussed: McGlone's lateralization hypothesis and Inglis and Lawson's differential problem-solving hypothesis. Turkheimer et al. (1993) analyzed the data of 33 males and 31 females using a complicated quantitative method for the assessment of covariation between IQ and location of the lesion—involving model-fitting to the Cartesian

coordinates of points in the patients' CT scans—to discern which hypothesis was supported.

The plausibility of the hypothesis that gender difference is largely the result of the degree of lateralization in males versus females (McGlone, 1977) was *not* supported by Turkheimer et al.'s results because a statistical model in which the genders have the same degree of lateralization fit the data as well as a model in which the genders were allowed to differ. In contrast, Turkheimer et al. found statistical support for Inglis and Lawson's (1982) hypothesis that females use verbal strategies in solving Performance IQ items. A single model of lesion effects accounted for deficits in V-IQ and P-IQ in females, but not in males. The results suggested that left-hemisphere lateral-posterior lesions caused the most severe deficits for male and female V-IQ, but the relationship between lesion location and P-IQ was considerably more complex for both genders.

Although support was found for Inglis and Lawson's (1982) hypothesis in Turkheimer et al.'s (1993) analysis of data based on a total of only 64 subjects, recall that summary data from Turkheimer and Farace's (1992) meta-analysis of 12 studies (Table 8.13) did *not* support predictions about V-IQ and P-IQ based on Inglis and Lawson's hypothesis (Table 8.15). In addition, Turkheimer et al. (1993) posit that there are multiple possible reasons for the patterns of deficit, not just the problem-solving strategies that were emphasized by Inglis and Lawson. Turkheimer et al. note that the strategy, brain organization, or both, could account for the patterns found for males and females. The most striking pattern that Turkheimer et al. found was that left-lesioned females had substantial P-IQ deficits related to lesion parameters, but left-lesioned males did not. Possible reasons for this discrepancy in gender patterns include the hypotheses that females have more nonverbal abilities relevant to P-IQ represented in the left hemisphere or that females use more verbal strategies in solving P-IQ items. Because P-IQ comprises more than one cognitive ability, ambiguity arises about the reasons underlying these patterns.

Turkheimer et al. suggest that the best way to determine whether problem-solving strategies or localization of function is responsible for the gender effects is to decompose the P-IQ items into more basic cognitive tasks. Certainly the four factor indexes yielded by the WAIS-III help achieve that goal to some extent, and future gender-based WAIS-III neuropsychological research that features the index profile may help resolve the reason for gender differences in lateralized lesion studies.

Summary of Evaluation of Hypotheses for Gender Differences in Lesioned Patients

Turkheimer et al.'s (1993) analysis lent more support to the Inglis/Lawson hypothesis than to McGlone's hypothesis, but Turkheimer et al. also recognized that more complex studies with larger samples are necessary for clarification. The results of empirical analyses discussed in earlier sections of this chapter and shown in Tables 8.13, 8.16, 8.17, and 8.18 generally contradict the Inglis/Lawson hypothesis and give more support to McGlone's (1977, 1978, 1980) notion of less asymmetry in the cerebral organization of female versus male brains. Anatomically, Witelson (1989) notes that right-handed males have greater cortical asymmetry than females in the temporal and parietal regions of the brain, and the part of the corpus callosum that connects these asymmetric regions is larger in females than males. Furthermore, the corpus callosum gets smaller for males with increasing age (between 25 and 68), but not for females (Lezak, 1995), which may make it less likely for older men than older women to use both sides of the brain to compensate for an injury to one hemisphere.

One reason for the failure of researchers to consistently find gender differences in cerebral organization may be that the difference resides in the *potential* for females to compensate for damage or dysfunction. Perhaps women tend to solve problems in a manner similar to men under ordinary circumstances. However, when the circumstances are extraordinary, such as having the type of brain dysfunction that might cause a learning disability or having a lateralized brain lesion associated with depressed Verbal or Performance IQ, females may be better equipped to spontaneously compensate for the deficit.

Many more boys than girls are learning disabled. Possibly girls respond better to the brain dysfunction; conceivably, girls may be able to compensate for a kind of brain dysfunction that in boys would lead to a learning disability. Even LD females may have better compensatory strategies than LD males. Indirect evidence for this hypothesis comes from an examination of subtest profiles of LD children, adolescents, and young adults. Some research suggests that the so-called ACID profile (see Chapter 9) associated with learning disabilities holds only for males; females perform poorly on three of the four ACID subtests, but tend to do quite well on Coding/Digit Symbol. The latter task has elements of both left-hemisphere and right-hemisphere processing and may be amenable to compensation from an intact part of the brain. Similarly, females with left-hemisphere lesions may show a smaller deficit in V-IQ than males with left lesions (and, analogously, females with right lesions may show a smaller deficit in P-IQ) because, subsequent to the damage, they may use their capacity for compensation when solving verbal (or nonverbal) problems.

This greater flexibility and capacity for compensation may result from a superior ability of females to demonstrate interhemispheric integration. Denckla (1974) has speculated that dyslexics may have faulty interhemispheric integration, and Witelson (1976, 1977) has also stressed the value of good integration for success in school-oriented activities. Because girls are far less likely than boys to be dyslexic, and women with lateralized lesions evidence less predictable V–P profiles than men with right versus left lesions, it may be that females surpass males in the ability to integrate the two cerebral hemispheres. Certainly cerebral integration is an important aspect of a complex psychomotor task like Digit Symbol.

Greater interhemispheric integration would be a plausible mechanism to explain McGlone's (1977/1978, 1980) suggestion that females have more lateralization of speech functions than males, and it also may relate to Inglis and Lawson's (1982) claim that women have a greater capacity than men to solve nonverbal problems via verbal mediation. Certainly, if females really do have a more efficient system for integrating strategies from the two hemispheres, one would expect women to demonstrate less cerebral asymmetry than men, at least under a circumstance (like an acute brain lesion) that prevents the application of an optimal problem-solving strategy.

The evidence presented here does not provide clear support for the Inglis/Lawson hypothesis in preference to McGlone's position or vice versa. Most of the evidence supporting McGlone's hypothesis is indirect, and it is unwise to discount either the criticisms of McGlone's (1980) conclusions (Hier & Kaplan, 1980; Inglis & Lawson, 1982; Kinsbourne, 1980) or the model-fitting evidence (Turkheimer et al., 1993) that was contrary to McGlone's hypothesis. The "verbal strategy" hypothesis advanced by Inglis and Lawson and by others (Bryden, 1980; Harris, 1980; Sherman, 1978) cannot be ignored, especially in light of the support recently advanced by Turkheimer et al. (1993). What is needed is a series of investigations of normal and brain-damaged males and females that evaluate directly and systematically possible gender differences in the application of verbal mediation to nonverbal problem solving (Kaufman, 1990).

ETHNICITY OF PATIENTS WITH LATERALIZED LESIONS

Researchers were slow to realize that gender differences among patients with unilateral lesions was a topic worthy of consideration. They have virtually ignored the issue of ethnic differences. To our knowledge, only one study has addressed this important issue, the doctoral dissertation investigation conducted by Munder (1976). Even though this study was executed quite well, included a substantial number of patients, and yielded provocative results, Munder's work has not been included in summaries of Wechsler research involving brain-damaged patients (Bornstein & Matarazzo, 1982, 1984; Inglis & Lawson, 1982; Matarazzo & Herman, 1985).

It is unusual, in fact, for investigators to indicate the ethnic breakdown of their samples, even for groups that are likely to include representative numbers of African Americans such as war veterans with missile wounds (e.g., Black, 1973, 1976). Even Lansdell, perhaps the earliest investigator to identify the importance of the variable of gender in brain lesion studies, failed to give the proportions of Caucasians and African Americans in his study of 150 men, many of whom had penetrating missile wounds (Lansdell & Smith, 1975).

Munder's Careful Investigation of V–P Differences for Caucasians and African Americans

Munder (1976) obtained her data by searching through psychological and medical records from a number of hospitals, selecting all brain-damaged males tested with a complete WAIS. Neurological diagnosis was arrived at independently of psychological test results for all patients based on some or all of the following criteria: EEG, brain scan surgery, autopsy. Patients with vision problems or incapacitating physical anomalies were not used in the study. Multiple analysis of covariance was used to control for age, years of education, and time interval between brain damage and date of testing.

The following numbers of male patients were investigated by Munder (1976): 25 Caucasians and 25 African Americans with left-hemisphere lesions, 25 Caucasians and 25 African Americans with right-hemisphere lesions, and 25 Caucasians and 25 African Americans with diffuse lesions (total sample size of 150). All patients were aged 18 or above, and no patient had known brain damage prior to age 18; Munder (1976) did not, however, provide the mean age or age range for the groups. There was no attempt made to control for type of lesion, either by etiology or specific location.

Table 8.19 summarizes the results of Munder's study, using Verbal and Performance IQs that have been adjusted for the covariates. As indicated, the Caucasian men demonstrated the expected patterns of P > V and V > P for lesions to the left and right hemispheres, respectively. As was true for most studies in Tables 8.1–8.3, the mean V–P discrepancy was larger for Caucasian patients with right-brain damage (+15.1 points) than for those with left damage (–5.2 points). African American male patients with right damage showed the expected pattern of V > P (by +10.4 points), but African Americans with left lesions did not. Instead, the latter sample of adults evidenced a V–P IQ difference of +5.7 points.

Regardless of ethnicity, patients with diffuse brain damage obtained a mean difference of about 5 points favoring the Verbal Scale. Thus, adult African American male patients with brain damage displayed a V > P profile regardless of the location of the lesion, the same result reported for the patients studied by Todd et al. (1977). Differences shown between African Americans and Caucasians in Table 8.19 were found by Munder (1976) to be statistically significant. Her analysis of covariance uncovered a significant interaction effect (.001 level) between ethnicity and location of brain damage on V- and P-IQs.

Subtest Patterns for Brain-Damaged Males by Race

Table 8.20 looks at the 11 WAIS subtests by race, comparing the mean scaled scores earned by patients with left lesions with the mean scaled scores earned by patients with right lesions. It was not meaningful to compare Caucasian patients with left lesions to African American patients with left lesions because the Caucasian patients scored significantly and substantially higher than African American patients on all WAIS IQs (Munder, 1976).

In Table 8.20, the scaled scores are different from the scores shown for the same groups in Table 8.9. The Table 8.9 scaled scores are the actual, observed values, which are appropriate to report for an accumulation of data across studies. For the present analysis, however, which aims to clarify to the degree possible an understanding of the interaction with ethnicity, it made more sense to control for extraneous variables; hence, the scaled scores shown in Table 8.20 have been

TABLE 8.19   V–P IQ discrepancies on the WAIS for separate groups of African American and Caucasian patients displaying localized or diffuse lesions

	Left Lesions			Right Lesions			Diffuse Lesions		
Group	Mean V-IQ	Mean P-IQ	V–P Diff.	Mean V-IQ	Mean P-IQ	V–P Diff.	Mean V-IQ	Mean P-IQ	V–P Diff.
Blacks	87.4	81.7	+5.7	91.5	81.1	+10.4	90.8	86.3	+4.5
Whites	92.5	97.7	–5.2	101.6	86.5	+15.1	97.5	91.2	+6.3
Total group	90.0	89.7	+0.3	96.5	83.8	+12.7	94.1	88.7	+5.4

NOTE: Data are from Munder (1976). The sample is composed of 150 adult males: 25 from each race in each brain-damage category. The mean IQs are adjusted values, based on a multiple analysis of covariance in which the following variables were covaried: chronological age, years of education, and time interval between the onset of the brain damage and the psychological testing.

TABLE 8.20   Mean scaled scores on the WAIS earned by African American males and Caucasian males with unilateral brain damage

| | Blacks | | | Whites | | |
Subtest	Left Lesion (N=25)	Right Lesion (N=25)	Mean Diff.	Left Lesion (N=25)	Right Lesion (N=25)	Mean Diff.
Verbal						
I	8.3	8.7	–0.4	9.5	9.9	–0.4
DSp	7.2	8.5	–1.3	7.4	8.6	–1.2
V	7.3	8.4	–1.1	8.6	10.3	–1.7
A	6.8	8.0	–1.2	8.5	9.7	–1.2
C	7.9	9.0	–1.1	8.3	10.9	–2.6
S	7.8	7.7	+0.1	8.7	10.4	–1.7
Performance						
PC	7.5	8.0	–0.5	10.4	8.0	+2.4
PA	6.7	6.7	0.0	8.8	6.9	+1.9
BD	5.7	5.8	–0.1	9.3	7.5	+1.8
OA	5.7	6.0	–0.3	8.9	6.4	+2.5
DSy	5.0	5.0	0.0	6.1	5.8	+0.3
Mean						
Verbal	7.6	8.4	–0.8	8.5	10.0	–1.5
Performance	6.1	6.3	–0.2	8.7	6.9	+1.8

NOTE: Mean Diff. = mean for left lesion minus mean for right lesion. Data are from Munder (1976). Mean scaled scores in this table are values that have been adjusted for three covariates: age, education, and interval between brain damage and date of testing. These values differ, therefore, from the unadjusted values presented in Table 8.9.

adjusted for three covariates: age, education, and interval between brain damage and date of testing.

The comparisons shown in Table 8.20 indicate that 9 of the 11 subtests behaved as predicted for Caucasians, but only four subtests (all Verbal) behaved as hypothesized for African Americans. That is to say, one would anticipate patients with left lesions to outscore patients with right lesions on Performance subtests, but to perform more poorly on Verbal subtests.

For Caucasians, substantial differences in the predicted directions were observed between the two patient groups on all tasks except Information and Digit Symbol. For African Americans, none of the Performance subtests distinguished between patients with left- or right-brain damage; left-lesion subjects did, however, outscore right-lesion subjects by about 1 scaled-score point on Comprehension, Vocabulary, Arithmetic, and Digit Span. Note that the latter two tasks are more associated with the Freedom from Distractibility or Working Memory factor than with the Verbal Comprehension factor.

Munder's (1976) covariance analyses with the separate subtests identified only three that produced significant interactions between ethnicity and location of brain damage (i.e., left, right, diffuse): Block Design, Picture Completion, Object Assembly. In her discriminant function analyses, the subtests with the highest coefficient weights for the ethnicity × location interaction were Picture Completion, Block Design, and Similarities. Therefore, Munder's statistical treatment of the data obtained on male brain-damaged patients suggests that African Americans and Caucasians may differ in the cerebral organization of their brains, with the biggest differences occurring for Similarities and the three most spatial or simultaneous subtests (the ones grouped together by Bannatyne, 1971, to form his Spatial Ability category, and the ones that have been most closely identified with the field independent/field dependent cognitive style; see Goodenough and Karp, 1961).

Bogen, DeZure, Tenhouten, and Marsh (1972) have speculated that, within our culture, African Americans may develop their right hemispheres more completely than their left hemispheres, a pattern opposite to that of Caucasians. Munder (1976) has cited the research of Bogen et al. (1972) and also of Levy (1972) to infer that African Americans are more bilateralized for language than Caucasians, and that African Americans have less asymmetry than Caucasians regarding verbal and spatial abilities. Interestingly, these are the same hypotheses advanced by McGlone (1977) regarding gender differences.

However, before hypothesizing about possible explanations for a potential ethnic difference in IQs or scaled scores, new research is needed. Patients from a diversity of ethnic groups, such as Caucasian, African American, Hispanic, Asian, and American Indian, need to be evaluated with the WAIS-III, and IQ, index, and scaled-score profiles for samples with lesions confined to a single hemisphere require careful scrutiny. Perhaps sophisticated statistical procedures such as the ones employed by Turkheimer et al. (1993) could be applied to try to determine both the presence of ethnic differences and the explanations for any observed differences.

AGE OF PATIENT SAMPLES

Brain Damage in Children and in Adults

Brain damage in children is different from brain damage in adults. The impact of lesions in early childhood on intelligence and neuropsychological functioning is often more profound and more generalized than lesions occurring during adulthood (Crockett, Clark, & Klonoff, 1981). However, "The consistent findings since the last century indicate not only significantly greater recovery from comparable brain insults in infants and children than in adults but also more severe and persisting sequelae in adults with advancing age" (Smith, 1983, p. 770). Also, adults with recent neurological problems tend to have more difficulty with immediate problem-solving ability than with memory, whereas children evidence the opposite pattern (Reed & Reitan, 1969).

Although V–P discrepancies in adults have generally been shown to relate predictably to the side of the lesion, particularly for patients with right lesions, such findings have not usually held for children (e.g., Fedio & Mirsky, 1969; Lewandowski & DeRienzo, 1985; Reed & Reitan, 1969). There are some data, however, that support the typical V–P discrepancies found in adults (Cohen, Branch, McKie, and Adams, 1994; Morris and Bigler, 1987). The equivocal nature of the pediatric lesion literature may be due to developmental trends in cerebral lateralization (Krashen, 1973), qualitatively different types of brain injuries in children and adults (Klonoff & Thompson, 1969), less rigorous criteria for determining locus of injury or type of pathology for children than adults (Fedio & Mirsky, 1969), greater plasticity in younger than older brains (Smith, 1983), or some combination of these and other reasons.

The nature of the discrepancies between studies of neurological injuries in children versus adults is a topic of some controversy (Satz &

Fletcher, 1981; Smith, 1983). Satz and Fletcher, for example, disputed the notion of greater plasticity in children's brains. The purpose of this section is not to try to resolve or even articulate these issues, but to examine the role of age as an intervening variable in adult studies of Wechsler V–P IQ discrepancies and side of lesion.

Empirical Analysis with Samples of Adolescents and Adults

Meyer and Jones (1957) correlated chronological age to the magnitude of verbal deficit for patients with epilepsy who had their left temporal lobe removed. The correlation for this group, which ranged in age from 12 to 46 years (mean = 27.7), was trivial and nonsignificant (.10). Snow, Freedman, and Ford (1986) also observed small, chance relationships between mean V-IQ versus P-IQ discrepancy and mean chronological age for numerous samples of left- or right-lesion patients tested on the WAIS ($r = .23$) or Wechsler-Bellevue ($r = .02$).

Reitan and Wolfson (1996) systematically investigated the effect of age on a sample of 50 brain damaged and 50 control subjects. The group with brain damage was composed of persons with definitive neurological diagnosis, but included a diversity of types and locations of cerebral disease or damage. Thus, no data were available on left- versus right-hemisphere damage. The mean age of the brain-damaged sample was 36.6 ($SD = 14.7$) and the mean age of the control sample was 35.8 ($SD = 11.5$). There were no significant differences between the mean ages or levels of education of the groups (education data are discussed in the section below).

Age correlated significantly with WAIS V-IQ (.48), P-IQ (.53), and FS-IQ (.52) for the brain-damaged sample, but only correlated significantly in the control group for P-IQ (.28). When the groups were each subdivided at the median for age, there were no significant correlations between age and IQ for the control group and

only minimal correlations for the brain-damaged group (i.e., the only significant correlation was for the older age brain-damage group between V-IQ and age, .41). When IQs were compared, the older controls showed a tendency to perform better than younger controls on all IQs (Verbal IQs differed by 5½ points and Performance IQs differed by 7 points). For subjects with brain damage, the discrepancy between IQs of younger and older groups was even more pronounced (Verbal IQs differed by 18 points and Performance IQs differed by 22½ points). Reitan and Wolfson (1996) suggest that the reason for these discrepancies may reflect sampling problems in their study or overly generous age adjustment in the Wechsler norms for older people (a problem with the WAIS, because it was only nationally normed through age 64, but not with the WAIS-R or WAIS-III). The younger controls performed significantly better than younger subjects with brain damage (17-point discrepancy on V-IQ and 26-point discrepancy on P-IQ), but the older groups did not differ significantly on any of the IQ variables. This finding suggested that among older subjects, IQ variance may be influenced more strongly by factors other than a diagnosis of brain damage.

EDUCATIONAL LEVEL OF PATIENT SAMPLES

More than other background variables, a person's level of education relates to his or her Verbal–Performance difference. This variable was previously discussed in Chapter 4 for several tests, based on data from large standardization samples. Clinicians and researchers should internalize the information presented in that chapter, notably the mean IQs earned by normal individuals with different amounts of formal education as a guide to expected level of functioning for patients with neurological damage, particularly in the absence of appropriate premorbid estimates of functioning. For example, from page 116, the average WAIS-III IQs were about 80–82 for elementary school dropouts, 98–100 for high school graduates, and 113–117 for those with some graduate school (data from Heaton et al., 2001; Manley, et al., 2000).

We constructed Table 8.21 from V-IQ and P-IQ means given by Heaton and his colleagues to provide expected V–P IQ discrepancies based on a person's level of educational attainment; in this table, we present the mean V–P discrepancy for each educational level between ≤ 7 and ≥ 17 years of formal schooling. Adults with 0–7 years of schooling displayed no meaningful V–P difference. However, adults with 8–13 years had a slight P > V profile of about 1½ to 2½ points; those with 2 to 4 years of college had a slight V > P profile of about 1½ to 3 points; and those with

at least 1 year of graduate study had a more substantial V > P pattern of about 4½ points.

Table 8.21 has clinical applications. For example, suppose a man who has completed a master's degree suffers a stroke that damages his left hemisphere, and he is subsequently found to have P > V of 6 points. From Table 8.21, we see that people with 17 or more years of education average V > P by 4.6 points. Hence, our best guess is that the brain-damaged man had a premorbid V–P difference of +5 points. Therefore, he probably went from +5 points before the stroke to –6 points after the cerebral lesion, a net shift of 11 points. This relative loss in nonverbal–spatial ability is thus far greater than the loss suggested by P > V of 6 points. The data in Table 8.21 provide a rough estimate of a neurological patient's premorbid V–P discrepancy based on the

TABLE 8.21   Mean WAIS-III Verbal minus Performance IQ discrepancy for normal adults by years of education, controlling for age, for adults ages 20 to 89 years ($N = 2{,}312$)

Years of Education	N	Mean V-IQ Minus P-IQ Difference
≤7	68	–0.6
8	294	–1.6
9	78	–2.0
10	96	–2.4
11	162	–1.8
12	736	–1.7
13	174	–1.4
14	207	+1.4
15	100	+2.8
16	261	+2.5
≥17	136	+4.6

NOTE: These data for ages 20–89 years are computed from age-corrected z scores, predicted by education, provided by Heaton, Manly, Taylor, and Tulsky (personal communication, September, 2000) with the permission of The Psychological Corporation. We converted the z scores to standard scores with mean = 100 and $SD = 15$. The sample of 2,312 includes 2,036 standardization cases plus 276 cases from an "education oversampling" (Manly, Heaton, & Taylor, 2000). The total sample has a mean age of 51.8 and mean education of 12.2 years; includes 53.5% females; and comprises 75.8% Caucasian, 13.0% African American, 7.7% Hispanic, and 3.5% "Other" (Manly et al., 2000).

background variable (educational level) that is most related to IQ. In addition, Barona, Reynolds, and Chastain (1984) developed regression tables for the WAIS-R that take into account several background variables in addition to education estimating premorbid V-, P-, or FS-IQ. However, we have not yet seen similar equations published for the WAIS-III. Nonetheless, even the most sophisticated equations for estimating premorbid intelligence on the Wechsler scales misclassify a person's intellectual category more than half the time (Silverstein, 1987a).

Research Implications of Base-Rate Education Data

The values shown in Table 8.21 are even more valuable for research purposes (applied to group data) than for clinical evaluation of a single patient, because there is great variability in the V–P discrepancies observed for the separate individuals within a sample.

The impact of education on the overall data presented for the numerous Wechsler studies of patients with unilateral brain damage summarized in Tables 8.1–8.3 is likely to be minimal. The reason is that nearly all the samples had a mean education level of 10 to 12 years. The mean or expected V–P discrepancy for individuals with a moderate amount of education is only about 2 points, in favor of P-IQ, as shown in Table 8.21.

However, the role of years of education is more sizable for samples with extremely high or low levels of education. Fitzhugh and Fitzhugh's (1964b) sample of 52 patients (about half male, half female) with chronic seizure activity (see Table 8.2) had a mean education level of about 5½ years and an average age of 37. On the WAIS, normal groups aged 35–44 with 8 or less years of education had a mean P > V profile of 3.7 points. Thus, our presumption is that Fitzhugh and Fitzhugh's left- and right-lesion samples each had a mean premorbid V–P discrepancy of –3.7 points.

Subsequent to their brain damage, the left-lesion sample had a V–P difference of –4.8 and

their right-lesion sample had a corresponding discrepancy of +4.5. However, if we take into account that the group likely had P > V of about 4 points before the lesion, then a P > V discrepancy of about 5 points after the lesion is really no change, i.e., no meaningful discrepancy at all! (If they had P > V of 3.7 points prior to the lesion, and 4.8 points following the lesion, then the net "increase" in the V–P discrepancy is only 1.1 point.)

In contrast, the V > P profile for the right-lesion patients is quite impressive considering that, as a group, they probably started with the opposite profile (P > V). Adjusting their mean V–P difference of +4.5 by the probable initial difference of –3.7 indicates a relative decrease in their nonverbal ability by about 8 points.

Thus, evaluating the data from Fitzhugh and Fitzhugh's (1964b) study without consideration of their sample's low educational level leads to the erroneous conclusion that the patterns for left- and right-lesion patients are equal and opposite in magnitude, mildly supporting predictions from the cerebral asymmetry literature. However, when the values are corrected for the likely premorbid V–P discrepancy, strong support for functional asymmetry is given for lesions to the right hemisphere, and no support is obtained for left lesions. The latter conclusion is consistent with the overview of all research on this topic using the WAIS or WAIS-R.

As early as the mid-1960s, Smith (1966a) was aware that Wechsler researchers investigating brain damage were remiss in ignoring the education level of the patients:

In addition to numerous ambiguities inherent in psychological studies of the effects of undifferentiated "brain lesions," comparisons of the mean education of the patients with lower verbal than performance aggregate weighted scores clearly illustrate one that has been consistently overlooked in such studies of effects of lateralized brain lesions. Wechsler (1944, p. 126) presented data for large samples showing that as mean [Wechsler-Bellevue] Full Scale IQ is decreased from 120 and above to 75 and below, the proportion of patients with higher performance than verbal IQ's increased from 21.0 percent to 74.3 percent. (p. 118)

Education Level and V–P for Brain-Damaged Samples

Table 8.22 summarizes all of the studies in Tables 8.1–8.3 that provided education information for the students' unilateral brain-damaged samples. The studies are grouped by mean education levels, cutting across other variables such as type of lesion, instrument used for assessment, gender, and so forth. The resultant composite samples range in size from 119 to 426, encompassing five levels of education: less than 10 years, 10 years, 11 years, 12 years, and 13–14 years.

These data show that the mean P > V profile that is anticipated for patients with left lesions is about 6–7 points for those samples that averaged 10 years of education or less, but is notably smaller (about 1–4 points) for those averaging 11 or more years of schooling. For patients with right-hemisphere lesions, the expected V > P profile is substantial (about 7–11 points) for patient samples averaging 12 or less years of schooling, but is only about 3 points for samples that averaged 1 or 2 years of college. Indeed, the latter sample is the only education group that tended *not* to show the characteristic pattern for either lesion group. However, the predicted patterns for each type of lesion resulted for the least educated samples, those with 0–9 years of schooling and those with 10 years. Consequently, based on these data:

(1) for patients with 0–10 years of schooling, expect a loss of verbal function for patients with left lesions and a loss in nonverbal function for those with right lesions; (2) for patients with 11–12 years of schooling, anticipate a nonverbal loss for those with right lesions, but don't expect P > V patterns for patients with left lesions; and (3) for patients with some college, do not expect either predicted profile to occur. However, the data in Table 8.22, and the guidelines derived from these data, are tentative because the education groups are not matched on gender, ethnicity, Wechsler scale, or type of lesion. Nonetheless, the overview shown in Table 8.22 for patient samples, when coupled with the education data for normal individuals presented in Table 8.21, indicates the importance of interpreting the results of a V–P IQ comparison in the context of the person's (or group's) level of formal education.

Herring and Reitan (1986) also noted the same type of relationship between level of education and V–P discrepancy indicated in Table 8.22 for patients with left lesions, based on unpublished studies in their laboratory: "[P]ersons with lower educational levels and left cerebral hemisphere lesions had relatively low VIQ compared with PIQ, whereas VIQs were only slightly lower than PIQs for persons with left cerebral hemisphere lesions when educational levels were higher" (p. 540).

TABLE 8.22   The relationship of mean education of brain-damaged sample to size of V–P IQ discrepancy for patients with left hemisphere and right hemisphere lesions

Mean Education Level of Sample (Years of School Completed)	Left Lesion		Right Lesion	
	N	*V–P Diff*	N	*V–P Diff*
<10 years	119	–7.2	130	+9.1
10 years	184	–5.6	199	+11.1
11 years	426	–3.7	423	+6.5
12 years	218	–1.1	168	+10.2
13–14 years	129	–3.8	128	+2.8

NOTE: These data are from all studies in Tables 8.1, 8.2, and 8.3 that indicated mean education level of the sample. However, like Tables 8.1, 8.2, and 8.3, overlapping samples are excluded. V–P Diff. Equals minus P–IQ.

Education as a Variable for Normal versus Brain-Damaged People

Reitan and Wolfson (1996a, 1996b) systematically investigated the role of education level on the intellectual and neuropsychological test performance of 50 patients with brain damage and 50 control subjects who were matched on age (36.5 years) and education (12.8 years). Although Reitan and Wolfson used the old WAIS and did not examine the side of the lesion as a variable (nor did they limit the study to those with unilateral damage), the results are instructive.

Reitan and Wolfson's (1996a, 1996b) main findings were that higher-educated subjects performed better on all IQs, but the finding was more consistent among controls than among subjects with brain damage and was not significant for the P-IQ within the patient sample. The correlations between education and each IQ distribution were significantly higher for the controls (rs of .66–.79) than for the patients with brain damage (rs of .35–.54). Reitan and Wolfson (1996b) identified an interesting interaction in the relationship of IQ and education, as shown in Table 8.23. Each sample (patients with brain damage, controls) was divided in half, based on educational attainment, and correlations were computed for each mini-sample. Dividing the control sample in half had no real influence on

the relationships of education to IQ, but splitting the sample of patients with brain damage had a striking effect. For control subjects in both halves of the sample, and for the "high-education" patient sample, IQ correlated substantially with V-IQ and FS-IQ (.64–.71) and moderately with P-IQ (.39–.57). However, correlations were nonsignificant and trivial (−.11–.26) for the "low-education" patient sample. The diminished role in the ability of educational attainment to predict IQ for relatively poorly educated patient samples suggests that, for such samples, the brain damage itself has a more potent effect on a patient's IQ than does his or her educational attainment.

Reitan and Wolfson (1996a) also looked at individual WAIS scaled scores to examine the effect of education on cognitive performance for patients with brain damage and for control subjects. Like the global results described above, level of education had a strong effect on subtest scores in the control group and a much lesser effect on scores in the patient group (see Table 8.24). In the group with brain damage, only three subtests produced significant differences ($p < .05$) between the high and low education subgroups (Information, Comprehension, and Vocabulary); however, in the control group, all subtests but two (Picture Completion and Object Assembly) had significant differences between the high and low education subgroups ($p < .05$). Likewise, correlations between education and subtest scores were larger

TABLE 8.23   Coefficients of correlation for education vs. V-IQ, P-IQ, and FS-IQ for patients with brain damage and control group, each subdivided at the median for education

Group	V-IQ	P-IQ	FS-IQ
Controls (N = 50)			
Education: Upper 50%	.71*	.39	.66*
Education: Lower 50%	.64*	.55*	.67*
Brain-Damaged (N = 50)			
Education: Upper 50%	.66*	.57*	.64*
Education: Lower 50%	.26	−.11	.07

*$p < .01$

NOTE: Data are from Reitan and Wolfson (1996b).

TABLE 8.24   Means on WAIS subtests for patients with brain damage and control group, each subdivided at the median for education

Subtest	Brain Damage (N = 50)		Control (N = 50)	
	Higher Education	*Lower Education*	*Higher Education*	*Lower Education*
Information	10.8*	8.6	12.5*	9.9
Comprehension	11.7*	9.4	13.1*	11.0
Arithmetic	8.6	6.9	12.5*	9.1
Similarities	10.8	8.5	13.8*	11.0
Digit Span	7.9	6.6	11.2*	7.8
Vocabulary	11.4*	8.1	13.6*	10.3
Digit Symbol	7.0	6.7	12.8*	9.2
Picture Completion	9.1	7.9	11.8	10.4
Block Design	8.2	7.7	13.0*	10.6
Picture Arrangement	7.6	7.2	10.8*	7.8
Object Assembly	7.7	8.2	11.7	10.5

*$p < .05$ (mean for higher education is significantly larger than mean for lower education)
NOTE: Data are from Reitan and Wolfson (1996a).

for the controls than the patient sample (mean *r*s for Verbal subtests were .65 and .46, respectively; mean *r*s for Performance subtests were .46 and .17, respectively). In fact, there were no significant correlations between education and Performance scaled scores for the patients with brain damage, but there were significant correlations for four of the five Performance subtests for the control group.

As noted previously, often age- and education-adjusted data based on normal samples are used to predict premorbid functioning of brain-damaged patients (e.g., Barona, Reynolds, and Chastain, 1984). Thus, Reitan and Wolfson (1996b) also used their education (and age) data from control patients to develop regression equations to determine its effectiveness in predicting the IQs of their sample with brain damage. Reitan and Wolfson's results showed that, when predictions of IQs for patients with brain damage were based on relationships of IQ with age and education for the *controls*, the predicted

IQ means for the patient sample differed significantly from the actual IQ means in each case. The authors conclude that the "use of relationships between the attribute variables of age and education versus IQ values, when based on control subjects, are subject to error when applied to brain-damaged subjects" (p. 302). They caution against adjusting IQs for patients with brain damage on the basis of normative data derived from nonbrain-damaged subjects (Reitan & Wolfson, 1996, 1997).

CLINICAL ISSUES IN THE INTERPRETATION OF A PATIENT'S V–P DIFFERENCE

The preceding sections of this chapter and Chapter 9 focus primarily on research findings for groups. Sometimes too much attention on typical group differences can obscure the interpretation of a given individual's discrepancy between his or her V- and P-IQs.

Individual versus Group Data

Matarazzo and his colleagues have consistently warned examiners to be aware of the huge difference between mean values obtained for groups and a set of scores earned by any particular individual; along with this wise and essential warning is Matarazzo's vital reminder to pay careful attention to base rates of differences that characterize a normal population, and always to compare the magnitude of observed differences (such as V–P discrepancies) to the normal or expected differences (Bornstein & Matarazzo, 1982, 1984; Matarazzo, 1972; Matarazzo & Herman, 1985). For example, the significant and persistent V > P pattern of about 9 points for patients with right lesions tested with the Wechsler-Bellevue, WAIS, or WAIS-R is statistically meaningful, and tells us much about groups of patients with right-brain damage; they do have a deficiency in the skill measured by Wechsler's Performance Scale, and that deficit is causally linked to the specific location of their brain lesion.

Grouped data, however, are much more reliable than the data for any one person in that sample. An 8-point WAIS-III V–P discrepancy is unusually large for a group, but for an individual that difference is not reliably different from zero at the .05 level. Further, even a V–P difference as large as 15 points is highly significant in a statistical sense, but it occurs fairly commonly in the normal population. Discrepancies of 15 or more points occur in about 18% of normal adults, far too common an occurrence to infer the presence of an abnormality such as brain damage.

Subsequent to their review of numerous unilateral brain damage studies, Bornstein and Matarazzo (1982) emphasized: "These findings suggest that groups of subjects with lateralized cerebral dysfunction tend to have greater discrepancies between V-IQs and P-IQs than would occur in a nonneurological population. Nevertheless it is important to stress that the evaluation of these Verbal–Performance differences must be determined for each individual patient in the context of base rates and also with respect to other neuropsychological measures" (p. 329).

For any individual, then, the precise V–P IQ difference obtained needs to be compared to the base rates provided for the WAIS-III (see Chapter 11 of this book or Table B.2 of the *WAIS-III Administration and Scoring Manual*; Wechsler, 1997). As a general rule of thumb, a WAIS-III V-IQ versus P-IQ difference of at least 19 points occurs in less than 10% of normal people, and is unusual enough to consider that the discrepancy may be related to a specific lesion, pending integration of the findings with other neurological data and pertinent background information (e.g., education level) or may be considered related to another typical profile such as those discussed in this chapter. However, the size of an abnormal difference, occurring less than 10% of the time on the WAIS-III, may be as little as 14 points for adults with Full Scale IQs below 80, or as much as 22 points for adults with superior ability (see Tables D.1–D.5 of the *WAIS-III/WMS-III Technical Manual*; Psychological Corporation, 1997).

Consideration of base rates or explanations of V–P differences other than brain damage is often lacking in the literature and, undoubtedly, in clinical practice as well. Balthazar and Morrison (1961), for example, investigated the hypothesis that "a difference of seven points or greater between Wechsler Verbal and Performance Subtest scales would be of diagnostic value in determining left-right and indeterminately unilateralized brain damage" (p. 161), and subsequently supported the experimental hypothesis. Whiddon (1978) stated: "Study 1 revealed that a VIQ–PIQ difference of more than 10 points could serve as a sign of brain damage" (p. 5051-B).

Fortunately, there are also researchers like Black (1974a), who used base-rate tables to select a criterion of 20 or more points to reflect possible neurological dysfunction and concluded that "seven per cent of the bilateral lesion Ss, 28 per cent of the right-hemisphere lesion Ss, and 14 per cent of left-hemispheric lesion Ss demonstrated such dysfunction" (p. 816).

Emotional Disturbance and Diffuse Brain Injury

Diamond, Barth, and Zillmer (1988) and others have suggested that psychological factors may be associated with head injury, which ultimately can complicate recovery. Along with the cognitive impairment noted in mild, moderate, and severe head injuries, emotional sequelae have been noted. Reported symptoms after head injury, both psychological and somatic, have included headache, fatigue, anxiety, emotional lability, and concentration impairment (Diamond et al., 1988).

Diamond et al. (1988) examined the overall level of psychological disturbance in 50 patients with minor head injury and 50 matched patients with documented brain damage. The authors excluded from their sample any patients with a history of major psychiatric disorders, neurological illness, or unemployment prior to their injuries. The subjects were administered the Minnesota Multiphasic Personality Inventory (MMPI). In order not to mask the effect of a variety of emotional reactions, Diamond et al. separated MMPI profiles into four discrete types. The results showed that patients with mild head injury showed significant emotional distress that was markedly similar to that of individuals with long-standing neurologic disease. Over half the sample reported an abnormal level of depression and had at least two MMPI scales that were elevated 2 standard deviations above normal. Not surprisingly, those who experienced significant emotional symptoms had the most difficulty resuming the pre-injury activities.

The results of a study that included 68 traumatically brain-injured patients further supported the association between head injury and emotional symptoms (Dicesare, Parente, Anderson-Parente, 1990). The primary problems reported after head injury were obsessive-compulsive behavior, interpersonal sensitivity, depression, and phobic anxiety. The results of Dicesare et al.'s study were obtained from self-report measures, but the authors noted that the self-reports were consistent with the observations of family members. Over time, the emotional symptoms may lessen, but Dicesare et al. remark that the client's premorbid personality may never return.

The interaction of cognitive and emotional dysfunctions after head injury was noted by Parker and Rosenblum (1996). They studied the cognitive and emotional sequelae in 33 mild head-injury patients. In their sample, the emotional consequences of minor head injury were extremely varied, including personality disorders, persistent altered consciousness, stress reactions, sexual disorders, and psychiatric diagnoses. Parker and Rosenblum hypothesized that the effect of the lesion itself can be exacerbated by the emotional consequences, making post-injury functioning more difficult.

Emotional Disturbance and Lateralized Lesions

Lezak (1995) and others (e.g., Heilman, Bowers, & Valenstein, 1985) have pointed out that lesions in the left versus right hemisphere are accompanied by different types of emotional reactions. Clinicians need to understand these differences to facilitate their interactions with patients having unilateral brain damage, especially when assessing these patients shortly after the damage has occurred.

Patients with Left Lesions

Damage to the left hemisphere is often accompanied by anxiety, undue cautiousness, oversensitivity to the impairment, and depression (Buck, 1968; Galin, 1974; Jones-Gotman & Milner, 1977; Lezak, 1995). Lezak notes: "Patients with left hemispheric lesions are more likely than those with right-sided brain damage to exhibit a *catastrophic* reaction (extreme and disruptive transient emotional disturbance). The catastrophic reaction may appear as acute—often disorganizing—anxiety, agitation, or tearfulness, disrupting the activity that provoked it. Typically, it occurs when patients are confronted with their limitations, as when taking a test" (p. 66). Goldstein (1948) first used the term *catastrophic reaction* to describe the profound depression accompanying left-hemisphere lesions; subsequent empirical investigations have supported the tendency for catastrophic reactions and depression to be more associated with left- than right-hemispheric damage (e.g., Gainotti, 1972; Gasparrini, Satz, Heilman, & Coolidge, 1977).

Depression, a common side effect of left-hemisphere damage, is often accompanied by numerous clinical presenting symptoms. These include "depressed mood and agitation;…psychomotor retardation; impaired immediate memory and learning abilities; defective attention, concentration, and tracking; impaired orientation; an overall shoddy quality to cognitive products; and listlessness with loss of interest in one's surroundings" (Lezak, 1995, p. 327).

Caine (1986), summarizing literature on depressed patients, stressed their impairments in sustaining attention, memory, learning ability, mental control, and motor performance. Based on these presenting clinical symptoms, it is not surprising that "[d]epressed people often have distinctly higher Verbal [than Performance] IQs" (Gregory, 1987, p. 72).

Gass and Russell (1985) studied the relationship of emotional adjustment (MMPI profile) to functional loss (WAIS Verbal IQ) in a study of 31 Caucasian male patients with carefully documented left-hemisphere damage. These investigators were critical of previous investigations of the emotional behavior in patients with left-brain lesions because of failure to control for premorbid status, to exclude aphasics, to exclude patients with right-hemisphere pathology, and to screen for inconsistent MMPI profiles.

Gass and Russell (1985) used state-of-the-art neurodiagnostic techniques to ensure that the patients' lesions were confined to the left hemisphere; they also controlled for education level in their multivariate data analysis. Their results showed that, regardless of the degree of impairment in verbal intelligence, the patients with right lesions consistently had MMPI profiles suggestive of the following emotional symptoms: "mild dysphoria, worry, and concerns or preoccupations with regard to one's physical condition" (p. 669). The implications of the left-lesion patients' MMPI emotional profiles are quite consistent with the stereotypical behaviors described previously for these patients.

Patients with Right Lesions

Patients with right-hemisphere damage typically have different emotional reactions than those with left lesions. The depression that accompanies left lesions can be simulated by inactivating the left hemisphere via the Wada technique, i.e., intracarotid injections of sodium amytal; in contrast, inactivation of the right hemisphere by this technique is likely to produce euphoria (Nebes, 1978). Also, "With left hemisphere damaged patients, depression seems to reflect awareness of deficit;…[w]hen the lesion is on the right, the emotional disturbance does not seem to arise from awareness of defects so much as from the secondary effects of the patient's diminished self-awareness and social insensitivity.… Depression in patients with right-sided cortical damage may take longer to develop than it does in patients with left hemisphere involvement[;]…however, it can be more chronic, more debilitating, and more resistive to intervention" (Lezak, 1995, p. 68).

The inappropriate indifference of right-lesion patients was first stressed in the early 1950s (Denny-Brown, Meyer, & Horenstein, 1952; Hecaen, Ajuriaguerra, & Massonet, 1951). This indifference was observed by Gainotti (1972) in patients with right damage, just as the catastrophic reaction was observed in left-damaged patients, in a study of 160 individuals with lateralized lesions. Whereas Gainotti considered the profound depression of patients with left lesions to be a normal response to severe cognitive deficits, "he felt the indifference reaction was an abnormal mood associated with denial of illness" (Valenstein & Heilman, 1979, p. 425).

In a study of 50 Caucasian male patients with right-hemisphere damage, Gass and Russell (1987) studied the relationship of emotional adjustment (MMPI profile) to functional loss (WAIS Performance IQ); this investigation was analogous to these authors' similar study, described previously, of patients with left lesions

(Gass & Russell, 1985). Gass and Russell (1987) again used sophisticated neurodiagnostic techniques and controlled for age and education level in their multivariate data analysis. Their results showed that, regardless of the degree of impairment in nonverbal intelligence, the patients with right lesions consistently had MMPI profiles suggestive of the following emotional symptoms: mildly depressed, pessimistic, and worried; discouraged and lacking initiative; somatic preoccupation; denial; and limited emotional insight. This profile sounds fairly consistent with clinical observations of right-lesion patients, but interpretation is hampered by the investigators' failure to report the degree of chronicity of the subjects' lesions, or to control for this important variable.

Even more consistent with the indifference and denial of right-lesion patients were the results of a creative study conducted by Anderson and Tranel (1989). They investigated 100 brain-damaged patients' awareness of their own cognitive deficits, as measured by a neuropsychological battery that included the WAIS-R. This sample included 32 acute stroke victims with lesions lateralized to the left ($N = 12$) or right ($N = 20$) hemisphere. Nearly all (90%) of the right-lesion patients demonstrated unawareness of cognitive deficits in intelligence, memory, or other areas, and five patients with right lesions—with substantial paralysis—even denied having motor problems. Significantly fewer (41%) of the patients with left lesions evidenced unawareness of a cognitive deficit; none of these patients with partial paralysis denied having motor difficulties.

Clinical Applications of the Emotional Component of Brain Damage

The generally different, predictable affective responses to damage to the left or right hemispheres must be taken into account when interpreting the V–P discrepancy studies involving patients with unilateral brain damage. The emotional behaviors accompanying left lesions, most notably anxiety, depression, carelessness, and low energy level, are likely to have their most significant impact on Wechsler's Performance IQ. Attention to detail is important to performance on Wechsler's nonverbal tasks such as Picture Arrangement, yet impaired and disordered attention in signal detection tasks has been documented in several investigations of depressed patients (Caine, 1986). Indeed, the V > P that often characterizes the profiles of depressed patients (Gregory, 1987) is opposite to the P > V that is anticipated for people with left-hemisphere lesions. This antagonistic influence on V–P differences may be a primary reason why patients with left lesions have demonstrated such trivial P > V profiles in so many studies of unilateral brain damage on the WAIS and WAIS-R. This hypothesis, however, is mere speculation; there are no data to support the contention that depression systematically lowers the P-IQs of patients with left lesions.

The emotional limitations of right-hemisphere patients may also affect their relative success on the Verbal and Performance Scales. Their difficulties with recognizing emotional tone in facial expressions, for example, may lead to lowered scores on Picture Arrangement, a social awareness task that measures this skill to some extent. Consequently, low scores on Picture Arrangement, for some patients with right-hemisphere damage, may have an emotional, rather than a visual–spatial, causality. Similarly, the indifference and lack of awareness of their mistakes that many subjects with right-brain lesions display may lead to low scores on the Block Design, Object Assembly, and Picture Arrangement subtests, which are dependent on the person's ability to benefit from visual, sensory-motor feedback.

Also, lack of awareness of mistakes and difficulty in comprehending the affective quality of speech can have a negative influence on success on the Verbals scale for a person with right-hemisphere damage, most notably in the patient's ability to improve ambiguous or incomplete responses after querying by the examiner. Finally, the possibility of a resistant-to-change depression in chronic (but not acute) patients with right-hemisphere lesions may lead to sizable V > P profiles in patients with long-standing right-brain damage. Although this discrepancy may have been absent during acute stages of the illness, its later appearance may be primarily a function of the depression than of any visual–spatial degeneration.

Although these potential emotional influences on the V–P discrepancies of patients with unilateral brain damage are speculative, they are quite important because of the consistency of the clinical observations across patients with diverse types of right- or left-brain lesions. When the right-hemisphere lesion response of indifference appears in a patient with a left lesion, this occurrence is so uncharacteristic that probably the most likely explanation is bilateral involvement of either a temporary or permanent nature (Lezak, 1995). Therefore, we need to be aware that some portion of the observed V > P differences in patients with right lesions may be due to emotional, not physiological or anatomical, characteristics associated with the location of the lesion; and the same explanation may be partly at the root of the failure of many studies to display the predicted P > V profile for patients with left-hemisphere damage.

V–P Interpretation in the Context of Patients' Behaviors

Merely identifying an abnormally large V–P IQ difference in a patient with unilateral brain damage is just the beginning of the interpretive procedure, as Bornstein and Matarazzo (1982) implied. The difference must next be evaluated in the context of other neurological data, behavioral observations, research findings, and background variables that interact with V–P differences such as age, gender, ethnicity, education level, and Full Scale IQ.

Observation is especially pertinent for neurologically impaired individuals because they are often characterized by sensory deficits, motor deficits, distractibility, depression (particularly those with left damage or chronic right damage), poor frustration tolerance, motivational defects, and a tendency to fatigue easily (Lezak, 1995).

For example, consider possible problems with fatigue. One solution is to test neurological patients in the early morning. With the Wechsler-Bellevue or WAIS, failure to respond to a patient's fatigue would likely have led to a depressed Performance IQ, because all Performance tasks were administered last. This occurrence might have produced V > P profiles for patients with right lesions that would have been interpreted wrongly as a visual–spatial deficit, but it is not a concern for current examiners because the WAIS-III administration procedures (like WAIS-R procedures) alternate Verbal and Performance subtests.

As another illustration, consider the role of sensory abilities, which, as discussed in Chapter 5 on aging, have been shown to correlate substantially with measures of intellectual processes (Baltes & Lindenberger, 1997; Lindenberger & Baltes, 1994, 1997); for elderly samples, astonishingly, more than 90% of the age-related variance in IQ can be accounted for by differences in sensory acuity. From a left-right hemisphere standpoint, Reitan and Fitzhugh (1971) administered a battery of tests that included several measures of somatosensory functioning (focusing on tactile, visual, and auditory imperception of simple stimuli under conditions of bilateral simultaneous stimulation). "In every instance, groups with left cerebral lesions performed more poorly on the right than left side of the body, and the reverse was true for groups with right cerebral lesions. The magnitude of these differences appeared to be smaller for auditory than tactile or visual deficits.... Lateralized deficiencies in perception of simultaneous tactile stimuli were more reliable in the group with left cerebral lesions, whereas the lateralized differences in the visual modality were more significant for the group with right cerebral damage" (pp. 220–221). Goldstein and Shelly (1973) likewise identified significant sensory impairments (auditory, visual, and tactile) in the hypothesized directions for their samples of patients with left or right lesions.

Also consider distractibility, often associated with brain damage (Lezak, 1995). When testing patients with known distractibility, it is often wise to test in a very quiet environment, with the examiner careful to avoid flashy, brightly colored clothing or jewelry. However, some patients will be distractible regardless of the examiner or testing environment, and the subtests composing the Working Memory Index are likely to be the ones most affected, with the Processing Speed tasks a close second. Poor performance on the WMI tasks due to distractibility leads to a very different interpretation from poor scores due to a verbal–sequential deficit. The latter cause of low scores reflects a deficit associated with the left hemisphere, whereas the former cause is not limited to either side of the brain.

Examiners must be alert to distractible behavior, and they need to assess its probable impact on test performance. Because the three WAIS-III subtests most influenced by distractibility are on the Verbal Scale, it is V-IQ that will most likely be artificially depressed for a distractible patient. Hence, examiners of left-lesion patients must be especially aware that some large P > V discrepancies, or some large differences between scores on the Perceptual Organization versus Working Memory factors, may be a deficit in distractible behavior rather than in left-hemisphere verbal/sequential/linear processing.

ILLUSTRATIVE CASE REPORT

A sample psychological case report follows: Walt H., a 21-year-old Caucasian male who suffered brain damage following a car accident at age 14. Walt has a striking V > P pattern, suggestive of damage that is exclusively or primarily confined to the right cerebral hemisphere. (This is an ac-

tual case, although the name and other identifying information have been altered to preserve anonymity.) We have modified the test interpretation sections of these reports (and of the other case reports that follow Chapters 9, 12, and 13) to conform to the specific interpretive procedures advocated in this book; however, these modifications affect only how the test results are communicated, not the basic findings themselves.

As is evident from the case reports in this book, report writing is as individual an endeavor as test administration. Competent interpretation of the WAIS-III depends on the examiner's ability to integrate the test data with data from other relevant tests, cognitive and otherwise. Further, test scores are interpretable only in the context of the person's specific background and clinically observed behaviors. The interpretive rules and guidelines elaborated throughout this text are useful to a point; however, competent interpretation often demands modifying the suggested procedures to fit a specific case.

Consequently, we are opposed to the computerized case reports that are so prevalent and easily available to clinicians. Some computerized techniques are available that simplify clerical procedures, such as determining significant strengths and weaknesses; we see no problem with that type of shortcut. However, we strongly oppose those computerized techniques that offer specific interpretations of IQ and subtest profiles and that generate canned reports. Nothing is more individual than the report that communicates the results of a psychological, neuropsychological, or psychoeducational evaluation to those who will potentially use the results for the person's benefit.

WALT H., AGE 21, HEAD INJURY

Referral and Background Information

Walt H. was referred to determine the current levels of his abilities and to make appropriate vocational suggestions for him. Walt is currently unemployed and lives at home with his mother and one younger sister. He has one older sister who no longer lives at home. He enjoys a good relationship with his stepfather, who is currently separated from his mother. Walt was involved in a car accident a few months before his 15th birthday. The accident resulted in partial paralysis of his left side and in a significant loss of vision. Vision in his right eye is limited to gross form discrimination peripherally and to light/dark awareness in his central vision. Central vision in his left eye is normal but peripheral vision is severely limited. Difficulties with both short-term and long-term memory were noted after the accident.

Prior to his accident, Walt was enrolled in public school and was placed in a learning disabilities resource room. Difficulties were noted in reading, spelling, and behavior. Both before and after the accident, Walt was taking Cylert for diagnosed hyperactivity. He is currently taking no medications.

Subsequent to the accident, Walt enrolled in a new public high school following his family's move to another state. Placement in a learning disabilities resource room was continued. During this period, presenting problems included severe motor deficits and limited vision. Partial paralysis continued to affect his left side, and his balance was tenuous. Walt was naturally left-handed and, consequently, was forced to learn to use his right hand for writing activities. His remaining vision permitted him to do most academic tasks; however, he experienced significant difficulties in tracking across a page or across the blackboard. Cognitively, Walt evidenced similar deficits to those noted prior to the accident. In addition, short-term memory was inconsistent and periods of confusion and disorientation were noted. Walt progressed steadily and was able to graduate from high school at age 19. During high school and subsequent to graduation, he received training through state vocational rehabilitation services. Training included job skills and a period of training at a nearby school for the deaf and blind.

He was administered a WISC-R at age 12, prior to his accident, and obtained a Full Scale IQ of 101 (Verbal and Performance IQs were not available). After his accident, Walt was administered a WAIS-R at age 17. That testing yielded a Verbal IQ of 91, a Performance IQ of 66, and a Full Scale IQ of 77. The large difference in favor of Verbal IQ over Performance IQ (25 points), the motor damage to the left side of Walt's body, and the precise nature of his visual problems all suggest that he suffered right cerebral damage—either primarily or exclusively—from his accident. This current testing was initiated in an effort to establish Walt's level of functioning and to isolate specific skill abilities and deficits. Walt has expressed a desire to determine career areas for which he is best suited.

Appearance and Behavioral Characteristics

Walt is a 21-year, 7-month-old Caucasian male with blond curly hair; he is heavyset and below average height. Walt was tested over the course of three sessions. The first session was in a psychologist's office at a high school; testing conditions were good. Subsequent sessions were at the University of Alabama under adequate testing conditions. Walt appeared to be at ease with all examiners and rapport was easily established and maintained throughout the testing. It is felt that these results represent a valid and reliable indication of his current level of functioning.

The effects of the accident were noted in his measured, somewhat rigid movement patterns. Physical posturing was used as an apparently effective accommodation to his limited vision. Walt presented himself as a friendly, highly verbal young man. He conversed freely with the examiners and did not seem to be intimidated by the situation. At times, he seemed to "search for words," but he nonetheless communicated his thoughts and feelings effectively. He appeared to be relaxed and frequently demonstrated a good sense of humor. When discussing the progress he had made, Walt appeared to be self-confident and seemed genuinely proud of what he had accomplished. He expressed a strong determination to continue his progress and indicated that he hoped some day to be able to help other people.

During the initial portions of the testing at the university, Walt evidenced a degree of disorientation. When asked to name the current date (April 15th), his response was delayed. After some thought, he responded, "I'm not sure. It's not January…April?" He was also uncertain as to what city or university he was in, even though this had been a frequent topic of conversation.

In general, Walt experienced difficulty on tasks that were abstract. When he encountered difficulty, he tended to persist and did not frustrate easily. Walt evidenced the ability to learn on tasks that were initially difficult for him. He tended to approach such problems with a trial-and-error method of problem solving and was most successful when accompanying instructions were ordered and step-by-step. Throughout the testing, Walt's processing skills appeared to be slow, and his answers tended to be measured and deliberate.

Tests Administered

- Bender-Gestalt Test of Visual-Motor Integration
- Peabody Picture Vocabulary Test—Third Edition (PPVT-III)
- Vineland Adaptive Behavior Scales (Expanded Form)
- Wechsler Adult Intelligence Scale—Third Edition (WAIS-III)[1]

Test Results and Interpretation

Walt H. earned a Full Scale IQ of 79 (8th percentile) on the WAIS-III, which classifies him in the Borderline range of intellectual functioning, ranking him at about the 8th percentile when compared to individuals his age. On the Peabody Picture Vocabulary Test-Third Edition (PPVT-III), Walt earned a standard score of 82, which ranks him at about the 13th percentile. These scores are consistent in categorizing Walt's cognitive functioning at the juncture of the Borderline and Low Average classifications of intelligence (a summary of all of Walt's scores is provided in Table 8.25).

Walt's Full Scale IQ does not provide the most meaningful estimate of his cognitive abilities because his verbal and nonverbal skills were highly discrepant. Specifically, a significant difference exists between his WAIS-III Verbal IQ of 93 (between 89–97 with 90% confidence; 32nd percentile; Average) and Performance IQ of 67 (between 63–75 with 90% confidence; 1st percentile; Extremely Low). This 26-point difference is significant at the .01 level and is abnormal, occurring very rarely (less than 1% of the time) among adults with IQs comparable to Walt's. The Verbal IQ, when compared to the other global scores, is less affected by Walt's brain damage because his accident seems to have primarily affected his right cerebral hemisphere. As such, it is felt that Walt's Verbal IQ of 93 (32nd percentile), is more representative of Walt's true intellectual functioning than other obtained scores. His low Performance IQ (1st percentile) undoubtedly reflects the impact of right cerebral damage suffered in the car accident. His high Verbal–low Performance profile was evident on the Woodcock-Johnson-III as well: Good performance on tests of verbal memory, concept formation, and reasoning; very deficient performance on visual–spatial, nonverbal reasoning, and timed tests.

Walt's WAIS-III Indexes paralleled the findings from his IQs. He had significantly more difficulty in the areas of visual–motor coordination and processing speed (Perceptual Organization Index of 72 and Processing Speed Index of 66) than in the areas of verbal conceptualization, memory, and sequencing (Verbal Comprehension Index of 91 and Working Memory Index of 88). The two indexes that comprise the Verbal IQ, Verbal Comprehension and Working Memory, were not significantly different from one another, and neither were the two indexes that comprise the Performance IQ, Perceptual Organization and Processing Speed. Thus, the Verbal IQ and Performance IQ provide meaningful estimates of his overall verbal and nonverbal abilities.

---

[1]This case originally included administration of a WAIS-R and PPVT-R in the first edition of this book. We decided to modify and update the scores from WAIS-R to WAIS-III in order to provide more valuable examples of how to interpret the most recent Wechsler test. However, the major findings from the original report remain unchanged.

TABLE 8.25   Psychometric summary of Walt H.'s test scores

Wechsler Adult Intelligence Scale—Third Edition (WAIS-III)

Scale	IQ	90% Confidence Interval	Percentile Rank
Verbal Scale	93	89–97	32
Performance Scale	67	63–75	1
Full Scale	79	75–82	7

Factor	Index	90% Confidence Interval	Percentile Rank
Verbal Comprehension	91	87–96	27
Perceptual Organization	72	68–80	3
Working Memory	88	83–94	21
Processing Speed	66	63–78	1

Subtest	Scaled Score	Percentile Rank	Subtest	Scaled Score	Percentile Rank
Vocabulary	8	25	Picture Completion	7	16
Similarities	9	37	Digit Symbol-Coding	2	0.5
Arithmetic	7	16	Block Design	5	5
Digit Span	8	25	Matrix Reasoning	4	2
Information	8	25	Picture Arrangement	5	5
Comprehension	14	91	Symbol Search	4	2
Letter-Number Sequencing	9	37	Object Assembly	5	5

Peabody Picture Vocabulary Test—Third Edition (PPVT-III)

	Standard Score	Percentile Rank
PPVT-III	82	13

Vineland Adaptive Behavior Scales (Expanded Form)

Domain	Standard Score (± 95% confidence)	Percentile Rank	Adaptive Level
Communication	84±10	14	Moderately low
Daily Living Skills	108±8	68	Adequate
Socialization	106±8	66	Adequate

(Continues)

TABLE 8.25   (Continued)

Vineland Adaptive Behavior Scales (Expanded Form)

Domain	Standard Score (± 95% confidence)	Percentile Rank	Adaptive Level
Motor (estimated)	61±12	0.5	Low (Mild Deficit)
Fine Motor (est.)	—	—	Moderately High
Gross Motor (est.)	—	—	Low
Adaptive Behavior Composite	69±5	2	Adequate

Bender-Gestalt Test of Visual-Motor Integration

Koppiz scoring errors	Developmental Age Equivalent
5	6.0 to 6.5 years

Throughout the entire testing, Walt approached tasks in an ordered, sequential manner. He experienced difficulties on tasks that required him to view stimuli as a whole rather than in parts. His strategy seemed to be a function of both his limited vision and his preferred mode of cognitive processing. On Picture Arrangement, Walt's restricted vision forced him to view each picture individually rather than scanning them as a whole. However, on tasks such as Block Design and Object Assembly, Walt was able to view the stimuli as a whole, but his solutions remained sequential in nature. Walt's performance on a novel nonverbal problem-solving task was further evidence for his difficulties with holistic tasks. On this task, which required him to complete a gridded pattern, he was challenged to see the "big picture" and scored at only the 2nd percentile. When presented with a Woodcock-Johnson-III task that involved reading sentences of symbolic figures, Walt again approached the task sequentially. He read figure by figure and was thus unable to make use of contextual clues. Woodcock-Johnson-III Concept Formation required Walt to view a series of geometric figures of varying sizes, shapes, and colors. The task involved determining rules that governed relationships among the figures. Walt tended to view each figure separately and evidenced difficulty in formulating global rules. Design reproduction on the Bender-Gestalt further evidenced an inability to maintain the gestalt and a reliance on sequential solutions.

Walt's performance further demonstrated a preference for concrete tasks and difficulties on items involving abstractions. Walt tended to do well on tasks that involved concrete solutions; this was noted on subtests requiring him to state how two words were alike, define vocabulary words, and answer questions about social rules or concepts, which all measure verbal conceptualization. A task measuring social awareness and judgment was Walt's highest score on the WAIS-III (91st percentile). He received maximum credit on all items on this Verbal subtest with the exception of two, which involved interpretation of abstract proverbs. On the Woodcock-Johnson-III Visual-Auditory Learning subtest, Walt generally was able to recall figures that were more concrete in nature. The figure representing "*and*" was an abstract grouping of three circles, and Walt was consistently unable to match the word to the symbol as he read. On tasks involving arithmetic from both the WAIS-III and the Woodcock-Johnson-III, Walt tended to subvocalize. He appeared to have difficulty visualizing solutions and relied on concrete manipulation of his fingers.

As noted previously, Walt was forced to switch to his right hand for writing tasks as a result of the accident. While generally slow and deliberate, Walt's writing and fine motor skills tend to be adequate. He did experience difficulties on tasks involving visual–motor integration, particularly when those items were timed. This timed visual–motor coordination deficit was most notable on a task requiring him to use a key to write symbols that are paired with numbers (less than 1st percentile), a test of psychomotor speed. His slow processing was also evident on another task requiring him to scan a series of symbols and mark with a pencil whether or not a target shape was present in the series (2nd percentile). Although not as much fine motor skill was necessary on this task, his slow speed of processing visual information seemed to impair his performance.

Evidence was noted of a degree of disorientation and of poor organizational skills. As noted previously, Walt was unable to easily recall the current month and the city that he was in. Walt has apparently developed strategies to assist in orientation. While trying to recall the month, Walt stated that he typically relied on his watch, but that the battery was dead and he had forgotten to replace it. Disorganization was noted on the overall order of his Bender-Gestalt performance.

Academically, Walt performed somewhat below the level to be expected when viewing his Verbal IQ as the best estimate of his potential. He did, however, achieve at a level commensurate with his scholastic aptitude in both reading and mathematics, as assessed by the relevant clusters on the Woodcock-Johnson-III Tests of Achievement. Indicated skill deficits in the areas of Word Attack (4.0 grade equivalent) and Letter-Word Identification (7.0 grade equivalent) may be a reflection of reading disabilities evidenced prior to his accident.

While Walt's physical limitations severely restrict his mobility, he appears to be functioning within an average range of adaptive behavior. He appears to possess adequate social skills and is generally able to care for personal needs independently.

SUMMARY AND RECOMMENDATIONS

Walt, a 21-year, 7-month-old Caucasian male of heavy build and below average height, was referred in an effort to obtain an evaluation of his current level of abilities and to make vocational recommendations. Walt earned a Full Scale IQ of 79 on the WAIS-III, placing him in the Borderline range of intellectual functioning. Similar performance was noted on the PPVT-III, as he scored 82 on this measure. A significant and striking discrepancy was noted on the WAIS-III between his Verbal IQ of 93 and the Performance IQ of 67. This discrepancy, significant at the .01 level and abnormal in its magnitude, appears to indicate that the Verbal IQ is a more representative reflection of Walt's intellectual abilities than are the three global scores or his Performance IQ. The WAIS-III Indexes reveal a similar pattern of performance with a significantly higher Verbal Comprehension Index than Perceptual Organization Index. The WAIS-III IQs obtained in this evaluation are nearly identical to the values obtained 2 years after his car accident. Hence, whatever improvement in Walt's visual perceptual functioning that one might expect to occur spontaneously was already completed 5 years ago. At this point, Walt's intellectual abilities, both verbal and nonverbal, are stable and not likely to change very much in the future.

Walt evidenced a preference for sequential problem solving rather than simultaneous problem solving and appeared to be more at ease on concrete tasks than on tasks involving abstractions. While Walt's vision is severely limited, he appears to have developed effective compensatory skills.

On this battery of tests, Walt demonstrated a relatively high level of verbal skill; his score was about Average for his age of 21. He evidenced good learning ability and persistence and flexibility in problem solving. He demonstrated good social skills and appeared to have a good self-concept. Walt presented himself as a very determined young man and expressed an interest in helping others. Deficits were noted in visual–motor skills and in his ability to function efficiently in timed situations. A degree of disorientation was also observed. Walt's academic achievement appears to be somewhat below the level to be expected from his evidenced Verbal IQ.

Walt's demonstrated skills and expressed desires would appear to be commensurate with jobs involving helping others. He is able to learn effectively when training procedures reflect step-by-step, organized instruction and patience. Problems involving transportation to and from work might be addressed by provision of an on-site residence. Therefore, possible job areas might include nursing homes, hospitals, residential treatment facilities, or facilities such as the Boys' Ranch. Vocational Rehabilitation services should be utilized in an effort to facilitate these recommendations.

Examiners and Report Writers:
Graduate students in Drs. Nadeen and Alan Kaufman's advanced assessment course at the University of Alabama: Buddy (James) Allen, Sandy Bennett, Jean Dalton, Susan Ervin, Bill Gilchrist, Debra Nix, Ella Shamblin, Margaret Webster, and Louise White.

Five-Month Follow-up Report: Walt

The results of Walt's evaluation were communicated to his mother and to Vocational Rehabilitation Services. Walt's file was activated by Vocational Rehabilitation, and he received a complete physical evaluation. Efforts were begun to locate appropriate employment. In the ensuing period Walt was hired as a night manager in a small convenience store. While he was able to handle most tasks individually, the complexity and need for rapid response proved to be too difficult.

Three months ago, Walt was hired in the housekeeping department of a local nursing home. His employers have proven to be patient and flexible. Walt needed time to orient himself to the physical plant, but his supervisor reports that Walt is currently performing well as a full-time employee. Walt says that he is comfortable with his duties and enjoys interacting with the residents.

Transportation continues to be problematic but Walt is currently able to ride with a fellow employee. Schedules have been rearranged by his employers to assist Walt in this area. While Walt is happy with his present position, he is anxious to move beyond his current duties. Possible alternative placements are currently being explored with his case worker at Vocational Rehabilitation Services.

SUMMARY

This chapter is the first of two on V–P IQ discrepancies and covers the following topics, all related to the neuropsychological interpretation of these verbal–nonverbal differences: (1) Wechsler-Bellevue, WAIS, WAIS-R, and WAIS-III V–P studies of neurological patients having damage confined to the left or right hemisphere; (2) WAIS-III studies of neurological patients with diffuse brain damage, focusing on the factor index profile; (3) relationship of the nature of brain damage (type, acuteness versus chronicity) to V–P discrepancy; (4) subtest patterns for patients with left or right lesions; (5) the interaction of gender and ethnicity with V–P discrepancies in brain damage; (6) the interaction of age and education with V–P discrepancies in brain damage.

The results of over 50 studies involving the testing of nearly 2,700 patients with unilateral brain damage on the W-B I, WAIS, and WAIS-R give basic support to the long-held contention that left-lesion patients have characteristic P > V profiles, while right-lesion patients show V > P discrepancies. However, the support is far more impressive for patients with right-hemisphere damage. Across all studies, the latter group averaged a 9-point Verbal IQ superiority compared to about a 3½-point Performance advantage for left-lesion patients. WAIS and WAIS-R studies were generally less impressive regarding the predicted V–P profiles than were the studies conducted with the W-B I. Most notably, left-lesion patients showed an average P > V difference of about 2 points on the WAIS and WAIS-R compared to a 7½-point discrepancy on the older battery. Because no data were available on the WAIS-III and lateralized lesions, we focused on the information available on diffuse brain injury and the WAIS-III. The most notable finding for recent (since 1988) studies of diffuse brain damage on the WAIS-R and WAIS-III was a V > P pattern. However, three studies of factor indexes on the WAIS-III produced even more provocative findings for patients with diffuse lesions as a result of traumatic brain injury, intact Perceptual Organization coupled with weak Processing Speed.

The degree to which predicted V–P discrepancies accompany left or right lesions depends on the type of lesion. Strokes tend to produce dramatic V–P differences in the predicted direction, especially for males. Patients with tumors in the right hemisphere display V > P profiles, but those with left-hemisphere tumors evidence no V–P difference. Patients with temporal lobe epilepsy show the predicted pattern for patients having lesions in the left as well as right hemisphere, although the mean discrepancies are modest in magnitude. Lateralized frontal lobe lesions, whether caused by missile wounds or tumors, have little impact on V–P discrepancies. Posterior lesions, especially in the right hemisphere, are more likely than frontal lesions to yield predictable profiles. Comparisons of the Wechsler test performance of patients with temporal lobe epilepsy have been made before surgery (when they have documented, lateralized lesions) and following surgery (after the lobe with the lesion has been removed). V–P differences were in the predicted directions for the left- and right-lesion samples of patients with epilepsy, but these differences were larger following the surgical removal of the temporal lobe.

Acuteness versus chronicity of lesions has long been considered a key variable in determin-

ing the magnitude of V–P discrepancies; however, the major study on which generalizations were based (i.e., acute patients have larger V–P differences in the predicted direction than do chronic patients) failed to match the patient groups on any variables. A compilation of research on this topic suggests that acute patients with right-hemisphere lesions display larger V > P profiles than chronic patients with right lesions. However, the acuteness–chronicity variable may not be meaningful for left-lesion patients.

Gender differences have been reported in some studies but not others. The predicted patterns of low Verbal IQ for left-lesion patients and low Performance IQ for right-lesion patients seem to be more characteristic of male than female patients. The cause of these apparent gender differences has been attributed by McGlone to greater cerebral asymmetry for males; Inglis and Lawson attribute the gender difference to the application by females of verbal strategies to solve nonverbal problems. Several analyses of WAIS and WAIS-R data argue for McGlone's cerebral asymmetry hypothesis while others argue for the Inglis/Lawson verbal mediation hypothesis.

One well-designed study found ethnic differences in whether males with brain damage display the predicted V–P patterns; Caucasian patients tended to evidence the predicted IQ relationships more so than African American patients. The latter finding requires cross-validation with a newer sample and with a diversity of ethnic groups.

Age as a variable in brain damage research has usually been approached by comparing lesions in children versus adults. In comparison to unilateral lesions in adults, lateralized lesions in children are less likely to produce equivocal results that show predictable V–P discrepancies. Although the possible reasons for this age-related difference are many, and disagreements abound among experts in the field, few investigations have systematically examined the relationship of chronological age to the V–P discrepancies observed for patients with lateralized lesions. In one well-matched study of patients with general brain damage and controls, when IQs were compared, the older controls showed a tendency to perform better than younger controls on all IQs; also, the discrepancy between IQs of younger and older groups was even more pronounced in the patient sample.

Educational attainment relates systematically to the size of a person's WAIS-III V–P IQ discrepancy. Those with less than a high school education, on the average, score 1–2 points higher on the Performance Scale; those with college degrees or higher score 2½ to 4½ points higher on the Verbal Scale. These relationships have important clinical implications for individual neuropsychological assessment, and provide valuable base-rate data for interpreting the results of V–P analyses in neuropsychological research studies. When the samples of patients with left hemisphere lesions are grouped by their mean education level, the mean P > V profile that is predicted for patients with left lesions is about 6–7 points for samples averaging 10 years of education or less, but is smaller (about 1–4 points) for those with 11 or more years of schooling. For patients with right-hemisphere lesions, the expected V > P profile is about 7 to 11 points for patient samples averaging 12 or less years of schooling, but is only about 3 points for samples that averaged 1 or 2 years of college. In fact, the latter sample (the most educated) is the only education group that tended *not* to show the characteristic pattern for either lesion group.

This chapter also discussed the clinical issues pertaining to individual neuropsychological assessment (as opposed to interpretation of research findings for groups of patients). When evaluating V–P differences for individuals instead of groups, extreme caution must be exercised. What are large differences between groups of patients may not even be statistically significant for a given individual. In addition, individual interpretation demands understanding of clinical phenomena associated with lateralized lesions. For example, patients with left lesions prototypically demonstrate a profound depression known as a *catastrophic reaction*, while patients with right lesions are more prone to euphoria or indifference. These opposite reactions are likely to affect the observed V–P discrepancy in different ways.

Other behavioral observations must also be considered when evaluating V–P differences. Fatigue, on the Wechsler-Bellevue or WAIS, for example, may have led to a depressed P-IQ because the six Verbal subtests are given first on those tests; the alternation of Verbal and Performance subtests on the WAIS-R and WAIS-III makes fatigue less of a problem for contemporary examiners' interpretation of V–P differences. Clinicians also need to understand sensory and attentional deficits associated with lesions in the left or right hemisphere to facilitate V–P analysis.

Verbal–Performance IQ Discrepancies: A Clinical Approach

This is the second of two chapters on V–P IQ discrepancies. Chapter 8 explored Verbal–Performance IQ discrepancies as related to brain damage. The patterns obtained by patients with left versus right lesions provided some insight into the greater sensitivity of the V–P IQ difference for patients with right damage (V > P of 9 points) compared to those with left damage (P > V of only 3½ points), and examined the relationship between patient variables and V–P discrepancy in adults with brain damage. This chapter focuses on Verbal–Performance discrepancies in various types of clinical profiles, such as learning disabilities, delinquency, bilingualism, autism, mental retardation, psychiatric disorders, alcoholism, multiple sclerosis, and dementia. The chapter will conclude with the presentation of clinical case reports that exemplify V–P discrepancies within a profile.

VARIABLES BELIEVED TO BE CORRELATES OF HIGH PERFORMANCE IQ

Individuals who obtain substantially higher Performance than Verbal IQs may do so because of strengths in fluid intelligence and visualization compared to weaknesses in crystallized intelligence and short-term memory (Horn, 1989; Horn & Cattell, 1967; Horn & Noll, 1997); strong Perceptual Organization skills in comparison with Verbal Comprehension abilities; a field-independent cognitive style (Goodenough & Karp, 1961); better developed simultaneous–holistic than analytic–sequential processing (Kaufman, 1994a); or for a number of other reasons.

Some adolescent and adult groups who characteristically obtain P > V profiles, or, more accurately, are generally believed to do so, are those who are learning disabled or illiterate, delinquent or psychopathic, bilingual, autistic, and mentally retarded. These topics are treated in the sections that follow.

Learning Disabilities

The diagnosis of learning disabilities is a complex process, but one that inevitably involves an IQ test and an achievement test. Although there has been recent controversy about the use of IQ tests in the diagnosis of learning disabilities (see Chapter 2), for the time being measures of intellectual ability play an integral role in diagnosis, and this featured role has been especially true for the Wechsler scales. Current diagnostic criteria for learning disabilities require "achievement, as measured by individually administered standardized tests…, that is substantially below that expected given the person's chronological age, measured intelligence, and age-appropriate education" (American Psychiatric Association, 1994, p. 50). There are two primary methods by which learning disabilities are determined: the simple difference method and the predicted difference method (Reynolds, 1984, 1990). The simple difference (subtracting the achievement score from the IQ) is used by many because it is straightforward and easily understood by parents as well as teachers. Most state education agencies have selected a discrepancy in the range of about 1½ standard deviations (18 to 22 standard score points) as a cut-off (Kamphaus, 1993). The problem with the simple discrepancy method is that it does not take into account the regression of achievement on intelligence (Reynolds, 1984, 1990). Thus, it can lead to overidentification of individuals with high IQs and underidentification of individuals with low IQs. The use of a regression model for identifying ability–achievement discrepancies, such as the one available in the WAIS-III manual for predicting WIAT scores based on WAIS-III IQs, evens out the probabilities that a child of any

intelligence level will be identified as having a severe discrepancy. Regardless, of the method used for determining learning disabilities, the IQ plays an important role in delineating the "ability" level at which a person is functioning. However, getting an IQ for use in an ability–achievement discrepancy is not as simple as it may seem.

As there are three separate IQs and four factor indexes yielded by the WAIS-III and WISC-III, it is not always a simple decision to choose one score to represent a person's ultimate ability level. In children and adults, for example, individuals with learning disablties often display P > V profiles on Wechsler instruments. Across many studies of adolescents and adults with various learning disabilities, a consistent pattern of a higher Performance IQ than Verbal IQ of about 7 to 19 points is present (e.g., Frauenheim & Heckerl, 1983; Sandoval, Sassenrath, & Penaloza, 1988). Some states have guidelines for deciding when the higher score can be used as the test of intelligence (Kamphaus, 1993). However, automatically using the highest available IQ to achieve a cutoff score for diagnosis does not encourage an in-depth understanding of the person being assessed. These issues of diagnosis are important to bear in mind when reviewing the literature on learning disabilities, as they affect subject selection and obviously affect individual children and adults in clinical practice. That being said, we turn our focus now to patterns within the Wechsler scales that are present for groups of individuals with learning disabilities.

The P > V pattern noted for individuals with learning disabilities is not that surprising because the Verbal tasks on Wechsler's scales are heavily achievement dependent. Several Verbal subtests tap information taken directly from school-learned knowledge. By definition, individuals with a learning disability are not good achievers. Thus, the P > V pattern in individuals with learning disabilities may be a reflection of their poor crystallized knowledge, and, more specifically, of their failure to learn in school. Looking beyond the V-IQ and P-IQ, the four factor indexes may provide the most useful information for understanding the cognitive abilities for most adolescents or adults with learning disabilities. These factors offer a purer measure of crystallized ability (Verbal Comprehension Index) than is available via the V-IQ, an amalgamation of verbal conceptual and memory tasks.

In samples of college students with learning disabilities, the P > V pattern has *not* been consistently found. College students more typically evidence the opposite pattern of V > P or have no V–P difference (Blalock, 1987; Gregg & Hoy, 1985; Kaufman, 1990; Morgan, Sullivan, Darden, & Gregg, 1997; Rogan & Hartman, 1976; Salvia, Gajar, Gajria, & Salvia, 1988; Sparks & Javorsky, 1999; Sparks, Philips, Ganschow, & Javorsky, 1999; Vogel, 1986). When college students with learning disabilities display V > P patterns, the discrepancies are typically small, about 4–5 points (Slate, Frost, & Cross, 1990, 1991).

The Verbal scale does measure achievement (crystallized abilities), and college students, even if learning disabled, have managed to achieve reasonably well. This achievement may be facilitated by compensatory strategies that have allowed the students to succeed educationally despite their disabilities. One study indicated that the attributes of self-awareness, proactivity, perseverance, emotional stability, goal setting, and the use of effective support systems are more predictive of the success of individuals with learning disabilities in adulthood than are either academic skills or IQ (Raskind, Goldberg, Higgins, & Herman, 1999). In another study of college students with learning disabilities, Cowles and Keim (1995) found that the longer students participated in special support services and the higher their IQs, the more likely they were to graduate from college (although it took the students with learning disabilities about a semester longer to graduate). Lefly and Pennington (1991) found that, in their sample of adult dyslexics, it was the *automaticity* with which dyslexics applied their reading skills, rather than their IQs or academic achievement, per se, that predicts whether

they are able to compensate for their learning difficulties.

Review of Research Findings on the P > V Profile

Because of the lack of consistency of a P > V profile in college students with learning disabilities, we focus here on individuals not in college. Learning-disabled adolescents (ages 13–18) tested on the relevant Wechsler scale displayed P > V profiles whether they were classified as delinquent (N = 25) or nondelinquent (N = 25); they outperformed the matched normal control group on the Performance Scale (Sobotowicz, Evans, & Laughlin, 1987). Similarly, McCue, Shelly, and Goldstein (1986) evaluated 75 male and 25 female learning-disabled adults (mean age = 24 years) referred for assessment by a state vocational rehabilitation agency and found a WAIS P-IQ superiority of 5 points (V-IQ = 87, P-IQ = 92).

Frauenheim and Heckerl (1983) tested 11 severely dyslexic adults on the WAIS-R at ages 25–30 (mean = 27) who had been previously diagnosed at age 10½. As children, they scored 21 points higher on the Performance Scale (WISC V-IQ = 84, P-IQ = 105); more than 15 years later, they earned almost identical mean scores on the WAIS-R (V-IQ = 85; P-IQ = 104) for a P > V discrepancy of 19 points as adults. Similarly, 30 learning adolescents with learning disabilities, ages 16–17, had a P > V profile on both the WAIS-R (V-IQ = 91; P-IQ = 102) and WISC-R (V-IQ = 90; P-IQ = 105), but these discrepancies of 11 and 15 points, respectively (Sandoval, Sassenrath, & Penaloza, 1988), may have been inflated to some extent by the fact that 60% of the sample was Hispanic.

Gold and Horn (1983) administered the WAIS to male inmates identified as illiterates. They divided their sample into low, medium, and high groups (mean FS-IQs of 70, 78, and 86, respectively), with sample sizes of about 13 per subsample. Each IQ group had P > V profiles ranging from 7 to 11 points. A small P > V discrepancy of only 3 points was found for 319 inmates identified as underachieving readers (Kender, Greenwood, & Conard, 1985), but this sample was neither illiterate nor learning-disabled.

Rack (1997) administered the WAIS-R to 14 adults with learning disabilities, ranging in age from 17 to 41 (mean age = 23.4 years). For his analyses, he calculated the Verbal Comprehension and Perceptual Organization factor scores. He found that 78% of his sample had a PO > VC pattern (average discrepancy = 9.7 points) and that 21% had a VC > PO pattern (average discrepancy = 2.7 points). He described his sample as "developmental phonological dyslexics," and noted that his results with the narrower factors seemed to follow what has been reported for the more global Verbal and Performance IQs.

The WAIS-III was administered to a sample of 24 adolescents diagnosed with a reading disability (Psychological Corporation, 1997). Looking just at the mean IQs (V-IQ of 96.7 and P-IQ of 102.1), the previously described P > V pattern is apparent, although the discrepancy of 5.4 points is smaller than P > V differences typically found for the WAIS-R. However, in examining the mean four factor indexes, different patterns emerged. A POI > VCI pattern was present, but the discrepancy (4.3 points) was even smaller than the P > V difference. But further examination revealed larger differences *within* each scale than between scales: VCI > WMI and POI > PSI, both by 6.6 points. Overall, 41.7% of the subjects with reading disabilities scored 15 or more points higher on the VCI than the WMI, in contrast to 13% of the standardization sample; and 30.4% earned higher POI than PSI scores by 15 or more points, about twice the 14% in the standardization sample.

Although the various studies have generally included small samples, the available data indeed suggest that adolescents and adults with learning disabilities—not in college—have a decided P > V profile. Deficiencies on the Verbal Scale are sensible because the WAIS-R, WAIS-III, WISC-R, and WISC-III Verbal tasks are heavily achievement oriented, and learning-disabled or illiterate adults are, by definition, poor achievers in read-

ing and related subject areas. However, more provocative than V–P discrepancies for future WAIS-III and WISC-III research with individuals diagnosed with reading or learning disabilities are the *within* scale discrepancies found by The Psychological Corporation (1997) when investigating the factor index profiles of their sample.

Clinical Implications of Research Findings

The implications of Wechsler research with children and adults diagnosed with learning disabilities are that the obtained IQs may be misleading. Low Verbal IQs are likely to reflect, at least to some extent, the poor school achievement of these individuals, along with impaired functioning in subtests associated with the Working Memory and Freedom from Distractibility factors. Whereas the Performance IQ is often the best estimate of LD children and adults' intellectual ability (except for those who attend or graduate from college despite their disability), this nonverbal estimate of intelligence is likely to be depressed by poor scores on the subtests that constitute the Processing Speed factor.

The best solution is to group the tasks in accordance with the WAIS-III's four factors (or three WAIS-R factors if examining WAIS-R data), or to apply Bannatyne's four groupings of subtests (Chapter 10): Spatial, Verbal Conceptualization, Sequential, and Acquired Knowledge. For many individuals with learning disabilities, the best evidence for intellectual potential will come from the Perceptual Organization index or Bannatyne's Spatial category. The Working Memory index or Sequential category reveals a possible attentional or processing deficit, and the Verbal Comprehension index or Acquired Knowledge grouping indicates a more specific achievement-related deficiency.

The ACID Profile in Individuals with Learning Disabilities

A large body of research, mainly with the WISC, WISC-R, or WISC-III, has explored subtest profiles of reading- and learning-disabled individuals and has identified reasonable consistency from study to study: Mean scores are highest for Bannatyne's Spatial category and lowest for his Sequential and Acquired Knowledge groupings (Gregg, Hoy, & Gay, 1996; Kaufman, 1979b; Kaufman, 1994a; Kaufman, Harrison, & Ittenbach, 1990; Rugel, 1974). Further, a pattern of low scaled scores on four of the subtests that define the Sequential and Acquired Knowledge categories has particularly shown resilience from one LD sample to another. This quartet makes up the ACID grouping because of the first initials of the four tasks, Arithmetic, Coding, Information, Digit Span. Even though Coding is called Digit Symbol-Coding on the WAIS-III, we will continue to refer to the profile as the ACID pattern inasmuch as that nickname has become entrenched in the literature and has been used by WAIS, WAIS-R, and WAIS-III researchers (Kaufman & Lichtenberger, 1999; Salvia et al., 1988; Vogel, 1986).

ACID and Bannatyne Patterns on the WAIS-R for Individuals with Learning Disabilities

Table 9.1 summarizes the results of six samples of adolescents and young adults tested on the WAIS-R, three samples are learning disabled, and three are included for comparison purposes. The table presents mean standard scores on the Bannatyne categories, the ACID profile, and the WAIS-R IQ scales. We computed the standard scores for the Bannatyne categories, entering the formulas presented in Kaufman (1990) with the relevant sum of scaled scores derived from group means. For the ACID profile, we derived a conversion formula using Tellegen and Briggs's (1967) simple method (ACID standard score = $1.6 X_{ss} + 36$) and substituted group means into the formula. Although these formulas are intended for use only with age-corrected scaled scores, we entered them with the regular scaled scores (the only ones provided) for the four samples having mean chronological ages within the

20- to 34-year age range encompassed by the WAIS-R reference group.

It would have been inappropriate to enter the formulas with the regular scaled scores for the LD sample of 16-year-olds (Sandoval, Sassenrath, & Penaloza, 1988) or for Salvia et al.'s (1988) 18.4-year-old control group of nonhandicapped college students. Scaled scores for these groups are simply not comparable to the regular scaled scores because of developmental factors as well as the questionable nature of the WAIS-R norms for adolescents. Consequently, we opted to estimate the age-corrected scaled scores for these two samples by using the mean values presented in the articles (mean subtest scores in the Sandoval article; mean Bannatyne and ACID clusters in the Salvia paper), along with scaled-score Tables 19 and 21 in the WAIS-R Manual (Wechsler, 1981). Although the precise standard scores for the ACID profile and Bannatyne clusters shown in Table 9.1 for the two adolescents samples are estimated values, we believe that they are fairly accurate and that the overall profiles depict each group's relative strengths and weaknesses.

As indicated in the table, Salvia et al.'s (1988) group of 74 college students with learning disabilities earned an ACID standard score of 101.6, about ½ standard deviation below their mean WAIS-R FS-IQ of 108.9. Also, the 11 dyslexic adults evaluated by Frauenhelm and Heckerl (1983) scored 76.3 on the ACID profile compared to their WAIS-R FS-IQ of 92 (a difference of more than 1 *SD*). Despite the small sample of adults with dyslexia, this result is given credence by previous test data: When tested on the WISC more than 15 years previously, they obtained virtually identical IQs and mean scaled scores on the Bannatyne groupings and ACID subtests.

Sandoval et al.'s sample of 30 16-year-olds with learning disabilities scored about ½ standard deviation lower on the ACID subtests than on the Full Scale. Like the data for the tiny sample of dyslexic adults, the results for the small group of 16-year-olds are given additional support by the appearance of a highly similar ACID profile on

TABLE 9.1   Mean Bannatyne, "ACID," and IQ scores of groups of learning-disabled adolescents and adults on the WAIS-R

	Learning-Disabled Samples			Comparison Samples		
				Prisoners[d]		
Category	*College Students*[a] *(N = 74)*	*Dyslexic Adults*[b] *(N = 11)*	*16 Year Olds*[c] *(N = 30)*	*Poor Readers (N = 319)*	*Adequate Readers (N = 246)*	*Normal College Students*[a] *(N = 74)*
Bannatyne						
Verbal Conceptualization	111.9	94.3	96.3	86.5	87.2	126.0
Spatial	105.3	111.4	108.3	91.9	92.1	117.0
Sequential	100.0	75.4	86.5	88.4	88.2	116.5
Acquired Knowledge	105.2	83.8	93.8	85.9	86.5	124.5
"ACID"	101.6	76.3	87.7	86.9	86.9	119.5
WAIS-R IQ						
Verbal	110.1	85	90.6	86.7	86.1	122.9
Performance	103.5	104	101.8	90.0	89.8	119.4
Full Scale	108.9	92	95.4	87.4	86.5	124.5

[a]Data from Salvia et al. (1988). Mean age = 22.2 years for LD college students and 18.4 years for the normal college students.
[b]Data from Frauenheim and Heckerl (1983). Mean age = 27 years.
[c]Data from Sandoval et al. (1988). Mean age = 16½ years.
[d]Data from Kender et al. (1985). Mean ages equal 31.5 years (poor readers) and 29.0 (adequate readers).
NOTE: Mean standard scores on Bannatyne categories were computed by entering the group mean sum of scaled scores on the WISC-R (the group was tested in counterbalanced order on both instruments). Further, comparable patterns were observed on the WAIS in McCue, Shelly, and Goldstein's (1986) investigation of 100 learning-disabled adults (mean age = 24.4); like the learning-disabled samples shown in Table 9.1, McCue et al.'s group performed relatively poorly on the ACID subtests (an estimated ½ SD below their Full Scale IQ of 88.6).

pertinent subtests into the appropriate formula. Mean ACID standard scores were computed in the same way using the formula: ACID = $1.6X_{ss}$ + 36. Mean age-corrected scaled scores were estimated from the regular scaled scores for Sandoval et al.'s (1988) 16-year-olds, and from the mean regular scaled scores on the Bannatyne and ACID groupings for Salvia et al.'s (1988) 18-year-old control group. For all other samples, the regular scaled scores were entered into the relevant formulas because their mean ages were within the 20- to 34-year range of the WAIS-R reference group.

The group with dyslexia (Frauenheim & Heckerl, 1983), the 16-year-old LD sample (Sandoval et al., 1988), and McCue et al.'s (1986) 100 adults with learning disabilities tested on the old WAIS each obtained highly similar Bannatyne patterns of Spatial > Verbal Conceptualization > Acquired Knowledge and Sequential. Such patterning accords well with much previous research on the WISC-R (Kaufman, Harrison, & Ittenbach, 1990). The poor performance by each of these groups on the ACID subtests actually reflects a merger of their consistent weaknesses in Sequential Ability and Acquired Knowledge. The Spatial superiority of Sandoval et al.'s adolescents with learning disabilities must be interpreted cautiously, however, because 40% of the sample was Hispanic, a group often characterized by P > V profiles on Wechsler's scales, especially when the samples are children and adolescents (Kaufman, 1994a; Valencia & Suzuki, 2001). (In contrast, Hispanic adults have not displayed a notable P > V profile on the WAIS-III; see Chapter 4.)

Despite the persistence of the Bannatyne and ACID patterns from childhood to adulthood for Frauenheim and Heckerl's (1983) group of adults with dyslexia and the occurrence of discrepancies of ½ to 1 SD between FS-IQ and ACID standard score, there is reason for caution: Spreen and Haaf (1986), in their investigation of LD subtypes of people followed up longitudinally, gave some evidence that, in individual cases, the ACID profile does not persist from childhood to adulthood.

Forty-six adults diagnosed with learning disabilities were administered the WAIS-III (Psychological Corporation, 1997). A proportion of this sample had depressed subtest scores on ACID subtests. Specifically, 24% exhibited a "partial ACID profile" and 6.5% exhibited a full ACID profile, both of which are proportions greater than seen in the normal population. However, the WAIS-III results obtained for the sample of adults with learning disabilities suggest that the discrepancies between indexes may be a more meaningful way to characterize their strengths and weaknesses. In the group with learning disabilities, the WMI was significantly lower than the VCI and the PSI was significantly lower than the POI for about 30 to 40% of the subjects. In light of these findings with indexes, a profile combining the WMI and PSI index may be useful in examining LD. A "SCALD" profile (Symbol Search, Coding, Arithmetic, Letter-Number-Sequencing, Digit Span) may be useful to investigate by clinicians and researchers working with adults with LD (Kaufman & Lichtenberger, 1999).

Exceptions among College Students with Learning Disabilities, Especially Females

Salvia et al.'s (1988) college students with learning disabilities performed relatively low on Ban-

natyne's Sequential grouping but—unlike samples of children with learning disabilities, or adults with learning disabilities who have not gone to college—their greatest strength was not the Spatial category. This college sample did best on WAIS-R Verbal Conceptualization, probably reflecting the fact that students with learning disabilities who attend college are the elite among LD samples and have achieved far more than others with a similar disability. Blalock's (1987) 91 adults with learning disabilities (36 either in college or college graduates) and Vogel's 31 female college students with learning disabilities also scored higher on Bannatyne's WAIS Verbal Conceptualization than Spatial category; a third sample of 57 college students with learning disabilities scored about equally well on both WAIS groupings (Cordoni, O'Donnell, Ramaniah, Kurtz, & Rosenshein, 1981). In addition, 211 applicants for a special college program for students with learning disabilities (161 given the WAIS, 50 given the WAIS-R) performed about equally well on the Verbal Conceptualization and Spatial categories, a finding that held for female as well as male applicants (Ackerman, McGrew, & Dykman, 1987). Both Cordoni et al.'s (1981) and Ackerman et al.'s (1987) samples performed extremely poorly on Bannatyne's Sequential and Acquired Knowledge categories and on the ACID profile; Blalock's (1987) group scored especially low on the Sequential category and ACID subtests; and Vogel's (1986) female sample with learning disabilities had decided weaknesses on Acquired Knowledge and the ACID profile.

With striking consistency in study after study of LD samples of adolescents and adults tested on the WISC, WISC-R, WAIS, or WAIS-R, the group means reflect substantial and occasionally striking decrements on the ACID profile and on Bannatyne's Sequential grouping. Deficits on Acquired Knowledge occur frequently but are less predictable, especially for college students with learning disabilities; again, better performance on verbal tasks, whether conceptual or achievement-oriented, is not overly surprising for individuals with learning disabilities who have managed to compensate for their disabilities sufficiently to aspire to higher education.

The one slightly maverick study is Vogel's (1986) sample of female college students with learning disabilities (mean age = 20), tested on the WAIS, who showed a marked weakness in Acquired Knowledge, a moderate weakness on the ACID profile, but only a small decrement on the Sequential category. Analysis of the separate subtests indicated that they obtained their three lowest mean scaled scores on Arithmetic, Information, and Digit Span (8.1–9.6), but earned their top scaled score in the fourth member of the ACID quartet: Digit Symbol (11.5). Females traditionally outperform males by a substantial amount on Coding and Digit Symbol (see Chapter 4), and Vogel's group composed of all female students with learning disabilities is a rarity; indeed, a huge majority of LD groups are predominantly male. Could the consistently low scores on Coding/Digit Symbol be partly a function of the maleness of most previous LD samples of children and adults and partly a function of their learning problems?

Fischer, Wenck, Schurr, and Ellen (1985) investigated this question for the WISC-R for 254 boys and 73 girls aged 9–14 years and found results that paralleled Vogel's. The boys earned mean scaled scores below 8.0 on the four ACID subtests while scoring about 9 or 10 on all other tasks except Vocabulary (mean = 8.3). The girls earned their three lowest scaled scores on Information, Arithmetic, and Digit Span (6.5–7.2), but did well on Digit Symbol (9.5). Comparing the Bannatyne profiles of LD and emotionally disturbed individuals, Fischer et al. found gender to be a more influential moderating variable than IQ or type of achievement discrepancy. Additionally, Vogel (1990), in a review of the literature for children, supported a clear gender difference on Coding for students with learning disabilities; this subtest was typically the second lowest for males with LD (Digit Span was lowest), but for females with learning disabilities, Coding "never fell into the lower third of the hierarchy" (p. 45).

Gender differences were not so apparent in Ackerman et al.'s (1987) investigation of 211 applicants to a special LD college program, of whom nearly one quarter were given the WAIS-R and the rest the WAIS. The authors tested about 150 males (38 on the WAIS-R) and 60 females (12 on the WAIS-R). They combined scores across instruments, despite observing the typical mean IQ difference of 5 to 6½ points in favor of the WAIS. Nonetheless, from their graph of WAIS/WAIS-R scaled scores for separate groups of male and female applicants with learning disabilities (Ackerman et al., 1987, Figure 1), it is evident that females did not do particularly well on Digit Symbol. The ACID profile was not quite as pronounced for females as for males, but Digit Symbol was only the seventh highest scaled score for females. Further studies, using only the WAIS-III, are needed to determine if the ACID profile, SCALD profile, or both, characterizes the patterns of both male and female individuals with learning disabilities.

Comparison of Learning-Disabled Samples to Other Samples

Table 9.1 presents data on three samples that might loosely be considered control populations. The most meaningful comparison group is the large sample of incarcerated adults who were grouped on the basis of their reading ability by Kender, Greenwood, and Conard (1985). These samples demonstrated a slight elevation in Spatial Ability but performed about equally well on the other three Bannatyne categories and on the ACID profile. Both samples earned FS-IQs that approximately equaled their ACID standard scores (means of 86–87). These results were in marked contrast to the difference of at least ½ standard deviation in favor of FS-IQ that characterized the profiles of several LD samples on the WAIS-R (see Table 9.1) and the WAIS (Cordoni et al., 1981; McCue et al., 1986).

The lack of deficiencies on Sequential and ACID groupings for the incarcerated adults suggests that these profiles may be more characteristic of LD samples than of behavior-disordered populations. In the WISC-R literature, differential diagnosis between these two exceptional groups has typically been unsuccessful (Clarizio & Bernard, 1981; Henry & Wittman, 1981); a review of many WISC-R studies reveals good performance on Spatial subtests and poor performance on Sequential and Acquired Knowledge subtests by both LD and emotionally disturbed samples (Fischer et al., 1985; Kaufman et al., in press, Tables 7 and 8). Kender et al.'s (1985) results with such large samples suggests that differential diagnosis may be possible with the WAIS-R, especially for students with learning disabilities who do not go to college. The group of poor ("underachieving") readers provides a particularly good comparison group for the LD samples because this group does not qualify as learning or reading-disabled. Whereas most reading- and learning-disabled samples of children and adults have been shown to perform relatively poorly on Bannatyne's Sequential category, Kender's sample of underachieving readers earned their highest two Verbal scaled scores on Digit Span and Arithmetic, and their Digit Symbol scaled score (though lower than other Performance subtests) surpassed their performance on all Verbal subtests.

Table 9.1 shows the WAIS-R profile of another comparison group, Salvia et al.'s (1988) nonhandicapped college students. Like most of the various samples of college students with learning disabilities discussed previously, this nonhandicapped sample scored highest on the Verbal Conceptualization category. However, their FS-IQ exceeded the ACID standard score by 5 points, not very different from the 7-point discrepancy observed for Salvia et al.'s college students with learning disabilities. The normal college students did perform about equally on the Spatial and Sequential groupings, though, in contrast to the Spatial > Sequential pattern observed consistently for all other samples of college students with learning disabilities tested on the WAIS or WAIS-R.

Salvia et al. (1988) compared the LD and normal college samples statistically and found that the normals performed significantly higher on three of the four Bannatyne categories (all but Verbal Conceptualization) and on the ACID subtests, while displaying less scatter on several scatter indexes. The scatter comparisons are legitimate, because scatter indexes have been shown to be independent of chronological age (McLean, Kaufman, & Reynolds, 1989). Unfortunately, the Bannatyne and ACID comparisons are meaningless because the control group was substantially younger than the students with learning disabilities (22.2 vs. 18.4 years). Contrasting the mean scaled scores (or their sums) is of little value because they are not comparable; the scaled scores for adolescents on the WAIS-R are especially questionable. Salvia et al. should have used age-corrected scaled scores for their Bannatyne and ACID analyses, and they should also have controlled for WAIS-R FS-IQ because the control group scored substantially higher than the students with learning disabilities (124.5 versus 108.9).

High Spatial versus Low Sequential

For virtually all adolescents or adults believed to be learning disabled, one might anticipate relatively good performance in Spatial Ability versus relatively poor performance in Sequential Ability. In Table 9.1 the college students with learning disabilities scored 5 points higher on Spatial than Sequential; the adults with dyslexia scored 36 points higher, and the 16-year-olds scored 22 points higher. The WAIS investigations produced similar findings: McCue et al.'s (1986) adults with learning disabilities scored 11 points higher on Spatial than Sequential; Blalock's (1987) adults with learning disabilities (40% with college experience) scored 7 points higher; and Cordoni et al.'s (1981) college students with learning disabilities scored 14 points higher. In the study that merged WAIS and WAIS-R data (Ackerman et al., 1987), males had a 15-point Spatial > Sequential differential, while the female applicants to a special LD college program had a 10-point discrepancy. Only Vogel's (1986) sample of female college students with learning disabilities showed a trivial difference in favor of Spatial Ability (2 points).

Among the comparison samples, the two groups of incarcerated adults scored 3½ to 4 points higher, while the normal college students earned virtually identical scores on the Spatial and Sequential categories. Cordoni et al.'s (1981) normal control group of 17 normal college students scored 1 point lower on Spatial Ability. Thus, high Spatial–low Sequential profiles are far more associated with adolescents and adults with learning disabilities (median discrepancy of 11 points for eight samples) than with pertinent comparison samples (median of 2 points for four samples).

High Spatial versus Low Acquired Knowledge

Vogel's (1986) sample of female college students with learning disabilities did show a more substantial 6-point difference when comparing Spatial Ability to Acquired Knowledge. Of the samples in Table 9.1, large discrepancies of about 15 or more points favoring Spatial Ability over Acquired Knowledge were observed for all LD samples except Salvia et al.'s (1987) college students, who performed equally on the two categories. Among samples tested on the WAIS or on both the WAIS and WAIS-R, Spatial > Acquired Knowledge differences of at least 10 points were found for McCue et al.'s (1986) adults with learning disabilities, Cordoni et al.'s (1981) college students with learning disabilities, Ackerman et al.'s (1987) males, and Ackerman et al.'s females. However, Blalock's (1987) adults with learning disabilities, many with college backgrounds, joined Salvia et al.'s college students with learning disabilities in demonstrating a trivial Spatial–Acquired Knowledge difference. Note, however, that Salvia et al.'s (1987) college control group evidenced an 8-point superiority in Acquired Knowledge over Spatial Ability; other comparison samples had small (3- to 6-point) differences in favor of Spatial Ability.

Overall, a deficiency in Acquired Knowledge is to be anticipated for adolescents and adults with learning disabilities, with the occasional exception of those in college. The median discrepancy in favor of Spatial Ability was 11 points for nine LD samples, compared to 4.5 points for four comparison groups.

The ACID Profile versus Bannatyne System or SCALD Profile

The ACID pattern represents a deficient area for adolescents and adults with learning disabilities, but the three LD samples shown in Table 9.1 scored even lower on the WAIS-R Sequential standard score than on the ACID score. On the WAIS, the same finding occurred for Blalock's (1987) adults with learning disabilities, whereas McCue et al.'s (1986), Cordoni et al.'s (1981), and Ackerman et al.'s (1987) LD samples earned closely similar means on the Sequential and ACID standard scores. Only Vogel's (1986) all-female sample of college students with learning disabilities scored lower on the ACID than Sequential score. (We computed standard scores for the WAIS studies as well, but preferred to report only WAIS-R data in Table 9.1. Using correlational data in the WAIS Manual for ages 25–34, we discovered that all formulas for the WAIS were identical to the ones for the WAIS-R.) We believe that the Bannatyne system is a better way to look for a "characteristic" Wechsler profile for adolescents and adults with learning disabilities. The ACID system does not seem to contribute anything over and above the Bannatyne groupings, so we suggest that it be dropped from consideration, except for research purposes. The Bannatyne approach permits systematic analysis of a person's strengths and weaknesses on the relevant categories, and is therefore preferable for the interpretation of individual profiles.

The SCALD profile, briefly mentioned above, is another that warrants consideration in investigating learning disabilities. This profile comprises the Working Memory and Processing Speed Indexes on the WAIS-III, and is analogous to the SCAD profile on the WISC-III (Kaufman, 1994a). In about 30 to 40% of the subjects with learning disabilities tested with the WAIS-III, the Working Memory and Processing Speed indexes were significantly lower than the Verbal Comprehension and Perceptual Organization indexes, respectively. The WISC-III SCAD profile has shown inconsistent validation in learning disabled samples. Prifitera and Dersh (1993) found a significantly higher proportion of individuals with learning disabilities having the SCAD profile than those in the WISC-III standardization sample, but others have not found it to be useful in distinguishing students with and without learning disabilities (Ward, Hatt, & Young, 1995; Watkins, Kush, & Glutting, 1997).

Perhaps the most useful method for evaluating the strengths and weaknesses of children, adolescents, and adults with learning disabilities will come from the four factor indexes yielded by the WAIS-III and WISC-III. The index profile will undoubtedly prove to be more useful than the V–P discrepancy (as is evident from several of the WAIS-III validity studies reported by The Psychological Corporation, 1997) and may prove more valuable than the Bannatyne system, or special combinations of subtests (ACID, SCAD, SCALD), pending the outcome of future investigations.

Implications for Examiners

When clinicians examine Bannatyne profiles on Wechsler scales for LD referrals, research suggests that they should anticipate strength in Spatial Ability contrasted with weakness in Sequential Ability and Acquired Knowledge. For college students, Verbal Conceptualization Ability may conceivably join Spatial Ability as an area of relative strength, and Acquired Knowledge may fail to emerge as a weakness. For females referred for learning disabilities, Sequential Ability may not emerge as a striking weakness because of good performance on Digit Symbol. In addition, there is some evidence that the Working Memory and Processing Speed indexes may

prove to be more depressed than the Perceptual Organization index in adolescents and adults with learning disabilities.

Although some of the profile patterns are reported fairly consistently for adolescents and adults with learning disabilities, these patterns are not powerful enough to make differential diagnosis. All of the previous discussions have been on group data, but clinical interpretation requires analysis of individual data, which are more unstable than group means. Thus, the profiles such as SCALD, Bannatyne's categories, or the four factor indexes may provide useful information about an individual's cognitive abilities on a case-by-case basis, but the profiles themselves cannot be used to justify making a diagnosis of learning disabilities. Similarly, a P > V profile cannot provide evidence of a learning disability in and of itself. A combination of many factors, such as performance on standardized measures of achievement, academic history, developmental history, medical history, family history, and behavioral observations, must be used to properly evaluate learning disabilities.

Delinquency and Psychopathic Behavior

Wechsler (1944) noted the P > V profile for delinquents, sociopaths, and psychopaths about a half century ago on the Wechsler-Bellevue. He considered this pattern to be a "sign" of psychopathic behavior, and a half generation later Wechsler (1958) stated, in regard to male adolescents and adults: "The most outstanding feature of the sociopath's test profile is his systematic high score on the Performance as compared to the Verbal part of the Scale. Occasional exceptions occur but these generally reflect some special ability or disability" (p. 176).

Validation of Wechsler's P > V Sign

Wechsler's general assertion about a P > V profile for male delinquents and psychopaths has generally been supported by group means on the Verbal and Performance scales of the Wechsler-Bellevue, WISC, WISC-R, WAIS, and WAIS-R (Andrew, 1974; Grace & Sweeney, 1986; Kaufman, 1979b, 1990, 1994a; Matarazzo, 1972).

For example, Matarazzo (1972, Table 14.1) summarizes mean IQs on several Wechsler scales for 29 samples from a variety of studies of adolescent and adult delinquents and psychopaths; the mean P > V profile ranged from 0.1 to 16.0 points for these numerous, variously defined, samples, with a median discrepancy of 6.0 points. However, Wechsler's strong statement about the power of the P > V sign for delinquents and psychopaths for individual cases is not supported by the moderate P > V discrepancies found in most studies of groups or in those investigations that explored the V–P patterns for specific individuals (Matarazzo, 1972).

Interactions with Age, Ethnicity, Wechsler Battery, and Reading Ability

The P > V sign seems to be more characteristic of adolescent delinquents aged 12½ to 15 years tested on the WAIS or WAIS-R (Andrew, 1974; Grace & Sweeney, 1986; Henning & Levy, 1967; Matarazzo, 1972, Table 14.1). There is inconsistent evidence that the pattern is more characteristic of whites than African Americans (Cornell & Wilson, 1992; Grace & Sweeney, 1986; Henning & Levy, 1967), and, when present, it may even be an artifact of other variables related to psychopathic behavior such as reading disabilities (Henning & Levy, 1967; Matarazzo, 1972; Nestor, 1992). Also, Groff and Hubble (1981) found larger P > V differences on the WISC-R for male delinquents with relatively high IQs (either V- or P-IQ > 89) than for those with low IQs (6.7 versus 2.6 points).

Regarding age and ethnicity, Henning and Levy (1967) found P > V profiles ranging from 3 to 10 points on the WISC (median = 5½) for 10 subsamples of Caucasian male delinquents aged 12 to 15 years, but found trivial V–P discrepancies of ±2 points for five subsamples of 16- to 17-year-old Caucasian male delinquents tested on

the WAIS (total sample = 1,250). For African American male delinquents (total sample = 1,111) in Henning and Levy's (1967) large-scale study, grouped into the same 15 age-samples, the WISC produced slight P > V profiles for 12- to 15-year olds (median difference = 2½ points) and the WAIS yielded small V > P discrepancies for each of five subsamples aged 16–17 years (median difference = 1 point).

Grace and Sweeney (1986), using the WISC-R and WAIS-R with 40 African Americans and 40 Caucasian male delinquents averaging about 16 years of age, also found age and ethnic differences regarding the P > V sign. They found larger P > V patterns for 14½-year-olds tested on the WISC-R than for 17-year-olds tested on the WAIS-R (11.1 versus 5.3 points), and they also identified greater P > V differences for Caucasians (9.0 points) than for African Americans (6.3 points) when data for both instruments were combined. Similarly, DeWolfe and Ryan (1984) administered the WAIS-R to 70 male felons or suspected felons (39 Caucasians and 31 African Americans, ranging from 16 to 73 years of age with a mean of 29 years) and found an ethnic difference that reached significance at the .10 level: 59% of the Caucasians, versus 39% of the African Americans, showed a P > V profile.

Grace (1986) reaffirmed the interaction with ethnicity, showing a more substantial P > V profile for Caucasian than African American 16-year-old male delinquents. But the results of his study raised the possibility of an instrument-related difference in the profiles rather than an age-related difference. Grace tested only 16-year-olds, assigning them randomly to be administered the WISC-R or WAIS-R. Caucasians given the WISC-R showed P > V of 13 points, but those given the WAIS-R had P > V of only 4 points. Similarly, African Americans displayed a P > V profile of 7 points on the WISC-R but had a V–P discrepancy of 0 points on the WAIS-R. As noted previously, Sandoval et al. (1988) also observed a more substantial P > V profile on the WISC-R (15 points) than on the WAIS-R (11 points) for their sample of adolescents with learning disabilities. Also, Hispanics have obtained larger P > V differences on Wechsler's children scales than on his adult scales (Kaufman, 1990; also, see Chapter 4), and 16-year-olds diagnosed as EMR had a larger P > V discrepancy on the WISC-R than on the WAIS (3.7 points; Nagle & Lazarus, 1979).

Cornell and Wilson (1992) assessed 44 Caucasian and 103 African American juvenile delinquents with either the WISC-R or WAIS-R (ages 12–17; mean = 15.2). Overall, their mean P-IQ (92.1) was significantly greater than their mean V-IQ (83.3), and approximately 35% of the juveniles had a P > V pattern that included at least a 12-point discrepancy. However, unlike previously cited research, when comparing the two ethnic groups, Cornell and Wilson found that there were no significant differences between Caucasians and African Americans in terms of the numbers of juveniles in each group that obtained a P > V pattern versus those who did not. They did, however, find that Caucasians, overall, scored significantly higher than African Americans on both the Verbal and Performance IQs. In addition, they found that more nonviolent offenders had P > V profiles than violent offenders (although this comparison was just short of being significant; $p = .053$). No difference was found between subjects who were administered the WISC-R versus the WAIS-R.

Adult prison inmates tested on the WAIS-R have evidenced relatively small P > V differences. Kender et al. (1985) found a difference of 3½ points for 565 incarcerated males and females ranging from 16 to 65 years (average age = 30). Although the P > V profile was almost identical for underachieving readers ($N = 319$) and adequate readers ($N = 246$) in Kender et al.'s investigation, Zinkus and Gottlieb (1979) did find a difference between adolescent males in the 13- to 18-year age range when this group was divided into those with adequate educational achievement and those with severe academic deficiencies: The former group had a slight (1-point) V > P profile, whereas the group with school learning problems had P > V by about 4 points. DeWolfe and Ryan (1984) also found a significant relationship between the P > V sign

and reading ability for their sample of adult male felons and suspected felons; among inmates with reading disabilities, 62% had P > V patterns compared to only 36% of inmates without reading disabilities.

As indicated previously, Gold and Horn (1983) found substantial mean WAIS IQ differences in favor of Performance IQ (7 to 11 points) for male illiterate prison inmates (82% African American) aged 16 to 51 with an average education level of 7.5. However, the P > V discrepancy might have been related to their psychopathic behavior, reading problem, low level of formal education, or some combination of these three variables. Indeed, the type of crime might have been a factor as well. DeWolfe and Ryan (1984) found the P > V pattern in 87% of the male inmates convicted of sex crimes compared to 33% of those incarcerated for murder or attempted murder.

Overview of Research Results with Delinquents and Psychopathic Behavior

The compilation of data during the past half century on delinquents and those demonstrating sociopathic behavior suggests that the P > V sign may be associated to some extent with the Wechsler profiles of younger adolescents tested on the WISC or WISC-R. The P > V pattern is occasionally found in older adolescent and adult populations of delinquents and psychopaths. For example, Lueger and Cadman (1982) found higher Performance IQs than Verbal IQs for 89 male delinquents aged 14–17 tested on the WISC, WISC-R, or WAIS. They discovered that 92% of the boys classified as recidivists (those who were convicted of a felony or lesser offense within 15 months after release from a residential treatment program) had higher Performance than Verbal IQ profiles, and they reported mean P > V profiles of 5½ to 9½ points for their groups of recidivists, nonrecidivists, and program-terminated delinquents.

In general, male delinquents who are recidivists seem to display significantly larger P > V mean differences on the WISC-R than delinquents with just one official adjudication (Bleker, 1983; Haynes & Bensch, 1981). There is also evidence that the WISC-R IQs of young delinquents were stable over a span of nearly 2½ years (coefficients of .86–.93); the group displayed P > V of 4.2 points on the first test and 7.6 points on the retest (Haynes & Howard, 1986).

In contrast to the typical WISC or WISC-R results, the P > V pattern on the WAIS and WAIS-R is not usually associated with delinquent or sociopathic behavior. When the mean profile does emerge for samples of older adolescents or adults, the likelihood is that the discrepancy is due to a confounding variable such as a reading disability or low level of education rather than to the delinquent behavior per se. It seems that Wechsler (1944, 1958) was incorrect to place so much faith in the P > V sign for delinquents and psychopaths, at least concerning his tests for older adolescents and adults.

It will be interesting to examine the WAIS-III and WISC-III factor index profiles obtained on future samples identified as delinquents or sociopaths to see if a characteristic profile emerges for these groups.

Bilingualism

An enormous number of investigations with bilingual children convincingly support the notion that Hispanics and American Indians obtain substantially higher Performance than Verbal IQs on the WPPSI, WISC, WISC-R, and WISC-III (Kaufman, 1979b, 1994a; McCullough, Walker, & Diessner, 1985; McShane & Cook, 1985; McShane & Plas, 1984a; Prifitera, Weiss, & Saklofske, 1998; Valencia & Suzuki, 2001). Data for adults are less available and less compelling.

Hispanic Children, Adolescents, and Adults

For children, Hispanics typically score about ½ to 1 SD IQ points higher on the Performance than Verbal scale (McShane & Cook, 1985; DiCerbo & Barona, 2000), although differences

are a bit smaller for the WISC-III standardization sample (5–6 points for P-IQ > V-IQ and POI > VCI) (Prifitera et al., 1998, Table 1.8; also see Chapter 4). Furthermore, nonverbal > verbal differences on the WISC-III are substantially larger for children of uneducated than educated parents, 8–9 versus 1–2 points (Prifitera et al., 1998).

McShane and Cook (1985) identified only a single WAIS study with Hispanics in their thorough review of transcultural intellectual assessment with the Wechsler scales (Murray, Waites, Veldman, & Heatly, 1973), and we have found one additional investigation (Whitworth & Gibbons, 1986). Murray et al. (1973) tested nearly 2,500 delinquent students aged 10–19, of whom 663 were Mexican American. The portion of these Mexican Americans below age 16 were given the WISC; they earned a mean V-IQ of 76, 12 points lower than their mean P-IQ of 87. On the WAIS, the Mexican American delinquents in the 16- to 19-year age range scored 8 points lower on the Verbal than Performance Scales (V-IQ = 83; P-IQ = 91). The smaller Hispanic discrepancy on the WAIS than WISC in the latter study is hard to interpret because the P > V pattern may have been related both to ethnicity and to the fact that the sample was composed of delinquents. Nonetheless, the Mexican Americans were the only group of 16- to 19-year-old delinquents who displayed the P > V pattern on the WAIS in Murray et al.'s (1973) sample; African Americans earned equal V- and P-IQs, and Caucasians had only a 2-point Performance IQ advantage.

Whitworth and Gibbons (1986) tested 25 Caucasian, 25 African American, and 25 Mexican American college students on the WAIS and WAIS-R using a combined administration technique (i.e., administration of one complete battery plus the additional items from the other battery). The Mexican Americans obtained a P > V discrepancy of nearly 7 points on the WAIS and 9 points on the WAIS-R. The Caucasians and African Americans each evidenced small (1 point) P > V profiles on the WAIS and 3½ point P > V discrepancies on the WAIS-R. Curiously, all three ethnic groups displayed about a 2-point increase in P > V when comparing the WAIS to the WAIS-R. As with adolescents identified as delinquents, however, generalization from college students is tenuous. Certainly, though, the results with the WAIS and WAIS-R reported by Murray et al. (1973) and Whitworth and Gibbons (1986) are consistent with the large body of data obtained for Hispanic children with the WISC, WISC-R, and WISC-III (McShane & Cook, 1985; Prifitera et al., 1998).

The best data for evaluating nonverbal > verbal profiles for Hispanic adults is provided for the WAIS-III by Manly et al. (2000) and Heaton et al. (in press) based on analyses of standardization data. Without a control for education or gender, but just an age control, the Hispanic sample (*N* = 163, ages 20–89) earned POI > VCI by about 5 points (Manly et al., 2000); comparable IQ data were not provided. When age, gender, and education were all controlled, the sample of Hispanic adults displayed a small P-IQ > V-IQ profile (3.3 points) and a trivial POI > VCI pattern (1.2 points) (Heaton et al., in press). The weak area for the Hispanic adults was on the WMI, not the VCI or V-IQ. The results of the WAIS-III analyses, briefly summarized here, are treated in depth in Chapter 4, which also presents data for other samples of Hispanic adults tested on the Binet-4, KAIT, and K-BIT.

Thus, WAIS-III P > V and POI > VCI profiles range from small to trivial, suggesting that the stereotypical high nonverbal–low verbal pattern for Hispanics—typically identified on Wechsler's children's scales, including the WISC-III (especially for the children of uneducated parents)—does not particularly apply to adults tested on the WAIS-III. Instead, data with the sample of normal Hispanic adults ages 20–89 suggests a relative weakness in the Working Memory subtests, coupled with a mean PSI of about 100.

American Indians

WAIS-III data are as yet unavailable for samples of American Indians, and adult data have been sparse, but for Wechsler's children's scales P > V discrepancies are sometimes monstrously large. Navajo children tend to score about 30 points (2 standard deviations!) higher on the WISC, WISC-R, or WISC-III Performance Scale; other tribes, such as Cree, Sioux, Tlingit, Ojibwa (Chippewa), Northern Cheyenne, Blackfeet, and Tohono O'odham—as well as groups identified just as "Native American" or "American Indian"—tend to have large P > V patterns, but the differences are usually in the ½ to 1½ *SD* range (Atkinson, 1995; Connelly, 1983; Kaufman & Kaufman, 1983b, Table 4.19; McCullough et al., 1985, Table 1; McShane & Berry, 1989; Salois, 1999; Shah, 1999; Tanner-Halverson, Burden, & Sabers, 1993). The differences of 2 standard deviations between the P- and V-IQs of Navajo children and adolescents have been found to hold for separate groups of learning-disabled, educationally disadvantaged, and nonhandicapped individuals (Teeter, Moore, & Petersen, 1982).

The results of a few WAIS studies with adolescents and adults have generally been similar (Crandall, 1969), although the differences in favor of Performance IQ for American Indians have not been as dramatic for the WAIS as was sometimes found for Wechsler's children's scales. McCullough et al. (1985) studied 75 adolescent American Indians from the Pacific Northwest (mostly Yakima), ages 12–19, attending a private junior and senior high school. Those administered the WISC-R (*N* = 42) scored 19 points higher on the Performance Scale (99 vs. 80); the 33 adolescents given the WAIS showed a 15-point difference (P-IQ = 106; V-IQ = 91).

Even Navajo 16- and 17-year-olds (*N* = 100) had a relatively moderate P > V difference of 10 points on the WAIS (Howell, Evans, & Donning, 1958), when compared to the 30-point differences typically identified for samples of Navajo children. The slightly smaller P > V pattern on the WAIS than WISC-R in McCullough et al.'s (1985) study, and the different magnitude of discrepancies for Navajo children versus adults, are consistent with WISC results reported by St. John, Krichev, and Bauman (1976) for 100 Cree and Ojibwa children and adolescents aged 7–15 years: The magnitude of P > V decreased with increasing age.

However, the evidence regarding the magnitude of V–P discrepancies for different age groups is not clear-cut (McShane & Plas, 1984a). Connelly (1983) detected the *opposite* pattern in his samples of Tlinget Indian children aged 6–10 versus Tlinget adolescents aged 11–16: The younger sample had P > V of 10.2 points, while the older sample had P > V of 17.5 points. An interesting finding in one of the few WAIS studies of American Indians is that the P > V profile may not reflect just diminished Verbal ability; Howell et al. (1958) found that his group of older adolescent Navajos had elevated scores on Block Design and Object Assembly compared to the normative sample.

In their review of American Indian studies, McShane and Plas (1984a) offered numerous potential explanations of the typical P > V pattern; these include physiological variables (e.g., otitis media and fetal alcohol syndrome), sociocultural factors (which emphasize nonverbal communication), and neurological considerations regarding lateralization of cerebral function. Brandt (1984) criticized many of the premises and conclusions of McShane and Plas (1984a); however, we agree wholeheartedly with McShane and Plas's (1984b) response to Brandt, and especially with their stress on treating their statements as hypotheses that need to be tested scientifically to help foster better understanding of the cognitive strengths and weaknesses of American Indians.

Autism

Autistic Disorder is a pervasive developmental disorder. The diagnostic criteria for Autistic Disorder as specified in the fourth edition of the *Diagnostic and Statistical Manual of Mental Disorders* (DSM-IV; American Psychiatric Association, 1994) include the following:

- qualitative impairment in social interaction (e.g., failure to make eye contact, failure to develop age-appropriate peer relationships, impaired expression of pleasure in others' happiness, lack of social reciprocity);

- qualitative impairment in communication (e.g., delay in the development of spoken language, marked impairment in ability to initiate or sustain conversation, repetitive use of language, lack of spontaneous make-believe play); and

- restricted repetitive and stereotyped patterns of behavior, interests, and activities (e.g., preoccupied with restricted patterns of interest, compulsive adherence to nonfunctional routines or rituals, stereotyped and repetitive motor mannerisms, persistent preoccupation with parts of objects).

The diagnostic criteria for Autistic Disorder also specify that there must be the delay or abnormal functioning before age three in either social interaction, language used in social communication, or symbolic or imaginative play. There are other disorders with features that are similar to Autistic Disorder that have not always been clearly distinguished in earlier research, for example, Asperger's Disorder or Pervasive Developmental Disorder-Not Otherwise Specified (PDD-NOS). It is important to be aware of these related conditions when evaluating the research on autism, as there is variability in the literature in terms of how well researchers have screened out other autism-related, yet different disorders from their samples of children and adults with Autistic Disorder.

The Wechsler profile of children and adults with autism has been characterized by higher Performance than Verbal IQ (P > V), with the highest score typically found on Block Design and the lowest on Comprehension (Lincoln, Courschesne, Kilman, Elmasian, & Allen, 1988; Rumsey, 1992; Yirmiya & Sigman, 1991). Lincoln et al. (1988) concluded that the P > V pattern is robust enough to be given particular consideration in the differential diagnosis of high-functioning individuals with autism (in combination with other supportive behavioral data and test results). Siegel and Minshew (1996) reviewed 16 samples reported in 15 studies that reported Wechsler IQ data from autism samples with a mean V-IQ or P-IQ > 70. The instruments used to assess IQ included the WISC, WISC-R, WAIS, and WAIS-R. In these studies, the P > V difference was found for 11 of the 16 samples, but the size of the discrepancy was highly variable, ranging from 1 to 29 points (e.g., Allen et al., 1991; Lincoln et al., 1988; Venter, Lord, & Schopler, 1992). One sample produced no V–P difference (Rumsey & Hamburger, 1990) and four others demonstrated the opposite (V > P) pattern, ranging from 4 to 9 points (e.g., Minshew, Goldstein, Muenz, & Payton, 1992). Thus, although the P > V profile has been accepted by many as characteristic of most individuals with autism, clearly it may lack sensitivity as it has not been found consistently across all research studies. Rumsey (1992) suggested that the P > V pattern may be small or nonexistent for samples of individuals with autism with IQs in the Average range.

Siegel, Minshew, and Goldstein (1996) investigated whether the P > V pattern would, in fact, hold up for samples of high-functioning children and adults who were rigorously diagnosed with autism. They collected WISC-R data from 45 children with autism, ranging from ages 6 to 16 ($M = 10.1$ years) and WAIS-R data from 36 adults with autism, ranging from ages 16 to 51 ($M = 26.5$ years). All subjects had FS-IQs or V-IQs of at least 70. Siegel et al. looked at the mean V-IQ and P-IQ results as well as the profiles of each individual subject. Overall, the children had a mean P > V discrepancy of only 0.4 points and the adults, on average, had a reverse pattern of V > P by 5.3 points. When they examined individual profiles, 40% of the children and 36% of the adults had a P > V pattern, whereas 58% of the children and 64% of the adults had a V > P pattern (2% of the children also had V = P). They found that a statistically significant WISC-R V–P discrepancy (12 or more points) was found in 20% of the children with P > V and 16% of the children with V > P. On the WAIS-R, a 10-point V–P difference is needed for significance, and

11% of the adults reached this magnitude of discrepancy for the P > V profiles, in contrast to 28% of the adults with the V > P profiles. Thus, in their sample of high-functioning children and adults with autism, Siegel et al. were unable to corroborate the P > V profile that has been put forth as typical for individuals with autism. When examining individual cases with significant V–P discrepancies, the differences appeared in both directions. However, the authors did find that, on average, both children and adults in their sample obtained their lowest scores on Comprehension and their highest on Block Design, consistent with previous research. Nonetheless, individual profiles showed a significant Block Design > Comprehension pattern in only 64% of the children and 44% of the adults.

Siegel et al. (1996) posit that the lack of consistency between their findings and some earlier reports of the P > V profile may be due to the general level of intellectual functioning of the groups. Other researchers, such as Rumsey and Hamburger (1990), who restricted the IQ range of their sample to include only those with V-IQs or P-IQs above 80, have also not found the P > V pattern for individuals with autism. They concluded that, in autism, V–P differences are associated with general intellectual ability and are, therefore, severity dependent. The relative lack of deficits in V-IQ in Siegel et al.'s sample is reflected in the absence of the P > V pattern, but these authors are careful to note that the Average V-IQ of their high-functioning sample does not indicate that their sample did not have significant language impairments. Rather, the V-IQ is not a sensitive measure of complex language abilities, which are often deficient in individuals with autsim.

In summary, the results of Siegel et al. (1996), along with the findings of numerous other studies of individuals with autism, indicate that this population can vary extensively with regard to V–P IQ discrepancy. The V–P patterns on the WISC-R and WAIS-R, and presumably the WISC-III and WAIS-III, have not been given adequate support as a valid tool in the differential diagnosis of Autistic Disorder (particularly for high-functioning individuals). The P > V pattern is not universally consistent in individuals of all ability levels with autism. These cautions about the use of IQ patterns in diagnosis notwithstanding, intellectual evaluations of individuals with Autistic Disorder are valuable, as they can aid in educational and vocational placement and planning. Thus, the WAIS-III and WISC-III should continue to be used as a component of a complete assessment battery for individuals with autism. Furthermore, it is still true that 11 of the 16 samples of individuals with autism reviewed by Siegel and Minshew (1996) displayed the P > V pattern, in some cases producing striking mean differences. Additionally, the high Block Design–low Comprehension profile remains prevalent across diverse samples of individuals diagnosed with Autistic Disorder.

Mental Retardation

Data from a standardized instrument measuring cognitive ability and a measure of adaptive functioning are typically used in making the diagnosis of mental retardation.[1] To be categorized as mentally retarded, a person must have an IQ of less than 70, in addition to having significantly impaired adaptive functioning (American Psychiatric Association, 1994). The American Association on Mental Retardation (AAMR) has a similar definition of mental retardation, emphasizing the necessity of *subaverage* intellectual functioning coexisting with limitations in adaptive skills (Luckason et al., 1992). According to Sara Sparrow (personal communication, March 26, 2001), "subaverage" refers to 2 standard deviations below the mean, with some leeway, meaning that the cutoff is usually an IQ of 70, but is sometimes 75.

The AAMR is more explicit than the American Psychiatric Association in its definition of problems with adaptive behavior skills, defining

them operationally as limitations in two or more of 10 areas (e.g., home living, social skills, health, and safety), and including the notion that "appropriate supports" affect the adaptive skill areas and—if provided over time—will improve the adaptive skill functioning of individuals with mental retardation (Luckason et al., 1992). In addition, whereas the American Psychiatric Association distinguishes between the level of severity of the mental retardation (e.g., mild retardation, corresponding to IQs in the 55–69 range, moderate IQs corresponding to the 40–54 range), the AAMR does not. Though the AAMR used to make such severity distinctions concerning both intellectual and adaptive functioning, it shifted its focus on distinctions based on the supports that are needed. Instead, they differentiate individuals with mental retardation based on the supports they need—ignoring considerable validity evidence of clear-cut theoretical and empirical differences between those diagnosed with "mild" mental retardation versus those diagnosed with more severe levels of retardation (MacMillan, Siperstein, & Gresham, 1996).

Consequently, definitions of mental retardation differ from governing body to governing body (American Psychiatric Association v. AAMR); they also vary from state to state. Not surprisingly, some of the studies in the literature that used populations of individuals with mental retardation did not adhere to the same criteria in their diagnoses. Some of the variability shown in the results of various studies with samples of children, adolescents, and adults diagnosed with mental retardation may be due to inconsistency across studies in their application of diagnostic criteria.

WAIS and WAIS-R IQ Profiles

The data available on the characteristic WAIS or WAIS-R profile of individuals who are mentally retarded do not yield a consistent V–P profile. Several studies support a P > V profile in developmentally disabled populations, but there are also those which support a V > P profile. Zim-

---

[1]Portions of this section on mental retardation are adapted from Chapter 15 of the first edition of this book (Kaufman, 1990, pp. 533–585), which was written by Patti L. Harrison.

merman and Woo-Sam (1973) summarized numerous correlational studies involving the WAIS and other tests. Included in the 14 tables in their Chapter 2 are 14 samples of adolescents and adults with mental retardation from 11 investigations for which they provide mean Verbal and Performance IQs. These samples included a total of 863 individuals—males and females and African Americans and Caucasians—whose mean chronological ages ranged from 16 to 47. Of the 14 samples, 10 had a P > V profile of 1 to 7 points, while four groups had V > P of 1 to 3 points. Overall, the weighted mean P > V discrepancy for the 14 samples equaled 2.7 points, suggesting a slight tendency for samples of adolescents and adults with mental retardation to score higher on the Performance than Verbal scale. However, three of the four samples showing the strongest P > V profiles (mean discrepancies of 7 points) had mean P-IQs of 84 to 86, suggesting that the definitions of retardation may be a bit lax in some investigations. For those appropriately diagnosed as mentally retarded, a P > V profile may be nonexistent.

Calvert and Crozier (1978) have offered some support for that supposition. They tested low-functioning adult males admitted for assessment in a hospital in England. This group included 22–23 males in each of five Full Scale IQ categories ranging from 40–49 to 80–89 (mean chronological age for each subsample was 23 to 28). Calvert and Crozier observed a P > V profile only for those individuals who scored above an IQ of 69, the cut-off typically used to denote retarded intellectual functioning. Of the 44 males with IQs in the 70–89 range, 59% earned higher P-IQs, 34% had higher V-IQs, and 7% scored equally on the two IQ scales; 68% of those with IQs clearly above the retarded level (80–89) earned P > V patterns.

In marked contrast, males with IQs below 70 tended to earn the opposite profile of higher Verbal IQs: 91% of those with mean IQs in the 40–49 range had higher Verbal IQs; for individuals with FS-IQs from 50–69, 57% had higher Verbal IQs,

30% had higher Performance IQs, and 13% had equal IQs. Thus, the P > V profile does not seem to be characteristic of adolescents and adults with mental retardation, and the opposite profile may well characterize individuals with IQs in the moderately or severely retarded range.

In more recent studies with subjects with mild mental retardation, small standard deviations in the IQs were found, which is typical for extreme populations, and a V > P pattern was reported (Mandes, Massimino, & Mantis, 1991; Rubin, Goldman, & Rosenfeld, 1990). The WAIS-R V > P difference in Mandes et al.'s (1991) sample of 34 individuals with mild mental retardation was 5.1 and the WAIS-R V > P difference for Rubin et al.'s (1990) sample of 43 individuals with mild mental retardation was 4.4. Atkinson (1992; Atkinson & Cyr, 1988) has reported that, in her investigations of mentally retarded populations, the factor structure of the WAIS-R was similar to that reported for the standardization sample and she also reported data that allows a clinician to examine pair-wise comparisons of subtests using data specific to this unique population.

WAIS-III IQ and Index Profiles

WAIS-III studies with individuals diagnosed as mentally retarded are presented in the WAIS-III Technical Manual (Psychological Corporation, 1997). Forty-six adults with mild mental retardation and 62 adults with moderate mental retardation were administered the WAIS-III. Individuals who were diagnosed with mild mental retardation earned a mean V-IQ of 60.1, a P-IQ of 64.0, and FS-IQ of 58.3, demonstrating a small P > V profile of about 4 points. Those diagnosed with moderate mental retardation earned a mean V-IQ of 54.7, a P-IQ of 55.3, and FS-IQ of 50.9, displaying approximately equal V and P IQs. The Psychological Corporation (1997) provided three of the four indexes for the two samples (excluding WMI), which yielded a small nonverbal superiority for both samples of retarded individuals: POI > VCI by 3.4 points for the "mild" sample and 2.1

points for the "moderate" group. Overall, the general impairment across the WAIS-III indexes and IQs was similar to that reported in earlier studies.

Clinical Implications of Findings on Individuals with Mental Retardation

Although revisions made from the WAIS-R to the WAIS-III improved the floor of the test to make it more appropriate for the assessment of adults with mental retardation, many mentally retarded samples still perform at the floor-level on the cognitively complex tasks of the WAIS-III. The WAIS-III's Verbal IQ scale and Verbal Comprehension index are both heavily loaded with questions that tap school-learned, crystal-lized abilities. Many schools place individuals with mental retardation in a "vocational-track" rather than an "academic-track" curriculum, which, in effect, makes the educational back-ground of individuals with mild mental retardation quite different from that of nondisabled individuals. Because of the discrepancies in educational experience of individuals with and with-out mental retardation, Verbal subtests may not provide the most helpful data in terms of under-standing cognitive processes to make appropriate recommendations. To better understand how a person with mental retardation can function adaptively in society, WAIS-III scores can be supplemented with a test that measures one's ability to apply crystallized knowledge to every-day situations, namely the Kaufman Functional Academic Skills Test (K-FAST; Kaufman & Kaufman, 1994a) for ages 15–85+ (see Chapter 15). A measure such as the Vineland Adaptive Behavior Scales (Sparrow, Balla, Cichetti, 1984a, 1984b) is necessary to provide additional infor-mation about other domains of adaptive func-tioning including communication, daily living skills, and socialization.

The most common use of intellectual assess-ment for adolescents with mental retardation in school is to determine the need for placement in special education classes. For adults and older adolescents with mental retardation, intelligence is assessed to determine eligibility for benefits, to determine competence or incompetence in han-dling themselves, to monitor functioning, and to assess employability or unemployability (Linde-mann & Matarazzo, 1984). Intelligence tests are useful as part of vocational planning for adoles-cents and adults with mental retardation (Capps, Levinson, & Hohenshil, 1985). Overall intellec-tual functioning is assessed to determine the level to which a person with mental retardation might progress in an occupation. Specific intellectual strengths and weaknesses are evaluated to deter-mine the potential to meet the various demands of a job (e.g., visual–spatial skills, verbal skills, memory). The research on IQ, specifically Wechsler IQ, has indicated that there is not one simple pattern of performance on IQ tests that is consistent across individuals with mental retarda-tion. Thus, without examination of an individ-ual's profile, assumptions about the functioning of an individual with mental retardation cannot be made on the basis of what is known from stud-ies using group data. In addition, although many think that adaptive behavior is equivalent to cog-nitive functioning (Coulter, 1980), this assump-tion is not true. Many professionals who work with adolescents and adults with mental retarda-tion often expect those with low intelligence to have low adaptive behavior and vice versa. Al-though adaptive behavior and cognitive function-ing are obviously related, the conceptualization and measurement of the two constructs differ in several respects (Meyers, Nihira, & Zetlin, 1979). Cognitive functioning is usually conceptualized as a thought process, while adaptive behavior em-phasizes everyday behavior. Tests of cognitive functioning are intended to measure optimal maximum performance, or potential, while adap-tive behavior scales measure typical performance. Intelligence is assumed to be stable, while adap-tive behavior is assumed to be modifiable. Thus, because of the differences between intelligence and adaptive behavior, the IQ profile of an indi-vidual should not be examined without the coin-ciding data from adaptive behavior measures. An

IQ profile is not sufficient to understand a person's vocational or educational needs.

Overview of Variables Believed to Be Correlates of High Performance IQ

A survey of research results of variables believed to be correlates of high P-IQ, covered in Chapter 8 as well as this chapter, provides little in the way of empirical validation. Patients with left-hemisphere lesions are anticipated to have P > V profile, but in most studies they do not. Patients with temporal lobe epilepsy in the left hemisphere, who undergo left lobectomies, display a decided postoperative P > V pattern on Wechsler's adult scales, including the WAIS-III, but within the neuropsychological literature, that is pretty much it. Across instruments and studies, based on more than 1,300 patients with left lesions, the P > V profile is only 3½ points. But that number is inflated by data obtained on old studies with the old Wechsler-Bellevue. Subtract those studies, and focus on the WAIS and WAIS-R investigations, and the P > V profile for $N = 967$ patients with left-hemisphere damage is an unimpressive 2 points.

The research reviews with adolescents and adults are no more compelling for several other variables long believed to be associated with high Performance IQ. Individuals with learning disabilities are defined more by their high and low areas of functioning when Wechsler subtests are regrouped by Bannatyne's system or by acronyms (e.g., ACID) than by V–P IQ discrepancy. Individuals with mental retardation do not show consistent P > V profiles, and neither do those with Autistic Disorder (especially if they are high functioning). Although Wechsler's children's scales, including the WISC-III, frequently yield substantial P > V patterns for Hispanic individuals, data from the WAIS-III reveal only small P > V IQ discrepancies, especially when Hispanics and other ethnic groups are matched on age, gender, and education; indeed, when these other

variables are controlled, the POI > VCI difference is only about 1 point. American Indians do display a substantial P > V profile for children and adults, but studies with adult samples are sparse, and nonexistent for the WAIS-III.

In general, none of the variables that are supposedly associated with high Performance IQ have been adequately validated for adult samples, and certainly not for the WAIS-III. The profile of four factor indexes holds the most hope for future research investigations, particularly because these indexes effectively subdivide both the Verbal and Performance scales into their major component abilities.

VARIABLES BELIEVED TO BE CORRELATES OF HIGH VERBAL IQ

In Chapter 8, right-hemisphere damage was shown, based on extensive data, to be associated with high Verbal IQ, relative to Performance IQ, a finding that also generally applied to patients with diffuse brain damage (including some samples tested on the WAIS-III). The following variables are also believed to be associated with V > P profiles for samples tested on Wechsler's adult scales: attendance at college, psychiatric disorders (e.g., schizophrenia, depression), alcohol abuse, motor coordination problems, Alzheimer's-type dementia, and having a Full Scale IQ of 110 or above.

The V > P profile for people who have attended, or graduated from, college was examined in Chapter 4 and again in Chapter 8 (see pages 115–116 and Table 8.21). The so-called characteristic profile only holds true for individuals who have completed one or more years of *graduate* school (V > P = 4.6 points), *not* one or more years of college. Those who have completed one year of college averaged about 1½ points *lower* on the Verbal scale, and those with 2, 3, or 4 years of college had a slight V > P pattern of 1.4–2.8

points. Among psychiatric patients, Loro and Woodward (1976) reported a 22-point Verbal superiority for those having 12+ years of formal schooling versus V–P discrepancies of 0–2 points for patients with less education (total sample = 214). However, whether that finding with the WAIS from a generation ago generalizes to other psychiatric samples tested in the present on the WAIS-III is unknown.

Several other variables believed to be associated with V > P profiles are discussed in the sections that follow.

Psychiatric Disorders

Depression, schizophrenia, bipolar disorder, and a variety of other psychiatric disorders are often believed to be associated with a V > P profile.

Depression and Bipolar Disorder

Depression often demonstrates itself in the cognitive profile with lower Performance than Verbal IQs (Gregory, 1987; Zimmerman & Woo-Sam, 1973). The reason for the higher Verbal IQ is generally believed to be due to impaired concentration, psychomotor retardation, anxiety, or low motivation. Indeed, some of the diagnostic signs of depression besides those of depressed mood include psychomotor retardation, fatigue, and diminished ability to concentrate or think (American Psychiatric Association, 1994). The size of the V–P pattern has not been consistent in the literature. This V > P pattern may be small, such as the 2.3-point difference on the WAIS for 21 patients with depression studied by Loro and Woodward (1976) or the 3.8-point difference on the WAIS-R for a sample of 62 adult patients with depression (Bornstein, Termeer, Longbrack, Heger, & North, 1989). However, it may average more than 15 points, as it did for Pernicano's (1986) sample of 12 male veterans hospitalized for depression who were administered the WAIS-R.

In a sample of unmedicated, medically healthy, middle-aged to elderly outpatients diagnosed with mild to moderate major depression, Boone et al. (1994) found a V > P pattern for three age groups from 46 to 85 years. Specifically, patients with depression ages 46–59 (N = 36), ages 60–69 (N = 23), and ages 70–85 (N = 14) were contrasted with patients who were not depressed in the same age range (Ns = 58, 54, and 41, respectively). All of the depressed samples showed a mean V > P pattern, with discrepancies of 3.3, 7.6, and 4.1 points, for the three respective age groups. The youngest two groups of controls (ages 46–59 and 60–69) also showed a V > P pattern, with discrepancies of 2.7 and 1.9 points, respectively. However, the 70 to 85-year-old controls showed the opposite pattern of P > V (3.3 points). Overall, the mean V > P difference for the depressed sample was 5 points and the corresponding difference for the controls was 0.5 points, which generally supports the association that is posited between depression and high Verbal IQ.

Inpatients and outpatients with bipolar disorder have also been shown to obtain a V > P pattern on the Wechsler tests (Hoff et al., 1990; Nair, Muller, Gutbrodt, Buffet, & Schwartz, 1979). A sample of 35 inpatients with bipolar disorder (46% male; mean age = 36.5 years; 29% not medicated, 71% on lithium or another medication) obtained a 5.8-point V > P profile (Hoff et al., 1990). Additionally, a sample of 21 outpatients with bipolar disorder (38% male, mean age = 50), all on lithium therapy, obtained an 11-point V > P profile (WAIS V-IQ = 97.7 and P-IQ = 86.9; Nair et al., 1979). The sample's worst performance was in Digit Symbol, although the most interesting finding was the significant negative correlation between Performance IQ and duration of lithium therapy (r = –.52). The lowest P-IQs were earned by patients with bipolar disorder who had been on lithium therapy for the longest time. Those on lithium for the longest time also tended to be characterized by mental slowness. This slowness, rather than diminished accuracy, may account for the depressed P-IQ (Judd, Hubbard, Janowsky, Huey, & Takashi, 1977). Nonetheless, evidence from animal behavior studies (Johnson & Barker, 1972) suggests that lithium's effects may emerge by "impairing central analysis of stimulus input whereby significance is attached to sensory information" (p. 666). Consistent with both proposed explanations are the significant negative correlations between length of lithium therapy and the success of patients with bipolar disorder on Picture Arrangement and Digit Symbol (Nair et al., 1979).

Because of the various hypotheses advanced for the relatively low P-IQs of patients with depression and bipolar disorder, for example, psychomotor retardation, fatigue, and mental slowness, the WAIS-III factor index profile on these samples of patients will be especially interesting to evaluate. Of particular interest will be the relationship of POI to PSI, and the relationship of each of these nonverbal scales to VCI.

Schizophrenia

Hoff et al. (1990) found a 9-point WAIS-R V > P profile in their 30 inpatients diagnosed with schizophrenia (70% male; mean age = 25). Eleven of Hoff et al.'s patients were off medication at the time of testing and 19 were on either neuroleptics, anticonvulsants, or lithium; however, the authors did not report the mean V–P differences for the patients on versus those off medication. The 17 outpatients with schizophrenia that were assessed on the WAIS-R by Morice and Delahunty (1996) showed a 7.4-point V > P profile, with the highest subtest score on Similarities and the lowest on Digit Symbol (sample was 59% male with a mean age of 32 years). Pernicano (1986) observed a 6½-point V > P profile on the WAIS-R for his sample of 15 patients hospitalized with schizophrenia. The 117 patients with schizophrenia assessed on the WAIS by Page and Steffy (1984) showed a similar 6-point V > P pattern, with the high Verbal profile observed for the 65 male (+7.3 points) and 52 female (+4.6 points) patients. Hawkins, Sullivan, and Choi (1997) found a 4.6-point WAIS-R V > P pattern in their sample of 17 patients with schizophrenia (59% male; mean age = 29.6). A smaller V > P pattern (2.8 points) was found by Goldman, Axelrod, Tandon,

and Berent (1993) in their sample of 40 hospitalized patients with schizophrenia (75% male, mean age 31). Loro and Woodward (1976) found a higher mean Verbal IQ for their sample of patients with well-defined schizophrenic disorders, but the discrepancy was only about 2 points.

In contrast to the studies above that reported V > P patterns for numerous schizophrenic samples, Gruzelier and Hammond (1976) found a substantial reduction in verbal ability on the WAIS compared to visual–spatial performance ability in a group of 19 chronic patients "diagnosed as unambiguously schizophrenic by the hospital psychiatrists" (p. 39). These authors interpreted the WAIS profile as supporting their hypothesized explanation of schizophrenia as being associated with left-hemisphere dysfunction, especially within the temporal–limbic system. Gruzelier and Hammond found further support for their hypothesis from the results of other measures administered to their sample of 19 patients with chronic schizophrenia, such as auditory temporal discrimination and skin conductance, and from previous research findings including WISC results for children at genetic risk for schizophrenia (Gruzelier & Mednick, 1976).

Although Gruzelier's hypothesis is interesting, and is supported by other researchers as well (Flor-Henry, 1976; Gur, 1978; Tucker, 1981), he seems to have overinterpreted the Wechsler data. Most other studies with samples diagnosed with schizophrenia have tended to show small V > P differences, not P > V profiles. Further, 21 patients with psychosis were significantly discriminated from 25 patients with borderline disorders on the WAIS V–P discrepancy, with the former group showing a more depressed Performance IQ (Hymowitz, Hunt, Carr, Hurt, & Spear, 1983). Finally, Gruzelier and Hammond (1976) did not report mean Verbal and Performance IQs for their sample, opting to present only age-corrected scaled scores for the separate subtests; the means for the 6 Verbal subtests (7.4) and 5 Performance subtests (7.9), estimated from a bar graph of the 11 scaled scores, were not strikingly different.

WAIS-III data have been reported for two samples of outpatients diagnosed with schizophrenia (Gold, Queern, Iannone, & Buchanan, 1999; Psychological Corporation, 1997). In a sample of 42 patients with schizophrenia (81% male; mean age = 38 years), a small 2.7-point V > P pattern was noted (Psychological Corporation, 1997), as was a small 3.7-point VCI > POI pattern. More noteworthy, however, was the overall index pattern, which indicated that both VCI and POI were the highest mean indexes earned by the sample of patients: VCI (93.3) > POI (89.6) > WMI (85.0) > PSI (83.4). Consequently, although the verbal > nonverbal discrepancy was small, the VCI > PSI difference was a substantial 10 points. Gold et al. (1999) administered the WAIS-III to a sample of 38 patients diagnosed with schizophrenia (71% male; mean age = 39.4 years). The authors only reported the WAIS-III Indexes, not the IQs. The pattern of performance on the Indexes was quite similar to the pattern reported by The Psychological Corporation (1997) cross-validating the findings: VCI (97.6) > POI (93.8) > WMI (89.7) > PSI (84.8). In addition to the very similar pattern of indexes, the VCI > POI discrepancy of 3.8 points and the VCI > PSI difference of almost 13 points resembled the discrepancies observed for The Psychological Corporation's (1997) sample. The index pattern is suggestive of relative impairment of performance of patients with schizophrenia on tasks requiring attention, processing speed, and working memory.

Generalized Psychiatric Samples

Apart from Gruzelier and Hammond's (1976) investigation, most Wechsler studies of previously defined psychiatric populations seem to produce V > P profiles. Todd, et al. (1977), identified a 4½ point V > P profile for their control group of psychiatric patients (N = 78, including 17 with depression and 15 with some form of psychosis). Page and Steffy (1984) likewise found high Verbal–low Performance patterns to characterize their sample of 429 adult inpatients with psychiatric disorders, which earned a mean V-IQ = 94.3 and a mean P-IQ = 88.9 (+5.4 discrepancy). The 6-point Verbal superiority for Page and Steffy's group of patients with schizophrenia was reported previously, but these investigators also observed a 7½-point V > P profile for 46 patients described as "neurotics," although they found a V–P difference of less than 1 point for 108 inpatients with personality disorders. In contrast to these V > P profiles, Hawkins, Sullivan, and Choi (1997) found a P = V profile for a mixed psychiatric group of 33 patients (18 with major depression or bipolar disorder, 8 with substance abuse problems, 4 with impulse control disorders, and three with assorted other disorders). The lack of a V > P pattern in Hawkins et al.'s mixed psychiatric group may be related to the diversity of diagnoses in the sample.

Generally, the results of the reviewed studies on depression, bipolar disorder, schizophrenia, and mixed psychiatric disorders support the finding of a V > P profile, although the results of the same basic WAIS-III factor index pattern for two groups of outpatients with schizophrenia (most notably VCI > PSI) is far more provocative than all of the previous studies with earlier editions of Wechsler's adult scales. The reasons for either the V > P or VCI > PSI profile have not been clearly defined, but some of the most compelling explanations include impaired concentration, psychomotor retardation, anxiety, or low motivation in these samples. The V > P or VCI > PSI profile is not evidence in and of itself of a psychiatric disorder, but it may be considered in treatment planning for these populations.

Alcohol Abuse

Alcohol abuse is characterized by a maladaptive pattern of alcohol use manifested by recurrent and significant adverse consequences related to the repeated use of alcohol (American Psychiatric Association, 1994). Cognitive impairments have also been shown in this population. For example, patients with intermediate-stage alcoholism have been shown to have a V > P profile on the Wechsler instruments. In reviewing the literature, Parsons (1996) notes that sober alcoholic patients are mildly to moderately impaired in "memory and learning, abstracting and problem solving, perceptual-spatial abilities, perceptual motor speed, and information processing speed" (p. 179). However, these same alcoholics usually have verbal abilities that are in the normal range. Barron and Russell (1992) showed that tasks of fluid ability are more impaired than overlearned tasks or tasks of crystallized ability in alcoholic patients. Therefore, on the WAIS-III, a V-IQ > P-IQ and VCI > POI pattern is predicted for alcoholic individuals.

The *WAIS-III/WMS-III Technical Manual* (Psychological Corporation, 1997) presented a study with 28 alcoholics who had recently undergone detoxification. The sample was nearly all male (96.4%) and predominantly Caucasian (89.3%), with a mean age of 53.3 years. Similarly to previous research, the sample's WAIS-III Verbal IQs were higher than the Performance IQs, with a 7.4-point V > P profile. Similarly, in the individual indexes, the average POI (102.0) was 7 points lower than the VCI (109.0), and the PSI (97.7) was 11.3 points lower than the VCI. WMI (104.6) was not as depressed as PSI, but was 4.4 points lower than VCI.

Motor Coordination Problems

Success on Wechsler's Performance Scale requires good nonverbal reasoning and concept formation, as well as the ability to demonstrate this nonverbal intelligence via well-coordinated motor behavior. The presumption is that individuals have adequate coordination to convey the level of their nonverbal thinking capacities, and P-IQ is intended to primarily reflect a person's nonverbal intelligence, not his or her ability to perform coordinated fine motor activities. When this assumption is violated during an administration of the WAIS-III (or WAIS or WAIS-R) because of a neurological disorder or a related reason, then noncognitive coordination difficulties "may serve to reduce the Performance IQ to an underestimate of nonverbal thinking" (Kaufman, 1979b, p. 36).

The Demands of the WAIS-III Performance Scale

The WAIS-III subtests vary in the demands placed on motor coordination. The least motor coordination is required for Matrix Reasoning and Picture Completion (two of the three Perceptual Organization Index subtests), indicating that the POI is not very dependent on motor coordination for success, not nearly to the degree as the P-IQ and PSI. Symbol Search requires paper-and-pencil coordination, although individuals with relatively poor coordination will often perform adequately on this subtest because only a slash through a box is required, and the slash can just barely nip the corner of the box for credit. The most pure fine-motor ability is required on Digit Symbol-Coding, like Symbol Search a component of the PSI. Picture Arrangement demands some motor coordination to move the pictures appropriately within the time limit, but, like Symbol Search, the scoring system is forgiving for uncoordinated adults: The pictures do not have to be spaced equally or arranged in a particularly straight line, and no bonus points are allotted for quick, perfect performance. Block Design and Object Assembly both place a premium on well-coordinated motor activity to arrange the blocks or puzzle pieces in their proper, precise alignment, and to earn bonus points for rapid solutions to the problems. WAIS-III Object Assembly probably places a greater premium on good motor coordination than does WAIS-III Block Design, because bonus points undoubtedly contribute more to an adolescent's or adult's scaled score on the former subtest than on the latter one. However, Object Assembly is a supplemental subtest and is not calculated in either the P-IQ or the POI.

The greater emphasis on speed for Object Assembly is probably related to the relative ease of solving the five puzzles within the generous time limits; because most people tend to solve nearly all puzzles correctly, the main discriminator between high and low scorers is the rapidity of the response. For Block Design, even well-coordinated individuals of average or below average intelligence fail several of the nine-block items within the relatively short time limits because of conceptual, not coordination, problems. Nonetheless, both Block Design and Object Assembly demand both nonverbal reasoning and coordination for successful performance. Digit Symbol-Coding is almost completely a psychomotor, clerical task because its cognitive component is small and the amount of actual conceptualization demanded of the person is limited. The new Digit-Symbol Incidental Learning procedures and Copy procedures help examiners determine whether cognitive demands (seen in Pairing and Free Recall) or speed of motor response (seen in Copy procedures) play a larger role in the overall Digit Symbol-Coding performance.

Other explanations may need to be considered for depressed Performance scores besides motor coordination. Fatigue is always a possibility, especially if the Verbal subtests showed the same declining trend and the person seemed to tire noticeably as the testing proceeded. Another potential explanation, at least for a person who earned a high Verbal IQ, is the application of verbal skills to Performance tasks. Such verbal compensation is most helpful on Picture Completion, because of verbal responding, and on Picture Arrangement and Matrix Reasoning, because of verbal mediation; verbalization of nonverbal strategies can sometimes be beneficial on Block Design and Object Assembly, but it is not very helpful on Digit Symbol-Coding. If behavioral observations suggest a notable motor problem, the person should probably be administered a thorough neuropsychological battery to assess his or her motor skills more fully.

Coordination Difficulties for Patients with Multiple Sclerosis

Studies have shown that adults with multiple sclerosis (MS) display the expected V > P profile, with Verbal IQ 5 to 12 points better (e.g., Heaton, Nelson, Thompson, Burks, & Franklin, 1985; Maurelli et al., 1992). The subtests that require the least amount of motor coordination are typically stronger for individuals with MS (e.g., Picture Completion), and the weakest performance is typically seen on the highly speeded subtests of Object Assembly and Digit Symbol.

Heaton et al. (1985) administered the WAIS and Halstead-Reitan Battery to 100 patients with MS. Of this sample, 57 patients had a relapsing–remitting disease course, and had been in remission for one month or longer when assessed, and 43 patients had a chronic–progressive form of MS, never experiencing significant remission. Both patient groups displayed the predicted V > P profile. As expected, however, the discrepancy was larger for the chronic–progressive sample (V-IQ = 110, P-IQ = 98, discrepancy = +12 points) than for the MS patients with remission (V-IQ = 111, P-IQ = 106, discrepancy = +5 points).

The subtest profile on the Performance Scale was not revealing for the relapsing–remitting patients, but for the chronic patients it conformed closely to the hypothesized pattern based on the supposed amount of motor coordination demanded by each WAIS-R Performance subtest: The chronic–progressive MS patients earned their highest mean Performance scaled score (10) on Picture Completion and their lowest (8½) on Object Assembly and Digit Symbol. The motor coordination difficulties of the MS patients were clearly documented by their performance on the Halstead-Reitan neuropsychological battery and by clinicians' ratings. Five of the neuropsychological subtests administered measure sensory–motor functioning without a clear-cut cognitive component. The total group of MS patients performed significantly more poorly than did 100 matched normal controls on all five sensory–motor tests, and the chronic–progressive MS patients scored significantly lower than the relapsing–remitting patients on three of the five tasks. Further, the clinicians' motor ratings classified 100% of the chronic patients as having motor impairment, compared to 77% of the patients in remission and 3% of the controls (Heaton et al., 1985).

Maurelli et al. (1992) administered the WAIS to a sample of 34 patients with MS who were in a clinically stable phase of the disease. Twenty-nine of the 34 patients had a relapsing–remitting course and 5 patients had a relapsing–progressive course. The sample was 32% male, with a mean age of 38.5 years, 9 years of education on average (range 5–18), and an average of 10 years since the onset of symptoms. The results showed that the mean V-IQ (94.9) was 5.1 points higher than the mean P-IQ (89.8), demonstrating the predicted V > P pattern. The highest mean scaled scores (10) were on Information and Similarities (both 10) and the lowest (6–7) were on Digit Symbol and Picture Arrangement. Maurelli et al. indicated that, in their sample, neither disease duration nor disability scores were related to cognitive functioning. Even patients with mild disability and who were in the early phases of the disease showed "disturbances in intelligence and memory functions" (p. 127).

With the addition of Matrix Reasoning to the WAIS-III, Picture Completion is no longer the only Performance subtest that does not require fine-motor skill. Add to the mix the fact that Object Assembly was bumped off the Performance scale, and it is likely that WAIS-III research on MS patients will produce V > P profiles smaller in magnitude than the ones found on the WAIS and WAIS-R. With the Processing Speed versus Perceptual Organization dichotomy within the Performance Scale, examiners are now able to separate out fine-motor skill and speed from perceptual organizational skill, which is quite useful in assessing those with motor difficulties, such as those who suffer from MS.

Performance Deficits in Huntington's Disease

Huntington's disease is associated with progressive motor deficits as well as symptoms of dementia and tends to be accompanied by V > P Wechsler profiles (Brandt et al., 1984; Butters, Sax, Montgomery, & Tarlow, 1978; Fedio, Cox, Neophytides, Canal-Frederick, & Chase, 1979; Josiassen, Curry, Roemer, DeBease, & Mancall, 1982; Randolph, Mohr, & Chase, 1993). Whereas the motor symptoms in this genetically transmitted disease involve "involuntary, spasmodic, often tortuous movements that ultimately become profoundly disabling" (Lezak, 1995, p. 231), the V > P profile emerges in the very early stages of the disease (Butters et al., 1978) and for patients suffering only minor movement disorders (Josiassen et al., 1982). In the Josiassen study, for example, the 13 Huntington's patients (mean age = 45.5 years, mean education = 12.7 years) scored 9.4 IQ points lower on the WAIS Performance than Verbal scale. Brandt et al.'s 13 patients with recent onset of chorea (abnormal movements) had V > P of 5.5 WAIS IQ points compared to a 9.4-point discrepancy for 44 patients with advanced chorea. The patients with advanced Huntington's disease showed significant decrements on the performance, but not the Verbal, subtests; nonetheless, intellectual differences between the recent and advanced patients were far more moderate in magnitude than differences in adaptive and social functioning (Brandt et al., 1984). Randolph et al.'s study of 36 patients with Huntington's disease showed a WAIS-R V > P pattern of 6.9 points.

In the studies by Butters et al. and Josiassen et al., the Huntington's patients earned their highest Performance scaled score on the nonmotoric Picture Completion subtest, while generally scoring low on visual–motor and timed tasks (including Arithmetic). Their deficiency on the Performance scale was matched by a clear-cut weakness on sequential subtests. Good performance on Picture Completion compared to the other nonverbal tasks may not only be related to the motor demands of Wechsler's subtests, however; Huntington's patients generally seem to have difficulty with tasks that lack familiarity and structure, are perceptually complex, or require a complex response (Aminoff, Marshall, Smith, & Wyke, 1975; Fedio et al., 1979; Lezak, 1995). Yet the motor component cannot be minimized. Brandt et al.'s (1984) advanced Huntington's patients and Randolph et al.'s (1993) Huntington's patients showed their greatest disabilities on the two subtests requiring the most motor coordination, Digit Symbol and Object Assembly.

Regardless of the patients' difficulties with non-verbal and sequential tasks, they clearly do best on skills that have been overlearned, like reading, writing, and Wechsler's Verbal Comprehension subtests (Lezak, 1995).

WAIS-III data on a small sample of 15 subjects with Huntington's Disease (33% male, mean age = 44.7 years) comes from the *WAIS-III/WMS-III Technical Manual* (Psychological Corporation, 1997). The group showed a striking 12.7-point V > P IQ profile. When examining the mean indexes, a similar pattern emerged (VCI > POI by 13.5 points), but the real story was the VCI > PSI discrepancy of 29.9 points (means of 98.4 and 69.3), demonstrating the degree to which the index profile shows enormous potential for neuropsychological assessment. The group earned similar means on the POI (84.0) and WMI (81.7). Thus, this sample showed relatively intact verbal abilities (although perhaps even lower than premorbid abilities), but severely affected visual–motor and processing speed skills, as well as deficits in visual–spatial ability, and either short-term memory or sequential processing skills.

Performance Deficits in Parkinson's Disease

The Psychological Corporation (1997) also reported WAIS-III data for a small sample of 10 patients with Parkinson's disease (mean age = 71.2, 80% male, 80% Caucasian), "a disease of involuntary movement characterized by resting tremors, reduced initiation of voluntary movements, shuffling gait, plastic rigidity, and impaired posture" (p. 152). Like MS, one would hypothesize V > P profiles for patients with Parkinson's disease, and, indeed, they had a 12.3-point discrepancy. Their index profile, though not as extreme as the MS sample concerning the PSI, was as follows: VCI (96.9) > WMI (89.6) > POI (84.7) > PSI (81.7). In addition to studying Huntington's patients (and patients with Alzheimer's disease), Randolph et al. (1993) obtained WAIS-R data on 59 patients with Parkinson's Disease (mean age 46), demonstrating a V > P IQ discrepancy of

14.9 points, similar to the value reported for the small WAIS-III sample of patients with Parkinson's disease.

Alzheimer's-Type Dementia

General intellectual deterioration is one of the hallmarks of individuals with Alzheimer's disease, but the cognitive deficiencies are complex. Memory impairment (both in learning new information and recalling old information) is part of the diagnostic criteria (American Psychiatric Association, 1994). Nonverbal measures appear to be affected to a greater extent than are verbal measures, commonly leading to a Wechsler profile of V > P.

The V > P Profile

Fuld (1984) was able to obtain valid WAIS data for 46 Alzheimer's patients; based on IQs prorated from four Verbal and three Performance subtests, she observed V > P profiles of 15 or more points in 24 (52%) of these patients. Intriguingly, Fuld also obtained dramatic V > P findings for 20 normal graduate and undergraduate students who were given drugs to induce experimentally the impaired cholinergic neurotransmitter functioning believed to characterize Alzheimer's patients. All 20 subjects demonstrated V > P patterns, with 15 (75%) showing differences of at least 15 points. To ensure that the V > P profile did not merely reflect the high educational attainment of the sample, Fuld administered placebos to a control group of 22 medical and undergraduate students. This group also tended to have higher Verbal IQs (16 individuals, or 73%, had V > P), but only 18% of the control subjects had a Verbal superiority by 15 or more points.

Brinkman and Braun (1984) also identified a WAIS V > P pattern in their sample of 23 adults suspected of Alzheimer's-type dementia. This group scored 7 points higher on the Verbal Scale (IQs of 97 and 90). However, it is unclear whether the V > P pattern that seems to be associated with Alzheimer's disease is useful in differentiating Alzheimer's patients from those with other types of dementia. In Brinkman and Braun's investigation, the 39 patients with multi-infarct dementia clearly did not evidence a substantial V > P pattern (V-IQ = 95, P-IQ = 94). However, Fuld (1984) found that 7 of her 11 multi-infarct dementia patients (64%) showed a V > P profile of 15+ points, very similar to the value of 52% obtained for the patients with Alzheimer's-type dementia.

Randolph et al. (1993) examined the WAIS-R scores of 53 patients with Alzheimer's disease (mean age 66), in addition to the samples of patients with Huntington's disease and Parkinson's disease, discussed previously. The patients with Alzheimer's disease and Huntington's disease were not significantly different in their global IQs, but the Parkinson's group IQ means were significantly higher than both the Alzheimer's and Huntington's groups. Randolph et al.'s results showed that all three groups had a V > P pattern; Alzheimer's patients had a mean V–P discrepancy of 8.2 points, a bit larger than the discrepancy for Huntington's patients, but considerably smaller than the V > P profile for Parkinson's patients. Overall, all three samples of patients with dementia were characterized by preservation of verbal knowledge and relative impairment on the Performance subtests, and, generally, the subtest profiles were remarkably similar.

Like the similarities found between dementing diseases such as Alzheimer's, Huntington's, and Parkinson's (Randolph et al., 1993), there are also many similarities between Alzheimer's-type dementia and multi-infarct dementia. In the early stages of both of these disorders, there are cognitive deficits, but some of the cognitive differences include greater impairment in abstract thinking and judgment for patients with Alzheimer's disease. In addition, overall memory is more preserved in multi-infarct dementia. Erker, Searight, and Peterson (1995) administered the WAIS-R to 62 patients diagnosed with Alzheimer's disease (mean age = 73.2 years, mean education = 9.9) and 20 patients with multi-infarct dementia (mean age = 74.5 years, mean education = 10.8). When Verbal and Performance IQs were examined for the two groups, no significant differences

were found. Both groups evidenced a V > P pattern, although the V–P discrepancy was twice as large for the multi-infarct dementia group (11 vs. 5.2 points). The groups had similar P-IQs, but the group with multi-infarct dementia had a higher V-IQ by 7 points. Despite the relatively similar V > P patterns, the multi-infarct dementia patients demonstrated better preserved memory in comparison to WAIS-R scores, relative to Alzheimer's patients. Erker et al.'s data on multi-infarct dementia patients produced results inconsistent with Brinkman and Braun's (1984) investigation, in which the 39 patients with multi-infarct dementia had essentially a V = P pattern.

McCurry, Fitz, and Teri (1994) administered the WAIS-R to 216 patients with probable Alzheimer's disease. All patients were aged 75 or older (mean = 79.9 years) with 51% having some formal education beyond high school. The sample was 62% female. McCurry et al. compared WAIS-R IQs based on four different sets of norms: (1) WAIS-R manual's norms for ages 70–74; (2) Ryan, Paolo, and Brungardt's (1990) norms for ages 75–79 and 80 or above; (3) Mayo's Older Americans Normative Studies (MOANS; Ivnik et al., 1992); and (4) Malec et al.'s (1992) age- and education-corrected MOANS norms. Despite notable differences between the four sets of norms, in all instances a V > P pattern was found for this elderly Alzheimer's sample, with differences ranging from 6.3 to 9.5 points.

WAIS-R IQs were reported in a sample of 32 patients with Alzheimer's disease (41% male, mean age = 71.6, mean education = 12.6) (Schopp, Callahan, Johnstone, & Schwake, 1998). The group as a whole had a 3.5-point V > P profile, although the discrepancy was larger for the portion of the sample ages 75 and above than for the younger part of the sample. Paque and Warrington (1995) administered a shortened version of the WAIS-R to 57 people with probable Alzheimer's disease on two occasions (about 10 months apart). A subset of 13 people was administered the WAIS-R on three occasions, separated by at least 10 months. The mean age at first assessment for the entire sample was 60.5 years (range 39–82). In both testings of the complete

Alzheimer's sample, a V > P profile was obtained—4.5 points the first time and 3 points the second time. The subset of 13 individuals with Alzheimer's disease who were tested on three occasions also produced consistent V > P patterns (first an 8-point discrepancy, then 6.3 points, and finally 4.6 points). The reduction in the V > P discrepancy for both the complete sample and the subset is undoubtedly partially a function of the differential practice effect for P-IQ versus V-IQ; nonetheless it is still noteworthy that the 13 Alzheimer's patients evidenced declines in *both* their V-IQs (15 points) and P-IQs from the first to third testing due to the degenerative nature of Alzheimer's disease.

The Psychological Corporation (1997) presented WAIS-III IQs and indexes for 35 individuals with probable mild Alzheimer's disease (mean age = 72.2 years, 88.6% Caucasian, 57.1% male). The group demonstrated the anticipated V > P profile of 10.5 points, but, once again, the index pattern provided more information about the skill areas of the group: VCI (93.0) > WMI (87.2) > POI (84.8) > PSI (79.6).

Overall, studies with the WAIS, WAIS-R, and WAIS-III support a consistent V > P profile, but this cognitive pattern is not good at differentially diagnosing Alzheimer-type dementia from other types of dementia (Nixon, 1996).

The Fuld Profile for Alzheimer's-Type Dementia

The Fuld profile (Fuld, 1983, 1984) has generated a growing amount of interest with a WAIS/WAIS-R profile that she believes to be characteristic of adults with Alzheimer's-type dementia. Most of the research has been quite positive, particularly in discriminating Alzheimer's patients from patients with other types of dementia.

The Fuld Profile

Fuld derived her WAIS profile from an earlier study (Drachman & Leavitt, 1974) and initially reported that an estimated 50% of Alzheimer's patients, compared to less than 1% of normal elderly adults, displayed the characteristic profile (Fuld,

1983). She and other investigators subsequently conducted careful research studies to systematically confirm or deny these clinical estimates.

The profile makes use of only seven WAIS-R subtests (actually, Fuld and most other researchers have used the WAIS), eliminating the four tasks "which are most likely to reflect cultural bias or difficulties in visual acuity" (Fuld, 1984, p. 382): Arithmetic, Comprehension, Picture Completion, and Picture Arrangement. The seven tasks are grouped as follows:

A = [Information + Vocabulary] divided by 2
B = [Similarities + Digit Span] divided by 2
C = [Digit Symbol + Block Design] divided by 2
D = Object Assembly

The Fuld profile, which is computed using age-corrected scaled scores on the previous editions of Wechsler's adult scales, is shown below.

$$A > B > C \leq D \text{ and } A > D$$

or

$$\frac{(I + V)}{2} > \frac{(S + DSp)}{2} > \frac{(DSy + BD)}{2} \leq (OA) \text{ and } \frac{(I + V)}{2} > (OA)$$

The profile has a neuropharmacological basis rather than a neuroanatomic basis and is related to neurotransmitter changes noted in Alzheimer's disease; Fuld (1984) noted that "a dramatic deficiency of the cholinergic system is the most severe neurochemical change known to occur in [Alzheimer's disease]" (p. 381). Fuld's WAIS-R profile is believed to show the patterning of abilities that results from cholinergic dysfunction. In a systematic investigation of the profile, Fuld (1984) studied normal college students, about half of whom had a chemically induced cholinergic deficiency that mimicked the chemically related dysfunction of Alzheimer's patients. Of the 19 drug subjects, 53% displayed the characteristic Fuld profile; in contrast, only 18% of the 22 college students receiving an injection of a placebo drug evidenced the profile. The difference was statistically significant.

Fuld (1984) investigated the WAIS profiles of a variety of dementia patients as well, studying only those who could be assessed validly on the seven WAIS tasks of interest. Of 138 eligible patients, only 77 usable protocols were obtained: 33 with a research diagnosis of Alzheimer's disease, 11 with probable Alzheimer's, 6 with a combination of Alzheimer's and multi-infarct dementia, 12 with multi-infarct dementia, and 15 with other types of dementia.

For data analysis, the 33 "pure" Alzheimer's patients were contrasted with the 12 multi-infarct dementia patients; 45% of the Alzheimer's patients displayed the Fuld profile compared to 8% of the multi-infarct dementia patients, a significant discrepancy. In fact, the percentage of Alzheimer's patients evidencing the profiles is about the same (44%) when the definition is expanded to include all 50 patients who manifested Alzheimer's disease to some extent (diagnosed Alzheimer's, probable Alzheimer's, and a combination of Alzheimer's and multi-infarct dementia). This percentage is significantly greater than the 4% found in the 27 patients with multi-infarct dementia or other dementias. Data from Fuld's (1984) study are presented in Table 9.2, along with data from the several attempts at cross-validation of the Fuld profile.

Fuld's (1984) initial research showed strong validity of her profile, demonstrating significant and substantial differences between college students with and without a drug-induced cholinergic dysfunction, and between multi-infarct dementia patients and those with other types of dementia. The data from cross-validation studies are not as strong as those reported in Fuld's initial study, as only one out of four patients with Alzheimer's disease displays the profile. Furthermore, as shown in Table 9.2, as many as 13% of patients with other types of dementia display the Fuld profile, along with 7% of normal elderly individuals. These values do not support the continued use of the Fuld profile.

In addition, there are other problems with the profile. Despite some favorable empirical findings (e.g., Alexander, Prohovnik, Stern, & Mayeux 1994; Brinkman & Braun, 1984), several studies have reported frankly negative results: (1) in one study of 44 Alzheimer's patients and 43 patients with depression, 7% of each group evidenced the Fuld profile (Logsdon, Teri, Williams, Vitiello, & Prinz, 1989); (2) in a second study, 16.7% of nondementia patients displayed the Fuld profile, not significantly different from the 21.9% for Alzheimer's patients (Filley, Kobayashi, & Heaton, 1987); (3) Gfeller and Rankin (1991) found the Fuld profile in 12% of the protocols of patients with multi-infarct dementia, not significantly different from the 15% identified for Alzheimer's patients; (4) Randolph et al. (1993) found that the Fuld profile in 19% of Huntington's Disease patients was identical to the percent found for patients with Alzheimer's disease; and (5) Ryan, Paolo, Oehlert, and Coker (1991) concluded from their analysis of data for 225 normal elderly individuals that, for persons with 12 or more years of education who were age 85 or older, the Fuld profile "lacks diagnostic significance" because it is "relatively common" (p. 451).

The problems with the Fuld formulas, especially for application with the WAIS-III are:

- ¾ of the patients with Alzheimer's disease do *not* display the Fuld profile, so its failure to emerge does not rule out Alzheimer's disease as a plausible diagnosis;

- all data have been obtained with the old WAIS or WAIS-R, so its generalization to the WAIS-III remains speculative;

- the formula places too much emphasis on Object Assembly, the least reliable (.68) and stable (.70) WAIS-R subtest and also the least reliable (.70) and least stable (.68) WAIS-III subtest, and a task with *inadequate subtest specificity* on both the WAIS-R and WAIS-III;

- WAIS-III Object Assembly is excluded from the Performance scale, Full scale, and POI, and is not even supposed to be administered to ages 75 and above;

- the profile will conceivably emerge for patients without Alzheimer's disease (e.g., those with Parkinson's disease) who are on anticholinergic

TABLE 9.2 Frequency of occurrence of the Fuld Profile for groups having Alzheimer-type dementia and for control populations

Percentage of Various Samples Evidencing the Fuld Profile

Study	Alzheimer-type dementia	Multi-infarct dementia	Other dementias	Head Injury	Nondementia Patients	Depressed	Normal Elderly[b]
Fuld (1984)	44% (N = 50)	8% (N = 12)	0% (N = 15)				
Brinkman & Braun (1984)	57% (N = 23)	5% (N = 39)					
Tuokko & Crockett (1987)							1% (N = 74)
Heinrichs & Celinski (1987)				10% (N = 50)			
Filley et al. (1987)	22% (N = 42)				17% (N = 30)[a]		2% (N = 42)
Satz et al. (1987)							13% (N = 149)
Satz et al. (1989)							
Ages:							
55–64							6% (N = 160)
65–69							6% (N = 160)
70–74							6% (N = 160)
Logsdon et al. (1989): Sample 1	22% (N = 67)						13% (N = 15)
Logsdon et al. (1989): Sample 2	7% (N = 45)					7% (N = 43)	7% (N = 54)
Bornstein & Share (1990)				5% (N = 79)[c]			
Satz et al. (1990)							
Education level:							
0–7							6% (N = 125)
8							4% (N = 134)
9–11							4% (N = 197)
12							5% (N = 462)
13–15							9% (N = 168)
16+							12% (N = 194)
Gfeller & Rankin (1991)	15% (N = 47)	12% (N = 16)					

Study							
Ryan et al. (1991)							8% (N = 225)
Education level:							
0–8							6% (N = 63)
9–11							5% (N = 43)
12							6% (N = 80)
≥13							18% (N = 39)
Age:							
75–79							8% (N = 115)
80–84							3% (N = 63)
≥85							15% (N = 47)
Randolph et al. (1993)	19% (N = 53)				19% (N = 36)		
Alexander et al. (1994)	36% (N = 28)				17% (N = 30)		5% (N = 21)
TOTALS	25% (N = 274)	7% (N = 67)	13% (N = 51)	7% (N = 129)	17% (N = 30)	7% (N = 43)	7% (N = 2,319)d

[a]The 30 nondementia patients included 13 with depression, 4 alcoholics, and 1–3 with a variety of disorders such as schizophrenia and stroke.

[b]The percentage of normal adolescents and adults (ages 16–74) in the WAIS-R standardization sample displaying the Fuld profile is 6.2 (Satz et al., 1989); no significant differences were observed for chronological age.

[c]The 79 head injury patients consisted of 43 with left temporal lobe epilepsy and 36 with right temporal lobe epilepsy.

[d]Only Ryan et al.'s (1991) total sample of 225 is summed in the total Normal Elderly sample because the data for age and education are simply a breakdown of Ryan et al.'s larger sample.

NOTE: Fuld (1984), Brinkman and Braun (1984), Tuokko and Crocket (1987), and Heinrichs and Celinski (1987) used the WAIS; Filley et al. (1987) used the WAIS or WAIS-R; all other studies used the WAIS-R. All profiles are based on age-corrected scaled scores.

349

medication (Fuld, 1984) or those with Huntington's disease (Randolph et al., 1993);

- the accuracy of the clinical diagnosis of Alzheimer's disease may not be enhanced very much by the formula because diagnostic accuracy is contingent on population base rates, and there is a "high incidence of [Alzheimer's disease] in comparison to other causes of dementia" (Fuld, 1984, p. 388); and

- limiting the WAIS-III administration to seven subtests eliminates the three new WAIS-III subtests, including the best measure of fluid intelligence (Matrix Reasoning) and working memory (Letter-Number Sequencing), both very important abilities to measure in all adults, including the elderly and those referred for dementia.

Our conclusion is to let the Fuld profile die for the WAIS-III. The four-index profile provides valid, reliable, and stable information about adults' abilities in four important areas of cognitive functioning. If a potentially diagnostic profile for patients with Alzheimer's disease is to be found, researchers should start with the index profile before examining other groupings of subtests. We recommend that clinicians who evaluate patients with Alzheimer's disease, or referrals for that disorder, administer the 11 subtests that are needed to compute the four indexes. That selection of tasks eliminates two of the four subtests that Fuld wanted to avoid because of possible issues concerning cultural bias or visual acuity: Comprehension and Picture Arrangement. However, examiners who believe that they can obtain valid data from patients with Alzheimer's disease on those two subtests would be wise to administer them as well. That will permit computation of the three IQs as well as the four indexes. The existing research still does support a V > P profile for patients with Alzheimer's disease, and by obtaining all IQs and standard scores, both clinicians and researchers can compare directly the relative value of the V–P discrepancy and the index profile.

High Average and Gifted Intellectual Functioning (Full Scale IQ of 110+)

Like the individuals who are mentally retarded, adolescents and adults with superior intellectual abilities represent a heterogeneous group of individuals who may be assessed by psychologists for a variety of purposes.[2] Bright adolescents may be evaluated for possible placement in gifted or honors programs or advanced placement in high school or college. Adults with exceptionally high intelligence may be assessed for occupational placement and planning. Although psychologists evaluate adolescents and adults with mental retardation more often than those with superior abilities (Harrison, Kaufman, Hickman, & Kaufman, 1988), the number of adults, particularly older adults, in our society is steadily growing and, with this change in the population, more emphasis is being placed on lifelong intellectual development and education beyond formal schooling (Burnham, 1982). More older adults are entering college and considering midlife career changes. Psychologists are likely to see more clients of average or superior intelligence who face occupational concerns, in addition to mental health concerns, and intellectual assessment of these individuals can be an important aspect of assisting them in decision making.

Gifted individuals have historically been identified by a cutoff score on an intelligence test (Sparrow & Gurland, 1998). Although this means of identification has recognizable problems such as cultural bias (Tyerman, 1986), ceiling effects (Harrington, 1982; Kaplan, 1992; Kaufman, 1993b), and an overemphasis on speed (Kaufman, 1992; Sternberg, 1982), psychologists typically do conduct an intellectual assessment if an individual (typically a child or adolescent) is

---

[2]Portions of this section on gifted intellectual functioning are adapted from Chapter 15 of the first edition of this book (Kaufman, 1990, pp. 533–585), which was written by Patti L. Harrison.

suspected of intellectual giftedness. The key to making appropriate decisions about giftedness is to consider more than a simple cutoff score (such as a Full Scale IQ of above 125 or 130). Important issues such as the appropriateness of a particular test for a person of a certain cultural background, the ceiling effects, the effect of speed on an individual's score, and the scatter within a person's profile must be considered.

WAIS-R and WAIS-III Patterns for Individuals with Full Scale IQ of 110 or Above

Consistent with the finding that highly educated adults (at least one year of graduate school; see Table 8.21) display higher scores on the Verbal than Performance scale is the finding that adolescents and adults with IQs in the High Average (Bright), Superior, and Very Superior ranges earn V > P profiles. Matarazzo and Herman (1985) combined data for the 1,880 individuals aged 16–74 in the WAIS-R standardization sample and grouped them into five IQ categories. Of the 177 people earning Full Scale IQs of 120 or more, about one fourth had V–P IQ discrepancies, in either direction, of 15+ points. Of this group with sizable discrepancies between their verbal and nonverbal abilities, 62% evidenced V > P profiles. A similar result emerged for the 312 people scoring 110–119 on the WAIS-R Full Scale; of the portion of this sample earning V–P differences of at least 15 points, 57% had V > P profiles. Using other criteria for determining large differences between V- and P-IQ (10, 13, or 22 points), Matarazzo and Herman (Table 5) showed that people in the 110–119 and 120+ IQ ranges consistently demonstrated V > P patterns more so than P > V profiles. None of the other IQ categories displayed characteristic V–P differences on the WAIS-R.

Although specific research on the WAIS-III has not yet been reported for individuals in the "gifted" range, from examination of the frequencies of differences between WAIS-III IQs in the standardization sample (N = 2,450), we can make some inferences. In the WAIS-III standardization sample, a WAIS-III V–P difference of 9 points is needed for significance at the .05 level. Adolescents and adults with Full Scale IQs of 120 or above achieved a 9-point V–P discrepancy (in either direction) in about 54% of the cases. In addition, a 17-point V–P discrepancy is considered abnormally large (i.e., it occurs less than 15% of the time in the overall standardization sample). However, a discrepancy of that magnitude occurs 20% of the time in individuals with Full Scale IQs of 120 or above, which implies that it is not, in fact, rare for individuals who function in the Superior or Very Superior range of intelligence. Likewise, even individuals who function in the High Average range of intelligence (FS-IQ of 110–119) quite frequently have significant WAIS-III V–P discrepancies (48% of the time) or abnormally large discrepancies (18% percent of the time). For a WAIS-III V–P discrepancy (in either direction) to be considered unusually or abnormally large in the Superior or Very Superior functioning individuals it would have to be 20 points or larger.

Similar findings characterize the WISC-III. Examination of the WISC-III standardization sample of 2,200 children and adolescents showed that 118 individuals had Full Scale IQs that were greater than or equal to 125 (a common cutoff point for determining giftedness); Sparrow and Gurland (1998) reported that 45.8% of those 118 children in the standardization sample had Verbal IQ versus Performance IQ discrepancies that were statistically significant at the .05 level (≥11 points). A difference of 16 or more points (p < .01) was found in 27.1% of the gifted sample.

Large V–P IQ discrepancies on any Wechsler test raise questions about whether the Full Scale IQ criteria for defining giftedness are adequate. Subtest scatter is reported in greater frequency in gifted samples than in the normative sample (Fishkin, Kampsnider, & Pack, 1996). Careful consideration always needs to be given as to whether the Full Scale IQ can be meaningfully interpreted for each individual child (e.g., Kaufman,

1994b; Kaufman & Lichtenberger, 1999, 2000; see Chapter 11).

Research on the WISC-R has shed light on a possible Wechsler profile using Bannatyne's categorizations. According to Bannatyne's system for categorizing Wechsler profiles (see Chapter 10), a characteristic profile on the WISC-R for gifted children and adolescents appears to be the Verbal Conceptualization > Acquired Knowledge > Spatial > Sequential pattern. Although many gifted individuals have higher Verbal than Performance IQs, the Verbal subtests appear to split into the two distinct and somewhat unexpected categories of Verbal Conceptualization and Acquired Knowledge. McGee and Brown (1984) also found that Comprehension scores were significantly higher than Information and Vocabulary scores on the WISC-R for children being considered for gifted placement and on the WAIS for bright college students, even though Comprehension scores are less dependent on formal education and other skills in which gifted individuals typically excel. Wilkinson (1993) found a WISC-R pattern of Verbal Comprehension > Perceptual Organization for 13% of her gifted third graders and 51% had Freedom from Distractibility factor scores that were lower than both the Verbal Comprehension and Perceptual Organization factors. Her research findings of (VC > PO > FD) lends support to the suggested Bannatyne profile in which sequential abilities are the weakest in comparison to spatial, verbal, or acquired knowledge. Future research will need to determine whether these patterns are also borne out in gifted samples on the WISC-III and WAIS-III.

Problems with the WAIS-III and WISC-III for High-Functioning Individuals

One of the commonly noted problems with the WAIS-III and the WISC-III (as well as the WPPSI-R) in the assessment of gifted individuals is the significant emphasis that each test places on the speed of response (Kaufman, 1992; Sparrow & Gurland, 1998). In addition to the Processing Speed subtests of the WAIS-III and WISC-III,

Block Design, Object Assembly, and Arithmetic (and Picture Arrangement on WISC-III) assign bonus points for speed, greatly affecting the scores of those who are slow to respond. For example, depending on the person's age, if he or she obtains a perfect performance but no bonus points for speed on the aforementioned WISC-III subtests, the maximum scaled score may be as low as 6 or 7 (Kaufman, 1993b). Individuals may respond slowly if they have a reflective problem-solving style or if they have a mild coordination problem, even if they are intellectually gifted. Thus, nonintellectual variables, such as fine-motor coordination or cognitive style, may influence the WISC-III and WAIS-III scores when a person's *cognitive* ability is supposedly measured. In situations where an individual's scores may have been influenced by his or her reflective style or coordination problems, appropriate steps may be taken to clarify why the scores are depressed (Kaufman & Lichtenberger, 2000). For example, supplementary tests may be given that do not emphasize speed of responding or tests of motor coordination may be administered to demonstrate what variables impacted performance on the Wechsler scales.

Considerations for Using Wechsler IQs in Gifted Assessment

The traditional use of intelligence test scores as the sole criterion for gifted functioning has been highly criticized. In the public schools, rigid criterion scores are frequently used to enable students with IQs of 131 to enter a gifted program but deny entrance to those with IQs of 129. Similar rigid cut-offs for cognitive test scores may be used for entrance to honors classes, advanced placement, or other activities for exceptional adolescents and adults. Cognitive test scores may be emphasized while other evidence, such as outstanding school achievement or creative accomplishment, is ignored.

Abusive practices such as these have led some professionals who work with the gifted to argue that identification of gifted individuals by using intelligence test scores is a serious mistake (e.g., Sternberg, 1986; Treffinger & Renzulli, 1986).

They argue that intelligence tests measure only one aspect of giftedness, academic giftedness, rather than other aspects, such as creative giftedness or practical giftedness (tacit knowledge). They suggest that intelligence, as measured by traditional intelligence tests, is an abstract, poorly defined concept, and that intelligence test scores represent only a limited sample of the dynamic, multifaceted functioning described in contemporary theories of intelligence.

Even proponents of using intelligence tests with gifted individuals agree with the arguments of the opponents and do not promote the sole use of intelligence tests to identify gifted functioning (e.g., Kaufman & Harrison, 1986; Robinson & Chamrad, 1986). They suggest, however, that intelligence tests have many positive characteristics that enhance gifted assessment, provide the most objective measure of gifted ability, and can be used intelligently with gifted individuals. They point out that intelligence tests have the best psychometric properties of any measure used with gifted individuals, are excellent predictors of academic achievement and success, and yield scores in several areas for a multifaceted interpretation of mental abilities. Psychologists who administer individual intelligence tests obtain qualitative information, in addition to scores, through careful administration and interpretation and clinical observation of the test taker. Some characteristics that may be observed by the acute examiner include problem-solving approach, language usage, self-concept, attention span, adaptation to change, anxiety, response to feedback, and reaction to novel tasks.

Intelligence tests can be used to identify gifted individuals who don't correspond to the stereotypical "gifted pattern" of extensive verbal ability and academic achievement and high motivation. Less objective methods of identifying gifted students, such as parent and teacher nominations, may result in a failure to identify gifted individuals with undeveloped potentials, handicapping conditions, low verbal ability, and lack of motivation who do not fit the "good student" pattern of striving, conforming, high achievers. Whitmore (1979, 1980, 1981) supplied evidence that underachieving and handicapped students often have talents that are not recognized until they are administered an individual intelligence test. Consult Valencia and Suzuki (2001) for excellent insight into giftedness among members of different minority groups, and culturally relevant suggestions for identifying gifted individuals within each subculture.

Thus, the WAIS-III and WISC-III are recommended for use in gifted assessment, but some aspects reveal a need for caution. One of the major drawbacks of these instruments in the assessment of giftedness is the overemphasis on speed of responding, and, for bilingual students, the heavy weight on verbal and culturally-based items. The scatter often reported in WAIS-III or WISC-III profiles of gifted samples suggests that caution should be used when interpreting global scores. Astute examiners will go beyond simple IQs and try to make sense of why an individual scored as he or she did. Observation of behaviors during testing, in combination with information from a child's background, can provide important clues to interpreting a profile. Psychologists and educators should take into account these issues, and support their WISC-III or WAIS-III data with supplementary tests, being careful not to interpret one IQ as *the* number that represents a person's ability (Kaufman 1994b; Kaufman & Lichtenberger, 1999, 2000).

Overview of Variables Believed to Be Correlates of High Verbal IQ

The overview of the variables believed to correlate with high Performance IQ was highlighted by *negative* findings; groups often believed to display P > V profiles were sometimes just as likely to yield no V–P discrepancy or the opposite discrepancy. The overview of would-be correlates of high Verbal IQ is filled with *positive* findings. The groups that were supposed to earn higher V-IQ than P-IQ invariably did so, namely those with damage to the right hemisphere (Chapter 8) as well as the groups discussed in this chapter: patients with psychiatric disorders (e.g., schizophrenia, depression, or bipolar disorder), alcohol abuse, motor coordination problems (multiple sclerosis, Huntington's disease, or Parkinson's disease), and Alzheimer's disease, plus those with high education and high Full Scale.

These positive findings mean that examiners of adolescents or adults who fit one or more of the groups shown to have V > P profiles should anticipate better-developed verbal than nonverbal skills when testing such individuals. The downside of the prevalence of V > P profiles in so many clinical samples reduces the effectiveness of this so-called sign for differential diagnosis. Once again, research with the four-factor index profile shows promise for understanding the cognitive patterns of clinical groups (Psychological Corporation, 1997, Chapter 4), more so than the V–P discrepancy, and may prove to have much value for differential diagnosis pending the outcome of future, much-needed research.

WHEN V–P IQ DISCREPANCIES ARE MEANINGLESS

There are several circumstances when the difference between a person's Verbal and Performance IQs is of little interpretive value, and may even be misleading. Four such factors are summarized here.

IQs Are Not Unitary Constructs

As explained in detail in the stepwise method for interpreting WAIS-III scores (Chapter 11), the V–P discrepancy is often not to be interpreted when one or both of the separate V and P IQ scales does not correspond to a unitary trait. The two main circumstances that cause the IQs not to be unitary are discussed in turn.

Indexes Are More Meaningful than IQs

When examiners look at the V–P IQ difference, they are interested in the person's underlying abilities within the verbal and nonverbal spheres, not the obtained scores per se. The discussion of the WAIS-III indexes in Chapter 11 indicates that often the Verbal scale will break apart into two distinct entities: Verbal Comprehension and Working Memory. Likewise the Performance scale may be comprised of discrepant scores on the Perceptual Organization Index and the Processing Speed Index.

Consequently, clinicians need to be aware of fluctuations in the subtest profile that relate to the WAIS-III factor indexes. An immediate clue is the splitting of the Verbal scale into two groups, with the Working Memory Index (WMI) emerging as either much lower or higher than the Verbal Comprehension Index (VCI). For example, a person may earn a WMI of 85 versus a Verbal Comprehension Index of 99. This disparity of scores is significantly different at the .01 level (see Chapter 11). Whenever an examiner discerns this particular pattern, or finds significantly discrepant scores between the Perceptual Organization Index and the Processing Speed Index, he or she should consider such findings as red flags that suggest the possible meaninglessness of the V–P discrepancy.

When either the Verbal IQ or the Performance IQ cannot be interpreted as meaningful, unitary constructs because of variability between the VCI and WMI or the POI and PSI, we recommend focusing on the VCI and POI for interpretation because the IQs and their difference are relatively meaningless. Only when the V-IQ versus P-IQ discrepancy is abnormally large (i.e., 17 points or more) do we suggest that it may be meaningfully interpreted despite significant differences between pairs of indexes (see Chapter 11).

Scatter in Verbal or Performance Subtest Profile

The use of summary scores such as IQs are based on the assumption that a unitary ability is being measured by the IQ scale. When a Verbal IQ is reported for a person, one assumes that the six Verbal subtests are primarily measuring verbal intelligence for that person. However, if a person was raised in a different culture, his or her low scores on Information and Comprehension may reflect that cultural difference rather than a verbal deficit, especially if the person performed at a much higher level on Similarities and Arithmetic. Analogous assumptions hold for the computation of Performance IQ; a highly anxious person who performs poorly on tasks like Symbol Search and Block Design, which place great emphasis on quick performance, may be exhibiting the negative impact of that anxiety rather than a deficiency in nonverbal intelligence.

The role of scatter in the Verbal or Performance Scale is discussed implicitly in the interpretive chapters of this book, such as in the stepwise interpretive procedure outlined in Chapter 11. One type of scatter has already been discussed: when the Verbal scale splits into VCI and WMI components, or when the Performance scale splits into POI and PSI portions. Scatter in the Verbal scale also occurs for a variety of other reasons, such as very low or high Digit Span for a person whose immediate memory is at a different level than his or her verbal comprehension and expression, a very low or high Arithmetic score for analogous reasons, or depressed scores on subtests that require spontaneous verbal expression for success (Vocabulary, Similarities, Comprehension). Variability in the Performance scale is common when scores on Picture Completion and Picture Arrangement are elevated due to a verbal compensation for a visual–motor deficit or due to special difficulty with abstractions, as opposed to the real-life stimuli used for the items in the two "Picture" subtests.

However, there does not have to be a known reason for the scatter; whenever there is significant scatter among a person's subtest scores on either the Verbal or Performance scale, for whatever reason, the IQ on that scale is less meaningful than if the scores were more unitary. If an individual's scaled scores on the Verbal scale range from a low of 2 to a high of 14, how meaningful is V-IQ as a summative statistic of the person's verbal intelligence? The same reasoning holds for wide scatter within the Performance

scale. When the obtained IQ is merely the midpoint of two or more different sets of skills, that IQ is not very meaningful.

When the Verbal and/or Performance IQ can be shown to be nothing more than a midpoint of distinct abilities, any comparisons involving the IQs (such as the V-IQ vs. P-IQ discrepancy) are usually meaningless. The examiner's goal then becomes the regrouping of subtests into alternative categories (see Chapters 10–12) to discern the person's specific areas of integrity and deficit. To enable the examiner to determine when the amount of profile variability within the Verbal or Performance Scale is significant or "marked," consult the discussion of this issue in Chapter 11.

Verbal Compensation for Performance Deficit

As discussed previously, some verbally bright individuals can score well on Wechsler's nonverbal tasks by using their well-developed verbal skills. Verbal responding on Picture Completion, verbal mediation on Picture Arrangement and Matrix Reasoning, and "thinking aloud" on Block Design and Object Assembly may be used as compensatory techniques for people with high verbal intelligence coupled with visual–motor deficits. Individuals who are particularly adept at this compensation can inflate their Performance IQs substantially, far beyond the level of their "true" nonverbal intelligence. Such individuals will conceivably still earn significantly higher Verbal than Performance IQs, but the discrepancy may be a "normal" 10 points instead of an extraordinary 25 points.

Obviously, the person who can spontaneously compensate for a nonverbal deficiency—especially in a highly structured, timed situation—has strong integrities and well-integrated brain functioning. That is the upside of the finding. The downside is that the person may truly have a visual–motor deficit requiring rehabilitation or remediation, such as a patient who has suffered a stroke in the right hemisphere; the failure for a sizable V > P or VCI > POI pattern to emerge may mask the real underlying deficits in the person's cognitive functioning. The alert clinician will be able to infer significant, and perhaps substantial, verbal–nonverbal discrepancies for a person who otherwise does not score remarkably differently on the Verbal and Performance scales. The things to look for are scaled scores on Picture Completion and Picture Arrangement (the most easily verbally mediated tasks) that are clearly above those on the remaining nonverbal tasks (and similar in magnitude to most Verbal scaled scores). These observations should be coupled with clear-cut behavioral observations of the use of verbal mediation when solving items on tasks like Picture Arrangement, Matrix Reasoning, and Block Design.

Effects of Retesting

There are several good intelligence tests for adolescents and adults, but the WAIS-III (or its predecessors) has usually been the test of choice whenever intellectual assessment is required. Thus, when a person requires a retest, for whatever reason, the same test battery is typically given. Because clinical and neurological patients are frequently assessed repeatedly to evaluate their current status, issues concerning retesting assume an important practical role. As discussed at length in Chapter 6, gains on the Performance scale are considerably larger than gains on the Verbal Scale for individuals ages 16–54 years. Gains for normal people on the WAIS-III over a 2- to 12-week interval average about 2½ points in V-IQ, 6½ points in P-IQ, and 4½ points in FS-IQ. Similar practice effects for earlier versions of Wechsler's adult scales have been observed for clinical populations (Hawkins & Sayward, 1994; Matarazzo, Carmody, & Jacobs, 1980; McSweeny, Naugle, Ghelune, Luders, 1993) and for children as well as adults (Kaufman, 1994b).

However, the 4-point *relative* gain in P-IQ (i.e., 6½ points in P-IQ minus 2½ points in V-IQ) is the average of results for several age groups. In fact, for adolescents and adults ages 16 to 54 years, the relative gain is 5–6 points. In contrast, for ages 55–74 the relative gain is about 3½ points, and for

ages 75–89, it is only about 1 point (see Table 6.5). Consequently, the effects of retesting on a person's V–P IQ discrepancy is primarily of concern for adults below the age of 55.

Thus, the average person between the ages of 16 and 54 will show a relative gain of about 5–6 points on the Performance scale when retested on the WAIS-III. Based on Catron's (1978; Catron & Thompson, 1979) retest study with the WAIS using five time intervals, one would expect the relative gain in P-IQ to be maintained for at least 4 months.

Impact of Retesting for Individual Assessment

The net result of this practice effect is to produce relatively higher Performance than Verbal IQs in individuals who are retested on a Wechsler Scale over an interval of a few months (which might even be as long as a year or more). A person between the ages of 16 and 54 who earns a P > V pattern by a nonsignificant 8 points on an initial testing of the WAIS-III would be expected to show a significant P > V profile by about 13–14 points on a retest, simply due to the predictable practice effect that leads to greater improvement in P-IQ than V-IQ. Similarly, a person with P > V of 16 points on the first administration is likely to have a striking discrepancy of about 21–22 points on the retest due to the practice effect. The practice effect works in reverse for people who initially show significant superiority on the Verbal Scale. A significant V > P profile of 12 points on the first test is likely to decline to a trivial 6–7 points on the retest, and so forth.

The overall conclusion is that V–P differences on a retest of the WAIS-III for persons in the 16–54 year age range are likely to be meaningless in most circumstances unless the initial test was invalid (e.g., because of the person's low motivation), or if at least a year has elapsed between administrations. V–P IQ discrepancies on a retest can only be interpreted in the context of the V–P differences observed on the first test. If the V–P discrepancies follow a lawful pattern, i.e., they show a shift on retesting in the direction of a relatively higher P-IQ, by perhaps 4 to 7 points, the V–P IQ difference on the retest should be considered artifactual. The V–P IQ discrepancy on the first testing probably gives a truer picture of the person's underlying verbal and nonverbal abilities than does the IQ difference on the second administration.

For individuals ages 55–74 tested twice on the WAIS-III, the relative gain on P-IQ is only 3½ points, as mentioned. Examiners need to take this value into account when interpreting V–P IQ discrepancies obtained on a retest for such individuals. However, its impact on the size of the retest V–P discrepancy will be notably less for this age range. For elderly adults, ages 75–89, the relative P-IQ gain of about 1 point is trivial and does not need to be taken into account at all. The magnitude of WAIS-III V–P IQ discrepancies for an elderly adult on a retest can be interpreted as meaningful.

Impact of Retesting for Research

The practice effect can have a significant impact on the interpretation of group data as well, as explained in more detail in the section on progressive error in Chapter 5 and in the section on practice effects in Chapter 6. For example, Juolasmaa et al. (1981) tested 60 cardiac patients pre- and post-open heart surgery on the WAIS (10-month interval) to evaluate the impact of heart surgery on intellectual performance. They observed a 4-point gain in P-IQ after surgery compared to a ½ point improvement in V-IQ, concluding: "In general, the rates of improvement exceeded those of impairment, the tests of visual functions showing the

highest rise" (p. 186). What they really observed was probably the practice effect in action. Similarly, Seidenberg et al. (1981) attempted to distinguish between practice effects and real cognitive changes in their group of epileptics by showing that those with reduced seizure frequency demonstrated the biggest intellectual gains. Nonetheless, the practice effect was clearly in evidence for patients who had improved in their seizures and for those who had not. Both samples showed V > P profiles on the initial WAIS administration of about 6 points; the relative Performance versus Verbal gain due to practice reduced the V–P IQ discrepancy on the retest to about zero for both subsamples of patients.

ILLUSTRATIVE CASE REPORTS

Two sample psychological case reports follow: Chester P., an African American adolescent male suspected of autism, and Robert N., a 36-year-old Caucasian man with mild mental retardation. Chester displays the anticipated P > V profile sometimes characteristic of individuals with autism or related language disorders, and Robert displays a V > P profile. (As stated in Chapter 8, the clients' names and other identifying information have been altered to preserve anonymity.) Both reports illustrate the integration of scores on intelligence tests and adaptive behavior measures as part of the assessment process.

CHESTER P., AGE 17, POSSIBLE AUTISM

Reason for Referral

Chester P., an African American male who just turned 17, was seen for reevaluation because his father has requested assistance with future planning for his son.

Background and Observations

Chester was last assessed at age 14. Psychological testing indicated a highly discrepant Verbal–Performance difference on the WISC-R, i.e., Verbal IQ of 65, Performance IQ of 101, and Full Scale IQ of 80. Errors on the Bender-Gestalt were not significant. He lives at home and continues to attend a therapeutic school. Mr. P. feels that his son is in a "caring situation" at the school, but they do not have a prevocational program and his concern is "where does he move from there." Chester's family is not interested in residential placement for him unless it could provide special benefits they could not provide at home. Most of Chester's social activities are with his family. His father voiced concern over Chester's poor socialization skills and the fact that he has no friends of his age where he lives.

Early developmental history, as reported by Mr. P., is sketchy and thus cannot support or rule out a possible diagnosis of primary autism. Chester was adopted when he was "less than 6 months old" through the Department of Children and Family Services. Nothing unusual was recalled in his birth or perinatal history. Problems were first noted when he was 2 years old, or perhaps 4 years old, as he exhibited delayed language development. Whether other areas of functioning were delayed could not be recalled by his father.

At the time of the present evaluation, Chester was quite cooperative despite a rather lengthy testing session. He exhibited delayed and immediate echolalia. Frequently, he would read from the examiner's manual at a distance of 3 to 5 feet (looking at the printed words upside down) and attempt to anticipate the next question and answer.

His answers were often verbal associations or functional descriptions rather than definitions or scorable responses.[3] Tasks that appeared more difficult for him, e.g., verbal questions about social situations, resulted in much agitated movement and irrelevant noises, e.g., teeth clicking. He was quite anxious to do the psychomotor tasks, e.g., WAIS-R Block Design, and he insisted on taking the test materials from the examiner so that he could set up the task himself. Several times when Chester could not answer, he would turn to the wall and in a booming, almost theatrical voice ask the question to a nonexistent person, for example, "Hey mister, could you tell me three kinds of blood vessels?" Chester did not respond when asked if there was really someone there; however, this examiner felt that Chester was playfully diverting attention away from his own lack of knowledge rather than hallucinating. Later he reportedly paced in the waiting room, repetitively saying, e.g., "to be or not to be, that is the question...to be or not to be that's the construction," and so on. He had begun this kind of behavior earlier during testing when asked to name United States presidents. Despite these bizarre verbalizations and his tendency toward aloofness, Chester did not appear to be exhibiting hallucinatory behavior and did not exhibit any systematized delusions.

During the evaluation, Chester complied with the examiner's request to draw a picture of himself; however, he first drew a full figure of himself standing next to a female figure, which he identified as the examiner. Later he drew another full figure of himself standing alone, and separate pictures of his face and the examiner's face. Chester seemed to accomplish these drawings with ease, and while they did not exhibit a great deal of detail, they were well proportioned, accurate, and without pathognomonic features.

Chester remained rather aloof during the evaluation, unable to respond to normal conversation with the examiner. Most responses were short phrases; however, his noncommunicative speech was more complex.

Tests Administered

(Table 9.3 provides a complete summary of scores)

- Bender-Gestalt Test of Visual-Motor Integration
- Kaufman Test of Educational Achievement (K-TEA)-Brief Form

---

[3] Unlike some of the case reports that we have included from the first edition of this book, Chester's case remains unchanged from the 1990 version, still using the WAIS-R. We decided not to modify Chester's scores because so much scatter exists in his profile that the WAIS-III Indexes would have been rendered uninterpretable. Thus, as was done with this WAIS-R report, we would have focused on his individual strengths and weaknesses had a WAIS-III been the main cognitive instrument administered.

TABLE 9.3   Chester P.: Tests Administered

Wechsler Adult Intelligence Scale—Revised (WAIS-R)

Verbal	Scaled Score	Age-Corrected Scaled Score	Performance	Scaled Score	Age-Corrected Scaled Score
Information	6	(8)	Picture Completion	9	(9)—W
Digit Span	15	(17)—S	Picture Arrangement	5	(5)—W
Vocabulary	4	(5)—W	Block Design	17	(18)—S
Arithmetic	3	(4)—W	Object Assembly	16	(18)—S
Comprehension	2	(3)—W	Digit Symbol	8	(8)—W
Similarities	12	(14)—S			

Age-Corrected Verbal Mean = 8   Age-Corrected Performance Mean = 12

  IQ (± 90% confidence)
  Verbal = 89 ± 5
  Performance = 113 ± 9
  Full Scale = 99 ± 5

Peabody Picture Vocabulary Test—Revised (PPVT-R), Form L

Receptive vocabulary standard score = 79 (8th percentile)
Age equivalent = 12–7

Bender-Gestalt Test of Visual-Motor Integration

Normal performance according to Koppitz scoring system

Kaufman Test of Educational Achievement (K-TEA), Brief Form

	Standard Score (±90%)	Percentile Rank	Grade Equivalent
Reading	96±10	39th	10.8
Spelling	96±11	39th	11.1
Mathematics	73±10	4th	6.4
Battery Composite	85±7	16th	8.8

Vineland Adaptive Behavior Scales (Expanded Form)
(Based on interview with Mr. P., Chester's father)

Domain	Standard Score[a]	Adaptive Level[a]	Age Equivalent	Percentile[a]
Communication	85±9	Adequate	14–0	16th
Daily Living Skills	61±7	Low (Mild Deficit)	9–4	<1st
Socialization	47±7	Low (Moderate Deficit)	5–10	<0.1st
Adaptive Behavior Composite	59±5	Low (Mild Deficit)	9–9	<1st

[a]Based on norms for ages 17–0 through 17–3 (standard scores are banded by 90% confidence interval).

- Peabody Picture Vocabulary Test-Revised (PPVT-R)
- Vineland Adaptive Behavior Scales (Expanded Form)
- Wechsler Adult Intelligence Test-Revised (WAIS-R)

Test Results and Interpretation

In contrast to the 36-point Verbal deficit that Chester displayed on the WISC-R at age 14 (P-IQ = 101, V-IQ = 65), he performed at a normal level of functioning on both WAIS-R scales at the present evaluation. His WAIS-R Performance IQ of 113±9 (High Average intelligence, 81st percentile) was still a significant 24 points greater than his Verbal IQ; further, differences as large as 24 points are abnormal, occurring less than 5% of the time in adolescents or adults with average intelligence. Yet his WAIS-R Verbal IQ of 89 ± 5 (23rd percentile) placed him at the juncture of the Low Average and Average categories, not within the deficient range of mental ability.

Based on the large V–P discrepancy, Chester's Average WAIS-R Full Scale IQ of 99 ± 5 (47th percentile) is meaningless; he clearly expresses his intellect far better nonverbally, with concrete materials, than via verbal comprehension and expression. However, the enormous scatter characterizing his subtest profile, within both the Verbal and Performance Scales, even reduces the meaningfulness of his high Performance–low Verbal pattern. Other explanations fit Chester's profile fluctuations better than Wechsler's verbal–nonverbal dichotomy.

Basically, Chester's WAIS-R profile is one of extremes, with scaled scores ranging from well below the 1st percentile (responding verbally to socially relevant problems) to the 99th percentile (rapidly constructing abstract designs out of blocks), when compared to other 17-year-olds. The degree of Verbal scatter, Performance scatter, and scatter among all 11 subtests is huge and striking, occurring less than 1% of the time in the normal population. Chester's greatest strength is in visual–constructive ability (above the 99th percentile), as he excelled in assembling cut-up picture puzzles as well as designs. His most deficient area is his ability to express his ideas with spontaneous verbalizations, whether defining words or solving questions of social relevance (2nd percentile). He displayed striking weakness, in general, with school-related, fact-oriented tasks (4th percentile) compared to his very superior visual–spatial skills (98th percentile). The latter strength was reinforced by his normal Bender-Gestalt performance (one minor error based on Koppitz's scoring system), indicating intact visual–motor integration.

All of these results are consistent with Chester's behaviors and possible diagnosis of autism. However, no comparison explains his assets and deficits better than a contrast of his success on tests of abstract thought (a verbal test of similarities, telling how two things are alike, plus the nonverbal abstract design test) versus tests of social comprehension (the verbal test of social problem solving, and a nonverbal task of arranging pictures to tell a meaningful story). Each category spans verbal and nonverbal content, and each involves high-level reasoning ability. Yet, Chester performed at the 98th percentile on the abstract thought tests, compared to the 2nd percentile on the measures of social understanding. Overall, Chester displayed a more broadly defined strength in fluid intelligence, the ability to solve novel problems with flexibility. This asset spanned verbal reasoning and short-term memory tests as well as a variety of nonverbal visual–spatial tests. Excluding the one fluid task with social content, Chester performed better than 96 out of 100 adolescents his age on measures of fluid intelligence.

On the PPVT-R, Chester earned a standard score of 79 (8th percentile), basically consistent with his Verbal IQ, but better than his WAIS-R scores on tasks requiring much verbal expression. When he is allowed to respond to school-related items nonverbally (as on the PPVT-R), or with just one or two words (as on a WAIS-R task of general information) he performs much better than when extra verbalization is required.

He evidenced this relative strength on an achievement battery as well, the K-TEA Brief Form. He earned Average standard scores of 96 (39th percentile) on both the Reading and

Spelling tests, performing about as well as one might expect from his WAIS-R IQs. The Reading test assesses word recognition as well as comprehension, but requires little verbalization; the Spelling test requires a written response. His Mathematics score of 73 (4th percentile) indicates a poor level of arithmetic concepts, reasoning, and computation skills (sixth-grade level), a finding that was underscored by his very low score on the WAIS-R Arithmetic subtest. He evidenced inadequate arithmetic performance with oral presentation (WAIS-R), with visual presentation and written response (the first half of the K-TEA), and with combined oral and visual presentation (the second half of the K-TEA).

On the Vineland Adaptive Behavior Scales (Expanded Form), based on Mr. P.'s report, Chester performed at about a 10-year-old level, demonstrating a mild deficit in his overall adaptive behavior. Despite his difficulty with WAIS-R verbal expressive tasks, Chester has a relative asset in communication, notably receptive and written; he also has all of the basic self-help skills. He reads on his own initiative, makes phone calls, and follows current events. Areas of relative deficit are in self-direction, socialization (interpersonal relationships, play and leisure time, coping skills), and expressive communication. Chester cannot make change for minor purchases nor does he go out unsupervised during the day. Most of his social activities are with the family, and he has few friends who are his peers in age and ability level. He helps around the house by cleaning his room, taking out the garbage, and assisting with the lawn chores.

Diagnostic Impression

Chester is a 17-year-old African American male who exhibits atypical patterns of development in terms of language and social skills. Currently his tested verbal abilities are much improved over his last evaluation; however, he still exhibits significantly poorer verbal than performance abilities. Interpretation of social situations on test materials and socialization skills in general continue to be areas of extreme difficulty for Chester. He exhibits loose associative verbalizations, which may not be predicted on the basis of his language disorder alone; however, no clear-cut mental illness appears evident to this examiner. He does display striking strengths in abstract thought, visual–spatial skills, and fluid intelligence (even within the verbal sphere) and has adequate reading and spelling abilities; arithmetic skills are poor, while adaptive behavior is inconsistent.

The unavailability of a clear developmental history makes a diagnosis of Autism impossible; however, Chester appears to be exhibiting an amelioration in left-hemisphere deficits, characteristic of adolescents with autism. He has distortions in the development of multiple basic psychological functions that are involved in the development of social skills and language.

Recommendations

Family conference with the father to discuss our recommendations for programming with Chester to include the following:

1. Socialization activities: Getting involved in organized activities such as art classes, or working with younger children as a volunteer, might be appropriate social activities.
2. Prevocational training
3. Independent living training
4. Encouragement of independent living activities by his family

The above recommendations may be most effectively carried out in a milieu therapy setting, such as The Group Home run by Mrs. H., which has been discussed with Mr. P. However, if the

P. family wishes to keep Chester at home on a full-time basis, other arrangements may be sought to provide these same programmatic needs.

Examiner: Judith Ivins, Psychologist III

ROBERT N., AGE 36, MILD RETARDATION

Reason for Referral

Robert N. was referred for a psychological evaluation by the Area Services for Work and Rehabilitation (ASWR).[4] An assessment of Robert's current level of functioning is needed to update his record. There is also some question as to whether neurological abnormalities may be present. Staff at the workshop feel that Robert is not working at his potential.

Background Information

Robert was born in a displaced persons camp in West Germany. The pregnancy and delivery were uncomplicated. Soon after his birth, an epidemic swept through the camp, affecting all who were living there. In addition to this, Robert had an upper respiratory ailment (possibly pneumonia) during infancy. His mother describes his development as normal during his first 2 years. At age 2, he reportedly began having temper tantrums and became increasingly active and unpredictable. When Robert was 5 years old, he and his family moved from Europe to a Ukrainian neighborhood in the Midwest, making it possible for them to maintain close cultural ties. Robert has two brothers (one of whom is retarded) and a sister.

Robert attended the local school for exceptional children from age 9 to 16. He was finally asked to leave the school because of unverified problems. He attended the local state school from age 17 to 24, and the Center for Developmentally Disabled (CDD) from age 25 to 33, before moving to the residential apartment facility where he currently resides. There is little information regarding his educational history; his work history is reportedly good. Robert was in a variety of vocational programs at CDD, where he received training in food and janitorial services. His work skills and attitude were described as good.

Psychological evaluations conducted through the years have consistently found Robert to function in the mildly retarded range of intelligence. A psychologist at the state school also found that he has difficulty expressing his emotions and tends to express his anger in a "passive–aggressive manner." Robert recently began therapy at a mental health clinic, focusing on increasing his ability to express emotion appropriately, as well as on social skills and assertiveness training. Ms. K., his therapist, feels that he is depressed.

Robert has a history of seizurelike activity and a chronic gastrointestinal disorder. His current medications are Tagamet, Gaviscon, and Colace. He lives in a workshop setting. No significant disturbances are currently being reported, but staff at the workshop feel that he is not working at a level consistent with his potential. Robert is described as withdrawn and as being somewhat of a loner. His father is deceased, and Robert has limited contact with family members. He reports that one of his brothers recently had a heart attack but is recovering nicely. This report could not be verified by Mr. R., on-site coordinator of the residential apartment facility.

---

[4]The case of Robert N. was adapted from Patti L. Harrison's chapter on Mental Retardation, Adaptive Behavior Assessment and Giftedness in the first edition of this book (Kaufman, 1990).

Observations and Impressions

Robert is an attractive 36-year-old Caucasian male of average height. He was neatly dressed in casual clothing and seemed adequately groomed, although some body odor was noticeable. His speech was clear and easily intelligible. He seemed somewhat clumsy (e.g., he had some difficulty seating himself). Robert avoided eye contact by gazing downward, and he seemed distant during much of the session. He would speak only when spoken to and then tended to answer in single words, although he was capable of formulating complete sentences. Although he was generally cooperative, he displayed occasional flashes of hostility when his responses were questioned by the examiner. Robert was wearing glasses but complained of having difficulty seeing some of the more detailed stimuli.

Test Results and Interpretation

Robert's performance on a standard measure of cognitive functioning (WAIS-III) places him within the mildly retarded range of intelligence (scores from all tests are listed in Table 9.4). His Full Scale IQ of 61 (59–66 with 90% confidence) indicates that he surpassed the mental functioning of only about 1% of the adults his age. Moreover, there was a significant difference between his Verbal IQ of 71 (3rd percentile) and Performance IQ of 55 (0.1st percentile). The 16-point discrepancy is not only significant but unusual; differences of that magnitude or greater occur less than 7% of the time in adults with IQs below 80. Robert's IQs indicate that he displays far better mental skills in the domain of verbal comprehension and expression than in nonverbal reasoning and visual–motor coordination. In the latter areas, he performed better than only 1 out of 1000 adults his age. His Verbal–Performance split is consistent with the results of previous testing. Given that Performance tasks generally require a greater expenditure of physical energy than do verbal tasks, his poor performance on such tasks may also reflect his depressed emotional state. Consistent with this hypothesis was his Processing Speed Index of 66 (1st percentile) and his Perceptual Organization Index of 58 (0.3rd percentile), which require visual–motor coordination and/or processing speed for success. His scores on these two nonverbal indexes were significantly lower than his performance on the Verbal Comprehension Index (74, 4th percentile), which measures verbal knowledge and expression. Robert's Working Memory Index of 73 did not provide a meaningful representation of his abilities as an abnormal amount of scatter was present among the subtests that comprise this index.

Robert's relative strengths and weaknesses in his profile indicate a relative strength in short-term auditory memory of stimuli that do not require processing of school-learned knowledge. His relative strength was evident in two tasks, one that required him to recall a series of orally presented numbers (25th percentile) and another that required him to track and orally repeat a sequence of letters and numbers (25th percentile). Particular deficits were noted on a verbal test of mental arithmetic (0.1st percentile). Compared to his overall performance at the 4th percentile on tasks of verbal expression and verbal conceptualization, he had significantly more difficulty on nonverbal measures involving the visual analysis and integration of social stimuli. Robert's approach to tasks calling for integration seemed to be to work piece-by-piece. He was unable to conceptualize a whole, and consistent with this difficulty in visual analysis and integration, Robert scored significantly below mental age expectancy on a separate measure of visual–motor integration (Bender-Gestalt). His drawings were characterized by distortions of shape, rotations, and an inability to integrate the designs, all of which are signs of possible organic involvement.

Robert's academic skills are also fairly consistent with what would be expected of someone with his global cognitive abilities. His academic skills were assessed with the Wide Range Achievement Test-Third Edition. His Reading (recognition only) standard score of 60 (0.4th percentile), Spelling standard score of 66 (1st percentile), and Arithmetic standard score of 68 (2nd percentile) were in the Extremely Low range of academic functioning. He can, for example,

TABLE 9.4   Robert N.: Tests Administered

Wechsler Adult Intelligence Scale—Third Edition (WAIS-III)

Scale	IQ	90% Confidence Interval	Percentile Rank
Verbal Scale	71	68–76	3
Performance Scale	55	52–63	0.1
Full Scale	61	58–65	0.5

Factor	Index	90% Confidence Interval	Percentile Rank
Verbal Comprehension	74	70–80	4
Perceptual Organization	58	55–67	0.3
Working Memory	73	69–80	3
Processing Speed	66	63–78	1

Subtest	Scaled Score	Percentile Rank	Subtest	Scaled Score	Percentile Rank
Vocabulary	5	5	Picture Completion	3	1
Similarities	5	5	Digit Symbol-Coding	3	1
Arithmetic	1 (W)	0.1	Block Design	3	1
Digit Span	8 (S)	25	Matrix Reasoning	2	0.5
Information	6	9	Picture Arrangement	2	0.5
Comprehension	6	9	Symbol Search	3	1
Letter-Number Sequencing	8 (S)	25	Object Assembly	2	0.5

Wide Range Achievement Test—Third Edition (WRAT3)

Scale	Standard Score	90% Confidence Interval	Percentile Rank
Reading	60	57–64	0.4
Spelling	66	63–70	1
Arithmetic	68	65–72	2

Vineland Adaptive Behavior Scales (Expanded Form)
(Self-report, corroborated by Mr. R., supervisor at residential apartment facility)

Domain	Standard Score	Adaptive Level	Age Equivalent	Percentile Rank[a]	Supplementary Percentile[b]
Communication	80±9	Moderately low	13-9	9	99
Daily Living Skills	65±7	Low (Mild Deficit)	10-10	1	70
Socialization	79±7	Moderately low	14-9	8	90
Adaptive Behavior Composite	69±5	Low (Mild Deficit)	13-1	2	95

[a]Based on norms for ages 18-8 through 18-11 and older (standard scores are banded by 90% confidence interval).
[b]Based on supplementary norms for adults with mental retardation, ages 18 and older, in nonresidential facilities.

Other Tests Administered:
Bender-Gestalt Test of Visual-Motor Integration
Thematic Apperception Test (TAT)
Rotter Incomplete Sentences Blank

recognize several common words and spell some three-letter words and words representing something in which he is interested (e.g., soccer). He is able to count and recognize written numbers but was unable to perform even the simplest computations in either verbal (Arithmetic, WAIS-III) or written (WRAT3) form. His academic achievement was commensurate with his cognitive potential, as evidenced from comparing his WAIS-III Full Scale IQ of 61 to his standard scores on the WRAT3.

According to self- and supervisor reports on the Vineland Adaptive Behavior Scales, Robert's social adaptive functioning, while still generally in the mild mentally retarded range (composite standard score = 69, with Domain scores ranging from 65 to 80), is notably above his cognitive functioning. Overall, Robert functioned at the approximate level of a 13-year-old in the adaptive domains of Communication, Daily Living Skills, and Socialization. His standard scores are just estimates, because norms are not available for those above the age of 18 years. Adaptive behavior strengths are in self-direction, independence, and use of leisure time. For example, Robert goes out unsupervised both during the day and at night, travels to distant points alone, and is fairly responsible about letting others know his whereabouts. Both Robert and his supervisor report that he is able to make change, manage his own spending money of $20 per week, buy his own clothing, and make major expenditures with assistance, but it should be noted that he was unable to make even the most basic computations in the current testing. Weaknesses were also evident in some aspects of his Written, Communication, Domestic, and Community skills (e.g., he does not communicate by letter or follow current events and is unable to use tools or utensils). When compared to other adults with mental retardation in nonresidential facilities, his adaptive behavior was exceptional, surpassing 95% of the individuals in this supplementary reference group in overall adaptive behavior.

In projective personality measures as well as in his general demeanor, Robert conveyed feelings of sadness and general lack of energy. He also seemed preoccupied with thoughts of death. These thoughts may stem from his feelings of sadness and anger regarding the loss of his father. He also seems concerned about his brother, whom he reported had recently suffered a heart attack. Whether or not the heart attack actually occurred, his mentioning it reflects his fear of potential losses. His fear of others breaking into his apartment, reported by his therapist, is consistent with this theme. Robert also seems to fear that he might die. In addition to these issues, he feels that he has failed to obtain competitive employment and this perceived failure seems to affect his self-esteem. His desire to make more money and his considerable appetite may reflect, at least in part, his emotional neediness. Staff at the residential apartments describe him as solemn and as somewhat of a loner. He tends to display resistance when demands are placed on him (e.g., at the workshop), which implies that there may be some complicity in his failure to obtain competitive employment. Robert is reportedly verbally aggressive and boastful with the few friends he does have, but is quiet and shy with people he doesn't know. He seems to have an appropriate level of sexual interest and reports socializing with women and having had a girlfriend in the past.

Summary

Robert is an attractive 36-year-old Caucasian male of average stature. He has a history of seizure-like activity and a chronic gastrointestinal disorder, which is being treated with medication. He is currently functioning overall in the mildly retarded range of intelligence (WAIS-III Full Scale IQ = 61), with significantly better verbal (V-IQ = 71) than nonverbal (P-IQ = 55) skills. Deficits displayed on various measures of visual–motor integration are consistent with possible organic involvement. His relative cognitive strengths are in the area of short-term memory (specifically with stimuli that are not academically related). Robert's academic skills are congruent with his overall level of cognitive ability (WRAT3 scores all ≤ 2nd percentile). According to self- and supervisor reports, his social adaptive functioning (13–1 year level), though deficient, is notably higher than his cognitive functioning. Strengths in this area are in self-direction, independence, and use of leisure time; weaknesses seemed present in some aspects of communication, domestic, and community skills. Personality assessment indicated feelings of sadness, lack of energy, preoccupation with death and loss in general, and insubstantial social relationships.

Diagnostic Impression

DSM-IV Classification

Axis I.   300.40 Dysthymic Disorder

Axis II.   317.00 Mild Mental Retardation

Axis III.   History of seizurelike behavior, chronic gastrointestinal disorder (by medical report)

Axis IV.   Psychosocial stressors: brother's heart attack

Axis V.   Highest level of adaptive functioning in past year: 45

Recommendations

Robert should continue therapy at the mental health clinic to deal with his emotional problems and build social skills. The therapist should be in touch with staff at the workshop to devise a program aimed at increasing his productivity.

It is recommended that Robert take courses in functional academic skills (e.g., reading, writing, arithmetic) at one of the area community colleges. Improved skills in these areas should increase his chances of obtaining competitive employment.

Examiner: Maria Nucci
Supervisor: Judith Ivins, Psychologist III

SUMMARY

The following variables are often believed to be associated with characteristically high P-IQs: learning disabilities or illiteracy, delinquency or psychopathic behavior, mental retardation, bilingualism, and autism.

Adolescents and adults diagnosed as learning-disabled, illiterate, or dyslexic often display a characteristic P > V profile of about 5 to 15 points. However, college students with learning disabilities are an exception; they usually evidence the opposite profile or have no V–P difference at all. Various profiles in the Wechsler subtests have been suggested for learning-disabled samples. We reviewed the ACID profile, the Bannatyne profile, and SCALD profile, and suggested that

Bannatyne's categories or the SCALD profile might be the most useful in assessing (although not necessarily diagnosing) learning disabilities. Better still will be application of the factor index profile, pending the outcome of future research. The P > V sign for delinquents and psychopaths was advocated by Wechsler over a half century ago. Whereas groups of delinquents and psychopaths sometimes average about 6 points higher on P-IQ than V-IQ, supporting Wechsler's generalization, many samples of adolescents and adults do not manifest this anticipated profile. Also, Wechsler's claim that the sign is useful for individual diagnosis has not been supported. Further, among delinquents and psychopaths, the P > V discrepancy tends to be larger for younger adolescents than for older adolescents and adults; larger on the WISC/WISC-R than on the WAIS/WAIS-R; sometimes larger for Caucasians than African Americans; and sometimes explainable by intervening variables like reading disabilities or number of criminal offenses. Mental retardation has sometimes been associated with P > V profiles; most studies with adolescents and adults, however, suggest only a slight profile (2–3 points), with the possibility that individuals with very low IQs may even display a high Verbal–low Performance profile. Numerous investigations have shown that bilingual Hispanic and American Indian children earn substantially higher Performance than Verbal IQs. This finding has been validated for American Indian adults, but not for Hispanic adults. Indeed, WAIS-III data reveal only a slight P > V profile for Hispanic adults, and a trivial POI > VCI discrepancy.

Research on individuals with Autistic Disorder is complicated by the presence of mental retardation in many of the subjects. Evidence from some studies of individuals with autism indicates a pattern of high Performance–low Verbal on Wechsler's scales and related tasks, but it may lack sensitivity as it has not been found consistently across all studies. In addition, when samples of relatively high-functioning individuals with Autistic Disorder are tested on a Wechsler scale, the opposite pattern of V > P sometimes emerges. Overall, the variables believed to be associated with P > V profiles (including left-hemisphere brain damage, discussed in Chapter 8) have not been associated with that pattern either consistently or of a magnitude that is large enough to be practically or clinically meaningful.

The following variables are believed to be associated with V > P profiles: high educational attainment, psychiatric disorders, motor coordination problems, Alzheimer's-type dementia, and high IQs. Individuals with at least one year of graduate school earn higher V-IQs, but that generalization does not necessarily apply to those who have attended college. Psychiatric patients, in general, display V > P profiles; this finding has been observed for patients with schizophrenia (although some have argued for low V-IQ in schizophre-

nia), depression, and bipolar disorder. The consistent finding has been explained by impaired concentration, psychomotor retardation, anxiety, or low motivation. Performance subtests range from the ones requiring little or no motor coordination (Picture Completion and Matrix Reasoning) to a test of psychomotor speed (Digit Symbol-Coding), with most of Wechsler's nonverbal tasks requiring good coordination for success. Groups with known motor problems (patients with multiple sclerosis, Huntington's disease, or Parkinson's disease) earn substantially higher V- than P-IQs. Among multiple sclerosis patients, discrepancies were larger for chronic than relapsing–remitting patients (12 vs. 5 points), with the chronic patients performing worst on the tasks most dependent on motor coordination. Analogous results were obtained when patients with advanced Huntington's disease were compared to those with a recent onset. Individuals who have abused alcohol show a higher V- than P-IQ, as do patients with Alzheimer's disease. The Fuld profile has been called a "marker" for Alzheimer's disease by many, but we are recommending that the Fuld formula be abandoned in favor of an emphasis on the WAIS-III profile of four factor indexes. In general, much research needs to be done with the index profile to help understand the cognitive assets and deficits of a variety of clinical samples. Data provided by the publisher of the WAIS-III in the technical manual for small samples of clinical patients suggest strongly that the index profile for different groups will provide information of much clinical value. For example, patients with Huntington's disease scored almost 2 standard deviations higher on their mean VCI than their mean PSI.

Gifted individuals often also show V > P discrepancies. When assessing individuals in the "gifted" or superior range of intelligence there is often not a consistent profile, but rather much scatter. It is important to incorporate multiple data sources in the evaluation of these individuals. Overall, the variables believed to be associated with V > P profiles were upheld in most studies, including patients with right-hemisphere brain damage (Chapter 8). These findings lead to expectancies regarding a patient's likely IQ profile based on his or background information, but the array of positive findings militates *against* the value of the V > P profile for differential diagnosis. Again, the factor index profile needs to be extensively researched to determine its clinical utility.

Clinicians need to be able to go beyond the computed Verbal and Performance IQs to determine when the discrepancy between the two may be misleading or meaningless. Illustrations include instances when the IQs do not correspond to a unitary ability because of differences between pertinent indexes (e.g., VCI vs. WMI), or because of marked subtest scatter within the V or P scale; when a person uses a verbal strength to compensate for a performance deficit; or when a person between the ages of 16 and 54 is retested on the WAIS-III after an interval of a few months.

CHAPTER 10

Profile Interpretation:
What the Subtests Measure

Chapters 10, 11, and 12 treat the crucial topic of WAIS-III profile interpretation by trying to integrate and explain the fluctuations that occur in each individual's subtest profile. Chapter 10 sets the foundation for this type of test interpretation by delineating the abilities and traits that each task measures and by indicating clinical, developmental, neuropsychological, and empirical aspects of each of the 14 separate subtests. Chapter 11 presents empirical methods to facilitate the identification of significant strengths and weaknesses in the WAIS-III profile, to assess the unusualness of the person's degree of subtest scatter, and to examine the results of empirical studies suggesting characteristic profiles for learning-disabled individuals and for adults with Alzheimer's-type dementia. Chapter 12 offers several rational and clinical approaches for generating meaningful hypotheses from the examinee's WAIS-III profile. Both Chapter 11 and Chapter 12 make full use of the raw materials presented in this chapter.

At the end of Chapter 10 are four *Examiner's Forms* to facilitate the clinician's task of evaluating the testing conditions and recording observations of the examinee's behaviors. Like the Examiner's Forms at the end of Chapters 9, 11 and 12, these forms may be copied without permission of the authors or publisher.

WAYS OF GROUPING
WAIS-III SUBTESTS

Wechsler (1939) opted for a two-pronged categorization of his Wechsler-Bellevue subtests into Verbal and Performance Scales. He maintained this organizational system for each succeeding version of his scales, although he readily admitted: "Of course, the abilities represented in the tests may also be meaningfully classified in other ways. But the Verbal vs. Performance subdivision remains a concurrent dichotomy regardless of other ways in which the tests are classified" (Wechsler, 1974, p. 9).

Some of the more clinically useful methods of recategorizing the WAIS-III subtests are covered briefly in the following sections to serve as a basis for understanding some of the terms and categories used later in the chapter in the subtest-by-subtest analysis of each task.

Factor Analysis

In Chapter 7, the WAIS-III factor structure was explored in detail, focusing on two-, three-, and four-factor solutions. The four-factor solutions correspond to the four indexes that should be routinely computed for virtually everyone assessed on the WAIS-III. The two-factor and three-factor solutions are discussed here briefly.

Two Factors

When two factors are rotated, the dimensions correspond generally to Wechsler's Verbal and Performance Scales (Kaufman, Lichtenberger, McLean, 2001). All seven Performance subtests loaded higher on the Performance than Verbal factor. Of the Verbal subtests, four loaded much higher on the Verbal than the Performance factor. However, Arithmetic loaded about equally on each factor and Digit Span and Letter-Number Sequencing loaded higher on the Performance factor. These WAIS-III factor-analytic findings represent the evidence for the construct validity of Wechsler's Verbal and Performance Scales, similar to that of the strong evidence of the construct validity of the 11 WAIS-R subtests that appeared in the last decade.

Three Factors

When three factors are rotated, based on data from Kaufman et al. (2001), the WAIS-III factors are best defined as shown in Table 10.1. Chapter 7 discusses when to interpret two or three factors for a given individual. Chapter 11 permits computation of standard scores on the three factors and describes an interpretive system.

TABLE 10.1   A three-factor structure of the WAIS-III

Verbal Comprehension	Perceptual Organization	Working Memory
Information	Picture Completion	Arithmetic
Vocabulary	Block Design	Digit Span
Similarities	Object Assembly	Letter-Number Sequencing
Comprehension	Matrix Reasoning	Digit Symbol-Coding
	Picture Arrangement	Symbol Search

NOTE: Based on varimax and oblimin rotations of 14 WAIS-III subtests at ages 16–89 (Kaufman et al., 2001).

Bannatyne's Categories

The four-pronged division of WISC subtests proposed by Bannatyne (1968, 1971) and subsequently modified (Bannatyne, 1974) has achieved widespread use for the assessment of children and adults (Kaufman, 1979b, 1990, 1994a). Numerous WISC, WISC-R, and WISC-III investigations of reading and learning-disabled children have revealed characteristic profiles for groups of children with learning difficulties; they perform relatively well on the Spatial triad, but demonstrate weaknesses in the Sequential and Acquired Knowledge areas (Kaufman, 1994a; Kaufman, Harrison, & Ittenbach, 1990; Rugel, 1974). WAIS and WAIS-R studies have also demonstrated the usefulness of this categorization system for organizing the profiles of adults with learning problems (e.g., Cordoni, O'Donnell, Ramaniah, Kurtz, & Rosenshein, 1981; Salvia, Gajar, Gajria, & Salvia, 1988). Indeed, some evidence suggests that learning-disabled adults also perform poorly on the subtests composing Bannatyne's Sequential and Acquired Knowledge groupings (see Chapter 11).

Bannatyne's recategorization of Wechsler tasks, as applied to the WAIS-III, is shown in

Table 10.2. We have categorized the new subtests of Matrix Reasoning and Letter-Number Sequencing based on our clinical judgment of what these tasks measure.

All WAIS-III tasks, except Picture Arrangement and Symbol Search, are included in Bannatyne's system, and two tasks (Vocabulary, Arithmetic) appear on two different scales. Picture Arrangement appears to measure skills akin to both Sequential and Spatial abilities; its exclusion from Bannatyne's approach again reinforces its maverick, subtest-specific nature. The Spatial Ability category corresponds to the Perceptual Organization factor in the WAIS-III three-factor solutions, to the subtests most associated with Witkin's field dependence/field independence cognitive style (Goodenough & Karp, 1961), and to the tasks most associated with the simultaneous processing of stimuli (Das, Kirby, & Jarman, 1979; Kaufman, 1979b; Kaufman & Kaufman, 1983a, 1983b; Naglieri & Das, 1997b).

The Sequential Ability grouping is related to the familiar Working Memory/Processing Speed factors, although for the WAIS-III, the quartet of Arithmetic–Digit Span–Digit Symbol-Coding–Letter-Number Sequencing seems like the best representation of this sequential factor. As Bannatyne's name for the category implies, it also reflects what has been referred to as the sequential processing of stimuli, and to what the Naglieri-Das-Luria model calls *successive processing*. Consequently, a comparison of Bannatyne's Spatial and Sequential categories for a given individual

may give insight into that person's mental processing preference, whether sequential or simultaneous. If the Luria (1980) model is extended one step further, the person's Picture Arrangement scaled score may give some clues to his or her planning ability.

The two categories composed only of Verbal subtests are also quite useful for profile analysis. The Acquired Knowledge grouping, in particular, often separates out from the remainder of the Verbal Scale for bright individuals who are dyslexic or who have completed only a little formal education, and for people of average or above average intelligence who have made the most of their ability through intellectual striving. The Acquired Knowledge grouping will be uncharacteristically low in the first case, and unusually high in the second.

A method for converting a person's scaled scores on the four different Bannatyne categories of WAIS-III tasks to standard scores (mean = 100, $SD = 15$) is given in Chapter 11, as is a simple empirical technique for computing strengths and weaknesses on the four Bannatyne categories.

Horn's Modified Fluid–Crystallized Model

Chapter 5 (on aging) revealed the importance of Horn's (1989) expansion and refinement of fluid–crystallized theory for interpreting age-related changes in intelligence across the adult

TABLE 10.2 Classification of WAIS-III subtests according to Bannatyne's model

Verbal Conceptualization Ability	Spatial Ability	Sequential Ability	Acquired Knowledge
Similarities	Picture Completion	Arithmetic	Information
Vocabulary	Block Design	Digit Span	Arithmetic
Comprehension	Object Assembly	Digit Symbol-Coding	Vocabulary
	Matrix Reasoning	Letter-Number Sequencing	

NOTE: Bannatyne's categorization includes the first three subtests listed in each column. Matrix Reasoning and Letter-Number Sequencing represent our classifications based on an understanding of Bannatyne's model.

life span. From the vantage point of the original Horn-Cattell two-pronged fluid–crystallized dichotomy, the Verbal Scale measures the kind of education-related abilities associated with crystallized thinking, while the Performance Scale assesses the novel problem solving associated with fluid thinking (Matarazzo, 1972).

Horn extended the fluid (*Gf*)–crystallized (*Gc*) model by identifying 9 to 10 broad abilities: Fluid intelligence, Crystallized intelligence, Short-Term Acquisition and Retrieval, Visual Intelligence, Auditory Intelligence, Long-Term Storage and Retrieval, Cognitive Processing Speed, Correct Decision Speed, and Quantitative Knowledge (Horn, 1991). We have grouped the WAIS-III subtests into five of the factors from the expanded *Gf–Gc* model, based on our understanding of the most recent version of the Horn model (Horn, 1989, 1991; Horn & Hofer, 1992, Horn & Noll, 1997; Kaufman & Horn, 1996; Woodcock, 1990): Crystallized Intelligence, Fluid Intelligence, Broad Visualization, Short-Term Acquisition and Retrieval, and Broad Speediness (see Table 10.3).

With the division of the WAIS-III subtests into these five categories, the three Verbal Comprehension tasks are considered measures of crystallized intelligence, along with Comprehension and the culture-loaded Picture Arrangement. In addition to its connection to *Gc*, Similarities is considered a measure of *Gf* as well because of its problem-solving component. The fluid category cuts across content areas by comprising two Verbal and four Performance sub-

tests, including one of the WAIS-III's new tasks, Matrix Reasoning. The Short-Term Acquisition and Retrieval category corresponds to the WMI, and Object Assembly (an optional WAIS-III subtest) joins the two PSI subtests to form the Speed category. See Chapter 11 for a method for converting Horn's five categories to standard scores and for identifying a person's strengths and weaknesses on the five categories.

Cattell-Horn-Carroll (CHC) Theory

There are striking similarities between Carroll's (1993) three-stratum model and the expanded Horn model, as well as notable differences. The Carroll model includes Stratum III, general or *g* ability, which has no place in Horn's theory (and no use to Horn). It also includes Stratum I, a wide diversity of specific, narrow abilities that are only tangentially related to the thrust of Horn's theory. However, the second level of Carroll's model—Stratum II (broad abilities)—includes the abilities of Fluid intelligence, Crystallized intelligence, General Memory and Learning, Broad Visual Perception, Broad Auditory Perception, Broad Retrieval Ability, Broad Cognitive Speediness, and Reaction Time/Decision Speed. This stratum is extremely similar both in terminology and concept to Horn's array of abilities that define his expanded and refined *Gf–Gc* theory. Because of these similarities, Horn's and Carroll's models were merged into the Cattell-

TABLE 10.3   Classification of WAIS-III subtests according to the *Gf–Gc* model

Crystallized Intelligence	Fluid Intelligence	Broad Visualization	Short-Term Memory	Broad Speediness
Information	Matrix Reasoning	Picture Completion	Arithmetic	Digit Symbol-Coding
Vocabulary	Block Design	Block Design	Digit Span	Symbol Search
Comprehension	Object Assembly	Object Assembly	Letter-Number	Object Assembly
Similarities	Similarities	Matrix Reasoning	Sequencing	
Picture Arrangement	Picture Arrangement			
	Arithmetic			

Horn-Carroll or CHC model (Flanagan, McGrew, & Ortiz, 2000; Flanagan & Ortiz, 2001; McGrew, 1997). This merger takes aspects of both Carroll's and Horn's theories that accord well, while eliminating Carroll's general ability stratum.

CHC theory emphasizes the broad and narrow abilities measured by cognitive tasks; each broad ability comprises numerous narrow abilities. Examples of narrow abilities associated with Crystallized intelligence are lexical knowledge and oral production and fluency, whereas the narrow abilities of induction and quantitative reasoning are subsumed under the broad ability of Fluid intelligence. Flanagan et al. (2000, Figure 2.4) list a total of 75 narrow abilities associated with 10 broad abilities (between 2 and 14 per broad ability) in their slight modification of CHC theory. The merger of the theories produced the following eight broad abilities, in addition to *Gf* and *Gc*: Quantitative Knowledge (*Gq*), Reading & Writing (*Grw*), Short-Term Memory (*Gsm*), Visual Processing (*Gv*), Auditory Processing (*Ga*), Long-Term Storage & Retrieval (*Glr*), Processing Speed (*Gs*), and Decision/Reaction Time/Speed (*Gt*) (Flanagan et al., 2000). See Flanagan et al. (2000), Flanagan and Ortiz (2001), and Chapter 14 of this book on the WJ III for more detail on CHC theory.

Based on Flanagan et al.'s (2000) analysis, the following broad abilities are measured by one or more WAIS-III subtests: *Gc* (VCI subtests plus Comprehension), *Gf* (Matrix Reasoning), *Gv* (Block Design, Object Assembly), *Gv/Gc* (Picture Completion, Picture Arrangement), *Gsm* (Digit Span, Letter-Number Sequencing), *Gq/Gf* (Arithmetic), and *Gs* (PSI subtests). In the subtest-by-subtest analysis, we list both the broad and narrow abilities measured by each of the 14 subtests, relying on the classifications made by Flanagan et al. (2000).

Baltes's Life Span Two-Component Model

A close conceptual and historical relative of the *Gf–Gc* model of intelligence is Baltes's (1999) two-component model of life span intellectual development. Baltes distinguishes between two main categories or components of intellectual functioning: the mechanics and the pragmatics of cognition.

- The *mechanics* of cognition are construed as an expression of the neurophysiological architecture of the mind as it evolved during biological evolution and unfolds during ontogenesis.
- The *pragmatics* of cognition are associated with acquired bodies of knowledge available from and mediated through culture.

Support for the two-component model comes from research on maintained and vulnerable intellectual abilities (see Chapter 5). Abilities that show roughly linear decline during adulthood, with further acceleration of decline in old age involve mechanics. Mechanics are abilities such as reasoning, spatial orientation, or perceptual speed. In contrast, abilities that show little relationship to age or that show decline in only very old age are the more pragmatic abilities. Pragmatic abilities are those such as verbal knowledge or numerical ability.

Thus, the mechanic and pragmatic abilities applied to the WAIS-III would lump subtests that are measures of reasoning (*Gf*), spatial orientation (*Gv*), and perceptual speed (*Gs*) all under mechanics, and subtests that are measures of verbal knowledge (*Gc*) and numerical ability (*Gq*) under pragmatics. All of the WAIS-III Performance subtests have either a component of reasoning, spatial orientation, or perceptual speed, and would be considered mechanical abilities, and all of the Verbal Subtests, except Digit Span and Letter-Number Sequencing, have either a component of verbal knowledge or numerical ability, and would be considered pragmatic abilities. Baltes's two-pronged theory, therefore, comes much closer to Wechsler's original, armchair division of subtests into two categories than it does to the more theory-based approaches of Horn (1989) and Carroll (1993) or the recent CHC merger of the pair of theories.

Osgood's Psycholinguistic Approach and the Information-Processing Approach

Kirk, McCarthy, and Kirk (1968) developed the Illinois Test of Psycholinguistic Abilities (IPA) based on Osgood's theory of communication. Although the ITPA was constructed to measure a child's language abilities, most of its component tasks are quite similar to the kinds of subtests that are included in Wechsler's intelligence batteries. Despite the ITPA's focus on children and language, the Osgood approach represents a useful way of regrouping WAIS-III subtests for adolescents and adults, especially when integrating the psycholinguistic model with Silver's (1993) information-processing model. (The latter model is discussed in Chapter 1 and depicted in Figure 1.2; as explained in the first chapter, its use for test interpretation is fundamental to the intelligent testing philosophy.)

The psycholinguistic model has three dimensions of cognitive abilities: channels of communication, levels of organization, and psycholinguistic processes. The major channels of communication, "the routes through which the content of communication flows" (Kirk et al., 1968, p. 7), are auditory–vocal and visual–motor. These are assessed quite well on the WAIS-III; all Verbal subtests are processed within the auditory–vocal channel, and all Performance tasks (with the possible exception of Picture Completion and Matrix Reasoning) are processed within the visual–motor channel. Picture Completion and Matrix Reasoning, for a person who verbalizes the response, are best categorized as visual–vocal subtests. Interpreting the WAIS-III from the vantage point of channels of communication recognizes that all WAIS-III tasks are a measure of communication ability as well as intelligence. If a person has a defective channel, perhaps because of a brain-related sensory–motor deficiency, either the Verbal or the Performance IQ will not be a valid measure of intelligence for that individual.

Osgood's levels of organization, the "degree to which habits of communication are organized

within the individual" (Kirk et al., 1968, p. 7), include representational and automatic. The former requires high-level, complex thinking, demanding the utilization of symbols and their meaning; in contrast, the automatic level requires less voluntary behavior and involves overlearned, highly organized habits. Automatic processing "is involved in such activities as visual and auditory closure, speed of perception, ability to reproduce a sequence seen or heard, rote learning, synthesizing isolated sounds into a word, and utilizing the redundancies of experience" (Kirk et al., 1968, p. 7).

Whereas one might immediately assume that any task included on a test of intelligence would, by definition, be at the representational level of organization, that is not quite the case. Certainly, most subtests are representational in nature. However, Digits Forward is clearly an automatic task, even though Digits Backward is representational. In addition, both Picture Completion and Digit Symbol-Coding have components of both automatic and representational tasks, and are best categorized as being at both levels of organization. Not infrequently, an individual will earn relatively high scores on Picture Completion and Digit Symbol-Coding while the remainder of the Performance scale is depressed. This pattern may well be associated with a person who, despite limited intelligence, has highly developed "automatic processing" skills. One might anticipate that person to have an average to good forward span (6 digits or more) as well.

Within each channel of communication, regardless of the level of organization, an individual must apply certain processes to the acquisition and use of the language: reception (recognizing and comprehending what is seen or heard); association (also called organization; mediating the information received by interpreting, organizing, or otherwise mentally manipulating the symbols); and expression (making a response, either vocally, gesturally, or manipulatively). All cognitive tasks have aspects of all three processes, although automatic-level tasks have little association or mediation. The ITPA includes representational subtests that stress a single process within either the auditory–vocal or visual–motor channel. In fact, their names reflect this goal: auditory reception, visual association, manual expression, and so forth.

Some WAIS-III subtests, most notably Comprehension and Block Design, are strong measures of all three psycholinguistic processes. Within the auditory–vocal channel, Comprehension requires excellent reception (because the questions are long and often complex), association (it is a high-level reasoning task), and expression (complex verbal responses are typically needed for 2-point answers). Similarly, the visual–motor Block Design subtest makes heavy demands on all three processes.

The three psycholinguistic processes correspond to three of the four components of Silver's (1993) information-processing model: Reception = Input, Association = Integration, and Expression = Output. However, the remaining component of the information-processing system—Storage— also needs to be considered. We have blended the Osgood and Silver models and have applied this merger to the WAIS-III subtests, as illustrated in Table 10.4. Whereas subtests like Block Design and Comprehension are quite complex in their psycholinguistic and information-processing demands, other WAIS-III subtests are a bit less complex and are able to fit into the grid we prepared in Table 10.4. The fits are not perfect, because mental ability tasks are necessarily multidimensional in what they measure, but we have assigned eight WAIS-III subtests to the grid, one occupying each slot in the 2 × 4 grid (2 channels × 4 processes).

Within the auditory–vocal channel, Information is a good measure of reception. The individual must interpret a fairly long oral question with a minimal amount of association (simply remembering a fact, not solving a problem) and expression (most responses require a single word). Similarly, Picture Completion assesses visual reception—interpreting the pictures—while making virtually no associative or expressive demands.

Similarities is mainly a test of relating or associating two concepts; the receptive demands are limited to the understanding of two words per item (e.g., DOG–LION) and even a person with unimpressive expressive abilities can earn 2 points on many items with just a single word. Matrix Reasoning is a good measure of visual association, but also demands receptive abilities to interpret the pictures or symbols. Nevertheless, Matrix Reasoning is primarily a reasoning test, putting the onus directly on the association aspect of the psycholinguistic model (or the integration aspect of the information-processing model). Its reliance on pointing to the correct response (or saying the letter of the answer) deemphasizes the expression component. In that sense, Matrix Reasoning is a far better fit to the grid than was Picture Arrangement, which was the best measure of visual association in the WAIS-R (Kaufman, 1990, Table 12.4). Despite the receptive demands of Matrix Reasoning, it is still well suited as a member of the grid shown in Table 10.4; even the ITPA Visual Association subtest (solving visual analogies) had the identical flaw of demanding considerable visual reception in addition to association.

Digit Span and Symbol Search adequately measure the storage component of the model for the auditory–vocal and visual–motor channels, respectively. Both tasks use stimuli that are limited

TABLE 10.4   WAIS-III subtests categorized by an integration of Osgood's psycholinguistic and the basic information-processing model

Channel	Input (Reception)	Integration (Association)	Storage (Memory)	Output (Expression)
Auditory–Vocal	Information	Similarities	Digit Span	Vocabulary
Visual–Motor	Picture Completion	Matrix Reasoning	Symbol Search	Digit Symbol-Coding

in their complexity, neither requires problem solving (Symbol Search may demand some planning ability), and neither places heavy demands on expression. Unlike the considerable visual–motor requirements for Digit Symbol-Coding, Symbol Search merely demands a slash through a "Yes" or "No" box, with no penalties given for sloppy pencil marks or for barely touching the correct box. Individuals with good visual memories will look at the Target Group once, scan the Search group, and respond, thereby earning high scores. Those with weak memories might go back and forth between the Target and Search groups, earning relatively poor scores because of the inefficient style of responding.

Vocabulary is a good measure of verbal expression; the individual has to understand just a single spoken word, and knowledge of each word must be retrieved from long-term storage, not figured out. The person's score depends heavily on how well he or she can spontaneously express the concept in words. Similarly, Digit Symbol-Coding makes minimal receptive demands (the symbols to be processed are quite simple) and requires little thinking. When operating from the Osgood model, it is essentially a test of psychomotor speed, or manual expression. In this respect, expression within the visual–motor channel requires excellent motor coordination, in contrast to the gestural communication necessary for success on the ITPA Manual Expression subtest (e.g., demonstrating gesturally the way to brush one's teeth).

Examiners who apply the Osgood/information-processing model model, especially for brain-injured or learning-disabled adolescents and adults, should be able to pinpoint the channel or level of organization that is dysfunctional, as well as the specific process that is deficient (reception, association, storage, expression).

Rapaport's Pioneering Clinical Model

The first generation of Wechsler clinicians grew up on Wechsler's own interpretations of the tests (his pattern analysis), along with Cohen's (1952a,

1952b) factor-analytic inferences and Rapaport's clinical model, which tried to bridge the gap between intellectual functioning and personality development (Mayman, Schafer, & Rapaport, 1951; Rapaport, Gill, & Schafer, 1945–46). From these sources, and perhaps especially from the clinical interpretive approach advocated by Rapaport and his colleagues, came the wealth of conventional clinical wisdom that has survived to the present day.

Rapaport preceded Hunt's (1961) important declaration that the IQ was neither fixed nor constant, and stressed the influence of personality, environmental stimulation, emotional stimulation, defensive styles, cultural predilections, psychopathology, and brain injury on the maturation and expression of intelligence. He predated modern approaches to systematic profile interpretation (for example, by urging examiners to evaluate deviations of each Wechsler-Bellevue subtest from the person's average of all subtests), and ensured that future generations of clinicians would interpret Wechsler intelligence profiles in the context of personality development and environmental influences.

We do not generally agree with a number of Rapaport's assertions, such as the notion that cognitive tests like Arithmetic or Picture Completion are primarily measures of the behavior of concentration. We also disagree with the pertinence of many of the Rapaport-Schafer hypotheses regarding the clinical interpretation of specific findings in individuals' profiles being associated with a variety of pathological conditions: for example, misses on easy Comprehension items conceivably reflecting schizophrenia or psychotic depression; decrements in Information, contrasted with adequate Comprehension, indicating a hysteric reaction; or increments in Picture Completion suggesting a possible paranoid trend (Gilbert, 1978). As Matarazzo (1972) noted a generation ago: "Little evidence in the way of validation for these or related hypotheses emerged" (p. 467). That statement remains true today.

Particularly indefensible, from the standpoint of psychometrics, are some of the inferences made by psychoanalytically oriented clinicians who have carried Rapaport's ideas to an extreme. For example, Allison, Blatt, and Zimet (1968) inferred from high Digit Symbol and low Digit Span a person "who seems to be controlling strong and pressing anxiety by excessive activity. When we find the reverse pattern, a high Digit Span and a low Digit Symbol, we are usually confronted with an essentially depressed person who is attempting to ward off recognition of depressive affect perhaps in a hypomanic way, usually via denial, but not necessarily through activity and acting out behavior" (p. 32).

Nonetheless, the Rapaport approach occupies a unique place in clinical history; it depended heavily on Wechsler's clinical insights and on considerable empirical data and has been influential in the clinical lore that has been passed on from generation to generation of clinicians. Further, Rapaport's analysis of Wechsler tasks in terms of the abilities and traits they measure represents a useful contemporary supplement for interpreting WAIS-III subtest profiles.

Basically, Mayman et al. (1951) posit five thought functions that affect differential performance on the Wechsler subtests: memory, concept formation, visual organization, visual–motor coordination, and orienting responses. Memory and Concept Formation facilitate the accumulation of experiences and memories, while visual organization (without essential motor activity) and visual–motor coordination deal with the key role of visual–perceptual processes in directing motor behavior and manipulations. The orienting category includes attention, concentration, and anticipation, each a crucial behavior that guides the selective orientation of each person in every reality situation. This category relates to Luria's (1980) Block 1 (attentional) and Block 3 (planning) operations, with attention and concentration considered a Block 1 function and anticipation a Block 3 function. In contrast, the remaining four Mayman-Schafer-Rapaport categories pertain primarily to Luria's Block 2, or coding, functions.

Each Wechsler task is considered to assess many functions, but one or two are considered primary for virtually every subtest. Comprehen-

sion does not fit directly into the five-pronged system. It measures the concept of judgment, which straddles the intellectual and emotional domains. Judgment is not quite concept formation, and not quite an orienting response, although it requires conceptual understanding and an "emotional–attitudinal orientation" that enables the individual to automatically select the relevant, appropriate aspects of each social situation. Table 10.5 shows how the remaining 13 WAIS-III tasks fit into Rapaport's scheme. We have used our clinical judgment to classify new subtests.

Rapaport's system has a number of benefits:

- It provides a sensible rationale for a common split that occurs in individuals' Performance profile (visual organization without essential motor activity versus visual–motor coordination).
- It provides a behavior-related explanation for the frequent split of Arithmetic and Digit Span from the remaining Verbal subtests.
- It provides possible behavioral explanations for low or high scores of many on the WAIS-III subtests.
- It shows the combination of the important cognitive and behavioral components of most Performance subtests.
- It offers behavioral hypotheses for two pairs of nonverbal tasks that may be uncharacteristically high or low for a given individual (anticipation–Picture Arrangement and Object Assembly; concentration–Picture Completion and Digit Symbol).
- It provides a rationale for a person's performance on Arithmetic or Block Design to be similar to his or her performance on tasks included in the opposite scale (concentration and concept formation, respectively).

Dean's Individual Ability Profile

Dean (1983) presented a system for regrouping WAIS-R subtests into 12 categories, which he

TABLE 10.5   Categorization of WAIS-III tasks based on Rapaport's system

Memory	Concept Formation	Visual Organization	Visual–Motor Coordination	Orienting Response
Information				
				Digit Span (attention)
Vocabulary	Vocabulary (verbal)			
				Arithmetic (concentration)
				Letter-Number Sequencing (concentration)
	Similarities (verbal)			
		Picture Completion		Picture Completion (concentration)
		Picture Arrangement		Picture Arrangement (anticipation)
	Matrix Reasoning (nonverbal)	Matrix Reasoning		
	Block Design (nonverbal)		Block Design	
			Object Assembly	Object Assembly (anticipation)
			Digit Symbol	Digit Symbol-Coding (concentration)
				Symbol Search (concentration)

referred to as his individual Ability Profile. Some of his categories overlap groupings discussed previously for other systems (most notably the factor-analytic trichotomy and Bannatyne's four-category system). Most of his remaining groupings augment profile interpretation in unique ways, and these are considered here:

General Ability—composed of the subtests that are the best measures of *g*, or general ability; except for people of limited formal education, for which this grouping must be interpreted cautiously, "[a] subject who performs poorly on this factor is seen as cognitively less able to compete within the dominant culture...performance here presents the best single measure of the subject's cognitive ability to deal

with the daily requirements of a technical, industrialized society" (Dean, 1983, p. 6). Dean included six tasks in this category, based on WAIS-R data, but we have selected a somewhat different set of tasks based on WAIS-III data. Specifically, we included the eight subtests whose *g* loadings are classified as "good" (unrotated first factor loadings ≥ .70), as categorized in Chapter 7, and listed in the Note to Table 10.6

Dean (1983) also groups several subtests together in ways that should aid WAIS-III interpretation (see Table 10.6). Although Dean's (1983) groupings were dyads, with the inclusion of new WAIS-III subtests, we have added subtests to his original WAIS-R groupings

TABLE 10.6   WAIS-III subtest groupings based on Dean's individual ability profile

Abstract Thought	Remote Memory	Visual Memory	Auditory Memory	Social Comprehension	Visual–Motor Speed
Similarities	Information	Picture Completion	Digit Span	Comprehension	Object Assembly
Block Design	Picture Completion	Digit Symbol-Coding	Arithmetic	Picture Arrangement	Digit Symbol-Coding
Matrix Reasoning		Symbol Search	Letter-Number Sequencing		Symbol Search

NOTE: The following subtests comprise the General Ability grouping: Vocabulary, Similarities, Information, Comprehension, Arithmetic, Block Design, Matrix Reasoning, Symbol Search.

based on the definitions that he provided of the six categories:

Abstract Thought—"[t]he ability to go beyond the concrete to the manipulation of concepts without a readily available referent in the environment…the abstraction and manipulation of components" (p. 6).

Remote Memory—"the recall or recognition of elements encoded greater than a month or two in the past…information which is assumed to have been overlearned in the remote past" (p. 7).

Visual Memory—"a compilation of long-term and short-term nonverbal memory components" (p. 8).

Auditory Memory—"reception and recall of information presented in the auditory mode… short-term auditory memory as a prerequisite to more complex processing…these subtests require not only auditory memory, but more specifically, verbal auditory memo" (p. 10).

Social Comprehension—"a measure of the individual's social understanding…the client's ability to apply customs, social knowledge, and mores to specific situations… Clients who score high on this factor are able to interpret and act upon environmental cues in a socially acceptable manner" (p. 12).

Visual–Motor Speed—"visual organization and continuous feedback in the motor execution of spatial tasks…the execution of these tasks [Digit Symbol and Object Assembly] requires significantly greater control over motor production than that required in either the Block Design or Picture Arrangement subtests" (p. 14).

The latter category, Visual–Motor Speed, was actually named Visual–Motor Coordination by Dean (1983). In addition, Dean included another grouping that he labeled Psychomotor Speed, composed of four Performance subtests (all but Picture Completion). We do not like Dean's Visual–Motor Coordination label for the Digit Symbol-Coding and Object Assembly dyad because it is the speed component that distinguishes this particular pair of Performance subtests; Digit Symbol-Coding is almost a pure test of speed (see Horn's classification of it), and perfect construction of the Object Assembly items, without any bonus points, yields a scaled score of 8 (25th percentile!). Similarly, the Psychomotor Speed label does not really fit the four WAIS-III Performance subtests because (1) it is an ability that is usually considered Digit Symbol-Coding's and Symbol Search's uniqueness, and (2) WAIS-III Picture Arrangement does not merit inclusion because bonus points are not given for quick, perfect performance. If Picture Arrangement is deleted from Dean's category, then the remaining triad is identical to Rapaport's Visual–Motor Coordination category. For simplicity and clarity, we have thus merged the names of Dean's two categories to produce Visual–Motor Speed.

Guilford's Structure-of-Intellect Model

Guilford's (1967) three-dimensional structure-of-intellect model has been applied to Wechsler's scales for years (Meeker, 1969; Sattler, 1974). Although it has been invaluable in a theoretical sense, clinicians have generally found it to be of limited value for profile interpretation. Nonetheless, we include it here because it sometimes represents the only way to make sense out of fluctuations in an individual's subtest profile. Table 10.7 shows brief definitions of the five Guilford operations, and the four types of Guilford content. (None of the WAIS-III tasks measures Divergent-production and only Picture Arrange-

ment might measure behavioral content.) Although Guilford (1977, 1988) modified his model, replacing Figural content with Auditory and Visual contents, and dividing Memory into short-term and long-term components, we have elected to define WAIS-III subtests from Guilford's original model. That original model remains more popular and is more familiar, and is probably more readily understood by clinicians, particularly those who have applied SOI theory to Wechsler profile interpretation in the past.

The third dimension of the model, the products (how the stimuli are organized), are of less general importance to WAIS-III interpretation and are not considered here; however, in the subtest-by-subtest analysis that follows, the products are indicated (except for Information, which includes several). Meeker (1969) classified Wechsler subtests according to the major abilities that each measures; obviously, all tasks involve cognition to some extent, but this operation is only listed for a task when it is of primary importance.

TABLE 10.7   Guilford's operations and contents

Operations (Intellectual Processes)	Description
Cognition (C)	Immediate awareness, recognition, or comprehension of stimuli
Memory (M)	Retention of information in the same form in which it was stored
Evaluation (E)	Making judgments about information in terms of a known standard
Convergent Production (N)	Responding to stimuli with the unique or "best" answer
Divergent Production (D)	Responding to stimuli where the emphasis is on a variety or quality of response (associated with creativity)

Contents (Nature of the Stimuli)	Description
Figural (F)	Shapes or concrete objects
Symbolic (S)	Numerals, single letters, or any coded symbol
Semantic (M)	Words and ideas that convey meaning
Behavioral (B)	Primarily nonverbal, involving human interactions with a stress on attitudes, needs, thoughts, and so on

The organization of WAIS-III subtests by operation and content is shown in Table 10.8, including our classifications of new subtests; only the major ability (semantic memory) is listed for Information, although scattered items assess other abilities as well.

Meeker's (1969) regrouping of Wechsler's subtests according to Guilford's structure-of-intellect model has several valuable features:

- An alternative explanation of the Working Memory factor and Bannatyne Sequential

category in terms of symbolic content (number ability).

- A rationale for Picture Arrangement's frequent concordance with a person's verbal rather than nonverbal abilities (according to Meeker, despite its use of pictures, it is the semantic meaning of the pictures that is manipulated mentally).

- An explanation for those profiles in which Comprehension is more in agreement with Performance than Verbal scores (a strength or weakness in the operation of evaluation).

TABLE 10.8   Classification of WAIS-III subtests in Guilford's model

WAIS-III Subtest	Cognition	Memory	Evaluation	Convergent-Production
Verbal Comprehension				
Vocabulary	Semantic			
Similarities	Semantic			
Information		Semantic		
Comprehension*			Semantic	
Perceptual Organization				
Picture Completion	Figural		Figural	
Block Design	Figural		Figural	
Matrix Reasoning			Figural	Figural
Picture Arrangement*			Semantic Figural Behavioral	Semantic Figural Behavioral
Object Assembly*	Figural		Figural	
Working Memory Index				
Arithmetic	Semantic	Symbolic		
Digit Span		Symbolic		
Letter-Number Sequencing		Symbolic		
Processing Speed				
Digit Symbol-Coding			Symbolic	Symbolic
Symbol Search			Figural	Figural

*Not included in the calculation of the WAIS-III factor indexes.

NOTE: Subtests are listed according to Meeker's categorization of Wechsler subtests into the Guilford model. Matrix Reasoning, Letter-Number Sequencing, and Picture Arrangement were modified according to our application of the Guilford model.

- A sensible reason for Arithmetic's loadings on both the verbal and the working memory factors (it measures both semantic cognition and symbolic memory).

ABILITIES MEASURED BY THE 14 WAIS-III SUBTESTS

Each of the 14 WAIS-III subtests is dissected in the pages that follow in terms of several analyses: Cognitive and Behavioral, Empirical, Aging, Clinical, and Neuropsychological. The seven Verbal subtests are listed first in their order of administration, followed by the seven Performance tasks, also in their order of administration.

Sources and Methods for Analyzing Each Subtest

Cognitive and Behavioral Analysis

Cognitive and behavioral analysis begins with a delineation of the abilities and traits assessed by each subtest in accordance with the various models discussed in the preceding sections of this chapter. These approaches include factor analysis, Bannatyne's categorizations, Horn's modification of the fluid–crystallized dichotomy, Osgood's psycholinguistic interpretation of cognitive tasks, Rapaport's clinical analysis, Dean's Individual Ability Profile, and Guilford's structure-of-intellect model. Next, other skills measured by each subtest, and the behavioral and background influences affecting test performance, are indicated. Finally, each subtest's specific contribution to the WAIS-III is shown.

The major sources for developing the lists of shared and unique abilities and traits for the 14 WAIS-III subtests (apart from the ones associated directly with Bannatyne, Horn, and so forth) were Kaufman (1994a, 1999); Kaufman and Lichtenberger (1999, 2000); Flanagan, McGrew, and Ortiz (2000); Matarazzo (1972);

Sattler (1992); Sattler and Ryan (1999); and Zimmerman and Woo-Sam (1985).

Aging, Clinical, and Neuropsychological Analyses

The aging analysis was based on data presented by Kaufman (2000) for the separate subtests, a study treated in depth in Chapter 5. This analysis presents adjusted mean scaled scores on each subtest for seven adult age groups (ages 16 through 89), after first equating for education level. The clinical analysis contains points stressed by Zimmerman and Woo-Sam (1985), Matarazzo (1972), and by Mayman, Schafer, and Rapaport (1951), as well as clinical inferences from our own experiences; Zimmerman and Woo-Sam's thorough analyses of each subtest were, however, the most important single source. For the neuropsychological analysis, we relied very heavily on Lezak's (1995) integration of research and clinical approach to the practical and brain-related aspects of cognitive tests; on the Boston process approach (Milberg, Hebben, & Kaplan, 1986); on Reitan's (1986) work; and on numerous articles in neuropsychological journals, including the many that we discussed in Chapters 8 and 9 on Verbal–Performance IQ discrepancies and brain damage.

Empirical Analysis

The empirical analysis includes thumbnail capsules of each subtest's *g* loadings (from Table 7.11); reliability and stability coefficients (from the WAIS-III Manual, Psychological Corporation, 1997, Tables 3.1 and 3.9) as well the magnitude of the practice effect (Table 6.6); subtest specificities (from Table 7.12); the primary and secondary oblimin factor loadings for each subtest (Tables 7.6 and 7.9; Sattler & Ryan, 1999, pp. 1216–1217; Psychological Corporation, 1997, pp. 108–109); and the subtest or subtests that each task is most and least related to (from the WAIS-III Manual, Psychological Corporation, 1997, Table 4.12). The analyses report values for the total standardization sample, ages 16–89 ($N = 2,450$); however, whenever pertinent, systematic differences due to chronological age are noted.

FACTOR LOADINGS.   The primary factor loading is listed for each subtest based on the oblimin-rotated 4-factor solution of the 14 WAIS-III subtests for ages 16–89, along with the secondary loading (defined for these analyses as ≥ .20) for some subtests. Data are from Table 7.6 for the three VCI subtests plus Comprehension. For the seven Performance subtests and the three Working Memory subtests, data are presented separately for ages 16–74 and 75–89 because of notable age-related differences in their factor loadings. For the elderly sample: (1) most Performance subtests had their primary factor loading on the Processing Speed factor, rather than the Perceptual Organization factor; and (2) the two Processing Speed subtests had secondary loadings on the Working Memory factor, creating a five-subtest dimension that resembles Barkley's (1997) construct of executive functioning. For all of the Performance subtests (except Object Assembly) and for the Working Memory subtests, mean factor loadings for ages 16–74 are based on data for four age groups (Psychological Corporation, 1997, pp. 108–109) and the values for ages 75–89 are from Table 7.9. Mean values for Object Assembly at ages 16–74 and 75–89 are based on oblimin-rotated factor loadings provided by Sattler and Ryan (1999, pp. 1216–1217)

for the 13 separate standardization age groups (Psychological Corporation, 1997, excluded Object Assembly from their analyses).

SUBTEST SPECIFICITY.   Each subtest has a proportion of variance that is unique only to it. This uniqueness is somewhat like the inverse of g, as it is a representation of the variance that is not shared with other subtests. Subtest specificity is important to know to determine now feasible it is to interpret the unique abilities or traits attributed to a subtest. It is justifiable to interpret a subtest's unique contributions to the overall test if its unique variance exceeds the error variance and is sufficient in magnitude. About 25% or more of the total variance is generally considered a sufficient amount to warrant "specific" interpretation, so long as the specific variance exceeds the error variance.

The specificity for each subtest was statistically calculated via an uncomplicated technique. The shared variance for each subtest was obtained (we used the squared multiple correlation), and then this common variance was subtracted from the subtest's reliability coefficient. The result of this calculation is the reliable unique variance (subtest specificity). To determine whether a task's uniqueness should be interpreted, the error variance for the subtest (one minus the reliability) was then compared to the specificity.

The levels of specificity are classified as "ample," "adequate," or "inadequate" in Table 10.9.

TABLE 10.9   WAIS-III subtests categorized by their specificity[a]

Ample Specificity	Adequate Specificity	Inadequate Specificity
Digit Span (.50/.10)	Picture Arrangement (.31/.26)	Symbol Search (.21/.23)
Matrix Reasoning (.39/.10)	Block Design (.27/.14)	Object Assembly (.24/.30)
Digit Symbol-Coding (.38/.16)	Information (.23/.09)	
Picture Completion (.35/.17)	Comprehension (.20/.16)	
Letter-Number Sequencing (.34/.18)	Similarities (.20/.14)	
Arithmetic (.30/.12)	Vocabulary (.19/.07)	

[a]Reliable unique variance is the first value in parentheses and subtest error variance the second.

Two values are listed for each subtest, first is the subtest specificity and second is the subtest's error variance. The subtests having the most ample amount of specificity include Digit Span, Matrix Reasoning, Digit Symbol-Coding, and Letter-Number Sequencing. This information on specificity indicates that all subtests have reliable and interpretable unique characteristics. However, interpretations of unique abilities should not always be made (see the steps of interpretation in Chapter 11).

Vocabulary

Cognitive and Behavioral Analysis for Vocabulary

ABILITIES SHARED WITH OTHER SUBTESTS

Factor Analysis:	Two-, three-, & four-factor solutions: Verbal Comprehension
Bannatyne:	Verbal Conceptualization Acquired Knowledge
Horn:	Crystallized Intelligence (*Gc*)
CHC:	Broad: Crystallized Intelligence (*Gc*) Narrow: Language Development, Lexical Knowledge
Baltes:	Pragmatics
Osgood:	Auditory–vocal channel of communication Representational level of organization Verbal expression
Rapaport:	Memory Concept formation (verbal)
Dean:	General ability
Guilford:	Cognition of semantic units
Other skills:	Fund of information Handling abstract verbal concepts Long-term memory Learning ability

INFLUENCES AFFECTING
VOCABULARY SUBTEST SCORES

- Cultural opportunities
- Foreign language background
- Intellectual curiosity and striving
- Interests
- Outside reading
- Reading ability (because a word list is presented to the examinee)
- Richness of early environment
- School learning

UNIQUE ABILITIES OR
TRAITS MEASURED BY VOCABULARY

- Language development
- Word knowledge

Empirical Analysis of Vocabulary

g loadings: *r* = .83 (best measure)

Reliability: split-half = .93, test-retest = .91

Practice effect: Trivial for ages 16–89 (gain of 0.2 scaled-score point)

Subtest specificity/Error variance: 19% vs. 7% (adequate specificity)

Primary Oblimin Factor Loading:
Verbal Comprehension factor = .89

Most related to: Information (*r* = .77)

Least related to: Object Assembly and Digit Symbol-Coding (*r* = .44)

Aging Analysis of Vocabulary

Mean scaled score across the adult age range (controlling for education at ages 20–89):

Age Group	Vocabulary Mean
16–17	8.6
18–19	9.2
20–24	9.5
25–29	10.0
30–34	10.5
35–44	10.7
45–54	11.4
55–64	10.8

Age Group	Vocabulary Mean
65–69	11.2
70–74	11.1
75–79	11.1
80–84	10.6
85–89	10.3

Aging patterns on the WAIS-R Vocabulary subtest showed gradually increasing mean scaled scores from ages 20–24 (mean = 9.7) all the way through the age span, with mean scaled scores of 10.7 and 11.1 for the 65–69 and 70–74 age groups, respectively.

Clinical Analysis of Vocabulary

- Those with repressive defensive styles may perform poorly by pushing out of consciousness any word meanings that are even mildly associated with conflict; repression impairs both the acquisition of the word knowledge and the recall of specific words that the person knows.

- High scores often reflect intellectual ambitiousness and striving, and may be associated with the defensive style of intellectualization.

- Content of responses lends itself to clinical analysis regarding the person's fears, preoccupations, feelings, interests, background, status, and possible bizarre thought processes; perseveration, clang associations (*ponder–yonder*, *assemble–resemble*), and incoherent strings of words are also observable.

- Responses need not be wrong to be clinically rich; of special clinical value are correct or partially correct responses that suffer from overelaboration (often containing trivial detail), ellipsis (omitting words, such as defining *breakfast* as "eggs and toast"), and self-reference (a sanctuary is "a safe place, far away from the ones who want to hurt you").

- Responses should be evaluated to distinguish between individuals who give overlearned, almost rote and mindless, answers, and those

with intellectual striving who approach the task with refreshing vigor by infusing responses with current experiences.

- Perseveration is sometimes evidenced when patients "give the same introduction to each response" (Milberg et al., 1986, p. 72).

Neuropsychological Analysis of Vocabulary

- Relatively insensitive to most types of psychopathology and even to many recent cerebral injuries, so it serves as a good estimate of premorbid intelligence.

- Sensitive to left-hemisphere lesions, but less so than most Verbal subtests; not very sensitive to diffuse or bilateral lesions.

- "Increased glucose metabolism occurs predominantly in and around the left temporal lobe while this test is taken, with a small metabolic increase appearing in the right temporal lobe" (Lezak, 1995, p. 540).

- Long administration time, compared to the unique information it yields, makes its cost-effectiveness questionable for known brain-damaged patients who may fatigue easily.

- The most likely WAIS-III subtest to distinguish between the diagnoses of brain damage and thought disorder because patients with the latter diagnosis "occasionally let down their guard on this innocuous-appearing verbal skill test to reveal a thinking problem in 'clangy' expressions, idiosyncratic associations, or personalized or confabulatory responses" (Lezak, 1995, p. 541).

Similarities

Cognitive and Behavioral Analysis of Similarities

ABILITIES SHARED WITH OTHER SUBTESTS

Factor Analysis:	Two-, three-, and four-factor solutions: Verbal Comprehension
Bannatyne:	Verbal Conceptualization

Horn: Crystallized Intelligence (*Gc*)
               Fluid Intelligence (*Gf*)

CHC: Broad: Crystallized Intelligence (*Gc*)
               Narrow: Language Development,
                  Lexical Knowledge

Baltes: Pragmatics

Osgood: Auditory–vocal channel
                  of communication
               Representational level
                  of organization
               Auditory association

Rapaport: Concept formation (verbal)

Dean: General ability
               Abstract thought

Guilford: Cognition of semantic content
                  (relations and transformations)

Other skills: Handling abstract verbal concepts
               Distinguishing essential from
                  nonessential details
               Reasoning (verbal)
               Verbal expression

INFLUENCES AFFECTING SIMILARITIES SUBTEST SCORES

- Flexibility
- Interests
- Negativism ("They're not alike")
- Overly concrete thinking
- Outside reading

UNIQUE ABILITIES OR TRAITS MEASURED BY SIMILARITIES

- Logical abstractive (categorical) thinking

Empirical Analysis of Similarities

g loadings: $r = .79$ (2nd best along with Information)

Reliability: split-half = .86, test-retest = .83

Practice effect: Small for ages 16–89 (gain of 0.5 scaled-score point)

Subtest specificity/Error variance: 20% vs. 14% (adequate specificity)

Primary Oblimin Factor Loading:
   Verbal Comprehension factor = .76

Most related to: Vocabulary ($r = .76$)

Least related to: Digit Symbol-Coding ($r = .40$) and Digit Span ($r = .45$)

Aging Analysis of Similarities

Mean scaled score across the adult age range (controlling for education at ages 20–89):

Age Group	Similarities Mean
16–17	9.1
18–19	9.2
20–24	9.5
25–29	10.0
30–34	10.5
35–44	10.7
45–54	11.4
55–64	10.8
65–69	11.2
70–74	11.1
75–79	11.1
80–84	10.6
85–89	10.3

Aging patterns on the WAIS-R Similarities subtest showed fairly maintained mean scaled scores, but gradual decline in the oldest age groups. After the scaled scores peak during ages 25–34 (mean = 10.2), decline occurs gradually with mean scaled scores of 9.5 and 9.0 for the 65–69 and 70–74 age groups, respectively.

Clinical Analysis of Similarities

- Responses should be evaluated to determine if they are abstract (table and chair are "furniture"), concrete (coat and suit are "made of cloth"), or functional (boat and automobile "take you where you want to go").

- Like Vocabulary responses, Similarities responses need not be wrong to be clinically rich; of special clinical value are correct or partially correct responses that suffer from overelaboration, ellipsis, and self-reference;

also interesting are overinclusive wrong responses (dog and lion both consist of cells or molecules, praise and punishment both start with the letter *p* and are both words) (Matarazzo, 1972, p. 490).

- Among Verbal Comprehension subtests, Similarities is the least affected by specific learning, formal education, background, and experience (hence, its fluid as well as crystallized classification in Horn's system); the emphasis is on finding the relationship (preferably abstract) between two concepts, but the actual concepts tend to be well known, even to retarded individuals (the hardest item is enemy–friend).

- Two-point responses to the first couple of two-point items (instruments, fruits) often reflect overlearned, everyday associations rather than true abstract thought.

- How a raw score is obtained tells much about a person's potential: A string of 1's suggests concretistic thinking and relatively limited potential, probably not due to maladjustment; a mixture of 2's and 0's implies the possibility of greater capacity for superior performance.

- "Personal preoccupations are rarely expressed and, therefore, are diagnostically meaningful when they invade this subtest" (Zimmerman & Woo-Sam, 1973, p. 93).

- Searching for relationships between the pairs of concepts sometimes evokes creative thinking and visual imagery; unlike Comprehension, the creativity does not invariably mean a wrong response.

- Responses "may reveal character trends: meticulousness, ostentation, sophistication" (Zimmerman & Woo-Sam, 1973, p. 94).

- Obsessive individuals may earn unusually high scores by giving numerous responses because a 2-point response is counted even if it is embedded in 1-point and 0-point answers (as long as the total response is not spoiled).

- Performance on this highly conceptual subtest is quite vulnerable to psychopathology.

Neuropsychological Analysis of Similarities

- Unlike Comprehension, Similarities is not affected by the impulsive behavior and lack of social appropriateness that are associated with some brain injuries.

- Brain-damaged patients often have difficulty giving abstract, conceptual responses that are worth 2 points.

- Similarities scores are very sensitive to left hemisphere lesions, especially in the left temporal and frontal lobes.

- Depressed Similarities scores are associated with bilateral damage to the frontal lobes, but not to damage to the right frontal lobe.

Arithmetic

Cognitive and Behavioral Analysis of Arithmetic

ABILITIES SHARED WITH OTHER SUBTESTS

Factor Analysis:	Two-factor solutions: Perceptual Organization and Verbal Comprehension (about equally)
	Three-factor solutions: Working Memory (primarily); Verbal Comprehension (secondarily)
	Four-factor solutions: Working Memory
Bannatyne:	Sequential
	Acquired Knowledge
Horn:	Fluid Intelligence (*Gf*)
	Short-Term Memory
CHC:	Broad: Quantitative Knowledge (*Gq*)
	Fluid Intelligence (*Gf*)
Baltes:	Pragmatics
Osgood:	Auditory–vocal channel of communication
	Representational level of organization
Rapaport:	Concentration
Dean:	General ability
	Auditory memory
Guilford:	Memory of symbolic implications
	Cognition of a semantic system

Other skills: Auditory sequencing
Encoding information for further
  cognitive processing
Facility with numbers
Mental alertness
Sequential (linear, left-brain)
  processing
Long-term memory
Reasoning (numerical)

INFLUENCES AFFECTING
ARITHMETIC SUBTEST SCORES

- Attention span
- Anxiety
- Concentration
- Distractibility
- Learning disabilities ("ACID" profile)
- School learning
- Working under time pressure

UNIQUE ABILITIES OR
TRAITS MEASURED BY ARITHMETIC

- Computational skill
- Quantitative Knowledge (*Gq*) (CHC broad ability)
- Mathematical Achievement (CHC narrow ability)
- Quantitative Reasoning (CHC narrow ability)

Empirical Analysis of Arithmetic

g loadings: *r* = .75 (5th best)

Reliability: split-half = .88, test-retest = .86

Practice effect: Small for ages 16–89 (gain of 0.4 scaled-score point)

Subtest specificity/Error variance: 30% vs. 12% (ample specificity at ages 16–17, 35–64, & 70–89, adequate at ages 18–34 & 65–69)

Primary Oblimin Factor Loading:

Ages 16–74: Working Memory factor = .47

Ages 75–89: Working Memory factor = .44

Secondary Oblimin Factor Loading:

Ages 16–34 (*not* 35–54): Verbal Comprehension factor = .31

Ages 75–89: Verbal Comprehension factor = .27; and Perceptual Organization factor = .21

Most related to: Vocabulary (*r* = .60) and Information (*r* = .63)

Least related to: Object Assembly (*r* = .39)

Aging Analysis of Arithmetic

Mean scaled score across the adult age range (controlling for education at ages 20–89):

Age Group	Arithmetic Mean
16–17	9.4
18–19	9.9
20–24	9.9
25–29	10.2
30–34	10.2
35–44	10.1
45–54	10.8
55–64	10.4
65–69	10.4
70–74	9.9
75–79	9.7
80–84	9.6
85–89	9.1

Aging patterns on the WAIS-R Arithmetic subtest showed maintained mean scaled scores across the age span, with a low mean scaled score of 9.9 at ages 20–24 and a high mean scaled score of 10.4 at ages 55–64.

Clinical Analysis of Arithmetic

- Because actual computational skills required for success are learned in elementary school and are, at most, seventh-grade level, failure is frequently due to temporary inability to attend or concentrate, "blocking" on mathematics items, nervousness at taking a school-like task without paper and pencil, a negativistic or defeatist attitude, and so forth.

- Wrong responses should be analyzed to infer whether the error was in computation, selection of the wrong operation, or failure to understand or attend to the question; for example, in response to the question about the number of hours it takes to walk 24 miles at the rate of 3 miles per hour, the answer "9" suggests an error in computational skill, while "27" reflects a reasoning mistake, and "1,000" is bizarre.

- Testing the limits without time pressure and with paper and pencil is often advised to help assess the roles of anxiety and concentration on test performance.

- Poor performance should be interpreted as a deficit in mathematical ability only after ruling out the wide range of behavioral and cognitive (e.g., short-term memory, sequencing) hypotheses that are known to have a strong impact on WAIS-III Arithmetic scores.

- For retarded individuals, the subtest measures a skill akin to social intelligence or adaptive behavior because the early items involve counting and handling money.

- The nature of the Arithmetic items commonly arouses anxiety in examinees; how they respond to the anxiety and possible frustration (by rejecting the test, by composing themselves and doing well, by acting agitated and distressed) is of clinical interest.

- Reflective, compulsive, obsessive, or neurologically impaired individuals with excellent arithmetic skills may perform relatively poorly compared to other Verbal subtests because of failure to respond within some time limits, and failure to earn any of the two possible bonus points. The impact of these behaviors was much greater for the WAIS-R Arithmetic, which allotted *five* possible bonus points.

Neuropsychological Analysis of Arithmetic

- Routinely administer Items 1–3 (block counting) to all individuals with known or suspected right-hemisphere lesions because they may have difficulty with the visual stimuli despite succeeding on much harder oral questions.

- Patients with immediate memory and related problems are not likely to display their true mathematical ability because of the oral nature of the task, and will conceivably experience great difficulty with the more complex, multistep items.

- The oral format prevents identification of the difficulties of patients whose spatial problems would be revealed on a paper-and-pencil test; also, "the examiner may remain ignorant of a figure or number alexia that would show up if the patient had to look at arithmetic symbols on paper" (Lezak, 1995, p. 644).

- Patients with damage to the left temporal or left parietal lobe have been reported to perform poorly on Arithmetic; so have some patients with right hemisphere lesions due to memory, attentional, or organizational difficulties.

Digit Span

Cognitive and Behavioral Analysis of Digit Span

ABILITIES SHARED WITH OTHER SUBTESTS

Factor Analysis:	Two-factor solutions: Perceptual Organization
	Three-factor solutions: Working Memory
	Four-factor solutions: Working Memory
Bannatyne:	Sequential
Horn:	Short-Term Memory (*Gsm*)
CHC:	Broad: Short-Term Memory (*Gsm*)
Osgood:	Auditory–vocal channel of communication
	Automatic level of organization (Digits Forward)
	Representational level of organization (Digits Backward)
Rapaport:	Attention
Dean:	Auditory memory

Guilford: Memory of symbolic content (units
              and systems)

Other skills: Auditory sequencing
               Encoding information for further
                 cognitive processing (Digits
                 Backward)
               Facility with numbers
               Mental alertness
               Sequential (linear, left-brain)
                 processing

INFLUENCES AFFECTING
DIGIT SPAN SUBTEST SCORES

• Ability to receive stimuli passively

• Attention span

• Anxiety

• Distractibility

• Flexibility (when switching from forward to backward span)

• Learning disabilities ("ACID" profile)

• Negativism (refusal to try to reverse digits, refusal to exert effort until the more challenging reversal task, or refusal to take a "meaningless" test)

UNIQUE ABILITIES OR
TRAITS MEASURED BY DIGIT SPAN

• Immediate rote recall

• Memory span (CHC narrow ability)

• Reversibility (Digits Backward)

Empirical Analysis of Digit Span

g loadings: $r = .57$ (worst)

Reliability: test-retest = .83, split-half = .90

Practice effect: Small for ages 16–74 (gains of 0.4–0.5 scaled-score point); Trivial for ages 75–89 (loss of 0.1 point)

Subtest specificity/Error variance: 50% vs. 10% (ample specificity)

Primary Oblimin Factor Loading:

  Ages 16–74: Working Memory factor = .74

  Ages 75–89: Working Memory factor = .58

Most related to: Letter-Number Sequencing ($r = .57$)

Least related to: Object Assembly ($r = .26$)

Aging Analysis of Digit Span

Mean scaled score across the adult age range (controlling for education at ages 20–89):

Age Group	Digit Span Mean
16–17	9.9
18–19	9.9
20–24	10.3
25–29	10.0
30–34	9.7
35–44	9.6
45–54	9.7
55–64	9.4
65–69	9.3
70–74	8.9
75–79	8.6
80–84	8.7
85–89	8.6

Aging patterns on the WAIS-R Digit Span subtest showed maintained mean scaled scores until the 55–64 age group, with high mean scaled score of 10.1 at ages 45–54 and a low mean scaled score of 9.4 at ages 65–74.

Clinical Analysis of Digit Span

• Testing the limits and recording responses is important to help discern whether failure is due to poor memory, sequencing problems, anxiety, inattention (perhaps caused by intrusions into consciousness of anxieties or emotionally laden ideas), distractibility, negativism, low motivation, inability to develop a strategy (such as "chunking"), or low intelligence in general.

• The average adult has a forward span of 6.4 and a backward span of 4.7 (Wechsler, 1997,

Table 8.6). Deviations from this norm—much longer forward than backward spans, or shorter forward than backward spans—are therefore clinically meaningful.

- Sensitive to testing conditions that fall short of the ideal.

- Good performance by a person whose psychopathology has disrupted success on other WAIS-III tasks may be demonstrating the "ability to rally to a simple task" (Zimmerman & Woo-Sam, 1973, p. 105).

- Hearing-impaired individuals and those with auditory discrimination problems are often unduly handicapped on this subtest.

- State anxiety (e.g., test anxiety), rather than trait or chronic anxiety, seems to disrupt the repetition of digits.

- Impulsivity may be noted by an individual who starts to respond before the examiner has completed the item or by one who repeats the digits very rapidly.

Neuropsychological Analysis of Digit Span

- The combination of forward and backward span into a single score reduces the task's neuropsychological value because brain injury often affects the two skills differently.

- Tasks like Digits Forward "tend to be more vulnerable to left hemisphere involvement than to either right hemisphere or diffuse damage" (Lezak, 1995, p. 360).

- Patients with left-hemisphere damage or visual–field defects have difficulty reversing digits (Lezak, 1995).

- Large differences (five or more digits) in favor of forward span occur rarely in normal people, but are more common in brain-damaged individuals.

- When interpreting raw scores on Digits Backward, examiners "should consider raw scores of 4 to 5 as *within normal limits*, 3 as *borderline defective* or *defective*, depending on

the patient's educational background..., and 2 to be *defective* for just about everyone" (Lezak, 1995, p. 367, italics in original).

- For neuropsychological purposes, the WAIS-III span, rather than the score (based on 1 point for each trial), is more diagnostic of possible brain damage because a person can achieve a low scaled score by passing only one trial per item but still have forward and backward spans that are average (Lezak, 1995).

- Digits Forward is a fairly stable skill that is generally resistant to most types of dementia, but Digits Backward "is very vulnerable to the kind of diffuse damage that occurs with solvent exposure...and in many dementing processes" (Lezak, 1995, p. 368); also, "[d]igit span backward is more sensitive to brain dysfunction than digit span forward" (Milberg et al., 1987, p. 72).

Information

Cognitive and Behavioral Analysis of Information

ABILITIES SHARED WITH OTHER SUBTESTS

Factor Analysis:	Two-, three-, and four-factor solutions: Verbal Comprehension
Bannatyne:	Acquired Knowledge
Horn:	Crystallized Intelligence (*Gc*)
CHC:	Broad: Crystallized Intelligence (*Gc*) Narrow: General Information
Baltes:	Pragmatics
Osgood:	Auditory–vocal channel of communication Representational level of organization Auditory reception
Rapaport:	Memory
Dean:	General ability Remote memory
Guilford:	Memory (primarily) of semantic content
Other skills:	Fund of information Long-term memory

INFLUENCES AFFECTING INFORMATION SUBTEST SCORES

- Alertness to the environment
- Cultural opportunities
- Foreign language background
- Intellectual curiosity and striving
- Interests
- Learning disabilities ("ACID" profile)
- Outside reading
- Richness of early environment
- School learning

UNIQUE ABILITIES OR TRAITS MEASURED BY INFORMATION

- Range of general factual knowledge

Empirical Analysis of Information

g loadings: $r = .79$ (2nd best)

Reliability: split-half = .91, test-retest = .94

Practice effect: Small for ages 16–89 (gain of 0.6 scaled-score point)

Subtest specificity/error variance: 23% vs. 9% (adequate specificity)

Primary Oblimin Factor Loading:

Verbal Comprehension factor = .81

Most related to: Vocabulary ($r = .77$)

Least related to: Digit Symbol Coding ($r = .38$)

Aging Analysis of Information

Mean scaled score across the adult age range (controlling for education at ages 20–89):

Age Group	Information Mean
16–17	9.7
18–19	10.1
20–24	10.0
25–29	10.1
30–34	10.3
35–44	10.7

Age Group	Information Mean
45–54	11.6
55–64	11.5
65–69	11.7
70–74	11.5
75–79	11.4
80–84	10.8
850–89	10.6

Aging patterns on the WAIS-R Information subtest showed maintained mean scaled scores across the age span, with a low mean scaled score of 9.9 at ages 20–24 and a high mean scaled score of 10.9 at ages 65–69.

Clinical Analysis of Information

- Items are emotionally neutral and nonthreatening.
- Easy to rationalize failures as due to limited experience or specialized knowledge.
- Those with chronic anxiety may suffer early failures and depressed scores in general; effortless, automatic responding facilitates good performance.
- Failure on easy items, coupled with success on harder items, suggests retrieval difficulties.
- Mentally retarded score especially low, but relatively high scores are sometimes obtained by individuals who have overlearned facts without true understanding.
- Bizarre responses are quite rare, hence noteworthy when they do occur (illustrations of bizarre responses from Matarazzo, 1972, p. 486: [1] an adolescent psychopath, asked for the distance from Paris to New York (an item excluded from the WAIS-III), replied, "I don't know, I never walked that far"; [2] a schizophrenic responded that the Koran is "like a chorus or a piece of cord"; [3] a manic depressive responded that the capital of Italy is "Rome, but it could have changed").
- Responses given with trivial, unnecessary detail suggest obsessiveness.

- Those with repressive defensive styles may perform poorly by pushing out of consciousness any facts that are even mildly associated with conflict; repression impairs both the acquisition of the facts and the recall of known faces; Information well below both Vocabulary and Comprehension may suggest repression.

- High scores often reflect intellectual ambitiousness, and may be associated with the defensive style of intellectualization.

- Low scores may sometimes reflect a tendency to give up easily, hostility toward a "schoolish" task, or a perfectionistic approach where no response is preferred to an imperfect answer.

Neuropsychological Analysis of Information

- Generally resistant to psychopathology and cerebral damage, so it serves as a good estimate of premorbid functioning.

- Limits should be tested with those having known or suspected brain damage to determine if failures reflect ignorance, loss of previously learned facts, or inability to retrieve the information.

- A markedly low score in the absence of a rational explanation (e.g., low education, cultural deprivation, foreign background), particularly in the context of relatively low scores on the other Verbal tests, suggests left-hemisphere involvement.

- "Temporal lobe epilepsy may result in specific impairment of this subtest" (Milberg et al., 1986, p. 70).

Comprehension

Cognitive and Behavioral Analysis of Comprehension

ABILITIES SHARED WITH OTHER SUBTESTS

Factor Analysis:	Two-, three-, and four-factor solutions: Verbal Comprehension
Bannatyne:	Verbal Conceptualization

Horn:	Crystallized Intelligence (*Gc*)
CHC:	Broad: Crystallized Intelligence (*Gc*) Narrow: Language Development, General Information
Baltes:	Pragmatics
Osgood:	Auditory–vocal channel of communication Representational level of organization
Rapaport:	Judgment
Dean:	General ability Social comprehension (social intelligence)
Guilford:	Evaluation of semantic implications
Other Skills:	Common sense (cause–effect relationships) Reasoning (verbal) Verbal expression

INFLUENCES AFFECTING COMPREHENSION SUBTEST SCORES

- Cultural opportunities
- Development of conscience or moral sense
- Negativism ("People shouldn't pay taxes," "You don't need a marriage license")
- Overly concrete thinking

UNIQUE ABILITIES OR TRAITS MEASURED BY COMPREHENSION

- Demonstration of practical information
- Evaluation and use of past experiences
- Generalization (proverbs items)
- Knowledge of conventional standards of behavior
- Social maturity
- Judgment

Empirical Analysis of Comprehension

g loadings: *r* = .77 (4th best)

Reliability: split-half = .84, test-retest = .81

Practice effect: Trivial for ages 16–89 (gain of 0.2 scaled-score point)

Subtest specificity/Error variance: 20% vs. 16% (adequate specificity)

Primary Oblimin Factor Loading:

   Verbal Comprehension factor = .80

Most related to: Vocabulary (*r* = .75)

Least related to: Digit Symbol-Coding (*r* = .37)

Aging Analysis of Comprehension

Mean scaled scores across the adult age range (controlling for education at ages 20–89):

Age Group	Comprehension Mean
16–17	8.9
18–19	9.7
20–24	9.7
25–29	10.2
30–34	10.8
35–44	10.7
45–54	11.5
55–64	11.2
65–69	11.4
70–74	11.1
75–79	10.9
80–84	9.9
85–89	9.5

Aging patterns on the WAIS-R Comprehension subtest showed maintained mean scaled scores across the age span, with a low mean scaled score of 9.9 at ages 20–24 that gradually increased to a high mean scaled score of 11.0 at ages 65–69.

Clinical Analysis of Comprehension

- Selecting the appropriate information needed to make relevant judgments demands a stable and balanced emotional–attitudinal orientation; hence, maladjustment of any sort often depresses scores.

- More than any other Wechsler subtest, Comprehension straddles the intellectual and emotional arenas.

- Conventional, rather than creative, problem-solving approaches are rewarded.

- Foreign-born subjects who have not assimilated U.S. culture are handicapped by many items, as are those from nonmainstream U.S. subcultures.

- The content of the responses is extremely valuable for indicating areas of current emotional conflict or concern; the following illustrations are taken from Zimmerman and Woo-Sam (1973, Table 4.1):

  - *Passive, dependent*—"Wait until found" if lost in forest; "My mother says to" wash clothes.
  - *Phobic*—wash clothes because "Germs kill you"; regarding deaf people, "It's a disease, from sex."
  - *Delinquent*—"Open it up and take the money," or "Throw it away," if find envelope.
  - *Unreflective*—"Go back the same way" if lost in forest.
  - *Alogical*—deaf people have "No tongue"; shallow brooks proverb means "Women talk a lot."
  - *Naive*—"Country land is better, pretty" compared to city land; marriage license "So no adultery."
  - *Contentious*—pay taxes to "Pay off politicians' graft"; "I prefer the country" to city land.

- To a much lesser extent than Vocabulary, the intrusion of emotional problems and conflicts on Comprehension responses is likely to lead to scores of zero.

- Routinely test the limits to infer the degree of real understanding when individuals (especially retarded or emotionally disturbed) give overlearned responses; stereotypes, bizarre thought processes, mere parroting, and coaching in socialization may underlie such answers.

- Provides "a rich sampling of the subject's coping ability. Active mastery versus passive dependency may be highlighted; the same applies to socialized versus antisocial behavior" (Zimmerman & Woo-Sam, 1973, p. 73).

- Responses offer clues regarding the disturbed patient's practicality and ability to behave appropriately in social situations; however, be cautious about generalizing from responses to single-issue questions because real-life adjustment is complex and multidimensional.

- Determine if pattern of successes and failures conforms to the types of questions that compose Comprehension: "personal and social behavior, general knowledge, and social obligations" (Milberg et al., 1986, p. 70).

- Obsessive individuals frequently give responses that are overlong and detailed.

Neuropsychological Analysis of Comprehension

- Patients with right hemisphere damage may score high, yet behave impractically and unreasonably.

- The most sensitive of any Wechsler Verbal subtest to left-hemisphere lesions.

- A good measure of premorbid intelligence for patients with right, bilateral, or diffuse lesions.

- Brain-related impulsivity in formerly bright individuals may evoke very different responses to various items: impulsive responses to the emotional movie and forest items; carefully reasoned answers to the city land or child labor item.

Letter-Number Sequencing

Cognitive and Behavioral Analysis of Letter-Number Sequencing

ABILITIES SHARED WITH OTHER SUBTESTS

Factor Analysis:	Two-factor solution: Perceptual Organization
	Three-factor solution: Working Memory
	Four-factor solution: Working Memory
Bannatyne:	Sequential
Horn:	Short-Term Memory (*Gsm*)

CHC:	Broad: Short-Term Memory (*Gsm*)
Osgood:	Auditory–vocal channel of communication
	Representational level of organization
	Auditory association
Rapaport:	Orienting response (verbal)
Dean:	Auditory Memory
Guilford:	Memory of symbolic content
Other skills:	Encoding information for further cognitive processing
	Facility with numbers
	Short-term memory (auditory)
	Learning ability
	Planning ability

INFLUENCES AFFECTING LETTER-NUMBER SEQUENCING SUBTEST SCORES

- Ability to receive stimuli passively
- Attention span
- Anxiety
- Concentration
- Distractibility
- Flexibility
- Illiteracy or dyslexia (does not know letters and alphabet at an automatic level)
- Learning Disabilities
- Attention Deficit-Hyperactivity Disorder (ADHD)
- Negativism (refusal to take a "meaningless" task)
- Persistence

UNIQUE ABILITIES OR TRAITS MEASURED BY LETTER-NUMBER SEQUENCING

- Facility with overlearned sequences
- Working Memory (CHC theory)

Empirical Analysis of Letter-Number Sequencing

g loadings: $r = .65$ (5th worst)

Reliability: split-half = .82, test-retest = .75

Practice effect: Small for ages 16–89 (gain of 0.4 scaled-score point)

Subtest specificity/Error variance: 34% vs. 18% (ample specificity)

Primary Oblimin Factor Loading:

Ages 16–74: Working Memory factor = .70

Ages 75–89: Working Memory factor = .62

Most related to: Arithmetic (r = .55) and Digit Span (r = .57)

Least related to: Object Assembly (r = .29)

Aging Analysis of Letter-Number Sequencing

Mean scaled score across the adult age range (controlling for education at ages 20–89):

Age Group	Letter-Number Sequencing Mean
16–17	10.6
18–19	10.2
20–24	10.4
25–29	10.1
30–34	9.6
35–44	9.5
45–54	9.4
55–64	8.9
65–69	8.7
70–74	7.8
75–79	7.1
80–84	6.6
85–89	5.8

Clinical Analysis of Letter-Number Sequencing

- Sequencing, poor short-term memory, inattention, distractibility, or anxiety may be causative factors for trouble on Letter-Number Sequencing. Similar to Digit Span, sequencing problems can be evident from correctly remembering the numbers and letters, but in the wrong sequence. Short-term memory may be implicated if part of the sequence is correct but some of the numbers or letters are forgotten.

- Observe the examinee for signs of "stimulus overload," which can lead to frustration. Statements such as "that is too much to remember at once" or "how about just the numbers" can be indicative of an examinee being overwhelmed with the amount of auditory stimuli.

- Digits Backward is more conceptually related to Letter-Number Sequencing than Digits Forward. Both the backward span and LNS require the examinee to mentally manipulate or visualize the stimuli. (Some examinees who rely on visualization strategies will close their eyes during the administration of the items and/or during their response.) If strategies were generated to respond to Digits Backward, the examinee may benefit from using those or similar strategies on LNS.

- As there are three trials for each item, subjects have an opportunity to develop and test strategies. Test the limits or question the examinee after the test is complete to gather information about any strategies that may have been generated to complete the task.

- Like Digit Span, the skills required for this test are impaired more by state (test) anxiety than by chronic anxiety.

- Whereas number sequences are automatic for most adolescents and adults, the precise alphabetic sequence has not been adequately "overlearned" for many individuals. Note whether some examinees consistently make errors on the letters but get all numbers right. Do these individuals have reading problems (e.g., illiteracy or dyslexia)?

- LNS is a novel task, not likely to be encountered in the real world, and requires a good flexible approach to succeed. Adolescents and adults who do poorly may display problems on other tasks that depend on fluid ability (e.g., Matrix Reasoning) or flexibility (e.g., Similarities).

Neuropsychological Analysis of Letter-Number Sequencing

- Auditory discrimination may be evident if a subject consistently mistakes similar sounding letters such as *T* for *D*.

- Examining patterns of errors may help to distinguish memory or sequencing problems from attentional problems. For example, an examinee who consistently fails to recall the last item in a number–letter series (e.g., responds "G-8-L" for the item "G-8-L-2") is quite different than a person who recalls the letters and numbers in a jumbled order (for "G-8-L-2" says "L-8-G-2"). Dropping a letter or number may be more indicative of an attentional problem, whereas mixing up the letters may be a sequencing or working memory problem.

Picture Completion

Cognitive and Behavioral Analysis of Picture Completion

ABILITIES SHARED WITH OTHER SUBTESTS

Factor Analysis:	Two-, three-, and four-factor solutions: Perceptual Organization Four-factor solution for ages 75–89: Processing Speed
Bannatyne:	Spatial
Horn:	Broad Visualization (*Gv*)
CHC:	Broad: Visual Processing (*Gv*) Crystallized Intelligence (*Gc*) Narrow: General Information
Baltes:	Mechanics
Osgood:	Visual–motor (or vocal) channel of communication Automatic and representational levels of organization Visual reception
Rapaport:	Visual organization (without essential motor activity) Concentration
Dean:	Remote memory Visual memory
Guilford:	Cognition of figural units Evaluation of a figural system
Other skills:	Simultaneous (holistic, right-brain) processing Distinguishing essential from nonessential details Visual closure Visual perception/processing of meaningful stimuli (people/things)

INFLUENCES AFFECTING PICTURE COMPLETION SUBTEST SCORES

- Ability to respond when uncertain
- Alertness to the environment
- Cognitive style (field dependence/field independence)
- Concentration
- Negativism ("Nothing's missing")
- Working under time pressure

UNIQUE ABILITIES OR TRAITS MEASURED BY PICTURE COMPLETION

- Flexibility of Closure (CHC theory)
- Visual alertness
- Visual recognition and identification (long-term visual memory)

Empirical Analysis of Picture Completion

g loadings: $r = .64$ (4th worst overall)

Reliability: split-half = .83, test-retest = .79

Practice effect: Very Large for ages 16–54 (gain of 2.3–2.4 scaled-score points); Large for ages 55–74 (gain of 1.6 point); Moderate for ages 75–89 (gain of 0.9 point)

Subtest specificity/Error variance: 35% vs. 17% (ample specificity)

Primary Oblimin Factor Loading:

Ages 16–74: Perceptual Organization factor = .55

Ages 75–89: Processing Speed factor = .62

Secondary Oblimin Factor Loading:

Ages 35–54: Processing Speed = .21

Ages 55–74: Verbal Comprehension factor = .23

Ages 75–89: Verbal Comprehension factor = .22

Most related to: Object Assembly ($r = .52$), and Block Design ($r = .52$)

Least related to: Digit Span ($r = .30$)

Aging Analysis of Picture Completion

Mean scaled score across the adult age range (controlling for education at ages 20–89):

Age Group	Picture Completion Mean
16–17	9.9
18–19	9.9
20–24	10.1
25–29	10.4
30–34	9.7
35–44	9.8
45–54	9.8
55–64	9.1
65–69	8.6
70–74	7.8
75–79	7.5
80–84	6.8
85–89	6.8

Aging patterns on the WAIS-R Picture Completion subtest showed declining mean scaled scores across the age span, with a high mean scaled score of 10.3 at ages 20–24 and a low mean scaled score of 7.4 at ages 70–74.

Clinical Analysis of Picture Completion

- Personality integration is sometimes revealed by Picture Completion performance: "The pointing out of tiny gaps in the lines of the sketch, the inability to identify simple objects, or the tendency to designate them in some bi-zarre scheme, all suggest distortion of reality" (Zimmerman & Woo-Sam, 1973, p. 134).

- The basically simple task of finding missing parts of common pictures is usually considered enjoyable and nonthreatening.

- The 20-second time limit is ample for most non-retarded and nonbrain-damaged individuals.

- A person's response rate is worth noting; quick, incorrect answers suggest impulsivity, while failure to respond within the limit (especially to easy items) is of potential diagnostic value.

- Confabulatory responses (stating that something not in the picture is missing, e.g., "the person" in the boat without an oarlock) are diagnostic of psychopathology when they occur several times during the subtest or are bizarre ("Her husband is missing" for the woman without a shadow; adapted from illustrations based on WAIS Picture Completion items; Matarazzo, 1972, p. 493).

- People who insist "Nothing is missing" for several items may be negative, hostile, or even phobic.

- Success "reflects not only alertness and attention to details but an aspect of reality testing that may figure only marginally in other subtests…[,] the kind of reality testing with which psychotic patients have so much difficulty" (Hymowitz et al., 1983, p. 594); consistent with this clinical hypothesis is schizophrenics' relatively weak Picture Completion score (Crookes, 1984; Wechsler, 1944), a decrement not found for patients suffering from depression or personality disorders (Crookes, 1984).

Neuropsychological Analysis of Picture Completion

- Extremely resilient to the impact of brain damage.

- Good indicator of premorbid intelligence, especially for patients with left hemisphere lesions with limited "ability to formulate the kinds of complex spoken responses needed for tests calling for a verbal response" (Lezak, 1995, p. 636).

- Patients with visual agnosia may completely fail to identify the stimulus.
- Note whether individuals consistently fail items where the missing part is embedded within the figure, but have "no difficulty when the important feature belongs to the contour" (Milberg et al., 1986, p. 73).

Digit Symbol-Coding

Cognitive and Behavioral Analysis of Digit Symbol-Coding

ABILITIES SHARED WITH OTHER SUBTESTS

Factor Analysis:	Two-factor solutions: Perceptual Organization
	Three-factor solutions: Working Memory
	Four-factor solutions: Processing Speed
Bannatyne:	Sequential
Horn:	Broad Speediness (Gs)
CHC:	Broad: Processing Speed (Gs)
	Narrow: Rate-of-test-taking
Baltes:	Mechanics
Osgood:	Visual–motor channel of communication
	Automatic and representational levels of organization
	Manual expression
Rapaport:	Visual–motor coordination
	Concentration
Dean:	Visual–motor speed
	Visual memory
Guilford:	Convergent-production of symbolic content (units and implications)
	Evaluation of symbolic units
Other skills:	Encoding information for further cognitive processing
	Facility with numbers
	Learning ability
	Reproduction of models; sequential (linear, left-brain) processing
	Visual perception of abstract stimuli (designs/symbols)
	Visual sequencing

INFLUENCES AFFECTING
DIGIT SYMBOL-CODING SUBTEST SCORES

- Anxiety
- Compulsive concern for accuracy and detail
- Distractibility
- Learning disabilities ("ACID" profile)
- Persistence
- Working under time pressure

UNIQUE ABILITIES OR TRAITS
MEASURED BY DIGIT SYMBOL-CODING

- Ability to follow directions
- Clerical speed and accuracy
- Paper-and-pencil skill
- Psychomotor speed
- Visual short-term memory

Empirical Analysis of Digit Symbol-Coding

g loading: $r = .59$ (2nd worst measure)

Reliability: test-retest = .86

Subtest specificity/Error variance: 38% vs. 16% (ample specificity)

Practice effect: Large for ages 16–54 (gain of 1.1–1.2 scaled-score points); Moderate for ages 55–89

(gains of 0.6–0.8)

Primary Oblimin Factor Loading:

Ages 16–74: Processing Speed factor = .71

Ages 75–89: Processing Speed factor = .52

Secondary Oblimin Factor Loading:

Ages 75–89: Working Memory factor = .39

Most related to: Symbol Search ($r = .65$)

Least related to: Object Assembly ($r = .33$)

Aging Analysis of Digit Symbol-Coding

Mean scaled score across the adult age range (controlling for education at ages 20–89):

Age Group	Digit Symbol-Coding Mean
16–17	9.9
18–19	10.4

Age Group	Digit Symbol-Coding Mean
20–24	10.3
25–29	9.9
30–34	9.8
35–44	9.4
45–54	8.8
55–64	7.6
65–69	6.8
70–74	6.6
75–79	5.6
80–84	5.6
85–89	5.2

Aging patterns on the WAIS-R Digit Symbol subtest showed a significant decline in mean scaled scores across the age span, with a high mean scaled score of 10.5 at ages 20–24 and a low mean scaled score of 5.5 at ages 70–74.

Clinical Analysis of Digit Symbol-Coding

- Visual impairment must be ruled out before interpreting a low score.

- Testing the limits by determining how many symbol pairs were committed to memory (either directly following the task or after administering Similarities, the last subtest given) provides useful information about a person's incidental learning and efficient application of an intelligent problem-solving strategy.

- Illiterates may be at a disadvantage because four of the symbols are letters (L, O, U, X); so may people who rarely write because of the pencil-and-paper aspect of the task.

- "The most common errors tend to be perseverative runs in the first line, the only place where sequences of any kind occur" (Zimmerman & Woo-Sam, 1973, p. 124).

- Individuals who have demonstrated perfectionistic or compulsive tendencies prior to Digit Symbol should be told during the sam-

ple items that they need to copy the symbols legibly, but not perfectly.

- Be attentive to changes in the person's response rate during the subtest (perhaps by noting progress at the end of each 30-second interval; Milberg et al., 1986) because such changes may relate to motivation, distractibility, fatigue, memorizing some or all of the symbols, boredom, and so forth.

- Scores are likely to be impaired for depressed individuals.

- Verbally encoding the symbols may facilitate performance; testing the limits (by asking the person about his or her strategy at the end of the subtest) should uncover this intelligent use of verbal mediation.

Neuropsychological Analysis of Digit Symbol-Coding

- Digit Symbol scores are extremely sensitive to cerebral damage, regardless of its localization in the right or left hemisphere; hence, it is of great use for indicating the presence of damage but useless for inferring lateralization of the lesion.

- Reitan (1986): Digit Symbol calls on functions of the left hemisphere when dealing with symbols, and on the right hemisphere "by the requirement of drawing various shapes" (p. 20); the task's various components, including the timed element, "combine to produce a test that is generally sensitive to the condition of the cerebral cortex" (p. 20). Therefore, it is not useful for determining the laterality of the lesion (Lezak, 1995).

- Digit Symbol is the WAIS-III task that is most sensitive to brain injury "in that its score is most likely to be depressed even when damage is minimal, and to be among the most depressed when other tests are affected as well" (Lezak, 1995, p. 378).

- Examine the symbols that are drawn: "Are they rotated, flipped upside down, or transformed into perceptually similar letters?... Does the patient use the box as part of the symbol,...consistently make incorrect substitutions, or skip spaces or lines of the task?" (Milberg et al., pp. 72–73).

Block Design

Cognitive and Behavioral Analysis of Block Design

ABILITIES SHARED WITH OTHER SUBTESTS

Factor Analysis:	Two-, three-, and four-factor solutions: Perceptual Organization Four factor solutions for ages 75–89: Processing Speed (primary), Perceptual Organization (secondary)
Bannatyne:	Spatial
Horn:	Fluid Intelligence (*Gf*) Broad Visualization (*Gv*)
CHC:	Broad: Visual Processing (*Gv*) Narrow: Spatial Relations, Visualization
Baltes:	Mechanics
Osgood:	Visual–motor channel of communication Representational level of organization
Rapaport:	Visual–motor coordination Concept formation (visual analysis and synthesis)
Dean:	General ability Abstract thought
Guilford:	Cognition of figural relations Evaluation of figural relations
Other skills:	Reproduction of models Simultaneous (holistic, right-brain) processing Synthesis Trial-and-error learning Visual perception/processing of abstract stimuli (designs/symbols)

INFLUENCES AFFECTING BLOCK DESIGN SUBTEST SCORES

- Cognitive style (field dependence/field independence)
- Visual–perceptual problems
- Working under time pressure

UNIQUE ABILITIES OR TRAITS MEASURED BY BLOCK DESIGN

- Analysis of whole into component parts
- Nonverbal concept formation
- Spatial visualization

Empirical Analysis of Block Design

g loading: $r = .72$ (6th best overall, best measure on Performance Scale, along with Matrix Reasoning)

Reliability: split-half = .86, test-retest = .82

Practice effect: Moderate to Large, ages 16–54 (gain of 0.7–1.0 scaled-score points); Trivial, ages 55–89 (gain of 0.2–0.3 point)

Subtest specificity/Error variance: 27% vs. 14% (adequate specificity)

Primary Oblimin Factor Loading:

Ages 16–74: Perceptual Organization factor = .67

Ages 75–89: Processing Speed factor = .51

Secondary Oblimin Factor Loading:

Ages 75–89: Perceptual Organization factor = .39

Most related to: Object Assembly ($r = .61$) and Matrix Reasoning ($r = .60$)

Least related to: Digit Span ($r = .36$)

Aging Analysis of Block Design

Mean scaled score across the adult age range (controlling for education at ages 20–89):

Age Group	Block Design Mean
16–17	9.9
18–19	10.1
20–24	10.2
25–29	10.3
30–34	10.1
35–44	9.7
45–54	9.0
55–64	8.7

Age Group	Block Design Mean
65–69	8.1
70–74	8.0
75–79	7.5
80–84	7.0
85–89	6.8

Aging patterns on the WAIS-R Block Design subtest showed declining mean scaled scores across the age span, with a high mean scaled score of 10.3 at ages 20–24 and a low mean scaled score of 7.2 at ages 70–74.

Clinical Analysis of Block Design

- Reflectivity or compulsivity can lower scores substantially because of 24 possible bonus points for quick, perfect responses; maximum scaled score for solving every item correctly while earning no bonus points is only 11 at ages 16–44.

- Observations of problem-solving approach may reveal a wide variety of behaviors: trial-and-error behavior versus a holistic and insightful attack, ability to establish and implement a learning set, persistence, motor coordination, hand preference, concentration, distractibility, anxiety (to stopwatch and time pressure), frustration tolerance, rigidity, perseveration, speed of processing, impulsiveness, carelessness, work habits, self-attitudes, ability to benefit from feedback, and cautiousness.

- Some individuals feel that the task is too much like a child's game and become defensive or negative when asked to put the blocks together.

- Visual–perceptual problems (e.g., figure–ground) can be detected during Block Design, especially with limit testing (recognizing, rather than constructing, correct and incorrect responses).

- Some individuals refuse to try and instead give up easily; others learn while taking the items and sometimes "catch on" just when

they discontinue (additional testing beyond that point is advised with such individuals, who may pass several items that do not "count" in the score, but are of great clinical value); reasons for catching on slowly, and only after early failures, may be "aging, a dementing process, frontal lobe disease, or head injury" (Lezak, 1995, p. 594).

- "Bizarre solutions (design constructed on top of the card, or made vertically) can indicate poor reality ties. Suspiciousness ('Not enough blocks,' 'can't be done') might reflect a projection of failure onto the material" (Zimmerman & Woo-Sam, 1973, p. 151); the so-called bizarre solutions may also indicate what Lezak (1995) refers to as the "stickiness" associated with the performance of some patients, like those with severe frontal lobe damage, or like Alzheimer's patients.

Neuropsychological Analysis of Block Design

- Brain-damaged patients (especially right hemisphere) with visual–spatial impairment have special difficulty with those items having extensive diagonals in the designs.

- Brain-damaged patients who are excessively slow in responding should be allowed to complete at least one design beyond the time limit to evaluate their persistence, frustration tolerance, ability to solve complex items with time constraints removed, and satisfaction with their possible success.

- Vulnerable to any kind of cerebral brain damage; it is "least affected when the lesion is confined to the left hemisphere, except when the left parietal lobe is involved" (Lezak, 1995, p. 592).

- Block Design scores are very sensitive to posterior lesions in the right hemisphere, especially the parietal lobes.

- Both hemispheres are essential for good Block Design performance because of both the analytic and synthetic nature of the task.

- Patients with right-hemisphere damage and concomitant visual–spatial deficits do best on designs that can be analyzed through verbalization; their errors are likely to be "disorientation, design distortions, and misperceptions …[and they may] lose sight of the squared or self-contained format of the design altogether" (Lezak, 1995, p. 592).

- Patients with left-hemisphere damage are able to maintain the gestalt of the designs, but may make errors in the smaller details, such as the orientation of a single block; left-lesion patients, especially parietal lobe, "tend to show confusion, simplification, and concrete handling of the design" (Lezak, 1995, p. 592).

- "Both right and left-hemisphere damaged patients make many more errors on the side of the design contralateral to the side of the lesion" (Lezak, 1995, p. 592).

- Note "whether the patient worked in the normally favored directions for a right hander (left to right and top to bottom)" (Milberg et al., 1986, p. 73).

Matrix Reasoning

Cognitive and Behavioral Analysis of Matrix Reasoning

ABILITIES SHARED WITH OTHER SUBTESTS

Factor Analysis:	Two-, three-, and four-factor solution: Perceptual Organization
Bannatyne:	Spatial Ability
Horn:	Fluid Intelligence (*Gf*) Broad Visualization (*Gv*)
CHC:	Broad: Fluid Intelligence (*Gf*)
Baltes:	Mechanics
Osgood:	Visual–motor channel of communication Representational level of organization Visual association
Rapaport:	Visual Organization
Dean:	General ability Abstract thought

Guilford:	Convergent-production Figural evaluation Figural cognition
Other skills:	Distinguishing essential from nonessential detail Holistic (right-brain) processing Learning ability Nonverbal reasoning Reasoning Simultaneous processing Spatial visualization Synthesis Visual Organization Visual perception of abstract stimuli

INFLUENCES AFFECTING
MATRIX REASONING SUBTEST SCORES

- Ability to respond when uncertain
- Cognitive style (field dependence/field independence)
- Color Blindness (for some items, the use of several colors may confuse color-blind individuals)
- Flexibility
- Motivation level
- Negativism ("None of them go there")
- Overly concrete thinking
- Persistence
- Visual–perceptual problems

UNIQUE ABILITIES OR TRAITS
MEASURED BY MATRIX REASONING

- Analogic reasoning
- Induction (CHC narrow ability)
- Nonverbal problem solving with no time limit

Empirical Analysis of Matrix Reasoning

g loadings: $r = .72$ (6th best, along with Block Design)

Reliability: split-half: .90, test-retest = .77

Practice effect: Trivial for ages 16–89 (gain of 0.1 scaled-score point)

Subtest specificity/Error variance: 39% vs. 10% (ample specificity)

Primary Oblimin Factor Loading:

    Ages 16–74: Perceptual Organization factor = .56

    Ages 75–89: Perceptual Organization factor = .42

Secondary Oblimin Factor Loading:

    Ages 16–19: Working Memory = .24

    Ages 20–34: Working Memory = .31

    Ages 55–74: Working Memory = .26

    Ages 75–89: Processing Speed factor = .30

Most related to: Block Design (r = .60)

Least related to: Digit Symbol-Coding (r = .40)

AGING ANALYSIS OF MATRIX REASONING. Mean scaled score across the adult age range (controlling for education at ages 20–89):

Age Group	Matrix Reasoning Mean
16–17	10.5
18–19	10.4
20–24	10.1
25–29	10.2
30–34	9.9
35–44	9.4
45–54	8.9
55–64	8.4
65–69	7.8
70–74	7.2
75–79	6.8
80–84	6.6
85–89	6.1

Clinical Analysis of Matrix Reasoning

- Because this subtest is not timed, response time may vary widely for adults. Those who are mentally retarded or neurologically impaired may take longer to respond. Impulsivity may be indicated by extremely quick, incorrect responses. Failure to respond within a reasonable amount of time (45 seconds) is of potential diagnostic value, as it may be indicative of reflective style, obsessiveness, or confusion.

- Some items have complex visual stimuli. Individuals with visual–perceptual problems may display "stimulus overload" in attempting to input the multicolored, spatially complex items.

- A holistic processing approach is most common in solving the matrices. Some individuals choose their answer to the problem with a trial-and-error approach by testing each of the possible choices one by one. Others may use a more planful approach to the problem, first mentally creating a solution to fill in the "?" and then searching the given responses to see if one matches the solution they had envisioned.

- Perseveration may be apparent on this subtests if an individual repeatedly chooses the same number response for each item (e.g., number 5).

- Color blindness must be ruled out as a potential cause for poor performance. If such information is not offered spontaneously by the examinee, consider probing for information on color blindness if there is less difficulty on items that depend on form (e.g., items 17, 19, 20, 21) versus those that depend on color (e.g., items 15, 16, 18, 22).

- Indecisiveness (e.g., "it is either 1 or 3") may indicate insecurity or need for feedback.

Neuropsychological Analysis of Matrix Reasoning

- Analysis of errors on Matrix Reasoning may indicate visual neglect if there is a differential frequency of errors on items in a given sector of visual space.

- If the client continually responds with an answer in the same location within the rows and columns of choices, this might suggest perseveration.

- If a piece is impulsively chosen that matches the details of the stimulus rather than one that completes the overall pattern, cognitive rigidity may be underlying the subject's responses.

- As a measure of *Gf*, the following neurological analysis might apply: "[T]he norepinephrine system of the brain, which centers around the locus coeruleus and branches largely into the hypothalamus and adjacent areas, is associated with neurological arousal such as is characteristic of *Gf*" (Horn & Noll, 1997, p. 81).

Picture Arrangement

Cognitive and Behavioral Analysis of Picture Arrangement

ABILITIES SHARED WITH OTHER SUBTESTS

Factor Analysis:	Two-factor solutions: Perceptual Organization (primary), Verbal Comprehension (secondary)
	Three-factor solutions: Perceptual Organization (primary), Verbal Comprehension (secondary)
	Four-factor solutions: Perceptual Organization
	Four-factor solutions at ages 75–89: Processing Speed
Bannatyne:	Uncategorized; has both a sequential and spatial component
Horn:	Fluid Intelligence (*Gf*)
	Crystallized Intelligence (*Gc*)
CHC:	Broad: Visual Processing (*Gv*)
	Crystallized Intelligence (*Gc*)
	Narrow: Visualization, General Information
Baltes:	Mechanics
Osgood:	Visual–motor channel of communication
	Representational level of organization; Visual association
Rapaport:	Visual organization (without essential motor activity); Anticipation
Dean:	Social comprehension (social intelligence)
Guilford:	Convergent-production of a semantic system
	Evaluation of semantic relations
Other skills:	Common sense (cause–effect relationships)
	Distinguishing essential from nonessential details

Reasoning (nonverbal)
Synthesis
Visual perception/processing of meaningful stimuli (people–things)
Visual sequencing

INFLUENCES AFFECTING PICTURE ARRANGEMENT SUBTEST SCORES

- Creativity
- Cultural opportunities
- Exposure to comic strips
- Working under time pressure

UNIQUE ABILITIES OR TRAITS MEASURED BY PICTURE ARRANGEMENT

- Anticipation of consequences
- Planning ability (comprehending and sizing up a total situation)
- Temporal sequencing and time concepts

Empirical Analysis of Picture Arrangement

g loading: *r* = .66 (6th worst)

Reliability: split-half = .74, test-retest = .69

Practice effect: Large, ages 16–74 (gain of 1.2 scaled-score points); Moderate, ages 75–89 (gain of 0.7 point)

Subtest specificity/Error variance: 31% vs. 26% (adequate specificity)

Primary Oblimin Factor Loading:

   Ages 16–74: Perceptual Organization factor = .51

   Ages 75–89: Processing Speed factor = .47

Secondary Oblimin Factor Loading:

   Ages 16–74: Verbal Comprehension factor = .26

   Ages 75–89: Verbal Comprehension factor = .30

Most related to: Vocabulary (*r* = .53), Information (*r* = .54)

Least related to: Digit Span (*r* = .33) and Digit Symbol-Coding (*r* = .37)

Aging Analysis of Picture Arrangement

Mean scaled score across the adult age range (controlling for education at ages 20–89):

Age Group	Picture Arrangement Mean
16–17	10.0
18–19	9.8
20–24	10.1
25–29	10.2
30–34	9.9
35–44	9.2
45–54	8.8
55–64	8.4
65–69	7.6
70–74	6.8
75–79	6.3
80–84	6.0
85–89	5.5

Aging patterns on the WAIS-R Picture Arrangement subtest showed declining mean scaled scores across the age span, with a high mean scaled score of 10.2 at ages 20–24 and a low mean scaled score of 6.6 at ages 70–74.

Clinical Analysis of Picture Arrangement

- Having the individual verbalize the stories, of both correct and incorrect sequences, is quite valuable for clinical understanding of the responses; however, the examiner should reconstruct the person's arrangements and request the verbalizations after completing the subtest to avoid violation of the norms and possibly giving the person a strategy for solving the harder items.

- Observing the person's process of handling the cards tells much about thought processes: trial-and-error versus insightful approach, reliance on visual feedback, impulsivity versus reflectivity, poor strategy generation.

- Examining thought processes via verbalizations "may reveal important aspects of the subject's cognition–precise or confused and tangential, socially oriented or self-oriented, realistic or bizarre, the ability or inability to relate verbal to visual–motor tasks" (Zimmerman & Woo-Sam, 1973, p. 156).

- Illustrations of verbalizations (of WAIS items) from Matarazzo (1972, pp. 492–493): FLIRT (Item 2), person charged with homicide: "A guy walks down the street with the head of a woman; he might have killed her"; FISH (Item 8), alcoholic with severe depression: "This guy didn't catch anything—he is cursing the water—he jumps in"; TAXI (Item 10), patient with a schizophrenic process: "The man carries a dummy—she changes into a woman in the taxi and he gets very hot and excited."

- Failure may be due to poor visual acuity or visual perception; adequate performance on Picture Completion will frequently rule out these factors as causes of a low Picture Arrangement score.

- The WAIS had two simple (three-card) items to ease the person into an unfamiliar task and ensure early success; the WAIS-III, like the WAIS-R, has only one such item, followed by some fairly complex five-card items, causing some low-functioning individuals to "fall off a cliff" and fail miserably at this task.

- Failure on occasional items may be related to the individual's cultural background, which may teach interpretations of social situations that are different from U.S. customs; surprisingly, however, this is not a pervasive problem.

- Performance on this logical, temporal task is impaired by serious psychopathology and bizarre thinking.

Neuropsychological Analysis of Picture Arrangement

- Picture Arrangement scores are vulnerable to brain damage in general, but are "specifically sensitive to the status of the right anterior temporal lobe" (Reitan, 1986, p. 21).

- Patients with frontal lobe damage have been reported "to shift the cards only a little if at all and to present this response (or nonresponse) as a solution" (Lezak, 1995, p. 639).

- Cards may need to be placed in a vertical column, instead of horizontally, for patients with "visual field and visual–spatial neglect deficits" (Milberg et al., 1986, pp. 73–74).

Symbol Search

Cognitive and Behavioral Analysis of Symbol Search

ABILITIES SHARED WITH OTHER SUBTESTS

Factor Analysis:	Two-factor solution: Perceptual Organization
	Three-factor solution: Working Memory (primarily), Perceptual Organization (secondarily)
	Four-factor solution: Processing Speed
Horn:	Broad Speediness (Gs)
CHC:	Broad: Processing Speed (Gs)
	Narrow: Rate-of-Test-Taking
Baltes:	Mechanics
Osgood:	Visual–motor channel of communication
	Automatic level of organization
	Visual reception
Rapaport:	Orienting response (concentration)
Dean:	General ability
	Visual–motor speed
Guilford:	Convergent-production and evaluation of figural stimuli
Other skills:	Clerical speed and accuracy
	Encoding information for further cognitive processing
	Integrated brain functioning (verbal–sequential and visual–spatial)
	Learning ability
	Paper-and-pencil skill
	Planning
	Short-term memory (visual)
	Spatial visualization
	Speed of mental processing
	Visual–motor coordination

INFLUENCES AFFECTING SYMBOL SEARCH SUBTEST SCORES

- Anxiety
- Distractibility
- Learning Disabilities/ADHD
- Motivation level
- Obsessive concern with accuracy and detail
- Persistence
- Visual–perceptual problems
- Working under time pressure

UNIQUE ABILITIES OR TRAITS MEASURED BY SYMBOL SEARCH

- Speed of visual search
- Perceptual speed (CHC theory)

Empirical Analysis of Symbol Search

g loadings: $r = .70$ (8th best)

Reliability: test-retest = .79

Practice effect: Large, ages 16–29 (gain of 1.0 scaled-score point); Small, ages 30–74 (gain of 0.5 point); Trivial, ages 75–89 (loss of 0.2 point)

Subtest specificity/Error variance: 21% vs. 23% (inadequate specificity)

Primary Oblimin Factor Loading:

Ages 16–74: Processing Speed factor = .66

Ages 75–89: Processing Speed factor = .59

Secondary Oblimin Factor Loading:

Ages 55–74: Perceptual Organization factor = .22

Ages 75–89: Working Memory factor = .37

Most related to: Digit Symbol-Coding ($r = .65$)

Least related to: Digit Span ($r = .41$)

Aging Analysis of Symbol Search

Mean scaled score across the adult age range (controlling for education at ages 20–89):

Age Group	Symbol Search Mean
16–17	10.1
18–19	10.5

Age Group	Symbol Search Mean
20–24	10.2
25–29	10.1
30–34	9.9
35–44	9.2
45–54	8.5
55–64	8.0
65–69	7.1
70–74	6.6
75–79	5.6
80–84	5.0
85–89	4.8

Clinical Analysis of Symbol Search

- Similar to many of the Performance subtests, visual impairment should be ruled out before interpreting a low Symbol Search score.

- It is important to be an astute observer during this task, as many observed behaviors can help to interpret the Symbol Search score. Concentration, distractibility, obsessive concern with detail, impulsiveness, reflectivity, motivation level, visual–perceptual problems, or anxiety are just some of the factors that may be inferred to be related to a person's performance on Symbol Search.

- As this is one of the last subtests administered, fatigue and boredom should be ruled out as possible explanations for a low score.

- After the entire test has been administered, you may test the limits to help discern why certain responses were made. Point to some items answered correctly and some that were wrong, and ask the adult to explain why they chose "yes" or "no."

Neuropsychological Analysis of Symbol Search

- A learning curve may be present on this test. Individuals who begin to answer later items

more quickly may have developed a plan or strategy after completing earlier items. To note whether speed of responding is, in fact, increasing, you can track how many items were answered during each of the four 30-second intervals during the subtest.

- Visual memory ability can sometimes be inferred from observations on this task. Some adults may look at the Target symbols only once and then find the response in the Search Group, and others may look back and forth several times between the Target and Search groups before marking "yes" or "no." The repeated referring back and forth between the symbols may be indicative of poor visual memory (or of insecurity).

Object Assembly

Cognitive and Behavioral Analysis of Object Assembly

ABILITIES SHARED WITH OTHER SUBTESTS

Factor Analysis:	Two-, three-, and four-factor solutions: Perceptual Organization
Bannatyne:	Spatial
Horn:	Fluid Intelligence (*Gf*) Broad Visualization (*Gv*)
CHC:	Broad: Visual Processing (*Gv*) Narrow: Spatial Relations
Baltes:	Mechanics
Osgood:	Visual–motor channel of communication Representational level of organization
Rapaport:	Visual–motor coordination; Anticipation
Dean:	Visual–motor speed
Guilford:	Cognition of figural content (systems and transformations) Evaluation of figural relations
Other skills:	Synthesis Simultaneous (holistic, right-brain) processing Trial-and-error learning Visual closure

INFLUENCES AFFECTING
OBJECT ASSEMBLY SUBTEST SCORES

- Ability to respond when uncertain
- Cognitive style (field dependence/field independence)
- Experience with puzzles
- Flexibility
- Persistence
- Working under time pressure

UNIQUE ABILITIES OR TRAITS
MEASURED BY OBJECT ASSEMBLY

- Ability to benefit from sensory–motor feedback
- Anticipation of relationships among parts
- Closure speed (CHC narrow ability)

Empirical Analysis of Object Assembly

g loading: $r = .62$ (3rd worst)
Reliability: split-half = .70, test-retest = .76
Practice effect: Very Large, ages 16–29 (gain of 2.3 scaled-score points); Large, ages 30–54 (gain of 1.6 points); Moderate to Large, ages 55–89 (gain of 0.9–1.0 point)
Subtest specificity/Error variance: 24% vs. 30% (inadequate specificity)
Primary Oblimin Factor Loading:
Ages 16–74: Perceptual Organization factor = .73
Ages 75–89: Perceptual Organization factor = .65
Most related to: Block Design ($r = .61$)
Least related to: Digit Span ($r = .26$) and Letter-Number Sequencing ($r = .29$)

Aging Analysis of Object Assembly

Mean scaled score across the adult age range (controlling for education at ages 20–89):

Age Group	Object Assembly Mean
16–17	9.9
18–19	10.2
20–24	10.2
25–29	10.2
30–34	10.2
35–44	9.5
45–54	8.7
55–64	8.3
65–69	7.6
70–74	7.4
75–79	6.9
80–84	6.2
85–89	6.1

Aging patterns on the WAIS-R Object Assembly subtest showed declining mean scaled scores across the age span, with a high mean scaled score of 10.3 at ages 20–24 and a low mean scaled score of 7.1 at ages 70–74.

Clinical Analysis of Object Assembly

- Reflectivity or compulsivity can lower scores substantially because of 15 possible bonus points for quick, perfect responses; maximum scaled score for solving every item correctly while earning no bonus points is only 11 at ages 16–44.
- As on Block Design, observations of problem-solving approach may reveal a wide variety of behaviors: trial-and-error behavior versus a holistic and insightful attack, persistence, motor coordination, hand preference, concentration, distractibility, anxiety (to stopwatch and time pressure), frustration tolerance, rigidity, perseveration, speed of processing, impulsiveness, work habits, self-attitudes, ability to benefit from feedback, and cautiousness; also of interest is when, during the problem-solving process, the individual realizes what object he or she is trying to assemble.
- Some individuals feel that the task is too much like a child's game and become defensive or negative when asked to solve the puzzles;

others become frustrated on the Elephant and Butterfly because of the virtual elimination of clues (i.e., the drawn-in cues on all puzzle pieces of the Man and Profile and most pieces of the House).

- Intense bodily concerns may lower scores on this task (Blatt's hypothesis, which is considered to be more valid for adults than children, e.g., Blatt, Baker, & Weiss, 1970; this hypothesis has been challenged, e.g., Turner & Horn, 1976).

- Individuals who try to "peek" behind the screen while the examiner is positioning the pieces may be revealing insecurity, impulsivity, or low moral development.

- "When the subject piles pieces one on top of another, reality ties can be questioned" (Zimmerman & Woo-Sam, 1973, p. 173).

Neuropsychological Analysis of Object Assembly

- Because bonus points affect greatly a person's scaled score, performance is particularly vulnerable to cerebral damage, most notably to posterior lesions, especially in the right-hemisphere; lowered scores for frontal lobe patients probably relate to the highly speeded nature of the task.

- Patients with left-hemisphere lesions are more likely to rely on "edge" contours when joining pieces, in contrast to those with right-hemisphere lesions who tend to match up "surface" details (Kaplan, Fein, Morris, & Delis, 1991).

- Patients with left-hemisphere damage may make errors on the details although they are able to maintain the overall contour and gestalt of the total puzzle.

- The concrete approaches of some brain-damaged patients may not affect Object Assembly performance (because of the construction of meaningful pictures), although it is likely to impair Block Design performance, notably when copying the abstract designs from the cards; in general, though, when brain damage hinders the patient's ability to construct the designs in Block Design, it also impairs his or her performance on Object Assembly.

- Individuals who consistently ignore puzzle pieces placed on one side or the other may have impairment in their visual fields.

- As on Picture Completion items, note whether errors occur more on details embedded within the object or on information provided by the contour.

SUMMARY

This chapter, the first of three on subtest profile interpretation, "sets the table" for profile analysis by providing specific information about each of the 14 subtests regarding the abilities it assesses and its clinical and neuropsychological significance. First, several methods of grouping Wechsler's subtests are described; then, each task is analyzed from the various perspectives. From factor analysis, two-factor solutions conform to Wechsler's division of the subtests into Verbal and Performance Scales; four-factor solutions produce the Verbal Comprehension, Perceptual Organization, Working Memory, and Processing Speed factors.

Bannatyne's system, commonly used with the WISC-III for learning disabilities assessment, applies to the WAIS-III as well. The four Bannatyne categories, which overlap to some extent, are Verbal Conceptualization, Spatial Ability, Sequential Ability, and Acquired Knowledge. Horn's extended fluid–crystallized model of intelligence also adds to clinicians' understanding of the major dimensions assessed by the WAIS-III. The crystallized grouping is identical to the Verbal Comprehension trio in addition to Comprehension and Picture Arrangement, while the fluid category merges two Verbal subtests (Arithmetic, Similarities) with four Performance tasks (Matrix Reasoning, Block Design, Object Assembly, and Picture Arrangement). In addition, Horn's system comprises a Short-Term Memory category (Digit Span, Arithmetic, Letter-Number

Sequencing) and a trio of subtests measuring speed (Digit Symbol-Coding, Symbol Search, and Object Assembly). CHC theory, a recent blend of Carroll's and Horn's theories, is also presented as a clinically valuable way of interpreting WAIS-III subtests in terms of their broad and narrow abilities.

Osgood's theory of communication offers several ways of categorizing the WAIS-III subtests: auditory–vocal (Verbal) versus visual–motor (Performance) channels of communication; representational versus automatic levels of organization; and receptive, associative, and expressive psycholinguistic processes; when merged with Silver's information-processing model, an additional process—storage—is added. Whereas all WAIS-III subtests are categorized at the representational level of (high-level, complex) organization, five tasks have automatic (overlearned) components: Digit Span, Letter-Number Sequencing, Picture Completion, Digit Symbol-Coding, and Symbol Search. Eight WAIS-III subtests fit nicely into the combined psycholinguistic/information-processing scheme, with four of these subtests measuring one process apiece within the auditory–vocal channel and four measuring one process apiece within the visual–motor channel.

Rapaport's clinical model stretches back nearly a half century, yet it still retains much that is useful for contemporary test interpretation. Some psychoanalytic interpretive techniques take Rapaport's methods to an extreme, but his basic division of subtests into five areas of cognition and behavior is valuable. Rapaport's categories include memory, concept formation (verbal and nonverbal), visual organization (without essential motor activity), visual–motor coordination, and orienting responses (attention, concentration, and anticipation).

Dean has assembled an eclectic approach to interpretation that subsumes many of the categories from other interpretive systems while adding some additional and interesting groupings. One category, General Ability, includes numerous tasks, while the others are groupings such as Abstract Thought (Similarities, Block Design, Matrix Reasoning), Remote Memory (Information, Picture Completion), and Social Comprehension (Comprehension, Picture Arrangement). Finally, Guilford's three-dimensional model of intelligence (operations or processes, contents, and products) offers novel ways of categorizing WAIS-III subtests that sometimes hold the key for competent profile analysis.

In the subtest-by-subtest analysis of each of the 14 WAIS-III tasks, the cognitive components and behavioral influences affecting test performance are derived primarily from the various systems just described. In addition, the following analyses are conducted systematically for the 14 subtests: (1) Aging, based on mean scaled scores earned by different adult age groups, controlled for differences in educational attainment at ages 20–89; (2) Clinical, with inferences derived primarily from leading authorities on the clinical assessment of intelligence; (3) Neuropsychological, based on leading authorities on neuropsychological assessment; and (4) Empirical, involving traditional considerations (e.g., reliability), plus the partitioning of each subtest's variance into the portions accounted for by each of the three factors, the portion that is separate from the major factors, and the portion that is due to errors.

WAIS-III Profile
Interpretation: Steps 1–7

This chapter begins by touching on recent criticisms of our approach to profile interpretation and then continues with a discussion of a step-by-step approach to interpreting the WAIS-III profile. Here we will provide a description of the first seven of nine steps of interpretation. In these steps we will lead you through an examination of the most global score (Step 1), to examination of the IQs (Steps 2 to 4) and then the factor indexes (Steps 5 to 7). The final two steps, which deal with determining the strengths and weakness in the profile (Step 8) and how to generate specific hypotheses from the statistically significant subtest strengths and weaknesses (Step 9), are discussed in Chapter 12. To aid in interpreting the global dimensions of the WAIS-III, we refer readers to the empirical research presented in Chapter 9 on characteristic profile patterns associated with learning disabilities (e.g., the ACID grouping), Alzheimer's-type dementia (Fuld profile), psychiatric disorders, multiple sclerosis, mental retardation, and giftedness.

CONSIDERATIONS ABOUT PROFILE INTERPRETATION

Before we present our approach to individual profile interpretation, we thought it important to address some of the criticism that has arisen from the approach we advocate (Kaufman, 1990, 1994a; Kaufman & Lichtenberger, 1999; Lichtenberger, Broadbooks, & Kaufman, 2000). Kaufman (1994a) summarizes some of the critic's reviews of profile interpretation as well as IQ tests in general. In a review of our recent brief treatment of the WAIS-III (Kaufman & Lichtenberger, 1999) that presents the same interpretive approach that we do in this chapter, Flanagan and Alfonso (2000) stated that, "Although only positive comments can be made about the contribution of Kaufman's psychometric profile analysis approach to the advancement of Wechsler test interpretation, the field of cognitive assessment appears to be gradually moving beyond this method and encouraging the application of current empirically supported theories in the interpretation process" (p. 529). They go on to say "Although Kaufman and Lichtenberger offer several theoretical categorizations of WAIS-III subtests, they are not based on confirmatory factor analyses or other empirical validation methods within a given paradigm" (p. 530). Flanagan and Alfonso conclude, "Notwithstanding the authors' cautionary statements regarding certain aspects of their interpretive approach, the [book's] major limitation may well prove to revolve around the fact that well-validated and contemporary theories of the structure of intelligence were not applied more vigorously in their interpretation guidelines" (p. 531). Their overall criticisms stem from the belief that the Kaufman approach to profile analyses is antiquated because it does not revolve around the very recent and strongly validated Cattell-Horn-Carroll (CHC) theory. The CHC theory does have much empirical support from factor-analytic studies (McGrew & Flanagan, 1998; see also Chapter 14) and is a useful framework for interpreting intelligence tests. Thus, Flanagan and Alfonso's comments made us stop and review again the approach we advocate. Is it truly antiquated and of little or no use to clinicians? Would we be doing a disservice to psychologists and students by presenting such an approach?

After pondering and discussing the contributions of the individual profile analysis, we concluded that the Kaufman-Lichtenberger method of Wechsler test interpretation is sound and defensible. One of the strongest arguments waged against our approach was that it does not have enough psychometric support in terms of factor-analytic data. All of the support from Flanagan and McGrew's cross-battery approach comes from group data. Although these factor-analytic data do provide empirical support for their approach, the approach we advocate examines each individual, not the performance of a group. The approaches that we present in our individual profile interpretation have either theoretical or clinical backing. We are looking for unique approaches to address individual profiles. The validity that comes from group data may never be

available for the individual profile approach that we advocate. For example, when you look at Digits forward and Digits backward, if you were to put them together in a factor analysis, they are almost always going to load together. However, this fact does not invalidate the practice of looking at the difference between them for an individual. Most people do, in fact, perform better on Digits forward than on Digits backward. Thus, it is very noteworthy, and clinically informative, when an individual scores higher on Digits backward or when the typical forward–backward discrepancy is unusually large. We have never advocated interpreting a WAIS-III profile or any other IQ test profile *in isolation*. Certainly such a practice would be of questionable validity and of questionable ethical practice. Thus, after careful consideration we feel that our individual profile interpretive approach is justifiable and valid.

Since the publication of our approach to the interpretation of the WAIS-III profile (Kaufman & Lichtenberger, 1999), we have received some specific questions about parts of our step-by-step approach from clinicians, students, and professors of psychology. The well-thought-out questions mainly focus on why we choose to take a certain step or focus on a particular area of interpretation. We welcomed these questions and thought it would be helpful for readers of this book who may have similar questions to see how we responded to the previously posed questions. Thus, throughout our description of the interpretive steps we have listed the questions and our responses in the relevant sections.

CONSIDERATIONS FOR APPLYING THE INTERPRETIVE STEPS WHEN ONLY 11 SUBTESTS WERE ADMINISTERED

In addition to the general considerations about profile interpretation discussed above are considerations for when only 11 subtests have been administered. There are two distinct sets of 11 subtests that may be administered rather than the entire 14-subtest WAIS-III battery: (1) 11 subtests needed to calculate the IQs, and (2) 11 subtests needed to calculate the Indexes. These two sets of 11 differ mainly in four subtests: Picture Arrangement, Comprehension, Symbol Search, and Letter-Number Sequencing. Nine subtests have to be administered whether the IQs or Indexes are calculated (i.e., Picture Completion, Vocabulary, Digit Symbol-Coding, Similarities, Block Design, Arithmetic, Matrix Reasoning, Digit Span, Information, and Picture Arrangement). However, if only the IQs are calculated, then the only remaining subtests that need to be administered are Picture Arrangement and Comprehension. In contrast, if only the Indexes are calculated then the only remaining subtests that need to be administered are Symbol Search and Letter-Number Sequencing. We believe that it is generally best to administer all 14 subtests whenever possible. However, we recognize that some examiners may need to shorten the battery to save time (in which case the 11 subtests needed to comprise the Indexes are your best bet because two of the longer subtests are not included: Picture Arrangement and Comprehension), and some examiners may simply need or want to derive only the IQs for interpretation (e.g., when comparing old WAIS-R IQs with new testing results). If saving time is really a crucial issue, consider using one of the brief batteries discussed in Chapter 15 (e.g., WASI, K-BIT, WRIT). In addition, some disorders, such as Alzheimer's dementia, warrant giving an abbreviated battery for specific reasons (see Chapter 9). Regardless of the reasons for only administering 11 subtests, some modifications will need to be made in our step-by-step approach to interpretation, which was designed to incorporate all 14 WAIS-III subtests. In each of the nine steps discussed in Chapters 11 and 12, we highlight where modifications need to be made to accommodate interpretation of an 11-subtest battery.

STEP 1: INTERPRET THE FULL SCALE IQ

The initial step in comprehensive analyses of WAIS-III profile fluctuations involves systematic statistical treatment of the most global score, Full Scale IQ. Following this initial step, proceed in a stepwise fashion to examination of the other IQs, Indexes, and, finally, specific subtests. Because the Full Scale IQ is the most reliable score in the battery (mean split-half coefficient of .98), it is the logical starting point in Wechsler profile interpretation. This score should be assigned an intellectual category, using Wechsler's (1997, Table 2.3, p. 25) classification system. The purpose of the verbal label is to facilitate communication, not to pigeonhole the subject, and most terms in Wechsler's system (e.g., Superior for IQs of 120–129 or Low Average for IQs in the 80s) communicate quite well to the professional and layperson alike. However, the terms used for IQs in the 70–79 range can be unclear. This range is called Borderline by Wechsler, and IQs of 69 and below are considered Extremely Low (formerly called Mentally Retarded). The term *Borderline* is indecisive, and may be confused with the *DSM-IV* psychiatric label of the same name. Examiners who are accustomed to Wechsler's classification system may wish to use it with a slight amendment: substituting Well Below Average for Borderline. We recommend examining the qualitative description for the confidence interval, not just the IQ alone. For example, if a FS-IQ is 108 and the 90% confidence interval is 104 to 113, then the person is functioning in the Average to High Average Range. Using such descriptive categories that correspond to the person's *range* of functioning helps to avoid pigeonholing an examinee, and provides a more accurate description of his or her abilities.

Next, the FS-IQ should be converted to a percentile rank, using Wechsler's (1997, pp. 197–198) Table A.5, which includes percentile ranks for every IQ. Finally, surrounding the Full Scale IQ with a band of error is essential to ensure that the IQ is perceived as a range rather than a specific number. Table A.5 in the *WAIS-III Administration and Scoring Manual* (Wechsler, 1997) presents bands of errors for FS-IQ at two levels of confidence (90% and 95%).

The confidence intervals provided in the WAIS-III *Administration and Scoring Manual* were derived from a method that uses the standard error of estimation (Psychological Corporation, 1997). This method uses an estimated true score rather than the observed score, which results in an asymmetrical interval around the observed score. This asymmetry is more noticeable on scores at the extremes of the bell curve (e.g., the 90% confidence interval for a V-IQ of 50 is 47–56) than on scores closer to the normative mean (e.g., the 90% confidence interval for a V-IQ of 100 is 96–104). This asymmetry exists because the estimated true score is always closer to the mean of the scale than is the observed score. Thus, a correction for true-score regression toward the mean is obtained when the confidence interval is based on the estimated true score and the standard error of estimation is used. Regardless of how the confidence intervals are calculated, it is important to utilize them to communicate, even to the novice, that scores on intelligence tests have a certain amount of built-in error. The *WAIS-III Interpretive Worksheet* presented at the end of Chapter 12 summarizes this step as well as all the others that follow.

The Role of Full Scale IQ in Profile Interpretation

The careful statistical treatment and categorization of the Full Scale IQ as the first interpretive step does not mean that it is holy, or even the most important result of the evaluation. As the most global score, it becomes the baseline of the individual's performance, the midpoint that establishes the person's own average level of functioning. This overall score then becomes the fulcrum for allowing the examiner to determine areas of strength and weakness within the total profile. The IQs are normative scores that rank the individual against a representative reference group and establish whether he or she is deficient or average or bright or superior in overall functioning. But the crux of profile interpretation is ipsative, the evaluation of strong and weak areas relative to the person's own midpoint. Ipsative and normative interpretations are one and the same only in those instances when the person's mean score equals the population mean.

FS-IQ is that midpoint and, as such, becomes the target for the astute clinician, a target at which to take careful aim in the search for both integrities and deficiencies within the cognitive and behavioral domains. The individual tested makes an unspoken plea to the examiner not to summarize his or her intelligence in a single, cold number; the goal of profile interpretation should be to respond to that plea by identifying hypothesized strengths and weaknesses that extend well beyond the limited information provided by the FS-IQ and that will conceivably lead to practical recommendations that help answer the referral questions.

STEP 2: ARE THE VERBAL IQ VERSUS THE PERFORMANCE IQ (OR THE VERBAL COMPREHENSION INDEX VERSUS THE PERCEPTUAL ORGANIZATION INDEX) SIGNIFICANTLY DIFFERENT?

The first challenge to the sanctity of the FS-IQ in profile interpretation comes from the V–P IQ discrepancy.[1] If it is found to be significant, FS-IQ immediately becomes less important than the distinction between the person's verbal and nonverbal

---

[1]If only the IQs are derived, then disregard the comparison between VCI and POI. Similarly, if only the Indexes are derived, then disregard the comparison between V-IQ and P-IQ.

intelligence in describing his or her cognitive functioning. The *WAIS-III Administration and Scoring Manual* (Wechsler, 1997, Table B.1) gives values for the significance of the difference between V-IQ and P-IQ. The overall values for the Verbal IQ versus the Performance IQ discrepancies are 9 points at the .05 level and 12 points at the .01 level. We feel the .15 level is too liberal for most testing purposes, as it contains too much built-in error; thus, only values at the .01 and .05 levels are presented.

Although we recommend first considering the V-IQ versus P-IQ differences in determining discrepancies in verbal and nonverbal abilities, it is wise also to examine these abilities via the Verbal Comprehension Index (VCI) and the Perceptual Organization Index (POI). We recommend that the V-IQ and the P-IQ be considered first because they are slightly more reliable and stable than the indexes and because the complete scales (5–6 regular subtests) measure a much wider array of abilities than the three-subtest VCI and POI. Specifically, the mean split-half reliability coefficients for the V-IQ and P-IQ are .97 and .94, respectively, in comparison to those of the VCI and POI (.96 and .93). The stability coefficients of the verbal constructs are .96 for the V-IQ and .95 for the VCI, and the stability coefficients of the nonverbal constructs are .91 and .88 for the P-IQ and the POI, respectively. For the WISC-III, the 5-subtest scales are not appreciably longer than the 4-subtest indexes. However, the curious decision by The Psychological Corporation (1997) to limit the WAIS-III VCI and POI to three subtests limits the generalizability of the attributes measured by the verbal and nonverbal indexes.

Because of the relative psychometric strength and clinical breadth of the V-IQ and P-IQ, if a statistically significant discrepancy exists between *both* the V-IQ versus P-IQ and the VCI versus POI, we suggest using the differences in the IQs to represent the discrepancy between overall verbal and nonverbal abilities. However, if a difference exists between the VCI and POI, but *not* the V-IQ and P-IQ, the VCI versus POI difference should be noted and an explanation for why this difference is present should be pro-

vided in the written report. The size of the difference between the VCI and POI needed for statistical significance is 10 points ($p < .05$) or 13 points ($p < .01$). The *WAIS-III Interpretive Worksheet* at the end of Chapter 12 summarizes all the values needed for significance for the various comparisons discussed in Step 2.

Psychometric treatment of a global verbal–nonverbal discrepancy must precede its clinical interpretation. If the V-IQ versus P-IQ difference or VCI versus POI difference is statistically significant, each of these IQs or indexes should be assigned a descriptive category, converted to a percentile rank, and banded with error. Tables A.3, A.4, A.6, and A.7 in the *WAIS-III Administration and Scoring Manual* (Wechsler, 1997) present confidence intervals for Verbal and Performance IQs and the Verbal Comprehension and Perceptual Organization Indexes. If, however, the V-IQ–P-IQ (or VCI–POI) discrepancy is not significant, it is usually unnecessary to give each IQ or index full statistical treatment. Sometimes such treatment will actually confuse the reader of a report because it seems contradictory; for example, explaining that a P-IQ of 94 is not significantly higher than a V-IQ of 87 will make little sense if the former is called Average and the latter Low Average. In fact, if neither a significant Verbal IQ versus Performance IQ nor Verbal Comprehension Index versus Perceptual Organization Index discrepancy is found, then you may assume that overall the examinee's verbal and nonverbal skills are fairly evenly developed. It is important to remember that the finding of nonsignificant discrepancies indicates that differences in scores occurred simply by chance. Thus, be careful to articulate clearly to readers of your report, for example, that if the VCI is not significantly bigger than the POI, then the examinee's ability to solve nonverbal problems involving motor coordination and visual perceptual skill are approximately equal to his or her ability to demonstrate verbal knowledge, verbal reasoning, and verbal expression. One should *not* speak of an "almost" significant difference or a "slight" preference for verbal or nonverbal thinking. If the difference is due to chance, then, for all practical purposes, it should be thought of as being zero.

The next steps in the interpretive process focus on determining whether the global verbal versus nonverbal discrepancy is interpretable. Thus, if any significant discrepancy is found in Step 2, you should proceed to Step 3. However, if no significant discrepancies are found in Step 2, it may not be necessary to complete the next three steps. **For examiners who are comfortable with the nuances of how the V-IQ, P-IQ, VCI, and POI function, you may skip the next three steps (Steps 3, 4, and 5) as they are specifically geared to determine whether the V-IQ versus P-IQ or VCI versus POI discrepancies can be meaningfully interpreted.** However, for the novice examiner, or for examiners who desire a deeper understanding of how the V-IQ, P-IQ, VCI, and POI are functioning, we recommend completing Steps 4 and 5, even if there are no significant verbal–nonverbal discrepancies. The information that can be gleaned from Steps 4 and 5 is useful for deciphering the meaningfulness of the global verbal and nonverbal constructs and the discrepancies between them. In fact, although

we state that you may skip these steps, most examiners find that valuable information is obtained when completing all of the steps sequentially, rather than skipping any. Figure 11.1 poses a reader's question about the issue of skipping steps after Step 2.

STEP 3: ARE THE VERBAL IQ VERSUS THE PERFORMANCE IQ (OR THE VERBAL COMPREHENSION INDEX VERSUS THE PERCEPTUAL ORGANIZATION INDEX) DIFFERENCES ABNORMALLY LARGE?

In Step 2 we presented values that determine whether a person's Verbal and Performance IQs or Verbal Comprehension Index and Perceptual

Reader's Question: "Step 2 states that if the VIQ (or VCI) is not significantly different from the PIQ (or POI), then the examiner should skip to step 6 and examine the minor WMI and PSI factors. Before examining these factors separately, I'm wondering why the examiner wouldn't first look at Step 4 to see if there is a significant difference between VCI and WMI, or a a significant difference between POI and PSI, then go on to explain the meaning of the indexes in relation to one another."

Our Response: "Regardless of whether a V–P discrepancy exists, we agree that it is important to know whether the V-IQ or the P-IQ are interpretable due to scatter or Index variability. As part of Step 7, interpreting the global verbal and nonverbal dimensions, we assume that individuals will discuss whether these factors are, indeed, interpretable. We often recommend to our students to complete the entire WAIS-III Interpretive Worksheet, and then use any aspects of the Steps that are informative in writing their report. Simply because the worksheet suggests to skip to Step 6, does not preclude you from looking within the IQs in the interim steps as well."

FIGURE 11.1

Reader's question regarding Step 2

Organization Index are significantly different, and Tables 11.1 and 11.2 provide empirical guidelines for determining whether the V-IQ versus P-IQ and VCI versus POI discrepancies are abnormal (i.e., unusually large).[2]

Values needed for statistically significant differences and for abnormal differences (at .15,

[2]If only the IQs are derived, then disregard the abnormality comparison between VCI and POI. Similarly, if only the Indexes are derived, then disregard the abnormality comparison between V-IQ and P-IQ.

.05, and .01 levels) for the total standardization sample produces the comparison figures shown in Table 11.3. For each level, the size of the discrepancy required to denote an abnormal difference is more than twice the value required for statistical significance.

The determination of statistical significance (Step 2) assesses only one aspect of a verbal–nonverbal discrepancy. Is it a chance fluctuation, or is it large enough to be meaningful ("real")? The levels of significance serve only to tell the clinician how confident to be in the reality or

TABLE 11.1   Size of WAIS-III V-IQ versus P-IQ discrepancy (regardless of direction) required to be abnormal at various levels of occurrence, by Full Scale IQ category

Frequency of Occurrence in Normal Population	WAIS-III Full Scale IQ					
	≤ 79	80–89	90–109	110–119	≥ 120	Total
<15%	12	15	17	18	20	17
<10%	14	17	19	20	22	19
<05%	17	20	22	26	25	22
<01%	22	27	29	38	38	29

NOTE: The values broken down by IQ-score ranges are based on frequency distributions provided in Table D.1 by The Psychological Corporation (1997, pp. 300–309) and the total values are based on frequency distributions provided in Table B.2 by Wechsler (1997, pp. 206–207).

TABLE 11.2   Size of WAIS-III VCI versus POI discrepancy (regardless of direction) required to be abnormal at various levels of occurrence, by Full Scale IQ category

Frequency of Occurrence in Normal Population	WAIS-III Full Scale IQ					
	≤ 79	80–89	90–109	110–119	≥ 120	Total
<15%	14	17	19	21	21	19
<10%	17	20	22	24	22	22
<05%	22	25	26	29	28	26
<01%	29	32	33	35	39	34

NOTE: The values broken down by IQ-score ranges are based on frequency distributions provided in Table D.1 by The Psychological Corporation (1997, pp. 300–309) and the total values are based on frequency distributions provided in Table B.2 by Wechsler (1997, pp. 206–207).

TABLE 11.3   Statistically significant and abnormal differences between V-IQ and P-IQ and VCI and POI (regardless of direction)

	V-IQ vs. P-IQ		VCI vs. POI	
Level	Statistically Significant	Abnormal	Statistically Significant	Abnormal
<15%	7	17	8	19
<05%	9	22	10	26
<01%	12	29	13	34

NOTE: As stated on page 416, we recommend using the $p < .05$ or $p < .01$ level for determining the significance of a discrepancy, as the $p < .15$ level is too liberal.

meaningfulness of the discrepancy. A V-IQ > P-IQ difference that is statistically significant at the 5% level means that the examiner can have 95% confidence that the observed discrepancy in favor of Verbal IQ is real and not due to chance. The 1% level of significance has an analogous interpretation. A person earning POI > VCI, for example, at the 1% level, is highly likely (99% confidence) to have a real or meaningful discrepancy between the two Indexes. The latter individual is simply better at expressing his or her intelligence nonverbally than verbally. This fact has nothing to do with how often people evidence similar discrepancies; it just doesn't address the issue of frequency of occurrence or abnormality.

The magnitudes of V–P differences required to indicate abnormally large discrepancies are unrelated to formulas or conventional notions of statistical significance. These values simply reflect the proportion of the individuals in the standardization sample who actually obtained V-IQ versus P-IQ or VCI versus POI discrepancies of a given size or greater—statements of fact, not of statistical probability. Hence, a 9-point V-IQ versus P-IQ discrepancy defines a *statistically significant* difference at the 5% level of significance but, in fact, a substantial 42.7% of normal individuals obtained discrepancies of 9 or more points (Wechsler, 1997, Table B.2). Similarly, for most adults, 13 points equals a significant VCI–POI difference at the 1% level, but 33% of normal

people displayed discrepancies of 12 or more points.

These findings show that V–P IQ differences of 9 or more and VCI–POI differences of 10 or more are *statistically* meaningful (they are real), but they are not *abnormal* because they occur too frequently (in about 40% of the normal population) to be of any concern. In order to determine whether a V–P discrepancy is truly abnormal, one must enter Tables 11.1 or 11.2 to find out which differences occurred rarely among the members of the standardization sample. The fact that so many people have differences of 9 or more points between their V-IQ and P-IQ underscores the fact that it is normal for people to differ significantly in how well they manifest their intelligence via verbal comprehension and expression versus the manipulation of concrete, nonverbal materials. This finding also characterized the children and adolescents in the WISC-III normative group (Kaufman, 1994a) and in the standardization sample of earlier editions of Wechsler's scales for children and adults (Kaufman, 1979b, 1990; Seashore, Wesman, & Doppelt, 1950).

Finding a statistically significant V-IQ versus P-IQ or VCI versus POI difference does *not*, by itself, have any diagnostic implications. To be potentially important diagnostically, the difference must be *abnormal*. It makes no sense to diagnose a person as having an abnormality based primarily on a WAIS-III V–P IQ (or VCI–POI) discrepancy unless that discrepancy is of a magnitude that is likewise abnormal. Consequently, after finding a statistically significant V–P difference, clinicians should routinely assess the abnormality of that meaningful discrepancy. Use Table 11.1 to determine whether the magnitude of the discrepancy denotes an unusual V-IQ > P-IQ or P-IQ > V-IQ profile, and use Table 11.2 to determine whether the VCI < POI or POI > VCI discrepancy is unusually large.

Marcella B., a 35-year-old female, obtained a Verbal IQ of 76, a Performance IQ of 93, and a Full Scale IQ of 83. The P > V difference of 17 points is significant at the 1% level (see Table 11.3). Entering Table 11.1 in the column denoting Full Scale IQs of 80–89 with the value of 17 points, one discovers that 10% or less of the normal population of individuals with Full Scale IQs in the Low Average range obtained V–P IQ discrepancies of 17 or more points. That empirical fact might be reported in Marcella's case report to indicate the precise frequency of occurrence of her V–P difference.

It is not important whether Tables 11.1, 11.2, and 11.3 presented in this text are used or if you prefer to use the more detailed tables presented in the WAIS-III Manual (Wechsler, 1997), but it is important that some base-rate table is used. The *WAIS-III Interpretive Worksheet* at the end of Chapter 12 also summarizes the size of the discrepancies necessary for abnormality. For a V–P difference to be of potential diagnostic significance, that difference must be *both* statistically significant *and* reasonably abnormal. The determination of abnormality should always be derived from the normal base-rate tables presented here or by Wechsler (1997). The decision about the unusualness of a particular Wechsler profile is an empirical issue, not a clinical one. Clinical acumen becomes important in selecting the most appropriate criterion of abnormality for a given assessment purpose in trying to interpret the meaning of the abnormal difference and in deciding what to do about it.

Matarazzo and Herman (1985) noted: "Data regarding the *statistical significance* (relative to a

'true' difference from zero) of an obtained V-IQ versus P-IQ difference have at times been misunderstood to reflect the actuarial *abnormality* of the difference. Too often the result has been conclusions about an examinee that are clinically unsound" (p. 925). They added: "[A] V-IQ versus P-IQ difference of 15 points is merely the *initial* datum that should stimulate the clinician to search for corroborating, extra test evidence from the *clinical or social history* that such a difference of 15 points is associated with a potentially significant diagnostic finding" (p. 928).

Some researchers have argued that base-rate tables for IQs and indexes that do not distinguish between the direction of the difference (e.g., P > V vs. V > P for IQ discrepancies) are primarily useful when examiners have no clinical hypotheses about the anticipated direction of the differences (Sattler, 2001; Tulsky, Zhu, & Vasquez, 1998). These researchers argue that, when there are valid hypotheses about directionality, then the tables that rely on absolute differences between IQs or indexes (regardless of direction) will lead clinicians to overestimate the frequency of occurrence of an observed discrepancy score. Their suggestions make sense in situations where examiners have a clear-cut notion of the direction of the discrepancy. For example, when assessing an adult with known brain damage to the right hemisphere, it is reasonable to hypothesize a V > P and VCI > POI profile; when testing a learning-disabled adolescent or adult, it is sensible to expect POI > WMI and POI > PSI profiles; when testing a lawyer or English professor as part of a clinical evaluation, one would anticipate V > P and VCI > POI; and so forth. In instances such as these, it is probably wise simply to *cut the WAIS-III base rates in half*, and use those values, rather than the larger values in the table. However, it does not seem necessary to refer to the special tables developed by Tulsky, Rolfhus, and Zhu (in press) for the WAIS-III and WMS-III, which reports the precise observed values for each direction of difference between IQs and indexes. Indeed, Tulsky et al. (in press) found no difference between the clinical application of their exact table versus the estimates obtained by dividing the absolute values in half. In general, for *most* clinical cases, where the examiner does not have a strong *a priori* idea of what the V–P or index pattern will be, do *not* use the "halved" base rates. For those occasional, select, clear-cut cases—probably most often with neuropsychological assessments—it is acceptable to divide the base rates in half.

The tables of statistical significance and abnormality presented in Chapter 11 will, we hope, discourage psychoanalytically oriented clinicians from making unfounded inferences from differences between the Verbal and Performance scales. For example, Allison, Blatt, and Zimet (1968) claimed: "An eight to ten point difference between Verbal and Performance IQs...indicates only a highly verbal subject with possible obsessive compulsive tendencies. When the Verbal IQ begins to have a marked imbalance over the Performance IQ (by greater than 15 points), more serious pathological trends may be considered" (p. 34). Even more outrageous in view of data for normal adults is Allison et al.'s (1968) proclamation that "a Performance IQ greater than a Verbal IQ in individuals of at least average intelligence is atypical. Three major diagnostic trends, all of which have acting out as a primary feature, are suggested by such a pattern: hysteric, narcissistic, and psychopathic character disorders" (p. 35).

The importance of base-rate data for assessing the abnormality of V-IQ versus P-IQ or VCI versus POI differences, presented here, is revealed in an illustrative case report. Robert N., a mildly retarded man (Chapter 9), displayed a WAIS-III V > P discrepancy of 16 points. Such a discrepancy occurs infrequently (less than 7% of the time) only for individuals earning FS-IQs below 70 (see Table D.1 of the *WAIS-III/WMS-III Technical Manual*), but is not considered unusual for someone who earns a Full Scale IQ of 115. Consequently, the difference is abnormal for Robert but not for an individual functioning in the High Average range of intelligence.

If a V-IQ versus P-IQ or VCI versus POI difference is large enough to be abnormal, the ex-

aminer should conclude that the adolescent or adult has a real preference for verbal or nonverbal expression of intelligence. *Even if* some scatter is found within the IQs or indexes, if an abnormally large difference exists it should be interpreted. This difference may relate to the best way to teach new material to a person or to remediate that person (e.g., a learning-disabled high school or college student); it may relate to recommendations regarding a person's occupational choice, or it may be pertinent to any decision about the person's clinical treatment that is affected by whether the person is more adept verbally or nonverbally. Simply put, when a discrepancy is abnormally large, we consider those too large to ignore for any reason. **In the decision box for Step 3 of our interpretive worksheet, we suggest that you may skip Steps 4 and 5 if either a V-IQ versus P-IQ or VCI versus POI discrepancy is found to be abnormally large (after, of course, the discrepancy is interpreted).** However, if you desire to gain more in-depth information about how the factor indexes are functioning and, thereby, impacting the IQs, you may find useful information in completing all steps, including 4 and 5. Figure 11.2 poses another reader's question regarding Step 3.

STEP 4: IS THE V-IQ VERSUS P-IQ DISCREPANCY INTERPRETABLE?

Determination of whether there was a significant discrepancy between either the V-IQ and P-IQ or the VCI and POI took place in Step 2.[3] However, if such discrepancies were not found to be abnormally large (Step 3), further investigation needs to take place before those discrepancies

---

[3] If only the IQs are derived, then disregard the VCI-WMI and POI-PSI comparisons, and instead just assess the level of subtest scatter in each of the IQs. If only the Indexes are derived, then just calculate the VCI-WMI and POI-PSI discrepancies and skip assessment of subtest scatter in the IQs.

Reader's Question: "Step 3 states that if the VIQ–PIQ difference is abnormally large, the examiner should explain this abnormally large difference (which makes sense to me), and then skip to Step 6 (looking at the minor WMI and PSI factors). My question is this: even if the VIQ–PIQ is abnormally large, wouldn't you still want to look at Step 4 to see if the VIQ scale splits apart into the VCI and WMI factors and to see if the PIQ scale splits apart into the POI and PSI factors. It seems that you could have an abnormally large VIQ–PIQ difference, but these scales might not hold together as unitary dimensions."

Our Response: "Our approach in this book was to let the reader know that the most reliable scales are always worth interpreting first and foremost, if possible. Thus, an abnormally large V–P difference is critical to interpret, regardless of whether there were differences between the other factors. So, that is really the bottom line. Remember, the six-subtest WAIS-III Verbal scale is twice as long as the three-subtest VC scale, and for the nonverbal scales the ratio is 5 to 3. Therefore, on the WAIS-III much more credence is given to to the V–P split than the VC–PO split. So if a WAIS-III V–P discrepancy is abnormally large, that finding is quite reliable and more important (to us) than the much smaller factor indexes. However, we believe that it is always reasonable to "investigate" hunches, both empirical and clinical, as well as fully understand how the factors look in comparison to each other. The heart of "intelligent testing" is to be a detective, not to be rigid, and to follow hunches. Our Steps or guidelines are just that—suggestions. They are not mandates. Always do what your "clinical heart" believes to be best, just be sure to have a rationale and not to ignore data completely."

FIGURE 11.2

Reader's question regarding Step 3

can be interpreted. For instance, if either the V-IQ or P-IQ is not measuring a unitary ability, then the V-P IQ discrepancies are not interpretable. In some instances, a clearer picture of an individual's verbal versus nonverbal skills will come from the "purer" Verbal Comprehension Index and Perceptual Organization Index, rather than the discrepancy between the IQ scales. Step 4 helps to determine whether the V-IQ versus P-IQ discrepancy is interpretable in a clinical or practical sense. **Note, however, that if Step 3 revealed an abnormally large V-IQ versus P-IQ (or VCI vs. POI) discrepancy, examiners should interpret this notable verbal–nonverbal difference regardless of the outcome of Step 4.** In addition, as stated at the end of Step 2,

experienced clinicians may choose to skip Step 4 (and Step 5 as well) if significant differences were not present between the V-IQ and P-IQ or the POI and PSI, unless they choose to gather more in-depth information about how the IQs and indexes are functioning.

The Verbal Scale of the WAIS-III is split into a pair of Indexes: Verbal Comprehension and Working Memory. The Performance Scale is also split into 2 Indexes: Perceptual Organization and Processing Speed. The abilities measured by each of these pairs of indexes are summarized in Table 11.4.

The V-IQ is not a very meaningful construct if the Verbal triad of Vocabulary–Similarities–Information is significantly different from the

TABLE 11.4   Abilities measured by pairs of factor indexes

Verbal IQ

Verbal Comprehension Index	*Working Memory Index*
Verbal conceptualization, knowledge, and expression. Answering oral questions that measure factual knowledge, word meanings, reasoning, and the ability to express ideas in words.	*Number ability and sequential processing.* Responding to oral stimuli that involve the handling of numbers and/or letters in a step-by-step, sequential fashion and require a good, nondistractible attention span for success.

Performance IQ

Perceptual Organization Index	*Processing Speed Index*
Nonverbal thinking and visual–motor coordination. Integrating visual stimuli, reasoning nonverbally, and applying visual–spatial and visual–motor skills to solve the kinds of problems that are not school-taught.	*Response speed.* Demonstrating extreme speed in solving an assortment of nonverbal problems (speed of thinking as well as motor speed).

NOTE: From *Essentials of WAIS-III assessment* (p. 121), by A. S. Kaufman & E. O. Lichtenberger, 1999, New York: Wiley.

Arithmetic–Digit Span–Letter-Number Sequencing triad. In such a situation, when the VCI is significantly greater or less than the WMI, the V-IQ is not a unitary construct. Likewise, if the Picture Completion–Block Design–Matrix Reasoning triad is significantly different from the Performance duo of Digit Symbol-Coding and Symbol Search, then the P-IQ is not meaningful and is not a unitary construct. Thus, a significant discrepancy between the POI and PSI yields a nonmeaningful P-IQ. Table 11.5 provides the discrepancy values necessary for the Indexes to be considered significantly different from one another.

Significant variability *between* the factor indexes making up the IQs creates IQs that are uninterpretable. However, even if the pairs of factor indexes do not differ significantly, the IQs still may not be interpretable if significant subtest scatter exists *within* the Verbal Scale or the Performance Scale. Beyond examination of

VCI–WMI discrepancies and POI–PSI discrepancies, to determine whether each IQ is measuring a unitary construct, the scaled-score range must be examined to determine the amount of subtest scatter. To compute the range, subtract the person's lowest Verbal subtest scaled score from his or her highest Verbal subtest scaled

TABLE 11.5   Size of discrepancies between pairs of factor indexes necessary for statistical significance

	Size of Discrepancy Necessary for Significance		
Factor Index Comparisons	*p* < .01	*p* < .05	**Not Significant**
VCI vs. POI	13 or more	10–12	0–9
VCI vs. WMI	13 or more	10–12	0–9
POI vs. PSI	17 or more	13–16	0–12

score (to obtain Verbal scale range). Similarly, subtract the person's lowest Performance subtest scaled score from his or her highest Performance subtest scaled score (to obtain Performance scale range). The range of subtest scaled score of the Verbal and Performance scales must each be 8 or more points to be considered abnormal (see Table 11.6). When computing these scaled-score ranges, include only the scaled scores of the six subtests that comprise the V-IQ and the scaled scores of the five subtests that comprise the P-IQ. If you have substituted a supplemental Verbal or Performance subtest in the calculation of one of the IQs, then that substituted subtest should be used in the calculation of the range of subtest scaled scores.

Scatter (i.e., abnormal variability) among Verbal subtests indicates that the client's Verbal IQ represents a summary of diverse abilities and does not represent a unitary entity. If an abnormal amount of scatter is present across subtest scores, a global verbal ability is not likely responsible for the individual's scaled scores. Similar logic applies to the Performance IQ. Thus, if unusually large scatter is present in either IQ scale, making at least one of the IQs uninterpretable, then the discrepancy between the V-IQ and P-IQ is not very meaningful or interpretable.

To determine when the V-IQ versus P-IQ discrepancy can be interpreted, four questions must be answered: two about the Verbal scale and two about the Performance scale. Table 11.7 outlines the questions to ask about each IQ scale. First, examine the difference between the VCI and WMI to determine whether the discrepancy is signifi-

cant (10-point discrepancy between indexes is necessary at the $p < .05$ level). Next, check the amount of scatter in the Verbal scale (a range of 8 scaled score points or more is considered abnormal variability between the six Verbal subtests). Then perform a parallel process for the Performance scale. Examine the POI versus PSI discrepancy to detect any significant differences (a 13-point discrepancy between indexes is necessary at the $p < .05$ level), and check Performance scatter (8 scaled-score points is abnormal subtest scatter). If either of the two questions about the Verbal scale indicate significant variability within the scale, then the Verbal IQ does not reflect a unitary construct for that person, and the V-IQ should probably not be interpreted. Likewise, if significant differences between indexes or significant subtest scatter are found in the Performance scale, then the Performance IQ does not reflect a unitary construct for that person, and the P-IQ probably should not be interpreted.

In summary, if all of the Step 4 questions are answered "no," then both the V-IQ and P-IQ are meaningful constructs, and, therefore, the V-IQ versus P-IQ difference provides a meaningful way to denote whether a child differs in verbal versus nonverbal intelligence. If the V-IQ versus P-IQ difference is statistically significant (see Step 2), then the examinee truly differs in his or her verbal and nonverbal intelligence. If the separate IQ scales are unitary, then the Verbal and Performance IQs merit interpretation. If the V-IQ and P-IQ are meaningfully interpretable, then these IQs are the best values to represent a client's global verbal and nonverbal abilities, rather than the

TABLE 11.6   Range of subtest scaled scores considered abnormal in Verbal and Performance IQs

Type of Scatter	Calculation of Range	Abnormal Scatter	Not Abnormal
Verbal Scale	High scaled score minus low scaled score of 6 Verbal IQ tests	8 or more	0–7
Performance Scale	High scaled score minus low scaled score of 5 Performance IQ tests	8 or more	0–7

TABLE 11.7 Four questions to ask in Step 4 before interpreting the V-IQ and P-IQ

Step 4 Question	How to Answer the Question

A. Is there a significant difference between VCI and WMI?

VCI	WMI	VCI–WMI Difference	Significant ($p < .01$)	Significant ($p < .05$)	Not Significant	Is there a significant difference?	
			13 or more	10–12	0–9	**YES**	**NO**

B. Is there abnormal verbal scatter?

High Scaled Score of 6 V-IQ Subtests	Low Scaled Score of 6 V-IQ Subtests	High–Low Difference	Abnormal Scatter	Abnormal Scatter	Not Abnormal	Is there abnormal scatter?	
				8 or more	0–7	**YES**	**NO**

C. Is there a significant difference between POI and PSI?

POI	PSI	POI–PSI Difference	Significant ($p < .01$)	Significant ($p < .05$)	Not Significant	Is there a significant difference?	
			17 or more	13–16	0–12	**YES**	**NO**

D. Is there abnormal performance scatter?

High Scaled Score of 5 P-IQ Subtests	Low Scaled Score of 5 P-IQ Subtests	High–Low Difference	Abnormal Scatter	Abnormal Scatter	Not Abnormal	Is there abnormal scatter?	
				8 or more	0–7	**YES**	**NO**

425

VC and PO Indexes. Thus, if the V–P IQ discrepancy is interpretable, you may choose to skip Step 5, which examines VCI and POI, and move ahead to Step 6.

However, if the answer to at least one of the Step 4 questions is "yes," then either the V-IQ, P-IQ, or both IQs are not interpretable. Therefore, the Verbal–Performance IQ discrepancy is probably also NOT interpretable, and the difference between V-IQ and P-IQ should usually not be considered a meaningful reflection of discrepant global verbal versus nonverbal abilities (see Step 4 Decision Box shown in Table 11.8). If either the V-IQ or P-IQ are uninterpretable, for whatever reason, move to Step 5, where the VCI and POI will be examined. The *WAIS-III Interpretive Worksheet* (Chapter 12) walks you through all of the questions posed in Step 4.

STEP 5: IS VCI VERSUS POI DIFFERENCE INTERPRETABLE?

The WAIS-III Verbal Comprehension Index and the Perceptual Organization Index provide examiners with an alternate pair of standard scores for comparing global verbal and nonverbal abilities, supplementing (and sometimes replacing) the all-encompassing V-IQ and P-IQ.[4]

[4]If only the IQs were derived, then skip Steps 5 and 6.

The factor indexes are sometimes considered "purer" measures of verbal and nonverbal intelligence. As detailed in Table 11.4, the VCI excludes the subtests that are thought to measure sequential processing, working memory, and number ability, and, instead, measures conceptual thought and verbal expression. The POI excludes the two subtests that tap mental and motor speed, and this index captures one's nonverbal thinking and application of visual–spatial skill. Figure 11.3 poses a reader's question about why we chose to focus only on certain WAIS-III index comparisons, such as the VCI versus POI.

To determine whether the VCI and POI are unitary constructs, the factor indexes need to be checked for subtest scatter or variability, just as the IQs were examined. Two parallel questions need to be asked about the factors to ascertain if either one is compromised by too much scatter: (1) Is there significant scatter among the VCI subtests, and (2) Is there significant scatter among the POI subtests? As noted in Table 11.9, a 5 or more point range between the scaled score of the highest and lowest VCI subtests is considered abnormal, and a 6 or more point range between scaled scores of the highest and lowest POI subtests is considered abnormal. The WAIS-III manual did not provide these ranges, so we computed them in the following way. The VCI and POI each includes three subtests. It is possible to compare pairs of scaled scores within each scale to determine if they are significantly different (data are provided in Wechsler, 1997, Table B.4). For VCI and POI, three pairwise comparisons

TABLE 11.8   Step 4 Decision Box

STEP 4 Outcome		Impact on V-IQ and P-IQ		How to Proceed
If ALL the answers to STEP 4 questions A, B, C, and D are **NO**	→	then V-IQ **versus** P-IQ discrepancy is interpretable	→	Explain the meaningful difference between V-IQ & P-IQ. **Then you may skip to STEP 6, if you choose.**
If the answer to one or more questions in STEP 4 is **YES**	→	then the V-IQ **versus** P-IQ difference should probably **not** be interpreted	→	Examine VCI **versus** POI discrepancy in **STEP 5**.

Reader's Question: "The Record Form for the WAIS-III has a section for comparing all possible combinations of the four indexes, yet the WAIS-II technical manual at this point recommends only comparisons between VCI and WMI, and between POI and PSI. I was wondering whether you have considered an approach looking at the mean of the four indexes, and then comparing each of the indexes to this mean to look for statistically significant index strengths or weaknesses. It seems as though this kind of approach, examining all possible index strengths and weaknesses, would be useful for both diagnostic and treatment planning purposes."

Our Response: "We were attempting to provide the most streamlined interpretive process that would provide the user with many useful hypotheses. Going from the global scales to specific subtests and examining the hypothesized abilities that underlie strengths and weaknesses is usually quite fruitful. Certainly, you may find additional means of uncovering hypotheses, such as examining other combinations of factor indexes. However, we find the factor discrepancies that are most theoretically and empirically informative are those that we suggest. We do recommend that you take from our system what is helpful, and modify it with what you find most clinically beneficial."

FIGURE 11.3

Reader's question regarding Step 6

are possible (for the VCI, these comparisons are Information vs. Similarities, Information vs. Vocabulary, and Similarities vs. Vocabulary). We decided that "abnormal scatter" on the VCI and POI would correspond to the smallest scaled-score range that ensured significant discrepancies ($p < .05$) between at least two of the three pairwise comparisons. For the VCI, that corresponded to a range of 5 points and, for the POI, to a range of 6 points. The *WAIS-III Interpretive Worksheet* (Chapter 12) also specifies these values.

Unless the discrepancy between the VCI and POI is abnormally large (see Step 3), if abnormal scatter is found in either the VCI or POI ("yes" answers to either question), then the VCI–POI discrepancy should probably *not* be interpreted. Abnormal scatter present in either of these factors

TABLE 11.9   Range of subtest scaled scores considered abnormal in VCI and POI

Type of Scatter	Calculation of Range	Abnormal Scatter	Not Abnormal
Verbal Conceptualization	High scaled score minus low scaled score of 3 Verbal Conceptualization Index subtests	5 or more	0–4
Perceptual Organization	High Scaled Score minus low scaled score of 3 Perceptual Organization Index subtests	6 or more	0–5

indicates that the Index cannot be meaningfully interpreted, as it is not a unitary factor. When neither the V–P IQ discrepancy nor the VC–PO Index discrepancy is interpretable, then the verbal and nonverbal constructs are not meaningful for that individual. However, if neither the VCI nor POI has abnormal scatter, then the two scales are interpretable and so is the significant discrepancy between them (see Table 11.10, which shows Step 5 from the *WAIS-III Interpretive Worksheet*). In either case, the next step in the interpretive process is to investigate the smallest factors on the WAIS-III (PSI and WMI). Figure 11.4 poses a reader's question regarding the Decision Boxes that appear prior to Step 6.

is 6 or more points, then the WMI should not be interpreted as a meaningful, unitary construct. (The same method for inferring abnormal scatter in the VCI and POI was used to obtain the 6-point value for WMI.) The absolute difference between the Symbol Search scaled score and Digit Symbol-Coding scaled score provides the range of scores on the Processing Speed Index. If the PSI scatter is 4 or more points (a significant discrepancy at the .05 level), then this Index does not represent a unitary construct and should not be interpreted. Table 11.11 and the *WAIS-III Interpretive Worksheet* in Chapter 12 review the values necessary to determine abnormal scatter on the WMI and PSI.

STEP 6: DETERMINE WHETHER THE WORKING MEMORY AND PROCESSING SPEED INDEXES ARE INTERPRETABLE

Examination of the V-IQ, P-IQ, VCI, and POI in Steps 4 and 5 helped to determine if they were unitary dimensions, and, in a similar vein, the smallest factors also need to be checked for abnormal scatter. The lowest scaled score of the three Working Memory Index subtests should be subtracted from the highest scaled score on this Index to obtain the range of scores. If the scatter

STEP 7: INTERPRET THE GLOBAL VERBAL AND NONVERBAL DIMENSIONS, AS WELL AS THE SMALL FACTORS, IF THEY WERE FOUND TO BE INTERPRETABLE

Steps 1 through 6 complete the empirical examination of the IQs and indexes. After examining the information gleaned from the first six steps we know which scores should, or perhaps should not, be interpreted. As you examine the results of

TABLE 11.10   Summary of Step 5

STEP 5 Outcome		Impact on VCI and POI		How to Proceed
If there is *not* an abnormal amount of scatter among either the VCI or POI subtests (i.e., the answers to STEP 5 questions A & B are both **NO**)	→	then VCI **versus** POI discrepancy is interpretable	→	Explain the meaningful difference between VCI & POI.
If there is an abnormal amount of scatter among either the VCI or POI subtests (i.e., the answer to either STEP 5 question A or B is **YES**)	→	then the VCI **versus** POI discrepancy should probably **not** be interpreted	→	Do *not* interpret VCI versus POI difference.

Reader's Question: "The students with whom I work like the linearity of your steps, but seem to get sidetracked and confused by some of the 'Decision Boxes' throughout the Steps that suggest that they skip steps here and there. Is it really important to 'skip' steps if the worksheet's decisions boxes say to do so?"

Our Response: "We recommend that you take from our system what is helpful, and modify it with what you find most clinically beneficial. To new examiners, the interpretive process can be confusing at times (as your students have expressed to you). In our Steps, we attempted to simplify the process as much as possible, but there are some aspects that must remain complex. Following the "cookbook approach" is a good start to interpretation, but students/clinicians must also integrate their conceptual and theoretical understanding of the instrument to create an in-depth understanding of the peaks and valleys in a profile. When we are instructing students who are newly learning the WAIS-III and how to interpret it, we suggest that they go through each of the interpretive Steps one-by-one, rather than skipping any. Completing these Steps in a linear fashion initially will help to develop a more in-depth understanding of how the instrument functions, and how to best describe the results to clients. As students become more familiar with the interpretation of the instrument, then they may find it more useful to skip steps as suggested in our Decision Boxes."

FIGURE 11.4

Reader's question regarding Decision Boxes prior to Step 6

the first six Steps, it is useful to conceptualize the structure of the WAIS-III as a hierarchy in which the bottom tiers impact the tiers above (see Figure 11.5 for a pictorial description of the tiers of the WAIS-III). For example, moving through the first six steps, you may find that variability in the lowest level of the WAIS-III tiered structure (the subtests) has rippling effects all the way to the interpretability of the Full Scale IQ (top tier). Figure 11.6 depicts how variability at the lowest level can impact the interpretability or meaningfulness of the levels above. Figure 11.6 shows an abnormal amount of variability among the Perceptual Organization subtests, which means that the POI is not a meaningful construct to interpret. Therefore neither the POI versus PSI comparison nor POI–VCI comparison can be meaningfully interpreted. This POI subtest scatter also impacts the interpretation of the P-IQ and, ultimately, the Full Scale IQ.

TABLE 11.11 Range of subtest scaled scores considered abnormal in WMI and PSI

Type of Scatter	Calculation of Range	Abnormal Scatter	Not Abnormal
Working Memory	High scaled score minus low scaled score of 3 Working Memory Index Subtests	6 or more	0–5
Processing Speed	High Scaled Score minus low scaled score of 2 Processing Speed Index subtests	4 or more	0–3

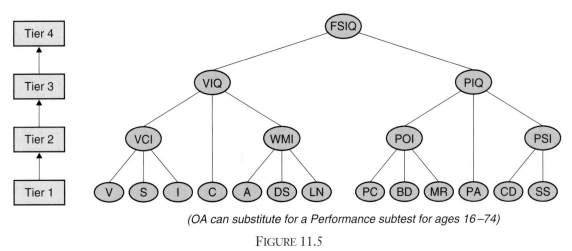

(OA can substitute for a Performance subtest for ages 16–74)

FIGURE 11.5

WAIS-III structure: Four-tier hierarchy

Although examination of Steps 1 through 6 is crucial in determining what scores to interpret, this process is different from actually interpreting them. Step 7 leads examiners to explore a variety of interpretive hypotheses derived from diverse theoretical, clinical, and research-based interpretations. The next few pages outline some of the possible interpretations of these global dimensions (also see Chapters 8 and 9 for information on global profiles in unique populations). We organize Step 7 into the following areas: (1) general interpretation of WAIS-III Indexes, and (2) Horn and Bannatyne formulations to interpret global verbal, global nonverbal, working memory, and processing speed dimensions.

GENERAL INTERPRETATION OF WAIS-III INDEXES

Verbal Conceptualization Index

The VCI, comprised of Vocabulary, Similarities, and Information, measures verbal reasoning and verbal acquired knowledge. Through answering questions, defining words, and determining how words are alike, the VCI provides a measure of factual knowledge, word knowledge, and verbal reasoning, as well as one's ability to express his or her ideas in words. The VCI is most similar to the Crystallized (Gc) dimension of the fluid–crystallized dichotomy (Horn, 1989). Although other subtests can be categorized under Gc, in addition to the three VCI subtests (most notably Comprehension), the VCI embodies the concept of crystallized skills (knowledge that is dependent on school-learned knowledge and acculturation). The VCI also shares conceptual similarities with two of Bannatyne's constructs: Verbal Conceptualization Ability and Acquired Knowledge. The Horn and Bannatyne constructs were discussed in more depth in Chapter 10 and formulas for creating standard-score comparisons of these constructs are provided later in this chapter.

Perceptual Organization Index

The POI, comprised of Picture Completion, Block Design, and Matrix Reasoning, measures visual–spatial problem solving, nonverbal reasoning, and visual–motor skills. Through copying three-dimensional designs, completing visual

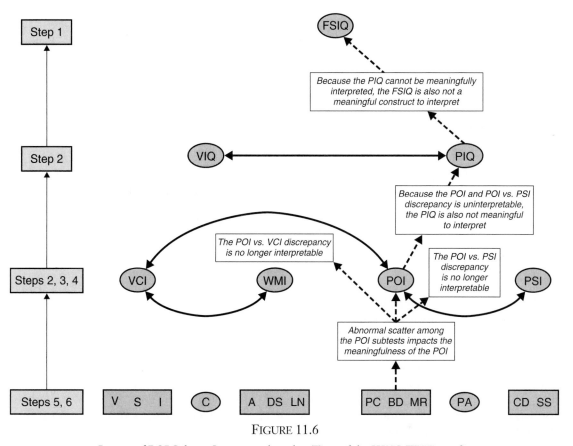

FIGURE 11.6

Impact of POI Subtest Scatter on the other Tiers of the WAIS-III Hierarchy

puzzles, and determining what is missing from a stimulus picture, the POI assesses one's ability to visually integrate information, motorically manipulate objects, and apply visual–spatial skills to problems that are not school-taught. The POI is most similar to the Broad Visualization (*Gv*) and Fluid (*Gf*) dimensions of Horn's expanded *Gf–Gc* model (Horn, 1989; Horn & Hofer, 1992; Horn & Noll, 1997). As we discuss elsewhere in this book, we don't view the POI as a "pure" measure of fluid ability, as visual–spatial abilities and visual–motor abilities are inextricably intertwined with the fluid components of the POI subtests. The POI also shares conceptual similarities with Bannatyne's Spatial Ability construct. Again, the

Horn and Bannatyne constructs were discussed in more depth in Chapter 10, and formulas for creating standard score comparisons of these constructs are provided later in this chapter.

Working Memory Index

The Arithmetic–Digit Span–Letter-Number Sequencing triad forms the WAIS-III Working Memory Index (WMI). It is similar to the WISC-III Freedom from Distractibility Factor, but contains an additional subtest and is more reliable. The name of this index, Working Memory, conveys one possible interpretation of the index's score. However, interpretation of the WMI score cannot be done on the basis of its name alone. Accurate interpretation of this index, and any other score, must integrate behavioral observations during testing, background information collected on the examinee, and the person's nuances of test performance (e.g., forward versus backward span on Digit Span). A wide range of interpretations may be applied to the WMI in addition to working memory, including attention, concentration, anxiety, sequencing ability, sequential processing, number ability, planning ability, short-term memory, executive processing or planning, and even visualization. The diverse interpretations of the WMI encompass both the cognitive and behavioral domains (see Table 11.12).

Behavioral explanations for a person's low WMI score (e.g., distractibility, inattention, low concentration, hyperactivity, anxiety) require clinical support. For example, if examinees frequently ask you to repeat questions during the testing session because they are unable to maintain attention, this observation would provide good clinical data to support an interpretation of inattention or distractibility. Additional sources of information to support interpretations may include the client's reason for referral or background information. For example, if a young executive who earned a low WMI came to you for an evaluation of ADHD because she found herself unable to concentrate for more than five minutes on paperwork or business meetings, such background information could provide good corroborating evidence of "short attention span" as an explanation of her low index. Even that referral information, though, ought to be reinforced by clinical observations of inattention during the administration of at least one Working Memory subtest.

When considering anxiety as an influence on the WMI score, examine the referral question to determine if it alludes to anxiety; again, integrate referral information with behavioral observations during rapport building and the test administration, noting whether signs of anxiety were present. Other subtests may have also been influenced by anxiety, especially highly speeded tasks on the Performance Scale. Anxiety may be manifested in excess motor activity, excessive talking, or distractibility during an assessment.

Difficulty with numbers sometimes is reflected in a low WMI. If a client has not adequately mastered computational skills, then behaviors such as counting on fingers or writing with fingers may be observed. Adolescents and adults with such difficulties may also report a history of struggling in math classes or experiencing anxiety about balancing their checkbook or performing daily activities related to numbers (shopping in a supermarket, following recipes). Often the Arithmetic subtest reveals such numerical difficulties, but the Digits backward portion of Digit Span may allude to difficulties as well. In contrast to Digits backward, performance on Digits forward may be adequate, as it involves simple rote memory. However, the backward span may be poorer as it involves manipulation of the numbers and is more complex. Letter-Number Sequencing may also be informative if examinees can correctly sequence the letters but not the numbers. Additional support for difficulty with symbolic representations (related to numbers) can be obtained from performance on Digit

TABLE 11.12   Possible WMI interpretations

anxiety
attention
concentration
executive processing or planning
number ability
planning ability
sequencing ability
sequential processing
short-term memory
visualization
working memory

NOTE: Adapted from *Essentials of WAIS-III assessment* (p. 136), by A. S. Kaufman & E. O. Lichtenberger, 1999, New York: Wiley.

Symbol-Coding. Note, also, that strong performance on the WMI needs explanation. For example, good number ability may sometimes explain high scores on WMI. To illustrate, consider accountants who earn a scaled score of 18 or 19 on Arithmetic and have an exceptional backward span for digits. These accountants were likely aided on the WMI by their history of manipulating numbers during the course of their occupational career, as well as by a facility with numbers that may have been instrumental in their occupational choice.

Given the name of the index, working memory ability (good or bad) is always a potential explanation for how a client performs on the WMI. One WMI task, in particular, is a prototypical measure of the cognitive function of working memory: Letter-Number Sequencing. Letter-Number Sequencing (LNS) requires an individual to hold letters and numbers in mind, reorganize them, and then repeat them sequentially. Like the Digits backward portion of Digit Span, LNS requires visualization and manipulation. Repeating digits in a forward order is more of an automatic task, and does not strain one's working memory. Arithmetic also requires manipulation and spatial visualization (in addition to knowledge of basic computational facts). Thus, if interpreting the WMI as a possible measure of working memory, we recommend that you examine the forward and backward portions of Digit Span separately and compare these with Arithmetic and Letter-Number Sequencing. Adults with weak working memory abilities may demonstrate poor performance on Digits *backward*, Letter-Number Sequencing, and Arithmetic, but may, at the same time, perform adequately on Digits *forward* because this rote recall task taps a different skill. If only the *total* Digit Span scaled score is considered, the possible discrepancy between the forward and backward span will be masked, and invaluable information lost. To further verify "memory" hypotheses, memory of Digit Symbol-Coding stimuli can be utilized. The supplemental Digit-Symbol Pairing and Free Recall procedures can

help determine how well individuals have held these visual stimuli in their memory.

Processing Speed Factor

Digit Symbol-Coding and Symbol Search comprise the Processing Speed Index (PSI). Although the name of the index suggests that interpretation of the PSI may be linked to processing speed, scores on this index may also denote good or poor fine motor coordination, motivation, visual memory, planning ability, or working memory; in addition poor scores are sometimes due to reflectivity or compulsiveness (Table 11.13).

To a considerable degree, Symbol Search taps *mental* speed, whereas Digit Symbol-Coding primarily measures *psychomotor* speed. Thus, to interpret the PSI, you need to discern whether mental or psychomotor speed is impacting the score (or whether both are contributing factors). Careful observation can provide information on motor coordination. For instance, take note of how an adolescent or adult holds the pencil during the PSI tasks. An awkward grip on the pencil or pencil strokes that are not fluid can be indicators of poor visual–motor coordination. Observation of visual–motor coordination during other subtests such as Block Design and Picture Arrangement, when a client is required to manipulate objects, also provides valuable supportive information. Visual–perceptual problems may also affect performance on the PSI. Such

TABLE 11.13   Possible PSI interpretations

---

compulsiveness
motivation
planning ability
processing speed
reflectiveness
visual memory
visual–motor coordination

NOTE: From *Essentials of WAIS-III assessment* (p. 139), by A. S. Kaufman & E. O. Lichtenberger, 1999, New York: Wiley.

difficulties may be evident in the quality of adults' drawing on The Digit Symbol-Coding subtest, in the nature of their errors on Block Design and Object Assembly items, and possible figure–ground problems or distortions on Picture Completion items. One of the supplemental Digit Symbol-Coding tasks, Digit-Symbol Copy, helps determine whether perceptual accuracy and speed are impacting a person's score (while ruling out the effect of memory).

Additional variables may also affect PSI scores, such as level of motivation, anxiety, perfectionism, and other noncognitive factors. For example, an individual's reluctance to try his or her best to work quickly (perhaps for fear of failing) can negatively affect PSI scores. Also, some people compulsively draw each symbol in Digit Symbol-Coding or draw a perfect diagonal through the Symbol Search boxes. Anxiety may disrupt a person's ability to remain focused on the PSI tasks, which may reduce PSI scores as well.

Planning ability and memory are two other variables to consider when interpreting PSI. Planning ability is especially apparent during Symbol Search, which requires efficient handling of two abstract symbols simultaneously and resembles the planning subtests on the Cognitive Abilities Scale (CAS; Naglieri & Das, 1997). Adults with strong planning ability (e.g., high Picture Arrangement) might score significantly higher on Symbol Search than on Digit Symbol-Coding. However, if planning skills are deficient, the reverse pattern may occur. A strong visual short-term memory can enhance the PSI score, and a poor one can hurt it, because both component subtests depend to a considerable extent on the ability to retain abstract visual stimuli for brief periods of time. On both Symbol Search and Digit Symbol-Coding, if adults can accurately remember the symbol, and not have to refer back to the key or the Target group, they will perform more efficiently. The supplemental Digit-Symbol Incidental Learning procedures (Pairing and Free Recall) provide invaluable information for determining how well a person has memorized the digit-symbol pairs and the symbols themselves. Administer these optional procedures routinely because the obtained scores can be compared to the national norms to permit meaningful interpretation of the results (cumulative percentage associated with raw scores can be obtained from *WAIS-III Administration and Scoring Manual*, Table A.11).

HORN'S AND BANNATYNE'S SYSTEMS FOR INTERPRETING GLOBAL VERBAL, NONVERBAL, WORKING MEMORY, AND PROCESSING SPEED DIMENSIONS

Two of the interpretive systems presented in Chapter 10—Bannatyne categories and Horn's fluid–crystallized approach—are quite popular and potentially valuable for generating meaningful hypotheses about an individual's cognitive functioning. The Bannatyne categories have reached the crest of their popularity during the past 15 or 20 years. They have been shown in study after study to yield characteristic WISC, WISC-R, and WISC-III profiles for reading- and learning-disabled children (Kaufman, 1979b, 1994a; Prifitera & Dersh, 1993; Rugel, 1974); the value of Bannatyne's system for adolescent and adult learning-disabled individuals (Salvia, Gajar, Gajria, & Salvia, 1988) has convinced us of its contributions to the WAIS-III. In addition, Horn's (1989) distinction adaption, refinement, and expansion of the original Horn-Cattell fluid–crystallized dichotomy has received wide attention in both clinical and theoretical circles, and is especially important for the assessment of intelligence across the adult life span using the WAIS-III (see Chapter 5).

We present these systems as *supplements* to the nine-step approach described in this chapter and the next, not as a replacement for it. Hence, the WAIS-III IQs and factor indexes should always form the first line of profile attack. Supplementary systems such as Horn's and Bannatyne's are useful when they *add* to the information yielded by the IQs and indexes, not when they merely echo the same results.

Assessment of Verbal Skills by the Two Approaches

The two interpretive approaches are similar. The WAIS-III factor indexes and Bannatyne categories each include two scales that assess, in "pure" form, the verbal and nonverbal dimensions of intelligence that Wechsler intended to measure when he first developed the Wechsler-Bellevue. The Verbal scale measures a person's ability to understand the spoken word and to respond orally. However, only four of the seven WAIS-III tasks—Comprehension plus the three (Information, Similarities, Vocabulary) that comprise the Verbal Comprehension Index—assess the essence of verbal intelligence: the ability to comprehend verbalizations, verbally mediate during the problem solving or retrieval process, and express one's thoughts in words. These same four subtests constitute Horn's crystallized intelligence grouping. In Bannatyne's system, only three subtests comprise his Verbal Conceptualization factor (Vocabulary, Comprehension, Similarities), because he legitimately considers Information to be more of a memory and achievement-oriented test than a measure of concept formation.

Assessment of Nonverbal Skills by the Two Approaches

Within the Performance domain, the WAIS-III factor indexes and the Bannatyne system both abbreviate the seven-subtest Performance Scale by deleting the factorially complex Picture Arrangement subtest, while retaining three tasks that cluster together conceptually and empirically: Picture Completion, Block Design, and Matrix Reasoning. This combination has been given various labels: Perceptual Organization (factor index),

Spatial Ability (Bannatyne also includes Object Assembly), simultaneous processing (Kaufman & Lichtenberger, 1999), and analytic thinking (field dependence/field independence cognitive style; Goodenough & Karp, 1961). Regardless of label, the combination reflects the blend of visual–perceptual skills, visual–motor coordination, and nonverbal reasoning that Wechsler probably intended to measure when he first sought to elevate nonverbal intelligence to the same exalted plateau as verbal intelligence.

The Horn model does not have a nonverbal component, but it does yield a scale with a distinct nonverbal flavor: fluid intelligence. This category intends to measure the kind of learning that is not specifically dependent on schooling and formal training, but one that is acquirable in less structured ways. To some extent, Wechsler considered Performance IQ to measure this type of fluid thinking, but Horn focused more on the process than the content of Wechsler's tasks when assigning them to be fluid or crystallized domains. Consequently, four of the Performance subtests are measures of fluid intelligence, but so are two Verbal tasks, namely Similarities and Arithmetic. Similarities is included in the crystallized grouping as well because of the verbal concepts that must be learned before one can uncover their relationships. Arithmetic is a complex task that is not only included in Horn's fluid grouping, but also in his quantitative reasoning (*Gq*) category and short-term memory (*Gsm*).

Assessment of Additional Skills by the Two Approaches

Both interpretive systems include a third component that involves memory to some extent and that fits well with the third WAIS-III factor index. The WAIS-III Working Memory index is composed of Letter-Number Sequencing, Arithmetic, and Digit Span. In our categorization of the WAIS-III subtests into Bannatyne's categories, Digit Symbol-Coding plus the Working Memory subtests triad form Bannatyne's Sequential Ability category, and our formulation of Horn's Short-Term Acquisition and Retrieval or short-term memory (*Gsm*) category is comprised of the same subtests as the Working Memory index.

Both Bannatyne's and Horn's systems have a fourth category. Horn's is a speed factor, analogous to the WAIS-III PSI but composed of three subtests—Digit Symbol-Coding, Symbol Search, and Object Assembly. Bannatyne's fourth category, Acquired Knowledge, represents a subgrouping of Verbal subtests, the ones that are most like achievement tests on other batteries (e.g., the Peabody Individual Achievement Test-Revised Normative Update; Markwardt, 1997). The combination of these three subtests (Information, Arithmetic, Vocabulary) does not emerge as a separate dimension in factor analysis (Sattler & Ryan, 1999), but it is, nonetheless, included in the Bannatyne interpretive system because it seems to be especially valuable in identifying an area of weakness in adults with dyslexia or learning disabilities, including females and those attending college (see Chapter 9).

Computing Standard Scores for the Bannatyne Categories and Horn Groupings

To be optimally meaningful, it is desirable to convert a person's scores on the subtests in each category to a standard score having the familiar mean of 100 and standard deviation of 15. We developed such formulas for each Bannatyne category and each Horn grouping. The formulas within each category were so similar from age group to age group across the 16–17 to 85–89 year range that we opted for simplicity: a single formula per category derived for the total standardization sample of 2,450 that will suffice for everyone between ages 16 and 89 years. These simple formulas are presented for each Bannatyne category and Horn grouping in Table 11.14. The only exception is Horn's Short-Term Memory category, which is identical to the Working Memory factor; therefore, the value of the WMI also serves as the standard score for Horn's *Gsm* grouping. For example, the formula to compute

TABLE 11.14   Formulas for converting WAIS-III sums of scaled scores of subtests composing various clusters to standard scores having a mean of 100 and *SD* of 15

Grouping	Formula	Component Subtests
Bannatyne Categories		
Verbal Conceptualization	$1.8\,X_{ss} + 46$	V + S + C
Spatial	$1.5\,X_{ss} + 40$	MR + BD + OA + PC
Sequential	$1.6\,X_{ss} + 36$	A + DS + CD + LNS
Acquired Knowledge	$1.9\,X_{ss} + 43$	I + A + V
Horn Groupings		
Fluid Intelligence	$1.1\,X_{ss} + 34$	MR + BD + OA + S + PA + A
Crystallized Intelligence	$1.2\,X_{ss} + 40$	I + V + C + S + PA
Broad Visualization	$1.5\,X_{ss} + 40$	MR + BD + OA + PC
Broad Speediness	$1.9\,X_{ss} + 43$	CD + SS + OA
Short-Term Memory	Same as WMI	A + DS + LNS

NOTE: Each formula applies to the entire 16- to 89-year age range. X_{ss} equals the sum of *the scaled scores for the subtests in each grouping*.

the Crystallized subtest grouping score in Horn's system is 1.2 X_{ss} + 40. X_{ss} equals the person's sum of scaled scores on the subtests that make up each category. For the Crystallized grouping, these subtests are Information, Vocabulary, Comprehension, Similarities, and Picture Arrangement. For example, Brandon Y. earned the following scaled scores on these five tasks: 11, 16, 12, 11, and 15, respectively. The sum of these scores equals 65; hence, substitute 65 for X_{ss} in the formula. 1.2 (65) + 40 = 78 + 40 = 118. This value becomes Brandon's Crystallized standard score.

Reliability of Bannatyne Categories and Horn Groupings

Table 11.15 presents reliability coefficients and standard errors of measurement for the four Bannatyne categories and five Horn groupings. For all separate categories in the two interpretive systems, reliabilities are excellent for adults, almost never falling below .90 (the one exception is Horn's Broad Speediness) and sometimes exceeding .95.

Determining Strengths and Weaknesses within Each System

Table 11.16 allows examiners to compute significant strengths and weaknesses among four Bannatyne categories and five Horn groupings. This table presents the size of the difference required for statistical significance when comparing a person's standard score on each factor to his or her own mean score on the several categories. The interpretive system presented here is similar to the one we describe for computing strengths and weaknesses on the 14 WAIS-III subtests: The person's average performance defines the baseline against which each separate cluster is compared. Standard scores significantly above the person's mean are relative strengths; scores be-

TABLE 11.15 Bannatyne categories and Horn groupings: Reliability and SE_M

Cluster	r_{xx}	SE_M
Bannatyne Categories		
Verbal Conceptualization		
V + S + C	.95	3.4
Spatial		
MR + BD + OA + PC	.93	4.0
Sequential		
A + DS + CD + LNS	.94	3.7
Acquired Knowledge		
I + A + V	.96	3.0
Horn Groupings		
Fluid Intelligence		
MR + BD + OA + S + PA + A	.95	3.4
Crystallized Intelligence		
I + V + C + S + PA	.96	3.0
Broad Visualization		
MR + BD + OA + PC	.93	4.0
Broad Speediness		
CD + SS + OA	.88	5.2
Short-Term Memory		
A + DS + LNS	.94	3.8

NOTE: SE_M's are in standard score units (SD = 15).

low the mean are relative weaknesses. Examiner Forms 11.1 and 11.2 (pp. 439–442) are intended to facilitate these computations.

The method of determining strengths and weaknesses is illustrated below for the Bannatyne system using the profile of Brandon Y., age 72, who suffered a stroke 2 years ago.

1. Compute Brandon's scaled scores.
2. Sum Brandon's three scaled scores for the subtests constituting the Verbal Conceptualization cluster. Brandon earned scores of 16 on Vocabulary, 11 on Comprehension, and 15 on

TABLE 11.16   Size of difference required for significance when comparing each separate cluster score to the person's own mean score on Horn and Bannatyne clusters

Cluster	DIFFERENCE FROM AVERAGE OF 5 HORN CLUSTERS		Cluster	DIFFERENCE FROM AVERAGE OF 4 BANNATYNE CLUSTERS	
	Significance Level			Significance Level	
	.01	.05		.01	.05
Fluid	9.2	7.5	Verbal Conceptualization	8.7	7.1
Crystallized	8.6	7.0	Spatial	9.7	7.9
Visualization	10.4	8.5	Sequential	9.2	7.5
Broad Speediness	12.9	10.5	Acquired Knowledge	8.1	6.6
Short-Term Memory	10.2	8.3			

NOTE: Each category score, after being converted to a standard score having a mean of 100 and SD of 15 (using the formulas in Table 11.14), is compared to the person's own mean on all categories in that particular system. All values for significant deviations have been corrected by the Bonferroni technique.

Similarities. His sum equals 42. Repeat this procedure for the other three Bannatyne categories. (Brandon's sums are 19 for Spatial, 20 for Sequential, and 37 for Acquired Knowledge.)

3. Enter each of Brandon's sums into the relevant formula (from Table 11.14), as the value of X_{ss}.

$$
\begin{aligned}
\text{Verbal Conceptualization} &= 1.8\,X_{ss} + 46 \\
&= 1.8(42) + 46 \\
&= 75.6 + 46 \\
&= 121.6, \text{ which rounds} \\
&\quad \text{to } 122 \\
\text{Spatial} &= 1.5\,X_{ss} + 40 \\
&= 1.5(19) + 40 \\
&= 28.5 + 40 \\
&= 68.5, \text{ which rounds} \\
&\quad \text{to } 69 \\
\text{Sequential} &= 1.6\,X_{ss} + 36 \\
&= 1.6(20) + 36 \\
&= 32 + 36 \\
&= 68 \\
\text{Acquired Knowledge} &= 1.9\,X_{ss} + 43 \\
&= 1.9(37) + 43
\end{aligned}
$$

$$
\begin{aligned}
&= 70.3 + 43 \\
&= 113.3, \text{ which rounds} \\
&\quad \text{to } 113
\end{aligned}
$$

4. Sum Brandon's standard scores (mean = 100, $SD = 15$ for the population at large) on the four Bannatyne categories, and divide by 4 to compute his average category score.

$$
\begin{aligned}
\text{Verbal Conceptualization} &= 122 \\
\text{Spatial} &= 69 \\
\text{Sequential} &= 68 \\
\underline{\text{Acquired Knowledge}} &= \underline{113} \\
\text{Sum} &= 372 \\
\text{Mean} &= 93
\end{aligned}
$$

5. Subtract Brandon's mean from each of the four standard scores.

$$
\begin{aligned}
\text{Verbal Conceptualization} &= 122 - 93 = +29 \\
\text{Spatial} &= 69 - 93 = -24 \\
\text{Sequential} &= 68 - 93 = -25 \\
\text{Acquired Knowledge} &= 113 - 93 = +20
\end{aligned}
$$

6. Compare these deviations to the size of the discrepancies required for statistical significance shown in Table 11.16. For Verbal Conceptualization at the $p < .05$ level, deviations of

EXAMINER FORM 11.1   Computing standard scores on Bannatyne's WAIS-III categories and determining significant strengths and weaknesses on the four categories (Developed by A. S. Kaufman and E. O. Lichtenberger)

Instructions for Calculating Bannatyne Standard Scores

Step 1.   Enter the person's scaled score for each subtest in the appropriate column.

Step 2.   Sum the four columns, entering each sum on the relevant line.

Step 3.   Multiply each sum by the value indicated for each category. Enter each product (to the nearest tenth).

Step 4.   Add the product to the constant indicated for each category. Enter this sum on the relevant line. These values equal the person's standard scores ($M = 100$, $SD = 15$) on the four categories.

Step 5.   Round each standard score to the nearest whole number.

Examinee's Name: _____   Date: _____

WAIS-III Subtest	Verbal Conceptualization	Spatial	Sequential	Acquired Knowledge
Verbal				
Vocabulary	V ____			V ____
Similarities	S ____			
Arithmetic			A ____	A ____
Digit Span			DS ____	
Information				I ____
Comprehension	C ____			
Letter-Number Seq.				
Performance				
Picture Completion		PC ____		
Digit Symbol-Coding			Cd ____	
Block Design		BD ____		
Matrix Reasoning		MR ____		
Picture Arrangement				
Symbol Search			SS ____	
Object Assembly		OA ____		
Sum =	____	____	____	____
Multiply Sum by	(1.8)	(1.5)	(1.6)	(1.9)
Product =	____	____	____	____
Add the Constant	+46	+40	+36	+43
Sum = Standard Score =	____	____	____	____
Rounded Standard Score =	____	____	____	____

(Continues)

EXAMINER FORM 11.1   (Continued)

Instructions for Calculating Strengths and Weaknesses of Bannatyne Standard Scores

Step 1. Enter the person's standard score for each of the four Bannatyne categories in the appropriate column.

Step 2. Compute the mean of the four standard scores, rounding the mean to the nearest whole number.

Step 3. Subtract the person's mean score from each of the four standard scores. Enter the difference scores in the column headed "Difference." Use negative signs to denote scores below the person's mean.

Step 4. Determine whether each difference is significant at the .05 level using the values provided. Differences that equal or exceed these values are significant strengths or weaknesses for the person.

Step 5. Enter an S or W in the column provided to denote significance.

			Size of Difference Needed for Significance		
Examinee's Name: _____			Date: _____		
Bannatyne Category	**Standard Score**	**Difference**	**($p < .05$)**	**($p < .01$)**	**S or W**
Verbal Conceptualization	_____	_____	±7	±9	_____
Spatial	_____	_____	±8	±10	_____
Sequential	_____	_____	±8	±9	_____
Acquired Knowledge	_____	_____	±7	±8	_____
Sum = _____					
Divide by 4					
Mean = _____					
Rounded Mean = _____					

at least 7 points are needed for significance, and at the .01 level at least 9 points are necessary. All of the deviations are clearly significant at the .01 level, although the .05 level provides ample significance for most interpretive purposes. Thus, Brandon (who had suffered right-hemisphere damage due to a stroke) displays relative strengths in both Verbal Conceptualization Ability and Acquired Knowledge, and relative weaknesses in Spatial Ability and Sequential Ability. Analogous steps to the six shown here can be used to determine a person's relative strengths and weaknesses among the factor scores of the three Horn groupings.

Strengths and Weaknesses within a Cluster

To perform more in-depth analysis of how a client is performing *within* any of the cvcvHorn or Bannatyne categories, compare the person's subtest scaled score on each subtest in a particular cluster

EXAMINER FORM 11.2   Computing standard scores on Horn's WAIS-III categories and determining significant strengths and weaknesses on the five categories (Developed by A. S. Kaufman and E. O. Lichtenberger)

Instructions for Calculating Horn Standard Scores

Step 1.   Enter the person's scaled score for each subtest in the appropriate column.

Step 2.   Sum the first four columns, entering each sum on the relevant line.

Step 3.   Multiply each sum by the value indicated for each category. Enter each product (to the nearest tenth).

Step 4.   Add the product to the constant indicated for each category. Enter this sum on the relevant line. These values equal the person's standard scores ($M = 100$, $SD = 15$) on the four categories.

Step 5.   Round each standard score to the nearest whole number.

Step 6.   Transfer the Working Memory Index score from the record form to the Short-Term Memory standard score.

Examinee's Name: _____   Date: _____

WAIS-III Subtest	Crystallized	Fluid	Broad Visualization	Broad Speediness	Short-Term Memory
Verbal					
Vocabulary	V _____				
Similarities	S _____	S _____			
Arithmetic		A _____			A
Digit Span					DS
Information	I _____				
Comprehension	C _____				
Letter-Number Seq.					LNS
Performance					
Picture Completion			PC _____		
Digit Symbol-Coding				Cd _____	
Block Design		BD _____	BD _____		
Matrix Reasoning		MR _____	MR _____		
Picture Arrangement	PA _____	PA _____			
Symbol Search				SS _____	
Object Assembly		OA _____	OA _____	OA _____	
	↓	↓	↓	↓	↓

	Crystallized	Fluid	Broad Visualization	Broad Speediness	Short-Term Memory
Sum =	_____	_____	_____	_____	
Multiply Sum by	(1.2)	(1.1)	(1.5)	(1.9)	
Product =	_____	_____	_____	_____	
Add the Constant	+40	+34	+40	+43	
Sum = Standard Score =	_____	_____	_____	_____	
Rounded Standard Score =	_____	_____	_____	_____	_____

(Continues)

EXAMINER FORM 11.2   (Continued)

Instructions for Calculating Strengths and Weaknesses of Horn Standard Scores

Step 1.   Enter the person's standard score for each of the four Horn categories in the appropriate column and transfer the Working Memory Index (WMI) to the Horn Short-Term Memory standard score.

Step 2.   Compute the mean of the five standard scores, rounding the mean to the nearest whole number.

Step 3.   Subtract the person's mean score from each of the four standard scores. Enter the difference scores in the column headed "Difference." Use negative signs to denote scores below the person's mean.

Step 4.   Determine whether each difference is significant at the .05 level using the values provided. Differences that equal or exceed these values are significant strengths or weaknesses for the person.

Step 5.   Enter an S or W in the column provided to denote significance.

Examinee's Name _____   Date: _____

Horn Category	Standard Score	Difference	Size of Difference Needed for Significance ($p < .05$)	Size of Difference Needed for Significance ($p < .01$)	S or W
Crystallized	_____	_____	±7	±9	_____
Fluid	_____	_____	±8	±9	_____
Broad Visualization	_____	_____	±9	±10	_____
Broad Speediness	_____	_____	±11	±13	_____
Short-Term Memory (= WMI)	_____	_____	±8	±10	_____

Sum = _____

Divide by   5

Mean = _____

Rounded Mean = _____

to that person's mean scaled score on all of the cluster subtests; enter the difference scores into Table 11.17 (Horn) or Table 11.18 (Bannatyne) to determine if they are significant. For example, to determine if a client's performance on the Information subtest is significantly different from his or her own mean performance on the Crystallized cluster, calculate the mean subtest scaled score for the Crystallized cluster (i.e., the average of the 5 Crystallized subtests) and subtract that from the Information subtest scaled score. The values in Table 11.17 inform us that a 2-point discrepancy between the mean Crystallized subtest scaled score and the Information subtest is necessary for significance at the .05 level and a 3-point (2.6 rounded up) discrepancy is needed for significance at the .01 level. Similar subtest-cluster discrepancies can be calculated

TABLE 11.17 Differences between single subtest scaled scores and mean scaled score on Horn Groupings: 1% and 5% level of significance

| | AVERAGE OF 6 FLUID SUBTESTS | | | AVERAGE OF 5 CRYSTALLIZED SUBTESTS | |
| | *Significance Level* | | | *Significance Level* | |
Subtest	.01	.05	Subtest	.01	.05
MR	2.8	2.3	I	2.6	2.1
BD	3.1	2.6	V	2.3	1.9
OA	4.3	3.5	C	3.1	2.6
S	3.1	2.5	S	3.0	2.4
PA	4.0	3.2	PA	3.7	3.1
A	2.9	2.4			

| | AVERAGE OF 3 BROAD SPEEDINESS SUBTESTS | | | AVERAGE OF 4 BROAD VISUALIZATION SUBTESTS | |
| | *Significance Level* | | | *Significance Level* | |
Subtest	.01	.05	Subtest	.01	.05
CD	3.2	2.6	MR	2.8	2.3
SS	3.4	2.8	BD	3.0	2.5
OA	3.7	3.0	OA	3.9	3.2
			PC	3.2	2.6

| | AVERAGE OF 3 SHORT-TERM MEMORY SUBTESTS | |
| | *Significance Level* | |
Subtest	.01	.05
A	2.6	2.1
DS	2.5	2.0
LNS	2.9	2.4

NOTE: Each subtest scaled score within a particular category is compared to the person's own mean subtest scaled score for that category. All values for significant deviations have been corrected by the Bonferroni technique.

for any of the Bannatyne or Horn clusters, and in Chapter 12 we discuss the analogous process for determining subtest strengths and weaknesses based on the WAIS-III Verbal–Performance dichotomy.

Selecting a System

Ordinarily, an examiner will supplement the "regular" nine-step analysis of IQs, Indexes, and subtests with only one of the two systems described

TABLE 11.18   Differences between single subtest scaled scores and mean scaled score on Bannatyne Groupings: 1% and 5% level of significance

	AVERAGE OF 3 VERBAL CONCEPTUALIZATION SUBTESTS			AVERAGE OF 4 SPATIAL SUBTESTS	
	Significance Level			Significance Level	
Subtest	.01	.05	Subtest	.01	.05
V	2.2	1.8	MR	2.8	2.3
S	2.6	2.1	BD	3.0	2.5
C	2.7	2.2	OA	3.9	3.2
			PC	3.2	2.6

	AVERAGE OF 3 ACQUIRED KNOWLEDGE SUBTESTS			AVERAGE OF 4 BROAD SEQUENTIAL SUBTESTS	
	Significance Level			Significance Level	
Subtest	.01	.05	Subtest	.01	.05
V	2.1	1.7	MR	2.7	2.2
A	2.4	1.9	BD	2.6	2.1
I	2.2	1.8	OA	3.0	2.4
			PC	3.2	2.6

NOTE: Each subtest scaled score within a particular category is compared to the person's own mean subtest scaled score for that category. All values for significant deviations have been corrected by the Bonferroni technique.

here. The systems overlap so much with each other (and with WAIS-III indexes) that it is not worthwhile to perform all of the computations for both systems. Further, the mound of data that will accumulate from such an effort—in addition to the wealth of data from the factor indexes and individual subtest strengths and weaknesses—may easily overwhelm examiners, causing confusion and clerical errors.

If examiners have a particular orientation toward one system or another, they may routinely employ it with each person they test. Examiners who find the fluid–crystallized model to be espe-cially valuable from either a theoretical or practical standpoint, or who consider Bannatyne's four categories to offer a useful regrouping of Wechsler's tasks, may give preference to one of these approaches. Indeed, Horn (1985, 1989) developed his refinement and expansion of *Gf–Gc* theory from a strong empirical and theoretical orientation. In contrast, Bannatyne (1968, 1971) developed his model from a strong clinical foundation, specifically based on his years of experience with a group he termed "genetic dyslexics." Conceivably, examiners with a more theoretical and empirical bent may often opt for Horn's approach, whereas those who consider themselves first and foremost as clinicians (as Wechsler did), may frequently choose Bannatyne's model.

The nature of the referral problem may also dictate the system of choice. A person believed or known to be learning-disabled may be best served by the Bannatyne system, inasmuch as his four categories have produced meaningful results in countless studies of learning-disabled children, adolescents, and adults (see Chapter 9), and his Acquired Knowledge category reflects school learning. Someone who may have dementia or other age-related diseases involving deterioration of cognitive abilities may display quite different functioning whether assessed by fluid, crystallized, memory, or speed tasks in view of the different characteristic aging patterns (see Chapter 5); for these individuals, Horn's model may be ideal. More specific recommendations for choosing among the Bannatyne, Horn, and other approaches are provided in the next chapter.

CHARACTERISTIC PROFILES IN UNIQUE POPULATIONS

Clinicians have long searched for characteristic subtest profiles associated with brain dysfunction and psychopathology with the same zeal that medical researchers apply to the search for biochemical patterns of cancer or AIDS patients, or that psychiatrists apply to the behavioral patterns of mass murderers. Mostly, these quests have not been fruitful, not unlike the quests of other scientists. Unforeseen and often unknown complexities frustrated Wechsler's search for a subtest profile associated with organic brain syndrome or the search of others for patterns that are pathognomonic of schizophrenia, psychotic depression, and countless other disorders. However, the fact that the search for characteristic profiles for *groups* has usually been unsuccessful does not alter the value of a diversity of theoretical and clinical approaches for gaining true in-

sight into the profiles of *individuals*. In addition to summarizing pertinent accumulated research for a wide array of clinical groups throughout this book, our other key goal is to offer a diversity of methods for gaining optimal understanding of the cognitive profile of every individual you assess.

SUMMARY

This chapter, the second of three on profile interpretation, stresses empirical treatment of the data, beginning with the most global score, the Full Scale IQ, and proceeding to the Indexes, and sets the stage for subtest interpretation in Chapter 12. The first seven steps of WAIS-III profile interpretation presented in this chapter guide you to determine whether the FS-IQ is a useful and meaningful construct to interpret or whether the V-IQ and P-IQ or the four indexes are more meaningfully interpreted. When the FS-IQ, V-IQ, P-IQ, and the indexes are interpreted, they should be banded with error and converted to an intelligence category and percentile rank. When significant differences are present between the indexes, these discrepancies can impact the interpretability of any or all of the three IQs. Significant subtest scatter in the indexes or V-IQ or P-IQ can also affect the meaningfulness of the IQs or indexes. Careful examination of the first seven steps will delineate which of the scores are the best to interpret in light of potential discrepancies and scatter within the profile.

The last of the interpretive steps presented in this chapter (Step 7) deals with interpretation of the global verbal and nonverbal dimensions, as well as the small factors. In the first six steps, we guided the reader through steps to determine what scores are meaningfully interpretable, but in Step 7, we led you through some potential interpretations based on theory, clinical experience, and research. The general interpretation of each of the four factor indexes is presented along with

Horn and Bannatyne formulations to interpret a variety of potentially meaningful dimensions.

In addition to the sequential steps that examine the IQs and indexes, a method for calculating standard scores (mean = 100, SD = 15) for alternative subtest configurations is provided in this chapter. Examiners who choose to use these standard scores for Bannatyne and Horn clusters will be able to apply the empirical system that is provided for determining significant strengths and weaknesses in a person's Horn or Bannatyne profile. Because the two interpretive approaches overlap to some extent, and both overlap with the four WAIS-III factor indexes, guidelines are discussed to help clinicians select the most appropriate system.

CHAPTER 12

WAIS-III Profile Interpretation: Steps 8 and 9

This chapter integrates the logical analysis of each WAIS-III subtest (Chapter 10) with the empirical treatment of the subtest profile to convert an individual's array of WAIS-III scaled scores into clinically meaningful hypotheses about his or her cognitive functioning. The two steps described in depth in this chapter (8 and 9) follow directly after Steps 1–7 presented in Chapter 11.

GENERATING WAIS-III HYPOTHESES

Our goal in this chapter is to structure the examiner's task of identifying meaningful cognitive hypotheses that may be embedded in a person's WAIS-III profile by restructuring and regrouping the component subtests. Where these hypotheses have reasonably consistent research support re-

garding their clinical, behavioral, or neuropsychological meaning, that support is indicated. Profile analysis is partitioned into two steps: 8 and 9 in the sections that follow, with emphasis on the identification—and not necessarily the clinical interpretation—of diverse strengths and weaknesses within the adolescent's or adult's cognitive and behavioral spectrum.

This chapter is organized in three sections, two of which reflect different approaches to WAIS-III profile attack, depending on the examiner's preferred processing style: (1) a sequential approach to profile attack—Steps 8 and 9 (to follow Steps 1–7 in Chapter 11); (2) a simultaneous approach to profile attack; and (3) illustrative case reports, which demonstrate the outcome of the various hypothesis generation methods and the integration of WAIS-III data with background information, test behaviors, and data from other tests.

THE NINE-STEP PROCESS

Our approach to examining the WAIS-III profile focuses on moving from the most global scores (i.e., the Full Scale IQ in Step 1 and Verbal and Performance IQs in Steps 2 and 3) to scores measuring more specific abilities (i.e., the four Indexes in Steps 4 through 7). As we described in Chapter 11, moving down the hierarchy of WAIS-III scores will at times lead you to realize that the most global scores are not necessarily the most meaningful ones to interpret. In fact, in some cases, variability in the subtest scaled scores will necessitate focusing on the pattern of scaled scores during interpretation rather than on the IQs or indexes. Examination of the pattern of subtest scaled scores is our focus in Steps 8 and 9 of the Kaufman-Lichtenberger approach to WAIS-III interpretation.

STEP 8: INTERPRET SIGNIFICANT STRENGTHS AND WEAKNESSES OF THE SUBTEST PROFILE

Unlike the traditional standard scores with a mean of 100 and SD of 15 that are used for the IQs and indexes, WAIS-III scaled scores are a special kind of standard score that have a mean set at 10 and SD set at 3; scaled scores on the WAIS-III can range from 1 to 19. These simple parameters have allowed clinicians to easily compare a person's performance from one subtest to another; to evaluate fluctuations in a person's scores on the same subtest from one time to another; and to relate the subtest scores of different people, regardless of their ages. The beauty of the scaled score for the WAIS-III, WISC-III, and WPPSI-R is that it always has the same meaning for an individual. No matter what the adolescent's or adult's age, or the particular subtest in question, the examiner has the interpre-

tive luxury of knowing that 10 is average, 7 is 1 SD below the mean, 16 is 2 SDs above the mean, and so forth.

Because the W-B I, WAIS, and WAIS-R derived scaled scores for everyone are based on subtest norms for ages 20–34, these earlier versions of Wechsler's adult scale did not enjoy the benefit of uniformity from age to age or from subtest to subtest. The farther the person was from the 20 to 34-year-old reference group, the lower the average scaled score was for his or her age group. Similarly, the degree to which subtests displayed different aging curves (such as Verbal versus Performance subtests; see Chapter 5) marked the degree to which the subtests would yield different mean scores for the same age group. Consider ages 65–69 on the WAIS-R. Relative to the reference group norms for ages 20–34, that age group earned an average Verbal scaled score, across the six Verbal subtests, of 8.9 and an average Performance scaled score of 6.8 (Wechsler, 1981, Table 7). Clinicians had to calculate a second set of scaled scores (age-corrected) if they wanted to restore the uniformity of the mean of 10 and SD of 3. The net result was confusion and extra opportunities for clerical errors. Happily, the WAIS-III avoided this problem by adopting procedures analogous to the ones used for decades for the children's scales, namely computing scaled scores separately for each age group. The result is the uniform, easy-to-interpret scaled score for everyone.

Step 8 details systematic ways of empirically attacking WAIS-III subtest profiles by determining significant relative strengths and weaknesses among the 14 separate subtests. We have previously endorsed a systematic, empirical system for determining significant strengths and weaknesses in the WAIS-III profile (Kaufman & Lichtenberger, 1999). The method avoids a comparison of myriad pairs of Wechsler subtests (e.g., Information versus Vocabulary, Comprehension versus Picture Arrangement) in favor of a more global approach to the problem: computing the significance of the difference between each Verbal scaled score and the pertinent mean score for that person (either the Verbal or Full Scale mean, depending on the size of the V–P IQ discrepancy), and then performing analogous computations for each Performance scaled score. This method involves seven comparisons per scale instead of an indeterminate number and invokes order in the process; the pairwise method exploits chance fluctuations, makes Type I errors likely (Knight & Godfrey, 1984), and produces a series of statements about pairs of specific tasks instead of a crisp overview of the person's strengths and weaknesses.

To compare an individual's mean performance to his or her performance on every individual subtest, you must first calculate a mean. **We suggest that you use the separate mean of all Verbal subtests and mean of all Performance subtests only when the V-IQ versus P-IQ discrepancy is abnormally large (i.e., 17 points); otherwise, use the mean scaled score of all subtests together as the point of comparison for each scaled score.**[1] Thus, if there is an abnormally large split between a person's verbal and nonverbal performance, then compare Verbal scale subtests to the mean of all Verbal subtests administered and the Performance scale subtests to the mean of all Performance subtests administered. However, if the verbal–nonverbal abilities are not *abnormally* discrepant (even if a significant V-IQ vs. P-IQ difference exists), then use the mean of all subtests (i.e., the mean scaled score of all WAIS-III subtests administered). Figure 12.1 poses a reader's question about selecting the mean score for ipsative comparisons.

Once the mean or means of the subtest scaled scores have been calculated, then you should round the mean(s) to the nearest whole number. This rounding procedure will simplify the next calculations and reduce the risk of clerical errors.

Next, calculate the differences between each of the 14 subtest scaled scores and the rounded mean scaled score. On the *WAIS-III Interpretive Worksheet* we have included a place to record both the mean scaled score as well as the difference between the individual subtest scaled scores and the mean. It is important to include a plus (+) or minus (–) sign in front of the difference score to indicate whether the scaled score was higher or lower than the mean score.

The size of the difference necessary for significance for each WAIS-III subtest varies, but is one of three values: ± 2, ± 3, or ± 4. We present rounded values for computing significant strengths and weaknesses within the Verbal and Performance Scales. Table 12.1 and Step 8 of our *WAIS-III Interpretive Worksheet*, adapted from the *WAIS-III Administration and Scoring Manual* (Wechsler, 1997, Table B3) summarizes the magnitudes of the differences needed for significance at the .05 level for each subtest when compared to the person's own mean score on the WAIS-III Verbal, Performance, and Full Scales. About half of the values at the .05 level are within about a half point of 3.0. Thus, when rounded, 8 subtests require ± 3 point discrepancies for significance, 1 subtest requires ± 2 point discrepancies for significance, and 5 subtests require ± 4 point discrepancies for significance.

We believe that 95% confidence is ample for nearly all assessment situations inasmuch as the reasons for identifying the strong and weak areas are to help generate hypotheses to explain a person's cognitive assets and liabilities, and to ensure some statistical order during the interpretive process, preventing examiners from declaring trivial differences to be meaningful. More stringent rules than the ones suggested would limit the generation of useful hypotheses and betray the purpose for giving the test battery in the first place.

Are exact values necessary? The WAIS-III record form and manual provide tables of specific values for each subtest at each age and encourage examiners to enter these tables to determine significance (Wechsler, 1997); in our Wechsler texts

---

[1]If only the 11 subtests that comprise the four indexes have been administered and the VCI–POI discrepancy is abnormally large (i.e., 19 points), then you should base your strengths and weaknesses on the *separate* means of verbal subtests versus the performance subtests. If the VCI is not abnormally discrepant from the POI, base your strengths and weaknesses on the mean of all 11 subtests administered.

Reader's Question: "I am curious as to why the decision was made to compare subtest scores to separate verbal and performance means only when the V–P split is abnormally large. In the past, Dr. Kaufman advocated the use of separate verbal and performance means if the V–P split was just significantly different, an approach that made a lot of sense to me because the full scale is not holding together as a unitary scale even if the split is just significantly different, rather than abnormally large."

Our Response: "One of the reasons we decided to recommend comparing subtest scores to individual V & P scales only when the V–P split is abnormal is in order to remain consistent with what was recommended by Kaufman (1994a, Intelligent Testing with the WISC-III) in interpreting the WISC-III. We imagined that many users of the WISC-III interpretive system may also follow suit with our WAIS-III interpretive system. Another reason is that we feel we can more strongly assume that separate global verbal and global nonverbal ability determine people's scores (as opposed to their General ability, g), when the V–P split is abnormal, rather than just significantly different."

FIGURE 12.1

Reader's question regarding Step 8

(Kaufman, 1990, 1994a; Kaufman & Lichtenberger, 1999, 2000), we encourage the application of rounded values. Why? Because the computation of strengths and weaknesses on the Wechsler tests involve manipulation of multiple numbers, which can lead to clerical errors. Consequently, we feel that performing calculations with rounded values, which does not force examiners to search out extra tables, will lead to fewer errors in empirical analysis and more accurate interpretation of Wechsler subtest profiles.

Some researchers prefer to use precise tabled values to compute strengths and weaknesses (Campbell & Wilson, 1986). To us, using precise values (rounded to the nearest tenth or hundredth!) to determine strengths and weaknesses, as proposed by Campbell and Wilson, ignores the realities of a clinician's task in making sense out of a subtest profile, as well as the problems encountered in scoring several of Wechsler's subtests. Apart from the administration and

scoring errors that are a built-in part of the Wechsler evaluation process (see Chapter 6), even conscientious examiners disagree about the distinction between 0-, 1-, and 2-point responses on several Verbal subtests. Examiners also differ in determining exactly when an individual has completed a Block Design or Object Assembly item—possibly affecting the number of bonus points given—and in questioning ambiguous verbal responses.

Consequently, we can find no rational defense for encouraging clinicians to use empirical rules that not only encourage additional clerical errors but that suggest a kind of psychometric precision that is just not obtainable in the clinical setting. Empirical rules and guidelines are needed to prevent interpretive chaos, but they should be simple and easily internalized. Further, they should not be so conservative that they impede the formulation of hypotheses about the person's cognitive and behavioral functioning.

TABLE 12.1   Magnitudes of the differences needed for significance for each subtest when compared to the person's own mean score on the WAIS-III Verbal, Performance, or Full Scales.

Verbal Subtest	Difference Needed for Significance
Vocabulary	±2
Similarities	±3
Arithmetic	±3
Digit Span	±3
Information	±3
Comprehension	±3
Letter-Number Sequencing	±4
Performance Subtest	
Picture Completion	±4
Digit Symbol-Coding	±3
Block Design	±3
Matrix Reasoning	±3
Picture Arrangement	±4
Symbol Search	±4
Object Assembly	±4

Illustration of Step 8: Ryan N. (see Table 12.2)

1. Ryan N. had a V-IQ versus P-IQ discrepancy of 19 points in favor of Verbal IQ. This value is statistically significant, exceeding by far the value of 12 points that is required for significance at the .01 level (see Table 11.3 and the *WAIS-III Interpretive Worksheet*). From Table 11.3, it is also evident that his discrepancy is abnormally large, as differences greater than 17 points are considered abnormal or unusual.

2. Because the V–P discrepancy is abnormally large, separate means were computed for the Verbal subtests and the Performance subtests. As indicated below Ryan's profile, his Verbal mean scaled score equals 13.86, which rounds to 14. His Performance mean is 10.28, which rounds to 10.

3. Ryan's scaled scores were entered next to their respective subtest into Step 8 of the WAIS-III Interpretive Worksheet.

4. Each of Ryan's Verbal scaled scores was compared, in turn, to his mean Verbal scaled score of 14. Using the values listed in the column "Difference Needed for Significance," we determined whether the obtained differences were large enough to be construed as significant strengths and weaknesses. Difference scores in Verbal profile revealed no relative strengths or weaknesses within the Verbal subtests. Thus, fluctuations in his Verbal scores may be attributed to chance.

5. This procedure was repeated for the Performance subtests. Relative strengths were observed in Block Design, Matrix Reasoning, and Picture Arrangement (his scaled scores of 14, 13, and 14 exceeded his Performance mean by 4, 3, and 4 points, respectively). Relative weaknesses were observed in Digit Symbol-Coding and Symbol Search (his scaled scores of 5 and 6 were 5 and 4 points below his Performance mean of 10). Fluctuations in the other Performance scaled scores are probably due to chance.

STEP 9: GENERATING HYPOTHESES ABOUT THE FLUCTUATIONS IN THE WAIS-III PROFILE

Before discussion of WAIS-III profiles can occur, the raw materials for interpretation, presented in Step 8, require systematic organization. While organizing the information about the peaks and valleys of the subtest profile, examiners must be good detectives and use not only evidence provided from analysis of strengths and weaknesses in a profile but also evidence gained from observed behaviors, background information, and supplemental testing as well, in order to

TABLE 12.2   Example of Step 8 using Ryan N's profile

V-IQ–P-IQ discrepancy				
			(After calculating means, round to the nearest whole number)	
0–16	Then use →	Mean of all subtests → administered	**Overall Mean**	**Rounded Mean**

17 or more	Then use →	Mean of all Verbal subtests administered → *and also use* Mean of all Performance subtests administered →	**Verbal Subtest Mean**	**Rounded Mean**
			13.86	*14*
			Performance Subtest Mean	**Rounded Mean**
			10.28	*10*

Verbal Subtest	Scaled Score	Rounded Mean	*Difference	Difference Needed for Significance	Strength or Weakness (S or W)	Percentile Rank
Vocabulary	*14*	*14*	*0*	±2	—	*91*
Similarities	*15*	*14*	*+1*	±3	—	*95*
Arithmetic	*15*	*14*	*+1*	±3	—	*95*
Digit Span	*13*	*14*	*–1*	±3	—	*84*
Information	*12*	*14*	*–2*	±3	—	*75*
Comprehension	*15*	*14*	*+1*	±3	—	*95*
Letter-Number Sequencing	*13*	*14*	*–1*	±4	—	*84*
Performance Subtest						
Picture Completion	*9*	*10*	*–1*	±4	—	*37*
Digit Symbol-Coding	*5*	*10*	*–5*	±3	W	*5*
Block Design	*14*	*10*	*+4*	±3	S	*91*
Matrix Reasoning	*13*	*10*	*+3*	±3	S	*84*
Picture Arrangement	*14*	*10*	*+4*	±4	S	*91*
Symbol Search	*6*	*10*	*–4*	±4	W	*9*
Object Assembly	*11*	*10*	*+1*	±4	—	*63*

*Use appropriate **rounded mean** in calculating the "scaled score–mean" difference.

confirm or disconfirm hypotheses. From these interpretations, validated by multiple pieces of data, strong and sensible recommendations can be made for intervention.

The starting point for creating hypotheses is the discovery of scores that deviate significantly from the examinee's own mean performance (Step 8). The challenge is to uncover hypotheses regarding abilities shared by *two or more subtests* or concerning influences that may have affected the test scores. Although some examiners take the easy road when writing reports, and simply regurgitate the textbook definitions of what each single subtest purportedly measures, this type of mindless recitation does not provide useful information about the individual adolescent or adult who was tested. For example, one examiner's report stated that the client "appears to have strong short-term memory" because the client had a high score on Digit Span. However, such a statement, made in isolation, neglects to incorporate the relative trouble that was evident from the person's poor performance on Letter-Number Sequencing and the comments noted by the person's caretaker about forgetfulness throughout the day.

The goal of the detective work involved in deciphering the strong and weak areas in the WAIS-III profile is to find information that is consistent across the entire profile. Specifically, strengths and weaknesses should be supported by two or more subtests and, whenever feasible, by clinical observations, background information, and supplementary cognitive or achievement measures. A subtest-specific hypothesis should only be used when the detective work to find global strengths or weaknesses is futile. At times a profile may be totally flat, evidencing no relative strengths or weaknesses. Examination of such flat profiles does not allow much detective work within the WAIS-III itself. In this case, a wise step to take to uncover more information about an adolescent's or adult's abilities is to administer supplementary subtests that measure abilities not well tapped by the WAIS-III (see, for example, Flanagan, McGrew, & Ortiz, 2000).

Before we present the details of how to attack the WAIS-III subtest profile, the next section spells out the rational postulates and axioms of the philosophy of profile interpretation inherent in "intelligent testing." These tenets are far more important for competent WAIS-III interpretation than any combination of tables or formulas.

BASIC TENETS OF THE PHILOSOPHY OF HYPOTHESIS GENERATION

1. Examiners must be detectives, actively attacking subtest profiles in systematic fashion. They need to group the subtests in new ways to best explain each individual's subtest-to-subtest fluctuations. Different theories of intelligence as well as practical and clinical approaches to assessment must be integrated to find the one best synthesis for each person tested.

2. As many subtests as possible should be grouped together to denote a person's areas of strength and weakness. Hypotheses generated from three subtests, for example, are usually more potent than hypotheses generated from two subtests. The more reliable the hypothesized strength or weakness, the more valuable it is for practical recommendations.

3. A corollary of the previous postulate is that subtest-specific hypotheses are usually to be avoided. A strength or weakness in a single subtest reflects a narrow area of asset or deficit, one that will not likely generalize to the real world. Some subtests have a considerable amount of reliable unique variance (e.g., Digit Symbol-Coding) and frequently do not pair up with any other WAIS-III task. In such instances, interpret the specific ability as the person's strength or weakness; however, such interpretations should be used only as a last resort.

4. A person who scores significantly high on a subtest does not have a strength in all of the abilities and traits measured by that subtest; a

person scoring very low does not have a weakness in every test component. The person is likely to be especially strong or weak in one or two abilities that the task assesses; the examiner's job is to determine the specific asset or liability by carefully evaluating the person's performance on other WAIS-III tasks that measure similar abilities.

5. The empirical determination of significant strengths and weaknesses is the starting point of test interpretation, not the end point. In essence, the existence of at least one significant fluctuation in the WAIS-III profile gives the examiner his or her "detective's license"—sanction to enter the profile to make sense out of the significant fluctuations. Without significant deviations, differences in the scaled scores are usually best interpreted as due to chance. When one or more scores deviate significantly from the person's mean, the other (nonsignificant) scaled scores become useful interpretive adjuncts for hypothesis testing, depending on whether they are above or below the individual's mean score.

6. When generating hypotheses, examiners should aggregate tasks. Just as subtest-specific interpretations are discouraged, so too are hypotheses that are derived by pitting one subtest against another. Some psychologists (e.g., Sattler, 1988) encourage this type of interpretation: "High Comprehension and low Arithmetic may suggest that reasoning ability is adequate in social situations but not in situations involving numbers" (p. 176). "High Object Assembly and low Picture Arrangement may suggest that visual inductive reasoning skills are better developed than visual sequencing skills" (p. 178). Most WAIS-III subtests, especially unstable tasks like Object Assembly and Picture Arrangement, are just not reliable enough to permit interpretation of differences between subtests.

Even reliable subtests like Information and Comprehension cannot support the kinds of diagnostic inferences that are sometimes attributed to them: "High Comprehension, especially coupled with lower Information,…is characteristic for hysterics. The reverse pattern…is generally seen in the obsessive-compulsive" (Allison, Blatt, & Zimet, 1968, p. 25). At the worst, such analyses can promote test abuse because of inadequate validation; at the best, they encourage overinterpretation of chance error.

7. Hypotheses generated from the shared abilities of WAIS-III subtests are just that—hypotheses. They are not facts but ideas about a person's cognitive and behavioral functioning that require external verification to be optimally meaningful. This type of cross-validation can come from background information (e.g., knowledge about the individual's cultural opportunities, behavioral descriptions by others who know the patient, nature of a head injury), clinical observations of the person's test-taking behavior, and scores on other pertinent subtests. This intelligent, scientific attitude toward hypothesis validation is also characteristic of clinicians, such as Allison et al. (1968) and Sattler (1988), who advocate interpretation of differences between specific subtests.

Never infer a behavioral or background hypothesis about a person based simply on a grouping of subtest scores. One should neither hypothesize distractibility because of low scores on Digit Span, Arithmetic, and Letter-Number Sequencing nor suggest a poor early environment because of deficits in Information and Vocabulary. Behavioral hypotheses require external support from the clinician's observations of test behavior, from behavioral rating scales filled out by others, and so forth. Background hypotheses demand reliable verification about the individual's environment as a child, adolescent, and adult.

8. The interpretive guidelines presented in Steps 8 and 9, as well as Steps 1–7, both empirical and rational, are not inviolable. They are intended as aids to interpretation and should not serve to hamper clinical inferences

from a WAIS-III administration. Rules, no matter what their empirical foundation, cannot replace good judgment and must not supersede clinical, neuropsychological, or psychoeducational insights. Rules are meant to be broken; however, violation of guidelines and principles should occur with full knowledge of "proper" interpretive procedures, not out of ignorance.

INTRODUCTION TO WAIS-III SUBTEST INTERPRETIVE TABLES

The abilities that are believed to underlie each WAIS-III subtest are organized in Table 12.3. The information included in the tables summarizes the material that was included in the subtest-by-subtest analysis in Chapter 10. The abilities and influences that are shared by at least two WAIS-III subtests are easy to pinpoint in the table. These tables are quite similar to tables that are presented for the WISC-III (Kaufman, 1994a).

Table 12.3 is organized by Silver's (1993) information-processing model: Input–Integration–Storage–Output. This model, which resembles Osgood's psycholinguistic model (see Chapter 10), considers more than just the content of the item. It denotes:

- What type of stimuli does the individual have to respond to?
- How is the information processed?
- How well is it remembered?
- How is the person required to respond?

This model takes into consideration that some aspects of the stimulus or the response may affect an adult's performance on certain subtests apart from the specific content or processes inherent in the task, and it makes allowances for the possibility

that the person may be unable to store the stimuli long enough to process them appropriately.

The shared abilities listed in Table 12.3 are not exhaustive; the information provided is intended to be illustrative and serve as a good guideline. Utilize this reference as a framework that is open to expansion. Incorporate your expertise as an examiner and the individuality of each person tested into the detective work involved in profile analysis.

RELIABILITY COEFFICIENTS OF SHARED ABILITIES

With each cluster of subtests listed are the split-half reliabilities and test-retest reliabilities. These values are based on the average reliabilities presented in the WAIS-III manual and on the average intercorrelations among subtests in each cluster. The formula for a composite was applied (Tellegen & Briggs, 1967). The test-retest and split-half reliabilities differ for most clusters; thus, both are provided. In general, clusters with reliability coefficients of .85 or above represent stable enough abilities or traits to support confident interpretation and the infrequent coefficients of .75 to .84 require more cautious interpretation. The reliability coefficients for most subtest combinations in Table 12.3 are quite outstanding, with numerous values at or above .95. The coefficients for adults dipped below .85 only for one performance dyad: planning ability.

HOW TO USE INFORMATION ABOUT SHARED ABILITIES

Table 12.3 shows how different abilities overlap in various subtests. Now, you ask, what do you do with all that information? Here we provide you with a sequential guide to generate hypotheses.

TABLE 12.3 Abilities shared by two or more WAIS-III subtests

Ability	I	S	A	V	C	D	LN	PC	Cd	PA	BD	OA	SS	MR	r_{xx}	r_{12}
Input																
Attention–concentration			A		C	D	LN	PC	Cd				SS		.95	.94
Auditory–vocal channel	I	S	A	V	C	D	LN								.97	.96
Complex verbal directions								PC	Cd	PA	BD		SS	MR	.94	.93
Distinguishing essential from nonessential detail		S						PC	Cd	PA			SS	MR	.94	.93
Encode information for processing			A			D	LN		Cd				SS		.95	.93
Simple verbal directions								PC				OA			.85	.84
Understanding long questions	I		A		C										.95	.94
Understanding words		S		V		D	LN								.95	.92
Visual–motor channel								PC	Cd	PA	BD	OA	SS	MR	.95	.94
Visual perception of abstract stimuli									Cd		BD		SS		.94	.93
Visual perception of complete meaningful stimuli								PC		PA					.86	.83
Visual perception of meaningful stimuli								PC		PA		OA			.88	.86
Integration/Storage																
Achievement	I	S	A	V	C										.97	.96
Acquired knowledge	I		A	V											.96	.95
Cognition	I	S	A	V				PC			BD	OA		MR	.96	.95
Common sense					C					PA					.86	.82
Concept formation		S		V							BD				.95	.92
Convergent-production									Cd	PA			SS		.92	.91
Crystallized ability	I	S		V	C					PA					.96	.95
Culture-loaded knowledge	I				C										.93	.92
Evaluation					C			PC	Cd	PA	BD	OA	SS	MR	.96	.95
Facility with numbers			A			D	LN		Cd						.94	.92
Figural cognition								PC			BD	OA		MR	.93	.91
Figural evaluation								PC			BD	OA	SS	MR	.94	.92
Fluid ability		S	A							PA	BD	OA		MR	.95	.93
Fund of information	I			V											.95	.95
General ability	I	S	A	V	C						BD			MR	.97	.96
Handling abstract verbal concepts		S		V											.94	.92

Verbal Subtests / *Performance Subtests* / *Reliability*[a]

Ability	Subtests (shared)		
Holistic (right-brain) processing	PC Cd PA BD OA MR	.90	.88
Integrated brain function	S V C SS	.92	.91
Language development (CHC)	V C Cd	.95	.93
Learning ability	V SS MR	.94	.93
Lexical knowledge (CHC)	S V Cd	.94	.92
Long-term memory	I A V D LN	.96	.95
Memory	I A D LN PA OA	.95	.92
Nonverbal reasoning	PA OA MR	.89	.85
Planning ability	PA SS	.83	.82
Reasoning	S A C PA OA MR	.95	.93
Reproduction of models	Cd BD OA	.89	.89
Semantic cognition	S A V	.95	.93
Semantic content	I S A V C PA	.97	.96
Sequential	A D LN Cd	.94	.92
Short-term memory (auditory or visual)	D LN Cd SS	.93	.91
Simultaneous processing	PC BD OA MR	.93	.91
Social comprehension	C PA OA	.86	.82
Spatial	PC BD OA	.90	.88
Spatial relations (CHC)	BD OA	.86	.83
Spatial visualization	BD SS MR	.92	.89
Symbolic content	A D LN Cd PA BD OA	.94	.92
Synthesis	PA BD OA MR	.92	.89
Trial-and-error learning	BD OA	.86	.83
Verbal concept formation	S V	.94	.92
Verbal conceptualization	S V C	.95	.93
Verbal reasoning	S C	.91	.89
Visualization (CHC)	PA BD	.87	.84
Visual memory	PC Cd	.88	.90
Visual processing	PC Cd BD OA MR	.93	.91
Visual sequencing	Cd PA	.85	.85

Output

Ability	Subtests (shared)		
Much verbal expression	S V C	.95	.93
Simple vocal expression	I A D LN	.95	.92

(Continues)

TABLE 12.3 (Continued)

Ability	Verbal Subtests							Performance Subtests							Reliability[a]	
	I	S	A	V	C	D	LN	PC	Cd	PA	BD	OA	SS	MR	r_{xx}	r_{12}
Output																
Visual organization								PC		PA				MR	.86	.83
Visual–motor coordination									Cd		BD	OA	SS		.92	.92
Influences Affecting Scores																
Ability to respond when uncertain								PC	Cd			OA		MR	.90	.88
Alertness to environment	I							PC							.91	.92
Anxiety			A						Cd				SS		.95	.93
Attention span			A			D	LN						SS		.94	.91
Cognitive style (field dependence)								PC			BD	OA		MR	.93	.91
Concentration			A				LN	PC	Cd				SS		.94	.94
Cultural opportunities	I			V	C				Cd	PA					.95	.94
Distractibility			A			D	LN		Cd				SS		.95	.93
Flexibility		S				D	LN					OA		MR	.94	.91
Foreign language background	I			V											.95	.95
Intellectual curiosity and striving	I			V											.95	.95
Interests	I	S		V											.96	.95
Learning disabilities	I		A	V		D	LN		Cd				SS		.97	.96
Motivation level									Cd				SS		.88	.91
Negativism		S			C	D	LN	PC							.95	.92
Obsessive concern with detail & accuracy									Cd				SS		.88	.91
Outside reading	I	S		V											.96	.95
Overly concrete thinking		S			C									MR	.94	.90
Persistence							LN		Cd			OA	SS		.91	.90
Rate-of-test-taking (CHC)									Cd				SS		.88	.91
Richness of early environment	I			V											.95	.95
School learning	I		A	V											.96	.95
Visual–perceptual problems									Cd		BD	OA	SS	MR	.94	.93
Work under time pressure			A					PC	Cd	PA	BD	OA	SS		.95	.94

[a] r_{xx} = Split-Half reliability; r_{12} = Test-Retest Reliability

From *Essentials of WAIS-III assessment*, by A.S. Kaufman & E. O. Lichtenberger, 1999, New York: Wiley.

To simplify this process of generating hypotheses, the information presented in Table 12.3 has been converted into worksheet forms (see Examiner Forms 12.1–12.14 on pp. 460–473), which may be photocopied without permission of the authors or publisher. The guidelines presented here will help identify potential strong and weak abilities evident from the WAIS-III profile. We will walk you through the process with Ryan N.'s subtest profile (see Table 12.2).

Guideline 1

Choose one of the strengths (S) or weaknesses (W) determined in Step 8. Write down all shared abilities (and influences affecting performance) that involve this subtest. If you choose to use the Examiner Forms on the following pages of this chapter, the shared abilities are outlined for you for each subtest.

We will go through each of these Guidelines using Ryan N.'s first relative weakness that was found in Step 8: Digit Symbol-Coding (p. 451). Figure 12.2 shows part of the Shared Abilities Worksheet for Digit Symbol-Coding that is incomplete.

Guideline 2

Determine how the examinee performed on the other subtest or subtests that also measure the identified abilities. Thus, one-by-one, consider each ability that may be related to the particular subtest at hand. In Step 8, you determined the relative strengths and weaknesses in the subtest profile by considering whether the score deviated significantly from the pertinent mean subtest score. In the process of deciding which abilities explain the strength, less stringent criteria have to be applied. Thus, consider whether a person scores above, below, or equal to their own mean score on all pertinent subtests for an ability. This information may be recorded on the Shared Abilities Worksheet (Examiner Forms 12.1–12.14) or

on your own list of shared abilities, by writing the following next to each subtest:

"–" (indicating performance below the individual's mean subtest scaled score)

"+" (indicating performance above the individual's mean subtest scaled score)

"0" (indicating performance exactly at the individual's mean subtest scaled score).

Continuing with the example of Ryan's relative weakness in Digit Symbol-Coding, Figure 12.3 demonstrates how to fill in the empty squares with plus (+), minus (–), or zero (0). For example, in the first row, Attention–concentration is listed as a hypothesized weak ability. The first blank square is found under the Arithmetic column, and, because Ryan's Arithmetic scaled score was one point above his Verbal scale mean scaled score (see Table 12.2), a "+" is placed in the box. Also listed with Attention–concentration are Digit Span, Letter-Number Sequencing, Picture Completion, and Digit Symbol-Coding. These boxes are filled with the appropriate pluses, minuses, or zeros according to the difference between each of Ryan's subtest scores and his mean scaled score. Figure 12.3 demonstrates this process further by showing this table partially completed.

Guideline 3

One-by-one determine whether each ability should be considered a strength or weakness. The rules for considering whether a shared ability should be construed as a strength or weakness are listed in Table 12.4.

In general, shared strengths will be those abilities for which a person has scored above his or her own mean score on all pertinent subtests, with at least one discrepancy reaching statistical significance. However, there are exceptions to this global rule for shared abilities that are described in Table 12.4. Rather than rigid principles, these guidelines should be considered rules

EXAMINER FORM 12.1   WAIS-III Shared Abilities Worksheet for ARITHMETIC

Ability	Verbal Subtests							Performance Subtests							S or W	
	I	S	A	V	C	D	LN	PC	Cd	PA	BD	OA	SS	MR	S	W
Input																
Attention–concentration			☐			☐	☐	☐	☐						S	W
Auditory–vocal channel		☐	☐	☐		☐	☐								S	W
Encode information for processing			☐	☐		☐	☐	☐	☐				☐		S	W
Understanding long questions	☐		☐		☐										S	W
Integration/Storage																
Achievement	☐	☐	☐	☐	☐	☐	☐	☐							S	W
Acquired knowledge	☐		☐	☐											S	W
Cognition				☐				☐			☐			☐	S	W
Facility with numbers			☐			☐	☐		☐						S	W
Fluid Ability	☐	☐	☐	☐						☐	☐	☐		☐	S	W
General Ability			☐		☐						☐			☐	S	W
Long-term memory	☐	☐	☐	☐											S	W
Memory		☐	☐			☐	☐								S	W
Reasoning	☐	☐	☐		☐					☐				☐	S	W
Semantic cognition				☐											S	W
Semantic content	☐	☐	☐	☐	☐					☐					S	W
Sequential						☐	☐		☐						S	W
Symbolic content	☐		☐			☐	☐		☐						S	W
Output																
Simple vocal expression	☐		☐			☐	☐								S	W
Influences Affecting Scores																
Anxiety			☐			☐	☐	☐	☐				☐		S	W
Attention span			☐			☐	☐		☐				☐		S	W
Concentration								☐	☐				☐		S	W
Distractibility						☐	☐		☐				☐		S	W
Learning disabilities	☐		☐	☐		☐	☐		☐				☐		S	W
School learning	☐		☐	☐											S	W
Work under time pressure			☐					☐		☐	☐	☐	☐	☐	S	W

EXAMINER FORM 12.2 WAIS-III Shared Abilities Worksheet for BLOCK DESIGN

Ability	Verbal Subtests							Performance Subtests							S or W	
	I	S	A	V	C	D	LN	PC	Cd	PA	**BD**	OA	SS	MR	S	W
Input																
Complex verbal directions								□		□	□			□	S	W
Visual perception of abstract stimuli									□		□	□			S	W
Visual–motor channel								□	□		□	□		□	S	W
Integration/Storage																
Cognition	□	□	□	□				□		□	□			□	S	W
Concept formation		□		□							□				S	W
Evaluation					□			□		□	□			□	S	W
Figural cognition								□		□	□		□	□	S	W
Figural evaluation								□		□	□	□	□	□	S	W
Fluid ability	□		□	□				□		□	□				S	W
General ability	□	□		□	□			□		□	□			□	S	W
Integrated brain function									□				□	□	S	W
Reproduction of models									□		□			□	S	W
Simultaneous processing								□			□			□	S	W
Spatial								□			□	□		□	S	W
Spatial relations (CHC)											□	□		□	S	W
Spatial visualization									□		□		□	□	S	W
Synthesis										□	□			□	S	W
Trial-and-error learning											□	□	□	□	S	W
Visualization (CHC)										□	□				S	W
Visual processing								□			□			□	S	W
Output																
Visual–motor coordination									□		□		□	□	S	W
Influences Affecting Scores																
Cognitive style (field dependence)								□			□	□		□	S	W
Visual–perceptual problems									□		□	□	□		S	W
Work under time pressure								□	□		□	□	□	□	S	W

EXAMINER FORM 12.3 WAIS-III Shared Abilities Worksheet for COMPREHENSION

Ability	Verbal Subtests							Performance Subtests							S or W
	I	S	A	V	C	D	LN	PC	Cd	PA	BD	OA	SS	MR	
Input															
Auditory–vocal channel	▣	▣	▣	⊞	⊞	▣	⊞								S W
Understanding long questions	▣	▣		⊞	⊞										S W
Integration/Storage															
Achievement	▣	▣	▣	⊞	⊞					⊞					S W
Common sense					⊞										S W
Crystallized ability	▣	▣	▣	⊞	⊞					⊞					S W
Culture-loaded knowledge	▣			⊞	⊞										S W
Evaluation	▣	▣	▣	⊞	⊞			⊞	⊞	⊞	⊞	⊞	⊞	⊞	S W
General ability	▣	▣	▣	⊞	⊞						⊞			⊞	S W
Language development (CHC)	▣	▣		⊞	⊞										S W
Reasoning		▣	▣		⊞					⊞		⊞		⊞	S W
Semantic content	▣	▣	▣	⊞	⊞					⊞					S W
Social comprehension										⊞					S W
Verbal conceptualization		▣	▣	⊞	⊞			⊞							Ⓢ W
Verbal reasoning		▣	▣		⊞										S W
Output															
Much verbal expression	▣	▣		⊞	⊞										Ⓢ W
Influences Affecting Scores															
Cultural opportunities	▣	▣		⊞	⊞					⊞					S W
Negativism		▣			⊞	▣	⊞	▣							S W
Overly concrete thinking	▣	▣	▣	⊞	⊞									⊞	Ⓢ W

462

EXAMINER FORM 12.4   WAIS-III Shared Abilities Worksheet for DIGIT SPAN

Ability	Verbal Subtests							Performance Subtests							S or W
---	I	S	A	V	C	**D**	LN	PC	Cd	PA	BD	OA	SS	MR	
Input															
Attention–concentration			□			□	□	□	□				□		S W
Auditory–vocal channel		□	□		□	□	□								S W
Encode information for processing			□			□	□	□	□				□		S W
Understanding words				□	□	□	□								S W
Integration/Storage															
Facility with numbers			□			□	□	□	□						S W
Memory	□		□			□	□								S W
Sequential			□			□	□	□	□						S W
Short-term memory (auditory or visual)						□	□		□				□		S W
Symbolic content			□			□	□	□	□						S W
Output															
Simple vocal expression	□		□			□	□	□							S W
Influences Affecting Scores															
Anxiety		□	□			□	□	□	□				□		S W
Attention span			□			□	□						□		S W
Distractibility			□			□	□	□	□				□		S W
Flexibility	□					□	□					□		□	S W
Learning disabilities	□		□	□		□	□	□	□				□		S W
Negativism	□				□	□	□	□							S W

463

EXAMINER FORM 12.5   WAIS-III Shared Abilities Worksheet for DIGIT SYMBOL-CODING

Ability	Verbal Subtests							Performance Subtests							S or W	
	I	S	A	V	C	D	LN	PC	*Cd*	PA	BD	OA	SS	MR	S	W
Input																
Attention–concentration		□						□	□				□	□	S	W
Complex verbal directions									□	□			□	□	S	W
Encode information for processing		□					□		□	□	□		□	□	S	W
Visual–motor channel								□	□	□	□	□	□		S	W
Visual perception of abstract stimuli								□	□	□	□		□	□	S	W
Integration/Storage																
Convergent-production		□				□	□	□	□	□	□		□	□	S	W
Evaluation					□	□	□		□	□	□		□	□	S	W
Facility with numbers		□				□	□	□	□	□	□		□		S	W
Integrated brain function									□	□	□		□	□	S	W
Learning ability				□					□						S	W
Reproduction of models									□		□				S	W
Sequential		□				□	□		□				□		S	W
Short-term memory (auditory or visual)						□	□						□		S	W
Symbolic content		□				□	□		□				□		S	W
Visual memory								□	□				□		S	W
Visual sequencing									□			□	□		S	W
Output																
Visual–motor coordination									□		□	□	□		S	W
Influences Affecting Scores																
Anxiety	□	□				□	□		□	□	□	□	□	□	S	W
Concentration		□				□			□				□		S	W
Distractibility		□		□		□	□	□	□				□		S	W
Learning disabilities	□			□		□	□		□				□		S	W
Motivation level									□				□		S	W
Obsessive concern with detail & accuracy									□			□			S	W
Persistence							□		□			□	□		S	W
Rate-of-test-taking (CHC)									□				□		S	W
Visual–perceptual problems								□	□	□	□	□	□	□	S	W
Work under time pressure						□		□	□				□		S	W

EXAMINER FORM 12.6 WAIS-III Shared Abilities Worksheet for INFORMATION

	Verbal Subtests							Performance Subtests							S or W
Ability	I	S	A	V	C	D	LN	PC	Cd	PA	BD	OA	SS	MR	
Input															
Auditory–vocal channel	□	□	□	□	□	□	□								S W
Understanding long questions	□		□		□	□									S W
Integration/Storage															
Achievement	□	□	□	□	□										S W
Acquired knowledge	□	□	□	□											S W
Crystallized ability	□			□	□					□					S W
Culture-loaded knowledge	□				□										S W
Fund of information	□	□	□	□	□										S W
General ability	□	□	□	□	□						□			□	S W
Long-term memory	□	□	□	□		□									S W
Memory	□		□			□	□								S W
Semantic content	□	□	□	□	□					□					S W
Output															
Simple vocal expression	□					□	□								S W
Influences Affecting Scores															
Alertness to environment	□	□						□							S S
Cultural opportunities	□	□		□						□					S W
Foreign language background	□	□	□	□											S W
Intellectual curiosity and striving	□			□	□										S W
Interests	□	□	□	□			□		□						S W
Learning disabilities	□	□											□		S W
Outside reading	□	□		□											S W
Richness of early environment	□			□											S W
School learning	□		□	□	□										S W

465

EXAMINER FORM 12.7 WAIS–III Shared Abilities Worksheet for LETTER-NUMBER SEQUENCING

Ability	Verbal Subtests							Performance Subtests							S or W
	I	S	A	V	C	D	LN	PC	Cd	PA	BD	OA	SS	MR	
Input															
Attention–concentration			□			□	□	□	□				□		S W
Auditory–vocal channel		□	□		□	□	□								S W
Encode information for processing			□			□	□		□				□		S W
Understanding words				□		□	□								S W
Integration/Storage															
Facility with numbers			□			□	□	□	□						S W
Memory	□		□			□	□								S W
Sequential			□			□	□		□						S W
Short-term memory (auditory or visual)						□	□		□				□		S W
Symbolic content		□				□	□		□						S W
Output															
Simple vocal expression	□		□			□	□		□						S W
Influences Affecting Scores															
Anxiety		□	□			□	□	□	□				□		S W
Attention span			□			□	□		□				□		S W
Concentration		□	□			□	□	□	□				□		S W
Distractibility				□		□	□	□	□				□		S W
Flexibility	□					□	□		□			□	□	□	S W
Learning disabilities	□		□			□	□	□	□				□		S W
Negativism		□			□	□	□	□	□						S W
Persistence				□		□	□		□			□	□		S W

466

EXAMINER FORM 12.8 WAIS-III Shared Abilities Worksheet for MATRIX REASONING

Ability	Verbal Subtests							Performance Subtests							S or W
	I	S	A	V	C	D	LN	PC	Cd	PA	BD	OA	SS	MR	
Input															
Complex verbal directions		☑												☑	Ⓦ / S
Distinguishing essential from nonessential detail														☑	W / S
Visual–motor channel								☑	☑	☑	☑	☑		☑	Ⓦ / S
Visual perception of abstract stimuli								☑						☑	W / S
Integration/Storage															
Cognition			☑	☑				☑		☑	☑	☑		☑	W / S
Convergent-production													☑	☑	W / S
Evaluation					☑			☑						☑	W / S
Figural cognition								☑				☑		☑	W / S
Figural evaluation								☑						☑	Ⓦ / S
Fluid ability		☑	☑											☑	W / S
General ability	☑	☑	☑	☑	☑			☑						☑	W / S
Holistic (right-brain) processing														☑	W / S
Learning ability					☑									☑	W / S
Nonverbal reasoning										☑				☑	W / S
Reasoning		☑	☑		☑					☑				☑	W / S
Simultaneous processing								☑						☑	W / S
Spatial visualization											☑	☑		☑	W / S
Synthesis										☑				☑	W / S
Visual processing														☑	W / S
Output															
Visual organization								☑		☑				☑	W / S
Influences Affecting Scores															
Ability to respond when uncertain								☑	☑					☑	W / S
Cognitive style (field dependence)								☑			☑			☑	W / S
Flexibility		☑					☑							☑	W / S
Overly concrete thinking		☑	☑				☑							☑	W / Ⓢ
Visual-perceptual problems									☑				☑	☑	Ⓦ / S

EXAMINER FORM 12.9 WAIS-III Shared Abilities Worksheet for OBJECT ASSEMBLY

Ability	Verbal Subtests							Performance Subtests							S or W
	I	S	A	V	C	D	LN	PC	Cd	PA	BD	OA	SS	MR	
Input															
Simple verbal directions															S / W
Visual–motor channel															S / (W)
Visual perception of meaningful stimuli															S / W
Integration/Storage															
Cognition															S / W
Evaluation															S / W
Figural cognition															S / W
Figural evaluation															S / (W)
Fluid ability															S / W
Holistic (right-brain) processing															S / W
Nonverbal reasoning															S / W
Reasoning															S / W
Simultaneous processing															S / W
Spatial															S / (W)
Spatial relations (CHC)															S / (W)
Synthesis															S / W
Trial-and-error learning															S / (W)
Visual processing															S / W
Output															
Visual–motor coordination															S / (W)
Influences Affecting Scores															
Ability to respond when uncertain															S / W
Cognitive style (field dependence)															S / W
Flexibility															S / W
Persistence															S / W
Visual–perceptual problems															S / (W)
Work under time pressure															S / (W)

468

EXAMINER FORM 12.10   WAIS-III Shared Abilities Worksheet for PICTURE ARRANGEMENT

Ability	Verbal Subtests							Performance Subtests							S or W
	I	S	A	V	C	D	LN	PC	Cd	PA	BD	OA	SS	MR	
Input															
Complex verbal directions									☐	☐			☐	☐	S ☐ W ☐
Distinguishing essential from nonessential detail		☐						☐	☐	☐			☐	☐	S ☐ W ☐
Visual–motor channel								☐	☐	☐	☐		☐	☐	S ☐ W ☐
Visual perception of complete meaningful stimuli								☐		☐					S ☐ W ☐
Visual perception of meaningful stimuli								☐		☐		☐		☐	S ☐ W ☐
Integration/Storage															
Common sensv					☐					☐					S ☐ W ☐
Convergent-production										☐					S ☐ W ☐
Crystallized ability	☐	☐		☐	☐					☐					S ☐ W ☐
Evaluation					☐			☐		☐				☐	S ☐ W ☐
Fluid ability		☐	☐							☐	☐				S ☐ W ☐
Integrated brain function									☐	☐					S ☐ W ☐
Nonverbal reasoning										☐		☐		☐	S ☐ W ☐
Planning ability										☐			☐		S ☐ W ☐
Reasoning	☐	☐	☐		☐					☐				☐	S ☐ W ☐
Semantic content		☐	☐	☐	☐					☐					S ☐ W ☐
Social comprehension					☐					☐					S ☐ W ☐
Synthesis										☐	☐				S ☐ W ☐
Visual sequencing									☐	☐					S ☐ W ☐
Visualization (CHC)											☐	☐			S ☐ W ☐
Output															
Visual organization								☐		☐					S ☐ W ☐
Influences Affecting Scores															
Cultural opportunities					☐					☐		☐	☐		S ☐ W ☐
Work under time pressure				☐						☐		☐	☐		S ☐ W ☐

EXAMINER FORM 12.11   WAIS-III Shared Abilities Worksheet for PICTURE COMPLETION

Ability	Verbal Subtests							Performance Subtests							S or W		
	I	S	A	V	C	D	LN	PC	Cd	PA	BD	OA	SS	MR			
Input																	
Attention–concentration			⊟			⊡	⊡	⊟	⊞				⊟		S	W	—
Distinguishing essential from nonessential detail		⊞						⊟		⊞			⊟	⊞	S	W	ⓦ
Simple verbal directions								⊟			⊟				S	Ⓦ	
Visual–motor channel								⊟	⊡	⊞	⊡	⊟	⊟	⊞	S	W	—
Visual perception of complete meaningful stimuli								⊟		⊞					S	W	—
Visual perception of meaningful stimuli								⊟		⊞		⊟			S	W	—
Integration/Storage																	
Cognition		⊞	⊟	⊞				⊟			⊡	⊟		⊞	S	W	—
Evaluation				⊞				⊟	⊞	⊞	⊡	⊟	⊟	⊞	S	W	—
Figural cognition								⊟			⊡	⊟		⊞	S	W	—
Figural evaluation								⊟			⊡	⊟	⊟	⊞	S	Ⓦ	
Holistic (right-brain) processing								⊟				⊟		⊞	S	W	—
Simultaneous processing								⊟			⊡	⊟		⊞	S	W	—
Spatial								⊟			⊡	⊟			S	Ⓦ	
Visual memory								⊟	⊞						S	W	—
Visual processing								⊟			⊡	⊟		⊞	S	W	—
Output																	
Visual organization								⊟		⊞					S	W	—
Influences Affecting Scores																	
Work under time pressure			⊟					⊟	⊞	⊞	⊡	⊟	⊡		S	W	?
Ability to respond when uncertain								⊟				⊟		⊞	S	W	
Alertness to environment	⊡							⊟							S	W	—
Cognitive style (field dependence)								⊟			⊡	⊟		⊞	S	W	—
Concentration			⊟				⊡	⊟	⊞				⊟		S	W	—
Negativism		⊞			⊞	⊡	⊡	⊟							S	W	—

EXAMINER FORM 12.12 WAIS-III Shared Abilities Worksheet for SIMILARITIES

Ability	Verbal Subtests							Performance Subtests							S or W
	I	S	A	V	C	D	LN	PC	Cd	PA	BD	OA	SS	MR	
Input															
Auditory–vocal channel	☐	☐	☐	☐	☐	☐	☐								S W
Distinguishing essential from nonessential detail		☐						☐		☐					S W
Understanding words	☐			☐	☐	☐	☐								S W
Integration/Storage															
Achievement	☐	☐	☐	☐	☐										S W
Cognition		☐	☐	☐	☐			☐			☐				S W
Concept formation	☐	☐		☐	☐						☐				S W
Crystallized ability	☐	☐		☐	☐					☐					S W
Fluid ability		☐	☐	☐	☐					☐	☐	☐		☐	S W
General ability	☐	☐	☐	☐	☐						☐				S W
Handling abstract verbal concepts		☐		☐	☐										S W
Language development (CHC)		☐		☐	☐										S W
Lexical knowledge (CHC)		☐	☐	☐											S W
Reasoning	☐	☐	☐	☐				☐				☐			S W
Semantic cognition	☐	☐	☐	☐	☐										S W
Semantic content		☐		☐	☐					☐					S W
Verbal concept formation		☐	☐	☐	☐										S W
Verbal conceptualization		☐		☐	☐										S W
Verbal reasoning		☐		☐	☐										S W
Output															
Much verbal expression		☐		☐	☐										S W
Influences Affecting Scores															
Flexibility		☐	☐	☐	☐	☐	☐					☐		☐	S W
Interests	☐	☐													S W
Negativism		☐		☐	☐	☐	☐	☐							S W
Outside reading	☐	☐	☐	☐											S W
Overly concrete thinking	☐	☐			☐									☐	S W

471

EXAMINER FORM 12.13   WAIS-III Shared Abilities Worksheet for SYMBOL SEARCH

Ability	Verbal Subtests							Performance Subtests							S or W	
	I	S	A	V	C	D	LN	PC	Cd	PA	BD	OA	SS	MR	S	W
Input																
Attention–concentration							☐	☐	☐				☐		S	W
Complex verbal directions									☐	☐				☐	S	W
Distinguishing essential from nonessential detail			☐					☐	☐	☐			☐		S	W
Encode information for processing						☐	☐	☐							S	W
Visual–motor channel								☐	☐		☐		☐		S	W
Visual perception of abstract stimuli								☐		☐			☐	☐	S	W
Integration/Storage																
Convergent production								☐	☐				☐	☐	S	W
Evaluation					☐			☐	☐	☐	☐		☐	☐	S	W
Figural evaluation								☐	☐	☐	☐		☐		S	W
Integrated brain function									☐	☐			☐		S	W
Learning ability				☐					☐						S	W
Planning ability										☐					S	W
Short-term memory (auditory or visual)						☐		☐	☐				☐		S	W
Spatial visualization											☐		☐		S	W
Output																
Visual–motor coordination									☐				☐		S	W
Influences Affecting Scores																
Anxiety	☐	☐	☐			☐	☐		☐				☐		S	W
Attention span	☐	☐	☐			☐	☐		☐						S	W
Concentration	☐	☐	☐			☐	☐	☐	☐				☐		S	W
Distractibility	☐	☐	☐			☐	☐		☐				☐		S	W
Learning disabilities	☐	☐	☐	☐		☐	☐		☐				☐		S	W
Motivation level									☐				☐		S	W
Obsessive concern with detail & accuracy									☐				☐		S	W
Persistence							☐		☐	☐			☐		S	W
Rate-of-test-taking (CHC)									☐				☐		S	W
Visual–perceptual problems									☐	☐	☐			☐	S	W
Work under time pressure								☐	☐	☐	☐		☐		S	W

Ability	Verbal Subtests							Performance Subtests							S or W
	I	S	A	V	C	D	LN	PC	Cd	PA	BD	OA	SS	MR	
Input															
Auditory-vocal channel	▨			▨	▨	▨	▨								S / W
Understanding words		▨		▨	▨	▨	▨								S
Integration/Storage															
Achievement	▨		▨	▨	▨										S / W
Acquired knowledge	▨		▨	▨											S / W
Cognition	▨	▨		▨	▨			▨			▨	▨		▨	S / W
Concept formation				▨						▨					S / W
Crystallized ability	▨			▨	▨										S / W
Fund of information	▨			▨											S / W
General ability	▨	▨		▨	▨						▨			▨	S / W
Handling abstract verbal concepts	▨	▨		▨											S / W
Language development (CHC)	▨			▨	▨				▨						S / W
Learning ability	▨			▨									▨		S / W
Lexical knowledge (CHC)	▨			▨											S / W
Long-term memory			▨	▨											S / W
Semantic cognition			▨	▨											S / W
Semantic content	▨	▨	▨	▨	▨					▨					S / W
Verbal concept formation				▨											S / W
Verbal conceptualization				▨	▨										S / W
Output															
Much verbal expression	▨			▨	▨					▨					S / W
Influences Affecting Scores															
Cultural opportunities	▨			▨	▨					▨					S / W
Foreign language background	▨			▨											S / W
Intellectual curiosity and striving	▨	▨		▨											S / W
Interests	▨			▨											S / W
Learning disabilities	▨	▨		▨		▨	▨						▨		S / W
Outside reading	▨	▨		▨											S / W
Richness of early environment	▨			▨											S / W
School learning	▨		▨	▨											S

473

FIGURE 12.2   Example of partial Shared Abilities Worksheet for Digit Symbol-Coding

Ability	Verbal Subtests							Performance Subtests							S or W	
	I	S	A	V	C	D	LN	PC	Cd	PA	BD	OA	SS	MR		
Input																
Attention–concentration			□			□	□	□	□				□		S	W
Complex verbal directions									□	□	□		□	□	S	W
Encode information for processing			□			□	□	□	□	□	□		□		S	W
Visual–motor channel								□	□		□	□	□	□	S	W
Visual perception of abstract stimuli								□	□		□	□	□	□	S	W
Integration/Storage																
Convergent-production								□	□	□	□		□	□	S	W
Evaluation					□			□	□	□	□		□	□	S	W
Facility with numbers			□			□	□	□	□	□	□		□		S	W
Integrated brain function									□	□	□		□	□	S	W
Learning ability	□							□	□				□	□	S	W

474

FIGURE 12.3 Example of partial Digit Symbol-coding Shared Abilities Worksheet with completed "−," "+," "o"

Ability	Verbal Subtests							Performance Subtests							S or W	
	I	S	A	V	C	D	LN	PC	Cd	PA	BD	OA	SS	MR		
Input																
Attention–concentration			+			−	−	−	−				−		S	W
Complex verbal directions									−	+	+			+	S	W
Encode information for processing			+			−	−		−	+	+	+	−	+	S	W
Visual–motor channel								−	−	+	+	+	−	+	S	W
Visual perception of abstract stimuli									−	+	+		−	+	S	W
Integration/Storage																
Convergent-production								−	−	−	+		−	+	S	W
Evaluation					+			−	−	+	+		−	+	S	W
Facility with numbers			+			−	−		−	+			−		S	W
Integrated brain function									−						S	W
Learning ability				o					−				−	+	S	W

TABLE 12.4   Rules for accepting and rejecting potential hypotheses

Number of Subtests Constituting a Shared Ability	Rule for Interpreting Ability as a Strength (at least one subtest is a significant strength)	Rule for Interpreting Ability as a Weakness (at least one subtest is a significant weakness)
2	*All* subtests must be **above** the mean.	*All* subtests must be **below** the mean.
3 or 4	*At least 2 or 3* subtests must be **above** the mean, and *only one* subtest may be **equivalent** to the mean.	*At least 2 or 3* subtests must be **below** the mean, and *only one* subtest may be **equivalent** to the mean.
5 or more	*At least 4* subtests must be **above** the mean, and *only one* subtest may be **equal** to the mean *or* **less than** the mean.	*At least 4* subtests must be **below** the mean, and *only one* subtest may be **equal to** the mean *or* **greater than** the mean.

of thumb. In instances when there is an over-abundance of other clinical information (from behavioral observations, background information, and supplementary testing data) that will support a shared ability as a strength or weakness, even if these rule-of-thumb guidelines are not met, the rules listed here should not preclude you from interpreting the strength or weakness.

Examiner Forms 12.1–12.14, which are essentially worksheets for determining shared abilities, list a place for strengths and weaknesses (S and W) to be circled once the rules of thumb have been applied. In Ryan's example of Digit Symbol-Coding shown in Figure 12.4, we examine each hypothesized ability (which are sometimes actually behaviors) to determine which ones may be considered strengths or weaknesses. "Attention–concentration" ability is considered to be underlying six subtests (A, D, LN, PC, Cd, and SS). Examining the pluses, minuses, and zeros filled in, we see that 5 subtests have minuses (indicating being below the mean) and one has a plus (indicating being above the mean). The rules for accepting and rejecting potential hypotheses (see Table 12.4) tell us that, for an ability to be considered a strength when there are five or more subtests, at least four subtests must be below the mean, and only one subtest may be equal to or greater than the mean. Thus, "Attention–concentration" may be considered a weak ability (and the "W" is circled on the worksheet).

The next ability examined in Ryan's profile is "Complex verbal directions." There are five subtests noted to have this underlying ability. On three of the subtests, Ryan earned scores that were above his own mean and on two he earned scores that were below his mean. Thus, because more than one test was above the mean, "Complex verbal directions" cannot be considered as a hypothesized weak ability. However, the next ability "Encode information for processing" follows the same pattern as "Attention–concentration" and can be considered a weak ability (and the "W" is circled on the worksheet).

Guideline 4

Repeat Guidelines 1, 2, and 3 for every other significant strength that has not been accounted for. Then follow analogous procedures for all significant weaknesses. Shown in Figure 12.5 is the next relative strength in Ryan's WAIS-III profile, Block Design. After filling in all of the pluses, minuses, and zeros in the Shared Ability Worksheet for Block Design, some hypothesized abilities appear to be possible explanations for Ryan's strength in Block Design: concept formation, fluid ability, and synthesis. Before including any of these abilities in Ryan's report, it is necessary to consider whether the behavioral observations, background information, and supplemental test data also support these hypotheses.

FIGURE 12.4 Example of Partial Digit Symbol-Coding Worksheet with strengths and weaknesses circled

	Verbal Subtests							Performance Subtests							S or W	
Ability	I	S	A	V	C	D	LN	PC	Cd	PA	BD	OA	SS	MR		
Input																
Attention–concentration			⊞			⊡	⊡	⊡	⊡				⊡		S	(W)
Complex verbal directions					⊞				⊡	⊞	⊞		⊡	⊞	S	W
Encode information for processing			⊞			⊡	⊡		⊡		⊡		⊡	⊡	S	(W)
Visual–motor channel								⊡	⊡	⊞	⊞	⊞	⊡	⊞	S	W
Visual perception of abstract stimuli								⊡	⊡	⊞	⊞		⊡	⊞	S	W
Integration/Storage																
Convergent-production								⊡	⊡	⊞	⊞		⊞	⊞	S	W
Evaluation					⊞				⊡	⊞	⊞	⊞	⊞	⊞	S	W
Facility with numbers					⊞	⊡		⊡	⊡	⊞	⊞		⊡		S	W
Integrated brain function									⊡	⊞				⊞	S	W
Learning ability				⊡				⊡	⊡		⊞		⊡	⊞	S	W

FIGURE 12.5 Example of completed Block Design Shared Abilities Worksheet with strengths and weaknesses indicated

Ability	Verbal Subtests							Performance Subtests							S or W
	I	S	A	V	C	D	LN	PC	Cd	PA	BD	OA	SS	MR	
Input															
Complex verbal directions									⊞	□	□	□	⊞	□	S W
Visual perception of abstract stimuli									⊞		□	□	⊞		S W
Visual–motor channel								⊞	⊞	□	□	□	⊞	□	Ⓢ W
Integration/Storage															
Cognition	⊞	□		⊡				⊞			□	□		□	
Concept formation	⊞	□		⊡							□	□			
Evaluation					⊞			⊞	⊞	□	□	□	⊞	□	S W
Figural cognition								⊞	⊞		□	□		□	Ⓢ W
Figural evaluation								⊞		□	□	□	⊞	□	S W
Fluid ability		□								□	□	□			S W
General ability	⊞	□		⊡	⊞						□	□		□	S W

NOTE: See Ryan N's score profile on p. 452 for details on how +, −, and 0s were determined. I = Information; S = Similarities; A = Arithmetic; V = Vocabulary; C = Comprehension; DS = Digit Span; LN = Letter-Number Sequencing; PC = Picture Completion; Cd = Digital Symbol-Coding; PA = Picture Arrangement; BD = Block Design; OA = Object Assembly; SS = Symbol Search; MR = Matrix Reasoning.

Guideline 5

If the process of examining shared abilities uncovers no hypothesized strengths or weaknesses, then interpret the unique abilities that are presumably measured by significantly high or low subtests. The primary focus for explaining significant discrepancies in a profile should be on shared abilities that link several subtests, especially when these hypothesized strengths and weaknesses are supported by background information, behavioral observations, and supplementary testing. However, at times no hypothesized strengths or weaknesses are apparent after examining the potential shared abilities. Subtest-specific interpretations may then have to be made. The unique abilities are listed in the subtest-by-subtest description of abilities listed in Chapter 10 (denoted with an asterisk) and in Table 12.5.

Before interpreting a unique ability on a subtest, consider its amount of specificity. Those with "ample" or "adequate" amounts of specificity may be interpreted (see Table 10.9 in Chapter 10). However, even if a subtest score deviates significantly from the mean and if that subtest has "ample" subtest specificity, do not automatically interpret the unique ability. Only when all hypotheses involving shared abilities prove useless should an examiner acquiesce to an interpretation of a unique and highly specific strength or weakness. When unique abilities are interpreted, other evidence from background data, behavioral observations, or supplemental testing is needed to support the interpretation of the ability.

SUMMARY OF SEQUENTIAL APPROACH TO WAIS-III INTERPRETATION

The ninth step presented above culminates our step-by-step approach to WAIS-III interpretation that began in Chapter 11 and is continued in this chapter. To more easily use these nine steps in clinical practice, we have formulated the *WAIS-III Interpretive Worksheet* that is at the end of this chapter. This worksheet can be photocopied directly from the book, and can be used in conjunction with Examiner Forms 12.1–12.14 that contain the shared abilities for each subtest. For those examiners who benefit from dual modes of processing—simultaneous and sequential—we have prepared a figure that summarizes the nine interpretive steps and depicts which tier of the WAIS-III hierarchy is addressed with each (see Figure 12.6).

A SIMULTANEOUS APPROACH TO HYPOTHESIS GENERATION

As noted in the previous section, hypothesis generation can be performed in a linear, sequential, "left-brained," scientific manner, which is what the nine-step approach in this chapter and Chapter 11 have detailed. However, we are sensitive to individual differences in the way adults may approach the same problem. For some people, the sequential, rule-governed methodology described previously conforms well to their typical processing approach; for others, it is a nightmare. Consequently, we are including an alternative method of hypothesis generation, one that might be preferable to individuals who prefer to rely more on simultaneous, holistic ("right-brained") problem-solving strategies. This approach also has sequential components, but it emphasizes configurations of subtests and the simultaneous treatment of two or three tasks at a time while deemphasizing mathematical computations and comparisons. Even the empirical determination of significant strengths and weaknesses in the subtest profile is optional.

Only one statistical application is mandatory: *After* the examiner reaches conclusions about contrasting strengths and weaknesses (e.g., high on visual–sequential—low on visual–spatial), *determine whether the difference is statistically significant*. The easiest way to make this comparison is

TABLE 12.5   Unique abilities measured by WAIS-III subtests and category of subtest specificity

Verbal Subtest	Unique Abilities	Subtest Specificity
Vocabulary	Language development Word knowledge	adequate
Similarities	Logical abstractive (categorical) thinking	adequate
Arithmetic	Computational skill Quantitative Knowledge (CHC theory) Mathematical Achievement (CHC theory) Quantitative Reasoning (CHC theory)	ample
Digit Span	Immediate rote recall Memory span (CHC theory)	ample
Information	Range of general factual knowledge	adequate
Comprehension	Demonstration of practical knowledge Evaluation and use of past experiences Knowledge of conventional standards of behavior	adequate
Letter-Number Sequencing	Facility with overlearned sequences Working memory	ample

Performance Subtest		
Picture Completion	Visual recognition without essential motor activity Flexibility of Closure (CHC theory)	ample
Digit Symbol-Coding	Psychomotor speed	ample
Block Design	Analysis of whole into component parts Nonverbal concept formation	adequate
Matrix Reasoning	Analogic reasoning Induction (CHC theory) Nonverbal problem solving with no time limit	ample
Picture Arrangement	Anticipation of consequences Temporal sequencing	adequate
Symbol Search	Perceptual speed (CHC theory) Speed of visual search	inadequate
Object Assembly	Ability to benefit from sensory–motor feedback Anticipation of relationships among parts Closure speed (CHC theory)	inadequate

to average the scaled scores for the subtests constituting the strength, and also average the scores for the subtests composing the weakness. If they differ by three points or more (a rule of thumb), the hypothesis is confirmed.

Basically, to interpret the WAIS-III in a simultaneous, holistic fashion, focus on configurations among the subtests, usually within each separate scale. First look for each scale to split into two recognizable halves; then see whether the profile re-

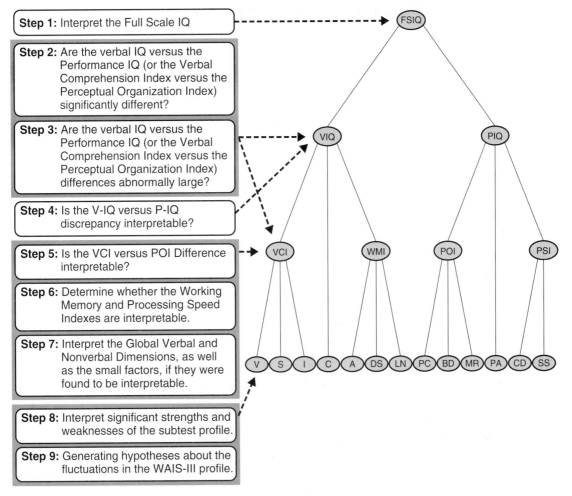

FIGURE 12.6

Summary of 9 WAIS-III Interpretative Steps and the WAIS-III tier that they each examine

veals a split between pairs of subtests that differ in an important way (e.g., a distinction between abstract and meaningful stimuli). Finally, if necessary, look for the coupling of subtests that often go together (e.g., the social comprehension dyad of Comprehension and Picture Arrangement).

The next several sections discuss common configurations of subtests within the Verbal and Performance Scales and a variety of WAIS-III dyads spanning both scales that frequently "pair

up" in an individual's profile. Table 12.6 lists common configurations of the WAIS-III scales.

Common Configurations of the WAIS-III Verbal Scale

Several global configurations involving five or all seven WAIS-III Verbal subtests occur frequently enough to warrant their internalization by examiners, especially those who prefer a holistic

TABLE 12.6   Common configurations of the WAIS-III scales

Configuration	Component Subtests
Verbal Configurations	
Memory/little verbal expression	I, DSP, A, LNS
Conceptualization/much verbal expression	V, C, S
Performance Configurations	
Visual organization	PC, PA, MR, SS
Visual–motor coordination	BD, OA, DSY
Visual perception/processing of abstract stimuli	BD, DSY
Visual perception/processing of complete meaningful stimuli	PC, PA
Visual perception/processing of meaningful stimuli	PC, PA, OA
Nonverbal reasoning	PA, OA, MR
Reproduction of models	BD, DSY
Simultaneous/visual–spatial	PC, BD, OA
Sequential/visual–sequential	PA, DSY
Visual closure	PC, OA
Visual sequencing	PA, DSY
Visual memory	PC, DSY
Synthesis	PA, BD, OA, MR
Both Scales	
Social comprehension	C, PA
Abstract thought	S, BD, MR
Fund of information	I, V
Visual Synthesis	BD, OA
Verbal reasoning	C, S
Nonverbal reasoning	PA, OA
Auditory memory	DSP, A, LNS
Visual memory	PC, DSY, SS
Auditory memory	DSP, A
Reproduction of models	BD, DSY
Auditory sequencing	DSP, A, LNS
Visual sequencing	PA, DSY

hypothesis generation strategy: Working Memory versus Verbal Comprehension; the amount of verbal expression required for successful performance; and fluid versus crystallized intelligence.

Working Memory versus Verbal Comprehension

The division of the Verbal indexes is probably one of the most common occurrences in a WAIS-III profile. A quick glance at the Verbal subtests commonly indicates that an individual's subtest fluctuations conform precisely to the results of countless factor structures: The three Verbal Comprehension subtests (Information, Vocabulary, Similarities) cluster together, with the person performing either substantially higher or lower on the Working Memory triad of Digit Span, Letter-Number Sequencing, and Arithmetic. Ideally, the person's scaled scores on Working Memory subtests will be above (or below) all Verbal Comprehension subtest scores to confirm a split in the Verbal profile. However, it is still the difference between the indexes that determines the meaningfulness of the dichotomization. When this difference is significant, examiners who are not offended by sequential strategies may wish to apply the systematic assessment of strengths and weaknesses on the three WAIS-III factors detailed in the nine steps.

Unfortunately, Comprehension is excluded from the WAIS-III VCI even though this subtest very often joins with the three component subtests, is included in the WISC-III VCI, and invariably loads with the three VCI subtests in virtually every factor analysis of Wechsler's scales since the W-B I. Therefore, check to see if Comprehension is consistent in magnitude with the three VCI subtests, especially for individuals who display a significant discrepancy between VCI and WMI. If so, then the Verbal Comprehension strength or weakness is given more credence and support from a quartet of subtests than by a trio. The exclusion of Comprehension from the VCI is a mystery.

Sometimes Information joins the Working Memory triad in splitting off from the rest of the Verbal Comprehension subtests. When this division of the Verbal scale into four and three subtests occurs (i.e., Comprehension joins with Similarities and Vocabulary; Information teams up with the WMI triad), the factor-related split must yield to a different interpretation: either the amount of verbal expression required for optimal task performance or memory versus conceptualization. The Comprehension–Similarities–Vocabulary grouping requires a good amount of verbal expression for successful performance, and all tasks measure verbal conceptualization or verbal reasoning. In contrast, Information and the WMI tasks all demand limited verbalization for success, and all involve memory (short-term memory for WMI, long-term retrieval for Information). This Verbal scale dichotomy is treated in more depth later in this chapter ("Amount of Verbal Expression Required").

When a bona fide Working Memory–Verbal Comprehension split occurs, the person's scaled scores on Digit Symbol-Coding or Symbol Search should be compared to his or her level of performance on the Working Memory triad. Are the PSI scores fairly consistent in magnitude to the depressed or elevated scores on Digit Span, Letter-Number Sequencing, and Arithmetic? If so, that finding further reinforces the importance of the Working Memory factor (perhaps as a measure of executive functioning) for understanding the profile fluctuations. See Chapter 7 for factor-analytic evidence for the merger of the two PSI subtests with the three WMI tasks. Yet, whether Working Memory is composed of just its usual three subtests or whether it merges with the Processing Speed dyad is of less concern than the *interpretation* given to the dimension. As is evident by scanning Table 12.3, an impressive variety of interpretations may be assigned to a strength or weakness on the Working Memory triad or Processing Speed dyad. The examiner's task is to narrow down the hypotheses to the degree possible.

The main points to consider are these: Is there crisp behavioral support, or reliable clinical reports, to justify distractibility, anxiety, or poor attention span as an explanation of poor performance? If memory is a plausible explanation of the dimension, is there *behavioral* evidence to support either a strength (memorizing the "code" halfway through Digit Symbol-Coding) or a weakness (needing frequent repetition of questions)? Is a sequencing problem evident on Picture Arrangement, and are any referral problems consistent with a sequential deficit ("Has difficulty following directions")? Is a strength or weakness in number ability consistent with background information about the person (works as an accountant; had a math block in school)?

Arithmetic, Digit Span, Letter-Number Sequencing, and sometimes Digit Symbol-Coding or Symbol Search may be interpreted from the factor-analytic model (Working Memory and Processing Speed), Bannatyne's approach (Sequencing Ability), the K-ABC neuropsychological model

(Sequential Processing), a Jensen (1982) Level I–Level II theory (auditory and visual memory, Level I abilities) or a Guilford structure-of-intellect framework (Symbolic Content). The theory doesn't matter; neither does the name given to the dyad or triad or pentad by the theorists. Only the interpretation of the factor for a given individual is of concern, and that task depends entirely on the clinician's acumen as an observer of behavior and integrator of data from numerous sources.

Memory versus Conceptualization

Each of the seven WAIS-III Verbal subtests makes demands on a person's memory and concept formation, although they differ considerably in the relative role assigned to each function. At one extreme is Digit Span, a test of short-term memory with a small conceptual component, the ability to reverse digits. Similarities occupies the opposite extreme of high conceptual–low memory. The ability to find the common, preferably abstract, element that unites two verbal concepts is perhaps a prototypical conceptual task. Memory is required to remember the examiner's question (short-term) and to retrieve the two concepts from storage (long-term), but the demands are minimal on both counts. The questions are short, and reduce to just two words, the concepts to be compared; further, the concepts themselves are simple, common, and usually overlearned.

Whereas dividing the Verbal scale into memory and conceptual halves is neither pure nor unequivocal, there has been some consensus on this type of dichotomy within the literature. In both Guilford's and Horn's models, the following subtests have a clear-cut memory component: Letter-Number Sequencing, Digit Span, and Arithmetic (Information is considered by Guilford to have a semantic memory component and involves long-term retrieval of facts). In contrast, Vocabulary, Comprehension, and Similarities are considered good measures of one or more of the following by Bannatyne, Guilford, Rapaport, or Dean: concept formation, judgment, cogni-

tion, evaluation, abstract thought, and social comprehension. Indeed, this triad of subtests composes Bannatyne's Verbal Conceptualization category.

Nonetheless, Arithmetic is classified by Guilford as a measure of cognition as well as memory, and Vocabulary is categorized by Rapaport as a dual measure of concept formation and memory. Hence, when examiners search for a memory–conceptualization split within the WAIS-III Verbal Scale, they must do so with flexibility and with the awareness that most Verbal subtests are complex.

Ben's Verbal profile (below) provides a good example of a clear-cut memory–reasoning split (conceptual subtests are in bold face).

Verbal Subtest	Scaled Score
Information	9
Digit Span	8
Vocabulary	**16**
Arithmetic	10
Comprehension	**11**
Similarities	**15**
Letter-Number Sequencing	10

Without computing significant strengths and weaknesses, and without following a systematic, sequential method of hypothesis generation, simultaneous processors should immediately detect a strength in conceptualization, contrasted with a generalized weakness in short- and long-term memory. Ben's highest memory score was one point less than his lowest conceptualization score. To ensure that this configuration is significant, compute his mean score in each category (14.0 in conceptualization—averaging Vocabulary, Similarities, and Comprehension, versus 9.3 in memory—averaging Digit Span, Arithmetic, Letter-Number Sequencing, and Information) and subtract these means (4.7 points, or 5 points after rounding the means to whole numbers). This value exceeds the rule of thumb of 3 points needed to denote a meaningful difference.

Of the Verbal subtests, Digit Span and Letter-Number Sequencing are generally the "cleanest" measures of memory, while Comprehension and Similarities are the "purest" tests of verbal conceptualization. Sometimes these two competing dyads will be considerably different from each other, in either direction, suggesting a possible difference in the person's memory and conceptual abilities; in this instance, examiners relying on a configuration approach to hypothesis generation need to be prepared to ignore the complex Arithmetic and Vocabulary subtests and focus on the best measures of each ability. As stated, whenever examiners use the configuration approach to subdivide a person's WAIS-III subtests into strong and weak areas, they should routinely confirm the significance of the finding by the simple procedure of verifying that the mean scaled scores differ by at least 3 points.

Further, the fact that the groupings discussed in this section have been labeled "memory" and "conceptualization" is no guarantee that an obvious split of a Verbal profile into these groups reflects differences in these skill areas. The interpretation of the person's strength and weakness must be verified with behavioral and background data, inasmuch as other explanations are possible, even conceivable. This point becomes apparent in the next section, which deals with a competing interpretation of the same Verbal scale dichotomy.

Amount of Verbal Expression Required

Three WAIS-III subtests demand individuals to put their ideas into words, to express their thoughts spontaneously via several well-chosen words. Each of these tasks has its own 2–1–0, somewhat subjective scoring system in the WAIS-III manual that is quite prone to examiner error, and makes up the category that Bannatyne calls Verbal Conceptualization Ability: Vocabulary, Comprehension, and Similarities. The remaining four Verbal subtests, composing the memory triad plus Information (considered semantic memory) and discussed in the previous section, are similar to each other apart from the memory component: Each requires the individual to give a brief verbal response, just a word or two, a number, or a series of numbers. People who have good ideas but who lack the facility to express them directly will be penalized on the three WAIS-III tasks that make the greatest demands on verbal expression.

Suppose that a person scores relatively high (or low) on Bannatyne's conceptual category. How does an examiner know whether to interpret the strength (or weakness) in terms of the conceptual or the expressive component of the triad? First, consider the person's verbal behavior during the test and the type of responses recorded on the record form. Poor expressive abilities are revealed by people who continually have difficulty explaining themselves, even during casual conversation or spontaneous verbalizations, or when they clearly understand the concepts being tested. In contrast, individuals with facility in verbal expression often demonstrate this skill by their directness in communication, use of pertinent and high-level vocabulary, and by responding to queries with appropriate elaboration. Frequently, good verbal expression and concept formation go hand in hand; the person who is able to communicate insightfully and directly has also mastered the concepts as well.

Sometimes, however, the strength is clearly conceptualization or expression. Good concept formation, in the absence of facile expressive skill, is evidenced by a person who responds tersely to items, gaining credit by use of pertinent abstractions and generalizations. The reverse pattern is demonstrated by someone who is extremely verbose (whose responses are written in the margins and all over the record form page), who consistently piles up 2-point responses on Similarities by giving several responses of varying quality, and who earns 2 points on Vocabulary and Comprehension items by an aggregation of 1-point answers, not by abstract thinking.

Low scores on Vocabulary, Similarities, and Comprehension are commonly due either to poor conceptualization or poor expressive abilities.

Again, many clues are found from behavioral observation and evaluation of the type of responses given. Usually, Similarities provides the best clue to the nature of the deficiency. Whereas Comprehension often involves explaining, and Vocabulary frequently demands elaboration, most Similarities items can be answered at a 2-point level by a single, well-chosen word or two ("Vehicles," "Senses," "Have life"). An extremely low score on Similarities compared to the other two conceptual tasks and/or a set of virtually all 1-point responses to Similarities items implicates poor conceptualization rather than expression as the primary cause of the failure. Analogously, extremely high Similarities for a person who does generally well on the other two tasks implies strong concept formation rather than verbal expressive abilities. The simple pattern of scores is not enough, though; corroboration is necessary from clinical observation of behaviors and background information. For example, autistic children and adults are known to have poor verbal expression and, in fact, earn by far their lowest Wechsler scaled scores on Vocabulary and Comprehension (see Kaufman, Kaufman, Lincoln, & Kaufman, 2000; Lincoln et al., 1988; Rutter, 1978).

Regardless of the interpretation given to a split between the low expression (memory) and high expression (conceptual) subtests on the Verbal scale, the occurrence of this configuration has some implications: (1) V-IQ becomes an inefficient summary of the person's verbal intelligence; (2) the Verbal Comprehension factor loses meaning, because Information splits off to join the memory triad; and (3) systematic evaluation based on Bannatyne's system (which includes the Verbal Conceptualization category) or Horn's system (which includes the Short-Term Memory grouping) is advised.

Fluid versus Crystallized Intelligence

Although Arithmetic and Similarities were described previously as being categorized separately in the memory–conceptual dichotomy, these two

Verbal subtests are united by their categorization in Horn's Fluid Intelligence grouping, along with four Performance tasks. Many of the remaining Verbal subtests are very dependent on specific learning, whether primarily at home (Comprehension) or at school (Information, Vocabulary). Similarities is also conceptualized as having a crystallized component (see Chapters 10 and 11). Horn (1985) *excluded* Arithmetic from his crystallized category based on his numerous research studies. Nonetheless, this task is included in Bannatyne's Acquired Knowledge grouping and is quite clearly related to formal school achievement. However, clinicians who prefer to operate consistently within the Horn system should eliminate Arithmetic from consideration in this analysis (see Chapters 10 and 11).

Common Configurations of the WAIS-III Performance Scale

Wechsler Performance subtests correlate lower with each other than do the Verbal subtests, and the WAIS-III Perceptual Organization Index is defined by only three of the seven Performance subtests: Block Design, Matrix Reasoning, and Picture Completion. Consequently, fluctuations among the Performance tasks are frequent, and the scale commonly splits in a number of ways. Most Performance subtests have long been known to be particularly sensitive to brain damage (see Chapter 8), tend to be lowered relative to Verbal subtests for psychiatric patients (see Chapter 9), and are commonly the best discriminators among neuropsychiatric patients with diverse pathologies (see Chapter 9). The specific divisions of Performance subtests and the interpretations assigned to the clusters, therefore, assume importance for clinical and neuropsychological evaluations.

The following configurations among four, or all five, Performance subtests are discussed in the next sections: (1) Rapaport's distinction between visual organization and visual–motor coordination, (2) the meaningfulness of the visual stimuli, (3) sequential versus simultaneous processing strategies, and (4) visual memory versus nonverbal thinking (synthesis).

Visual Organization versus Visual–Motor Coordination

A frequent performance dichotomy, easy to spot, conforms to Rapaport's distinction between visual organization (without essential motor activity) and visual–motor coordination. The tasks *least* dependent on motor coordination are Matrix Reasoning and Picture Completion and the most motor-oriented subtest is Digit Symbol-Coding. Symbol Search and Picture Arrangement could legitimately be placed in either category. For most individuals, in our clinical opinion, they are best classified as Visual Organization (without essential motor activity). Both place heavy emphasis on visual scanning strategies and planning ability, and Picture Arrangement, especially, requires reasoning. Neither task greatly penalizes poor coordination (sloppy marking of "Yes" and "No" boxes is okay for Symbol Search, and awkward alignments of Picture Arrangement series are acceptable); also, the latter task does not award bonus points for speed on the WAIS-III (it does on the WISC-III). Therefore, the Rapaport dichotomy produces a configuration that splits the Performance subtests into groupings of three and four: those primarily requiring visual organization—Picture Completion, Matrix Reasoning, Symbol Search, and Picture Arrangement—and those heavily dependent on visual–motor coordination—Digit Symbol-Coding, Block Design, and Object Assembly.

Ben's Performance profile (below) provides a good example of a clear-cut visual organization–visual-motor coordination split (visual organization subtests are in bold face).

Performance Subtest	Scaled Score
Picture Completion	**9**
Digit Symbol-Coding	2
Block Design	6
Matrix Reasoning	**8**

Picture Arrangement	**8**
Symbol Search	**9**
Object Assembly	5

He earned scaled scores of 8 or 9 on Picture Completion, Matrix Reasoning, Symbol Search, and Picture Arrangement (mean = 8.5) compared to scores of only 2 to 6 on the visual–motor triad (mean = 4.3). The difference between the mean subtest scores for the visual organization subtests and the visual–motor coordination was larger than our ±3 rule of thumb.

Because so many variables affect a person's success on the visual–motor triad in addition to coordination, any deficiency in this area must be corroborated with other test scores, behaviors, and information before concluding that the person has a visual–motor deficit. High visual organization/low visual–motor coordination implies that the individual has adequate or better nonverbal intelligence, but is unable to express it on tasks that make heavy demands on motor coordination and motor speed. That interpretation suggests that the obtained P-IQ underestimates nonverbal intelligence. Yet coordination may not be the culprit; as discussed in the next section, the person with poor visual–motor performance may be handicapped by an inability to process abstract stimuli. Alternatively, the person may simply be a slow problem solver, truly denoting limited nonverbal intelligence. Such slowness will tend to depress scores on the highly speeded Block Design, Object Assembly, and Digit Symbol-Coding subtests. Less affected are scores on Matrix Reasoning, which is not timed, and Picture Completion and Picture Arrangement, neither of which offers bonus points for rapid solutions. Although Symbol Search is a timed test and part of the Processing Speed Index, the speed of processing necessary is more mental speed than visual–motor speed.

If the speed component, rather than the visual–motor coordination element, leads to low visual–motor coordination scores, the examiner must try to discern whether the slowness is due to a cognitive limitation or a behavioral trait such as apathy, compulsiveness, or anxiety. If the low scores are related either to the affective domain or the psychomotor domain, the visual organization cluster may offer the best estimate of the individual's nonverbal intelligence. Good clinical skills are essential.

Meaningful versus Abstract Stimuli

Picture Completion and Picture Arrangement use pictures of people and things, whereas Matrix Reasoning, Block Design, Symbol Search, and Digit Symbol-Coding require the perception and processing of abstractions: complex designs, simple designs, and numbers. Object Assembly doesn't fit neatly into either category. For the WISC-III, we classified Object Assembly with the two "Picture" subtests because the final product to be assembled is meaningful (Kaufman & Lichtenberger, 2000). However, the first two WISC-III puzzles are named for the child, and almost all puzzles have at least one large piece that makes the object to be constructed obvious to all but the severely impaired. For the WAIS-III, none of the puzzles is named, and some individuals are unaware of the nature of what they are constructing for the Elephant and, especially, the Butterfly. Consequently, we have categorized Object Assembly as measuring visual perception of *meaningful stimuli* but only Picture Completion and Picture Arrangement are categorized as measuring visual perception of *complete meaningful stimuli*. The WAIS-III puzzle pieces may be seen as meaningful by many people, but are likely to be processed as abstractions by others, for example, by some neurological patients because they are not "complete" meaningful stimuli.

Because of the complexity of the Performance tasks in general—Matrix Reasoning, Block Design, Symbol Search, and Digit Symbol-Coding in particular—it is necessary to cross-validate any hypothesis regarding an individual's discrepancy between perceiving or processing meaningful versus abstract stimuli. More likely than not, the person will evidence better performance in mean-

ingful than abstract stimuli; the reverse pattern is not as explainable from a neuropsychological framework and is less valuable in a diagnostic sense. If Matrix Reasoning, Block Design, Symbol Search, and Digit Symbol-Coding are high relative to the "picture" dyad, other explanations may be necessary. Possibly the person is threatened by the social stimuli, especially in Picture Arrangement, and feels more comfortable with neutral stimuli. Or the difference may be more related to the *imitative* aspect of Digit Symbol-Coding and Block Design (both involve reproduction of models), a skill that may be better developed than problem solving without a model.

The latter hypothesis requires consideration of Object Assembly rather than Picture Completion performance. Picture Arrangement and Object Assembly are each nonverbal-reasoning, problem-solving tasks; unlike Block Design and Digit Symbol-Coding, neither reasoning subtest provides the individual with a model to copy. Some individuals perform better when a model is provided, and others do better without one. When Picture Arrangement pairs with Object Assembly (or also with Matrix Reasoning), in contrast to a different level of performance on the two nonverbal imitative tasks, the examiner should entertain a reasoning versus imitation hypothesis. Additional support for this hypothesis may reside within the configuration of the Verbal profile. An individual with better imitative than reasoning skills within the visual–motor sphere, for example, might well display a comparable profile of high memory–low reasoning within the auditory–vocal channel.

But, when the pattern does not involve Object Assembly, and the nonverbal configuration clearly implies a deficiency in perceiving or processing abstract stimuli compared to meaningful stimuli, verification of the hypothesis can take several forms. Is there any evidence of brain damage, either diffuse or in the posterior regions of the right cerebral hemisphere? Did the individual have difficulty on Verbal subtests that use numerical symbols (Digit Span, Arithmetic, Letter-Number Sequencing)? Did he or she do better on the more meaningful, context-related Verbal subtests (Information, Comprehension) than on the ones that require responses to isolated verbal concepts (Vocabulary, Similarities)? Matrix Reasoning can help assess if a person is able to reason effectively with abstract stimuli. If Matrix Reasoning scores are discrepant from poor performance on Block Design and Digit Symbol-Coding, some other variable (speed, coordination, imitation), but not the abstractness of the stimuli, may have affected performance.

Simultaneous versus Sequential Processing

The four subtests that make up Bannatyne's Spatial Ability category (three of which compose the Perceptual Organization index) are also measures of simultaneous processing, the kind of gestalt–holistic problem-solving approach that cerebral specialization researchers associate with the right hemisphere and Luria adherents attribute to the occipital–parietal regions of the brain. Of the remaining Performance subtests, analytic, linear, left-brain processing is best measured by Digit Symbol-Coding. Other measures of sequential processing are found on the Verbal scale: Digit Span, Letter-Number Sequencing, and Arithmetic. Consequently, a possible configuration of the Performance scale is for the four simultaneous processing subtests to split off as a cluster, with the individual performing about equally well on Digit Symbol, Symbol Search, and Picture Arrangement (either substantially higher or lower than on Picture Completion–Block Design–Matrix Reasoning–Object Assembly).

The occurrence of this sequential–simultaneous dichotomy may be checked by investigating the individual's level of performance on the Verbal tasks that measure sequential processing (Digit Span, Letter-Number Sequencing, and Arithmetic). Do not accept a processing explanation as viable for an apparent visual–spatial (simultaneous) versus visual–sequential dichotomy of the Performance scale unless the person evidenced a similar level of functioning (either high

or low) on the verbal–sequential dyad. Further, examiners should not conclude that the individual has a simultaneous strength or weakness unless there is behavioral support for that contention. For example, did the person use a trial-and-error, sequential method of constructing puzzles and designs and placing pictures, or was an insightful, reflective, holistic problem-solving approach evident?

If verification of a processing interpretation of the Performance scale is lacking (from Verbal Scale scores or from clinical observations), one should explore other options. Even if Digit Symbol-Coding and Picture Arrangement pair up, this occurrence may be coincidental. Remember that each of these subtests has much subtest specificity (as does Matrix Reasoning). Hence, assigning unique or chance interpretations to fluctuations on Digit Symbol or Picture Arrangement may be defensible (an exception to our bias against subtest-specific inferences).

Relatively high scores on visual–spatial–simultaneous compared to visual–sequential tasks characterize autistic individuals. Lincoln et al.'s (1988) 33 nonretarded autistic children, adolescents, and adults (age range 8½ to 29, mean age = 17½ years), tested on the WISC-R or WAIS-R, had a mean scaled score of close to 9 on the spatial triad versus a mean of about 6 on Picture Arrangement and Digit Symbol-Coding. The differential was similar in Rutter's (1978) autistic sample (means of about 6⅔ and 3⅓, respectively). In Rutter's sample, the deficiency on visual–sequential tasks was comparable to the group's deficit in verbal expression, although the nonretarded autistic group studied by Lincoln et al. showed its most striking weakness in expressive skills.

A group of 21 manic-depressives on lithium therapy performed poorly on WAIS visual–sequential tasks, especially Digit Symbol; the lowest scores on Picture Arrangement and Digit Symbol were obtained by patients who had been on lithium the longest (Nair et al., 1979). In addition, high simultaneous–low sequential Performance profiles have been found fairly consistently for patients with Huntington's disease. Consistencies among several samples of patients with this genetic disease imply that they truly have a strength in simultaneous processing coupled with a weakness in sequential processing. Huntington's patients typically earn their highest performance scaled score on Picture Completion, while evidencing depressions in Digit Symbol, Picture Arrangement, Arithmetic, and Digit Span (Brandt et al., 1984; Butters et al., 1978; Josiassen et al., 1982; Randolph et al., 1993).

The spatial–simultaneous grouping of subtests (excluding Matrix Reasoning, because none of the studies were based on the WAIS-III) has also been found to be of clinical significance for a different sample with motor coordination problems: patients with multiple sclerosis (Heaton et al., 1985; Maurelli et al., 1992). All five WAIS-R Performance subtests (versus only two of six Verbal tasks) discriminated significantly between normal adults and patients having multiple sclerosis. But only Block Design, Object Assembly, and Picture Completion significantly discriminated between two samples of multiple sclerosis patients, one with relapsing–remitting symptoms, the other having chronic–progressive multiple sclerosis. Interpretation of the simultaneous subtests requires some caution. Although performance on the tasks has been positively associated with a field-independent cognitive style (Goodenough & Karp, 1961), there is some evidence, based partly on WAIS Block Design data, that the two constructs (spatial ability, field-independent cognitive style) are indistinguishable from one another (MacLeod, Jackson, & Palmer, 1986). Further, as discussed in Chapter 4 on individual differences, there is a significant gender difference, favoring males, in visualization.

Sometimes Block Design is a maverick subtest regarding its processing demands. Matrix Reasoning, Picture Completion, and Object Assembly stress the synthetic, visual closure skills that are so closely associated with a simultaneous processing approach to problem solving. Block Design demands this synthetic ability, but it also makes heavy demands on analytic ability, especially when constructing the designs from the two-dimensional cards with the guidelines removed. On these items, individuals must first effectively analyze the design into its component parts before they can synthesize a solution. The relevance of both processing styles has been demonstrated both in neuropsychological research and practice (Lezak, 1995). Matarazzo (1972) noted: "Oddly enough, individuals who do best on the test are not necessarily those who see, or at least follow, the pattern as a whole, but more often those who are able to break it up into small portions" (p. 212).

Support for Block Design's analytic component comes from experimental psychology research conducted by Schorr, Bower, and Kiernan (1982) with 10 undergraduate students from Stanford included in each of three studies. These authors distinguished between two types of strategies, one more simultaneous (synthetic), the other more sequential (analytic). The synthetic style involves holistic pattern matching; the analytic style demands mentally segmenting each block in the design. Results of each study indicated the predominant application of analytic problem-solving strategies. Although Royer (1984) challenged the use of the analytic–synthetic typology by Schorr et al., these investigators responded cogently to Royer's criticisms (Kiernan, Bower, & Schorr, 1984). Although one cannot generalize much from data obtained on a group of undergraduate students at a highly rated university, it is clear that Block Design items can be solved efficiently by sequential approaches, simultaneous approaches, or a combination of the two.

Sometimes, therefore, Block Design must be deleted when conducting a processing analysis of the Performance scale. Like Picture Arrangement and Digit Symbol-Coding, Block Design may be solved sequentially or by an integration of processes; and, like the two visual–sequential subtests, Block Design demands good verbal comprehension of lengthy verbal directions read by the examiner. Matrix Reasoning also has an analytic component that comes into play when dealing with each stimulus separately, and verbal mediation is a common strategy for solving the abstract reasoning problems. Picture Completion and Object Assembly, by contrast, depend more heavily on the gestalt function with minimal emphasis on analysis or on the so-called left-brain function of interpreting lengthy verbalizations or verbal mediation. Examiners should be alert for the emergence of the Picture Completion–Object Assembly dyad in Performance profiles. Should the appropriate configuration be detected, this visual closure dyad should be contrasted to the visual–sequencing subtests (Picture Arrangement, Digit Symbol-Coding) and, perhaps, to the pair of tasks that emphasize an integration of sequential and simultaneous processing (Block Design, Matrix Reasoning).

Luria's Block 1, Block 2, and Block 3 Functions

Luria (1980) posited the existence of three "blocks" or "functional units" in the brain: Block 1 concerns arousal or attention; Block 2 deals with successive and simultaneous coding functions, and pertains directly to the sequential–simultaneous dichotomy just discussed; and Block 3 involves higher-level planning processes (Luria, 1980; Naglieri, 1999; Naglieri & Das, 1988, 1997). Digit Symbol-Coding, apart from its sequential component, is for Rapaport a measure of concentration and is often a member of the distractibility/working memory grouping; therefore, it may be thought of as a measure of arousal, a Block 1 function that "maintains a proper state of arousal or cortical tone…[which] is also important for effective performance because too much or too little interferes with proper processing of information" (Naglieri & Das, 1988, p. 36). In addition, Picture Arrangement has long been considered a measure of planning ability, of anticipation of consequences, and, by inference, of Luria's third functional unit.

From this perspective, an individual's performance on Digit Symbol-Coding (and perhaps Digit Span, a measure of attention according to

Rapaport) may reflect arousal or orientation toward the tasks in general; scores on Arithmetic, Letter-Number Sequencing, and Digit Span may denote successive or sequential processing; success or failure on the Spatial triad may indicate simultaneous processing; and Picture Arrangement and Symbol Search performance may denote planning, the ability to develop strategies, to generate hypotheses, and generally to program, regulate, and verify activity (Naglieri & Das, 1988, 1997).

From Naglieri's (1999; Naglieri and Das, 1988, 1997) research, one might treat Picture Arrangement, Symbol Search, and Digit Symbol-Coding as measures of the Block 3, or planning, ability. Naglieri and Das (1997) interpret as planning ability a scale on the Cognitive Assessment System (CAS) that includes several highly speeded tasks, each of which resembles traditional measures of processing speed. Naglieri (1999) has provided some construct validity evidence for the CAS Planning scale, including research findings that support the need to generate problem-solving strategies to perform well on the CAS measures of planning ability. From this vantage point, it seems reasonable to hypothesize a Luria-based Block 3 "planning ability" interpretation of high or low scores on the Processing Speed Index, especially for those individuals whose score on Picture Arrangement is consistent with the PSI (whether high or low). Whereas the clerical, psychomotor Digit Symbol-Coding subtest is questionable as a measure of Luria's Block 3, both Picture Arrangement and Symbol Search seem to embrace the essence of Naglieri and Das's (1987) description of Block 3 characteristics: "planning entails the aptitude for asking new questions, solving problems, and self-monitoring, which…may represent one of the most complex forms of human behavior" (p. 355).

Visual Memory versus Nonverbal Thinking

One other configuration involving the entire Performance scale is easily and immediately recognizable: High scores on Picture Completion,

Digit Symbol-Coding, and Symbol Search conceivably indicate a good visual memory, because the former tests long-term visual memory and the latter two assess short-term visual memory (although Digit Symbol-Coding does so to a lesser extent than perceptual speed; Laux & Lane, 1985). Other Performance subtests measure nonverbal thinking and problem solving, as opposed to memory: Block Design assesses nonverbal concept formation, and Matrix Reasoning, Picture Arrangement, and Object Assembly are good measures of nonverbal reasoning. Together, the latter four tasks measure synthesis, assembling parts into a whole, either temporally (Picture Arrangement) or spatially.

According to Osgood's communication theory, the visual memory dyad assesses skills that are at least partially at the automatic, overlearned level of organization. In contrast, the thinking group comprises high-level, representational measures of adult intelligence. Some subjects who are low in nonverbal thinking will be able to perform adequately, or even exceptionally, on the three visual memory subtests; the Picture Completion/Digit Symbol-Coding dyad, in particular, makes fewer demands on higher intellectual processes. Although some individuals have the reverse pattern of high thinking–low memory, we suspect that alternative hypotheses are necessary to explain the profile. For example, in Rapaport's system, Picture Completion, Digit Symbol-Coding, and Symbol Search are classified as measures of concentration. Individuals with low scores on these tasks may have difficulty concentrating, a hypothesis that may be confirmed or rejected by behavioral observation.

Configurations of Both Scales

Clinicians who apply the configuration method of generating hypotheses should be alert to a few patterns that involve dyads or triads on both the Verbal and Performance scales. Several comparisons involve cross-validation of a finding from one scale to the other regarding memory, imitation, sequencing ability, and reasoning. If a person reasons well or poorly on the Verbal Scale (Similarities, Comprehension), does this strength or weakness maintain on the Performance scale (Picture Arrangement, Object Assembly, Matrix Reasoning)? A number of these comparisons are included in Table 12.6 to allow examiners to compute averages on categories that are assessed in similar fashion both verbally and nonverbally. The ±3 rule of thumb may be used to assess their similarity.

In addition, two specific comparisons involving the Verbal and Performance scale are of sufficient importance to warrant separate discussion: social comprehension versus abstract thought and fund of information versus visual synthesis.

Social Comprehension versus Abstract Thought

Two of Dean's (1983) clusters provide an interesting contrast for WAIS-III examiners to consider: Social Comprehension (Comprehension–Picture Arrangement) and Abstract Thought (Similarities–Block Design–Matrix Reasoning). Each category holds fairly constant the content to be processed (by including both Verbal and Performance subtests); all five tasks assess high-level reasoning or conceptual processes.

The Social Comprehension dyad combines the two subtests that have interpersonal themes, socially oriented items, and real-world problem-solving situations. They are believed to measure social judgment and common sense and may tentatively be thought of as a crude measure of social intelligence. As Dean (1983) stated: "Both subtests examine the client's ability to apply customs, social knowledge, and mores to specific situations" (p. 12). Some psychologists (e.g., Sattler, 1988) explore differences between the two subtests to infer specific modes of social functioning: "High Picture Arrangement coupled with low Comprehension may suggest sensitivity to interpersonal nuances, but a disregard for social conventions" (p. 177). We find little validity in such interpretations, but consider it useful to combine an individual's performance on the two socially oriented WAIS-III tasks to get a better estimate of social understanding.

The abstract thought triad represents an ideal point of comparison. Similarities presents verbal concepts totally out of social context (even Arithmetic incorporates a social setting for each item), requiring abstract reasoning with each pair of concepts. Further, the abstract designs and figures that constitute the Matrix Reasoning and Block Design items are about as far removed as possible from the socially relevant stimuli in Picture Arrangement.

Dean (1983), in speaking about the Similarities–Block Design dyad that constituted the Abstract Thought category on the WAIS-R, said: "Although basic concrete knowledge may be required, each subtest requires the subject to go beyond that knowledge level to the abstraction and manipulation of components" (p. 6); that statement applies as well to Matrix Reasoning. How well a person solves problems in an abstract setting versus a social setting is, therefore, of considerable clinical value regarding inferences about a person's personality, intellectual potential in quite different circumstances, and neuropsychological integrity.

The best validation of the Abstract Thought–Social Comprehension differential comes from Browning and Quinlan's (1985) study of the Wechsler profiles of 91 adolescent and young adult psychiatric patients (45 females, 46 males) ranging in age from 13 to 30 years (mean = 19). These patients were administered Loevinger's Sentence Completion Test (SCT) for measuring ego development (Loevinger & Wessler, 1970), along with either the WISC-R (*N* = 16), WAIS (*N* = 46), or the WAIS-R (*N* = 29). The SCT is meant to measure an aspect of personality functioning akin to social intelligence: "The exercise of social judgment and the capacity for anticipation and planning may be compared to Loevinger's description of ego development as a 'complexly interwoven fabric of impulse control, character, interpersonal relations, conscious preoccupations and cognitive complexity'" (Browning & Quinlan, p. 261).

These investigators grouped the patients into three ego development categories based on the SCT: preconformist (the lowest level), protoconformist, and postconformist (the highest level). We entered each group's mean sum of scaled scores on the two pertinent categories into the formulas to produce standard scores (we had to use a formula based on the Similarities–Block Design dyad because all of the Wechsler tests in the study predated Matrix Reasoning). The results require cautious interpretation because of the merger of data from three Wechsler batteries and the inability to convert the WAIS and WAIS-R values to age-corrected scaled scores; nonetheless, the findings are intriguing. The largest deficiency in Social Comprehension was evidenced by the group with the lowest level of ego development, with the discrepancy narrowing with increased ego functioning. Browning and Quinlan (1985) also found that Comprehension correlated highest with the SCT among the 11 subtests (.44), and that the correlation remained a significant .34 after partialling out FS-IQ. Although Picture Arrangement failed to correlate significantly with Loevinger's ego development test, according to Browning and Quinlan, "[t]he hypothesis of some association was partially supported" (p. 262).

In general, studies of the social intelligence hypothesis pertaining to the two Social Comprehension tasks have produced mixed findings. Schill (1966) and his associates (Schill, Kahn, & Muehleman, 1968a, 1968b) showed that WAIS Picture Arrangement related positively to measures of extroversion, such as the MMPI Social Introversion scale, for three samples of college students; Johnson (1969) found the opposite pattern in psychiatric patients. Terry and Berg (1984) reconciled these discrepant findings by demonstrating a significant interaction with the MMPI Psychopathic Deviance (PD) scale. High WAIS Picture

Arrangement was related to high extroversion only in psychiatric patients with high PD.

Turner and Horn (1976) failed to find any support for a social intelligence hypothesis in their MMPI–WAIS correlational study, using data from 400 adoptive parents (mean age = 37 for mothers, 40 for fathers). Picture Arrangement did not consistently relate to MMPI items on the Social Introversion scale or to other socially relevant items for males or females; and the MMPI items that consistently correlated with Comprehension were no more socially pertinent than the items that were significant correlates of Vocabulary. In contrast to Turner and Horn's negative findings, Edinger's (1976) investigation of 15 male process schizophrenics (mean age = 21.5 years) yielded positive results: WAIS Picture Arrangement correlated significantly with the Phillips Premorbid Adjustment Scale, even after partialling out FS-IQ.

WAIS-R investigations have been just as contradictory as the WAIS studies. Nobo and Evans (1986) found trivial, nonsignificant correlations involving the two Social Comprehension subtests and any of the five measures of social behavior (including the MMPI Social Introversion scale) for 37 college students. In contrast, Sipps, Berry, and Lynch (1987) used the California Psychological Inventory (CPI) scales to predict raw scores on WAIS-R Comprehension and Picture Arrangement for 85 normal adults (mean age = 29) and obtained positive results. The CPI scales of Capacity for Status and Flexibility (in thinking and social behavior) were significant predictors for both subtests. Both subtests were significantly related to CPI measures of social behavior, even after partialling out Vocabulary score; Sipps et al. concluded that there is "substantial evidence in support of the notion that Comprehension and Picture Arrangement are to some degree measures of social intelligence" (p. 503).

Despite the optimism of the latter team of researchers, the construct validity of the WAIS-III Social Comprehension category remains speculative: None of the studies have used the WAIS-III

version of Picture Arrangement, and generalizations from the WAIS and WAIS-R versions of the subtest to the WAIS-III version are tenuous because the subtest has undergone great changes from version to version (resulting in relatively poor correlations between different Picture Arrangement subtests); the studies have reported mixed results; the samples vary widely, are too dependent on college student populations, and are sometimes haphazard; the criteria are often dubious at best. (Are socially intelligent people necessarily extroverted?) We also question whether the correlational approach is the best methodology for investigating the issue. We find the Browning and Quinlan (1985) criterion of ego development the most compelling, and their methodology the most direct. But, despite their generally favorable findings, the validity of Social Comprehension is primarily face validity (the test items *seem* to measure the intended aptitude) rather than criterion-related or construct validity.

Far less pertinent research has been conducted with the Abstract Thought category (again, because all pertinent research was conducted prior to the WAIS-III, this category excludes Matrix Reasoning for all studies). Psychosurgery (frontal lobe or limbic–hypothalmic regions) has reportedly led to deficient abstract thinking, as measured by Wechsler's Block Design and Similarities (Jurko & Andy, 1973) and Kohs's Block Design test (Walsh, 1977). But a summary of pertinent research has led Joschko (1986) to conclude that "deficits in abstract thinking following psychosurgery either are not permanent or cannot be dissociated from factors related to long-term psychiatric illness" (p. 310). From the perspective of the Personality Assessment System (Krauskopf & Davis, 1973; Winne and Gettinger, 1973), "[i]ndividuals who achieve relatively low Block Design and Similarities scores are termed 'flexible, compensated' and considered as someone who... 'denies and punishes sensitivity'; rejects the subtle...[and is] [e]xplosively emotional under stress" (Kunce, Ryan, & Eckelman, 1976, p. 44). The PAS might predict violent behavior from some individuals low in Abstract Thought, and some evidence to support the association of low Similarities scores with violent behavior was provided by Kunce et al. for Caucasian males court-committed as criminally insane. Kunce et al. cross-validated their finding with a second sample of Caucasian males from the same institution, and Hays and Solway (1977) obtained comparable results with the WISC for a racially mixed group of violent and nonviolent juvenile delinquents. Yet, the generalizability of this theory-supported relationship was challenged when the *opposite* finding (relatively high Similarities) was observed on the WAIS with young African American offenders (Lira, Fagan, & White, 1979).

Fund of Information versus Visual Synthesis and Novel Problem Solving

Information and Vocabulary are so correlated with each other (.77) that exploring differences between them is a feeble exercise. As a team, however, this "fund of information" dyad reflects a formidable combination for evaluating a person's intellectual accomplishments in culturally relevant verbal arenas. This pair of subtests has much to recommend it: Information and Vocabulary are the most reliable WAIS-III subtests, both in terms of internal consistency and stability; they typically emerge as the best measures of *g* and of the Verbal Comprehension factor; they are the highest correlates of educational attainment among the WAIS-III tasks; they are resilient to the impact of aging (see Chapter 5 as well as the aging analyses for each subtest in Chapter 10); and they often remain as intact strengths for patients with organic or functional disorders.

An individual's fund of information has been shown empirically to have a definite cultural component (Cernovsky, 1986; Holland & Watson, 1980), in contrast to the Performance triad of Block Design–Matrix Reasoning–Object Assembly, which reflects a blend of Horn's (1989) *Gf* and *Gv*. Just as Information and Vocabulary are the best exemplars of the Verbal Compre-

hension factor, the nonverbal triad captures the essence of Perceptual Organization (see factor analysis in Chapter 7). All three tasks involve a visual synthesis and often novel problem solving. In contrast, visual synthesis and novel problem solving have no place in the Information–Vocabulary dyad; these types of problems are familiar—often learned in school—not novel. Unlike the Verbal dyad, the Performance tasks relate relatively weakly to education level; they decrease dramatically with age (even after controlling for education); and they are typically among the subtests most likely to reveal deficits in individuals with a wide variety of neuropsychiatric disorders (see Chapters 8 and 9). Consequently, the comparison of the "fund of information" dyad with the Block Design–Matrix Reasoning–Object Assembly triad affords examiners a crisp overview of a person's verbal and nonverbal skills (or crystallized knowledge versus fluid/visualization; or acquired knowledge versus spatial ability); the difference may be related to the referral problem and may help pinpoint areas of asset and deficit that might otherwise be obscured by other fluctuations within the Verbal and Performance scales.

Clinicians may also wish to compare performance on Information–Vocabulary with the person's success on either the Social Comprehension or Abstract Thought category. Some tentative WAIS research suggests that such comparisons may be made cautiously in certain diagnostic circumstances. McMullen and Rogers (1984) examined the traditional clinical hypothesis that obsessive personality styles are associated with a high score on the fund of information dyad and low Comprehension, whereas the reverse cognitive pattern is associated with hysteric personality styles. They found a significant interaction in the predicted direction, in support of the clinical hypothesis, for the 16 most extreme scorers among their sample of 65 college students.

For the Abstract Thought category, evidence was provided, and then cross-validated, in support of the notion that scores on the fund of information dyad and on Similarities may distinguish among temporal lobe and generalized epileptic patients (Milberg, Greiffenstein, Lewis, & Rourke, 1980). These investigators postulated that generalized seizure patients would have high scores on WAIS Information + Vocabulary, contrasted with a relatively low Similarities score, and that temporal lobe seizure patients would display good Similarities performance and a poor fund of information. Milberg et al. applied discriminant function analysis and reported excellent "hit" rates of 77% (initial sample of 39 patients) and 79% (for a cross-validation sample of 39 patients). A second experiment with the WAIS (Bolter, Veneklasen, & Long, 1981), however, found considerably lower hit rates (a median

of about 54% for several comparisons); Bolter et al. concluded that "the WAIS seizure index may be of limited diagnostic utility in the assessment of seizure patients" (p. 552).

ILLUSTRATIVE CASE REPORTS

The following three case reports illustrate the methods and procedures for WAIS-III interpretation described in the nine interpretive steps. These techniques are also exemplified in the case reports at the end of Chapters 8, 9, and 13.

NICOLE H., AGE 34, LEARNING PROBLEM

Referral and Background Information

Nicole (Nikki) volunteered for testing and evaluation available through the psychoeducational assessment class as she has been concerned about her poor performance on tests in a college-level statistics course, inconsistent performance in her college coursework, test anxiety, and a possible learning disability. She is interested in finding out if she has the ability to complete a degree from the University of Alabama. Nikki has been aware of a problem since grade school (she repeated the 7th grade). Her particular problems are with numbers and details. She has noticed that she reverses numbers (as well as some letters, but to a lesser extent).

She knows number concepts but makes mistakes with her checkbook, for example, despite good concentration. She took only one math course in high school; she took college algebra at the University of Alabama and failed it. She indicates that she is frustrated because she knows something is wrong, but she does not know what it is. She wants to know what the problem is and how to deal with it.

Nikki reports that she was diagnosed 8 years ago as having Grave's disease (hyperthyroidism with one or more of the following: goiter, exophthalmos, pretibial myxedema). The disease is not controlled at the present time, although she has had isotope therapy, which resulted in the reverse condition (hypothyroidism). Side effects of the disease and/or treatment, according to Nikki, include memory problems and emotional side effects such as nervousness and irritability.

Nikki is married and has two daughters (aged 2 and 11). Her husband is about to finish his Ph.D. program in physical education. She returned to school after more than 10 years and is now a junior in home economics at the University of Alabama, majoring in food and nutrition. One of her stated reasons for returning to school was to be a good mother to her older child, who is "gifted." Nikki is currently taking Introductory Statistics, Economics, and two classes in nutrition. While doing well in nutrition courses, she is having great difficulty with statistics and economics. Nikki works part-time at a local child development center. Although she is undertaking a great deal, she does not report a great deal of support from either her husband or parents.

Nikki says that she wants to be a county health counselor and work with pregnant teenagers regarding their prenatal care. She likes to read and play the piano.

Appearance and Behavioral Characteristics

Nikki, a 34-year-old Caucasian female, wears glasses and is of medium height and weight. She was cooperative and a willing worker throughout the testing session, although she was shy at the beginning.

It was evident throughout the session that Nikki was highly motivated. On a task requiring her to define a word she gave a string of responses until she felt comfortable with her answer. On a task of immediate recall of digits she closed her eyes and tried to concentrate on the task.

One of Nikki's outstanding characteristics was her excellent verbal ability (rich vocabulary and expressions). On a task requiring her to define words she frequently gave a few synonyms (e.g., *terminate* is 'to end,' 'complete,' and 'finish') or long elaborations. Nikki successfully used trial-and-error strategy to solve verbal questions. Asked to explain the meaning of the saying, "One swallow doesn't make a summer," on a task testing her commonsense understanding of social situations, she was puzzled at first, asking, "One swallow?" She did not seem to be familiar with the saying. She began to describe the migration of swallows. While giving trial responses, she was able to find the proper answer. It should be noted that, when she faced a hard question, she often laughed, saying, "Oh, boy," before trying. Laughing seemed to be her strategy for coping with anxiety.

Nikki exhibited her poor facility with numbers and her fear of them. On a test of general information, her responses to two questions requiring numerical answers (e.g., the population of the United States) were not even "in the ballpark." She also had extreme difficulty in repeating digits in their reverse order. When solving oral arithmetic problems, she was so nervous that she could not correct her responses even when she was aware that she was giving wrong answers. After the task she gave a sigh of relief.

Nikki showed her poor short-term memory, having to check with the key very often on a task requiring her to copy symbols that are paired with numbers. Though she tried to be careful, she made several mistakes, for example, copying the symbol for the number 3 in the box for the number 4.

Test Results and Interpretation

On the WAIS-III, Nikki earned a Verbal IQ of 106, a Performance IQ of 99, and Full Scale IQ of 103, scores that place her in the Average classification of intelligence and rank her at about the 50th–66th percentile for people her age (scores from all tests are listed in Table 12.7). Although her Verbal and Performance appear similar on the surface, Nikki's highly consistent scores on the three IQs mask the high degree of variability that characterized her subtest profile. Because of that variability, neither the Full Scale IQ nor the Verbal IQ provide a meaningful representation of her overall abilities. The Verbal scale is comprised of two indexes: Verbal Comprehension and Working Memory. In Nikki's case, these two indexes were significantly different from one another, rendering the Verbal IQ useless as a meaningful representation of her overall verbal skills. Examination of these indexes separately is much more informative. Nikki earned a Verbal Comprehension Index of 118 (88th percentile; 113–122 with 90% confidence) and a Working Memory Index of 82 (12th percentile; 77–89 with 90% confidence). The discrepancy between the indexes that comprise her Verbal scale indicate that Nikki's verbal conceptualization, knowledge, and expression are much stronger than her number ability and sequential processing. In addition, Nikki's Verbal Comprehension Index (118) was also significantly higher than her Perceptual Organization Index of 103 (58th percentile; 85–100 with 90% confidence). The discrepancy between these two indexes indicates that Nikki's ability to answer oral questions measuring factual knowledge, word meanings, and verbal expression is much stronger than her ability to integrate visual stimuli, reason nonverbally, and apply visual–motor skills to solve problems.

The variability in Nikki's WAIS-III profile was also evident in her pattern of relative subtest strengths and weaknesses. Similar to her overall High Average abilities depicted by her Verbal

TABLE 12.7   Nicole H.: Tests administered

Wechsler Adult Intelligence Scale—Third Edition (WAIS-III)

Scale	IQ	90% Confidence Interval	Percentile Rank
Verbal Scale	106	102–110	66
Performance Scale	99	93–105	47
Full Scale	103	100–106	58

Factor	Index	90% Confidence Interval	Percentile Rank
Verbal Comprehension	118	113–122	88
Perceptual Organization	103	97–109	58
Working Memory	82	77–89	12
Processing Speed	91	85–100	27

Subtest	Scaled Score	Percentile Rank	Subtest	Scaled Score	Percentile Rank
Vocabulary	13	84	Picture Completion	9	37
Similarities	13	84	Digit Symbol-Coding	8	25
Arithmetic	8	25	Block Design	13	84
Digit Span	6	9	Matrix Reasoning	10	50
Information	14	91	Picture Arrangement	10	50
Comprehension	13	84	Symbol Search	9	37
Letter-Number Sequencing	7	16	Object Assembly	9	37

Selected Clusters from the Woodcock-Johnson—Third Edition (WJ III): Tests of Achievement

Scale	Standard Score	90% Confidence Interval	Percentile Rank
Broad Math	99	95–103	47
Math Calculation Skills	101	97–105	53
Broad Written Language	110	106–114	75
Basic Writing Skills	106	102–110	66
Written Expression	112	107–116	79

Strong-Campbell Interest Inventory

Highest Rated Occupations

Occupational Therapist

Physical Therapist

Registered Nurse

Comprehesion Index, her subtest scores indicated that she has a relative strength in crystallized knowledge (acquired knowledge), her fund of knowledge, verbal reasoning, and verbal expression. These strengths were evident in her strong performance on a task of general information (91st percentile), as well as tasks requiring her to define words, describe how two words are alike, and use judgment and common sense to answer questions (all 84th percentile).

In contrast to these strong abilities, Nikki demonstrated relative weaknesses in her number ability and short-term memory. These areas of poor ability were notable in her depressed performance on a task requiring her to remember and repeat a series of numbers presented orally (9th percentile). Nikki's attention and concentration during the entire test were optimal, so her poor performance cannot be explained by distractibility. Rather, her weakness seems to be primarily in auditory short-term memory and number manipulation, which was further supported by her performance on tasks of sequencing letters and numbers (16th percentile) and oral arithmetic (25th percentile).

It should be noted that her incorrect responses on the task of oral arithmetic were frequently very close to correct ones (e.g., $0.38 in place of $0.36, $1.85 in place of $1.86), implying that Nikki has weaknesses in the mental manipulation of numbers and computation rather than in quantitative reasoning. This finding accords well with her statement that she knows number concepts but still makes mistakes. Her weakness with numbers was observed even on a test of general information; Nikki failed some quantitative factual items (e.g., "How far is it from Paris to New York?") despite responding correctly to all of the more difficult nonnumerical items. Further, she performed at a relatively low level in a task requiring the rapid copying of abstract symbols that are paired with numbers. Performance on this task is influenced by short-term memory and number ability (plus other variables).

To contrast Nikki's cognitive aptitude (WAIS-III) with her achievement in mathematics and written language, clusters were administered from the Woodcock-Johnson—Third Edition (WJ III) Tests of Achievement. On the Broad Math cluster, involving problem solving, number facility, automaticity, and reasoning, Nikki earned a scaled score of 99 (47th percentile). On the Math Calculation Skills cluster, involving basic mathematical skills, including computation skills and automaticity with basic math facts, she earned a standard score of 101 (53rd percentile). When comparing her achievement in mathematics to her cognitive potential or aptitude, we see a person who had High Average aptitude (Verbal Comprehension Index of 118), but who is achieving in the Average range of mathematics. The discrepancy is large, indicating that she has not been able to apply her cognitive potential to acquire computational and problem-solving skills. However, the discrepancy is not of sufficient magnitude to be categorized as a learning disability.

On the Written Language Clusters of the WJ III Tests of Achievement, Nikki ranked at the 75th percentile for people her age on Broad Written Language (standard score = 110) and performed similarly on Written Expression (112, 79th percentile), but had slightly lower scores on Basic Writing Skills (106; 66th percentile). Across the written tasks she performed most poorly on a task requiring her to respond in writing to a variety of questions demanding knowledge of punctuation, spelling, and usage. However, she was able to produce Average to High Average quality writing that required meaningful written expression and fluency in her overall written language. Thus, overall, Nikki's performance on the Written Language Clusters was commensurate with her aptitude as shown on the WAIS-III Verbal Comprehension Index. These results, coupled with the finding that Nikki has excellent verbal comprehension and oral expression, suggest that she has the potential to do better than she currently reports doing in school on tasks that demand written language.

Nikki was given the Strong-Campbell Interest Inventory (SCII), a measure of interests (not aptitudes) that provides general prediction of occupations in which she may find satisfaction. The results of the SCII suggest that Nikki may be happiest when she works with people for the welfare of others in less structured settings and gets many opportunities for self-expression. The areas she is most interested in are music/drama, art, domestic arts, and nature. The occupations she may enjoy most include occupational therapist, physical therapist, and registered nurse. Her goal of becoming a county health counselor and working with pregnant adolescents seems to fit her interests very well; so does her choice of college major (food and nutrition).

Summary and Conclusion

Concerned about her poor performance on tests and a possible learning disability, Nikki, a 34-year-old female, volunteered for evaluation to find out whether she can graduate from the University of Alabama, what her learning problems are, and how she can deal with them. She was a hard worker, using trial-and-error strategies to solve verbal items successfully. Nikki performed in the Average to High Average range on the WAIS-III, earning a Verbal Comprehension Index of 118, a Perceptual Organization Index of 103, a Working Memory Index of 82, and a Processing Speed Index of 91. Examination of the discrepancies between her Indexes indicated that her Full Scale and Verbal IQ do not provide meaningful representations of her overall ability, so our interpretation focused on the Indexes and the strengths and weaknesses in her subtest profile.

Further examination of the test results showed that she has strengths in verbal comprehension and expression and relative weaknesses in numbers, short-term memory, and nonverbal reasoning. The test results of selected clusters from the Woodcock-Johnson III: Tests of Achievement revealed that Nikki has Average to High Average achievement in written language and Average achievement in mathematics. Nikki's own report of her skills indicates that she has not been able to apply these academic areas of knowledge to acquire writing skills and computational skills in the "real world." Nikki's Strong-Campbell Interest Inventory results conform well with her college major and her choice of occupation.

It is apparent from the evaluation that Nikki has the ability to complete her college degree. Although the discrepancy between her ability and achievement in mathematics is fairly large, it is not sufficient to suggest a learning disability. Instead, her poor performance in mathematics seems to stem in part from the quality of math education she has received and in part from her being away from school for more than 10 years.

Nikki seems to try to accomplish too much at once: taking four courses, working part-time, and taking care of her family as a wife and mother of two children. This overload, in the face of little support from her husband and parents, seems to be making her extremely anxious and may be related to her inconsistent performance in her college courses. She needs to learn that she doesn't have to be perfect. Nikki's goal of becoming a county health counselor to help deliver prenatal care to pregnant teenagers is consistent with her interests and abilities.

Recommendations

1. Nikki should cut back on her workload. She should take fewer university courses each semester and should take more time to complete her college education.

2. Nikki should find time to get away from the house to concentrate on studying.

3. Nikki should take remedial math courses or go to the Learning Skills and Tutorial Center, where she can get tutorial service for free. Her tutor needs to help with the specific subject matter.

4. Nikki should take remedial grammar courses (such as Basic Writing) or go to the Writing Center, where she can get tutorial service on grammar and writing for free. The center has many returning students who are able to learn in a nonthreatening atmosphere.

5. In an effort to accommodate her memory difficulties, Nikki should study over several short periods of time, rather than in a block of, say, three straight hours. Nikki should also

use a tape recorder, taping classes and talking into the tape recorder so that she can listen again and again to what she is trying to learn.

6. She should make learning more active to study effectively. The following suggestions are recommended.

   a. Make a test for herself and practice it under no pressure.

   b. Make fact sheets and quiz herself.

   c. Try to teach her gifted daughter the subject matter of her courses and have her daughter try to teach her or quiz her.

   d. Make every effort to make her studying gamelike and challenging.

Examiners and Report Writers:
Graduate students in Drs. Nadeen and Alan Kaufman's advanced assessment course at the University of Alabama; Peggy Connell, Ellen Dossett, Elizabeth Eller, Toshinorl Ishikufna, Marcia O'Neal, and Gwen Wilson.

AIMÉE L., AGE 26, MEMORY CONCERNS

Reason for Referral

Aimée L., a 26-year-old Caucasian female, was self-referred for an evaluation because she was concerned about recent difficulty she was experiencing in one of her classes. She is enrolled in a social work graduate program. Specifically, Aimée expressed a desire to know more about her strengths and weaknesses to facilitate her performance in her classes. She had specific concerns about one of her courses that involves a lot of rote memorization. The main goals of this evaluation are to inform Aimée about her particular learning styles and to explain the difficulty she is experiencing in her class in order to improve her performance.

Background Information

Aimée is currently in her first year of a graduate program in social work. She reported liking many of her classes and has enjoyed her program thus far. Aimée grew up in Northern California, where she lived with her parents in an upper-middle-class neighborhood. She said she had a "pretty good" relationship with all of her family members, but has remained independent from them since entering college. Aimée discussed how her younger sister still lives with her parents and attends a nearby college. Aimée reported working a limited number of hours at an office job. Her father is in business and her mother is a homemaker and teaches part-time in a local high school. She told the examiner that her developmental course was normal with no marked delays or impairments.

Aimée reported that her grades were at the "A" level throughout high school, but have slipped a little down to some B's since she has been in college. She did not express much concern about this, and seemed relatively content with her performance in graduate school. Aimée also discussed her involvement with a wide variety of friends. She said that she is particularly close to her roommate, who she said is her best friend, and that she also has a wide circle of friends in her graduate program. She reported that she likes running for exercise and relaxing at home when she is not in school or working.

Aimée reported having had a physical exam eight months ago and was told by her physician that she is in excellent health. She denied having been in therapy, and reported that none of her family members has a history of psychiatric problems. Her most recent reported concern is the stress involved with work and balancing the hours between her school program and extracurricular activities.

Appearance and Behavioral Characteristics

Aimée, a 26-year-old, Caucasian, upper-middle-class female, attended the evaluation casually dressed, wearing jeans and a blouse. Her hair was short and appeared well kept. She was verbal and cooperative during the testing session, and rapport was established and maintained within the first few minutes. She was also quite humorous and made light of many different things throughout the examination. She did not appear anxious at any time during the testing process, and appeared motivated on most of the subtests. She seemed to enjoy most tasks that required her to express herself verbally, such as those requiring her to define various vocabulary words and manipulate pictures to make a logical story. She appeared to enjoy talking about the pictures both while she was arranging them and after she was finished doing so. She did not appear discouraged by her failures throughout the examination, but rather reacted to her failures by laughing and telling jokes.

One strategy that was evident throughout the testing process was Aimée's verbal mediation of nonverbal tasks. This strategy allowed her to think through her responses to focus on the task. For example, this approach was evident when she arranged pictures to tell a logical story. When she talked about the various elements of the story, she appeared to form a clearer picture of what was occurring, which helped her on her task. This was further demonstrated in a subtest requiring Aimée to arrange puzzle pieces to make a complete object. Again, she talked herself through what she thought the objects were supposed to be, and this helped facilitate her performance. Aimée talked throughout the examination and on many occasions her self-talk appeared to expedite her ability to work on various subtests.

Throughout the evaluation, Aimée was very determined and able to concentrate on tasks for long periods of time. Her high level of focus was particularly evident on a task that required her to put puzzle pieces together. Even though she did not seem to know where to start with one of the most difficult of the puzzles, she continually looked down and intently pondered what to do next. In this case, the examiner suggested moving on to the next subtest when the time expired. She refused the suggestion, and continued to try to figure out what she was doing wrong. Her determination was further demonstrated during a subtest that required that Aimée put together blocks to match a model. She had difficulty on one of the designs and did not want to give up trying to figure out the arrangement of the blocks until the examiner suggested that the next design should be tried. Overall, Aimée was determined and did not give up on difficult tasks.

Another notable characteristic was Aimée's quick processing style. Aimée answered many of the questions rapidly, and was able to think through a wide variety of tasks very quickly. This speed was evident on a subtest requiring Aimée to provide verbal responses to arithmetic problems that were presented orally. She answered about half of the problems instantly without any apparent deliberate thinking. On all other problems she was able to report answers very quickly and did well. Her quick processing was further demonstrated on a task requiring Aimée to define a series of vocabulary words. She defined almost all of the vocabulary words almost instantly, and reported them with thorough and complete responses. A final example of her style was on a subtest that required Aimée to find what was missing in a picture. She responded to almost all of the pictures within a few seconds, and seemed to take pride in her ability to think through the missing element with speed. Overall, Aimée's processing speed during many facets of the testing was very quick.

A final characteristic that was seen throughout the examination was her use of humor. She appeared to be able to use humor both in response to her difficulty with items as well as when facing relatively easy tasks. Via her humor, she was able to effectively break the uncomfortable feelings she may have been experiencing as the testing process began, as well as when the shifts were made to different subtests. For example, when Aimée was drawing a person, she made light of her difficulty with artwork, and was able to make fun of her drawing and laugh about it. She also laughed while she was doing an easier subtest that involved finding what was missing in the picture. She made fun of something related to the picture, which allowed her to proceed through some of the more mundane tasks smiling. Overall, Aimée used humor in a wide variety of situations, and her ability to do so helped her to relax and maintain her motivation.

When considering Aimée's observed behaviors during the testing, such as humor, quick processing style, concentration, and determination reflected in many subtests, these results should be interpreted as a valid measure of Aimée's cognitive functioning.

Tests Administered (scores are listed in Table 12.8)

- Wechsler Adult Intelligence Scale-Third Edition (WAIS-III)
- Kaufman Functional Academic Skills Test (K-FAST)

Test Results and Interpretation

The Wechsler Adult Intelligence Scale—Third Edition (WAIS-III), which is an individually administered test of intellectual ability of a person's strengths and weaknesses, measures two types of abilities. The first ability is measured by the Verbal scale, which assesses both school-learned knowledge as well as problem-solving skills involving words and numbers. The Performance scale measures largely nonverbal abilities that are assessed by tasks that require one to find patterns, complete a sequence or missing elements in pictures, and problem-solve using blocks or symbols. When a 90% confidence interval was used, Aimée obtained a Verbal IQ ranging from 118–128 (IQ = 124; 95th percentile), a Performance IQ ranging from 109–123 (IQ = 117; 87th percentile), and a Full Scale IQ ranging from 118–127 (IQ = 123; 94th percentile). These IQs place her in the High Average to Superior range of cognitive functioning.

However, significant variability was present in Aimée's Verbal IQ, Full Scale IQ, and Verbal Comprehension Index, which diminished the meaningfulness of these global scores. Specifically, there was wide disparity within her performance on the subtests comprising the Verbal IQ: She earned a score at the 99.9th percentile on a vocabulary defining task and a score at the 50th percentile on a rote recall task. Similar disparity was seen across her performance on tasks that comprise the Verbal Comprehension Index: Her scores ranged from 99.9th percentile (defining vocabulary) to the 75th percentile (determining how two words are alike). Thus, because neither the Full Scale IQ, Verbal IQ, nor Verbal Comprehension index can be meaningfully interpreted as measures of her global functioning, we focus instead on the remaining three WAIS-III Indexes as well as her unique subtest strengths and weaknesses.

The three indexes that meaningfully represent Aimée's global performance were the Perceptual Organization Index (POI), on which she scored 123 (94th percentile), the Processing Speed Index (PSI), on which she scored 114 (82nd percentile), and the Working Memory Index, on which she scored 115 (84th percentile). The POI subtests require one to integrate visual stimuli, reasoning ability, and to apply visual–spatial and visual–motor skills to solve the kind of problems that are not taught in school. The PSI comprises various tasks that required Aimée to solve nonverbal problems at a rapid pace. Aimée's abilities were consistently Above Average on both the POI and PSI. Aimée also performed at a similar High Average level on tasks that required

TABLE 12.8   Aimée L.'s psychometric summary

Wechsler Adult Intelligence Scale—Third Edition (WAIS-III)

Scale	IQ	90% Confidence Interval	Percentile Rank
Verbal Scale	124	118–128	95
Performance Scale	117	109–123	87
Full Scale	123	118–127	94

Factor	Index	90% Confidence Interval	Percentile Rank
Verbal Comprehension	129	122–133	97
Perceptual Organization	123	114–129	94
Working Memory	115	107–121	84
Processing Speed	114	103–121	82

Subtest	Scaled Score	Percentile Rank	Subtest	Scaled Score	Percentile Rank
Vocabulary	19	99.9	Picture Completion	15	95
Similarities	12	75	Digit Symbol-Coding	11	63
Arithmetic	14	91	Block Design	12	91
Digit Span	10	50	Matrix Reasoning	14	91
Information	14	91	Picture Arrangement	11	63
Comprehension	14	91	Symbol Search	14	91
Letter-Number Sequencing	14	91	Object Assembly	10	50

Kaufman Functional Academic Skills Test (K-FAST)

Scale	Standard Score	90% Confidence Interval	Percentile Rank
Reading	111	101–121	77
Arithmetic	108	98–118	70
Composite	114	107–121	82

short-term memory, concentration, and the ability to mentally manipulate information. These skills were evident from her score at the 84th percentile on the Working Memory Index.

Aimée's subtest profile revealed a relative strength in acquired knowledge. She had a wide variety of skills in many different areas, which was evident in numerous subtests. This was apparent in two subtests that required her to perform tasks that were very different from each other. She was able to do well on subtests involving manipulating arithmetic problems in her head (91st percentile) as well as defining various vocabulary words (99.9th percentile). She was able to easily change the way she solved a task depending on what the problem required. She seemed comfortable doing a wide variety of tasks, and she completed most questions without any demonstrated anxiety. Acquired knowledge was also established in a task requiring Aimée to answer a series of questions designed to tap into the knowledge of common events, objects, and people (91st percentile).

Her strength in acquired knowledge was also shown in Aimée's consistent performance on the Kaufman Functional Academic Skills Test (K-FAST). This is a test of functional academic skill, which is related to one's ability to apply academic knowledge to real-life situations. Overall, her performance was in the Average to Superior range, as she exhibited a consistent high capacity for knowledge with her Composite standard score of 114±7 (82nd percentile). The K-FAST has two sections: Reading and Arithmetic, and Aimée's abilities were relatively equal in both areas. She scored 108±10 (70th percentile) on mathematics and 111±10 (77th percentile) on reading. Her flexibility in being able to shift to solve a variety of tasks added to her ability to reason, thereby facilitating her performance. Her K-FAST scores were not significantly different than one another, which supports the idea that her academic abilities are well rounded. Her scores on the K-FAST were also commensurate with the overall scores Aimée earned on the WAIS-III.

A relative strength closely related to acquired knowledge was Aimée's ability to hold information in long-term memory. This strong ability was evident during a subtest requiring Aimée to define vocabulary words (99.9th percentile), as well as during a subtest requiring her to solve mental arithmetic problems (91st percentile). This skill was further exemplified in her performance on a subtest that required Aimée to remember many different common events, objects, places, and people (91st percentile). Finally, Aimée's strong long-term memory was supported by how detailed and specifically she recalled information about her background history and presenting problem.

A final relative strength of Aimée was her learning ability. This strength was evident in high scores on subtests that required her to learn before performing the tasks. This was particularly demonstrated in her ability work on a novel task of nonverbal problem solving. She was also able to learn this task's demands that required her to learn the pattern and figure out where various shapes belong (91st percentile). She was very flexible and remained focused on the directions and what the task required. She seemed very willing to learn new subtests, and was able to excel at tasks that were novel and required learning.

In summary, when Aimée utilized her verbal strengths to articulate the process she used to solve problems, her score was positively affected. On the WAIS-III, this was most evident when she excelled on a task requiring her to define various vocabulary words (99.9th percentile). She was extremely thorough when defining the words, and seemed to have the ability to easily think through the meanings and verbalize them very quickly. She was very specific on many of the words, and this contributed to her high score. Aimée was further able to utilize her strong verbal ability to help in her performance on nonverbal tasks. This skill was evident on a task requiring her to put together a group of cards in order of logical progression (63rd percentile). She made many comments throughout the process of figuring out the arrangement, which allowed her to increase her understanding as well as her score. Overall, Aimée's verbal expression was very strong.

In contrast to Aimée's relative strengths in her subtest profile, was one relative weakness. This weakness was in a very specific skill: rote recall of auditorally presented information, and was evident on a subtest requiring Aimée to repeat a series of numbers either forward or backward (50th percentile). She appeared to be unable to utilize her verbal strength with this subtest to help her performance, and, thus, difficulty was exhibited. The stimuli for this task are not meaningful strings of numbers or words, and, although Aimée was focused during the task, she admitted afterward that it bored her. Her relative weakness is also corroborated by her reported difficulty in her graduate course that requires much rote memorization of information. This weakness is very specific to rote recall, as overall her short-term memory skills are intact and in the High Average range (evidenced by her Working Memory Index of 115; 84th percentile).

Summary and Diagnostic Impressions

Aimée is a 26-year-old female self-referred because of concern with her performance in one of her graduate courses that demands much rote recall of information. She wanted to identify cognitive strengths and weaknesses to determine how she can utilize her skills to overcome her deficits. Aimée was motivated and focused throughout the examination. She also tended to work very quickly and prided herself on this aspect of her work. She used humor as a means to relax herself and maintain her focus.

On the WAIS-III, Aimée obtained a Perceptual Organization Index of 117 (94th percentile), a Processing Speed Index of 114 (82nd percentile), and a Working Memory Index of 115 (84th percentile). These scores placed her in the High Average to Superior range of cognitive functioning. The three WAIS-III IQs and Verbal Comprehension Index did not meaningfully represent Aimée's global cognitive abilities due to significant variability in her performance on subtests that comprise these scales; therefore, our interpretation focused on the three remaining Indexes and her relative subtest strengths and weaknesses.

Aimée's relative strengths included her acquired knowledge, long-term memory, and her learning ability. These strengths also relate to her strong academic ability, which was apparent from her Average to Superior performance on the K-FAST. She earned an overall K-FAST Composite standard score of 114 (82nd percentile), Arithmetic standard score of 108 (70th percentile), and Reading standard score of 111 (77th percentile).

These verbal strengths were in contrast to her only relative weakness: rote recall. Although she performed in the High Average range overall on tasks of short-term memory and tasks requiring mental manipulation of information, she had more difficulty on a specific task that demanded rote recall of a series of numbers. She was not able to implement her strong verbal ability to facilitate her performance on this task. Her unique weakness in rote recall on the WAIS-III supports her reported problems in her graduate course that also requires rote memorization of facts.

From all indications, Aimée appeared to be an engaging, humorous, and personable woman whose abilities are in the Average to Superior range of intelligence and achievement. She is a verbal woman, who is particularly good at using verbal mediation, which helps her performance. She appeared to thrive when engaged in a wide variety of tasks, and was very determined and focused on some of the tasks that caused her difficulty. Her reported difficulties at school have been validated by this assessment. Recommendations are made below to help Aimée utilize her strengths to help her compensate for her areas of deficit.

Recommendations

The following recommendations are suggested to assist Aimée with her difficulties on tasks of rote recall, such as those in her challenging graduate course:

1. Aimée should try to use her strong verbal ability when learning and memorizing information. By verbalizing her thought processes, it may help her performance on a wider variety of tasks.

2. Tasks that are tedious or boring to Aimée, such as memorizing seemingly needless or unrelated facts or figures, should be worked on in small increments of time. For example, instead of memorizing 10 pages of information at one sitting, Aimée should focus on one or two pages at a time. Then, before she moves on to new material, she should review what she has learned. Such distributed review will lessen the monotony of rote memorization.

3. Mnemonic devices, such as pairing a word or fact with another more meaningful word, may benefit Aimée. For example, when trying to memorize a list of 10 facts, Aimée should try pairing each fact with a more meaningful word or list.

4. Another mnemonic strategy is to take the first letter of each word in a list that is to be remembered and create a meaningful sentence from it. For example, to remember "**c**arrots, **a**pples, **p**otatoes, **r**ice, **t**hyme, **w**atermelon," Aimée could associate the C, A, P, R, T, and W with the following sentence: "**C**ats **a**nd **p**igeons **r**ule **t**he **w**orld."

5. Working with a friend or personal tutor on assignments related to her difficult course would be beneficial. Because Aimée is so verbal, speaking out loud while trying to recall information will be beneficial. Also, creating a dialog with another person about the information to be remembered will help her to remember the topics she is trying to recall.

Douglas Johnson
Psychological Intern

Elizabeth O. Lichtenberger, Ph.D.
Clinical Supervisor

LAUREN J., AGE 57, DECLINE IN JOB PERFORMANCE

Reason for Referral

Lauren J. was referred by her current employer for a psychoeducational evaluation in order to assess her cognitive strengths and weaknesses. Her employer is an agency that employs part-time substitute teachers and sends them out to teaching assignments at private schools to fill in for master teachers in their absence. Lauren has been employed by this company for four years and has received countless accolades from the schools she has taught at about her superior performance as a substitute teacher. However, Lauren expressed concern to her supervisor that recently she has begun to feel inept in certain classrooms. For example, she stated that she feels unqualified and uncomfortable when she has to teach a math lesson. Oftentimes, the students can figure out the problem before Lauren is able to, which had never previously happened, and this causes her a lot of embarrassment. The supervisor empathized with her situation and suggested that a psychoeducational evaluation be performed to achieve an accurate assessment of her cognitive strengths and weaknesses. She would also like Lauren to receive recommendations about what subjects and grade levels she is qualified to teach and how to improve on her weaker skill areas.

Background Information

Lauren is married and has two daughters, twenty-five and twenty-three years of age. She currently lives with her husband and works part-time as a substitute teacher. Mr. C. is the vice president of a major corporation and is not at home very often.

In speaking about her educational history, Lauren stated that, in high school, she did not "live up to her full potential" and consequently had to attend a junior college because her grades were not good enough to be directly accepted into a university. Lauren reported that she worked very hard during her first year of junior college. She achieved superior grades and was then able to transfer to a university where she continued to perform well. She received a bachelor's degree in History with a minor in English Literature. She commented to the examiner that she believes this is one of her biggest accomplishments in life.

After she graduated from the university, Lauren was employed as a flight attendant for one of the major airline carriers. She continued in this occupation for ten years and resigned when she married and decided to have children. She stated that she has worked in many different vocational settings over the years including retail sales, secretarial work, and as a teacher in the private school system. She commented that her present employment is extremely satisfying and she has a very good relationship with her colleagues and supervisors. Lauren remarked that she has received complements from school administrators and other teachers that she is "the best" and "a godsend" because she does great work as a substitute teacher and is always willing to go the extra mile to get the job done. Lauren stated that one of the best features of her job is that she gets to choose the days she wishes to work, which gives her the opportunity to enjoy social time with friends and family and ample time to "take care of the household."

Lauren's medical history is relatively unremarkable. She is farsighted and, therefore, requires the use of reading glasses. During a recent physical examination, her physician found her hearing to be excellent and no medical conditions were noted. Lauren has had no major illnesses, injuries, or hospitalizations. She does not use nicotine or illegal drugs. When asked about her pattern of alcohol use, Lauren stated that she enjoys a glass of wine every night with dinner, but never drinks large quantities at a time. She added that her eating habits are a bit erratic and her diet is not balanced enough. She also expressed a concern about not getting enough sleep on a daily basis and that to get a "really good night of sleep," she has to take an over-the-counter sleep aid such as Sominex, but no other medications were noted.

Lauren reported no history of learning problems in her family, but she does have a history of psychological disorders in her family. Her mother suffered from a severe case of menopausally-related depression at the age of 51. She was treated for her disorder and, after fighting the disorder for thirteen years, regained her psychological health. However, after a fifteen-year period of remission, her mother's depression recently resurfaced. She was admitted to a psychiatric hospital just a few weeks ago. Lauren stated that this has been a severe stressor in her life and has dictated her daily activities for the past few weeks. She has been unable to teach on a regular basis, as her mother's condition demands the availability of constant care. She remarked that she feels lucky to have a very strong support system to help her through this tough time. She has a close relationship with her husband and her two daughters, and a good friend who lives next door. Luckily, her other siblings live close by and her father lives with her mother, so they have been able to share the responsibilities of her mother's care.

Lauren stated that she enjoys jogging and working in her garden during her free time. Lauren believes her strengths to be that she is skilled in organizing her time and activities and she is a very caring and giving mother to her two daughters. Lauren stated rather frankly that her weaknesses are her poor self-image and low self-esteem.

Appearance and Behavioral Characteristics

Lauren, a 57-year-old Caucasian female, is of medium height and weight and appears younger than her stated age. Lauren arrived for the evaluation dressed casually in a cotton dress and low-heeled shoes. She was well-groomed and wore subtle makeup on her face.

Lauren was very pleasant and polite throughout the examination. She chatted casually with the examiner at the beginning of the evaluation, but was very attentive and receptive to the intake questions asked of her. She appeared very comfortable in answering all of the background questions and she seemed to want to cooperate by providing a sufficient amount of detail for the examiner to record. Therefore, rapport was very easily established during the intake interview, and a comfortable relationship between Lauren and the examiner continued throughout the testing administration.

Lauren was extremely articulate in her verbal responses, but she appeared to be apprehensive in answering certain verbal questions that were difficult. Her attention remained focused throughout the evaluation. Extreme concentration was evident from her intense facial expressions. Her tension was noticed in her tight grip on the pencil during written tasks and her habit of holding her hand up to her mouth but not engaging in nail-biting behavior. During a task in which she was required to copy a design of a figure with blocks, she burst out in laughter during one of the constructions because she thought it was "so mind-boggling." Though this distracted her from performing well on this particular item, she quickly regained her composure and proceeded to work diligently through the rest of the items.

Certain problem-solving tactics were evident during Lauren's evaluation. She used verbal mediation to talk out the answers to certain tasks. She demonstrated a planning approach in several tasks, and therefore was not impulsive in her responses. She frequently checked her answers on tasks that were more difficult and ambiguous to her. Comments were made about certain subtests such as, "Oh, this is awful," but she still appeared motivated and challenged by the tasks she had stated that she disliked. In fact, Lauren demonstrated a keen interest in performing well on all the subtests. She seemed to be very excited and proud of herself when she knew that she got a difficult question correct, but she also appeared a little discouraged and embarrassed by her failures on certain items. Self-disparaging comments were made such as "Oh, I should have known that one." However, these failures did not seem to affect her performance or motivation on successive tasks.

On the basis of Lauren's above behaviors, the results of this assessment are considered a valid indication of her current level of cognitive and academic functioning.

Tests Administered

(test scores are listed in Table 12.9)

- Kaufman Functional Academic Skills Test (K-FAST)
- Kinetic Family Drawing
- Wechsler Adult Intelligence Scale—Third Edition (WAIS-III)
- Woodcock-Johnson—Third Edition (WJ III): Tests of Achievement-Selected Subtests

Test Results and Interpretation

Lauren was administered the Wechsler Adult Intelligence Scale—Third Edition (WAIS-III), which is an individually administered test of a person's intellectual ability and cognitive strengths and weaknesses. The WAIS-III is comprised of fourteen separate subtests and measures both verbal skills and specific performance abilities including constructing designs with blocks and arranging pictures to tell a story. On the WAIS-III, Lauren earned a Verbal IQ (VIQ) score of 114. This score has a 90% chance of falling in the range of 109 and 118. She earned a Performance IQ (PIQ) score of 100, with a 90% likelihood that her true performance score lies between 94 and 106. Lauren earned a Full-Scale IQ (FS-IQ) of 108, and there is a 90% likelihood that her true Full-Scale IQ lies between the scores of 104 and 111. These scores place her in the Average ability range and the 70th percentile for an individual her age. However, because there was a significant variability between the indexes that comprise her Full-Scale IQ and Performance IQ, both the FS-IQ and P-IQ are rendered meaningless and cannot be interpreted as meaningful representations of Lauren's overall performance. An examination of the components of the test is required.

The Verbal scale of the WAIS-III is made up of two indexes, termed the Verbal Comprehension (VC) Index and the Working Memory (WM) Index. The one-point difference in scaled scores for these indexes (VCI = 112 and WMI = 111), indicates that Lauren performs about equally well on all verbal tasks, regardless of whether they depend on acquired knowledge and verbal expression or the use of working memory to perform operations with numbers.

TABLE 12.9   Psychometric summary of Lauren J.'s test scores

Wechsler Adult Intelligence Scale—Third Edition (WAIS-III)

Scale	IQ	90% Confidence Interval	Percentile Rank
Verbal Scale	114	109–118	82
Performance Scale	100	94–106	50
Full Scale	108	104–111	70

Factor	Index	90% Confidence Interval	Percentile Rank
Verbal Comprehension	112	107–116	79
Perceptual Organization	105	99–111	63
Working Memory	111	105–116	77
Processing Speed	86	80–95	18

Subtest	Scaled Score	Percentile Rank	Subtest	Scaled Score	Percentile Rank
Vocabulary	14–S	91	Picture Completion	11	63
Similarities	11	63	Digit Symbol-Coding	08–W	25
Arithmetic	14–S	91	Block Design	10	50
Digit Span	11	63	Matrix Reasoning	12	75
Information	12	75	Picture Arrangement	10	50
Comprehension	12	75	Symbol Search	07–W	16
Letter-Number Sequencing	11	63	Object Assembly	15-S	95

Kaufman Functional Academic Skills Test (K-FAST)

Scale	Standard Score	90% Confidence Interval	Percentile Rank
Reading	110	104–116	75
Arithmetic	117	109–124	87
Composite	112	106–118	79

Selected Subtests from the Woodcock-Johnson—Third Edition (WJ III): Tests of Achievement

Scale	Standard Score	90% Confidence Interval	Percentile Rank
Mathematics			
Applied Problems	107	101–113	68
Calculation	94	90–98	34
Reading			
Reading Fluency	103	98–108	58
Passage Comprehension	106	100–112	66
Written Language			
Spelling	99	93–105	47

The Performance scale is comprised of two indexes, termed Perceptual Organization (PO) and Processing Speed (PS). A significant difference (19 points) was found between the scaled scores of the PO Index (105) and the PS Index (86). This large discrepancy indicates that Lauren performs better on performance tasks that require nonverbal reasoning than on performance tasks of visual processing speed. Due to this significant difference between the two indexes of the performance scale, the V-IQ versus P-IQ difference cannot be interpreted as a meaningful representation of Lauren's abilities on verbal versus performance tasks. To achieve a better understanding of her assets and deficits, specific comparisons between the indexes of the two scales must be performed.

Lauren performs equally well on verbal conceptualization tasks (79th percentile) and nonverbal reasoning tasks (63rd percentile), as evident from her performance on the Verbal Comprehension Index (112) and Perceptual Organization Index (105). Comparing the Working Memory Index (111) of the Verbal Scale with the Processing Speed Index (86) of the Performance Scale manifests a significant difference of 25 points between these two indexes. This gives support to the idea that Lauren does well (77th percentile) on tasks that require performing various operations with numbers (e.g., computing arithmetic problems, repeating sequences of numbers, and ordering numbers and letters in numerical and alphabetical order). This also supports a hypothesis of a possible deficit in processing speed. She scored in the 18th percentile on the PS Index (comprised of two timed subtests), coding and copying symbols in one task and searching for target symbols in a search group in another task. A possible interpretation for her poor performance on these subtests is that her excessive planning and very methodical and deliberate processing slow her work on certain tasks. She was never impulsive in her answers to any subtest; however, her so-called strength of organization was detrimental to her scores on tasks that required fast performance.

Perhaps the most meaningful representation of Lauren's overall abilities is found through examination of her individual strengths and weaknesses. In terms of her processing style, Lauren evidenced a significant relative strength in holistic, right-brain processing and a relative weakness in her integrated brain functioning. In other words, Lauren's preferred way to process information is using primarily gestaltlike processing, or interpreting information as a whole. This holistic processing approach was evidenced by her superior performance (95th percentile) on a task that required her to assemble puzzle pieces of common objects into an integrated whole and a task that required her to complete a series of incomplete gridded patterns by choosing the correct response from a set of five choices. In contrast, Lauren evidenced a significant relative weakness on tasks that required integrated brain functioning, using both sides of the brain to solve tasks. Integrated brain functioning requires both analytic and sequential processing characteristic of the left hemisphere of the brain, as well as the visual–spatial and nonverbal components of the right hemisphere. Integrated brain functioning examines bits and pieces of the information in a problem, rather than simply looking at the information as a big picture. Lauren's weakness in integrated brain functioning was evidenced by her performance on a task that required her to arrange a set of pictures to create a logical story sequence and a task in which she constructed geometric patterns with blocks. This weakness was further evidenced by her performance on a task (25th percentile) in which she examined a key of hieroglyphiclike symbols paired with numbers and she reproduced the symbols corresponding to the numbers, and a task in which she searched for target symbols in a search group of symbols (16th percentile). Though one viable hypothesis for these low scores is her tendency to apply a holistic processing approach, it is also worth noting that both of these tasks were timed. Her low scaled score on the tasks comprising the Processing Speed Index warrants slow processing speed as a possible hypothesis for her poor performance on the subtests described here.

Lauren also demonstrated a significant relative strength in semantic cognition, the ability to use words and ideas to convey meaning. This ability was evidenced by her performance on subtests in which she gave definitions of words (91st percentile), explained similarities between objects (63rd percentile), and solved arithmetic problems mentally (91st percentile). This was also noted in the description given to the examiner of the components of her Kinetic Family Drawing. In this supplementary test, Lauren was provided with a pencil and paper and asked to draw a picture of her family doing something. She worked on the drawing for five minutes and then was asked to explain the components of her drawing. Lauren presented an elaborate story of her family in which she clearly articulated the behaviors, thoughts, and feelings of all of her family members. Her explanation exhibited her strength in semantic cognition as she used her words and ideas to convey meaning to her drawing.

Lauren demonstrated significant relative strengths in both her acquired knowledge and her fund of information. These abilities were evidenced by her performance on a subtest in which she demonstrated her knowledge of common events, objects, places, and people and a second subtest in which she gave definitions of words. These subtests, as well as her performance on a subtest in which she solved arithmetic problems orally, are also evidence for her strength in long-term memory, as they tapped into her knowledge of information and concepts that Lauren probably learned decades ago. The fact that she is now fifty-seven years old and is able to re-member this information demonstrates her vast fund of acquired knowledge and her impressive long-term memory abilities.

In line with her strengths in semantic cognition, acquired knowledge, and fund of informa-tion, were Lauren's scores on tests of achievement. Lauren was administered selected subtests from the Woodcock-Johnson—Third Edition (WJ-III): Tests of Achievement, which is an indi-vidually administered battery of tests measuring academic achievement. She was administered subtests in the areas of mathematics, reading, and spelling. The WJ III subtests were adminis-tered to Lauren in response to her referral question with the hopes that the results might con-tribute further information about Lauren's strengths and weaknesses in academically related domains, in contrast to the cognitive domains that are assessed by the WAIS-III alone.

Lauren performs better on tasks in which the information is meaningful to her in some way. This concept was demonstrated by her performance on two WJ III subtests. A comparison of Lauren's mathematics Applied Problems standard score (107) and her mathematics Calculation standard score (94) revealed a significant difference (13 points) between these two skill areas. The arithmetic problems that she was asked to solve that were more applicable to daily life and encap-sulated some meaning for her (Applied Problems) were solved with much more success than those that were strictly computations of mathematics with no practical significance (Calculation).

Further evidence for the above skill in solving applied problems as well as strength in ac-quired knowledge was found in Lauren's performance on the Kaufman Functional Academic Skills Test (K-FAST), an individually administered test of achievement given to individuals ranging in age from 15 to 85 years. The K-FAST is not an IQ test, but is, instead, intended to be an achievement-based test that yields a composite score of Functional Academic Skills and subtest scores on Arithmetic and Reading. Lauren performed in the Above Average range on the K-FAST (79th percentile), earning a scaled Functional Academic Skills score of 112. There is a 90% chance that this composite score lies somewhere between 106 and 118. The K-FAST measured how well Lauren could apply her mental ability and past learning to realistic situations that dealt with arithmetic and reading. The majority of items on the K-FAST had practical significance. For example, items on the arithmetic subtest included telling time on a clock, counting numbers of objects, and reading graphs. Lauren chose, initially, not to use the pencil and paper that were offered to her for the Mathematics subtest. She said that she wanted to try to see if she could do the computations in her head. She successfully solved the problems mentally until she reached the last few items that required more complicated arithmetic. This style of problem solving fur-ther supports the hypothesis that she performs better on mathematical applications than on pure computation because analyzing the problem in her head has more "practical" significance for her as a teacher than simply performing the operations of the problem. The reading subtest included items such as describing the meaning of signs and symbols, interpreting recipes, and defining abbreviations. Lauren seemed to enjoy the K-FAST test. Her Above Average performance on this test provides further evidence of her strength in acquired knowledge, long-term memory, and fund of information.

In addition to her strong abilities on school-related tasks, Lauren demonstrated specific relative strengths in both the integration of verbal concepts and the output of verbal expression. These strengths were evidenced by her performance on three WAIS-III verbal subtests that required her to solve arithmetic problems orally, explain the similarities between objects, and articulate social rules and concepts or provide solutions to everyday problems. Articulate verbalization was further noted in her explanation of her Kinetic Family Drawing (previously discussed), and her ease of verbalization with the examiner during the intake interview. Though she evidenced strengths in verbal conceptualization and expression, Lauren demonstrated that her spelling abilities were less well developed. This was noted by her performance (47th percentile) on the Spelling subtest of the WJ III (previously discussed). Familiar words such as *loyalty*, *obedience*, and *prejudice* were misspelled by Lauren. As is true for many adults, her spelling skills may have declined over the years due to the fact that Lauren has been out of school for several years, and usually depends on her computer's spell-check rather than worrying about correcting errors herself. Lauren also commented to the examiner at the beginning of this subtest that she "hates spelling…I always just use a dictionary or my spell-check to spare myself the agony."

In contrast to the strengths described above, Lauren demonstrated significant relative weaknesses in both visual memory and visual sequencing. These weaknesses were noted in a task that required her to pair numbers with their hieroglyphic symbols presented in a key. Her weakness in visual memory was further noted in two tasks: one in which Lauren had to examine pictures of objects and settings and determine important parts that were missing in the picture, and in another in which she examined a group of symbols to determine if it contained one of the symbols present in a target pair. Lauren was not able to quickly retrieve the visual images required to perform well on these tasks. Her visual sequencing weakness was noted in a task in which she had to rearrange sets of mixed-up pictures to create a logical story sequence. Her weaknesses in both visual memory and visual sequencing supports her weakness in sequential processing, which is in contrast to her strong holistic processing style (interpreting visual–spatial relationships as a whole rather than in parts).

Summary and Conclusion

Concerned about her feeling of inadequacy as a substitute teacher for certain subjects and grade levels, Lauren, a 57-year-old female, was referred by her employer for a psychoeducational evaluation to assess her cognitive strengths and weaknesses. Lauren was interested in determining what grade levels and academic subjects she is qualified to substitute for and she wanted specific recommendations to enhance her performance as a teacher.

Lauren's WAIS-III profile contained significant variability among her Indexes, which rendered her Verbal IQ and Full Scale IQ meaningless as a representation of her overall ability, and warrants interpretation of the individual Indexes and her subtest strengths and weaknesses.

As evident from her performance on the Verbal Comprehension Index (112) and Perceptual Organization Index (105), Lauren performs equally well on verbal conceptualization tasks (79th percentile) and nonverbal reasoning tasks (63rd percentile). In addition, Lauren's Verbal Comprehension and Working Memory indexes were almost identical, indicating that she performs equally well on all types of verbal tasks including those dependent on acquired knowledge as well as tasks of performing operations with numbers. The 19-point discrepancy found between her Perceptual Organization Index and her Processing Speed Index indicates that Lauren performs better on performance tasks that require nonverbal reasoning than on performance tasks of visual processing speed. Lauren tended to use a methodical, planning approach in her performance work and, therefore, tended to work slower on the performance tasks.

A significant relative strength was noted in Lauren's holistic processing and a significant relative weakness was found in her integrated brain functioning. Taken together, this means that Lauren tends to process information by predominantly using the right side of her brain and examining information as an integrated whole. Lauren demonstrated a significant relative strength in semantic cognition evidenced by several subtests of the WAIS-III, as well as her explanation of her Kinetic Family Drawing and her higher scores on the mathematics Applied Problems versus Calculation subtest on the WJ-III. Other relative strengths include her level of acquired knowledge, fund of information, and use of long-term memory. These strengths were demonstrated on several of the WAIS-III verbal subtests (describing similarities between objects, defining vocabulary words, and articulating social rules and solutions to problems), as well as her above-average performance on the K-FAST. Lauren also manifested strengths in the integration of verbal concepts and the output of verbal expression exhibited on three WAIS-III subtests, her Kinetic Family Drawing explanation, and her articulate conversation with the examiner. In contrast to these verbal strengths, Lauren was weaker in her spelling ability, indicated by her performance on the Spelling subtest of the WJ III. Other relative weaknesses of Lauren included poor visual memory, visual sequencing, and short-term memory.

Overall, Lauren is an intelligent woman who seems very dedicated to her occupation as a substitute teacher and places importance on performing well. She may be at a slight disadvantage in her job because of her age and the number of years she has been out of school. This may account for some of her relative weaknesses in visual memory, spelling, and processing speed. Her concerns about teaching mathematics were unfounded in this evaluation, but she performs best on mathematics tasks when she can apply the problem in a practical way to her daily life. Lauren is skilled in verbal tasks and has a vast knowledge base. Therefore, it is apparent from this evaluation that she is qualified to substitute teach for a variety of grade levels and subjects. She needs to realistically recognize her weaknesses but also give herself credit for the many strong abilities she possesses.

Recommendations

1. Though Lauren is qualified to teach at a high level in mathematics, to relieve some of her anxiety surrounding this subject she would benefit from being able to examine the specific lesson plan and calculations prior to teaching the concepts to a class. It is recommended that her employer make special arrangements with the schools that Lauren substitutes in to provide her with preparation materials for the mathematics classes that she is asked to teach.

2. Based on Lauren's mathematics scores in this evaluation, she might benefit from employing an application problem-solving approach to difficult mathematics questions that she encounters in the classroom. This means that she should try to apply the arithmetic question to her daily life or a practical situation to make it more meaningful and interesting to her. She may also be able to increase her speed in solving mathematics problems with extra practice on timed tasks in her spare time.

3. Lauren's difficulties with spelling might be remedied by an intensive review of commonly misspelled words. There are several books available that contain spelling exercises to help individuals brush up on their skills in this area. It is recommended that Lauren acquire one of these books and start reviewing the proper spelling of some commonly used words.

4. Lauren might also be able to improve her visual memory by simply attempting to exercise it more in her daily life. For example, instead of writing down a phone number after seeing it in the phone book, she should try to hold it in her short-term memory long enough

to dial the number, and then later try to write down the number on a piece of paper. Successfully using her memory more often may also give her more confidence in her abilities.

5. It is recommended that Lauren consider brief psychotherapy to work on her poor self-image and low self-esteem. She might also benefit from a support group for relatives of family members who have a psychological disorder. Such supportive environments may help her to better cope with her mother's depression and would give her extra social support from other individuals who are dealing with the same issues.

Megan Lucas
Examiner

Elizabeth O. Lichtenberger, Ph.D.
Supervisor

SUMMARY

Chapter 12, the third of three profile interpretation chapters, focuses on the generation of valid hypotheses for explaining significant fluctuations in WAIS-III subtest profiles. As described throughout Steps 8 and 9 of our interpretive approach, the raw ingredients for this combined rational and empirical endeavor are the abilities measured by two or more subtests and the influences that affect performance on several tasks. For convenience, these "shared" abilities and influences are organized into a table and worksheets that constitute the raw materials for hypothesis generation. The reliability of these clusters appears in the table.

The following basic rules for examiners apply for the generation of hypotheses: (1) work like a detective, regrouping tasks in different ways; (2) group as many tasks as possible together when forming hypotheses; (3) avoid subtest-specific hypotheses, if possible; (4) identify the specific aspect of a task that is strong or weak; (5) recognize that finding significant profile fluctuations is the starting point, not the goal, of interpretation; (6) aggregate tasks when forming hypotheses rather than pitting one subtest against another; (7) cross-validate hypotheses with data from other tests, background information, and clinical observations of behavior; (8) apply interpretive rules as guidelines, but use clinical inferences liberally.

Two methods of hypothesis generation are offered, one sequential and one simultaneous. The sequential, step-by-step approach begins with Steps 1–7 in Chapter 11 and continues with Steps 8 and 9 in this chapter. The simultaneous method affords examiners with a holistic processing orientation the chance to develop hypotheses by observing various configurations within the subtest profile. After detecting meaningful configurations, simple empirical checks are advised to ensure that the apparent differences in skill areas are real. A discussion of common configurations to anticipate within the Verbal scale, within the Performance scale, and across both scales is presented.

Common Verbal configurations include Working Memory versus Verbal Comprehension, memory versus conceptualization, the amount of verbal expression required, and fluid versus crystallized intelligence. The subtests requiring much verbal expression are also the ones demanding good conceptualization skills. Some groups, such as autistic individuals, characteristically do not perform well on these tasks; good clinical skills are needed to infer the reason for a person's high or low scores on the pertinent subtests.

Common Performance scale configurations are: (1) visual organization versus visual–motor coordination, (2) meaningful versus abstract stimuli,

(3) simultaneous versus sequential processing, and (4) visual memory versus nonverbal thinking. Picture Arrangement and Digit Symbol, along with the spatial–simultaneous tasks, permit WAIS-III interpretation from the vantage point of Luria's Blocks 1, 2, and 3. Block Design, though primarily a simultaneous task, is quite complex and has important analytic components as well.

Two configurations that comprise both the Verbal and Performance scales are Social Comprehension versus Abstract Thought and Fund of Information versus Visual–Spatial and Nonverbal Problem Solving.

WAIS-III INTERPRETIVE WORKSHEET

Client Name _____

Age _____

Date _____

STEP 1: Interpret the Full Scale IQ

Scale	IQ	Confidence Interval 90%/95% (circle one)	Percentile Rank	Descriptive Category
Verbal				
Performance				
Full Scale				

NOTE: If there **IS** a **significant difference** between the component parts of the FS-IQ (i.e., V-IQ & P-IQ or VCI & POI), the FS-IQ should **not** be interpreted as a meaningful representation of the individual's **overall** performance.

STEP 2: Are the V-IQ versus P-IQ or VCI versus POI Significantly Different?

V-IQ	P-IQ	Difference	Significant ($p < .01$)	Significant ($p < .05$)	Not Significant	Is there a significant difference?	
			12 or more	9–11	0–8	**YES**	**NO**

VCI	POI	Difference	Significant ($p < .01$)	Significant ($p < .05$)	Not Significant	Is there a significant difference?	
			13 or more	10–12	0–9	**YES**	**NO**

STEP 2 Decision Box

If the answers are both **NO**, there are not significant differences between EITHER the V-IQ and P-IQ or the VCI and POI	→	First explain the meaning of the scales not being significantly different. Then you may **Skip to Step 6.**
If either answer is **YES**, there is a significant difference between either the V-IQ and P-IQ **or** between VCI and POI	→	Continue on to **Step 3.**

STEP 3: Are the V-IQ versus P-IQ or VCI versus POI Differences Abnormally Large?

V-IQ versus P-IQ Difference	Size of difference needed for abnormality	Does size meet abnormality criteria? (circle one)	
	17	YES	NO

VCI versus POI Difference	Size of difference needed for abnormality	Does size meet abnormality criteria? (circle one)	
	19	YES	NO

NOTE: Exact point values according to ability level are available in Technical Manual Appendix D (Wechsler, 1997, pp. 300–309).

STEP 3 Decision Box

If **ANY abnormal** differences are found	→	then this **abnormally** large discrepancy should be interpreted	→	Explain the **abnormally** large Verbal and Performance differences. Then you may **Skip to Step 6.**
If **NO abnormal** differences are found	→	then you must determine if the noted differences are interpretable	→	Go on to Step 4.

STEP 4: Is V-IQ versus P-IQ Discrepancy Interpretable?

VERBAL SCALE
A. Is there a significant difference between VCI and WMI?

VCI	WMI	Difference	Significant (p < .01)	Significant (p < .05)	Not Significant	Is there a significant difference?	
			13 or more	10–12	0–9	YES	NO

B. Is there abnormal verbal scatter?

High Scaled Score of 6 V-IQ Subtests	Low Scaled Score of 6 V-IQ Subtests	High–Low Difference	Abnormal Scatter	Not Abnormal	Is there abnormal scatter?	
			8 or more	0–7	YES	NO

PERFORMANCE SCALE
C. Is there a significant difference between POI and PSI?

POI	PSI	Difference	Significant (p < .01)	Significant (p < .05)	Not Significant	Is there a significant difference?	
			17 or more	13–16	0–12	YES	NO

D. Is there abnormal Performance scatter?

High Scaled Score of 5 P-IQ Subtests	Low Scaled Score of 5 P-IQ Subtests	High–Low Difference	Abnormal Scatter	Not Abnormal	Is there abnormal scatter?	
			8 or more	0–7	YES	NO

STEP 4 Decision Box

If ALL STEP 4 questions A, B, C, and D are **NO**	→ then V-IQ **versus** P-IQ discrepancy is interpretable	→ Explain the meaningful difference between V-IQ and P-IQ. **Then skip to STEP 6.**
If 1 or more questions in STEP 4 is **YES**	→ then the V-IQ **versus** P-IQ difference should probably **not** be interpreted	→ Examine VCI **versus** POI discrepancy in **STEP 5.**

STEP 5: Is VCI versus POI Difference Interpretable?

A. Is there significant scatter in VCI subtests?

High Scaled Score of 3 VCI Subtests	Low Scaled Score of 3 VCI Subtests	High–Low Scaled Score Difference	Abnormal Scatter	Not Abnormal	Is there abnormal scatter?	
			5 or more	0–4	**YES**	**NO**

B. Is there significant scatter in POI subtests?

High Scaled Score of 3 POI Subtests	Low Scaled Score of 3 POI Subtests	High–Low Scaled Score Difference	Abnormal Scatter	Not Abnormal	Is there abnormal scatter?	
			6 or more	0–5	**YES**	**NO**

STEP 5 Decision Box

If STEP 5 questions A and B are **NO**	→ then VCI **versus** POI discrepancy is interpretable	→ Explain the meaningful difference between VCI and POI.
If answer to either A or B is **YES**	→ then the VCI **versus** POI discrepancy should probably **not** be interpreted	→ Do not interpret VCI versus POI difference.*

*The verbal and nonverbal constructs are not interpretable if you reach this point.

STEP 6: Determine whether the Working Memory and Processing Speed Indexes Are Interpretable
A. Is WMI factor interpretable?

Arithmetic	Digit Span	Letter-Number Sequencing	Difference between High and Low Scaled Score	Abnormal Scatter	Not Abnormal
				6 or more *(don't interpret)*	0–5 *(ok to interpret)*

B. Is PSI factor interpretable?

Symbol Search	Digit Symbol-Coding	Difference between High and Low Scaled Score	Abnormal Scatter	Not Abnormal
			4 or more *(don't interpret)*	0–3 *(ok to interpret)*

Step 7: Interpret the Global Verbal and Nonverbal Dimensions, as well as the Small Factors, if they were found to be Interpretable

For interpretive suggestions of these dimensions, study the information and procedures presented in Chapter 11

STEP 8: Interpret Significant Strengths and Weaknesses of Profile

1. Determine which mean you should use to calculate strengths and weaknesses:

V-IQ–P-IQ discrepancy			(After calculating means, round to the nearest whole number)

0–16 →	Then use →	Mean of all subtests → administered	**Overall Mean**	**Rounded Mean**

17 or more →	Then use →	Verbal Scale Mean →	**V-IQ Mean**	**Rounded Mean**
		and also use		
		Performance Scale Mean →	**P-IQ Mean**	**Rounded Mean**

Verbal Subtest	Scaled Score	Rounded Mean	Difference*	Difference Needed for Significance	Strength or Weakness (S or W)	Percentile Rank
Vocabulary				±2		
Similarities				±3		
Arithmetic				±3		
Digit Span				±3		
Information				±3		
Comprehension				±3		
Letter-Number Sequencing				±4		
Performance Subtest						
Picture Completion				±4		
Digit Symbol–Coding				±3		
Block Design				±3		

Verbal Subtest	Scaled Score	Rounded Mean	Difference*	Difference Needed for Significance	Strength or Weakness (S or W)	Percentile Rank
Matrix Reasoning				±3		
Picture Arrangement				±4		
Symbol Search				±4		
Object Assembly				±4		

*Use appropriate **rounded mean** in calculating the "Scaled score–mean" difference.

STEP 9: Generating Hypotheses about the Fluctuations in the WAIS-III Profile

Review the information presented in Chapter 12 that details how to reorganize subtest profiles to systematically generate hypotheses about strengths and weaknesses. Examiner Forms 12.1 through 12.14 present an organized system for creating hypothetical strong or weak abilities based on the findings in Step 8.

Supplemental Table for Converting Scaled Scores to Percentile Ranks
for WAIS-III Interpretive Worksheet

Percentile Rank	Scaled Score	Percentile Rank	Scaled Score
99.9	19	37	9
99.6	18	25	8
99	17	16	7
98	16	9	6
95	15	5	5
91	14	2	4
84	13	1	3
75	12	0.4	2
63	11	0.1	1
50	10		

19-16 VS
15-14 S
13-12 HA
11-9 A
8-7 LA
6-5 B
4-1 EL

CHAPTER 13

Kaufman Adolescent and Adult Intelligence Test (KAIT)

KAIT THEORY

Alan and Nadeen Kaufman focused on several goals during the development of the Kaufman Adolescent and Adult Intelligence Test (KAIT).[1] The Kaufmans wanted to construct a test battery based on intellectual theory that would account for developmental changes in intelligence, and also wanted their test to provide important clinical and neuropsychological information for those tested with the instrument (Kaufman & Kaufman, 1993).

Three cognitive and neuropsychological theories provide the foundation for the KAIT: (1) Horn and Cattell's (1966, 1967) theory of fluid (*Gf*) and crystallized (*Gc*) intelligence; (2) Luria's (1966, 1980) definition of planning ability; and (3) the formal operational stage of

development in Piaget's (1972) theory. Because these theories are described in detail elsewhere in this book, we summarize them here and indicate their relevance to the KAIT.

Horn-Cattell Theory in the KAIT

The Horn-Cattell theory is the foundation for organizing and interpreting the KAIT subtests. The theory used in the KAIT is the original formulation of the fluid–crystallized distinction, referred to as the *Gf–Gc* theory (Horn & Cattell, 1966). Recall that fluid ability measures one's adaptability and flexibility when solving new problems, using both verbal and nonverbal stimuli, whereas crystallized ability measures acquired concepts, facts, and problem-solving ability using stimuli that are dependent on schooling, acculturation, and verbal conceptual development for success. The KAIT scales were designed to measure broader, more general versions of *Gf* and *Gc*

[1]The authors would like to thank Debra Y. Broadbooks, Ph.D. for her contribution to this chapter.

than Horn's extended ability model, which divides cognitive abilities into nine discrete abilities (Horn, 1989; Horn & Hofer, 1992). Kaufman and Kaufman believed that assessing the broader *Gf–Gc* abilities would enhance the value of the KAIT as a clinical measure of adolescent and adult problem-solving ability. They contended that assessing each ability distinctly in its purest form (as is done in Horn's extended model) would serve to decrease the practical utility of the test by making the tasks less relevant to problems encountered in real life (Kaufman & Kaufman, 1997). Furthermore, they adhered to David Wechsler's deep-seated belief that the best way to develop a clinically rich instrument is to offer complex measurement of a few broad constructs rather than many narrow constructs (Kaufman, 2000). Wechsler asserted that too much fragmentation of constructs led to narrow abilities that are not optimally suited for assessing human intelligence. Because Wechsler was Alan Kaufman's primary mentor (Alan worked closely with him in the 1970s during the development and standardization of the WISC-R), Wechsler's approach influenced the decision to use the broad *Gf–Gc* constructs. However, Alan and Nadeen's deep interest in theory also led to the choice of how to organize the scales. Their research interests in aging and IQ across the life span indicated that *Gf–Gc* theory was the most pertinent theory for explaining observed patterns of growth and decline across the age span covered by the KAIT. As detailed in Chapter 5 of this book, a large body of research indicates that *Gc* abilities are mostly maintained throughout the adult life span whereas *Gf* abilities peak in the late teens and early 20s before declining steadily throughout the aging process (Kaufman, 1990, Chapter 7; Kaufman & Horn, 1996).

The Theories of Luria and Piaget in the KAIT

Both Luria's (1980) definition of planning ability and Piaget's (1972) stage of formal operations

also helped to guide the development of the KAIT. Certain developmental changes in the brain that emerge at the ages of 11 or 12 are associated with Luria's (1973, 1980) notion of planning ability (Block 3). Similarly, Piaget's formal operational stage also begins to emerge at ages 11 or 12. Furthermore, Luria's definition of planning ability involves decision making, evaluation of hypotheses, and flexibility in problem solving, which is quite similar to Piaget's concept of formal operations. Piaget conceptualized the stage of formal operations as hypothetico–deductive reasoning, or having the ability to use abstractions and solve novel problems using higher-level reasoning. Thus, Kaufman and Kaufman decided that their adolescent and adult test should assess intelligence in individuals beginning at age 11, as this is a theoretically meaningful age distinction, given the developmental changes occurring during this period. Likewise, from a neuropsychological perspective, ages 11–12 are meaningful because they coincide with the maturation of the tertiary areas of the prefrontal cortex, structures believed to be intimately associated with Luria's concept of planning ability. Because the Kaufmans used the Piaget and Luria theories as "entry-level" requirements for a task's inclusion in the KAIT, that further ensured that the KAIT would meet its goal of measuring broad, complex constructs; even the Crystallized subtests deliberately measure some reasoning ability in order to be advanced enough to measure formal operations and planning ability (Kaufman, 2000).

COMPOSITION OF THE KAIT

The KAIT is a standardized measure of old (crystallized) and new (fluid) learning for individuals ages 11 to over 85. The combination of these two types of abilities may be considered general intelligence. As shown in Figure 13.1, the KAIT is organized into a Core Battery and an Extended Battery. The Core Battery is comprised

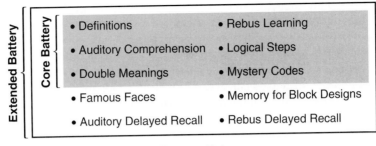

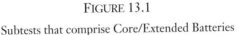

FIGURE 13.1

Subtests that comprise Core/Extended Batteries

of two scales: Fluid and Crystallized, which contain three subtests each. The Extended Battery is comprised of 10 subtests. It includes the Fluid and Crystallized scales mentioned above, two additional subtests (one Fluid and one Crystallized), and two delayed recall subtests. The delayed recall subtests allow for a comparison of performance on Immediate and Delayed Recall tasks. Furthermore, the inclusion of delayed recall tasks—which are administered without prior warning about 25 and 45 minutes after the administration of the original, related subtests—expands the Horn (1989) abilities measured by the KAIT whenever the Expanded Battery is given. In addition to the broad *Gf* and *Gc* abilities measured by the IQ scales, the delayed recall subtests offer reasonably pure measurement of an ability that Horn (1985, 1989) calls TSR (Long-Term Storage and Retrieval). This long-term memory ability, labeled *Glr* in the Woodcock-Johnson—Revised (WJ-R), "involves the storage of information and the fluency of retrieving it later through association" (Woodcock, 1990, p. 234). The KAIT also includes a supplemental Mental Status exam, a standardized, normed test that is utilized for people with neurological impairment. Although the mental status exam is not included in the composite scores with the other KAIT subtests, it may provide important neuropsychological information.

OTHER TESTS AND THE KAIT

KAIT and the Wechsler Scales

In developing the KAIT, the Kaufmans wanted their test's Fluid Scale to measure planning ability and problem solving based on higher-level reasoning rather than broad visualization. Although Wechsler's Performance Scale has often been considered a measure of fluid ability, Horn noted that the Performance IQ emphasizes visualization (Horn & Hofer, 1992) and Woodcock (1990) demonstrated that the Performance IQ measures broad visualization (*Gv*), not simply fluid intelligence. To determine the overlap between the KAIT and the Wechsler scales in adolescents and adults, Kaufman and Kaufman (1993) conducted joint factor analyses of the KAIT with WAIS-R. Table 13.1 summarizes the three factors characterizing the joint analysis of the KAIT and WAIS-R data. Overlap between the two scales occurs for the Crystallized/Verbal factor, as is shown in the figure. However, a crucial finding is that the KAIT Fluid scale measures a markedly different construct than the Wechsler Performance scale. In fact, the Fluid and Perceptual Organization factors correlate about as highly with each other as they do with the Crystallized/Verbal factor.

TABLE 13.1   Highest loading KAIT and WAIS-R subtests in the joint factor analysis

Crystallized/Verbal	Perceptual Organization	Fluid
Vocabulary	Object Assembly	Memory for Block Designs[a]
Information	Block Design	Rebus Learning[a]
Comprehension	Digit Symbol	Logical Steps[a]
Famous Faces[a]	Picture Arrangement	Mystery Codes[a]
Auditory Comprehension[a]	Picture Completion	Double Meanings[a]
Definitions[a]		
Similarities		
Double Meanings[a]		
Arithmetic		

[a]KAIT subtest. From *Kaufman Adolescent and Adult Intelligence Test Manual* (p. 93), by A. S. Kaufman and N. L. Kaufman, 1993, Circle Pines, MN: American Guidance Service. Copyright 1993 American Guidance Service.
NOTE: $N = 338$. Subtests are listed in the order of their loading.

KAIT and WJ III

The Horn-Cattell (Horn, 1991) model has been used as a theoretical framework for the revised edition and third edition of the Woodcock-Johnson Tests of Cognitive Ability (WJ-R; Woodcock & Johnson, 1989; WJ III; Woodcock, McGrew, & Mather, 2000), in addition to the KAIT (see Chapter 14). McGrew (1997) applied the broad abilities of the expanded Horn-Cattell model to both the KAIT and WJ-R. In Table 13.2, we adapted McGrew's classification of the subtests to include the new WJ III subtests. McGrew reported that his classification of the KAIT's subtests in this framework is based on Flanagan and McGrew's (1998) confirmatory factor study.

The WJ III was designed to measure a wide array of the broad cognitive abilities. Thus, in addition to the fluid, crystallized, long-term memory, and short-term memory abilities into which McGrew (1997) classifies the KAIT subtests, the WJ III also has subtests classified in visual–spatial thinking, auditory processing, and processing speed. Future joint confirmatory factor analysis will provide more definitive information about the relationships between the subtests of the KAIT and the WJ III (see Chapter 14).

TYPES OF SCORES ON THE KAIT

There are several types of scores that are yielded from the KAIT, including raw scores, scaled scores, and IQs. Raw scores are not norm-referenced, and are, therefore, not interpretable. Thus, it is necessary to transform the raw scores into some kind of standard scores (in this case either scaled scores or IQs). Scaled scores are the standard scores for each subtest; they have a mean of 10 and a standard deviation of 3. IQs are obtained by adding the scaled scores and transforming them into a standard score for each IQ scale (Fluid, Crystallized, Composite). The IQs have a mean of 100 and standard deviation of 15.

KAIT's STANDARDIZATION AND PSYCHOMETRIC PROPERTIES

The KAIT's standardization sample was composed of 2,000 adolescents and adults, selected

TABLE 13.2   KAIT and WJ III in Horn's expanded model

Broad Cognitive Factor	WJ-III Subtest	KAIT Subtest
Comprehension Knowledge (*Gc*)	Verbal Comprehension General Information	Definitions Auditory Comprehension Double Meanings Famous Faces Auditory Delayed Recall
Long-Term Retrieval (*Glr*)	Visual–Auditory Learning Retrieval Fluency Visual–Auditory Delayed	Auditory Delayed Recall Rebus Learning Delayed Recall Rebus Learning
Visual–Spatial Thinking (*Gv*)	Spatial Relations Picture Recognition Planning (*Gv/Gf*)	
Auditory Processing (*Ga*)	Sound Blending Auditory Attention Incomplete Words	
Fluid Reasoning (*Gf*)	Concept Formation Analysis–Synthesis	Logical Steps Mystery Codes
Processing Speed (*Gs*)	Visual Matching Decision Speed Rapid Picture Naming Pair Cancellation	
Short-Term Memory (*Gsm*)	Numbers Reversed Memory for Words Auditory Working Memory	Auditory Comprehension Memory for Block Designs

NOTE: WJ-III subtest groupings are based on Woodcock, McGrew, & Mather's (2000) classifications, and KAIT subtest groupings are based on McGrew's (1997) classifications.

according to 1988 U.S. Census data. The sample was stratified on the variables of gender, race/ethnic group, geographic region, and socioeconomic status (educational attainment). The large sample was divided into fourteen age groups with 100 to 250 subjects in each age group between the ages of 11 and 85+. The mean split-half reliability coefficients for the IQs for the total normative sample were strong, ranging from .95 for both Crystallized IQ and Fluid IQ to .97 for Composite IQ (see Table 13.3 for split-half and test-retest reliability coefficients for all subtests). Mean split-half reliabilities for individ-

ual subtests ranged from .79 for Memory for Block Designs to .93 for Rebus Learning; median values were .90 for the four Crystallized subtests and .88 for the four Fluid subtests. Test-retest data were based on a subset of the standardization sample (*N* = 153) in three age groups (11–19, 20–54, 55–85+) who were retested after a 1-month interval; mean test-retest reliability coefficients were .94 for Crystallized IQ, .87 for Fluid IQ, and .94 for Composite IQ. Median test-retest reliabilities for the eight subtests ranged from .72 on Mystery Codes to .95 on Definitions (median = .78).

TABLE 13.3   KAIT split-half and test-retest reliability

KAIT Subtest or IQ Scale	Split-Half Reliability	Test-Retest Reliability[a]
Definitions	.90	.95
Auditory Comprehension	.89	.77
Double Meanings	.89	.79
Famous Faces	.92	.84
Rebus Learning	.93	.81
Logical Steps	.90	.76
Mystery Codes	.87	.72
Memory for Block Designs	.79	.73
Rebus Delayed Recall	.91	.80
Auditory Delayed Recall	.71	.63
Crystallized	.95	.94
Fluid	.95	.87
Composite Intelligence	.97	.94

[a]These reliability coefficients were corrected for the variability of the norm group, based on the standard deviation obtained on the first testing, using Guilford's (1954, p. 392) formula.

NOTE: The data are from *Kaufman Adolescent and Adult Intelligence Test Manual* (pp. 80–81), by A. S. Kaufman and N. L. Kaufman, 1993, Circle Pines, MN: American Guidance Service.

KAIT INTERPRETATION

Like the approach we present for WAIS-III interpretation, the step-by-step approach outlined here provides the reader with a systematic way to make sense of the multiple scores obtained from the KAIT. This approach examines the most global scores first (Composite Intelligence scale), then explores more specific subtest scores, as well as detailed aspects of the test (strengths and weaknesses; memory comparisons).

To illustrate our step-by-step approach to KAIT interpretation, we will be discussing the case of Dafne M. throughout this section of the chapter. Dafne is a 51-year-old woman who was referred for an assessment for vocational guidance and symptoms of depression. Dafne revealed in an interview to collect her background history that she is married and has two grown children. Until the age of 45, she was a full-time housewife and mother. However, when her last child graduated from high school, Dafne obtained employment in the field of real estate sales. Thus, although she only completed 10 years of formal schooling, Dafne has worked in real estate for 6 years. Her employment career has been somewhat unstable, as she was recently fired from her second job in nine months. Her husband is in the Navy, and Dafne reported that she is "self-sufficent" when he is away. During the testing session itself, Dafne appeared to be attentive, reflective, mildly anxious, and lethargic. Her KAIT profile follows (see Table 13.4).

Step 1: Interpret the KAIT Composite IQ

The Composite IQ is the most global and reliable measure of the KAIT. Beginning interpretation with the most reliable score of a test is a very sensible approach. After scoring the KAIT, including completing the bottom of the front page of the Individual Test Record form, which contains confidence intervals, the percentile ranks, and the descriptive categories, you can begin interpretation. Often, the percentile ranks and descriptive categories are more helpful and more descriptive to clients and other professionals for communicating the meaning of the IQ. In Dafne's case her Composite IQ of 112 is where we would begin the process of profile interpretation. This level of overall performance on the KAIT falls within the 108 to 116 confidence interval, which signifies performance in the Average to Above Average Range. Her Composite IQ is in the 78th percentile, indicating that she scores at or above 78 percent of adults her age.

TABLE 13.4   Dafne M.'s KAIT profile

Composites	Standard Score	90% Confidence Interval	Percentile Rank
Fluid Scale	132	126–136	98
Crystallized Scale	93	88–98	31
Composite	112	108–116	78

Fluid Subtests	Scaled Scores	Percentile Rank	Crystallized Subtests	Scaled Scores	Percentile Rank
Rebus Learning	14	91	Definitions	6	9
Logical Steps	17	99	Auditory Comprehension	9	37
Mystery Codes	16	98	Double Meanings	11	63
Memory for Block Designs	10	50	Famous Faces	7	16
Rebus Delayed Recall	11	63	Auditory Delayed Recall	5	5

Although the Composite IQ is the most global and reliable measure, it is not always the most meaningful estimate of the individual's cognitive functioning. For instance, if there is significant variability in the various subtests or scales that make up the Composite IQ, the global Composite IQ would simply be a measure of discrepant abilities rather than of the individual's overall intellectual abilities. Continuing through the interpretive steps will help you determine if the Composite IQ is meaningful, and generate hypotheses for a person's specific profile.

Step 2: Examine the KAIT Crystallized IQ versus the Fluid IQ

A combination of the Crystallized and Fluid IQs produces the Composite IQ. Thus, to help determine if the Composite IQ is meaningful, the difference between the Crystallized IQ versus the Fluid IQ must be examined. The chart on the KAIT record form can be used to determine whether the IQs are discrepant enough to be

considered significantly different. An 11-point discrepancy is needed for significance (.05 level) for individuals age 14 or younger; the point value is less as individuals become older.

If the Crystallized IQ–Fluid IQ difference is not statistically significant, then the difference is considered due to chance, and the individual's crystallized and fluid abilities should be viewed as equivalent. However, if the difference is statistically significant, then there is likely a real difference between the individual's ability to solve problems that are dependent on school learning or acculturation (crystallized intelligence) and his or her ability to solve novel problems requiring reasoning (fluid intelligence). However, the presence of a significant difference between the Crystallized and Fluid IQs may not translate into a *clinically* important finding.

In the case of Dafne, there was a Fluid–Crystallized discrepancy of 39 points. With her Fluid IQ of 132 and her Crystallized IQ of 93, the large significant discrepancy indicates that there is a real difference between her ability to solve novel problems requiring reasoning and her ability to solve problems that are dependent on school learning. Such a discrepancy indicates that Dafne's Composite IQ is not a meaningful representation of her global cognitive abilities.

Step 3: Is the KAIT Crystallized IQ versus Fluid IQ Difference Abnormal?

Although a significant Crystallized IQ versus Fluid IQ discrepancy indicates that there are meaningful differences in a person's abilities, merely having a difference in one's abilities is not uncommon. In fact, the average Crystallized–Fluid IQ discrepancy in the standardization sample was approximately 9 points. Thus, average people demonstrate a statistically significant difference in their abilities. The rarity or unusualness of a discrepancy indicates whether or not it is *clinically* meaningful.

The frequency with which a discrepancy occurs in the normal population can be found in Table 5.3 of the *KAIT Administration and Scoring Manual* (Kaufman & Kaufman, 1993, p. 49). As a general guideline, the value needed for an abnormal Crystallized IQ–Fluid IQ discrepancy is 16 points. Table 13.5 shows the size of discrepancy needed to be considered abnormally large at each age level. This defines *abnormal* as occurring in the extreme 15% of the normal population

TABLE 13.5 Size of Fluid–Crystallized IQ discrepancy needed for abnormality

Age	*Percentage*				
	15	10	5	2	1
11–14	16	19	23	28	33
15–19	16	18	22	28	32
20–34	17	19	22	26	31
35–54	17	20	24	29	33
55–69	16	19	24	28	33
70–85+	16	18	22	28	30

tion (15% corresponds to one standard deviation from the mean). Thus, if the individual has a discrepancy of at least 16 points, not only is this difference statistically significant, it is also uncommon, in that it occurs in less than 15% of the normal population.

Even by just eyeballing Dafne's 39-point Fluid–Crystallized IQ discrepancy, without checking the discrepancy chart, you might have guessed that it was abnormally large. In fact, a discrepancy the magnitude of Dafne's occurs in less than 1% of the U.S. population. Given its rarity, we can clearly assume that the discrepancy in her profile is clinically meaningful. Exploring the rest of the profile and supplemental tests will help to determine why such a discrepancy occurred.

Step 4: Determine if the Crystallized and Fluid IQs Are Interpretable

In order to interpret the Crystallized and Fluid scales in a meaningful way, each of the scales must be measuring a single construct. That is, merely because the scale is called the Crystallized Scale does not necessarily indicate that it is a good assessment of each individual's crystallized abilities. One way to determine if the Crystallized and Fluid scales are interpretable is to examine the amount of scatter among the subtests comprising either the Crystallized or Fluid scale. Scatter is calculated by taking the difference between the individual's highest and lowest subtest scaled scores on a particular IQ scale.

The amount of intrascale scatter within the normal population is used to determine whether an examinee's range of scaled scores is abnormally large, and, therefore, clinically meaningful. Using the occurrence rate in the extreme 15% of the normal population, the following point values may be used as a guideline: If the individual was administered the Core Battery (six subtests), a difference of 5 points between the highest and lowest scaled scores of the three Crystallized IQ subtests is needed to be considered abnormal, whereas a difference of 6 points is needed to be considered abnormal among the three Fluid IQ subtests. If the Expanded Battery was administered (eight subtests, this does not include the delayed recall subtests), the difference is 6 and 7 points among the four Crystallized IQ and four Fluid IQ scales, respectively (see Table 13.6). A more thorough examination of the frequency differences between highest and lowest scaled scores can be found in Table 5.4 of the *KAIT Administration and Scoring Manual* (Kaufman & Kaufman, 1993, p. 50).

The scatter within Dafne's profile was examined to determine whether it was abnormally large. The subtest scaled scores on the Crystallized scale ranged from 6 to 11, indicating a 5-point scatter. Because a 6-point range is necessary to be considered abnormal for the four Crystallized subtests from the Expanded Battery, we can interpret the Crystallized scale as a meaningful entity. On the other hand, the Fluid Scale subtests range from 10 to 17, with a scatter of 7 points. This amount of variability is sufficient to be considered abnormal scatter for the four Fluid subtests from the Expanded Battery. Therefore, the Fluid scale is rendered a meaningless estimate of Dafne's Fluid abilitlies. Likewise, the 11-point scatter on the KAIT Composite IQ indicates that this IQ is not interpretable (which we had already deduced based on the unusually large discrepancy between the Fluid and Crystallized IQs).

If significant scatter is found in the Crystallized Scale, then neither the Crystallized Scale nor the Crystallized–Fluid difference is interpretable. Likewise, if significant scatter is found in the Fluid Scale, then neither the Fluid Scale nor the Crystallized–Fluid difference is interpretable. The presence of significant variability among the subtests that comprise the larger scale (Fluid, Crystallized) indicates that the subtests are measuring discrepant abilities rather than a unitary skill or construct. However, if there is an abnormally large difference between the Fluid IQ and Crystallized IQ (see Table 13.4), then the Fluid–Crystallized IQ discrepancy may be interpreted regardless of existing scatter within the Fluid or Crystallized scales anyway because the difference is too large to ignore and likely suggests a clinically meaningful distinction in the person's abilities in those two areas.

Step 5: Interpret the Meaning of the Crystallized and Fluid Scales

If there is not significant scatter or variability among the subtests that comprise each scale (Steps 3 & 4), then the scales are likely measuring a unitary ability. Thus, the examiner should articulate what these scales mean and if there is a significant difference between them. For example, in the case of an examinee who has performed significantly better on the Fluid Scale than on the Crystallized Scale (without significant scatter within either scale), you should ex-

TABLE 13.6   Summary of size of subtest scatter necessary for abnormality

Core Battery (Number of Subtests)			Expanded Battery (Number of Subtests)		
Crystallized (3)	Fluid (3)	Composite (6)	Crystallized (4)	Fluid (4)	Composite (8)
5	6	8	6	7	9

NOTE: The values for scatter were taken from Table 5.4 of the *KAIT Administration and Scoring Manual* (p. 50) and indicate differences between highest and lowest subtest scaled scores that occurred in only 15 percent of the standardization sample.

plain that the examinee does significantly better in solving novel problems than in solving problems dependent on schooling and acculturation. On the other hand, if there is significant scatter within one or both of the scales, you should indicate that the particular scale or scales are not interpretable due to the variability within the scale. However, there is an exception to the rule of scatter indicating that a scale is not interpretable. As mentioned previously, if an abnormally large discrepancy exists between the Fluid and Crystallized Scales (as in Dafne's case), you may interpret the discrepancy between the scales because such an abnormally large difference is likely *clinically* meaningful, regardless of the presence of significant variability among the subtests in either one of the scales.

Step 6: Interpret KAIT Strengths and Weaknesses

To gain a more thorough understanding of an individual's abilities, it is helpful to look at the strengths and weaknesses within the profile. Many adolescents and adults show variability within their subtest profile, so it is important to determine whether the variability within the profile is statistically significant. This process involves calculating statistically significant strengths and weaknesses within the subtest scaled scores.

There are typically two modes of determining strengths and weaknesses: comparing a person's scores to those of the normative population, and comparing them to the individual's own mean score (an ipsative comparison). The calculations used as part of the profile analysis, which is completed on the backside of the Individual Record Form, produce ipsative strengths and weaknesses. That is, the strengths and weaknesses found deviate from the person's own average performance. Before computing the strengths and weaknesses portion of the profile analysis, you must first transfer the individual subtest scaled scores to their corresponding space in the

Subtests section. (You may also want to graph the scores on the Subtest Scaled-Score Profile at this time). Also transfer the examinee's IQs, including their confidence intervals, and graph them under the IQ Profile. (See page 45 of the *KAIT Administration and Scoring Manual* for an example of a profile analysis page.) Next, determine which mean scaled score to use for calculating strengths and weaknesses. If there is no significant difference between the Crystallized and Fluid IQs, use the mean score for the Composite Intelligence Scale. If there is a significant difference between the Crystallized and Fluid IQs, use the separate mean scaled scores for the Crystallized Scale and Fluid Scale, respectively (see Figure 7.2 for determining significant differences). After determining which mean scaled score to use, transfer the appropriate score(s) to the back page of the record form.

To determine strengths and weaknesses, calculate the difference between each subtest scaled score and the appropriate mean scaled score. Remember, the appropriate mean scaled score is determined by the discrepancy between the Crystallized and Fluid IQs. If there is not a significant discrepancy between the Crystallized–Fluid IQs, the difference between each subtest scaled score and the mean scaled score for the Composite Scale would be calculated. If there is a significant Crystallized–Fluid IQ discrepancy, the difference between each Crystallized subtest scaled score and the mean scaled score for the Crystallized Scale would be calculated; the difference between each Fluid subtest scaled score and the mean scaled score for the Fluid Scale would be calculated. If the difference score is equal to or exceeds the difference required for significance at the .05 level, which is listed on the record form, then it is either a significant strength or weakness. It is a strength if the value is positive, a weakness if the value is negative. However, these strengths and weaknesses may or may not deviate from the average of the normative population. Thus, it is also important to examine the standard scores. Sometimes a person's performance on a subtest is a strength or weakness compared to his or her own mean score, but not compared to the normative population. In this case, the strength or weakness is referred to as a *relative* strength or weakness be-cause it is relative to the individual's performance, but not to the average population.

The process of determining subtest strengths and weaknesses is exemplified in Figure 13.2 us-

		Mean Scaled Score								
		Crystallized Scale	Fluid Scale	Composite Intelligence Scale						
		9	16	- - -						
	Subtest Scaled Score	Difference Required for Significance at .05 Level[c]								S/W
		Crystallized[a]			Fluid[a]			Composite Intelligence[a]		
		Age 11–14	15–34	35+	Age 11–14	15–34	35+	Age 11–14	15–34	35+	
Crystallized Subtests										
1. Definitions	6	3	2	2				3	2	2	W
4. Auditory Comprehension	9	3	2	2				3	2	2	
6. Double Meanings	11	3	2	2				3	3	2	S
10. Famous Faces[b]	7	4	3	2				3	3	2	W
Fluid Subtests										
2. Rebus Learning	14				2	2	2	2	2	2	W
3. Logical Steps	17				2	2	3	3	2	3	
5. Mystery Codes	16				3	2	2	3	3	2	
9. Memory for Block Designs[b]	10				4	4	4	4	4	4	W

[a] Numbers indicate significant differences (p<.05) by age between the person's obtained subtest scaled scores and mean scaled score for the indicated IQ scale.

[b] If subtest was used as alternate for IQ calculation, examiners may wish to use the values in Tables B.2, B.3, and B.4.

[c] All values for significant differences between scores on this page have been adjusted for multiple simultaneous comparisons.

FIGURE 13.2

Dafne's KAIT strengths and weaknesses

ing Dafne's KAIT profile. The 39-point difference between her Crystallized and Fluid IQs is significant, so separate mean scaled scores for the Fluid and Crystallized scaled are used to compute strengths and weaknesses. In this case, Dafne's mean Fluid scaled score is 9 and her Crystallized mean scaled score is 16. Comparing the scaled scores she earned on each subtest with her mean scaled score, we find that she has one significant strength on Double Meanings. (There is a 2-point difference between her scaled score of 11 on Double Meanings and her mean Crystallized scaled score of 9.) She has four significant weaknesses: Definitions, Famous Faces, Rebus Learning, and Memory for Block Designs. The next steps will describe how to interpret her strengths and weaknesses.

Step 7: Generate Hypotheses about Fluctuations in the KAIT Profile

It is important to go beyond examination of the Crystallized–Fluid dichotomy when interpreting an individual's unique KAIT profile. This step helps interpret the individual's strengths and weaknesses in a meaningful way. In addition to examining different theoretical and research models to generate hypotheses, it is also necessary to integrate many other sources of information, such as background information about the examinee, the examinee's behaviors during the testing, and supplemental testing results. If additional sources of data do not support the hypothesis, it should be rejected.

In generating hypotheses about fluctuations in the profile, you will begin by looking at those fluctuations that are statistically significant (significantly strong or weak subtest scaled scores). Many examiners simply list the unique abilities measured by the subtest in question as the individual's strengths or weaknesses. However, it is much more reliable and meaningful to examine the person's performance on the subtest in question *combined* with his or her performance on

other subtests that assess overlapping abilities. Thus, our model of interpretation involves examining abilities shared by two or more subtests. Only if no shared abilities are uncovered to explain a significant strength or weakness do we advise you to turn to the *unique abilities* measured by the subtest.

The guidelines (A–F) in Table 13.7 are provided to assist in a step-by-step approach for generating hypotheses from an individual's relative strengths and weaknesses and in examining abilities shared by two or more subtests. Dafne's case is used to exemplify these guidelines (see the right column of the table).

To find supportive or disconfirming evidence for Dafne's hypothesized relative strong and weak abilities, we need to examine the WAIS-III data in combination with the KAIT data, as suggested in Guideline F of Step 7 (see Table 13.7). We determined that one possible explanation for her strong performance on the KAIT's Double Meanings subtest was a strength in her hypothetico–deductive reasoning ability (also supported by her performance on Logical Steps = 99th percentile, Mystery Codes = 98th percentile, and global Fluid IQ = 98th percentile). Examination of her WAIS-III profile also shows support for this hypothesis with her relatively strong performance on both Matrix Reasoning (95th percentile) and Similarities (84th percentile). We would next investigate her complete background to see if there were any other data supporting this hypothesis. Another hypothesis to explain her strong performance on Double Meanings is her reflective cognitive style. First, we look to the behavioral observations of Dafne during the testing, which do support the fact that she tended to be reflective in processing information rather than impulsive. Second, we look at her performance on the WAIS-III. Dafne tended not to do as well on speeded tests such as those in the Processing Speed Index (32nd percentile) and Object Assembly (16th percentile), which may be due, in part, to her reflective style. Thus, the hypotheses that we investigated to explain her relative strength in KAIT Double Meanings seem to

TABLE 13.7 Guidelines for developing hypotheses

Step 7 Guidelines	Example of How to Use the Guideline
A. Select one of the statistically significant subtest strengths or weaknesses calculated in Step 6.	A. Double Meanings is selected as a significant strength for Dafne calculated in Step 6.
B. Look at each ability and influence involved in that subtest (see Table 13.8) one at a time, and consider the person's performance on every subtest that involves that ability or influence. For each subtest that shares the ability, write a "−" next to the subtest to indicate that performance was below the individual's own subtest scaled-score mean; write a "+" next to the subtest to indicate that performance was above the individual's own subtest scaled-score mean; write a "0" to indicate that performance was the same as the individual's subtest scaled-score mean (see Table 13.9 for an example of Guideline B).	B. As shown in Table 13.9, for all subtests that share an ability with Double Meanings, either a "−", "+", or "0" was placed next to each subtest, as appropriate, indicating whether the scaled score was above, below, or equivalent to the mean scaled score of Dafne's Crystallized subtests.
C. Examine each ability and influence and assess whether it is considered a shared strength or weakness. When examining shared abilities and influences, the shared subtests do not need to deviate significantly from the mean to support a shared strength or weakness. Rules to follow are that all scores should be above the person's mean for a strength, or below the person's mean for a weakness. Table 13.10 provides rules that should be used for accepting and rejecting potential hypotheses. There are some exceptions to these rules, which are also noted in Table 13.10.	C. The rules in Table 13.10 were used to determine which abilities were accepted as potential hypothetical explanations for Dafne's strength. In this case, we see that hypothetico–deductive reasoning is a hypothesized strong ability for Dafne, and a reflective cognitive style is a hypothesized influence affecting her performance.
D. Repeat the guidelines A, B, and C for all subtests that were relative strengths and weaknesses.	D. Definitions is the next subtest to examine to determine which abilities are potential explanations for Dafne's relatively poor performance on this subtest. Thus, you would work through Guidelines A–C for Definitions and each of the remaining relative weaknesses.
E. If no shared abilities or influences are apparent after completing these guidelines, interpret the unique ability for the significant subtest strengths and weaknesses (see Table 13.11).	E. Because there were shared abilities and influences present in the profile, it was not necessary to interpret the unique abilities for any subtest in Dafne's case.
F. Examine all accepted hypotheses for shared abilities and influences to determine if they are viable hypotheses by integrating other sources of data you have, such as background information, behavioral observations, and supplemental testing data.	F. Data from the WAIS-III (Table 13.12) should be examined along with her background information and behavioral observations to support these hypothesized strong and weak abilities. Integration of Dafne's KAIT and WAIS-III profiles is discussed in more depth in the chapter.

TABLE 13.8 Abilities shared by two or more KAIT subtests

Ability	Crystallized Subtests				Fluid Subtests				Reliability[a]	
	D	AC	DM	FF	RL	LS	MC	MBD	r_{xx}	r_{12}
Fund of information	D		DM	FF					.96	.94
Verbal concept formation	D	AC	DM						.95	.94
Verbal memory		AC		FF					.94	.88
Word Knowledge	D	AC	DM						.94	.92
Acquired (school-learned) knowledge	D	AC	DM	FF					.97	.94
Crystallized intelligence	D	AC	DM	FF					.97	.94
Long-term memory (tertiary or remote memory)	D	AC	DM	FF					.97	.94
Hypothetico–deductive reasoning (planning) with novel stimuli						LS	MC		.93	.83
New learning efficiency					RL	LS	MC		.95	.87
Perceptual organization							MC	MBD	.89	.82
Simultaneous processing					RL		MC	MBD	.93	.88
Spatial visualization						LS		MBD	.89	.83
Visual memory of newly learned information					RL			MBD	.91	.85
Visual–motor coordination							MC	MBD	.89	.82
Fluid intelligence					RL	LS	MC	MBD	.95	.91
Visual perception/processing of abstract or symbolic stimuli					RL	LS	MC	MBD	.95	.91
Abstract reasoning		AC	DM			LS	MC		.96	.91
Cross-modal integration				FF	RL	LS	MC		.96	.90
Distinguishing essential from nonessential details			DM				MC		.92	.84
Hypothetico–deductive reasoning (planning)			DM		RL	LS	MC		.95	.88
Long-term memory (secondary memory of newly learned information)		AC			RL			MBD	.93	.88
Sequencing ability		AC			RL				.94	.86
Short-term memory		AC			RL			MBD	.93	.88
Speed of mental processing			DM	FF		LS	MC	MBD	.95	.90
Verbal comprehension	D	AC	DM	FF		LS			.97	.95

(Continues)

TABLE 13.8 (Continued)

Ability	Crystallized Subtests				Fluid Subtests				Reliability[a]	
	D	AC	DM	FF	RL	LS	MC	MBD	r_{xx}	r_{12}
Verbal expression	D	AC	DM	FF					.97	.95
Visual memory				FF	RL			MBD	.93	.89
Visual perception/processing of meaningful stimuli				FF			MC		.93	.84
Visual perception/processing of numbers, letters, or words	D		DM			LS			.95	.92
Word storage and retrieval	D		DM		RL				.96	.93
Influences Affecting Performance										
Ability to respond when uncertain					RL	LS	MC			
Ability to work under time pressure						LS	MC	MBD		
Alertness to the environment		AC		FF						
Anxiety		AC			RL	LS	MC	MBD		
Attention span		AC			RL	LS		MBD		
Cognitive style (reflective/impulsive)			DM			LS	MC			
Concentration		AC			RL	LS	MC	MBD		
Cultural opportunities	D	AC	DM	FF						
Distractibility		AC				LS	MC			
Flexibility		AC	DM			LS				
Foreign language background	D	AC	DM	FF	RL	LS	MC			
Frustration tolerance					RL					
Intellectual curiosity & striving	D		DM	FF						
Interests	D	AC	DM	FF						
Outside reading	D	AC		FF						
Reading disability/illiteracy	D		DM							
Richness of early environment	D	AC	DM	FF						
School learning	D		DM	FF						

NOTE: D = Definitions; AC = Auditory Comprehension; DM = Double Meanings; FF = Famous Faces; RL = Rebus Learning; LS = Logical Steps; MC = Mystery Codes; MBD = Memory for Block Designs
[a]r_{xx} = Split-half reliability; r_{12} = Test-retest reliability

TABLE 13.9 Example of Guideline B of Interpretation Step 7

Ability	Crystallized Subtests				Fluid Subtests				Reliability[a]	
	D	AC	DM	FF	RL	LS	MX	MBD	r_{xx}	r_{12}
Fund of information	D –		DM +	FF –					.96	.94
Verbal concept formation	D –	AC O	DM +						.95	.94
Word Knowledge	D –		DM +						.94	.92
Acquired (school-learned) knowledge	D –	AC O	DM +	FF –					.97	.94
Crystallized intelligence	D –	AC O	DM +	FF –					.97	.94
Long-term memory (tertiary or remote memory)	D –	AC O	DM +	FF –					.97	.94
Abstract reasoning		AC O	DM +			LS +	MC O		.96	.91
Distinguishing essential from nonessential details			DM +				MC O		.92	.84
Hypothetico–deductive reasoning (planning)			DM +			LS +	MC O		.95	.88
Speed of mental processing			DM +			LS +	MC O	MBD –	.95	.90
Verbal comprehension	D –	AC O	DM +	FF –		LS +			.97	.95
Verbal expression	D –	AC O	DM +	FF –	RL –				.97	.95
Visual perception/processing of numbers, letters, or words	D –		DM +			LS +			.95	.92
Word storage and retrieval	D –		DM +		RL –				.96	.93
Influences Affecting Performance										
Cognitive style (reflective/impulsive)			DM +			LS +	MC O			
Cultural opportunities	D –	AC O	DM +	FF –						
Flexibility		AC O	DM +			LS +	MC O			
Foreign language background	D –	AC O	DM +	FF –						
Intellectual curiosity & striving	D –	AC O	DM +	FF –						
Interests	D –	AC O	DM +	FF –						
Reading disability/illiteracy	D –		DM +							
Richness of early environment	D –	AC O	DM +	FF –						
School learning	D –	AC O	DM +	FF –						

TABLE 13.10   Rules for accepting and rejecting potential hypotheses

Number of Subtests Constituting a Shared Ability	Rule for Interpreting Ability as a Strength (at least one subtest is a significant strength)	Rule for Interpreting Ability as a Weakness (at least one subtest is a significant weakness)
2	• *All* subtests must be **above** the mean.	• *All* subtests must be **below** the mean.
3 or 4	• *At least 2 or 3* subtests must be **above** the mean, • and *only one* subtest may be **equivalent** to the mean.	• *At least 2 or 3* subtests must be **below** the mean, • and *only one* subtest may be **equivalent to** the mean.
5 or more	• *At least 4* subtests must be **above** the mean, • and *only one* subtest may be **equal to** the mean *or* **less than** the mean.	• *At least 4 subtests* must be **below** the mean, • and *only one* subtest may be **equal to** the mean *or* **greater than** the mean.

TABLE 13.11   Unique abilities associated with each KAIT subtest

Subtest	Unique Abilities
Crystallized	
Definitions	Inferring semantic part–whole relationships; visual closure
Auditory Comprehension	Auditory sequencing; listening comprehension
Double Meanings	Semantic flexibility
Famous Faces	Range of general factual knowledge
Fluid	
Rebus Learning	Paired associate learning; visual sequencing
Logical Steps	Syllogistic reasoning; facility with numbers
Mystery Codes	Planning speed
Memory for Block Designs	Nonverbal concept formation

hold up with the help of supporting data from the WAIS-III, behavioral observations, and background information.

One of Dafne's relative weaknesses on the KAIT was found on the Definitions subtest. Her pattern of scores did not uncover many shared abilities among subtests. In fact the only one that we found was that her outside reading may have affected her performance on this subtest. However, this lack of shared abilities seemed mainly to be due to her strong performance on Double Meanings, which, although a Crystallized subtest, also has a loading on the Fluid factor (see Table 13.1). Thus, her strong fluid reasoning skills likely helped her on Double Meanings, but her relatively low level of educational attainment may have negatively influenced her performance on Definitions. To determine whether this is a plausible interpretation of the dissociation within her Crystallized scale, we can turn to her

TABLE 13.12   Dafne M.'s WAIS-III Profile

Wechsler Adult Intelligence Scale—Third Edition (WAIS-III)

Scale	IQ	90% Confidence Interval	Percentile Rank
Verbal Scale	99	95–103	47
Performance Scale	110	104–115	75
Full Scale	104	100–107	61

Factor	Index		
Verbal Comprehension	93	89–98	32
Perceptual Organization	116	109–121	86
Working Memory	108	102–113	70
Processing Speed	93	86–101	32

Subtest Scaled Scores

Subtest	Scaled Score	Percentile Rank	Subtest	Scaled Score	Percentile Rank
Vocabulary	(W) 7	16	Picture Completion	(S) 14	91
Similarities	(S) 13	84	Digit Symbol-Coding	9	37
Arithmetic	10	50	Block Design	37	37
Digit Span	(S) 15	95	Matrix Reasoning	(S) 15	95
Information	(W) 6	9	Picture Arrangement	11	63
Comprehension	9	37	Symbol Search	37	37
Letter-Number Sequencing	9		Object Assembly	16	16

NOTE: (W) = relative weakness compared to her overall subtest mean scaled score; (S) = relative strength compared to her overall subtest mean scaled score.

WAIS-III Verbal subtests. In that profile, we have support for a relatively weak fund of acquired knowledge, with her relatively weak performance on Vocabulary (16th percentile) and Information (9th percentile). Thus, although at first glance at the KAIT shared abilities table, Dafne's relative weakness on the Definitions subtest did not seem to be readily explained, when we delved into the KAIT subtests on a deeper level (e.g., Double Meanings' joint Fluid–Crystallized loadings) in combination with the WAIS-III profile, we uncovered a plausible explanation for her profile scores.

Alternative KAIT Subtest Groupings

At times a search for shared abilities or influences within the KAIT profile is fruitless, so examiners may want to regroup the subtests according to other theories or aspects of the test. Thus, examiners can explore the individual's performance based on the psycholinguistic aspects of the test. Table 13.13 provides a list of the psycholinguistic aspects of each KAIT subtest.

KAIT Memory Comparisons

In further generating hypotheses about an individual's performance, the examiner may find it useful to look at an individual's performance on memory tasks. If an individual has evidenced possible memory problems either during the testing or perhaps as part of a presenting problem, more in-depth memory analysis may be warranted. Examiners can make comparisons between an individual's ability to remember information immediately after its presentation versus the ability to remember the material after a mod-

erate period of time has passed (typically 25 to 45 minutes). Thus, significant differences in immediate versus delayed recall of information can be examined by comparing the individual's performance on Rebus Learning versus Rebus Delayed Recall and Auditory Comprehension versus Auditory Delayed Recall.

However, to make comparisons between the immediate and delayed recall memory performance, the Expanded Battery must be administered. If only the Core Battery is administered or the delayed recall tasks are omitted for some reason, this step cannot be completed.

To calculate the differences between the immediate and delayed recall subtests, look at the Memory Comparisons section on the bottom of the backside of the Individual Record Form.

TABLE 13.13   Psycholinguistic aspects of KAIT subtests

	Vocal/Auditory	Visual	Motor
Input	Rebus Learning Logical Steps Auditory Comprehension Double Meanings Famous Faces	Rebus Learning Logical Steps Mystery Codes Double Meanings Memory for Block Designs Famous Faces	
Integration		Logical Steps Mystery Codes Double Meanings	
Storage	Rebus Learning Auditory Comprehension Famous Faces	Rebus Learning Memory for Block Designs Famous Faces	
Output	Rebus Learning Logical Steps Auditory Comprehension Mystery Codes (easel items) Double Meanings Famous Faces		Mystery Codes (booklet items) Memory for Block Designs

Calculate the difference between the scores (Rebus Learning from Rebus Delayed Recall and Auditory Comprehension from Auditory Delayed Recall). To determine if the difference score is statistically significant, refer to the table in the bottom right corner of the Record Form. If the difference is statistically significant (and, therefore, not due to chance), check the .05 box, but if the difference is not statistically significant, check the NS box (not significant). Figure 13.3 shows Dafne M.'s Memory Comparisons.

To accurately interpret the memory scores, determine both the direction of the difference (whether the person does better in recalling information immediately after its presentation or in recalling information after a period of delay) as well as the type of material (auditory or visual) a person retains or forgets. This information, along with background information and behavioral observations, can be used in the process of differential diagnosis and making recommendations for remediation.

KAIT RESEARCH ON CLINICAL PROFILES

In this section, we will focus on five common applications of the KAIT: (1) assessment of learning disabilities, (2) utility for understanding

Alzheimer's-type Dementia, (3) assessment of clinical depression and pseudodementia, (4) personality and interests as they pertain to career decisions, and (5) construct validity of the KAIT for African Americans and Hispanics.

Assessment of Learning Disabilities

Learning Disorders (LD) are diagnosed when an individual's performance on standardized achievement tests is substantially below what is expected for his or her age, schooling, and level of intelligence (American Psychiatric Association, 1994). "Substantially below" is typically defined as a discrepancy of 1½ to 2 or more standard deviations between one's IQ and achievement. The majority of the research on LDs continues to be with children, whereas information about the cognitive functioning of adults with LDs remains limited (Gregg, Hoy, & Gay, 1996). This may, in part, be due to the fact that there are limited measures to assess the achievement of adults. Despite the difficulties defining and assessing adult achievement, researchers continue to search for profiles of individuals with learning disabilities on the various intelligence tests. For instance, research with the Wechsler Adult Intelligence Scale—Revised (WAIS-R; Wechsler, 1981) and the Wechsler Intelligence Scale for Children—Third Edition (WISC-III; Wechsler,

Memory Comparisons (Expanded Battery)

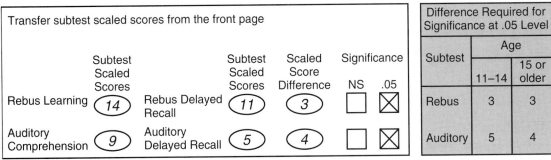

FIGURE 13.3

Example of Dafne M.'s Memory Comparisons

1991) has shown the ACID (Arithmetic, Digit Symbol-Coding, Information, Digit Span) profile to be commonly associated with LDs, as these subtests are the lowest scores for individuals who are learning disabled (Gregg, Hoy, & Gay, 1996). Moreover, findings from the data reported in the *WAIS-III and WMS-III Technical Manual* (Psychological Corporation, 1997), based on 46 adults with LDs, demonstrated that discrepancies among the various index scores exist. Specifically, the Working Memory Index was significantly lower than the Verbal Comprehension Index and the Processing Speed Index was significantly lower than the Perceptual Organization Index.

Although individuals with learning disabilities have not been heavily researched using the KAIT, the research thus far is noteworthy. Kaufman & Kaufman (1993) found no differences in KAIT profiles between a small sample ($N = 14$) of adolescents with reading disabilities and a sample of matched controls. However, they did report a trend in which the Fluid scale was significantly higher than the Crystallized scale. This makes sense given that individuals with LDs would likely have more difficulty with tasks based on school learning. Morgan, Sullivan, Darden, and Gregg (1997) investigated 60 college students with and without learning disabilities on both the KAIT and the WAIS-R. They found no significant differences between the two groups or the two tests. Both groups performed similarly on the WAIS-R Full Scale IQ, Verbal IQ, and Performance IQ as well as on the KAIT Composite, KAIT Crystallized IQ, and KAIT Fluid IQ. However, in comparing the scales of the KAIT to the scales of the WAIS-R, minor differences were found such that students both with and without learning disabilities earned significantly higher Performance IQs than Fluid IQs. The authors noted as possible explanations for the differences, (1) the Fluid subtests are more novel than the Performance subtests, and (2) the drop in scores may be due to the effect of the KAIT's newer norms. These results, which show that there are no significant differences between tests in assessing learning disabilities, indi-

cate that the KAIT is a viable new option for the assessment of learning disabilities. Moreover, in some instances (e.g., for individuals with expressive language problems, those who have already been tested several times with Wechsler tests) the KAIT is the preferred instrument.

McIntosh, Waldo, and Koller's (1997) examined the KAIT and the Wechsler Memory Scale—Revised (WMS-R; Wechsler, 1987) with 59 individuals with learning disabilities. Given that many individuals who are learning disabled often show various types of memory difficulties (John & Rattan, 1991; Swanson, 1993; Waldron & Saphire, 1992), the authors wanted to explore the overlap between the two tests in assessing persons with LDs. Their sample of adolescents and adults with learning disabilities performed in the Average range on KAIT Composite, Crystallized, and Fluid IQs, but in the Below Average to Well Below Average range on four of five WMS-R subtests. This finding is consistent with previous research, which demonstrates that individuals who are learning disabled do show memory impairments. However, the researchers in this study used only the six Core subtests of the KAIT, not the Extended Battery. (All four subtests of the Extended Battery have a memory component.) It is unclear why the authors did not utilize the Extended Battery in their research. It would be consistent with the above results if individuals with LDs were found to perform better on the Core Battery subtests than on the Extended Battery subtests due to the memory components of the latter tasks; however, without additional research, this question remains unanswered. For clinical practice, administration of the Extended Battery is still recommended when conducting psychoeducational assessments, although it may be warranted to include an additional measure of memory, such as the Wechsler Memory Scale—Third Edition (WMS-III; Wechsler, 1997), or the Wide Range Assessment of Memory and Learning (WRAML; Sheslow & Adams, 1990).

Although studies with the KAIT and LDs are limited, the research suggests that the KAIT is a good alternative instrument to use in assessing learning disabilities. Based on the above-mentioned findings, when using the KAIT in the assessment of LDs, clinicians may expect to see the following results on the KAIT (summarized in Table 13.14): (1) individuals with higher Fluid scale performance than Crystallized Scale performance, (2) lower scores on the subtests requiring memory, particularly on the Expanded Battery of the KAIT, and (3) some differences between the KAIT and other batteries, such as the WISC-III or WAIS-III. Specific differences between the KAIT and Wechsler tests would typically be between the KAIT Fluid Scale and the Wechsler Performance IQ (P-IQ). This difference is likely due to the fact that the P-IQ is not measuring simply fluid ability, as is often assumed. Rather, the P-IQ also appears to measure broad visualization (*Gv*) (Kaufman, Ishikuma, & Kaufman, 1994) in addition to having a strong emphasis on processing speed (*Gs*). Initial research gives evidence that individuals with LDs might perform better on the P-IQ than on the Fluid scale; however, additional studies will need to be done before any stronger conclusions can be drawn.

Assessment of Alzheimer's-Type Dementia

Dementia is characterized by the development of multiple cognitive deficits, with the essential fea-

TABLE 13.14 Hypothesized KAIT results for clients with learning disabilities

- Higher scores on Fluid scale than Crystallized scale
- Lower scores on the subtests requiring memory: Rebus Delayed Recall, Auditory Delayed Recall, Memory for Block Designs, Rebus Learning, Auditory Comprehension
- Differences between the KAIT and WISC-III or WAIS-III: KAIT Fluid scale higher than Wechsler Performance IQ (P-IQ)

ture of this syndrome being memory impairment along with one or more additional disturbances in cognitive functions (APA, 1994). These other affected functions may include orientation, abstraction, and problem solving, judgment, visual–spatial performance, and language, in addition to changes in personality (Nixon, 1996). In Alzheimer's-type Dementia, the most common form of dementia, there is a gradual deterioration in cognitive functioning (American Psychiatric Association, 1994). In order to diagnose Alzheimer's-type Dementia, all other causes of the symptoms must first be ruled out because it is technically not diagnosed until an autopsy is conducted to identify neuritic plaques and neurofibrillary tangles. Thus, the primary purpose of intelligence and memory testing in individuals with suspected Alzheimer's is to track the level of deterioration against one's premorbid level of functioning (Psychological Corporation, 1997).

The research with the KAIT and patients with Alzheimer's-type Dementia is limited to analyses conducted by Kaufman and Kaufman (1993) and to a doctoral dissertation study by Petterson (1998). In Kaufman and Kaufman's work, they compared a small sample of Alzheimer's patients ($N = 10$) to a matched control group during standardization of the KAIT. They found that the control group performed better than the Alzheimer's patients on five of the subtests (Auditory Comprehension, Auditory Delayed Recall, Famous Faces, Rebus Delayed Recall, and Logical Steps). This difficulty with the delayed recall tasks is consistent with the literature, which shows that tasks of delayed recall are most sensitive in the detection of the disease (Welsh, Butters, Hughes, Mohs, & Heyman, 1991; Welsh et al., 1992). Kaufman & Kaufman (1993) also found that the Alzheimer's patients, in addition to a combined sample of neurologically impaired individuals, performed significantly worse on the Mental Status Exam. In fact, 42% of the neurologically impaired and Alzheimer's patients ($N = 52$) were classified in the Lower Extreme or Below Average on the Mental Status Exam, whereas only 4% of the matched controls were classified in either of these two categories.

Petterson's (1998) study compared the cognitive deficit patterns of nondementia elderly subjects at high risk for developing Alzheimer's-type Dementia due to the presence of the ∈ 4 allele of the Apolipoprotein E ($N = 29$) with nondementia elderly who had tested negative for the ∈ 4 allele ($N = 31$). In addition, she had a group of 10 patients diagnosed as being in the early stages of Alzheimer's-type Dementia. Although both groups of nondementia elderly subjects (one at high risk and one at low risk for developing Alzheimer's-type Dementia) obtained similar absolute KAIT Fluid IQs, the group at high risk for developing Alzheimer's showed a larger discrepancy between Crystallized and Fluid IQ's relative to the low-risk group. The group in the early stages of Alzheimer's also demonstrated significantly larger discrepancies between the two IQs than the low-risk group. Petterson's findings lend support to Horn's theory regarding differential susceptibility of fluid abilities to neurological problems. Additionally, it suggests that measures of fluid/crystallized abilities may be used to demonstrate preclinical cognitive decline. Petterson also found that, contrary to expectation, measures of delayed recall did not discriminate between the high-risk and low-risk nondementia groups. However, delayed recall deficits were found in the Alzheimer's group. These findings suggest that, while the KAIT delayed recall subtests may not be as sensitive to preclinical cognitive deficits, they are sensitive to the cognitive impairment of individuals with Alzheimer's. This data, and the results from the Kaufman and Kaufman analyses, while only tentative, provide initial evidence for the clinical utility of the KAIT for assessing patients with Alzheimer's-type Dementia.

Although studies using the KAIT with Alzheimer's are limited, we can look to research with other instruments for clues as to what we may predict regarding performance on the KAIT. In addition, research with other new instruments can provide important information about the cognitive functioning of these patients. In a small sample ($N = 35$) of Alzheimer's patients using the WAIS-III and WMS-III, it was found that the patients performed worse on the WAIS-III Performance IQ than on the Verbal IQ and that the Perceptual Organization and Processing Speed Indexes showed the largest decrements of all the indexes (Psychological Corporation, 1997). This was not surprising, given that the Performance Scale measures more "vulnerable" abilities, which are not only vulnerable to aging but to brain dysfunction. Furthermore, on the WMS-III, these patients had mean scores on all the indexes, with the exception of Working Memory, that were clearly impaired (i.e., standard scores < 70). A closer look at their performance demonstrated problems with encoding and impaired storage of new information, but no significant retrieval deficits.

When these initial research findings are combined with what is known about the disease (its symptomatology), we can attempt to predict how we would expect these patients to perform on other cognitive batteries, in this case the KAIT. First, we know that Alzheimer's patients typically become impaired in their ability to learn new information or they forget previously learned material (APA, 1994). Therefore, we would expect these individuals to do poorly on Auditory Comprehension, Rebus Learning, Auditory Delayed Recall, Rebus Delayed Recall, and Memory for Block Designs. Second, these patients often have difficulty producing names of individuals and objects (APA, 1994). This might translate into difficulties on the Faces and Places subtest. Third, individuals with Alzheimer's may have executive dysfunction, which may cause problems in planning, shifting mental sets, or performing complex tasks. Thus, it is likely that they would have more trouble with the tasks requiring fluid ability (e.g., Mystery Codes, Logical Steps, Double Meanings). Last, those patients with attention and orientation problems would likely do worse on the Mental Status Exam. Overall, patients might not perform better on the Crystallized Scale than the Fluid scale, even though a V-IQ > P-IQ was noted on the WAIS-III. This is likely because some of the Crystallized subtests require fluid skills (e.g., Double Meanings) or memory (e.g., Faces and Places), and the Fluid subtests do not emphasize motor speed as do the Wechsler Performance Scale subtests. It is important to mention that, until more research is conducted to provide evidence for the diagnostic validity of the KAIT in assessing individuals with Alzheimer's, the above conclusions (highlighted in Table 13.15) remain tentative. Examiners must always use their clinical judgment, observations of patients' behavior, and supplementary testing data, in combination with their knowledge of the research.

Depression and Pseudodementia

The essential feature of major or clinical depression is either depressed mood or the loss of interest or pleasure in nearly all activities during a period of at least 2 weeks (APA, 1994). Additional symptoms that may be present include sleep and/or eating disturbances, psychomotor retardation or agitation, loss of energy, difficulties in thinking or concentration, and suicidal ideation. Typically, intelligence tests are not used as the primary assessment tool in diagnosing depression; however, they can be useful to this end. For instance, many individuals with learning disabilities also have major depression (APA, 1994; Culbertson & Edmonds, 1996). Additionally, it can be difficult, particularly in elderly persons, to determine whether cognitive symptoms are due to dementia or to a major depressive episode (APA, 1994). In fact, the literature suggests that the cognitive symptoms associated with depression are the most common type of "pseudodementia" and the most easily misdiagnosed (Lishman, 1987). Thus, neuropsychological testing and other tests assessing cognitive abilities can be helpful in the differential diagnosis of depression versus other disorders.

Although research with the KAIT and depressed patients is limited, an initial study found that a sample of patients with clinical depression ($N = 44$) did not differ from their matched controls on any subtest of the KAIT (Kaufman & Kaufman, 1993; Grossman, Kaufman, Mednitsky, Scharff, & Dennis, 1994). One significant difference between depressed and nondepressed subjects was found regarding the size of the discrepancy between scores on Auditory Comprehension and Auditory Delayed Recall (tasks of

TABLE 13.15 Hypothesized KAIT results for clients with Alzheimer's-type dementia

Symptom	→	Hypothesized Effect on KAIT
Impairment in ability to learn new information or forgetting previously learned material	→	Relatively poor performance on Auditory Comprehension, Rebus Learning, Auditory Delayed Recall, Rebus Delayed Recall, and Memory for Block Designs
Difficulty producing names of individuals and objects	→	Difficulties on the Faces and Places
Problems in planning, shifting mental sets, or performing complex tasks	→	Trouble on Mystery Codes, Logical Steps, Double Meanings
Attention and orientation problems	→	Lowered score on Mental Status Exam
General cognitive impairment	→	Because some of the Crystallized subtests require fluid skills (e.g., Double Meanings) or memory (e.g., Faces and Places), a Crystallized IQ > Fluid IQ may not be present

immediate versus delayed recall). Specifically, the discrepancy between these two subtests was significantly larger for the depressed group than for the control group and the depressed group scored higher on the delayed task than the immediate task. Given that depressed individuals often have difficulties with concentration and problems in encoding and learning, the lower score on the initial Auditory Comprehension task is not surprising. The overall lack of findings in this KAIT study between the depressed and control samples is not consistent with prior research on other cognitive instruments. For example, prior research has shown that depressed patients have problems with memory (Gruzelier, Seymour, Wilson, Jolley, & Hirsch, 1988), planning and sequential abilities (Burgess, 1991), psychomotor tasks (Pernicano, 1986), and cognitive tasks requiring sustained effortful responding (Golinkoff & Sweeney, 1989). Given that the KAIT requires sustained effortful responding in addition to assessing many of the above-mentioned skills, the absence of differences between the depressed and control samples is surprising. However, Kaufman and Kaufman (1997) noted that the conclusions based on prior research regarding depressed patients' deficiencies may have been drawn prematurely "in part because of weaknesses in experimental design and inappropriate applications of statistics." They further noted that the one area of weakness that may reflect true deficiencies may be psychomotor retardation, which is sometimes reflected in lower Performance IQs than Verbal IQs on Wechsler tests (Kaufman, 1990). Similar findings on the KAIT would not be expected because the KAIT minimizes visual–motor speed. However, it should be mentioned that the depressed sample in Grossman et al. (1994) earned their lowest scaled scores on Memory for Block Designs, one of the KAIT subtests requiring the most visual–motor coordination and speed.

No research to date has been conducted on pseudodementia using the KAIT. However, neuropsychological studies utilizing other cognitive tasks have been conducted. Thus, we can use the available research to help us understand and predict KAIT profiles. For these studies, *pseudodementia* refers to the "coexistence of a psychiatric disorder and dementia," with the dementia symptomatology being treatable or reversible (Nixon, 1996). A study of patients with pseudodementia associated with depression ($N = 14$) versus patients with dementia ($N = 28$) was conducted by Reynolds et al. (1988). The results showed that those with pseudodementia performed better on Mini Mental Status Exams than those with dementia, whereas the groups did not differ on measures of short-term recall or repetition. In a longitudinal study of patients referred for differential diagnosis of dementia versus pseudodementia ($N = 37$), the following tests were differentially sensitive to early organic dementia: WAIS-R Block Design (Wechsler, 1981), Temporal Orientation Questionnaire (Benton, Hamsher, Varney, & Spreen, 1983), and Revised Visual Retention Test (RVRT; Benton, 1974). Specifically, patients with pseudodementia performed well on these tests, whereas patients with dementia performed poorly. Another study compared patients with dementia, depression, and controls on a variety of tests assessing memory, language, abstraction, calculation, judgment, praxis, and gnostic functions. In this study, Chaves and Izquierdo (1992) found significant differences among the groups such that the patients with depression showed significantly better memory functioning than the patients with dementia.

As can be seen from the above research, profiles differentiating depression or pseudodementia from organic dementia are not consistent and have not yet been identified. However, the research can provide us with information both to increase our understanding of these disorders and to help us predict performance on other cognitive batteries. Given that most patients with depression or pseudodementia do not show significant impairment in orientation, naming, or other tasks associated with mental status exams, it is likely that these patients will perform in the normal range on the KAIT Mental Status Exam. Moreover, if psychomotor retardation is present for the depressed individual, he or she may do poorly on Memory for Block Designs. Because the memory difficulties in depressed people are suggestive of problems in encoding and learning, as opposed to retention or retrieval of information, we might see poorer performance on the KAIT immediate recall tasks (Rebus Learning, Auditory Comprehension) and better performance on the delayed recall tasks (Rebus Delayed Recall, Auditory Delayed Recall). Certainly, it is important to observe patients' behaviors during testing and to attempt to determine if there are any additional factors affecting performance, such as poor concentration or motivation. Moreover, as was mentioned in the previous section on Alzheimer's disease, more research is needed to give evidence of the diagnostic validity of the KAIT for use with these special populations. Until that time, examiners must be cautious in applying these conclusions (summarized in Table 13.16), always integrating test scores with multiple sources of data.

Personality and Interests as They Pertain to Career Choices

Assisting individuals to make academic and career choices by assessing their vocational interests and personality style has been a traditional role for counselors and clinical psychologists (Lowman, 1991). School psychologists have also begun to participate in this type of assessment (Bernard & Naylor, 1982; Shepard & Hohenshil, 1983). Given the widely held belief that personality and intellectual processes are closely re-

TABLE 13.16   Hypothesized KAIT results for clients with depression or pseudodementia

---

- Score in normal range on Mental Status Exam
- Relatively lower score on Memory for Block Designs
- Rebus Learning scaled score lower than Rebus Delayed Recall
- Auditory Comprehension scaled score lower than Auditory Comprehension Delayed Recall

---

lated, understanding the relationships between personality style, interests, and intellectual level is important to better assist individuals with their curricular and career decisions.

The relationship between interests, measured by the Strong Interest Inventory (SII; Hansen & Campbell, 1985), and intelligence, measured by the KAIT, was examined in 936 individuals aged 16 to 65 years (Kaufman & McLean, 1998). IQ level was significantly related to two of the General Occupational Themes (GOTs) and several of the Basic Interest Scales (BISs) yielded by the SII. Specifically, individuals with higher IQs were more Investigative and more Artistic than those with average IQs or low IQs. According to the authors, this relationship between high IQ and Investigative interests is sensible, as the Investigative person is interested in science and in solving abstract problems. Furthermore, the results are consistent with prior research, which has shown that high IQs are associated with high Investigative vocational interests (Lowman, 1991). The relationship between IQ and individuals with Artistic interests was unexpected. However, when the influence of the Investigative interests was accounted for statistically, the effect size for the Artistic interests was quite small. A fluid–crystallized discrepancy was also examined with regard to vocational interests. Although several relationships between fluid and crystallized intelligence and interests exist (i.e., Crystallized > Fluid IQs related to higher scores on the Writing Scale; high Crystallized IQs related to highest scores on the Music/Dramatics scale; and Fluid < Crystallized IQs related to low interest on the Mechanical Activities scale), the authors concluded that "the constructs of fluid and crystallized intelligence do not seem to relate in a meaningful way to the SII's constructs, but intelligence level does" (Kaufman & McLean, 1998, p. 293).

The KAIT and the Myers-Briggs Type Indicator (MBTI; Briggs & Myers, 1983), a personality test yielding scores on four Jung-inspired indexes, were also recently investigated in a sample of 1,297 individuals aged 14 to 94 years (Kaufman, McLean, & Lincoln, 1996). IQ was significantly related to only one of the four dimensions of the MBTI, Sensing–Intuition, with higher KAIT Composite IQs related to the Intuitive pole (preference for perceiving via reporting possibilities and relationships). This finding is consistent with previous results, which indicated that the Sensing–Intuition dimension was related to performance on tests such as the SAT and National Teacher's Examination, and to grade-point average (Hengstler, Reichard, Uhl, & Goldman, 1981; Myers & McCaulley, 1985; Pratt, Uhl, Roberts, & DeLucia, 1981; Schurr, Ruble, Henriksen, & Alcorn, 1989). When taking both studies together, IQ was closely related to the following three personality and interest variables: Intuitive on the MBTI, and Investigative and Artistic on the SII. Given that the relationship between the MBTI and SII includes a positive correlation between the Sensing–Intuition dimension and the Artistic and Investigative GOTs (Apostal, 1991; Dillon & Weissman, 1987), the relationships between these two measures and the KAIT do not seem surprising.

Most vocational and academic counseling is likely to be conducted with school-aged individuals. Thus, examining the relationship between interests, personality style, and intelligence with young samples is important. These factors and their relationship to intelligence have been examined in preadolescents, adolescents, and young adults. McLean and Kaufman (1995) explored the relationship of the Harrington-O'Shea Career Decision-Making System (CDM; Harrington & O'Shea, 1982), an interest inventory used to assess career interests, and the KAIT in a sample of 12- to 22-year-olds (N = 254). In this sample of adolescents and young adults, intellectual level was not significantly related to career interests. Similarly, no significant relationship between intelligence (measured by the KAIT) and personality style, measured by the Murphy-Meisgeier Type Indicator for Children (Meisgeier & Murphy, 1987), a downward extension of the MBTI, was found in a group of 263 children ages 11 to 15 (Kaufman & McLean, 1994). Thus, the relation-

TABLE 13.17   KAIT subtests' factor loadings on the crystallized and fluid factors for Caucasians, African Americans, and Hispanics

Subtest	Caucasian		African American		Hispanic	
	Gc	*Gf*	*Gc*	*Gf*	*Gc*	*Gf*
Crystallized						
Definitions	*79*	06	*67*	20	*72*	22
Auditory Comprehension	*65*	15	*70*	17	*76*	16
Double Meanings	*66*	17	*51*	35	*90*	–06
Famous Faces	*80*	–10	*83*	–14	*74*	12
Fluid						
Rebus Learning	26	*54*	13	*67*	28	*45*
Logical Steps	13	*64*	30	*52*	09	*58*
Mystery Codes	07	*67*	03	*67*	14	*65*
Memory for Block Designs	–08	*71*	–06	*68*	06	*57*

NOTE: Results are from a promax rotation. Sample included 1,535 Caucasians, 226 African Americans, and 140 Hispanics. *Gc* = Crystallized, *Gf* = Fluid. Decimal points are omitted, and loadings ≥ .40 are italicized. Adapted from "Factor structure of the Kaufman Adolescent and Adult Intelligence Test (KAIT) for whites, African Americans, and Hispanics," by A. S. Kaufman, J. C. Kaufman, and J. E. McLean, 1995, *Educational and Psychological Measurement, 55*, pp. 365–376. Copyright 1995 by Sage Publications. Adapted with permission of the author.

ships found in adults between intelligence, personality, and interests were not found in children and adolescents (Kaufman & McLean, 1998; Kaufman, McLean, & Lincoln, 1996).

In summary, it appears that the variable of intelligence does not need to be considered when interpreting interests and personality style as they pertain to career choices for preadolescents and young adults (ages 11 to 22). However, for adults, intellectual level interfaces in a meaningful, yet limited way with interests and personality style. Therefore, when clinically assessing an adult client's personality style or interests, insights may be gained by integrating information about the client's intellectual functioning.

KAIT's Construct Validity for African Americans and Hispanics

The KAIT Manual (Kaufman & Kaufman, 1993) provides strong evidence for the construct validity of the scale using the entire standardization sample. However, because people from different ethnic groups often perform differently on tests of intelligence, it is important to extend the construct validity of the KAIT to examine the differential construct validity for separate ethnic groups. Here we discuss the KAIT's construct validity in samples of Caucasians, African Americans, and Hispanics (Kaufman, Kaufman, & McLean, 1995).

The construct validity of the overall KAIT standardization sample is evident from the results of factor analysis, which identified clear-cut crystallized (*Gc*) and fluid (*Gf*) factors across the entire KAIT age range. The individual KAIT Crystallized and Fluid subtests most strongly load on the Crystallized and Fluid factors, respectively. Kaufman, Kaufman, and McLean (1995) analyzed a sample of 1,535 Caucasians, 226 African Americans, and 140 Hispanics to determine whether the validity of the crystallized and fluid constructs would hold for the groups separately. Consistent results were found across analyses using different types of factor-analytic rotational procedures. For each of the three ethnic group samples, all KAIT Crystallized subtests loaded primarily on the *Gc* factor, and all KAIT Fluid subtests loaded primarily on the *Gf* factor. With both the varimax and promax rotations, there were secondary loadings for some subtests in the different ethnic groups. Specifically, in the varimax rotation, the Double Meanings subtest was weighted .60 on *Gc* and .53

TABLE 13.18 Coefficients of congruence between unrotated *g* factors and rotated crystallized and fluid factors for Caucasians, African Americans, and Hispanics

Name of Factor	Caucasians × African Americans	Caucasians × Hispanics	African Americans × Hispanics
Unrotated "g"	.999	.994	.992
Varimax			
Crystallized	.993	.994	.986
Fluid	.991	.974	.973
Promax			
Crystallized	.987	.985	.954
Fluid	.976	.983	.962

NOTE: Coefficients of congruence across rotated factors (Crystallized with Fluid), both within and across race/ethnic groups, ranged from .753 to .870 (median = .882) for the varimax solutions and from .342 to .488 (median = .399) for the promax solutions. Sample included 1,535 Caucasians, 226 African Americans, and 140 Hispanics. Adapted from "Factor structure of the Kaufman Adolescent and Adult Intelligence Test (KAIT) for whites, African Americans, and Hispanics," by A. S. Kaufman, J. C. Kaufman, and J. E. McLean, 1995, *Educational and Psychological Measurement*, 55, pp. 365–376. Copyright 1995 by Sage Publications. Adapted with permission of the authors.

on *Gf* for African Americans. For Hispanics, Rebus Learning had about equal loadings on both factors (.53 on *Gf* and .42 on *Gc*). However, the promax rotation gave more decisive splits for the subtests on each of the factors (see Table 13.17). Considerable congruence between the pairs of factors indicated that the empirically defined dimensions were quite similar for all three subject groups (see Table 13.18). Thus, the results of this study support the construct validity of the KAIT for separate groups of Caucasians, African Americans, and Hispanics.

KAIT CASE STUDY

How to progress through the steps of KAIT interpretation was presented earlier in the chapter, but in this section we exemplify how all the KAIT data is integrated by presenting a case report. The goal of this example is to bring together the key points of the chapter in an applied format, to illustrate how the KAIT may be used as part of a comprehensive test battery. This case report will demonstrate how hypotheses are cross-validated with multiple sources of information (behavioral observations, background information, supplemental tests) and how all this information can be integrated and communicated in an understandable format. For the purposes of this book, the psychometric summary of scores is provided at the beginning of each report. As with other cases presented throughout the book, all pertinent identifying information in the case report has been modified to protect the confidentiality of the client.

JEFF H., AGE 17, POSSIBLE LEARNING DISABILITY

Reason for Referral

Jeff H. was referred for an evaluation due to his parents' concern about the presence of a possible learning disability. His parents also wanted information to determine if there was any way to help Jeff get into college, and to succeed once he enters college. Mr. and Mrs. H. stated that Jeff has difficulty with "comprehension of written passages, processing information and coming out with an appropriate response, vocabulary, and self motivation." Jeff's parents developed questions about his ability and a potential learning disability after he received low scores on the SAT exam he recently took (Verbal 260, Math 260). Jeff stated that he is able to remember vocabulary for a test, but cannot remember it later. He also stated concern over the fact that it is sometimes difficult for him to concentrate well enough to fully comprehend what he is reading.

Background Information

Jeff is the youngest of two children in his family. He currently lives alone with his parents, as his sister is attending college out-of-state. Mr. and Mrs. M. both work in the computer industry.

Mrs. M. reported that Jeff's prenatal and birth history were unremarkable. She had a normal, full-term pregnancy, and gave birth to Jeff through a normal delivery. Jeff weighed 7 pounds, 3 ounces at birth and was 20 inches long. According to his mother, Jeff's medical history includes having tubes placed in his ears at age 3, due to repeated ear infections. He also had chicken pox at age 5, and is currently affected mildly by hay fever. No other major illnesses or injuries were reported. His parents indicated that he has a physical exam annually for his participation in school athletics.

With the exception of his speech development, Mr. and Mrs. M. reported that all of Jeff's developmental milestones were reached within the normally expected time frame. He sat up at age

4 months, walked at 13 months, and was completely toilet-trained by around age 3. Jeff's parents reported that, in his early language development, his language was very "indistinct." Thus, he received language therapy from ages 3 to 5. His parents stated that the language difficulty was remediated through this treatment.

Jeff's educational history began when he entered preschool at age 3. He attended preschool until he was 5 years old, and his parents reported that he enjoyed it. In first grade Jeff participated in a special language program to help him with vocabulary and comprehension. His parents stated that they thought this program helped him because he tested too high at the end of the year on a test to qualify to continue in the program.

Jeff has attended his current high school since ninth grade. He will be beginning the twelfth grade in less than one month. According to his report card, his overall grade-point average is equivalent to a "B." Jeff reported that he does not like math and science, but he does like history. The lowest grades he has obtained in high school have been in Spanish, English, Biology, and Chemistry.

He is an active participant in extracurricular sports such as soccer and basketball. Jeff and his parents both report that they hope he may be able to receive an athletic scholarship for college. Mr. and Mrs. M. stated that sports take up much of Jeff's time after school. To complete all of his homework, his parents indicated that they must help motivate him or push him to do it. They stated that he seems to do better when he has an example in front of him from which to work.

Appearance and Behavioral Characteristics

Jeff is an athletic-looking 17-year-old. He is a tall young man, with short blonde hair. He dressed comfortably and appropriately for each of the evaluation sessions, wearing shorts, a T-shirt, and tennis shoes. Jeff was responsible for making appointments and getting himself to each of his evaluation sessions. He demonstrated his responsibility by his prompt arrival at the clinic after driving himself to each of his appointments.

On initially meeting the examiner, Jeff did not seem nervous or anxious, but was somewhat apprehensive about the testing process. He was quiet at first, but always responded to questions asked by the examiner. As rapport developed through initial conversation with the examiner, he began to engage in conversation more spontaneously, and even shared with the examiner what some of his concerns were about his ability. During the testing itself, he was very focused on the tasks at hand and seldom initiated dialogue unless asked a question by the examiner.

Jeff's face and body were rather expressionless during the evaluation. He rarely smiled, frowned, grinned, or grimaced, and he sat still in his chair with no excess body movement. Occasionally, when he was presented with a problem that he thought looked difficult, his initial response before attempting to solve it was "whew" or "wow." He never took breaks offered to him by the examiner; he just wanted to keep going through each part of the evaluation. Jeff was socially appropriate, pleasantly friendly, and cooperative.

Jeff showed a strong ability to concentrate and focus on each task presented to him. His attention never drifted, even on tasks that were somewhat boring for him to do. He also demonstrated stamina and persistence working on tasks that were quite challenging to him. For example, on a task that required him to recreate an example geometric design with colored blocks, Jeff had difficulty making the correct design but kept on trying and attempted to complete the design. On other tasks, if he did not know the answer to a problem he said, "I don't know," but would not let his inability to answer one question interfere with his attempting the next question.

While attempting more school-related tasks, Jeff stated occasionally, "I know that answer, I learned it in school...I can't remember." He appeared momentarily frustrated, but then just continued on with the next problem. Jeff appeared to try his hardest on each item. When asked by the examiner whether his performance was an accurate assessment of his abilities, he agreed that it was. Because of his level of motivation to do his best, and his aforementioned behaviors and good concentration, the results of this evaluation are considered a valid estimate of his current cognitive and academic abilities.

Tests Administered

Developmental Test of Visual–Motor Integration (VMI)
Kaufman Adolescent and Adult Intelligence Test (KAIT)
Kaufman Functional Academic Skills Test (K-FAST)
Kaufman Test of Educational Achievement (K-TEA)-Comprehensive Form
Kinetic Family Drawing
Peabody Picture Vocabulary Test—Third Edition (PPVT-III)
Wechsler Adult Intelligence Scale—Third Edition (WAIS-III)
Wechsler Individual Achievement Test (WIAT): Selected Subtest
Woodcock Johnson—Revised (WJ-R): Tests of Achievement: Selected Subtests
Woodcock Johnson—Revised (WJ-R): Tests of Cognitive Ability: Selected Subtest

Test Results and Interpretation

Cognitive Abilities

Jeff was administered both the Wechsler Adult Intelligence Scale—Third Edition (WAIS-III) and the Kaufman Adolescent and Adult Intelligence Test (KAIT), which are individually administered tests of a person's intellectual ability and cognitive strengths and weaknesses (scores from all tests are listed in Table 13.19). The WAIS-III groups an individual's abilities into two global areas: verbal and nonverbal. The most global measures of Jeff's abilities, the Verbal IQ of 85, Performance IQ of 73, and Full Scale IQ of 77 do not provide the most meaningful estimate of his abilities because of the variability within the subtests and indexes that comprise these IQs. Significant scatter was present in both sets of subtests comprising Jeff's verbal and nonverbal abilities. For example, on the Verbal scale, his scores showed discrepant abilities with subtest scores ranging from the 1st percentile to the 63rd percentile, and on the Performance scale his subtest scores ranged from the 2nd percentile to the 50th percentile. Thus, his IQs only represent the numerical average of these many very discrepant abilities. Because of the significant amount of variability within his scores, it is more meaningful to look at his WAIS-III Index scores, as well as his individual strengths and weaknesses, to gain a better understanding of his cognitive abilities. His Verbal Comprehension Index of 80 (9th percentile; Low Average) was significantly higher than his Perceptual Organization Index of 69 (2nd percentile; Extremely Low), indicating that he is able to solve problems better when they are presented auditorally and require a verbal response, such as answering a question or defining a word, than when problems are presented visually and require a nonverbal or motor response, such as manipulating objects or reasoning visually. Jeff also performed significantly better on his Working Memory Index (94, 34th percentile) than his Verbal Comprehension Index, indicating that he may have relative strengths in short-term memory, especially rote recall. Jeff's Processing Speed Index (93, 32nd percentile) was significantly higher than his Perceptual Organization Index, indicating that he is better able to work rapidly and process simple visual symbols quickly than to use reasoning in solving visual–spatial problems.

Another measure of Jeff's cognitive abilities was obtained through the Kaufman Adolescent and Adult Intelligence Test (KAIT). The KAIT groups an individual's cognitive abilities into two global areas: Fluid and Crystallized. Jeff obtained a scaled score of 87±5 (20th percentile) on the Fluid Scale, which measures one's ability to solve novel problems, and he earned a scaled score of 84±5 (15th percentile) on the Crystallized Scale, which measures one's ability to solve problems that are dependent on schooling and acculturation for success. His individual subtest

TABLE 13.19   Psychometric Summary of Jeff H.'s Test Scores

Kaufman Adolescent and Adult Intelligence Test (KAIT)

Composites	Standard Score ±90% Confidence Interval	Percentile Rank
Fluid Scale	87±5	20
Crystallized Scale	84±5	15
Total Composite Scale	85±4	15

Fluid Scale Subtests	Scaled Scores	Percentile Rank	Crystallized Scale Subtests	Scaled Scores	Percentile Rank
Rebus Learning	5	5	Definitions	7	16
Logical Steps	9	37	Auditory Comprehension	9	37
Mystery Codes	9	37	Double Meanings	5	5
Memory for Block Designs	4	2	Famous Faces	9	37
Delayed Recall					
Rebus Delayed Recall	5	5			

Wechsler Adult Intelligence Scale—Third Edition (WAIS-III)

Scale	IQ	90% Confidence Interval	Percentile Rank
Verbal Scale	85	81–90	16
Performance Scale	73	69–80	4
Full Scale	77	74–81	6

Factor	Index	90% Confidence Interval	Percentile Rank
Verbal Comprehension	80	76–86	9
Perceptual Organization	69	65–77	2
Working Memory	94	89–100	34
Processing Speed	93	86–101	32

Subtest	Scaled Score	Percentile Rank	Subtest	Scaled Score	Percentile Rank
Vocabulary	8	25	Picture Completion	4	2
Similarities	8	25	Digit Symbol-Coding	10	50
Arithmetic	9	37	Block Design	5	5

(Continues)

TABLE 13.19   (Continued)

Subtest	Scaled Score	Percentile Rank	Subtest	Scaled Score	Percentile Rank
Digit Span	11	63	Matrix Reasoning	5	5
Information	3	1	Picture Arrangement	4	2
Comprehension	6	9	Symbol Search	8	25
Letter-Number Sequencing	7	16	Object Assembly	4	2

Kaufman Functional Academic Skills Test (KFAST)

Subtest	Standard Score	90% Confidence Interval	Percentile Rank
Arithmetic	81	74–90	10
Reading	80	72–90	9
Composite	80	75–87	9

Kaufman Test of Educational Achievement (K-TEA): Comprehensive Form

Composite	Standard Score ±90% Confidence Interval	Percentile Rank
Reading Composite	93±6	32
Mathematics Composite	82±6	12
Battery Composite	97±4	27
Subtest		
Mathematics Applications	75±8	5
Reading Decoding	103±7	58
Spelling	110±8	75
Reading Comprehension	85±8	16
Mathematics Computation	91±8	27

Peabody Picture Vocabulary Test—Third Edition (PPVT-III)

	Standard Score	Percentile Rank
PPVT-III	74	4

(Continues)

TABLE 13.19   (Continued)

Selected Subtest of the Wechsler Individual Achievement Test (WIAT)

Subtest	Standard Score	Percentile Rank
Written Expression	80	9

Developmental Test of Visual-Motor Integration (VMI)

	Standard Score	Percentile Rank
VMI	86	18

Selected Subtests of the Woodcock-Johnson—Revised (WJ-R) Tests of Cognitive Ability

Subtest	Standard Score	Percentile Rank
Visual Closure	93	32
Memory for Names	107	68
Analysis–Synthesis	73	3

Selected Subtests of the Woodcock-Johnson—Revised (WJ-R): Tests of Achievement

	Standard Score	Percentile Rank
Broad Knowledge	*66*	*1*
Science	77	6
Social Studies	75	5
Humanities	61	0.5

scores on each of the two scales were not unusually variable, and the two global scales were not significantly different from one another. Thus, his ability to solve new problems and his ability to solve problems using school-learned knowledge are equally well developed. His overall KAIT Composite standard score of 85±5 (15th percentile; Below Average) represents the average of all his abilities.

One of Jeff's relative cognitive strengths is in the area of rote memory and recall. He performed well on a WAIS-III task that required him to concentrate, remember, and repeat sequences of numbers that were presented to him auditorally (63rd percentile). He also performed well on another WAIS-III task that required him to copy a code of symbols (50th percentile). On both of these tasks, Jeff used his strong attention and incorporated his rote memory and sequencing abilities to succeed. Similarly, his good short-term memory abilities were evident in a Woodcock Johnson—Revised Test of Cognitive Ability (WJ-R) task that required him to learn and remember the unusual names of numerous visually presented cartoon space creatures, such as "Plik" and "Delton." Jeff performed at the 63rd percentile on this task by using his memory and rote recall abilities.

Another relative cognitive strength of Jeff's was his ability to use planning and reasoning. Such reasoning is used when different premises are presented and a logical conclusion is found from them. This strength was evident on two KAIT tasks, one that required Jeff to respond to a question by making use of logical premises (37th percentile), and another that required him to figure out the code of a novel pictorial stimulus (37th percentile). In a separate, but related logic task on the WJ-R, Jeff did not perform as well. On this task, in which Jeff had to complete a logic puzzle, he scored at only the 3rd percentile. His lower performance on this task, in comparison to the two KAIT reasoning tasks, seemed to be due to the fact that he had difficulty when the task quickly became more and more complex. Jeff could reason out the one-step problems, but had much more difficulty when he had to integrate more steps to solve the problems.

Jeff demonstrated some relative cognitive weaknesses in the verbal realm. His basic fund of general information, including knowledge obtained through formal schooling and knowledge obtained through acculturation and general awareness of one's environment, is low compared to his other abilities and others his age (1st percentile). This weakness was further supported by three achievement subtests of the Woodcock-Johnson—Revised (WJ-R-Ach.). On subtests measuring his knowledge in the areas of science, social studies, and humanities, Jeff obtained scores in the 6th, 5th, and 0.5th percentiles, respectively. In contrast to this, on a KAIT task measuring knowledge of general factual information from history, literature, sports, entertainment, science, and art, which one acquires through television, magazines and newspapers, Jeff scored higher (37th percentile). The difference appears to be in the way the information was presented to Jeff. He performed better on the task that presented a verbal cue about a famous face shown, which he had to identify, than on tasks that simply required him to answer questions about facts. The use of verbal and pictorial clues encourages integration of facts and concepts, and makes the task more of a problem-solving exercise than just purely a long-term memory task. Thus, it appears that Jeff is not adequately able to use purely his long-term memory to retrieve the broad base of general information that is presented to him in and out of academic settings.

Although Jeff's verbal comprehension skills were relatively well developed in comparison to his visual–spatial skills, compared to the others his age, his abilities fall in the Low Average range or below. This difficulty was paralleled by his performance on the Reading Comprehension subtest of the Kaufman Test of Educational Achievement (KTEA). This subtest required him to read short passages and answer brief questions about what he had read. He performed at the Below Average Level (16th percentile) on this task. Similarly, on a task from the Kaufman Functional Academic Skills Test (K-FAST) that required Jeff to understand written material used in everyday situations, such as signs, labels, recipes, and abbreviations, his difficulty was apparent because he earned a score at the 9th percentile. However, in contrast to these difficulties, he performed at the Average Level (37th percentile) on a related KAIT task that required him to listen to a mock radio news broadcast and answer questions about it. On tasks that are more school-like, requiring reading and answering questions, rather than listening to news on the radio, he has less confidence and weaker ability. Two, on tasks that require him to make inferences or use more than just basic rote recall about what he has heard or read, he has more difficulty.

Related to his Low Average abilities in verbal comprehension, Jeff demonstrated a weakness in word storage and retrieval through paired associate learning. On a KAIT task that simulates reading and is like learning a new language, Jeff scored at the 5th percentile. This is similar to his performance on a WAIS-R vocabulary task and KAIT task of word knowledge and concept formation, in which he earned scores at the 16th percentile. In addition, Jeff earned a standard score of 74 (4th percentile) on the Peabody Picture Vocabulary Test—Third Edition (PPVT-III), a test of receptive vocabulary.

Visual–Motor Abilities

Overall, Jeff's abilities to perceive and visually organize material are weaker than his global verbal abilities. This was evident on most of the WAIS-III Performance Scale Subtests, including those requiring him to identify the missing part of a picture, arrange picture cards in the correct sequential order, copy a geometric design with blocks, and solve a puzzle. His scores on these tasks ranged from the 2nd to 5th percentiles. Supportive evidence for his perceptual organization and visual organization difficulties was present in a similar KAIT task of replicating a design with blocks from memory (he earned a score at the 2nd percentile). Likewise, on a task of visual–motor skill, he performed at a Below Average level (VMI standard score of 86, 18th percentile). To rule out a potential deficit in simultaneous processing, or holistic processing, a WJ-R subtest was administered. This subtest required Jeff to identify a drawing or picture that is distorted, has missing lines, or has a superimposed pattern. His performance was higher (32nd percentile) on this task than on perceptual–organizational tasks previously mentioned, indicating that his difficulties are not likely due to a weakness in holistic processing.

Achievement Abilities

Jeff's achievement abilities were thoroughly evaluated, in addition to his cognitive abilities. Some of his achievement scores have been discussed previously in conjunction with his cognitive abilities, but all achievement scores will be discussed in detail in the following paragraphs. Jeff was administered multiple separate tests of achievement to assess his reading ability, both comprehension and decoding, his mathematics computation and applied abilities, his written expression ability, his receptive vocabulary, his spelling ability, and his basic knowledge skills. In general, his achievement abilities were at a level commensurate with his cognitive abilities, with the exception of his spelling and reading decoding, which were higher than would be predicted from his cognitive scores. This indicates that Jeff does not have a learning disability, and, in fact, it is clear that he works very hard to achieve at the level he does academically as evidenced by his current GPA ("B" average).

On the Kaufman Test of Educational Achievement-Comprehensive Form (KTEA), Jeff earned Spelling and Reading Decoding Scores at the 75th and 58th percentiles, respectfully. Given his overall performance on the tests of cognitive ability and intelligence (KAIT and WAIS-III), ranging from the 2nd percentile on WAIS-III Perceptual Organization to the 20th percentile on KAIT Fluid IQ and 34th percentile on WAIS-III Working Memory, he appears to be overachieving in these particular academic areas. On closer inspection, it seems that Jeff is using his strong rote memory abilities to perform strongly on spelling words and on word pronunciation. He appears to have a good understanding and memory of the phonics involved in word pronunciation, which enables him to sound out words with which he may not be familiar.

Jeff's low score on the SAT Verbal exam (260), reported by his parents, was paralleled by his KTEA Reading Comprehension score at the 16th percentile, his Kaufman Functional Academic Skills Test (K-FAST) Reading score at the 9th percentile, and his PPVT-III receptive vocabulary score at the 4th percentile. Commensurate with these verbal scores is his written expression ability (Wechsler Individual Achievement Test, WIAT, 9th percentile). On this task of written expression, points may be earned in the areas of vocabulary, organization, ideas and development, sentence structure, grammar, and capitalization and punctuation. His achievement abilities on this testing also appear to be in line with his lower grades obtained at school in English and Spanish.

Like his SAT Math score (260), in the area of mathematics Jeff earned significantly lower scores on tasks that were applied and required problem solving in everyday situations than in the computation of written mathematics problems. On the K-TEA Mathematics Applications and K-FAST Arithmetic, he earned scores at the 5th and 10th percentiles, respectively. However, on the K-TEA Mathematics Computation he earned a higher score at the 27th percentile. This discrepancy is analogous to his performance on the aforementioned reasoning tasks: He was able to solve simple, one-step problems, but had much more difficulty with increasingly complex problems, such as the applied math problems.

Summary and Diagnostic Impressions

Jeff H. is a 17-year-old student who is about to enter his senior year in high school. He was referred for an evaluation because of his parents' concern about his academic abilities and a possible learning disability. This evaluation was performed to answer Mr. and Mrs. H.'s questions about whether there is any way to help Jeff with academic difficulties he has that may hinder him once he enters college. Cognitive, achievement, and supplemental tests were administered over the course of four sessions. Jeff demonstrated good concentration and attention during the entire evaluation. He was persistent and motivated to try his best, even on very challenging tasks. Detailed behavioral observations of the testing, as well as information provided by a clinical interview with Jeff and his parents, and academic records, gave further insight into Jeff's strengths and weaknesses.

Jeff's cognitive abilities were assessed by two instruments, the WAIS-III and the KAIT. On the WAIS-III, Jeff performed significantly better on tasks requiring answering questions verbally than on solving problems that are presented visually and require a nonverbal, or motor, response. He earned a WAIS-III Verbal Comprehension Index of 80 (Low Average Range) and a Perceptual Organization Index of 69 (Extremely Low Range). Because of the significant variability within his different IQ scales, Jeff's cognitive abilities are most meaningfully represented by his Index scores and individual strengths and weakness on the WAIS-III. On the KAIT, Jeff's performance did not show a significant amount of variability, indicating that his measured abilities were evenly developed. He earned a Fluid IQ of 87±5 (Below Average Range) and a Crystallized IQ of 84±5 (Below Average Range), indicating that he solves problems equally well whether they are novel problems or problems dependent on schooling and acculturation for success.

Jeff's relative cognitive strengths were evident in two areas: his rote memory and recall abilities, and his ability to use planning and reasoning in solving uncomplicated, one-step problems. However, when more complex reasoning is involved in problems requiring the integration of multiple steps, Jeff has much more difficulty. Overall, Jeff generally had more difficulty on tasks that required visual organization and perceptual organization than those that required only verbal abilities. Specific areas of weakness were found in Jeff's general fund of knowledge. It appears that Jeff's ability to learn, store, and retrieve information from his long-term memory is below average. Jeff has less difficulty when he can use pictorial or visual cues in addition to verbal cues, but has much more trouble when he is required to answer questions about facts that are presented in a written or oral format, such as is most commonly done in an academic setting. Jeff also demonstrated a weakness in verbal comprehension of both academic material and written material used in everyday situations. In comprehension, Jeff again was found to perform much better when he was able to use basic rote memory, but is quite challenged when required to utilize more complex processes, such as making an inference from what he hears or reads.

There were no significant discrepancies between Jeff's cognitive abilities, indicated by his IQs, and his achievement abilities, indicated by his achievement standard scores, which demonstrates that he does not have a learning disability. Jeff's scores on the individually administered achievement tests were commensurate with his scores on the SAT exam. In two areas, word pronunciation and spelling words, Jeff achieved scores that were better than what his global IQ would have predicted. It seems that, in these two areas, Jeff is able to use his strong rote memory to succeed. Similar to what was found in the cognitive testing, Jeff performed significantly better on math problems that involved only calculation of written problems than on applied problems, which were more complex and involved multiple steps. Jeff's achievement in the verbal area ranged from the 4th percentile in receptive vocabulary to the 9th percentile in written expression to the 16th percentile in reading comprehension.

Jeff's high school "B" grade-point average seems to be quite representative of the diligence, effort, and persistence that he applies to his academic work. It is likely that academic work is more difficult for Jeff than other students his age. Through his performance at school, as evidenced by his grades and comments by his teachers, such as "conscientious worker and excellent attitude," it appears that Jeff is able to compensate well for his weaknesses.

Recommendations

The following recommendations have been made to assist Jeff and his parents to best utilize his strengths in areas that are more challenging for him, both in and out of academic settings.

1. As Jeff was found not to have a learning disability, he will not qualify for special academic programs at a college or university to help with learning problems. However, Jeff may still find that he will have difficulty with college courses that are more complex and challenging than high school academics. Because such advanced courses may be harder for him than other students, it is recommended that he and/or his parents look into academic programs that offer tutoring support. This may include peer tutoring or teaching by advanced students. Information may be obtained by calling or writing student affairs or student services departments of various universities or community colleges.

2. In choosing a college or university, Jeff and his parents may want to consider the size of classes. In making the transition to higher education, sometimes students who struggle academically get lost in big lecture courses that are often found at large universities. Jeff will likely benefit from smaller classes in which one-on-one interaction with the professor/ teacher is possible. This will allow him easier access to having his questions answered, and place him at lower risk for being lost in the crowd of students.

3. If Jeff decides to enter a school for pursuing his athletic interests, such as football, he will want to consider how rigorous the athletic schedule will be. In college, he will have to set his own study schedule, and the time taken by athletic practice and games should be factored in as a potential conflict. Choosing a program that allows enough time for studying and tutoring, if necessary, will be critical to Jeff's academic success beyond high school.

4. As Jeff demonstrated difficulty in his fund of general information, it is recommended that Jeff gain more enrichment from his environment. This may include activities such as watching documentary movies, going to museums and concerts, and trying new things such as following a recipe to cook a meal or similar activities.

5. Jeff has difficulty retrieving information that is stored long term. To help him better remember such information, several things are recommended. Jeff may benefit from taping lectures and listening to them more than once. He will also benefit from having new information presented so that he can hear and see what he is expected to learn. This may be made possible by speaking with his professors and asking if they will use overheads or videos in addition to lectures. If possible, he will also benefit from gaining information through other channels such as touch and movement. Using concrete objects to illustrate concepts will be beneficial. Thus, when available, Jeff will benefit from laboratory classes, or classes that provide hands-on work.

6. Learning new information is easier if it is clearly associated with something one already knows. Therefore, Jeff will benefit from forming relationships, organizing information and integrating information with prior knowledge. For example, when reading a new text on a scientific concept like gravity, Jeff will benefit form visualizing a familiar object, like a baseball being pitched, to figure out how the new concept is applied. Thus, using various strategies, like visualization, can help increase his retention of information.

7. Jeff reported that he has difficulty staying focused on reading for an extended period of time and remembering and comprehending what he has already read. Jeff may benefit from reading a passage by breaking it down into smaller parts, making sure that he understands each small part as he goes along. He should stop and ask himself questions about what he has read periodically. Highlighting important text and taking notes in the margin are also effective strategies for enhancing comprehension. He should allow himself extra time while reading so he can take breaks to avoid fatigue and boredom.

Elizabeth O. Lichtenberger, Ph.D.
Carren J. Stika, Ph.D.

SUMMARY

This chapter presents information on the Kaufman Adolescent and Adult Intelligence Test (KAIT). The KAIT is a standardized measure of old (crystallized) and new (fluid) learning for individuals ages 11 to over 85. Three cognitive and neuropsychological theories provide the foundation for the KAIT: (1) Horn and Cattell's (1966, 1967) theory of fluid (Gf) and crystallized (Gc) intelligence; (2) Luria's (1966, 1980) definition of planning ability; and (3) the formal operational stage of development according to Piaget's (1972) theory. Each of these theories is briefly discussed in this chapter.

The KAIT is organized into a Core Battery and an Extended Battery. The Core Battery is comprised of two scales: Fluid and Crystallized, which contain three subtests each. The Extended Battery is comprised of 10 subtests. It includes the Fluid and Crystallized scales mentioned above, two additional subtests (one Fluid and one Crystallized), and two delayed recall subtests.

The standardization and psychometric properties of the KAIT were strong. The KAIT's standardization sample was composed of 2,000 adolescents and adults, selected according to 1988 U.S. Census data. The sample was stratified on the variables of gender, race/ethnic group, geographic region, and socioeconomic status (educational attainment). The large sample was divided into fourteen age groups with 100 to 250 subjects in each age group between the ages of 11 and 85+.

In addition to general information about the organization and development of the KAIT, an approach to interpreting the KAIT is also presented in this chapter. This approach examines the most global scores first (Composite Intelligence Scale), then explores more specific subtest scores, as well as detailed aspects of the test (strengths and weaknesses, memory comparisons). The philosophy underlying this approach is similar to that which we advocate for the WAIS-III.

Also related to interpretation is a section in which five common applications of the KAIT are presented: (1) assessment of learning disabilities, (2) utility for understanding Alzheimer's-type Dementia, (3) assessment of clinical depression and pseudodementia, (4) personality and interests as they pertain to career decisions, and (5) construct validity of the KAIT for African Americans and Hispanics.

This chapter culminates with an illustrative case report of a young man with possible learning difficulties. His case helps to bring to life how the KAIT functions as a clinical tool.

The Woodcock-Johnson Battery—Third Edition (WJ III)

KEVIN S. MCGREW
University of Minnesota

RICHARD WOODCOCK
Measurement/Learning/Consultants

LAURIE FORD
University of South Carolina

HISTORY AND EVOLUTION OF THE WJ III

Original Woodcock-Johnson (WJ)

The Woodcock-Johnson—Third Edition (WJ III; Woodcock, McGrew, & Mather, 2001) is the most recent revision of a battery of tests first published in 1977 as the Woodcock-Johnson Psycho-Educational Battery (WJ; Woodcock & Johnson, 1977). The WJ was the first comprehensive co-normed battery of tests of cognitive abilities, achievement, and interests. The WJ was normed

The authors express their appreciation for the constructive received feedback from Dr. Fred Schrank and Dr. Dawn Flanagan. We also wish to express our thanks to Jeff Evans and Julie Evans for their assistance in the preparation of the tables and the editing of the text.

on 4,732 subjects from ages three through 80+ and provided both age- and grade-based norm scores.

The WJ Tests of Cognitive Ability (COG) included 12 individual tests designed to represent a sampling of cognitive abilities ordered from lower- to higher-level cognitive processing (Woodcock, 1978). The 12 COG tests were combined into a differentially weighted estimate of g or general intelligence (Broad Cognitive Ability cluster), the first differentially weighted g-score provided with an individually administered battery of cognitive tests. The WJ COG included four cognitive ability factors (Reasoning, Verbal Ability, Memory, Perceptual Speed) that were empirically derived from a series of exploratory factor and cluster analyses. As such, the WJ COG factors were not based on any particular structure-of-intellect model of intelligence available at that time.

Four Scholastic Aptitude (SAPT) clusters were also included in the WJ. The SAPT clusters were the cornerstone of one component of the WJ's featured *pragmatic decision-making model*, a model that utilized a decision-based test design strategy (McGrew, 1986; Woodcock, 1984a, 1984b). Briefly, the WJ was designed to provide the data necessary for practitioners needing to make important psychoeducational decisions (McGrew, 1986). Each SAPT cluster was composed of the best differentially weighted combination of four cognitive tests that predicted a respective achievement domain. The SAPT clusters were pivotal in the quantification of aptitude/achievement discrepancies via the aptitude/achievement Relative Performance Indexes (RPIs). Within-cognitive and within-achievement discrepancies comprised the intra-cognitive and intra-achievement components of the pragmatic decision-making model, and were operationalized via comparison of test/cluster confidence bands.

The WJ Tests of Achievement (ACH) were comprised of 10 tests and resultant clusters organized around the curricular areas reading, mathematics, written language, and knowledge. Broad cluster scores were provided in each of these achievement domains. The Tests of Interest Level provided scores for the measurement of Scholastic (Reading, Mathematics, and Written Language) and Nonscholastic (Physical and Social) Interests. A Spanish version (Woodcock, 1982) included 10 of the cognitive tests and 7 of the achievement tests. In 1984 the battery was linked to the Scales of Independent Behavior (Bruininks, Woodcock, Hill, & Weatherman, 1985) as part of the WJ/SIB Assessment System.

Woodcock-Johnson—Revised (WJ-R)

In 1989 a revised and re-standardized WJ-R battery was published (Woodcock & Johnson, 1989a, 1996b). The primary goal of the WJ-R was to expand the diagnostic capabilities of the test and to complement the pragmatic decision-making model with a validated structure-of-intellect model (viz., Cattell-Horn *Gf–Gc* theory) (McGrew, 1994; McGrew et al., 1991). The WJ Tests of Interest were dropped and the WJ-R was divided into two main batteries: Tests of Cognitive Ability (WJ-R COG) and Tests of Achievement (WJ-R ACH), each with standard and supplemental battery. The complete norm sample was comprised of 6,359 subjects from age two through 90+. For the first time, separate college/university norms were provided.

The WJ-COG was enhanced by the addition of new tests and clusters grounded in the Cattell-Horn *Gf–Gc* theory of cognitive abilities. The WJ-R COG was the first of the major intelligence test batteries to utilize a *multiple intelligences* approach with several (seven) empirically supported cognitive ability factors. The WJ-R ACH was extended from 10 to 14 tests with several new tests of reading, written language, and mathematics added. Broad achievement clusters were supplemented with subdomain clusters (e.g., Basic Reading Skills and Reading Comprehension) in reading, math, and written language. Parallel, alternative forms (Forms A & B) were also introduced to the Tests of Achievement. A complete Spanish version of both the WJ-R COG and WJ-R ACH were made available in 1996 (Woodcock & Munoz-Sandoval, 1996a, 1996b).

A number of the WJ interpretation features were refined and other new features added to the WJ-R. In response to concerns about the complexity of hand-scoring the WJ, the differential weighting of the SAPT and the BCA clusters were replaced with equally weighted clusters (McGrew, 1994). A major improvement was the development of actual norm-based scores for evaluating the intra-cognitive and intra-achievement discrepancies. Finally, an extensive technical manual (McGrew, Werder, & Woodcock, 1991) provided detailed information that supported the construct validity of the *Gf–Gc* structure-of-intellect model for the battery.

The current WJ III has benefited from 23 years of development and ongoing revision. Detailed historical information regarding the development and evolution of the WJ to the WJ-R, as well as a synthesis of related research literature and independent reviews, can be found in a number of sources (Hessler, 1982, 1993; McGrew, 1986, 1994; McGrew et al., 1991). The presentation of an overview of the latest version of the WJ battery (WJ III), with a particular emphasis on its characteristics and use with adolescents and adults, is the purpose of this chapter.

THEORETICAL FOUNDATIONS OF THE WJ III

The validity of psychological tests hinges on the degree to which empirical evidence and theory support the use and interpretation of the test scores. Over time, a number of prominent measurement experts (Benson, 1998; Cronbach, 1971; Cronbach & Meehl, 1955; Loevinger, 1957; Messick, 1989; Nunnally, 1978) have, in one way or another, outlined a three- or four-source validity framework, a framework that now serves as the foundation for most of the validity standards in the joint APA, AERA, NCME *Standards on Educational and Psychological Testing* (1999). As per the joint *Test Standards*, substantive, internal, and external validity evidence is the cornerstone of a strong program of construct validity.

The *substantive* stage of construct validity defines the *theoretical* and *measurement* (empirical) domains of the theoretical constructs. In the current context, the substantive question to be answered is *"How should intelligence be defined and operationally measured by the WJ III?"* According to Benson (1998), a strong psychological theory maximizes substantive (content) validity vis-à-vis the specification of a well-bounded construct domain, which, in turn, guides the development of measures in the empirical domain. The Cattell-Horn-Carroll (CHC) Theory of Cognitive Abilities served this function for the WJ III. The theory and its use as the WJ III test-design blueprint is described here.

The Cattell-Horn-Carroll (CHC) Theory of Cognitive Abilities

CHC theory evolved from the psychometric tradition of defining intelligence (Flanagan et al., 2000; McGrew & Flanagan, 1998). The psychometric approach is the oldest and most well-established approach to describing the structure of intelligence, dating back to Galton's attempt, in the late 1800s, to measure intelligence with psychophysical measures. Correlation and factor-analytic methods are employed typically to analyze scores from psychological tests in an attempt to objectively identify the primary dimensions that form the structure of individual differences in cognitive ability.

CHC theory is a *strong* psychological theory, as it represents one of the best examples of cumulative science in applied psychology. The original roots of CHC theory can be traced to Spearman's (1904, 1927) presentation of the general or *g*-factor theory of intelligence, a development some consider the formal birth of the psychometric research tradition. The fundamental premise of Spearman's theory is that a single *g* or general intelligence ability accounts for the performance of individuals on most tasks of cognitive ability. Spearman's work was followed by decades of correlation and factor-analytic investigations by researchers who were committed to "slicing and dicing" the construct of intelligence into a taxonomy of cognitive abilities.

One of these researchers, Raymond Cattell, diverged from Spearman's single *g*-factor model to propose the existence of two general types of intelligence: fluid intelligence (*Gf*) and crystallized intelligence (*Gc*) (Cattell, 1941). *Fluid Intelligence (Gf)* is influenced by both biological and neurological factors and incidental learning through interaction with the environment and includes inductive and deductive reasoning as hallmark *Gf* indicators (Taylor, 1994). In contrast, *Crystallized Intelligence (Gc)* is comprised of abilities that reflect the influences of acculturation (viz., verbal–conceptual knowledge; Taylor,

1994; Gustafsson, 1994). Over the next 30 to 40 years, a variety of individual scholars (Carroll & Horn, 1981; Ekstrom, French, & Harmon, 1979; Horn, 1965, 1968, 1985, 1988, 1991; Thurstone, 1935, 1938; Thurstone & Thurstone, 1941) applied factor-analytic methods to a diverse array of ability measures in a wide array of samples. These efforts produced a number of empirically-based human cognitive ability taxonomies, the most notable being the *Well Replicated Common Factors (WERCOF)* (Ekstrom et al., 1979) and *Thurstone's Primary Mental Abilities (PMA)* model (1938). Collectively, these structure-seeking research activities indicated that human intellectual ability is best represented by a multitude of abilities that vary by degree of breadth or generality.

Cattell-Horn *Gf–Gc* Model

As reflected in Figure 14.1, by the early 1980s, John Horn, a student of Cattell's, articulated the relatively "complete" *Gf–Gc* model of intelligence that included eight broad abilities, which, in turn, subsumed the WERCOF and PMA abilities. Horn, like Cattell, continued to dismiss the notion of *g* and posited the broad abilities of fluid intelligence (*Gf*), crystallized intelligence (*Gc*), visual processing (*Gv*), auditory processing (*Ga*), short-term acquisition and retrieval (*SAR*, later referred to as short-term memory or *Gsm*), tertiary storage and retrieval (*TSR*, later referred to as long-term storage and retrieval or *Glr*), processing speed (*Gs*), and correct decision speed (*CDS*) (Horn, 1991).

In a series of publications between 1981 and 1991, Horn presented evidence for a broad quantitative knowledge ability (*Gq*) and sketched the faint outlines of a broad "English language usage" ability. The latter language factor was formally defined and described by Woodcock (1994) as a broad reading and writing ability (*Grw*). By 1994, contemporary Cattell-Horn *Gf–Gc* theory included 9 to 10 broad abilities. Although the Cattell-Horn *Gf–Gc* model was derived heavily from structural or factor-analytic

research, support for the model comes from a number of divergent sources. Horn and Noll (1997) summarize the developmental, heritability, neurocognitive, and external/outcome validity evidence that also support the structure of the model.

Carroll's Three-Stratum Model

Aside from the specification of the 9 to 10 broad ability Cattell-Horn model, the most important influence in applied intelligence testing during the past decade has been Carroll's (1993) meta-analysis integration of the extant psychometric factor-analytic research (see Figure 14.1). Briefly, Carroll retrieved, sampled, and then factor-analyzed (via exploratory "let the data speak for themselves" methods) the reported correlation coefficients or raw data from 461 post-1925 data sets, including four sets drawn from the 1977 WJ norming sample. Carroll (1993, 1997) articulated a hierarchical *three-stratum theory*. Sixty-nine specific, or *narrow*, abilities were identified and classified as *Stratum I* abilities. The narrow abilities were subsumed under *broad* categories of cognitive ability (*Stratum II*), which he labeled Fluid Intelligence (*Gf*), Crystallized Intelligence (*Gc*), General Memory and Learning (*Gy*), Broad Visual Perception (*Gv*), Broad Auditory Perception (*Gu*), Broad Retrieval Ability (*Gr*), Broad Cognitive Speediness (*Gs*), and Processing Speed (*Gt*). At the apex of his model (*Stratum III*), Carroll identified a higher-order factor above the broad factors, which he interpreted as General Intelligence, or *g*.

Notwithstanding the differences between the Cattell-Horn and Carroll models, the two models are very similar. Carroll (1993) reached the same conclusion when, after reviewing all the major theories of intelligence, he described the *Gf–Gc* model as the best available model of the structure of human intellect:

The Cattell-Horn model, as summarized by Horn (1985, 1988), is a true hierarchical model covering all major domains of intellectual functioning. Numerous

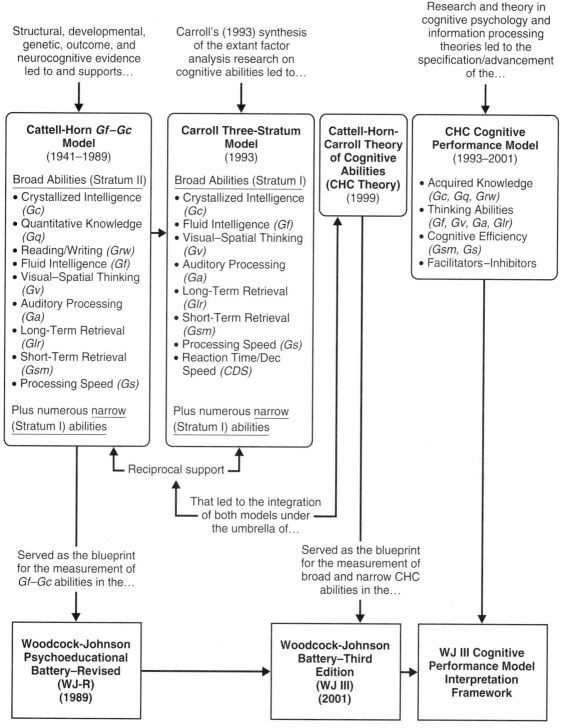

Structural, developmental, genetic, outcome, and neurocognitive evidence led to and supports…

Carroll's (1993) synthesis of the extant factor analysis research on cognitive abilities led to…

Research and theory in cognitive psychology and information processing theories led to the specification/advancement of the…

Cattell-Horn *Gf–Gc* Model
(1941–1989)

Broad Abilities (Stratum II)

- Crystallized Intelligence (*Gc*)
- Quantitative Knowledge (*Gq*)
- Reading/Writing (*Grw*)
- Fluid Intelligence (*Gf*)
- Visual–Spatial Thinking (*Gv*)
- Auditory Processing (*Ga*)
- Long-Term Retrieval (*Glr*)
- Short-Term Retrieval (*Gsm*)
- Processing Speed (*Gs*)

Plus numerous <u>narrow</u> (Stratum I) abilities

Carroll Three-Stratum Model
(1993)

Broad Abilities (Stratum I)

- Crystallized Intelligence (*Gc*)
- Fluid Intelligence (*Gf*)
- Visual–Spatial Thinking (*Gv*)
- Auditory Processing (*Ga*)
- Long-Term Retrieval (*Glr*)
- Short-Term Retrieval (*Gsm*)
- Processing Speed (*Gs*)
- Reaction Time/Dec Speed (*CDS*)

Plus numerous <u>narrow</u> (Stratum I) abilities

Cattell-Horn-Carroll Theory of Cognitive Abilities (CHC Theory)
(1999)

CHC Cognitive Performance Model
(1993–2001)

- Acquired Knowledge (*Gc, Gq, Grw*)
- Thinking Abilities (*Gf, Gv, Ga, Glr*)
- Cognitive Efficiency (*Gsm, Gs*)
- Facilitators–Inhibitors

⌐ Reciprocal support ⌐

That led to the integration of both models under the umbrella of…

Served as the blueprint for the measurement of *Gf–Gc* abilities in the…

Served as the blueprint for the measurement of broad and narrow CHC abilities in the…

Woodcock-Johnson Psychoeducational Battery–Revised (WJ-R)
(1989)

Woodcock-Johnson Battery–Third Edition (WJ III)
(2001)

WJ III Cognitive Performance Model Interpretation Framework

FIGURE 14.1

The evolution of Cattell-Horn-Carroll (CHC) theory and the Woodcock-Johnson III *details remain to be filled in through further research, but among available models it appears to offer the most well-founded and reasonable approach to an acceptable theory of the structure of cognitive abilities. The major reservation I would make about it is that it appears not to provide for a third-order g factor to account for correlations among the broad second-order factors. (p. 62)*

The most significant contribution of Carroll's work was that it circumscribed the *Gf–Gc* ability domain and imposed a systematic taxonomic structure, particularly at the narrow ability level. Carroll has provided the field of intelligence a common set of terms and definitions (i.e., a standard nomenclature), a critical development for any field of science. The *CHC Table of Cognitive Elements* is analogous to the Table of Periodic Elements in chemistry and should serve to facilitate communication among professionals and guard against test misinterpretations (Flanagan et al., 2001; McGrew & Flanagan, 1998).

Integration of the Cattell-Horn and Carroll Models

The first published attempt to integrate the Cattell-Horn and Carroll models was presented by McGrew (1997), and was later refined by McGrew and Flanagan (1998) and Flanagan et al. (2000). The resultant "Synthesized Cattell-Horn/Carroll *Gf–Gc*" model used the broad ability structure outlined in the Cattell-Horn model and organized the narrow abilities from the Carroll model to fit the broader structure. Subsequently, as indicated in Figure 14.1, in 1999 Horn and Carroll agreed that both of their frameworks should be considered as two slightly different models within the same theoretical domain (J. B. Carroll and J. L. Horn, personal communication, July 1999). The result was the agreement that both were operational models of the *Cattell-Horn-Carroll (CHC) Theory of Cognitive Abilities.*

For the WJ III, the answer to the substantive validity question (How should intelligence be defined and operationally measured?) was: "It

should be defined and measured as per CHC theory." Therefore, consistent with the *Test Standards*, the WJ III is based on a strong psychological theory that provides a well-specified and bounded domain of constructs for test development. The broad and narrow CHC abilities used in the revision of the WJ III are summarized in Table 14.1. Finally, Figure 14.1 indicates that recent attempts have been made to integrate psychometric CHC theory with information-processing theory. Woodcock's (1993, 1997) Cognitive and Academic Performance Models will be described later in this chapter.

Use of the CHC Theory as the WJ III Design Blueprint

The WJ III has benefited from two rounds of formal test development guided by the CHC theory. Between 1985 and 1986, Woodcock and McGrew independently applied confirmatory factor-analytic methods to the 1977 WJ battery. The Cattell-Horn *Gf–Gc* model drove the specification and evaluation of the structural models tested. Concurrently, Horn and Carroll independently factor-analyzed the same data. As outlined in Figure 14.1, these four sets of independent analyses were synthesized to produce the WJ-R test design blueprint (McGrew et al., 1991). Briefly, the WJ-R blueprint identified *Gf–Gc* abilities that were either adequately represented in the 1977 WJ (e.g., *Gf* by the Analysis–Synthesis and Concept Formation tests) or underrepresented (e.g., *Glr* represented only by the Visual–Auditory Learning test).

By the time the WJ III revision began, certain WJ-R *Gf–Gc* cognitive clusters were suggested to be too narrow (i.e., inadequate construct representation) by Carroll's (1993) work, Woodcock's (1990) cross-battery confirmatory factor analysis of all the major intelligence batteries, and the narrow ability analysis of the WJ-R (and all other major intelligence test batteries) (McGrew, 1997; McGrew & Flanagan, 1998). For example, the WJ-R *Ga* cluster was com-

TABLE 14.1   Broad and narrow CHC abilities incorporated into the WJ III revision

Narrow Stratum I Name (Code)	CHC Broad Stratum II Ability Definition
Acquired Knowledge	
Verbal Comprehension Knowledge (Gc)	***Breadth and depth of a person's acquired knowledge of a culture and the effective application of this knowledge***
Language Development (LD)	General development, or the understanding of words, sentences, and paragraphs (not requiring reading) in spoken native language skills
Lexical Knowledge (VL)	Extent of vocabulary that can be understood in terms of correct word meanings
Listening Ability (LS)	Ability to listen to and comprehend oral communications
General (verbal) Information (KO)	Range of general knowledge
Information about Culture (K2)	Range of cultural knowledge (e.g., music, art)
General Science Information (K1)	Range of scientific knowledge (e.g., biology, physics, engineering, mechanics, electronics)
Geography Achievement (AS)	Range of geography knowledge
Reading and Written Language (Grw)	***Store of knowledge that includes basic reading and writing and skills required for the comprehension of written language and the expression of thought in writing***
Reading Decoding (RD)	Ability to recognize and decode words or pseudowords in reading
Reading Comprehension (RC)	Ability to comprehend connected discourse during reading
Cloze Ability (CZ)	Ability to supply words deleted from prose passages that must be read
Spelling Ability (SG)	Ability to spell (not clearly defined by existing research)
Writing Ability (WA)	Ability to write with clarity of thought, organization, and good sentence structure (not clearly defined by existing research)
English Usage Knowledge (EU)	Knowledge of writing in the English language with respect to capitalization, punctuation, usage, and spelling
Reading Speed (RS)	Time required to silently read a passage as quickly as possible
Quantitative Knowledge (Gq)	***Store of mathematical knowledge; the ability to use quantitative information and to manipulate numeric symbols***
Mathematical Knowledge (KM)	Range of general knowledge about mathematics
Mathematical Achievement (A3)	Measured mathematics achievement
Thinking Abilities	
Visual–Spatial Thinking (Gv)	***The ability to generate, perceive, analyze, synthesize, store, retrieve, manipulate, transform, and think with visual patterns and stimuli***
Visualization (Vz)	Ability to mentally manipulate objects or visual patterns and to "see" how they would appear under altered conditions

(Continues)

TABLE 14.1   (Continued)

Narrow Stratum I Name (Code)	CHC Broad Stratum II Ability Definition
	Thinking Abilities
Spatial Relations (SR)	Ability to rapidly perceive and manipulate visual patterns or to maintain orientation with respect to objects in space
Visual Memory (MV)	Ability to form and store a mental representation or image of a visual stimulus and then recognize or recall it later
Spatial Scanning (SS)	Ability to accurately and quickly survey a spatial field or pattern and identify a path through the visual field or pattern
Auditory Processing (Ga)	*Ability to perceive, analyze, and synthesize patterns among auditory stimuli and discriminate subtle nuances in patterns of sound and speech*
Phonetic Coding: Analysis (PC:A)	Ability to segment larger units of speech sounds into smaller units of speech sounds
Phonetic Coding: Synthesis (PC:S)	Ability to blend smaller units of speech together into larger units of speech
Speech Sound Discrimination (US)	Ability to detect differences in speech sounds under conditions of little distraction or distortion
Resistance to Auditory Stimulus Distortion (UR)	Ability to understand speech that has been distorted or masked in one or more ways
Long-Term Retrieval (Glr)	*Ability to store information in and fluently retrieve new or previously learned information from long-term memory*
Associative Memory (MA)	Ability to recall one part of a previously learned but unrelated pair of items when the other part is presented (i.e., paired-associative learning)
Meaningful Memory (MM)	Ability to recall a set of items in which there is a meaningful relation between items or the items create a meaningful story or connected discourse
Ideational Fluency (FI)	Ability to rapidly produce a series of ideas, words, or phrases related to a specific condition or object
Naming Facility (NA)	Ability to rapidly produce names for concepts
Fluid Reasoning (Gf)	*Mental operations involved when faced with novel tasks that cannot be performed automatically, including forming and recognizing concepts, drawing inferences, comprehending implications, problem solving, and extrapolating*
General Sequential Reasoning (RG)	Ability to start with stated rules, premises, or conditions and to engage in one or more steps to solve a problem
Induction (I)	Ability to discover the underlying characteristic (e.g., rule, concept, process, trend, class membership) that governs a problem or a set of materials
Quantitative Reasoning (RQ)	Ability to inductively and deductively reason with concepts involving mathematical relations and properties

TABLE 14.1   (Continued)

Narrow Stratum I Name (Code)	CHC Broad Stratum II Ability Definition
	Cognitive Efficiency
Processing Speed (Gs)	*Ability to fluently and automatically perform cognitive tasks, especially when under pressure to maintain focused attention and concentration*
Perceptual Speed (P)	Ability to rapidly search for and compare visual symbols presented side-by-side or separated in a visual field
Rate-of-Test-Taking (R9)	Ability to rapidly perform tests that are relatively easy or that require very simple decisions
Number Facility (N)	Ability to rapidly and accurately manipulate and deal with numbers, from elementary skills of counting and recognizing numbers to advanced skills of adding, subtracting, multiplying, and dividing numbers
Semantic Processing Speed (R4)	Speed of making a decision that requires some encoding and mental manipulation of stimulus content
Short-Term Memory (Gsm)	*Ability to apprehend and hold information in immediate awareness and to use it within a few seconds*
Memory Span (MS)	Ability to attend to and immediately recall temporally ordered elements in the correct order after a single presentation
Working Memory (MW)	Ability to hold information in mind for a short time while performing some operation on it; requires divided attention and the management of the limited capacity of short-term memory

NOTE: Narrow abilities not listed here can be found in Flanagan, McGrew, and Ortiz (2001).

From D. P. Flanagan, K. S. McGrew, and S. O. Ortiz, *The Wechsler intelligence scales and Gf-Gc theory: A contemporary approach to interpretation.* Copyright © 2000 by Allyn and Bacon. Adapted by permission.

prised of the Sound Blending and Incomplete Words tests. Both of these tests are indicators of a single narrow *Ga* ability, namely, Phonetic Coding (PC). Instead of representing a broad *Ga* domain, the WJ-R *Ga* cluster was in reality an index of a single narrow ability (PC) within *Ga*.

These analyses resulted in a revision that focused on selecting the tests that would improve the construct domain coverage of each WJ III CHC cognitive cluster. Special attention was paid to Carroll's hierarchical ability taxonomy to determine which narrow abilities should be measured. Each broad WJ III CHC cluster is now comprised of two qualitatively different narrow,

or Stratum I, abilities. For example, the WJ III *Glr* cluster includes a measure of associative memory (Visual–Auditory Learning) and a measure of ideational fluency (Retrieval Fluency); the *Gv* cluster includes a measure of visualization (Spatial Relations) and a measure of visual memory (Picture Recognition). This blueprint for the WJ III had, as a primary goal, the assurance of adequate construction representation of the WJ III cognitive clusters and the minimization of construct-irrelevant variance in the tests. The process has resulted in a battery of individually administered tests that operationalizes the three-stratum CHC model of cognitive abilities.

DESCRIPTION AND ORGANIZATION OF THE WJ III TESTS AND CLUSTERS

Organization

The WJ III is a comprehensive collection of individually administered co-normed tests organized as two distinct test batteries. The Woodcock-Johnson Tests of Cognitive Abilities (WJ III COG) and the Woodcock-Johnson Tests of Achievement (WJ III ACH) are designed to measure a wide array of cognitive, oral language, and academic achievement abilities for individuals ages two through the geriatric population.

Each battery consists of two separate easel books organized into a Standard and Extended battery that can be used independently, together,

or in conjunction with other tests. Tables 14.2 and 14.3 list the 20 Tests of Cognitive Abilities and the 22 Tests of Achievement. The cognitive tests are organized by both the broad CHC clusters and by three broader categories related to cognitive performance: verbal ability, thinking ability, and cognitive efficiency. The achievement tests are organized by curricular area (reading, mathematics, written language, and academic knowledge) and oral language and by clusters within these areas, with additional groupings for special purpose clusters. Examiners would rarely administer all tests but are, instead, encouraged to be *selective* in their testing. As examiners become more familiar and skilled with the tests in the battery, they can craft better referral-specific assessments by selecting different evaluation *tools* from their chest of tests. Different referral questions may require different tools for assessment.

TABLE 14.2   Organization of the WJ III Tests of Cognitive Abilities

Cognitive Performance Category/ CHC Ability Factor	Standard Battery Tests	Extended Battery Tests
Verbal Ability		
Comprehension–Knowledge (*Gc*)	Test 1: Verbal Comprehension	Test 11: General Information
Thinking Ability		
Long-Term Retrieval (*Glr*)	Test 2: Visual–Auditory Learning *Test 10: Visual–Auditory Learning-Delayed*	Test 12: Retrieval Fluency *Test 18: Rapid Picture Naming*
Visual–Spatial Thinking (*Gv*)	Test 3: Spatial Relations	Test 13: Picture Recognition *Test 19: Planning*
Auditory Processing (*Ga*)	Test 4: Sound Blending *Test 8: Incomplete Words*	Test 14: Auditory Attention
Fluid Reasoning (*Gf*)	Test 5: Concept Formation	Test 15: Analysis–Synthesis
Cognitive Efficiency		
Processing Speed (*Gs*)	Test 6: Visual Matching	Test 16: Decision Speed *Test 20: Pair Cancellation*
Short-Term Memory (*Gsm*)	Test 7: Numbers Reversed *Test 9: Auditory Working Memory*	Test 17: Memory for Words

NOTE: Italic font designates supplemental tests.

TABLE 14.3   Organization of the WJ III Tests of Achievement

Curricular Area/CHC Ability Factor	Standard Battery Tests	Extended Battery Tests
Reading (*Grw*)		
Basic Reading Skills	Test 1: Letter–Word Identification	Test 13: Word Attack *Test 21: Sound Awareness*
Reading Fluency	Test 2: Reading Fluency	
Reading Comprehension	Test 9: Passage Comprehension	Test 17: Reading Vocabulary
Oral Language (*Gc*)		
Oral Expression	Test 3: Story Recall *Test 12: Story Recall-Delayed*	Test 14: Picture Vocabulary
Listening Comprehension	Test 4: Understanding Directions	Test 15: Oral Comprehension
Mathematics (*Gq*)		
Math Calculation Skills	Test 5: Calculation	
Math Fluency	Test 6: Math Fluency	
Math Reasoning	Test 10: Applied Problems	Test 18: Quantitative Concepts
Written Language (*Grw*)		
Basic Writing Skills	Test 7: Spelling	Test 16: Editing *Test 20: Spelling of Sounds* *Test 22: Punctuation & Capitalization*
Writing Fluency	Test 8: Writing Fluency	
Written Expression	Test 11: Writing Samples *H: Handwriting Legibility Scale*	
Knowledge (*Gc*)		Test 19: Academic Knowledge

NOTE: Italic font designates supplemental tests.

The Cognitive Battery

The Tests of Cognitive Abilities (WJ III COG) consists of 20 tests: a Standard Battery (Tests 1–10) and an Extended Battery (Tests 11–20), with each test designed to measure a different aspect of cognitive abilities. The 20 tests in the WJ III COG provide a wide variety of clusters useful for clinical and diagnostic purposes. The WJ III COG provides measurement of seven broad CHC factors described previously in this chapter. While each of the 20 tests is an independent test, interpretation of the individual tests serves primarily to understand the broader clusters. The clusters provide the primary basis for test interpretation. Assessment time will vary based on the choice of clusters and the resultant number of tests selected for administration. Most tests in the cognitive battery take about 5 to 10 minutes to administer, with the seven tests needed to get a General Intellectual Ability-Standard score (GIA-Std) requiring approximately 45 minutes and the GIA-Extended (GIA-Ext) taking about 75 to 90 minutes.

The broad abilities from the CHC model are represented by clusters in the WJ III COG. Each test (1–20) was designed to measure a narrow ability within its broad ability. The tests in the WJ III COG were revised from the WJ-R or were newly designed to decrease sources of variance that are irrelevant to the narrow ability measured by the test and to insure adequate construct representation for each broad *Gf–Gc* cluster (McGrew & Woodcock, 2001). Table 14.4 describes the broad and narrow CHC abilities measured by the WJ III COG tests.

The WJ III General Intellectual Ability (GIA) score is a measure of *g* or general intelligence and is the best single predictor of a performance, *on average*, across a wide variety of academic and cognitive outcomes. The GIA score is a differentially weighted combination of tests of seven broad CHC abilities. The test weightings for the GIA-Std score are derived from the first principal components analysis of Tests 1 through 7 (one indicator of each CHC factor). The GIA-Ext test weights are similarly calculated using Tests 1 through 7 and Tests 11 through 17 (two indicators of each CHC factor). While both have strong reliabilities throughout the life span, the broader mix of CHC narrow abilities assessed makes the GIA-Ext the single best measure of theoretical *g*. A Brief Intellectual Ability (BIA) cluster comprised of three tests (Verbal Comprehension, Concept Formation, and Visual Matching) is appropriate for screening purposes. Unlike the weighted GIA scores, the BIA is an arithmetic average of the three tests.

The *Predicted Achievement* scores are differentially weighted combinations of WJ III COG-Std Tests 1 through 7 and are used to predict achievement in reading, mathematics, written language, oral language, and academic knowledge. Each of the five Predicted Achievement scores is based on a differential weighting procedure that produces the best prediction for the achievement criterion in the near term. The seven tests are differentially weighted by age to allow for the best prediction in an academic area without including tests that overlap with the achievement criteria. The design

and use of the GIA and Predicted Achievement options in ability/achievement comparisons are discussed later in this chapter.

The Achievement Battery

Like the WJ III COG, the WJ III ACH tests are organized into a Standard Battery (Tests 1–12) and an Extended Battery (Tests 13–22). A primary goal of the revision of the WJ-R was to enhance the diagnostic capabilities of the battery. Both breadth and depth have been added to the WJ III ACH, improving the utility of many of the tests from the WJ-R for use with young children. In addition, a number of new "special purpose clusters" were added in each curricular area.

The 22 tests and 20 clusters provided by the WJ III ACH allow for a comprehensive or selective diagnostic assessment. Seven of the clusters on the WJ III ACH are aligned with the seven areas of Learning Disability specified in the Individuals with Disabilities Education Act (IDEA, 1997). In addition, the WJ III includes an important eighth area of disability, expressive oral language. Of particular relevance to assessments of students at the secondary level are the fluency measures in reading, mathematics, and written language and the Academic Fluency cluster. The movement of the oral language tests from the WJ III COG also adds increased diagnostic utility to the WJ III ACH battery. Testing time will vary, depending on the age of the person evaluated, the reason for referral, and the number of tests administered. The 22 tests in the WJ III ACH are described in Table 14.5.

Broad cluster scores are available in all three academic areas (Reading, Mathematics, and Written Language), and an Oral Language—Standard score is also available by administering tests in the Standard Battery. Additional cluster scores in each academic area and oral language are available by administering additional tests in the Extended Battery. A general academic proficiency cluster score, Total Achievement, is available, based on nine tests in the standard battery.

TABLE 14.4 WJ III COG CHC ability construct and content coverage of the individual tests

Test	Primary Broad CHC Factor	Narrow CHC Ability	Task Requirement
Test 1: Verbal Comprehension	Comprehension–Knowledge (Gc)	Lexical Knowledge Language development	Naming pictures; knowledge of synonyms and antonyms; completing verbal analogies
Test 2: Visual–Auditory Learning	Long-Term Retrieval (Glr)	Associative memory	Learning and recalling pictographic representations of words
Test 3: Spatial Relations	Visual–Spatial Thinking (Gv)	Visualization Spatial relations	Identifying the subset of pieces needed to form a complete shape
Test 4: Sound Blending	Auditory Processing (Ga)	Phonetic coding: Synthesis	Synthesizing language sounds (phonemes)
Test 5: Concept Formation	Fluid Reasoning (Glr)	Induction	Identifying, categorizing, and determining rules for a set of objects
Test 6: Visual Matching	Processing Speed (Gs)	Perceptual Speed	Rapidly locating and circling identical numbers from sets of numbers
Test 7: Numbers Reversed	Short-Term Memory (Gsm)	Working memory	Holding a span of numbers in immediate awareness while reversing the sequence
Test 8: Incomplete Words	Auditory Processing (Ga)	Phonetic coding: analysis	Identifying words with missing phonemes
Test 9: Auditory Working Memory	Short-Term Memory (Gsm)	Working memory	Holding a mixed set of numbers and words in immediate awareness while reporting the sequence of words, then numbers
Test 10: Visual–Auditory Learning–Delayed	Long-Term Retrieval (Glr)	Associative Memory	Recalling and relearning pictographic representations of words from 30 minutes to 8 days later
Test 11: General Information	Comprehension–Knowledge (Gc)	General (verbal) information	Identifying where objects are found and what people typically do with an object
Test 12: Retrieval Fluency	Long-Term Retrieval (Glr)	Ideational Fluency	Naming as many examples as possible from given categories
Test 13: Picture Recognition	Visual–Spatial Thinking (Gv)	Visual memory	Identifying a subset of previously presented pictures within a field of distracting pictures
Test 14: Auditory Attention	Auditory Processing (Ga)	Speech-sound discrimination Resistance to auditory stimulus distortion	Identifying auditorily presented words amid increasingly intense background noise

(Continues)

573

TABLE 14.4 (Continued)

Test	Primary Broad CHC Factor	Narrow CHC Ability	Task Requirement
Test 15: Analysis–Synthesis	Fluid Reasoning (*Gf*)	General sequential (deductive) reasoning	Analyzing puzzles (using symbolic formulations) to determine missing components
Test 16: Decision Speed	Processing Speed (*Gs*)	Semantic processing speed	Locating and circling two pictures most similar conceptually in a row
Test 17: Memory for Words	Short–Term Memory (*Gsm*)	Memory span	Repeating a list of unrelated words in correct sequence
Test 18: Rapid Picture Naming	Processing Speed (*Gs*)	Naming facility	Recognizing objects, then retrieving and articulating their names rapidly
Test 19: Planning	Visual–Spatial Thinking (*Gv*) Fluid Reasoning (*Gf*)	Spatial scanning General sequential reasoning	Tracing a maze pattern without removing the pencil from the paper or retracing any lines
Test 20: Pair Cancellation	Processing Speed (*Gs*)	Attention and concentration	Identifying and circling instances of a repeated pattern rapidly

TABLE 14.5 WJ III ACH CHC ability construct and content coverage of the individual tests

Test	Primary Broad CHC Factor	Narrow CHC Ability	Test Requirement
Test 1: Letter–Word Identification	Reading & Writing (*Grw*)	Reading decoding	Identifying printed letters and words
Test 2: Reading Fluency	Reading & Writing (*Grw*) Processing Speed (*Gs*)	Reading speed	Reading printed statements rapidly and responding true or false (Yes or No)
Test 3: Story Recall	Comprehension–Knowledge (*Gc*) Long-term Retrieval (*Glr*)	Language development Listening ability Meaningful memory	Listening to and recalling details of stories
Test 4: Understanding Directions	Comprehension–Knowledge (*Gc*)	Listening ability Language development	Listening to a sequence of instructions and then following the directions
Test 5: Calculation	Quantitative Knowledge (*Gq*)	Math achievement	Performing various mathematical calculations
Test 6: Math Fluency	Quantitative Knowledge (*Gq*) Processing Speed (*Gs*)	Math achievement Number fluency	Adding, subtracting, and multiplying rapidly
Test 7: Spelling	Reading & Writing (*Grw*)	Spelling ability	Spelling orally presented words
Test 8: Writing Fluency	Reading & Writing (*Grw*) Processing Speed (*Gs*)	Writing speed	Formulating and writing simple sentences rapidly
Test 9: Passage Comprehension	Reading & Writing (*Grw*)	Reading Comprehension Verbal (printed) language comprehension Cloze ability	Identifying a missing key word that makes sense in the context of a written passage
Test 10: Applied Problems	Quantitative Knowledge (*Gq*)	Quantitative reasoning Math achievement Math knowledge	Performing math calculations in response to orally presented problems
Test 11: Writing Samples	Reading & Writing (*Grw*)	Writing ability	Writing meaningful sentences for a given purpose
Test 12: Story Recall-Delayed	Long-Term Retrieval (*Glr*)	Meaningful memory	Recalling previously presented story elements
Test 13: Word Attack	Reading & Writing (*Grw*)	Reading decoding Phonetic coding: Analysis & synthesis	Recalling phonically regular nonwords
Test 14: Picture Vocabulary	Comprehension–Knowledge (*Gc*)	Language development Lexical knowledge	Naming pictures

(Continues)

TABLE 14.5 (Continued)

Test	Primary Broad CHC Factor	Narrow CHC Ability	Test Requirement
Test 15: Oral Comprehension	Comprehension–Knowledge (*Gc*)	Listening ability	Identifying a missing key word that makes sense in an oral passage
Test 16: Editing	Reading & Writing (*Grw*)	Language development English usage	Identifying and correcting errors in written passages
Test 17: Reading Vocabulary	Reading & Writing (*Grw*) Comprehension–Knowledge (*Gc*)	Verbal (printed) language comprehension Lexical knowledge	Reading words and supplying appropriate meanings
Test 18: Quantitative Concepts	Quantitative Knowledge (*Gq*) Fluid Reasoning (*Gf*)	Math knowledge Quantitative reasoning	Identifying math terms and formulae Identifying number patterns
Test 19: Academic Knowledge	Comprehension–Knowledge (*Gc*)	General information Science information Cultural information Geography achievement	Responding to questions about science, social studies, and humanities
Test 20: Spelling of Sounds	Reading & Writing (*Grw*) Auditory Processing (*Ga*)	Spelling ability Phonetic coding: Analysis & synthesis	Letter combinations that are regular patterns in written English
Test 21: Sound Awareness	Auditory Processing (*Ga*)	Phonetic coding: Analysis & synthesis	Providing rhyming words, removing, substituting, and reversing parts of words to make new words
Test 22: Punctuation & Capitalization	Reading & Writing (*Grw*)	English usage	Applying punctuation and capitalization rules

INTERPRETIVE FEATURES OF THE WJ III

As a comprehensive co-normed battery, the WJ III provides a wide array of interpretive features, some not typically available in other test batteries. Four levels of interpretive information are available for the tests and clusters. While each of the four levels provides unique information about the person's test performance, the levels of information cannot be used interchangeably. Table 14.6 provides a summary of the levels of interpretation available on the WJ III. At *Level One*, qualitative aspects of the subject's performance are noted, including test session observations and error pattern analysis. *Level Two* provides information from the raw scores about the individual's stage or level of development. At *Level Three*, the quality of a person's performance on criterion tasks at different difficulty levels is indicated. Normative comparisons to peers in the standardization sample are available at *Level Four*.

Both age- and grade-based norms are available. Grade norms are available for students in Grades K through 12, two-year colleges, and four-year colleges, including graduate school. Age norms are available for individuals age two through 95+. While the age and grade equivalents are not affected by selection of age or grade-based norms, relative proficiency index, standard score, and percentile rank are affected by an examiner's choice of norms. While the decision of which norms should be used is left to the examiner, if age norms are used to score the WJ III ACH, then age norms also should be used to score the WJ III COG and vice versa.

TABLE 14.6   Level of interpretive information available on the WJ III

Level	Type of Information	Basis	Information & Scores
1	Qualitative (Criterion-Referenced)	Observation during testing and analysis of responses	Description of the subject's reaction to the test situation Performance on finely defined skills at the item content level
2	Level of Development (Norm-Referenced)	Sum of item scores Age or grade level in the norming sample at which the average is the same as the subject's score	Raw Score Rasch Ability Score (W Score) Age Equivalent (AE) Grade Equivalent (GE)
3	Proficiency (Criterion-Referenced)	Subject's distance on a Rasch scale from an age or grade reference point	Quality of performance on reference tasks Rasch Difference score Relative Proficiency Index (RPI) CALP Level Developmental or Instructional Zone
4	Relative Standing in a Group (Norm-Referenced)	Relative position (a transformation of a difference score, such as dividing by the standard deviation of the reference group)	Rank Order Standard Score (SS) (including T score, z score, NCE, Discrepancy SD DIFF) Percentile Rank (PR) (including Discrepancy PR)

Types of Scores

A variety of scores are provided by the WJ III, including age and grade equivalents, relative proficiency indexes (RPI), cognitive–academic language proficiency (CALP) levels, percentile ranks, and standard scores. It is not possible to obtain any derived scores by hand except estimated age and grade equivalents. All scores are obtained through the use of the *WJ III Compuscore and Profiles Program* (Schrank & Woodcock, 2001). The program provides a number of special and unique features that would not be possible if scoring were done by hand. Several of the scores provided on the WJ III are discussed below.

W Score

All raw scores are converted to *W* scores, which are a special transformation of the Rasch ability scale (Rasch, 1960; Wright & Stone, 1979). The equal interval properties of the *W* scale make it a useful intermediate step in test interpretation and for measuring growth. The *W* scale for each test is centered on a value of 500 (the approximate average performance of a ten-year-old). Cluster scores are the average of the *W* scores for the individual tests in the cluster (Mather & Woodcock, 2001).

Age and Grade Equivalents

The WJ III provides both age (AE) and grade equivalent (GE) scores. An AE or GE reflects the subject's performance in terms of the age or grade level in the norming sample at which the median score is the same as the subject's score. The WJ III AE and GE scores have advantages over AE or GE scores reported on many other test batteries. One frequently cited criticism of grade (or age) scores is that they are not useful for instructional planning because they do not reflect the student's ability. It is not always recognized that this common criticism of GE's applies to tests that are composed primarily of items with a limited range of difficulty, such as the multilevel tests of many group achievement batteries. For example, if a third-grade student earns a grade equivalent of 6.5 on a test that is designed for students in grade 3, it does not mean that the student will be successful on tasks associated with the mid-sixth-grade level. Rather, it means that the student got a high percentage of the items on a third-grade test correct, the same percentage of items correct that an average sixth-grade student received. In this case, the student's score is a reflection more of the student's accuracy than of the grade level of task difficulty that this student can perform.

The "just say 'no' to grade equivalents" mantra does not apply when test items are: (1) distributed uniformly over a wide range of difficulty, (2) when individuals are administered the subset of items centered on their level of ability, and (3) when the test has been normed on an appropriately selected sample of individuals across a wide grade range (McGrew et al., 1991). The latter three conditions characterize the WJ III AE and GE scores. The WJ III AE and GE scores do, in fact, reflect the level of task difficulty an individual can perform and thus may be useful in instructional planning.

Relative Proficiency Index

The relative proficiency index (RPI), formerly called the RMI (relative mastery index) on the WJ-R, is a valuable score in better understanding a subject's quality of performance relative to peers in the normative sample. The score reads like the index used with Snellen charts to describe visual acuity. A 90 is always written in the denominator. An RPI score of 90/90 means that the subject demonstrated 90% proficiency on tasks where the average person in the comparison group (same age or grade) would also obtain 90%. The Developmental Zone (called the Instructional Zone on the WJ III ACH), is a special application of the RPI provided to help understand the subject's range of functioning on tasks from "easy" (independent level) to "difficult" (frustration level). The Developmental and Instructional Zone profiles are printed when using the *Compuscore and Profiles Program.*

CALP Levels

Cognitive Academic Language Proficiency (CALP) is described by Cummins (1984) as language used in academic situations and those that result from formal schooling. A CALP level can be reported for both the WJ III COG, using the Verbal Ability clusters, and the WJ III ACH, using the Academic Knowledge cluster and several oral and written language tests and clusters. The availability of this CALP score is valuable for examiners working with students who are non-native English speakers. The five CALP levels (1 = Negligible to 5 = Advanced) provide examiners with information useful in describing English language proficiency in academic settings. These levels also may provide information to help a nonbilingual examiner make informed referrals for evaluation by a bilingual evaluator.

Percentile Rank

Percentile ranks are provided for all tests and clusters. They are useful in describing the person's relative standing in the population. A unique feature of the WJ III percentile ranks is the extended percentile ranks at the upper and lower ends of the scale. The extension of the scale adds approximately one and one-half standard deviation units to the range of the traditional percentile rank scale.

Standard Score

The standard score scale for the WJ III is based on a mean of 100 and a standard deviation of 15. The standard score is the score most commonly reported in clinical practice. The WJ III provides standard scores from 1 to greater than 200. In addition, the *Compuscore and Profiles Program* provides an option to select a z-score, T-score, NCE, or stanine.

Types of Profiles

The use of the *Compuscore and Profiles Program* in scoring the WJ III provides the opportunity to plot the *Age/Grade Profile* or the *Standard Score/ Percentile Rank Profile*. These profiles provide a visual display of the person's Developmental Zone for the WJ III COG (called Instructional Zone on the WJ III ACH) and normative comparisons. The *Age/Grade Profile* is particularly useful when the examiner needs to explain the person's test performance for instructional planning. The left end of the shaded zone on a graphic bar represents the age or grade level where the subject would perceive the tasks as *easy* (RPI = 96/90). The right end of the zone represents the age or grade level at which the subject would perceive the tasks as *difficult* (RPI = 75/ 90). An easy level represents a person's independent level for instructional purposes while the difficult level would represent the frustration level. The width of the band will vary, as some zones will appear narrow while others appear wide. The width of the band reflects how rapidly or slowly the underlying skill or ability changes over age or grade (see section on WJ III CHC growth curves later in this chapter). A wide band reflects a slow rate of change while a narrow band indicates a rapid rate of change over time.

The *Standard Score/Percentile Rank Profile* provides a plot of the confidence band surrounding the standard score and percentile for a given test and/or cluster. The confidence band represents the region within which the subject's true score on a test or cluster most likely falls. The software program provides for the option to select three different levels of confidence (68%, 90%, 95%). The 68% confidence interval is recommended for profile interpretation. While statistical procedures are available to interpret differences in scores, guidelines are provided that allow for a visual interpretation of the display.

Clinical and Selected Special Purpose Clusters

Additional cluster scores are available to provide more comprehensive diagnostic information from both the Tests of Cognitive Abilities and the Tests of Achievement. While these clusters are likely not part of the typical test battery an examiner may give for initial evaluations, they do provide valuable special clinical and diagnostic information. Five *clinical clusters* are available on the WJ III COG. The *Phonemic Awareness* cluster measures the ability to attend to the phonemic structure of language by analyzing and synthesizing speech sounds. This ability is important to early reading as well as spelling acquisition. Scores on phonemic awareness measures have a strong relationship with reading achievement (Flanagan et al., 2001). In addition to the two-test Phonemic Awareness cluster available on the WJ III COG, a Phonemic Awareness III cluster is available by combining the Incomplete Words and Sound Blending tests (both from the WJ III COG) and the Sound Awareness test from the WJ III ACH.

Broad Attention is a special clinical cluster that provides a global measure of attention. Frequently, attention and concentration difficulties are measured using external behavior observation measures. However, more recent ADHD research points to the importance of examining cognitive indicators in addition to traditional behavior indicators (Barkley, 1996). The four tests that comprise the Broad Attention cluster—Auditory Working Memory, Numbers Reversed, Auditory Attention, and Pair Cancellation—each measure a qualitatively different aspect of attention (see neuropsychological applications section later in this chapter for more information). The *Working Memory* cluster provides additional information about a person's ability to hold information in immediate awareness while performing operations on it. The two tests comprising the Working Memory cluster (Auditory Working Memory, Numbers Reversed) require divided attention and the management of the limited capacity of short-term memory.

The *Cognitive Fluency* cluster is comprised of three tests that collectively measure a person's ability to quickly and fluently perform simple to complex cognitive tasks: speed of retrieval from stored knowledge (Retrieval Fluency); speed of

forming simple concepts (Decision Speed); and speed of lexical (vocabulary) access (Rapid Picture Naming). Finally, the COG battery also provides an *Executive Processing* cluster that provides information regarding a person's ability to effectively control and implement cognitive processes for the purpose of integrating short-term and long-term future goals (Eslinger, 1996). The Planning, Pair Cancellation, and Concept Formation tests tap different aspects of central executive control, namely, strategic planning (forward thinking), proactive interference control, and the ability to repeatedly shift mind-set (cognitive flexibility).

Four special purpose clusters are available on the WJ III ACH. The *Academic Skills* cluster is obtained from three skills tests (one in each academic area). Formerly known as *Basic Skills* on the WJ-R, the Academic Skills cluster provides useful information about the examinee's abilities in basic academic skills, including sight word recognition, spelling, and math calculation. In contrast, *Academic Applications* is a cluster that includes measures of academic reasoning in the three curricular areas. For some persons referred for evaluation, basic academic skills may be well developed in all academic areas, but they have difficulty with the more complex academic applications that require reasoning skills. Others may do well in all academic areas in both skills and applications, but they may have difficulty in their ability to work smoothly and efficiently with their abilities. The *Academic Fluency* cluster measures efficiency and the ability to work in the reading, math, and written language areas with ease. The Academic Fluency cluster may provide particularly relevant information when evaluating special accommodation requests for extended time on tasks. The *Phoneme/Grapheme Knowledge* cluster is a potentially clinically useful feature of the WJ III ACH, especially when this cluster is used in conjunction with the *Phonemic Awareness* cluster from the WJ III COG. The Phoneme/Grapheme Knowledge cluster is comprised of the Word Attack and Spelling of Sounds tests, tests in which examinees are asked to read and spell non-words with regular English spelling patterns.

The Cognitive and Achievement Performance Models

The *Cognitive and Achievement Performance Models (CA-PM)* are another set of frameworks that can assist in interpreting an individual's performance on the WJ III. The CA-PM are based largely on logical and theoretical considerations rather than empirical data (Woodcock, 1993, 1997). Based on the CA-PM frameworks, additional clusters are provided for diagnostic information. The models indicate that four overarching factors can impact a person's "real-world" cognitive and academic performance. Indicators of three of the four CA-PM domains can be obtained from the WJ III. Figure 14.2 illustrates the relationship between

the four indicators and cognitive and achievement performance.

The conceptual roots of the CA-PM framework can be traced back to Spearman, who, in *The Abilities of Man*, stated that "the process of cognition cannot possibly be treated apart from those of conation and affection, seeing that all these are inseparable aspects in the instincts and behavior of a single individual, who himself, as the very name implies, is indivisible" (Spearman, 1927, p. 2). David Wechsler was similarly convinced that a variety of *nonintellectual factors* (e.g., persistence, curiosity, and motivation) influenced the expression of intelligent behavior (Zachary, 1990). Snow's (1989) work on *aptitude complexes* and Ackerman's more recent *intelligence-as-process,*

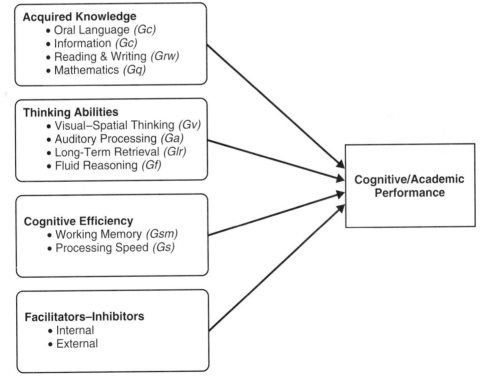

FIGURE 14.2

The WJ III cognitive and achievement performance models

personality, interests, intelligence-as-knowledge (PPIK) theory (Ackerman, 1996; Rolfhus & Ackerman, 1999) represent other attempts to integrate non-cognitive constructs into a larger theoretical framework to explain variations in cognitive and academic performance. The CA-PM is conceptually useful for bridging psychometric perspectives on test interpretation (such as the CHC model) and information-processing models of cognitive and academic functioning

Briefly, the CA-PM stores of acquired procedural and declarative knowledge are represented by the *Verbal Abilities* clusters (Std or Ext) on the WJ III COG and the respective WJ III ACH math (*Gq*) and reading and written language (*Grw*) clusters. In the cognitive model, the WJ III Verbal Abilities cluster provides a measure of language development that includes the comprehension of individual words and the comprehension of relationships among words. The tests comprising this cluster include measures of comprehension–knowledge and are influenced by the person's experience and English-language development. Verbal abilities are an important requirement for cognitive performance, especially when it involves oral language development in English. According to the CA-PM framework, "things you know" is one area that impacts cognitive and academic performance.

The WJ III *Thinking Abilities* clusters (Std or Ext) provide a sampling of different thinking processes that may be invoked when information in short-term memory cannot be processed automatically. These abilities are likely at the center of what most laypeople consider intelligence (McGrew & Woodcock, 2001). The *Thinking Abilities* cluster is comprised of measures of long-term retrieval (*Glr*), visual–spatial thinking (*Gv*), auditory processing (*Ga*), and fluid reasoning (*Gf*). According to the CA-PM, a person could "know things" yet not be able to "think" or reason with that knowledge well. Thus, thinking abilities impact cognitive performance.

Short-term memory and processing speed influence the efficiency of a person's cognitive performance. The WJ III *Cognitive Efficiency* clusters (Std or Ext) measure this aspect of the CA-PM.

These two aspects of automatic cognitive processing (*Gs* and *Gsm*) represent the capacity of the cognitive system to process information automatically. This automatic processing facilitates complex cognitive functioning. In the CA-PM, people must be able to "work efficiently" with their "knowledge" and "thinking" skills to demonstrate their best cognitive and academic performance. Finally, *facilitators–inhibitors* to cognitive performance modify cognitive and academic performance for better or worse. These noncognitive factors may be *internal* to the person (e.g., emotional state, health, and motivation) or *external* to the person in the environment (e.g., auditory distractions) or the result of situational variables (e.g., the teaching method). Woodcock (1993, 1997) and Dean and Woodcock (1999) have presented a more detailed and complex *CHC Information Processing Model* that is not presented here.

PSYCHOMETRIC CHARACTERISTICS

The development of the original WJ and WJ-R followed many traditional test development stages and procedures. In addition to traditional procedures, new concepts introduced in latent-trait or item-response theory (IRT) and the analysis of data by the Rasch model were extensively employed. Similar procedures, as well as the application of recent developments in IRT and multivariate statistics (e.g., structural equation modeling), were applied to the WJ III data. In addition, particular attention was paid to the *Test Standards* (AERA, APA, & NCME, 1999) during the test development process. The WJ III norm, reliability, and validity characteristics resulting from these test development procedures are summarized here, with a particular focus on the adolescent and adult age ranges.

Norms

The WJ III norms were calculated on the largest standardization sample of any individually administered battery of cognitive and achievement tests. A total of 8,818 individuals, from age 24 months to age 95+ years, living in more than 100 geographically and economically diverse communities in the United States, were assessed. The norm subjects were randomly selected via a stratified sampling plan that controlled for 10 specific individual (e.g., parent SES for school-age subjects; occupational status and level for adults) and community (e.g., community size, SES, etc.) variables. The preschool sample includes 1,143 children from 2 to 5 years of age (not enrolled in kindergarten). The kindergarten to 12th-grade sample is composed of 4,783 students, the college/university sample is based on 1,165 students, and the adult sample includes 1,843 individuals.

Although the distribution of norming subjects approximated the U.S. population distribution, individual subject weighting was applied during data analysis to obtain a distribution of WJ III data that was exactly proportioned to the community and individual sampling variables from year 2000 U.S. Census statistics. This exact weighting removed the potential bias effects that might result from having approximate, rather than exact, proportional representation in each cell of the sampling design. The sample and norming procedures are described in detail in McGrew and Woodcock (2001). Continuous age norms (Zachary & Gorsuch, 1985; Woodcock, 1987b) are provided at one-month intervals from 2–0 to 18–11 years of age and one-year intervals from 19 to 95+.

The combined adult and college/university sample is comprised of 3,008 individuals. In addition to the standard census variables of sex, race, Hispanic origin, and census region, individual-level information was also collected (and used in the adult subject weighting) on number of years of education, occupational/employment status, and occupational job category or status (e.g., white collar, service worker, etc.). Unique to the WJ, WJ-R, and WJ III, when compared to traditional norming plans, was the collection and use of community characteristic information in the selection of communities. The community

SES characteristics included the distribution of the population in each community according to years of education, household income, labor force characteristics (i.e., percent employed, unemployed, and not in the labor force), and occupational characteristics (i.e., percent in white-collar, service, etc., job categories).

The WJ III provides grade-based norms for subjects in kindergarten through high school and for adults enrolled in postsecondary institutions. New to the WJ III is the provision of *separate* continuous grade norms (13.0 to 18.0) for subjects in two-year and four-year postsecondary institutions.[1] This provides the ability to compare an adult subject enrolled in a postsecondary institution against a representative sample of peers at similar institutions. For example, a 27-year-old with an obtained WJ III Broad Reading *W*-score of 524 would be at the 20th percentile (standard score [SS] = 87) when compared to other 27-year-olds. If this individual was in his or her second year of instruction at a two-year community college (grade = 14.0), that same reading performance would be at the 12th percentile (SS = 82) for that population. This level of performance would be at the 6th percentile rank (SS = 76) for students in their second year of coursework at a four-year institution. This could be particularly useful information for a subject if he or she were considering a transfer to a four-year postsecondary institution. Adult subject performance on the WJ III cognitive can be scored in reference to three different normative reference groups (viz., age norms; two-year college grade norms; four-year college/university grade norms).

Reliability

Reliability and standard error or measurement (SEM) statistics are reported in the technical manual for all WJ III tests and clusters across their range of intended use (McGrew & Woodcock, 2001). The reliabilities for all but the

---

[1]Grade 18.0 represents the beginning of the year for second-year graduate students.

speeded tests and tests with multiple-point scoring systems were calculated using the split-half procedure (odd and even items) and corrected for publication test length using the Spearman-Brown correction formula. The reliabilities for the multiple-point and speeded tests were calculated using the unique standard error of measurement for each subject from Rasch analysis (McGrew & Woodcock, 2001). The reliability of cluster scores were calculated by a formula from Mosier (1943; McGrew & Woodcock, 2001). One-day interval test-retest reliabilities are reported for 165 subjects on the eight WJ III speeded tests. Test-retest correlation studies with an interval of less than one year to 10 years, involving more than 1,600 subjects, are also reported.

The WJ III test and cluster median reliabilities for eight adolescent and adult age ranges are presented in Tables 14.7 and 14.8.[2] As summarized in Table 14.7, 18 of the cognitive test median reliabilities meet or exceed the .80 level standard and 12 meet or exceed the .90 standard. All 22 achievement test median reliabilities exceed .80 and 11 meet or exceed the more stringent .90 standard. Across the WJ III cognitive and achievement batteries almost all of the 42 clusters meet or exceed the .90 reliability standard (Table 14.8). The WJ III cognitive and achievement clusters, the recommended unit for interpretation and decision making for the WJ III, possess strong reliabilities across the adolescent and adult age ranges.

Validity

Validity is the most important consideration in test development, evaluation, and interpretation and "refers to the degree to which evidence and theory support the interpretations of test scores entailed by proposed uses of tests" (AERA, 1999). Furthermore, validity is not a single-point event; it involves accumulating multiple sources of validity evidence over time.

[2]A detailed breakdown of reliabilities by specific age groups can be found in the WJ III technical manual (McGrew & Woodcock, 2001).

For many WJ III tests and clusters, validity evidence has accumulated across three different versions of the battery. For example, five of the Standard COG tests (Visual–Auditory Learning, Sound Blending, Concept Formation, Visual Matching, and Numbers Reversed) have retained the same general format across all three versions of the battery. Two additional tests (Spatial Relations and Incomplete Words) have two generations of accumulated research evidence. The remaining test (Verbal Comprehension) is comprised of four subtests for which validity data is present across all three versions.

Summarizing all generations of validity evidence presented in the respective technical manuals (McGrew, Werder, and Woodcock, 1991; McGrew & Woodcock, 2001; Woodcock, 1978) and by independent researchers is beyond the scope of this chapter. Much of this information can be found in the three respective technical manuals and other publications (McGrew, 1986, 1994). Instead, the current chapter will focus on summarizing WJ III-specific validity evidence for the adolescent and adult age ranges. Post-WJ III publication validity research (with subjects from the adolescent and adult age ranges) is also presented.

Content Validity

Although content validity has been a focus in all three editions of the WJ III, content validity evidence derived from a theoretically based test design specification framework received special attention during the WJ III revision. As described previously, the CHC theory served as the test-design blueprint for the WJ III (see Figure 14.1). The use of the strong CHC theory, a theory based on evidence accumulated over nearly 60 years of research, maximizes the substantive (content) validity vis-à-vis the specification of a well-bounded construct domain. Although confirmatory factor analysis and developmental evidence are presented in the technical manual to support the WJ III test narrow ability classifications, the WJ III narrow ability test classifications rest primarily on expert and logical task

TABLE 14.7   Median WJ III cognitive and achievement test reliabilities across eight adolescent/adult age groups (from 14 to 80+ years)

Standard Cognitive Battery Tests	Median Reliability	Standard Achievement Battery Tests	Median Reliability
Test 1: Verbal Comprehension	0.95	Test 1: Letter–Word Identification	0.94
Test 2: Visual–Auditory Learning	0.91	Test 2: Reading Fluency	0.90
Test 3: Spatial Relations	0.83	Test 3: Story Recall	0.88
Test 4: Sound Blending	0.92	Test 4: Understanding Directions	0.89
Test 5: Concept Formation	0.95	Test 5: Calculation	0.89
Test 6: Visual Matching	0.92	Test 6: Math Fluency	0.91
Test 7: Numbers Reversed	0.90	Test 7: Spelling	0.95
Test 8: Incomplete Words	0.88	Test 8: Writing Fluency	0.92
Test 9: Auditory Working Memory	0.86	Test 9: Passage Comprehension	0.86
Test 10: Visual–Auditory Delayed Recall	0.94	Test 10: Applied Problems	0.94
		Test 11: Writing Samples	0.90
		Test 12: Story Recall-Delayed	0.82

Extended Cognitive Battery Tests	Median Reliability	Extended Achievement Battery Tests	Median Reliability
Test 11: General Information	0.94	Test 13: Word Attack	0.87
Test 12: Retrieval Fluency	0.91	Test 14: Picture Vocabulary	0.90
Test 13. Picture Recognition	0.79	Test 15: Oral Comprehension	0.89
Test 14: Auditory Attention	0.88	Test 16: Editing	0.89
Test 15: Analysis–Synthesis	0.94	Test 17: Reading Vocabulary	0.92
Test 16: Decision Speed	0.90	Test 18: Quantitative Concepts	0.94
Test 17: Memory for Words	0.85	Test 19: Academic Knowledge	0.91
Test 18: Rapid Picture Naming	0.97	Test 20: Spelling of Sounds	0.82
Test 19: Planning	0.74	Test 21: Sound Awareness	0.83
Test 20: Pair Cancellation	0.84	Test 22: Punctuation and Capitalization	0.88

analyses, including expert consensus-based task analyses of the WJ III tests.

Structural Validity: Norm-Based Studies

The design of both the WJ-R and WJ III paid particular attention to the extent to which the relations among test scores (and/or their components) conformed to the relations implied by the CHC theoretical construct domain. This is typically referred to as internal or structural validity (AEAR, 1999; Benson, 1998). Structural validity research focuses on answering the question: "*Do the observed measures behave in a manner consistent with the theoretical domain definition of intelligence?*" Although it would be possible to report and discuss the patterns of test and cluster correlations

TABLE 14.8   Median WJ III cognitive and achievement cluster reliabilities across eight adolescent/adult age groups (from 14 to 80+ years)

Standard Cognitive Battery Clusters	Median Reliability	Standard Achievement Battery Clusters	Median Reliability
General Intellectual Ability (Std)	0.98	Total Achievement	0.98
Brief Intellectual Ability	0.97	Oral Language (Std)	0.92
Verbal Ability (Std)	0.95	Broad Reading	0.94
Thinking Ability (Std)	0.97	Broad Mathematics	0.96
Cognitive Efficiency (Std)	0.94	Broad Written Language	0.97
Phonemic Awareness	0.94	Academic Skills	0.97
Working Memory	0.93	Academic Fluency	0.94
		Academic Applications	0.96

Extended Cognitive Battery Clusters	Median Reliability	Extended Achievement Battery Clusters	Median Reliability
General Intellectual Ability (Ext)	0.99	Oral Language (Ext)	0.95
Verbal Ability (Ext)	0.97	Oral Expression	0.91
Thinking Ability (Ext)	0.98	Listening Comprehension	0.94
Cognitive Efficiency (Ext)	0.95	Basic Reading Skills	0.95
Comprehension–Knowledge (*Gc*)	0.97	Reading Comprehension	0.94
Long-Term Retrieval (*Glr*)	0.93	Math Calculation Skills	0.94
Visual–Spatial Thinking (*Gv*)	0.85	Mathematics Reasoning	0.97
Auditory Processing (*Ga*)	0.94	Basic Writing Skills	0.95
Fluid Reasoning (*Gf*)	0.97	Written Expression	0.94
Processing Speed (*Gs*)	0.95	Phoneme/Grapheme Knowledge	0.90
Short-Term Memory (*Gsm*)	0.92		
Broad Attention	0.94		
Cognitive Fluency	0.97		
Executive Processes	0.95		
Delayed Recall	0.93		
Knowledge	0.97		
Phonemic Awareness 3	0.95		

reported for the adolescent and adult age ranges, factor analysis is typically used to objectively evaluate the structural validity of a battery of ability tests. In this regard, the WJ III structural evidence has the advantage of building on the internal exploratory and confirmatory factor analysis of the 1977 WJ and the WJ-R norm data (McGrew et al., 1991), as well as a series of joint cross-battery analyses with all other major intelligence batteries (see Flanagan & Ortiz, 2001, for the most recent synthesis). The extant structural analyses research supports the CHC broad factor structure of the WJ-R (McGrew, 1994; McGrew et al., 1991). Given that the design of the WJ III extended and refined the previously validated broad CHC ability structure of the WJ-R, confirmatory factor analyses (CFA) studies were used almost exclusively in the evaluation of the structural validity of the WJ III.

Across the entire standardization sample, the WJ III operational CHC measurement model was determined to be the best fitting model when compared to six alternative models (McGrew & Woodcock, 2001). The six alternative models included a null, g-only, dichotomous *Gf–Gc*, and three four-factor models that operationalized the intelligence measurement models represented by the PASS, SB-IV, and WAIS-III. The factor loadings for the best fitting CHC models for one adolescent and two adult norm samples are presented in Table 14.9. In all three samples, the WJ III CHC measurement model was the best fitting model (McGrew & Woodcock, 2001). Similar to the WJ-R CFA analyses, the models reported for the oldest samples (ages 40–100) were the poorest fitting models (in an absolute sense). These findings suggest that additional research is needed to determine if alternative models may better represent the CHC structure of cognitive functioning during middle to late adulthood.

The results summarized in Table 14.9 indicate that, in general, most WJ III tests are relatively strong and invariant indicators of the same CHC abilities across the adolescent and adult age ranges. A few exceptions are noted. First, in the *Gc* domain, the Understanding Direction test is a mixed measure of *Gc* (LS, listening ability) and *Gsm* (MW, working memory) during the adolescent and young adult age ranges, but taps more *Gsm* (MW) during middle to late adulthood. Similarly, the Quantitative Concepts test is a consistent mixed indicator of *Gq* (KM, mathematical knowledge) and *Gf* (RQ, quantitative reasoning) during the adolescent and young adult age ranges, with a greater emphasis on *Gf* during middle to late adulthood. Although some

age-related changes are observed for a few WJ III reading and writing (viz., Reading Vocabulary and Spelling of Sounds) and *Glr* (Story Recall and Retrieval Fluency) tests, these changes appear unsystematic in nature.

The only *Gv* test that changes noticeably across the three age groups is Planning. The Planning test demonstrates a slight increase in *Gv* (SS, Spatial Scanning) with age. However, it is important to note that this test has more unique than common variance (at all age ranges) and is likely measuring other variables outside the boundaries of the WJ III CHC construct domain (e.g., cognitive style; planning; attention and concentration). With the possible exception of the Auditory Attention test (which appears to increase in *Ga* variance with age), all WJ III *Ga* and *Gf* tests are relatively invariant CHC-domain specific indicators.

The WJ III *Gs* tests demonstrate the most interesting variations with age. In general, the Visual Matching, Decision Speed, and Pair Cancellation tests show increased reliance on *Gs* abilities with increasing age, particularly after age 40. This is particularly noticeable for Pair Cancellation, a test deliberately designed to assess sustained concentration or vigilance. This finding suggests that the Pair Cancellation test may become an increasingly important diagnostic test for detecting changes in cognitive efficiency during the later adult years. In the case of Visual Matching, the increase in *Gs* ability (P, perceptual speed) is associated with a decrease in a minor *Gq* (N, number facility) influence. Finally, Rapid Picture Naming appears to be a relatively moderate indicator of *Gs* (R9, rate-of-test-taking) and a weak indicator of *Glr* (NA, naming facility) during the adolescent and young adult ages, with the *Glr* abilities measured diminishing after age 40. Given the prominent role processing speed (*Gs*) plays in theories of changes in adult intelligence (Bashore, Ridderinkhof, & van der Molen, 1998; Kail, 1991a, 1991b; Kail & Salthouse, 1994; Salthouse, 1996), the findings for Pair Cancellation and Rapid Picture Naming are particularly interesting. Additional research

TABLE 14.9   WJ III broad CHC test factor loadings in adolescent and two adult norm samples

Broad CHC Factors by Age Groups

Tests	Gc			Gq			Grw			Glr		
	14–19	20–39	40+	14–19	20–39	40+	14–19	20–39	40+	14–19	20–39	40+
Verbal Comprehension	0.92	0.94	0.95									
General Information	0.89	0.93	0.93									
Understanding Directions (Ach)	0.41	0.30	0.17								0.18	
Picture Vocabulary (Ach)	0.82	0.84	0.89									
Oral Comprehension (Ach)	0.75	0.81	0.79									
Academic Knowledge (Ach)	0.89	0.90	0.93									
Calculation (Ach)				0.85	0.87	0.89						
Math Fluency (Ach)				0.46	0.47	0.41						
Applied Problems (Ach)	0.19	0.23	0.23	0.53	0.57	0.54						
Quantitative Concepts (Ach)				0.51	0.59	0.39						
Letter–Word Identification (Ach)	0.12	0.15	0.12				0.77	0.76	0.80			
Reading Fluency (Ach)							0.45	0.42	0.35			
Passage Comprehension (Ach)	0.48	0.50	0.46				0.32	0.32	0.43			
Word Attack (Ach)							0.73	0.76	0.81			
Reading Vocabulary (Ach)	0.66	0.82	0.63				0.18		0.30			
Spelling (Ach)							0.83	0.85	0.90			
Writing Fluency (Ach)							0.47	0.46	0.52			
Writing Samples (Ach)							0.73	0.78	0.84			
Handwriting (Ach)							0.25	0.25	0.36			
Editing (Ach)							0.75	0.76	0.85			
Spelling of Sounds (Ach)							0.36	0.49	0.32			
Visual–Auditory Learning										0.77	0.71	0.86
Visual–Auditory Learning: DR										0.74	0.68	0.80
Retrieval Fluency										0.31	0.55	0.37
Story Recall (Ach)	0.59		0.41							0.10	0.59	0.28
Story Recall: DR (Ach)	0.57	0.42	0.44									
Memory for Names										0.65	0.62	0.79
Memory for Names: DR										0.61	0.56	0.72

Broad CHC Factors by Age Groups

Gv			Ga			Gf			Gs			Gsm		
14–19	20–39	40+	14–19	20–39	40+	14–19	20–39	40+	14–19	20–39	40+	14–19	20–39	40+
												0.35	0.34	0.64
									0.47	0.40	0.51			
						0.25	0.16	0.18						
						0.48	0.42	0.56						
									0.48	0.45	0.54			
									0.36	0.38	0.35			
			0.37	0.26	0.50									
									0.35	0.08	0.40			

(Continues)

TABLE 14.9   (Continued)

| | Broad CHC Factors by Age Groups | | | | | | | | | | | |
| | Gc | | | Gq | | | Grw | | | Glr | | |
Tests	14–19	20–39	40+	14–19	20–39	40+	14–19	20–39	40+	14–19	20–39	40+
Spatial Relations												
Picture Recognition												
Planning												
Visual Closure												
Block Rotation												
Sound Blending												
Incomplete Words												
Auditory Attention												
Sound Awareness (Ach)												
Sound Patterns												
Analysis–Synthesis												
Concept Formation												
Numerical Reasoning				0.34	0.39							
Visual Matching				0.22	0.21	0.12						
Decision Speed												
Rapid Picture Naming										0.17	0.21	0.08
Pair Cancellation												
Cross Out												
Numbers Reversed												
Auditory Working Memory												
Memory for Words												
Memory for Sentences	0.33	0.42	0.38									
Factor loading on g	0.90	0.91	0.92	0.71	0.66	0.85	0.90	0.91	0.91	0.80	0.95	0.89

NOTE: Italic font designates WJ III Research tests used during the development of the WJ III (McGrew & Woodcock, 2001).
Copyright © 2001 by The Riverside Publishing Company. Adapted from the Woodcock-Johnson® III (WJ III™) by Richard W. Woodcock, Kevin S. McGrew and Nancy Mather, with permission of the publisher. All rights reserved.

is needed to determine if these two WJ III *Gs* tests may have special diagnostic utility (above and beyond the other WJ III *Gs* tests) in the assessment of the effects of aging on cognitive performance.

All WJ III *Gsm* tests are factorially pure and strong indicators of the *Gsm* domain. There is a trend for the Auditory Working Memory (MW, working memory) and Memory for Words (MS, memory span) tests to change slightly in *Gsm* characteristics after adolescence, with the former increasing in *Gsm* and the latter decreasing in *Gsm* starting at age 20.

Broad CHC Factors by Age Groups

Gv			Ga			Gf			Gs			Gsm		
14–19	20–39	40+	14–19	20–39	40+	14–19	20–39	40+	14–19	20–39	40+	14–19	20–39	40+
0.71	0.75	0.73												
0.47	0.43	0.55												
0.33	0.43	0.54				0.09								
0.37	0.46	0.55												
0.53	0.65	0.61												
			0.67	0.72	0.66									
			0.51	0.61	0.61									
			0.34	0.44	0.48									
			0.79	0.83	0.85									
			0.35	0.47	0.55									
						0.74	0.80	0.83						
						0.77	0.79	0.79						
						0.56	0.56	0.86						
									0.70	0.71	0.81			
									0.69	0.73	0.78			
									0.48	0.41	0.59			
									0.59	0.73	0.82			
0.24	0.26	0.27							0.66	0.67	0.67			
												0.75	0.71	0.78
												0.73	0.82	0.82
												0.70	0.69	0.64
												0.42	0.38	0.37
0.77	0.79	0.85	0.87	0.96	0.97	0.92	0.92	0.94	0.49	0.51	0.75	0.83	0.86	0.92

Brief Comments on "Good" Factors

As more intelligence test batteries pay closer attention to sampling a greater breadth of narrow abilities within each CHC theoretical construct domain, some of the established "rules of thumb" regarding what constitutes a *strong* or *good* factor loading for a cognitive construct may need to change. Reviewers often relate the strength of a factor (and its indicators) to the absolute magnitude and consistency of the factor loadings. McGrew and Woodcock (2001) argue that, in some situations, excessively high test factor loadings may be a counter indicator of good construct validity.

For example, in the WJ-R, the *Glr* cluster was comprised of the Visual–Auditory Learning and Memory for Names tests. Both tests consistently demonstrated high *Glr* factor loadings. In contrast, the WJ III *Glr* cluster is comprised of the Visual–Auditory Learning and Retrieval Fluency tests. These two WJ III tests demonstrate markedly less consistent *Glr* factor loadings in Table 14.9, with the Retrieval Fluency loading being much lower (.31 to .51) than Visual–Auditory Learning (.71 to .86). Did the WJ-R *Glr* factor (and its two tests) represent a more valid factor than the WJ III *Glr* factor? McGrew and Woodcock (2001) argue that, when *all* forms of validity evidence are combined, the WJ III *Glr* factor is more valid than the WJ-R *Glr* construct. Why?

It is not often recognized that, when indicators of different aspects of a broad construct domain are sampled adequately, a factor with all moderate factor loadings may, in fact, be a more valid factor. This is referred to as the *attenuation paradox* in the reliability literature (Boyle, 1991; Clark & Watson, 1995; Loevinger, 1954), where it has long been recognized that if the inter-item correlation increases among items too much, a test may become very homogeneous and reliable, but at the expense of narrow content coverage that compromises validity. The same principle holds for the correlation of test factor indicators. Maximizing the absolute magnitude of indices of factor homogeneity (e.g., factor loadings) may occur at the expense of factor breadth (construct validity). One may end up with a very narrow factor with test indicators that may tap very similar abilities, rather than a factor that more adequately samples different aspects of the construct domain. Post-WJ-R content validity and hierarchical CFA studies that included narrow and broad factors suggested that the relatively high and tight WJ-R *Glr* factor loadings were reflecting a narrow ability (viz., MA, Associative Memory) and not the intended broad *Glr* ability (Flanagan et al., 2000; McGrew & Flanagan,

1998; McGrew & Woodcock, 2001). McGrew and Woodcock (2001) present logical and empirical evidence (e.g., content validity; hierarchical narrow and broad CFA analyses; differential developmental growth curve trajectories) that supports the divergent WJ III *Glr* factor loadings for Visual–Auditory Learning and Retrieval Fluency as reflecting a more valid factor and set of indicators. A review of the factor loadings in Table 14.9, in the context of other forms of validity evidence, suggests that the WJ III *Glr*, *Ga*, and *Gv* clusters are also exemplars of broader and more valid CHC construct measures.

Structural Validity: Special Study Analysis

The WJ III technical manual describes a study (Gregg/Hoy 1985 study) based on a sample of 204 university students who were administered a wide array of cognitive and achievement measures. Recently, McGrew et al., (2001) subjected the WJ III, WAIS-III, WMS-III, and KAIT test scores from this study to a set of CHC-organized broad and broad plus narrow ability CFAs. The broad and narrow CHC classifications for the most viable broad factor CHC model are presented in Table 14.10.

The pattern of findings summarized in Table 14.10 is nearly identical to those summarized in Table 14.9 and will not be repeated here. The cross-battery CFA results provide additional structural validity evidence for the WJ III tests included in the analysis. A number of findings in Table 14.10 are of particular interest with regard to the structural validity of the WJ III and cross-battery applications (to be discussed later). More detailed discussion and interpretation of this CFA study can be found in McGrew et al. (2001).

First, the modification of four prior WJ-R tests to serve as four *subtests* for the Verbal Comprehension composite test appears to have produced a strong single test indicator of *Gc*. McGrew et al. (2001) report that the WJ III Verbal Comprehension test demonstrated the highest *Gc* factor loading (.85), followed next by the

TABLE 14.10 WJ III, WAIS-III, WMS-III, KAIT broad and narrow classifications based on Gregg/Hoy university sample CFA (McGrew et al., 2001)

Battery	Tests	Gc	Gq	Grw	Glr	Gv	Ga	Gf	Gs	Gsm
WJ III	**Verbal Comprehension**	LD/VL								
WAIS-III	Information	K0								
WAIS-III	Comprehension	LD/K0								
WAIS-III	Vocabulary	VL								
WAIS-III	Similarities	LD/K0								
WMS-III	Logical Memory I	LS								
WMS-III	Logical Memory II	ls			mm					
KAIT	Definitions	vl/ld		SG/RD						
KAIT	Double Meanings	VL		v						
KAIT	Auditory Comprehension	LD/LS								
WJ III	**Math Fluency (Ach)**		A3							
WAIS-III	Arithmetic		A3							
WJ III	**Letter–Word Identification (Ach)**			rd			pc			
WJ III	**Reading Fluency (Ach)**			RS					r4/r9	
WJ III	**Passage Comprehension (Ach)**			cz				rq		
WJ III	**Visual–Auditory Learning**				MA					
WJ III	**Retrieval Fluency**				fi				r4/r9	
WJ III	*Memory for Names*				MA					
KAIT	Rebus Learning				MA					
WMS-III	Family Pictures I				ma	mv				
WMS-III	Family Pictures II				ma					
WMS-III	Spatial Span					mv				ms
WMS-III	Faces I				mm					
WMS-III	Faces II				mm					
WMS-III	Verbal-Paired Associates I				MA					
WMS-III	Verbal-Paired Associates II				MA					
WJ III	**Spatial Relations**					Vz/SR				
WJ III	**Picture Recognition**					mv				
WJ III	*Block Rotation*					Vz/SR				
WJ III	*Visual Closure*					cs				
WAIS-III	Picture Completion					CF				
WAIS-III	Picture Arrangement					vz				
WAIS-III	Block Design					SR/Vz				

(Continues)

TABLE 14.10   (Continued)

Battery	Tests	Gc	Gq	Grw	Glr	Gv	Ga	Gf	Gs	Gsm
WJ III	**Sound Blending**						PC:S			
WJ III	**Incomplete Words**						PC:A			
WJ III	**Auditory Attention**						us/ur			
WJ III	*Sound Patterns*						U3			
WJ III	**Analysis-Synthesis**							RQ		
WJ III	**Concept Formation**							I		
WAIS-III	Matrix Reasoning							I		
KAIT	Mystery Codes							I		
KAIT	Logical Steps							RQ		
WJ III	**Visual Matching**								P	
WJ III	**Decision Speed**								R4	
WJ III	**Rapid Picture Naming**								na	
WJ III	*Cross Out*					ss			P	
WAIS-III	Digit Symbol-Coding								R9	
WAIS-III	Symbol Search								P/R9	
WJ III	**Numbers Reversed**									MW
WJ III	**Auditory Working Memory**									MW
WJ III	**Memory for Words**									MS
WJ III	*Memory for Sentences*	ld								Ms
WAIS-III	Letter–Number Sequencing									MW
WMS-III	Letter–Number Sequencing									MW

NOTE: Bold font = WJ III tests; italic font = WJ III Research tests (McGrew & Woodcock, 2001). Significant factor loadings have been replaced with the narrow CHC ability classifications proposed by McGrew et al. (2001). See Table 14.1 for the names and definitions corresponding to each narrow ability code/abbreviation. Capitalized narrow ability codes designate significant factor loadings > .49. Lower-case narrow ability codes designate significant factor loadings < .50. Significant residuals were reported between WMS-III Family Pictures I & II, WMS-III Logical Memory I & II, WAIS-III/WMS-III Letter–Number Sequencing; WMS-III Faces I & II; WMS-III Verbal Paired-Associates I & II; WJ III Decision Speed & Rapid Picture Naming; WJ III Visual Matching and Math Fluency; WJ III Math Fluency & WAIS-III Digit Symbol; WJ III Math Fluency and Reading Fluency.

WAIS-III Vocabulary test (.83). The WJ III Verbal Comprehension test has a distinct advantage over the other *Gc* tests reported in Table 14.10 in that it is comprised of four tests that together tap lexical knowledge (VL) and general language development (LD, which subsumes VL). Unfortunately, the WJ III General Information test was not included in this study. Second, consistent with a prior joint WJ-R/KAIT CFA study (Flanagan & McGrew, 1998), two of the KAIT *Gc* tests (Definitions and Double Meanings) were found to be mixed measures of *Gc* and *Grw*. The influence of reading and writing achievement variance on these two *Gc* tests, and the Definitions test in particular (*Grw* loading = .80), although consistent with Carroll's definition of

Gc, suggests that these two *Gc* tests must be interpreted with caution when assessing adolescents and adults with learning difficulties in reading or writing skills.

Third, the results continue to reinforce the conclusion that two of the original 1977 WJ tests (Analysis–Synthesis and Concept Formation) have withstood the test of time as two of the best available tests of *Gf* abilities. The results in Table 14.10 also indicate that the KAIT Mystery Codes and Logical Steps are also excellent tests for the assessment of *Gf* abilities. Fourth, given the historical prominence of the WAIS series in the assessment of adolescent and adult intelligence, it is important to note that the results in Table 14.10 indicate that the long-overdue addition of a *Gf* test (viz., Matrix Reasoning) to the WAIS-III has successfully plugged the WAIS-III *Gf* hole (McGrew, 1997; McGrew & Flanagan, 1996, 1998; Woodcock, 1990), at least with one test. More importantly, the strong loading of the WAIS-III Block Design on *Gv* (.80; McGrew et al., 2001), in the absence of any significant loading on the robust *Gf* factor, adds one more nail to the coffin of the traditional clinical interpretation of WAIS-III Block Design as a measure of "reasoning," particularly abstract fluid reasoning. These results, plus the extant CHC cross-battery factor-analysis research of the Wechsler series of tests (see Flanagan et al., 2001, for the most recent synthesis), should put to rest the notion that the WAIS-III (and WISC-III) Block Design test can be used to draw inferences about *Gf* abilities. The WJ III and KAIT *Gf* tests appear to be much more valid tests for measuring the *Gf* abilities of adolescents and adults.

Fifth, the interpretation of the WJ III Retrieval Fluency test as a good indicator of *Glr* requires the use of a hierarchical model in which Retrieval Fluency and Rapid Picture Naming form a narrow naming facility (NA) factor, which, in turn, has a moderate loading on *Glr*. The broad *Glr* factor also subsumes the narrow abilities of meaningful memory (MM) and associative memory (MA) (see McGrew and Woodcock, 2001, for a detailed explanation). Sixth, the

KAIT Rebus Learning (MA, Associative Memory) and many WMS-III tests provide for additional coverage of *Glr*. Two of the WMS-III tests (Family Pictures I and Spatial Span) appear to be factorially complex measures, a situation that clouds their diagnostic interpretation. Seventh, the WJ III is the only major intelligence battery for use with adolescents and adults that includes strong indicators of *Ga*.

Finally, although imposing near-identical task requirements on subjects, the WJ III Auditory Working Memory test (MW, working memory) appears to be a stronger *Gsm* (.81) indicator than the WAIS-III and WMS-III Letter-Number Sequencing tests (with .67 *Gsm* loadings for both) (McGrew et al., 2001). The less complex WJ III *Gsm* tests of memory span (MS, Memory for Words and Memory for Sentences) displayed more moderate factor loadings when compared to the working memory tasks. Of note for the WAIS-III Working Memory Index (a combination of Digit Span, Letter-Number Sequencing, and Arithmetic) is the finding that Arithmetic loads on a *Gq* factor and *not* on the *Gsm* factor with other tests of working memory. These findings suggest that the WJ III Working Memory cluster is a more valid measure of working memory (MW) than is the WAIS-III Working Memory Index. The WAIS-III Working Memory Index is confounded with construct irrelevant *Gq* variance.

External Validity

External validity focuses on the external relations among the focal constructs and their measures and other constructs and/or subject characteristics (AERA, 1999; Benson, 1998). The question posed is "*Do the focal constructs and observed measures fit within a network of expected construct relations (i.e., the nomological network)?*" The adolescent- and adult-specific external validity evidence for the WJ III COG presented in the WJ III technical manual is summarized here. The reader is referred to McGrew and Woodcock (2001) for external validity evidence at other age groups. In addition to summarizing the studies presented in the WJ III technical manual, a recently completed group differentiation analysis with the special Gregg/Hoy LD/non-LD university sample will be presented later in this chapter.

Concurrent Validity: WJ III Ability Cluster Correlations with Achievement and Other Intelligence Batteries

The WJ III GIA scores displayed concurrent correlations in the .70s with the general composite scores across all age samples and instruments (WPPSI-R, WISC-III, WAIS-III, DAS, KAIT, and SB-IV; McGrew & Woodcock, 2001). These studies provide concurrent validity evidence that the WJ III GIA-Std and GIA-Ext clusters are valid indicators of general intelligence, as operationalized by other intelligence batteries.

The single adult-specific concurrent study that presented correlations with the composite scores of other intelligence batteries was the Gregg/Hoy university sample (1985) described previously. Given the selective nature of the two adult subgroups included in this study, the combined sample exhibited significant restriction of range in scores, a situation that dampened the resultant correlations. Thus, the relative comparisons of concurrent correlations are important here, not the absolute magnitude of the correlations. Given this caveat, the .67 and .75 correlations (reported in Table 14.11) with the WAIS-III Full Scale and KAIT Composite IQ, respectively, reinforce the validity of the WJ III COG as a valid measure of general intellectual functioning with adults.

Also presented in Table 14.11 are select correlations that allow for the comparison of the relative concurrent validity of the WJ III, WAIS-III, and KAIT composite scores in the prediction of basic reading, math, and writing achievement. Across and within achievement domains, the WJ III Predicted Achievement and GIA-Standard clusters outperformed both the WAIS-III Full Scale and KAIT composite IQs in the concurrent prediction of achievement. The superiority

of the WJ III Predicted Achievement option was again borne out in these data. It is particularly interesting to note that the KAIT demonstrated a median correlation (.51) with achievement much closer to the WJ III GIA-Standard (.56) and WJ III Predicted Achievement (.60) options than did the WAIS-III (.36). It is hypothesized that this is because the KAIT (although only providing *Gf* and *Gc* composite scores) includes a much greater breadth of CHC abilities than does the WAIS-III, but not as great a breadth as does the WJ III. The prior discussion of the joint WJ III, WAIS-III, WMS-III, KAIT CFA study and the Flanagan and McGrew (1998) study support this interpretation. These data suggest that CHC-designed intelligence batteries, and the WJ III in particular, may hold a distinct advantage over the venerable WAIS-III when investigating the academic functioning of adolescents and adults.

A more circumscribed study described in the WJ III technical manual (Norton Study; see McGrew & Woodcock, 2001) involved 50 adults attending a California community college. As part of a study focused on understanding math achievement, the adult subjects were administered a select set of eight WJ III Cognitive tests, five WJ III research tests, and two WJ III math achievement tests. They were also administered select tests from the KAIT and WAIS-III. The specific cognitive tests selected from each battery were those from the CHC ability domains (i.e., *Gf*, *Gv*, *Gs*, *Glr*) that prior research suggested were the most related to math achievement (Flanagan et al., 2000; McGrew & Flanagan, 1998).

In the Norton Community College sample, the simple correlations between all *Gf* tests (WJ III Analysis–Synthesis and Concept Formation; WAIS-III Matrix Reasoning; KAIT Logical Steps and Mystery Codes) and math achievement were consistently higher than the correlations between the *Glr*, *Gs*, and *Gv* tests and math achievement. Stepwise multiple regression found the combination of the WJ III Concept Formation and Analysis–Synthesis tests (regression

TABLE 14.11 Select WJ III, WAIS-III, and KAIT concurrent validity correlations in LD/Not-LD university sample

Cognitive Measures	Reading Achievement				Writing Achievement			Fluency	Median Correlations
	WJ III Broad Reading	*WJ III Basic Reading Skills*	*WRAT-III Reading*	*Nelson Denny Reading Comp.*	*WJ III Basic Writing Skills*	*OWLS Written Expression*	*WRAT-III Spelling*	*WJ III Academic Fluency*	
WJ III General Intellectual Ability—Standard	.56	.56	.61	.61	.62	.49	.47	.48	**.56**
WJ III Predicted Achievement	.66	.62	.60	.60	.63	.52	.49	—	**.60**
Wechsler Adult Intelligence Scale III Full Scale	.35	.39	.43	.47	.38	.36	.27	.27	**.36**
Kaufman Adolescent & Adult Intelligence Composite	.57	.53	.58	.59	.51	.47	.37	.49	**.51**
N	206	185	204	191	200	102	204	205	
Mean	94.7	92.2	107.6	219.1	95.9	93.2	104.5	103.6	
Standard Deviation	12.4	12.9	9.6	23.9	14.0	13.4	13.7	13.3	

NOTE: WJ III General Intellectual Ability Standard correlated .67 and .75 with WAIS-III Full Scale and KAIT Composite scores, respectively.

weights = .41 to .36, respectively), followed to a lesser extent by KAIT Mystery Codes (weight = .22), provided the best prediction of adult math achievement (R^2 = .66). This study suggests that the WJ III *Gf* tests of Concept Formation and Analysis–Synthesis may be particularly useful for predicting and explaining mathematics achievement in a postsecondary education setting. Together, the Gregg/Hoy and Norton postsecondary education studies provide support for the concurrent validity of the WJ III COG tests and ability clusters, particularly when compared to other intelligence batteries suitable for this population.

Concurrent Validity: WJ III Ability and Achievement Cluster Correlations

The average concurrent WJ III ability–achievement correlations across the adolescent and adult age ranges (McGrew & Woodcock, 2001) are reported in Table 14.12. A review of Table 14.12 leads to a number of conclusions. First, the three WJ III Cognitive ability options (Predicted

TABLE 14.12   Average (median) correlations between WJ III ability cluster options and WJ III achievement clusters across the adolescent and adult norm samples

	Median Correlations			
Achievement Cluster	**Predicted Achievement**	**General Intellectual Ability (GIA) Standard**	**General Intellectual Ability (GIA) Extended**	**Oral Language**
Reading				
Broad Reading	0.85	0.81	0.84	0.76
Basic Reading Skills	0.79	0.76	0.78	0.74
Reading Comprehension	0.82	0.76	0.79	0.81
Mathematics				
Broad Mathematics	0.77	0.75	0.76	0.67
Math Calculation Skills	0.72	0.69	0.61	0.57
Math Reasoning	0.79	0.77	0.78	0.73
Written Language				
Broad Written Language	0.83	0.81	0.83	0.73
Basic Writing Skills	0.81	0.77	0.79	0.74
Written Expression	0.80	0.78	0.80	0.69
Language & Knowledge				
Oral Language (Std.)	0.77	0.82	0.86	
Oral Language (Ext.)	0.77	0.80	0.83	
Oral Expression	0.67	0.73	0.77	
Listening Comprehension	0.77	0.81	0.83	
Academic Knowledge	0.87	0.77	0.80	0.84

Achievement; GIA-Std; GIA-Ext) are consistently better predictors of achievement than the Oral Language ability option. The three WJ III COG ability options are the preferred measures when making predicted/actual achievement comparisons during the adolescent and adult age ranges. Second, as expected, the ability option that uses optimal differential weights of the seven standard COG tests to predict achievement (Predicted Achievements) outperforms a combination of the same seven tests when they are differentially weighted to approximate g or general intelligence (GIA). Third, although there is a minor trend for the GIA-Ext cluster to correlate slightly higher with achievement than does the GIA-Std, these differences are not practically significant.

When in-depth diagnostic information is not necessary, the seven-test GIA-Std offers prediction equal to that of the more in-depth 14-test GIA-Ext. Finally, when predictions are necessary regarding an adolescent or adult oral language functioning, the GIA clusters are consistently better predictors. This is not surprising given that the GIA clusters include measures of Gc, a construct domain that subsumes oral language. The design of the oral language Predicated Achievement score option eliminates this predictor/criterion overlap by fixing the Gc test weights to zero. The decision on which ability score to use when making oral language expected/actual performance comparisons depends on the nature of the specific referral questions (McGrew & Woodcock, 2001).

Group Membership Differentiation: LD/Normal Mean Score Comparisons

The final set of external validity evidence available for the adolescent and adult population was a comparison of test performance of the LD and Not-LD (Normal) subjects in the Gregg/Hoy university sample (McGrew & Woodcock, 2001). Mean score LD/Not-LD comparisons were presented for 16 WJ III COG clusters and 6 WJ III ACH clusters. Even after the applica-

tion of the Bonferroni adjustment to control for overall experiment-wise error rate, all but 3 of the 22 t-tests were significant at the .05 level of significance. As would be expected, given the prominence achievement plays in the identification and classification of individuals with learning disabilities, the largest mean score differences were on five of the six achievement clusters. With the Normal subject mean scores ranging primarily in the average to above average ranges (98.2 for Basic Reading Skills to 112.0 for Academic Fluency), the LD subjects scored approximately one standard deviation lower on Basic Writing Skills (–17.8), Academic Fluency (–17.3), Broad Reading (15.8), Basic Reading Skills (–14.0), and Phoneme/Grapheme Knowledge (–13.5). Oral Expression scores were not significantly different.

The LD subjects were also –11.8 points lower on the GIA-Std cluster. The largest differences on the cognitive clusters occurred in domains related to the efficiency of cognitive processing and Ga abilities. In particular, the largest mean score differences were noted for the Cognitive Efficiency (–11.8 for Standard and –10.4 for Extended), Auditory Processing (–11.7), Phonemic Awareness (–11.3), and Working Memory (–11.1) clusters. The only cognitive clusters that did not differentiate the two groups were the Long-term Retrieval (Glr), Visual–Spatial Thinking (Gv), and Cognitive Fluency (Gs) clusters. Collectively, the mean score comparisons suggest that the WJ III COG and ACH batteries provide useful information for the differentiation of adult university subjects with and without learning disabilities. These largely descriptive findings suggest that adult university students with learning disabilities, as a group, are characterized by: significantly lower achievement (across all areas); lower general intellectual functioning: and relatively larger specific cognitive deficits in the auditory processing domains and the efficiency of cognitive processing (particularly working memory). More refined analyses of these data with specialized group-differentiation methodology are described in the next section of this chapter.

SPECIAL APPLICATIONS AND USE WITH SPECIAL POPULATIONS

Assessment of Learning Disabilities

The WJ III includes a variety of cluster scores and interpretive options that can be useful in the assessment and identification of learning disabilities (LD). As described previously in this chapter, the breadth of measures included in the WJ III provides diagnosticians with a large theory-based tool chest for surveying many of the cognitive and achievement abilities associated with comprehensive LD assessments. The WJ III also provides a set of discrepancy-based interpretive features that facilitate the norm-based identification of within-person cognitive and achievement strengths and weaknesses, a practice that has been at the core of LD assessment and identification since the field's inception. Three different discrepancy models for evaluating the strengths and weaknesses between and among WJ III cluster scores are presented. These discrepancy models are then followed by the presentation of preliminary research that identifies potentially important WJ III clusters for the identification of adults with LD.[3]

General Intellectual Ability–Achievement Discrepancy Model

Ninety-eight percent of all states, and most federal agencies servicing adolescents and adults, have followed the lead of federal law and have in-

corporated the notion of a learning disability being defined by a discrepancy between a person's actual (measured) and expected achievement (usually predicted from general intellectual ability) (Flanagan et al., 2001). The WJ III provides reliable and valid procedures that can contribute useful information for use in these procedures. The GIA Ability–Achievement Model and the Predicted Achievement Model are both presented in Figure 14.3.

It is important to note that *neither the WJ III GIA or PA discrepancy procedures were designed for the diagnosis of LD*, if the intent is to identify a specific learning disorder. The GIA and PA approaches are intended to answer the question, "*Given the person's present cognitive abilities, is he/she achieving as well as could be expected?*" The WJ III GIA Model is straightforward. Either the differentially weighted WJ III GIA-Std or GIA-Ext *g* standard scores are used to provide a prediction of what a person's achievement standard score would be, given their level of general intellectual ability and age or grade. As portrayed in Figure 14.3, the individual's expected achievement (e.g., predicted Basic Reading Skills standard score) is then subtracted from the person's actual Basic Reading Skills standard score, producing an ability–achievement standard score discrepancy. The WJ III is unique with respect to three major features of this model.

- The WJ III provides a true *g* score for use in the ability–achievement calculations. Other major intelligence batteries rely on an arithmetic average of test scores, an average that implies an equally weighted general intelligence score. Thus, a more theoretically sound general ability index is used in the WJ III GIA ability–achievement discrepancy procedures.

- The WJ III predicted (sometimes referred to as "expected") achievement score accounts for regression-to-the-mean in a manner that captures the developmental changes in ability–achievement correlations. The regression-to-the-mean effect is greatest for predicted achievement scores that diverge the farthest

---

[3]It is important to note that space limitations do not allow a detailed explanation of all caveats related to the use of the different WJ III discrepancy procedures in the "art and science" of LD decision making and classification. Comprehensive models that encompass a broader array of variables are required. A particularly interesting comprehensive model grounded in the CHC theory has recently been outlined by Flanagan, Ortiz, Alfonso, and Mascolo (in press).

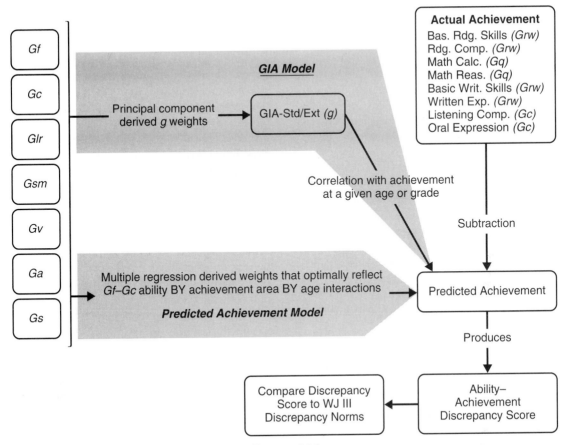

FIGURE 14.3

WJ III GIA (*g*) and predicted achievement ability–achievement discrepancy

from the mean. This occurs because the correlation between any combination of ability and achievement measures is less than perfect.

- The WJ III capitalizes on the co-norming of the WJ III COG and ACH to provide slightly different regression adjustments across age or grade when generating the predicted achievement score. The developmental changes in the ability–achievement correlations observed in the WJ III norm data are incorporated into the prediction equations. A common practice, particularly when an intelligence test is not co-normed with the administered achievement test, is to select a single point correlation (e.g., .65) and use this value to correct for regression effects via a formula for all ages. The predicted score in the WJ III GIA Ability–Achievement Model is based on a developmentally sensitive regression-to-the-mean adjustment procedure.

- The WJ III GIA ability–achievement discrepancy scores are compared against *real* discrepancy norms (end box in Figure 14.3; McGrew, 1994; McGrew et al., 1991; McGrew & Woodcock, 2001; Mather & Schrank, 2001; Woodcock, 1978). Predicted achievement scores in all relevant achievement domains were generated for all norming subjects. Each subject's predicted and actual achievement difference scores in the same domain produced ability–achievement discrepancy scores for the WJ III norm file. The distributional characteristics of each ability–achievement discrepancy score distribution were used to produce the WJ III GIA ability–achievement discrepancy norms just as age- or grade-specific norms are determined for any test or cluster.

In summary, whenever a WJ III GIA ability–achievement discrepancy score is calculated, this score incorporates the developmentally appropriate degree of regression-to-the-mean and is then compared against the actual distributions of discrepancy scores in the norming sample. The WJ III GIA ability–achievement discrepancy scores may be interpreted in three different metrics (standard score discrepancy, percentile rank, and standard deviation units; McGrew & Woodcock, 2001) as the examiner chooses.[4]

Predicted Achievement–Achievement Discrepancy Model

The WJ III Predicted Achievement (PA) Model for ability–achievement discrepancy calculation is also portrayed in Figure 14.3. A similar model was present in the WJ and WJ-R in which the differential Scholastic Aptitude clusters were used as the predictor measures. The Scholastic Aptitude clusters were used to provide predicted achievement scores based on the best combination of four cognitive tests that predicted different achievement domains (McGrew, 1986, 1994; McGrew et al., 1991; Woodcock, 1978).

As portrayed in Figure 14.3, in the WJ III PA Model the standard seven WJ III COG tests are placed into equations that differentially weight each tests' contribution to the prediction of the target achievement domain. Not only do the weights for the same test differ by achievement

domain (e.g., Sound Blending [*Ga*] has a near zero weight for the prediction of math achievement but a significant weight for the prediction of Basic Reading Skills), but the weights also change systematically as a function of developmental status. For example, although Sound Blending is important in the prediction equation for Basic Reading Skills during the formative years, its contribution drops appreciably past the elementary school ages. In contrast, the Verbal Comprehension (*Gc*) weight increases with age in the prediction of Basic Reading Skills. The utilization of computer-scoring technology provides the ability to implement this *developmental/purpose-focused/optimal test weighting* prediction method. This method better captures the complex nuances of human development via predictions that reflect achievement domain, by developmental status, by CHC ability domain interactions.

Similar to the GIA Model, the PA Model also implicitly accounts for regression-to-the-mean. Also, an individual's resultant discrepancy score is compared against real distributions of discrepancy norms. Not surprisingly, the WJ III PA Model provides a better estimate of a person's predicted (expected) achievement than does the GIA Model (McGrew & Woodcock, 2001). The PA Model optimally weights the seven standard COG tests to "wring out" as much variance as possible in the prediction of achievement. In comparison, the WJ III GIA score is developed to "wring out" as much general intelligence variance as is possible from the 7- or 14-test combinations of tests; optimal weighting for the prediction of achievement is not included in the differential GIA *g*-weighting.[5]

---

[4]An additional ability–achievement discrepancy procedure that is identical to the GIA Model, with the exception being the substitution of the WJ III ACH Oral Language (*Gc*) cluster as the ability measure, is not described here.

[5]Although true, as described by McGrew and Woodcock (2001), one of the major criteria used to select tests for the WJ III COG-Std was which respective CHC test was a better predictor of achievement. For example, both the Analysis–Synthesis and Concept Formation *Gf* were found to be equally strong indicators of *Gf*. Concept Formation was found to be a slightly better predictor of achievement across all domains and ages and, therefore, was selected to be the featured *Gf* test in the WJ III COG-Std. This insured that the GIA-Std score, although not weighted to best predict achievement, included those tests from each CHC ability domain (when all other psychometric factors were judged to be relatively equal) that best predicted achievement.

Given the different design goals and philosophies, the WJ III GIA and PA ability–achievement discrepancy models provide different and complementary information. The calculation of ability–achievement discrepancies with either the GIA-Std or GIA-Ext may be useful when a generalized measure of cognitive functioning or intelligence is required for eligibility purposes (Schrank & Mather, 2001). In contrast, the WJ III PA option is intended to determine if a person is performing as well as one would expect, *given his or her measured levels of associated cognitive abilities*, not necessarily to diagnose a learning disability (Schrank & Mather, 2001). The PA discrepancy procedure will be particularly useful for making the most accurate predictive statements possible concerning an individual's anticipated levels of current achievement. It should be informative for setting short-term goals.

Because the strong PA prediction is achieved via the inclusion and higher weighting of certain tests that measure cognitive abilities that may be a significant weakness for a person, and that may reflect an intrinsic cognitive or processing disorder, it may not be appropriate (in many cases), nor was it ever intended to be used, for determining a specific learning disability. The PA's predict how an individual will perform, on the *average*, in a variety of situations requiring that particular subset of abilities, otherwise known as "aptitude."[6]

Intra-Ability Discrepancy Model

Unique to the WJ III are three types of norm-based within-person discrepancy score procedures that have the potential to better identify the unique patterns of cognitive abilities and achievements in individuals with LD. Collectively the intra-cognitive, intra-achievement, and intra-individual (cognitive and achievement combined) discrepancies are called the *intra-ability discrepancies*. The intra-ability discrepancies allow examiners to analyze an individual's cognitive and academic strengths and weaknesses across the cluster scores of the WJ III COG and WJ III ACH. These discrepancies, and the combined COG and ACH procedure in particular (intra-individual), can assist in the identification of a learning disability by providing information that complements (but does not supplant) the information provided by the GIA and PA ability–achievement discrepancies.

The logic of intra-ability discrepancies is simple. Using the intra-cognitive discrepancies as an example, the standard score for each of the seven CHC cognitive clusters is first isolated (the target cluster) from the six remaining clusters, which are then averaged. The average of the "other" cognitive clusters then functions similarly to the ability cluster in the GIA Ability–Achievement Model previously described and presented in Figure 14.3. The average of the "others" generates a predicted score for the isolated target cluster. A discrepancy between the target cluster standard score and the predicted standard score is calculated and the result compared against the distribution of discrepancy norms for the target cluster. The same discrepancy evaluation scores (percentile rank and standard deviation units) provided for the GIA and PA Models are used to interpret the importance of the intra-cognitive discrepancy. The intra-achievement and intra-individual (achievement and cognitive clusters combined) discrepancy norms are derived from similar procedures.

Schrank and Mather (2001) believe that the intra-individual discrepancy procedure may be particularly useful in the identification of a specific learning disability when the examiner needs to determine what is "specific" about the problem. The intra-individual procedure is conceptually similar to recent recommendations to identify an individual with a learning disability via the evaluation of domain-specific achievement skills conjointly with their related cognitive abilities (Brackett & McPherson 1996; Fletcher et al., 1998). For example, an adolescent referred for long-standing problems with math

[6]The term *aptitude* has come to be misunderstood in much of psychological practice. Snow (1991) provides an excellent summary of the history of how the original connotation has changed (for the worse) over time. The term *aptitude* is used here in the classic sense as described by Snow.

who demonstrates relative intra-individual weaknesses (less than -1 *SD*) on the WJ III ACH Math Calculation and Math Reasoning clusters with concurrent deficits on the WJ III COG Working Memory (*Gsm*), Long-term Retrieval (*Glr*), Processing Speed (*Gs*), and Fluid Reasoning (*Gf*) clusters would be exhibiting a constellation of deficits consistent with a domain-specific disability in mathematics (Carroll, 1996; Geary, 1993; Geary, Hamson, & Hoard, 2000; Geary, Hoard, & Hamson, 1999). The intra-individual discrepancy procedure can be used with several combinations of clusters depending on which sets of WJ III COG and ACH tests are administered.

Preliminary Research on Adult LD Identification with the WJ III

Preliminary research evidence on potentially important diagnostic patterns of WJ III scores in adult university subjects was recently extracted from the Gregg/Hoy LD/Normal university sample previously described in this chapter. The results, briefly summarized here, demonstrate the potential of the WJ III in the identification of adolescents and adults with or without learning disabilities.

Select WJ III COG and ACH data from the Gregg/Hoy university sample was subjected to the *Classification and Regression Tree (CART)* program, a robust set of decision-tree procedures for "data mining" and predictive modeling (Salford Systems, 1999, 2000). Briefly, CART uses computer-intensive and complex data-searching algorithms to identify important patterns and relations in data. CART can uncover hidden structure in very large and highly complex data, even data that may be difficult to analyze with traditional statistical methods (e.g., when a set of variables are highly multicollinear).

Using the dependent categorical variable of LD versus Not-LD (Normal), the CART analyses "grew" a large decision-making tree that resulted in the optimal classification of 204 subjects

with scores from the complete set of WJ III COG and ACH clusters. The initial LD/Not-LD decision-tree was set aside by CART and a tenfold internal cross-validation procedure produced 10 new independent trees that were then combined and used to "prune" the original tree. The complete sample was then classified based on the final pruned tree. The results of these analyses, which identify two Normal (Not-LD) and three LD classification groups (called terminal nodes), are presented in Figure 14.4.

The first decision point in the tree indicates that the WJ III Academic Fluency cluster is the single most important variable in differentiating LD from Not-LD university students in this sample. Subjects with WJ III Academic Fluency scores greater than 107 are most likely not LD. Terminal Node 5 includes 81 normal subjects and 13 LD subjects. Thus, this first decision rule results in 86.2% of these 94 subjects correctly classified as Not-LD, and 13.8 % of the LD subjects misclassified (included in Terminal Node 5). Conversely, a WJ III Academic Fluency score less than or equal to 107 produces three other decision-making points and four other terminal nodes (Nodes 1 through 4). Nodes 1 through 4 have classification accuracy figures ranging from 81.0% (Node 2) to 95.4% (Node 1). The complete decision tree indicates the following for university subjects:

- A subject with a WJ III Academic Fluency score greater than 107 is most likely not previously diagnosed as LD. This classification was accurate 86.2% of the time.

- A subject with a WJ III Academic Fluency score less than 107 and a WJ III Basic Writing Skills cluster score less than or equal to 96 is most likely LD (95.4% accuracy).

- A subject with a WJ III Academic Fluency score less than or equal to 107, a WJ III Basic Writing Skills cluster score greater than 96, and a WJ III Verbal Ability-Std cluster (same as the Verbal Comprehension test) score less than or equal to 104 is most likely LD (81.0% accuracy).

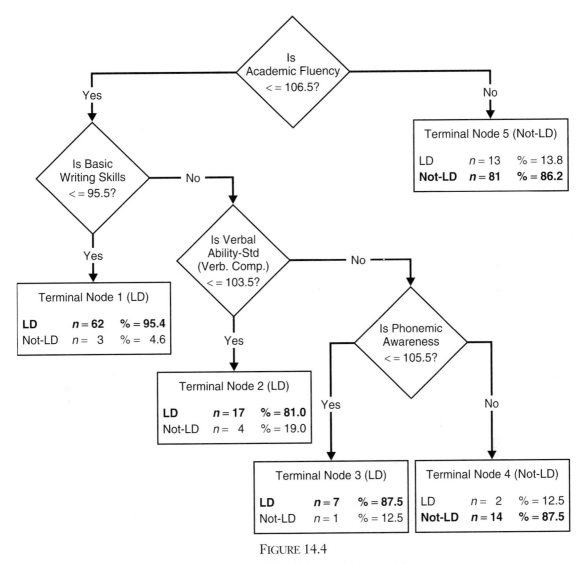

FIGURE 14.4

WJ III university subject LD/Not-LD classification and decision tree
(Gregg/Hoy study, 2001)

- A subject with a WJ III Academic Fluency score less than or equal to 107, a WJ III Basic Writing Skills cluster score greater than 96, a WJ III Verbal Comprehension test score greater than 104, and a WJ III Phonemic Awareness (*Ga*) cluster score less than or equal to 106 is most likely LD (87.5% accuracy).

- Finally, a subject with a WJ III Academic Fluency score less than or equal to 107, a WJ III Basic Writing Skills cluster score greater than 95.5, a WJ III Verbal Comprehension test score greater than 104, and a WJ III Phonemic Awareness (*Ga*) cluster score greater than 106 is most likely not LD (87.5% accuracy).

Using the above WJ III-based decision-tree rules, the cross-validation classification table revealed classification accuracy rates of 81% (LD) and 85% (Normal). Given that the initial sample was almost equally divided between LD ($n = 101$) and Not-LD ($n = 103$) subjects, this classification agreement rate suggests that the WJ III COG and ACH variables included in Figure 14.3 can improve over a 50% chance base-rate classification of newly referred university subjects by approximately 30%. This indicates that the WJ III COG and ACH batteries include measures that may be particularly helpful in the identification of adults with learning difficulties.

Although CART procedures are atheoretical and empirically driven, post-hoc interpretation of the results in Figure 14.4 presents a number of interesting theoretical hypotheses. First, the pivotal WJ III Academic Fluency cluster, which is comprised of the WJ III Reading, Math, and Writing Fluency tests, suggests that, if an individual reaches a state of automaticity in basic academic functioning, this may be a strong indicator that the person does not have any specific disabilities. Academic fluency can be considered the "end state" of academic performance that results from the successful acquisition and integration of basic academic and related cognitive abilities, much like the expert state in the novice/expert cognitive psychology literature. Second, three subgroups of adults with LD may be identified via the inspection of domain-specific constellations of cognitive and achievement abilities. One group (Terminal Node 1) may be subjects with poor automaticity in general academic functioning and low basic skills in writing, with no apparent associated cognitive deficits. The second group (Terminal Node 2) may display poor academic automaticity associated with a weakness in general verbal knowledge or comprehension (*Gc*). The third group also displays poor academic automaticity, but, instead of relative *Gc* deficits, they have associated cognitive problems in phonemic awareness (*Ga*).

An additional source of useful information regarding the WJ III COG and ACH clusters in this study is the CART *variable importance* output table (Table 14.13). The most important variable is assigned an index score of 100, and all other variables are scaled in relative terms to this anchor point. Variable importance is related to both the potential and actual splitting behavior of a variable, and it is possible for a variable to be very important but not included in the final decision tree (the variable may be a constant "bridesmaid" at each splitting point in the data). This information helps identify possible explanations for the structure in the data and also identifies "surrogate" variables that may be used to make decisions at critical points when a subject is missing data on the decision variable.

The most obvious conclusion from an inspection of Table 14.13 is that a number of variables were lurking just below the surface at critical decision points and, if used as replacements for the critical WJ III variables, may produce similar classification accuracy. A number of substantive conclusions are gleaned from Table 14.13. First, deficient achievement in the language arts domains (reading and writing) is the most obvious characteristic that differentiates university subjects with and without LD. Second, the cognitive and achievement domains that differentiate LD and Not-LD university subjects are primarily those dealing with auditory–linguistic achievement (WJ III Broad Reading, Basic Writing Skills, Basic Reading Skills) and cognitive abilities (WJ III Phoneme/Grapheme Knowledge, Phonemic Awareness, Auditory Processing), and efficient/automatic cognitive and achievement functioning (WJ III Academic Fluency, Cognitive Efficiency, Processing Speed, Short-Term Memory, and Working Memory). This information, in addition to the practical decision-rule tree, suggests that the WJ III COG and ACH clusters that tap these abilities should receive significant attention when evaluating adults for possible learning difficulties. The high level of accuracy achieved via these analyses is most likely a function of the power of the CART procedures combined with a battery of cognitive and achievement measures (WJ III) that cover a wide

TABLE 14.13   WJ-III relative importance variable ratings for LD/Not-LD university sample CART analysis

WJ III Cluster	CHC Ability Domain	Relative Importance
Broad Reading	*Grw*	100.0
Academic Fluency	*Grw, Gq*	97.8
Basic Writing Skills	*Grw*	92.1
Basic Reading Skills	*Grw*	78.5
Cognitive Efficiency-Std	*Gs, Gsm*	37.1
Processing Speed	*Gs*	27.3
General Intellectual Ability-Std	*g*	27.1
Phoneme/Grapheme Knowledge	*Grw*	23.3
Phonemic Awareness	*Ga*	19.8
Thinking Abilities-Std	*Glr, Gv, Ga, Gf*	12.7
Auditory Processing	*Ga*	11.6
Short-Term Memory	*Gsm*	9.7
Verbal Ability-Std	*Gc*	9.3
Fluid Reasoning	*Gf*	8.7
Working Memory	*Gsm*	8.4
Long-Term Retrieval	*Glr*	7.3
Oral Expression	*Gc*	5.6
Visual–Spatial Thinking	*Gv*	0.0
Cognitive Fluency	*Gs, Glr*	0.0

and theoretically valid breadth of human abilities. These results also demonstrate the strong research potential of the WJ III.

Neuropsychological Applications

One distinguishing characteristic of neuropsychological assessment is its emphasis on the identification and measurement of psychological deficits.... Neuropsychological assessment is also concerned with the documentation and description of preserved functions—the patient's behavioral competencies and strengths. (Lezak, 1995, p. 97)

Neuropsychological assessment is concerned with evaluating brain–behavior relations. His-

torically, there have been two approaches to neuropsychological assessment. The *quantitative* (structural) approach has focused on the development of psychometric test batteries that allow for the identification of aberrant neurological conditions. In contrast, a more *qualitative* approach, often associated with Luria (1966), has focused more on "pathognomonic signs" (Dean & Woodcock, 1999). Regardless of the research tradition, contemporary neuropsychological assessment has been largely an atheoretical approach that has employed an eclectic mix of measurement tools that have been normed at different dates and with different subjects (Dean & Woodcock, 1999; Flanagan et al., 2000; Wilson, 1992).

This section provides a brief glimpse at current and future applications of the WJ-R/WJ III to neuropsychological assessment. Although the WJ III does not cover all aspects required for a comprehensive neuropsychological evaluation, it provides more coverage for the assessment and description of deficits and preserved neurocognitive functions than any other single nationally standardized and norm-referenced source battery. Furthermore, the WJ III provides a coherent and empirically based framework (viz., CHC theory) that can be used to ground contemporary neuropsychological cognitive assessment and interpretation. The WJ III also provides for evaluation of performance on a common integrated set of norms (Dean & Woodcock, 1999).

In this section, the WJ III CHC-classified tests are cross-referenced to a more traditional neuropsychological taxonomy that includes the constructs of attention, visual and auditory perception/processing, memory and learning, language, reasoning and problem solving, and academic achievement. The breadth of coverage and wide age range of the WJ III make it particularly suited for use as a neuropsychological instrument, either as the primary battery or as a resource of supplemental measures. Efforts are currently underway to integrate the WJ-R and WJ III batteries into a comprehensive neuropsychological assessment system that would also include measures of sensory and motor functioning, a structured interview, and a mental status exam. The *Dean-Woodcock Neuropsychological Assessment System (D-WNAS)* (Dean & Woodcock, 1999) uses the WJ-R/WJ III to integrate CHC and neuropsychological constructs within an information-processing framework.

Several features of the WJ III enhance its usefulness as a neuropsychological instrument:

- The wide age range of application spans from 2 to 90+ years.

- All tests are normed and used across almost the entire life span.

- All major areas of cognitive functioning and academic achievement can be assessed without the need to "cross" batteries.

- The wide range of item difficulty within each test allows the documentation of strengths and superior performance as well as deficits.

- To foster standardized administration, critical auditory stimuli tests (e.g., auditory memory span, phonological processing, and listening comprehension) are presented by recorded audiotape. The WJ III COG is the only norm-referenced intelligence battery to provided co-normed measures of auditory processing.

- The selective or focused testing principle allows any single test or combination of tests to be selected for use and interpreted on a common norm base.

- Special college- and university-level norms are provided that differentiate performance by type of postsecondary education institution.

- Significance of any aptitude–achievement, intra-cognitive, or intra-achievement discrepancies is reported and is based on real discrepancy norms.

- Computerized scoring and a narrative report program are available.

- Parallel test batteries are available in English and Spanish.

- Equivalent forms of the achievement battery are available for situations requiring frequent retesting.

Application of the WJ III to Neuropsychological Assessment

Why should a practicing neuropsychologist spend time studying new models of cognitive abilities and, in particular, CHC theory? As outlined earlier in this chapter, a primary reason is that the CHC model represents the best of current research into the structure of intellect. A second reason is that the CHC organization offers an empirically derived taxonomic classification of cognitive abilities that is characterized by a high level of functional independence among the categories. Traditional ability classifications used in neuropsychology have evolved primarily from clinical practice and have broadly defined areas of special interest. As a result, the classification constructs sometimes overlap and, at other times, may be a mix of two or three distinctly different types of functions as defined by current cognitive science. The efforts of Dean and Woodcock (1999) coincide with other recent attempts to integrate neuropsychological assessment paradigms with CHC theoretical constructs (Pallier, Roberts, & Stankov, 2000).

Toward the goal of urging the integration of CHC theory into current neuropsychological thought, the following material describes how the CHC-organized WJ III can measure deficits and preserved functions in the context of a traditional neuropsychological organization. Table 14.14 illustrates the relationships between these two systems of classifying neurocognitive functions. As presented in Table 14.14, the WJ III provides measures across a wide spectrum of the traditional neuropsychological functional categories. The reader will note that several tests appear in more than one category of functions. This reflects the less precise and largely atheoretical nature of a traditional neuropsychological classification.

Assessment of Attention (*Gs, Gsm, Ga, Gf*)

During the past several decades, researchers have recognized that attention is not a unitary construct. This has resulted in the specification of multidimensional models of the construct of attention (Carroll, 1993; Lezak, 1995; Mirsky, Anthony, Duncan, Ahearn, & Kellam, 1991). The WJ III does not measure all of the important aspects of this broad construct; however, four aspects—selective attention, divided attention, sustained attention, and attention capacity—are measured by eight WJ III tests listed in Table 14.15.

Briefly, *attentional capacity* is the ability to hold information in immediate awareness while performing some action on the information. The task requirements (see Table 14.4) of the WJ III Numbers Reversed test, and to a lesser degree the Memory for Words test, suggest these two tests may shed light on an individual's attentional capacity. *Sustained attention*, or the capacity to stay on task in a vigilant manner, is measured by Pair Cancellation. The WJ III Pair Cancellation test requires a subject to rapidly identify a certain instance of a repeated pattern under conditions in which he or she must maintain a constant focus on the target condition in the presence of similar distracting stimuli. The clerical speed ability required by Visual Matching may also tap sustained attention, but under conditions that require less vigilance.

The WJ III Auditory Attention test, a test that requires making simple sound discriminations under increasing stimulus background noise distor-

TABLE 14.14 Comparison of traditional neuropsychological ability with CHC broad ability categories

Traditional Neuropsychological Categories	CHC Broad Abilities								
	Gsm	Gs	Gc	Gq	Grw	Gv	Ga	Glr	Gf
Attention	•	•					•		•
Visual Perception/Processing						•			
Auditory Perception/Processing							•		
Memory and Learning	•		•			•		•	
Language			•						
Reasoning and Problem Solving				•					•
Academic Achievement			•	•	•				

TABLE 14.15   Attention dimensions tapped by eight WJ IIII COG tests

WJ III Test	Type of Stimuli	Attention Dimension			
		Selective Attention	Shifting/ Divided Attention	Vigilance/ Sustained Attention	Attentional Capacity
Auditory Attention (*Ga*)	Auditory	•			
Auditory Working Memory (*Gsm*)	Auditory		•		
Concept Formation (*Gf*)	Visual		•		
Pair Cancellation (*Gs*)	Visual	•		•	
Decision Speed (*Gs*)	Visual		•		
Visual Matching (*Gs*)	Visual			•	
Numbers Reversed (*Gsm*)	Auditory				•
Memory for Words (*Gsm*)	Auditory				•

NOTE: Bold font designates tests comprising the WJ III Broad Attention cluster.

tion, measures *selective attention*, or the ability to focus attention when distracting stimuli are present. The sheer mass and repeated occurrences of the same visual stimuli on the Pair Cancellation test also may require the "selective" filtering of relevant and irrelevant stimuli for successful performance. Finally, the WJ III Auditory Working Memory test requires an individual to retain and rearrange information placed in short-term memory to form two distinct sequences (a form of mental "juggling"). The Auditory Working Memory and Numbers Reversed tests may also be combined to form a *Working Memory* cluster. This cluster measures the ability to hold information in immediate awareness while performing a mental operation on it.

Assessment of Visual Perception/Processing (Gv)

Visual–spatial measures have had a long and prominent history in neuropsychological assessment. Visual perceptual–spatial skills are part of everyday life and enable individuals to receive, process, integrate, and synthesize information that is seen or manipulated "in the mind's eye." As presented in Table 14.14, the WJ III provides three measures of visual perception–processing.

These include Spatial Relations (Vz, visualization), Picture Recognition (MV, visual memory), and, to a lesser extent, Planning (SS, Spatial Scanning).

Assessment of Auditory Perception/Processing (Ga)

Neuropsychologists have long recognized the importance of assessing auditory perception/processing. Auditory processing involves the ability to perceive, discriminate, process, and synthesize both speech and nonspeech sounds. The WJ III is the only intelligence battery to provide for comprehensive assessment of certain aspects of the auditory domain recognized by neuropsychologists. The Sound Blending and Incomplete Words tests are measures of phonological awareness or phonemic knowledge (PC, or phonetic coding as per the CHC taxonomy). A third WJ III COG test, Auditory Attention, is a measure of the ability to discriminate speech sounds (US) under distracting conditions (UR). The WJ ACH battery also includes the Sound Awareness test, a *Ga* test that may prove to be a particularly good *Ga* screener because of the diversity of auditory skills required (e.g., sound deletion, substitution, and rhyming).

Assessment of Memory and Learning (*Gsm, Gv, Glr, Gf,* and *Gc*)

Memory and learning tests constitute the broadest category of tests in a traditional neuropsychological classification. From the perspective of CHC theory, three factorially distinct cognitive abilities (*Gsm, Glr, Gc*) fall within this broad category. The clinical assessment of memory deficits typically involves evaluation of the ability to actively learn and remember new material presented in both auditory and visual modalities. The adequacy of both short-term memory (immediate recall) and long-term retention (delayed recall) are typically assessed. Indexes of remote memory may also be helpful with persons of advanced age and other clinical populations. Eleven WJ III tests are identified as good measures of various aspects of memory or learning. Tests of auditory short-term memory (*Gsm*) include Numbers Reversed (MW), Auditory Working Memory (MW), and Memory for Words (MW). Picture Recognition (*Gv*) is an indicator of immediate visual recall (MV).

Three other tests are identified as measures of long-term retrieval (*Glr*). Visual–Auditory Learning is a visual–auditory associational learning task. The task requires learning new material with corrective feedback provided whenever the examinee makes an error. There is a delayed recall version of the test, Delayed Recall-Visual–Auditory Learning, which measures the ability to recall, from 30 minutes to 8 days later, the just-learned associations. This test is among the few clinical memory tests that include standardized and normed delay procedures extending more than 24 hours beyond initial administration. Retrieval Fluency (*Glr*) is a measure of ideational fluency (FI) or the ability to fluently recall related items from memory within a short time. Finally, the Story Recall and Delayed Recall-Story Recall tests from the WJ III ACH battery can provide information regarding meaningful memory (MM).

Two other WJ III tests can be characterized as new learning tasks. Concept Formation (*Gf*-I) and Analysis–Synthesis (*Gf*-RG) are controlled learning paradigms that both require learning a

series of procedures to solve inductive and deductive logic problems. Corrective feedback for errors and reinforcement for correct responses are provided, two essential characteristics of many real-world learning situations. These two tests will be identified again in the discussion of Reasoning and Problem-Solving tasks.

Some neuropsychologists include tests of learned or acquired information (sometimes called long-term memory or remote memory) among their assessment procedures. The WJ III General Information (*Gc*-K0) and Academic Knowledge (K0, K1, K2, A5) tests are of this type.

Assessment of Language (*Gc*)

The ability to communicate through language is typically assessed through an examination of both receptive and expressive language. The three traditional broad divisions of language are oral language, reading, and writing. Verbal Comprehension (*Gc*), consisting of four subtests (Picture Vocabulary, Synonyms, Antonyms, and Analogies), is the primary measure of oral language (LD, language development; VL, lexical knowledge) in the WJ III COG. Several other tests of oral language, as well as the tests of reading and writing, are included in the WJ III ACH (see Table 14.5). Reading and writing are generally considered skills that are learned primarily through formal schooling. Therefore, those tests will be mentioned again in a later section on academic achievement. Additionally, as reflected in the test descriptions in Table 14.5, the four WJ III ACH oral language tests can provide language-related information regarding receptive language (Understanding Directions, LS, listening ability; Oral Comprehension, LS, listening ability) and expressive language (Picture Vocabulary, VL, lexical knowledge; Story Recall, LD, language development).

Assessment of Reasoning and Problem Solving (*Gf, Gv*)

Problem solving, or the ability to arrive at solutions in novel and unpracticed situations, involves a complex set of cognitive processes. Abstract thinking and adequate concept formation are required to formulate flexible ideas and strategies and to apply them across a variety of situations. Neuropsychological test batteries have employed a wide variety of tasks (e.g., Halstead Categories; Tower of London; Wisconsin Card Sorting Test) to tap different aspects of reasoning and problem solving.

Two WJ III tests are strong measures of abstract reasoning (*Gf*-Concept Formation), primarily a measure of inductive reasoning (I), and Analysis–Synthesis, primarily a measure of sequential or deductive reasoning (RG). Planning (*Gv*) is also a measure of sequential reasoning (RQ), although it also taps an aspect (SS, spatial scanning) of visual processing (*Gv*). The Quantitative Concepts test on the WJ ACH battery, which consists of 50% number series items, can provide additional insights into quantitative reasoning (RQ).

Assessment of Academic Achievement (*Grw, Gq, Gc*)

An important advantage of the WJ III, when the goal is to provide for psychometrically sound neuropsychological assessment, is the inclusion of a number of co-normed tests that measure learned skills associated with formal schooling. These tests all appear in the WJ III ACH and are only mentioned briefly (see Table 14.5 for additional information). The five tests of reading measure a spectrum of reading abilities from identifying letters and words in isolation to the comprehension of written text. The five tests of writing ability measure several writing abilities, ranging from spelling to the writing of sentences, that must meet certain requirements. The four tests of mathematics measure skills from basic calculation to mathematics reasoning. The WJ III ACH also contains a test of Academic Knowledge (Science, Social Studies, and Humanities). All of these tests were described earlier as possible measures of remote memory.

Assessment of Handwriting

The WJ III includes a normed scale of handwriting legibility. An individual's quality of handwriting may provide useful information about fine-motor hand coordination. This may be particularly useful if premorbid samples of the patient's handwriting are also available for evaluation. Although this procedure is usually applied to the written output from the WJ III Writing Samples test, the scale can be applied to any handwritten product.

Interpretation

Focused norms are currently being prepared for use in neuropsychological applications of the WJ III (Dean & Woodcock, 1999). Focused norms allow an individual's performance to be compared to others of the same age, education, and gender in the norming sample. This scoring system adjusts the WJ III age-based standard scores into standard scores based jointly on age, education, and gender. Thus, these demographics for individual patients can be taken into account when classifying patients as "normal" or "impaired." Conceptually, the *D-WNAS* focused norms are similar to recent efforts to incorporate both development (age) and the effects of schooling into norms for a Hebrew-language version of the WISC-R (Cahan, 2000).

Examples of score adjustment via the focused norms procedure follow. In one instance, a 40-year-old woman with 6 years of college obtained a standard score of 85 on the *Gs* (processing speed) cluster. A score of 85 is one standard deviation below the mean for all persons in the norming sample of the same age. When the score is adjusted by also taking into account gender and education, the focused norm standard score is 78. The adjusted score indicates that her performance is 1.6 standard deviations below the mean when compared to others in the norming sample most like herself. Thus, the deficit in performance is now seen as more significant than if age alone had been the basis for the standard score. In another instance, an 80-year-old man with only one year of schooling had a standard score of 76 on the *Gs* cluster. After adjustment via the focused norms procedure, his standard score was 103. These two examples are somewhat extreme; however, such cases may be encountered in neuropsychological practice.

Table 14.16 presents a suggested modification for the verbal labels used in Table 4-2 of the Examiner's Manuals for the WJ III. These labels are more appropriate for reporting levels of deficit or preserved function in neuropsychological reports. The functional level indices, derived from Rasch scaling (McGrew & Woodcock, 2001), are particularly useful in neuropsychological settings for describing the degree of deficit or preservation of functions demonstrated by the patient.

WJ-R Neuropsychological Research Data

Dean and Woodcock (1999) have presented a preliminary report on the validity of the *D-WNAS*.[7] This report includes information on: (1) descriptive statistics for a wide variety of clinical groups organized as per *DSM-IV* or *ICD-9* (total N = 1,315 subjects from 5 to 81 years of age), (2) factor analysis of the WJ-R cognitive tests in these samples, (3) factor analysis of the

[7]A copy of the report (*The WJ-R and Bateria-R in Neuropsychological Assessment: Research Report Number 3*) can be downloaded free at *www.IAPsych.com*.

D-WNAS sensory and motor batteries, (4) predictive validity studies focused on predicting the presence and location of brain damage, and (5) four clinical case studies. Space limits the presentation of these extant data in detail in this chapter. Instead, a sample of the type of data and samples on which these data are being gathered is presented in Table 14.17. Inspection of the relative ordering of WJ-R *Gf-Gc* cluster scores within each clinical sample in Table 14.17 suggest is a number of interesting hypotheses. The reader is referred to the original report (Dean & Woodcock, 1999) for more detailed analysis and interpretation of these data.

The available *D-WNAS* validity evidence suggests possibilities for improving the "state-of-the art" of neuropsychological assessment through the combination of the CHC model of cognitive abilities, a co-normed battery of cognitive and achievement tests designed as per the CHC model (i.e., the WJ III), and supplementary and traditional neuropsychological (sensory, motor, interview, and mental status) assessments. Additional research data are currently being gathered and analyzed, and will be forthcoming.

CHC Abilities across the Life Span

A basic premise in science is that meaningful comparison of any two instances of a phenomenon requires use of the

TABLE 14.16   Functional level/deficit descriptions for WJ III scores used in neuropsychological assessments

RMI	W Difference Score	Functional Level	Patient Will Find the Demands of Related Age Level Tasks:
97/90 to 100/90	+11 and above	Advanced	Very Easy
75/90 to 96/90	−10 to +10	Adequate	Manageable
25/90 to 74/90	−30 to −11	Mildly Impaired	Very Difficult
4/90 to 24/90	−50 to −31	Moderately Impaired	Extremely Difficult
0/90 to 3/90	−51 and below	Severely Impaired	Impossible

TABLE 14.17   WJ-R *Gf–Gc* cluster score pattern by type of sample as reported for the *D-WNAS:* Ages 5 to 81

Sample	*n*		BCA	|| *Gf–Gc* Cluster by Standard Score Order						
				1	2	3	4	5	6	7
Reference Samples:										
WJ-R Norming Sample	5470	Cluster:	BCA	*Gv*	*Gc*	*Gf*	*Ga*	*Gs*	*Glr*	*Gsm*
		Mdn:	100	100	100	100	100	100	100	100
		SD:	16	16	16	15	15	16	16	16
Total Clinical Sample	1315	Cluster:	BCA	*Gs*	*Glr*	*Gc*	*Ga*	*Gf*	*Gsm*	*Gv*
		Mdn:	90	87	91	92	93	93	94	98
		SD:	18	18	15	18	15	17	18	17
Gifted	84	Cluster:	BCA	*Gv*	*Gsm*	*Ga*	*Glr*	*Gf*	*Gs*	*Gc*
		Mdn:	120	105	110	111	112	116	118	120
		SD:	11	13	15	13	16	11	14	13
Clinical Samples:										
Deficits in Acquired Knowledge										
Knowledge <70	56	Cluster:	BCA	*Gc*	*Gf*	*Gs*	*Gsm*	*Glr*	*Ga*	*Gv*
		Mdn:	56	58	65	68	70	72	73	76
		SD:	11	10	12	15	12	16	11	16
Math <70	122	Cluster:	BCA	*Gs*	*Gc*	*Gf*	*Gsm*	*Glr*	*Ga*	*Gv*
		Mdn:	64	68	68	72	77	78	80	82
		SD:	14	15	16	12	14	15	13	16
Oral Language <70	63	Cluster:	BCA	*Gc*	*Gsm*	*Gf*	*Gs*	*Glr*	*Ga*	*Gv*
		Mdn:	59	60	70	70	71	73	74	77
		SD:	10	10	11	11	12	12	11	15
Reading <70	133	Cluster:	BCA	*Gc*	*Gs*	*Gsm*	*Gf*	*Glr*	*Ga*	*Gv*
		Mdn:	66	69	72	75	76	77	82	89
		SD:	15	16	13	15	14	13	13	16
Written language <70	164	Cluster:	BCA	*Gs*	*Gc*	*Glr*	*Gsm*	*Gf*	*Ga*	*Gv*
		Mdn:	70	75	76	78	78	80	83	89
		SD:	15	14	16	12	15	14	13	16
Anxiety Spectrum Disorders	100	Cluster:	BCA	*Gs*	*Glr*	*Ga*	*Gc*	*Gf*	*Gsm*	*Gv*
		Mdn:	95	91	94	94	96	97	97	100
		SD:	16	17	15	15	17	16	16	15
Attention Deficit/Hyperactivity Disorders, Mixed	494	Cluster:	BCA	*Gs*	*Glr*	*Ga*	*Gc*	*Gf*	*Gsm*	*Gv*
		Mdn:	95	90	93	94	96	96	97	100
		SD:	16	17	14	14	16	15	17	15
Brain Tumors, Mixed	32	Cluster:	BCA	*Gs*	*Gc*	*Glr*	*Gsm*	*Ga*	*Gf*	*Gv*
		Mdn:	90	90	92	93	94	94	96	97
		SD:	15	20	17	12	14	11	14	16

TABLE 14.17 (Continued)

Sample	n		BCA	Gf–Gc Cluster by Standard Score Order						
				1	2	3	4	5	6	7
Clinical Samples:										
Depressive Spectrum Disorder	150	Cluster:	BCA	Gs	Ga	Gf	Gsm	Glr	Gc	Gv
		Mdn:	95	92	94	96	96	97	98	100
		SD:	16	18	13	14	17	14	17	15
Hydrocephalus	18	Cluster:	BCA	Gs	Gc	Gf	Glr	Ga	Gsm	Gv
		Mdn:	62	66	69	76	78	81	82	89
		SD:	19	18	20	14	22	14	16	21
Impulsive/Disruptive Spectrum Disorders	73	Cluster:	BCA	Gs	Gc	Gf	Ga	Gsm	Glr	Gv
		Mdn:	87	86	87	90	91	92	94	98
		SD:	16	19	14	16	14	17	14	17
Infectious Processes	23	Cluster:	BCA	Gs	Gc	Ga	Gsm	Glr	Gf	Gv
		Mdn:	79	68	82	82	85	87	89	93
		SD:	20	20	20	12	16	17	21	22
Language Disorders	48	Cluster:	BCA	Gsm	Gc	Ga	Gs	Gf	Glr	Gv
		Mdn:	78	81	82	82	84	86	88	100
		SD:	15	14	16	11	15	17	15	14
Learning Disorders, Mixed	584	Cluster:	BCA	Gs	Glr	Gc	Ga	Gf	Gsm	Gv
		Mdn:	88	86	89	91	92	93	93	98
		SD:	15	17	14	16	14	15	17	16
Mental Retardation, Mild to Profound	81	Cluster:	BCA	Gc	Gf	Gs	Gsm	Ga	Glr	Gv
		Mdn:	56	62	66	68	71	74	75	80
		SD:	13	12	13	16	13	13	15	17
Motor Impairment	52	Cluster:	BCA	Gs	Glr	Ga	Gf	Gv	Gsm	Gc
		Mdn:	93	90	90	95	96	96	101	102
		SD:	17	16	18	13	16	18	20	18
Neurofibromatosis	11	Cluster:	BCA	Gsm	Ga	Gc	Glr	Gs	Gf	Gv
		Mdn:	84	85	87	87	88	89	89	97
		SD:	14	10	14	11	9	19	13	19
Pervasive Developmental Disorders	13	Cluster:	BCA	Gs	Gf	Ga	Gsm	Gc	Glr	Gv
		Mdn:	75	72	80	80	81	87	88	93
		SD:	20	29	16	11	19	18	16	20
Seizure Disorders/Epilepsy	57	Cluster:	BCA	Gc	Gs	Glr	Gf	Gsm	Ga	Gv
		Mdn:	83	84	85	89	89	91	92	93
		SD:	17	18	17	15	14	16	16	15
Traumatic/Closed Head Injury	170	Cluster:	BCA	Gs	Gc	Glr	Gsm	Ga	Gf	Gv
		Mdn:	92	89	94	95	95	96	96	96
		SD:	19	21	17	18	16	15	16	18

(Continues)

TABLE 14.17   (Continued)

Sample	n		BCA	Gf–Gc Cluster by Standard Score Order						
				1	2	3	4	5	6	7
Samples with Known Lesion Localization:										
Left Hemisphere Only	56	Cluster:	BCA	Gs	Glr	Gc	Ga	Gsm	Gf	Gv
		Mdn:	85	84	86	87	92	92	95	97
		SD:	18	19	15	15	17	14	18	18
Right Hemisphere Only	64	Cluster:	BCA	Gs	Glr	Gc	Gsm	Gv	Gf	Ga
		Mdn:	88	83	90	92	92	93	93	93
		SD:	18	23	19	17	18	18	14	14
Bilateral Diffuse Brain Damage	36	Cluster:	BCA	Gs	Glr	Gc	Gf	Ga	Gv	Gsm
		Mdn:	89	88	89	90	94	95	95	96
		SD:	20	21	15	20	19	16	14	15
Anterior Cortical Lesions, Mixed	68	Cluster:	BCA	Gs	Gc	Glr	Ga	Gsm	Gf	Gv
		Mdn:	90	86	91	92	95	96	96	98
		SD:	20	24	18	20	16	17	17	21
Posterior Cortical Lesions, Mixed	78	Cluster:	BCA	Gs	Glr	Gc	Gsm	Gf	Ga	Gv
		Mdn:	88	82	87	89	91	92	93	94
		SD:	18	20	15	17	17	16	17	17
Frontal Lobe Lesions, Mixed	22	Cluster:	BCA	Gs	Gc	Gv	Glr	Gf	Ga	Gsm
		Mdn:	85	76	85	85	88	88	89	90
		SD:	24	34	18	29	24	17	17	22
Temporal Lobe Lesions, Mixed	52	Cluster:	BCA	Gs	Glr	Gc	Gf	Gsm	Ga	Gv
		Mdn:	88	85	87	87	93	93	93	97
		SD:	15	17	14	16	13	15	16	15
Parietal Lobe Lesions, Mixed	20	Cluster:	BCA	Gs	Glr	Gc	Gsm	Ga	Gf	Gv
		Mdn:	78	72	78	78	83	84	86	92
		SD:	16	22	14	12	16	13	15	19
Subcortical/Brain Stem Lesions	17	Cluster:	BCA	Gs	Glr	Gv	Gf	Ga	Gc	Gsm
		Mdn:	83	73	86	86	86	88	89	95
		SD:	16	18	14	15	9	11	17	17

Key to Cluster Abbreviations: BCA = Broad Cognitive Ability; *Gsm* = Short-Term Memory; *Gs* = Processing Speed; *Glr* = Long-Term Retrieval; *Gv* = Visual Processing; *Gc* = Comprehension–Knowledge; *Ga* = Auditory Processing; *Gf* = Fluid Reasoning.

same measurement scale. (Strauss, Spreen & Hunter, 2000, p. 242)

The study of developmental patterns of cognitive growth and change has fascinated cognitive and developmental psychologists for decades (see Chapter 5). Although longitudinal data are typically viewed as the best source for investigating developmental changes in intelligence, large-scale longitudinal data sets are expensive and are few and far between. Not unexpectedly, cross-sectional normative data from nationally standardized measures of cognitive abilities have played a prominent role in this research. As noted by Gustafsson and Undheim (1996), most of the research on changes in cognitive abilities, particularly during adulthood, "has been tied largely to *Gf–Gc* theory" (p. 221). This section highlights some of the limitations of the extant cross-sectional intelligence research and then describes how the WJ III can help overcome these limitations. Finally, potential new insights into the growth and decline of human intelligence are presented via select cross-sectional WJ III CHC growth curves.

Some Limitations of the Available Intelligence Growth Curve Research

Various iterations of the Wechsler series' norm data have played a central role in the analysis of intellectual development, primarily because of the relatively similar format of most of the individual tests in the three separate Wechsler batteries. Notwithstanding the important contribution of the analyses of the various Wechsler standardization samples, these data suffer from a number of significant limitations that raise questions about the accuracy of some of the conclusions derived from this research.

First, and foremost, despite tests with common names and test formats (e.g., WPPSI-R, WISC-III, and WAIS-III Similarities test), "substantial differences in content are present, and the pattern of performance for a given participant across subtests may not be particularly consistent

between tests" (Strauss et al., 2000, p. 238). Attempts to apply decision rules derived from the analyses of test scores and subtest patterns on one version of the Wechsler may not be applicable when using a different version (Bornstein, 1987; Chelune, Eversole, Kane, & Talbott, 1987).

Second, as outlined in this chapter and by others (Flanagan et al., 2001; McGrew & Flanagan, 1998; Woodcock, 1990), most of the Wechsler-based developmental research has used tests that are "impure from the perspective of Horn's theory" (Kaufman, Kaufman, Chen, & Kaufman, 1996, p. 161). The questioning of the validity of some of the Wechsler tests as indicators of CHC abilities has significant implications. For example, the confidence that has been placed in the interpretation of the Wechsler Performance Scale as an indicator of *Gf* is now being questioned. Wang and Kaufman (1993) pointed out the significant implications of this now-recognized Performance Scale misinterpretation when they observed:

> *analyses conducted by Woodcock (1990) and Stone (1992) that offer empirical evidence that Wechsler's Performance Scale may, indeed, be primarily a measure of* Gv.... *The possibility remains that the numerous research investigations of aging and intelligence that have involved the WAIS and WAIS-R may have attested to the rapid and early decline of* Gv—*or, more likely, an amalgam of* Gv *and* Gf—*instead of just* Gf. *(p. 30)*

The aforementioned confounded interpretation of the Wechsler Performance Scale is problematic as it is axiomatic in science that the measurement of a phenomenon requires a unidimensional measurement scale in which the resultant scores reflect individual differences on a single common dimension (Hattie, 1985; Lumsden, 1961; Reise, Waller, & Comrey, 2000). "If a scale is multidimensional (i.e., has multiple correlated dimensions), then not only is the total score more challenging to interpret but different aspects of the scale (e.g., its content facets) may have different correlations with external variables" (Reise et al., 2000, p. 293).

Third, as described in the cross-battery section of this chapter, the Wechsler batteries, as well as most other major intelligence batteries, have been unable to shed light on a number of important CHC abilities because of inadequate construct representation. With the exception of the WAIS-III Matrix Reasoning tests, none of the Wechsler batteries have been able to shed valid light on the developmental patterns for *Gf*. Other constructs that have not been reflected in the extant Wechsler cognitive developmental literature are *Glr* and *Ga*. Fortunately, recent analyses of the developmental change in valid *Gf* and *Glr* test scores from other nationally normed instruments (viz., K-BIT, K-FAST, K-SNAP, and KAIT) have been reported (Kaufman et al., 1996; Wang & Kaufman, 1993). Fourth, even for the Wechsler tests that are valid indicators of a CHC ability (e.g., Arithmetic as an indicator of *Gq*), the availability of only one test or indicator for a CHC construct limits the generalizability of some of the research findings (Kaufman et al., 1996).

Finally, the lack of an equal-interval measurement scale *across* the three Wechsler batteries has necessitated some creative methodological "trickery" to analyze scores across ages. For example, Kaufman (1990) employed a procedure with the WAIS-R data in which the individual test scores for all seven adult age groups in the standardization sample were equated to a reference norm group. All WAIS-R norm subject individual test raw scores were converted to subtest scaled scores ($M = 10$; $SD = 3$) using the "target" norm age group of 25–34. This provided for the ability to analyze the change in standard scores in reference to a common standard.

Another creative approach reported by Kaufman et al. (1996) was to convert the raw scores for all norm subjects between ages 15 and 94 on seven tests from the Kaufman family of instruments to z-scores ($M = 100$; $SD = 15$) calculated on the entire sample ($N = 1,193$). The resultant standard scores, which are referenced to the mean and standard deviation of the entire sample, were then analyzed. At the level of individual tests, the latter approach provides for more precision in the measurement of change than the WAIS-R approach. The WAIS-R subtest scaled scores only provide for three points of measurement for every standard deviation on the scale, regardless of which normative reference group is used. In contrast, the Kaufman et al. (1996) approach placed the individual tests on a scale that allowed for five times the degree of ability differentiation (15 points are covered for each standard deviation on the scale). All subjects with a scaled score of 12 on a WAIS-R subtest are not all likely to be at the same ability level and would cover a range of scores on a scale with a standard deviation of 15.

Regardless of the creative methods used to obtain a score suitable for analyses across age groups, this has only provided a partial *within*-battery metric solution. Without a common equal-interval growth scale, the analyses of cognitive change *across* similar batteries from the same family of tests (e.g., Wechsler or Kaufman family of related instruments) is extremely difficult and fraught with potential error. These measurement limitations result in lost opportunities for more comprehensive and informative analyses of cross-sectional CHC-based data.

Advantages of the WJ III in Measuring Growth and Change

The WJ III is particularly well suited for the measurement of growth and change both in clinical practice and for developmental research. A number of characteristics of the WJ III address the previously described limitations of measures.

First, the WJ III includes the same tests across all developmental age groups. Although only certain tests provide norms below age five, almost all of the 20 WJ III COG and 24 ACH tests provide measurement starting at age 5 or 6 and extending up through 95+ years of age. The use of the same tests across most of the life span removes the potential of "method" effects (i.e., different test content across tests in different batteries) confounding the interpretation of the resultant change scores. Second, when the focus is on changes in CHC abilities across the life span, the WJ III provides two-test clusters that maximize construct relevant variance. As described previously, each WJ III CHC COG cluster is comprised of two tests of qualitatively different narrow abilities (therefore insuring adequate construction representation) within each respective *Gf–Gc* domain. No other individually administered battery provides empirically validated cluster scores for the major cognitive constructs included in contemporary CHC theory.

Finally, and probably more important in the context of the current discussion, is the fact that all WJ III tests are grounded in unidimensional and equal-interval *growth* scales. All WJ III tests incorporate the *W*-scale, a transformation and application of the Rasch measurement model (Woodcock, 1978; Woodcock & Dahl, 1971). Each test's *W*-score is centered on a value of 500, which is the approximate average performance of 10-year-olds. Cluster scores represent the arithmetic mean (average) of the tests comprising the cluster. Although the *W*-scores are test- or cluster-specific (*W*-scores cannot be compared *across* measures), changes in scores can be compared. That is, a change of 1 *W* point represents the same amount of unit change within any of the WJ III tests or clusters. More importantly, within a test or cluster, growth can be measured from the preschool years through late adulthood on a single common scale.[8]

For the above reasons, the WJ III battery is particularly well suited to the measurement and evaluation of cognitive growth and change. Examples of the potential research benefits accrued from using a battery designed like the WJ III have been demonstrated in research with the WJ-R. For example, McArdle and Woodcock (1997; also see test-retest study by McArdle & Woodcock reported in McGrew et al., 1991) presented a series of longitudinal test-retest designs with developmental time-lag components that focused on decomposing the sources of change in test scores over time (e.g., test score variance due to practice and retention, growth or maturation, trait stabil-

ity, and test unreliability). Using the WJ-R standardization data, Salthouse (1998a) investigated the extent to which age-related differences in cognitive abilities should be interpreted as reflecting either a general developmental mechanism or an ability-specific mechanism.

WJ III CHC Growth Curves

The norm-based growth curves for 11 WJ III clusters are presented in Figures 14.5a–k.[9] Included are the curves for the GIA-Ext (Figure 14.5a), seven CHC cognitive clusters (*Gc, Glr, Gv, Ga, Gf, Gs, Gsm*, Figure 14.5b–h), and three broad achievement clusters (reading, math, and written language, Figure 14.5i–k). Each figure includes three smoothed curves (average score and standard deviations) based on the WJ III norms. We believe these figures represent the first time a complete set of *Gf–Gc* growth curves based on measures with strong construct validity (adequate construct representation) have been presented across most of the life span. The following discussion of the curves will be descriptive. Appropriate data-analytic methods need to be applied to these data to empirically evaluate the trends and to compare the results with the extant literature on the development of CHC abilities. These growth curves should be systematically compared to the analyses of the WAIS-III and other measures (WAIS, WAIS-R, Kaufman tests) presented in detail in Chapter 5, especially regarding the different aging patterns for different abilities within Horn's expanded *Gf–Gc* framework. However, note that the data are not directly comparable because (1) the WJ III analyses use *W*-scores and the Chapter 5 analyses use

---

[8]See Woodcock (1978) for a thorough treatment of the development and application of the Rasch-based *W*-score metric.

[9]See McGrew and Woodcock (2001) for a description of how the growth curves were centered at the same starting point to allow for a comparison of relative changes across the curves. The *W*-scores on the x-axis do *not* represent the normative values as a different constant has been subtracted from all values for each curve. Furthermore, ideally it would be optimal to present an additional set of curves of the same data using a logarithmic transformation of the age scale. This would allow for a closer examination of the changes occurring during the early years. Space limitations preclude the presentation of both sets of figures.

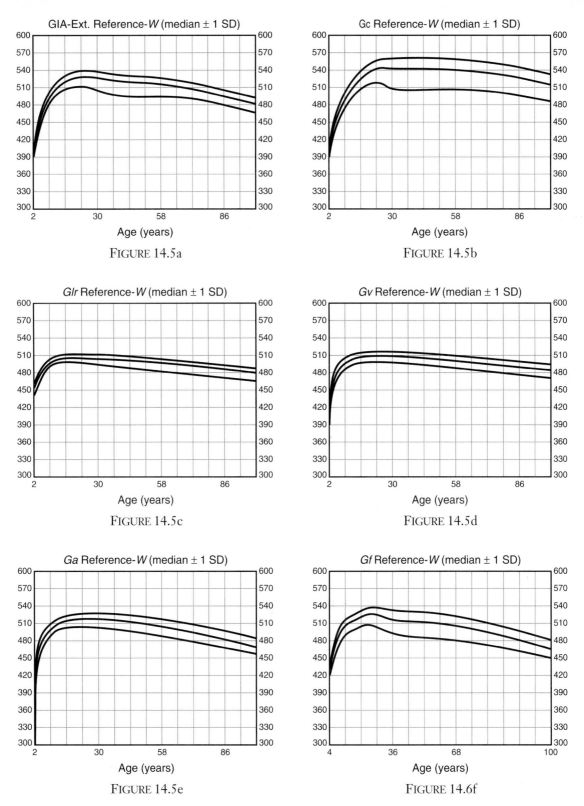

FIGURE 14.5a — GIA-Ext. Reference-*W* (median ± 1 SD)

FIGURE 14.5b — Gc Reference-*W* (median ± 1 SD)

FIGURE 14.5c — *Glr* Reference-*W* (median ± 1 SD)

FIGURE 14.5d — *Gv* Reference-*W* (median ± 1 SD)

FIGURE 14.5e — *Ga* Reference-*W* (median ± 1 SD)

FIGURE 14.6f — *Gf* Reference-*W* (median ± 1 SD)

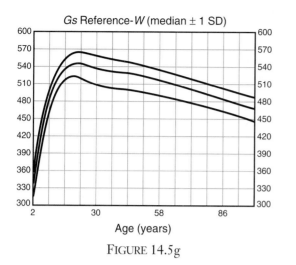

FIGURE 14.5g

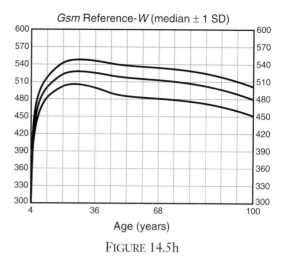

FIGURE 14.5h

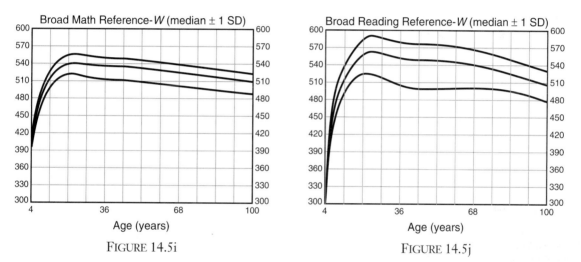

FIGURE 14.5i

FIGURE 14.5j

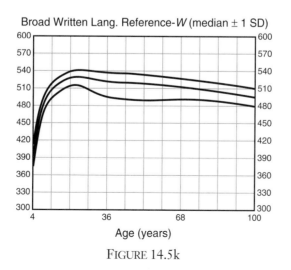

FIGURE 14.5k

standard scores; and (2) the WJ III data presented here are not corrected for educational attainment across the adult age groups, raising the possibility that some of the observed declines with age for WJ III abilities are more due to educational differences in the age groups than in real age-related decline.

Before examining the curves, it is important to understand how they are constructed, because the construction of the WJ III norms differs slightly from most other standardized measures of cognitive abilities. First, the middle smoothed curve represents the average (median) *W*-score for an age group. These are referred to as the WJ III Reference *W*-score values (Ref *W*). The curves above and the Ref *W* curve represent *unique* standard deviations for the separate halves of the distribution above and below the Ref *W* (McGrew & Woodcock, 2001).

It has long been noted that the *observed* distribution of cognitive test scores typically does not adhere to the *theoretical* normal or Gaussian distribution (Brody & Brody, 1976; Burt, 1963; Matarazzo, 1972; McNemar, 1942). The WJ III is unique in psychoeducational assessment in that, via a set of special norm procedures (see McGrew et al., 1991, and McGrew & Woodcock, 2001, for explanation), the shape of the original distribution of traits is *not* transformed to conform to the normal curve. Instead, the use of separate standard deviations above and below the Ref *W* retains the "real-world" distribution of ability traits. We believe this procedure provides scores that better mirror the reality of human cognitive abilities.

Inspection of the curves in Figure 14.5a–k, as well as review of the actual Ref *W* and SD values (not reported here), suggest the following general conclusions:

- The pattern of growth and decline for CHC abilities differs markedly, an observation attesting to the uniqueness of the CHC constructs.
- Most CHC abilities reach an asymptote at approximately age 25. *Glr* and *Gf* abilities reached an earlier apex at ages 20 and 22, re-

spectively. The early peaks for the *Glr* and *Gf* curves are typical of cognitive abilities based more on processing abilities that are developed more through informal and indirect learning (often referred to as *process*-dominant abilities). Conversely, *Gc* shows a markedly different pattern of growth, with a peak at approximately age 45.[10] The *Gc* curve is more representative of cognitive abilities that are more influenced by formal training and learning and that continue to develop over a longer period of time through the crystallization of learning experiences (*product*-dominant abilities). The peak ages for abilities such as *Glr* and *Gf* accord well with the findings for Wechsler and Kaufman tests (Chapter 5), as does the peak at about age 45 for *Gc*; again, however, these WJ III data have not been corrected for educational attainment differences across the adult portion of the age range.

- All cognitive abilities influenced more by formal learning and instruction (*Gc*, reading, math, written language) show extremely steep rates of growth during the childhood years (up to approximately age 12). These trends most likely represent the significant influence of schooling on the rapid acquisition of new acquired knowledge and skills during the early school years. Conversely, a number of more process-dominant abilities (*Glr*, *Gv*, *Ga*, *Gf*) display a much briefer and less rapid rate of growth during the formative years. It is interesting to note that two largely process-dominant abilities classified as cognitive efficiency constructs in the CPM model (*Gs* and *Gsm*) also demonstrate steep rates of development during the childhood and adolescent years (especially *Gs*). This observation is intriguing in light of the information-processing-theory-based *developmental cascade* model,

---

[10]The slight dip at age 30 in Figure 14.5b is a result of a less than perfect curve smoothing process used in the development of the figures for this chapter and does not represent a real change in abilities or the actual WJ III *Gc* norms.

which posits that, with increasing age and maturation, processing speed (*Gs*) and working memory (*Gsm*, MW) may be responsible for most increases in general intellectual functioning (Fry & Hale, 1996, 2000; Miller & Vernon, 1996). According to Fry and Hale (1996, p. 30), "virtually all of the effect of the age-related increase in speed on intelligence appears to be mediated through the effect of speed on working memory."

- The variability (as reflected in the two standard deviation curves) for CHC cognitive abilities is markedly different. The process-dominant abilities of *Glr*, *Gv*, and *Ga* show a much narrower range of variability. Conversely, reading abilities demonstrate an extremely wide range of normal variability in the population, particularly starting and continuing after adolescence. In contrast, math achievement, an acquired trait that is probably the most linked to formal instruction, is much less variable in comparison to *Grw*. One possible explanation for the significant difference in *Grw*/Math (*Gq*) variability may be that many people continue to read during their everyday life experiences once they leave school and, thus, continue to develop better reading abilities, while fewer people continue to learn new math skills via everyday learning experiences.

- One of the most significant WJ III contributions to the developmental literature is the presentation of the asymmetrical SD values in Figures 14.5a–k. These unique SD values provide potential insights into the distribution of human cognitive abilities not previously recognized. Inspection of the exact ratio of the two SDs at each age (not reported here) reveals a number of interesting findings that will benefit from additional research and study. Of interest are the observations that:

  - With a few exceptions, all CHC abilities are characterized by positively skewed distributions. There is a greater portion of the population below the average or median value than above.

- *Glr* shows significant swings in distributional characteristics. The distribution is positively skewed until approximately age 6, after which the shape shifts to a more normal distribution. However, starting at approximately the beginning of adolescence, the distribution systematically shifts in the direction of positive skew and becomes extremely skewed after approximately age 30. Given the prominence of memory decline in descriptive and theoretical studies of aging, this finding warrants further exploration.

- Acquired knowledge abilities (*Gc*, *Grw*, *Gq*) also display a significant shift toward more individuals being below than above average after approximately age 25. There is an observed swing back toward normality for *Grw* (reading and writing) starting at approximately age 75.

- The process-dominant *Gf* and *Ga* abilities show interesting patterns that vary from other CHC abilities. Although approximating normality beginning at age 8, the *Ga* distribution begins a systematic and monotonically increasing trend toward a negatively skewed distribution starting at approximately age 30. Around age 65 to 70, the *Ga* distribution becomes increasingly negatively skewed in shape. The relation between this observation and the age-related changes in hearing acuity warrants further exploration. The trend for *Gf* abilities roughly mirrors that for *Ga*, although the observed SD ratio suggests a positively skewed distribution of abilities from approximately age 13 through age 75, after which it systematically shifts into a more normal distribution.

In summary, the WJ III CHC growth curves presented here provide intriguing insights into the growth and development of human cognitive abilities. Additional research with appropriate analytic methods is necessary to "tease out" the possible explanations of the observations noted above (for example, controlling for educational attainment within the adult age groups to rule out the possible role of educational differences as an explanation for a portion of the apparent age-related declines; see Chapter 5). Although there is a risk in simply presenting the WJ III CHC growth curves in the absence of structured data analyses, we believe that the presentation of the WJ III CHC ability curves may serve to stimulate new research, dialogue, and insights into understanding and explaining the growth and development of human intelligence. In particular, the presentation of data that maintains the "real-world" distributional characteristics of CHC constructs has the potential to impact thinking on how human cognitive abilities should be properly measured and described. Similar to recent research that has simultaneously examined the population distributions at the extremes (viz., individuals with mental retardation or who are gifted), the WJ III approach to maintaining the asymmetrical characteristics of human cognitive abilities is consistent with the suggestion that we should "reevaluate our concept of intelligence as necessarily conforming to the expected normal curve distribution" (Robinson, Zigler, & Gallagher, 2000, p. 1415). In other words, it may be time to "redraw the normal curve" (Robinson et al., 2000).

CHC Cross-Battery Applications

CHC Cross-Battery (CB) assessment is a *"time efficient method of intellectual assessment that allows practitioners to measure validly a wider range (or a more in-depth but selective range) of cognitive abilities than that represented by any one intelligence battery in a way consistent with contemporary psychometric theory and research on the structure of intelligence"* (McGrew & Flanagan, 1998, p. 357; italics original). The goal of CB assessment is to guide practitioners, via a set of systematic principles, steps, and procedures, to design assessments that are organized vis-à-vis the CHC theory of intelligence. For most test batteries, this serves as a

form of *CHC post-hoc validity repair* (Flanagan, McGrew, & Ortiz, 2001). That is, with the exception of the WJ-R and WJ III, all available individually administered intelligence batteries have not used the CHC theory as their test-design blueprint. This results in the need to supplement the other intelligence batteries with additional measures to increase their coverage of CHC abilities. The primary objective of CB assessments is to combine two or more tests of different narrow CHC abilities to provide a composite score to represent a broad CHC ability. In this regard, tests that are relatively factorially pure measures of constructs are favored.

The birth of CHC CB assessments can be traced to Woodcock's (1990) CHC-organized joint confirmatory factor analysis of the then-available major intelligence batteries. Woodcock's analyses resulted in the classification of the individual tests from each intelligence battery into the broad *Gf–Gc* abilities of the CHC model. McGrew (1997) extended this work by classifying all tests at both the narrow *and* broad ability strata. This led to a detailed specification of the CB approach (Flanagan & McGrew, 1997; McGrew & Flanagan, 1998). A Wechsler-specific application of the CB approach followed (Flanagan, McGrew, & Ortiz, 2001). The most recent refinement of the CB approach is that articulated by Flanagan and Ortiz (2001).

The purpose of this section is threefold. First, the focus is on the application of the CB approach with adolescents and adults. The second focus is on how the WJ III battery can be used as the primary "tool chest" for supplementing other major intelligence batteries. Finally, approaches to supplementing the WJ III cognitive battery will be discussed.

The Big Three

Only three intelligence batteries provide coverage of the complete adolescent and adult age ranges. The Kaufman Adolescent and Adult Intelligence Test (KAIT; Kaufman & Kaufman, 1993) can be used from ages 11 through 85+. The WAIS-III/

WMS-III (Wechsler, 1997a, 1997b) span ages 16 to 89. Finally, as described previously, the WJ III spans ages 2 through 95+. Although other cognitive batteries (i.e., CAS, DAS, SB-IV) provide coverage of the adolescent age range, norms are not provided for assessing adults. The KAIT, WAIS-III/WMS-III, and WJ III have the most current set of test norms with publication dates of 1993, 1997, and 2001, respectively. For these reasons, plus the desire to adhere to the CB principle of minimizing the number of norm groups "crossed" when designing a CB assessment, the current discussion will be limited to these three batteries. Information on the selective and judicious use of individual tests from the remaining intelligence batteries for adolescents can be gleaned from other sources (Flanagan et al., 2000; Flanagan & Ortiz, 2001; McGrew & Flanagan, 1998).

Supplementing the WAIS-III/WMS-III with the WJ III[11]

Table 14.10 provides a summary of the broad and narrow CHC ability classifications of the individual tests in the WAIS-III, WMS-III, KAIT, and WJ III based on McGrew et al. (2001). A review of Table 14.10 indicates that the WAIS-III has adequate construct coverage (i.e., at least two tests of two qualitatively different narrow CHC abilities) of Gc, Gv, Gs, and Gsm. Supplementing the WAIS-III in these broad ability domains is not necessary, unless in-depth assessment of specific narrow abilities is suggested. For example, if a subject's fund of general information (K0) is a concern, the WJ III General Information test could be administered. The WJ III General Information and WAIS-III Information tests could be combined, as per CB procedures (see Flanagan & Ortiz, 2001), into a general information (K0) composite score. The WJ III should also be con-

sidered when additional information is required in the domain of listening ability (LS), particularly given that the WMS-III Logical Memory I test is a factorially complex measure (and, thus, is a diagnostically indeterminate measure of Gc and Glr). The WAIS-III Verbal Comprehension Index would appear to be a good score to use as an indicator of the broad ability of Gc.

The WAIS-III Processing Speed Index (PSI) can be interpreted as a valid measure of the broad Gs given its coverage of the narrow abilities of perceptual speed (P) and rate-of-test-taking (R9). The WJ III battery includes measures of the same narrow Gs abilities. In addition, the WJ III Decision Speed test is believed to be a measure of an aspect of semantic processing speed (R4).

The WAIS-III version of the Perceptual Organization Index (POI), when viewed from the perspective of CHC theory, is a step backwards. The WAIS-III POI consists of one good indicator each of Gv (Block Design, SR/Vz) and Gf (Matrix Reasoning, I), and a factorially complex indicator of Gv (CF) and Gc (Picture Completion).[12] The interpretation of the POI index is, therefore, diagnostically complex and indeterminate. If valid coverage of the broad Gv ability is required, it is suggested that the WAIS-III Block Design test be supplemented with the WAIS-III Object Assembly test (CS) and the WJ III Picture Recognition test (MV). This would provide for coverage of three different narrow Gv abilities (viz., Vz, CS, and MV). The WJ III Spatial Relations test would be useful if in-depth measurement of the highly related SR/Vz abilities is necessary.

The WAIS-III provides for adequate coverage of Gsm via measures of memory span (MS) and working memory (MW). However, the CHC-organized CB research consistently suggests that the WAIS-III Working Memory Index (WMI) contains a significant proportion of construct-irrelevant Gq variance. The WAIS-III

---

[11]The interpretations provided in this section also draw on the extant CB factor-analysis research for Wechsler as summarized by Flanagan et al. (2001), particularly for the WAIS-III tests not included in the analysis reported in Table 14.10.

[12]Although not reported in Table 14.10, the extant Wechsler factor-analysis research has consistently found the Picture Completion test to load on both a visual (Gv) and verbal (Gc) factor.

Arithmetic test is considered a good indicator of *Gq*, not *Gsm*. In addition to providing additional measures of memory span and working memory from the WMS-III and WJ III, the WJ III has the advantage of providing a relatively factorially pure norm-based composite score for working memory (Working Memory cluster).

The greatest benefit offered by the WJ III in WAIS-III CB assessments is the number of factorially pure indicators of the broad CHC abilities in the WJ III. The WJ III is also the only significant source for the assessment of *Ga* in adolescents and adults. *Glr* abilities are also completely underrepresented on the WAIS-III. As presented in Table 14.10, clinicians can turn to either the WMS-III or the WJ III to measure *Glr* abilities. The unique contribution of the WJ III comes from the Retrieval Fluency and Rapid Picture Naming tests, tests that provide for the measurement of ideational fluency (FI) and naming facility (NA; often referred to as RAN, or rapid automatic naming, in the reading literature).

The addition of Matrix Reasoning to the WAIS-III was a useful move that addresses prior criticisms that the various Wechsler batteries have never contained an appreciable measure of *Gf* (Flanagan et al., 2000; Flanagan & Ortiz, 2001; McGrew & Flanagan, 1996; McGrew & Flanagan, 1998; Woodcock, 1990). The WJ III Analysis–Synthesis test, which is classified as a measure of general sequential (deductive) reasoning (RG), would be an ideal CB supplement to Matrix Reasoning, which measures induction (I). However, this combination does not provide a score based on actual norms. If a norm-based *Gf* score is desired, then both the WJ III Concept Formation (I) and Analysis–Synthesis (RG) tests can be administered to obtain the broad WJ III Fluid Reasoning cluster.[13]

---

[13]The KAIT Logical Steps and Mystery Codes tests can provide a norm-based *Gf* score. The KAIT can also be viewed as a battery to use to supplement the WAIS-III. This function, as well as the possibility of using the WAIS-III to supplement the KAIT, is not addressed directly in this chapter. Table 14.10 can be inspected to perform these functions.

Supplementing the KAIT with the WJ III

Table 14.10 can also be used in a similar manner for KAIT CB assessments. The WJ III can address the KAIT's construct underrepresentation of *Gv*, *Ga*, *Gs*, and *Gsm*. In contrast, the KAIT provides for valid measurement of *Gf*. The WJ III *Gf* tests could help examiners if there is a need for in-depth narrow ability assessment of inductive and deductive abilities or if a sampling of quantitative reasoning (RQ) is necessary. Similarly, the WJ III Visual–Auditory Learning and Delayed Recall-Visual–Auditory Learning could be used to supplement the KAIT Rebus Learning test in the pursuit of an associative memory (MA) narrow ability composite score. Similar to the case of WAIS-III/WMS-III CB assessment, the WJ III can make a unique contribution to KAIT CB assessments in the measurement of ideational fluency (FI) and naming facility (NA).

Supplementation of the KAIT *Gc* tests would depend on the specific circumstances of the assessment. As reported in Table 14.10, the KAIT Definitions and Double Meanings tests, although displaying *Gc* factor loadings, also contain construct irrelevant *Grw* (reading and spelling) variance. If a strict Carroll (1993) model were followed, this extraneous *Grw* variance would not necessarily be considered a weakness of these two tests. Carroll includes *Grw* abilities under *Gc*. From Carroll's theoretical perspective, the KAIT *Gc* tests would be viewed as good indicators of *Gc* for most adolescents and adults. However, if an examinee has problems with reading and spelling, and more importantly, if the referral is for academic/learning problems, the KAIT *Gc* tests may be inappropriately impacted by reading and writing deficiencies. In such situations, the WJ III *Gc* tests could be added to a KAIT CB assessment.

Supplementing the WJ III

As previously described, the WJ III COG was designed to provide two or more qualitatively different narrow abilities within each broad

CHC domain. When viewed from the perspective of CHC CB assessment, the WJ III cognitive battery requires little, if any, supplementing in order to provide adequate ability coverage at the broad *Gf–Gc* level. This can be ascertained by reviewing the number and variety of narrow abilities measured by the WJ III in Table 14.10.

The WAIS-III/WMS-III and KAIT could be used to broaden the WJ III's *Gv* coverage via the addition of a measure of closure speed (WAIS-III Object Assembly). The WJ III *Glr* coverage might also benefit from a measure of free recall memory (WMS-III Word Lists I & II). Additionally, the WJ III Quantitative Concepts achievement test may not be an optimal indicator of quantitative reasoning (*Gf*, RQ), given that half of the test measures math knowledge (*Gq*, KM). The primary area in which the WJ III may benefit from CB supplemental testing is the addition of tests for in-depth exploration at the narrow ability level, a topic not discussed in detail here (see Flanagan & Ortiz, 2001, for a detailed explanation of these procedures).

SUMMARY

This chapter provides an overview of one of the newest revisions of a comprehensive test of intelligence: the Woodcock-Johnson III. A brief history of the family of Woodcock-Johnson tests is provided, which helps to explain how the changes for the test's third edition came into existence. The WJ III's theoretical foundation is the Cattell-Horn-Carroll (CHC) theory of cognitive abilities. This theory is described in some detail, as well as its application to the WJ III.

The WJ III is a comprehensive collection of individually administered co-normed tests organized as two distinct test batteries. The Woodcock-Johnson Tests of Cognitive Abilities (WJ III COG) and the Woodcock-Johnson Tests of Achievement (WJ III ACH) are designed to measure a wide array of cognitive, oral language,

and academic achievement abilities for individuals age 2 through the geriatric population. Although the focus of this book and this chapter is on cognitive abilities, the WJ III ACH tests play a significant role in the conceptual framework of the overall WJ III; thus, they are included here. The WJ III includes 20 Tests of Cognitive Abilities and 22 Tests of Achievement, each of which are described and categorized within tables in the chapter. The cognitive tests are organized by both the broad CHC clusters and by three broader categories related to cognitive performance: verbal ability, thinking ability, and cognitive efficiency. The achievement tests are organized by curricular area (reading, mathematics, written language, and academic knowledge) and oral language and by clusters within these areas, with additional groupings for special purpose clusters.

Interpretation of the WJ III involves careful examination of the multiple scores that the test yields. A variety of scores are provided by the WJ III, including age and grade equivalents, relative proficiency indexes (RPI), cognitive–academic language proficiency (CALP) levels, percentile ranks, and standard scores. The WJ III's scores were derived from an exceptionally large standardization sample: a total of 8,818 individuals, from age 24 months to 95+ years, living in more than 100 geographically and economically diverse communities in the United States, were assessed. The psychometric properties of the WJ III are quite strong. Eighteen of the cognitive test median reliabilities meet or exceed the .80 level standard and 12 meet or exceed the .90 standard. All 22 achievement test median reliabilities exceed .80 and 11 meet or exceed the more stringent .90 standard. Across the WJ III cognitive and achievement batteries almost all of the 42 clusters meet or exceed the .90 reliability standard. Support for the validity of many WJ III tests and clusters has accumulated across three different versions of the battery. The evidence that specifically pertains to WJ III is summarized in this chapter.

The latter half of the chapter presents special applications and use with special populations, including applications with individuals with learning disabilities, neuropsychological applications, CHC abilities across the life span, and CHC cross-battery applications. The cross-battery section focuses on how the WJ III may be used in conjunction with other comprehensive intelligence tests such as the WAIS-III and the KAIT.

Brief Tests of
Intelligence and Related Abilities

Examiners want to save time. Many clinicians want to measure a child's or adult's IQ quickly, without devoting too much time to psychometric evaluations. They want to obtain a reliable and valid estimate of the person's intelligence but prefer to spend their valuable time on therapy or personality assessment, not on the standardized administration of a comprehensive test battery, which, they erroneously believe, provides only a few IQ scores. Some of these examiners are content to obtain IQ estimates from a quick-and-dirty measure—never mind the psychometric stuff—that can be given by their receptionist or secretary. Most clinicians, however, see the value of a thorough battery and use brief tests only under circumstances that justify them.

BRIEF HISTORY
OF BRIEF ASSESSMENT

In many cases, administration of a short test may be wise because the time with an individual may be limited and a short IQ test may help optimize how that time is spent. Time limitations are especially pervasive in institutional settings (Klett, Watson, & Hoffman, 1986).

The Terman-Merrill Innovation

Terman and Merrill (1937) recognized this need more than a half century ago when they identified four tasks at each level to be given as an abbreviated form of the Stanford-Binet, "when limitations of time make it necessary" (p. 31). Their proposed short form saved the examiner about one third of the testing time and yielded an IQ that "is still reliable enough for most purposes" (p. 31). Terman and Merrill developed the shortened Binet with care and sophistication: "The…tests have been selected so as to be as representative of the entire scale as possible with respect to variety, difficulty, interest to subject, sex differences, and validity as measured by correlation with total score" (pp. 31–32).

The Role of the Slosson, Shipley-Hartford, and Other Early Brief Tests

Unfortunately, for years, many developers of brief intelligence tests did not heed this lesson. Several tried to meet clinicians' needs for brief intelligence tests, but their products were often inferior; some test developers believed that the word *brief* was supposed to apply to the test construction efforts as well as the administration time. When brief intellectual assessment was called for, some clinicians, perhaps naively, administered short tests with imaginary psychometric properties; some examiners even used the Bender-Gestalt to assess IQ, while many others relied on the IQs generated by the Slosson Intelligence Test (Slosson, 1982), a brief, mostly verbal, test organized in the format of the old Binet. The 1963 version of the Slosson was quite popular despite its use of the outmoded ratio IQ; the restandardized, but not revised, 1981 norms edition continued to offer this psychometric dinosaur, although tables of standard scores became available subsequent to Richard Slosson's death (Jensen & Armstrong, 1985). For the 1981 edition, norms were based on subjects who "were not selected at random. They were persons in the northeastern part of the United States, specifically New England" (Jensen & Armstrong, p. 133). Quite clearly, the Slosson got by on its brevity, not its merit. Oakland assailed it as hav-

ing a standardization sample that "is meager, narrow, and unrepresentative of the U.S." (p. 1403), and as "including numerous statements in the test manual and norm tables [that] are misleading or incorrect" (p. 1402). Reynolds (1985) stated flatly that the Slosson "remains a psychometrically poor measure of general intelligence …[T]he extant problems still inherent in this test…[are] cause for ethical concern regarding its utilization beyond a limited application as a preliminary screening measure" (p. 1404).

Astonishingly, despite the obvious flaws, the Slosson ranked as the fifth most popular test in the 1970s (Brown & McGuire, 1976) and as the eighth most popular in the 1980s (Harrison et al., 1988). The Slosson wasn't the only culprit. Other brief tests were commonly used as IQ substitutes, some that were too narrow in scope and others that rivaled the Slosson for psychometric weakness. An illustration of the narrow-scope brief test is the Peabody Picture Vocabulary Test (PPVT; Dunn, 1959) and its revisions, the PPVT-R and PPVT-III (Dunn & Dunn, 1981, 1997). The Shipley Institute of Living Scale (also called Shipley-Hartford; Shipley, 1940; Zachary, 1986) exemplifies the popular, but psychometrically weak, tests.

The PPVT and its successors are one-skill tests that were never intended to be substituted for an intelligence test. In the PPVT-R manual, the authors stated clearly, "The PPVT-R is designed primarily to measure a subject's receptive (hearing) vocabulary.… It is *not*, however, a comprehensive test of general intelligence" (Dunn & Dunn, 1981, p. 2). Yet, the PPVT or PPVT-R has been included in a variety of large-scale, epidemiological studies as a measure of IQ, typically the mothers of the subjects (e.g., Bellinger, Stiles, & Needleman, 1992; Ernhart, Morrow-Tlucak, Wolf, Super, & Drotar, 1989). The PPVT had poor norms, but the PPVT-R and PPVT-III have excellent psychometric data. For that reason, we have included the PPVT-III among the excellent brief measures discussed later in this chapter. However, despite its strong points, the PPVT-III is not a substitute for an IQ test and should not be used as a replacement for a Wechsler scale or other comprehensive intelligence test.

And the Shipley-Hartford, which ranked among the five most commonly used tests for assessing adults (Harrison et al., 1988), rivals the Slosson as a weak instrument. Although originally developed to assess impaired mental functioning, the Shipley attained popular use, especially in institutions, as a brief measure of IQ for adolescents and adults. Ironically, despite these origins, Zachary (1986) noted that the Shipley "is not appropriate for use with individuals who have suspected mental retardation or have suffered profound cognitive deterioration due to neurological or severe psychological disturbances. Rather, [it] is intended as a screening device for the broad band of near-average intelligence" (p. 2). The Shipley, which comprises two self-administered subtests (Vocabulary and the nonverbal Abstraction task), has low stability (.62–.65 for subtests, .73 for Total Score) and an inappropriate normative sample composed of a mixed sample of 290 *psychiatric* patients whose data were reported in an old study (Paulson & Lin, 1970). Zachary (1986) has written a sophisticated and comprehensive manual for the Shipley, and the series completion items that comprise the Abstraction subtest are clever and enjoyable. However, unfortunately, this "palace" has been built on a swamp; the norms are awful, stability is weak, and Dalton, Pederson, and McEntyre (1987) obtained better prediction from one or two WAIS-R subtests than from the Shipley, in about half the time that it takes to administer the Shipley.

Reynolds, Willson, and Clark (1983) admonished clinicians who selected tests like the Slosson or Shipley in situations where brief intellectual assessment is appropriate: "Short forms of major intelligence scales are clearly superior to such measures: they are typically better normed, more reliable, [and] have greater depth and breadth of research backing" (p. 111).

And, indeed, short forms, especially of Wechsler's tests, have been developed throughout the years by an extensive number of researchers and have been used by clinicians in myriad assessments, by examiners engaged in large-scale screening, and by researchers who needed a reliable IQ but not a separate cognitive profile.

Silverstein's Contributions to Wechsler Short Forms

Probably the most prodigious and innovative researcher in this field was Arthur Silverstein, who developed Wechsler short forms during the 1960s, 1970s, and 1980s, and was instrumental in advancing psychometric technology in this area (Silverstein, 1971, 1984a, 1984b, 1985b).

He proposed the use of two different abbreviated WAIS-Rs (Silverstein, 1982a), both of which had rich clinical histories based on previous Wechsler scales; both his two-subtest and four-subtest abbreviated tests were among the most popular WAIS-R short forms in evoking research studies (e.g., Thompson, 1987) and as the instrument of choice in many large-scale research investigations (e.g., Dietrich, Berger, Succop, Hammond, & Bornschein, 1993; Lansdown, Yule, Urbanowicz, & Hunter, 1986).

The first Silverstein short form is the Vocabulary-Block Design dyad, composed of the one Verbal and one Performance subtest that has traditionally been the most reliable task, and the best measures of *g*, on its respective scale. This very abbreviated Wechsler battery has been used in numerous large-scale investigations conducted by the Public Health Service (e.g., Sells, 1966) and was investigated for the 1949 WISC and 1955 WAIS by Silverstein (1967a, 1967b).

The second Silverstein WAIS-R short form adds one Verbal and one Performance subtest to the popular dyad to maintain the equality of verbal and nonverbal skills in the assessment of intelligence: Vocabulary–Arithmetic–Block Design–Picture Arrangement (V–A–BD–PA). This particular combination of four subtests is identical to the tetrad selected by Doppelt (1956) for the 1955 WAIS, and by Kaufman (1976a) for the WISC-R.

Silverstein (1982a) noted that his chosen four-subtest short form did not even rank among the top 10 tetrads, but he selected it anyway because of its clinical, practical, historical, and empirical virtues. In the past, many researchers selected a short form simply because it was the very highest correlate of Full Scale IQ, even if that combination of tasks was a clinical hodgepodge (composed, for example, of one Performance and three Verbal tasks). Silverstein pointed out that the validity of V–A–BD–PA trailed the coefficient of the very best tetrad by less than .01, a difference of no practical consequence.

Aside from factor analysis, the abbreviation of Wechsler's multitask batteries has received the most attention from psychometric researchers, even as far away as South Africa (Pieters & Sieberhagen, 1986) and Denmark (Kandel et al., 1988). Indeed, articles on short forms by Silverstein (1982a) and Reynolds et al. (1933) appeared in print before most clinicians were aware that the WAIS-R was available for use! Nonetheless, the proliferation of examiners who used brief tests with poor norms (like the Slosson) during the last quarter of the twentieth century is reason enough to be thankful to the Wechsler short form researchers.

One of us (A. S. K.), too, has always had an interest in developing short forms, starting with the WPPSI about 30 years ago (Kaufman, 1972) and extending to the present day with the K-ABC, WAIS-R, and WISC-III (Kaufman & Applegate, 1988; Kaufman, Kaufman, Balgopal, & McLean, 1996; Kaufman, Ishikuma, & Kaufman-Packer, 1991). While working for a test publisher in the 1970s, A. S. K. once attended a meeting to determine the fate of a would-be publication. He suggested that they publish only four of the six subscales of the proposed battery for infants, believing that two of the subscales assessed maturational development, not intelligence. He was quickly admonished facetiously by Dr. Alexander Wesman, Director of Test Development, to "please wait until after we publish the test before developing a short form for it" (Al Wesman, 1968, coined the phrase, "Intelligent Testing").

Trends in Short-Form Development for WAIS and Its Successors

There have been subtle changes in the predominant type of short-form research conducted on the 1955 WAIS and its subsequent revisions. Many WAIS short-form articles involved efforts to discover the "best" brief battery for specialized populations such as psychiatric inpatients (Robertson, Steinmeyer, & Goff, 1980; Stricker, Merbaum, & Tangeman, 1969). That approach was flawed because short forms developed for a specific, atypical population do not generalize well to other specific populations, even ones with the same "label" but from a different part of the country or spanning a different age range.

WAIS-R researchers have tended to validate with special populations specific brief tests with known psychometric properties, selected by conscientious researchers (Reynolds et al., 1983; Silverstein, 1982d) from data on the large, normal standardization sample. They tended to focus on a variety of issues when selecting the best short forms besides the simple statistical question of "which form correlated best with the Full Scale." For example, some WAIS-R short-form researchers pointed out that short-form validity (i.e., correlation with Full Scale) had been stressed to the point of ignoring the reliability of the abbreviated form (Brooker & Cyr, 1986; Cyr & Brooker, 1984), something they remedied in their WAIS-R research.

In his early work, Kaufman (1972, 1976b) criticized most previous short-form researchers who focused exclusively on the size of the validity coefficients, without concern for the "clinical sense" of the grouping of selected tasks; the tasks he chose met a variety of practical, clinical, and conceptual criteria, as well as psychometric criteria. More recently, Kaufman and his colleagues (Kaufman et al., 1991; Kaufman et al., 1996) have addressed the *length* of the short form, asking the sensible question, "If the aim of short forms is to save time, why do so many short forms include subtests that take a long time to give (e.g., Picture

Arrangement) or score (e.g., Comprehension)?" They examined brief short forms (two to four subtests) of the WAIS-R (and, later, of the WISC-III) and discovered that reliable and valid IQ estimates resulted from groupings of subtests that are short to administer and score, such as Picture Completion and Arithmetic.

Despite this focus on brevity, which attracted considerable research attention in the mid-1990s (e.g., McCusker, 1994; Nagle & Bell, 1995), more recent WAIS-III researchers have done an about-face, shifting the focus away from brevity by advocating the use of *seven* subtests, instead of the more traditional two to four, to estimate IQs (Ryan, 1999; Ryan & Ward, 1999) and even factor indexes (Axelrod, Dingell, Ryan, & Ward, 2000).

The Future of Short Forms

Short forms have continued to proliferate in diverse forms and formats, being developed at a rapid pace for the WAIS-R (Kaufman et al., 1991; McPherson, Buckwalter, Tingus, Betz, & Back, 2000) and WAIS-III (e.g., Axelrod et al., 2000; Pilgrim, Meyers, Bayless, & Whetstone, 1999; Ryan, Lopez, & Werth, 1999). The steady accumulation of short forms for the WAIS-III, and subsequent validation of these brief batteries, has continued into the new millennium and shows no sign of abating. But it is time to stop.

Reynolds et al.'s (1983) admonition to use short forms instead of brief tests like the Slosson was true in the 1980s, but it is no longer true. There are now several excellent brief tests available that have much more to recommend them than any short form can possibly match, most notably the Wechsler Abbreviated Scale of Intelligence (WASI; Psychological Corporation, 1999), Kaufman Brief Intelligence Test (K-BIT; Kaufman & Kaufman, 1990), and Wide Range Intelligence Test (WRIT; Glutting, Adams, & Sheslow, 2000).

James Kaufman and Alan Kaufman (in press) have appealed to clinicians and researchers to stop developing and stop using short forms of intelligence tests. We endorse that position, for reasons

that are set out in the next section. Then we systematically discuss the three best short forms for yielding global IQs plus verbal–nonverbal splits (WASI, K-BIT, and WRIT), as well as a number of other brief, well-constructed tests that fill more specific clinical or research needs (e.g., measures of nonverbal ability, receptive vocabulary, and functional intelligence).

LET'S STOP DEVELOPING AND USING SHORT FORMS OF LONG TESTS

J. Kaufman and A. Kaufman (in press) argue against the need for short forms in the present, conceding that they served a useful purpose up until about 1990, but are now antiquated because clinicians and researchers now have access to three brief tests (WASI, K-BIT, and WRIT) that are well-normed, reliable, stable, and valid; and, equally importantly, short forms of long tests have built-in flaws, mostly statistical, that prevent them from competing effectively with the newer brief tests.

Later in this chapter, we discuss many of the best available brief tests, including the three brief tests of high quality that measure both verbal and nonverbal ability. Now we turn our attention to the major problems with short forms that were pointed out by J. Kaufman and A. Kaufman (in press): (1) short-form norms, which are invariably derived from norms for the complete battery and not from an administration of the abbreviated battery, are not necessarily valid; (2) there are statistical problems involving the development and validation of abbreviated forms, such as the fact that short-form validity coefficients are often spuriously high because of correlated error variances. The first limitation, the problem of basing short-form estimates of IQs on norms obtained for the complete battery, affects both major types of short forms that are typically developed: a selection of several subtests—historically two or four, but, more recently, seven—to estimate Full Scale IQ; and the administration of every second or third item in some subtests, followed by the prorating of raw scores to obtain estimated scaled scores and IQs (the "Satz-Mogel" approach).

Short forms have been developed for a variety of cognitive tests, such as the Kaufman Assessment Battery for Children (Applegate & Kaufman, 1989; Kaufman & Applegate, 1988), McCarthy Scales of Children's Abilities (Harrington & Jennings, 1986), and Stanford-Binet Intelligence Scale: Fourth Edition (Prewett, 1992c). However, most short forms have been based on Wechsler's many test batteries, and most statistical and research issues about short-form development and validation have been conducted with diverse Wechsler short forms. Consequently, the discussion that follows focuses on short versions of Wechsler's comprehensive tests.

The Normative Issue, Part I: Thompson's Key Research

Thompson (1987) and his colleagues (Thompson, Howard, & Anderson, 1986) have contributed greatly to the validation of Silverstein's (1982a) short forms and delineated the range of their usefulness by conducting a long-needed study that needs replication but that still has dramatic implications for clinicians. Researchers have long conducted short-form research after the fact. Rather than administer just the two or four subtests constituting the brief battery to a fresh sample, the investigators (A. S. K. included) have analyzed data from samples administered a complete test in the usual order. The various possible short forms are then evaluated against the criterion of the whole battery, but always on a "what if" basis: What if only the V–BD dyad had been given? What if a particular tetrad had been given? But Thompson was the first to carefully research the question of what might happen differently if just the short form were given. Will the subject have a different level of motivation when taking only a few subtests than when tested for an

hour and a half? What about the ability to sustain attention and concentration for a short period of time compared to a long testing session? Exactly how much time is saved when particular short forms are given? These are precisely the questions that Thompson et al. (1986) addressed when they compared the validity of Silverstein's (1982a) two- and four-subtest short forms with a psychiatric sample of 90 inpatients.

Thompson and his colleagues divided their sample of 45 males and 45 females into three subsamples of 30 patients each. To one subsample, they administered V–BD as the first two subtests, followed by the remaining nine WAIS-R subtests in standard order; to a second subsample, they gave V–A–BD–PA as the first four tasks, followed by the rest of the WAIS-R; and to the third subsample they administered a standard WAIS-R. *They found that the patients who were given V–BD as the first two subtests obtained significantly overestimated short-form IQs when compared to their actual Full Scale IQs.* There was some overestimation, but significantly less, when Vocabulary and Block Design were embedded in the total WAIS-R (i.e., given in the standard order as the fifth and sixth subtests, respectively).

Thompson et al. inferred from these results that the patients were more motivated and attended better to the task at hand when given just the two short form subtests. However, when V–BD were given in the standard format, precisely in the middle of the 11-subtest WAIS-R, their attention, concentration, and, perhaps, motivation lagged to some extent. If these results are replicated, then the V–BD dyad—when given alone as an abbreviated Wechsler battery—will yield uncharacteristically high estimated IQs. This overestimate may be especially large for groups who are known to fatigue easily or have difficulty sustaining attention, such as elderly people or those with brain damage (Thompson, 1987).

Interestingly, this bias due to order of administration was not found by Thompson et al. (1986) for Silverstein's (1982a) four-subtest WAIS-R short form. However, V–A–BD–PA overestimated IQ significantly more for males (four points) than females (one point). Thompson's separate validation of the WAIS-R short forms for females and males was another important contribution inasmuch as most previous WAIS-R studies (often conducted in VA hospitals) included a preponderance of men.

The Normative Issue, Part II: The Satz-Mogel Approach

Satz and Mogel (1962) abbreviated the WAIS by administering Digit Span and Digit Symbol in their entirety, while giving every third item on Information, Picture Completion, and Vocabulary and every second item on the remaining six subtests. This approach to short-form development has been commonly researched (Dinning & Craft, 1983; Evans, 1985; McPherson et al., 2000; Nelson, Edinger, & Wallace, 1978) and has probably been used fairly widely in clinical practice (Cella, Jacobsen, & Hymowitz, 1985). Unlike the method of selecting several subtests for a short form, which usually yields a single IQ (estimated FS-IQ), the Satz-Mogel approach yields estimated V-, P-, and FS-IQs and a complete profile of scaled scores.

Silverstein (1982c) reported correlations of .95 between estimated and actual WAIS-R Full Scale IQs for the standardization sample when using the Satz-Mogel short form, along with .94 and .89 correlations for the V- and P-IQs, respectively. He reported similar values for the 1955 WAIS. Evans (1985) found virtually the identical correlations for a sample of 81 normal adults tested by graduate students in an assessment course, and also reported coefficients between the curtailed and complete subtests. These values ranged from .66 to .88 (median = .80). Coefficients were lowest for Picture Arrangement (.66) and Similarities (.74).

The Satz-Mogel method of abbreviating Wechsler's tests is questionable, a point Kaufman (1979b, pp. 206–207) has discussed elsewhere regarding Yudin's (1966) similar abbreviation of the WISC. It is highly unlikely that norms obtained on a complete administration of a Wechsler battery are applicable to scores produced by administering every second or third item of a subtest. Thompson et al. (1986) showed that subjects do better on the V–BD dyad when these subtests are given first rather than in their usual position midway through the WAIS-R. They speculated that motivation and attention are more nearly optimal when the short form is given alone than when it is embedded in the complete battery. In effect, they are suggesting that the WAIS-R norms for Vocabulary and Block Design are valid for these tasks when they are given as part of the long, complete battery but not when the dyad is given in isolation.

Perhaps the norms for several Wechsler subtests are likewise invalid when only one half or one third of the relevant items are given. But instead of being too "soft," like the V and BD norms when these tasks are administered first, the norms for the shortened subtests are probably too "steep." Some Wechsler subtests function as "learning" tasks during a test administration. Practice on easy items facilitates performance on harder items. Progressing gradually from easy to hard items helps ensure success on each more difficult item. This learning takes place most clearly on subtests that do not emphasize knowledge of facts, but, instead, require the examinee to learn how to solve different types of items. The best examples are Similarities, Picture Arrangement, Block Design, Picture Completion, and Digit Span (and Matrix Reasoning, as well, on the WAIS-III). All but Digit Span are abbreviated in the Satz-Mogel short form.

Thus, examinees who are administered every third Picture Completion item or every second Block Design item may not do as well when they come to the harder items as they would have if they were shaped gradually to learn the response set by taking every item. This question is answerable by a good research design, but no studies have focused on administration of only a Satz-Mogel short form to subjects; as with the dyad or tetrad methodology, research on the split-half short forms of the WAIS, WAIS-R, or

WAIS-III invariably analyzes data obtained on complete test batteries.

One of us (A. S. K.) did come across some informal support for my contention when conducting a WISC-R study with a colleague. We were trying to identify a common core of items from the 1949 WISC that were retained intact in the WISC-R in order to compare how the WISC and WISC-R standardization samples performed on identical items (Doppelt & Kaufman, 1977). This methodology helped us determine the magnitude of WISC/WISC-R IQ differences.

However, we found that Similarities items could not be included in this common core, even though numerous items were retained in the WISC-R (e.g., Beer–Wine). This was because some items were much more difficult on the WISC than WISC-R due to their place in the administration sequence. For example, consider the item Cat–Mouse. On the 1949 WISC, this was the *second* item of its type (i.e., In what way are ___ and ___ alike?) to be administered. On the WISC-R, it was the *seventh* item given (because several new, easy items in the same format were added to provide a "bottom" for the WISC-R Similarities subtest). Cat–Mouse was a much easier item on the WISC-R than the WISC because it appeared after the individual had "practiced" six times with comparable items.

Because of this probable practice effect on several Wechsler subtests, the validity of Satz-Mogel short forms is doubtful when their psychometric properties and estimated scores are based on data obtained for the complete battery. In addition, the split-half methodology fosters interpretation of V–P IQ discrepancies and subtest fluctuations although the correlations between the short-form and long-form IQs and scaled scores do *not* support profile analysis of any sort.

Evans (1985) warned that "with the exception of only a few subtests (such as Arithmetic and Vocabulary), Satz-Mogel estimates of individual subtests do not appear to yield the accuracy needed to discuss them interpretively in a psychological report" (p. 103). That is not a particularly stern warning, and Evans didn't even address the issue of interpreting V–P discrepancies, also an inadvisable practice in view of the data. But if IQ and scaled-score profiles are derived and then reported based on a Satz-Mogel administration, examiners will interpret them. (We have never understood what "cautious interpretation" means, and doubt that it means much in practice.) In sum, if examiners want to administer a brief WAIS-III (ignoring our plea to abandon short forms altogether), it is preferable to use a dyad, triad, or tetrad—or the seven-subtest "short" form—rather than a split-half short form. These preferred abbreviated batteries produce only a single IQ; if examiners choose to interpret the separate scaled scores or the scatter among the subtests, they are at least using scores from tasks that have been administered in their entirety, under standard conditions, without a loss of reliability or validity.

Despite these sane reasons for avoiding Satz-Mogel short forms, they continue to proliferate (McPherson et al., 2000; Ryan et al., 1999), and the Satz-Mogel approach is not the only one that ignores the way that norms were obtained in the first place. For example, Vincent (1979) suggested a different type of abbreviation for the WAIS, recommending that the examiner save 15 to 20 minutes of testing time by adjusting the starting points of five subtests. If a person answers the first 10 Information items correctly, the examiner is instructed to begin Comprehension at Item 6, Arithmetic at Item 10, Vocabulary at Item 13, Block Design at Item 4, and Picture Arrangement at Item 3. This modified WAIS spurred other adjustments to Vincent's method (Himelstein, 1983) to enable clinicians to further shorten the WAIS. (Why save time only with examinees who can respond correctly to the first 10 Information items?)

These articles generated validation research, for example, with patients at a medical center (Jeffrey & Jeffrey, 1984) and elderly war veterans referred for psychological evaluation (Cargnello & Gurekas, 1987). All studies showed high correlations (.99+) between IQs obtained on the modified and regular WAIS. And, naturally, all studies, including Vincent's (1979), were *ex post facto* research designs—rescoring WAIS protocols from the files to see what would have happened if.... Has anyone ever actually administered a modified WAIS to a real person?

Cella (1984) integrated Vincent's and Himelstein's methods and applied them to the WAIS-R. Further, he added Similarities and Picture Completion to Vincent's list of five subtests so that, in Cella's approach, a total of seven WAIS-R tasks are truncated based on a person's success on Information. Following Himelstein's (1983) lead, the clinician administers Information under standard conditions and determines an examinee's scaled score. If a person obtains an Information scaled score of 7, for example, then the examiner starts that person on Item 8 for Picture Completion, Item 6 for Similarities, and so forth.

All modified starting points correspond to the Information scaled score earned by the person, in this case, 7. Examinees who answer the starting item correctly for any subtest are given full credit for all earlier items; those who fail it are administered items in reverse order until two perfect scores are obtained. This procedure permits modification of the seven WAIS-R subtests for anyone who earns a scaled score of 4 or above on Information. Cella (1984) reported correlations of .995 to .998 between the modified and actual IQs earned by 50 psychiatric patients *who were given the WAIS-R under standard conditions.* Naturally.

All of the concerns expressed about the use of Satz-Mogel short forms apply to the modified WAIS-R, and with even greater emphasis. Learning sets are built up for the subtests; if the clinician starts Comprehension at Item 9 or Picture Arrangement at Item 4, examinees are unlikely to catch on right away without the benefit of success on easy items. Further, how can one expect individuals who earn a scaled score of 6 or 8 on Information to earn at least that scaled score on six other subtests, including some on the Performance Scale? Research on scatter suggests otherwise (Kaufman, 1976b; McLean, Kaufman, & Reynolds, 1989).

Why would any examiner with clinical sense start a low-functioning individual with an ad-

vanced item, depriving him or her of the confidence that comes from experiencing success? The rule allowing the administration of easier items if the starting item is failed does not help enough. Confidence may erode when an examinee fails the first item given in a new subtest, leading to possible disrupted performance on easier items. Going back to Item 1 might have been more acceptable, but administering items in reverse order may totally destroy a person's confidence before they ever reach the "confidence-building" items.

If Cella or others who advocate saving time by modifying WAIS-R starting points insist on continuing in this line of research with the WAIS-III, we implore them to start *administering* the modified WAIS-III to determine empirically how this altered administration compares to the standard administration in the scores yielded. With even greater fervor, we implore clinicians who do not heed our advice to abandon short forms altogether to, at least, avoid *modified* or Satz-Mogel short forms of the WAIS-III. Yet, despite similar warnings in the first edition of this book, Satz-Mogel short forms continue to be developed (Ryan et al., 1999) and evaluated (McPherson et al., 2000).

The Statistical Issue: Correlated Error Variance

Silverstein has published numerous articles on sophisticated statistical techniques concerning short form development, for example, linear equating to obtain norms and computing standard errors (Silverstein, 1984a, 1984b). One set of articles has provoked mild controversy, namely the correction of short-form validity coefficients for the spuriousness that enters into the coefficients when the short-form scores are derived from a complete administration of a Wechsler battery (Kaufman, 1977; McNemar, 1974; Silverstein, 1971, 1975).

Correlations between short form and full scale, when obtained from a single administration of the battery, violate a basic assumption underlying computation of the coefficients: that the respective error variances are uncorrelated. Silverstein's (1971) formula corrects for the slight spuriousness. Silverstein (1977b) concurs with Kaufman's (1977) proposed resolution to the question of whether short-form validity coefficients should be corrected: They should be adjusted when the short form is used as a replacement for the total battery (when administered in research studies, for example), but *not* when the brief version is used for screening purposes such that individuals "flagged" by the short form are likely to be given the remaining Wechsler subtests.

In the preceding sections, any mention of validity coefficients has referred only to the *uncorrected* coefficients because most clinicians who use a Wechsler short form do so for clinical or screening purposes and give the complete battery if the short-form score (or scatter among the component subtests, or clinical observations during the brief administration) arouse any concern. In such instances, the uncorrected coefficients are the relevant indexes of validity.

If, however, examiners use short forms with no intention of giving the remainder of the battery, the obtained (uncorrected) validity coefficients are a bit high. For Silverstein's (1982a, 1985b) dyad and tetrad, the correction is only .01; for less reliable brief Wechsler short forms, the correction is likely to be about .02 to .03. The correction is, thus, slight, but is something more psychometrically oriented examiners should know.

Other statistical topics have also been the subject of debate, and, occasionally, controversy, such as the advantages of using linear equating techniques rather than multiple regression analysis for estimating the IQs from the sums of the short-form scaled scores (Tellegen & Briggs, 1967). Neither the issue of correlated error variance nor the question of the best method of obtaining estimated IQs is of vital magnitude. But such topics point to the fact that the development of short forms from data obtained on comprehensive batteries is filled with a variety of problems that, ultimately, militates against their use in preference to the new group of brief tests that were normed appropriately and specifically developed to stand on their own feet.

Appropriateness of the New Brief Tests for African Americans and Hispanics

Silverstein's (1982d) Vocabulary–Block Design (V–BD) WAIS-R short form was hypothesized to underestimate IQs for African Americans (Kaufman, 1990) because the two component subtests typically produce among the largest differences between Caucasians and African Americans (see Chapter 4 section on ethnic differences). That hypothesis was given some support in two studies that compared Wechsler short forms that included V–BD with short forms that excluded them (Cravens, 1999; Paolo, Ryan, Ward, & Hilmer, 1996). In addition, short forms that include measures of vocabulary are conceivably unfair to Hispanics as well. These criticisms are pertinent to J. Kaufman and A. Kaufman's (in press) strong suggestion to abandon short forms in favor of the new breed of brief tests and to our endorsement of that position. The WASI and WRIT each include Vocabulary and Block Design (or a Block Design clone) among their four component subtests, and the K-BIT includes a vocabulary subtest along with a matrices task.

The inclusion of matrices tasks in both the two-subtest and four-subtest versions of the WASI, in the WRIT, and in the K-BIT helps neutralize the influence of vocabulary measures, to some extent, regarding assessment of African Americans and Hispanics because of evidence that ethnic differences on this type of task tend to be relatively small (Kaufman & Kaufman, 1983b, Table 4.35; Kaufman & Wang, 1992; Vincent, 1991; see Chapter 4).

When examining the WAIS-III ethnic-difference data analyzed by Heaton et al. (2001) and summarized in Chapter 4 (controlling for age, gender, and education), it is evident that Block Design yields the largest difference between Caucasians and African Americans, and Vocabulary ranks among the four most discriminating subtests. However, Matrices ranks in the middle of the pack. When the WASI 2-subtest version is administered (Vocabulary–Matrix Reasoning), the average difference between Caucasians and African Americans is 0.67 *SD*, not very different from the median effect size of 0.63 *SD* for all 14 subtests. For the four-subtest version of the WASI (which adds Similarities and Block Design to the two-subtest version), the mean effect size is 0.69 *SD*, also not very different from the median value for all subtests. Consequently, both versions of the WASI seem appropriate for African Americans and are not likely to underestimate the IQs they likely would have obtained on the complete WAIS-III. In contrast, the V–BD short form (the one Silverstein has advocated) has a median effect size of 0.76 *SD*, which is substantially greater than the median value for all 14 WAIS-III subtests.

When similar analyses are conducted for Caucasians versus Hispanics on the WAIS-III (again, based on data by Heaton et al., in press, summarized in Chapter 4), the results are interesting. The median effect size is 0.34 *SD* for the seven Verbal subtests and 0.16 *SD* for the seven Performance subtests. Vocabulary actually had the second *smallest* effect size for Caucasians versus Hispanics (0.27 *SD*) and the combination of Similarities and Vocabulary (in the four-subtest WASI) has a median effect size of 0.32 *SD*, close to the median of all Verbal subtests. Matrices and Block Design had similar effect sizes (0.14–0.16 *SD*), and the average of the two is likewise very close to the median. Therefore, neither the two-subtest nor the four-subtest WASI will underestimate the WAIS-III IQs of Hispanics. However, when testing a Hispanic individual, or anyone who is bilingual, the validity or fairness of verbal ability tests does not rest on group data. That decision has to be made separately for each bilingual person. In those instances in which a brief test is sensible for a bilingual person, but verbal skills are perceived to be an unfair measure of intelligence, we suggest giving only the nonverbal portions of the WASI or WRIT (both of which include two nonverbal subtests), or administering one of the well-constructed nonverbal brief tests discussed later in this chapter (e.g., General Abilities Measure for Adults) (GAMA; Naglieri & Bardos, 1997). Another good alternative is either the two-subtest (Abbreviated Battery) or four-subtest (Standard Battery) version of the excellent Universal Nonverbal Intelligence Test (Bracken & McCallum, 1998).

Ethnic-difference analyses of the K-BIT versus the pertinent comprehensive IQ test, the KAIT, are not so favorable (Kaufman, McLean, & Kaufman, 1995; Kaufman & Wang, 1992), as summarized in the ethnic-differences section of Chapter 4. When controlling for education, differences in favor of Caucasians versus African Americans on the two K-BIT subtests averaged about 0.90 *SD*, substantially larger than comparable values for the KAIT Fluid and Crystallized subtests. Similarly, the Caucasians–Hispanic education-controlled discrepancies of 1.02 *SD* and 0.44 *SD* on K-BIT Vocabulary and Matrices, respectively, are higher than the average values for KAIT Crystallized (0.50 *SD*) and Fluid (0.25 *SD*) subtests. The K-BIT ethnic differences for African Americans and Hispanics are also larger than comparable Verbal and Performance subtest effect sizes obtained for the WAIS-III. Consequently, when the K-BIT is used in place of either the KAIT or WAIS-III with these ethnic groups, it might underestimate their IQs.

Based on the Heaton et al. (2001) ethnic-difference data, the WASI seems appropriate for African American and Hispanic adolescents and adults, and not likely to underestimate the WAIS-III IQs for either ethnic group. Comparable data are not available for the WISC-III. Analyses of K-BIT data suggest that this brief test not be used with African Americans or Hispanics when reduction in testing time is warranted, because the obtained IQ is likely to underestimate their KAIT IQs. Glutting et al. (2000, Table 8.10) demonstrated that the WRIT was construct-valid for separate groups of Caucasians, African Americans, and Hispanics, based on factor analyses that produced highly congruent factors for the three ethnic groups, but they failed to provide mean–difference ethnic data. Pending such data for the WRIT, the WASI would seem to be the brief test of choice for African Americans and Hispanics.

Although there is reason to avoid the V–BD WAIS-III short form for African Americans because of its possible underestimation of Full Scale IQs, that logic clearly does not apply to the WASI. Therefore, we recommend all three brief tests for Caucasians, and the WASI for Caucasians, African Americans, and Hispanic; and we suggest the abandonment of short forms for all ethnic groups.

The Seven-Subtest WAIS-III

Some researchers have been making a strong push for a seven-subtest short form of the WAIS-III (e.g., Ryan & Ward, 1999). The seven-subtest abbreviated version was developed for the WAIS-R (Ward, 1990), and recent research has mushroomed with the WAIS-III (Axlerod et al., 2000; Pilgrim, Meyers, Bayless, & Whetstone, 2000; Ryan & Ward, 1999). Ward's (1990) initial seven subtests included four Verbal subtests (Information, Digit Span, Arithmetic, Similarities) and three Performance subtests (Picture Completion, Block Design, Digit Symbol). Recently, Ryan and Ward (1999) compared that WAIS-III seven-subtest short form with a similar one that substituted Matrix Reasoning for Block Design, and found them both to be extremely reliable and valid. These authors also praised the seven-subtest short forms for their fairness and utility with neurological patients.

But every study we have seen with these seven-subtest short forms has been after the fact—analyses based on administration of the complete WAIS-R or WAIS-III. No one ever evaluates the reliability or validity of the seven subtests based on an administration of just the short form; no one has normed this short form.

Why would anyone choose to use it? If you can give seven subtests, then you can give 11. If you want to save time, then don't give all 13 or 14 subtests. Pick the 11 "regular" subtests and you obtain IQs. Choose a slightly different set of 11, and you obtain the four factor indexes. No prorating or estimating is necessary. If time is an issue, then select the 11 subtests that yield the indexes. That means you eliminate the long (about 11-minute) Picture Arrangement and Comprehension subtests (excluded from the indexes) and replace them with the 4-minute Letter-Number Sequencing and Symbol Search subtests (see Table 6.1).

If you want short, then use a two-subtest WASI or K-BIT or use a four-subtest WASI or WRIT. Don't give 7 when, with a little more time, you can give 11.

WHEN TO ADMINISTER BRIEF TESTS

As J. Kaufman and A. Kaufman (in press) emphasize, we are proposing the use of the three new brief tests to replace short forms. We are not saying or implying that the new brief tests should be used to replace comprehensive IQ tests. In most clinical situations, clinicians should administer a comprehensive IQ test to achieve a competent evaluation, often including the IQ test as part of a larger neuropsychological, clinical, or psychoeducational battery.

When assessing adolescents and adults, clinicians sometimes have legitimate reasons to spend a half hour or less on an intellectual evaluation. Perhaps the individual was referred for a psychiatric disturbance, and only a global estimate of IQ is needed in the context of a complete personality evaluation. Or the person was given a thorough clinical or neuropsychological evaluation within the past several years, and a quick check of current intellectual status is desired. Perhaps large groups of individuals need to be screened for potential educational or neurological impairment to determine which areas need a thorough follow-up. Or the time spent with a client is limited by practical constraints, and intelligence is but one of several areas (vocational interests, educational achievement, adaptive behavior, special abilities, personality development) requiring evaluation. Or any similar circumstances in which the clinicians' goals are *not:* (1) to categorize the individual's intelligence into a specific level of functioning such as retarded, gifted, or (in the case of learning-disabilities assessment) "normal"; (2) to make neuropsychological or clinical inferences about the person's ability profile; or (3) to diagnose cognitive disorders. Brief tests are also ideal for use in research investigations, when an individual's precise score is less important than group performance. But King and King (1982) far overstate the case, in our opinion, when they argue that "perhaps the most valuable and only justifiable use of short forms is for research purposes" (p. 436).

And, in all of the circumstances that might dictate reduced time for assessing IQ, we suggest that the diversity of short forms that have been developed and studied—almost always based on data obtained with the complete battery—be set aside. Use one of the new brief tests that were specifically developed as brief tests, normed as brief tests, and validated as brief tests.

That is our professional opinion. Other professionals will continue to endorse short forms (Ryan & Ward, 1999) or pan them (Smith, McCarthy, & Anderson, 2000). Still others believe that brief IQ tests can be used instead of comprehensive IQ tests for virtually any testing purpose. A case in point is Joe Glutting, the first author of the WRIT, who wrote in an E-mail that "although the WRIT clearly is a short test, we do not believe it is a 'brief' measure of intelligence ...and all that implies in the field of individual intelligence testing. Rather, we believe it is just as good diagnostically as any other IQ test" (Glutting, personal communication, March 1, 2000). We disagree with that statement, but do agree that the WRIT is a good instrument for brief assessment.

THREE WELL-NORMED RECENT BRIEF TESTS OF VERBAL AND NONVERBAL INTELLIGENCE

In this section of the chapter, we discuss the three recent, well-normed brief tests of verbal and nonverbal intelligence that have already been discussed to some extent: the WASI (Psychological Corporation, 1999), K-BIT (Kaufman & Kaufman, 1990), and WRIT (Glutting et al., 2000). These three tests share in common that they (1) provide a valid measure of intelligence for children, adolescents, adults, and the elderly; (2) yield measures of global verbal (crystallized) and nonverbal (fluid) abilities; (3) have exceptional normative samples and strong psychometric properties.

Wechsler Abbreviated Scale of Intelligence (WASI)

Overview and Description

The WASI (Psychological Corporation, 1999) was developed in order to meet the needs for an abbreviated scale of intelligence for clinical, psychoeducational, and research settings. It can be used to assess a broad age range, from ages 6 through 89 years. It consists of four subtests: Vocabulary, Block Design, Similarities, and Matrix Reasoning, which are similar to the subtests of the same name on the WAIS-III and the WISC-III (exception Matrix Reasoning, which does not appear on the WISC-III). According to the WASI Manual (Psychological Corporation, 1999), these four subtests were chosen for their strong association with general cognitive functioning (these are the subtests with the highest g loadings) and for their relationship to the constructs of verbal and performance intelligence and fluid and crystallized intelligence. The WASI Verbal subtests provide good measures of crystallized intelligence or acquired knowledge whereas the WASI

Performance subtests are good measures of both fluid intelligence and visualization (Horn, 1989; Horn & Hofer, 1992; Kaufman, 1994a).

Administration of the four WASI subtests takes approximately 30 minutes. A two-subtest form of the WASI (Vocabulary and Matrix Reasoning) takes approximately 15 minutes to administer. Individuals who have completed some formal graduate or professional-level training in psychological assessment, or individuals with a bachelor's degree in psychology, education, counseling, speech therapy, and occupational therapy who have received training in standardized testing procedures are considered qualified examiners for the WASI.

A Full Scale IQ can be obtained either from the administration of all four WASI subtests or just two subtests. The shorter form of the test, comprising Vocabulary and Matrix Reasoning, yields only a Full Scale IQ. However, the four subtests together yield Verbal and Performance IQs in addition to the Full Scale IQ. Vocabulary and Similarities compose the Verbal scale and yield a Verbal IQ, while Block Design and Matrix Reasoning compose the Performance scale and yield a Performance IQ. Each IQ scale has a mean of 100 and a standard deviation of 15, as is typical for most tests of intelligence. However, the WASI subtests yield age-corrected T-scores, with a mean of 50 and SD of 10, which is unlike the scaled-score metric used for all other Wechsler subtests (mean of 10 and SD of 3). The Psychological Corporation (1999) explains that their choice to use T-scores rather than scaled scores was based on the fact that the T-score has a wider range of score points, and can, therefore, better differentiate the level of ability reflected by the subtest raw scores. The WASI manual provides a table for converting WASI subtest T-scores into the more widely used subtest scaled scores (Psychological Corporation, 1999, Table A.2).

Standardization and Psychometric Properties

The WASI normative sample included 2,245 children and adults highly representative of the English-speaking U.S. population aged 6 years to 89 years and was well stratified on gender, race/ethnicity, and educational level. To ensure that the sample was representative by geographic region, the number of participants from each of four regions of the United States were chosen to be closely proportionate to the population in each region, according to the 1997 census data. The standardization sample was divided into 23 age groups, each with a sample size of 100, except the last three age groups (75–79, 80–84, and 85–89), which had samples of 85, 85, and 75, respectively. When stratifying according to education, the participants under age 20 were stratified according to their parent's educational level and those age 20 and above were stratified according to their own educational level.

The overall psychometric qualities of the WASI are quite strong. Generally, the reliability coefficients for the adult sample were slightly higher than those for the children's sample. The mean internal consistency reliability coefficients for children ages 6 to 16 are .93, .94, .96, and .93 for the V-IQ, P-IQ, FS-IQ (four subtests), and FS-IQ (two subtests), respectively. Comparable values for adults ages 17–89 are .96, .96, .89, and .96. At the subtest level, the reliability coefficients for ages 6–16 range from .86 to .93 for Vocabulary (mean = .89), from .83 to .91 for Similarities (mean = .87), from .84 to .93 for Block Design (mean = .90), and from .86 to .96 for Matrix Reasoning (mean = .92). Comparable values for adults ages 17–89 are Vocabulary (.90–.98, mean = .94), Similarities (.90–.94, mean = .92), Block Design (.88–.96, mean = .92), and Matrix Reasoning (.84–.96, mean = .94). A summary of mean reliability coefficients for children and adults is listed in Table 15.1.

The test-retest method was used to examine the stability of scores over an interval of 2 to 12 weeks, with a mean retest interval of 31 days. The samples retested comprised 116 children ages 6–16 and 106 adults ages 17–89. For children, the mean stability coefficients of the IQs ranged from .85 (FS-IQ two subtests) to .93 (FS-IQ four subtests). And for adults the range was .88 (FS-IQ two subtests) to .92 (FS-IQ four sub-

CHAPTER 15 BRIEF TESTS OF INTELLIGENCE AND RELATED ABILITIES   **643**

TABLE 15.1 Summary of mean WASI reliability coefficients for children and adults

Subtest/Scale	Split-Half Reliability		Test-Retest Reliability	
	Ages 6–16	Ages 17–89	Ages 6–16	Ages 17–89
Vocabulary	.89	.94	.85	.90
Similarities	.87	.92	.86	.88
Block Design	.90	.92	.81	.86
Matrix Reasoning	.92	.94	.77	.79
V-IQ	.93	.96	.92	.92
P-IQ	.94	.96	.88	.87
FS-IQ (4-subtest)	.96	.98	.93	.92
FS-IQ (2-subtest)	.93	.96	.85	.88

NOTE: Data are from The Psychological Corporation (1999). The samples used to obtained the stability coefficients were from the total standardization sample (1,100 children ages 6–16 and 1,145 adults ages 17–89). $N = 116$ in children's test-retest sample and $N = 106$ in adult's test-retest sample.

tests and V-IQ). Exact values for stability of IQ scales and subtests are listed in Table 15.1. In children, the mean stability coefficients ranged from .77 (Matrix Reasoning) to .86 (Similarities) and in adults from .79 (Matrix Reasoning) to .90 (Vocabulary). Interscorer reliability coefficients, obtained from four trained raters, were in the high .90s for all subtests.

The practice effect for children ages 6–16 from the test-retest study averaged about 6 points for P-IQ and 3 points for V-IQ; for the FS-IQ, retest gains were about 5 points and 2½ points for the four-subtest and two-subtest versions, respectively. For adults, as was true for the WAIS-III (see Chapter 6), practice effects were larger for younger than older adults. For ages 17–54 years, approximate retest gains were as follows: V-IQ (2 points), P-IQ (5 points), FS-IQ-4 (4 points), and FS-IQ-2 (2½ points). For ages 55–89, comparable values were: V-IQ (1½ points), P-IQ (3 points), FS-IQ-4 (2½ points), and FS-IQ-2 (2 points).

Studies measuring the content, construct, convergent, discriminant, and clinical validity of the WASI are cited in the manual (Psychological Corporation, 1999) and provide evidence for the validity of the WASI as a quick screening measure of general intellectual ability. The WASI FS-IQ-4 is highly consistent with the FS-IQs of the Wechsler full batteries and accounts for 76% and 85% of the variance of the WISC-III and WAIS-III FS-IQs, respectively (Psychological Corporation, 1999). The correlations between the WASI and WISC-III were obtained from a sample of 176 children and 248 adults that provided the correlational data between the WASI and the WAIS-III. As shown in Table 15.2, the strongest associations between the WASI and the WISC-III and WAIS-III were between the FS-IQs of the tests.

Joint factor analyses between the WASI and WISC-III ($N = 176$) and WAIS-III ($N = 248$) supported the WASI's construct validity (Psychological Corporation, 1999). The results of exploratory joint factor analysis with the WASI and WAIS-III resulted in the four WASI subtests loading strongly on the expected factors. WASI Vocabulary and Similarities had loadings of .90

TABLE 15.2 WASI correlations with WISC-III and WAIS-III

Subtest/Scale	WASI vs. WISC-III	WASI vs. WAIS-III
Vocabulary	.72	.88
Similarities	.69	.76
Block Design	.74	.83
Matrix Reasoning	—	.66
V-IQ	.82	.88
P-IQ	.76	.84
FS-IQ (4-subtest)	.87	.92
FS-IQ (2-subtest)	.81	.87

NOTE: Data are from The Psychological Corporation (1999). $N = 176$ in WASI-WISC-III comparison and $N = 248$ in WASI-WAIS-III comparison.

and .75, respectively, on the Verbal Comprehension factor and WASI Block Design and Matrix Reasoning had loadings of .73 and .68, respectively, on the Perceptual Organization factor. The findings from the joint factor analysis with the WISC-III were similar, but not quite as robust: WASI Vocabulary and Similarities had loadings of .87 and .66, respectively, on the Verbal Comprehension factor, and WASI Block Design and Matrix Reasoning had loadings of .60 and .54, respectively, on the Perceptual Organization factor.

Evidence for the WASI's validity as a quick screening measure of general intellectual functioning for certain clinical populations was provided with several small studies of individuals with mental retardation, attention deficit-hyperactivity disorder, learning disabilities, and traumatic brain injury (Psychological Corporation, 1999). As noted in the WASI manual, although an accurate estimate of general intellectual functioning for these special groups is obtainable through this measure, it cannot provide some of the important clinical information necessary for diagnosis and placement; the comprehensive tests are advised.

Evaluation

Our overall impressions of the WASI are quite favorable. It is a well-developed and well-standardized instrument with strong psychometric properties and good clinical utility. The four chosen subtests offer a nice array of abilities and form a cohesive clinical unit. As opposed to short forms of the WISC-III or WAIS-III, the normative data for the WASI were collected from a nationally representative sample, independent of the standardization data of the related full Wechsler batteries. As we stated earlier, the lack of independent norms for the short forms of the WISC-III and WAIS-III has been a problem for these short forms, making the WASI a better choice than a Wechsler short form.

The WASI's familiar subtests and format will be easy for most examiners to learn and use. The constructs were shown to be similar to those of the full Wechsler batteries with correlational and factor-analytic data. Another advantage of the WASI is the broad age range that can be assessed with the test, which is advantageous for making valid comparisons when an individual is tested over time. For example, when testing an individual under age 16 and later over age 16, the WASI can be used in both instances, rather than having to use the WISC-III and then the WAIS-III. This consistency in the instrument used makes the two obtained test scores more comparable. However, examiners need to keep the practice effects in mind when interpreting retests, especially for children and adults ages 17–54 years. Another advantage of the WASI is the option of administering either a four-subtest or a two-subtest battery. When time is truly of the essence, the 15-minute administration of the two WASI Full Scale subtests will offer a reliable and valid estimate of a child's or adult's intelligence. The links between the WASI and the WISC-III and WAIS-III are advantageous, as the scores between the brief and full batteries are quite comparable. In fact, the WASI manual provides tables for determining WISC-III and WAIS-III FS-IQ score ranges from the WASI FS-IQ four-subtest scores (Psychological Corporation, 1999, Tables B.1 and B.2).

There were few disadvantages to the WASI that we could find. One minor inconvenience is the use of T-scores for the subtests rather than scaled scores. Although psychologists and other professionals evaluating the WASI scores will surely be familiar with the T-score metric (mean = 50, SD = 10), it is inconvenient to have to look up scores in yet another table to translate the T-scores into the scaled scores. Requiring additional tables introduces another possible place for errors to occur. Also, no place is listed on the WASI record form for the T-score-to-scaled score translation to be recorded. Although the WASI has been shown to be a valid estimate of general IQ, the fact that it doesn't include subtests tapping the constructs of working memory or processing speed (as are found in the full batteries) makes it much less clinically useful than a complete battery. Clearly, the WASI cannot be used alone to make diagnoses or educational placement decisions, and should not be used to replace more comprehensive measures of intelligence.

Kaufman Brief Intelligence Test (K-BIT)

Overview and Description

The Kaufman Brief Intelligence Test (K-BIT, Kaufman & Kaufman, 1990) is a brief, individually administered test of verbal and nonverbal intelligence for individuals ages 4 to 90 years. The K-BIT includes two subtests: Vocabulary (both Expressive Vocabulary and Definitions) and Matrices. The Vocabulary subtest measures verbal, school-related skills via the assessment of word knowledge and verbal concept formation. Matrices measures nonverbal reasoning by assessing the ability to perceive relationships and complete analogies. Administration time for the K-BIT is quite short, taking approximately 15 to 30 minutes to administer.

Standardization and Psychometric Properties

The K-BIT was standardized on a sample of 2,022 subjects ages 4 to 90 years. The sample was stratified within 14 age groups by gender, geographic region, socioeconomic status, and race/ethnic group. The sample sizes for each of the age groups between ages 4 and 10 were between 105 and 122, whereas the sample sizes for each of the age groups between ages 11 and 54 were larger (Ns ranged from 148 to 207). The oldest age group (55–90 years) comprised 155 people. The sample closely approximated the 1990 U.S. Census data (however, 1985 U.S. Census data were used if 1990 projections were not available). The K-BIT was co-normed and codeveloped with the KAIT, which allows for easy interpretation of the instruments when used together.

The mean split-half reliability coefficients for both subtests and the K-BIT IQ Composite were excellent for adults (ages 20–90) and good for children (ages 4–19) (see Table 15.3 for median reliability coefficients for children and adults). For children, the reliability coefficients ranged from .89–.93 for Vocabulary, .74–.92 for Matrices, and .88–.95 for the Composite. For adults, the reliability coefficients ranged from .96–.98 for Vocabulary, .93–.95 for Matrices, and .96–.98 for the Composite. The sample used to obtain information on test-retest reliability included 232 children and adults ages 5 to 89 years. The test-retest interval ranged from about two weeks to four months, and the average interval was three weeks. Adequate test-retest reliability was found for the two subtests and the composite. The mean values of the coefficients across all ages for the Vocabulary and Matrices subtests were .94 and .85, respectively, and for the composite .94 (see Table 15.3). Practice effects were generally small in magnitude, though they were a bit larger for ages 5–12 and 13–19 (2½ to 4 points) than for ages 20–54 and 55–89 (1½ to 2½ points).

The K-BIT's validity has been demonstrated in multiple criterion-related validity studies with tests of intelligence and achievement. The *K-BIT manual* (Kaufman & Kaufman, 1990) provides complete results of correlational studies involving the K-BIT and the K-ABC, WISC-R, and WAIS-R. In brief, the average correlation between the K-BIT and WISC-R FS-IQ was .80 and between the K-BIT and WAIS-R Full Scale IQ was .75. In summary, the correlation coefficients presented between the K-BIT and tests of cognitive ability offer good support for the K-BIT's concurrent validity.

Correlational studies with achievement tests such as the Kaufman Test of Educational Achievement (K-TEA Brief or Comprehensive Form; Kaufman & Kaufman, 1985a, 1985b) and Wide Range Achievement Test—Revised (WRAT-R; Jastak & Wilkinson, 1984) were also conducted, including five with normal samples, three with learning-disabled groups, and one with school dropouts. Again, for detailed results of the studies, refer to the *K-BIT Manual* (Kaufman & Kaufman, 1990, Table 5.10, pp. 69–70). Of the

TABLE 15.3   K-BIT split-half and test-retest reliability coefficients

	Median Split-Half Reliability Coefficients					Mean Test-Retest Reliability Coefficients				
	Age Group					*Age Group*				
Subtest	4	5–12	13–19	20–54	55–89	4	5–12	13–19	20–54	55–89
Vocabulary	0.92	0.91	0.92	0.96	0.98	N/A	0.86	0.96	0.97	0.95
Matrices	0.80	0.85	0.88	0.93	0.95	N/A	0.83	0.8	0.86	0.92
Composite	0.91	0.92	0.94	0.96	0.98	N/A	0.92	0.93	0.95	0.95

NOTE: Adapted from *Kaufman Brief Intelligence Test Manual* (pp. 56–57), by A. S. Kaufman and N. L. Kaufman, 1990, Circle Pines, MN; American Guidance Service. Copyright 1990 by American Guidance Service. Adapted with permission.

studies using the K-TEA (either Brief or Comprehensive Form), the K-BIT IQ Composite had a mean correlation of .73 with the K-TEA Battery Composite. The average K-BIT–K-TEA correlation was about the same for the normal samples versus the learning-disabled samples. Low to moderate correlations were found between the K-BIT and the WRAT-R for the learning-disabled and normal young adult samples (ranging mostly from .30s to .40s). In summary, the correlation coefficients presented between the K-BIT and tests of achievement offer strong evidence of the K-BIT's concurrent validity.

Additional Research Studies

The K-BIT has achieved wide popularity and much K-BIT research has accumulated. Lichtenberger et al. (2000) summarized the K-BIT research relevant to the topics of gender, ethnicity, and SES differences, age-related patterns, and assessment of clinical populations such as learning-disabled, mentally retarded, or neuropsychological samples. Here we highlight some of the major findings on clinical populations, as the other topics have been discussed at length in Chapter 5 (aging) and Chapter 6 (gender, ethnicity, SES), and ethnic differences were reviewed earlier in this chapter.

K-BIT research conducted on samples of individuals with learning disabilities or mental retar-

dation has supported the K-BIT's use as a screening tool for such individuals (Lichtenberger et al., 2000). In these populations, the correlations between the K-BIT Composite and global IQs from comprehensive batteries of intelligence range from .78 to .82 (Canivez, 1996; Prewett, 1992a, 1992b, 1995; Prewett & McCaffrey, 1993; Slate, Graham, & Bower, 1996). In addition, the K-BIT has been shown to be a promising instrument for patients referred for neuropsychological assessment (Lichtenberger et al., 2000). In patients referred for neuropsychological evaluation, the K-BIT has proven its ability to adequately estimate WAIS-R IQs (Axelrod & Naugle, 1998; Einstein & Englehart, 1997).

Evaluation

Reviews of the K-BIT have been positive (Jirsa, 1994; Miller, 1995; Young, 1995). The test has several strengths and only minor weaknesses, according to reviewers, both of which we discuss here briefly.

One of the advantages of the K-BIT is that it was co-normed and codeveloped with a comprehensive measure of intelligence, the KAIT, which allows for easy interpretation of the instruments when used together. These tests' standardization samples overlap considerably, but are not identical. Overall, the K-BIT standardization sample is well stratified on age, gender, geographic region, SES, and race/ethnicity, and the size of the normative group is large (2,022) (Jirsa, 1994). The stability and internal consistency coefficients for the test are very good and the K-BIT's reliability is higher than those typical of short forms of other scales (Anastasi & Urbina, 1997). The validity data for the K-BIT are extensive and well presented. Age trend data are consistent with Horn's (1985, 1989) findings for fluid and crystallized abilities (Jirsa, 1994).

Like the WASI, the K-BIT assesses a wide age range (4 to 90), which is especially useful when retesting needs to be completed across age groups that typically require different tests for an assessment (e.g., the WISC-III at age 12 versus the WAIS-III at age 18 or the K-ABC at age 11 and the KAIT at age 20). The small practice effect for all ages, and especially for adults ages 20–89, facilitates interpretation of the retest data as well as changes in intellectual functioning from the first to the second testing. The K-BIT subtests measure similar constructs as major intelligence tests, which makes the test translate well to widely used intelligence tests. The format of the K-BIT is well designed and logically laid out, which leads to smooth administration (Jirsa, 1994). The K-BIT subtests do not require motor responses, so the test is good for individuals with physical impairments. The scoring of all items is objective and straightforward and the scoring process is clearly presented in the manual (Miller, 1995).

One of the disadvantages of the K-BIT is that it may not provide the best estimate of intelligence for individuals with known or suspected visual–perceptual problems, due to its substantial reliance on visual stimuli (Miller). The test should also not be used as an estimate of intelligence for nonreaders because of the reading component required on part of the Vocabulary subtest. And, as noted, ethnic differences in studies of Caucasians versus African Americans and Hispanics are larger than for other instruments when education is controlled.

Although the overall standardization sample is excellent, the norm samples were small for the older age groups: 55–59 (N = 27), 60–64 (N = 21), 65–69 (N = 24), 70–74 (N = 19), 75–79 (N = 12), and 80+ years (N = 12). Therefore, caution should be used when interpreting standard scores for older subjects because of the use of small N's in the norming (Miller, 1995). Although the K-BIT has high g loadings and high correlations with popular IQ tests, it should not be considered commensurate with an intelligence test. In fact, the test authors discuss throughout the manual that the K-BIT should be used as a screening instrument and not to replace more comprehensive assessment (Jirsa, 1994; Miller, 1995).

Wide Range Intelligence Test (WRIT)

Overview and Description

The Wide Range Intelligence Test (WRIT; Glutting et al., 2000) is an individually administered test of brief intelligence designed for people ages 4 through 85 years. The WRIT has four subtests and three IQs, all of which yield standard scores with means of 100 and standard deviations of 15. The three IQs are Verbal (Crystallized), Visual (Fluid), and General. Unlike the WASI, there is no two-subtest version. The WRIT manual uses the parenthetical description of the IQs "as a reminder that the Verbal and Visual IQs can be conceptualized according to several common theoretical orientations such as the verbal/performance dichotomy associated with the Wechsler tests…or crystallized–fluid dyad of Horn and Cattell…" (Glutting et al., 2000, p. 4). The Verbal IQ comprises two subtests: Verbal Analogies and Vocabulary. The Visual IQ also comprises two subtests: Matrices and Diamonds.

The Verbal Analogies subtest requires participants to orally provide a word that best completes a verbally presented analogy (e.g., Cow is to calf, as cat is to ____.). The Vocabulary subtest requires examinees to verbally define an orally presented word. For Matrices, individuals select a picture from among several alternatives in order to complete an implied visual–perceptual relationship. The Diamonds subtest requires examinees to reproduce a two- and three-dimensional pattern using chips shaped as single or multiple diamonds.

Depending on the subject's age, abilities, and work style, the administration time for the WRIT ranges from 20 to 30 minutes. The subtests are presented in alternating order of visual–verbal–visual–verbal to maintain the interest and motivation of the participants. The WRIT manual cautions that, as with all intelligence tests, the WRIT should be used as part of a larger evaluation so that history and other psychometric data can be integrated with the results in order to make clinical decisions.

Standardization and Psychometric Properties

A large number of individuals (N = 2,285) from ages 4 to 85 comprised the standardization sample for the WRIT. These subjects were stratified according to age, gender, ethnicity, educational level, and regional residence, and closely matched the 1997 U.S. Census data. Twenty-three age groups were used with Ns ranging from 87 to 125 (most groups had 100 individuals). The overall gender of the standardization sample was 48.9% male and the overall ethnic composition of the sample was 69% Caucasian, 15% African American, 11%, Hispanic, and 6% "other."

The reliability of the WRIT is quite strong. The average internal consistency coefficients for the General, Verbal, and Visual IQs were .95, .94, and .92, respectively. The internal consistency coefficients for the subtests were likewise strong: Vocabulary (.91), Verbal Analogies (.84), Matrices (.90), and Diamonds (.93). The stability of the WRIT was measured by testing 100 individuals from the standardization sample on two occasions, with a 6- to 115-day interval separating the testings (M = 30.5 days). Overall stability coefficients for the IQs were good: .91 for General IQ, .90 for Verbal IQ, and .83 for Visual IQ. The average stability coefficients were good for Vocabulary (.83) and Verbal Analogies (.90), but

weak for the two nonverbal subtests, Matrices (.70) and Diamonds (.69). Practice effects were substantial for children ages 4–18 years on the three IQs (about 7½ points for Visual IQ, 5 points for Verbal IQ, and 7 points for General IQ) and moderate for adults ages 19–85 (4–5 points, with only a ½-point differential for visual vs. Verbal).

The validity of the WRIT was demonstrated through factor analysis as well as correlations with other measures of intelligence. Glutting et al. (2000) performed a principal axis factor analysis with a promax rotation to determine if the WRIT's subtests would load on their hypothesized factors. With their forced two-factor solution, support for the Verbal and Visual IQs was apparent. The factor loadings for the Verbal subtests on the Verbal factor were .81 and .68 and the factor loadings for the Visual subtests on the Visual factor were .59 and .44. The General IQ was also supported in the unrotated factor solution resulting in a single dimension. The four subtests had fair to good g loadings (.64 for Diamonds and .72–.82 for the other three tasks). Glutting et al. also reproduced their factor-analytic findings separately in males and females, indicating that the test's two factors provide similar assessments across gender (coefficients of congruence were .992 for the Verbal factor and .995 for the Visual factor). Similarity of construct validity was also assessed across Caucasian, African American, and Hispanic groups. Substantial coefficients of congruence, ranging from .997 to .985, supported the use of the WRIT's constructs across these three groups. Similar analyses were conducted for educational level, and the results again demonstrated the WRIT's structure across these various groups. The final set of replications reported were to determine if the WRIT's two-factor solution held across the entire age span. Seven age groups were formed for the analyses. The mean coefficients of congruence across the age groups showed sufficient congruence for the Verbal factor (.900), but insufficient congruence for the Visual factor (.808). Glutting et al. suggested that the lack of replication in the Visual factor was the result of the "Visual factor wanting to merge with the Verbal factor for adolescents (i.e., ages 13 through 19 years) to form a single, *g* dimension" (p. 111).

Concurrent validity was assessed by administering the WRIT with the WISC-III, WAIS-III, and the Wide Range Achievement Test—Third Edition (WRAT3). A sample of 100 children ages 6–16 were administered the WISC-III and WRIT and a sample of 100 adults ages 16–79 were administered the WAIS-III and WRAT3. Table 15.4 lists the correlations between the WISC-III and WRIT as well as the WAIS-III and WRIT.

The correlations between the WRIT General IQ and the Full Scale IQs of the WISC-III and WAIS-III were appreciable (.90 and .91, respectively), as were other coefficients. *However, all of these values are spuriously high because standard deviations were in excess of 15, sometimes very much in excess, and the test authors failed to make the appropriate corrections for heterogeneity of variance; SDs for the Wechsler IQs were 18.0–20.5 and SDs for WRIT IQs were 16.0–22.4.* Until these values are

corrected for variability, and until samples of more appropriate variability are tested, the true magnitude of the correlations with Wechsler's scales remains a question. The authors also gave apparently good evidence of factorial congruence with Wechsler's scales, but, again, the extreme variability of the samples makes interpretation of the results difficult. It is probably fair to say that the WRIT IQs relate moderately to substantially to the corresponding Wechsler IQs based on the data provided, but exactly how close the relationship is is indeterminate.

Additional correlational data were presented for the WRIT and an achievement test, the WRAT3, composed of Reading, Math, and Spelling. For individuals ages 19 and older, the WRIT General IQ score correlated .54–.56 with each subtest. Correlations between the WRIT Verbal IQ and WRAT3 Reading and Spelling were slightly stronger (*r*s = .60 and .57, respectively). These moderately high relationships between the WRIT and a test of achievement provide further indication of the WRIT's validity. However, the test authors failed to provide means and *SD*s for the WRIT IQs and WRAT3 standard scores, so the accuracy of these relationships cannot be verified.

TABLE 15.4   Correlations between the WRIT and WISC-III, and WRIT and WAIS-III

	WRIT General IQ	WRIT Verbal IQ	WRIT Visual IQ
WISC-III FS-IQ	.90	.85	.80
WISC-III V-IQ	.88	.85	.76
WISC-III P-IQ	.85	.78	.78
WAIS-III FS-IQ	.91	.89	.85
WAIS-III V-IQ	.88	.90	.80
WAIS-III P-IQ	.86	.80	.85

NOTE: From Tables 8.22 and 8.24 of Glutting, Adams, and Sheslow (2000, pp. 127 & 129). *These coefficients are spuriously inflated by very large standard deviations for WRIT and Wechsler IQs that ranged from 16.0 to 19.1 in the WISC-III study and from 18.8 to 22.4 in the WAIS-III study. The test authors failed to make appropriate statistical corrections for the extreme heterogeneity of variance.*

Evaluation

The WRIT is a recently published test of general cognitive ability and visual and verbal skill. It was developed with multiple theoretical frameworks in mind (i.e., Wechsler and Horn-Cattell). The factor-analytic data in the manual offer support for these dimensions in the WRIT's Verbal (Crystallized) and Visual (Fluid) scales. The test was well standardized with a large sample and has strong reliability for the IQs and subtests. Stability was strong for the IQs and Verbal subtests, but weak for the Performance subtests. The manual is quite comprehensive in its presentation of reliability and validity data. However, the important validity data with the WISC-III and WAIS-III preclude easy interpretation because the authors inexplicably failed to correct the values for unusually large *SD*s for the samples tested. The WRIT IQs undoubtedly relate moderately to substantially to corresponding Wechsler IQs, but the exact magnitude of the relationships are indeterminate. The authors also failed to supply data in the manual on clinical samples; because it is such a recent instrument, there are no other published data to support its use in non-normal clinical samples.

One strength of the WRIT is the extensive differential factorial validity offered to provide excellent evidence of the constructs measured by the WRIT for males and females, three ethnic groups, and four education levels. An additional strength is the WRIT manual's detailed section on interpretation. The authors describe interpretation of each of the levels of the test, including Visual–Verbal discrepancies and the possible interpretation of the individual subtests. Data for identifying IQ-achievement discrepancies based on WRIT–WRAT3 values are also provided.

Thus, overall, the WRIT is a useful measure of general intelligence that can be administered in a brief amount of time. However, as with the other brief measures of intelligence that we have discussed, it should not be used alone to make diagnoses or educational placement decisions, and should not be used to replace more comprehensive measures of intelligence in such situations.

BRIEF TESTS OF EITHER NONVERBAL OR VERBAL ABILITY

In this section of the chapter, we present information on three brief tests with generally good psychometric properties that measure specific abilities, either verbal or nonverbal. One verbal test is discussed, a popular brief test of semantic knowledge, the Peabody Picture Vocabulary Test—Third Edition (PPVT-III; Dunn & Dunn, 1997); we also discuss two nonverbal tests: the General Abilities Measure for Adults (GAMA; Naglieri &

Bardos, 1997) and Matrix Analogies Test (MAT; Naglieri, 1985a, 1985b).

Peabody Picture Vocabulary Test—Third Edition (PPVT-III)

Overview and Description

The Peabody Picture Vocabulary Test—Third Edition (PPVT-III; Dunn & Dunn, 1997) is similar in format to the original and revised editions published in 1959 and 1981. The PPVT-III is an individually administered test of receptive vocabulary (of standard English) for children and adults ages 2.5 to 90. It is an untimed test that requires individuals to examine four drawings and choose which one best represents the meaning of a stimulus word that is presented orally by the examiner. Only nonverbal responses are required. Four training items are provided at the beginning of the test, and test items are presented subsequently in order of increasing difficulty. Two parallel forms are provided in the PPVT-III. The total administration time for either form is between 10–15 minutes, because individuals are only administered item sets that are of appropriate difficulty for them. Items that are far too easy or too difficult are not administered. The test yields standard scores (*M* = 100; *SD* = 15), percentile ranks, age equivalents, and descriptive categories.

Some notable differences exist between the 1981 PPVT-R and the 1997 PPVT-III. One is an increase in the number of items on the test. The PPVT-III has 204 test items, which are grouped into 17 sets of 12. These groupings also served to modify the basal and ceiling rules in the PPVT-III. The content of the PPVT-III was modernized with new illustrations and the PPVT-III kit itself was packaged in a manner that facilitates transporting materials.

Standardization and Psychometric Properties

The PPVT-III was standardized on a stratified sample of 2,725 persons, including 2,000 children ages 2.5–19 and 725 adults over age 19. The alternate-forms reliability coefficients for the PPVT-III standard scores, based on the entire standardization sample, ranged from .88 to .96 with a median value of .94. The split-half reliability coefficients were also high, ranging from .86 to .97, with a median reliability of .94 for both forms of the PPVT-III. The PPVT-III is more reliable than the PPVT-R, which had a median split-half reliability coefficient of .81. The stability of the PPVT-III was also very strong, as determined in a sample of 226 subjects who were administered the test twice (with approximately a one-month interval between testings). Test-retest reliability coefficients were all in the .90s, and ranged from .91 to .93.

The validity of the PPVT-III was shown in its correlations with measures of intellectual ability as well as other measures of verbal ability. The K-BIT Vocabulary, Matrices, and Composite scales correlated .82, .65, and .78, respectively, with the PPVT-III in a sample of 80 individuals. The PPVT-III also was administered concurrently with the Oral and Written Language Scales (OWLS; Carrow-Woolfolk, 1995) to a sample of 43 children. The correlation between the OWLS Oral Composite score and the PPVT-III was .75.

For special populations, such as incarcerated individuals, the PPVT-R has been shown to be an effective screening tool. Carvajal, Shaffer, and Weaver (1989) showed that the PPVT-R was highly correlated with the WAIS-R FS-IQ ($r = 80$) in a sample of 29 male inmates (ages 24–36) at a maximum security penitentiary. Across three different studies assessing the correlation between the WAIS-R and PPVT-R in normal samples, the PPVT-R correlated .68 with the FS-IQ and V-IQ and .50 with the P-IQ (Dunn & Dunn, 1997). However, Altepeter and Johnson (1989) cautioned that the PPVT-R overestimates the WAIS-R FS-IQ and V-IQ in individuals who function in the lower ability ranges and the PPVT-R underestimates mean WAIS-R IQs in individuals who function in the upper ability ranges. Similar research using the PPVT-III and WAIS-III needs

to be conducted to determine if these relationships hold in the most recent versions of the tests.

Evaluation

Overall, the PPVT-III is a solid measure of receptive vocabulary. It is an easy and quick task to administer and score. The revisions of the last edition have made scoring easier because of the new basal and ceiling rules. As a measure of a single ability, the PPVT-III cannot be equated with an intelligence test. Therefore, it should not be used alone as a criterion for diagnosis or placement in assessment, but is a helpful component in a more comprehensive battery of tests.

There is some evidence that PPVT-R may provide a useful estimate of premorbid ability for patients with brain damage with greater than high school education (Snitz, Bieliauskas, Crossland, Basso, & Roper, 2000). The PPVT-R was administered to a clinical sample of 150 elderly patients (ages 43 to 95) with known or suspected brain damage. Although the PPVT-R was vulnerable to increasing levels of cognitive impairment among patients with less than a high school education, the PPVT-R was stable across mild to moderate levels of impairment for patients with greater than 12 years of education. In patients that were considered "cognitively intact," the PPVT-R standard score correlated substantially with a WAIS-R estimated FS-IQ ($r = .61$). In fact, the PPVT-R was less likely to overestimate the WAIS-R FS-IQ in the cognitively intact patients than the Barona equation estimation of FS-IQ (Barona et al., 1984).

In addition to being useful as an estimate of premorbid functioning, the PPVT-R has been shown to be a useful tool for identifying malingered intellectual impairment. Morrison (1994) found that, by calculating the probability that particularly low scores could be achieved by guessing, the results obtained on the PPVT-R could be used to establish malingering. Thus, a standardized instrument such as the PPVT-R or PPVT-III may be a useful component in a thorough battery to assess possible malingering in cases related to litigation or in other circumstances when client's benefit from feigning low scores.

In all, the PPVT-III measures a limited aspect of intellectual functioning, but it does it well.

General Abilities Measure for Adults (GAMA)

Overview and Description

The General Abilities Measure for Adults (GAMA; Naglieri & Bardos, 1997) is a timed paper-and-pencil test that allows 25 minutes to complete it. The test is comprised of four subtests (Matching, Analogies, Sequences, and Construction), all of which tap visual–spatial reasoning skills. The GAMA, which requires examinees to choose the correct abstract design from among six alternative responses, yields a global IQ that is obtained from the sum of the scaled scores on the four subtests. The IQ has a mean of 100 and standard deviation of 15 and each of the four subtests yields a mean of 10 and standard deviation of 3.

In the Matching subtest, the examinee is required to choose the correct option that matches the stimulus by color, shape, and configuration. Verbal analogy tests are similar to the GAMA Analogies subtest, except for the fact that the GAMA's test uses abstract designs for the stimulus and response rather than words. The stimulus items consist of a completed pair of designs and an incomplete pair. The examinee must recognize the relationship between the first stimulus pair and then select the design that completes the second pair from the alternatives provided. The same conceptual relationship presented in the first design pair must be maintained in the second pair of designs.

The items in the Sequences subtest each present a series of geometric designs across the printed page. The geometric designs change in a logical sequence from left to right across the page. The examinee must identify the succession of change and select the option that best fits the pattern of change.

In the Construction subtest, the examinee must determine how several colored shapes can be combined to produce a design. Each stimulus item consists of a variety of shapes of different colors that are presented in disarray. The goal is to analyze the spatial attributes of the colored shapes in order to mentally reconfigure and synthesize them into a whole design, and then accurately match the stimulus item.

Standardization and Psychometric Properties

The GAMA was standardized with a sample of 2,360 adults ages 18 to 96 that was stratified to closely match the 1990 U.S. Census data. The internal consistency of the GAMA IQ score was strong; across 11 age intervals the reliability coefficients ranged from .79 to .94 (the average was .90). The internal consistency coefficients for the individual subtests are adequate for Analogies (.81) and Sequences (.79) and low for Matching (.66) and Construction (.65) (Naglieri & Bardos, 1997). Two studies have reported the test-retest reliability of the GAMA (Lassiter & Matthews, 1999; Naglieri & Bardos, 1997). The test-retest data in the GAMA manual are based on a sample of 86 adults who were group-administered the GAMA twice in a 2- to 6-week interval (mean interval 25 days). The test-retest coefficient for GAMA's Full Scale IQ was .67. Stability coefficients for the four subtests were generally poor: .55 for Matching, .65 for Analogies, .74 for Sequences, and .38 for Construction. Lassiter and Matthews replicated the test-retest study with a sample of 25 college students (77% male). The subjects were administered the GAMA twice in a 22- to 48-day interval (mean interval 35 days). The stability coefficients were even lower than those reported in the GAMA manual and were quite unimpressive (.62 for Full Scale IQ and .31–.54 for subtests).

The concurrent validity of the GAMA has been assessed by its correlation with several other measures of global cognitive ability, such as the WAIS-III, WAIS-R, WJ-R, KAIT, K-BIT,

Shipley-Hartford, and Wonderlic Personnel Test. A sample of 60 college students (83% male) were administered the GAMA and WAIS-III in counterbalanced order (Lassiter, Bell, Hutchinson, & Matthews, in press). Overall, the GAMA IQ was significantly lower than the mean WAIS-III FS-IQ, V-IQ, POI, and VCI, but was significantly higher than PSI. There were no significant differences between the GAMA IQ and WAIS-III P-IQ and WMI. GAMA IQ correlated .59–.78 with WAIS-III IQs, with the highest value (as expected) obtained with P-IQ. The relationship between the GAMA and P-IQ was significantly stronger than GAMA's relationship with the V-IQ. GAMA IQ correlated .80 with POI and .41–.50 with the other three indexes. Lassiter et al. also found that, for individuals with Low Average to Average IQ on the WAIS-III, the GAMA IQs were within 4 points of the WAIS-III FS-IQ and P-IQ. However, for individuals with Superior or Very Superior WAIS-III FS-IQs, the GAMA IQ mean was approximately 8 to 14 standard-score points lower than the WAIS-III FS-IQ or P-IQ. Thus, the GAMA may not provide an accurate estimate of WAIS-III FS-IQ and P-IQ for individuals who are functioning in the Superior to Very Superior range of intelligence on the WAIS-III.

A sample of 80 college students with learning difficulties was used to examine the validity of the GAMA in comparison with the WAIS-R (Lassiter, Leverett, and Safa, 2000). Similar to the findings with the WAIS-III and college students without learning difficulties, the GAMA correlated most strongly with the WAIS-R P-IQ (.69) and least with the V-IQ (.36). The GAMA–WAIS-R FS-IQ correlation was .60. The GAMA IQ more accurately predicted the ability of individuals with learning difficulties who scored within the Average and High Average ranges on the WAIS-R. In contrast, the GAMA underestimated the WAIS-R IQs of those who fell in the Superior to Very Superior ranges of intelligence.

The relationship between the GAMA and Woodcock-Johnson—Revised Tests of Cognitive Ability (WJ-R) was examined in a sample of 62 male college students (Nagy, Lassiter, & Leverett, in press). Three of the WJ-R's composite scores were compared to the GAMA IQ, including Processing Speed, Visual Processing Speed, and Auditory Processing. There was no significant relationship between WJ-R Auditory Processing and the GAMA IQ, but the WJ-R Processing Speed and Visual Processing Composites were moderately correlated with the GAMA IQ ($r = .55$ and .49, respectively). The results of this study indicate that the GAMA can accurately be viewed as a measure of processing speed and visual ability, but does not measure other aspects of cognitive ability such as auditory processing.

Maher, Lassiter, Matthews, and Bell (in press) studied the relationship of the GAMA to the KAIT in a sample of 77 college students. Two of the KAIT scales showed moderate correlations with the GAMA: Fluid IQ ($r = .47$) and Composite IQ ($r = 44$). Although the correlation between KAIT Crystallized IQ and GAMA IQ was significant, it was of very small magnitude ($r = .28$). Thus, similar to findings on the WAIS-III and WAIS-R, the GAMA appears to have a small relationship to measures of verbal or crystallized ability, contrasted with moderate relationships to fluid abilities and nonverbal reasoning skills. Also, parallel to findings on the WAIS-III and WAIS-R, the GAMA underestimated the KAIT Composite IQ of individuals who scored above average or better on the KAIT.

Naglieri and Bardos (1997) reported that the GAMA had significant correlations with the K-BIT Composite, Matrices subtest, and Vocabulary subtest ($r = .70$, .72, and .54, respectively). Leverett, Matthews, Bell, and Lassiter (in press) reported a moderate correlation between the GAMA IQ and Wonderlic Personnel Test ($r = .46$). Overall, the relationship with the GAMA to each of these brief measures of cognitive ability further supports the validity of the GAMA as a measure of general intelligence.

Evaluation

Overall the GAMA seems to be a good measure of nonverbal ability, but its reliability and stability are fairly weak and the IQs it yields do not correspond very well to the IQs yielded by comprehensive tests, especially for high-functioning adults. The subtest reliability and stability are too low to permit meaningful profile interpretation; only the global score should be interpreted. Validity studies indicate that it may be best characterized as a measure of perceptual organization, visual–spatial skill, fluid ability, and processing speed. It bears little relationship to verbal abilities as measured by other tests of cognitive ability. The fact that it can be group-administered can be beneficial in many settings, especially in research. Much of the research conducted to date on the GAMA has been with predominantly male samples, so the instrument would benefit from additional data using more female subjects.

Matrix Analogies Test (MAT)

Overview and Description

The Matrix Analogies Test (MAT; Naglieri, 1985a, 1985b) is a figural matrices test, similar to others of like names (e.g., K-ABC Matrix analogies, K-BIT Matrices, WAIS-III Matrix Reasoning). The MAT comes in two forms: a group-administered short form that consists of 34 multiple-choice items and an expanded form that consists of 64 individually administered multiple-choice items. The test consists of abstract designs printed two per page, in the colors of black, white, blue, and yellow. The nature of the test is abstract reasoning with four item types: pattern completion, reasoning by analogy, serial reasoning, and spatial visualization. The MAT Short and Expanded forms are designed for administration to individuals ages 5 through 18 years. Because of the minimal language involvement in the test, the MAT is particularly well suited to assessing the intelligence of individuals whose native language is not English, and of those with hearing impairments or learning disabilities.

The raw scores obtained on the expanded form of the MAT can be converted into standard scores with a mean of 100 and standard deviation of 15. Age equivalents and percentile ranks are also provided. The raw scores obtained on the short form of the MAT can be converted to percentile ranks, stanines, and age equivalents.

Standardization and Psychometric Properties

A very large sample was used in the standardization of the MAT (N = 5,718). The sample was stratified according to U.S. Census data by race, gender, age, geographic region, community size, and socioeconomic status. The match between the actual sample and Census statistics was adequate.

The MAT Expanded Form's reliability is generally high. Internal consistency coefficients range from .88 to .95, although the test-retest reliability of the total test score over a 1-month interval was only .77. The validity of the MAT has been assessed with correlations between the MAT Expanded Form and tests of intelligence and achievement. The MAT Expanded Form standard score correlated .41 with WISC-R FS-IQ for a normal sample of 82 children and .68 for a sample of hearing-impaired children. Correlations for the MAT Short Form and WISC-R are generally in the same moderate range. Generally, the MAT Expanded form has produced lower scores than the WISC-R Performance IQ, by about 10 points (Naglieri & Prewett, 1990). In a variety of studies, the MAT short form correlated .67 with WISC-III Full Scale IQ (Prewett, 1995), .73 with Binet-4 Composite, and .38–.44 with Math, Reading, and Spelling achievement on the Kaufman Test of Educational Achievement (Prewett & Farhney, 1994). Mean correlation between the K-ABC Mental Processing Composite and the MAT Expanded Form was .53, and the MAT scores were approximately 0.5 SD lower than the K-ABC Mental Processing Composite (Smith, 1988). The MAT and K-BIT Matrices subtest correlated .62 in a sample of juvenile delinquents (Hayes, 1999).

Evaluation

As a single subtest, the MAT is a good screener for intelligence. The Expanded form is particularly useful in samples that have communication problems or motor problems, or in samples for whom English is not their first language. As a brief measure, it has been shown to be comparable to the K-BIT in terms of its usefulness as a screening tool (Hayes, 1999; Prewett, 1995). The MAT is modern in its appearance, and has a large normative sample. The MAT Expanded form has an advantage over the Short form in that it produces standard scores, which are beneficial when comparing MAT scores to other tests of intelligence or achievement.

BRIEF TESTS FOR SPECIALIZED ABILITIES

In this section, two brief tests of special abilities are featured: the Kaufman Short Neuropsychological Assessment Procedure (K-SNAP; Kaufman & Kaufman, 1994b), a neuropsychological screening test; and the Kaufman Functional Academic Skills Test (K-FAST, Kaufman & Kaufman, 1994a), a measure of cognitive–adaptive functioning.

Kaufman Short Neuropsychological Assessment Procedure (K-SNAP)

Overview and Description

The Kaufman Short Neuropsychological Assessment Procedure (K-SNAP; Kaufman & Kaufman, 1994b) is a brief, individually administered test that assesses mental functioning at three levels of cognitive complexity for individuals ages 11 to over 85 years. Four subtests comprise the K-SNAP, organized by level of complexity. Typically, administration time for the K-SNAP is 20 to 30 minutes.

The Mental Status subtest (low complexity) assesses attention and orientation; the Number Recall and Gestalt Closure subtests (medium complexity) measure simple memory and perception skills, respectively; Four-Letter Words

(high complexity) assesses reasoning and planning ability. The subtests are also intended to be interpreted from the vantage point of Luria's (1980) neuropsychological model: Block 1, Attention (Mental Status); Block 2, Coding functions (Number Recall, Gestalt Closure); and Block 3, planning ability (Four-Letter Words).

The Mental Status subtest consists of 10 items that are questions asked by the examiner that probe for information about the patient's mental status. A person's alertness, attention, and orientation to the environment are ascertained. The Gestalt Closure subtest consists of 25 items. In each item, the examinee is shown a partially completed "inkblot" and the examinee must name the object that is depicted. This subtest assesses visual closure and simultaneous processing. The Number Recall subtest consists of 16 items that require the examinee to repeat out loud a series of numbers said by the examiner. It assesses sequential processing and short-term auditory memory. The Four-Letter Words subtest consists of 22 items. For each item, the examinee tries to guess a "secret" word from the stimuli, which consist of a series of four-letter words, along with the number of letters in each word that are included in the "secret" word. This subtest assesses planning and problem-solving ability.

The K-SNAP Composite is a standard score with mean = 100 and SD = 15. Scaled scores (mean = 10, SD = 3) are yielded by each subtest except Mental Status, which yields a raw score that is concerted to a category, and by the Recall/Closure Composite (Number Recall + Gestalt Closure). The K-SNAP also yields an Impairment Index.

Standardization and Psychometric Properties

Standardization of the K-SNAP included a sample of 2,000 subjects ages 11 to 94 years, which was stratified within each of 13 age groups by gender, geographic region, socioeconomic status, and race/ethnic group. The K-SNAP standardization sample closely approximated 1988 U.S. Census data.

The mean split-half reliability coefficients were strong: .82–.84 for the subtests (excluding Mental Status), .85 for the Recall/Closure Composite, and .89 for the K-SNAP Composite (see Table 15.5). Test-retest reliability was based on data from 132 normal adolescents and adults ages 11–91 years tested twice with an average test-retest of 30 days (see Table 15.5). Good test-retest reliability was found for the two composites (in the .80s), but the subtest reliabilities were mediocre, ranging from the mid-60s for Four-Letter Words to the high 70s for Number Recall and Gestalt Closure. Reliability for the Mental Status subtest was based on data from 54 subjects aged 55 or older, as this subtest is primarily intended for clinical populations and middle-aged or elderly populations; the mean stability coefficient was .74.

Results of factor analyses and age trend data provide excellent support for the construct validity for the K-SNAP. In a joint factor analysis of the K-SNAP, K-FAST, and KAIT ($N = 1,270$), clearly defined crystallized (Gc) and fluid (Gf) factors were identified in two-factor solutions (Kaufman & Kaufman, 1993). The K-SNAP Four-Letter Words subtest was associated with the Fluid factor, consistent with the notion that it measures higher-level reasoning and planning ability. And, as hypothesized, none of the K-SNAP subtests were closely associated with the Crystallized factor; that is sensible because the K-SNAP tasks do not assess the types of tasks formally taught in school.

An additional factor-analytic study of the K-SNAP, K-FAST, KAIT, and WAIS-R produced a meaningful four-factor solution (Kaufman, Ishikuma, & Kaufman, 1994). The four factors produced by the sample of 225 were Gc, Gv/Gf (broad visualization and fluid abilities), Gf, and Gsm (Horn's short-term memory). The three K-SNAP subtests were each associated with different factors, with each substantial factor loading entirely consistently with the rationale for the K-SNAP's development: Four-Letter Words loaded on the Gf factor, Number Recall was associated with the Gsm factor, and Gestalt Closure loaded on the Gv/Gf factor. Thus, these factor-analytic studies suggest that the construct validity of the K-SNAP is supported by its relationship to the Horn constructs (fluid, broad visualization, and short-term memory).

The age-related patterns of performance on the K-SNAP also support its construct validity (Kaufman & Kaufman, 1994b; Kaufman, Kaufman, Chen, & Kaufman, 1996); these data are reported in Chapter 5.

Evaluation

Overall, the K-SNAP appears to have many positive characteristics, as noted by reviewers of the

TABLE 15.5   K-SNAP split-half and test-retest reliability

K-SNAP Scale or Composite	Split-Half Reliability	Test-Retest Reliability[a]
Gestalt Closure	.82	.78
Number Recall	.83	.79
Four-Letter Words	.84	.65
Recall/Closure Composite	.85	.83
K-SNAP Composite	.89	.82
Impairment Index	—	.68

[a]These reliability coefficients were corrected for the variability of the norm group, based on the standard deviation obtained on the first testing, using Guilford's (1954, p. 392) formula.

NOTE: The data in columns 1 & 2 are from *Kaufman Short Neurological Procedure Manual* (pp. 51–52), by A. S. Kaufman and N. L. Kaufman, 1994, Circle Pines, MN: American Guidance Service.

test (Geller, 1998; Herbert, 1998). Lichtenberger, Broadbooks, and Kaufman (2000) also summarize the test's strengths and weaknesses based on the test's reviews, and we highlight many of those here.

The K-SNAP assesses mental functioning at varying levels of cognitive complexity, allowing for a range of abilities to be measured across a wide age range (11 to 85+; Herbert, 1998). The well-normed Mental Status test is more beneficial than many commonly used measures of mental status that are not well standardized (Geller, 1998). The test yields reliable standard scores at the extremes (three standard deviations above and below the mean), allowing for accurate and stable measurement of individuals in both the low and high cognitive ability range.

There are many positive aspects to the administration of the K-SNAP. It is easy and quick to administer with a well-designed easel format (Geller, 1998; Herbert, 1998). Teaching is allowed during administration (except on the Mental Status test) to ensure that examinees understand the task. Responses are acceptable in foreign languages, sign language, or slang. In addition, scoring is objective with little subjectivity.

Because the K-SNAP was co-normed and developed with the KAIT, K-BIT, and K-FAST, interpretation is not difficult when they are used conjointly (Geller, 1998). K-SNAP profiles can be interpreted in the context of several neuropsychological theories as well as Horn's expanded crystallized–fluid theory. The test is a good measure of the abilities "vulnerable" to the effects of aging and brain damage (Gf, Gv, and SAR).

One of the K-SNAP's weaknesses is that it is only somewhat useful in identifying the need for follow-up testing, as it does not accurately identify patients who do not need more comprehensive assessment (Geller, 1998). One subtest in particular is not useful for assessing individuals with learning disabilities: Because of the reading necessary to complete Four-Letter Words, this subtest should not be administered to individuals with a reading disability or who cannot read.

There is needed research on the validity of the K-SNAP. No validity studies with comprehensive neuropsychological batteries have been conducted. Also problematic is that a majority of patients with documented unilateral brain damage had Impairment Index scores within the normal range, indicating that this Index may not be effective in distinguishing such patients from normal individuals (Herbert, 1998). It also does not discriminate well between the normal population and those with depression (Grossman, Chan, Parente, & Kaufman, 1994).

Because the K-SNAP only measures a discreet and narrow aspect of cognitive functioning, it should be used to supplement other norm-referenced cognitive and neuropsychological tests.

Kaufman Functional Academic Skills Test (K-FAST)

Overview and Description

The Kaufman Functional Academic Skills Test (K-FAST; Kaufman & Kaufman, 1994a) is a brief, individually administered test of cognitive–adaptive behavior that assesses functional reading and math abilities of individuals ages 15 to over 85 years. It assesses acquired knowledge of basic reading and math skills and the ability to apply those skills to everyday problems, which is an aspect of adaptive behavior.

The K-FAST comprises two untimed subtests: Arithmetic and Reading. K-FAST administration takes approximately 15 to 25 minutes. The Arithmetic subtest consists of 25 items that assess numerical reasoning, computation skill, and mathematical concepts through questions paired with pictorial stimuli that depict real-life content. The Reading subtest consists of 29 items that assess the ability to recognize and understand frequently used symbols, abbreviations, and phrases by asking examinees to interpret the meaning of rebuses, abbreviations, and words or sentences that are seen in commonplace situations.

The K-FAST is similar in some aspects to the more traditional achievement batteries, just as it resembles aspects of intelligence tests and adaptive behavior scales; however, care was taken in developing the items to remove those items that were too school-like or minimized practical application. In fact, unlike most reading achievement tests, the K-FAST Reading subtest does not assess pronunciation or the ability to recognize multisyllabic or phonetically irregular words. Moreover, the K-FAST Arithmetic subtest uses pictorial stimuli along with its verbally presented questions to lessen the influence of reading. Thus, the K-FAST provides a unique, standardized way to briefly measure functional intelligence and achievement.

Standardization and Psychometric Properties

The K-FAST was standardized on a sample of 1,424 subjects ages 15 to 85+ years. The sample was stratified within each age group by gender, geographic region, socioeconomic status, and race/ethnic group. The sample closely approximates the 1988 U.S. Census data. The mean split-half reliability coefficients for both subtests and the Functional Academic Skills Composite (all standard scores with mean = 100 and *SD* = 15) were strong for all age groups: Reading (.90), Arithmetic (.88), and Composite (.94) (see Table 15.6). Test-retest reliability was based on data from 116 adolescents and adults ages 15–91 years who were tested twice on the K-FAST (average test-retest interval was 33 days). Very good test-retest reliability was found for the two subtests and the composite; the mean values of the coefficients across all ages for Arithmetic and Reading were .84 and .88, respectively, and the mean stability coefficient for the Composite was .91 (see Table 15.6).

Multiple studies with the K-FAST and tests of intelligence provide evidence of the test's criterion validity, but relatively few studies include tests of achievement and adaptive functioning. The K-FAST manual provides complete results of correlational studies involving the K-FAST and the WISC-R, WAIS-R, SB-IV, and the KAIT (Kaufman & Kaufman, 1994a, Tables 6.8–6.10, pp. 52–56) in addition to studies involving the K-FAST and brief measures, including the K-BIT,

TABLE 15.6   K-FAST split-half and test-retest reliability

Age	Split-Half Reliability		
	Arithmetic	**Reading**	**Composite**
15–16	.88	.89	.93
17–19	.89	.87	.93
20–24	.83	.89	.92
25–34	.89	.89	.94
35–44	.86	.86	.92
45–54	.89	.90	.94
55–59	.91	.94	.96
60–64	.85	.91	.93
65–69	.94	.94	.97
70–74	.92	.95	.96
75–85+	.85	.93	.94
Mean Split-Half Reliability	.88	.90	.94
Mean Test-Retest Reliability	.87	.88	.91

NOTE: Adapted from Lichtenberger, Broadbooks, and Kaufman (2000).

PPVT-R, and K-SNAP (Kaufman & Kaufman, 1994a, Tables 6.11–6.12). The K-FAST Composite correlated .71 with WISC-R and WAIS-R Full Scale IQs, .84 with Binet-4 Composite, and .80 with KAIT Composite IQ. It correlated .84 with K-BIT IQ Composite, .77 with PPVT-R standard score (ages 15–40), and .64 with K-SNAP Composite. In addition, initial correlational studies with a traditional achievement test (K-TEA Brief Form) were conducted with two clinical populations, one group with mental retardation and one with reading disabilities. The K-FAST Composite standard score correlated .54 with the K-TEA Composite for the sample of individuals with mental retardation (*N* = 24), and .76 for the sample of individuals with reading disabilities (*N* = 34). The results indicate that the types of academic abilities measured by the K-FAST are different from the more traditional academic skills assessed by the K-TEA. Correlations with a group of people with mental retardation ($N = 60$) were also conducted on the K-FAST Reading and Arithmetic subtests and the Vineland Adaptive Behavior Scales, Survey Form (Stinson, 1988). However, Stinson's results need to be interpreted in light of the fact that, when the data were collected, the K-FAST subtests were in their standardization form in which each subtest was composed of 44 items. Moreover, half the sample was younger than the age of 15, which now is the youngest age for the K-FAST norms. The K-FAST raw scores for the Arithmetic and Reading Subtests (norms were not available when Stinson conducted her study) correlated .30 and .41 with the Vineland Adaptive Behavior Composite. Similar to the above results with the K-TEA, these results suggest that the K-FAST measures different aspects of adaptive behavior than the Vineland.

Additional validity data for the K-FAST is found in factor-analytic studies and studies on aging patterns. A joint factor analysis of the K-SNAP, K-FAST, and KAIT ($N = 1,270$) yielded crystallized (Gc) and fluid (Gf) factors (Kaufman & Kaufman, 1993). The K-FAST Reading and Arithmetic subtests were associated with the crystallized factor, which was hypothesized as they both depend on formal education and acculturation for success. In Kaufman et al.'s (1994) joint factor analysis of several tests—including the WAIS-R—that produced four factors, the K-FAST's two subtests were associated with Gc (Reading & Arithmetic), Gf (Arithmetic), and Gsm (Arithmetic) factors. The fact that Reading is associated with Gc, and that Arithmetic is multifactorial, are both consistent with Horn's (1989) expanded Gf–Gc theory.

The aging patterns on the K-FAST subtest are similar to the maintained patterns seen on other tests of crystallized ability (see Chapter 5), joining the results of factor analysis in providing support for the construct validity of the test.

Evaluation

Generally, the published reviews of the K-FAST (Shaw, 1998; Williams, 1998) are quite positive.

Lichtenberger et al. (2000) provide detailed lists of the test's strengths and weaknesses, many of which we highlight here. In contrast to other widely used measures of adaptive functioning, the K-FAST directly assesses adaptive functioning, rather than requiring a parent or teacher to describe the examinee's abilities. However, the K-FAST only measures a very limited aspect of adaptive functioning (Shaw, 1998).

K-FAST subtests require application of skills to everyday situations, not simply regurgitation of school-learned knowledge. All K-FAST items are untimed, which allows measurement of functional intelligence without speed as a central component. Examinees are allowed to use paper and pencil, which makes the testing situation more like everyday life. Accurate and stable measurement of individuals with low cognitive ability can be ascertained with the K-FAST.

Several facets of the K-FAST's administration are positive. K-FAST scoring is objective and straightforward and the discontinue rule is the same for both subtests, which simplifies the administration process (Williams, 1998). Examinees are allowed to respond in foreign language, sign language, or slang, which is beneficial to those with disabilities or those for whom English is a second language. In addition, pronunciation on the Reading subtest is not penalized as it is on many other academic reading tests.

The standardization and psychometric properties of the K-FAST also are quite good (Shaw, 1998). The K-FAST was co-normed and developed with the KAIT, K-BIT, and K-SNAP, which allows for easy interpretation of the instruments when they are used together. The large standardization sample is well stratified on age, gender, geographic region, SES, and race/ethnicity. Reliability and validity were well demonstrated in the manual (Shaw, 1998).

Because the K-FAST manual includes a description of suggested interpretive steps, examiners will find interpretation to be uncomplicated (Williams, 1998). The test provides a good assessment of crystallized ability, making it a good supplemental measure for the elderly, who often do poorly on fluid tasks and are assumed to be unable to function independently based on those results. Generally the K-FAST Composite is a good measure of g (general ability); Reading is strongly associated with crystallized ability and Arithmetic with fluid ability, crystallized ability, and short-term memory.

In addition to the advantages that we have described for the K-FAST, there are some disadvantages. For example, the test measures only one of eight areas reported by Harrison (1990) that are found in most adaptive behavior inventories, applied cognitive skills (Shaw, 1998). Because of the reading required on some items, the K-FAST should not be used as an estimate of functional intelligence for individuals with known or suspected learning disabilities in reading or math or for nonreaders. The test does not discriminate among those who score high on the K-FAST as it only yields scores up to two standard deviations above the mean (Williams, 1998).

Although the overall standardization sample was strong, the norm samples for certain age groups were relatively small: ages 65–69 (N = 81), ages 70–74 (N = 93), and ages 75–85+ (N = 103) (Shaw, 1998). A clinically depressed sample scored better than the normal sample, indicating that the test does not discriminate well between normal and depressed populations. The manual presents only one validity study with adaptive behavior scales and achievement tests.

In summary, the advantages of the K-FAST seem to outweigh its disadvantages. Some of its most positive aspects include the ease and brevity of administration and scoring, its excellent psychometric properties and standardization sample (it has outstanding reliability for such a brief test), and its outstanding use with lower functioning examinees. Even though the K-FAST has high g-loadings and correlates highly with popular IQ tests, it should not be interpreted as an intelligence test. Rather, it should be used to supplement other norm-referenced academic tests, intelligence tests, or adaptive behavior measures, as the K-FAST measures a limited subset of adaptive behavior—academic achievement and intelligence.

SUMMARY

In this chapter, we review the history of assessment with short forms and other brief tests. We discuss reasons why short forms, typically of Wechsler's scales, used to be a much better choice for brief assessment, but that is no longer the case. In past times, the available, commonly used brief tests, primarily the Slosson and Shipley-Hartford, were of poor psychometric quality. The Slosson Intelligence Test, a mostly verbal test organized in the format of the old Binet, has been commonly used for decades, but it has largely unknown psychometric properties and a poor standardization sample. The Shipley-Hartford, a self-administered test that contains two subtests (Vocabulary and Abstraction) comes equipped with an outstanding manual, yet has a thoroughly inadequate normative sample and unimpressive stability data.

Present-day brief tests, notably the WASI, K-BIT, and WRIT, are well normed, reliable and stable, and valid. This new breed of brief test is preferable to the use of short forms because of built-in limitations of short forms, as J. Kaufman and A. Kaufman (in press) have argued. These limitations include issues involving norms for short forms that are derived from an administration of the complete battery and statistical problems that occur because of correlated error variance.

One of the problems with short-form norms pertains to research conducted by Thompson and colleagues. They explored the impact of estimated IQs obtained just from administration of Silverstein's short forms versus the IQs estimated from these same brief tests embedded in the complete WAIS-R. Such studies are sorely needed because virtually all short-form research has come from after-the-fact studies of complete intelligence tests, not from separate administrations of the abbreviated batteries. Silverstein's dyad (V–BD) was found by Thompson to yield overestimates of IQ when administered in isolation. A second problem with norms concerns the Satz-Mogel split-half abbreviations of Wechsler's tests. These kinds of short forms have been common research topics, and continue to evoke investigations in the twenty-first century, but it is highly questionable whether norms based on a complete administration of the WAIS-R or WAIS-III are applicable to IQs obtained when every second or third item is administered. Cella's "modified" WAIS-R, which adjusts the starting points of numerous subtests to save administration time, has flaws similar to the Satz-Mogel procedure.

The statistical issue surrounding short-form use concerns the fact that, when validity coefficients are obtained (correlation of short form with Full Scale) based on a single administration of the complete battery, there is spuriousness due to correlated error variance. Depending on the purposes of administering a short form, it is sometimes advisable to apply Silverstein's "correction" to validity coefficients and sometimes advisable to interpret the obtained coefficients. In any case, we argue that the problems with norms and the statistical concerns are all based on the fact that both norms and validity coefficients are based on administration of the complete battery, and not on a separate administration of just the short form.

Some researchers have argued that Silverstein's V–BD Wechsler short form is unfair to African Americans because the component subtests produce among the largest ethnic differences. Similar concerns might apply to Hispanics because of the inclusion of Vocabulary. Consequently, our suggestion to abandon short forms in favor of the new breed of brief tests required careful consideration for their applicability to these two ethnic groups; both the WASI and WRIT include V and BD, and the K-BIT includes a measure of vocabulary. Data on the

WAIS-III versions of WASI subtests suggest that both the two-subtest and four-subtest versions of the WASI are fair to administer to African Americans and Hispanics. K-BIT versus KAIT ethnic-difference data, however, suggest not using the K-BIT in place of the KAIT or the WAIS-III with these ethnic groups. No pertinent ethnic data are available for the WRIT.

Since 1990, Ward, Ryan, and others have supported the use of a seven-subtest WAIS-R or WAIS-III short form. We argue against this short form and in favor of the new brief tests because no norms are available only for the seven-subtest short form. We urge examiners to administer the 11 WAIS-III subtests that are needed to yield the four factor indexes (eliminating the long Comprehension and Picture Arrangement subtests if time is an issue), but not to give the seven-subtest short form.

The use of brief intelligence tests is justified under certain conditions, for example, for screening, so long as the scores are not used for categorization, diagnosis, or drawing neuropsychological inferences. Otherwise, comprehensive IQ tests should be administered.

The remainder of the chapter reviews several available brief tests, all having excellent psychometric properties. The brief tests are organized as follows: (1) the best brief tests that yield measures of *both* verbal and nonverbal intelligence; (2) the best measures of *either* verbal or nonverbal ability; (3) specialized brief tests, for example, of functional intelligence.

The WASI, K-BIT, and WRIT are all brief measures of intellectual ability that provide a global IQ as well as a verbal/crystallized score and a visual/fluid score. All three instruments have strong psychometric properties and were standardized on large, highly representative samples. Their correlations with more comprehensive measures of IQ are generally impressive and support their valid use in most assessment situations where a brief test is justified.

PPVT-III is a solid measure of receptive vocabulary, which has also been used by many (wrongly) to estimate intelligence. It is an easy and quick task to administer and score. Although the PPVT-III correlates moderately to substantially with tests of intelligence, it cannot be used interchangeably with an intelligence test. Therefore, it should not be used alone as a criterion for diagnosis or placement in assessment, but it is a helpful component in a more comprehensive battery of tests.

The GAMA and MAT are both nonverbal brief tests of visual–spatial, perceptual organization ability. They provide a viable alternative means to test individuals for whom verbal communication is difficult. For example, individuals who do not speak English as their primary language, individuals with hearing impairments, or individuals with learning impairments may be suited for administration of these instruments.

The K-SNAP and K-FAST are two brief specialized tests in what they measure and the purposes for which they are applicable. The K-SNAP measures neuropsychological functioning across various levels of complexity, and the K-FAST measures functional intelligence and achievement, as well as specific facets of adaptive behavior. These two instruments were co-normed and have strong psychometric properties. The validity of these instruments is supported by factor-analytic data that shows the K-FAST to measure primarily crystallized abilities and the K-SNAP to measure primarily fluid and visualization skills.

REFERENCES

Abel, E. L. (1980). Fetal alcohol syndrome: Behavioral technology. *Psychological Bulletin, 87,* 29–50.

Abrahams, J. P. (1976). Health status as a variable in aging research. *Experimental Aging Research, 2,* 63–71.

Ackerman, P. L. (1996). A theory of adult intellectual development: Process, personality, interests, and knowledge. *Intelligence, 22,* 229–259.

Ackerman, P. L., & Heggestad, E. D. (1997). Intelligence, personality and interests: Evidence for overlapping traits. *Psychological Bulletin, 121*(2), 219–245.

Ackerman, P. T., McGrew, M. J., & Dykman, R. A. (1987). A profile of male and female applicants for a special college program for learning-disabled students. *Journal of Clinical Psychology, 43,* 67–78.

Adams, G. L. (1984a). *Comprehensive Test of Adaptive Behavior examiner's manual.* Columbus, OH: Charles E. Merrill.

Adams, G. L. (1984b). *Normative Adaptive Behavior Checklist examiner's manual.* Columbus, OH: Charles E. Merrill.

Adams, K. M. (1980). In search of Luria's battery: A false start. *Journal of Consulting and Clinical Psychology, 48,* 511–516.

Adams, R. L. (1985). Review of the Luria-Nebraska Neuropsychological Battery. In J. V. Mitchell (Ed.), *The ninth mental measurements yearbook* (pp. 878–881). Lincoln, NE: Buros Institute of Mental Measurement, University of Nebraska Press.

Aiken, L. R. (1987). *Assessment of intellectual functioning.* Boston: Allyn & Bacon.

Albert, M. S., & Kaplan, E. (1980). Organic implications of neuropsychological deficits in the elderly. In L. W. Poon, J. L. Fozard, L. S. Cermak, D. Ehrenberg, & L. W. Thompson (Eds.), *New directions in memory and aging.* Proceedings of the George Talland Memorial Conference. Hillsdale, NJ: Erlbaum.

Alekoumbides, A., Charter, R. A., Adkins, T. G., & Seacat, G. F. (1987). The diagnosis of brain damage by the WAIS, WMS, and Reitan battery utilizing standardized scores corrected for age and education. *International Journal of Clinical Neuropsychology, 9,* 11–28.

Alexander, G. E., Prohovnik, I., Stern, Y., & Mayeux, R. (1994). WAIS-R subtest profile and cortical perfusion in Alzheimer's disease. *Brain and Cognition, 24,* 24–43.

Allen, J. G., Coyne, L., & David, E. (1986). Relation of intelligence to ego functioning in an adult psychiatric population. *Journal of Personality Assessment, 50,* 212–221.

Allen, M. H., Lincoln, A. J., & Kaufman, A. S. (1991). Sequential and simultaneous processing abilities of high-functioning autistic and language-impaired children. *Journal of Autism and Developmental Disorders, 21,* 483–502.

Allison, J., Blatt, S. J., & Zimet, C. N. (1968). *The interpretation of psychological tests.* New York: Harper & Row.

Altepeter, T. S., & Johnson, K. A. (1989). Use of the PPVT-R for intellectual screening with adults: A caution. *Journal of Psychoeducational Assessment, 7,* 39–45.

Alvarez, E. R. (1962). Comparison of depressive and brain injured subjects on the trail making test. *Perceptual and Motor Skills, 14,* 91–96.

American Educational Research Association (AERA), American Psychological Association (APA), and National Council on Measurement in Education (NCME). (1999). *Standards for educational and psychological testing.* Washington, DC: Author.

American Psychiatric Association (1994). *Diagnostic and statistical manual of mental disorders.* (4th ed.). Washington, D.C.: Author.

Aminoff, M. J., Marshall, J., Smith, E. M., & Wyke, M. A. (1975). Pattern of intellectual impairment in Huntington's chorea. *Psychological Medicine, 5,* 169–172.

Amolsch, T. J., & Henrichs, T. F. (1975). Behavioral correlates of WAIS profile patterns: An exploratory study. *Journal of Personality Assessment, 39,* 55–63.

Anastasi, A., & Urbina, S. (1997). *Psychological testing* (7th ed.). Upper Saddle River, NJ: Prentice-Hall.

Andersen, A. L. (1950). The effect of laterality localization of brain damage on Wechsler-Bellevue indices of deterioration. *Journal of Clinical Psychology, 6,* 191–194.

Andersen, A. L. (1951). The effect of laterality localization of focal brain lesions on the Wechsler-Bellevue subtests. *Journal of Clinical Psychology, 7,* 149–153.

Anderson, S. W., & Travel, D. (1989). Awareness of disease states following cerebral infarction, dementia, and head trauma: Standardized assessment. *Clinical Neuropsychologist, 3,* 327–339.

Andrew, J. M. (1974). Delinquency, the Wechsler P > V sign, and the I-level system. *Journal of Clinical Psychology, 30,* 331–335.

Angoff, W. H. (1988). The nature–nurture debate, aptitudes, and group differences. *American Psychologist, 43,* 713–720.

Apostel, R. A. (1991). College students' career interests and sensing–intuition personality. *Journal of College Student Development, 32,* 4–7.

Applegate, B., & Kaufman, A. S. (1989). Short form of K-ABC sequential and simultaneous processing for research and screening. *Journal of Clinical Child Psychology, 18*(4), 305–313.

Arbuckle, T. Y., Gold, D., Andres, D., Schwartzman, A. E., & Chaikelson, J. (1992). The role of psychosocial context, age, and intelligence in memory performance of older men. *Psychology and Aging, 7,* 25–36.

Arcenaux, J. M., Cheramie, G. M., & Smith, C. W. (1996). Gender differences in age-corrected scaled scores. *Perceptual and Motor Skills, 83,* 1211–1215.

Archer, R. P., Maruish, M., Imhof, E. A., & Piotrowski, C. (1991). Psychological test usage with adolescent clients: 1990 survey findings. *Professional Psychology: Research and Practice, 22,* 247–252.

Armentrout, J. A. (1976). Bender Gestalt recall: Memory measure or intelligence estimate? *Journal of Clinical Psychology, 32,* 832–834.

Armstrong, E. J. (1982). The extent of bias for the WAIS-R for Chicano and white high school students. (Doctoral dissertation, University of North Colorado, 1982, Order No. DA8301133). *Dissertation Abstracts International, 43* (9-A), p. 2971.

Asarnow, R. F., Tanguay, P. E., Bott, L., & Freedman, B. J. (1987). Patterns of intellectual functioning in non-retarded autistic and schizophrenic children. *Journal of Child Psychology and Psychiatry, 28,* 273–280.

Atkinson, L. (1992). Mental Retardation and WAIS-R scatter analysis. *Journal of Intellectual Disability Research, 36,* 433–448.

Atkinson, L., & Cyr, J. J. (1984). Factor analysis of the WAIS-R: Psychiatric and standardization samples. *Journal of Consulting and Clinical Psychology, 52,* 714–716.

Atkinson, L., & Cyr, J. J. (1988). Low IQ samples and WAIS-R factor structure. *American Journal of Mental Deficiency, 93,* 278–282.

Atkinson, M. H. (1995). Comparison of volunteer and referred children on individual measures of assessment: A Native American sample. (Doctoral dissertation, University of Arizona, 1995) *Dissertation Abstracts International, 56* (1-A).

Ausubel, D. P., & Sullivan, E. V. (1970). *Theory and problems of child development* (2nd ed.). New York: Grune & Stratton.

Axelrod, B. N., Dingell, J. D., Ryan, J. J., & Ward, L. C. (2000). Estimation of Wechsler Adult Intelligence Scale-III index scores with the 7-subtest short form in a clinical sample. *Assessment, 7,* 157–161.

Axelrod, B. N., & Naugle, R. I. (1998). Evaluation of two brief and reliable estimates of the WAIS-R. *International Journal of Neuroscience, 94* (1–2), 85–91.

Backman, L., Hill, R. D., Herlitz, A., Robins-Wahlin, T.-B., Wahlin, A., & Winblad, B. (1998). Predictors of change in verbal and nonverbal episodic memory performance in a 2-year longitudinal study of optimally healthy very old adults. *Journal of Mental Health and Aging, 4,* 139–154.

Backman, L., Small, B. J., Wahlin, A., & Larsson, M. (2000). Cognitive functioning in very old age. In F. I. M. Craik & T. A. Salthouse (Eds.), *The handbook of aging and cognition* (2nd ed.; pp. 499–558). Mahwah, NJ: Erlbaum.

Bailey, B. S. (1979). Differential perceptions of children's adaptive behavior. (Doctoral dissertation, University of Georgia, 1979) *Dissertation Abstracts International, 40,* 159A.

Bailey, K. G., & Millbrook, J. M. (1984). "Primitiveness" and "advancedness" of pleasures and aversions in relation to WAIS indices. *Journal of Clinical Psychology, 40,* 295–299.

Bajema, C. J. (1968). A note on the interrelations among intellectual ability, educational attainment, and occupational achievement: A follow-up study of a male Kalamazoo public school population. *Sociology of Education, 41,* 317–319.

Bak, J. S., & Greene, R. L. (1981). A review of the performance of aged adults on various Wechsler Memory Scale subtests. *Journal of Clinical Psychology, 37,* 186–188.

Baker, H. J., & Leland, B. (1967). *Detroit Tests of Learning Aptitude: Examiner's handbook.* Indianapolis, IN: Bobbs-Merrill.

Balinsky, B. (1941). An analysis of the mental factors of various age groups from nine to sixty. *Genetic Psychology Monographs, 23,* 191–234.

Ball, J. D., Archer, R. P., & Imhof, E. A. (1994). Time requirements of psychological testing: A survey of practitioners. *Journal of Personality Assessment, 63,* 239–249.

Baltes, P. B. (1997). On the incomplete architecture of human ontogeny: Selection, optimization, and compensation as foundation of developmental theory. *American Psychologist, 52,* 366–380.

Baltes, P. B., & Lindenberger, U. (1997). Emergence of a powerful connection between sensory and cognitive functions across the adult life span: A new window to the study of cognitive aging? *Psychology & Aging, 12,* 12–21.

Baltes, P. B., & Mayer, K. U. (Eds.). (1999). *The Berlin Aging Study: Aging from 70 to 100.* New York: Cambridge University Press.

Baltes, P. B., & Schaie, K. W. (1976). On the plasticity of adult and gerontological intelligence: Where Horn and Donaldson fail. *American Psychologist, 31,* 720–725.

Baltes, P. B., Staudinger, U. M., & Lindenberger, U. (1999). Lifespan psychology: Theory and application to intellectual functioning. *Annual Review of Psychology, 50,* 471–507.

Baltes, P. B., & Willis, S. L. (1982). Enhancement (plasticity) of intellectual functioning in old age: Penn State's Adult Development and Enrichment Project (ADEPT). In F. I. M. Craik & S. E. Trehub (Eds.), *Aging and cognitive processes* (pp. 353–389). New York: Plenum.

Balthazar, E. E., & Morrison, D. H. (1961). The use of Wechsler Intelligence Scales as diagnostic indicators of predominant left-right and indeterminate unilateral brain damage. *Journal of Clinical Psychology, 17,* 161–165.

Banken, J. A. (1985). Clinical utility of considering digits forward and digits backward as separate components of the Wechsler Adult Intelligence Scale-Revised. *Journal of Clinical Psychology, 41,* 686–691.

Banken, J. A., & Banken, C. H. (1987). Investigation of Wechsler Adult Intelligence Scale-Revised short forms in a sample of vocational rehabilitation applicants. *Journal of Psychoeducational Assessment, 5,* 281–286.

Bannatyne, A. (1968). Diagnosing learning disabilities and writing remedial prescriptions. *Journal of Learning Disabilities, 1,* 242–249.

Bannatyne, A. (1971). *Language, reading, and learning disabilities.* Springfield, IL: Charles C. Thomas.

Bannatyne, A. (1974). Diagnosis: A note on recategorization of the WISC scaled scores. *Journal of Learning Disabilities, 7,* 272–274.

Barclay, A. G., Giray, E. F., & Altkin, W. M. (1977). WAIS subtest score distribution of institutionalized retardates. *Perceptual and Motor Skills, 44,* 488–490.

Barkley, R. A. (1996). Critical issues in research on attention. In G. R. Lyon & N. A. Krasnegor (Eds.), *Attention, memory and executive function* (pp. 45–96). Baltimore, MD: Brookes.

Barkley, R. A. (1997). Behavioral inhibition, sustained attention, and executive functions: Constructing a unifying theory of ADHD. *Psychological Bulletin, 121,* 65–94.

Barnett, W. S. (1995). Long-term effects of early childhood programs on cognitive and school outcomes. *The Future of Children, 5 (3),* 25–50.

Baroff, G. S. (1986). *Mental retardation: Nature, cause, and management* (2nd ed.). New York: Hemisphere.

Barona, A., Reynolds, C. R., & Chastain, R. (1984). A demographically based index of premorbid intelligence for the WAIS-R. *Journal of Consulting and Clinical Psychology, 52,* 885–887.

Barron, J. H., & Russell, E. W. (1992). Fluidity theory and neuropsychological impairment in alcoholism. *Archives of Clinical Neuropsychology, 7,* 175–188.

Bartak, L., & Rutter, M. (1976). Differences between mentally retarded and normally intelligent autistic children. *Journal of Autism and Childhood Schizophrenia, 6,* 109–122.

Bartz, W. R., & Loy, D. L. (1970). The Shipley-Hartford as a brief I.Q. screening device. *Journal of Clinical Psychology, 26,* 74–75.

Bashore, T. R., Ridderinkhof, R., & van der Molen, M. W. (1997). The decline of cognitive processing speed in old age. *Current Directions in Psychological Science, 6(6),* 163–169.

Basso, A., Capitani, E., & Moraschini, S. (1982). Sex differences in recovery from aphasia. *Cortex, 18,* 469–475.

Bastian, H. C. (1898). *Aphasia and other speech deficits.* London: H. K. Lewis.

Battersby, W. S., Bender, M. B., Pollack, M., & Kahn, R. L. (1955). Unilateral "spatial agnosia" ("inattention") in patients with cortical lesions. *Brain, 79,* 68–93.

Bauer, C. A., Schlottmann, R. S., Kane, R. L., & Johnsen, D. E. (1984). An evaluation of the Digit Symbol component of the Russell, Neuringer, and Goldstein average impairment rating. *Journal of Consulting and Clinical Psychology, 52,* 317–318.

Baumeister, A. A. (1967). The effects of dietary control on intelligence in phenylketonuria. *American Journal of Mental Deficiency, 71,* 840–847.

Bayley, N. (1969). *Manual for the Bayley Scales of Infant Development.* San Antonio: The Psychological Corporation.

Beck, N. C., Horwitz, E., Seidenberg, M., Parker, G., & Frank, R. (1985). WAIS-R factor structure in psychiatric and general medical patients. *Journal of Consulting and Clinical Psychology, 53,* 402–405.

Bellinger, D. C., Stiles, K. M., & Needleman, H. L. (1992). Low-level lead exposure, intelligence and academic achievement: A long-term follow-up study. *Pediatrics, 90,* 855–861.

Benbow, C. P., & Stanley, J. C. (1980). Sex differences in mathematical ability: Fact or artifact? *Science, 210,* 1262–1264.

Benbow, C. P., & Stanley, J. C. (1982). Consequences in high school and college of sex differences in mathematical reasoning ability: A longitudinal perspective. *American Educational Research Journal, 19,* 598–622.

Benbow, C. P., & Stanley, J. C. (1983). Sex differences in mathematical reasoning ability: More facts. *Science, 222,* 1029–1031.

Bengtson, V. L., Reedy, M. N., & Gordon, C. (1985). Aging and self-conceptions: Personality processes and social contexts. In J. E. Birren and K. W. Schaie (Eds.), *Handbook of the psychology of aging* (2nd ed.; pp. 544–593). New York: Van Nostrand Reinhold.

Bengtson, V. L., & Schaie, K. W. (Eds.). (1999). *Handbook of theories of aging.* New York: Springer.

Benson, J. (1998). Developing a strong program of construct validation: A test anxiety example. *Educational Measurement: Issues and Practice, 17,* 10–16, 22.

Benton, A. L. (1950). *Right-left discrimination and finger localization: Development and pathology.* New York: Hoeber.

Benton, A. L. (1962). Clinical symptomatology in right and left hemispheric lesions. In V. B. Mountcastle (Ed.), *Interhemispheric relations and cerebral dominance* (pp. 253–263). Baltimore, MD: Johns Hopkins.

Benton, A. L. (1963). *The Revised Visual Retention Test: Clinical and experimental applications* (3rd ed.). Iowa City, IA: The State University of Iowa.

Benton, A. L. (1974). *The Revised Visual Retention Test: Clinical and experimental application* (4th ed.). New York: The Psychological Corporation.

Benton, A. L. (1980). The neuropsychology of facial recognition. *American Psychologist, 35,* 176–186.

Benton, A. L. (1982). Child neuropsychology: Retrospect and prospect. In J. de Wit & A. L. Benton (Eds.), *Perspectives in child study* (pp. 41–61). Lisse, the Netherlands: Swets and Zeitlinger.

Benton, A. L., & Fogel, M. L. (1962). Three-dimensional constructional praxis: A clinical test. *Archives of Neurology, 7,* 347–354.

Benton, A. L., Hamsher, K., Varney, N. R., & Spreen, O. (1983). *Contributions to neuropsychological assessment: A clinical manual.* New York: Oxford.

Benton, A. L., Van Allen, M. W., & Fogel, M. L. (1964). Temporal orientation in cerebral disease. *Journal of Nervous and Mental Disease, 139,* 110–119.

Berg, C. A. (2000). Intellectual development in adulthood. In R. J. Sternberg (Ed.), *Handbook of intelligence* (pp. 117–137). New York: Cambridge University Press.

Berger, A. (1985). Review of the Watson-Glaser Critical Thinking Appraisal. In J. V. Mitchell (Ed.), *The ninth mental measurements yearbook* (pp. 1692–1693). Lincoln, NE: Buros Institute of Mental Measurements, University of Nebraska Press.

Berger, L., Bernstein, A., Klein, E., Cohen, J., & Lucas, G. (1964). Effects of aging and pathology on the factorial structure of intelligence. *Journal of Consulting Psychology, 28,* 199–207.

Berkowitz, B., & Green, R. F. (1963). Changes in intellect with age: I. Longitudinal study of Wechsler-Bellevue scores. *Journal of Genetic Psychology, 103,* 3–21.

Bernard, M. E., & Naylor, F. D. (1982). Vocational guidance consultation in school settings. In T. R. Kratochwill (Ed.),

Advances in school psychology (Vol. 2; pp. 203–243). Hillsdale, NJ: Erlbaum.

Berrueta-Clement, J. R., Schweinhart, L. J., Barnett, W. S., Epstein, A. S., & Weikart, D. P. (1984). Changed lives: The effects of the Perry Preschool Program on youths through age 19. *Monographs of the High/Scope Educational Research Foundation. Number Eight.* Ypsilanti, MI: High/Scope Press.

Berry, K. K., & Sherrets, S. A. (1975). A comparison of the WISC and WISC-R scores of special education students. *Pediatric Psychology, 3,* 14.

Bieliauskas, L., & Boll, T. (1984). Division 40/INS Task Force on Education, Accreditation and Credentialing. *APAD Newsletter, 40.*

Bigler, E. D., Johnson, S. C., Jackson, C., & Blatter, D. D. (1995). Aging, brain size, and IQ. *Intelligence, 21,* 109–119.

Binder, L. M. (1987). Appropriate reporting of Wechsler IQ and subtest scores in assessments for disability. *Journal of Clinical Psychology, 43,* 144–145.

Binet, A. (1890a). Recherches sur les mouvements de quelques jeunes enfants. *La Revue Philosophique, 29,* 297–309.

Binet, A. (1890b). Perceptions d'enfants. *La Revue Philosophique, 30,* 582–611.

Binet, A. (1911). Nouvelle recherches sur la mesure du niveau intellectual chez les enfants d'école. *L'Année Psychologique, 17,* 145–210.

Binet, A., & Henri, V. (1895). La psychologie individuelle. *L'Année Psychologique, 2,* 411–465.

Binet, A., & Simon, T. (1905). Méthodes nouvelles pour le diagnostic du niveau intellectual des anormaux. *L'Année Psychologique, 11,* 191–244.

Binet, A., & Simon, T. (1908). Le développement de l'intelligence chez les enfants. *L'Année Psychologique, 14,* 1–94.

Birren, J. E., & Morrison, D. F. (1961). Analysis of the WAIS subtests in relation to age and education. *Journal of Gerontology, 16,* 363–369.

Birren, J. E., & Schaie, K. W. (1985). (Eds.). *Handbook of the psychology of aging* (2nd ed.). New York: Van Nostrand Reinhold.

Birren, J. E., Schaie, K. W., Abeles, R. P., Gatz, M., & Salthouse, T. A. (Eds.). (1996). *Handbook of the psychology of aging* (4th ed.). San Diego, CA: Academic Press.

Black, F. W. (1973). Memory and paired-associate learning of patients with unilateral brain lesions. *Psychological Reports, 33,* 919–922.

Black, F. W. (1974a). Cognitive effects of unilateral brain lesions secondary to penetrating missile wounds. *Perceptual and Motor Skills, 38,* 387–391.

Black, F. W. (1974b). The cognitive sequelae of penetrating missile wounds of the brain. *Military Medicine, 139,* 815–817.

Black, F. W. (1976). Cognitive deficits in patients with unilateral war-related frontal lobe lesions. *Journal of Clinical Psychology, 32,* 366–372.

Black, F. W. (1980). WAIS Verbal–Performance discrepancies as predictors of lateralization in patients with discrete brain lesions. *Perceptual and Motor Skills, 51,* 213–214.

Black, F. W. (1986a). Digit repetition in brain-damaged adults: Clinical and theoretical implications. *Journal of Clinical Psychology, 42,* 770–782.

Black, F. W. (1986b). Neuroanatomic and neuropsychologic correlates of Digit Span performance by brain-damaged adults. *Perceptual and Motor Skills, 63,* 815–822.

Black, F. W., & Strub, R. L. (1978). Digit repetition performance in patients with focal brain damage. *Cortex, 14,* 12–21.

Blackburn, J. A. (1984). The influence of personality, curriculum, and memory correlates on formal reasoning in young adults and elderly persons. *Journal of Gerontology, 39,* 207–209.

Blackstock, G. (1978). Cerebral asymmetry and the development of early infantile autism. *Journal of Autism and Childhood Schizophrenia, 8,* 339–353.

Blaha, J., Mandes, E., & Swisher, C. W. (1987). The hierarchical factor structure of the WAIS-R for learning disabled adults. *Journal of Clinical Psychology, 43,* 280–286.

Blaha, J., & Vance, H. (1979). The hierarchical factor structure of the WISC-R for learning disabled children. *Learning Disabilities Quarterly, 2,* 71–75.

Blaha, J., & Wallbrown, F. H. (1982). Hierarchical factor structure of the Wechsler Adult Intelligence Scale-Revised. *Journal of Consulting and Clinical Psychology, 50,* 652–660.

Blakey, W., Fantuzzo, J., Gorsuch, R., & Moon, G. (1987). A peer mediated, competency based training package for administering and scoring the WAIS-R. *Professional Psychology: Research and Practice, 18,* 17–20.

Blakey, W., Fantuzzo, J., & Moon, G. (1985). An automated competency-based model for teaching skills in the administration of the WAIS-R. *Professional Psychology: Research and Practice, 16,* 641–647.

Blalock, J. (1987). Intellectual levels and patterns. In D. Johnson & J. Blalock (Eds.), *Young adults with learning disabilities: Clinical studies.* Orlando, FL: Grune & Stratton.

Blatt, S. J., Baker, B. L., & Weiss, J. (1970). Wechsler Object Assembly subtest and bodily concern: A review and replication. *Journal of Consulting and Clinical Psychology, 34,* 269–274.

Blatt, S. J., & Quinlan, P. (1967). Punctual and procrastinating students: A study of temporal parameters. *Journal of Consulting Psychology, 31,* 170–174.

Bleker, E. G. (1983). Cognitive defense style and WISC-R P > V sign in juvenile recidivists. *Journal of Clinical Psychology, 39,* 1030–1032.

Bloom, A. S., Hersh, J. H., Podruch, P. E., Weisskopf, B., Topinka, C. W., & Reese, A. (1986). Developmental characteristics of recognizable patterns of human malformation. In J. M. Berg (Ed.), *Science and service in mental retardation* (pp. 34–51). London: Methuen.

Bloom, B. L. (1959). Comparison of the alternate Wechsler Memory Scale forms. *Journal of Clinical Psychology, 15,* 72–74.

Blusewicz, M. J., Schenkenberg, T., Dustman, R. E., & Beck, R. E. (1977). WAIS performance in young normal, young alcoholic, and elderly normal groups: An evaluation of organicity and mental aging indices. *Journal of Clinical Psychology, 33,* 1149–1153.

Bogen, J. E., DeZure, R., Tenhouten, N., & Marsh, J. (1972). The other side of the brain: IV. The A/P ratio. *Bulletin of the Los Angeles Neurological Society, 37,* 49–61.

Boll, T. J. (1974). Right and left cerebral hemisphere damage and tactile perception: Performance of the ipsilateral and contralateral sides of the body. *Neuropsychologia, 12,* 235–238.

Boll, T. J. (1981). The Halstead-Reitan Neuropsychology Battery. In S. B. Filskov & T. J. Bolla (Eds.), *Handbook of clinical neuropsychology* (pp. 577–607). New York: Wiley.

Boll, T. J. (1983). Minor head injury in children—out of sight but not out of mind. *Journal of Clinical Child Psychology, 12,* 74–80.

Boll, T. J. (1985). Developing issues in clinical neuropsychology. *Journal of Clinical and Experimental Neuropsychology, 7,* 473–485.

Boll, T. J., Heaton, R. K., & Reitan, R. M. (1974). Neuropsychological and emotional correlates of Huntington's chorea. *Journal of Nervous and Mental Disease, 158,* 61–69.

Boll, T. J., & Reitan, R. M. (1973). Effect of age on performance on the Trail Making Test. *Perceptual and Motor Skills, 36,* 691–694.

Bolter, L., Veneklasen, J., & Long, C. J. (1981). Investigation of WAIS effectiveness in discriminating between temporal and generalized seizure patients. *Journal of Consulting and Clinical Psychology, 49,* 549–55 3.

Bolton, B. (1980). Personality (16 PF) correlates of WAIS scales: A replication. *Applied Psychological Measurement, 4,* 399–401.

Boomsma, D. I., & van Baal, G. C. M. (1998). Genetic influences on childhood IQ in 5- and 7-year-old Dutch twins. *Developmental Neuropsychology, 14,* 115–126.

Boone, K. B., Lesser, I., Miller, B., Wohl, M., Berman, N., Lee, A., Palmer, B. (1994). Cognitive functioning in a mildly to moderately depressed geriatric sample: Relationship to chronological age. *Journal of Neuropsychiatry, 6,* 267–272.

Bornstein, R. A. (1982). Effects of unilateral lesions on the Wechsler Memory Scale. *Journal of Clinical Psychology, 38,* 389–392.

Bornstein, R. A. (1983a). Relationship of age and education to neuropsychological performance in patients with symptomatic carotid artery disease. *Journal of Clinical Psychology, 139*, 470–478.

Bornstein, R. A. (1983b). Verbal IQ–Performance IQ discrepancies on the Wechsler Adult Intelligence Scale-Revised in patients with unilateral or bilateral cerebral dysfunction. *Journal of Consulting and Clinical Psychology, 51*, 779–780.

Bornstein, R. A. (1984). Unilateral lesions and the Wechsler Adult Intelligence Scale-Revised: No sex differences. *Journal of Consulting and Clinical Psychology, 52*, 604–608.

Bornstein, R. A. (1987). The WAIS-R in neuropsychological practice: Boon or bust? *The Clinical Neuropsychologist, 1*, 185–190.

Bornstein, R. A., Baker, G. B., & Douglass, A. B. (1987). Short-term retest reliability of the Halstead-Reitan battery in a normal sample. *Journal of Nervous and Mental Disease, 175*, 229–232.

Bornstein, R. A., & Chelune, G. J. (1988). Factor structure of the Wechsler Memory Scale-Revised. *Clinical Neuropsychologist, 2*, 107–115.

Bornstein, R. A., & Matarazzo, J. D. (1982). Wechsler VIQ versus PIQ differences in cerebral dysfunction: A literature review with emphasis on sex differences. *Journal of Clinical Neuropsychology, 4*, 319–334.

Bornstein, R. A., & Matarazzo, J. D. (1984). Relationship of sex and the effects of unilateral lesions on the Wechsler Intelligence Scales: Further considerations. *Journal of Nervous and Mental Disease, 172*, 707–710.

Bornstein, R. A., & Share, D. (1990). Prevalence of the Fuld profile in temporal lobe epilepsy. *Journal of Clinical and Experimental Neuropsychology, 12*, 265–269.

Bornstein, R. A., Suga, L., & Prifitera, A. (1987). Incidence of Verbal IQ–Performance IQ discrepancies at various levels of education. *Journal of Clinical Psychology, 43*, 387–389.

Bornstein, R. A., Termeer, J., Longbrake, K., Heger, M., & North, L. (1989). WAIS-R cholinergic deficit profile in depression. *Psychological Assessment 1*, 342–344.

Botwinick, J. (1967). *Cognitive processes in maturity and old age.* New York: Springer.

Botwinick, J. (1977). Intellectual abilities. In J. E. Birren & K. W. Schaie (Eds.), *Handbook of the psychology of aging* (pp. 580–605). New York: Van Nostrand Reinhold.

Botwinick, J. (1981). Neuropsychology of aging. In S. B. Filskov & T. J. Boll (Eds.), *Handbook of clinical neuropsychology.* New York: Wiley.

Bouchard, T. J., Jr. (1998). Genetic and environmental influences on adult intelligence and special mental abilities. *Human Biology, 70*, 257–279.

Bouchard, T. J., Jr. (1996). Galton lecture: Behaviour genetic studies of intelligence, yesterday and today: The long jour-

ney from plausibility to proof. *Journal of Biosocial Science, 28*, 527–555.

Bouchard, T. J., Jr., & McGue, M. (1981). Familial studies of intelligence: A review. *Science, 212*, 1055–1059.

Bouchard, T. J., Jr., & Segal, N. L. (1985). Environment and IQ. In B. B. Wolman (Ed.), *Handbook of intelligence* (pp. 391–464). New York: Wiley.

Boucher, M. L., Dewan, M. J., Donnelly, M. P., Pandurangi, A. K., Bartell, K., Diamond, T., & Major, L. F. (1986). Relative utility of three indices of neuropsychological impairment in a young, schizophrenic population. *Journal of Nervous and Mental Disease, 174*, 44–46.

Bowers, T. G., Washburn, S. E., & Livesay, J. R. (1986). Predicting neuropsychological impairment by screening instruments and intellectual evaluation indices: Implications for the meaning of Kaufman's factor III. *Psychological Reports, 59*, 487–493.

Boyle, G. J. (1991). Does item homogeneity indicate internal consistency or item redundancy in psychometric scales? *Personality and Individual Differences, 12*(3), 291–294.

Bracken, B., & Barnett, D. (1987). The technical side of preschool assessment: A primer of critical issues. *Preschool Interests, 6–7,* 9.

Bracken, B. A., & McCallum, R. S. (1998). *Universal Nonverbal Intelligence Test (UNIT).* Itasca, IL: Riverside.

Brackett, J., & McPherson, A. (1996). Learning disabilities diagnosis in postsecondary students: A comparison of discrepancy-based diagnostic models. In N. Gregg, C. Hoy, & A. F. Gay (Eds.), *Adults with learning disabilities: Theoretical and practical perspectives* (p. 68–84). New York: Guilford Press.

Braden, J. P., & Paquin, M. M. (1985). A comparison of the WISC-R and WAIS-R Performance scales. *Journal of Psychoeducational Assessment, 3*, 285–290.

Bradley, R. H., & Caldwell, B. M. (1981). The HOME inventory: A validation of the preschool scale for black children. *Child Development, 52*, 708–710.

Bradway, K. P., Thompson, C. W., & Cravens, R. B. (1958). Preschool IQs after twenty-five years. *Journal of Educational Psychology, 49*, 278–281.

Brandt, E. A. (1984). The cognitive functioning of American Indian children: A critique of McShane and Plas. *School Psychology Review, 13*, 74–82.

Brandt, J., Strauss, M. E., Larus, J., Jensen, B., Folstein, S. E., & Folstein, M. F. (1984). Clinical correlates of dementia and disability in Huntington's disease. *Journal of Clinical Neuropsychology, 6*, 401–412.

Breteler, M. M. B., Claus, J. J., Grobbee, D. E., & Hofman, A. (1994). Cardiovascular disease and distribution of cognitive function in elderly people: The Rotterdam Study. *British Medical Journal, 308*, 164–168.

Bridgeman, B., & Wendler, C. (1991). Gender differences in predictors of college mathematics performance and in college mathematics course grades. *Journal of Educational Psychology, 83*, 275–284.

Briggs, G. G., Nebes, R. D., & Kinsbourne, M. (1976). Intellectual differences in relation to personal and family handedness. *Quarterly Journal of Experimental Psychology, 28*, 591–601.

Briggs, K. C., & Myers, I. B. (1983). *Myers-Briggs Type Indicator.* Palo Alto, CA: Consulting Psychologists Press.

Briggs, P. F. (1960). The validity of WAIS performance subtests completed with one hand. *Journal of Clinical Psychology, 16*, 318–320.

Brinkman, S. D., & Braun, P. (1984). Classification of dementia patients by a WAIS profile related to central cholinergic deficiencies. *Journal of Clinical Neuropsychology, 6*, 393–400.

Brinkman, S. D., Largen, J. W., Gerganoff, S., & Pomara, N. (1983). Russell's revised Wechsler Memory Scale in the evaluation of dementia. *Journal of Clinical Psychology, 39*, 989–993.

Broca, P. (1861). Nouvelle observation d'aphemie produite par un élision de la multe postérieure des deuxieme et troisieme circonvolutions frontales. *Bulletin de la Société Anatomique de Paris, 36*, 398–407.

Brodal, A. (1973). Self-observations and neuroanatomical consideration after a stroke. *Brain, 96*, 675–694.

Brody, E. B., & Brody, N. (1976). *Intelligence: Nature, determinants, and consequences.* New York: Academic Press.

Brody, N. (1985). The validity of tests of intelligence. In B. B. Wolman (Ed.), *Handbook of intelligence* (pp. 353–389). New York: Wiley.

Broman, S. H., Nichols, P. L., & Kennedy, W. A. (1975). *Preschool IQ: Prenatal and early developmental correlates.* Hillsdale, NJ: Erlbaum.

Brooker, B. H., & Cyr, J. J. (1986). Tables for clinicians to use to convert WAIS-R short forms. *Journal of Clinical Psychology, 42*, 982–986.

Brophy, A. L. (1986). Confidence intervals for true scores and retest scores on clinical tests. *Journal of Clinical Psychology, 42*, 989–991.

Brown, G. G., Baird, A. D., & Shatz, M. W. (1986). The effects of cerebral vascular disease and its treatment on higher cortical functioning. In I. Grant & K. M. Adams (Eds.), *Neuropsychological assessment of neuropsychiatric disorders* (pp. 384–414). New York: Oxford University Press.

Brown, W. R., & McGuire, J. M. (1976). Current psychological assessment practices. *Professional Psychology, 7*, 475–484.

Browning, D. L., & Quinlan, D. M. (1985). Ego development and intelligence in a psychiatric population: Wechsler subtest scores. *Journal of Personality Assessment, 49*, 260–263.

Bruininks, R. H., & McGrew, K. (1987). *Exploring the structure of adaptive behavior* (Report Number 87-1). Minneapolis, MN: University of Minnesota, Department of Educational Psychology.

Bruininks, R. H., Thurlow, M., & Gilman, C. J. (1987). Adaptive behavior and mental retardation. *Journal of Special Education, 21*, 69–88.

Bruininks, R. H., Woodcock, R. W., Hill, B. K., & Weatherman, R. F. (1984). *Scales of Independent Behavior examiner's manual.* Allen, TX: DLM/Teaching Resources.

Bruininks, R. H., Woodcock, R. W., Hill, B. K., & Weatherman, R. F. (1985). *Development and standardization of the Scales of Independent Behavior.* Allen, TX: DLM/Teaching Resources.

Bruininks, R. H., Woodcock, R. W., Weatherman, R. F., & Hill, B. K. (1984). *Scales of Independent Behavior: Woodcock-Johnson Psycho-Educational Battery: Part Four.* Allen, TX: DLM/Teaching Resources.

Bryant, D. M., & Maxwell, K. (1997). The effectiveness of early intervention for disadvantaged children. In M. J. Guralnick (Ed.), *The effectiveness of early intervention* (pp. 23–46). Baltimore: Paul H. Brookes.

Bryden, M. P. (1979). Evidence for sex-related differences in cerebral organization. In M. A. Wittig & A. C. Peterson (Eds.), *Sex related differences in cognitive functioning.* New York: Academic Press.

Bryden, M. P. (1980). Sex differences in brain organization: Different brains or different strategies? *Behavioral and Brain Sciences, 3*, 230–231.

Buchanan, M., & Wolf, J. S. (1986). A comprehensive study of learning disabled adults. *Journal of Learning Disabilities, 19*, 34–38.

Buck, M. (1968). *Dysphasia.* Englewood Cliffs, NJ: Prentice-Hall.

Buffery, A. W. H. (1974). Asymmetric lateralization of cerebral functions and the effects of unilateral brain surgery in epileptic patients. In S. J. Dimond & J. G. Beaumont (Eds.), *Hemispheric function in the human brain,* London: Elek Science.

Buffery, A. W. H., & Gray, J. (1972). Sex differences in the development of perceptual and linguistic skills. In C. Ounsted & D. Taylor (Eds.), *Gender differences: Their ontogeny and significance.* London: Churchill.

Burchinal, M. R., Campbell, F. A., Bryant, D. M., Wasik, B. M., & Ramey, C. T. (1997). Early intervention and mediating processes in intellectual development among low-income African American children. *Child Development, 68*, 935–954.

Burdick, J. A., Johnson, L. C., & Smith, J. W. (1970). Measurements of change during alcohol withdrawal in chronic alcoholics. *British Journal of Addiction, 65*, 273–280.

Burgess, J. W. (1991). Neurocognition in acute and chronic depression: Personality disorder, major depression, and schizophrenia. *Biological Psychiatry, 30*, 305–309.

Burks, B. S. (1928). The relative influence of nature and nurture upon mental development: A comparative study of foster parent–offspring child resemblance and true parent–true child resemblance. *Yearbook of the National Society for the Study of Education, 27*, 219–316.

Burnham, L. B. (1982). Adults. Not grown up children. *Community and Junior College Journal, 53*, 22–26, 46.

Burt, C. (1963). Is intelligence distributed normally? *British Journal of Statistical Psychology, 16*, 175–190.

Butters, N., & Cermak, L. S. (1980). *The alcoholic Korsakoff's syndrome: An information processing approach to amnesia.* New York: Academic Press.

Butters, N., Salmon, D. P., Cullum, M., Cairns, P., Troster, A. I., Jacobs, D., Moss, M., & Cermak, L. S. (1988). Differentiation of amnestic and demented patients with the Wechsler Memory Scale-Revised. *Clinical Neuropsychologist, 2*, 133–148.

Butters, N., Sax, D., Montgomery, K., & Tarlow, S. (1978). Comparison of the neuropsychological deficits associated with early and advanced Huntington's disease. *Archives of Neurology, 35*, 585–589.

Cahan, S. (2000, Fall). Schooling and the norming of intelligence test scores. *Educational Measurement: Issues and Practice,* 26–32.

Caine, E. D. (1986). The neuropsychology of depression: The pseudodementia syndrome. In I. Grant & K. M. Adanis (Eds.), *Neuropsychological assessment of neuropsychiatric disorders* (pp. 221–243). New York: Oxford University Press.

Caine, E. D., Bamford, K. A., Schiffer, R. B., Shotilson, I., & Levy, S. (1986). A controlled neuropsychological comparison of Huntington's disease and multiple sclerosis. *Archives of Neurology, 43*, 249–254.

Calvert, E. J., & Crozier, W. R. (1978). An analysis of Verbal–Performance intelligence quotient discrepancies in the Wechsler Adult Intelligence Scale results of mentally subnormal hospital patients. *Journal of Mental Deficiency Research, 22*, 147–153.

Camara, W. J., Nathan, J. S., Puente, A. E. (2000). Psychological test usage: Implications in professional psychology. *Professional Psychology: Research and Practice, 31*, 141–154.

Campbell, B., & Wilson, B. J. (1986). An investigation of Kaufman's method for determining scatter on the WISC-R. *Journal of School Psychology, 24*, 373–380.

Campbell, F. A., Pungello, E. P., Miller-Johnson, S., Burchinal, M., & Ramey, C. T. (in press). The development of cognitive and academic abilities: Growth curves from an early childhood educational experiment. *Developmental Psychology.*

Campbell, F. A., & Ramey, C. T. (1986). High risk infants: Environmental risk factors. In J. M. Berg (Ed.), *Science and service in mental retardation* (pp. 23–33). London: Methuen.

Campbell, F. A., & Ramey, C. T. (1994). Effects of early intervention on intellectual and academic achievement: A follow-up study of children from low-income families. *Child Development, 65*, 684–698.

Campbell, F. A., & Ramey, C. T. (1995). Cognitive and school outcomes for high-risk African American students in middle adolescence: Positive effects of early intervention. *American Educational Research Journal, 32*, 743–772.

Campbell, I. A. (1985). Review of Vineland Adaptive Behavior Scales. In J. V. Mitchell, (Ed.), *The ninth mental measurements yearbook* (pp. 1660–1662). Lincoln, NE: Buros Institute of Mental Measurements, University of Nebraska Press.

Campbell, V., Smith, R., & Wool, R. (1981). Adaptive Behavior Scale differences in scores of mentally retarded individuals referred for institutionalization and those never referred. *American Journal of Mental Deficiency, 86*, 425–528.

Candler, A. C., Maddux, C. D., & Johnson, D. L. (1986). Relationship of scores on PPVT-R and WISC-R with special education children and youth. *Perceptual and Motor Skills, 62*, 417–418.

Canivez, G. L. (1996). Validity and diagnostic efficiency of the Kaufman Brief Intelligence Test in reevaluating students with learning disability. *Journal of Psychoeducational Assessment, 14*, 4–19.

Capps, C. F., Levinson, E. M., & Hohenshil, T. H. (1985). Vocational aspects of psychological assessment: Part III. *NASP Communique, 13*(5), 5–6.

Cargnello, J. C., & Gurekas, R. (1987). The clinical use of a modified WAIS procedure in a geriatric population. *Journal of Clinical Psychology, 43*, 286–290.

Carroll, J. B. (1993). *Human cognitive abilities: A survey of factor-analytic studies.* New York: Cambridge University Press.

Carroll, J. B. (1996). Mathematical abilities: Some results from factor analysis. In R. J. Sternberg & T. Ben-Zeev (Eds.), *The nature of mathematical thinking* (pp. 3–25). Mahwah, NJ: Erlbaum.

Carroll, J. B. (1997). The three-stratum theory of cognitive abilities. In D. P. Flanagan, J. L. Genshaft, & P. L. Harrison (Eds.), *Beyond traditional intellectual assessment: Theories, tests, and issues* (pp. 122–130). New York: Guilford Press.

Carroll, J. B., & Horn, J. L. (1981). On the scientific basis of ability testing. *American Psychologist, 36*, 1012–1020.

Carrow-Woolfolk, E. (1995). *Oral and Written Language Scales: Listening Comprehension and Oral Expression.* Circle Pines, MN: American Guidance Service.

Carsrud, A. L., Carsrud, K. B., Dodd, B. G., Thompson, M., & Gray, W. K. (1981). Predicting vocational aptitude of mentally retarded persons: A comparison of assessment systems. *American Journal of Mental Deficiency, 86*, 275–280.

Caruso, J. C., & Cliff, N. (1999). The properties of equally and differentially weighted WAIS-III factor scores. *Psychological Assessment, 11*, 198–206.

Carvajal, H., Gerber, J., Hewes, P., & Weaver, K. A. (1987). Correlations between scores on the Stanford-Binet IV and Wechsler Adult Intelligence Scale-Revised. *Psychological Reports, 61*, 83–86.

Carvajal, H., Gerber, J., & Smith, P. D. (1987). Relationship between scores of young adults on Stanford-Binet IV and Peabody Picture Vocabulary Test-Revised. *Perceptual and Motor Skills, 65*, 721–722.

Carvajal, H., Shaffer, C., & Weaver, K. A. (1989). Correlations of scores of maximum security inmates on Wechsler Adult Intelligence Scale-Revised. *Psychological Reports, 65*, 268–270.

Carvajal, T. I., Lane, M., & Gay, D. A. (1984). Longitudinal comparisons of Wechsler's scales in educable mentally handicapped children and adults. *Psychology in the Schools, 21*, 137–140.

Catron, D. W. (1978). Immediate test-retest changes in WAIS scores among college males. *Psychological Reports, 43*, 279–290.

Catron, D. W., & Catron, S. S. (1977). WISC-R vs. WISC: A comparison with educable mentally retarded children. *Journal of School Psychology, 15*, 264–266.

Catron, D. W., & Thompson, C. C. (1979). Test-retest gains in WAIS scores after four retest intervals. *Journal of Clinical Psychology, 35*, 352–357.

Cattell, R. B. (1941). Some theoretical issues in adult intelligence testing. *Psychological Bulletin, 38*, 592.

Cattell, R. B. (1963). Theory of fluid and crystallized intelligence: A critical experiment. *Journal of Educational Psychology, 54*, 1–22.

Cella, D. (1984). The modified WAIS-R: An extension and revision. *Journal of Clinical Psychology, 40*, 801–804.

Cella, D., Jacobsen, P. B., & Hymowitz, P. (1985). A comparison of the intertest accuracy of two short forms of the WAIS-R. *Journal of Clinical Psychology, 41*, 544–546.

Cernovsky, Z. (1986). Masculinity-femininity scale of the MMPI and intellectual functioning of female addicts. *Journal of Clinical Psychology, 42*, 310–312.

Chalke, F., & Ertl, J. (1965). Evoked potentials and intelligence. *Life Sciences, 4*, 1319–1322.

Chance, J., Overcast, T., & Dollinger, S. J. (1978). Aging and cognitive regression: Contrary findings. *Journal of Psychology, 98*, 177–183.

Chapman, L. F., & Wolff, H. G. (1959). The cerebral hemispheres and the highest integrative functions of man. *A.M.A. Archives of Neurology, 1*, 357–424.

Chastain, R., & Joe, G. W. (1987). Multidimensional relations between intellectual abilities and demographic variables. *Journal of Educational Psychology, 79*, 323–325.

Chaves, M. L. F., & Izquierdo, I. (1992). Differential diagnosis between dementia and depression: A study of efficiency increment. *Acta Neurologica Scandinavica, 85*, 378–382.

Chelune, G. J. (1982). A reexamination of the relationship between the Luria-Nebraska and Halstead-Reitan batteries: Overlap with the WAIS. *Journal of Consulting and Clinical Psychology, 50*, 578–580.

Chelune, G. J., & Bornstein, R. A. (1988). WMS-R patterns among patients with unilateral lesions. *Clinical Neuropsychologist, 2*, 121–132.

Chelune, G. J., Eversole, C., Kane, M., & Talbott, R. (1987). WAIS versus WAIS-R subtest patterns: A problem of generalization. *Clinical Neuropsychologist, 1*, 235–242.

Chelune, G. J., Naugle, R. I., Luders, H., Sedlak, J., & Awad, I. A. (1993). Individual change after epilepsy surgery: Practice effects and base-rate information. *Neuropsychology, 7*, 41–52.

Chen, T., Kaufman, A. S., & Kaufman, J. C. (1994). Examining the interaction of age x race pertaining to Black–White differences at ages 15 to 93 on six Horn abilities assessed by K-FAST, K-SNAP, and KAIT subtests. *Perceptual and Motor Skills, 79*, 1683–1690.

Childs, D. F. (1982). A study of the adaptive behavior of retarded children and the resultant effects of this use in the diagnosis of mental retardation. *Education and Training of the Mentally Retarded, 77*, 109–113.

Chmielewski, C., & Golden, C. (1980). Alcoholism and brain damage: An investigation using the Luria-Nebraska Neuropsychological Battery. *International Journal of Neuroscience, 10*, 99–105.

Christensen, A. L. (1975). *Luria's neuropsychological investigation.* New York: Spectrum.

Christensen, A. L. (1979). *Luria's neuropsychological investigation.* Munkesgaard: Copenhagen.

Christensen, H., Henderson, A. S., Griffiths, K., & Levings, C. (1997). Does ageing inevitably lead to declines in cognitive performance? A longitudinal study of elite academics. *Personality & Individual Differences, 23*, 67–78.

Christian, W. P., Jr., & Malone, D. R. (1973). Relationships among three measures used in screening mentally retarded for placement in special education. *Psychological Reports, 33*, 415–418.

Cicchetti, D. V., & Sparrow, S. S. (1986). False conclusions about Vineland standard scores: Silverstein's Type I errors and other artifacts. *American Journal of Mental Deficiency, 91*, 5–9.

Clampit, M. K., Adair, J., & Strenio, J. (1983). Frequency of discrepancies between deviation quotients on the WISC-R: A table for clinicians. *Journal of Consulting and Clinical Psychology, 51*, 795–796.

Clarizio, H., & Bernard, R. (1981). Recategorized WISC-R scores of learning disabled children and differential diagnosis. *Psychology in the Schools, 18*, 5–12.

Clark, C., Crockett, D., Kionoff, H., & MacDonald, J. (1983). Cluster analysis of the WAIS on brain-damaged patients. *Journal of Clinical Neuropsychology, 5*, 149–158.

Clark, L., & Watson, D. (1995). Constructing validity: Basic issues in objective scales development. *Psychological Assessment*, 7(3), 309–319.

Clausen, J. (1972). The continuing problem of defining mental deficiency. *Journal of Special Education*, 6, 97–106.

Clayton, G. A., Sapp, G. L., O'Sullivan, P., & Hall, L. (1986). Comparative validity of two WAIS-R short forms with vocational rehabilitation clients. *Perceptual and Motor Skills*, 63, 1303–1308.

Coffman, W. E. (1985). Review of Structure of Intellect Learning Abilities Test. In J. V. Mitchell (Ed.), *The ninth mental measurements yearbook* (pp. 1486–1488). Lincoln, NE: Buros Institute of Mental Measurements, University of Nebraska Press.

Cohen, J. (1952a). A factor-analytically based rationale for the Wechsler-Bellevue. *Journal of Consulting Psychology*, 16, 272–277.

Cohen, J. (1952b). Factors underlying Wechsler-Bellevue performance of three neuropsychiatric groups. *Journal of Abnormal and Social Psychology*, 47, 359–365.

Cohen, J. (1957a). A factor-analytically based rationale for the Wechsler-Adult Intelligence Scale. *Journal of Consulting Psychology*, 6, 451–457.

Cohen, J. (1957b). The factorial structure of the WAIS between early adulthood and old age. *Journal of Consulting Psychology*, 21, 283–290.

Cohen, J. (1959). The factorial structure of the WISC at ages 7–6, 10–6, and 13–6. *Journal of Consulting Psychology*, 23, 285–299.

Cohen, J. (1977). *Statistical power analysis for the behavioral sciences* (Rev. ed.). New York: Academic.

Cohen, M. J., Branch, W. B., McKie, V. C., & Adams, R. J. (1994). Neuropsychological impairment in children with sickle cell anemia and cerebrovascular accidents. *Clinical Pediatrics*, 517–524.

Cohen, R. J., Montague, P., Nathanson, L. S., & Swerdlik, M. E. (1988). *Psychological testing: An introduction to tests and measurement*. Mountain View, CA: Mayfield.

Colby, K., & Parkinson, C. (1977). Handedness in autistic children. *Journal of Autism and Childhood Schizophrenia*, 7, 3–9.

Coleman, M., Jorgenson, C., & Evans, M. H. (1988). The WISC-R and Detroit Tests of Learning Aptitude: 2. A Comparative study. *Journal of Psychoeducational Assessment*, 6, 341–346.

Colsher, P. L., & Wallace, R. B. (1991). Longitudinal application of cognitive function measures in a defined population of community-dwelling elders. *Annals of Epidemiology*, 1, 215–230.

Cone, J. D. (1984). *The pyramid scales*. Austin, TX: PRO-ED.

Cone, J. D. (Ed.). (1986). *The pyramid system: Comprehensive assessment and programming for handicapped persons*. Morgantown, WV: Pyramid Press.

Conley, J. J. (1984). The hierarchy of consistency: A review and model of longitudinal findings on adult individual differences in intelligence, personality and self-opinion. *Personality and Individual Differences*, 5, 11–26.

Connelly, J. B. (1983). Recategorized WISC-R score patterns of older and younger referred Tlingit Indian children. *Psychology in the Schools*, 20, 271–275.

Connor, R., Kamphaus, R. W., & Harrison, P. L. (1988, April). *Testing the independence of intelligence and adaptive behavior constructs*. Paper presented at the meeting of the National Association of School Psychologists, Chicago, IL.

Conroy, J., Efthimlou, J., & Lemanowicz, J. (1982). A matched comparison of the developmental growth of institutionalized and deinstitutionalized mentally retarded clients. *American Journal of Mental Deficiency*, 86, 581–587.

Cordoni, B. K., O'Donnell, J. P., Ramaniah, N. V., Kurtz, J., & Rosenshein, K. (1981). Wechsler Adult Intelligence Scale patterns for learning-disabled young adults. *Journal of Learning Disabilities*, 14, 404–407.

Cornell, D. G., & Wilson, L. A. (1992). The PIQ>VIQ discrepancy in violent and nonviolent delinquents. *Journal of Clinical Psychology*, 48, 256–261.

Cornell, E. L., & Coxe, W. W. (1934). *A performance ability scale: Examination manual*. New York: World.

Costa, L. D. (1975). The relation of visuospatial dysfunction to digit span performance in patients with cerebral lesions. *Cortex*, 11, 31–36.

Coulter, W. A. (1980). Adaptive behavior and professional disfavor: Controversies and trends for school psychologists. *School Psychology Review*, 9, 67–74.

Courville, C. B. (1966). *Effects of alcohol on the nervous system of man*. Los Angeles: San Lucas Press.

Cowles, J. R., & Keim, M. C. (1995). The graduation rate, intellectual functioning level, and matriculation time of university students with learning disabilities. *College Student Journal*, 29, 145–149.

Craft, N. P., & Kronenberger, E. J. (1979). Comparability of WISC-R and WAIS IQ scores in educable mentally handicapped adolescents. *Psychology in the Schools*, 16, 502–506.

Craig, D. L. (1979). Neuropsychological assessment in public psychiatric hospitals: The current state of practice. *Journal of Clinical Neuropsychology*, 1, 1–7.

Craik, F. I. M., & Salthouse, T. A. (Eds.). (2000). *The handbook of aging and cognition* (2nd ed.). Mahwah, NJ: Erlbaum.

Crandall, F. (1969). *A cross-cultural study of Ahtan Indian and non-Indian high school students in Alaska on selected value orientations and measured intellectual ability*. Unpublished doctoral dissertation, Clark University, Worcester, MA.

Cravens, T. B. (1999). Evaluation of Kaufman, Ishikuma, and Kaufman-Packer's short forms for use with psychiatric African

Amercian children. *Journal of Psychoeducational Assessment, 17,* 332–342.

Crawford, J. R., & Allan, K. M. (1997). Estimating premorbid WAIS-R IQ with demographic variables: Regression equations derived from a UK sample. *Clinical Neuropsychologist, 11,* 192–197.

Critchley, M. (1953). *The parietal lobes.* London: Edward Arnold.

Crockett, D., Clark, C., & Klonoff, H. (1981). Introduction: An overview of neuropsychology. In S. B. Filskov & T. J. Boll (Eds.), *Handbook of clinical neuropsychology* (pp. 1–37). New York: Wiley.

Cronbach, L. J. (1970). *Essentials of psychological testing* (3rd ed.). New York: Harper & Row.

Cronbach, L. J. (1971). Construct validation after thirty years. R. Linn (ed.), *Intelligence: Measurement, theory, and public policy: Preceedings of a symposium in honor of Lloyd Humphreys* (pp. 147–167). Urbana, IL: University of Chicago Press.

Cronbach, L. J. (1984). *Essentials of psychological testing* (4th ed.). New York: Harper & Row.

Cronbach, L. J., & Meehl, P. E. (1955). Construct validity in psychological tests. *Psychological Bulletin, 52,* 281–302.

Crookes, T. G. (1984). A cognitive peculiarity specific to schizophrenia. *Journal of Clinical Psychology, 40,* 893–896.

Croxon, S. C. M., & Jagger, C. (1995). Diabetes and cognitive impairment: A community-based study of elderly subjects. *Age and Aging, 24,* 421–424.

Culbertson, J. L., & Edmonds, J. E. (1996). Learning disabilities. In R. Adams, O. A. Parsons, J. L. Culbertson, & S. J. Nixon (Eds.), *Neuropsychology for clinical practice: Etiology, assessment, and treatment of common neurological disorders.* Washington, DC: American Psychiatric Association.

Cummings, J. A. (1985). Review of the Woodcock-Johnson Psycho-Educational Battery. In J. V. Mitchell (Ed.), *The ninth mental measurements yearbook* (pp. 1759–1762). Lincoln, NE: Buros Institute of Mental Measurements, University of Nebraska Press.

Cummings, J. A., & Simon, M. S. (1988). Review of the Scales of Independent Behavior. *Journal of Psychoeducational Assessment, 6,* 315–320.

Cummins, J. C. (1984). *Bilingual and special education: Issues in assessment and pedagogy.* Austin, TX: Pro-Ed.

Cummins, J. P., & Das, J. P. (1980). Cognitive processing, academic achievement, and WISC-R performance in EMR children. *Journal of Consulting and Clinical Psychology, 49,* 777–779.

Cunningham, T., & Presnall, D. (1978). Relationship between dimensions of adaptive behavior and sheltered workshop productivity. *American Journal of Mental Deficiency, 82,* 386–393.

Cunningham, W. R., Clayton, Z. & Overton, W. (1975). Fluid and crystallized intelligence in young adulthood and old age. *Journal of Gerontology, 30,* 53–55.

Cunningham, W. R., & Owens, W. A. (1983). The Iowa State study of the adult development of intellectual abilities. In K. W. Schaie (Ed.), *Longitudinal studies of adult psychological development* (pp. 20–39). New York: Guilford.

Cyr, J. J., & Brooker, B. H. (1984). Use of appropriate formulas for selecting WAIS-R short forms. *Journal of Consulting and Clinical Psychology, 52,* 903–905.

Dalton, J. E., Pederson, S. L., & McEntyre, W. L. (1987). A comparison of the Shipley vs. WAIS-R subtests in predicting WAIS-R Full Scale IQs. *Journal of Clinical Psychology, 43,* 278–280.

Daniel, M. H. (1989). *Differential ability scales: Research notes.* San Antonio, TX: The Psychological Corporation.

Das, J. P., Kirby, J., & Jarman, R. F. (1979). *Simultaneous and successive cognitive processes.* New York: Academic Press.

Davis, F. B. (1959). Interpretation of differences among averages and individual test scores. *Journal of Educational Psychology, 50,* 162–170.

Davis, F. B. (1971). The measurement of mental ability through evoked potential recording. *Educational Record Research Bulletin, 1.*

Davison, L. A. (1974). Current status of clinical neuropsychology. In R. M. Reitan & L. A. Davison (Eds.), *Clinical neuropsychology: Current status and applications* (pp. 325–362). Washington, DC: V. H. Winston & Sons.

Dawson, G., Warrenburg, S., & Fuller, P. (1982). Cerebral lateralization in individuals diagnosed as autistic in early childhood. *Brain and Language, 15,* 353–368.

Dean, J. (1985). A multivariant assessment and treatment technique for alcohol problems. *International Journal of the Addictions, 20,* 1281–1290.

Dean, R. S. (1983). *Manual: Report of individual evaluation for use with WAIS/WAIS-R.* Orlando, FL: Psychological Assessment Resources.

Dean, R. S. (1988). Comment on "IQ: R.I.P." *NASP Communique, 17*(4), 4.

Dean, R. S., & Woodcock, R. W. (1999). *The WJ-R and Bateria-R in Neuropsychological Assessment.* Chicago: Riverside.

Deary, I. J., Starr, J. M., & MacLennan, W. J. (1998). Fluid intelligence, memory, and blood pressure in cognitive aging. *Personality & Individual Differences. 25,* 605–619.

Deaux, K. (1984). From individual differences to social categories: Analysis of a decade's research on gender. *American Psychologist, 39,* 105–116.

DeCroly, I. (1914). Epreuve nouvelle pour l'examination mental. *L'Année Psychologique, 20,* 140–159.

Delaney, H. D., Norman, R. D., & Miller, D. A. (1981). An exploration of the verbal encodability hypothesis for sex differences in the Digit-Symbol (symbol-digit) test. *Intelligence, 5,* 199–208.

Dells, D. C., & Kaplan, E. (1982). The assessment of aphasia with the Luria-Nebraska Neuropsychological Battery: A case critique. *Journal of Consulting and Clinical Psychology, 50,* 32–39.

Dells, D. C., & Kaplan, E. (1983). Hazards of a standardized neuropsychological test with low content validity: Comment on the Luria-Nebraska Neuropsychological Battery. *Journal of Consulting and Clinical Psychology, 51,* 396–398.

DeMyer, M. K. (1975). The nature of neuropsychological disability in autistic children. *Journal of Autism and Childhood Schizophrenia, 5,* 109–128.

Denckla, M. B. (1974). Development of motor coordination in normal children. *Developmental Medicine and Child Neurology, 16,* 729–741.

Dennerll, R. D. (1964). Prediction of unilateral brain dysfunction using Wechsler test scores. *Journal of Consulting Psychology, 28,* 278–284.

Denney, N. W. (1982). Aging and cognitive changes. In B. B. Wolman (Ed.), *Handbook of developmental psychology* (pp. 807–827). Englewood Cliffs, NJ: Prentice-Hall.

Dennis, M. (1985a). Intelligence after early brain injury: I. Predicting IQ scores from medical variables. *Journal of Clinical and Experimental Neuropsychology, 7,* 526–554.

Dennis, M. (1985b). Intelligence after early brain injury: II. IQ scores of subjects classified on the basis of medical history variables. *Journal of Clinical and Experimental Neuropsychology, 7,* 555–576.

Denny-Brown, D., Meyer, J. S., & Horenstein, S. (1952). The significance of perceptual rivalry resulting from parietal lesions. *Brain, 75,* 434–471.

Derner, G. F., Aborn, M., & Canter, A. H. (1950). The reliability of the Wechsler-Bellevue subtests and scales. *Journal of Consulting Psychology, 14,* 172–179.

Devlin, B., Daniels, M., & Roeder, K. (1997). The heritability of IQ. *Nature, 388,* 468–471.

DeWolfe, A. S., Barrell, R. P., Becker, B. C., & Spaner, F. E. (1971). Intellectual deficit in chronic schizophrenia and brain damage. *Journal of Consulting and Clinical Psychology, 36,* 197–204.

DeWolfe, A. S., & Ryan, J. J. (1984). Wechsler Performance IQ > Verbal IQ index in a forensic sample: A reconsideration. *Journal of Clinical Psychology, 40,* 291–294.

Diamond, R., Barth, J. T., & Zillmer, E. A. (1988). Emotional correlates of mild closed head trauma: The role of the MMPI. *International Journal of Clinical Neuropsychology, 10,* 35–41.

DiCerbo, K. E., & Barona, A. (2000). A convergent validity study of the Differential Ability Scales and the Wechsler Intelligence Scale for Children-Third Edition, with Hispanic Children. *Journal of Psychoeducational Assessment, 18,* 344–352

DiCesare, A., Parente, R., & Anderson-Parente, J. (1990). Personality change after traumatic brain injury: Problems and solutions. *Cognitive Rehabilitation, 8*(2), 14–18.

Dickinson, D. J. (1986). Test review: Kaufman Test of Educational Achievement, Brief Form. *Journal of Psychoeducational Assessment, 4,* 333–336.

Dickstein, L. S., & Blatt, S. J. (1967). The WAIS Picture Arrangement subtest as a measure of anticipation. *Journal of Projective Techniques and Personality Assessment, 31,* 32–38.

Dietrich, K. N., Berger, O. G., Succop, P. A., Hammond, P. B., & Bornschein, R. L. (1993). The developmental consequences of low to moderate prenatal and postnatal lead exposure: Intellectual attainment in the Cincinnati lead study cohort following school entry. *Neurotoxicology and Teratology, 15,* 37–44.

Dillon, H. J. (1949). *Early school learners: A major educational problem.* New York: National Child Labor Committee.

Dillon, M., & Weissman, S. (1987). Relationship between personality types on the Strong-Campbell and Myers-Briggs instruments. *Measurement and Evaluation in Counseling and Development, 20,* 68–79.

Dinning, W. D., & Kraft, W. A. (1983). Validation of the Satz-Mogel short form for the WAIS-R with psychiatric inpatients. *Journal of Consulting and Clinical Psychology, 51,* 781–782.

Dixon, R. A., Kramer, D. A., & Baltes, P. B. (1985). Intelligence: A life-span developmental perspective. In B. B. Wolman (Ed.), *Handbook of intelligence* (pp. 301–350). New York: Wiley.

Dodrill, C. B., & Clemmons, D. (1984). Use of neuropsychological tests to identify high school students with epilepsy who later demonstrate inadequate performances in life. *Journal of Consulting and Clinical Psychology, 52,* 520–527.

Dodrill, C. B., & Troupin, A. S. (1975). Effects of repeated administrations of a comprehensive neuropsychological battery among chronic epileptics. *Journal of Nervous and Mental Disease, 161,* 185–190.

Doehring, D. G., & Reitan, R. M. (1961). Certain language and nonlanguage disorders in brain-damaged patients with homonymous visual field defects. *Archives of Neurological Psychiatry, 132,* 227–233.

Doehring, D. G., Reitan, R. M., & Klove, H. (1961). Changes in patterns of intelligence test performance associated with homonymous visual field defects. *Journal of Nervous and Mental Disease, 132,* 227–233.

Doll, E. A. (1935). A generic scale of social maturity. *American Journal of Orthopsychiatry, 5,* 180–188.

Doll, E. A. (1940). The social basis of mental diagnosis. *Journal of Applied Psychology, 24,* 160–169.

Doll, E. A. (1941). The essentials of an inclusive concept of mental deficiency. *American Journal of Mental Deficiency, 46,* 214–219.

Doll, E. A. (1953). *Measurement of social competence.* Circle Pines, MN: American Guidance Service.

Doll, E. A. (1965). *Vineland Social Maturity Scale*. Circle Lines, MN: American Guidance Service.

Doll, E. A. (1966). Recognition of mental retardation in the school age child. In I. Phillips (Ed.), *Prevention and treatment of mental retardation*. New York: Basic Books.

Donlon, T. F. (Ed.). (1984). *The College Board technical handbook for the Scholastic Aptitude Test and achievement tests*. New York: College Entrance Examination Board.

Doppelt, J. E. (1956). Estimating the Full Scale score on the Wechsler Adult Intelligence Scale from scores on four subtests. *Journal of Consulting Psychology, 20*, 63–66.

Doppelt, J. E., & Kaufman, A. S. (1977). Estimation of the differences between WISC-R and WAIS IQs. *Educational and Psychological Measurement, 37*, 417–424.

Doppelt, J. E., & Wallace, W. L. (1955). Standardization of the Wechsler Adult Intelligence Scale for older persons. *Journal of Abnormal and Social Psychology, 51*, 312–330.

Drachman, D. A., & Arbit, J. (1966). Memory and the hippocampal complex: Is memory a multiple process? *Archives of Neurology, 15*, 52–61.

Drachman, D. A., & Leavitt, J. (1974). Human memory and the cholinergic system: A relationship to aging? *Archives of Neurology, 30*, 113–121.

Dubois, P. H. (1970). *A history of psychological testing*. Boston: Allyn & Bacon.

Duckro, P. N., Longstreet, A., & McLaughlin, L. J. (1982). A selection of short forms of the WAIS for use with a low SES psychiatric population. *Journal of Clinical Psychology, 38*, 847–852.

Dudek, F. J. (1979). The continuing misinterpretation of the standard error of measurement. *Psychological Bulletin, 86*, 335–337.

Dukes, L., & Buttery, T. J. (1982). Comparison of two screening tests: Gesell Developmental Test and Meeting Street School Screening Test. *Perceptual and Motor Skills, 54*, 1177–1178.

Duncan, D. R., & Barrett, A. M. (1961). A longitudinal comparison of intelligence involving the Wechsler-Bellevue I and WAIS. *Journal of Clinical Psychology, 17*, 318–319.

Dunn, L. M. (1959). *Peabody Picture Vocabulary Test Manual*. Circle Pines, MN: American Guidance Service.

Dunn, L. M., & Dunn, L. (1981). *Manual for the Peabody Picture Vocabulary Test-Revised (PPVT-R)*. Circle Pines, MN: American Guidance Service.

Dunn, L. M., & Dunn, L. (1997). *Manual for the Peabody Picture Vocabulary Test-Third Edition (PPVT-III)*. Circle Pines, MN: American Guidance Service.

Durham, T. W. (1982, August). The relationship of the Vineland Adaptive Behavior Scales to intelligence among the institutionalized mentally retarded. In J. C. Childers (Chair), *Vineland Adaptive Behavior Scales: A measure of adaptive functioning*. Symposium conducted at the meeting of the American Psychological Association, Washington, DC.

Dye, J. (1982). Factor structure of the Wechsler Memory Scale in an older population. *Journal of Clinical Psychology, 38*, 163–166.

Eckhardt, M. J., & Matarazzo, J. D. (1981). Test-retest reliability of the Halstead Impairment Index in hospitalized alcoholic and nonalcoholic males with mild to moderate neuropsychological impairment. *Journal of Clinical Neuropsychology, 3*, 257–269.

Edinger, J. D. (1976). WAIS picture arrangement and premorbid social competence among process schizophrenics. *Journal of Personality Assessment, 40*, 52–53.

Edinger, J. D., Shipley, R. H., Watkins, C. E., & Hammett, E. B. (1985). Validity of the Wonderlic Personnel Test as a brief IQ measure in psychiatric patients. *Journal of Consulting and Clinical Psychology, 53*, 937–939.

Edwards, B. T., & Klein, M. (1984). Comparison of the WAIS and the WAIS-R with Ss of high intelligence. *Journal of Clinical Psychology, 40*, 300–302.

Einstein, N., & Engelhart, C. I. (1997). Comparison of the K-BIT with short forms of the WAIS-R in a neuropsychological population. *Psychological Assessment, 9*(1), 57–62.

Eisdorfer, C., Busse, E. W., & Cohen, L. D. (1959). The WAIS performance of an aged sample: The relationship between Verbal and Performance IQs. *Journal of Gerontology, 14*, 197–201.

Eisdorfer, C., & Wilkie, F. (1973). Intellectual changes with advancing age. In L. E. Jarvik, C. Eisdorfer, & J. E. Blum (Eds.), *Intellectual functioning in adults*. New York: Springer.

Ekstrom, R. B., French, J. W., & Harman, H. H. (1979). Cognitive factors: Their identification and replication. *Multivariate Behavioral Research Monographs, 79*(2), 3–84.

Ekstrom, R. B., French, J. W., Harman, H. H., & Dermen, D. (1978). *Kit of Factor Referenced Cognitive Tests*. Princeton, NJ: Educational Testing Service.

Elardo, R., Bradley, R., & Caldwell, B. M. (1977). A longitudinal study of the relation of infants' home environments to language development at age three. *Child Development, 48*, 596–603.

Elliott, C. D. (1990). *Differential Ability Scales (DAS) administration and scoring manual*. San Antonio, TX: The Psychological Corporation.

Elliott, C. D. (in press). *Manual for the Differential Ability Scales*. San Antonio, TX: The Psychological Corporation.

Elliott, R. (1987). *Litigating intelligence*. Dover, MA: Auburn House.

Elliott, S. N. (1985). Review of AAMD Adaptive Behavior Scale. In J. E. Mitchell (Ed.), *The ninth mental measurements yearbook* (pp. 2–4). Lincoln, NB: Buros Institute of Mental Measurements, University of Nebraska Press.

Elliott, S. N., Piersol, W. C., Witt, J. C., Argulewicz, E. N., Gutkin, T. B., & Galvin, G. A. (1985). Three-year stability of WAIS-R IQs for handicapped children from three racial/ethnic groups. *Journal of Psychoeducational Assessment, 3,* 233–244.

Engel, R., & Henderson, N. B. (1973). Visual evoked responses and I.Q. scores at school age. *Developmental and Medical Child Neurology, 15,* 136–145.

Erickson, R. C., & Scott, M. L. (1977). Clinical memory testing: A review. *Psychological Bulletin, 84,* 1130–1149.

Erker, G. J., Searight, H. R., & Peterson, P. (1995). Patterns of neuropsychological functioning among patients with multi-infarct and Alzheimer's dementia: A comparative analysis. *International Psychogeriatrics, 7,* 393–406.

Ernhart, C. B., Morrow-Tlucak, M., Wolf, A. W., Super, D., & Drotar, D. (1989). Low level exposure in the prenatal and early preschool periods: Intelligence prior to school entry. *Neurotoxicology and Teratology, 11,* 161–170.

Ertl, J. (1971). Fourier analysis of evoked potentials and human intelligence. *Nature, 230,* 525–526.

Ertl, J., & Schafer, E. (1969). Brain response correlates of psychometric intelligence. *Nature, 223,* 421–422.

Eslinger, P. J. (1996). Conceptualizing, describing, and measuring components of exective functions: A summary (pp. 327–348). In G. R. Lyon & N. A. Krasnegor (Eds.), *Attention, memory, and executive function.* Baltimore: Brookes.

Estes, W. K. (1974). Learning theory and intelligence. *American Psychologist, 29,* 740–749.

Estes, W. K. (1982). Learning, memory, and intelligence. In R. J. Sternberg (Ed.), *Handbook of human intelligence* (pp. 170–224). New York: Cambridge.

Ettinger, G. E. (1963). Defective identification of fingers. *Neuropsychologia, 41,* 39–45.

Evans, R. G. (1985). Accuracy of the Satz-Mogel procedure in estimating WAIS-R IQs that are in the normal range. *Journal of Clinical Psychology, 41,* 100–103.

Eyman, R. K., Demaine, G. C., & Lei, T. J. (1979). Relationship between community environments and resident changes in adaptive behavior: A path model. *American Journal of Mental Deficiency, 83,* 330–338.

Eysenck, H. J. (1982). Is intelligence? An epilogue. In H. J. Eysenck (Ed.), *A model for intelligence.* Berlin: Springer-Verlag.

Eysenck, H. J., & Barrett, P. (1985). Psychophysiology and the measurement of intelligence. In C. R. Reynolds & V. L. Willson (Eds.), *Methodological and statistical advances in the study of individual differences* (pp. 1–49). New York: Plenum.

Falconer, D. S. (1960). *Introduction to quantitative genetics.* London: Oliver and Boyd.

Fantuzzo, J., Sisemore, T., & Spradlin, W. (1983). A competency-based model for teaching skills in the administration of intelligence tests. *Professional Psychology, 14,* 224–231.

Faulstich, M., McAnulty, D., Gresham, F., Veltia, M., Moore, J., Bernard, B., Waggoner, C., & Lowell, R. (1986). Factor structure of the WAIS-R for an incarcerated population. *Journal of Clinical Psychology, 42,* 369–371.

Fawcett, A. J., Nicolson, R. I., & Maclagan, F. (2001). Cerebellar tests differentiate between groups of poor readers with and without IQ discrepancy. *Journal of Learning Disabilities, 34,* 119–135.

Fedio, P., Cox, C. S., Neophytides, A., Canal-Frederick, G., & Chase, P. N. (1979). Neuropsychological profile of Huntington's disease: Patients and those at risk. In P. N. Chase, N. S. Wexler, & A. Barbeau (Eds.), *Advances in neurology* (Vol. 23). New York: Raven Press.

Fedio, P., & Mirsky, A. F. (1969). Selective intellectual deficits in children with temporal lobe or centrencephalic epilepsy. *Neuropsychologia, 7,* 287–300.

Feingold, A. (1950). *A psychometric study of senescent twins.* Unpublished doctoral dissertation, Columbia University.

Feingold, A. (1982). The validity of the Information and Vocabulary subtests of the WAIS. *Journal of Clinical Psychology, 38,* 169–174.

Feingold, A. (1983a). Extracting maximum validity from the WAIS. *Journal of Clinical Psychology, 39,* 994–997.

Feingold, A. (1983b). The validity of the Information and Vocabulary subtests of the WAIS for predicting college achievement. *Educational and Psychological Measurement, 43,* 1127–1131.

Feingold, A. (1984). The reliability of score differences on the WAIS, WISC-R, and WAIS-R. *Journal of Clinical Psychology, 40,* 1060–1063.

Feingold, A. (1988). Cognitive gender differences are disappearing. *American Psychologist, 43,* 95–103.

Feuerstein, R. (1979). *The dynamic assessment of retarded performers: The learning potential assessment device, theory, instruments, and techniques.* Baltimore, MD: University Park Press.

Field, D., Schaie, K. W., & Leino, E. Z. (1988). Continuity in intellectual functioning: The role of self-reported health. *Psychology and Aging, 3,* 385–392.

Field, G. E., & Sisley, R. (1986). IQ score differences between the WAIS and the WAIS-R: Confirmation with a New Zealand sample. *Journal of Clinical Psychology, 42,* 986–988.

Fields, F. R. J., & Whitmyre, J. W. (1969). Verbal and Performance relationships with respect to laterality of cerebral involvement. *Diseases of the Nervous System, 30,* 177–179.

Filley, C. M., Kobayashi, J., & Heaton, R. K. (1987). Wechsler intelligence scale profiles, the cholinergic system, and

Alzheimer's disease. *Journal of Clinical and Experimental Neuropsychology, 9,* 180–186.

Filskov, S. B., & Goldstein, S. G. (1974). Diagnostic validity of the Halstead-Reitan battery. *Journal of Consulting and Clinical Psychology, 42,* 382–388.

Filskov, S. B., & Lell, D. A. (1981). Assessment of the individual in neuropsychological practice. In S. B. Filskov & T. J. Boll (Eds.), *Handbook of clinical neuropsychology,* New York: Wiley.

Finkel, D., Pederson, N. L., McGue, M., & McClearn, G. E. (1995). Heritability of cognitive abilities in adult twins: Comparison of Minnesota and Swedish data. *Behavior Genetics, 25,* 421–431.

Finlayson, M. A. J., Johnson, K. A., & Reitan, R. M. (1977). Relationship of level of education to neuropsychological measures in brain-damaged and non-brain-damaged adults. *Journal of Consulting and Clinical Psychology, 45,* 536–543.

Fisch, R. O., Bilek, M. K., Horrobin, J. M., & Chang, P. N. (1976). Children with superior intelligence at 7 years of age. *Archives of American Journal of Diseases of Children, 130,* 481–487.

Fischbein, S. (1980). IQ and social class. *Intelligence, 4,* 51–63.

Fischer, J. S. (1988). Using the Wechsler-Memory Scale-Revised to detect and characterize memory deficits in multiple sclerosis. *Clinical Neuropsychologist, 2,* 149–172.

Fischer, W. E., Wenck, L. S., Schurr, K. T., & Ellen, A. S. (1985). The moderating influence of gender, intelligence, and specific achievement deficiencies on the Bannatyne WISC-R recategorization. *Journal of Psychoeducational Assessment, 3,* 245–255.

Fisher, A. T. (1978, August). *Adaptive behavior in nonbiased assessment: Effects on special education.* Paper presented at the meeting of the American Psychological Association, Toronto.

Fisher, D. C., Ledbetter, M. F., Cohen, N. J., Marmor, D., & Tulsky, D. S. (2000). WAIS-III and WMS-III profiles of mildly to severely brain-injured patients. *Applied Neuropsychology, 7,* 126–132.

Fisher, M. (1956). Left hemiplegia and motor impersistence. *Journal of Nervous and Mental Disease, 123,* 201–213.

Fishkin, A. S., Kampsnider, J. J., & Pack, L. (1996). Exploring the WISC-III as a measure of giftedness. *Roeper Review, 18,* 226–231.

Fitzhugh, K. B., Fitzhugh, L. C., & Reitan, R. M. (1962). Wechsler-Bellevue comparisons in groups with "chronic" and "current" lateralized and diffuse brain lesions. *Journal of Consulting Psychology, 26,* 306–310.

Fitzhugh, K. B., Fitzhugh, L. C., & Reitan, R. M. (1964). Influence of age upon measures of problem solving and experiential background in subjects with long-standing cerebral dysfunction. *Journal of Gerontology, 19,* 132–134.

Fitzhugh, K. H., & Fitzhugh, L. C. (1964). WAIS results for subjects with longstanding, chronic, lateralized and diffuse cerebral dysfunction. *Perceptual and Motor Skills, 19,* 735–739.

Fitzhugh, K. H., Fitzhugh, L. C., & Reitan, R. M. (1961). Psychological deficits in relation to acuteness of brain dysfunction. *Journal of Consulting Psychology, 25,* 61–66.

Fitzhugh, L. C., Fitzhugh, K. B., & Reitan, R. M. (1965). Adaptive abilities and intellectual functioning of hospitalized alcoholics. *Quarterly Journal of Studies on Alcohol, 26,* 402–411.

Fitzhugh, L. C., & Fitzhugh, K. H. (1964). Relationships between Wechsler-Bellevue Form I and WAIS performances of subjects with long-standing cerebral dysfunction. *Perceptual and Motor Skills, 19,* 539–543.

Flanagan, D. P., & Alfonso, V. C. (2000). Essentially, Essential for WAIS-III Users. *Contemporary Psychology: APA Review of Books, 45,* 528–533.

Flanagan, D. P., Genshaft, J. L., & Harrison P. L. (Eds.). (1997). *Contemporary intellecual assessment: Theories, tests, and issues.* New York: Guilford.

Flanagan, D. P., & McGrew, K. S. (1997). A cross-battery approach to assessing and interpreting cognitive abilities: Narrowing the gap between practice and science. In D. P. Flanagan, J. L. Genshaft, & P. L. Harrison (Eds.), *Contemporary intellectual assessment: Theories, tests, and issues* (pp. 314–325). New York: Guilford.

Flanagan, D. P., & McGrew, K. S. (1998). Interpreting intelligence tests from contemporary *Gf–Gc* theory: Joint confirmatory factor analyses of the WJ-R and KAIT in a non-white sample. *Journal of School Psychology, 36,* 151–182.

Flanagan, D. P., McGrew, K. S., & Ortiz, S. O. (2000). *The Wechsler intelligence scales and* Gf-Gc *theory.* Boston: Allyn & Bacon.

Flanagan, D. P., & Ortiz, S. O. (2001). *Essentials of cross-battery assessment.* New York: Wiley.

Flanagan, D. P., Ortiz, S. O., Alfonso, V. C., & Mascolo, J. T. (in press). *The Achievement test desk reference (ATDR): Comprehensive assessment and learning disabilities.* Boston: Allyn & Bacon.

Flaugher, R. L. (1978). The many definitions of test bias. *American Psychologist, 33,* 671–679.

Fletcher, J. M., Francis, D. J., Shaywitz, S. E., Lyon, G. R., Foorman, B. R., Stuebing, K. K., & Shaywitz, B. A. (1998). Intelligent testing and the discrepancy model for children with learning disabilities. *Learning Disabilities Research & Practice, 13,* 186–203.

Flor-Henry, P. (1976). Lateralized temporal-limbic dysfunction and psychopathology. *Annals of New York Academy of Sciences, 280,* 777–795.

Flynn, J. R. (1983). Now the great augmentation of the American IQ. *Nature, 301,* 655.

Flynn, J. R. (1984). The mean IQ of Americans: Massive gains 1932 to 1978. *Psychological Bulletin, 95,* 29–51.

Flynn, J. R. (1986). Sociobiology and IQ trends over time. *Behavioral and Brain Sciences, 9,* 192.

Flynn, J. R. (1987). Massive gains in 14 nations: What IQ tests really measure. *Psychological Bulletin, 101,* 171–191.

Flynn, J. R. (1998a). IQ gains over time: Toward finding the causes. In U. Neisser (Ed.), *The rising curve: Long-term gains in IQ and related measures* (pp. 25–66). Washington, DC: American Psychological Association.

Flynn, J. R. (1998b). Rising IQ scores: Implications for the elderly. *Australian Journal on Ageing, 17,* 106–107.

Flynn, J. R. (1998c). WAIS-III and WISC-III IQ gains in the United States from 1972 to 1995: How to compensate for obsolete norms. *Perceptual and Motor Skills, 86,* 1231–1239.

Fogel, M. L. (1965). The Proverbs Test in the appraisal of cerebral diseases. *Journal of General Psychology, 72,* 169–275.

Forsyth, A., Gaddes, W. J., Reitan, R. M., & Tryk, H. E. (1971). *Intellectual deficit in multiple sclerosis as indicated by psychological tests* (Research Monograph No. 23). Victoria, BC, Canada: University of Victoria.

Fowler, P. C., Richards, F. C., & Boll, T. J. (1980). WAIS factor patterns of epileptic and normal adults. *Journal of Clinical Neuropsychology, 2,* 115–123.

Fowles, G. P., & Tunick, R. (1986). WAIS-R and Shipley estimated IQ correlations. *Journal of Clinical Psychology, 42,* 647–649.

Foy, A., O'Connell, D., Henry, D., Kelly, J., Cocking, S., & Halliday, J. (1995). Benzodiazepine use as a cause of cognitive impairment in elderly hospital inpatients. *Journal of Gerontology: Medical Sciences, 50,* 99–106.

Fraboni, M., Saltstone, R., Baines, G. H., & Cooper, D. (1988). WAIS-R factor structure in a vocational rehabilitational sample: Additional support for a third factor in special populations. *Psychological Reports, 63,* 819–822.

Franklin, M., Stillman, P., Burpeau, M., & Sabers, D. (1982). Examiner error in intelligence testing: Are you a source? *Psychology in the Schools, 19,* 563–569.

Frauenheim, J. G., & Heckerl, J. R. (1983). A longitudinal study of psychological and achievement test performance in severe dyslexic adults. *Journal of Learning Disabilities, 16,* 339–347.

Frederiksen, N. (1986). Toward a broader conception of human intelligence. *American Psychologist, 41,* 445–452.

Freedman, B. J., Lucas, J. C., Forness, S. R., & Ritvo, E. R. (1985). Cognitive processing of high-functioning autistic children: Comparing the K-ABC and the WISC-R. *Journal of Psychoeducational Assessment, 4,* 357–362.

Fry, A. F., & Hale, S. (1996). Processing speed, working memory, and fluid intelligence: Evidence for a developmental cascade. *Psychological Science, 7*(4), 237–241.

Fry, A. F., & Hale, S. (2000). Relationships among processing speed, working memory, and fluid intelligence in children. *Biological Psychology, 54,* 1–34.

Fryers, T. (1984). *The epidemiology of severe intellectual impairment.* London: Academic Press.

Fryers, T. (1986). Factors affecting prevalence of severe mental retardation. In J. M. Berg (Ed.), *Science and service in mental retardation* (pp. 3–14). London: Methuen.

Fuld, P. A. (1983). Psychometric differentiation of the dementias: An overview. In B. Relsberg (Ed.), *Alzheimer's disease: The standard reference* (pp. 201–210). New York: Free Press.

Fuld, P. A. (1984). Test profile of cholinergic dysfunction and of Alzheimer-type dementia. *Journal of Clinical Neuropsychology, 6,* 380–392.

Gainotti, G. (1972). Emotional behavior and hemispheric side of lesion. *Cortex, 8,* 41–55.

Galin, D. (1974). Implications for psychiatry of left and right cerebral specialization. *Archives of General Psychiatry, 31,* 78–82.

Gallagher, A. M., & De Lisi, R. (1994). Gender differences in scholastic aptitude tests: Mathematics problem solving among high ability students. *Journal of Educational Psychology, 86,* 204–211.

Gallagher, A. M., De Lisi, R., Holst, P. C., McGillicuddy-De Lisi, A. V., Morely, M., & Cahalan, C. (2000). Gender differences in advanced mathematical problem solving. *Journal of Experimental Child Psychology, 75,* 165–190.

Galton, F. (1869). *Hereditary genius: An inquiry into its laws and consequences.* London: Macmillan.

Galton, F. (1883). *Inquiries into human faculty and its development.* London: Macmillan.

Gardner, H. (1993a). *Frames of mind: The theory of multiple intelligences* (10th anniversary ed.). New York: Basic Books.

Gardner, H. (1993b). *Multiple intelligences: Theory in practice.* New York: Basic Books.

Garfield, J. C. (1963). *Motor impersistence in normal and brain-damaged children.* Unpublished doctoral dissertation, University of Iowa.

Garfield, J. C. (1964). Motor impersistence in normal and brain-damaged children. *Neurology, 14,* 623–630.

Garfinkle, A. S. (1982). Genetic and environmental influences on the development of Piagetian logico-mathematical concepts and other specific cognitive abilities: A twin study. *Acta Geneticae Medicae et Gemeltologiae, 31,* 10–61.

Gasparrini, W., Satz, P., Heilman, K. M., & Coolidge, F. (1977, February). *Hemispheric asymmetries of affective processing as determined by the Minnesota Multiphasic Personality In-*

ventory. Paper presented at the meeting of the International Neuropsychological Society, Santa Fe, NM.

Gass, C. S., & Russell, E. W. (1985). MMPI correlates of verbal–intellectual deficits in patients with left hemisphere lesions. *Journal of Clinical Psychology, 41*, 664–670.

Gass, C. S., & Russell, E. W. (1987). MMPI correlates of performance intellectual deficits in patients with right hemisphere lesions. *Journal of Clinical Psychology, 43*, 484–489.

Gass, R. O. (1981). Comparative validity of the Verbal IQ as a short form of the WAIS. *Journal of Clinical Psychology, 37*, 843–846.

Gatton, F. (1869). *Hereditary genius: An inquiry into its laws and consequences.* London: Macmillan.

Geary, D. C. (1993). Mathematical disabilities: Cognitive, neuropsychological, and genetic components. *Psychological Bulletin, 114*(2), 345–362.

Geary, D. C., Hamson, C. O., & Hoard, M. K. (2000). Numerical and arithmetical cognition: A longitudinal study of process and concept deficits in children with learning disability. *Journal of Experimental Child Psychology, 77*(3), 236–263.

Geary, D. C., Hoard, M. K., & Hamson, C. O. (1999). Numerical and arithmetical cognition: Patterns of functions and deficits in children at risk for a mathematical disability. *Journal of Experimental Child Psychology, 74*(3), 213–239.

Geller, K. (1998). Kaufman Short Neuropsychological Assessment Procedure. In J. C. Impara & B. S. Plake (Eds.), *The thirteenth mental measurements yearbook* (pp. 572–573). Lincoln, NE: Buros Institute of Mental Measurements, University of Nebraska Press.

Gerstmann, J. (1924). Fingeragnosie: Eine unschriebene storting der orientierung am eigerst korper. *Wein Klin. Wchnsfchr, 37*, 1010–1012.

Gfeller, J. D., & Rankin, E. J. (1991). The WAIS-R profile as a cognitive marker of Alzheimer's disease: A misguided venture? *Journal of Clinical and Experimental Neuropsychology, 13*, 629–636.

Ghannani, J., Javornisky, G., & Smith, A. (1979, February). *Diaschisis in adult chronic aphasics with left hemisphere infraction.* Paper presented at the meeting of the International Neuropsychology Society, San Francisco.

Ghiselli, E. E. (1966). *The validity of occupational aptitude tests.* New York: Wiley.

Ghiselli, E. E. (1973). The validity of aptitude tests in personnel selection. *Personnel Psychology, 26*, 461–477.

Gilandas, A., Touzy, S., Beumont, P. J. V., & Greenberg, H. P. (1984). *Handbook of neuropsychological assessment.* Orlando, FL: Grune & Stratton.

Gilbert, J. (1978). *Interpreting psychological test data: Volume I. Test response antecedent.* New York: Van Nostrand Reinhold.

Gilleard, C. J. (1980). Wechsler Memory Scale performance of elderly psychiatric patients. *Journal of Clinical Psychology, 36*, 958–960.

Gilmore, G. C., Royer, F. L., & Gruhn, J. J. (1983). Age differences in symbol–digit substitution performance. *Journal of Clinical Psychology, 39*, 114–123.

Glanotti, G., & Tiacel, C. (1973). The unilateral forms of finger agnosia. *Confina Neurologica, 35*, 271–284.

Glasser, A. J., & Zimmerman, I. L. (1967). *Clinical interpretation of the Wechsler Intelligence Scale for Children (WISC).* New York: Grune & Stratton.

Glutting, J. J., Adams, W., & Sheslow, D. (2000). *Wide Range Intelligence Test Manual.* Wilmington, DE: Wide Range.

Glutting, J. J., & Kaplan, D. (in press). Stanford-Binet Intelligence Scale: Fourth Edition: Making the case for reasonable interpretations. In C. R. Reynolds & R. W. Kamphaus (Eds.), *Handbook of psychological and educational assessment of children: Volume 1. Intelligence and achievement.* New York: Guilford.

Goddard, H. H. (1911). A revision of the Binet scale. *Training School, 8*, 56–62.

Goh, D. S., Teslow, C. J., & Fuller, G. B. (1981). The practice of psychological assessment among school psychologists. *Professional Psychology, 12*, 696–706.

Gold, J. M., Queern, C., Iannone, V. N., & Buchanan, R. W. (1999). Repeatable battery for the Assessment of Neuropsychological Status as a Screening Test in Schizophrenia: I. Sensitivity, reliability, and validity. *American Journal of Psychiatry, 12*, 1944–1950.

Gold, P. C., & Horn, P. L. (1983). Intelligence and achievement of adult illiterates in a tutorial project: A preliminary analysis. *Journal of Clinical Psychology, 39*, 107–113.

Golden, C. J. (1977). Validity of the Halstead-Reitan Neuropsychological Battery in mixed psychotic and brain-impaired populations. *Journal of Consulting and Clinical Psychology, 45*, 1043.

Golden, C. J. (1979). Identification of specific neurological disorders using double discrimination scales derived from the standardized Luria neuropsychological battery. *International Journal of Neuroscience, 10*, 51–56.

Golden, C. J. (1981). *Diagnosis and rehabilitation in clinical neuropsychology.* Springfield, IL: Charles C. Thomas.

Golden, C. J., Ariel, R. N., Moses, J. A., Jr., Wilkening, G. N., McKay, S. E., & MacInnes, W. D. (1982). Analytic techniques in the interpretation of the Luria-Nebraska Neuropsychological Battery. *Journal of Consulting and Clinical Psychology, 50*, 40–48.

Golden, C. J., & Berg, R. A. (1980b). Interpretation of the Luria-Nebraska Neuropsychological Battery by item intercorrelation: The rhythm scale. *Journal of Clinical Neuropsychology, 2*, 153–156.

Golden, C. J., & Berg, R. A. (1980a). Interpretation of the Luria-Nebraska Neuropsychological Battery by item intercorrelation: Items 1–24 of the Motor Scale. *Journal of Clinical Neuropsychology, 2,* 66–71.

Golden, C. J., & Berg, R. A. (1980c). Interpretation of the Luria-Nebraska Neuropsychological Battery by item intercorrelation: The writing scale. *Journal of Clinical Neuropsychology, 2,* 8–12.

Golden, C. J., Berg, R. A., & Graber, H. (1982). Test-retest reliability of the Luria-Nebraska Neuropsychological Battery in stable, chronically impaired patients. *Journal of Consulting and Clinical Psychology, 50,* 452–454.

Golden, C. J., Fross, K. H., & Graber, B. (1981). Split-half reliability and item–scale consistency of the Luria-Nebraska Neuropsychological Battery. *Journal of Consulting and Clinical Psychology, 49,* 304–305.

Golden, C. J., Graber, B., Moses, J. A., Jr., & Zatz, I. M. (1980). Differentiation of chronic schizophrenics with and without ventricular enlargement by the Luria-Nebraska Neuropsychological Battery. *International Journal of Neuroscience, 11,* 131–138.

Golden, C. J., Hammeke, T., Osmon, D., Sweet, J., Purisch, A., & Graber, B. (1981). Factor analysis of the Luria-Nebraska Neuropsychological Battery: IV. Intelligence and pathognomonic scales. *International Journal of Neuroscience, 13,* 87–92.

Golden, C. J., & Kuperman, S. K. (1980). Training opportunities in neuropsychology at APA-approved internship settings. *Professional Psychology, 11,* 907–918.

Golden, C. J., Osmon, D., Sweet, J., Graber, B., Purisch, A., & Hammeke, T. (1980). Factor analysis of the Luria-Nebraska Neuropsychological Battery: III. Arithmetic, memory, left, and right. *International Journal of Neuroscience, 11,* 309–315.

Golden, C. J., Purisch, A., Sweet, J., Graber, B., Osmon, D., & Hammeke, T. (1980). Factor analysis of the Luria-Nebraska Neuropsychological Battery: II. Visual, receptive, expressive, and reading scales. *International Journal of Neuroscience, 11,* 227–236.

Golden, C. J., Sweet, J., Hammeke, T., Purisch, A., Graber, B., & Osmon, D. (1980). Factor analysis of the Luria-Nebraska Neuropsychological Battery: I. Motor, rhythm, and tactile scales. *International Journal of Neuroscience, 11,* 91–99.

Goldman, J. (1987). Differential WAIS/WAIS-R IQ discrepancies among institutionalized mentally retarded persons. *American Journal of Mental Deficiency, 91,* 633–635.

Goldman, R. S., Axelrod, B. N., Tandon, R., & Berent, S. (1993). Spurious WAIS-R cholinergic profiles in schizophrenia. *Clinical Neuropsychologist, 7,* 171–178.

Goldstein, G., & Shelly, C. (1972). Statistical and normative studies of the Halstead-Reitan neuropsychological test battery, relative to a neuropsychiatric hospital setting. *Perceptual and Motor Skills, 34,* 603–620.

Goldstein, G., & Shelly, C. (1973). Univariate versus multivariate analysis in neuropsychological test assessment of lateralized brain damage. *Cortex, 9,* 204–216.

Goldstein, G., & Shelly, C. (1984). Discriminative validity of various intelligence and neuropsychological tests. *Journal of Consulting and Clinical Psychology, 52,* 383–389.

Goldstein, K. (1948). *Language and language disturbances.* New York: Grune & Stratton.

Goldstein, K. (1952). The effects of brain damage and personality. *Psychiatry, 15,* 245–260.

Goldstein, K., & Scheerer, M. (1941). Abstract and concrete behavior: An experimental study with special tests. *Psychological Monographs, 53,* Whole No. 239.

Goldstein, S. G., Deysach, R., & Kleinkiieclit, R. A. (1973). Effect of experience and amount of information on identification of cerebral impairment. *Journal of Consulting and Clinical Psychology, 41,* 30–34.

Golinkoff, M., & Sweeney, J. A. (1989). Cognitive impairments in depression. *Journal of Affective Disorders, 17,* 105–112.

Gonen, J. Y., & Brown, L. (1968). Role of vocabulary in deterioration and restitution of mental functioning. *Proceedings of the 76th Annual Convention of the American Psychological Association, 3,* 469–470. (Summary).

Goodenough, D. R., & Karp, S. A. (1961). Field dependence and intellectual functioning. *Journal of Abnormal and Social Psychology, 63,* 241–246.

Goodglass, H., & Kaplan, E. (1979). Assessment of cognitive deficit in the brain-injured patient. In M. S. Ciazzaniga (Ed.), *Handbook of behavioral neuropsychology.* New York: Plenum.

Goolishian, H. A., & Ramsay, R. (1956). The Wechsler-Bellevue Form I and the WAIS: A comparison. *Journal of Clinical Psychology, 12,* 147–151.

Gordon, M., Greenberg, R. D., & Gerton, M. (1983). Wechsler discrepancies and the Rorschach experience balance. *Journal of Clinical Psychology, 39,* 775–779.

Gordon, N. G. (1977). Base rates and the decision-making model in clinical neuropsychology. *Cortex, 13,* 3–10.

Gorsuch, R. L., & Zachary, R. A. (1985). Continuous norming: Implication for the WAIS-R. *Journal of Clinical Psychology, 41*(1), 86–94.

Gottfredson, L. S. (1984). *The role of intelligence and education in the division of labor* (Report No. 355). Baltimore, MD: Johns Hopkins University, Center for Social Organization of Schools.

Gottfredson, L. S. (1997). Why g matters: The complexity of everyday life. *Intelligence, 24,* 79–132.

Gottfredson, L. S., & Brown, V. C. (1981). Occupational differentiation among white men in the first decade after high school. *Journal of Vocational Behavior, 19,* 251–289.

Grace, W. C. (1986). Equivalence of the WISC-R and WAIS-R in delinquent males. *Journal of Psychoeducational Assessment, 4*, 257–262.

Grace, W. C., & Sweeney, M. E. (1986). Comparisons of the P > V sign on the WISC-R and WAIS-R in delinquent males. *Journal of Clinical Psychology, 42*, 173–176.

Grady, C. L., McIntosh, A. R., Horwitz, B., Maisog, J. M., Ungerleider, L. G., Mentis, M. J., Pietrini, P., Schapiro, M. B., & Haxby, J. V. (1995). Age-related reduction in human recognition memory due to impaired encoding. *Science, 269*, 218–221.

Graham, F. K., & Kendall, B. S. (1960). Memory-for-Designs Test: Revised general manual. *Perceptual and Motor Skills, 11*, 147–188.

Granick, S., Kleban, M. H., & Weiss, A. D. (1976). Relationships between hearing loss and cognition in normally hearing aged persons. *Journal of Gerontology, 31*, 434–440.

Grant, I., & Adanis, K. M. (Eds.). (1986). *Neuropsychological assessment of neuropsychiatric disorders.* New York: Oxford University Press.

Gray, S. W., Ramsey, B. K., & Klaus, R. A. (1982). *From 3 to 20: The Early Training Project.* Baltimore, MD: University Park Press.

Green, R. F. (1969). Age–intelligence relationship between ages sixteen and sixty-four: A rising trend. *Developmental Psychology, 1*, 618–627.

Gregg, N., & Hoy, C. (1985). A comparison of the WAIS-R and the Woodcock-Johnson tests of cognitive ability with learning-disabled college students. *Journal of Psychoeducational Assessment, 3*, 267–274.

Gregg, N., Hoy, C., & Gay, A. F. (1996). *Adults with learning disabilities: Theoretical and practical perspectives.* New York: Guilford.

Gregory, R. J. (1987). *Adult intellectual assessment.* Boston: Allyn & Bacon.

Gresham, F. M., & Elliott, S. N. (1987). The relationship between adaptive behavior and social skills: Issues in definition and assessment. *Journal of Special Education, 21*, 167–182.

Gribbon, K., Schaie, K. W., & Parham, I. (1980). Complexity of life style and maintenance of intellectual abilities. *Journal of Social Issues, 36*, 47–61.

Gridley, B. E., & Roid, G. H. (1998). The use of the WISC-III with achievement tests. In A. Prifitera & D. H. Saklofske (Eds). *WISC-III clinical use and interpretation: Scientist-practitioner perspectives* (pp. 249–288). San Diego, CA: Academic Press.

Griffin, P. T., & Heffernan, A. (1983). Digit Span, forward and backward: Separate and unequal components of the WAIS Digit Span. *Perceptual and Motor Skills, 56*, 335–338.

Grigorenko, E. L. (2000). Heritability and intelligence. In R. J. Sternberg (Ed.), *Handbook of intelligence* (pp. 53–91). New York: Cambridge University Press.

Grigorenko, E. L., & Carter, A. S. (1996). Co-twin, peer and mother–child relationships and I.Q. in a Russian adolescent twin sample. *Journal of Russian & East European Psychology, 34*, 59–87.

Groff, M. G., & Hubble, L. M. (1981). Recategorized WISC-R scores of juvenile delinquents. *Journal of Learning Disabilities, 14*, 515–516.

Groff, M. G., & Hubble, L. M. (1982). WISC-R factor structures of younger and older youth with low IQs. *Journal of Consulting and Clinical Psychology, 50*, 148–149.

Grossman, F. M. (1983). Percentage of WAIS-R standardization sample obtaining Verbal–Performance discrepancies. *Journal of Consulting and Clinical Psychology, 51*, 641–642.

Grossman, F. M., Herman, D. O., & Matarazzo, J. D. (1985). Statistically inferred versus empirically observed VIQ–PIQ differences in the WAIS-R. *Journal of Clinical Psychology, 41*, 268–272.

Grossman, I., Chan, T., Parente, A., & Kaufman, A. S. (1994). Validation of two new brief cognitive tests with a WAIS-R short form using a hospitalized depressed sample. *Perceptual and Motor Skills, 78*, 107–111.

Grossman, I., Kaufman, A. S., Mednitsky, S., Scharff, L., & Dennis, B. (1994). Neurocognitive abilities for a clinically depressed sample versus a matched control group of normal individuals. *Psychiatry Research, 51*, 231–244.

Grossman, J. (Ed.) (1973). *Manual on terminology and classification in mental retardation* (1973 revision). Washington, DC: American Association on Mental Deficiency.

Grossman, J. (1983). *Classification in mental retardation.* Washington, DC: American Association on Mental Deficiency.

Groth-Marnat, G. (Ed.). (2000). *Neuropsychological assessment in clinical practice: A guide to test interpretation and integration.* New York: Wiley.

Groth-Marnat, G., Gallagher, R. E., Hale, J. B., & Kaplan, E. (2000). The Wechsler intelligence scales. In G. Groth-Marnat (Ed.), *Neuropsychological assessment in clinical practice: A guide to test interpretation and integration* (pp. 129–194). New York: Wiley.

Gruelich, W. W. (1957). A comparison of the physical growth and development of American-born and Japanese children. *American Journal of Physical Anthropology, 15*, 489–515.

Gruzelier, J., & Hammond, N. V. (1976). Schizophrenia: A dominant hemisphere temporal-limbic disorder? *Research Communications in Psychology, Psychiatry and Behavior, 1*, 33–72.

Gruzelier, J. H., & Mednick, S. (1976). WISC profiles of children at genetic risk for psychopathology: A neuropsychological interpretation. Unpublished manuscript cited by J. F. Gruzelier & N. V. Hammond (1976). Schizophrenia: A dominant hemisphere temporal-limbic disorder? *Research Communications in Psychology, Psychiatry and Behavior, 1*, 3–72.

Gruzelier, J., Seymour, K., Wilson, L., Jolley, A., & Hirsch, S. (1988). Impairments on neuropsychologic tests of temporohippocampal and frontohippocampal functions and word fluency in remitting schizophrenia and affective disorders. *Archives of General Psychiatry, 45*, 623–629.

Guilford, J. D. (1980). Fluid and crystallized intelligences: Two fanciful concepts. *Psychological Bulletin, 88*, 406–412.

Guilford, J. P. (1954). *Psychometric methods.* New York: McGraw-Hill.

Guilford, J. P. (1967). *The nature of human intelligence.* New York: McGraw-Hill.

Guilford, J. P. (1977). *Way beyond IQ: Guide to improving intelligence and creativity.* Buffalo, NY: Barely Limited.

Guilford, J. P. (1985). The structure-of-intellect model. In B. B. Wolman (Ed.), *Handbook of intelligence* (pp. 225–266). New York: Wiley.

Guilford, J. P. (1988). Some changes in the structure-of-intellect model. *Educational and Psychological Measurement, 48*, 1–4.

Gur, R. (1978). Left hemisphere dysfunction and left hemisphere overactivation in schizophrenia. *Journal of Abnormal Psychology, 87*, 226–238.

Gustafsson, J. E. (1994). General intelligence. R. J. Sternberg (Ed.), *Encyclopedia of human intelligence* (pp. 469–475). New York: Macmillan.

Gustafsson, J.-E., & Undheim, J. O. (1992). Stability and change in broad and narrow factors of intelligence from ages 12 to 15 years. *Journal of Educational Psychology, 84*(2), 141–149.

Gustafsson, J.-E., & Undheim, J. O. (1996). Individual differences in cognitive functions. In D. C. Berliner & R. C. Calfer (Eds.), *Handbook of educational psychology* (pp. 186–242). New York: MacMillan.

Gutkin, T. B. (1979a). WISC-R scatter indices: Useful information for differential diagnosis? *Journal of School Psychology, 17*, 368–371.

Gutkin, T. B. (1979b). The WISC-R verbal comprehension, perceptual organization, and freedom from distractibility deviation quotients: Data for practitioners. *Psychology in the Schools, 16*, 356–360.

Gutkin, T. B., & Reynolds, C. R. (1981a). Examination of the Selz and Reitan scatter index of neurological dysfunction with a nationally representative sample of normal children. *Journal of Clinical Neuropsychology, 3*, 38–41.

Gutkin, T. B., & Reynolds, C. R. (1981b). Factorial similarity of the WISC-R for white and black children from the standardization sample. *Journal of Educational Psychology, 73*, 227–231.

Gutkin, T. B., Reynolds, C. R., & Galvin, G. A. (1984). Factor analysis of the Wechsler Adult Intelligence Scale Revised

(WAIS-R): An examination of the standardization sample. *Journal of School Psychology, 22*, 83–93.

Haaland, K. Y., & Delaney, H. D. (1981). Motor deficits after left or right hemisphere damage due to stroke or tumor. *Neuropsychologia, 19*, 17–27.

Hager, P. C. (1985). Woodcock-Johnson Psycho-Educational Battery. In D. J. Keyser & R. C. Sweetland (Eds.), *Test critiques* (Vol. IV; pp. 683–703). Kansas City, MO: Test Corporation of America.

Halpern, A. S., Raffeld, P., Irvin, L., & Link, R. (1975). Measuring social and prevocational awareness in mildly retarded adolescents. *American Journal of Mental Deficiency, 80*, 81–89.

Halpern, D. F. (2000). *Sex differences in cognitive abilities* (3rd ed.). Mahwah, NJ: Erlbaum.

Halstead, W. C. (1947). *Brain and intelligence: A quantitative study of the frontal lobes.* Chicago: University of Chicago Press.

Halstead, W. C., & Wepman, J. M. (1949). The Halstead-Wepman aphasia screening test. *Journal of Speech and Hearing Disorders, 14*, 9–13.

Hamm, H., Wheeler, J., McCallum, S., Herrin, M., Hunter, D., & Catoe, C. (1976). A comparison between the WISC and WISC-R among educable mentally retarded students. *Psychology in the Schools, 13*, 4–8.

Hammeke, T., Golden, C. J., & Purisch, A. (1978). A standardized short and comprehensive neuropsychological test battery based on the Luria neuropsychological evaluation. *International Journal of Neuroscience, 8*, 135–141.

Hammill, D. D. (1985). *Detroit Tests of Learning Aptitude (DTLA-2).* Austin, TX: PRO-ED.

Hamsher, K., Benton, A. L., & Digre, K. (1980). Serial digit learning: Normative and clinical aspects. *Journal of Clinical Neuropsychology, 2*, 39–50.

Hamsher, K., Levin, H. S., & Benton, A. L. (1979). Facial recognition in patients with focal brain lesions. *Archives of Neurology, 36*, 837–839.

Handbook of mental delinquency: Psychological theory and research (2nd ed.; pp. 483–531). Hillsdale, NJ: Erlbaum.

Hansen, J. C., & Campbell, D. P. (1985). *Manual for the Strong Vocational Interest Blank-Strong-Campbell Interest Inventory* (4th ed.). Stanford, CA: Stanford University Press (distributed by Consulting Psychologists Press).

Harlow, H. F. (1938). Recovery of pattern discrimination in monkeys following occipital lobe lesions. *Psychological Bulletin, 35*, 686–687.

Harnqvist, K. (1968). Relative changes in intelligence from 13 to 18. *Scandinavian Journal of Psychology, 9*, 50–64.

Harrington, R. G. (1982). Caution: Standardized testing may be hazardous to the educational programs of intellectually gifted children. *Education, 103*, 112–117.

Harrington, R. G., & Jennings, V. (1986). A comparison of three short forms of the McCarthy Scales of Children's Abilities. *Contemporary Educational Psychology, 11*(2), 109–116.

Harrington, T. F., & O'Shea, A. J. (1982). *Manual for the Harrington-O'Shea Career Decision-Making System.* Circle Pines, MN: American Guidance Service.

Harris, A. B. (1980). Structural and chemical changes in experimental epileptic foci. In J. S. Lockard & A. A. Ward, Jr. (Eds.), *Epilepsy: A window to brain mechanisms* (pp. 149–164). New York: Raven Press.

Harris, L. J. (1980). Lateralized sex differences: Substrate and significance. *Behavioral and Brain Sciences, 3,* 236–237.

Harrison, P. L. (1987a). Research with adaptive behavior scales. *Journal of Special Education, 21,* 37–68.

Harrison, P. L. (1987b). *Review of the Wide Range Achievement Test-Revised.* Accession number AN-10010263, Buros Institute Data Base (Search Label MMYSXD), BRS Information Technologies.

Harrison, P. L. (1990). Mental retardation, adaptive behavior assessment, and giftedness. In A. S. Kaufman (Author), *Assessing adolescent and adult intelligence* (pp. 533–585). Boston, MA: Allyn & Bacon.

Harrison, P. L., Flanagan, D. P., Genshaft, J. L. (1997). An integration and synthesis of contemporary theories, tests, and issues in the field of intellectual assessment. In In D. P. Flanagan, J. L. Genshaft, & P. L. Harrison (Eds.), *Beyond traditional intellectual assessment: Contemporary and emerging theories, tests, and issues* (pp. 533–561). New York: Guilford.

Harrison, P. L., & Kamphaus, R. W. (1984, April). *Comparison between the K-ABC and Vineland Adaptive Behavior Scales.* Paper presented at the meeting of the National Association of School Psychologists, Philadelphia, PA.

Harrison, P. L., Kaufman, A. S., Hickman, J. A., & Kaufman, N. L. (1988). A survey of tests used for adult assessment. *Journal of Psychoeducational Assessment, 6,* 188–198.

Haskins, R. (1986). Social and cultural factors in risk assessment and mild mental retardation. In D. C. Farran & J. D. McKinney (Eds.), *Risk in intellectual and psychosocial development* (pp. 29–60). Orlando, FL: Academic Press.

Hattie, J. (1985). Methodology Review: Assessing unidimensionality of tests and items. *Applied Psychological Measurement, 9*(2), 139–164.

Haug, J. O. (1968). Pneumoencephalographic evidence of brain damage in chronic alcoholics. *Acta Psychiatrica Scandinavica (Supplement), 203,* 135–143.

Hauser, R. M. (1998). Trends in Black–White test-score differentials I: Uses and misuses of NAEP/SAT data. In U. Neisser (Ed.), *The rising curve: Long-term gains in IQ and related measures* (pp. 219–250). Washington, DC: American Psychological Association.

Hawkins, K. A. (1998). Indicators of brain dysfunction derived from graphic representations of the WAIS-III/WMS-III Technical Manual clinical samples data: A preliminary approach to clinical utility. *Clinical Neuropsychologist, 12,* 535–551.

Hawkins, K. A., & Sayward, H. K. (1994). Examiner judgment and actual stability of psychiatric inpatient intelligence quotients. *Clinical Neuropsychologist, 8,* 394–404.

Hawkins, K. A., Sullivan, T. E., & Choi, E. J. (1997). Memory deficits in schizophrenia: Inadequate assimilation or true amnesia? Findings from the Wechsler Memory Scale-Revised. *Journal of Psychiatry and Neuroscience, 22,* 169–179.

Hayes, S. C. (1999). Comparison of the Kaufman Brief Intelligence Test and the Matrix Intelligence Test-Short Form in an adolescent forensic population. *Psychological Assessment, 11,* 108–110.

Haynes, J. P. (1983). Comparative validity of three Wechsler short forms for delinquents. *Journal of Clinical Psychology, 39,* 275–278.

Haynes, J. P. (1985). Comparative validity of two WAIS-R short forms with clients of low IQ. *Journal of Clinical Psychology, 41,* 282–284.

Haynes, J. P., & Bensch, M. (1981). The P > V sign on the WISC-R and recidivism in delinquents. *Journal of Consulting and Clinical Psychology, 49,* 481.

Haynes, J. P., & Howard, R. C. (1986). Stability of WISC-R scores in a juvenile forensic sample. *Journal of Clinical Psychology, 42,* 534–537.

Haynes, J. P., Howard, R. C., & Haynes, S. M. (1987). Internal reliability of the WISC-R with male juvenile delinquents. *Journal of Clinical Psychology, 43,* 496–499.

Hays, J. R., & Solway, K. S. (1977). Violent behavior and differential Wechsler Intelligence Scale for Children characteristics. *Journal of Consulting and Clinical Psychology, 45,* 1187.

Hayslip, B., & Sterns, H. L. (1979). Age differences in relationships between crystallized and fluid intelligences and problem solving. *Journal of Gerontology, 34,* 404–414.

Head, H. (1926). *Aphasia and kindred disorders of speech.* London: Cambridge University Press.

Heath, C. P., & Obrzut, J. E. (1986). Adaptive behavior: Concurrent validity. *Journal of Psychoeducational Assessment, 4,* 53–59.

Heaton, R. K., Chelune, G. J., Talley, J. L., Kay, G. G., & Curtis, G. (1993). *Wisconsin Card Sorting Test manual.* Odessa, FL: Psychological Assessment Resources.

Heaton, R. K., Grant, I., & Matthews, C. G. (1986). Differences in neuropsychological test performance associated with age, education, and sex. In I. Grant & K. M. Adams (Eds.), *Neuropsychological assessment of neuropsychiatric disorders* (pp. 100–120). New York: Oxford University Press.

Heaton, R. K., Manly, J. J., Taylor, M. J., & Tulsky, D. S. (2001). Association between demographic characteristics on WAIS-III and WMS-III. Manuscript in preparation.

Heaton, R. K., Nelson, L. M., Thompson, D. S., Burks, J. S., & Franklin, G. M. (1985). Neuropsychological findings in relapsing–remitting and chronic–progressive multiple sclerosis. *Journal of Consulting and Clinical Psychology, 53,* 103–110.

Heaton, R. K., Schmitz, S. P., Avitable, N., & Lehman, R. A. W. (1987). Effects of lateralized cerebral lesions on oral reading, reading comprehension, and spelling. *Journal of Clinical and Experimental Neuropsychology, 9,* 711–722.

Heber, R. F. (1961). A manual on terminology and classification in mental retardation. *American Journal of Mental Deficiency, 1959, 64,* Monograph Supplement (Revised ed.).

Heber, R. F., & Garber, H. (1970). *An experiment in the prevention of cultural–familial retardation.* Paper presented at the Second Congress of the International Association for the Scientific Study of Mental Deficiency, Warsaw, Poland.

Hecaen, H., Ajuriaguerra, J. de, & Massonet, J. (1951). Les troubles visuoconstructifs par lésion parieto-occipitale droit. *Encephale, 40,* 122–179.

Hecaen, H., & Angelergues, R. (1962). Agnosia for faces (prosopagnosia). *Archives of Neurology, 7,* 92–100.

Heilbrun, A. B. (1956). Psychological test performance as a function of lateral localization of cerebral lesions. *Journal of Comparative and Physiological Psychology, 49,* 10–14.

Heilman, K. M., Bowers, D., & Valenstein, F. (1985). *Clinical neuropsychology* (2nd ed.). New York: Oxford University Press.

Heimburger, R. F., & Reitan, R. M. (1961). Easily administered written test for lateralizing brain lesions. *Journal of Neurosurgery, 18,* 301–312.

Heinemann, A. W., Harper, R. G., Friedman, E. C., & Whitney, J. (1985). The relative utility of the Shipley-Hartford scale: Prediction of WAIS-R IQ. *Journal of Clinical Psychology, 41,* 547–551.

Heinrichs, R. W., & Celinski, M. J. (1987). Frequency of occurrence of a WAIS dementia profile in male head trauma patients. *Journal of Clinical and Experimental Neuropsychology, 9,* 187–190.

Helmstadter, G. C. (1985). Review of Watson-Glaser Critical Thinking Appraisal. In J. V. Mitchell (Ed.), *The ninth mental measurements yearbook* (pp. 1693–1694). Lincoln, NE: Buros Institute of Mental Measurements, University of Nebraska Press.

Hengstler, D. D., Reichard, D. J., Uhl, N. P., & Goldman, B. A. (1981, May). *Prediction of academic success with the Myers-Briggs Type Indicator (MBTI).* Paper presented at the 21st annual forum of the Association for Institutional Research, Minneapolis, MN. (ERIC Document Reproduction Service No. ED 205 129).

Henning, J. J., & Levy, R. H. (1967). Verbal–performance IQ differences of white and Negro delinquents on the WISC and WAIS. *Journal of Clinical Psychology, 23,* 164–168.

Henrichs, T. F., & Amolsch, T. J. (1978). A note on the actuarial interpretation of WAIS profile patterns. *Journal of Personality Assessment, 42,* 418–420.

Henrichs, T. F., Krauskopf, C. J., & Amolsch, T. J. (1982). Personality descriptions from the WAIS: A comparison of systems. *Journal of Personality Assessment, 46,* 544–549.

Henry, S. A., & Wittman, R. D. (1981). Diagnostic implications of Bannatyne's recategorized WISC-R scores for learning disabled children. *Journal of Learning Disabilities, 14,* 517–520.

Henson, F. O., & Bennett, L. M. (1985). Kaufman Test of Educational Achievement. In D. J. Keyser & R. C. Sweetland (Eds.), *Test critiques* (Vol. IV; 368–375). Kansas City, MO: Test Corporation of America.

Herbert, M. (1998). Kaufman Short Neuropsychological Assessment Procedure. In J. C. Impara & B. S. Plake (Eds.), *The thirteenth mental measurements yearbook* (pp. 573–575). Lincoln, NE: Buros Institute of Mental Measurements, University of Nebraska Press.

Herman, D. O. (1988). Development of the Wechsler Memory Scale-Revised. *Clinical Neuropsychologist, 2,* 102–106.

Hermelin, B., & O'Connor, N. (1970). *Psychological experiments with autistic children.* New York: Pergamon.

Herring, J. P. (1922). *Herring revision of the Binet-Simon tests: Examination manual-Form A.* London: World Book.

Herring, S., & Reitan, R. M. (1986). Sex similarities in Verbal and Performance IQ deficits following unilateral cerebral lesions. *Journal of Consulting and Clinical Psychology, 54,* 537–541.

Herrnstein, R. J., & Murray, C. (1994). *The bell curve.* New York: Free Press.

Hertzog, C. (1989). Influences of cognitive slowing on age differences in intelligence. *Developmental Psychology, 25,* 636–651.

Hertzog, C., & Schaie, K. W. (1988). Stability and change in adult intelligence: Simultaneous analysis of longitudinal means and covariance structures. *Psychology and Aging, 3,* 122–130.

Hertzog, C., Schaie, K. W., & Gribbin, K. (1978). Cardiovascular disease and changes in intellectual functioning from middle to old age. *Journal of Gerontology, 33,* 872–883.

Hessler, G. L. (1982). *Use and interpretation of the Woodcock-Johnson Psycho-Educational Battery.* Chicago: Riverside.

Hessler, G. L. (1993). *Use and interpretation of the Woodcock-Johnson Psycho-Educational Battery-Revised.* Chicago: Riverside.

Hetherington, E. M., & Parke, R. D. (1986). *Child psychology* (3rd ed.). New York: McGraw-Hill.

Hier, D. B., & Kaplan, J. (1980). Are sex differences in cerebral organization clinically significant? *Behavioral and Brain Sciences, 3,* 238–239.

Hightower, M. G., & Anderson, R. D. (1986). Memory evaluation of alcoholics with Russell's revised Wechsler Memory Scale. *Journal of Clinical Psychology, 42,* 1000–1005.

Hill, A. L. (1978). WAIS subtest score characteristics of institutionalized mentally retarded samples. *Perceptual and Motor Skills, 47,* 131–134.

Hill, T. D., Reddon, J. R., & Jackson, D. N. (198S). The factor structure of the Wechsler scales: A brief review. *Clinical Psychology Review, 5,* 287–306.

Hilliard, A. G., III. (1979). Standardization and cultural bias as impediments to the scientific study and validation of "intelligence." *Journal of Research and Development in Education, 12,* 47–58.

Hiltonsmith, R. W., Hayman, P. M., & Kleinman, D. (1984). Predicting WAIS-R scores from the Revised Beta for low functioning minority group offenders. *Journal of Clinical Psychology, 40,* 1063–1066.

Hiltonsmith, R. W., Hayman, P. M., & Ursprung, A. W. (1982). Beta-WAIS comparisons with low functioning minority group offenders: A cautionary note. *Journal of Clinical Psychology, 38,* 864–866.

Himelstein, P. (1983). An additional modification for the rapid calculation of the WAIS Verbal IQ. *Journal of Clinical Psychology, 39,* 259–260.

Hoff, A. L., Shukla, S., Aronson, T., Cook, B., Ollo, C., Baruch, S., Jandorf, L., & Schwartz, J. (1990). Failure to differentiate bipolar disorder from schizophrenia on measures of neuropsychological function. *Schizophrenia Research, 3,* 253–260.

Holland, T. R., & Watson, C. G. (1980). Multivariate analysis of WAIS-MMPI relationships among brain-damaged, schizophrenic, neurotic, and alcoholic patients. *Journal of Clinical Psychology, 36,* 352–359.

Hollinger, C. L., & Sarvis, P. H. (1984). Interpretation of the PPVT-R: A pure measure of verbal comprehension? *Psychology in the Schools, 21,* 97–102.

Holman, J., & Bruininks, R. (1985). Assessing and training adaptive behaviors. In K. C. Lakin & R. H. Bruininks (Eds.), *Strategies for achieving community integration of developmentally disabled citizens* (pp. 73–104). Baltimore, MD: Paul H. Brookes.

Hom, J., & Reitan, R. M. (1982). Effect of lateralized cerebral damage upon contralateral and ipsilateral performances. *Journal of Clinical Neuropsychology, 4,* 249–268.

Hom, J., & Reitan, R. M. (1984). Neuropsychological correlates of rapidly vs. slowly growing intrinsic neoplasms. *Journal of Clinical Neuropsychology, 6,* 309–324.

Honzik, M. D., Macfarlane, J. W., & Allen, E. (1948). The stability of mental test performance between two and eighteen years. *Journal of Experimental Education, 17,* 309–324.

Hooper, F. H., Fitzgerald, J., & Papalia, D. (1971). Piagetian theory and the aging process: Extensions and expectations. *Human Development, 2,* 3–20.

Hooper, F. H., Hooper, J. O., & Colbert, K. K. (1985). Personality and memory correlates of intellectual functioning in adulthood: Piagetian and psychometric assessments. *Human Development, 28,* 101–107.

Horn, E., & Fuchs, D. (1987). Using adaptive behavior assessment and intervention: An overview. *Journal of Special Education, 21,* 11–26.

Horn, J. L. (1965). *Fluid and crystallized intelligence: A factor analytic and developmental study of the structure among primary mental abilities.* Unpublished doctoral dissertation, University of Illinois, Urbana-Champaign.

Horn, J. L. (1968). Organization of abilities and the development of intelligence. *Psychological Review, 75,* 242–259.

Horn, J. L. (1970). Organization of data on life-span development of human abilities. In L. R. Goulet & P. B. Baltes (Eds.), *Life-span developmental psychology: Research and theory* (pp. 424–466). New York: Academic Press.

Horn, J. L. (1978). Human ability systems. In P. B. Baltes (Ed.), *Life-span development and behavior* (Vol. 1; pp. 211–256). New York: Academic Press.

Horn, J. L. (1982). The theory of fluid and crystallized intelligence in relation to concepts of cognitive psychology and aging in adulthood. In F. I. M. Craik & S. Trehub (Eds.), *Advances in the study of communication and affect: Volume 8. Aging and cognitive processes* (pp. 237–278). New York: Plenum.

Horn, J. L. (1985). Remodeling old models of intelligence. In B. B. Wolman (Ed.), *Handbook of intelligence* (pp. 267–300). New York: Wiley.

Horn, J. L. (1988). Thinking about human abilities. In J. R. Nesselroade (Ed.), *Handbook of multivariate psychology* (pp. 645–685). New York: Academic Press.

Horn, J. L. (1989). Cognitive diversity: A framework of learning. In P. L. Ackerman, R. J. Sternberg, & R. Glaser (Eds.), *Learning and individual differences* (pp. 61–116). New York: Freeman.

Horn, J. L. (1991). Measurement of intellectual capabilities: A review of theory. In K. S. McGrew, J. K. Werder, & R. W. Woodcock, *WJ R technical manual* (pp. 197–232). Chicago: Riverside.

Horn, J. L., & Cattell, R. B. (1966). Refinement and test of the theory of fluid and crystallized intelligence. *Journal of Educational Psychology, 57,* 253–270.

Horn, J. L., & Cattell, R. B. (1967). Age differences in fluid and crystallized intelligence. *Acta Psychologica, 26,* 107–129.

Horn, J. L., & Donaldson, G. (1976). On the myth of intellectual decline in adulthood. *American Psychologist, 31,* 701–719.

Horn, J. L., & Donaldson, G. (1977). Faith is not enough: A response to the Baltes-Schaie claim that intelligence will not wane. *American Psychologist, 32,* 369–373.

Horn, J. L., & Donaldson, G. (1980). Cognitive development, II: Adulthood development of human abilities. In O. G. Brim & J. Kagan (Eds.), *Constancy and change in human development: A volume of review essays* (pp. 445–529). Cambridge, MA: Harvard University Press.

Horn, J. L., Donaldson, G., & Engstrom, R. (1981). Apprehension, memory, and fluid intelligence decline in adulthood. *Research on Aging, 3,* 33–84.

Horn, J. L., & Hofer, S. M. (1992). Major abilities and development in the adult period. In R. J. Sternberg & C. A. Berg (Eds.), *Intellectual development* (pp. 44–99). Boston, MA: Cambridge University Press.

Horn, J. L., Loehlin, J. C., & Willerman, L. (1979). Intellectual resemblance among adoptive and biological relatives: The Texas adoption project. *Behavior Genetics, 9,* 177–207.

Horn, J. L., & McArdle, J. J. (1980). Perspectives on mathematical/statistical model building (MASMOB) in research on aging. In L. W. Poon (Ed.), *Aging in the 1980s: Psychological issues* (pp. 503–541). Washington DC: American Psychological Association.

Horn, J. L., & Noll, J. (1997). Human cognitive capabilities: *Gf-Gc* theory. In D. P. Flanagan, J. L. Genshaft, & P. L. Harrison (Eds.), *Contemporary intellectual assessment: Theories, tests and issues* (pp. 53–91). New York: Guilford.

Horn, J. L., & Risberg, J. (1989). Blood flow in the brain and adulthood aging of cognitive function. In H. Wold (Ed.), *Theoretical empiricism: A general rationale for scientific model-building* (pp. 201–233). New York: Paragon House.

Howell, R. J., Evans, L., & Donning, L. H. (1958). A comparison of test scores for a 16- to 17-year-old age group of Navajo Indians with standardization norms for the Wechsler Adult Intelligence Scale (Arizona and New Mexico). *Journal of Social Psychology, 47,* 355–359.

Huber, S. J., Paulsen, G. W., Shuttleworth, E. C., Chakeres, D., Clapp, L. E., Pakalnis, A., Weiss, K., & Rammohan, K. (1987). Magnetic resonance imaging correlates of dementia in multiple sclerosis. *Archives of Neurology, 44,* 732–736.

Hughes, H. H., & Converse, H. D. (1962). Characteristics of the gifted: A case for a sequel to Herman's study. *Exceptional Children, 29,* 179–183.

Hultsch, D. F., Hammer, M., & Small, B. (1993). Age differences in cognitive performance in later life: Relationships to self-reported health and activity life style. *Journal of Gerontology: Psychological Sciences, 48,* 1–11.

Hultsch, D. F., Hertzog, C., Small, B. J., & Dixon, R. A. (1999). Use it or lose it: Engaged lifestyle as a buffer of cognitive decline in aging? *Psychology and Aging, 14,* 245–263.

Humphreys, L. G. (1986). Commentary. *Journal of Vocational Behavior, 29,* 421–427.

Hunsley, J. (1996). Assessment practices of clinical psychologists. *The Forum, 27,* 315–316.

Hunt, J. McV. (1961). *Intelligence and experience.* New York: Ronald.

Hunter, J. E. (1986). Cognitive ability, cognitive aptitudes, job knowledge, and job performance. *Journal of Vocational Behavior, 29,* 340–362.

Hunter, J. E., & Hunter, R. F. (1984). Validity and utility of alternate predictors of job performance. *Psychological Bulletin, 96,* 72–98.

Husen, T. (1951). The influence of schooling upon IQ. *Theoria, 17,* 61–68.

Hutton, J. B., Bubes, R., & Muir, S. (1992). Assessment practices of school psychologists: Ten years later. *School Psychology Review, 21,* 271–284.

Hyde, J. S. (1981). How large are cognitive gender differences? A meta-analysis using w2 and d. *American Psychologist, 36,* 892–901.

Hyde, J. S., & Linn, M. C. (1988). Are there sex differences in verbal abilities? A meta-analysis. *Psychological Bulletin, 104,* 53–69.

Hymowitz, P., Hunt, H. F., Carr, A. C., Hurt, S. W., & Spear, W. E. (1983). The WAIS and Rorschach test in diagnosing borderline personality. *Journal of Personality Assessment, 47,* 588–596.

Hynd, G. W. (1988a). *Neuropsychological assessment in clinical child psychology.* Newbury Park, CA: Sage.

Hynd, G. W. (1988b). R.I.P. (or ripping) IQ: A reaction. *NASP Communique, 17,*(4), 4–5.

Hynd, G. W., & Willis, W. G. (1988). *Pediatric neuropsychology.* Orlando, FL: Grune & Stratton.

Inglis, J., & Lawson, J. S. (1981). Sex differences in the effects of unilateral brain damage on intelligence. *Science, 212,* 693–695.

Inglis, J., & Lawson, J. S. (1982). A meta-analysis of sex differences in the effects of unilateral brain damage on intelligence test results. *Canadian Journal of Psychology, 36,* 670–683.

Inglis, J., & Lawson, J. S. (1986). A principal components analysis of the Kaufman Assessment Battery for Children (K-ABC): Implications for the test results of children with learning disabilities. *Journal of Learning Disabilities, 19,* 80–85.

Inglis, J., Ruckman, M., Lawson, J. S., MacLean, A. W., & Monga, T. N. (1982). Sex differences in the cognitive effects of unilateral brain damage. *Cortex, 18,* 257–276.

Ingram, F., Caroselli, J., Robinson, H., Hetzel, R. D., Reed, K., & Masel, B. E. (1998). The PPVT-R: Validity as a quick screen of intelligence in a postacute rehabilitation setting for brain-injured adults. *Journal of Clinical Psychology, 54,* 877–884.

Insua, A. M. (1983). WAIS-R factor structures in two cultures. *Journal of Cross-Cultural Psychology, 14,* 427–438.

Irvin, L. K., Halpern, A. S., Reynolds, W. M. (1977). Assessing social and prevocational awareness in mildly and moderately retarded individuals. *American Journal of Mental Deficiency, 82,* 266–272.

Ishikuma, T., Applegate, B., & Kaufman, A. S. (1989). *WAIS-R interpretation from the factor-analytic, Bannatyne, and Horn models.* Unpublished manuscript. University of Alabama, Tuscaloosa.

Ishikuma, T., Moon, S., & Kaufman, A. S. (1988). Sequential–simultaneous analysis of Japanese children's performance on the Japanese McCarthy Scales. *Perceptual and Motor Skills, 66,* 355–362.

Isingrini, M., & Taconnat, L. (1998). Alterations de l'intelligence fluide et de la mémoire épisodique au cours du vieillissement: Des mécanismes independants? [Changes in fluid intelligence and episodic memory during aging: Are the mechanisms independent?] *Année Psychologique, 98,* 61–60.

Isingrini, M., & Vazou, F. (1997). Relation between fluid intelligence and frontal lobe functioning in older adults. *International Journal of Aging & Human Development, 45,* 99–109.

Ivnik, R. J., Malec, J. F., Smith, G. E., Tangalos, E. G., Petersen, C., Kokmen, E., & Kurland, L. T. (1992). Mayo's Older Americans Normative Studies: WAIS-R norms for ages 56 to 97. *Clinical Neuropsychologist, 6* (Suppl.), 1–30.

Ivnik, R. J., Sharbrough, F. W., & Laws, E. R., Jr. (1987). Effects of anterior temporal lobectomy on cognitive function. *Journal of Clinical Psychology, 43,* 128–137.

Jacklin, C. N. (1989). Female and male: Issues of gender. *American Psychologist, 44,* 127–133.

Jackson, J. H. (1878). On affections of speech from disease of the brain. *Brain, 1,* 304–330.

Jackson, R. H. (1981). Other genetic disorders. In J. E. Lindemann (Ed.), *Psychological and behavioral aspects of physical disability* (pp. 69–116). New York: Plenum.

Jaffe, L. S. (1983). *A study of various factors influencing examiner scoring reliability on WAIS-R Vocabulary, Comprehension, and Similarities subtests.* Unpublished doctoral dissertation, California School of Professional Psychology, San Diego.

Jarvik, L. F., & Bank, L. (1983). Aging twins: Longitudinal psychometric data. In K. W. Schaie (Ed.), *Longitudinal studies of adult psychological development* (pp. 40–63). New York: Guilford.

Jarvik, L. F., Kallman, F. J., & Falek, A. (1962). Intellectual changes in aged twins. *Journal of Gerontology, 17,* 289–294.

Jastak, S., & Wilkinson, G. S. (1984). *WRAT-R: Wide Range Achievement Text administration manual.* Los Angeles: Western Psychological Services.

Jeffrey, T. B., & Jeffrey, L. K. (1984). The utility of the modified WAIS in a clinical setting. *Journal of Clinical Psychology, 40,* 1067–1069.

Jencks, C., Smith, M., Acland, H., Bane, M. J., Cohen, D., Gintis, H., Heyns, B., & Michelson, S. (1972). *Inequality: A reassessment of the effect of family and schooling in America.* New York: Basic Books.

Jensen, A. R. (1969). How much can we boost IQ and scholastic achievement? *Harvard Educational Review, 39,* 1–123.

Jensen, A. R. (1973). *Educability and group differences.* New York: Harper & Row.

Jensen, A. R. (1980). *Bias in mental testing.* New York: Free Press.

Jensen, A. R. (1982a). Level I/Level II: Factors or categories? *Journal of Educational Psychology, 74,* 868–873.

Jensen, A. R. (1982b). The chronometry of intelligence. In R. J. Sternberg (Ed.), *Recent advances in research on intelligence.* Hillsdale, NJ: Erlbaum.

Jensen, A. R. (1984). The black–white difference on the K-ABC: Implications for future tests. *Journal of Special Education, 18,* 377–408.

Jensen, A. R. (1985a). Methodological and statistical techniques for the chronometric study of mental abilities. In C. R. Reynolds & V. L. Willson (Eds.), *Methodological and statistical advances in the study of individual differences* (pp. 51–116). New York: Plenum.

Jensen, A. R. (1985b). The nature of the black–white difference on various psychometric tests: Spearman's hypothesis. *Behavioral and Brain Sciences, 8,* 193–219.

Jensen, A. R. (1987). The *g* beyond factor analysis. In R. R. Ronning, J. C. Conoley, J. A. Glover, & J. C. Witt (Eds.), *The influence of cognitive psychology on testing: Buros-Nebraska Symposium on Measurement and Testing* (Vol. 3; pp. 87–142). Hillsdale, NJ: Erlbaum.

Jensen, A. R. (1998). *The g factor: The science of mental ability.* Westport, CT: Praeger.

Jensen, A. R., & Figueroa, R. A. (1975). Forward and backward digit-span interaction with race and IQ. *Journal of Educational Psychology, 67,* 882–893.

Jensen, A. R., & Reynolds, C. R. (1982). Race, social class and ability patterns on the WISC-R. *Personality and Individual Differences, 3,* 423–438.

Jensen, A. R., & Reynolds, C. R. (1983). Sex differences on the WISC-R. *Personality and Individual Differences, 4,* 223–226.

Jensen, J. A., & Armstrong, R. J. (1985). *Slosson Intelligence Test (SIT) for children and adults: Expanded norms tables application and development.* East Aurora, NY: Slosson Educational Publications.

Jester, R. E., & Guinagh, B. J. (1983). The Gordon Parent Education Infant and Toddler Program. In Consortium for Longitudinal Studies (Eds.), *As the twig is bent…lasting effects of preschool programs* (pp. 103–132). Hillsdale, NJ: Erlbaum.

Jirsa, J. E. (1994). Kaufman Brief Intelligence Test. In D. Keyser & R. Sweetland (Eds.), *Test critiques* (Vol. 10; pp. 340–349). Austin, TX: Pro-Ed.

John, K., & Rattan, G. (1991). A comparison of short-term memory tests as predictors of reading achievement for learning disabled and educable mentally retarded students. *Journal of School Psychology, 29*(4), 309–318.

Johnson, D. T. (1969). Introversion, extraversion, and social intelligence: A replication. *Journal of Clinical Psychology, 25,* 181–183.

Johnson, D. L., & Walker, T. (1991). A follow-up evaluation of the Houston Parent–Child Development Center: School performance. *Journal of Early Intervention, 15*(3), 226–236.

Johnson, F. N., & Barker, G. J. (1972). Effects of lithium chloride on learned responses. *Diseases of the Nervous System, 33,* 664–666.

Jones, C. L. (1992). Recovery from head trauma: A curvilinear process? In C. J. Long & L. K. Ross (Eds.), *Handbook for head trauma: Acute care to recovery* (pp. 247–270). New York: Plenum.

Jones, H. E., & Conrad, H. S. (1933). The growth and decline of intelligence: A study of a homogeneous group between the ages of ten and sixty. *Genetic Psychology Monographs, 13,* 223–298.

Jones, R. S., & Torgesen, J. K. (1981). Analysis of behaviors involved in performance of the Block Design subtest of the WISC-R. *Intelligence, 5,* 321–328.

Jones-Gotman, M., & Milner, B. (1977). Design fluency: The invention of nonsense drawings after focal cortical lesions. *Neuropsychologia, 15,* 653–674.

Joschko, M. (1986). Clinical and neuropsychological outcome following psychosurgery. In I. Grant & K. M. Adams (Eds.), *Neuropsychological assessment of neuropsychiatric disorders* (pp. 300–320). New York: Oxford University Press.

Josiassen, R. C., Curry, L., Roemier, R. A., DeBease, C., & Mancall, E. L. (1982). Patterns of intellectual deficit in Huntington's disease. *Journal of Clinical Neuropsychology, 4,* 173–183.

Joynt, R. J., Benton, A. E., & Fogel, M. (1962). Behavioral and pathological correlates of motor impersistence. *Neurology, 12,* 876–881.

Judd, L. L., Hubbard, B., Janowsky, D. S., Huey, L. Y., & Takahashi, K. I. (1977). The effect of lithium carbonate on the cognitive functions of normal subjects. *Archives of General Psychiatry, 34,* 355–357.

Juolasmaa, A., Outakoski, J., Hirvenoja, R., Tienari, P., Sotanlemi, K., & Takkunen, J. (1981). Effect of open heart surgery on intellectual performance. *Journal of Clinical Neuropsychology, 3,* 181–197.

Jurko, M. F., & Andy, O. J. (1973). Psychological changes correlated with thalamotomy site. *Journal of Neurology, Neurosurgery, and Psychiatry, 36,* 846–852.

Kagin, E. F. (1968). Adaptive behavior and mental retardation during the Renaissance and Reformation. *Proceedings of the 76th Annual Convention of the American Psychological Association, 687–688.*

Kail, R. (1991a). Development of processing speed in childhood and adolescence. *Advances in Child Development and Behavior, 23,* 151–184.

Kail, R. (1991b). Developmental change in speed of processing during childhood and adolescence. *Psychological Bulletin, 109,* 490–501.

Kail, R., & Salthouse, T. A. (1994). Processing speed as a mental capacity. *Acta Psychologica, 86,* 199–225.

Kaiser, S. M. (1986). *Ability patterns of black and white adults on the Wechsler Adult Intelligence Scale-Revised independent of general intelligence and as a function of socioeconomic status.* Unpublished doctoral dissertation, Texas A & M University.

Kalmar, K., Massoth, N. A., Gallagher, D., Westerveld, M., & Lanzi, A. (1985, October). *Wechsler subtest differences and similarities among right-handed torque and non-torque subjects for the WAIS-R, WISC-R and WPPSI intelligence scales.* Paper presented at National Academy of Neuropsychology, Philadelphia, Pa.

Kamin, L. J. (1974). *The science and politics of IQ.* Pontiac, MD: Erlbaum.

Kamphaus, R. W. (1987). Conceptual and psychometric issues in the assessment of adaptive behavior. *Journal of Special Education, 21,* 27–36.

Kamphaus, R. W. (1993). *Clinical assessment of children's intelligence.* Boston: Allyn & Bacon.

Kamphaus, R. W., & Reynolds, C. R. (1987). *Clinical and research applications of the K-ABC.* Circle Pines, MN: American Guidance Service.

Kandel, E., Mednick, S. A., Kirkegaard-Sorensen, L., Hutchings, B., Knop, J., Rosenberg, R., & Schulsinger, F. (1988). IQ as a protective factor for subjects at high risk for antisocial behavior. *Journal of Consulting and Clinical Psychology, 56,* 224–226.

Kane, R. L., Parsons, O. A., & Goldstein, G. (1985). Statistical relationships and discriminative accuracy of the Halstead-Reitan, Luria-Nebraska, and Wechsler IQ scores in the identification of brain damage. *Journal of Clinical and Experimental Neuropsychology, 7,* 211–223.

Kaplan, C. (1992). Ceiling effects in assessing high-IQ children with the WPPSI-R. *Journal of Clinical Child Psychology, 21,* 403–406.

Kaplan, E., Fein, D., Morris, R., & Delis, D. (1991). *WAIS-R as a neuropsychological instrument.* San Antonio, TX: The Psychological Corporation.

Karnes, F. A., & Brown, K. E. (1980). Factor analysis of the WISC-R for the gifted. *Journal of Educational Psychology, 72,* 197–199.

Karson, S., Pool, K. B., & Freund, S. L. (1957). The effects of scale and practice on WAIS and W-B I test scores. *Journal of Consulting Psychology, 21,* 241–245.

Karzmark, P., Heaton, R. K., Grant, I., & Matthews, C. G. (1984). Use of demographic variables to predict Full Scale IQ and level of performance on the Halstead-Reitan battery. *Journal of Consulting and Clinical Psychology, 52,* 663–665,

Kasper, J., Throne, F., & Schulman, J. (1968). A study of the inter-judge reliability in scoring the responses of a group of mentally retarded boys to three WISC subscales. *Educational and Psychological Measurement, 28,* 469–477.

Kaufman, A. S. (1972). A short form of the Wechsler Preschool and Primary Scale of Intelligence. *Journal of Consulting and Clinical Psychology, 39,* 361–369.

Kaufman, A. S. (1973). The relationship of WPPSI IQs to SES and other background variables. *Journal of Clinical Psychology, 29,* 354–357.

Kaufman, A. S. (1975). Factor analysis of the WISC-R at 11 age levels between 6½ and 16½ years. *Journal of Consulting and Clinical Psychology, 43,* 135–147.

Kaufman, A. S. (1976a). A four-test short form of the WISC-R. *Contemporary Educational Psychology, 1,* 180–196.

Kaufman, A. S. (1976b). A new approach to the interpretation of test scatter on the WISC-R. *Journal of Learning Disabilities, 9,* 160–168.

Kaufman, A. S. (1976c). Verbal–performance IQ discrepancies on the WISC-R. *Journal of Consulting and Clinical Psychology, 44,* 739–744.

Kaufman, A. S. (1977). Should short-form validity coefficients be corrected? *Journal of Consulting and Clinical Psychology, 45,* 1159–1161.

Kaufman, A. S. (1979a). *Intelligent testing with the WISC-R.* New York: Wiley.

Kaufman, A. S. (1979b). The role of speed on WISC-R performance across the age range. *Journal of Consulting and Clinical Psychology, 47,* 595–597.

Kaufman, A. S. (1983a). Comparison of the performance of matched groups of black children and white children on the Wechsler Preschool and Primary Scale of Intelligence. *Journal of Consulting and Clinical Psychology, 41,* 186–191.

Kaufman, A. S. (1983b). Intelligence: Old concepts–new perspectives. In G. W. Hynd (Ed.), *The school psychologist: An introduction* (pp. 95–117). Syracuse, NY: Syracuse University Press.

Kaufman, A. S. (1985a). Review of Wechsler Adult Intelligence Scale-Revised. In J. V. Mitchell (Ed.), *The ninth mental measurements yearbook* (pp. 1699–1703). Lincoln, NE: Buros Institute of Mental Measurements, University of Nebraska Press.

Kaufman, A. S. (1985b). Review of Woodcock-Johnson Psycho-Educational Battery. In J. V. Mitchell (Ed.), *The ninth mental measurements yearbook* (pp. 1762–1765). Lincoln, NE: Buros Institute of Mental Measurements, University of Nebraska Press.

Kaufman, A. S. (1988). Funeral oration for a long-dead corpse: A reply to Lezak. *National Association of School Psychologists Communique, 17*(4), 5.

Kaufman, A. S. (1990). *Assessing adolescent and adult intelligence.* Boston, MA: Allyn & Bacon.

Kaufman, A. S. (1992). Evaluation of the WISC-III and WPPSI-R for gifted children. *Roeper Review, 14,* 154–158.

Kaufman, A. S. (1993a). Joint exploratory factor analysis of the Kaufman Assessment Battery for Children and the Kaufman Adolescent and Adult Intelligence Test for 11- and 12-year-olds. *Journal of Clinical Child Psychology, 22,* 355–364.

Kaufman, A. S. (1993b). King WISC the third assumes the throne. *Journal of School Psychology, 31,* 345–354.

Kaufman, A. S. (1994a). *Intelligent testing with the WISC-III.* New York: Wiley.

Kaufman, A. S. (1994b). Practice effects. In R. J. Sternberg (Ed.), *Encyclopedia of intelligence* (Vol. II; pp. 828–833). New York: Macmillan.

Kaufman, A. S. (1999). Genetics of childhood disorders: Genetics and intelligence II. *Journal of the American Academy of Child and Adolescent Psychiatry, 38,* 626–628.

Kaufman, A. S. (2000a). Seven questions about the WAIS-III regarding differences in abilities across the 16- to 89-year life span. *School Psychology Quarterly, 15,* 3–29.

Kaufman, A. S. (2000b). Tests of Intelligence. In R. J. Sternberg (Ed.), *Handbook of intelligence* (pp. 445–476). New York: Cambridge University Press.

Kaufman, A. S. (2001). WAIS-III IQs, Horn's theory, and generational changes from young adulthood to old age. *Intelligence, 29,* 131–167.

Kaufman, A. S., & Applegate, B. (1988). Short forms of the K-ABC Mental Processing and Achievement scales at ages 4 to 12½ years for clinical and screen purposes. *Journal of Clinical Child Psychology, 17*(4), 359–369.

Kaufman, A. S., & Doppelt, J. E. (1976). Analysis of WISC-R standardization data in terms of the stratification variables. *Child Development, 47,* 165–171.

Kaufman, A. S., & Harrison, P. L. (1986). Intelligence tests and gifted assessment: What are the positives? *Roeper Review, 8,* 154–159.

Kaufman, A. S., Harrison, P. L., & Ittenbach, R. F. (1990). Intelligence testing in the schools. In T. Gutkin & C. R. Reynolds (Eds.), *The handbook of school psychology* (2nd ed.; pp. 289–327). New York: Wiley.

Kaufman, A. S., & Horn, J. L. (1996). Age changes on tests of fluid and crystallized ability for women and men on the

Kaufman Adolescent and Adult Intelligence Test (KAIT) at ages 17–94 years. *Archives of Clinical Neuropsychology, 11,* 97–121.

Kaufman, A. S., & Ishikuma, T. (1989). *Amazingly short forms of the WAIS-R.* Unpublished manuscript. University of Alabama, Tuscaloosa.

Kaufman, A. S., Ishikuma, T., & Kaufman, N. L. (1994). A Horn analysis of the factors measured by the WAIS-R, Kaufman Adolescent and Adult Intelligence Test (KAIT), and two new brief cognitive measures for normal adolescents and adults. *Assessment, 1,* 353–366.

Kaufman, A. S., Ishikuma, T., & Kaufman-Packer, J. L. (1991). Amazingly short forms of the WAIS-R. *Journal of Psychoeducational Assessment, 9,* 4–15.

Kaufman, A. S., Kaufman, J. C., Balgopal, R., & McLean, J. E. (1996). Comparison of three WISC-III short forms: Weighing psychometric, clinical, and practical factors. *Journal of Clinical Child Psychology, 25*(1), 97–105.

Kaufman, A. S., Kaufman, J. C., Chen, T., & Kaufman, N. L. (1996). Differences on six Horn abilities for fourteen age groups between 15–16 and 75–94 years. *Psychological Assessment, 8,* 161–171.

Kaufman, A. S., Kaufman, J. C., Lincoln, A. J., & Kaufman, J. L. (2000). Intellectual and cognitive assessment. In M. Herson & R. T. Ammerman (Eds.), *Advanced abnormal child psychology* (2nd ed.; pp. 153–175). Hillside, NJ: Erlbaum.

Kaufman, A. S., Kaufman, J. C., & McLean, J. E. (1995). Factor structure of the Kaufman Adolescent and Adult Intelligence Test (KAIT) for Whites, African-Americans, and Hispanics. *Educational and Psychological Measurement, 55,* 365–376.

Kaufman, A. S., & Kaufman, N. L. (1977). *Clinical evaluation of young children with the McCarthy Scales.* New York: Grune & Stratton.

Kaufman, A. S., & Kaufman, N. L. (1975). Social–class differences on the McCarthy Scales for black and white children. *Perceptual and Motor Skills, 41,* 205–206.

Kaufman, A. S., & Kaufman, N. L. (1983a). *K-ABC administration and scoring manual.* Circle Pines, MN: American Guidance Service.

Kaufman, A. S., & Kaufman, N. L. (1983b). *K-ABC interpretive manual.* Circle Pines, MN: American Guidance Service.

Kaufman, A. S., & Kaufman, N. L. (1985a). *Manual for the Kaufman Test of Educational Achievement (K-TEA) Brief Form.* Circle Pines, MN: American Guidance Service.

Kaufman, A. S., & Kaufman, N. L. (1985b). *Manual for the Kaufman Test of Educational Achievement (K-TEA) Comprehensive Form.* Circle Pines, MN: American Guidance Service.

Kaufman, A. S., & Kaufman, N. L. (1990). *Manual for Kaufman Brief Intelligence Test (K-BIT).* Circle Pines, MN: American Guidance Service.

Kaufman, A. S., & Kaufman, N. L. (1993). *Kaufman Adolescent and Adult Intelligence Test (KAIT) manual.* Circle Pines, MN: American Guidance Service.

Kaufman, A. S., & Kaufman, N. L. (1994a). *Manual for Kaufman Functional and Academic Skills Test (K FAST).* Circle Pines, MN: American Guidance Service.

Kaufman, A. S., & Kaufman, N. L. (1994b). *Manual for Kaufman Short Neuropsychological Assessment Procedure (K-SNAP).* Circle Pines, MN: American Guidance Service.

Kaufman, A. S., & Kaufman, N. L. (1997). The Kaufman Adolescent and Adult Intelligence Test (KAIT). In D. P. Flanagan, J. L. Genshaft, & P. L. Harrison (Eds.), *Contemporary intellectual assessment: Theories, tests, and issues* (pp. 209–229). New York: Guilford.

Kaufman, A. S., & Kaufman, N. L. (2001a). Assessment of specific learning disabilities in the new millennium: Issues, conflicts, and controversies. In A. S. Kaufman & N. L. Kaufman (Eds.), *Specific learning disabilities and difficulties in children and adolescents: Psychological assessment and evaluation* (pp. 433–461). (Included in the Series, Cambridge Monographs in Child and Adolescent Psychiatry.) Cambridge, England: Cambridge University Press.

Kaufman, A. S., & Kaufman, N. L. (Eds.). (2001b). *Specific learning disabilities: Psychological assessment and evaluation.* (Included in the Series, Cambridge Monographs in Child and Adolescent Psychiatry.) Cambridge, England: Cambridge University Press.

Kaufman, A. S., & Lichtenberger, E. O. (1999). *Essentials of WAIS-III assessment.* New York: Wiley.

Kaufman, A. S., & Lichtenberger, E. O. (2000). *Essentials of WISC-III and WPPSI-R assessment.* New York: Wiley.

Kaufman, A. S., Lichtenberger, E. O., & McLean, J. E. (2001). Two- and three-factor solutions of the WAIS-III. *Assessment, 8,* 267–280.

Kaufman, A. S., & McLean, J. E. (1994). The relationship of the Murphy-Meisgeier Type Indicator for Children to sex, race, and fluid-crystallized intelligence on the KAIT at ages 11 to 15. *Research in the Schools, 1,* 37–47.

Kaufman, A. S., & McLean, J. E. (1998). An investigation into the relationship between interests and intelligence. *Journal of Clinical Psychology, 54*(2), 279–295.

Kaufman, A. S., McLean, J. E., Ishikumia, T., & Moon, S. (1988). Integration of the literature on the intelligence of Japanese children and analysis of the data from a sequential simultaneous perspective. *School Psychology International, 10,* 173–183.

Kaufman, A. S., McLean, J. E., & Kaufman, J. C. (1995). The fluid and crystallized abilities of white, black, and Hispanic adolescents and adults, both with and without an education covariate. *Journal of Clinical Psychology, 51,* 637–647.

Kaufman, A. S., McLean, J. E., & Lincoln, A. (1996). The relationship of the Meyers-Briggs Type Indicator to IQ level and fluid-crystallized discrepancy on the Kaufman Adolescent and Adult Intelligence Test (KAIT). *Assessment, 3,* 225–239.

Kaufman, A. S., McLean, J. E., & Reynolds, C. R. (1988). Sex, race, residence, region, and education differences on the WAIS-R subtests. *Journal of Clinical Psychology, 44,* 231–248.

Kaufman, A. S., McLean, J. E., & Reynolds, C. R. (1990). Empirical test of the Inglis and Lawson hypothesis about sex differences in WAIS and WAIS-R brain-damage studies. *Journal of Clinical and Experimental Neuropsychology, 12,* 281–285.

Kaufman, A. S., McLean, J. E., & Reynolds, C. R. (1991). Analyses of WAIS-R factor structure by race and sex. *Journal of Clinical Psychology, 47,* 548–557.

Kaufman, A. S., & O'Neal, M. (1988a). Analysis of the cognitive, achievement, and general factors underlying the Woodcock-Johnson Psycho-Educational Battery. *Journal of Clinical Child Psychology, 17,* 143–151.

Kaufman, A. S., & O'Neal, M. (1988b). Factor structure of the Woodcock-Johnson cognitive subtests from preschool to adulthood. *Journal of Psychoeducational Assessment, 6,* 35–48.

Kaufman, A. S., Reynolds, C. R., & McLean, J. E. (1989). Age and WAIS-R intelligence in a national sample of adults in the 20- to 74-year age range: A cross-sectional analysis with educational level controlled. *Intelligence, 13,* 235–253.

Kaufman, A. S., & Van Hagen, J. (1977). Investigation of the WISC-R for use with retarded children: Correlation with the 1972 Stanford-Binet and comparison of WISC and WISC-R profiles. *Psychology in the Schools, 14,* 10–14.

Kaufman, A. S., & Wang, J. J. (1992). Gender, race, and education differences on the K-BIT at ages 4 to 90. *Journal of Psychoeducational Assessment, 10,* 219–229.

Kaufman, A. S., & Wang, J. J. (1993). Changes in fluid and crystallized intelligence across the 20- to 90-year age range on the K-BIT. *Journal of Psychoeducational Assessment, 11,* 29–37.

Kaufman, J. C., Chen, T., & Kaufman, A. S. (1995). Ethnic group, education, and gender differences on six Horn abilities for adolescents and adults. *Journal of Psychoeducational Assessment, 13,* 49–65.

Kaufman, J. C., & Kaufman, A. S. (in press). Time for the changing of the guard: A farewell to short forms of IQ tests. *Journal of Psychoeducational Assessment.*

Kausler, D. H. (1982). *Experimental psychology and human aging.* New York: Wiley.

Kausler, D. H. (1991). *Experimental psychology, cognition, and human aging.* New York: Springer-Verlag.

Kavale, K. A., & Forness, S. R. (2000). What definitions of learning disability say and don't say: A critical analysis. *Journal of Learning Disabilities, 33,* 239–256.

Keith, T. Z., Cool, V. A., Novak, C. G., White, L. J., & Pottebaum, S. M. (1988). Confirmatory factor analysis of the Stanford-Binet fourth edition: Testing the theory–test match. *Journal of School Psychology, 26,* 253–274.

Keith, T. Z., Fehrmann, P. G., Harrison, P. L., & Pottebaum, S. M. (1987). The relationship between adaptive behavior and intelligence: Testing alternative explanations. *Journal of School Psychology, 25,* 31–43.

Keith, T. Z., Harrison, P. L., & Ehly, S. (1987). Effects of adaptive behavior on achievement: Path analysis of a national sample. *Professional School Psychology, 2,* 205–216.

Keller, W. K. (1971). *A comparison of two procedures for assessing constructional praxis in patients with unilateral cerebral disease.* Unpublished doctoral dissertation, University of Iowa.

Kelly, M. D., Montgomery, M. L., Felleman, E. S., & Webb, W. W. (1984). Wechsler Adult Intelligence Scale and Wechsler Adult Intelligence Scale-Revised in a neurologically impaired population. *Journal of Clinical Psychology, 40,* 788–791.

Kender, J. D., Greenwood, S., & Conard, E. (1985). WAIS-R performance patterns of 565 incarcerated adults characterized as underachieving readers and adequate readers. *Journal of Learning Disabilities, 18,* 379–383.

Kessel, C., & Linn, M. C. (1996). Grades or scores: Predicting future college mathematics performance. *Educational Measurement: Issues and Practice, 15,* 10–14.

Khatena, J., & Torrance, E. P. (1976). *Khatena-Torrance Creative Perception Inventory.* Chicago: Stoelting.

Kiernan, R., Bower, G. H., & Schorr, D. (1984). Stimulus variables in the Block Design task revisited: A reply to Royer. *Journal of Consulting and Clinical Psychology, 52,* 705–707.

Kiernan, R. J., & Matthews, C. G. (1976). Impairment index versus T-score averaging in neuropsychological assessment. *Journal of Consulting and Clinical Psychology,* 951–957.

Kimura, D. (1963). Right temporal lobe damage. *Archives of Neurology, 8,* 264–271.

King, L. A., & King, D. W. (1982). Wechsler short forms: A brief status report. *Psychology in the Schools, 19,* 433–438.

Kinsbourne, M. (1980). If sex differences in brain lateralization exist, they have yet to be discovered. *Behavioral and Brain Sciences, 3,* 241–242.

Kirk, S. A., McCarthy, J. J., & Kirk, W. D. (1968). *Examiner manual: Illinois Test of Psycholinguistic Abilities.* Urbana, IL: University of Illinois Press.

Kirkpatrick, E. A. (1903). *Fundamentals of child study: A discussion of instincts and other factors in human development with practical applications.* New York: Macmillan.

Kite, E. S. (1916). *Translation of A. Binet & T. Simon, The development of intelligence in children.* Baltimore, MD: Williams and Wilkins.

Kleist, K. (1923). Kriegsverlertzungen des Gehirns in lhrer Bedeutung fur die Hirnlokalisation und Hirnpathologie. In O. von Schjerning (Ed.), *Handbuch der aerztlichen Erfahrung im Weltkriege 1914/1918: Bd. IV, Geistes-und Nervenkrankheiten.* Leipzig: Barth.

Klett, W. G., Watson, C. G., & Hoffman, P. T. (1986). The Henmon-Nelson and Slosson tests as predictors of WAIS-R IQ. *Journal of Clinical Psychology, 42*, 343–347.

Kliegl, R., Smith, J., & Baltes, P. B. (1990). On the locus and process of magnification of age differences during mnemonic training. *Developmental Psychology, 26*, 894–904.

Kljajic, I. (1984). The predictive utility of a significantly lower WAIS PIQ with psychiatric inpatients. *Journal of Clinical Psychology, 40*, 571–576.

Kljajic, I., & Berry, D. (1984). Brain syndrome and WAIS PIQ-VIQ difference scores corrected for test artifact. *Journal of Clinical Psychology, 40*, 271–277.

Klonoff, H., Fibiger, C. H., & Hutton, G. H. (1970). Neuropsychological pattern in chronic schizophrenia. *Journal of Nervous and Mental Disease, 150*, 291–300.

Klonoff, H., & Thompson, G. (1969). Epidemiology of head injuries in adults: A pilot study. *Canadian Medical Association Journal, 100*, 235–241.

Klove, H. (1959). Relationship of differential electroencephalographic patterns to distribution of Wechsler-Bellevue scores. *Neurology, 9*, 871–876.

Klove, H., & Fitzhugh, K. B. (1962). The relationship of differential EEG patterns to the distribution of Wechsler-Bellevue scores in a chronic epileptic population. *Journal of Clinical Psychology, 18*, 334–337.

Klove, Z. H., & Reitan, R. M. (1958). Effect of dysphasia and spatial distortion on Wechsler-Bellevue results. *Archives of Neurology and Psychiatry, 80*, 708–713.

Knight, R. G. (1983). On interpreting the several standard errors of the WAIS-R: Some further tables. *Journal of Consulting and Clinical Psychology, 51*, 671–673.

Knight, R. G., & Godfrey, H. P. D. (1984). Assessing the significance of differences between subtests on the Wechsler Adult Intelligence Scale-Revised. *Journal of Clinical Psychology, 40*, 808–810.

Kodama, H., Shinagawa, F., & Motegi, M. (1978). *Manual for the Wechsler Intelligence Scale for Children-Revised* (Standardized in Japan). Tokyo: Nihon Bunka Kagakusha.

Kohs, S. C. (1923). *Intelligence measurement.* New York: Macmillan.

Kolb, D., & Whishaw, I. Q. (1980). *Fundamentals of human neuropsychology.* San Francisco: W. H. Freeman.

Kornhaber, M., & Krechevsky, M. (1995). Expanding definition of learning and teaching: Notes from the MI underground. In P. W. Cookson & B. Schneider (Eds.), *Transforming schools* (pp. 118–208). New York: Garland.

Korten, A. E., Henderson, A. S., Christensen, H., Jorm, A. F., Rodgers, B., Jacomb, P., & MacKinnon, A. J. (1997). A prospective study of cognitive function in the elderly. *Psychological Medicine, 27*, 919–930.

Kraiuhin, C., Shores, E. A., & Roberts, C. (1996). Sensitivity of the WAIS-R verbal–performance IQ difference and inter-subtest scatter to traumatic brain injury. *Brain Injury, 10*, 677–685.

Kramer, J. J., Henning-Stout, M., Ullman, D. P., & Schellenberg, R. P. (1987). The viability of scatter analysis on the WISC-R and the SBIS: Examining a vestige. *Journal of Psychoeducational Assessment, 5*, 37–48.

Krashen, S. D. (1973). Lateralization, language learning, and the critical period: Some new evidence. *Language Learning, 23*, 63–74.

Krashen, S. D. (1975). The left hemisphere. *UCLA Educator, 17*, 23.

Krauskopf, C. J., & Davis, K. G. (1973). Studies of the normal personality. *JSAS Catalog of Selected Documents in Psychology, 3*, 85 (Ms. No. 415).

Krohn, E. J., & Traxler, A. J. (1979). Relationship of the McCarthy Scales of Children's Abilities to other measures of preschool cognitive, motor, and perceptual development. *Perceptual and Motor Skills, 49*, 783–790.

Kunce, J. T., Ryan, J. J., & Eckelman, C. C. (1976). Violent behavior and differential WAIS characteristics. *Journal of Consulting and Clinical Psychology, 44*, 42–45.

Kunce, J. T., & Schmidt de Vales, E. (1986). Cross-cultural factor analytic similarity of Wechsler intelligence scores for Mexican adults. *Journal of Clinical Psychology, 42*, 165–169.

Kupferman, I. (1985). Genetic determinants of behavior. In E. R. Kandel & J. H. Schwartz (Eds.), *Principles of Neural Science* (2nd ed.; pp. 795–804). New York: Elsevier.

Kupke, T., & Lewis, R. (1985). WAIS and neuropsychological tests: Common and unique variance within an epileptic population. *Journal of Clinical and Experimental Neuropsychology, 7*, 353–366.

Kurlan, R., & Como, P. (1988). Drug-induced Alzheimerism. *Archives of Neurology, 45*, 356–357.

Labouvie-Vief, G. (1985). Intelligence and cognition. In J. E. Birren & K. W. Schaie (Eds.), *Handbook of the psychology of aging* (2nd ed.; pp. 500–530). New York: Van Nostrand Reinhold.

Lally, J. R., Mangione, P. L., & Honig, A. S. (1988). The Syracuse University Family Development Research Program: Long-range impact on an early intervention with low-income children and their families. In I. E. Sigel (Series Ed.) & D. R. Powell (Vol. Ed.), *Annual advances in applied developmental psychology: Volume 3. Parent education as early childhood intervention: Emerging directions in theory, research, and practice* (pp. 79–104). Norwood, NJ: Ablex.

Lambert, N. M. (1981). *AAMD Adaptive Behavior Scale: School edition: Diagnostic and technical manual.* Monterey, CA: Publishers Test Service.

Lambert, N. M., & Windmiller, M. (1981). *AAMD Adaptive Behavior Scale: School edition*. Monterey, CA: Publishers Test Service.

Lambert, N. M., Windmiller, M., Cole, L., & Figueroa, R. (1975). *Manual of the AAMD Adaptive Behavior Scale: Public school version*. Washington, DC: American Association on Mental Deficiency.

Landesman-Dwyer, S., & Butterfield, E. C. (1983). Mental retardation: Developmental issues in cognitive and social adaptation. In M. Lewis (Ed.), *Origins of intelligence* (2nd ed.; pp. 479–519). New York: Plenum.

Langone, J., & Burton, T. A. (1987). Teaching adaptive behavior skills to moderately and severely handicapped individuals: Best practices for facilitating independent living. *Journal of Special Education, 21*, 149–166.

Lansdell, H. (1962). A sex difference in effect of temporal-lobe neurosurgery on design preference. *Nature, 194*, 852–854.

Lansdell, H. (1968). The use of factor scores from the Wechsler-Bellevue scale of intelligence in assessing patients with temporal lobe removals. *Cortex, 4*, 257–268.

Lansdell, H., & Smith, F. J. (1975). Asymmetrical cerebral function for two WAIS factors and their recovery after brain injury. *Journal of Consulting and Clinical Psychology, 43*, 923.

Lansdown, R., Yule, W., Urbanowicz, M. A., & Hunter, J. (1986). The relationship between blood-lead concentrations, intelligence, attainment and behaviour in a school population: The second London study. *International Archives Occupational Environmental Health, 57*, 225–235.

Larrabee, G. J., Kane, R. L., & Schuck, J. R. (1983). Factor analysis of the WAIS and Wechsler Memory Scale: An analysis of the construct validity of the Wechsler Memory Scale. *Journal of Clinical Neuropsychology, 5*, 159–168.

Larrabee, G. J., Largen, J. W., & Levin, H. S. (1985). Sensitivity of age-decline resistant ("hold") WAIS subtests to Alzheimer's disease. *Journal of Clinical and Experimental Neuropsychology, 7*, 497–504.

Lashley, K. S. (1929). *Brain mechanisms and intelligence: A quantitative study of injuries to the brain*. Chicago: University of Chicago Press.

Lashley, K. S. (1950). In search of the engram. *Symposia of the Society for Experimental Biology, 4*, 454–482.

Lassiter, K. S., Bell, N. L., Hutchinson, M. B., & Matthews, T. D. (in press). College student Performance on the General Ability Measure for Adults and the Wechsler Intelligence Scale for Adults-Third Edition. *Psychology in the Schools*.

Lassiter, K. S., Leverett, J. P., & Safa, T. A. (2000). The validity of the General Ability Meaure of Adults: Comparison with WAIS-R IQ scores in a sample of college students with academic difficulties. *Assessment, 7*, 63–72.

Lassiter, K. S., & Matthews, T. D. (1999). Test-retest reliability of the General Ability Measure for Adults. *Perceptual and Motor Skills, 88*, 531–534.

Laux, L. F., & Lane, D. M. (1985). Information processing components of substitution test performance. *Intelligence, 9*, 111–136.

Law, J. G., Box, D., & Moracco, J. D. (1980). A validation study of recategorized WISC-R scores of learning disabled children. *Education, 101*, 195–199.

Lawson, J. S., & Inglis, J. (1983). A laterality index of cognitive impairment after hemispheric damage: A measure derived from a principal-components analysis of the Wechsler Adult Intelligence Scale. *Journal of Consulting and Clinical Psychology, 51*, 832–840.

Lawson, J. S., & Inglis, J. (1984). The psychometric assessment of children with learning disabilities: An index derived from a principal-components analysis of the WISC-R. *Journal of Learning Disabilities, 17*, 513–576.

Lawson, J. S., Inglis, J., & Stroud, T. W. F. (1983). A laterality index of cognitive impairment derived from a principal-components analysis of the WAIS-R. *Journal of Consulting and Clinical Psychology, 51*, 841–847.

Lawton, M. P., & Salthouse, T. A. (Eds.). (1998). *Essential papers on the psychology of aging*. New York: New York University Press.

Laycock, F. (1979). *Gifted children*. Glencoe, IL: Scott, Foresman.

Leahy, B. J., & Lam, C. S. (1998). Neuropsychological testing and functional outcome for individuals with traumatic brain injury. *Brain Injury, 12*, 1025–1035.

Leckliter, I. N., Matarazzo, J. D., & Silverstein, A. B. (1986). A literature review of factor analytic studies of the WAIS-R. *Journal of Clinical Psychology, 42*, 332–342.

Lees-Haley, P. R., Smith, H. H., Williams, C. W., & Dunn, J. T. (1996). Forensic neuropsychological test usage: An empirical survey. *Archives of Clinical Neuropsychology, 11*, 45–51.

Lefly, D. L., & Pennington, B. F. (1991). Spelling errors and reading fluency in compensated adult dyslexics. *Annals of Dyslexia, 41*, 143–162.

Lehman, H. C. (1953). *Age and achievement*. Princeton, NJ: Princeton University Press.

Lehman, H. C. (1954). Men's creative production rate at different ages and in different countries. *Scientific Monthly, 78*, 321–326.

Leland, H. (1983). Assessment of adaptive behavior. In K. D. Paget & H. A. Bracken (Eds.), *The psychoeducational assessment of preschool children* (pp. 191–206). New York: Grune & Stratton.

Leland, H., Shellhaas, N., Nihira, K., & Foster, R. (1967). Adaptive behavior: A new dimension on the classification of the mentally retarded. *Mental Retardation Abstracts, 4*, 359–387.

Leli, D. A., & Filskov, S. H. (1979). Relationship of intelligence to education and occupation as signs of intellectual deterioration. *Journal of Consulting and Clinical Psychology, 47,* 702–707.

Leli, D. A., & Filskov, S. B. (1981a). Actuarial assessment of Wechsler Verbal–Performance scale differences as signs of lateralized cerebral impairment. *Perceptual and Motor Skills, 53,* 491–496.

Leli, D. A., & Filskov, S. B. (1981b). Actuarial detection and description of brain impairment with the W-B Form 1. *Journal of Clinical Psychology, 37,* 615–622.

Leli, D. A., & Filskov, S. H. (1981c). Clinical–actuarial detection and description of brain impairment with the W-B Form 1. *Journal of Psychology, 37,* 623–629.

Leli, D. A., & Scott, E. H. (1982). Cross-validation of two indexes of intellectual deterioration on patients with Alzheimer's disease. *Journal of Consulting and Clinical Psychology, 50,* 468.

Leton, D. A. (1985). Review of Structure of Intellect Learning Abilities Test. In J. V. Mitchell (Ed.), *The ninth mental measurements yearbook* (pp. 1488–1489). Lincoln, NB: Buros Institute of Mental Measurements, University of Nebraska Press.

Leverett, J. P., Matthews, T. D., Bell, N. L., Lassiter, K. S. (in press). Validity comparison of the General Ability Measure for Adults with the Wonderlic Personnel Test. *Personnel Psychology.*

Levin, H. (1973a). Motor impersistence in patients with unilateral cerebral disease: A cross-validating study. *Journal of Consulting and Clinical Psychology, 41,* 287–290.

Levin, H. (1973b). Motor impersistence and proprioceptive feedback in patients with unilateral cerebral disease. *Neurology, 23,* 833–841.

Levin, H., & Benton, A. L. (1975). Temporal orientation in patients with brain disease. *Applied Neuropsychology, 38,* 56–60.

Levy, J. (1972). Lateral specialization of the brain: Behavioral manifestations and possible evolutionary basis. In J. A. Kiger, Jr. (Ed.), *The biology of behavior.* Corvallis, OR: Oregon State University Press.

Lewandowski, L. J. (1986). Test review: Kaufman Test of Educational Achievement. *Journal of Reading, 30,* 258–261.

Lewandowski, L. J., & DeRienzo, P. J. (1985). WISC-R and K-ABC performances of hemiplegic children. *Journal of Psychoeducational Assessment, 3,* 215–222.

Lewis, G. P., Golden, C. J., Moses, J. A., Jr., Osmon, D. C., Purisch, A., & Hammeke, T. (1979). Localization of cerebral dysfunction with a standardized version of Luria's neuropsychological battery. *Journal of Consulting and Clinical Psychology, 47,* 1003–1019.

Lewis, G. P., Golden, C. J., Purisch, A., & Hammeke, T. (1979). The effects of chronicity of disorder and length of hospitalization on the standardized version of Luria's neuropsychological battery in a schizophrenic population. *Journal of Clinical Neuropsychology, 1,* 13–18.

Lewis, M. L., & Johnson, J. J. (1985). Comparison of the WAIS and WAIS-R IQs from two equivalent college populations. *Journal of Psychoeducational Assessment, 3,* 55–60.

Lezak, M. D. (1983). *Neuropsychological assessment* (2nd ed.). New York: Oxford University Press.

Lezak, M. D. (1988a). IQ: R. I. P. *Journal of Clinical and Experimental Neuropsychology, 10,* 351–361.

Lezak, M. D. (1988b). The last but hardly final word on the issue. *NASP Communique, 17*(4), 6.

Lezak, M. D. (1995). *Neuropsychological assessment* (3rd ed.). New York: Oxford University Press.

Lezak, M. D., & Newman, S. P. (1979). *Verbosity and right hemisphere damage.* Paper presented at the second European Conference of the International Society, Noordvijkerhout, Holland.

Lichtenberger, E. O., Broadbooks, D. Y., & Kaufman, A. S. (2000). *Essentials of cognitive assessment with KAIT and other Kaufman measures.* New York: Wiley.

Likert, R., & Quasha, W. (1970). *The Revised Minnesota Paper Form Board Test.* New York: The Psychological Corporation.

Lin, Y. (1979). Note on WAIS Verbal–Performance differences in IQ. *Perceptual and Motor Skills, 79,* 888–890.

Lincoln, A. J., Courchesne, E., Kilman, B. A., Elmasian, R., & Allen, M. (1988). A study of intellectual abilities in high-functioning people with autism. *Journal of Autism and Developmental Disorders, 18,* 505–524.

Lindemann, J. E., & Matarazzo, J. D. (1984). Intellectual assessment of adults. In G. Goldstein & M. Hersen (Eds.), *Handbook of psychological assessment* (pp. 77–99). New York: Pergamon.

Lindenberger, U., & Baltes, P. B. (1994). Sensory functioning and intelligence in old age: A strong connection. *Psychology & Aging, 9,* 339–355.

Lindenberger, U., & Baltes, P. B. (1997). Intellectual functioning in old and very old age: Cross-sectional results from the Berlin Aging Study. *Psychology & Aging, 12,* 410–432.

Lindgren, S. D., & Benton, A. E. (1980). Developmental patterns of visuospatial judgement. *Journal of Pediatric Psychology, 5,* 217–225.

Linn, R. L. (1986). Comments on the *g* factor in employment testing. *Journal of Vocational Behavior, 29,* 438–444.

Lippold, S., & Claiborn, J. M. (1983). Comparison of the Wechsler Adult Intelligence Scale and the Wechsler Adult Intelligence Scale-Revised. *Journal of Consulting and Clinical Psychology, 51,* 3–15.

Lira, F. T., Fagan, T. J., & White, M. J. (1979). Violent behavior and differential WAIS characteristics among black prison inmates. *Psychological Reports, 45,* 356–358.

Lishman, W. A. (1987). *Organic psychiatry: The psychological consequences of cerebral disorder* (2nd ed.). Oxford, England: Blackwell Scientific.

Little, A. J., Templer, D. I., Persel, C. S., & Ashley, M. J. (1996). Feasibility of the neuropsychological spectrum in prediction of outcome following head injury. *Journal of Clinical Psychology, 52*, 455–460.

Livesay, J. R. (1986). Clinical utility of Wechsler's deterioration index in screening for behavioral impairment. *Perceptual and Motor Skills, 63*, 619–626.

Lockyer, L., & Rutter, M. (1970). A five- to fifteen-year follow-up study of infantile psychosis: IV. Patterns of cognitive ability. *British Journal of Social and Clinical Psychology, 9*, 152–163.

Loehlin, J. C., Horn, J. M., & Willerman, L. (1994). Differential inheritance of mental abilities in the Texas Adoption Project. *Intelligence, 19*, 325–336.

Loehlin, J. C., Horn, J. M., & Willerman, L. (1997). Heredity, environment, and IQ in the Texas Adoption Project. In R. J. Sternberg & E. Grigorenko (Eds.), *Intelligence, heredity, and environment* (pp. 105–125). New York: Cambridge University Press.

Loevinger, J. (1954). The attenuation paradox in test theory. *Psychological Bulletin, 51*(5), 493–504.

Loevinger, J. (1957). Objective tests as instruments of psychological theory. *Psychological Reports, 3*, 635–694.

Loevinger, J., & Wessler, R. (1970). *Measuring ego development* (Vol. I). San Francisco: Jossey-Bass.

Logsdon, R. G., Teri, L., Williams, D. E., Vitiello, M. V., & Prinz, P. N. (1989). The WAIS-R profile: A diagnostic tool for Alzheimer's disease? *Journal of Clinical and Experimental Neuropsychology, 11*, 892–898.

Long, C. J., & Brown, D. A. (1979, September). *Analysis of temporal cortex dysfunction by neuropsychological techniques.* Paper presented at the meeting of the American Psychological Association, New York City.

Longstreth, L. E. (1984). Jensen's reaction-time investigations of intelligence: A critique. *Intelligence, 8*, 139–160.

Lorge, I. (1936). The influence of test upon the nature of mental decline as a function of age. *Journal of Educational Psychology, 27*, 100–110.

Lorge, I. (1945). Schooling makes a difference. *Teachers College Record, 46*, 483–492.

Loro, B., & Woodward, J. A. (1976). Verbal and Performance IQ for discrimination among psychiatric diagnostic groups. *Journal of Clinical Psychology, 32*, 107–114.

Louttit, C. M., & Browne, C. G. (1947). Psychometric instruments in psychological clinics. *Journal of Consulting Psychology, 11*, 49–54.

Lowitzer, A. C., Utley, C. A., & Baumeister, A. A. (1987). AAMD's 1983 Classification in Mental Retardation as uti-lized by state mental retardation/developmental disabilities agencies. *Mental Retardation, 25*, 287–291.

Lowman, R. L. (1991). *The clinical practice of career assessment.* Washington, DC: American Psychological Association.

Lubin, B., Larsen, R. M., & Matarazzo, J. D. (1984). Patterns of psychological test usage in the United States: 1935–1982. *American Psychologist, 39*, 451–454.

Lubin, B., Larsen, R. M., Matarazzo, J. D., & Seever, M. (1986). Psychological assessment services and psychological test usage in private practice and in military settings. *Psychotherapy in Private Practice, 4*, 19–29.

Luckason, R., Coutler, D. L., Polloway, E. A., Reiss, S., Schalock, R. L., Snell, M. E., Spitalnik, D. M., & Stark, J. A. (1992). *Mental retardation: Definition, classification, and systems of support* (9th ed.). Washington, DC: American Association on Mental Retardation.

Lueger, R. J., & Cadman, W. (1982). Variables associated with recidivism and program termination of delinquent adolescents. *Journal of Clinical Psychology, 38*, 861–863.

Lumsden, J. (1961). The construction of unidimensional tests. *Psychological Bulletin, 58*, 121–131.

Luria, A. R. (1966a). *Higher cortical functioning in man.* New York: Basic Books.

Luria, A. R. (1966b). *Human brain and psychological processes.* New York: Harper & Row.

Luria, A. R. (1973). *The working brain: An introduction to neuropsychology.* New York: Basic Books.

Luria, A. R. (1980). *Higher cortical functions in man* (2nd ed.). New York: Basic Books.

Luria, A. R., & Majovski, L. V. (1977). Basic approaches used in American and Soviet clinical neuropsychology. *American Psychologist, 32*, 959–968.

Lynn, R. (1982). IQ in Japan and the United States shows a growing disparity. *Nature, 297*, 222–223.

Lynn, R. (1983). IQ in Japan and the United States. *Nature, 306*, 292.

Lynn, R. (1987). The intelligence of the Mongoloids: A psychometric, evolutionary and neurological theory. *Personality and Individual Differences, 8*, 813–844.

Lynn, R., & Hampson, S. (1986a). The rise of national intelligence: Evidence from Britain, Japan, and the U.S.A. *Personality and Individual Differences, 7*, 23–32.

Lynn, R., & Hampson, S. (1986b). Intellectual abilities of Japanese children: An assessment of 2-1/8–1/2 year olds derived from the McCarthy Scales of Children's Abilities. *Intelligence, 10*, 41–58.

Lynn, R., & Hampson, S. (1986c). The structure of Japanese abilities: An analysis in terms of the hierarchical model of intelligence. *Current Psychological Research and Review, 4*, 309–322.

Maccoby, E. E., & Jacklin, C. N. (1974). *The psychology of sex differences.* Stanford, CA: Stanford University Press.

MacEachron, A. E. (1983). Institutional reform and adaptive functioning of mentally retarded persons: A field experiment. *American Journal of Mental Deficiency, 88,* 2–12.

MacLeod, C. M., Jackson, R. A., & Palmer, J. (1986). On the relation between spatial ability and field dependence. *Intelligence, 10,* 141–151.

MacMillan, D. L., Siperstein, G. N., & Gresham, F. M. (1996). A challenge to the viability of mild mental retardation as a diagnostic category. *Exceptional Children, 62,* 356–371.

MacMillan, D. L., & Speece, D. L. (1999). Utility of current diagnostic Categories for research and practice. In R. Gallimore, L. P. Bernheimer, D. L. MacMillan, D. L. Speece, & S. Vaughn (Eds.), *Developmental perspectives on children with high-incidence disabilities* (pp. 111–113). Mahweh, NJ: Erlbaum.

Madison, L. S., George, C., & Moeschler, J. B. (1986). Cognitive functioning in the Fragile-X syndrome: A study of intellectual, memory and communication skills. *Journal of Mental Deficiency Research, 30,* 129–148.

Maher, C. M., Lassiter, K. S., Matthews, T. D., & Bell, N. N. (in press). The General Ability Measure of Adults as a measure of fluid intelligence: Comparison with the Kaufman Adolescent and Adult Intelligence Test.

Majeres, R. L. (1983). Sex differences in symbol-digit substitution and speeded matching. *Intelligence, 7,* 313–327.

Malec, J. F., Ivnik, R. J., Smith, G. E., Tangalos, E. G., Peterson, C., Kokmen, E., & Kurland, L. T. (1992). Mayo's Older Americans Normative Studies: Utility of corrections for age and education for the WAIS-R. *Clinical Neuropsychologist, 6* (Suppl.), 31–47.

Malgady, R. S., Barcher, P. R., Davis, J., & Towner, G. (1980). Validity of the Vocational Adaptation Rating Scale: Prediction of mentally retarded workers' placement in sheltered workshops. *American Journal of Mental Deficiency, 84,* 633–640.

Malone, D. M. (1985). Comparability of scores earned on the Wechsler Adult Intelligence Scale-Revised and on the Wechsler Adult Intelligence Scale by educable mentally handicapped high school students. *Dissertation Abstracts International, 45,* (8-A), 2453.

Mandes, E., Massimino, C., & Mantis, C. (1991). A comparison of borderline and mild mental retardates assessed on the memory for designs and the WAIS-R. *Journal of Clinical Psychology, 47,* 562–567.

Mangiaracina, J., & Simon, M. J. (1986). Comparison of the PPVT-R and WAIS-R in state hospital psychiatric patients. *Journal of Clinical Psychology, 42,* 817–820.

Manly, J. J., Heaton, R. K., & Taylor, M. J. (2000, August). The effects of demographic variables and the development of demographically adjusted norms for the WAIS-III and WMS-III. In D. S. Tulsky & D. Saklofske (Chairs), *The clin-ical interpretation of the WAIS-III and WMS-III: New research findings.* Symposium presented at the meeting of the American Psychological Association, Washington, DC.

Margolis, R. B., Taylor, J. M., & Greenlief, C. E. (1986). A cross-validation of two short forms of the WAIS-R in a geriatric sample suspected of dementia. *Journal of Clinical Psychology, 42,* 145–146.

Margolis, R. H., & Scialfa, C. T. (1984). Age differences in Wechsler Memory Scale performance. *Journal of Clinical Psychology, 40,* 1442–1449.

Markwardt, F. C. (1989). *Manual for the Peabody Individual Achievement Test-Revised (PIAT-R).* Circle Pines, MN: American Guidance Service.

Markwardt, F. C. (1997). *Manual for the Peabody Individual Achievement Test-Revised Normative Update (PIAT-R NU).* Circle Pines, MN: American Guidance Service.

Martin, T. A., Donders, J., & Thompson, E. (2000). Potential of and problems with new measures of psychometric intelligence after traumatic brain injury. *Rehabilitation Psychology, 45,* 402–408.

Matarazzo, J. D. (1972). *Wechsler's measurement and appraisal of adult intelligence* (5th and enlarged ed.). New York: Oxford University Press.

Matarazzo, J. D. (1985). Review of Wechsler Adult Intelligence Scale-Revised. In J. V. Mitchell (Ed.), *The ninth mental measurements yearbook* (pp. 1703–1705). Lincoln, NE: Buros Institute of Mental Measurements, University of Nebraska Press.

Matarazzo, J. D., Bornstein, R. A., McDermott, P. A., & Noonan, J. V. (1986). Verbal IQ versus Performance IQ difference scores in males and females from the WAIS-R standardization sample. *Journal of Clinical Psychology, 42,* 965–974.

Matarazzo, J. D., Carmody, T. D., & Jacobs, L. D. (1980). Test-retest reliability and stability of the WAIS: A literature review with implications for clinical practice. *Journal of Clinical Neuropsychology, 2,* 89–105.

Matarazzo, J. D., Daniel, M. H., Prifitera, A., & Herman, D. O. (1988). Intersubtest scatter in the WAIS-R standardization sample. *Journal of Clinical Psychology, 44,* 940–950.

Matarazzo, J. D., & Herman, D. O. (1984a). Base rate data for the WAIS-R: Test-retest stability and VIQ–PIQ differences. *Journal of Clinical Neuropsychology, 6,* 351–366.

Matarazzo, J. D., & Herman, D. O. (1984b). Relationship of education and IQ in the WAIS-R standardization sample. *Journal of Consulting and Clinical Psychology, 52,* 631–634.

Matarazzo, J. D., & Herman, D. O. (1985). Clinical uses of the WAIS-R: Base rates of differences between VIQ and PIQ in the WAIS-R standardization sample. In B. B. Wolman (Ed.), *Handbook of intelligence* (pp. 899–932). New York: Wiley.

Matarazzo, J. D., Matarazzo, R. G., Weins, A. N., Gallo, A. E., & Kionoff, H. (1976). Retest reliability of the Halstead Impairment Index in a normal, a schizophrenic, and two samples of organic patients. *Journal of Nervous and Mental Disease, 158,* 37–49.

Matarazzo, J. D., & Prifitera, A. (1989). Subtest scatter and premorbid intelligence: Lessons from the WAIS-R standardization sample. *Psychological Assessment: A Journal of Consulting and Clinical Psychology, 1,* 186–191.

Matarazzo, J. D., Weins, A. N., Matarazzo, R. G., & Goldstein, S. G. (1974). Psychometric and clinical test-retest reliability of the Halstead Impairment Index in a sample of healthy, young, normal men. *Journal of Nervous and Mental Disease, 158,* 37–49.

Matarazzo, R. G., Matarazzo, J. D., Gallo, A. E., & Wiens, A. N. (1979). IQ and neuropsychological changes following carotid endarterectomy. *Journal of Clinical Neuropsychology,* 97–116.

Mather, N., & Schrank, F. A. (2001). Use of the WJ III discrepancy procedures for learning disabilities identification and diagnosis. *Assessment Service Bulletin No. 3.* Itasca, IL: Riverside.

Mather, N., & Woodcock, R. W. (2001). Application of the Woodcock-Johnson Tests of Cognitive Ability-Revised to the diagnosis of learning disabilities. In A. S. Kaufman & N. L. Kaufman (Eds.), *Specific learning disabilities and difficulties in children and adolescents: Psychological assessment and evaluation* (pp. 55–96). (Included in the Series, Cambridge Monographs in Child and Adolescent Psychiatry.) Cambridge, England: Cambridge University Press.

Matheson, D. W., Mueller, H. M., & Short, R. H. (1984). The validity of Bannatyne's acquired knowledge category as a separate construct. *Journal of Psychoeducational Assessment, 2,* 279–291.

Matthews, C. G. (1981). Neuropsychological practice in a hospital setting. In S. B. Filskov & T. J. Boll (Eds.), *Handbook of clinical neuropsychology* (pp. 645–685). New York: Wiley.

Matthews, C. G., Shaw, D., & Klove, G. (1966). Psychological test performances in neurological and "pseudoneurologic" subjects. *Cortex, 2,* 244–253.

Mattis, P. J., Hannay, H. J., & Meyers, C. A. (1992). Efficacy of the Satz-Mogel short form WAIS-R for tumor patients with lateralized lesions. *Psychological Assessment, 4,* 357–362.

Mattis, P. J., Hannay, H. J., Plenger, P. M., & Pollock, L. (1994). Head injury and the Satz-Mogel type short form WAIS-R. *Journal of Clinical Psychology, 50,* 605–614.

Maurelli, M., Marchioni, M., Cerretano, R., Bosone, D., Bergamaschi, R., Citterio, A., Martelli, A., Sibilla, L., & Savoldi, F. (1992). Neuropsychological assessment in MS: Clinical, neuropsychological and neuroradiological relationships. *Acta Neurologica Scandinavica, 86,* 124–128.

Mayfield, K. L., Forman, S. G., & Nagle, R. J. (1984). Reliability of the AAMD Adaptive Behavior Scale, Public School Version. *Journal of School Psychology, 22,* 53–61.

Mayman, M., Schafer, R., & Rapaport, D. (1951). Interpretation of the WAIS in personality appraisal. In H. H. Anderson & G. L. Anderson (Eds.), *An introduction to projective techniques* (pp. 541–580). New York: Prentice-Hall.

McArdle, J. J., & Prescott, C. A. (1997). Contemporary models for the biometric genetic analysis of intellectual abilities. In D. P. Flanagan, J. L. Genshaft, & P. L. Harrison (Eds.), *Beyond traditional intellectual assessment: Contemporary and emerging theories, tests, and issues* (pp. 403–436). New York: Guilford.

McArdle, J. J., Prescott, C. A., Hamagami, F., & Horn, J. L. (1998). A contemporary method for developmental-genetic analysis of age changes in intellectual abilities. *Developmental Neuropsychology, 1,* 69–114.

McArdle, J. J., & Woodcock, R. W. (1997). Expanding test-retest designs to include developmental time-lag components. *Psychological Methods, 2*(4), 403–435.

McCall, R. B. (1977). Childhood IQ's as predictors of adult educational and occupational status. *Science, 197,* 482–483.

McCallum, R. S. (1985). Review of the Peabody Picture Vocabulary Test-Revised. In J. V. Mitchell (Ed.), *The ninth mental measurements yearbook* (pp. 1126–1127). Lincoln, NE: Buros Institute of Mental Measurements, University of Nebraska Press.

McCarthy, D. (1972). *Manual for the McCarthy Scales of Children's Abilities.* New York: The Psychological Corporation.

McCarty, S. M., Logue, D. E., Power, D., Ziesat, H. A., & Rosenstiel, A. K. (1980). Alternate-form reliability and age-related scores for Russell's revised Wechsler Memory Scale. *Journal of Consulting and Clinical Psychology, 48,* 296–298.

McLean, J. E., Kaufman, A. S., & Reynolds, C. R. (1989). Base rates of WAIS-R subtest scatter as a guide for clinical and neuropsychological assessment. *Journal of Clinical Psychology, 45,* 919–926.

McClearn, G. E., Johansson, B., Berg, S., Pedersen, N. L., Ahern, F., Petrill, S. A., & Plomin, R. (1997). Substantial genetic influence on cognitive abilities in twins 80 or more years old. *Science, 276,* 1580–1585.

McCue, P. M., Shelly, C., & Goldstein, G. (1986). Intellectual, academic and neuropsychological performance levels in learning disabled adults. *Journal of Learning Disabilities, 19,* 233–236.

McCullough, C. S., Walker, J. E., Diessner, R. (1985). The use of Wechsler scales in the assessment of Native Americans of the Columbia River Basin. *Psychology in the Schools, 22,* 23–28.

McCurry, S. M., Fitz, A. G., & Teri, L. (1994). Comparison of age-extended norms for the Wechsler Adult Intelligence Scale-Revised in patients with Alzheimer's disease. *Psychological Assessment, 6,* 231–235.

McCusick, V. A. (1986). *Mendelian inheritance in man* (8th ed.). Baltimore, MD: Johns Hopkins University Press.

McCusker, P. J. (1994). Validation of Kaufman, Ishikuma, and Kaufman-Packer's Wechsler Adult Intelligence Scale-Revised short forms on a clinical sample. *Psychological Assessment, 6*(3), 246–248.

McDowd, J. M., & Shaw, R. J. (2000). Attention and aging: A functional perspective. In F. I. M. Craik & T. A. Salthouse (Eds.), *The handbook of aging and cognition* (2nd ed.; pp. 499–558). Mahwah, NJ: Erlbaum.

McEchron, W. D. (1980). Interrelationships among discrepancy scores on the Wechsler scales and performance on the MMPI and BPC. *Dissertation Abstracts International, 41*, (6-B), 2335.

McGee, S., & Brown, C. (1984). A split in the verbal comprehension factor in WAIS and WISC-R profiles. *Journal of Clinical Psychology, 40*, 580–583.

McGlone, J. (1977). Sex differences in the cerebral organization of verbal functions in patients with unilateral brain lesions. *Brain, 100*, 775–793.

McGlone, J. (1978). Sex differences in functional brain asymmetry. *Cortex, 14*, 122–128.

McGlone, J. (1980). Sex differences in human brain asymmetry: A critical survey. *Behavioral and Brain Sciences, 3*, 215–227.

McGlone, J., & Davidson, W. (1973). The relationship between speech and laterality and spatial ability with special reference to sex and hand preference. *Neuropsychologia, 11*, 105–113.

McGlone, J., & Kertesz, A. (1973). Sex differences in cerebral processing of visuospatial tasks. *Cortex, 9*, 313–320.

McGowan, R. J., & Johnson, D. L. (1984). The mother–child relationship and other antecedents of childhood intelligence: A causal analysis. *Child Development, 55*, 810–820.

McGrew, K. S. (1986). *Clinical interpretation of the Woodcock-Johnson Tests of Cognitive Ability.* Boston: Allyn & Bacon.

McGrew, K. S. (1987). Exploratory factor analysis of the Woodcock-Johnson Tests of Cognitive Ability. *Journal of Psychoeducational Assessment, 5*, 200–216.

McGrew, K. S. (1994). *Clinical interpretation of the Woodcock-Johnson Tests of Cognitive Ability-Revised.* Boston: Allyn & Bacon.

McGrew, K. S. (1997). Analysis of the major intelligence batteries according to a proposed comprehensive *Gf-Gc* framework. In D. P. Flanagan, J. L. Genshaft, & P. L. Harrison (Eds.), *Contemporary intellectual assessment: Theories, tests, and issues* (pp. 151–179). New York: Guilford.

McGrew, K. S., & Flanagan, D. P. (1996). The Wechsler performance scale IQ debate: Fluid intelligence (*Gf*) or visual processing (*Gv*)? *NASP Communique, 24*(6), 14–16.

McGrew, K. S., & Flanagan, D. P. (1998). *The Intelligence Test Desk Reference (ITDR): Gf-Gc cross-battery assessment.* Boston: Allyn & Bacon.

McGrew, K. S., Gregg, N., Hoy, C., Stennett, R., Davis, M., & Knight, D., Coleman, C., & Ford L. (2001). *Cattell-Horn-Carroll confirmatory factor analysis of the WJ III, WAIS-III, WMS-III and KAIT in a university sample.* Manuscript in preparation.

McGrew, K. S., Untiedt, S. A., & Flanagan, D. P. (1996). General factor and uniqueness characteristics of the Kaufman Adolescent and Adult Intelligence Test (KAIT). *Journal of Psychoeducational Assessment, 14*, 208–219.

McGrew, K. S., Werder, J. K., & Woodcock, R. W. (1991). *Woodcock Johnson Psycho Educational Battery-Revised technical manual.* Itasca: Riverside.

McGrew, K. S., & Woodcock, R. W. (2001). *Technical Manual. Woodcock-Johnson III.* Itasca, IL: Riverside.

McGue, M., Bouchard, T. J., Jr., Iacono, W. G., & Lykken, D. T. (1993). Behavior genetics of cognitive ability: A life-span perspective. In R. Plomin & G. E. McClearn (Eds.), *Nature, nurture and psychology* (pp. 59–76). Washington, DC: American Psychological Association.

McIntosh, D. E., Waldo, S. L., & Koller, J. R. (1997). Exploration of the underlying dimensions and overlap between the Kaufman Adolescent and Adult Intelligence Test and the Wechsler Memory Scale-Revised. *Journal of Psychoeducational Assessment, 15*, 15–26.

McKay, S., & Golden, C. J. (1979a). Empirical derivation of experimental scales for localizing brain lesions using the Luria-Nebraska Neuropsychological Battery. *Clinical Neuropsychology, 1*, 19–23.

McKay, S., & Golden, C. J. (1979b). Empirical derivation of neuropsychological scales for the lateralization of brain damage using the Luria-Nebraska Neuropsychological Test Battery. *Clinical Neuropsychology, 1*, 1–5.

McKay, S., & Golden, C. J. (1981). The assessment of specific neuropsychological skills using scales derived from factor analysis of the Luria-Nebraska Neuropsychological Battery. *International Journal of Neuroscience, 14*, 189–204.

McLean, J. E. (1995). *Improving education through action research.* Thousand Oaks, CA: Corwin.

McLean, J. E., & Kaufman, A. S. (1995). The Harrington-O'Shea Career Decision-Making System (CDM) and the Kaufman Adolescent and Adult Intelligence Test (KAIT): Relationship of interest scale scores to fluid and crystallized IQs at ages 12 to 22 years. *Research in the Schools, 2*, 63–73.

McLean, J. E., Kaufman, A. S., & Reynolds, C. R. (1988a). The canonical relationship between the WAIS-R Verbal and performance scales. *Perceptual and Motor Skills, 66*, 432–434.

McLean, J. E., Kaufman, A. S., & Reynolds, C. R. (1988b, November). What role does formal education play in the IQ–age relationships across the adult life-span. *Mid-South Educational Researcher, 17*(1), 6–8, 13–18.

McLean, J. E., Kaufman, A. S., & Reynolds, C. R. (1989). Base rates of WAIS-R subtest scatter as a guide for clinical and neuropsychological assessment. *Journal of Clinical Psychology, 45*(6), 919–926.

McMullen, L. M., & Rogers, D. E. (1984). WAIS characteristics of nonpathological obsessive and hysteric styles. *Journal of Clinical Psychology, 40*, 577–579.

McNemar, Q. (1942). *The revision of the Stanford-Binet Scale.* Boston: Houghton Mifflin.

McNemar, Q. (1974). Correction to a correction. *Journal of Consulting and Clinical Psychology, 42*, 145–146.

McPherson, S., Buckwalter, J. G., Tingus, K., Betz, B., & Back, C. (2000). The Satz-Mogel short form of the Wechsler Adult Intelligence Scale-Revised: Effects of global mental status and age on test-retest reliability. *Journal of Clinical and Experimental Neuropsychology, 22*, 545–553.

McQuaid, M. M., & Spreen, O. (1989, February). *Cognitive changes over 15 years in a person with a learning disability, as reflected by the Wechsler intelligence scale.* Paper presented at the meeting of the International Neuropsychological Society, Vancouver, British Columbia.

McShane, D. A., & Berry, J. W. (1989). Native North American Indians: Indians and intuitive abilities. In S. H. LeVine & J. W. Berry (Eds.), *Cultural context of human abilities* (pp. 385–426). New York: Wiley.

McShane, D. A., & Cook, V. (1985). Transcultural intellectual assessment: Performance by Hispanics on the Wechsler scales. In B. B. Wolman (Ed.), *Handbook of intelligence* (pp. 737–785). New York: Wiley.

McShane, D. A., & Plas, J. M. (1984a). The cognitive functioning of American Indian children: Moving from the WISC to the WISC-R. *School Psychology Review, 13*, 61–73.

McShane, D. A., & Plas, J. M. (1984b). Response to a critique of the McShane and Plas review. *School Psychology Review, 13*, 83–88.

McSweeny, A. J., Naugle, R. I., Chelune, G. J., & Luders, H. (1993). "T scores for change": An illustration of a regression approach to depicting change in clinical neuropsychology. *Clinical Neuropsychologist, 7*, 300–312.

Meacham, F. R. (1985). A comparable study of the WISC-R and WAIS-R Performance IQ scores of 16-year-old hearing impaired students in a residential program. *Dissertation Abstracts International, 45*, (7-A), 2042–2043.

Meacham, F. R., Kline, M. M., Stovall, J. A., & Sands, D. I. (1987). Adaptive behavior and low incidence handicaps: Hearing and visual impairments. *Journal of Special Education, 21*, 183–196.

Mealor, D. J. (1984). *An analysis of intellectual functioning and adaptive behavior of behaviorally disordered students.* Unpublished manuscript, University of Central Florida, Orlando.

Mealor, D. J., & Richmond, B. O. (1980). Adaptive behavior: Teachers and parents disagree. *Exceptional Children, 46*, 386–389.

Meeker, M. N. (1969). *The structure of intellect.* Columbus, OH: Charles E. Merrill.

Meeker, M. N. (1985). Toward a psychology of giftedness: A concept in search of measurement. In B. B. Wolman (Ed.), *Handbook of intelligence* (pp. 787–800). New York: Wiley.

Meeker, M. N., & Meeker, R. (1981). *Structure of Intellect Learning Abilities Test.* Segundo, CA: SOI Institute.

Meier, M. J. (1981). Education for competency assurance in human neuropsychology: Antecedents, models, and directions. In S. B. Filskov & T. J. Boll (Eds.), *Handbook of clinical neuropsychology* (pp. 754–781). New York: Wiley.

Meier, M. J. (1985). Review of the Halstead-Reitan Neuropsychological Test Battery. In J. V. Mitchell (Ed.), *The ninth mental measurements yearbook* (pp. 646–649). Lincoln, NB: Buros Institute of Mental Measurements, University of Nebraska Press.

Meier, M. J., & French, I. A. (1966). Longitudinal assessment of intellectual functioning following unilateral temporal lobectomy. *Journal of Clinical Psychology, 22*, 22–27.

Meisgeier, C., & Murphy, E. (1987). *Murphy-Meisgeier Type Indicator for Children manual.* Palo Alto, CA: Consulting Psychologists Press.

Mercer, J. R. (1973). *Labeling the mentally retarded.* Berkeley: University of California Press.

Merritt, H. H. (1979). *Textbook of neurology* (6th ed.). Philadelphia: Lea & Febiger.

Messick, S. (1980). Test validity and the ethics of assessment. *American Psychologist, 35*, 1012–1027.

Messick, S. (1989). Validity. In R. L. Linn (Ed.), *Educational Measurement* (3rd ed., Vol. 2, pp. 13–103). New York: MacMillan.

Meyer, V., & Jones, H. G. (1957). Patterns of cognitive test performance as functions of the lateral localization of cerebral abnormalities in the temporal lobe. *Journal of Mental Science, 103*, 758–772.

Meyers, C. E., Nihira, K., & Zetlin, A. (1979). The measurement of adaptive behavior. In N. R. Ellis (Ed.), *Handbook of mental deficiency: Psychological theory and research* (2nd ed; pp. 215–253). Hillsdale, NJ: Erlbaum.

Milberg, W. P., Cummings, J., Goodglass, H., & Kaplan, E. (1979). Case report: A global sequential processing disorder following head injury: A possible role for the right hemisphere in serial order behavior. *Journal of Clinical Neuropsychology, 1*, 213–225.

Milberg, W. P., Greiffenstein, M., Lewis, R., & Rourke, D. (1980). Differentiation of temporal lobe and generalized seizure patients with the WAIS. *Journal of Consulting and Clinical Psychology, 48*, 39–42.

Milberg, W. P., Hebben, N., & Kaplan, E. (1986). The Boston process approach to neuropsychological assessment. In I. Grant & K. M. Adams (Eds.), *Neuropschological assessment of neuropsychiatric disorders* (pp. 65–86). New York: Oxford University Press.

Miles, C. C., & Miles, W. R. (1932). The correlation of intelligence scores and chronological age from early to late maturity. *American Journal of Psychology, 44*, 44–78.

Miller, L. T., & Vernon, P. A. (1997). Developmental changes in speed of information processing in young children. *Developmental Psychology, 33*(3), 549–554.

Miller, M. D. (1995). Kaufman Brief Intelligence Test. In J. C. Conoley & J. C. Impara (Eds.), *The twelfth mental measurements yearbook* (pp. 533–534). Lincoln, NE: Buros Institute of Mental Measurements, University of Nebraska Press.

Milner, H. (1954). Intellectual function of the temporal lobes. *Psychological Bulletin, 51*, 42–62.

Minshew, N. J., Goldstein, G., Muenz, L. R., & Payton, J. B. (1992). Neuropsychological functioning in non-mentally retarded autistic individuals. *Journal of Clinical and Experimental Neuropsychology, 14*, 749–761.

Mirsky, A. F., Anthony, B. J., Duncan, C. C., Ahearn, M. B., & Kellam, S. G. (1991). Analysis of the elements of attention: A neuropsychological approach. *Neuropsychology Review, 2*, 109–145.

Mishra, S. D., & Brown, K. H. (1983). The compatibility of WAIS and WAIS-R IQs and subtest scores. *Journal of Psychology, 39*, 754–757.

Mitchell, R. E., Grandy, T. G., & Lupo, J. V. (1986). Comparison of the WAIS and the WAIS-R in the upper ranges of IQ. *Professional Psychology: Research and Practice, 17*, 82–83.

Mitchell, S. W., Morehouse, G., & Keen, W. W., Jr. (1864). *Reflex paralysis, article 6*. Washington, DC: Surgeon General's Office.

Mittenberg, W., & Ryan, J. J. (1984). Effects of omitting one to five subtests on WAIS-R Full Scale reliability. *Perceptual and Motor Skills, 58*, 563–565.

Mohs, R. C., Kim, Y., Johns, C. A., Dunn, D. D., & Davis, K. E. (1986). Assessing changes in Alzheimer's disease: Memory and language. In L. W. Poon (Ed.), *Clinical memory assessment of older adults* (pp. 149–155). Washington, DC: American Psychological Association.

Moon, G. W., Blakey, W. A., Gorsuch, R. L., & Fantuzzo, J. W. (1991). Frequent WAIS-R administration errors: An ignored source of inaccurate measurement. *Professional Psychology: Research and Practice, 22*, 256–258.

Moon, G. W., Fantuzzo, J., & Gorsuch, R. (1986). Teaching WAIS-R administration skills: Comparison of the MASTERY model to other existing clinical training modalities. *Professional Psychology: Research and Practice, 17*, 31–35.

Moon, S. (1988). *A cross-cultural validity study of the Kaufman Assessment Battery for Children*. Unpublished doctoral dissertation, University of Alabama.

Moore, A. D., Stambrook, M., Hawryluk, G. A., Peters, L. C., Gill, D. D., & Hymans, M. M. (1990). Test-retest stability of the Wechsler Adult Intelligence Scale-Revised in the assessment of head-injured patients. *Psychological Assessment: A Journal of Consulting and Clinical Psychology, 2*, 98–100.

Morgan, A. W., Sullivan, S. A., Darden, C., & Gregg, N. (1997). Measuring the intelligence of college students with learning disabilities: A comparison of results obtained on the WAIS-R and the KAIT. *Journal of Learning Disabilities, 30*, 560–565.

Morice, R., & Delahunty, A. (1996). Frontal/executive impairments in schizophrenia. *Schizophrenia Bulletin, 22*, 125–137.

Morris, J. M., & Bigler, E. D. (1987). Hemispheric functioning and the Kaufman Assessment Battery for Children: Results in the neurologically impaired. *Developmental Neuropsychology, 3*, 67–79.

Morrison, M. W. (1994). The use of psychological tests to detect malingered intellectual impairment. *American Journal of Forensic Psychology, 12*, 47–64.

Moses, J. A., & Golden, C. J. (1979). Cross validation of the discriminative effectiveness of the standardized Luria neuropsychological battery. *International Journal of Neuroscience, 9*, 149–155.

Mosier, C. I. (1943). On the reliability of a weighted composite. *Psychometrika, 8*(3), 161–168.

Muhs, P. J., Hooper, F. H., & Papalia-Finlay, D. (1979–80). Cross-sectional analysis of cognitive functioning across the life-span. *International Journal of Aging and Human Development, 10*, 311–333.

Munder, L. (1976). Patterns of deficit in black and white men with brain damage to the left, right and both hemispheres. *Dissertation Abstracts International, 37 (I-B)*, 442–443 (University Microfilms No. 76–14, 816).

Murphy, G. (1968). Psychological views of personality and contributions to its study. In E. Norbeck, D. Price-Williams, & W. M. McCord (Eds.), *The study of personality* (pp. 15–40). New York: Holt, Rinehart and Winston.

Murray, M. E., Waltes, L., Veldman, D. J., & Heatly, M. D. (1973). Differences between WISC and WAIS scores in delinquent boys. *Journal of Experimental Education, 42*, 68–72.

Myers, I. B., & McCaulley, M. H. (1985). *Manual: A guide to the development and use of the Myers-Briggs Type Indicator*. Palo Alto, CA: Consulting Psychologists Press.

Nagle, R. J., & Bell, N. L. (1995). Clinical utility of Kaufman's "amazingly" short forms of the WAIS-R with educable mentally retarded adolescents. *Journal of Clinical Psychology, 51*, 396–400.

Nagle, R. J., & Lazarus, S. C. (1979). The comparability of the WISC-R and WAIS among 16-year-old EMR children. *Journal of School Psychology, 17*, 362–367.

Naglieri, J. A. (1979). *A comparison of McCarthy GCI and WISC-R IQ scores for educable mentally retarded, learning disabled, and normal children.* Unpublished doctoral dissertation, University of Georgia.

Naglieri, J. A. (1982). Two types of tables for use with the WAIS-R. *Journal of Consulting and Clinical Psychology, 50,* 319–321.

Naglieri, J. A. (1985a). *Matrix Analogies Test-Expanded form.* San Antonio, TX: The Psychological Corporation.

Naglieri, J. A. (1985b). *Matrix Analogies Test-short form.* San Antonio, TX: The Psychological Corporation.

Naglieri, J. A. (1988a). Comment on "IQ: R.I.P." *National Association of School Psychologists Communique, 17*(4), 4–5.

Naglieri, J. A. (1988b). Interpreting area score variation on the fourth edition of the Stanford-Binet scale of intelligence. *Journal of Clinical Child Psychology, 17,* 225–228.

Naglieri, J. A. (1999). *Essentials of CAS assessment.* New York: Wiley.

Naglieri, J. A., & Bardos, A. N. (1997). *The manual of the General Ability Measure for Adults.* Minneapolis, MN: National Computer Scoring Systems.

Naglieri, J. A., & Das, J. P. (1987). Construct and criterion-related validity of planning, simultaneous, and successive cognitive processing tasks. *Journal of Psychoeducational Assessment, 5,* 353–363.

Naglieri, J. A., & Das, J. P. (1997a). *Cognitive assessment system administration and scoring manual.* Chicago, IL: Riverside.

Naglieri, J. A., & Das, J. P. (1997b). *Cognitive Assessment System interpretive handbook.* Itasca, IL: Riverside.

Naglieri, J. A., & Das, J. P. (1988). Planning-Around-Simultaneous-Successive (PASS): A model for assessment. *Journal of School Psychology, 26,* 35–48.

Naglieri, J. A., & Kaufman, A. S. (1983). How many factors underlie the WAIS-R? *Journal of Psychoeducational Assessment, 1,* 113–119.

Naglieri, J. A., & Prewett, P. N. (1990). Nonverbal intelligence measures: A selected review of instruments and their use. In C. R. Reynolds & R. W. Kamphaus (Eds.), *Handbook of psychological and educational assessment of children: Intelligence and achievement* (pp. 348–370). New York: Guilford.

Nagy, K., Lassiter, K. S., & Leverett, J. P. (in press). *A validity study of the General Abilities Measure for Adults.* Paper presented at the 45th annual meeting of the Southeastern Psychological Association, Savannah, GA.

Nair, N. P. V., Muller, H. F., Gutbrodt, E., Buffet, L., & Schwartz, G. (1979). Neurotropic activity of lithium: Relationship to lithium levels in plasma and red blood cells. *Research Communications in Psychology, Psychiatry and Behavior, 4,* 169–180.

Narita, T., & Koga, Y. (1987). Neuropsychological assessment of childhood autism. *Advances in Biological Psychiatry, 16,* 156–170.

Nathan, M., Millham, J., Chilcutt, J., & Atkinson, B. (1980). Mentally retarded individuals as informants for the AAMD Adaptive Behavior Scale. *Mental Retardation, 18,* 82–84.

Nebes, R. D. (1978). Direct examination of cognitive function in the right and left hemispheres. In M. Kinsbourne (Ed.), *Asymmetrical function of the brain,* Cambridge: Cambridge University Press.

Neisser, U. (Ed.). (1998). *The rising curve: Long-term gains in IQ and related measures.* Washington, DC: American Psychological Association.

Neisser, U., Boodoo, G., Bouchard, T. J., Jr., Boykin, A. W., Brody, N., Ceci, S. J., Halpern, D. F., Loehlin, J. C., Perloff, R., Sternberg, R. J., & Urbina, S. (1996). Intelligence: Knowns and unknowns. *American Psychologist, 51,* 77–101.

Nelson, W. M., Edinger, J. D., & Wallace, J. (1978). The utility of two Wechsler Adult Intelligence Scale short forms with prisoners. *Journal of Personality Assessment, 42,* 302–311.

Nesselroade, J. R., & Labouvie, E. W. (1985). Experimental design in research on aging. In J. E. Birren & K. W. Schaie (Eds.), *Handbook of the psychology of aging* (2nd ed.; pp. 35–60). New York: Van Nostrand Reinhold.

Nestor, P. G. (1992). Neuropsychological and clinical correlates of murder and other forms of extreme violence in a forensic psychiatric population. *Journal of Nervous and Mental Disease, 180,* 418–423.

Neuringer, C. (1963). The form equivalence between the Wechsler-Bellevue Intelligence Scale Form I and the Wechsler Adult Intelligence Scale. *Educational and Psychological Measurement, 23,* 755–763.

Newcombe, F. (1969). *Missile wounds of the brain.* London: Oxford University Press.

Newman, H. H., Freeman, F. N., & Holzinger, K. H. (1937). *Twins: A study of heredity and environment.* Chicago: University of Chicago Press.

Nichols, P. L. (1984). Familial mental retardation. *Behavior Genetics, 14,* 161–170.

Nichols, R. (1978). Twin studies of ability, personality, and interests. *Homo, 29,* 158–173.

Nicholson, R. I. (1996). Developmental dyslexia: Past, present and future. *Dyslexia, 2,* 190–207.

Nihira, K. (1985). Assessment of mentally retarded individuals. In B. B. Wolman (Ed.), *Handbook of intelligence* (pp. 801–824). New York: Wiley.

Nihira, K., Foster, R., Shellhaas, M., & Leland, H. (1969). *Adaptive Behavior Scales Manual.* Washington, DC: American Association on Mental Deficiency.

Nihira, K., Foster, R., Shellhaas, M., & Leland, H. (1975). *AAMD Adaptive Behavior Scale.* Monterey, CA: Publishers Test Service.

Nixon, S. J. (1996). Alzheimer's disease and vascular dementia. In R. L. Adams, O. A. Parsons, J. L. Culbertson, & S. J. Nixon (Eds.), *Neuropsychology for clinical practice: Etiology, assessment, and treatment of common neurological disorders* (pp. 65–106). Washington, DC: American Psychological Association.

Nobo, J., & Evans, R. G. (1986). The WAIS-R Picture Arrangement and Comprehension subtests as measures of social behavior characteristics. *Journal of Personality Assessment, 50,* 90–92.

Nunnally, J. S. (1978). *Psychometric theories.* New York: McGraw-Hill.

Oakland, T. (1980). An evaluation of the ABIC, pluralistic norms, and estimated learning potential. *Journal of School Psychology, 18,* 3–11.

Oakland, T. (1983). Joint use of adaptive behavior and IQ to predict achievement. *Journal of Consulting and Clinical Psychology, 51,* 298–301.

Oakland, T. (1985). Review of Slosson Intelligence Test. In J. V. Mitchell (Ed.), *The ninth mental measurements yearbook* (pp. 1401–1403). Lincoln, NE: Buros Institute of Mental Measurements, University of Nebraska Press.

Oakland, T., & Houchins, S. (1985). A review of the Vineland Adaptive Behavior Scales, Survey Form. *Journal of Counseling and Development, 63,* 585–586.

Oakland, T., & Parmelee, R. (1985). Mental measurement of minority group children. In B. B. Wolman (Ed.), *Handbook of intelligence* (pp. 699–736). New York: Wiley.

Oakland, T., & Zimmerman, S. (1986). The course on individual mental assessment: A national survey of course instructors. *Professional School Psychology, 1,* 51–59.

Oakman, S., & Wilson, B. (1988). Stability of WISC-R intelligence scores: Implications for 3-year reevaluations of learning disabled students. *Psychology in the Schools, 25,* 118–120.

Oas, P. (1984). Validity of the Draw-A-Person and Bender Gestalt tests as measures of impulsivity with adolescents. *Journal of Consulting and Clinical Psychology, 52,* 1011–1019.

Obringer, S. J. (1988, November). *A survey of perceptions of the Stanford-Binet IV.* Paper presented at the meeting of the Mid-South Educational Research Association, Louisville, KY.

Oden, M. G. (1968). The fulfillment of promise: 40-year follow-up of the Terman gifted group. *Genetic Psychology Monographs, 77,* 3–93.

O'Donnell, J. P., Kurtz, J., & Ramanaiah, N. V. (1983). Neuropsychological test findings for normal, learning disabled, and brain-damaged young adults. *Journal of Consulting and Clinical Psychology, 51,* 726–729.

O'Grady, K. E. (1983). A confirmatory maximum likelihood factor analysis of the WAIS-R. *Journal of Consulting and Clinical Psychology, 51,* 826–831.

Ohta, M. (1987). Cognitive disorders of infantile autism: A study employing the WISC, spatial relationship conceptualization, and gesture imitations. *Journal of Autism and Developmental Disorders, 17,* 45–62.

Okun, M. A. (1976). Adult age and cautiousness in decision: A review of the literature. *Human Development, 19,* 220–233.

Okun, M. A., Siegler, I. C., & George, L. K. (1978). Cautiousness and verbal learning in adulthood. *Journal of Gerontology, 33,* 94–97.

Orgel, S. A., & McDonald, R. D. (1967). An evaluation of the trail making test. *Journal of Consulting Psychology, 31,* 77–79.

Orzeck, A. Z. (1964). *The Orzeck Aphasia Evaluation.* Los Angeles: Western Psychological Services.

Osmon, D., Golden, C. J., Purisch, A., Hammeke, T., & Blume, H. (1979). The use of a standardized battery of Luria's tests in the diagnosis of lateralized cerebral dysfunction. *International Journal of Neuroscience, 9,* 1–9.

Overall, J. E., Hoffmann, N. G., & Levin, H. (1978). Effects of aging, organicity, alcoholism, and functional psychopathology on WAIS subtest profiles. *Journal of Consulting and Clinical Psychology, 46,* 1315–1322.

Owens, W. A. (1953). Age and mental abilities: A longitudinal study. *Genetic Psychology Monographs, 48,* 3–54.

Owens, W. A. (1959). Is age kinder to the initially more able? *Journal of Gerontology, 14,* 334–337.

Owens, W. A. (1966). Age and mental ability: A second adult follow-up. *Journal of Educational Psychology, 57,* 311–325.

Ownby, R. L., & Carmin, C. N. (1988). Confirmatory factor analysis of the Stanford-Binet Intelligence Scale, fourth edition. *Journal of Psychoeducational Assessment, 6,* 331–340.

Ownby, R. L., & Matthews, C. G. (1985). On the meaning of the WISC-R third factor: Relations to selected neuropsychological measures. *Journal of Consulting and Clinical Psychology, 53,* 531–534.

Page, S., & Steffy, R. (1984). WAIS and WISC-R "VP" scores: Sampling characteristics from three psychiatric populations. *Canadian Journal of Behavioral Science, 16,* 99–106.

Pallier, G., Roberts, R. D., & Stankov, L. (2000). Biological versus psychometric intelligence: Halstead's (1947) distinction revisited. *Archives of Clinical Neuropsychology, 15*(3), 205–226.

Paniak, C. E., Silver, K., Finlayson, M. A. J., & Tuff, L. P. (1992). How useful is the WAIS-R in closed head injury assessment? *Journal of Clinical Psychology, 48,* 219–225.

Paolo, A. M., & Ryan, J. J. (1995). Selecting WAIS-R norms for persons 75 years and older. *Clinical Neuropsychologist, 9,* 44–49.

Paolo, A. M., Ryan, J. J., Ward, L. C., & Hilmer, C. (1996). Different WAIS-R short forms and their relationship to ethnicity. *Personality and Individual Differences, 6,* 851–856.

Papalia, D. E. (1972). The status of several conservation abilities across the life-span. *Human Development, 15,* 229–243.

Paque, L., & Warrington, E. K. (1995). A longitudinal study of reading ability in patients suffering from dementia. *Journal of the International Neuropsychological Society, 1,* 517–524.

Park, D. C., & Schwarz, N. (Eds.). (2000). *Cognitive aging: A primer.* Philadelphia, PA: Psychology Press/Taylor & Francis.

Parker, J. C., Granberg, B. W., Nichols, W. K., Jones, J. C., & Hewett, J. E. (1983). Mental status outcomes following carotid endarterectomy. *Journal of Clinical Neuropsychology, 5,* 345–353.

Parker, K. C. H. (1983). Factor analysis of the WAIS-R at nine age levels between 16 and 74 years. *Journal of Consulting and Clinical Psychology, 51,* 302–308.

Parker, K. C. H. (1986). Changes with age, year-of-birth cohort, age by year-of-birth interaction, and standardization of the Wechsler adult intelligence tests. *Human Development, 29,* 209–222.

Parker, R. S., & Rosenblum, A. (1996). IQ loss and emotional dysfunctions after mild head injury incurred in a motor vehicle accident. *Journal of Clinical Psychology, 52,* 32–43.

Parkin, A. J., & Java, R. I. (1999). Deterioration of frontal lobe function in normal aging: Influences of fluid intelligence versus perceptual speed. *Neuropsychology, 13,* 539–545.

Parsons, O. A. (1996). Alcohol abuse and alcoholism. In R. L. Adams, O. A. Parsons, J. L. Culbertson, & S. J. Nixon (Eds.), *Neuropsychology for clinical practice: Etiology, assessment and treatment of common neurological disorders* (pp. 175–201). Washington, DC: American Psychological Association.

Parsons, O. A., Vega, A., Jr., & Burn, J. (1969). Different psychological effects of lateralized brain damage. *Journal of Consulting and Clinical Psychology, 33,* 551–557.

Paulson, M. J., & Lin, T. (1970). Predicting WAIS IQ from Shipley-Hartford scores. *Journal of Clinical Psychology, 26,* 453–461.

Pederson, N. E., McGlearn, C. E., & Friberg, I. (1985). Separated fraternal twins: Resemblance for cognitive authorities. *Behavior Genetics, 15,* 407–419.

Pederson, N. E., Plomin, R., Nesselroade, J. R., & McClearn, C. E. (1992). A quantitative genetic analysis of cognitive abilities during the second half of the life span. *Psychological Science, 3,* 346–353.

Perez, S. A., Schlottmann, R. S., Holloway, J. A., & Ozolins, M. S. (1996). Measurement of premorbid intellectual ability following brain injury. *Archives of Clinical Neuropsychology, 11,* 491–501.

Perlmutter, M., & Nyquist, L. (1990). Relationships between self-reported physical and mental health and intelligence performance across adulthood. *Journal of Gerontology: Psychological Sciences, 45,* 145–155.

Pernicano, K. M. (1986). Score differences in WAIS-R scatter for schizophrenics, depressives, and personality disorders: A preliminary analysis. *Psychological Reports, 59,* 539–543.

Petrill, S. A., Saudino, K., Cherny, S. S., Emde, R. N., Fulker, D. W., Hewitt, J. K., & Plomin, R. (1998). Exploring the genetic and environmental etiology of high general cognitive ability in fourteen- to thirty-six-month-old twins. *Child Development, 69,* 68–74.

Petterson, P. L. (1998). Intellectual deficit patterns in APOE-e4 Individuals at risk for Alzheimer's disease. Unpublished doctoral dissertation, California School of Professional Psychology.

Phelps, L., Rosso, M., & Falasco, S. (1984). Correlations between the Woodcock-Johnson and the WISC-R for a behavior disordered population. *Psychology in the Schools, 21,* 442–446.

Phelps, L., Rosso, M., & Falasco, S. (1985). Multiple regression data using the WISC-R and the Woodcock-Johnson Tests of Cognitive Ability. *Psychology in the Schools, 2,* 63–69.

Phillips, L. H., & Della Sala, S. (1998). Aging, intelligence, and anatomical segregation in the frontal lobes. *Learning & Individual Differences, 10,* 217–243.

Piaget, J. (1972). Intellectual evolution from adolescence to adulthood. *Human Development, 15,* 1–12.

Pickering, J. W., Johnson, D. L., & Stary, J. E. (1977). Systematic VIQ/PIQ differences on the WAIS: An artifact of this instrument? *Journal of Clinical Psychology, 33,* 1060–1064.

Piersma, H. L. (1986). Wechsler Memory Scale performance in geropsychiatric patients. *Journal of Clinical Psychology, 42,* 323–327.

Pieters, H. C., & Sieberhagen, J. J. (1986). Evaluation of two shortened forms of the SAWAIS with three diagnostic groups. *Journal of Clinical Psychology, 42,* 809–815.

Pilgrim, B. M., Meyers, J. E., Bayless, J., & Whetstone, M. M. (1999). Validity of the Ward seven-subtest WAIS-III short form in a neuropsychological population. *Applied Neuropsychology, 6,* 243–246.

Pinneau, S. R. (1961). *Changes in intelligence quotient: Infancy to maturity.* Boston: Houghton-Mifflin.

Pintner, R., & Paterson, D. D. (1925). *A scale of performance tests.* New York: Appleton & Co.

Piotrowski, C., & Keller, J. W. (1989). Psychological testing in outpatient mental health facilities: A national study. *Professional Psychology: Research and Practice, 20,* 423–425.

Piotrowski, R. J., & Siegel, D. J. (1984). Interpreting WISC-R profiles: Reliability of subtest composites. *Journal of Psychoeducational Assessment, 2,* 183–190.

Plake, B. S., Gutkin, T. B., Wise, S. L., & Kroeten, T. (1987). Confirmatory factor analysis of the WAIS-R: Competition of models. *Journal of Psychoeducational Assessment, 3,* 267–272.

Plake, B. S., Reynolds, C. R., & Gutkin, T. H. (1981). A technique for the comparison of the profile variability between independent groups. *Journal of Clinical Psychology, 37,* 142–146.

Plomin, R. (1983). Developmental behavioral genetics. *Child Development, 54,* 253–259.

Plomin, R. (1986). *Development, genetics, and psychology.* Hillsdale, NJ: Erlbaum.

Plomin, R. (1988). The nature and nurture of cognitive abilities. In R. J. Sternberg (Ed.), *Advances in the psychology of human intelligence* (Vol. 4; pp. 1–33). Hillsdale, NJ: Erlbaum.

Plomin, R. (1989). Environment and genes: Determinants of behavior. *American Psychologist, 43,* 105–111.

Plomin, R. (1997). Identifying genes for cognitive abilities and disabilities. In R. J. Sternberg & E. Grigorenko (Eds.), *Intelligence, heredity, and environment* (pp. 89–104). New York: Cambridge University Press.

Plomin, R., & DeFries, J. C. (1980). Genetics and intelligence: Recent data. *Intelligence, 4,* 15–24.

Plomin, R., Fulker, D. W., Corley, R., & DeFries, J. C. (1997). Nature, nurture, and cognitive development from 1 to 16 years: A parent–offspring adoption study. *Psychological Science, 8,* 442–447.

Plomin, R., Pederson, N. L., McClearn, G. E., Nesselroade, J. R., & Bergenian, C. S. (1988). EAS temperaments during the last half of the life span: Twins reared apart and twins reared together. *Psychology and Aging, 3,* 43–50.

Plomin, R., & Petrill, S. A. (1997). Genetics and intelligence: What's new? *Intelligence, 24,* 53–77.

Plotrowski, Z. (1937). The Rorschach inkblot method in organic disturbances of the central nervous system. *Journal of Nervous and Mental Disease, 86,* 525–537.

Pollack, M. (1955). *Effects of brain tumour on perception of hidden figures, sorting behavior, and problem solving performance.* Unpublished doctoral dissertation, New York University.

Pollingue, A. (1987). Adaptive behavior and low incidence handicaps: Use of adaptive behavior instruments for persons with physical handicaps. *Journal of Special Education, 21,* 117–126.

Poon, L. W. (1985). Differences in human memory with aging: Nature, causes, and clinical implications. In J. E. Birren and K. W. Schaie (Eds.), *Handbook of the psychology of aging* (2nd ed.; pp. 427–462). New York: Van Nostrand Reinhold.

Poon, L. W. (Ed.). (1980). *Aging in the 1980s: Psychological issues.* Washington DC: American Psychological Association.

Poon, L. W. (Ed.). (1986). *Clinical memory assessment of older adults.* Washington, DC: American Psychological Association.

Pratt, L. K., Uhl, N. P., Roberts, A. R., & DeLucia, S. (1981, May). *The relationship of the Myers-Briggs Type Indicator to scores on the National Teacher's Examination.* Paper presented at the 21st annual forum of the Association for Institutional Research, Minneapolis, MN. (ERIC Document Reproduction Service No. ED 205 128).

Prewett, P. N. (1992a). The relationship between the Kaufman Brief Intelligence Test (K-BIT) and the WISC-R with incarcerated juvenile delinquents. *Educational and Psychological Measurement, 52,* 977–982.

Prewett, P. N. (1992b). The relationship between the Kaufman Brief Intelligence Test (K-BIT) and the WISC-R with referred students. *Psychology in the Schools, 29,* 25–27.

Prewett, P. N. (1992c). Short forms of the Stanford-Binet Intelligence Scale: Fourth Edition. *Journal of Psychoeducational Assessment, 10*(3), 257–264.

Prewett, P. N. (1995). A comparison of two screening tests (the Matrix Analogies Test-Short Form and the Kaufman Brief Intelligence Test) with the WISC-III. *Psychological Assessment, 7*(1), 69–72.

Prewett, P. N., & Farhney, M. R. (1994). The concurrent validity of the Matrix Analogies Test-Short Form with the Stanford-Binet: Fourth Edition and KTEA-BF. *Psychology in the Schools, 31,* 20–25.

Prewett, P. N., & McCaffrey, L. K. (1993). A comparison of the Kaufman Brief Intelligence Test (K-BIT) with the Stanford-Binet, a two subtest short form, and the Kaufman Test of Educational Achievement (K-TEA) Brief Form. *Psychology in the Schools, 30,* 299–304.

Prifitera, A., & Dersh, J. (1993). Base rates of WISC-III diagnostic subtest patterns among normal, learning disabled, and ADHD samples. *Journal of Psychoeducational Assessment* [Monograph Series: WISC-III Monograph], 43–55.

Prifitera, A., & Ryan, J. J. (1983). WAIS-R/WAIS comparisons in a clinical sample. *Journal of Clinical Neuropsychology, 5,* 97–99.

Prifitera, A., Weiss, L. G., & Saklofske, D. H. (1998). The WISC-III in context. In A. Prifitera & D. Saklofske (Eds.), *WISC-III clinical use and interpretation* (pp. 1–39). San Diego, CA: Academic Press.

Prigitano, G. P., & Parsons, O. A. (1976). Relationship of age and education to Halstead test performance in different patient populations. *Journal of Consulting and Clinical Psychology, 44,* 527–533.

Prout, H. T., & Schwartz, J. F. (1984). Validity of the Peabody Picture Vocabulary Test-Revised with mentally retarded adults. *Journal of Clinical Psychology, 40,* 584–587.

Psychological Corporation (1992). *WIAT manual.* San Antonio, TX: Author.

Psychological Corporation (1997). *WAIS-III/WMS-III technical manual*. San Antonio, TX: Author.

Psychological Corporation (1999). *Manual for the Wechsler Abbreviated Scale of Intelligence*. San Antonio, TX: Author.

Puente, A. E., & Salazar, G. D. (1998). Assessment of minority and culturally diverse children. In A. Prifitera & D. Saklofske (Eds.), *WISC-III clinical use and interpretation* (pp. 227–248). San Diego, CA: Academic Press.

Purisch, A., Golden, C. J., & Hammeke, T. (1978). Discrimination of schizophrenic and brain-injured patients by a standardized version of Luria's neuropsychological tests. *Journal of Consulting and Clinical Psychology, 46*, 1266–1273.

Quattrocchi, M., & Sherrets, S. (1980). WISC-R: The first five years. *Psychology in the Schools, 17*, 297–312.

Rabbitt, P. (1993). Baseline changes in cognitive performance with age. In R. Levy & R. Howard (Eds.), *Treatment and care in old age psychiatry* (pp. 11–30). Petersfield, England, UK: Wrightson Biomedical.

Rabbitt, P., Bent, N., & McInnes, L. (1997). Health, age and mental ability. *Irish Journal of Psychology, 18*, 104–131.

Rabbitt, P., Donlan, C., Watson, P., McInnes, L., & Bent, N. (1995). Unique and interactive effects of depression, age, socioeconomic advantage, and gender on cognitive performance of normal healthy older people. *Psychology and Aging, 10*, 307–313.

Rack, J. (1997). Issues in the assessment of developmental dyslexia in adults: Theoretical and applied perspectives. *Journal of Research in Reading, 20*, 66–76.

Radencich, M. C. (1986a). Test review: Detroit Tests of Learning Aptitude (DTLA-2). *Journal of Psychoeducational Assessment, 4*, 173–181.

Radencich, M. C. (1986b). Test update: Kaufman Test of Educational Achievement (K-TEA). *Academic Therapy, 21*, 619–622.

Radencich, M. C. (1988). Test review: Woodcock Reading Mastery Tests-Revised. *Journal of Psychoeducational Assessment, 6*, 168–173.

Ramey, C. T., & Campbell, F. A. (1984). Preventive education for high-risk children: Cognitive consequences of the Carolina Abecedarian Project. *American Journal of Mental Deficiency, 88*, 515–523.

Ramey, C. T., Campbell, F. A., & Ramey, S. L. (1999). Early intervention: Successful pathways to improving intellectual development. *Developmental Neuropsychology, 16*, 385–392.

Ramey, C. T., & Haskins, R. (1981a). Early education, intellectual development, and school performance: A reply to Arthur Jensen and J. McVicker Hunt. *Intelligence, 5*, 41–48.

Ramey, C. T., & Haskins, R. (1981b). The modification of intelligence through early experience. *Intelligence, 5*, 5–19.

Ramey, C. T., McGinness, G. D., Cross, L., Collier, A. M., & Barrie-Blackley, S. (1982). The Abecedarian approach to social competence: Cognitive and linguistic intervention for disadvantaged preschoolers. In K. Borman (Ed.), *The social life of children in a changing society* (pp. 145–174). Hillsdale, NJ: Erlbaum.

Randolph, C., Mohr, E., & Chase, T. N. (1993). Assessment of intellectual function in dementing disorders: Validity of WAIS-R short forms for patients with Alzheimer's, Huntington's, and Parkinson's disease. *Journal of Clinical and Experimental Neuropsychology, 15*, 743–753.

Rapaport, D., Gill, M., & Schafer, R. (1945–1946). *Diagnostic psychological testing, 2 vols*. Chicago: Year Book.

Rasch, G. (1960). *Probabilistic models for some intelligence and attainment tests*. Chicago: MESA Press.

Raskind, M. H., Goldberg, R. J., Higgins, E. L., & Herman, K. L. (1999). Patterns of change and predictors of success in individuals with learning disabilities: Results from a twenty-year longitudinal study. *Learning Disabilities Research and Practice, 14*, 35–49.

Raven, J., Raven, J. C., & Court, J. H. (1993). *Manual for Raven's Progressive Matrices and Vocabulary Scales* (Section 1). Oxford, England: Oxford Psychologists Press.

Raven, J. C., Court, J. H., & Raven, J. (1983). *Manual for Raven's Progressive Matrices and Vocabulary Scales* (Section 3)-*Standard Progressive Matrices*. London: Lewis.

Raybourn, R. E. (1983). The Wechsler Adult Intelligence Scale (WAIS) and the WAIS-Revised: A comparison and a caution. *Professional Psychology: Research and Practice, 14*, 357–361.

Raz, N. (2000). Aging of the brain and its impact on cognitive performance: Integration of structural and functional findings. In F. I. M. Craik & T. A. Salthouse (Eds.), *The handbook of aging and cognition* (2nd ed.; pp. 1–90). Mahwah, NJ: Erlbaum.

Reed, H. B. C., Jr., & Reitan, R. M. (1963a). Changes in psychological test performance associated with the normal aging process. *Journal of Gerontology, 18*, 271–274.

Reed, H. B. C., Jr., & Reitan, R. M. (1963b). A comparison of the effects of the normal aging process with the effects of organic brain damage on adaptive abilities. *Journal of Gerontology, 18*, 177–179.

Reed, H. B. C., Jr., & Reitan, R. M. (1963c). Intelligence test performances of brain damaged subjects with lateralized motor deficits. *Journal of Consulting Psychology, 27*, 102–106.

Reed, J. C. (1985). The contributions of Ward Halstead, Ralph Reitan and their associates. *International Journal of Neuroscience, 25*, 289–293.

Reed, J. C., & Reitan, R. M. (1969). Verbal and Performance differences among brain-injured children with lateralized motor deficits. *Perceptual and Motor Skills, 29*, 747–752.

Reese, H., & Rodeheaver, D. (1985). Problem solving and complex decision making. In J. E. Birren and K. W. Schaie

(Eds.), *Handbook of the psychology of aging* (2nd ed.; pp. 474–499). New York: Van Nostrand Reinhold.

Reid, N. (1986). Testing the test: Wide Range Achievement Test: 1984 Revised edition. *Journal of Consulting and Development, 64*, 538–539.

Reilly, T. F., Wheeler, L. J., & Ettinger, L. E. (1985). Intelligence versus academic achievement: A comparison of juvenile delinquents and special education classifications. *Criminal Justice and Behavior, 12*, 193–208.

Reinert, G. (1970). Comparative factor analytic studies of intelligence throughout the human life-span. In L. R. Goulet & P. B. Baltes (Eds.), *Life-span developmental psychology: Research and theory* (pp. 467–484). New York: Academic Press.

Reise, S. P., Waller, N. G., & Comrey, A. L. (2000). Factor analysis and scale revision. *Psychological Assessment, 12*(3), 287–297.

Reitan, R. M. (1955a). *Instructions and procedures for administering the neuropsychological test battery used at the Neuropsychology Laboratory, Indiana University Medical Center.* Unpublished manuscript.

Reitan, R. M. (1955b). Investigation of the validity of Halstead's measures of biological intelligence. *A.M.A. Archives of Neurology and Psychiatry, 73*, 28–35.

Reitan, R. M. (1955c). Certain differential effects of left and right cerebral lesions in human adults. *Journal of Comparative and Physiological Psychology, 48*, 474–477.

Reitan, R. M. (1958). Validity of the Trail Making Test as an indication of organic brain damage. *Perceptual and Motor Skills, 8*, 271–276.

Reitan, R. M. (1959). The comparative effects of brain damage on the Halstead Impairment Index and the Wechsler-Bellevue Scale. *Journal of Clinical Psychology, 15*, 281–285.

Reitan, R. M. (1960). The significance of dysphasia for the intelligence and adaptive abilities. *Journal of Psychology, 60*, 355–376.

Reitan, R. M. (1966). Diagnostic inferences of brain lesions based on psychological test results. *Canadian Psychologist, 7*, 386–392.

Reitan, R. M. (1974). Methodological problems in clinical neuropsychology. In R. M. Reitan & L. A. Davison (Eds.), *Clinical neuropsychology: Current status and applications* (pp. 19–46). New York: Wiley.

Reitan, R. M. (1976). Neurological and physiological basis of psychopathology. *Annual Review of Psychology, 27*, 189–216.

Reitan, R. M. (1985). Relationships between measures of brain functions and general intelligence. *Journal of Clinical Psychology, 41*, 245–253.

Reitan, R. M. (1986). Theoretical and methodological bases of the Halstead-Reitan Neuropsychological Test Battery. In I. Grant & K. M. Adams (Eds.), *Neuropsychological assessment of neuropsychiatric disorders* (pp. 3–30). New York: Oxford University Press.

Reitan, R. M., & Boll, T. J. (1971). Intellectual and cognitive functions in Parkinson's disease. *Journal of Consulting and Clinical Psychology, 37*, 364–369.

Reitan, R. M., & Fitzhugh, K. B. (1971). Behavioral deficits in groups with cerebral vascular lesions. *Journal of Consulting and Clinical Psychology, 37*, 215–223.

Reitan, R. M., Reed, J. C., & Dyken, M. L. (1971). Cognitive, psychomotor, and motor correlates of multiple sclerosis. *Journal of Nervous and Mental Disease, 153*, 218–224.

Reitan, R. M., & Wolfson, D. (1985). *The Halstead-Reitan Neuropsychological Test Battery: Theory and clinical interpretation.* Tucson, AZ: Neuropsychology Press.

Reitan, R. M., & Wolfson, D. (1996). Relationships of age and education to Wechsler Adult Intelligence Scale IQ values in brain-damaged and non-brain-damaged groups. *Clinical Neuropsychologist, 10*, 293–304.

Reitan, R. M., & Wolfson, D. (1997). The influence of age and education on neuropsychological performances of persons with mild head injuries. *Applied Neuropsychology, 4*, 16–33.

Reivich, M., Jones, S., Castano, T., Crowe, W., Ginsberg, M., & Greenberg, J. (1977). Cerebral function, metabolism, and circulation. In D. H. Ingvar & N. A. Lassen (Eds.), *A model of diaschisis using middle cerebral artery occlusion.* Copenhagen: Munksgaard.

Reschly, D. J. (1981). Evaluation of the effects of SOMPA measures on classification of students as mildly mentally retarded. *American Journal of Mental Deficiency, 86*, 16–20.

Reschly, D. J. (1982). Assessing mild mental retardation: The influence of adaptive behavior, sociocultural status, and prospects for nonbiased assessment. In C. R. Reynolds & T. B. Gutkin (Eds.), *The handbook of school psychology* (pp. 209–242). New York: Wiley.

Reschly, D. J. (1985). Best practices: Adaptive behavior. In A. Thomas & J. Grimes (Eds.), *Best practices in school psychology* (pp. 353–368). Stratford, CT: National Association of School Psychologists.

Reschly, D. J., & Jipson, F. J. (1976). Ethnicity, geographic locale, age, sex, and urban–rural residence as variables in the prevalence of mild retardation. *American Journal of Mental Deficiency, 81*, 154–161.

Resnick, L. B. (1987). The 1987 Presidential Address: Learning in school and out. *Educational Researcher, 16*, 13–20.

Resnick, R. J., & Entin, A. D. (1971). Is an abbreviated form of the WISC valid for Afro-American children? *Journal of Consulting and Clinical Psychology, 36*, 97–99.

Retzlaff, P., Slicner, N., & Gibertini, M. (1986). Predicting WAIS-R scores from the Shipley Institute of Living Scale in a homogeneous sample. *Journal of Clinical Psychology, 39*, 357–359.

Reynolds, C. F., III, Hoch, C. C., Kupfer, D. J., Buysse, D. J., Houck, P. R., Stack, J. A., & Campbell, D. W. (1988). Bedside differentiation of depressive pseudodementia from dementia. *American Journal of Psychiatry, 145*, 1099–1103.

Reynolds, C. R. (1982). The problem of bias in psychological assessment. In C. R. Reynolds & T. B. Gutkin (Eds.), *The handbook of school psychology* (pp. 178–208). New York: Wiley.

Reynolds, C. R. (1984). Critical measurement issues in learning disabilities. *Journal of Special Education, 18*, 451–476.

Reynolds, C. R. (1986a, March). K-TEA terrific! *Information/Edge, 2*(1), 1, 4. Bensalem, PA: Buttonwood Farms.

Reynolds, C. R. (1986b). Wide Range Achievement Test (WRAT-R), 1984 edition. *Journal of Counseling and Development, 64*, 540–541.

Reynolds, C. R. (1987a). Playing IQ roulette with the Stanford-Binet, 4th edition. *Measurement and Evaluation in Counseling and Development, 20*, 139–141.

Reynolds, C. R. (1987b). Raising intelligence: Clever Hans, Candides, and the miracle in Milwaukee. *Journal of School Psychology, 25*, 309–312.

Reynolds, C. R. (1988). Of straw men and the practice of the ancients: Commentary on Lezak. *National Association of School Psychologists Communique, 17*(4), 6.

Reynolds, C. R. (1990). Conceptual and technical problems in learning disability diagnosis. In C. R. Reynolds and R. W. Kamphaus (Eds.), *Handbook of psychological and educational assessment of children: Intelligence and achievement* (pp. 571–592). New York: Guilford.

Reynolds, C. R., & Brown, R. T. (Eds.). (1984). *Perspectives on bias in mental testing.* New York: Plenum.

Reynolds, C. R., Chastain, R. L., Kaufman, A. S., & McLean, J. E. (1987). Demographic characteristics and IQ among adults; Analysis of the WAIS-R standardization sample as a function of the stratification variables. *Journal of School Psychology, 25*, 323–342.

Reynolds, C. R., & Fletcher-Janzen, E. (1989). *Handbook of clinical child neuropsychology.* New York: Plenum.

Reynolds, C. R., & Gutkin, T. B. (1979). Predicting the premorbid intellectual status of children using demographic data. *Clinical Neuropsychology, 1*, 36–38.

Reynolds, C. R., & Gutkin, T. B. (1981). Test scatter on the WPPSI: Normative analysis of the WPPSI. *Journal of Learning Disabilities, 14*, 460–464,

Reynolds, C. R., Kamphaus, R. W., & Rosenthal, B. L. (1988). Factor analysis of the Stanford-Binet-Fourth edition for ages 2 through 23 years. *Measurement and Evaluation in Counseling and Development, 21*, 52–63.

Reynolds, C. R., Willson, V. L., & Clark, D. L. (1983). A four-test short form of the WAIS-R for clinical screening. *Journal of Clinical Neuropsychology, 5*, 111–116.

Reynolds, W. M. (1979). A caution against the use of the Slosson Intelligence Test in the diagnosis of mental retardation. *Psychology in the Schools, 16*, 77–79.

Reynolds, W. M. (1985). Review of Slosson Intelligence Test. *The ninth mental measurements yearbook* (pp. 1403–1404). Lincoln, NE: Buros Institute of Mental Measurements, University of Nebraska Press.

Rhudick, P. J., & Gordon, C. (1973). The Age Center of New England Study. In L. F. Jarvik, C. Eisdorfer, & J. F. Blunt (Eds.), *Intellectual functioning in adults* (pp. 7–12). New York: Springer.

Roberts, F. (1988, December). Test review: Kaufman Test of Educational Achievement. *National Association of School Psychologists Communique, 17*, 30.

Roberts, J. A. F. (1952). The genetics of mental deficiency. *Eugenics Review, 44*, 71–83.

Robertson, D. U., Steinmyer, C. H., & Goff, C. P. (1980). Decision-theoretic approach for WAIS short forms with an inpatient psychiatric population. *Journal of Consulting and Clinical Psychology, 48*, 657–658.

Robertson, G. J., & Eisenberg, J. L. (1981). *Peabody Picture Vocabulary Test-Revised: Technical supplement, Forms L and M.* Circle Pines, MN: American Guidance Service.

Robinson, A., Bender, B., Borelli, J., Puck, M., Salsenblati, J., & Webber, M. L. (1982). Sex chromosomal abnormalities (SCA): A prospective and longitudinal study of newborns identified in an unbiased manner. *Birth Defects: Original Article Series, 18*(4), 7–39.

Robinson, N. M., & Chamrad, D. E. (1986). Appropriate uses of intelligence tests with gifted children. *Roeper Review, 8*, 160–162.

Robinson, N. M., Zigler, E., & Gallagher, J. (2000). Two tails of the normal curve: Similarities and differences in the study of mental retardation and giftedness. *American Psychologist, 55*(12), 1413–1424.

Rogan, L., & Hartman, L. (1976). *A follow-up study of learning disabled children as adults.* Initial report. Evanston, IL: Cove School (ERIC Document Reproduction Service No. ED 163 728).

Rogers, D. L., & Osborne, D. (1984). Comparison of the WAIS and WAIS-R at different ages in a clinical population. *Psychological Reports, 54*, 91–95.

Rogers, R. C., & Simensen, R. J. (1987). Fragile X syndrome: A common etiology of mental retardation. *American Journal of Mental Deficiency, 91*, 445–449.

Roid, G. H., Prifitera, A., & Ledbetter, M. (1988). Confirmatory analysis of the factor structure of the Wechsler Memory Scale-Revised. *Clinical Neuropsychologist, 2*, 116–120.

Rolfhus, E. L., & Ackerman, P. L. (1999). Assessing individual differences in knowledge: Knowledge, intelligence, and related traits. *Journal of Educational Psychology, 91*(3), 511–526.

Rose, R. J., Uchida, I. A., & Christian, J. C. (1981). Placentation effects on cognitive resemblance of adult monozygotes. *Twin Research 3: Intelligence, Personality, and Development*, 35–41.

Rosenthal, B. L., & Kamphaus, R. W. (1988). Interpretive tables for test scatter on the Stanford-Binet Intelligence Scale: Fourth edition. *Journal of Psychoeducational Assessment*, 6, 359–370.

Rosenthal, R., & Ruben, D. B. (1982). Further meta-analytic procedures for assessing cognitive gender differences. *Journal of Educational Psychology*, 74, 708–712.

Ross, A. T., & Reitan, R. M. (1955). Intellectual and affective functions in multiple sclerosis. *A.M.A. Archives of Neurology and Psychiatry*, 73, 663–677.

Ross, E. D. (1981). The Aprosodias: Functional-anatomic organization of the affective components of language in the right hemisphere. *Archives of Neurology*, 38, 561–569.

Ross, E. D. (1984). Right hemisphere's role in language, affective behavior and emotion. *Trends in Neurosciences*, 7, 342–346.

Ross, J. D., & Ross, C. M. (1979). *Ross Test of Higher Cognitive Processes*. Novato, CA: Academic Therapy.

Roszkowski, M. J. (1983). The freedom-from-distractibility factor: An examination of its adaptive behavior correlates. *Journal of Psychoeducational Assessment 1*, 285–297.

Roszkowski, M. J., & Bean, A. G. (1980). The Adaptive Behavior Scale (ABS) and IQ: How much unshared variance is there? *Psychology in the Schools*, 17, 452–459.

Roth, D. L., Hughes, C. W., Monkowkski, P. G., & Crossen, B. (1984). Investigation of validity of WAIS-R short forms for patients suspected to have brain impairment. *Journal of Consulting and Clinical Psychology*, 52, 722–723.

Rourke, B. P., & Adams, K. M. (Eds.). (1988). [Special issue on the Wechsler Memory Scale-Revised]. *Clinical Neuropsychologist*, 2(2). Lisse, the Netherlands: Swets.

Rowe, D. C., Jacobson, K. C., & Van den Oord, E. J. C. G. (1999). Genetic and environmental influences on vocabulary IQ: Parental education level as moderator. *Child Development*, 70, 1151–1162.

Royer, F. L. (1977). Information processing in the Block Design task. *Intelligence*, 1, 32–50.

Royer, F. L. (1978). Sex differences in symbol-digit substitution task performance. *Intelligence*, 2, 145–151.

Royer, F. L. (1984). Stimulus variables in the Block Design task: A commentary on Schorr, Bower, and Kiernan. *Journal of Consulting and Clinical Psychology*, 52, 700–704.

Rubin, H. H., Goldman, J. J., & Rosenfeld, J. G. (1985). A comparison of WISC-R and WAIS-R IQs in a mentally retarded residential population. *Psychology in the Schools*, 22, 392–397.

Rubin, H. H., Goldman, J. J., & Rosenfeld, J. G. (1990). A follow-up comparison of WISC-R and WAIS-R IQs in a residential mentally retarded population. *Psychology in the Schools*, 27, 309–310.

Rubin, K. H., Attewell, P. W., Tierney, M. C., & Tumolo, P. (1973). Development of spatial egocentrism and conservation across the life span. *Developmental Psychology*, 9, 432.

Ruchalla, E., Schalt, E., & Roger, F. (1985). Relations between mental performance and reaction time: New aspects of an old problem. *Intelligence*, 9, 189–205.

Rugel, R. P. (1974). WISC subtest scores of disabled readers: A review with respect to Bannatyne's recategorization. *Journal of Learning Disabilities*, 7, 48–55.

Rumsey, J. M. (1992). Neuropsychological studies of high-level autism. In E. Schopler & G. B. Mesibov (Eds.), *High-functioning individuals with autism* (pp. 41–64). New York: Plenum.

Rumsey, J. M., & Hamburger, S. D. (1988). Neuropsychological findings in high-functioning men with infantile autism, residual state. *Journal of Clinical and Experimental Psychology*, 10, 210–221.

Rumsey, J. M., & Hamburger, S. D. (1990). Neuropsychological divergence of high-level autism and severe dyslexia. *Journal of Autism and Developmental Disorders*, 20, 155–168.

Russell, E. W. (1972). WAIS factor analysis with brain-damaged subjects using criterion measures. *Journal of Consulting and Clinical Psychology*, 39, 133–139.

Russell, E. W. (1975). A multiple scoring method for the assessment of complex memory functions. *Journal of Consulting and Clinical Psychology*, 43, 800–809.

Russell, E. W. (1980). Fluid and crystallized intelligence: Effects of diffuse brain damage on the WAIS. *Perceptual and Motor Skills*, 51, 121–122.

Russell, E. W. (1988). Renorming Russell's version of the Wechsler Memory Scale. *Journal of Clinical and Experimental Neuropsychology*, 10, 235–249.

Rust, J. O., Barnard, D., & Oster, G. D. (1979). WAIS Verbal–Performance differences among elderly when controlling for fatigue. *Psychological Reports*, 44, 489–490.

Rutter, M. (1978). Language disorder and infantile autism. In M. Rutter & E. Schopler (Eds.), *Autism: A reappraisal of concepts and treatment* (pp. 85–104). New York: Plenum.

Rutter, M. (1979). Language, cognition and autism. In R. Katzman (Ed.), *Congenital and acquired cognitive disorders* (pp. 247–264). New York: Raven.

Ryan, J. J. (1983). Clinical utility of a WAIS-R short form. *Journal of Clinical Psychology*, 39, 261–262.

Ryan, J. J. (1985). Application of a WAIS-R short form with neurological patients: Validity and correlational findings. *Journal of Psychoeducational Assessment*, 3, 61–64.

Ryan, J. J. (1999). Two types of tables for use with the seven-subtest short forms of the WAIS-III. *Journal of Psychoeducational Assessment, 17*(2), 145–151.

Ryan, J. J., Abraham, E., Axelrod, B. N., & Paolo, A. M. (1996). WAIS-R Verbal–Performance IQ discrepancies in persons with lateralized lesions: Utility of a seven-subtest short form. *Archives of Clinical Neuropsychology, 11,* 207–213.

Ryan, J. J., Dai, X., & Zheng, L. (1994). Psychological test usage in the Peoples Republic of China. *Journal of Psychoeducational Assessment, 12,* 324–330.

Ryan, J. J., Georgemiller, R. J., Geisser, M. E., & Randall, D. M. (1985). Test-retest stability of the WAIS-R in a clinical sample. *Journal of Clinical Psychology, 41,* 552–556.

Ryan, J. J., Georgemiller, R. J., & McKinney, B. E. (1984). Application of the four-subtest WAIS-R short form with an older clinical sample. *Journal of Clinical Psychology, 40,* 1033–1036.

Ryan, J. J., & Lewis, C. V. (1988). Comparison of normal controls and recently detoxified alcoholics on the Wechsler Memory Scale-Revised. *Clinical Neuropsychologist, 2,* 173–180.

Ryan, J. J., Lopez, S. J., & Werth, T. R. (1998). Administration time estimates for WAIS-III subtests, scales, and short forms in a clinical population. *Journal of Psychoeducational Assessment, 16,* 315–323.

Ryan, J. J., Lopez, S. J., & Werth, T. R. (1999). Development and preliminary validation of a Satz-Mogel short form of the WAIS-III in a sample of persons with substance abuse disorders. *International Journal of Neuroscience, 98,* 131–140.

Ryan, J. J., Nowak, T. J., & Geisser, M. E. (1987). On the comparability of the WAIS and the WAIS-R: Review of the research and implications for clinical practice. *Journal of Psychoeducational Assessment, 5,* 15–30.

Ryan, J. J., Paolo, A. M., & Brungardt, T. M. (1990). Standardization of the Wechsler Adult Intelligence Scale-Revised for persons 75 years and older. *Psychological Assessment, 2,* 404–411.

Ryan, J. J., Paolo, A. M., & Dunn, G. (1995). Analysis of WAIS-R old-age normative sample in terms of gender, years of education, and preretirement occupation. *Assessment, 2,* 225–231.

Ryan, J. J., Paolo, A. M., Oehlert, M. E., & Coker, M. C. (1991). Relationship of sex, race, age, education, and level of intelligence to the frequency of occurrence of a WAIS-R marker for dementia of the Alzheimer's type. *Developmental Neuropsychology, 7,* 451–458.

Ryan, J. J., Prifitera, A., & Larsen, J. (1982). Reliability of the WAIS-R with a mixed patient sample. *Perceptual and Motor Skills, 55,* 1277–1278.

Ryan, J. J., Prifitera, A., & Powers, L. (1983). Scoring reliability on the WAIS-R. *Journal of Consulting and Clinical Psychology, 51,* 149–150.

Ryan, J. J., Prifitera, A., & Rosenberg, S. J. (1983). Interrelationships between factor structures of the WAIS-R and WAIS in a neuropsychological battery. *International Journal of Neuroscience, 21,* 191–196.

Ryan, J. J., & Rosenberg, S. J. (1983). Relationship between WAIS-R and Wide Range Achievement test in a sample of mixed patients. *Perceptual and Motor Skills, 56,* 623–626.

Ryan, J. J., & Rosenberg, S. J. (1984a). Administration time estimates for WAIS-R subtests and short forms. *Journal of Psychoeducational Assessment, 2,* 125–129.

Ryan, J. J., & Rosenberg, S. J. (1984b). Validity of the Verbal IQ as a short form of the Wechsler Adult Intelligence Scale-Revised. *Journal of Clinical Psychology, 51,* 306–308.

Ryan, J. J., Rosenberg, S. J., & DeWolfe, A. S. (1984). Generalization of the WAIS-R factor structure with a vocational rehabilitation sample. *Journal of Consulting and Clinical Psychology, 52,* 311–312.

Ryan, J. J., Rosenberg, S. J., & Heilbronner, R. L. (1984). Comparative relationships of the Wechsler Adult Intelligence Scale-Revised and the Wechsler Adult Intelligence Scale (WAIS) to the Wechsler Memory Scale (WMS). *Journal of Behavioral Assessment, 6,* 37–43.

Ryan, J. J., Rosenberg, S. J., & Prifitera, A. (1983). On substituting the WAIS-R for the WAIS in neuropsychological assessment: A caution for clinicians. *Journal of Psychology, 115,* 131–134.

Ryan, J. J., & Schneider, J. A. (1986). Factor analysis of the Wechsler Adult Intelligence Scale-Revised (WAIS-R) in a brain-damaged sample. *Journal of Clinical Psychology, 42,* 962–964.

Ryan, J. J., & Ward, L. C. (1999). Validity, reliability, and standard errors of measurement for two seven-subtest short forms of the Wechsler Adult Intelligence Scale-III. *Psychological Assessment, 11*(2), 207–211.

Salford Systems (1999). *Data mining with decision trees: An introducton to CART.* San Diego, CA: Author.

Salford Systems (2000). *CART for Windows users guide: A Salford Systems implementation of the original CART program.* San Diego, CA: Author.

Salois, K. A. (1999). A comparative study of the Wechsler Intelligence Scale for Children-Third Edition (WISC-III) test performance: Northern Cheyenne and Blackfeet Reservation Indian children with the standardization sample. *Dissertation Abstracts International, 60* (4-B).

Salthouse, T. A. (1984, August). *Speculations of the what, when, and why of mental aging.* Paper presented at the meeting of the American Psychological Association, Toronto.

Salthouse, T. A. (1985). Speed of behavior and its implications for cognition. In J. E. Birren & K. W. Schaie (Eds.), Handbook of the psychology of aging (2nd ed; pp. 400–426). New York: Van Nostrand Reinhold.

Salthouse, T. A. (1991). *Theoretical perspectives on cognitive aging*. Hillsdale, NJ: Erlbaum.

Salthouse, T. A. (1992). *Mechanisms of age–cognition relations in adulthood*. Hillsdale, NJ: Erlbaum.

Salthouse, T. A. (1996). The processing-speed theory of adult age differences in cognition. *Psychological Review, 103*(3), 403–428.

Salthouse, T. A. (1998a). Independence of age-related influences on cognitive abilities across the life span. *Developmental Psychology, 34*(5), 851–864.

Salthouse, T. A. (1998b). Relation of successive percentiles of reaction time distribution to cognitive variables and adult age. *Intelligence, 26*(2), 153–166.

Salthouse, T. A. (2000). Methodological assumptions in cognitive aging research. In F. I. M. Craik & T. A. Salthouse (Eds.), *The handbook of aging and cognition* (2nd ed.; pp. 467–498). Mahwah, NJ: Erlbaum.

Salthouse, T. A., Fristoe, N., McGurthry K. E., & Hambrick D. Z. (1998). Relation of task switching to speed, age, and fluid intelligence. *Psychology and Aging, 13*(3), 445–461.

Salthouse, T. A., Hambrick, D. Z., & McGuthrey, K. E. (1998). Shared age-related influences on cognitive and non-cognitive variables. *Psychology and Aging, 13*, 486–500.

Salthouse, T. A., Hancock, H. E., Meinz, E. J., & Hambrick, D. Z. (1996). Interrelations of age, visual acuity, and cognitive functioning. *Journal of Gerontology: Psychological Sciences, 51*, 81–84.

Salthouse, T. A., Kausler, D. H., & Saults, J. S. (1988). Utilization of path analytic procedures to investigate the role of processing resources in cognitive aging. *Psychology and Aging, 3*, 158–166.

Salthouse, T. A., Kausler, D. H., & Saults, J. S. (1990). Age, self-assessed health status, and cognition. *Journal of Gerontology: Psychological Sciences, 45*, 156–160.

Salvia, J., Gajar, A., Gajria, M., & Salvia, S. (1988). A comparison of WAIS-R profiles of nondisabled college freshmen and college students with learning disabilities. *Journal of Learning Disabilities, 21*, 632–636.

Salvia, J., & Ysseldyke, J. E. (1988). *Assessment in special and remedial education* (4th ed.). Boston: Houghton Mifflin.

San Diego, E. A., Foley, J. M., & Walker, R. E. (1970). WAIS scores for highly educated young adults from the Philippines and the United States. *Psychological Reports, 27*, 511–515.

Sandoval, J., & Irvin, M. G. (1988). Review of the Stanford-Binet Intelligence Scale: Fourth edition. *Professional School Psychology, 3*, 157–161.

Sandoval, J., Sassenrath, J., & Penaloza, M. (1988). Similarity of WISC-R and WAIS-R scores at age 16. *Psychology in the Schools, 25*, 373–379.

Sapp, G. L., Chissoni, B., & Graham, E. (1985). Factor analysis of the WISC-R for gifted students: A replication and comparison. *Psychological Reports, 57*, 947–951.

Sattler, J. M. (1974). *Assessment of children's intelligence* (Rev. ed.). Philadelphia: Saunders.

Sattler, J. M. (1982). Age effects on Wechsler Adult Intelligence Scale-Revised. *Journal of Consulting and Clinical Psychology, 50*, 785–786.

Sattler, J. M. (1988). *Assessment of children* (3rd ed.). San Diego, CA: Author.

Sattler, J. M. (1992). *Assessment of children: WISC-III and WPPSI-R Supplement*. San Diego, CA: Author.

Sattler, J. M. (2001). *Assessment of children: Cognitive applications* (4th ed.). San Diego, CA: Author.

Sattler, J. M., & Covin, T. M. (1986). Comparison of the Slosson Intelligence Test, revised norms, and WISC-R for children with learning problems and for gifted children. *Psychology in the Schools, 23*, 259–264.

Sattler, J. M., & Gwynne, J. (1982). White examiners generally do not impede the intelligence test performance of black children. *Journal of Consulting and Clinical Psychology, 50*, 196–208.

Sattler, J. M., Polifka, J. C., Polifka, S., & Hilsen, D. E. (1984). A longitudinal study of the WISC-R and WAIS-R with special education students. *Psychology in the Schools, 21*, 294–295.

Sattler, J. M., & Ryan, J. J. (1999). *Assessment of children: Revised and updated third edition. WAIS-III Supplement*. San Diego, CA: Author.

Sattler, J. M., & Winger, B. M. (1970). Intelligence testing procedures as affected by expectancy and IQ. *Journal of Clinical Psychology, 26*, 446–448.

Satz, D. (1966). Specific and nonspecific effects of brain lesions in man. *Journal of Abnormal Psychology, 71*, 65–70.

Satz, D., & Fletcher, J. M. (1981). Emergent trends in neuropsychology: An overview. *Journal of Consulting and Clinical Psychology, 49*, 851–865.

Satz, D., Hynd, G. W., D'Elia, L., Daniel, M., Van Gorp, W., & Conner, R. (1989). *A WAIS-R marker for accelerated aging and dementia, Alzheimer's type? Base rates of the Fuld Formula in the WAIS-R standardization sample*. Manuscript submitted for publication.

Satz, P., Hynd, G. W., D'Elia, L., Daniel, M. G., Van Gorp, W., & Connor, R. (1990). A WAIS-R marker for accelerated aging and dementia, Alzheimer's type?: Base rates of the Fuld formula in the WAIS-R standardization sample. *Journal of Clinical and Experimental Neuropsychology, 12*, 759–765.

Satz, P., & Mogel, S. (1962). Abbreviation of the WAIS for clinical use. *Journal of Clinical Psychology, 18*, 77–79.

Satz, P., Richard, W., & Daniels, A. (1967). The alteration of intellectual performance after lateralized brain-injury in man. *Psychonomic Science, 7,* 369–370.

Satz, P., Van Gorp, W., Soper, H. V., & Mitrushina, M. (1987). WAIS-R marker for dementia of the Alzheimer type? An empirical and statistical induction test. *Journal of Clinical and Experimental Neuropsychology, 9,* 767–774.

Scarr, S. (1981). Genetics and the development of intelligence. In S. Scarr (Ed.), *Race, social class, and individual differences in IQ* (pp. 3–59). Hillsdale, NJ: Erlbaum.

Scarr, S. (1997). Behavior-genetic and socialization theories of intelligence: Truce and reconciliation. In R. J. Sternberg & E. Grigorenko (Eds.), *Intelligence, heredity, and environment* (pp. 3–41). New York: Cambridge University Press.

Scarr, S., & Barker, W. (1981). The effects of family background: A study of cognitive differences among black and white twins. In S. Scarr (Ed.), *Race, social class, and individual differences in IQ* (pp. 261–315). Hillsdale, NJ: Erlbaum.

Scarr, S., & Carter-Saltzman, I. (1982). Genetics and intelligence. In R. J. Sternberg (Ed.), *Handbook of human intelligence* (pp. 792–896). Cambridge, England: Cambridge University Press.

Scarr, S., & Grajek, S. (1982). Similarities and differences among siblings. In M. E. Lamb & B. Sutton-Smith (Eds.), *Sibling relationships.* Hillsdale, NJ: Erlbaum.

Scarr, S., & Weinberg, R. A. (1976). IQ test performance of black children adopted by white families. *American Psychologist, 31,* 726–739.

Scarr, S., & Weinberg, R. A. (1978). The influence of "family background" on intellectual attainment. *American Sociological Review, 43,* 674–692.

Scarr-Salapatek, S. (1971). Unknowns in the IQ equation. *Science, 174,* 1223–1228.

Schachter, D. L., & Crovitz, H. F. (1977). Memory function after closed head injury: A review of the quantitative research. *Cortex, 13,* 150–176.

Schaie, K. W. (1958). Rigidity-flexibility and intelligence: A cross-sectional study of the adult life-span from 20 to 70. *Psychological Monographs, 72* (9, Whole No. 462).

Schaie, K. W. (Ed.). (1983a). *Longitudinal studies of adult psychological development.* New York: Guilford.

Schaie, K. W. (1983b). The Seattle Longitudinal Study: A 21-year exploration of psychometric intelligence in adulthood. In K. W. Schaie (Ed.), *Longitudinal studies of adult psychological development* (pp. 64–135). New York: Guilford.

Schaie, K. W. (1983c). What can we learn from the longitudinal study of adult psychological development? In K. W. Schaie (Ed.), *Longitudinal studies of adult psychological development* (pp. 1–19). New York: Guilford.

Schaie, K. W. (1984). Midlife influences upon intellectual functioning in old age. *International Journal of Behavior Development, 7,* 463–478.

Schaie, K. W. (1994). The course of adult intellectual development. *American Psychologist, 49,* 304–313.

Schaie, K. W. (1996). *Intellectual development in adulthood: The Seattle Longitudinal Study.* New York: Cambridge University Press.

Schaie, K. W., & Hertzog, C. (1983). Fourteen-year cohort-sequential analyses of adult intellectual development. *Developmental Psychology, 19,* 531–543.

Schaie, K. W., & Hertzog, C. (1985). Measurement in the psychology of adulthood and aging. In J. E. Birren & K. W. Schaie (Eds.), *Handbook of the psychology of aging* (2nd ed.; pp. 61–92). New York: Van Nostrand Reinhold.

Schaie, K. W., & Hertzog, C. (1986). Stability and change in adult intelligence: Analysis of longitudinal covariance structures. *Psychology and Aging, 1,* 159–171.

Schaie, K. W., & Labouvie-Vief, G. (1974). Generational vs. ontogenetic components of change in adult cognitive behavior: A fourteen-year cross-sequential study. *Developmental Psychology, 10,* 305–320.

Schaie, K. W., & Schaie, J. D. (1977). Clinical assessment and aging. In J. E. Birren & K. W. Schaie (Eds.), *Handbook of the psychology of aging* (pp. 692–723). New York: Van Nostrand Reinhold.

Schaie, K. W., & Strother, C. R. (1968). The cross-sequential study of age changes in cognitive behavior. *Psychological Bulletin, 70,* 671–680.

Schaie, K. W., & Willis, S. L. (1986). Can decline in intellectual functioning be reversed? *Developmental Psychology, 22,* 223–232.

Schaie, K. W., & Willis, S. L. (1993). Age difference patterns of psychometric intelligence in adulthood: Generalizability within and across ability domains. *Psychology & Aging, 8,* 44–55.

Schiff, M. M., Kaufman, A. S., & Kaufman, N. E. (1981). Scatter analysis of WISC-R profiles for learning disabled children with superior intelligence. *Journal of Learning Disabilities, 14,* 400–404.

Schill, T. (1966). The effect of MMPI social introversion on the WAIS PA performance. *Journal of Clinical Psychology, 22,* 72–74.

Schill, T., Kahn, M., & Muehleman, T. (1968a). WAIS PA performance and participation in extracurricular activities. *Journal of Clinical Psychology, 24,* 95–96.

Schill, T., Kahn, M., & Muehleman, T. (1968b). Verbal conditionability and Wechsler Picture Arrangement scores. *Journal of Consulting and Clinical Psychology, 32,* 718–721.

Schiller, F. (1947). Aphasia studied in patients with missile wounds. *Journal of Neurology, Neurosurgery and Psychiatry, 10,* 183–197.

Schinka, J. A. (1974). *Performances of brain damaged patients on tests of short-term and long-term verbal memory.* Unpublished doctoral dissertation, University of Iowa.

Schmidt, F. L., & Hunter, J. E. (1998). The validity and utility of selection methods in personnel psychology: Practical and theoretical implications of 85 years of research findings. *Psychological Bulletin, 124,* 262–274.

Schmidt, H. P. J., & Saklofske, D. H. (1983). Comparison of the WISC-R patterns of children of average and exceptional ability. *Psychological Reports, 53,* 539–544.

Schmitz-Sherzer, R., & Thomae, H. (1983). Constancy and change of behavior in old age: Findings from the Bonn Longitudinal Study on Aging. In K. W. Schaie (Ed.), *Longitudinal studies of adult psychological development* (pp. 191–221). New York: Guilford.

Schneider, S. G., & Asarnow, R. F. (1987). A comparison of cognitive/neuropyschoogical impairments of nonretarded autistic and schizophrenic children. *Journal of Abnormal Child Psychology, 15,* 29–46.

Schooler, C. (1987). Psychological effects of complex environments during the life span: A review and theory. In C. Schooler & K. W. Schaie (Eds.), *Cognitive functioning and social structure over the life course* (pp. 24–49). Norwood, NJ: Ablex.

Schooler, C. (1990). Psychosocial factors and effective cognitive functioning in adulthood. In J. E. Birren & K. W. Schaie (Eds.), *Handbook of the psychology of aging* (pp. 347–358). San Diego, CA: Academic Press.

Schooler, D. L., Beebe, M. C., & Koepke, T. (1978). Factor analysis of WISC-R scores for children identified as learning disabled, educable mentally impaired, and emotionally impaired. *Psychology in the Schools, 15,* 478–485.

Schopp, L. H., Callahan, C. D., Johnstone, B., & Schwake, C. J. (1998). Utility of a seven-subtest version of the WAIS-R among an Alzheimer's disease sample. *Archives of Clinical Neuropsychology, 13,* 637–643.

Schorr, D., Bower, G. H., & Klienman, R. (1982). Stimulus variables in the Block Design task. *Journal of Consulting and Clinical Psychology, 50,* 479–487.

Schrank, F. A., & Woodcock, R. W. (2001). WJ III Compuscore and Profiles Program [computer software] [Woodcock-Johnson III]. Itasca, IL: Riverside.

Schreiber, D. J., Goldman, H., Kleinman, K. M., Goldfaber, P. R., & Snow, M. Y. (1976). The relationship between independent neuropsychological detection and localization of cerebral impairment. *Journal of Nervous and Mental Disease, 162,* 360–365.

Schretlen, D., Pearlson, G. D., Anthony, J. C., Aylward, E. H., Augustine, A. M., Davis, A., & Barta, P. (2000). Elucidating the contributions of processing speed, executive ability, and frontal lobe volume to normal age-related differences in fluid intelligence. *Journal of the International Neuropsychological Society, 6,* 52–61.

Schultz, N. R., Jr., Dineen, J. T., Elias, M. F., Pentz, C. A., & Wood, W. G. (1979). WAIS performance for different age groups of hypertensive and control subjects during the administration of a diuretic. *Journal of Gerontology, 34,* 246–253.

Schultz, N. R., Jr., Elias, M. F., Robbins, M. A., Streeten, D. H. P., & Blakeman, N. (1986). A longitudinal comparison of hypertensives and normotensives on the Wechsler Adult Intelligence Scale: Initial findings. *Journal of Gerontology, 41,* 169–175.

Schurr, K. T., Ruble, V. E., Henriksen, L. W., & Alcorn, B. K. (1989). Relationships of National Teacher Examination communication skills and general knowledge scores with high school and college grades, Myers-Briggs type indicator characteristics, and self-reported skill ratings and academic problems. *Educational and Psychological Measurement, 49,* 243–252.

Schuster, T. L., & Butler, E. B. (1986). Learning, mild mental retardation, and long-range social adjustment. *Sociological Perspectives, 29,* 461–483.

Schwean, V. L., & Saklofske, D. H. (1998). WISC-III assessment of children with attention deficit/hyperactivity disorder. In A. Prifitera & D. Saklofski (Eds.), *WISC-III clinical use and interpretation* (pp. 91–118). San Diego, CA: Academic Press.

Schweinhart, L. J., Barnes, H. V., & Weikart, D. P. (1993). Significant benefits: The High/Scope Perry Preschool study through age 27. *Monographs of the High Scope Educational Research Foundation* (Number 10). Ypsilanti, MI: High/Scope.

Scott, K. G., & Carran, D. I. (1987). The epidemiology and prevention of mental retardation. *American Psychologist, 42,* 801–804.

Sears, P. S., & Barbee, A. H. (1977). Career and life satisfaction among Terman's gifted women. In J. C. Stanley, W. C. George, & C. H. Solano (Eds.), *The gifted and the creative: Fifty-year perspective* (pp. 28–65). Baltimore: Johns Hopkins University Press.

Sears, R. R. (1977). Sources of life satisfactions of the Terman gifted men. *American Psychologist, 32,* 119–128.

Seashore, H. G., Wesman, A. G., & Doppelt, J. E. (1950). The standardization of the Wechsler Intelligence Scale for Children. *Journal of Consulting Psychology, 14,* 99–110.

Segal, N. L. (1997). Same-age unrelated siblings: A unique test of within-family environmental influences on IQ similarity. *Journal of Educational Psychology, 89,* 381–390.

Segal, N. L. (1999). *Entwined lives: Twins and what they tell us about human behavior.* New York: Dutton.

Segal, N. L. (2000). Virtual twins: New findings on within-family environmental influences on intelligence. *Journal of Educational Psychology, 92,* 442–448.

Seidenberg, M., O'Leary, D. S., Giordani, B., Berent, S., & Boll, T. J. (1981). Test-retest IQ changes of epilepsy patients:

Assessing the influence of practice effects. *Journal of Clinical Neuropsychology, 3*, 237–255.

Seitz, V., Rosenbaum, L. K., & Apfel, N. H. (1985). Effects of family support intervention: A ten-year follow-up. *Child Development, 56*, 376–391.

Sells, S. B. (1966). *Evaluation of psychological measures used in the health examination survey of children ages 6–11.* Washington, DC: U.S. Department of Health, Education, and Welfare, Public Health Service, Vital and Health Statistics, Publication No. 1000 (Series 2, No. 15).

Selz, M., & Reitan, R. M. (1979). Rules for neuropsychological diagnosis: Classification of brain function in older children. *Journal of Consulting and Clinical Psychology, 47*, 258–264.

Shah, M. G. (1999). Verbal and visual learning in a sample of Native American children: A study of the effects of practice on memory. *Dissertation Abstracts International, 59* (8-A).

Shapiro, B. A. (1982). Relation of facial expressions and activities: A study of attensity differences in events. *Perceptual and Motor Skills, 54*, 1199–1211.

Sharp, S. E. (1898–99). Individual psychology: A study in psychological method. *American Journal of Psychology, 10*, 329–391.

Shatz, M. W. (1981). Comment: WAIS practice effects in clinical neuropsychology. *Journal of Clinical Neuropsychology, 3*, 171–179.

Shaw, D. J. (1966). The reliability and validity of the Halstead Category Test. *Journal of Clinical Psychology, 22*, 176–180.

Shaw, S. R. (1998). Kaufman Functional Academic Skills Test. In J. C. Impara & B. S. Plake (Eds.), *The thirteenth mental measurements yearbook* (pp. 568–570). Lincoln, NE: Buros Institute of Mental Measurements, University of Nebraska Press.

Shellenberger, S. (1977). *A cross-cultural investigation of the Spanish version of the McCarthy Scales of Children's Abilities for Puerto Rican children.* Unpublished doctoral dissertation, University of Georgia, Athens.

Shellenberger, S., & Lachterman, T. (1979). Cognitive and motor functioning on the McCarthy Scales by Spanish-speaking children. *Perceptual and Motor Skills, 49*, 863–866.

Shepard, J., & Hohenshil, T. H. (1983). Career development functions of practicing school psychologists: A national study. *Psychology in the Schools, 20*, 445–449.

Shepherd, M. J. (2001). History lessons. In A. S. Kaufman & N. L. Kaufman (Eds.), *Specific learning disabilities and difficulties in children and adolescents: Psychological assessment and evaluation* (pp. 3–28). (Included in the Series, Cambridge Monographs in Child and Adolescent Psychiatry.) Cambridge, England: Cambridge University Press.

Sherman, E. M. S., Strauss, E., Spellacy, F., & Hunter, M. (1995). Construct validity of WAIS-R factors: Neuropsychological test correlates in adults referred for evaluation of possible head injury. *Psychological Assessment, 7*, 440–444.

Sherman, J. A. (1978). *Sex-related cognitive differences: An essay on theory and evidence.* Springfield, IL: Charles Thomas.

Sherman, J. A. (1980). Sex-related differences in human brain asymmetry: Verbal functions-no; spatial functions-maybe. *Behavioral and Brain Sciences, 3*, 248–249.

Sheslow, D., & Adams, W. (1990). *Wide Range Assessment of Memory and Learning.* Wilmington, DE: Jastak Assessment Systems.

Shimamura, A. P., Berry, J. M., Mangels, J. A., Rusting, C. L., & Jurica, P. J. (1995). Memory and cognitive abilities in university professors: Evidence for successful aging. *Psychological Science, 6*, 271–277.

Shinn, M., Algozzine, B., Marston, D., & Ysseldyke, J. E. (1982). A theoretical analysis of the performance of learning disabled students on the Woodcock-Johnson Psycho-Educational Battery. *Journal of Learning Disabilities, 15*, 221–226.

Shipley, C. (1953). The Shipley Institute of Living Scale for measuring intellectual impairment. In A. Weider (Ed.), *Contributions toward medical psychology: Vol. 2. Theory and diagnostic methods* (pp. 751–756). New York: Ronald.

Shipley, W. C. (1940). A self-administering scale for measuring intellectual impairment and deterioration. *Journal of Psychology, 9*, 371–377.

Shouksmith, G. (1970). *Intelligence, creativity and cognitive style.* New York: Wiley.

Shuecy, A. M. (1966). *The testing of Negro intelligence* (2nd ed.). New York: Social Science Press.

Shure, G. H., & Halstead, W. C. (1958). *Cerebral localization of intellectual processes.* Psychological Monogaphs, 72 (12, Whole No. 465).

Siegel, D. J., & Minshew, N. J. (1996). Wechsler IQ profiles in diagnosis of high-functioning autism. *Journal of Autism and Developmental Disorders, 26*, 389–406.

Siegel, D. J., Minshew, N. J., & Goldstein, G. (1996). Wechsler IQ profiles in diagnosis of high-functioning autism. *Journal of Autism and Developmental Disorders, 26*, 389–406.

Siegel, L. S. (1989). IQ is irrelevant to the definition of learning disabilities. *Journal of Learning Disabilities, 22*, 469–479.

Siegel, L. S. (1999). Issues in the definition and diagnosis of learning disabilities: A perspective on *Guckenberger v. Boston University. Journal of Learning Disabilities, 32*, 304–319.

Siegler, I. (1983). Psychological aspects of the Duke Longitudinal studies. In K. W. Schaie (Ed.), *Longitudinal studies of adult psychological development* (pp. 136–190). New York: Guilford.

Siegler, I., & Botwinick, J. (1979). A long-term longitudinal study of intellectual ability of older adults: The matter of selective subject attrition. *Journal of Gerontology, 34*, 242–245.

Sigelman, C. K., Schoenrock, C. J., Winer, J. L., Spanhel, C. L., Hromias, S. G., Martin, P. W., Budd, E. C., & Bensberg, G. J. (1981). Issues in interviewing mentally retarded persons: An empirical study. In R. H. Bruininks, C. E. Meyers, B. B. Sigford, & K. C. Lakin (Eds.), *Deinstitutionalization and community adjustment of mentally retarded people.* Washington, DC: American Association on Mental Deficiency.

Silver, L. B. (Ed.). (1993). *Child and adolescent psychiatric clinics of North America, 2,* 181–353.

Silverstein, A. B. (1967a). A short short form of the WISC and WAIS for screening purposes. *Psychological Reports, 21,* 692.

Silverstein, A. B. (1967b). A short short form of Wechsler's scales for screening purposes. *Psychological Reports, 21,* 842.

Silverstein, A. B. (1969). An alternative factor analytic solution for Wechsler's Intelligence Scales. *Educational and Psychological Measurement, 29,* 763–776.

Silverstein, A. B. (1971). A corrected formula for assessing the validity of WAIS, WISC, and WPPSI short forms. *Journal of Clinical Psychology, 27,* 212–213.

Silverstein, A. B. (1973). Note on prevalence. *American Journal of Mental Deficiency, 77,* 380–382.

Silverstein, A. B. (1975). A reply to McNemar. *Journal of Consulting and Clinical Psychology, 43,* 423–424.

Silverstein, A. B. (1977a). Comparison of two criteria for determining the number of factors. *Psychological Reports, 41,* 387–390.

Silverstein, A. B. (1977b). Comment on Kaufman's "Should short form validity coefficients be corrected?" *Journal of Consulting and Clinical Psychology, 45,* 1162–1163.

Silverstein, A. B. (1982a). Factor structure of the Wechsler Adult Intelligence Scale-Revised. *Journal of Consulting and Clinical Psychology, 50,* 661–664.

Silverstein, A. B. (1982b). Note on the constancy of the IQ. *American Journal of Mental Deficiency, 87,* 227–228.

Silverstein, A. B. (1982c). Pattern analysis as simultaneous statistical inference. *Journal of Consulting and Clinical Psychology, 50,* 234–240.

Silverstein, A. B. (1982d). Two- and four-subtest short forms of the Wechsler Adult Intelligence Scale-Revised. *Journal of Consulting and Clinical Psychology, 50,* 415–418.

Silverstein, A. B. (1982e). Validity of random short forms. *Perceptual and Motor Skills, 55,* 411–414.

Silverstein, A. B. (1982f). Validity of Satz-Mogel-Yudin-type short forms. *Journal of Consulting and Clinical Psychology, 50,* 20–21.

Silverstein, A. B. (1984a). Estimating Full Scale IQs from short forms of Wechsler's scales: Linear scaling versus linear regression. *Journal of Consulting and Clinical Psychology, 52,* 919.

Silverstein, A. B. (1984b). Standard errors for short forms of Wechsler's Intelligence scales with deviant subjects. *Journal of Consulting and Clinical Psychology, 52,* 913–914.

Silverstein, A. B. (1985a). An appraisal of three criteria for evaluating the usefulness of WAIS-R short forms. *Journal of Clinical Psychology, 41,* 676–680.

Silverstein, A. B. (1985b). Two- and four-subtest short forms of the WAIS-R: A closer look at validity and reliability. *Journal of Clinical Psychology, 41,* 95–97.

Silverstein, A. B. (1985c). Cluster analysis of the Wechsler Adult Intelligence Scale-Revised. *Journal of Clinical Psychology, 41,* 98–100.

Silverstein, A. B. (1985d). Verbal–Performance IQ discrepancies on the WAIS-R: Estimated vs. empirical values. *Journal of Clinical Psychology, 41,* 694–697.

Silverstein, A. B. (1986a). Discrepancies between composite quotients on the Detroit Tests of Learning Aptitude. *Journal of Psychoeducational Assessment, 4,* 239–242.

Silverstein, A. B. (1986b). Nonstandard standard scores on the Vineland Adaptive Behavior Scales: A cautionary note. *American Journal of Mental Deficiency, 91,* 1–4.

Silverstein, A. B. (1987a). Accuracy of estimates of premorbid intelligence based on demographic variables. *Journal of Clinical Psychology, 43,* 493–495.

Silverstein, A. B. (1987b). Multidimensional scaling versus factor analysis of Wechsler's intelligence scales. *Journal of Clinical Psychology, 43,* 381–386.

Silverstein, A. B. (1987c). Unusual test score combinations and unusual test score differences. *Journal of Clinical Psychology, 43,* 490–492.

Simon, C. L., & Clopton, J. R. (1984). Comparison of WAIS and WAIS-R scores of mildly and moderately mentally retarded adults. *American Journal of Mental Deficiency, 89,* 301–303.

Simons, M. R., & Goh, D. S. (1982). Relationships between McCarthy Scales of Children's Abilities and teacher's ratings of school achievement. *Perceptual and Motor Skills, 54,* 1159–1162.

Simpson, C. D., & Vega, A. (1971). Unilateral brain damage and patterns of age-corrected WAIS subtest scores. *Journal of Clinical Psychology, 27,* 204–208.

Sipps, G. J., Berry, G., & Lynch, E. M. (1987). WAIS-R and social intelligence: A test of established assumptions that uses the CPI. *Journal of Clinical Psychology, 43,* 499–504.

Sisemore, T. A. (1985). A comparison of the WISC-R and WAIS-R in exceptional adolescents. Fuller Theological Seminary, 1984. *Dissertation Abstracts International, 45* (12-B, Pt. 1), 3962.

Slate, J. R. (1986). A reaction to the revised Stanford-Binet Intelligence Scale: New does not necessarily mean better. *National Association of School Psychologists Communique, 15*(1), 3.

Slate, J. R., & Fawcett, J. (1996). Gender differences in Wechsler Performance scores of school-age children who are deaf or hard of hearing. *American Annals of the Deaf, 141,* 19–23.

Slate, J. R., Frost, J., & Cross, B. (1990). Comparability of WISC-R and WAIS-R scores for a sample of college students with learning disabilities. *Learning Disability Quarterly, 13,* 205–208.

Slate, J. R., Frost, J., & Cross, B. (1991). WAIS-R stability for college students with learning disabilities. *Learning Disability Quarterly, 14,* 2–6.

Slate, J. R., & Hunnicutt, E. C. (1988). Examiner errors on the Wechsler scales. *Journal of Psychoeducational Assessment, 6,* 280–288.

Slate, J. R., Graham, L. S., & Bower, J. (1996). Relationship of the WISC-R and K-BIT for an adolescent clinical sample. *Adolescence, 31,* 777–782.

Slate, J. R., Jones, C. H., & Murray, R. A. (1991). Teaching administration and scoring of the Wechsler Adult Intelligence Scale-Revised: An empirical evaluation of practice administrations. *Professional Psychology: Research and Practice, 22,* 375–379.

Slosson, R. E. (1982). *Slosson Intelligence Test* (2nd ed.). East Aurora, NY: Slosson Educational Publications.

Small, L. (1980). *Neuropsychodiagnosis in psychotherapy.* New York: Brunner/Mazel.

Smith, A. (1962). Ambiguities in concepts and studies of "brain damage" and "organicity." *Journal of Nervous and Mental Diseases, 135*(3), 11–326.

Smith, A. (1966a). Certain hypothesized hemispheric differences in language and visual functions in human adults. *Cortex, 2,* 109–126.

Smith, A. (1966b). Intellectual functions in patients with lateralized frontal tumours. *Journal of Neurology, Neurosurgery and Psychiatry, 29,* 52–59.

Smith, A. (1966c). Verbal and nonverbal test performances of patients with "acute" lateralized brain lesions (tumors). *Journal of Nervous and Mental Disease, 141,* 517–523.

Smith, A. (1981). Principles underlying human brain functions in neuropsychological sequelae of different neuropathological processes. In S. H. Filskov & T. J. Boll (Eds.), *Handbook of clinical neuropsychology* (pp. 175–226). New York: Wiley.

Smith, A. (1983). Overview or "underview"? Comment on Satz and Fletcher's "Emergent trends in neuropsychology: An overview." *Journal of Consulting and Clinical Psychology, 51,* 768–775.

Smith, C. R., & Knoff, H. M. (1981). School psychology and special education students' placement decisions: IQ still tips the scale. *Journal of Special Education, 15,* 55–63.

Smith, D. (1982). *Recognizable patterns of human malformation.* Philadelphia: Saunders.

Smith, D. K. (1988, April). *The Matrix Analogies Test: A validity study with the K-ABC.* Paper Presented at the Annual Meeting of the National Association of School Psychologists, Chicago, IL.

Smith, G. T., McCarthy, D. M., & Anderson, K. G. (2000). On the sins of short-form development. *Psychological Assessment, 12*(1), 102–111.

Smith, H. H., & Smith, L. S. (1977). WAIS functioning of cirrhotic and noncirrhotic alcoholics. *Journal of Clinical Psychology, 33,* 309–313.

Smith, R. S. (1983). A comparison study of the Wechsler Adult Intelligence Scale and the Wechsler Adult Intelligence Scale-Revised in a college population. *Journal of Consulting and Clinical Psychology, 51,* 414–419.

Snitz, B. E., Bielkaukskas, L. A., Crossland, A., Basso M. R., & Roper, B. (2000). PPVT-R as an estimate of premorbid intelligence in older adults. *Clinical Neuropsychologist, 14,* 181–186.

Snow, J. H., Koller, J. R., & Roberts, D. (1987). Adolescent and adult learning disability subgroups based on WAIS-R performance. *Journal of Psychoeducational Assessment. 5,* 7–14.

Snow, R. E. (1989). Toward assessment of cognitive and conative structures in learning. *Educational Researcher, 18,* 8–14.

Snow, R. E. (1991). The concept of aptitude. In R. E. Snow & D. E. Wiley (Eds.), *Improving inquiring in social science* (pp. 249–284). Hillsdale, NJ: Erlbaum.

Snow, W. G., Freedman, L., & Ford, E. (1986). Lateralized brain damage, sex differences, and the Wechsler intelligence scales: A reexamination of the literature. *Journal of Clinical and Experimental Neuropsychology, 8,* 179–189.

Snow, W. G., & Sheese, S. (1985). Lateralized brain damage, intelligence, and memory: A failure to find sex differences. *Journal of Consulting and Clinical Psychology, 53,* 940–941.

Snyderman, M., & Rothman, S. (1987). Survey of expert opinion on intelligence and aptitude testing. *American Psychologist, 42,* 137–144.

Sobotowicz, W., Evans, J. R., & Laughlin, J. (1987). Neuropsychological function and social support in delinquency and learning disability. *International Journal of Clinical Neuropsychology, 9,* 178–186.

Sommer, R., & Sommer, B. A. (1983). Mystery in Milwaukee: Early intervention, IQ, and psychology textbooks. *American Psychologist, 38,* 982–985.

Souchay, C., Isingrini, M., & Espagnet, L. (2000). Aging, episodic memory feeling-of-knowing, and frontal functioning. *Neuropsychology, 14,* 299–309.

Sparks, R. L., & Javarskey, J. (1999). Students classified as LD and the college foreign language requirement: Replication and comparison studies. *Journal of Learning Disabilities, 32,* 329–349.

Sparks, R. L., Philips, L., Gahshaw, L., & Javarskey, J. (1999). Students classified as LD and the college foreign language requirement: A quantitative analysis. *Journal of Learning Disabilities, 32,* 566–580.

Sparling, J. J., & Lewis, I. (1979). *Learningames for the first three years: A guide to parent–child play.* New York: Walker.

Sparling, J. J., & Lewis, I. (1984). *Learningames for threes and fours: A guide to adult and child play.* New York: Walker.

Sparrow, S. S., Balla, D. A., & Cicchetti, D. V. (1984a). *Vineland Adaptive Behavior Scales, Expanded Form manual.* Circle Pines, MN: American Guidance Service.

Sparrow, S. S., Balla, D. A., & Cicchetti, D. V. (1984b). *Vineland Adaptive Behavior Scales, Survey Form manual.* Circle Pines, MN: American Guidance Service.

Sparrow, S. S., & Cicchetti, D. V. (1987). Adaptive behavior and the psychologically disturbed child. *Journal of Special Education, 21,* 89–100.

Sparrow, S. S., & Gurland, S. T. (1998). Assessment of gifted children with the WISC-III. In A. Prifitera & D. Saklofske (Eds.), *WISC-III clinical use and interpretation* (pp. 59–72). San Diego, CA: Academic Press.

Spearman, C. E. (1904). "General Intelligence," objectively determined and measured. *American Journal of Psychiatry, 15,* 201–293.

Spearman, C. E. (1927). *The abilities of man: Their nature and measurement.* London: Macmillan.

Sperry, R. W. (1968). Hemispheric deconnection and unity in conscious awareness. *American Psychologist, 23,* 723–733.

Spiers, D. A. (1981). Have they come to praise Luria or to bury him? The Luria-Nebraska Battery controversy. *Journal of Consulting and Clinical Psychology, 49,* 331–431.

Spiers, P. A. (1982). The Luria-Nebraska Neuropsychological Battery revisited: A theory in practice or just practicing? *Journal of Consulting and Clinical Psychology, 50,* 301–306.

Spitz, E., Carlier, M., Vacher-Lavenu, M., Reed, T., Moutier, R., Busnel, M., & Roubertoux, P. (1996). Long-term effect of prenatal heterogeneity among monozygotes. *Cahiers Psychologie Cognitive (Current Psychology of Cognition), 15,* 283–308.

Spitz, H. (1986). *The raising of intelligence: A selected history of attempts to raise retarded intelligence.* Hillsdale, NJ: Erlbaum.

Spivack, G. M. (1980, April). *The construct of adaptive behavior: Consistency across raters and instruments.* Paper presented at the meeting of the National Association of School Psychologists, Washington, DC.

Sprandel, H. Z. (1985). *The psychoeducational use and interpretation of the Wechsler Adult Intelligence Scale-Revised.* Springfield, IL: Charles C. Thomas.

Spreen, O. (1987). *Learning disabled children growing up: A follow-up into adulthood.* New York: Oxford University Press.

Spreen, O., & Gaddes, W. H. (1969). Developmental norms for 15 neuropsychological tests age 6 to 15. *Cortex, 5,* 171–191.

Spreen, O., & Haaf, R. G. (1986). Empirically derived learning disability subtypes: A replication attempt and longitudinal patterns over 15 years. *Journal of Learning Disabilities, 19,* 170–180.

Spreen, O., Tupper, D., Risser, A., Tuokko, H., & Edgell, D. (1984). *Human developmental neuropsychology.* New York: Oxford University Press.

Springer, S. P., & Deutsch, G. (1985). *Left brain, right brain.* New York: W. H. Freeman.

Spruill, J. (1984). Wechsler Adult Intelligence Scale-Revised. In D. J. Keyser & R. C. Sweetland (Eds.), *Test critiques* (Vol. I; pp. 728–739). Kansas City, MO: Test Corporation of America.

Spruill, J. (1988). Two types of tables for use with the Stanford-Binet Intelligence Scale: Fourth edition. *Journal of Psychoeducational Assessment, 6,* 78–86.

Spruill, J., & Beck, B. (1986). Relationship between the WAIS-R and Wide Range Achievement Test-Revised. *Educational and Psychological Measurement, 46,* 1037–1040.

Squire, L. R. (1986). The neuropsychology of memory dysfunction and its assessment. In I. Grant & K. M. Adanis (Eds.), *Neuropsychological assessment of neuropsychiatric disorders* (pp. 268–299). New York: Oxford University Press.

St. John, J., Krichev, A., & Bauman, E. (1976). Northwestern Ontario Indian children and the WISC. *Psychology in the Schools, 13,* 407–411.

Stankov, L. (1988). Aging, attention, and intelligence. *Psychology and Aging, 3,* 59–74.

Stanovich, K. E. (1986). Matthew effects in reading: Some consequences of individual differences in the acquisition of literacy. *Reading Research Quarterly, 21,* 360–407.

Stanovich, K. E. (1989). Has the learning disabilities field lost its intelligence? *Journal of Learning Disabilities, 22,* 487–492.

Stanovich, K. E. (1991). Discrepancy definitions of reading disability: Has intelligence led us astray? *Reading Research Quarterly, 26,* 7–29.

Stanovich, K. E. (1994). Does dyslexia exist? *Journal of Child Psychology and Psychiatry, 35,* 579–595.

Stanovich, K. E. (1999). The sociopsychometrics of learning disabilities. *Journal of Learning Disabilities, 32,* 350–361.

Stanovich, K. E. (2000). *Progress in understanding reading: Scientific foundations and new frontiers.* New York: Guilford.

Steelman, L. C., & Doby, J. T. (1983). Family size and birth order as factors on the IQ performance of black and white children. *Sociology of Education, 56,* 101–109.

Sternberg, R. J. (1982). Lies we live by: Misapplication of tests in identifying the gifted. *Gifted Child Quarterly, 26,* 157–161.

Sternberg, R. J. (1985). *Beyond IQ: A triarchic theory of human intelligence.* New York: Cambridge University Press.

Sternberg, R. J. (1986). Identifying the gifted through IQ: Why a little bit of knowledge is a dangerous thing. *Roeper Review, 8,* 143–147.

Sternberg, R. J. (Ed.). (1982). *Handbook of human Intelligence.* New York: Cambridge University Press.

Sternberg, R. J. (Ed.). (1988). *Advances in the psychology of human intelligence* (Vol. 4). Hillsdale, NJ: Erlbaum.

Sternberg, R. J., & Grigorenko, E. (1997). *Intelligence, heredity, and environment.* New York: Cambridge University Press.

Sternberg, R. J., Wagner, R. K., Williams, W. M., & Horvath, J. A. (1995). Testing common sense. *American Psychologist, 50,* 912–927.

Stevenson, H. W., & Azuma, H. (1983). IQ in Japan and the United States. *Nature, 306,* 291–292.

Stevenson, H. W., Stigler, J. Lee, S., Lucker, G., Kitamura, S., & Hsu, C. (1985). Cognitive performance and academic achievement of Japanese, Chinese, and American children. *Child Development, 56,* 718–734.

Stevenson, J. D. (1986). Alternate form reliability and concurrent validity of the PPVT-R for referred rehabilitation agency adults. *Journal of Clinical Psychology, 42,* 650–653.

Stewart, D. D. (1981). Scatter comparability, and form equivalence of the verbal scales of the Wechsler-Bellevue, Form I, and the WAIS-R. *Dissertation Abstracts International, 42,* (2-B), 788–789.

Stewart, K. D., & Jones, E. C. (1976). Validity of the Slosson Intelligence Test: A ten-year review. *Psychology in the Schools, 13,* 372–380.

Stinson, M. (1988). *Validity of the adaptive intelligence scale, of the Kaufman Adolescent and Adult Intelligence Test for a sample of educable mentally retarded students.* Unpublished doctoral dissertation, University of Alabama, Tuscaloosa.

Stone, B. J. (1992). Joint confirmatory factor analysis of the DAS and WISC-R. *Journal of School Psychology, 30,* 185–195.

Storandt, M. (1976). Speed and coding effects in relation to age and ability level. *Developmental Psychology, 12,* 177–178.

Storandt, M. (1977). Age, ability level, and method of administering and scoring the WAIS. *Journal of Gerontology, 32,* 175–178.

Storandt, M., Botwinick, J., & Danziger, W. L. (1986). Longitudinal changes: Patients with mild SDAT and matched healthy controls. In L. W. Loon (Ed.), *Clinical memory assessment of older adults* (pp. 277–284). Washington, DC: American Psychological Association.

Strauss, E., Spreen, O., & Hunter, M. (2000). Implications of test revisions for research. *Psychological Assessment, 12*(3), 237–244.

Stricker, G., Merbaum, M., & Tangeman, P. (1969). WAIS short forms, information transmission and approximations of Full Scale IQ. *Journal of Clinical Psychology, 25,* 170–172.

Sutter, P., Mayeda, T., Gall, T., Yanagi, G., & Yee, S. (1980). Comparison of successful and unsuccessful community-placed mentally retarded persons. *American Journal of Mental Deficiency, 85,* 262–267.

Swanson, H. (1993). Individual differences in working memory: A model testing and subgroup analysis of learning disabled and skilled readers. *Intelligence, 17*(3), 285–332.

Swenson, W. M., & Lindgren, E. (1952). The use of psychological tests in industry. *Personnel Psychology, 5,* 19–23.

Szatmari, P., Tuff, L., Finalyson, M. A. J., & Bartolucci, G. (1990). Asperger's syndrome and autism: Neurocognitive aspects. *Journal of the American Academy of Child and Adolescent Psychiatry, 29,* 130–136.

Tambs, K., Sunder, J. M., & Magnus, D. (1984). Heritability analysis of the WAIS subtests: A study of twins. *Intelligence, 8,* 283–293.

Tamkin, A. S., & Jacobsen, R. H. (1987). Age-corrected norms for Shipley Institute of Living Scale scores derived from psychiatric inpatients. *Journal of Clinical Psychology, 43,* 138–142.

Tannenbaum, A. J. (1983). *Gifted children.* New York: Macmillan.

Tanner, J. M. (1962). *Growth at adolescence* (2nd ed.). Oxford: Blackwell.

Tanner-Halverson, P., Burden, T., & Sabers, D. (1993). WISC-III normative data for Tohono O'odham Native American children. In B. A. Bracken & R. S. McCallum (Eds.), *Wechsler Intelligence Scale for Children: Third edition. Journal of Psychoeducational Assessment. Advances in psychoeducational assessment* (pp. 125–133). Brandon, VT: Clinical Psychology.

Taylor, J. R. (1976). A comparison of the adaptive behavior of retarded individuals successfully and unsuccessfully placed in group living homes. *Education and Training of the Mentally Retarded, 11,* 56–64.

Taylor, R. E. (1989). *Assessment of exceptional children* (2nd ed.). Englewood Cliffs, NJ: Prentice-Hall.

Taylor, T. R. (1994). A review of three approaches to cognitive assessment, and a proposed integrated approach based on a unifying theoretical framework. *South African Journal of Psychology, 24*(4), 183–193.

Teeter, A., & Moore, C. L. (1982). Verbal–Performance IQ discrepancies and subtest scatter on the WISC-R for Native American learning-disabled students. *Journal of Psychological Research, 2,* 1–13.

Teeter, A., Moore, C. L., & Petersen, J. D. (1982). WISC-R Verbal and Performance abilities of Native American students referred for school learning problems. *Psychology in the Schools, 19,* 39–44.

Tellegen, A., & Briggs, D. (1967). Old wine in new skins: Grouping Wechsler subtests into new scales. *Journal of Consulting Psychology, 31,* 499–506.

Telzrow, C. (1988). Summary of "IQ: R.I.P." *NASP Communique, 17*(4), 4.

Terdal, L. G. (1981). Mental Retardation. In J. E. Lindemann (Ed.), *Psychological and behavioral aspects of physical disability* (pp. 179–216). New York: Plenum.

Terman, L. D. (1916). *The measurement of intelligence*. Boston: Houghton Mifflin.

Terman, L. M. (1925). *Genetic studies of genius* (Vol. 1). Stanford, CA: Stanford University Press.

Terman, L. M. (1954). The discovery and encouragement of exceptional talent. *American Psychologist, 9,* 221–230.

Terman, L. M., & Childs, H. G. (1912). A tentative revision and extension of the Binet-Simon measuring scale of intelligence. *Journal of Educational Psychology, 3,* 61–74; 133–143; 198–208; 277–289.

Terman, L. M., & Merrill, M. A. (1937). *Measuring intelligence*. Boston: Houghton Mifflin.

Terman, L. M., & Merrill, M. A. (1960). *Stanford-Binet Intelligence Scale*. Boston: Houghton Mifflin.

Terman, L. M., & Merrill, M. A. (1973). *Stanford-Binet Intelligence Scale: 1972 Norms Editions*. Boston: Houghton Mifflin.

Terman, L. M., & Oden, M. H. (1947). *The gifted child grows up*. Stanford, CA: Stanford University Press.

Terman, L. M., & Oden, M. H. (1959). *The gifted child at mid-life: Vol. V. Genetic studies of genius*. Stanford, CA: Stanford University Press.

Terman, L. M., et al. (1925). *Mental and physical traits of a thousand gifted children: Vol. I. Genetic studies of genius*. Stanford, CA: Stanford University Press.

Terry, R. L., & Berg, A. J. (1984). The relationship between WAIS Pa and MMPI Si is mediated by MMPL Pd. *Journal of Clinical Psychology, 40,* 970–971.

Teuber, H. L. (1964). The riddle of frontal lobe function in man. In J. M. Warren & K. Akert (Eds.), *The frontal granular cortex and behavior* (pp. 410–444). New York: McGraw-Hill.

Thiel, G. W. (1981). Relationship of IQ, adaptive behavior, age, and environmental demand to community placement success of mentally retarded adults. *American Journal of Mental Deficiency, 86,* 208–211.

Thienes, C. H., & Haley, T. J. (1972). *Clinical toxicology* (5th ed.). Philadelphia: Lea & Febiger.

Thompson, A. P. (1987). Methodological issues in the clinical evaluation of two- and four-subtest short forms of the WAIS-R. *Journal of Clinical Psychology, 43,* 142–144.

Thompson, A. P., Howard, D., & Anderson, J. (1986). Two- and four-subtest short forms of the WAIS-R: Validity in a psychiatric sample. *Canadian Journal of Behavioral Science, 18,* 287–293.

Thompson, A. P., & Hodgins, C. (1994). Evaluation of a checking procedure for reducing clerical and computational errors on the WAIS-R. *Canadian Journal of Behavioural Science, 26,* 492–504.

Thompson, R. J. (1980). The diagnostic utility of WISC-R measures with children referred to a developmental evaluation center. *Journal of Consulting and Clinical Psychology, 48,* 440–447.

Thompson, T., & Carey, A. (1980). Structured normalization: Intellectual and adaptive behavior changes in a residential setting. *Mental Retardation, 18,* 193–197.

Thorndike, R. L. (1972). Review of the Wide Range Achievement Test. In O. K. Buros (Ed.), *The seventh mental measurement yearbook* (pp. 37–38). Highland Park, NJ: Gryphon.

Thorndike, R. L. (1975). Mr. Binet's test 70 years later. *Educational Researcher, 4,* 3–7.

Thorndike, R. L., Hagen, E. P., & Sattler, J. M. (1986a). *Stanford-Binet Intelligence Scale: Fourth Edition*. Chicago: Riverside.

Thorndike, R. L., Hagen, E. P., & Sattler, J. M. (1986b). *Technical manual for the Stanford-Binet Intelligence Scale: Fourth Edition*. Chicago: Riverside.

Thurstone, L. L. (1935). *The vectors of the mind*. Chicago: University of Chicago Press.

Thurstone, L. L. (1938). Primary mental abilities. *Psychometric Monographs*, (1).

Thurstone, L. L., & Thurstone, T. G. (1941). Factorial studies of intelligence. *Psychometric Monographs*, 2.

Thurstone, L. L., & Thurstone, T. G. (1949). *Examiner's manual for the SRA Primary Mental Abilities Test*. Chicago: Science Research Associates.

Tien, A. Y., Schlaepfer, T. E., Orr, W., & Pearlson, G. D. (1998). SPECT brain blood flow changes with continuous ligand infusion during previously learned WCST performance. *Psychiatry Research: Neuroimaging, 82,* 47–52.

Tittemore, J. A., Lawson, J. S., & Inglis, J. (1985). Validation of a learning disability index (LDI) derived from a principal components analysis of the WISC-R. *Journal of Learning Disabilities, 18,* 449–454.

Todd, J., Coolidge, F., & Satz, P. (1977). The Wechsler Adult Intelligence Scale Discrepancy Index: A neuropsychological evaluation. *Journal of Consulting and Clinical Psychology, 45,* 450–454.

Torrance, E. P. (1980). Growing up creatively gifted: A 22-year longitudinal study. *Creative Child and Adult Quarterly, 5,* 148–158.

Torrance, E. P. (1981). Predicting the creativity of elementary school children (1958)—and the teacher "who made a difference." *Gifted Child Quarterly, 25,* 55–61.

Torrance, E. P. (1984). *Torrance tests of creative thinking*. Bensenville, IL: Scholastic Testing Service.

Torrance, E. P., Khatena, J., & Cunningham, B. F. (1973). *Thinking creatively with sounds and words*. Bensenville, IL: Scholastic Testing Service.

Treffinger, D. J. (1985). Review of the Torrance Tests of Creative Thinking. In J. M. Mitchell (Ed.), *The ninth mental measurements yearbook* (pp. 1632–1634). Lincoln, NB: Buros Institute of Mental Measurenients, University of Nebraska Press.

Treffinger, D. J., & Renzulli, J. S. (1986). Giftedness as potential for creative productivity: Transcending IQ scores. *Roeper Review, 8*, 150–154.

Tucker, D. (1981). Lateral brain function, emotion, and conceptualization. *Psychological Bulletin, 89*, 19–46.

Tuddenham, R. (1948). Soldier intelligence in World Wars I and II. *American Psychologist, 5*, 54–56.

Tulsky, D. S., & Ledbetter, M. F. (2000). Updating to the WAIS-III and WMS-III: Considerations for research and clinical practice. *Psychological Assessment, 12*, 253–262.

Tulsky, D. S., Rolfhus, E. L., & Zhu, J. (2000). Two-tailed versus one-tailed base rates of discrepancy scores on the WAIS-III. *The Clinical Neuropsychologist, 14*, 451–460.

Tulsky, D. S., Zhu, J., & Prifitera, A. (2000). Assessing adult intelligence with the WAIS-III. In G. Goldstein and M. Herson (Eds.), *Handbook of psychological assessment* (3rd ed.) (pp. 97–129). New York: Pergamon.

Tulsky, D. S., Zhu, J., & Vasquez, C. (1998). Patterns of WAIS-III subtests, IQ and index scores in samples of individuals with a variety of neuropsychological disorders. *Journal of the International Neuropsychological Society, 4*, 52.

Tulving, E. (1983). *Elements of episodic memory.* New York: Oxford University Press.

Tuokko, H., & Crockett, D. (1987). Central cholinergic deficiency WAIS profiles in a nondemented aged sample. *Journal of Clinical and Experimental Neuropsychology, 9*, 225–227.

Turkheimer, E., & Farace, E., (1992). A reanalysis of gender differences in IQ scores following unilateral brain lesions. *Psychological Assessment, 4*, 498–501.

Turkheimer, E., Farace, E., Yeo, R. A., & Bigler, E. D. (1993). Quantitative analysis of gender differences in the effects of lateralized lesions on Verbal and Performance IQ. *Intelligence, 17*, 461–474.

Turnbull, W. W. (1985). *Student change, program change: Why the SAT scores kept falling* (College Board Rep. 85–2). New York: College Entrance Examination Board.

Turner, R. G., & Horn, J. M. (1976). MMPI item correlates of WAIS subtest performance. *Journal of Clinical Psychology, 32*, 583–594.

Turner, R. G., & Horn, J. M. (1977). Personality scale and item correlates of WAIS abilities. *Intelligence, 1*, 281–297.

Turner, R. G., & Willerman, L. (1977). Sex differences in WAIS item performance. *Journal of Clinical Psychology, 33*, 795–797.

Turner, R. G., Willerman, L., & Horn, J. M. (1976). Personality correlates of WAIS performance. *Journal of Clinical Psychology, 32*, 349–354.

Tyerman, M. J. (1986). Gifted children and their identification: Learning ability not intelligence. *Gifted Education International, 4*, 81–84.

Tymchuk, A. J., Simmons, J. Q., & Neafsey, S. (1977). Intellectual characteristics of adolescent childhood psychotics with high verbal ability. *Journal of Mental Deficiency Research, 21*, 133–138.

Urbina, S. P., Gooden, C. J., & Ariel, R. N. (1982). WAIS/WAIS-R: Initial comparisons. *Journal of Clinical Neuropsychology, 4*, 145–146.

Uzzell, B. P., Zimmerman, R. A., Dolinskas, C. A., & Obrist, W. D. (1979). Lateralized psychological impairment associated with CT lesions in head injured patients. *Cortex, 15*, 391–401.

Valencia, R. R., & Suzuki, L. A. (2001). *Intellectual testing and minority students.* Thousand Oaks, CA: Sage.

Valenstein, E., & Heilman, K. M. (1979). Emotional disorders resulting from lesions of the central nervous system. In K. M. Heilman & F. Valenstein (Eds.), *Clinical neuropsychology* (pp. 413–438). New York: Oxford University Press.

Van Hagen, J., & Kaufman, A. S. (1975). Factor analysis of the WISC-R for a group of mentally retarded children and adolescents. *Journal of Consulting and Clinical Psychology, 43*, 661–667.

Vance, H. R., Brown, W., Hankins, N., & Furgerson, S. C. (1987). A comparison of the WISC-R and the WAIS-R with special education students. *Journal of Clinical Psychology, 43*, 377–380.

Vance, H. R., Hankins, N., Wallbrown, F., Engin, A., & McGee, H. (1978). Analysis of cognitive abilities for mentally retarded children on the WISC-R. *Psychological Record, 28*, 391–397.

Vance, H. R., Kitson, D., & Singer, M. (1983). Further investigation of comparability of WISC-R and PPVT-R for children and youth referred for psychological services. *Psychology in the Schools, 20*, 307–310.

Vandenberg, S. G., & Vogler, C. P. (1985). Genetic determinants of intelligence. In B. B. Wolman (Ed.), *Handbook of intelligence* (pp. 3–57). New York: Wiley.

Vane, J. R., & Motta, R. W. (1984). Group intelligence tests. In G. Goldstein & M. Hersen (Eds.), *Handbook of psychological assessment* (pp. 100–116). New York: Pergamon.

Varney, N. R. (1982). Pantomime recognition defect in aphasia: Implications for the concept of asymbolia. *Brain and Language, 15*, 32–39.

Vega, A., Jr., & Parsons, O. A. (1967). Cross-validation of the Halstead-Reitan tests for brain damage. *Journal of Consulting Psychology, 31*, 619–623.

Vega, A., Jr., & Parsons, O. A. (1969). Relationship between sensory–motor deficits and WAIS Verbal and Performance scores in unilateral brain damage. *Cortex, 5,* 229–241.

Vellutino, F. R., Scanlon, D. M., & Lyon, G. R. (2000). Differentiating between difficult-to-remediate and readily remediated poor readers: More evidence against the IQ-achievement discrepancy definition of reading disability. *Journal of Learning Disabilities, 33,* 223–238.

Venter, A., Lord, C., & Schopler, E. (1992). A follow-up study of high functioning autistic children. *Journal of Child Psychology and Psychiatry, 33,* 489–507.

Verhaaren, P., & Conner, F. P. (1981). Physical disabilities. In J. M. Kauffman & D. P. Hallahan (Eds.), *Handbook of special education.* Englewood Cliffs, NJ: Prentice-Hall.

Verhaeghen, P. (1993). *Teaching old dogs new tricks: Plasticity in episodic memory performance in old age.* Leuven, Belgium: Catholic University of Leuven.

Vernon, D. A. (1983). Speed of information processing and general intelligence. *Intelligence, 7,* 53–70.

Vernon, D. A., & Kantor, L. (1986). Reaction time correlations with intelligence test scores obtained under either timed or untimed conditions. *Intelligence, 10,* 315–330.

Vernon, P. A., Nador, S., & Kantor, E. (1985). Group differences in intelligence and speed of information processing. *Intelligence, 9,* 137–148.

Vincent, K. R. (1979). The modified WAIS: An alternative to short forms. *Journal of Clinical Psychology, 35,* 624–625.

Vincent, K. R. (1991). Black/white IQ differences: Does age make the difference? *Journal of Clinical Psychology, 47,* 266–270.

Vining, D. R. (1983). Mean IQ differences in Japan and the United States. *Nature, 301,* 738.

Vining, D. R. (1986). Social versus reproductive success: The central theoretical problem of human sociobiology. *Behavioral and Brain Sciences, 9,* 167–187.

Vogel, S. A. (1986). Levels and patterns of intellectual functioning among LD college students: Clinical and educational implications. *Journal of Learning Disabilities, 19,* 71–79.

Vogel, S. A. (1990). Gender differences in intelligence, language, visual–motor abilities, and academic achievement in students with learning disabilities: A review of the literature. *Journal of Learning Disabilities, 23,* 44–52.

Von Monakow, C. V. (1911). Lokalization der hirnfunktionen. *Journal fur Psychologie und Neurologie, 17,* 185–200.

Waber, D. P., Carlson, D., Mann, M., Merola, J., & Moylan, D. (1984). SES-related aspects of neuropsychological performance. *Child Development, 55,* 1878–1886.

Wadsworth, S. J., Olson, R. K., Pennington, B. F., & De-Fries, J. C. (2000). Differential genetic etiology of reading disability as a function of IQ. *Journal of Learning Disabilities, 33,* 192–199.

Wagner, E. E., & McCormick, M. K. (1982). Relationships between WAIS Verbal versus Performance decrements and Bender-Gestalt errors. *Perceptual and Motor Skills, 54,* 1259–1263.

Wagner, R. K., & Sternberg, R. J. (1990). Street smarts. In K. E. Clark & M. B. Clark (Eds.), *Measures of leadership* (pp. 493–504). West Orange, NJ: Leadership Library of America.

Wainer, H. (1988). How accurately can we assess changes in minority performance on the SAT? *American Psychologist, 43,* 774–778.

Waldron, K., & Saphire, D. (1992). Perceptual and academic patterns of learning disabled/gifted students. *Perceptual and Motor Skills, 74*(2), 599–609.

Walker, N. W. (1987). The Stanford-Binet 4th edition: Haste does seem to make waste. *Measurement and Evaluation in Counseling and Development, 20,* 135–138.

Walsh, K. W. (1977). Neuropsychological aspects of modified leucotomy. In W. H. Sweet (Ed.), *Neuropsychological treatment in psychiatry* (pp. 163–174). Baltimore, MD: University Park Press.

Walton, J. R. (1987). Today's kids, tomorrow's nations. *National Association of School Psychologists Communique, 15*(5), 6–7.

Waltz, A. G. (1972). Cortical blood flow of opposite hemisphere after occlusion of the middle cerebral artery. *Transamerican Neurological Association, 92,* 293–294.

Wang, J., & Kaufman, A. S. (1993). Changes in fluid and crystallized intelligence across the 20- to 90-year age range on the K-BIT. *Journal of Psychoeducational Assessment, 11,* 29–37.

Ward, L. C. (1990). Prediction of Verbal, Performance, and Full Scale IQs from seven subtests of the WAIS-R. *Journal of Clinical Psychology, 46,* 436–440.

Ward, L. C., Ryan, J. J., & Axelrod, B. N. (2000). Confirmatory factor analysis of the WAIS-III standardization data. *Psychological Assessment, 12,* 341–345.

Ward, L. C., Selby, R. B., & Clark, B. L. (1987). Subtest administration times and short forms of the Wechsler Adult Intelligence Scale-Revised. *Journal of Clinical Psychology, 43,* 276–278.

Ward, S. B., Ward, T. J., Hatt, C. V., & Young, D. L. (1995). The incidence and utility of the ACID, ACIDS, and SCAD profiles in a referred population. *Psychology in the Schools, 32,* 267–276.

Warner, M. H. (1983). *Practice effects, test-retest reliability, and comparability of WAIS and WAIS-R: Issues in the assessment of cognitive recovery in detoxified alcoholics.* Unpublished doctoral dissertation, University of Georgia, Athens.

Warner, M. H., Ernst, J., & Townes, H. D. (1986). Comparison of WAIS and WAIS-R factor structure for neuropsychiatric patients. *Psychological Reports, 59,* 715–720.

Warner, M. H., Ernst, J., Townes, B. D., Peel, J., & Preston, M. (1987). Relationships between IQ and neuropsychological measures in neuropsychiatric populations: Within-laboratory and cross-cultural replications using WAIS and WAIS-R. *Journal of Clinical and Experimental Neuropsychology*, 9, 545–562.

Warrington, F. K., & James, M. (1967). Disorders of visual perception in patients with localized cerebral lesions. *Neuropsychologia*, 5, 253–266.

Wasserstein, J. (1980). *Differentiation of perceptual closure implications for right hemisphere functions.* Unpublished doctoral dissertation, City University of New York.

Wassing, H. E. (1965). Cognitive functioning in early infantile autism: An examination of four cases by means of the Wechsler Intelligence Scale for Children. *Acta Paedopsychiatrica*, 32, 122–135.

Watkins, C. E., Campbell, V. L., Nieberding, R., & Hallmark, R. (1995). Contemporary practice of psychological assessment by clinical psychologists. *Professional Psychology: Research and Practice*, 26, 54–60.

Watkins, M. W., Kush, J. C., & Glutting, J. J. (1997). Prevalence and diagnostic utility of the WISC-III SCAD profile among children with learning disabilities. *School Psychology Quarterly*, 12, 235–248.

Watson, C. G., Kiett, W. G., Kucala, T., Nixon, Schaefer, A., & Gasser, B. (1981). Prediction of the WAIS scores from the 1973 Henmon-Nelson revision. *Journal of Clinical Psychology*, 37, 840–842.

Watson, C. G., Thomas, R., Anderson, D., & Felling, J. (1968). Differentiation of organics from schizophrenics at two chronicity levels by use of the Reitan-Halstead organic test battery. *Journal of Consulting and Clinical Psychology*, 32, 679–684.

Watson, G., & Glaser, E. M. (1980). *Watson-Glaser Critical Thinking Appraisal.* New York: The Psychological Corporation.

Wechsler, D. (1928). Psychometric tests. In I. S. Wechsler (Ed.), *A textbook of clinical neurology* (pp. 104–116). Philadelphia: W. B. Saunders.

Wechsler, D. (1939). *Measurement of adult intelligence.* Baltimore, MD: Williams & Wilkins.

Wechsler, D. (1944). *The measurement of adult intelligence* (3rd ed.). Baltimore, MD: Williams & Wilkins.

Wechsler, D. (1945). A standardized memory scale for clinical use. *Journal of Psychology*, 19, 87–95.

Wechsler, D. (1946). *The Wechsler-Bellevue Intelligence Scale, Form II.* New York: The Psychological Corporation.

Wechsler, D. (1949). *Manual for the Wechsler Intelligence Scale for Children.* New York: The Psychological Corporation.

Wechsler, D. (1950). Cognitive, conative and non-intellective intelligence. *American Psychologist*, 5, 78–83.

Wechsler, D. (1955). *Manual for the Wechsler Adult Intelligence Scale (WAIS).* San Antonio, TX: The Psychological Corporation.

Wechsler, D. (1958). *Measurement and appraisal of adult intelligence* (4th ed.). Baltimore, MD: Williams & Wilkens.

Wechsler, D. (1974). *Manual for the Wechsler Intelligence Scale for Children-Revised (WISC-R).* San Antonio, TX: The Psychological Corporation.

Wechsler, D. (1981). *Manual for the Wechsler Adult Intelligence Scale-Revised* (WAIS-R). San Antonio, TX: The Psychological Corporation.

Wechsler, D. (1987). *Manual for the Wechsler Memory Scale-Revised (WMS-R).* San Antonio, TX: The Psychological Corporation.

Wechsler, D. (1989). *Manual for the Wechsler Preschool and Primary Scale of Intelligence-Revised (WPPSI-R).* San Antonio, TX: The Psychological Corporation.

Wechsler, D. (1991). *Manual for the Wechsler Intelligence Scale for Children-Third Edition (WISC-III).* San Antonio, TX: The Psychological Corporation.

Wechsler, D. (1997). *Manual for the Wechsler Adult Intelligence Scale-Third Edition (WAIS-III).* San Antonio, TX: The Psychological Corporation.

Weinberg, J., Diller, L., Gerstman, L., & Schulman, P. (1972). Digit span in right and left hemiplegics. *Journal of Clinical Psychology*, 28, 361.

Weinberg, R. A. (1989). Intelligence and IQ: Landmark issues and great debates. *American Psychologist*, 43, 98–104.

Weller, C., & Strawser, S. (1987). Adaptive behavior of subtypes of learning disabled individuals. *Journal of Special Education*, 21, 101–116.

Welsh, K., Butters, N., Hughes, J., Mohs, R., & Heyman, A. (1991). Detection of abnormal memory decline in mild cases of Alzheimer's disease using CERAD neuropsychological measures. *Archives of Neurology*, 48, 278–281.

Welsh, K., Butters, N., Hughes, J., Mohs, R., & Heyman, A. (1992). Detection and staging of dementia in Alzheimer's disease: Use of the neuropsychological measures developed for the consortium to establish a registry for Alzheimer's disease. *Archives of Neurology*, 49, 448–452.

Werner, E. E. (1986). A longitudinal study of perinatal risk. In D. C. Farran & J. D. McKinney (Eds.), *Risk in intellectual and psychosocial development* (pp. 3–27). Orlando, FL: Academic Press.

Wernicke, C. (1874). *Der aphasiche symptomenkomplex.* Breslau: Cohn and Weigert.

Wesman, A. G. (1968). Intelligent testing. *American Psychologist* 23, 267–274.

Wheaton, P. J., & Vandergriff, A. F. (1978). Comparison of WISG and WISC-R scores of highly gifted students in public school. *Psychological Reports, 43,* 627–630.

Wheeler, L., Burke, C. J., & Reitan, R. M. (1962). An application of discriminant functions to the problem of predicting brain damage using behavioral variables. *Perceptual and Motor Skills, 16* (Monograph Supplement), 417–440.

Wheeler, L., & Reitan, R. M. (1962). The presence and laterality of brain damage predicted from responses to a short Aphasia Screening Test. *Perceptual and Motor Skills, 15,* 783–799.

Whelan, T. B., & Walker, M. L. (1988). Effects of sex and lesion locus on measures of intelligence. *Journal of Consulting and Clinical Psychology, 56,* 633–635.

Whiddon, M. F., Sr., (1978). Identification and validation of a subtest pattern on the Wechsler Adult Intelligence Scale that will separate brain damaged, schizophrenic, and normal subjects by means of a discriminant function analysis. (University of Southern Mississippi, 1977). *Dissertation Abstracts International, 38,* (10-B), 5051.

Whitmore, J. R. (1979). The etiology of underachievement in highly gifted young children. *Journal for the Education of the Gifted, 3,* 38–51.

Whitmore, J. R. (1980). *Giftedness, conflict, and underachievement.* Boston: Allyn & Bacon.

Whitmore, J. R. (1981). Gifted children with handicapping conditions: A new frontier. *Exceptional Children, 48,* 106–114.

Whitworth, R. H., & Gibbons, R. T. (1986). Cross-racial comparison of the WAIS and WAIS-R. *Educational and Psychological Measurement, 46,* 1041–1049.

Wigdor, A. K., & Garner, W. R. (Eds.). (1982). Ability testing: Uses, consequences, and controversies. Washington, DC: National Academy Press.

Wiig, E. H. (1985). Review of the Peabody Picture Vocabulary Test-Revised. In J. V. Mitchell (Ed.), *The ninth mental measurement yearbook* (pp. 1127–1128). Lincoln, NE: Buros Institute of Mental Measurements, University of Nebraska Press.

Wildman, R. W., & Wildman, R. W. (1977). Validity of Verbal IQ as a short form of the Wechsler Adult Intelligence Scale. *Journal of Consulting and Clinical Psychology, 45,* 171–172.

Wilkinson, S. C. (1993). WISC-R profiles of children with superior intellectual ability. *Gifted Child Quarterly, 37,* 84–91.

Williams, R. L. (1974). Scientific racism and IQ: The silent mugging of the black community. *Psychology Today, 7,* 32–41.

Williams, R. T. (1998). Kaufman Functional Academic Skills Test. In J. C. Impara & B. S. Plake (Eds.), *The thirteenth mental measurements yearbook* (pp. 570–572). Lincoln, NE: Buros Institute of Mental Measurements, University of Nebraska Press.

Willis, S. L. (1985). Towards an educational psychology of the older adult learner: Intellectual and cognitive bases. In J. E. Birren and K. W. Schaie (Eds.), *Handbook of the psychology of aging* (2nd ed.; pp. 818–847). New York: Van Nostrand Reinhold.

Willoughby, R. R. (1927). Family similarities in mental-test abilities. *Genetic Psychology Monographs, 2,* 239–277.

Willson, V. L., & Reynolds, C. R. (1985). Normative data on the WAIS-R for Selz and Reitan's index of scatter. *Journal of Clinical Psychology, 41,* 254–258.

Wilson, M. S., & Reschly, D. J. (1996). Assessment in school psychology training and practice. *School Psychology Review, 25,* 9–23.

Wilson, R. S. (1983). The Louisville twin study: Developmental synchronies in behavior. *Child Development, 54,* 298–316.

Wilson, W. M. (1992). The Stanford-Binet: Fourth Edition and from L-M in the assessment of young children with mental retardation. *Mental Retardation, 80*(2), 81–84

Wing, L. (1971). Perceptual and language development in autistic children: A comparative study. In M. Rutter (Ed.), *Infantile autism: Concepts, characteristics, and treatments.* London: Churchill-Livingston.

Winne, J., & Gittinger, J. (1973). An introduction to the Personality Assessment System. *Journal of Clinical Psychology* (Monograph Supplement 38).

Wissler, C. (1901). The correlation of mental and physical tests. *Psychological Review, 3* (Monograph Supplement 16).

Witelson, S. F. (1976). Sex and the single hemisphere: Specialization of the right hemisphere for spatial processing. *Science, 193,* 425–427.

Witelson, S. F. (1977). Developmental dyslexia: Two right hemispheres and none left. *Science, 195,* 309–311.

Witelson, S. F. (1989). Hand and sex differences in the isthmus and genu of the human corpus callosum. *Brain, 112,* 799–835.

Witt, J. C., & Martens, B. K. (1984). Adaptive behavior: Tests and assessment issues. *School Psychology Review, 13,* 478–484.

Witt, S. J. (1981). Increase in adaptive behavior level after residence in an intermediate care facility for mentally retarded persons. *Mental Retardation, 19,* 75–79.

Wolman, B. B. (1985). Intelligence and mental health. In B. B. Wolman (Ed.), *Handbook of intelligence* (pp. 849–872). New York: Wiley.

Woodcock, R. W. (1978). *Development and standardization of the Woodcock-Johnson Psycho-Educational Battery.* Allen, TX: DLM/Teaching Resources.

Woodcock, R. W. (1982). *Bateria Woodcock Psico-Educativa en Espanol.* Allen, TX: DLM.

Woodcock, R. W. (1984a). A response to some questions raised about the Woodcock-Johnson: I. The mean score discrepancy issue. *School Psychology Review, 13,* 342–354.

Woodcock, R. W. (1984b). A response to some questions raised about the Woodcock-Johnson: II. Efficacy of the aptitude clusters. *School Psychology Review, 13,* 355–362.

Woodcock, R. W. (1987a). Who should use the Woodcock-Johnson: A response from Richard Woodcock. *NASP Communique, 15*(8), 4.

Woodcock, R. W. (1987b). *Woodcock Reading Mastery Tests-Revised: Examiner's manual.* Circle Pines, MN: American Guidance Service.

Woodcock, R. W. (1988, August). *Factor structure of the Tests of Cognitive Ability from the 1977 and 1989 Woodcock-Johnson.* Paper presented at the ACER Seminar on Intelligence, Melbourne, Australia.

Woodcock, R. W. (1990). Theoretical foundations of the WJ-R measures of cognitive ability. *Journal of Psychoeducational Assessment, 8,* 231–258.

Woodcock, R. W. (1993). An information processing view of *Gf-Gc* theory. *Journal of Psychoeducational Assessment, Monograph Series: WJ R Monograph,* 80–102.

Woodcock, R. W. (1994). Measures of fluid and crystallized intelligence. In R. J. Sternberg (Ed.), *The encyclopedia of intelligence* (pp. 452–456). New York: Macmillan.

Woodcock, R. W. (1997). *The Woodcock-Johnson Tests of Cognitive Ability Revised.* New York: Guilford.

Woodcock, R. W., & Dahl, M. N. (1971). A common scale for the measurement of person ability and test item difficulty. *AGS Paper No. 10.* Circle Pines, MN: American Guidance Service.

Woodcock, R. W., & Johnson, M. B. (1977). *Woodcock-Johnson Psycho-Educational Battery.* Itasca, IL: Riverside.

Woodcock, R. W., & Johnson, M. B. (1989). *Woodcock-Johnson Psycho-Educational Battery-Revised.* Itasca, IL: Riverside.

Woodcock, R. W., & Mather, N. (1989). WJ-R Tests of Cognitive Ability-Standard and Supplemental Batteries: Examiner's manual. In R. W. Woodcock & M. B. Johnson, *Woodcock-Johnson Psycho-Educational Battery-Revised.* Allen, TX: DLM/Teaching Resources.

Woodcock, R. W., McGrew, K. S., & Mather, N. (2000). *Woodcock-Johnson Psycho-Educational Battery Third Edition (WJ-3).* Chicago: Riverside.

Woodcock, R. W., McGrew, K. S., & Mather, N. (2001). *Woodcock-Johnson III.* Itasca, IL: Riverside.

Woodcock, R. W., & Munoz-Sandoval, A. F. (1996a). *Batteria Woodcock-Munoz Pruebas de aprovechamiento-Revisada.* Chicago, IL: Riverside.

Woodcock, R. W., & Munoz-Sandoval, A. F. (1996b). *Batteria Woodcock-Munoz Pruebas de habiliadad cognoscitiva-Revisada.* Chicago, IL: Riverside.

Worthington, C. F. (1987). Testing the test: Kaufman Test of Educational Achievement, Comprehensive Form and Brief Form. *Journal of Counseling and Development, 65,* 325–327.

Wright, B. D., & Stone, M. H. (1979). *Best test design.* Chicago: MESA Press.

Yerkes, R. M. (1917). The Binet versus the point scale method of measuring intelligence. *Journal of Applied Psychology, 1,* 111–122.

Yirmiya, N., & Sigman, M. (1991). High functioning individuals with autism: Diagnosis, empirical findings, and theoretical issues. *Clinical Psychology Review, 11,* 669–683.

Yoakum, C. S., & Yerkes, R. M. (1920). *Army mental tests.* New York: Henry Holt.

Young, J. W. (1995). Kaufman Brief Intelligence Test. In J. C. Conoley & J. C. Impara (Eds.), *The twelfth mental measurements yearbook* (pp. 534–535). Lincoln, NE: Buros Institute of Mental Measurements, University of Nebraska Press.

Yudin, L. W. (1966). An abbreviated form of the WISC for use with emotionally disturbed children. *Journal of Consulting Psychology, 30,* 272–275.

Zachary, R. A. (1986). *Shipley Institute of Living Scale: Revised manual.* Los Angeles: Western Psychological Services.

Zachary, R. A. (1990). Wechsler's intelligence scales: Theoretical and practical considerations. *Journal of Psychoeducational Assessment, 8,* 276–289.

Zelinski, E. M., & Burnight, K. P. (1997). Sixteen-year longitudinal and time-lag changes in memory and cognition in older adults. *Psychology and Aging, 12,* 503–513.

Zimmerman, I. L., Covin, T. M., & Woo-Sam, J. M. (1986). A longitudinal comparison of the WISC-R and WAIS-R. *Psychology in the Schools, 23,* 148–151.

Zimmerman, I. L., & Woo-Sam, J. M. (1972). Research with the WISC, 1960–1970. *Journal of Clinical Psychology Monograph Supplement, 33,* 1–44.

Zimmerman, I. L., & Woo-Sam, J. M. (1973). *Clinical interpretation of the Wechsler Adult Intelligence Scale.* New York: Grune & Stratton.

Zimmerman, I. L., & Woo-Sam, J. M. (1985). Clinical applications. In B. B. Wolman (Ed.), *Handbook of Intelligence* (pp. 873–898). New York: Wiley.

Zimmerman, I. L., &, Woo-Sam, J. M. (1990, April). *The interchangeability of major measures of intelligence.* Paper presented at Western Psychological Association Convention, Los Angeles, CA.

Zimmerman, I. L., & Woo-Sam, J. M. (1997). Review of the criterion-related validity of the WISC-III: The first five years. *Perceptual and Motor Skills, 85,* 531–546.

Zimprich, D. (1998). Geschwindigkeit der Informationsverarbeitung und fluide Intelligenz im hoeheren Erwachsenenalter: Eine Sekundaranalyse des Datenmaterials der Bonner Laengsschnittstudie des Alterns anhand von "Latent Growth Curve Models." [Speed of information processing and fluid intelligence in the elderly.] *Zeitschrift Fuer Gerontologie und Geriatrie, 31,* 89–96.

NAME INDEX

SUBJECT INDEX